STRATEGY & STRATEGISTS

JAMES CUNNINGHAM & BRIAN HARNEY

STRATEGY & STRATEGISTS

Great Clarendon Street, Oxford, OX2 6DP,
United Kingdom

Oxford University Press is a department of the University of Oxford. It furthers the University's objective of excellence in research, scholarship, and education by publishing worldwide. Oxford is a registered trade mark of Oxford University Press in the UK and in certain other countries

Impression: 1

British Library Cataloguing in Publication Data
Data available

Library of Congress Cataloging in Publication Data
Data available

ISBN 978–0–19–921971–1

Printed in Italy on acid-free paper by
L.E.G.O. S.p.A.—Lavis TN

Foreword

One of the main tenets of the field of strategic management is that a firm should differentiate itself from its competitors. The authors have attempted to take this fundamental notion to heart in the design of their book. As a long-time strategy professor who has taught thousands of business students and managers, I see their book as distinctive and valuable in three important ways. First, I believe that both students and executives need to have an understanding of a 'complete' strategic management framework and how it can contribute to the design and management of firms. Our field has been criticized at various times for simply being a hodgepodge of concepts and tools or as too narrowly focused on the resource-based view of the firm. A complete framework does not have to be complex, but it should be comprehensive. It should show, fundamentally, that a firm interacts with many dynamic environments, that it must develop the capabilities and resources to succeed in those environments, and that other firms are competing against it for customers and resources. The student or practitioner of strategy should feel comfortable analysing changing situations by using a wide lens—one that encompasses the ideas of evolutionary processes, systems thinking, and the alignment of organizations with their environments. Moreover, a complete framework should place as much emphasis on 'management' as it does on 'strategy'—for example, by adopting a stakeholder management approach, which implies using a 'balanced scorecard' to measure a firm's performance. There is little value, it seems to me, in presenting new, creative, or sophisticated strategies without also showing how they can be pursued through appropriate organization designs and management approaches. *Strategy and Strategists* attempts to develop a comprehensive understanding of strategic management by providing a broad conceptual framework early on in the book. Later, a chapter on 'critical' strategy allows students to wrestle philosophically with what strategy can and cannot do for a firm.

Another differentiating factor in this book is its focus on 'strategists': who they are; the roles they play; and the activities they perform. Historically, our field has placed responsibility for the formulation of strategy on top management, either through the chief executive officer (CEO) as master strategist or through the entire top management team. These are the executives who have the best vantage point from which to see the entire company and how it operates in its various environments. Although there have been periodic calls about the desirability of spreading strategic and entrepreneurial thinking throughout a firm, the actual mechanisms for doing so have been slow to develop. As a consequence, most members of a given organization are unaware of the current thinking of their top managers and of where the organization is or might be headed.

Strategy and Strategists uses the emerging 'strategy as practice' perspective to explore who the producers of strategy really are and what they do. The authors argue that strategists can—and should—be found anywhere in the organization and that good strategists reflect characteristics of entrepreneurship, leadership, and management. The authors emphasize that the key understanding of any strategist is that of the total company and how it relates to its stakeholders. Such an understanding can be enhanced by incorporating the thinking of relevant individuals and groups outside the organization, including customers, bankers, venture capitalists, consultants, and government officials. Hopefully, ongoing research on network organizations and knowledge management systems will soon be integrated with that on 'strategy as practice', and we will have a clear picture of how firms can use both their own and others' resources to spread strategic thinking and action throughout an organization.

Lastly, *Strategy and Strategists* places an appropriate amount of emphasis on strategy implementation. Many years ago, I attended a conference at which Tom Peters was the keynote speaker. This was when Peters was still a McKinsey consultant—but soon to become a best-selling author and management guru. One of the many interesting comments that he made in that talk referred to strategy implementation. He said that of all the failed business strategies that he had seen among McKinsey's client companies, 90 per cent of them were due to poor implementation: 'If you put managers in a room and give them enough time and information, they will come up with good strategies. It's trying to carry out those strategies that is the hard part.'

Both students and managers, of course, need to understand the concepts and tools that will allow them to formulate sound business strategies, and *Strategy and Strategists* covers this material well. Managers, however, operate on the front lines of business, and they need all of the help they can get in seeing that the strategies for which they are responsible are carried out successfully. Successful implementation of a strategic initiative in an ongoing enterprise requires thoughtful and often quite sophisticated managerial behaviour. Strategy implementation essentially involves change: changing people's attitudes and behaviours; changing the organization's structure or processes; and so on. Teaching students how to create and sustain organizational change is difficult; indeed, some have argued that it is impossible until they have had a substantial amount of experience in actual organizations.

Strategy and Strategists addresses the subject of implementation by providing insights into the levers of strategic control and empowerment, as well as the configurations of structures, management systems, and people management that may facilitate in enabling success and realizing advantage. Central to the approach is stimulating debate around the utility and viability of various concepts and tools, rather than offering prescriptive 'cookbook', quick-fix approaches. In addition, by focusing on the way in which advantage is sustained though change management and innovation, the book comes full circle on the process of strategic management—recognizing that strategy never stands still, and that the task of the strategist in formulating and implementing strategy is a continuous one. My hope and belief is that *Strategy and Strategists* can play a valuable role in this process, especially by conveying to students and future managers knowledge about formulating and implementing strategies for firms and other types of organization.

Professor Charles Snow
Penn State University, 2011

Contents in brief

Section 7 **Long cases**

Detailed contents

How to use this book

Theoretical debates

Each chapter contains a synthesis of theoretical debates and critical reflections on key issues that have shaped strategic management research and practice.

Strategy spotlight

Key issues discussed in the chapter are considered in the context of contemporary examples.

Spotlight How CSOs think about their role

As companies struggle to meet the challenges of today's complex business environment by developing short-term and long-term strategic visions, the role of CSO has become increasingly prominent. Although CEOs remain ultimately responsible for strategic decisions, they regularly look to the CSOs to craft and implement successful strategies. But the

Annabel Spring, managing director in charge and execution at the investment bank Morgan S J. F. Van Kerckhove, vice president of corpora at the e-commerce company eBay.

Some of the panellists say that they have on corporate suite and the other deep in the bu

Implications for strategy practice

Explore the key challenges and opportunities that a strategist may face.

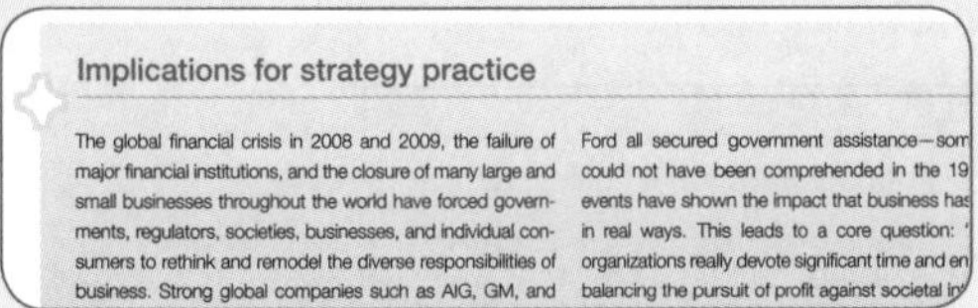
Implications for strategy practice

The global financial crisis in 2008 and 2009, the failure of major financial institutions, and the closure of many large and small businesses throughout the world have forced governments, regulators, societies, businesses, and individual consumers to rethink and remodel the diverse responsibilities of business. Strong global companies such as AIG, GM, and

Ford all secured government assistance—som could not have been comprehended in the 19 events have shown the impact that business has in real ways. This leads to a core question: organizations really devote significant time and en balancing the pursuit of profit against societal in

Mini case study

Real-life examples help generate discussion, reflection, and debate.

Mini case study Fairtrade: making a difference?

The Fairtrade label can be found on an increasing number of product ranges—more than 1,500 products in retail stores and coffee shops (see the box below). According to Fairtrade (2010), by 2008, Fairtrade-certified sales amounted to approximately €3.8bn worldwide, a 22 per cent year-on-year increase and nearly 40 per cent average growth per

in community development. Including families ar ants, Fairtrade Labelling Organizations Internati the umbrella organization for the eighteen nation organizations, estimates that 6 million people dire from Fairtrade (Fairtrade, 2010). In the UK, bet and 2007, there was a 47 per cent increase in ye

Discussion questions

Each chapter contains discussion questions to help you consider the role of the strategist and develop your own insights and conclusions.

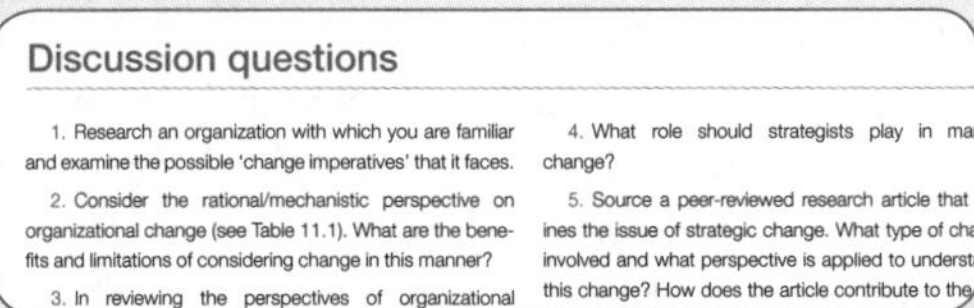
Discussion questions

1. Research an organization with which you are familiar and examine the possible 'change imperatives' that it faces.
2. Consider the rational/mechanistic perspective on organizational change (see Table 11.1). What are the benefits and limitations of considering change in this manner?
3. In reviewing the perspectives of organizational
4. What role should strategists play in mar change?
5. Source a peer-reviewed research article that ines the issue of strategic change. What type of cha involved and what perspective is applied to underst this change? How does the article contribute to the

Practitioner reflections

Reflecting on the issues debated within the chapters, executives consider their own business experiences and share their views and insights.

Readings

Readings for each chapter are grouped at the end of each section. You'll also find links to more readings on the Online Resource Centre accompanying this book. The readings range from seminal articles to contemporary contributions, and explore the key debates which have informed the dynamic field of strategy.

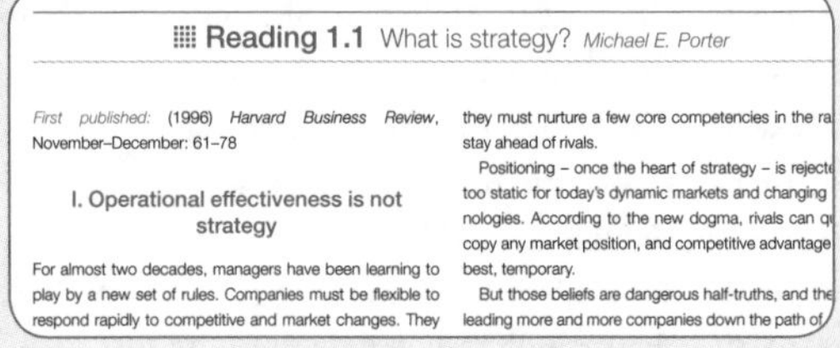
Reading 1.1 What is strategy? *Michael E. Porter*

First published: (1996) *Harvard Business Review*, November–December: 61–78

I. Operational effectiveness is not strategy

For almost two decades, managers have been learning to play by a new set of rules. Companies must be flexible to respond rapidly to competitive and market changes. They

they must nurture a few core competencies in the ra stay ahead of rivals.

Positioning – once the heart of strategy – is rejecte too static for today's dynamic markets and changing nologies. According to the new dogma, rivals can qu copy any market position, and competitive advantage best, temporary.

But those beliefs are dangerous half-truths, and the leading more and more companies down the path of

Long cases

Section 7 provides a bank of long cases to help you engage with, explore, and debate the many strategic tensions.

Case 4 The Ethical Trading Initiative Michael Blowfield, Teaching Fellow Organizational Behaviour, London Business School

About the Online Resource Centre

www.oxfordtextbooks.co.uk/orc/cunningham_harney/

Resources include:

- Links to online readings
- Strategy tools: offers further information on strategy tools, methodologies, and models.

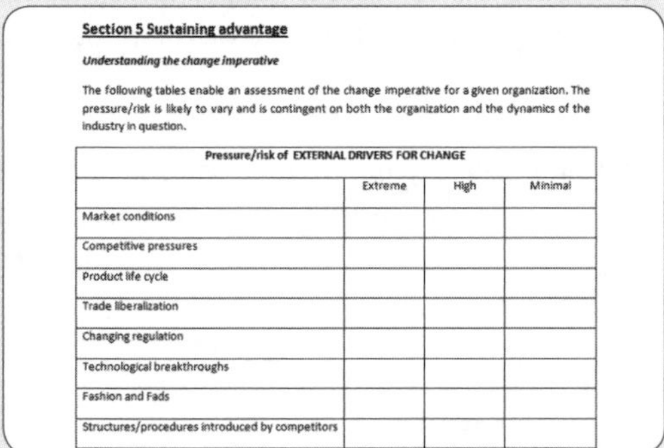

Section 5 Sustaining advantage

Understanding the change imperative

The following tables enable an assessment of the change imperative for a given organization. The pressure/risk is likely to vary and is contingent on both the organization and the dynamics of the industry in question.

Pressure/risk of EXTERNAL DRIVERS FOR CHANGE			
	Extreme	High	Minimal
Market conditions			
Competitive pressures			
Product life cycle			
Trade liberalization			
Changing regulation			
Technological breakthroughs			
Fashion and Fads			
Structures/procedures introduced by competitors			

For registered adopters of the book

- Customizable PowerPoint slides for each chapter
- Test bank: a fully customizable electronic assessment resource
- Teaching notes for mini cases and long cases
- Guidance for answering discussion questions
- Links to online readings

Acknowledgements

We owe a long-standing debt of gratitude to all the students of strategy and strategy practitioners that we have worked with over the years. The insights, experiences, and challenges they have imparted to us form the foundation of this text. We also wish to acknowledge the on-going support and encouragement of many colleagues and friends, especially those in the Management Discipline at the J.E. Cairnes School of Business and Economics, National University of Ireland Galway, at the Judge Business School, University of Cambridge, and at Dublin City University Business School.

In completing the text we would like to thank all those who contributed a case study or spotlight piece: Dr William Geoghegan, Professor Thomas Lawton, Dr Denis Harrington, Grace Walsh, Dr Conor O'Kane, Damien Organ, Dr Anne Torres, Ann Brehony, Michael Blowfield, Ranjani Jagannathan, Vivek Gupta, Sophie Cacciaguidi-Fahy, Dr Martin Fahy, Dr Kerrie Fleming, Dr Ciara Fitzgerald, and Mishko Hansen. From a practitioner's perspective, we appreciate the time and effort taken by Dr Richard Schroth, Dr Chris Coughlan, Padraig O'Ceidigh, and Mike Devane in contributing their insights. We also thank Professor Charles Snow for contributing the Foreword for this text. Finally, we would like to acknowledge all the reviewers who meticulously provided us with feedback on draft chapters.

The professional support that we have received from Oxford University Press has been outstanding. We would like to wholeheartedly thank Sacha Cooke, Nicki Sneath, Alex Lazarus-Priestley, Siân Jenkins, Fiona Goodall, and Tristan Jones. We are particularly indebted to Sarah Lodge, our senior development editor, for her invaluable support, advice, and patience in seeing this project through to completion. Finally, on a personal note James dedicates this book to his wonderful wife Sammi. Brian dedicates the book to his parents, Breda and Charlie, for their unwavering support and encouragement.

We hope that you enjoy reading and using this book. We hope it will provide a platform for a deeper understanding and appreciation of strategy and strategists. We welcome your feedback, comments, perspectives, and ideas.

James Cunningham (james.cunningham@nuigalway.ie) and
Brian Harney (brian.harney@dcu.ie)
March 2012

Section 1

Discovering strategy and strategists

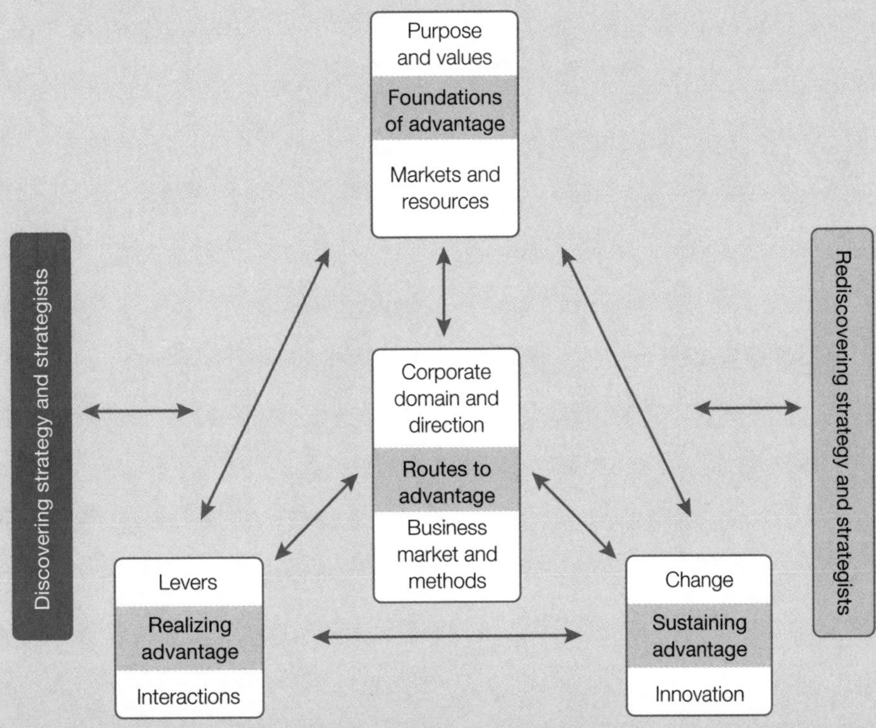

Discovering strategy

You ask, what is our aim? I can answer in one word. It is victory. Victory at all costs—victory in spite of all terrors—victory, however long and hard the road may be, for without victory there is no survival.

(Winston Churchill, House of Commons, London, 13 May 1940)

Introduction

Nearly a decade after Napster's peer-to-peer file-sharing software horrified the music **industry**, individual artists are attempting to use technology to their benefit. Notably, Radiohead launched their album, *In Rainbow*, through their website and made it available for download at prices nominated by fans. If adopted by other bands, this pay-what-you-want download strategy has the potential to dramatically alter the music industry's revenue model. Other artists have similarly embraced technology to try out new and innovative ways in which to engage consumers: the Arctic Monkeys are among a number of bands who have generated attention for their music through social networking sites and by exploiting online viral marketing, while in June 2011 the Kaiser Chiefs offered their fans a chance to make their own customized album, including the album's artwork, by choosing downloads from twenty tracks streamed on their website.

These developments are changing the way in which new, emerging musical talent is entering the music industry and developing its fan base. Even though technological **innovation** has long been recognized as having the potential to destroy the traditional model of how music is delivered and used, record companies have largely stood still rather than embrace these challenges. The void left by this inaction has been filled by innovative firms such as Apple, which, through its online iTunes Store, has cleverly linked software and hardware to create an integrated distribution system. Sony, Amazon, and even Wal-Mart have quickly followed suit, while new online **business models** such as music streaming service Spotify are constantly emerging. The result is a frantic search for strategies that will best capture the innate potential of the digital age and achieve a competitive advantage over rivals.

This is not an isolated trend. YouTube and Skype have similarly revolutionized the television and telecommunication industries. Not only are the lines between traditional industries blurring, so too are the lines between the creators and distributors of media content and the makers of hardware. In light of such developments, how do traditional players in music retailing, television, or telecommunications best compete? Confronted by this technological convergence, can they develop value propositions that are unique and sustainable? Can they ride the wave of technological change or will they be drowned by new, previously unrelated competitors encroaching on their competitive space? Such questions, which impinge on the very viability of a business, are questions of strategy. As the eminent strategy specialist Michael Porter (1991: 95) has noted, 'the reasons why firms succeed or fail is perhaps the central question in strategy'.

The task of formulating a successful strategy is made all the more difficult by the rapid pace of environmental change that confronts organizations, in what D'Aveni (1994) has termed the era of 'hypercompetition'. The competitive landscape is being dramatically altered by the interlinked forces of globalization, information technology, and scientific developments, coupled with the shifting balance of global power from the West to the East (March, 2007). At the same time, firms are faced with increasingly sophisticated consumers and pressure to produce 'greener' strategies. Changes to the environment in which strategy is played out are therefore dynamic and profound. Those who stand still risk not only losing out, but also falling further behind. In major strategic moves away from their origins, IBM no longer makes PCs, Tesco aims to sell more non-retail than retail products, and football clubs such as Manchester United obtain a large proportion of their revenue from the provision of hospitality and financial services. For these and many other organizations, success is critical—or, as the opening quotation from Churchill puts it, the focus must be on victory in order to ensure survival.

Strategy provides the means to understand the implications of such changes in terms of how organizations can compete; while a carefully considered strategy cannot guarantee organizational success, it can provide a safeguard against organizational failure (Thomas and Pruett, 1993). In this chapter, we will attempt, first, to put some parameters around what we mean by 'strategy'. Too easily, strategy can become a catchword for everything and thereby lose meaning. We begin the chapter by exploring the purpose of strategy; in doing so, we examine strategy in its historical and contemporary contexts. Here, we attempt to find a broad consensus of what strategy is—and, by implication, what it is not. We build upon this by highlighting key strategic challenges that confront each and every organization—the orientation challenge, the **trade-off** challenge, the relevance challenge, and the continuous-change challenge—before outlining the overall structure of the book. We conclude with a spotlight feature on **evidence-based management** and its implications for strategy practice. Overall, the discussion in this chapter helps to illustrate that the meaning of the term 'strategy' is far from simple, and is hotly contested. This is a critical point that underpins how we will approach the concept of strategy and the process of strategic management. After all, if strategy were anything other than complex, **strategists** would simply have to follow a step-by-step process—a cookbook approach—and, inevitably, would not be paid half as much as they are (Whittington, 1993).

The purpose of strategy

There is very little agreement about what strategy actually is (Markides, 2004). Even one of the founding fathers of strategy notes that 'strategy is an elusive and somewhat abstract concept' (Ansoff, 1987: 104). Yet if we are asked to identify organizations with successful strategies, we will usually not have much difficulty. Lists will typically include 'celebrity' organizations that we hear about regularly or encounter in our daily lives, such as Nike, Starbucks, Apple, Amazon, Wal-Mart, Singapore Airlines, and Johnson and Johnson. Yet while it is not too difficult to identify a successful organization, it is much more difficult to unpack the key building blocks of its success. We must therefore distinguish simple identification of successful strategies from in-depth explanation and understanding of success. This becomes critical when we remember that success is the exception rather than the rule. The task for the student of strategy is therefore to understand what strategists have to do in order to create and sustain the conditions for 'winning' in the game of business. In short, strategy is about developing an understanding of what makes for a successful organization: 'at a minimum, strategy is what makes a firm unique, a winner, or a survivor' (Thomas and Pruett, 1993: 4).

In strategy, winning centres on creating what is termed a **sustainable competitive advantage**. This is a unique advantage that is still obtained despite competitors' constant attempts at replication. It is typically a proven value-based proposition positively received by end users, and delivered by the integration of organizational components in a way that competitors find hard to imitate; they may find it hard even to identify the basis of success (Barney, 1991). For example, business folklore has it that management at Toyota were happy to open their doors to interested parties who wished to observe the lean production systems at their manufacturing plants. It would seem that Toyota was well aware that while others could copy techniques such as just-in-time production and team working, they would never be able to replicate the culture embedded within Toyota—the culture that made the operation of these techniques so successful in delivering cost savings and quality enhancements. Indeed, although leading proponents of Toyota's techniques argued that 'the conversion to lean production will have a profound effect on human society—it will truly change the world' (Womack *et al.*, 1990: 7–8), the reality is that this did not come to pass. Yet strategists are continuously trying to deliver advantage by applying new techniques and delivering value in different ways. That this quest for competitive advantage takes place under constant media, **stakeholder**, and stock market scrutiny makes the task all the more arduous. By the same token, these factors make the individual and organizational rewards for achieving success all the more significant.

With this understanding of the ultimate purpose of strategy and the quest for competitive advantage, we can begin to appreciate why strategy is always spoken of with some reverence. Yet in the attempt to emphasize its importance and impress organizational stakeholders, there is a risk that strategy is latched on to everything and so becomes meaningless. Whereas strategy is supposed to emphasize difference and uniqueness, all too often the language of strategy can foster the impression of convergence and similarity—the exact opposite of its original purpose. This is ably illustrated in the following boxed feature.

Indistinctive strategy talk

Understanding and utilizing the correct language can be important in communicating strategy to organizational stakeholders. Yet if taken too far and communicated in a segmented manner rather than as a coherent line of thinking, strategy talk will not serve to differentiate. For example, we may ask the typical chairman: what is your company's strategy?

To be competitive and profitable. And your brands? Leading. And your services? Top quality. Your market share? Growing or highest. Your profits will . . . ? Increase. Your strategy is also to have operations that are highly efficient and cost-competitive? Correct. Your strategic approach to achieve this? Further rationalization; constant improvement.

Your people are . . . ? Our greatest assets. Why? Because they are highly motivated, skilled, and enthusiastic. What does your strategy say about sales? Grow them. About investors? Value them. About management? Reward them. About competitors? Compete with them, effectively, and when we're feeling aggressive, beat them. The business environment? It poses challenges and opportunities, and a few threats.

What choices do you face? Difficult ones. How does the future look? Bright. How will it all happen? If we all pull together.

Communicated in this manner, intentions quickly become meaningless. Are you likely to remember this hypothetical chairman and his organization's strategy? We think not.

Source: O'Connor (1998)

Strategy in its historical context: the origins and evolution of strategy

At the heart of strategy is the aim of defeating and gaining victory over competitors or enemies. Given this, it is probably unsurprising that the concept of strategy has its origins in military warfare. The word derives from the Greek term *strategos*, denoting a commander elected by the citizens of Athens to assume leadership in time of war (Cummings, 2002). The concept formed a central element in the military treatise *The Art of War* by Chinese General Sun Tzu, which appeared around 500 BC. At this time, war was spreading from small family feuds to state battles. Consequently, there was a requirement to deal with this increasing complexity and facilitate the deployment of large numbers of **resources**. In *The Art of War*, Sun Tzu offered a detailed treatment of military planning and deliberation, stressing the importance of clarity of conception and depth of design. The incorporation of strategy into the business lexicon some 2,450 years later reflected similar concerns. By the 1950s in the USA, corporations were becoming more diverse, geographically as well as in terms of their activities. Complex operations, large staff numbers, and the separation of ownership and control mandated some form of overarching thinking. Managerial specialisms were no longer deemed appropriate to coordinate and guide the activities of organizations effectively (Hafsi and Thomas, 2005). What was required necessitated a move beyond the simple integration of functional areas; consideration had to be given to the markets in which the firm would compete and, equally critically, *how* it would compete (Rumelt *et al.*, 1991). Academics at Harvard Business School, including Kenneth Andrews (1971), introduced the notion of 'business policy' to address these concerns. In keeping with Sun Tzu's ideas, business policy retained the distinct separation of the conception of strategy by the chief executive officer (CEO)—the commander—from the execution of strategy by the shop floor—the troops on the battlefield. Mirroring these developments, consultancy firms were developing tools that 'fuelled the impression that strategy was a rigorous scientific endeavour' (Hambrick and Chen, 2008: 42).

The term **corporate strategy** was introduced by Igor Ansoff as the title of his text in 1965. The subtitle, 'An analytical approach to business policy for growth and expansion' is telling, as it reflects the emphasis on developing new administrative structures to accommodate growth that was at the centre of Chandler's (1962) earlier research on the emergence of the multi-divisional firm. Chandler's research at US firms DuPont, General Motors, Standard Oil, and Sears illustrated the development of large enterprises and, in particular, how strategic change leads to structural change. This was captured in the dictum 'Structure follows strategy' (Hoskisson *et al.*, 1999). In these early approaches, the implementation of strategy was largely seen to be an administrative task and so was accorded limited importance. Once soundly conceptualized, the transfer of plans into practice was deemed unproblematic. For Ansoff, corporate strategy was a 'common thread' aligning the firm with opportunities and threats posed by its environment. Ansoff made the distinction between objectives as the ends that the firm was seeking to obtain and strategy as 'the means to these ends' (Ansoff, 1987: 104). This definition of strategy as means to an end is probably its most simplistic and easily communicated meaning—although it does beg the question of what or whose ends. Along with a relative neglect of implementation, the focus of this early work was very much on the external environment: 'strategic decisions are primarily concerned with external, rather than internal, problems of the firm and specifically with the selection of the product-mix which the firm will produce and the markets to which it will sell' (ibid: 24).

Over time, it was acknowledged that strategic planning was much too important to be left to chance and that formal analytical processes for the development of strategy were critical to organizational success. The result was a proliferation of dedicated strategic planning departments within organizations, as strategic planning evolved from a budgetary activity to a dedicated profession. Definitions of strategy also evolved, with a landmark text by Hofer and Schendel (1978) bringing previous work together and providing a definition of strategy as 'the fundamental pattern of present and planned resource deployments and environment interactions that indicates how the organization will achieve its objectives' (ibid: 25). Critical here was the notion of resource deployments, which Chandler had originally stressed, but which had been given insufficient attention in the subsequent definitions provided by Ansoff and Andrews. By drawing attention to resource endowments, Hofer and Schendel also foresaw the **resource-based view** of the firm that would become dominant in the 1990s:

> [W]e have included resource deployments (distinctive competencies) as a strategy component because it is clear that no actions or goal achievements can take place unless some basic skills are created and resources obtained and deployed in ways that cannot be duplicated easily by others ... the fact is that scope can be limited by weak resources or poor positioning of resources.
>
> (Hofer and Schendel, 1978: 25)

However, before strategy scholars came explicitly to recognize and embrace the importance of internal organizational resources, the pendulum was to swing in the opposite direction. During the 1980s, the work of Harvard academic Michael Porter moved to centre stage (Hoskisson *et al.*,

1999). Porter's work was grounded in industrial organization (IO) economics, and had its external focus on industry structure and competitive positioning. With its solid grounding in economics, Porter's work, especially his book *Competitive Strategy* (1980), provided the much-needed theoretical underpinning with which to confirm strategy as a truly academic discipline. Strategy's time had arrived and the language of competitive analysis, competitive advantage, and competitive strategies became commonplace in both the classroom and the boardroom. Strategic planning became strategic positioning as Porter put forward the idea of three generic strategies of cost leadership, differentiation, and focus—closely echoing Miles *et al.*'s (1978) defender, prospector, and analyser strategies—as the key strategic routes available to organizations.

During this period, strategy, implicitly at least, remained true to its military origins, focusing on competitive analysis and competitive manoeuvring. The centre of attention was the strategist as the key strategy commander. Table 1.1 captures the key dimensions of the historical view of strategy. Here, strategy is very much focused on what organizations should do; it assumes a relatively static, evolutionary, and predictable organizational environment in which organizations should strive to best position themselves. Consequently, and following Ansoff's notion of 'common thread', it holds that alignment between the organization and its environment should be one of best fit—that is, matching existing resources to existing market opportunities. Overall, this approach is grounded in the rigour of economics with its assumptions of profit maximization and rational, sequential analysis.

Yet cracks in this overall mode of thinking soon began to appear. Long-term planning floundered in the face of sudden changes in the environment, such as the oil-price shocks of the 1970s, while planning departments were increasingly seen as isolated units that might not be able to adequately grasp competitive realities. Similarly, during the 1980s, Porter's positioning perspective was increasingly judged to be static and limited in its ability to cope with changing and undefined industry boundaries. In order to reflect the evolution from a static, industrial-based era to a more dynamic, knowledge-based era, perhaps a new conception of strategy was required. Change, social dynamics, and strategy implementation needed to be adequately accommodated. The (re)discovery of the importance of resources, as in Hofer and Schendel's early definition and the even earlier writings of Edith Penrose (1959) and Selznick (1957), was the catalyst for such an approach.

Table 1.1 Discovering strategy in context

	Strategy in historical context (historical view of strategy)	Strategy in present context (contemporary view of strategy)
Era	Industrial	Knowledge-based
Purpose	Prescriptive: what organizations should do	Descriptive: what organizations actually do
Environment	Static; evolutionary; predictable	Dynamic; revolutionary; unpredictable
Strategy as:	strategic planning	strategic management
Strategy–environment alignment	Best fit	Unique fit
Key theories	Economics	Hypercompetition
	Positioning	Resource-based and knowledge-based view
	Game theory	Organizational learning
		Complexity theory
Key tools	BCG portfolio matrix	Value chain
	Five Forces	Core competencies
	Strategic group maps	Dynamic capabilities
	SWOT	Architecture building
Strategists	Top management commanders	Multiple levels, including third parties, e.g. consultants

Strategy in its present context: progression of strategy and strategic management

In an attempt to deal with a more complex and changing environment, strategy had to be founded on a more stable basis than positioning the firm in its existing environment. To focus merely on positioning was to make the inappropriate assumption that the future would be just like the past. Yet in the light of innovative and nimbler competitors—most famously, Japanese firms entering the US market in the 1980s—industry standards were increasingly being challenged. The fusing of technological developments, globalization, and increasing customization meant that competition was increasingly seen to be about knowledge, learning, and capabilities rather than the economies of scale and scope that had defined the industrial era. The result was that strategy literature began to consider that the basis for competitive advantage might reside within the firm (Kiechel, 2010; Prahalad and Hamel, 1990; see Figure 1.1 for a strategy timeline). Early mainstream recognition of this came from Peters and Waterman's hugely successful *In Search of Excellence: Lessons from America's Best-run Companies* (1982), which stressed the importance of human capital and culture in arguing that 'the crucial problems in strategy are most often those of execution and continuous adaptation; getting it done and staying flexible' (ibid: 4).

The emergence of the importance of an internal focus was crystallized in an article by Wernerfleft (1984), which redirected attention towards the writings of Edith Penrose (1959). Penrose had defined the firm as a 'bundle of productive resources'. Jay Barney (1991), among others, made this work more managerially relevant by emphasizing the conditions under which resources could yield competitive advantage; this could be, for example, when they were valuable, rare, and difficult to imitate. This resource-based view of strategy turned the positioning view on its head. From the resource-based perspective, what really matters is the internal resource endowments of a firm and, critically, how they are deployed. In the dynamic and unpredictable environment of the 1990s, building a foundational base of capabilities that fostered innovation, flexibility, adaptability, and organization learning was a much more secure basis on which to gain advantage. Classic examples included the logistic capabilities of FedEx, the core competencies of miniaturization at Sony, technological prowess at Intel, or optics at Canon. Properly nurtured, such competencies could form the foundation for new product development and capture latent demand (Hamel and Prahalad, 1990; Teece, 2007). Consequently, the focus of strategy altered from the notion of best fit with an existing environment—the mainstay of Porter's positioning view—to the notion that organizations could achieve unique fit by creating their own environment or by doing things in a completely different way. In support of this view, commentators pointed to revolutionary organizations such as Dell, Swatch, The Body Shop, or easyJet, which had reconfigured their value chains or dramatically altered the way in which value was delivered (Hamel, 1996).

Figure 1.1 Strategy timeline

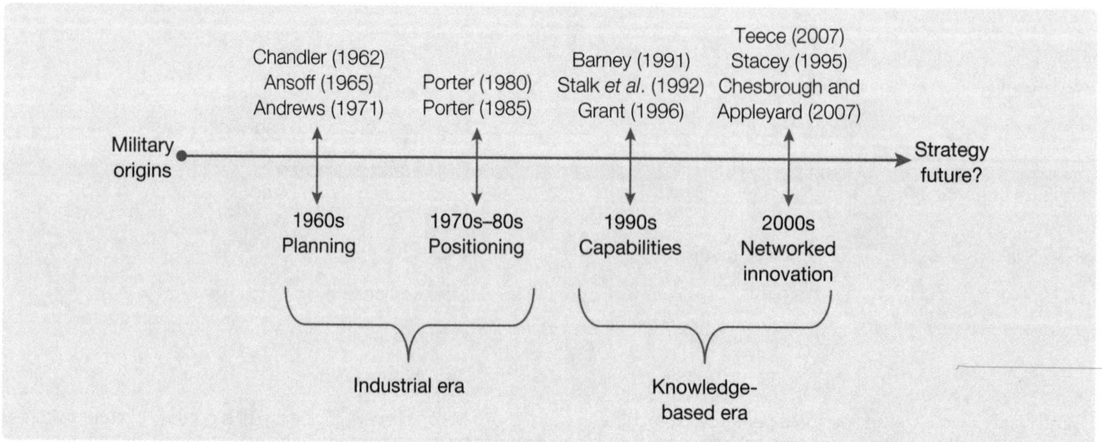

In the so-called knowledge-based era, it became harder to prescribe what organizations should do to be successful. Instead, strategy progressed to more descriptive accounts of what successful organizations actually did and to an understanding of why they were successful. Likewise, the concept of strategy had evolved into 'strategic management'. This bridged **formulation** and implementation, and introduced the human dimension, which had been noticeably absent in the rationality of the planning-based and positioning-based perspectives. Strategic planning was not about strategy; it was about programming strategy (Minztberg, 1994). In practice, the trajectory of strategy development is fluid, iterative, and shaped by chance and intuition as much as by clipboards and formal meetings. The title of Mintzberg's contribution in the mid-1990s—*The Rise and Fall of Strategic Planning*—aptly captures the extent of the shift in thinking. Long-term, detailed planning was judged to be too rigid, inhibiting the flexibility deemed necessary for competitive success. The foreword to a revised edition of Igor Ansoff's classic text, *Corporate Strategy*, some decades after its original publication, captures much of the criticism:

> If there is a weakness in the book [*Corporate Strategy*], it is the emphasis on methodology and the lack of emphasis on the fact that the way in which the strategy is developed is, in itself, a means of promoting the best opportunity by which the strategy itself will be followed. It is perhaps as well for all of us who have made our lives in business that there is still room for flair, intuition, perception, foresight and luck. Without these no business will succeed and without these the development of strategies could be safely left to Professor Ansoff's excellent book.
>
> (Sir John Harvey Jones' Foreword, in Ansoff, 1987: 12)

At the same time, the image of the aloof commander ploughing through data and contemplating move and countermove in isolation was judged outdated. Strategic management, by contrast, was seen to be very much about living the battle, blending the art and science aspects of strategy. Strategy was not the exclusive reserve of the CEO or top management team, but instead was informed in its development and implementation by a multitude of players, some of whom were external to the organization. Nuances of temperament, uncertainty, and the unexpected outcomes that generally characterize dealing with people came to the fore. After all, strategy is never simply a stand-alone plan; it is always enacted in real-life events through people. While strategic planning in its classic sense was about a fixed destination and calculating the best means to get there, strategic management involved engaging people on a journey; the best route was never certain, learning and adaptability were key, and even the destination itself was subject to change (Mintzberg, 1994). Equally critical, allowing multiple voices to inform strategy facilitated rapid diffusion of trends and ideas. With knowledge said to be a critical competitive weapon (Grant, 1996), the days of the isolated strategic planning departments became ancient history; real-time insights and understanding were the air that allowed strategy to breathe most productively.

Yet, at this juncture, perhaps strategists could once again have learnt from military warfare. The more descriptive accounts of the knowledge-based era matched those that had been put forth by the Prussian general Carl von Clausewitz, in his treatise *On War*, published in 1832. According to von Clausewitz, 'real' war was a dynamic process of constant interactions. In this context, no prescription could ever be complete: war was dictated by chaos and chance, and knowledge was cultivated through experience. Likewise, von Clausewitz recognized how the impact of human factors of fear, fatigue, and confusion on men in battle rendered even the simplest action difficult and unpredictable. He stressed the uniqueness of situations as opposed to attempting to prescribe a best type of fit. From this perspective, success stemmed from developing capabilities in exploration, being adept and flexible, and following instinct (von Ghyczy *et al.*, 2001). Von Clausewitz's ideas were most famously invoked by Jack Welch of General Electric:

> Von Clausewitz summed up what it had all been about in his classic, *On War*. Men could not reduce strategy to a formula. Detailed planning necessarily failed, due to the inevitable frictions

> encountered: chance events, imperfections in execution, and the independent will of the opposition. Instead, the human elements were paramount: leadership, morale, and the almost instinctive savvy of the best generals.
>
> (Welch, 2001: 448)

While Stalk *et al.* (1992) speak of leveraging capabilities in a 'war of movement' (see Table 1.2), the military metaphor does not sit easily with the most recent manifestation of the knowledge-based era, which highlights the value of collaborative networks. Here, the logic of competitive battle is misplaced, if not destructive, as it provides strategy with a language of rivalry, division, and a win–lose mentality (Patel, 2005). Instead, trends suggest that firms are engaging in a more dynamic set of win–win relations driven by concepts such as open innovation, wikinomics, intellectual commons, and peer production (Chesbrough and Appleyard, 2007: 60). In this space, the distinction between producer and consumer is not simply becoming more blurred; it is vanishing altogether. Enabled by technological developments and mandated by the rapid pace of change, organizations are working increasingly with their customers and competitors, as cooperation is seen as one of the key ways in which to keep up with the game (McIntyre and Subramaniam, 2009; Michel *et al.*, 2008: 49). Indeed, the very ability to innovate comes from a skill that is underused in most companies and underdeveloped in theory: collaboration (Miles *et al.*, 2000).

Similarly, the military legacy of an organization having control and being able to predict future occurrences is questioned by the basic premises of chaos theory, with its emphasis on non-linear progression and an emergent order. Chaos theory holds that organizations are systems that co-evolve far from equilibrium in a self-organizing manner, towards unpredictable long-term outcomes. The strategist is urged simply to 'let go' and be attentive to emergent patterns (Beinhocker, 1997). We discuss this further in Chapter 9 on organizational change. From a network perspective, strategy is about dynamic manoeuvring—'moves and counter-moves'—rather than 'static positioning, such as resources, routines, capabilities, generic strategy, industry structure, **strategic groups**, etc.' (D'Aveni *et al.*, 2010: 1371). By way of summary, Table 1.2 presents sample quotations from key contributions reflecting the varying origins and eras that have characterized the evolution of thinking on strategy.

Despite the apparent evolution of strategy as we have highlighted it, a recent review claimed that strategy was 'groping out of adolescence for direction, role, respect and contribution' (McKiernan and Carter, 2004: 3), while from another perspective it is in 'crisis' (Volberda, 2004). One fruitful addition to the debate is no doubt a clearer idea and accommodation of who strategists (whether depicted as forecasters, planners, analysts, composers, conductors, or innovators) actually are and what are the activities that they conduct in practice. This is a key feature of an emerging **strategy-as-practice** perspective (Jarzabkowski and Wilson, 2006), which we examine in Chapter 2. For our present purposes, we will try to make sense of diversity by reviewing the common challenges that characterize the strategic management process.

The challenges of strategic management

Strategic management is the process by which organizations develop a long-term orientation, and deploy and animate resources to facilitate the realization of this, with the overall purpose of realizing value through changing circumstances. This definition is similar to the consensual definition held by strategy scholars: 'the field of strategic management deals with the major intended and emergent initiatives taken by general managers on behalf of owners, involving utilization of resources, to enhance the performance of firms in their external environments' (Nag *et al.*, 2007: 944). Strategic management therefore consists of formulating strategies and designing a firm's capability, as well as managing the implementation of strategies and capabilities (Ansoff, 1987:

Table 1.2 Discovering strategy: the theory

Military origins of strategy

... all men can see the tactics whereby I conquer, but what none can see is the strategy out of which victory is evolved.

(Sun Tzu, *The Art of War*, 500 BC)

... theory should guide the future commander in his process of self-education, but it should not accompany him onto the battlefield.

(Von Clausewitz, 1832)

Industrial era

Planning

[Strategy is] the determination of basic long term goals and objectives of an enterprise, and the adoption of courses of action and allocation of resources necessary for carrying out those goals.

(Chandler, 1962: 13)

Positioning

Competitive strategy is about being different. It means deliberately choosing a different set of activities to deliver a unique mix of value ...

(Porter, 1996: 64)

Knowledge-based era

Capabilities

When the economy was relatively static, strategy could afford to be static ... competition was a 'war of position' in which companies occupied competitive space like squares on a chessboard. In this dynamic business environment competition is now 'a war of movement' ... a process more akin to an interactive video game than to chess. In such an environment the essence of strategy is not the structure of a company's products and markets but the dynamics of its behaviour.

(Stalk *et al.*, 1992: 62)

Networked Innovation

If we are to make strategic sense of innovation communities, ecosystems, networks, and their implications for competitive advantage, we need a new approach to strategy—what we call 'open strategy'. Effective open strategy balances value capture and value creation ... Items that were of central importance in earlier strategy treatments, such as ownership, entry barriers, switching costs, and intra-industry rivalry are of secondary importance.

(Chesbrough and Appleyard, 2007: 58–62)

265). Since Andrew's (1971) distinction, strategic management issues are held to operate at two major levels:

- at the corporate level, the organization will consider the key *domain question* 'What business should we be in?' (see Chapter 7);
- at the business level, the organization will ask *the market-orientated question* 'How will we compete in this business?' (often termed 'competitive strategy'; see Chapter 8).

The value of strategic management is that it encourages a holistic perspective of the business and its environment, and how key elements fit together (Wilson, 1998). The most successful organizations are those with a coherency and consistency within and between their objectives and activities. Strategy is a tight, internally coherent statement of what a company is and where it wants to be (Kiechel, 2010: 1).

Yet if the key elements of strategic management can be highlighted so easily, the actual process is remarkably complex—and even comparatively similar organizations delivering similar types of product can turn out to be remarkably different in terms of their scope, activities, and ultimate success. Virgin, which operates in businesses as diverse as retail, travel, financial services, entertainment, and hospitality, obviously answers the domain question 'What business should we be in?' in a dramatically different fashion from organizations such as Hilton Worldwide, which operates exclusively in one domain: namely, hospitality. Contrast the stances of Ryanair and easyJet. With their no-frills services, both have answered the market-based question 'How will we compete in this business?' in a similar fashion. However, while Ryanair answers the domain question by focusing largely on the airline industry (admittedly while using clever **alliances** to provide insurance and financial services options as well), easyJet has moved into completely different businesses such as easyCinema, easyCruise, and easyCafe. Underpinning these divergent routes is the notion that strategy constitutes *a firm's theory* of how to gain competitive advantage (Barney and Hesterly, 2006). This captures the idea that a firm's strategy is something that is based on the unique perspective held by each individual firm.

A firm's strategic posture is underpinned and informed by a series of *firm-unique* assumptions about its values and purpose, and about the nature of its external and internal environment. These in turn dictate decisions about what to do and what not to do, as well as define what an organization considers meaningful results (Drucker, 1994). This idea also helps us to understand why simply having a strategy does not automatically yield corporate success: the firm's idea of how best to deliver value must match and keep up with what the market requires and consumers demand. Not all strategies lead to competitive advantage: 'strategy is a firm's best bet about how the competition is going to evolve' (Barney and Hesterly, 2006: 5). As noted by Mintzberg, 'strategy *is* a theory—a cognitive structure and filter to simplify and explain the world, and thereby to facilitate action' (Mintzberg, 1987: 29). The task of strategic analysis is therefore not only to unpack the routes to advantage—*what* corporate and business strategies are being pursued by the firm (Chapters 7 and 8)—but also the foundations of advantage—that is, the assumptions about values, purpose, markets, and resources that underpin *why* these are being pursued (Chapters 5 and 6). This is represented in Figure 1.2, which also highlights the key elements of the strategic management process and links them to the chapters in this text. At the centre is the idea that strategy constitutes a firm's theory about how best to compete.

The differences between organizations stem not only from their underlying assumptions and values, but also from *how* they execute their strategy. Strategy implementation is not a mechanical process, and while a firm's theory of how to compete may be superior to those of its competitors, unless it can realize this advantage through the implementation of its strategy, competitive advantage will remain a dream in the heads of its executives. 'Too much attention to getting the strategy right can divert attention away from building the capability to operate effectively' (Pfeffer and Sutton, 2006: 146); only through sound execution can advantage be realized. This, as we have noted, was something that early writing on strategy failed to grasp. Nowadays, the focus is almost reversed, with some commentators arguing that sound execution of even a poor strategy will yield a greater advantage than weak execution of a better one. Consequently the book focuses on the critical tasks of both realizing (Chapters 9 and 10) and sustaining advantage (Chapters 11 and 12).

The final section of this book, on rediscovering strategy and strategists (Chapters 13 and 14), will question how key ideas may differ in various contexts. We have spoken about delivering value and, implicitly at least, assumed that this is for the corporate purpose of maximizing profits or returns to shareholders. But what about strategy in the public sector, where value is hard to measure and strategy creation is fraught with political wrangling? What about smaller organizations, which may lack time and resources for strategic management? What about not-for-profit firms, for which a specific mission must take precedent? Finally, the last chapter of this book takes a critical look at the key agents of the strategy process, including consultants and academics, as well as the language, or **discourse**, of strategy, critically questioning whose interests strategy may serve.

Figure 1.2 illustrates how realizing and sustaining an advantage is a very complex and demanding process. Expanding upon our earlier definition of strategic management helps to capture the nature of the challenges that organizations confront as they attempt to devise and realize their own overall theories of how best to compete. Specifically, strategic management is a process by which organizations develop a long-term orientation (*orientation challenge*), deploy and animate

Figure 1.2 Overview of strategy and strategists

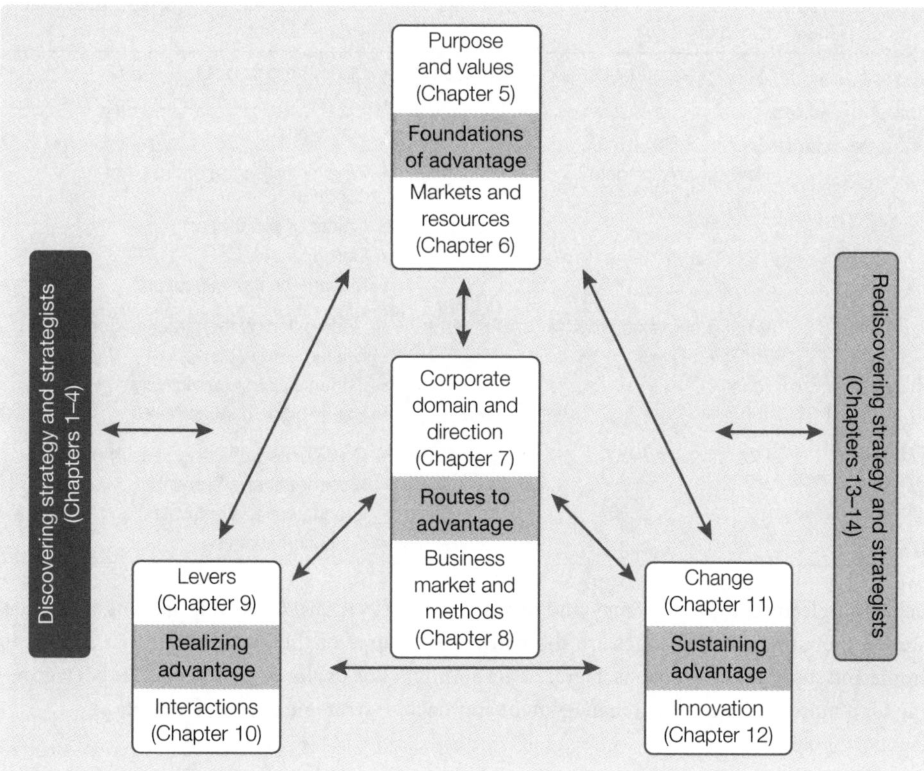

resources to facilitate the realization of this (*trade-off challenge*), with the overall purpose of realizing value (*relevance challenge*) through changing circumstances (*continuous-change challenge*). Addressing these challenges should enable an organization to have a competitive advantage over rivals in a competitive market arena. In Table 1.3, we outline what we see as the key questions and dimensions of these four strategic management challenges. Exploring strategy as a process of confronting key challenges is particularly appropriate, as articulated by Rumelt (2009: 35):

> By strategy, I mean a cohesive response to a challenge. A real strategy is neither a document nor a forecast but rather an overall approach based on a diagnosis of a challenge. The most important element of a strategy is a coherent viewpoint about the forces at work, not a plan.

In making strategic decisions, deciding what not to do is as important as deciding what to do. As the Roman poet Virgil observed, 'we are not all capable of everything'. Of course, the distinction between the challenges that we have identified is one of conceptual elegance. For the most part, questions that are truly strategic will spread across a range of challenges. Take, as an example, an issue of geographical scope, such as whether to move from being a national organization to one that has a more international focus. This might involve consideration of: *orientation*—who the organization is; consideration of what *trade-offs* are involved; whether the organization has the necessary capabilities; *relevance*—how the organization's customer appeal will transfer to a different context; and assessment of the overall change that such a move might imply in terms of execution, the likelihood of stability in customer demand, and so on. This helps us to distinguish between strategic questions, which will directly impact the long-term viability of the organization, and operational, short-term, day-to-day issues. While there is no clear dividing line, short-term decisions are those that can be made by individuals and do not generally require 'clearance' (Penrose, 1959), while strategic issues have fundamental implications, opening up or closing off opportunities for months and years to come (Courtney, 2008: 6). In the absence of strategy, the motivations and logistics of narrow functional areas would guide

Table 1.3 Strategic management challenges and key dimensions

Strategic management challenge	Key question	Key dimensions
Orientation challenge	Who we are and where do we compete?	• Clear strategic position • Coherency in communication and actions • Leadership
Trade-off challenge	How do we compete?	• What activities to conduct, not to conduct • Nature of capabilities • Consistency • Management of execution
Relevance challenge	What is our value proposition? And for whom?	• Understanding the target customer • Customer offering/appeal • Communication of message • Stakeholder management
Continuous change challenge	How do we adapt?	• Continuously challenge assumptions • Monitor the environment • Experiment and innovate • Execution activities

behaviour, leading to incoherency and chaos (Porter, 1991: 96). Critical in gaining an understanding of strategic challenges are the nature and source of the information that is used to frame and support key decisions. Here, as the Spotlight box explores, preference has been growing for a more evidence-based management approach to **strategic decision making**.

Spotlight Evidence-based management: a cure-all for strategy practice?

> If doctors practised medicine the way many companies practise management, there would be far more sick and dead patients, and many more doctors would be in jail.
>
> (Pfeffer and Sutton, 2006: 5)

Apparently all is not well with the practice of strategy. Organizations are accused of simply trudging after one another, blinded by the seduction of the 'next big thing'. Strategists scramble to consume the 'strategy concept of the day', in order to be seen to be ahead of the game. For example, strategists have happily digested and regurgitated concepts such as 'offshoring' and its sidekicks, 'nearshoring' and 'farshoring', spreading these ideas freely across their operations. Yet the result of uncritically adopting 'next practice' is convergence: instead of becoming different, companies become more and more alike (Porter, 1996—Reading 1.1). Consequently, strategists are often depicted as all marching to the same beat. According to Pfeffer and Sutton (2006: 22), their guiding tune is composed of at least one of three 'bum notes' or flawed assumptions: simply benchmarking what others have done; assuming that the future will be like the past; and following 'deeply held yet unexamined ideologies'.

Evidence-based management

Such is the concern about strategy's ill health that some have turned to the idea of evidence-based management in hope of a cure. Evidence-based management stresses the importance of rigorous and systematic assessment of the best available scientific evidence in the process of decision making. This approach has its roots in clinical medicine (particularly appropriate, therefore, to cure the ills of current managerial practice). In *Hard Facts, Dangerous Half Truths and Total Nonsense: Profiting from Evidence-based Management*, Pfeffer and Sutton (2006) argue that strategy should not be shaped by imitation, fear, and deeply held assumptions; instead, strategists should 'face hard facts and act on the best evidence', thereby promoting healthy scepticism about what is currently being flaunted as 'best managerial practice'.

For Pfeffer and Sutton, evidence-based management involves the dual criteria of 'putting aside belief and conventional wisdom' and 'committing to gather facts and information to make more informed decisions'. It follows that a number of questions should be asked before introducing a new business idea: for example, its underlying assumptions, whether these assumptions intuitively make sense and/or can be tested, and whether alternative solutions exist (ibid: 22). Overall, the evidence-based management movement suggests that strategy practitioners should heed the advice of Sherlock Holmes, who highlighted the importance of using hard data to inform theories, the alternative being that 'insensibly one begins to twist facts to suit theories, instead of theories to suit facts' (Conan Doyle, 1891: 163). The evidence-based management approach certainly seems attractive and is intuitively appealing—so why are there not more organizations practising it? Is it realistic to expect that we can make strategy practice into a science of cold calculation and detailed factual analysis?

Strategy: all science and no art?

Others hold that strategy does not fit easily into the straitjacket of scientific analysis. We cannot assume that diagnosis is as straightforward as it is in medical practice. How does an organization decide what is 'the *best* evidence available'? Henry Mintzberg (1994) refers to the 'soft underbelly of hard data', noting that 'much information important for strategy never becomes hard fact. The expression on a customer's face, the mood in the factory, the tone of voice of a government official—all of this can be important information' (ibid: 258). In addition, organizations are inherently political, and a multitude of perspectives bear on every decision that is made, while information is rarely available freely and consistent in the first place. Instead of behaving like clinical doctors, perhaps strategists are more like detectives, acting on clues and hunches, trying to understand the accounts of multiple witnesses and attempting to piece a story together based on limited information. At the same time, in terms of practicalities, it may prove difficult to combine rigorous and time-consuming analysis with the adaptability necessary for competitive success.

Strategy may not be all about number-crunching, detailed consideration of facts, and evaluation of alternatives. The risk in such an approach is that the strategist becomes a hermit, isolated, with time to reflect on the extensive data that surrounds him or her. In reality, strategy may require something quite different. Perhaps answers come from action rather than isolated thinking. Evidence-based management leaves little room for intuition, risk-taking, visionary leadership, and learning by experience. Yet increasingly these are the very factors deemed vital for competitive success. Indeed, the symbolic actions of leaders in animating and engendering commitment to a vision or broad path of strategic action (think of individuals such as Mother Teresa or Richard Branson) may be equally as, if not more, important as detailed orientation. Evidence-based management does not leave scope for the art of creating a vision, the power of raw emotion and commitment, and the significance of action and experimentation. Karl Weick's account of an incident that happened during military manoeuvres in Switzerland makes the point nicely:

> The young lieutenant of a small Hungarian detachment in the Alps sent a reconnaissance unit out into the icy wilderness. It began to snow immediately, snowed for two days, and the unit did not return. The lieutenant suffered, fearing that he had dispatched his own people to death. But the third day the unit came back. Where had they been? How had they made their way? Yes, they said, we considered ourselves lost and waited for the end. And then one of us found a map in his pocket. That calmed us down. We pitched camp, lasted out the snowstorm, and then with the map we discovered our bearings. And here we are. The lieutenant borrowed this remarkable map and had a good look at it. He discovered to his astonishment that it was not a map of the Alps but of the Pyrenees.
>
> (Weick, 2001: 345–346)

One wonders if the troops would have made it down from the mountain safely if they had had to rely on the techniques of evidence-based management? In this case, it would appear that the sense of security provided by even false 'evidence' (the map) was enough to get the unit up and moving. Here, acting was just as important as a detailed plan or blueprint, while animation stemmed from a common objective. The standard moral often drawn from this story is 'When you are lost, any map will do!' (Mintzberg *et al.*, 1998: 160). Perhaps the only way to see the full path ahead is to start moving. In this case, strategy is as much about experimentation as it is about foresight and analysis (Hamel, 1997).

The leading management thinker Peter Drucker (1994) also favoured the medical metaphor. For example, he stressed the importance of 'preventative care'—that is, building into the organization systematic monitoring and testing of its theory of the business. Following this logic, perhaps the lieutenant should never have dispatched the unit so unprepared in unfamiliar terrain in such terrible weather conditions; maybe early diagnosis would have halted the incident. At the same time, Drucker emphasizes the importance of effective action in order to 'bring the organization's behavior in line with the new realities of its environment'. While a strategy process may start out with rigorous diagnosis and analysis, it must be appreciated that change often demands a serious rethinking of one's early prescriptions. Finally, Drucker stresses the importance of the surgeon's time-tested principle and one of the oldest principles of effective decision making: 'a degenerative disease will not be cured by procrastination. It requires decisive action!' (ibid: 103).

Implications for strategy practice

A key purpose of strategy is to act as a compass, pointing the organization in the right direction. Without it, an organization is like a lost traveller, without bearing or sense of direction, and so unable to chart the best way forward. Yet it is important for those practising strategy to note the varying purposes that strategy can serve. Why do organizations have strategies and engage in the process of strategic management? A series of different arguments can be put forward.

1. **Rational: maximize choice (strategy as blueprint)**
The classic understanding is that strategy allows for the assessment of a wide range of alternatives and a holistic understanding of what the organization is and does. A systematic review of the factors influencing strategy might never occur if it were not for the strategy process. Strategy development provides a means of adaptive thinking that results in a broader range of perspectives and solutions being entertained (Miller and Cardinal, 1994), and ultimately produces better alignment and financial results than can trial-and-error analysis or learning (Ansoff, 1991).

2. **Cathartic: provide identity and motivation (strategy as guiding light)**
Strategy also has a strong power to motivate individuals and to leverage their energy towards a common goal. The notion of 'strategic intent' (Prahalad and Hamel, 1990) or 'big hairy audacious goals' (BHAGs; Collins and Porras, 1994) captures the idea of a goal that might not even be reachable, yet which can galvanize an entire organization. Selznick (1957) stressed that goals can be ideological weapons to overcome resistance. Often, individuals relate to an organization's identity: for example, graduates applying for jobs might be attracted to an organization such as Google or Yahoo because of its exciting, innovative, and youthful culture. Indeed, emotional buy-in, often obtained through involvement in strategy conversations, is often the unheralded champion of strategic success (Stern, 2007).

3. **Symbolic: provide legitimacy (strategy as security blanket)**
A glance through an annual report will quickly reveal that strategy is a critical tool for communicating with organizational stakeholders. The language of strategy conveys importance and rigour, and is associated with successful initiatives. Strategy therefore performs a symbolic function, and strategy actors are more likely to obtain interest and legitimacy from audiences—public; customers; investors; suppliers—if they conform to the etiquette of strategy talk. At the same time, this strategy talk provides a security blanket for strategists, allowing them to simplify reality and be seen to conform with expectations; perception might be as important as content. This is the same for governments that speak of 'moving up the value chain', 'creating knowledge economies', and 'sustainability'.

4. **Validation: justification for action (strategy as lever)**
Strategy provides a means for post-rationalization of events that have occurred through chance, luck, or emergence. The language of strategy implies deliberateness and purposeful activities, and can be used to cement down emergent initiatives or to claim credit for past events. For example, investors would much prefer to hear—or think at least—that Viagra was discovered through a process of extensive and deliberate research and development rather than as a result of unexpected side effects on patients being treated for angina (De Rond and Thietart, 2007). It is human nature to try to provide a rational and linear explanation for events, and in business, strategy provides just this mechanism. Strategy can also be used by people in powerful positions, or by powerful interest groups, to force through a set of activities that are in their interest; here, strategy provides a perfect gift-wrap for power plays. By stressing that a course of action is necessary to 'deal with competition' or as a result of the 'changes in the competitive environment', specific interests and responsibility can be absolved. Strategy provides a language that means that decisions and actions can be perceived as neutral.

5. **Performative: evaluate performance (strategy as benchmark)**
Strategy objectives provide a benchmark by which the organization and individuals therein can assess their performance. Without this overarching framework, it would be difficult to assess individual contributions. At higher levels, in particular, performance appraisal is inherently related to the achievement of certain objectives, be it expansion objectives at Wal-Mart, innovation objectives at Intel, or continuous improvement objectives at Motorola. Strategy is, of course, also the self-imposed benchmark by which external stakeholders will assess the performance of an organization; institutional investors in particular will be quick to ask: 'Did it meet its benchmarks and expectations for this quarter? Is its strategy viable? Is the top management team leading in the right direction and in the right manner?' Involving up-and-coming managers in strategy development sessions can also be a way of providing an early assessment of long-term career prospects, hence auditing the organization for quality of human resources.

Inevitably, strategy serves multiple purposes (Scott, 2003). In addition to the above, at the level of the individual, strategy can also be used to ask some tough questions. Carly Fiorina, former CEO of Hewlett-Packard, challenged a graduation class of 2001 to self-reflect: 'Am I acting out a role, or am I living the truth? Am I still making choices, or have I simply stopped choosing? Am I in a place that engages my mind and captures my heart? Am I stuck in the past, or am I defining my future?'

Introduction to readings

Reading 1.1 is taken from the now-classic work by Michael Porter, 'What is strategy?' (1996). Writing in the mid-1990s, Porter offers a hard-hitting defence of his early positioning view against the capabilities approach, which, as the strategy timeline shows, superseded his positioning perspective. He offers a view of strategy that centres on being unique and different; focusing on operational efficiency will lead only to convergence. Critically, for Porter, the unit of analysis of strategy should be the activities conducted by the firm, because these bridge the external environment and the internal workings of the firm. The essence of strategy is therefore about trade-offs: deciding which activities to conduct and which not to conduct. Illustrating his points with examples such as the SouthWest Airlines model, which companies in Europe such as Ryanair were quick to follow, Porter offers a robust argument. But is strategy all science and no art, and how well does Porter capture the continuous change challenge? Is this really an external positioning view that can be contrasted with a capabilities approach—is the distinction valid? What of the critical task of implementation?

Reading 1.2 is from 'Strategy as simple rules' by Eisenhardt and Sull (2001). This article looks at the high-velocity environments that characterize the knowledge-based era. The authors focus on how organizations can best deal with chaos and complexity. Instead of the exploitation of stable positions or resources, they advocate the role of simple rules in enabling organizations to seize fleeting opportunities. Following simple rules allows organizations to retain sufficient flexibility to respond rapidly to changing circumstances. What does this mean for planning, positioning, and capabilities perspectives? Given the high-technology companies on which Eisenhardt and Sull focus, does their argument hold in other contexts? The article cites Enron before its dramatic fall from grace: perhaps Enron had too few rules and followed too many opportunities. Can strategy be simple rules?

Our final reading for this chapter, to which a link is provided on the Online Resource Centre that accompanies this book, is by Volberda (2004) and is entitled 'Crisis in strategy: fragmentation, integration or synthesis'. It reviews the state of play in strategic management. The field is judged to be fragmented and in urgent need of focus. Three perspectives on strategic management are highlighted: the classical, which follows the line of argument of our planning and positioning scholars; the modern perspective, which suggests that strategy is more like an emergent activity; and what is labelled a 'postmodern' approach, which focuses on how individuals interact with the environment. But are these perspectives mutually exclusive? Volberda calls for synthesis in the field of strategy, stressing three schools of synthesis—the boundary, dynamic capabilities, and configurational schools—but are these new and novel insights? What will determine their value or will they only limit thinking into categories? Moreover, what does this mean for the practitioner strategist?

Mini case study Hyundai: rewriting global automotive history

Will Geoghegan

In 1999, Mong-Koo Chung took control of Hyundai from his father Chung Ju-Yung. He immediately set about changing the focus of the motor business from quantity to quantity *and* quality. This renewed focus on quality has propelled Hyundai to its position as the world's fourth-largest car manufacturer, selling over 4 million cars in 2009 (OICA, 2010). This leaves only Toyota, General Motors (GM), and Volkswagen with more sales than Hyundai in the world auto market. As one industry observer put it, 'the old Hyundai didn't build cars you wanted to drive; it built cars you could afford'; while now 'the new Hyundai makes cars you want and can afford' (Krebs, 2010a).

Hyundai has come a long way to engender its core ethos of safety, design, and quality since its first offering to the US market. In 1986, the much-parodied Hyundai Excel entered the US marketplace priced at US$4,995 and sold 126,000 models in its first year. It looked as though Hyundai had made a master play to gain market share in its attempt to secure a lasting foothold in the US marketplace. However, the Excel was the cause of a lasting slur on Hyundai's perceived quality. It was sold to many non-creditworthy buyers, who soon defaulted on their loans. Ironically, the Excel was so poorly built that the repossessed cars were usually worth less than what was owed (Taylor III, 2010).

Quality and America's best warranty

The initial failure of the Excel served to drive Hyundai to put concerted effort into the quality of future products. It might be said that the company moved from the mass production of average cars to the mass production of good cars. Key to restoring consumer faith in the company was the new warranty that it offered. This ten-year, or 100,000 miles, powertrain warranty is what Hyundai now calls 'America's best warranty' (Hyundai, 2010a). This warranty included six years of bumper-to-bumper cover, and ten years of engine and transmission cover, and, as some analysts reported, helped to 'take the fear out of buying a Hyundai' (Warner, 2002).

In the car industry, a manufacturer cannot offer a comprehensive warranty-and-insurance programme unless it believes that its product will stand up to the challenge. This appeared to be a risky strategy given Hyundai's relative failure with the Excel. However, Hyundai had already put the wheels in motion to improve the quality of its offering. It accomplished this through a rigorous quality improvement campaign, benchmarking against Toyota and introducing the 'Six Sigma' (Taylor III, 2010). Allied to this, it replaced many of its manager-level positions with engineers to bring a more concerted and qualified focus on quality. The impact was obvious. One magazine article in 2002 highlighted that: 'Hyundai drivers are no longer the butt of jokes—they're smart consumers with an eye for great design and an appreciation of excellent quality at a good price' (Warner, 2002).

The design factor

Quality, however, means very little in the car market unless you have aesthetically pleasing models. Nowadays, many would say that the quality of a car is taken for granted, and that car manufacturers now need to compete on the design of the car and the added extras within. With this in mind, Hyundai invested heavily in design during the beginning of the last decade, establishing the Hyundai Kia Motors Design and Technical Centre in Irvine, California. The design element needed a complete overhaul, because many saw the 'old' Hyundai as 'baroque and fussy' (Taylor III, 2010). Hyundai enrolled international designers to help to develop more fluid lines with more elegant designs. This is particularly evident in the television advertising for the 2011 Hyundai Tucson, which emphasizes its unique and innovative design. Hyundai has also decided to build a global design network, connecting cities in the USA, Europe, Japan, and the newly emerging economies. Hyundai states that this design centre 'will spearhead even more original and innovative designs to raise our profile as a global leading automaker' (Hyundai, 2010b).

Aggressiveness and speed

'Whereas Toyota thrives on consistency and Honda (HMC) on innovation, Hyundai is all about aggressiveness and speed' (Taylor III, 2010). Similarly to Toyota's first failed offering to the US market (the Toyopet), the Excel helped to focus Hyundai not only on quality at a low price, but also on producing these products at a higher speed to capture as much of the market as possible. In its first year, for example, the Excel sold well in the USA. Although deemed a failure, it showed the market that Hyundai could satisfy a large demand in a foreign marketplace.

Speed to market and responsiveness are key strengths for Hyundai. The Sonata was unveiled seven weeks ahead of schedule and, in August 2010, US production plants were working to a thirty-seven-day line-wide supply compared with the industry average of sixty days (Ganz, 2010). Hyundai's capacity in 2010 was 5.8 million cars and trucks, which it hopes to grow to 6.5 million by 2012 (Taylor III, 2010). One can also point to the company's meteoric rise in becoming the world's fourth-largest auto manufacturer as an example of how Hyundai has embraced change, whether these be external market forces or the need to develop new internal competences to become a world leader.

Marketing and a customer-centred approach

Hyundai has emphasized its core strengths of quality, design, and responsiveness with some interesting ploys to position its product. The ten-year, 100,000 miles, powertrain warranty was revolutionary in its conception and helped to change the mindset of many consumers. Such was its impact that other manufacturers have followed suit, offering an extended warranty and other similar guarantees to attract consumers. For example, Chrysler Corporation rolled out a scheme to fix gasoline prices at US$2.99, calling the programme 'Let's refuel America' (Holstein, 2009).

Hyundai was also the first to offer an innovative incentive for consumers in recognition of the market uncertainty caused by the global financial crisis. The company basically told consumers: 'If you lose your job within the first year of your Hyundai purchase, we will let you walk out of the credit agreement without it affecting your credit rating.' It employed a company called Walkaway USA that allowed financially troubled auto buyers to be released from their financial commitment. This not only appealed to people who perceived their jobs to be at risk, but also engendered goodwill for the company: the public now saw Hyundai as a firm that cared. Joel Ewanick, the vice president for marketing in Hyundai, explained: 'In focus groups we noticed that more and more consumers were putting off vehicle purchases because they were worried about losing their jobs. We had a consumer insight ... People were pulling back because of their long-term financial outlooks' (Holstein, 2009).

Other companies have since followed suit. Ford offered a two-month incentive plan (the 'Ford Advantage Plan'), which covered the loan payments on the consumer's vehicle for up to a year if he or she lost his or her job. GM offered a similar deal (the 'Total Confidence Plan'), which gave the consumer a nine-month period of grace, with GM paying the auto loans during that period if the customer became unemployed (Holstein, 2009). Hyundai reaped huge rewards for being the first mover with its initiative and, as a result, greatly enhanced its sales during difficult economic circumstances.

Geographic markets

Hyundai sold 4,952,021 units in 2009, a strong figure in the context of the total 61 million cars that were sold worldwide that year. The main markets in which Hyundai operates are Europe, North America, and Korea. It has made significant strides in all three of these core markets over the past ten years.

In Korea, Hyundai and Kia accounted for almost 80 per cent of the auto sales in 2009 (Holstein, 2009). The company's hold on the Korean market has been questioned by some industry observers as not necessarily being driven by consumers' patriotism. One study has shown that buyers bought Korean out of fear of tax audits and assault, with some even believing that they would be a target for traffic police if they were to drive a foreign-manufactured car (*The Economist*, 2010).

In the US market, Hyundai capitalized on the US government's 'Cash for Clunkers' programme and held a 8.2 per cent market share at March 2010 (Krebs, 2010b). It has taken advantage of many of the US policy incentives to stimulate the auto market, increasing its sales by an impressive 46 per cent in 2009.

To help to complete the global perspective that Hyundai has embraced, it has developed ten manufacturing plants throughout the globe, including plants in Korea, the USA, the Czech Republic, India, China, Brazil, and Russia. It also has eleven research centres and more than 6,000 sales networks throughout the world. This will allow it to match anticipated global demand through the next decade.

The future?

New products

In early 2011 Hyundai launched the Equus, a premium luxury car expected to compete with Audi, BMW, and Mercedes Benz. It retails at a relatively low price and even comes with an iPad instead of the traditional car manual. This is a bold, ambitious move by Hyundai, appealing to a customer segment to which it has not looked before. It will cost the consumer about US$20,000 less than the more established brands—but the question remains: will consumers wish to make this saving and lose the status of a German premium brand name? As one article suggested, 'depending on your point of view, the introduction of the Equus is either ambitious, arrogant, or ignorant' (Taylor III, 2010).

Hyundai has also finally decided to enter the electric car market. The BlueOn was announced on 9 September 2010 and will initially be tested in various Korean governmental organizations before a mass-market push. BlueOns will compete in the eco-friendly car market with cars such as the Toyota Prius, Nissan Leaf, and Mitsubishi i-MiEV. The BlueOn will have a maximum speed 80.6 mph, travel 87 miles on a single charge, and top up its battery to 80 per cent charge in 25 minutes (Schwartz, 2010).

New and mature markets

It is not only new products that may allow Hyundai to grow, but also new and existing markets. Throughout 2008 and 2009, there was a lull in car sales worldwide due to the economic downturn, but many analysts expect a reversal of fortunes in the coming years. Haddock and Jullens (2009) expect growth to come from three main areas:

1. the rapidly emerging economies (REEs)—Brazil, Russia, India, and China, allied to Malaysia, Argentina, Mexico, Turkey, Thailand, Iran, and Indonesia;

2. the lower-growth economies (compared to REEs), which consist of about a hundred nations—although these nations are impoverished at present, some of their political leaders are interested in building up the middle classes and see personal mobility as a major stepping stone; and

3. the mature economies—Europe, North America, and Japan—through population growth and vehicle replacement.

Hyundai is ideally placed to take full advantage of the idiosyncrasies that each of these segments requires. It has developed rapidly over the past ten years and can continue to do so by harnessing distinctive customer demand patterns in each of the different classifications. 'Years ago Toyota used to say that Hyundai was the company it feared most. Today those fears have grown into a nightmare' (Taylor III, 2010); the key question is whether Hyundai will be able to maintain this competitive momentum. Recent product recalls at Toyota also provide important lessons about the potential perils of the quest for speed and dramatic growth and how these can compromise quality. The future intent for Hyundai is best summed up by Mong-Koo Chung (2010):

> Since its establishment, Hyundai has placed customer satisfaction as its highest priority—achieved only through meeting challenges head-on with our undying passion. Now, Hyundai Motor Company will raise its future competitive edge through innovative ideas. We encourage you to continue your interest [in] and support [for] Hyundai Motor Company as we rewrite global automotive history and become a top global company. We promise to continue providing the highest standards in customer satisfaction.

Questions

1. Outline the orientation challenges that Hyundai faces as it attempts to rewrite global automotive history to become a top global company.

2. What triggered Hyundai's change of trade-off strategies between quantity and quality? As it seeks to become a top global company, what other trade-offs might Hyundai have to deal with to achieve its ambitions?

3. Outline Hyundai's value proposition. How sustainable is it? Would you suggest any further changes?

4. Describe Hyundai's strategy. Do you think that it will change in the next five years? If so, what key factors may cause changes in Hyundai's strategy?

Summary

In this chapter, we began by outlining what strategy is and its purpose, and then examined the origins and evolution of strategy. We turned our focus to exploring strategy in its present-day context and outlined the challenges of strategic management. Strategy is a complex activity. While the key characteristics driving success might be quite obvious—for example, a clear strategy, sound execution, ability to adapt (Nohria *et al.*, 2003)—achieving these in practice is far from straightforward. Overall, the competitive threats facing organizations have never been so great, while at the same time 'opportunities multiply as they are seized' (Sun Tzu, 1912). Yet how do organizations stay on top, or at least keep up with the game? Developing such understanding is the essence of strategy. Current challenges do not diminish the need for strategic thinking; in fact, they enhance it. Questions fundamental to strategy—such as who you are and what you do—have never been more important (Rosenzweig, 2007; Rumelt, 2009). Indeed, Hamel (1997) suggests that strategizing should itself be the critical capability that organizations leverage and nurture: 'it is not a one year rain dance nor is it a decade long consultancy project' (ibid: 73). Getting the best out of strategy requires a sustained commitment, an understanding of its complexity, and a harnessing of strategic opposites (Wilson, 1998: 511). Ultimately, strategy is a way of thinking, not a procedural exercise or a set of frameworks (Bradley *et al.*, 2011: 1)

There is no straightforward formula for success. Too often, the search for clear-cut answers is destructive to our process of understanding strategy. The difficulty with a 'one best way' is that it mitigates the opportunity for unique advantage. Equally, there is doubt over whether any advantage can ever be fully sustainable (D'Aveni *et al.*, 2010). Thinking along these lines may well prove to be a strategic trap that blinds strategists to the requirement for change, renewal, and reinvention (Oliver, 1992). Instead, we should direct our attention to understanding the conditions under which certain practices are successful and the conditions under which they are not. In an era in which prediction is difficult, if not impossible, understanding and explanation become critical. The best strategists are those who are wise to this (the focus of Chapter 2). Knowledge and insight into the strategic management process is best created through strategic conversations and confronting difficult truths (Beer and Eisenstat, 2004: 83). In Table 1.4, we consider the strategic questions that underpin each chapter of this book and the typical elements of strategic

Table 1.4 The structure of *strategy and strategists* and corresponding strategic questions

Section	Chapter	Strategic question	Strategic conversations
Discovering strategy and strategists	Chapter 1 Discovering strategy	What is strategy?	Planning, positioning, capabilities, and networked innovation Challenges of strategic management (orientation; trade-off; relevance; continuous change)
	Chapter 2 Discovering strategists	Who are the strategists?	CEOs, middle managers, individual or collectivity Top-down or bottom-up strategy
	Chapter 3 The process of strategizing	How are strategic decisions made?	Balancing strategic thinking, decision making, and leadership
	Chapter 4 Dynamics of strategy formulation	How is strategy formulated?	Deliberate, emerging, cognition, or chaos
Foundations and routes to advantage	Chapter 5 Purpose and values	What are our key values and responsibilities?	Profit and/or people, accountability, corporation vs community
	Chapter 6 Market-based and resource-based approaches	How do we best analyse the environment?	Best fit with environment or unique fit; play by rules or make own rules
	Chapter 7 Corporate and global strategy	What is our strategic scope/the domain(s) in which we operate?	Domain: nature and spread of businesses in which we operate Direction: extent of diversification; focus versus diversification; global versus local
	Chapter 8 Business and network strategies	How do we best compete in a given market?	Market: cost and/or quality; broad or focused Method: alone or together; organic strategic alliances; joint venture, merger, or acquisition
Realizing and sustaining advantage	Chapter 9 Levers for implementing strategy	What levers can we use to implement strategy?	Empowerment and/or control, flexibility vs commitment
	Chapter 10 Interactions in executing strategy	What configurations can we use to implement strategy?	Structure, people, technology and customer mix
	Chapter 11 Strategic change	How and why do we change?	Revolutionary or evolutionary change Appropriate lens: rational, emergent, cultural/political, or complexity
	Chapter 12 Innovation and corporate entrepreneurship	How and why do we innovate?	Balancing creative freedom with control, technology push or market control, deliberate or emergent
Rediscovering strategy and strategists	Chapter 13 Managing strategy in context	How does context matter?	Application of strategy and role of strategists in the public sector, for not-for-profits, and small firms
	Chapter 14 The role of strategy agents	Who is strategy really for?	Key agents in the strategy process Strategy fashion and fads, and role of discourse

conversation that might ensue. Ultimately, strategy should be a home for multiple competing perspectives, because 'good science is good conversation' (Mahoney, 1993; Nag *et al.*, 2007: 952). That these conversations should be ongoing is not surprising; after all, strategy is a journey, not an end destination.

Discussion questions

1. Consider the following quote about strategic planning:

> For the better part of a year, they [corporate planners] collect financial and operational data, make forecasts, and prepare lengthy presentations with the CEO and other senior managers about the future direction of the business. But at the end of this expensive and time-consuming process, many participants say they are frustrated by its lack of impact on either their own actions or the strategic direction of the company.
>
> (Dye and Sibony, 2007: 40)

Why do you think this might this be the case?

2. Choose a successful organization and attempt to identify the reason for its success. How does it deal with each of the challenges of strategic management?

3. What would be the arguments for and against an organization being explicit in writing and communicating its strategy?

4. Is there such a thing as a sustainable competitive advantage?

5. Based on what you have read in this chapter, how would you define 'strategy'?

Further reading

For a useful overview of the development of the field as a pendulum swinging from an internal to external focus see R. E. Hoskisson, M. A. Hitt, and W. Wan (1999) 'Theory and research in strategic management: swings of a pendulum', *Journal of Management*, 25(3): 417–456.

R. Whittington (1993) *What is Strategy and Does it Matter?*, London: Routledge, presents an extremely accessible and well-crafted account of different theoretical perspectives in strategy.

For a more detailed account of the nature and key elements of strategy, see D. Hambrick and J. Fredrickson (2005) 'Are you sure you have a strategy?', *Academy of Management Executive*, 19(4): 51–62.

More academic, the first edition of the *European Management Review* (2004) provides a number of articles reviewing the current state of play of strategic management.

R. Rumelt (2011) *Good Strategy/Bad Strategy*, London: Profile Books, is a fine overview text by one of strategy's key scholars. It draws on a range of company examples, intertwined with personal tales from the battlefield, to present a realistic, problem-focused view of strategy. Similar to the focus in this chapter, for Rumelt, the essence of strategy involves confronting and managing key challenges.

visit the Online Resource Centre that accompanies this book to access more learning resources on this chapter topic at www.oxfordtextbooks.co.uk/orc/cunningham/

References

Andrews, K. R. 1971. ***The Concept of Corporate Strategy***. Homewood, IL: Irwin.

Ansoff, I. 1987. ***Corporate Strategy: An Analytical Approach to Business Policy for Growth and Expansion.*** Rev'd edn. London: Penguin Books.

Ansoff, I. 1991. Critique of Henry Mintzberg's 'The design school: reconsidering the basic premises of strategic management'. ***Strategic Management Journal***, 12(6): 174–187.

Barney, J. 1991. Firm resources and sustained competitive advantage. ***Journal of Management***, 17(1): 99–120.

Barney, J. and Hesterly, W. 2006. ***Strategic Management and Competitive Advantage***. Saddle River, NJ: Pearson Education.

Beer, M. and Eisenstat, R. 2004. How to have an honest conversation about your business strategy. ***Harvard Business Review***, Feb: 82–89.

Beinhocker, E. 1997. Strategy as the edge of chaos. ***McKinsey Quarterly***, 1: 25–39.

Bradley, C., Hirt, M., and Smit, S. 2011. Have you tested your strategy lately? ***McKinsey Quarterly***, 1–13.

Bughin, J., and Chui, M. 2010. The rise of the networked enterprise: Web 2.0 finds its payday. ***McKinsey Quarterly***, Dec: 1–9.

Chandler, A. D. 1962. ***Strategy and Structure***. Cambridge, MA: MIT Press.

Chesbrough, H. and Appleyard, M. 2007. Open innovation and strategy. ***California Management Review***, 50(1): 57–76.

Chung, M.-K. 2010. Hyundai corporate message. Available online at http://worldwide.hyundai.com/company-overview/ceo-message.html

Collins, J. and Porras, J. 1994. ***Built to Last: Successful Habits of Visionary Companies***. New York: Harper Collins.

Conan Doyle, A. 1891. A scandal in Bohemia. Reprinted in A. Conan Doyle. 2001. ***The Complete Adventures and Memoirs of Sherlock Holmes***. London: Random House.

Courtney, H. 2008. A fresh look at strategy under uncertainty. ***McKinsey Quarterly***, Dec: 1–8.

Cummings, S. 2002. ***ReCreating Strategy***. London: Sage.

D'Aveni, R. A. 1994. ***Hypercompetition: Managing the Dynamics of Strategic Maneuvering***. New York: Free Press.

D'Aveni, R. A., Dagnino, G., and Smith, K. G. 2010. The age of temporary advantage. ***Strategic Management Journal***, 31: 1371–1385.

De Rond, M. and Thietart, R.-A. 2007. Choice, chance and inevitability in strategy. ***Strategic Management Journal***, 28: 535–551.

Drucker, P. F. 1994. The theory of the business. ***Harvard Business Review***, September/October: 95–105.

Dye, R. and Sibony, O. 2007. How to improve strategic planning. ***McKinsey Quarterly***, 3: 40–49.

The Economist. 2010. One-way street. 8 July.

Fiorina, C. 2001. The process of distillation: getting to the essence of things. Speech given at the Stanford University Commencement Ceremony, Palo Alto, CA, 17 June. Available online at http://www.hp.com/hpinfo/execteam/speeches/fiorina/stanford_01.html

Ganz, A. 2010. Hyundai to boost US production capacity. ***The Left Lane News***. Available online at http://www.leftlanenews.com/hyundai-to-boost-u-s-production-capacity.html

Grant, R. M. 1996. Towards a knowledge theory of the firm. ***Strategic Management Journal***, 17: 109.

Haddock, R. and Jullens, J. 2009. The best years of the auto industry are still to come. ***Strategy + Business***, 55: 2–12.

Hafsi, T. and Thomas, H. 2005. The field of strategy: in search of a walking stick. ***European Management Journal***, 23(5): 507–519.

Hambrick, D. and Chen, M.-J. 2008. New academic fields as admittance-seeking social movements: the case of strategic management. ***Academy of Management Review***, 33(1): 32–54.

Hambrick, D. and Fredrickson, J. 2005. Are you sure you have a strategy? ***Academy of Management Executive***, 19(4): 51–62.

Hamel, G. 1996. Strategy as revolution. ***Harvard Business Review***, July/Aug: 69–82.

Hamel, G. 1997. Killer strategies that make shareholders rich. ***Fortune***, 135: 70–84.

Harvey-Jones, S. J. 1987. Introduction to corporate strategy. In I. Ansoff (ed.) ***Corporate Strategy***. London: Penguin.

Hofer, C. W. and Schendel, D. 1978. ***Strategy Formulation: Analytical Concepts***. New York: West Publishing Company.

Holstein, W. 2009. Convincing consumers to spend again. ***Strategy + Business***, 54: 1–5.

Hoskisson, R. E., Hitt, M. A., and Wan, W. 1999. Theory and research in strategic management: swings of a pendulum. ***Journal of Management***, 25(3): 417–456.

Hyundai. 2010a. America's best warranty. Available online at http://www.hyundaiusa.com/warranty.aspx

Hyundai. 2010b. Hyundai innovation—design. Available online at http://worldwide.hyundai.com/innovation/design.html

Jarzabkowski, P. and Wilson, D. 2006. Actionable strategy knowledge: a practice perspective. ***European Management Journal***, 24(5): 348–367.

Kiechel, W. 2010. Seven chapters of strategic wisdom. ***Strategy and Business***, 58: 1–7.

Krebs, M. 2010a. Who'd buy a $55,000 Hyundai? Surprising answers. ***Edmunds AutoObserver***. Available online at http://www.autoobserver.com/2010/05/whod-buy-a-55000-hyundai-surprising-answers.html

Krebs, M. 2010b. Toyota's woes open the door even wider for Hyundai, AutoObserver analysis shows. ***Edmunds AutoObserver***. Available online at http://www.autoobserver.com/2010/03/toyotas-woes-open-the-door-even-wider-for-hyundai-autoobserver-analysis-shows.html

Mahoney, J. 1993. Strategic management and determinism: sustaining the conversation. ***Journal of Management Studies***, 30: 173–191.

March, J. G. 2007. The study of organizations and organizing since 1945. ***Organization Studies***, 28(1): 9–19.

Markides, C. 2004. What is strategy and how do you know if you have one? ***Business Strategy Review***, 15(2): 5–12.

McIntyre, D. and Subramaniam, M. 2009. Strategy in network industries: a review and research agenda. ***Journal of Management***, 35(6): 1494–1517.

McKiernan, P. and Carter, C. 2004. The millennium nexus: strategic management at the cross-roads. ***European Management Review***, 1: 3–13.

Michel, S., Brown, S., and Gallan, A. 2008. Service-logic innovations: how to innovate customers, not products. ***California Management Review***, 50(3): 49–65.

Miles, R., Snow, C., and Miles, G. 2000. TheFuture.org. ***Long Range Planning***, 33: 300–321.

Miles, R., Snow, C., Meyer, A., and Coleman, H. 1978. Organisation strategy, structure and process. ***Academy of Management Review***, 3: 546–662.

Miller, C. and Cardinal, L. 1994. Strategic planning and firm performance: a synthesis of more than two decades of research. ***Academy of Management Journal***, 37(6): 1649–1665.

Mintzberg, H. 1987. The strategy concept II: another look at why organizations need strategies. ***California Management Review***, Fall: 25–32.

Mintzberg, H. 1994. ***The Rise and Fall of Strategic Planning***. New York: Free Press.

Mintzberg, H., Ahlstrand, B., and Lampel, J. 1998. ***Strategy Safari: The Complete Guide through the Wilds of Strategic Management***. London: FT Prentice Hall.

Nag, R., Hambrick, D., and Chen, M.-J. 2007. What is strategic management, really? Inductive derivation of a consensus definition of the field. ***Strategic Management Journal***, 28: 935–955.

Nohria, N., Joyce, W., and Robertson, B. 2003. What really works. ***Harvard Business Review***, 81(7): 12–26.

O'Connor, O. 1998. Strategic plan must be clear. ***Irish Times***, 3 July.

Oliver, R. 1992. Sustainable competitive advantage. ***Journal of Business Strategy***, 21(6): 7–10.

Organisation Internationale des Constructeurs d'Automobiles [International Organization of Motor Vehicle Manufacturers] (OICA). 2010. World motor vehicle production by manufacturer: world ranking of manufacturers 2009. Available online at http://oica.net/wp-content/uploads/ranking-2010.pdf

Patel, K. 2005. ***The Master Strategist: Power, Purpose and Principle***. London: Arrow Books.

Penrose, E. 1959. ***Theory of the Growth of the Firm***. Oxford: Oxford University Press.

Peters, H. 2010. Europe car sales to fall; Toyota woes benefit Hyundai. ***Reuters***. Available online at http://www.reuters.com/article/2010/03/02/us-toyota-idUSTRE6210OV20100302

Peters, T. J. and Waterman, R. H. 1982. ***In Search of Excellence: Lessons from America's Best-Run Companies***. London: Harper and Row.

Pfeffer, J. and Sutton, R. 2006. ***Hard Facts, Dangerous Half Truths, and Total Nonsense***. Boston, MA: Harvard Business School Press.

Porter, M. 1980. ***Competitive Strategy***. New York: Free Press.

Porter, M. 1985. ***Competitive Advantage***. New York: Free Press.

Porter, M. 1991. Toward a dynamic theory of strategy. ***Strategic Management Journal***, 12: 95–117.

Porter, M. 1996. What is strategy? ***Harvard Business Review***, December: 61–78.

Prahalad, C. and Hamel, G. 1990. The core competencies of the corporation. ***Harvard Business Review***, May/June(3): 79–91.

Rosenzweig, J. 2007. Misunderstanding the nature of company performance: the halo effect and other business delusions. *California Management Review*, 49(4): 6–19.

Rumelt, R. 2009. Strategy in a 'structural break'. *McKinsey Quarterly*, 1: 35–42.

Rumelt, R., Schendel, D., and Teece, D. 1991. Strategic management and economics. *Strategic Management Journal*, 12: 5–29.

Schwartz, A. 2010. Hyundai goes electric. *Fast Company*. Available online at http://www.fastcompany.com/1687906/hyundai-takes-on-asian-rivals-with-its-first-ev

Scott, R. W. 2003. *Organizations: Rational, Natural and Open Systems*. 5th edn. Englewood Cliffs, NY: Pearson International.

Selznick, P. 1957. *Leadership in Administration*. Evanston, IL: Row, Peterson.

Stacey, R. D. 1995. The science of complexity: an alternative perspective for strategic change process. *Strategic Management Journal*, 12: 477–495.

Stalk, G., Evans, P., and Schulman, L. 1992. Competing on capabilities: the new rules of corporate strategy. *Harvard Business Review*, March/April: 57–69.

Stern, S. 2007. Wanted: more emotion and less rationality about strategy, *Financial Times*, 19 Feb: 9.

Sun Tzu. 1912. *The Art of War*. Trans L. Giles. Puppet Press Classic.

Taylor III, A. 2010. Hyundai smokes the competition. *CNNMoney*. Available online at http://money.cnn.com/2010/01/04/autos/hyundai_competition.fortune/index.htm

Teece, D. 2007. Explicating dynamic capabilities: the nature and microfoundations of (sustainable) enterprise performance. *Strategic Management Journal*, 28: 1319–1359.

Teece, D., Pisano, G., and Shuen, A. 1997. Dynamic capabilities and strategic management. *Strategic Management Journal*, 18: 509–533.

Thomas, H. and Pruett, M. 1993. Introduction to the special issue: perspectives on theory building in strategic management. *Journal of Management Studies*, 30(1): 3–10.

Volberda, H. 2004. Crisis in strategy: fragmentation, integration or synthesis. *European Management Review*, 1(1): 35–42.

von Ghyczy, T., von Oetinger, B., and Bassford, C. (eds) 2001. *Clausewitz on Strategy: Inspiration and Insight from a Master Strategist*. Chichester: John Wiley and Sons.

Wallace, V. and Herrick, A. 2009. What banking needs to become. *Strategy and Business*, 57: 1–12.

Warner, F. 2002. Finbarr O'Neill is not a car guy. *Fast Company*. Available online at http://www.fastcompany.com/magazine/64/oneill.html

Weick, K. E. 2001. *Making Sense of the Organization*. Oxford: Blackwell.

Welch, J. 2001. *Jack: What I've Learned Leading a Great Company and Great People*. London: Headline Book Publishing.

Wernerfelt, B. 1984. A resource-based view of the firm. *Strategic Management Journal*, 5: 171–180.

Whittington, R. 1993. *What is Strategy and Does it Matter?* London: Routledge.

Wilson, I. 1998. Strategic planning for the millennium: resolving the dilemma. *Long Range Planning*, 31(4): 507–513.

Womack, J. P., Jones, D., and Roos, D. 1990. *The Machine that Changed the World.* New York: Rawson Associates.

2

Discovering strategists

I sometimes feel like I'm behind the wheel of a race car ... One of the biggest challenges is that there are no road signs to help navigate. And, in fact, no one has yet determined which side of the road we're supposed to be on.

(Stephen M. Case, Former chairman, AOL Time Warner)

Introduction

In the previous chapter, we explored what strategy is. The focus of this chapter is to examine those people in organizations who are actively involved in crafting and implementing strategy: namely, organizational **strategists**. Every day of our lives, strategists influence the nature of the services and products that we purchase, from the cereal that we eat for breakfast, the mode of transport that we use to get around, the way in which we access music and news, to the beverages that we consume. In the airline **industry**, strategists such as Herb Kelleher of Southwest Airlines have developed and perfected a low-cost **business model** that has revolutionized the way in which people travel, how they purchase travel, and how they think about travelling. Building upon this, Michael O'Leary CEO of Ryanair has disaggregated the different elements of airline travel and maximized the value from each: baggage; ticket booking; and so on (Porter, 1996—Reading 1.1). Strategy is not something that simply exists as words on a page; it is embedded in the behaviours, activities, and actions of those who make up an organization (Whittington, 2007). It is a social process involving multiple interactions with a wide variety of people, both internal and external to the organization (Birkinshaw, 2010; Hunsicker, 1980). Strategy is a process of shaping behaviour—something you *do* rather than something you *have* (Ghoshal and Bartlett, 1995: 94). For this reason, strategists are critical to continuously crafting, evaluating, and implementing strategy, ultimately shaping the competitive rivalry of their industry, the performance of their company, and how the company is perceived in the minds of consumers. Strategists are centrally involved in dealing with the strategic management challenges of orientation, **trade-off**, relevance, and continuous change.

Despite the importance of strategists, accounts of who they actually are and what they do are difficult to unearth. The strategy field remains surprisingly silent about strategists, often providing heroic fairy-tale accounts of high-performing organizations that leave the observer wondering: 'What do we do to get to this beautifully crafted strategy? Who is actually involved? What skills are required?'

One key debate is whether there is only one strategist in the organization—usually the chief executive officer (CEO)—or whether everyone in the organization can be a strategist. The strategist's responsibility to make prudent and sustainable decisions about the direction of a business can be daunting, while ensuring that the desired strategy is executed effectively is a significant task. Stephen Case's quote that opened this chapter gives us a sense of the enormity of the challenge faced by strategists and the lack of structured guidance that there can be in crafting strategy. Over the course of this chapter, we will address these issues at a macro level by tracing the historical roots of the strategist's role, and examining who strategists are and their key characteristics, before considering in detail factors at a more micro level, including the key roles, skills, motivations, and formation of strategists, as outlined in Figure 2.1.

Figure 2.1 Overview of strategists

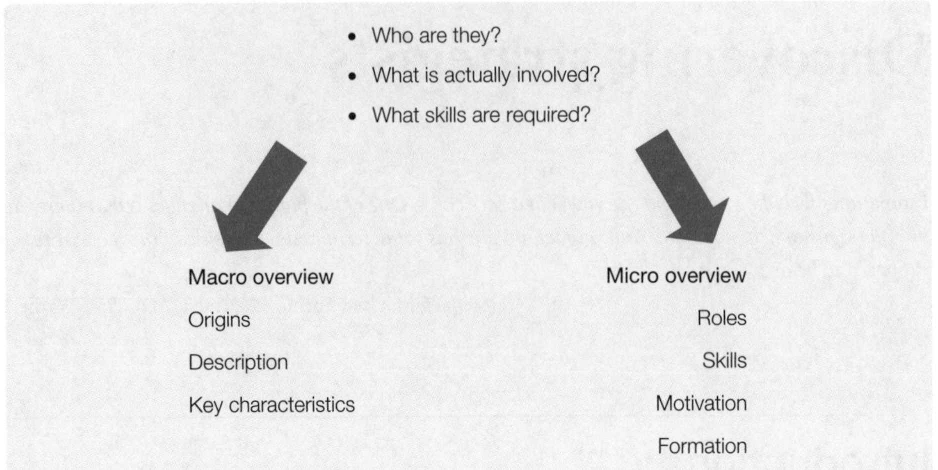

In search of strategists: tracing their origins and characteristics

We saw in Chapter 1 that the concept of strategy and strategists has its genesis in military warfare and the politics of engaging in battle. Cummings (1993—Reading 1.3) states that the word 'strategy' is derived from the Greek word *strategos*, which described a commanding role in the army, and the successful deployment and governance of troops. The historical focus on the strategist's leadership role and the perceived separation between the army general devising military plans (**formulation**) and front-line soldiers enacting them through battle (implementation) were retained as the idea of strategy entered the business lexicon after the Second World War. During this period, authors such as Chandler, Ansoff, and Andrews engaged in a search for the universal principles of business policy—what would become strategic management. Central to these efforts, and borrowing heavily from the military origins of the concept, each of these authors attributed to it the characteristics of leadership, coordination, and control, and afforded the CEO a critical position in strategy formulation.

One can argue that modern strategists can learn much from the military origins of strategy. Like the army generals of 500 BC, strategists today should be consumed by ambition and an obsession with winning, and a focus on understanding the external environment and competition, while at the same time exploiting their organization's own unique strengths and capabilities. Paying attention to the human dynamics of battle, von Clausewitz captured how the most successful generals formed powerful coalitions and controlled obligatory points of passage, while also engendered wide-ranging support through motivational speeches and convincing rhetoric (Carter *et al.*, 2008: 93). Von Clausewitz also stressed the importance of adaptability, noting how theories of war and strategy must evolve as social and political conditions change (Jacobides, 2010: 84). The relevance of these insights for our understanding of the activities of organizational strategists are limited by the relative paucity of accounts capturing what contemporary strategists actually do, and how they deliver value through their activities. There is something of a paradox here: strategists have remained invisible or silent beings, with their roles simply assumed, or glossed over, despite the importance of their rational and analytical capabilities. Indeed, many organizations designate strategy roles at executive level or as part of their top management team. Among the FTSE 100 companies of 2005, forty-one had senior formal organizational positions with the word 'strategy' in their title (see Table 2.1). Similar formal roles have been created in many other private and public organizations.

Table 2.1 Selected strategy job titles from FT listing

Company	FT ranking 2005	Specific strategy job titles
Microsoft	3	Advanced strategies and policy officer Corporate strategy, planning, and analysis officer Consumer strategy and partnerships officer
Citigroup	4	Chief financial officer and head of strategy Strategy and business development officer
Pfizer	9	Vice president, corporate policy and strategic planning
Vodafone	10	Commercial strategy analyst
IBM	11	Senior vice president for IBM strategy
Intel Corporation	12	Director, manufacturing strategic support Director of strategic investment Director of technology strategy Director of equipment strategy

It is interesting to note the variations in the use of 'strategy' in the designation of executive posts. In Microsoft, for example, there were three specific strategy titles—but, from reading them, it is not clear what each post entails. By contrast, IBM designated only one vice president for strategy. The variety in titles reflects the intertwined forces of the Internet age, new organizational forms, new types of collaboration across industries, and globalization—factors that have altered the skill set and positioning of the strategist within an organization (Angwin *et al.*, 2009). Consequently, some commentators suggest that the received military analogy of the strategist's role as a general is only partly appropriate, or even that it is distorted. In practice, the question of who actually constitutes the strategist(s) of an organization and the roles and activities that they conduct are not so clear-cut. To add to the confusion, the literature uses multiple terms as proxies for strategists: 'CEO'; 'president'; 'manager'; 'top leaders'; 'top management team'; 'strategic thinkers'; and 'corporate entrepreneur' (Ericson *et al.*, 2001: 66–68; Garvin and Levesque, 2006; Mintzberg, 1991).

Describing strategists: who are they?

Descriptions and definitions of leaders, managers, and entrepreneurs are well developed in management literature and management practice. However, if we were to ask managers at different organizational levels who the strategist is for their organization, we would probably get a variety of answers. From the 1950s through to the 1970s, the number of corporate planners rapidly expanded. These individuals were responsible for the corporate planning activities of organizations, but also became involved in shorter-term operational planning, as well as other issues at the behest of top management. In 1970, Steiner took note of this change:

> Today's corporate planner is a rather different person—in status and function—from his predecessor of ten years. In another ten years I think he will be much different from what he is today. He will be closer to, and have a deeper involvement with, top management in the strategic planning of his company. In a number of cases he will also provide the coordination, technical expertise, and specialized skills needed in planning throughout the company.
>
> (Steiner, 1970: 139)

Since 2000, there has been a resurgence of dedicated strategy posts, with many Fortune 500 companies employing chief strategy officers (CSOs). In contrast to the corporate planning department of old, the CSO role requires relevant experience, direct engagement with organizational realities, and a track record of leading success. Breene *et al.* (2007: 87) offer a description of CSOs as follows:

> These executives are not, for example, pure strategists, conducting long-range planning in relative isolation. And they are not specialists who have breathed in only the rarefied air of strategy over long careers of thinking rather than doing. Rather they are seasoned executives with a strong strategy orientation who have typically led major initiatives or businesses and worn many operating hats before taking on the role.

Still, despite this significance, the role of strategists in the strategy process has been implied rather than made explicit. Cummings (1993—Reading 1.3), in his discussion of the origins of strategy, draws on a description of a Xenophon commander as one who 'must be ingenious, energetic, careful, full of stamina, and presence of mind, loving and tough, straightforward and crafty, alert and deceptive, ready to gamble everything and wishing to have everything, generous and greedy, trusting and suspicious' (ibid: 134). This description presents complex and contradictory traits that all human beings are capable of exhibiting. Implicit is the political capability of the strategist and the ability to keep going no matter what the circumstances and irrespective of the risks. This leads to a number of issues that have yet to be resolved: namely, how to identify the strategists or strategy actors that are actually involved in the process, and whether a single individual with all of these personality traits and characteristics really exists, or whether these traits are spread among the board and senior members of an organization, with the result that its strategic leadership can include a group and even external agents.

The 'strategy as practice' research perspective is one attempt to explore who the producers of strategy actually are and what they do (Johnson *et al.*, 2003; Whittington, 2002). This research agenda has highlighted the fact that there is much confusion and disagreement in the strategy literature regarding who is actually involved in and responsible for crafting and implementing strategy. The earliest academic accounts of strategists argued that 'the responsibility of control and consciousness must rest with the CEO; *that person is the strategist*' (Andrews, 1971: 19, emphasis added). This seems logical, because there can be only one ultimate decision maker in a company. Other academics posit senior managers and top management teams as the most likely strategists (Gopinath and Hoffman, 1995; Hambrick and Mason, 1984). This would involve the CEO and the chief financial officer, perhaps with the board of directors, working together as the strategists for the company.

A counter perspective suggests that strategy is not only the concern of senior management, but also has a broader remit; consequently, additional members of the company become involved in strategic issues and hence could be described as 'strategists' (Mintzberg, 1973).

For some, it is the middle manager who plays a key role in the strategy process, serving as an intermediary between top management and operational activity (Nonaka, 1988; Wooldridge *et al.*, 2008: 1192). Hamel (1996) and Markides (2000) point to the innovative contribution that can be made by anyone, at any level in the organization. Mintzberg *et al.* (1998: 178) capture this succinctly:

> an informed individual anywhere in the organization can contribute to the strategy process. A strategist can be a mad scientist working in a far-flung research laboratory who comes up with a better product. A group of sales people who decide to promote one product and not others can redirect a company's market positions. Who better to influence the strategist than a foot soldier on the firing line, closest to the action?

Beyond this others note that outsiders, renegades, and strangers may have an influence on strategy in practice (Carter *et al.*, 2008).

The inherent risk of a broad conception of strategists is that, in becoming everyone's domain, the term loses meaning and has less analytical purchase (Angwin *et al.*, 2009). Clarification of who the strategists are and their descriptions is not facilitated by the fact that there is limited research on how strategy and planning actually take place at board level, top management level, with the involvement of lower management levels or professional strategy staff, or via interventions by strategy consultants (Jarzabkowski and Balogun, 2009). Research by Paroutis and Pettigrew (2007) focused on strategy teams at multiple levels and showed that 'acting and knowing of these teams is dynamic, collective and distributed within the multi-business firm across two interrelated levels: within the team and across teams, each involving both recursive and adaptive activities' (ibid: 99). This highlights the intensity and complexity of interaction both within and across teams in multi-business firms. The work of Henry Mintzberg is instructive in this regard. He argues that strategy is something that can be crafted, rather than the scientific process implied in the military metaphors. For Mintzberg (1987—Reading 1.5), the role of the strategist is best captured in the metaphor of the potter who utilizes intuition, creativity, judgement, learning, and experience to create strategies, often with emergent aspects to respond to changing circumstances. Much of the previous literature had focused on the science of strategy, viewing the strategist as a technical architect (Andrews, 1971). This was at the expense of paying attention to the creative aspects of strategy in which judgement, wisdom, and risk-taking are integral elements. In order to explore such tensions further, it is important to capture the full range of possible descriptions of the strategist's role.

In mapping ten different schools of thought in strategy, Mintzberg provides us with insights into who constitutes the strategist and gives us a broad snapshot of the various strategist behaviours, all of which may be evident in managerial practice. In Table 2.2, each of the ten schools of thought is linked to a specific conception of strategy and an associated strategist role. Mintzberg further enhances our understanding by introducing animal metaphors that best describe the likely behaviour of the strategist in this role.

From this, it is clear that the strategist can be a combination of many people (as in the learning school), or the role can be the sole remit of the CEO (as in the design school). As we progress down through the various schools, the role of the strategist and his or her formal power base diminish, thereby moving from more traditional prescriptive depictions reminiscent of strategy's military origins (design; planning; positioning) to more contemporary descriptive interpretations that provide a more fluid integration of the formulation and implementation of strategy (cognitive; learning; cultural). The wolf metaphor, associated with the entrepreneurship school, may be best to describe Richard Branson, founder of Virgin. Organizations in which strategists attempt to foster innovative working environments may be associated with the monkey metaphor of the learning school, such as IDEO, a global design consulting firm. The peacock metaphor of the cultural school may best represent government departments and **public sector organizations**. Strategists can clearly take on many roles: some quite proximate to the terms' military legacy and some far removed from it; some individual in orientation and some more collective; some rational and others more symbolic or power-driven; some proactive and others more reactive. Mintzberg's metaphors provide powerful labels to capture, or foster debate, around the nature and role of strategists

Table 2.2 Mintzberg's strategy schools and metaphors for the strategist

School	Conception of strategy	Strategist as...	Metaphor
Design	Strategy as a process of *conception*	CEO	Spider
Planning	Strategy as a *formal* process	CEO and planning department	Squirrel
Positioning	Strategy as an *analytical* process	CEO in principle; also analysts	Water buffalo
Entrepreneurial	Strategy as a *visionary* process	Entrepreneur; visionary leader	Wolf
Cognitive	Strategy as a *mental* process	Individual or group	Owl
Learning	Strategy as an *emergent* process	Many potential strategists	Monkey
Power	Strategy as a process of *negotiation*	Micro-individual; macro-organization	Lion
Cultural	Strategy as a *collective* process	Organization collectivist dimension of social process	Peacock
Environmental	Strategy as a *reactive* process	Passive, reactive role	Ostrich
Configurational	Strategy as a process of *transformation*	Multiple strategists and roles	Chameleon

in any organization. Exploring possible commonalities across different roles, the next section examines key characteristics of the strategist.

Key characteristics of the strategist

The earliest descriptions of strategists emphasized their leadership characteristics. But if the strategist is to ensure constant refinement and **innovation** of the organization's value proposition, he or she will also require entrepreneurial and managerial characteristics. Arguably, the exaggeration of one characteristic leads to a dangerous neglect of others. For Birkinshaw (2010), recent focus on leadership activity has served to downplay the importance of managerial activity, with consequences evident in corporate scandals, company bankruptcies, and the financial crisis. In a similar vein, Mintzberg (2009) argues that there is little benefit in a leader who cannot manage or a manager who cannot lead. For the strategist, the characteristics of management and leadership are both equally important, like two horses pulling the same cart (Birkinshaw, 2010); the issue is one of balance. Pitcher (1993) contends that you need artists, craftsmen, and technocrats, in the right doses and in the right places. You need someone with a vision, but you also need someone who can develop the people, structures, and systems to make the vision a reality.

The characteristics of strategists can be said to be a combination of the characteristics of entrepreneurship, leadership, and management. Thus, in mapping the day-to-day activities of strategists, it may be useful to relate them to the various modes of thinking and characteristics of entrepreneurs, leaders, or managers, as indicated in Table 2.3. A strategist requires the independence of thought of an entrepreneur, the task logic and technical expertise of a manager, and the intensity of persistence of a leader. Combining these characteristics in crafting strategy may occur on an airplane en route to an executive meeting, in the boardroom, or on the shop floor on a plant visit. The strategist's characteristics enable them to see and understand the broader environmental, industry, and corporate-level issues alongside micro, organizational level, issues. In crafting strategy, entrepreneurial characteristics come to the fore in terms of seeking new opportunities.

Leadership characteristics are needed to convey the crafted strategy in order to elicit company and shareholder support. The managerial characteristics of strategists are essential to the effective

Table 2.3 Entrepreneurs, leaders, and managers

	Entrepreneur	Leader	Manager	Strategist
Relationship with people	Favour independence	Intense and personal; emotional	Task logic, technical	Empathetic: people and contexts
Goals	Individualistic, daring	Active and personal; wise	Passive, impersonal, methodical	Focus on journey rather than destination goals
Motivation, actions based on...	Impulse, need for achievement: see, decide, exploit	Desires, shaping of ideas: see, feel, inspire, change	Analysis; necessities of existing business: analyse, think, change	Achievement orientation, sense of challenge, passion for what he or she does
Choice and risk	Bold, seek new opportunities	Opening up options; encourage risk taking	Limit choice, reduce risk; organized	Intuitive, analytical, seeking to secure uniqueness
Role	Opportunists: exploit opportunities as they emerge	Creators: masters of change and emotions	Conservators: regulators of the existing state of affairs	Politician/communicator Networker/leader Entrepreneur/thinker Decision maker/planner Self-developer
Pitcher's typology	Artist	Craftsman	Technocrat	Film director

Sources: Cunningham *et al.* (2005); Pitcher (1993); Zaleznik (1977)

functioning of the formulation process, the building of coalitions, and the implementation of an organization's strategy. In addition, a management mindset enables considered and realistic evaluation of strategy (Rumelt, 1979—Reading 1.6). The questions are whether strategists embody some unique mix of these ideal types, as outlined in Table 2.3, and if so, which elements and under which circumstances. In order to broaden their thinking, organizations often rely on external strategists, who may shape the broad parameters for micro action or may assist or influence the crafting, formulation, and implementation of strategy. These strategy actors may be management or strategy consultants, such as McKinsey & Co. and the Boston Consulting Group, or they may be bankers, venture capitalists, or state agencies.

A skill necessary for the successful strategists is devising a top management team or strategy group that has an optimal configuration of entrepreneurial, leadership, and managerial characteristics. Many entrepreneurial ventures fail to realize their potential as a result of entrepreneurs who are unable to complement their intrinsic entrepreneurial capabilities with necessary management and leadership skills. Successful strategists therefore integrate key characteristics seamlessly, like a tapestry of woven threads. This does not necessarily imply bringing together the brightest and most technically gifted people, but rather understanding what configuration of people and ideas will work best together (de Rond, 2008). This is what makes the task of the strategist so complex and the ability to deliver value in this domain so unique.

A capable CSO has the ability to visualize and implement strategy across his or her organization through a combination of skills and experience. Reflecting our discussion of key characteristics, Breene *et al.* (2007) found that the CSO should at once be:

- deeply trusted by the CEO;
- a master of multitasking;
- a jack of all trades;
- a star player;
- a doer, not only a thinker;
- the guardian of horizon two (the medium term);
- an influencer, not a dictator;
- comfortable with ambiguity; and
- objective.

The job summary, main duties, and responsibilities outlined in a job specification for a CSO for Stroke-on-Trent NHS Primary Care Trust illustrates the diversity of the role, involving strategy formulation, implementation, and change management activities. Main duties identified include:

> • Drive decision making to sustain organizational change, ensure robust strategic planning processes are in place within the organization and across partners to enable rapid and effective decision making, execution, and delivery of plans both within the PCT and across partnerships.
>
> • Establish a focus and discipline throughout the organization which continually checks whether decisions and actions are aligned with overall strategic goals and will deliver intended results.
>
> • Establish, embed and, clearly articulate the strategic goals and vision of the organization, ensuring all departments and functions understand the detail of the strategic plan and how their work connects to the PCT strategic goals and contributes to becoming world-class commissioners.
>
> • Horizon-scan to pre-empt and interpret highly complex strategic issues confronting Trust board, directors, and senior managers, and problem solve to address these.
>
> (CSO job specification, Stoke-on-Trent NHS)

This job specification highlights that the CSO has to work across organizational boundaries and not only focus on one activity or business unit. This job specification also reflects the multi-dimensional nature of the CSO role and the need to have strong soft and hard skills, with a specific focus on communications skills. Specifically, the CSO must combine managerial analytical decision making and evaluation, visionary leadership to embed ideas, and entrepreneurial insight to 'horizon-scan', and to address opportunities and challenges as they emerge.

Overall, the ultimate objective should be to create a strategist who has the ability to synthesize complex issues based on in-depth analysis. In addressing these issues, it is necessary to unpack the concept of the strategist further to explore more micro, psychological issues likely to inform the success of strategists, including their role and skills, as well as their motivation and formation.

Role, skills, motivation, and formation of the strategist

The strategy literature presents little detailed research as to the role, skills, formation, and motivation of the strategist, which means that there is a significant gap in our understanding of the strategist. Directing attention to the nature of the strategist is critical, and means that strategy may be conceived as being essentially a human process of interpreting events and actions. This view has gathered momentum over recent years, drawing on classic work in the 1950s and 1960s about behavioural theories of the firm, as well as on classic work on strategy decision making in the 1970s and 1980s (McGee *et al.*, 2005: 3). While strategy literature has paid vast attention to analysing industry forces, understanding key success factors (KSFs) and disaggregating value chain activities, much less attention has been paid to analysing, understanding, or disaggregating the key factors that constitute a successful strategist (Whittington, 1996). To facilitate this task, Figure 2.2 outlines the roles, skills, motivation, and formation of the strategist.

Role of the strategist

The role of the strategist is to think, act, and manage the business strategically. This involves seeking to control the future competitive landscape by whatever means are most effective to ensure that the uniqueness of the company is maintained. This can prove a difficult task if the strategist's attention is constantly focused on operational issues. Garratt (1991: 164) describes the role of the strategist as:

> managing the conjunction of the political world or 'polity', with the more day-to-day routines of tactics and trying to keep them sufficiently in balance without allowing ossification. It is, therefore, essential for a director to have the ability to rise above the daily and weekly tactical detail so that he or she can project and direct the business campaigns.

The strategist can fulfil multiple roles in a company context. As Garret noted, the political role of a strategist is not limited to internal action, but also involves dealing with competitors, collaborators, and regulators. The strategist's role is to take ownership of the strategy, to simplify its key messages, and to cascade them through the organization. The strategist must take a leadership role in driving strategy implementation as well as crafting strategy. More importantly, the strategist has to keep the balance and the link between the hands and minds of the organization through his or her role as a networker, thinker, and entrepreneur. To do this effectively, strategists need to maintain a network of information sources, particularly as managers progress up the ladder of an organization (Wrapp, 1967). Successful strategists seek to be at the centre of several formal and informal communication networks, functioning as nodes and nerve centres that monitor and learn from a continually changing information field (Schoemaker, 1993).

Figure 2.2 Roles, skills, motivation, and formation of strategists (cunningham *et al.*, 2005)

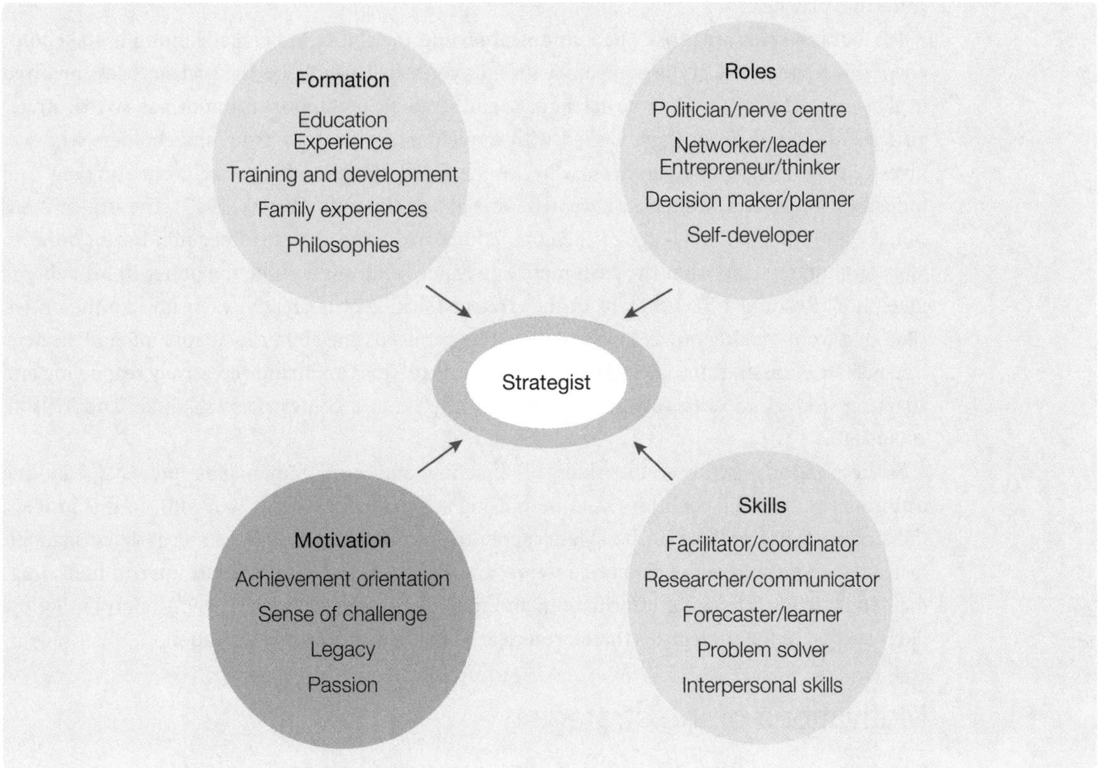

Invariably, the strategist is central to the decision-making process. Effective strategists are not people who abstract themselves from the daily detail, but those who *immerse* themselves in it while being able to abstract the strategic *messages* from it. The strategist's role therefore involves a combination of orientation (direction) and animation (action) (Jarzabkowski and Wilson, 2002). Drucker (1954) viewed the manager as someone who creates order out of chaos. In the metaphor of a symphony or orchestra, at any one time the strategist can be composer and/or conductor (Schoemaker, 1993: 114). In the case of the CSO, Breene *et al.* (2007) outline the key roles as:

- engendering commitment to clear strategic plans;
- driving immediate change; and
- driving decision making that sustains organizational change.

While there is some debate over the nature and mix of strategist roles, ultimately these have to be judged in the context of the overall responsibility that the role confers upon individuals. As the late C. K. Prahalad reminded us, strategists are 'custodians of society's most powerful institutions. They must therefore hold themselves to a higher standard' (Prahalad, 2010: 36).

Skills of the strategist

Despite the recognized role of human capital in generating advantage (Kraaijenbrink *et al.*, 2010: 356; Wright and McMahan, 2011), we still know little in terms of the skills of the strategist. Some empirical research carried out by Cunningham *et al.* (2005) highlighted the key skills as being interpersonal, problem solving, forecasting, communicating, researching, facilitating, and coordinating. A structured and analytical mind is crucial, as is an understanding of the discipline and the need for process (Mintzberg, 1994). Such clichés as 'thinking outside the box' and 'lateral thinking' come into play here.

Further key skills are those of communication and the ability to persuade multiple **stakeholders** of the desired view of the company within its context. This reflects the social process involved in all aspects of strategy. The role of language and **strategic metaphors** is important, so that strategists secure buy-in from those tasked with implementing strategy, from shareholders who will invest equity, and from customers, who are the final arbitrors of success. From company and industry perspectives, strategists have to be able to 'talk the walk' (Weick, 1995). The strategist has to have an intimate knowledge of the competitive arena and the customer mindset in order to know and understand what the customer really values and wants—like the potter in Mintzberg's metaphor (Reading 1.5). Inherent in the strategist's skill set is creativity. Again like the potter, changing from making bowls to vases, the strategist needs the ability to adapt and craft strategy irrespective of organizational and competitive context. This can include creatively reapplying and adapting strategy tools to suit his or her own purpose and context (Jarzabkowski and Wilson, 2006: 360).

Strategy clearly involves the skills of enacting and doing: managing projects; handling disturbances; building coalitions; and mobilizing support (Mintzberg, 2009: 48). In this process, the strategists are unlikely to be able to apply their craft uninterrupted in an isolated manner; instead, they must have the patience, reserve, and ability to deal with multiple interruptions, fragmented activities, changing information, and multiple power plays (ibid: 19). Underpinning the likely success of the strategist is therefore a clear sense of purpose and motivation.

Motivations of the strategist

Key motivations of the strategist include achievement orientation, sense of challenge, and passion for what they do (Cunningham *et al.*, 2005). These motivations are reflective of the human condition of striving to develop, to succeed, and to get to the next level. Strategists have a responsibility to grow the business year on year—but they also gain personal satisfaction in attempting to achieve something different and in doing so on a continual basis. The strategist's passion for the business, like that of an entrepreneur, can be infectious. Further issues that may motivate strategists include status and the legacy that they may leave with their company. Frequently, we associate periods of an organization's success with the individuals and teams involved. This is why strategy may dominate their attention: 'served by hordes of underlings, their huge desks uncluttered by the daily minutiae of business, they often consider strategy as their most valuable contribution' (*The Economist*, 1993, cited in Mintzberg *et al.*, 2005).

Formation of the strategist

For professions such as accountancy, human resource management, and marketing, there are clear paths in terms of educational and professional attainment; to become a strategist, the path is less clear. So how does one become a strategist? Are strategists born? Does entry via a graduate placement programme help? The simple answer is that there is no definable career path to becoming a strategist. In the traditional conception of strategy, strategic planning was judged to be guided by a cadre of highly educated planners (Mintzberg *et al.*, 1998: 48). This placed education and the teaching and dissemination of strategy principles as key to the formation of the strategist. Thus education, experience, training and development, family experiences, philosophies (business and personal), as well as the individual's values, can shape the individual in becoming a strategist (Cunningham *et al.*, 2005; Hartman, 2000). Individuals' mental models are most affected by education, experience, and age (Markides, 1997). Managerial mental models are simplified knowledge structures or cognitive representations about how the business environment works (Gary and Wood, 2001).

In understanding the background of the strategist, Breene *et al.*'s (2007: 88) research found that:

> Less than one-fifth of our survey respondents spent the bulk of their careers (pre-CSO) on strategic planning. Most reported significant line-management and functional experience in disparate areas, including technology management, marketing, and operations.

The route to the strategic summit of an organization is not necessarily one based on objective assessment of talent. Research indicates that top managers are more likely to pick people similar to them in personality, thinking, and characteristics, while it remains the case that women remain massively under-represented in strategist positions. As an example, Helfat and colleagues estimate that only 6 per cent of the Fortune 1000 will have women CEOs by 2016 (Helfat *et al.*, 2011: 42).

Overall, far from being straightforward and rational, this focus on the strategist suggests that strategy is, in fact, interpreted by managers according to their own frames of reference (Johnson, 1988). Relational, political, and emotive considerations typically present at the micro level will almost inevitably influence strategic decisions outcomes (Johnson *et al.*, 2003). Each strategy may then be best judged as reflective of the strategist's cognitive perspective, which is interpreted, shaped, and synthesized by his or her formation, his or her role within the company, his or her skill set, and his or her motivation. This draws attention to the importance of cognition, strategic thinking, and decision making, which are explored in more detail in the next chapter.

Spotlight How CSOs think about their role

As companies struggle to meet the challenges of today's complex business environment by developing short-term and long-term strategic visions, the role of CSO has become increasingly prominent. Although CEOs remain ultimately responsible for strategic decisions, they regularly look to the CSOs to craft and implement successful strategies. But the role's relative novelty raises critical questions about its function and the degree of ownership that it carries.

McKinsey brought together CSOs from several high-profile companies to discuss the challenges of the job—starting with its definition and what it entails. The panel included: Edward C. Arditte, senior vice president of strategy and investor relations at the multi-industry company Tyco International; Stuart Grief, vice president of strategy and business development at the aircraft, industrial, and finance group Textron; Marius A. Haas, senior vice president of strategy and corporate development at the technology company HP; Dan Simpson, vice president, office of the chairman, at the cleaning-products group Clorox; Annabel Spring, managing director in charge of strategy and execution at the investment bank Morgan Stanley; and J. F. Van Kerckhove, vice president of **corporate strategy** at the e-commerce company eBay.

Some of the panellists say that they have one foot in the corporate suite and the other deep in the business units. Others believe that while communication with the business units is very important, a CSO's primary concern is the development of high-level strategy. In that capacity, CSOs grapple with the challenge of balancing short-term and long-term goals: handling the multifaceted demands of an increasingly global business environment, they strive to focus on growth without losing sight of productivity. All panel members agree that a close relationship with the CEO is vital for instigating change, but they voice different views on other issues, such as how to interact with the finance function.

Renée Dye, a consultant based in McKinsey's Atlanta office, moderated the panel discussion.

The Quarterly: **How well defined is the role of the CSO?**

Dan Simpson: The role of the CSO is poorly defined, much like the discipline of strategy itself. Most other C-level executives have high levels of control over their disciplines, fairly clear ownership, and a large staff. But that isn't true for the CSO. Many things affect the role, from the nature of the industry or company to the CSO's reporting relationship. But the biggest factor is the style of the CEO, the true chief strategy officer.

Stuart Grief: The CEO makes the ultimate decisions, but it's our job to explore the facts and alternatives around an issue. We make sure CEOs have a clear understanding of the implications of various choices so that they can make informed decisions.

J. F. Van Kerckhove: The CEO is the ultimate owner of corporate strategy. A good strategy process finds the right balance between top-down and bottom-up engagement in developing strategy, building on the collective wisdom, and exposing its main assumptions. While the formulation of strategy often goes through specific planning milestones, its development is ongoing—at times explicit and at times not. The CSO plays an important role in helping to coordinate and inject knowledge in the more formal strategy process, as well as fostering an environment for more spontaneous strategy creation. The latter often finds its roots in a close collaboration with the business units or field operations at the forefront of experimentation and learning. In a fast-paced industry like ours, the ability to rapidly learn from the field is a true competitive advantage.

Ed Arditte: That depends on your organizational structure and how many lines of business you have. In a more monolithic type of company, it's easier to identify issues around which people can rally. For more diversified companies, like Tyco, strategy is driven by the businesses, with appropriate input and guidance from the corporate centre. That has proved to be a better approach for us than approaching it from the centre outward.

Annabel Spring: I absolutely agree. Our role is to get feedback from the business units, overlay the global trends, and make sure that everybody has identified the right issues. We then prioritize the opportunities across the business units and provide a strategic element for that prioritization. Feedback from the business units is also critical for maintaining that entrepreneurial edge. Morgan Stanley is so specialized and yet complex and global, which is hard to balance.

Marius Haas: The CSO's role is dependent on CEOs not only because they have the final sign-off on strategy decisions, but also because of their skill sets, tendencies, and way of managing the business. The question becomes: how do you complement the CEO's strengths and weaknesses? My job at HP is to lay out the key initiatives we need to focus on in order to execute the plan. What are the initiatives that could build extra capacity, enhance our plan, or bring incremental operating profits or revenues? We go through those questions to get a sense of which ones need to mature and which ones are clearer from an execution standpoint.

Annabel Spring: The market also affects the CSO's role. When the market is up, the role addresses long-term vision and investment. When the market is down, it requires restructuring strategy. You have to be able to move with the market and with the CEO.

Dan Simpson: Is it your role per se that varies according to market conditions, or does the difference lie more in the issues you address?

Annabel Spring: 'Role' is somewhat of an amorphous word. When the market is growing, it's easier to see the big picture, sit back, and prioritize across opportunities. In a market downturn, it is very much a tighter, hand-holding role with the business units, and a much more operational one.

Stuart Grief: I find Textron going in the opposite position, which may highlight the difference between industrial and financial companies. When the company is struggling, there's a need to step back and re-examine things. When the company performs very well, people sometimes believe the good times will continue forever.

The Quarterly: How does a company's performance modify what the CSO does?

Dan Simpson: Performance changes the issue set, not the role. During performance shortfalls, consistency and conviction become more important—horizons are closer and you focus all the water on short-term fires. But it's not uncommon for short-term fixes to create long-term problems. A downward spiral develops momentum and becomes harder to turn around. While nearly everyone focuses on the near term, a CSO must be an advocate for long-term health.

Marius Haas: That makes sense, but in our situation at HP, when the company wasn't performing well, the solution required restructuring. The people running the business were so close to the business that they weren't able to think outside of the box. The fundamental pieces were broken. We felt that driving for operational excellence was going to deliver more value for us in that period of time.

Stuart Grief: If a company's doing poorly, one of the first worthwhile diagnoses is an assessment of the quality of the strategy and its execution. If you're happy with the strategy, you just need to focus operationally to get it done. I wasn't at Textron at the time, but in 2000 and 2001, the leadership realized, 'We've got a dead business model. We have to rebuild the company and transform it fundamentally.' It was a strategic issue in need of rewriting.

Marius Haas: I was in a corporate-strategy team at Compaq about eight years ago, where the team spent way too much time focusing on the strategic, long-term view. The CEO liked this model, but none of the other executives felt there was any deliverable value. When I got into the role of CSO, I tried to build a bridge between the CEO and the executives in the business units. I wanted a model that pulled from all of them. You need to be able to dive into a business unit and become a core part of its strategy-setting and operational-excellence initiatives.

The Quarterly: **How do you ensure that strategy is executed well?**

Ed Arditte: At Tyco, it's very clear. It is the responsibility of the businesses to act upon the plan, and it's our responsibility, at the corporate centre, to challenge and evaluate the plan. Once it's approved, our job is to watch it and make sure the right people are being put on the bigger issues.

The Quarterly: **When we surveyed 800 executives on strategic planning in 2006, one of the most striking results was that only 36 per cent of them said that the strategic plan was meaningfully integrated with human-resources processes—incentive, evaluation, and compensation systems. Does strategy play a role in evaluations?**

Ed Arditte: The responsibility is both in the short and long-term results. There has to be a balance, but there's never a perfect answer for how you balance them. You need a dialogue that aligns **resource** allocation, people, and money with both the short and the long term.

Stuart Grief: Balancing the short versus the long term is the biggest challenge we have. How do you balance the trade-off between the short-term compensation lift from near-term performance and the investments—and therefore the depressed economics, short term—that make the long-term strategies pay off?

Marius Haas: An implementation plan that has clear milestones and owners is a must. Execution sits in the business units. At HP, we won't make the hand-off until the business owner understands, accepts ownership, and acknowledges the need to deliver. As to the strategic plan as a whole, we've gotten a lot more disciplined. Now we can say, 'Here are the levers within our plan that we need to execute in order to deliver. We know the plan, the capacity, and what we can do incrementally. If you're going to show me a number, you've got to tell me how you're going to get there.' Management has changed how people's performance was going to be measured at a granular level.

The Quarterly: **What's the dialogue like, though, when a business unit presents a plan that doesn't have steadily increasing margins, because the unit wants to make a long-term investment that won't pay off until beyond the current planning period?**

Marius Haas: We ask the business unit heads to build capacity in the plan and then reinvest that into areas they believe will be longer-term growth areas. Most of them have now divvied up their portfolios into three areas: emerging market opportunities and initiatives; mature but current businesses; and investments that help generate the required cash flow. We constantly look at that life cycle to see if those investments are in the right areas to generate longer-term growth.

The Quarterly: **Is there any advantage to having a closer relationship with the finance function?**

Annabel Spring: I think there is a significant advantage to being close to the CFO. I understand the budgeting and am involved in the process, both within the business units and at the corporate level. I'm part of the dialogue—which is critical for credibility and understanding the business. For Morgan Stanley in particular, being close to the CFO is important, given the number of transactions we do for the firm on a principal basis, because you need that back-and-forth relationship in order to be effective.

Ed Arditte: There's always a debate about who owns the strategy process—accountants, financial-planning people, or business people? But it shouldn't be a question of where it's owned, but of who is involved in the process. Do they work together? Are they able to achieve alignment? Alignment is key to the process: it defines what you want to do and, more important, makes sure that everybody understands the priorities. Then you can allocate the resources, evaluate the progress regularly, and provide support when necessary.

Dan Simpson: People commonly confuse strategy and planning. Planning is primarily internal resource allocation and budgeting, which is clearly tied to finance. Resource allocation has to be driven by strategy, but isn't strategy in and of itself. Strategy should be focused on the marketplace and on customers and consumers. You must improve your position in the marketplace and have a clear idea about why people choose your products or services over someone else's. At Clorox, we try to separate those conversations. One of the things we've done in the past is to bar financial components and exhibits from the first rounds of strategy meetings. That way, the discussion focuses on market competitiveness rather than on internal resource allocation.

Stuart Grief: One of the challenges we used to face at Textron, though, was that without finance being deeply involved in the strategic discussions early on, we risked the CFO undoing the strategy three months down the road. A personal relationship with the CFO is really critical—more than reporting to the CFO. Alignment is vital on the road to execution.

Marius Haas: Our plans require three things to be aligned: efficiency productivity, accelerating growth, and capital strategy, both financial and human. We've often taken resources out of the capital strategy to tackle inefficiency, generating capacity so we can invest in growth. In those cases, the triangulation of those key areas has been critical.

Dan Simpson: Execution problems are often symptoms of trouble upstream in the strategy-development process—the strategy process has failed to realistically assess current reality, to honestly understand organizational capabilities, to align key players with those who do real work, or, at the end of the day, to create a compelling, externally driven vision of success.

Ed Arditte: It depends on your organization and how centralized it is, but the more a strategic initiative is owned by the business units, the greater the chance of success. Many great corporate ideas fail in the business units because of a lack of ownership.

The Quarterly: What are the most important issues facing strategists today?

Stuart Grief: An important challenge is engaging with the businesses to think differently about what they do by helping them consider different business models, challenging the status quo, and avoiding complacency. It's hard but necessary in an environment where competitors are more aggressive and diverse than ever.

Marius Haas: The biggest challenge for us is transitioning from an efficiency–productivity focus to a growth focus without dropping the ball on the execution of the efficiency–productivity side. The second challenge lies in migrating external influences and forces to our mainstream thinking. If the customer and technology are evolving, we're facing an environment of accelerated consolidation in the competitive landscape. Getting ahead of the pack and being the ones consolidating—versus having to react to actions taken by our competitors—is very important.

Annabel Spring: I would echo the short-term versus long-term balance issues but add a layer of globalization. Short-term profit opportunities are abundant in the developed world, as long-term opportunities are in the developing world. You have to do both to get the continuous-growth profile we all need, but managing the timing is a very tricky thing—not to mention a core component of our role in terms of project prioritization, resource allocation, and long-term strategy.

J. F. Van Kerckhove: Given rising customer expectations for the online experience, the high pace of innovation, and the emergence of new business models, we need to sharpen our game continuously and faster than ever, as well as assess what elements of our past success we need to strengthen and from which we need to depart. In that context, our main challenge is strengthening our core business while rapidly scaling our new growth platforms and developing new operational and organizational muscles for our future success. Just as our company has grown rapidly, so has its organizational complexity. We are focusing on simplifying how we do business, creating alignment behind a few clear priorities, and stepping up our organizational agility and effectiveness.

Ed Arditte: As is probably true for everyone here, our businesses are exceedingly complex and growing more so every day. It doesn't matter if this is driven by developed markets, emerging markets, financial markets, or technology—there are so many changes, and the pace has gotten much faster over the years. Taking a complex set of business issues and simplifying them is a key part of this role. We can't do it individually, but we have to be facilitators of that process and get alignment around the truly important issues that will drive performance.

Dan Simpson: Externally, our toughest strategic issue at Clorox is the consolidation and globalization of both the upstream cost structure and the downstream retail trade, offset by extreme fragmentation in the media environment. Change in the last 20 years has been extraordinary, and the implications for brand equity and value creation and distribution are profound.

Internally, the toughest issues are exposing orthodoxies that constrain our thinking and options, as well as spreading priorities and resources across time horizons and business unit boundaries. Part of strategy's role is to define external imperatives at a higher level so that investments spanning different time horizons or organizational units actually reinforce each other.

Source: Dye (2008)

Implications for strategy practice

Strategy is messy and unstructured, and can involve high levels of risk and uncertainty. Not everyone excels in or adapts or responds well to these conditions. However, in becoming a strategist, one has to reflect on one's own strengths and weaknesses to understand how they can be developed and honed further. As we have seen in the chapter thus far, having a leadership and entrepreneurial mindset is critical; along with this are the ability to be creative and, given the social nature of strategy, the possession of good interpersonal skills. Being a strategist is about relating to and understanding people's behaviour as much as it is about organizational processes and activities.

The ability to understand the competitive environment and to develop mindshare with customers in different markets are two of the core capabilities of a strategist. The strategy of the business has to positively impact and influence potential purchase in a competitive marketplace. For example, how would you, as a strategist in a retail environment, ensure that customers come into your store and buy as many products as possible? Contrast this with the role of a strategist in, say, Medtronic, a global company specializing in medical devices. The experiences of the two roles will be different, but the strategic challenges that they face are similar. As a strategist, you have to reflect on your own strengths and capabilities. When you work in a team, what skills and other attributes do you bring? How do you behave during meetings? How persuasive are your arguments? By definition, this should also involve an objective acknowledgement and understanding of key weaknesses and how these may be addressed or countered.

Being a strategist requires effective interpersonal skills, so you may have conversations with people on the shop floor, in the boardroom, with customers, competitors, or shareholders. This requires the strategist to have a holistic understanding of the company, how it works, and the formal and informal aspects, as well as a clear understanding of the competitive dynamics that are at play. This knowledge is enhanced by hard evidence-based analysis. Being a strategist requires clarity of thought, and the ability to persuade and implement. In practice, this is difficult to achieve; organizational politics can sap an organization's strength, and the strategist may have to deal with several organization filters and become a master of impression management. Despite all, the strategist has to make strategy personal for everyone, by getting them involved in the strategy process, through personal interactions via meetings, and by putting in place a reward and performance system that is equitable, but which challenges people.

Who creates and who implements the strategy in any organization are fundamental issues. It is critical that organizations identify the key group of people who contribute towards the formulation and implementation of strategy. By identifying them, effort can be made to encourage, acknowledge, and reward their behaviours, as well as to ensure that appropriate communication channels are in place so that the strategy message diffuses throughout the organization and becomes a reality. For successful strategy execution, influencers within the organization have to take ownership of the strategy. Further, by considering the motivation and skill set required of strategists, organizations can assess whether they have an appropriate balance in terms of entrepreneurs, leaders, and managers, and whether they have the people with the necessary experience to continually drive organizational performance while ensuring flexibility and adaptability. At an organizational level, it is important to foster a culture that encourages the debate of different perspectives throughout the organization, and which can challenge core assumptions about the organization and the competitive environment.

Nowadays, employees and other stakeholders often have an involvement with strategy workshops and strategy development at different levels of the organization. After such experiences, they may be sceptical about the value of strategy and strategists. The democratization of strategy in organizations is essential and strategists have to be mindful of managing people's expectations, as well as overcoming their cynicism about the process. While very little academic literature has explored how strategy and strategy tools are used in practice by strategy actors, it is important that organizations provide space and freedom for the social processes of strategy to evolve. This may be through formal events such as strategy workshops, team-building exercises, or round-table discussions, but strategists should also use informal mechanisms to discuss and reflect on the reality of strategy for the organization.

For many organizations, the business case for hiring a CSO or a strategic planner is still a difficult one to make, given uncertainty about what actual tangible value they contribute to organizational performance. On a practical level, the business must consider what the core tasks and responsibilities would be of a designated strategist. However, the reality for many organizations is that the short-term planning horizon and objectives pervade organizational efforts and thinking. Even in organizations that have a formal strategy role, it is inevitable that a significant allocation of the individual's time will be spent on operational activities. This raises the question of who in the organization is considering the medium-to-longer-term horizon. When the organization finds itself in a crisis, the cost of having a designated strategist or strategy department may not seem high or organizationally onerous.

Introduction to readings

Reading 1.3, by Stephen Cummings (1993), intricately details the deep historical and political origins of strategists, which stem all the way back to 400 BC. In providing a historical overview of the origin of strategy, Cummings documents the relevance of this to those engaging in strategic activities and decision making in organizations today, including the criteria for identifying an excellent strategist and the best methods for learning strategy. The questions then become: how applicable are these principles today? Can they be identified? And what are the implications? If all of the issues addressed in this book are age-old, what further lessons can be learnt from reflection on historical episodes? Cummings' review suggests the importance of political acumen, practical intelligence, and experience at the coalface, as well as directing and taking part in the thick of the battle. This may suggest that the perceived separation of formulation and implementation, which the strategic management literature often associates with its military underpinnings, may need to be revisited.

Our second reading for this chapter, to which a link is provided on the Online Resource Centre that accompanies this book, is Michael Porter's 'The CEO as strategist' (2005), in which Porter takes up the inheritance of an emphasis on the military general and the leadership role in developing and promoting strategy—in this case, examining the role of the CEO. Reflecting his emphasis on positioning in strategic management, Porter attributes the central strategy-making role to the CEO, arguing that the 'chief strategist of any organization has to be the leader—the CEO'. In advancing his view (similar in tone to Reading 1.1), Porter contends that the CEO is critical in choosing and defending the trade-offs that enable a firm to sustain its unique position over time. Consequently, he associates exceptionally good strategies and exceptionally good leaders. He leaves open the impact of various contexts and contingencies that may influence the role and impact of a leader's direction. Is Porter's perspective a universal panacea for managing strategy? If the role of the strategist is to 'teach' as opposed to 'coach', is it all about science and no art? And does this assume an ability and willingness of those at a lower level to learn and thus implement?

The final reading for the chapter, also accessible through a link on the Online Resource Centre, is by Richard

Whittington (1996) and offers 'Strategy as practice' as a theoretical lens that may enable an understanding of how strategy practitioners really act and interact. Whittington argues that the key question should be: 'What does it take to be an effective practitioner?' He argues that the practice perspective on strategy facilitates a focus on strategists and strategizing, as opposed to the traditional focus on organizations and strategies. He leaves a number of questions unresolved, such as: who actually constitutes a strategist; how the strategist's roles and activities are determined; what motivates the strategist; whether there is value in an overarching theory such as 'strategy as practice'; and whether it is useful to distinguish strategists from managers, leaders, or entrepreneurs.

Approaches such as those of Mintzberg and Whittington clearly complicate issues and question more traditional approaches to understanding the role of the strategist. In so doing, they also set up the debate for the next chapter, which considers in more depth the key processes of strategizing and the activities of strategists including strategic thinking, decision making, and leadership.

Mini case study U2: even better than the real thing? *Professor Tom Lawton, Cranfield School of Management, Dr Denis Harrington, Waterford Institute of Technology, and Dr James Cunningham*

Bono, The Edge, Adam Clayton, and Larry Mullen, Jr. The name recognition may not be as instant or universal as for John, Paul, George, and Ringo, but for fans in Cape Town or Dublin, Toronto or Tokyo, the music that these four make is equally entertaining and uplifting. Ever since breaking onto the international stage in the early 1980s, the quartet has inspired rock music lovers across the world. It is rare that an artist or band maintains a premier position in the business for more than a few short years. Some endure, but lose much of the critical acclaim and commercial appeal that they once possessed; a rarefied few last the course, consistently delivering innovative, attention-grabbing music, and delighting both fans and critics alike. Over the course of the last thirty years, Irish rock group U2 has stood head and shoulders above most of their contemporaries. The numbers are impressive: a dozen albums; more than 145 million copies sold worldwide; twenty-two Grammy awards; and sold-out concerts from London to Los Angeles.

From Mount Temple

U2 started in 1976 with an advert posted on the bulletin board of Mount Temple High School in Dublin, Ireland, by 14-year-old Larry Mullen. The band's first break came in 1978, winning IR£500 in a talent contest on St Patrick's Day (17 March) in Limerick. A judge at the show, Jackie Hayden, worked for CBS Records and helped the band to produce their first demo. Live performances led to a modest following and their first release, *U2–Three*, was independently released in 1979 by CBS Ireland as a three-song EP. One important fan of the U2 style was Bill Graham, a journalist with the music paper *Hot Press*. Graham was an early champion of the band and introduced them to their manager, Paul McGuinness—often referred to as the 'fifth member' of U2. The EP did not do well outside Ireland (where it topped the charts), but U2 toured to promote it and landed a contract with Island Records in 1980. Their live performances were a key part of their early success: their shows were energetic and, thanks to Bono's charisma, people began to notice them. Between 1980 and 1983, they released three albums—*Boy*; *October*; and *War*—with reasonable sales. *War* gave them their first number-one hit and ensured that the band became mainstream.

The band of the 1980s and style changes

In 1984, the band gave a show-stealing performance at the Live Aid concert, which coupled with the critical and commercial success of their latest album, *The Unforgettable Fire*. Despite the consequent global success, the group did not rest on their laurels and continued going from strength to strength. *The Unforgettable Fire* was eclipsed by the release of *The Joshua Tree* in 1987. Probably U2's best-known recording, their fifth album (named after a small town in California's Death Valley, the album cover featuring a photo of one such tree from the area) went platinum in the UK 48 hours after being released, winning the band Grammy awards and the front cover of *Time* magazine.

In the 1980s, U2 started to hint about reinventing themselves. The result was the radical departure of 1991's *Achtung Baby* album, inspired in part by the excitement of Berlin around the time of the fall of the Wall. The 1990s saw a transformation in this political rock band from guitars and idealism to electronica, starting with the *Achtung Baby* album and going right though to *Pop* and the single 'Lemon'. *Achtung Baby* hit the right chord with fans and critics. The subsequent tour, 'ZooTV', was a huge extravaganza, which was purposefully as much about the show as the songs. The show was built around a stage backed up with hundreds of TV screens, flashing satellite-TV images, and subliminal messages to an enthralled audience. Inspired by the dramatic TV footage of the Gulf War, U2 used the technology to capture what was happening in the world and feed it back to its audience.

Achtung Baby was followed by *Zooropa* in 1993 and was a further change for the band, embracing a more electronic, techno style. *Zooropa* was less commercially successful than other albums and is illustrative of U2's experimentation period. In 1997, the *Pop* album was as far away from classic U2 as was possible and was a difficult album to record because of time pressure. Another world tour followed, again with extravagance, computer generation, and a giant rotating lemon and huge olive on a 100-foot cocktail stick. The tour itself was the second-highest grossing tour in 1997, with revenues of US$80m; it had cost US$100m to produce. Change was inevitable and essential. The group would have to go back to basics. This they would successfully do, but it took them several years to pull it off.

Conquering the twenty-first century

Every release from U2 represents an evolution of their sound. *All That You Can't Leave Behind*, released in 2000, returned to what the band was about and is the spiritual follow-up to *The Joshua Tree*. Returning to their guitar-driven sound, they sold more than 10 million copies. The tour accompanying the album (the 'Elevation' tour) was a scaled-down affair compared with their more recent forays and their eighty US shows grossed revenues of US$110m—the second-highest total ever, behind only The Rolling Stones' 'Voodoo Lounge' tour in 1994. After the tour had ended, U2 performed at the half-time show during Super Bowl XXXV, with a fully live rendition of 'Where the streets have no name', in which they paid tribute to the victims of the 9/11 terrorist attacks some months earlier. The album subsequently won four Grammy awards.

Their 2005 album, *How to Dismantle an Atomic Bomb*, falls squarely into the category of a band in mid-transformation. Its debut track, 'Vertigo', has seen much overexposure thanks to Apple's iPod marketing campaign, for which the band cleverly received no royalties. In its first week, the album sold 840,000 copies in the USA (a record for the band) and topped the charts in thirty-two countries. The 'Vertigo' tour that followed the album was a huge success, generating US$260m in revenue and drawing more than 3 million people to ninety concerts, all of which were sell-outs. The European leg of the tour ended in August 2005 in Portugal, where the country's president, Jorge Sampaio, presented the band with the Order of Liberty—the country's most prestigious honour—because of their work for action in Africa and worldwide to combat poverty. This award had never before been presented to a foreign music group.

New dimensions, new directions

While other big acts felt threatened by the new music download culture, U2 were busy working on a new business model. As early as 2000, they had opened an extensive website, with an index to every song and album, lyrics, tour news refreshed nightly, and subscriber features that allowed access to tickets, exclusive content, and streaming downloads of every song and video the band has ever made.

In November 2005, U2 struck a deal with Apple to offer an iPod music player special edition model tied to the group. Apple also introduced the iPod Photo, which stored digital photographs along with music. The group partnered with Apple to promote the iPod, performing 'Vertigo', on an iPod TV commercial, and releasing the track as a single exclusively through Apple's online music download service, iTunes. The collaboration with Apple gave visibility to the band at a time when most radio station playlists did not extend much beyond a narrow selection of pop singers.

Following a relatively unsuccessful period with producer Rick Rubin, U2's twelfth studio album, *No Line on the Horizon*, saw the band work once more with creative producers Brian Eno and Daniel Lanois. The album was more experimental than previous work. While generally well received by critics, album sales were comparatively low by U2 standards and the album did not contain a U2 staple hit single. Unperturbed, U2 once again innovated with technology and embarked on a hugely successful 360-degree tour. The 360-degree design meant a staging/audience configuration allowing the band to completely sell out stadiums; with the stage centrally placed, fans were able to surround from all sides. As the tour progressed, the band played less of their *No Line on the Horizon* material. Nonetheless, having played to over 7 million people in addition to a headline Glastonbury set, few will doubt it has been another successful tour when they eventually come off the road in July 2011.

Paul McGuinness: the fifth member of U2

At the core of U2, Paul McGuinness has been part of the band since the early days and, as long-time manager and confidant, is widely regarded as the band's fifth member. His management of the band over the decades has ensured that U2 maintain a commercial and temporal relevance as a result of his ability to create and think about the future, and his courage to take bold decisions that would allow the band to exploit their creative talents. McGuinness recognized the importance of being outwardly focused in creative terms to take advantage of business opportunities, but at the same time he identified the need for the band to keep a firm handle on operations. As he pointed out in an interview with the *New York Times*:

> The band members and I were always aware that it would be pathetic to be good at music but bad at business. They shared my understanding that great rock'n' roll is a complex equation involving art, commerce, advertising, fashion, sex, politics and all sorts of things.
>
> (Olsen, 2005)

While McGuinness has honed his business and management talents with U2, he has also represented acts such as PJ Harvey and Sinead O'Connor. He has also diversified into other ventures such as his Celtic Heartbeat label, established with former Clannad manager David Kavanagh and Barbara Galavan. From the start, McGuinness had a clear sense of how U2 might develop strategically. As he has pointed out, in 1983, during the early days of MTV, U2 were achieving a reputation as a live band, but had not yet had a hit album. He decided to produce a TV programme at the Red Rocks Amphitheatre in Denver, Colorado, and use the film to illustrate U2's emerging status in the USA. McGuinness remarked on the importance of using the concert footage 'to try and get on MTV'. The band subsequently invested all available resources in the programme. On the day of the show, the rain poured down, but, as the *New York Times* reported, 'luckily the rain and fog concealed the fact that the show was not sold out. There were only about 2,000 people in the audience, but it looked like there were 10,000'.

While other bands have had difficult relationships with their managers, McGuinness's thirty-year tenure as U2's manager is widely regarded as one of the most successful in the music industry. His ability to think about, and deliver on, the band's evolution over the long term has been a significant and often overlooked asset possessed by U2.

And what of the future?

Any rumours of the band's demise are certainly overstated: U2 are far from finished, and continue to reinvent and refresh. During the 'Vertigo' tour, they delighted fans by including some of their earlier work from albums such as *Boy*. The release of a U2 3D film based on revolutionary digital 3D technology used in sporting events is another sign of the band's ability to harness music and technology to enhance their appeal and longevity. 2011 saw the twentieth anniversary of their defining album *Achtung Baby*, which was remastered and packaged for the occasion. Thirty years on from Larry Mullen's school noticeboard advert, U2 remain at the top of their industry and have no intention of passing on the rock crown any time soon.

? Questions

1. How would you assess U2 in relation to Cummings' description of a Xenophon commander (see Reading 1.3)?
2. How have U2 maintained their relevance through the decades?
3. How would you assess U2 as strategists? Who are the key players?
4. What strategic challenges do U2 face going forward?
5. If you were the strategist for U2, what recommendations would you have as they seek to continue their appeal and longevity?

Summary

In this chapter, we began by tracing the origins and characteristics of strategists. We then turned our focus to the role, skills, motivations, and formations of the strategist, and saw, from the academic literature, that there is a dearth of research focusing on strategists. Being a strategist in any context is fraught with difficulties, uncertainties, and unexpected events that can be an exciting, enjoyable, frustrating, and rewarding experience. The chapter has shown that definitions of strategists and of the nature of their roles and activities are difficult to come by. The inherited military analogy presents a very narrow and traditional top-down view of the strategist. Strategists come from different backgrounds in organization settings, and it is not always the case that the CEO is the strategist. In contrast, Mintzberg's animal metaphors serve as a useful tool in capturing the potential diversity in terms of nature, sources, and behaviour of strategists. The characteristics required by strategists will vary by context, often involving some sort of interplay between managerial, leadership, and entrepreneurial roles. Underpinning this diversity, however, is commonality in terms of the skills and roles that strategists are expected to exhibit, as well as their formation and motivation. This commonality often coalesces around a driving sense of purpose and the desire to create an identity associated with success, thereby leaving a legacy in the company.

To date, considerations of strategy have largely dehumanized the function, speaking of organizational action and industry forces to the neglect of those who actually decide the action and define the forces (Sayles, 1970: 27). For strategy researchers, there is much to do to understand who strategists are and what they actually do. At present, there appears to be little room in mainstream strategy for the living beings whose emotions, motivations, and actions shape strategy (Jarzabkowoski and Spee, 2009: 69). Research suggests that what makes for successful strategists will vary, involving different styles of motivation and different ways of building relationships (Buckingham and Coffman, 1999). Factors that will stand you in good stead in dealing with any issue as a strategist include: being open to new ideas and perspectives within and outside the organization; having an analytical perspective; finely honed interpersonal skills; and an understanding of human behaviour and organizational process. Successful strategists are those who merge ideas, order, and craft (Mintzberg, 2009).

Discussion questions

1. Do the military origins of the strategist hold true for today's organization?
2. Define and discuss the role of a CSO, using the 'Spotlight' box.
3. Is the strategist the same person for every organization? Can a top management team be the strategists for any given organization? Does context matter in defining the role of the strategist in an organization?
4. Based on the readings and mini case study, what do you think it takes to be an effective strategy practitioner?
5. What strategic outcomes can be used to compare the role of strategists?
6. What are the methodological implications of each of the readings for the study of strategy and strategists?
7. Take a well-known strategist and examine his or her role, activities, formation, and motivation. How do they compare with those in Figure 2.2? Which reading do you feel best captures his or her activities?

Further reading

A special 2003 issue of the *Journal of Management Studies*, 40(7), and the first 2003 issue of the *European Management Review* focus on the emerging theme of strategy as practice. For a comprehensive review of this perspective, its emergence, and its implications, see G. Johnson, A. Langley, and R. Whittington (2007) *Strategy-as Practice: Research Directions and Resources*, Cambridge: Cambridge University Press.

R. Burgelman (2001) *Strategy is Destiny: How Strategy-Making Shapes a Company's Future*, New York: Simon and Schuster, draws on Burgelman's extensive research into Intel. In this text, the author presents an in-depth analysis of the decisions made by Intel's key strategist as the company evolved from being a memory-chip company to a firm the product of which is now a central building block of the Internet. In contrast to dominant actor–rational depictions of strategy and the role of the strategists, Burgelman uncovers an approach that is more adaptable and attuned to context.

H. Mintzberg (2009) *Managing*, London: FT Prentice Hall, revisits the terrain of his classic 1973 study to provide what is another rare insight into practice. Mintzberg spent a day with twenty-nine managers, directly observing and documenting their key tasks and activities. The result is a series of in-depth insights into the day-to-day dynamics and untold complexities of the managerial job, recounted in an accessible and informative manner.

visit the Online Resource Centre that accompanies this book to access more learning resources on this chapter topic at www.oxfordtextbooks.co.uk/orc/cunningham/

References

Andrews, K. R. 1971. *The Concept of Corporate Strategy*. New York: McGraw-Hill.

Angwin, D., Paroutis, S., and Mitson, S. 2009. Connecting up strategy: are senior strategy directors missing a link?. *California Management Review*, 51(3): 74–94.

Birkinshaw, J. 2010. *Reinventing Management*. Chichester: John Wiley & Sons.

Breene, T., Nunes, P., and Shill, W. 2007. The chief strategy officer. *Harvard Business Review*, 85(10): 84–93.

Buckingham, M. and Coffman, C. 1999. *First, Break all the Rules: What the World's Greatest Managers Do Differently*. New York: Simon and Schuster.

Carter, C., Clegg, C., and Kornberger, M. 2008. Soapbox: editorial essays—strategy as practice? *Strategic Organization*, 6(1): 83–99.

Chandler, A. D. 1962. *Strategy and Structure: Chapter in the History of the Industrial Enterprise*. Cambridge, MA: MIT Press.

Cummings, S. 1993. The first strategists. *Long Range Planning*, 26(3): 133–135.

Cunningham, J. 2002. Understanding the strategist: the strategist as a corporate back packer. Paper presented at Strategic Management Mini Conference on Strategic Thinking, Rotterdam, 28–30 August.

Cunningham, J., Harney, B., and O'Dea, E. 2005. In search of the strategist: lessons from Travel Co. Paper presented at the British Academy of Management Conference, Oxford University, 14–16 September.

de Rond, M. 2008. *The Last Amateurs: To Hell and Back with the Cambridge Boat Race Crew*. London: Icon Books.

Drucker, P. F. 1954. *The Practice of Management*. New York: Harper & Row.

Dye, R. 2008. Strategy spotlight: how chief strategy officers think about their role. *McKinsey Quarterly*, May: 1–8.

Ericson, T. Melander, A., and Melin, L. 2001. The role of the strategist. In H. Volberda and T. Elfring (eds) *Rethinking Strategy*. London: Sage.

Garratt, B.1991. *Learning to Lead*. London: HarperCollins.

Garvin, D. and Levesque, L. 2006. Meeting the challenge of corporate entrepreneurship. *Harvard Business Review*, October: 102–112.

Gary, M. S. and Wood, R. 2001. Mental models, decision rules and performance heterogeneity. *Strategic Management Journal*, 32(6): 569–594.

Ghoshal, S. and Bartlett, C. 1995. Changing the role of top management: beyond structure to processes. *Harvard Business Review*, Jan/Feb: 86–96.

Gopinath, G., and Hoffman, R. 1995. The relevance of strategy research: Academic and Practitioner Viewpoints. *Journal of Management Studies*, 32(5).

Hambrick, D. C. 1987. The top management team: key to strategic success. *California Management Review*, 30: 88–109.

Hambrick, D. C. and Mason, P. A. 1984. Upper echelons: the organization as a reflection of its top managers. *Academy of Management Review*, 9: 193–206.

Hamel, G. 1996. Strategy as revolution. *Harvard Business Review*, July/Aug: 69–82.

Hartman, M. 2000. Class-specific habitus and the social reproduction of the business elite in Germany and France. *Sociological Review*, 48(2): 241–261.

Helfat, C., Harris, D., and Wolfson, P. 2011. The pipeline to the top: women and men in the top executive ranks of US corporations. *Academy of Management Perspectives*, Nov: 42–64.

Hunsicker, Q. 1980. Can top managers be strategists? *Strategic Management Journal*, 1(1): 77–83.

Jacobides, M. 2010. Strategy tools for a shifting landscape. *Harvard Business Review*, Jan/Feb: 77–84.

Jarzabkowski, P. and Balogun, J. 2009. The practice and process of delivering integration through strategic planning. *Journal of Management Studies*, 46(8): 1255–1288.

Jarzabkowski, P. and Spee, A. P. 2009. Strategy-as-practice: a review and future directions for the field. *International Journal of Management Reviews*, 11(1): 69–95.

Jarzabkowski, P. and Wilson, D. 2002. Top management teams and strategy in a UK university. *Journal of Management Studies*, 39(3): 355–381.

Jarzabkowski, P. and Wilson, D. 2006. Actionable strategy knowledge: a practice perspective. *European Management Journal*, 24(5): 348–367.

Johnson, G. 1988. Rethinking incrementalism. *Strategic Management Journal*, 9(1): 75–91.

Johnson, G., Melin, L., and Whittington, R. 2003. Micro strategy and strategizing: towards an activity-based view. *Journal of Management Studies*, 40(7): 3–22.

Kraaijenbrink, J., Spender, J. C., and Groen, A. 2010. The resource-based view: a review and assessment of its critiques. *Journal of Management*, 36(1): 349–372.

Markides, C. 1997. Strategic innovation. *Sloan Management Review*, Spring: 9–23.

Markides, C. 2000. Strategy and management: Constantinos Markides discusses strategic innovation. *European Management Journal*, 18: 356–366.

McGee, J., Thomas, H., and Wilson, D. 2005. *Strategy Analysis and Practice*. London: McGraw-Hill.

Mintzberg, H. 1973. *The Nature of Managerial Work*. New York: Harper Row.

Mintzberg, H. 1987. Crafting strategy. *Harvard Business Review*, 65: 66–76.

Mintzberg, H. 1991. Strategy thinking as 'seeing'. In J. Nasi (ed.) *Arenas of Strategic Thinking, Foundation for Economic Education*. Helsinki: Foundation for Economic Education.

Mintzberg, H. 1994. *The Rise and Fall of Strategic Planning*. New York: Prentice Hall.

Mintzberg, H. 2009. Rebuilding companies as communities. *Harvard Business Review*, July/Aug: 140–143.

Mintzberg, H., Ahlstrand, B., and Lampel, J. 1998. *Strategy Safari: A Guided Tour Through the Wilds of Strategic Management*. London: The Free Tree Press.

Mintzberg, H., Ahlstrand, B., and Lampel, J. (eds). 2005. *Strategy Bites Back*. London: FT Prentice Hall.

Nonaka, I. 1988. Toward middle-up down management: accelerating information creation. *Sloan Management Review*, 29(3): 9–18.

Paroutis, S. and Pettigrew A. 2007. Strategy in multi-business firm: strategy teams at multiple levels and over time. *Human Relations*, 60(1): 99–135.

Pitcher, P. 1993. Balancing personality types at the top. *Business Quarterly*, Winter: 46–57.

Porter, M. 1996. What is strategy? *Harvard Business Review*, Dec: 61–78.

Prahalad, C. 2010. Thought leader interview by Art Kleiner. *Strategy + Business*, August.

Rumelt, R. P. 1979. Evaluation of strategy: theory and models. In D. Schendel and C. W. Hofer (eds) *Strategic Management: A New View of Business Policy and Planning*. Boston, MA: Little Brown.

Sayles, L. 1970. Whatever happened to management? *Business Horizons*, Apr: 25–34.

Schoemaker, P. 1993. Strategic decisions in organizations: rational and behavioural views. *Journal of Management Studies*, 30(1): 107–129.

Steiner, G. A. 1970. Rise of the corporate planner. *Harvard Business Review*, Sept/Oct: 138–139.

Weick, K. (1995) *Sensemaking in Organisations*. London: Sage.

Whittington, R. 1996. Strategy as practice. *Long Range Planning*, 29(5): 731–735.

Whittington, R. 2002. Practice perspectives on strategy: unifying and developing a field. *Academy of Management Proceedings*, OMT: C1.

Whittington, R. 2007. Strategy practice and strategy process: family differences and the sociological eye. *Organization Studies*, 28(10): 1575–1586.

Wooldridge, B., Schmid, T., and Floyd, S. W. 2008. The middle management perspective on strategy process: contributions, synthesis and future research. *Journal of Management*, 34(6): 1190–1221.

Wrapp, E. 1967. Good managers don't make policy decisions. *Harvard Business Review*, Sept/Oct: 91–99.

Wright, P. and McMahan, G. 2011. Exploring human capital: putting human back into strategic human resource management. *Human Resource Management Journal*, forthcoming.

Zaleznik, A. 1977. Managers and leaders: are they different? *Harvard Business Review*, May/June: 67–68.

3

The process of strategizing

Strategic thinking, decision making, and leadership

Some men see things as they are and say: 'Why?' I dream things that never were and say: 'Why not?'
(George Bernard Shaw)

Introduction

In the last chapter, our focus was on who **strategists** *are*. We now turn our attention to what strategists *do* by examining the process of strategizing. This involves considering the nature of strategic thinking, the process of decision making, and the role of strategic leadership. Consider the degree to which the functionality of the mobile phone has increased over the last decade. Once we used a mobile phone solely for conversation; now we use it for email, for downloading music, for checking the news, and as a camera, organizer, and web browser. Over the next decade, its capability will undoubtedly be enhanced further with new devices and additional functionality. One of the key challenges for strategists is to predict next-generation devices and functionality. This calls for strategic thinking, marrying factual information and intuition about future developments, decision making about the best options and channels to pursue, and leadership to guide the process and ensure clarity around objectives. Each of these elements is critical to the process of strategizing.

Successfully navigating the strategizing process is by no means an easy task. If you had predicted over a decade ago that one day you would be able to make a living selling second-hand goods as a trader on the Internet, very few people would have believed you. Very few might also have believed that there would be sales chart lists for mobile phone ringtones based on popular tunes, or that you would have to pay for your baggage when you travel on an airline. Individuals think differently, and the strategist's role is to constantly search for novelty, uniqueness, and difference while ensuring relevance to key **stakeholders**, particularly customers, in order to ensure the sustainable competitiveness of the organization. As George Bernard Shaw puts it in the opening quote, strategists have to focus not only on the 'why', but also on the 'why not'.

The strategist's ability to think differently is critical, but equally important is his or her capability to translate this thinking into specific strategies that can be evaluated and implemented, and which will ultimately influence buyer behaviour. In the strategy field, we have only just begun the research that delves into the mind of the strategist. How does he or she think? When does thinking become strategic? What informs thinking and acting? How can we understand the process of **strategic decision making**, and how do strategists ensure communication and ownership of their ideas?

Too often, when discussing strategy, there is a tendency to jump ahead to consider the tools and mechanics of strategy **formulation**, neglecting the fact that it is *people*, not companies, who craft and implement strategies, as we explored in Chapter 2. Over the course of this chapter, we will address this issue by considering the key elements of the process of strategizing: namely, the contribution of strategic thinking, the nature of decision making, and the role of strategic leadership—and in particular the way in which strategists convey strategy through the use of **strategic metaphors**.

Figure 3.1 The Process of strategizing

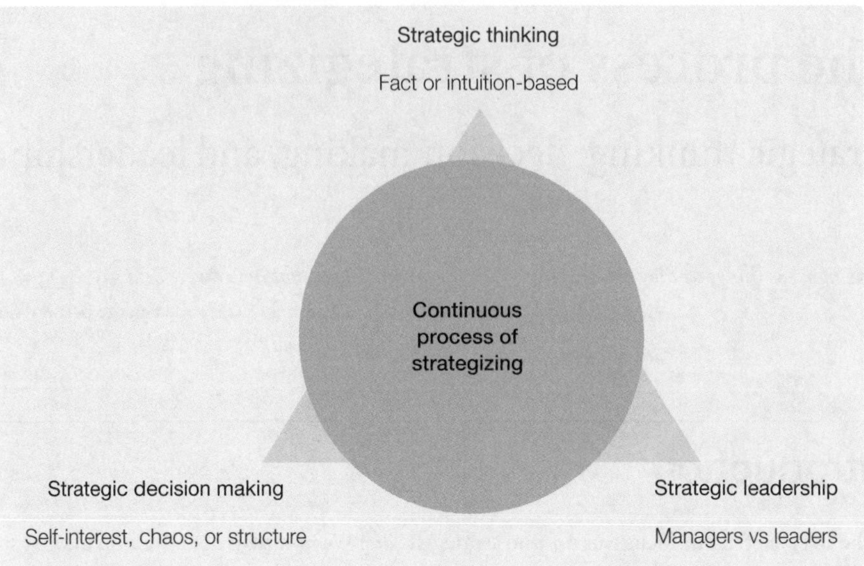

As Figure 3.1 illustrates, the process of strategizing is a richly interactive, continuous process that will be heavily shaped by the context in which it is conducted. The nature of thinking, decision making, and leadership will be very different in a local government agency dealing with child protection, in a high-tech software start-up, and in a plastic component manufacturing firm entering the mature stage of its **industry** life cycle. Despite such differences, in all cases it is the interaction and meshing of these three elements in a consistent and coherent manner that produces optimal strategizing—that is, they are mutually reinforcing. Narrow and rational 'in the box' thinking tends to be associated with a conservative leadership style and slow decision making based on political consensus and conformity, while the opposites of these qualities will characterize a creative 'out of the box' approach. These differences faced by strategists will become clearer as we explore each of the elements of Figure 3.1 in more depth, along with the key debates and tensions inherent in each element. In the case of strategic thinking, one of the key debates is whether it is based on fact or intuition. In the case of strategic decision making, the debate centres on self-interest, chaos, or structure. Finally, when considering leadership, the debate focuses on the differences between managers and leaders.

Strategic thinking

Successful strategic thinking allows key decision makers in the organization to achieve the organization's purpose, or political will, while avoiding the mistakes of the past (Garratt, 1991: 3). Gavetti and Rivkin (2005: 54) put it even more bluntly: 'Strategy is about choice. The heart of a company's strategy is what it chooses to do and not to do. The quality of the thinking that goes into such choices is a key driver of the quality and success of a company's strategy.' Thus thinking strategically involves understanding the activities that an organization should not pursue as well as those that it should pursue. In Chapter 1, we termed this the **trade-off** challenge (see Porter, 1996—Reading 1.1). Given the complexity and the imposing nature of competitive environments, leaders rarely have sufficient time to reflect on future business directions or opportunities. Nonetheless, strategic thinking is essential for competitive survival. As we saw in Chapter 2, appointing a chief strategy officer may afford a leader some additional support to consider the long-term direction of his or her organization; in Chapter 1, we termed this the 'orientation' challenge. Yet while the importance of negating the trade-off challenge and having a clear orientation is well recognized, the strategy literature offers much less insight about the processes by which this may be achieved (Hodgkinson and Healey, 2012). Reflecting this, Mintzberg *et al.* (1998) argue that 'we could do well to drop the term strategic planning altogether and to talk instead about strategic thinking connected to acting' (ibid: 72).

In order to better understand strategic thinking, it is important to explore its key dimensions and levels.

The key dimensions and levels of strategic thinking

Increasingly, it is recognized that a key skill for strategists is the ability to think about their own thinking (Rumelt, 2011: 260). The process of strategic thinking has been likened to painting a picture: the vision is conveyed through the painting, while the frame of the picture provides a mechanism for the organization to assess strategic options (Robert, 2005). Strategic thinking can involve: visualization of what the strategist wants his or her organization to become; the repositioning of resources to compete in markets; assessing the risk, revenues, and costs of strategic options; identifying and thinking about the questions the strategic plan must answer; and thinking logically and systematically about the planning steps and model that the strategist will use to activate his or her strategic thinking in the company's operation (Zabbriskie and Huellmantel, 1991).

Strategic thinking consists of three dimensions: time (the strategist thinks across time—past, present, and future); substance (the strategist thinks in both concrete and abstract terms); and cardinality (Boar, 1997: 67). Cardinality involves thinking about multiple issues concurrently. From this perspective, synthesis rather than analytical decomposition lies at the heart of strategic thinking. While a scientist will explain phenomenon by dissecting and pulling apart into smaller segments, the strategists organizes known principles and insights into larger systems of understanding (Simon, 1967: 14). Seeing ahead, behind, down, below, beside, and beyond—and seeing a scenario through—leads to strategic thinking as a visionary process (Mintzberg, 1991). To begin to think strategically, the strategist needs a good basis for analysis. So a strategist seeking, say, to understand new opportunities in men's retail fashion would seek to interpret industry data from multiple sources and perhaps by experiencing competitors' offerings in different retailing formats (Davenport, 2006). This involves three kinds of thinking process: mechanical systems thinking, leading to rearrangement of elements (that is, an analytical understanding of the context); intuition, leading to local optimization (seeing the trees, not only the forest, and in which the strategist's gut feeling plays a role); and strategic thinking, leading to transformation or changed configuration (Ohmae, 1982).

In undertaking strategic thinking, mental models, visualization, and the strategist's imagination are also critical (Lorenz, 1995). In using a mental models approach for strategic thinking purposes, mental faculties, operations, processes, and vocabulary are important (Garratt, 1991). Garratt (1995: 97) suggests: 'Anyone who consistently ignores certain of his or her mental faculties is obviously vulnerable in situations where those particular faculties are vital. Less obvious is that excessive fondness for any particular mental faculty can make someone quite dangerous.' The global financial crisis of 2007–11 provided a painful reminder of the dangers of cognitive bias, which leads to overconfidence about the current state of affairs and future predictions (Courtney, 2008: 7).

Strategic thinking can be explored at a number of different levels, including individual, team, organizational, and even industry. From an individual perspective, strategic thinking is influenced by the strategist's personality, education, experience, context, and the norms of his or her profession. An appreciation of the competitive context, the future direction of the organization, and the individual's own role are necessary elements for effective strategic thinking. If you are a Nokia software engineer, ideally you will have a strong sense of identity and ideas on how to improve the performance of Nokia in the areas in which you operate, as well as a broad understanding of the challenges facing the mobile communications sector and Nokia specifically. At a team level, strategic thinking can be shaped by team composition: for example, age, experience, gender, and cultural diversity. Firms looking to expand internationally or have a global presence purposefully populate top management teams with people from diverse cultural backgrounds. At an organizational level, strategic thinking involves harnessing all of the creativity of individuals collectively and using appropriate organization structures to achieve cross-functional discussion anchored in a common vision of the future. For the Nokia software engineer, organizational strategic thinking may take the form of being a member of a cross-functional committee and participating actively in organization mechanisms designed to harness and implement new ideas. Clearly, when multiple actors are involved in strategic thinking, it is a social situation, and the group's thinking and action are likely to be influenced by group norms, power relations, and social interaction (Leonard *et al.*, 2005: 121). One of the key tensions that a strategist has to manage is the bias towards self-interest at both individual and organizational levels, which can impede progress, reduce competitiveness, and ultimately lead to suboptimal outcomes for the organization. The strategist also has to ensure that those responsible for strategy implementation take ownership of the strategy over which they have influence. In addition, strategists have to appreciate the momentum and impact, not only of individual thought processes, but also of collective cognition.

Creating a conceptual glue and challenging the industry recipe

Strategy is a social process. Ongoing dialogue (formal and informal) within an organization creates common cognitive structures among top management; these in turn shape beliefs about the environment, strategy, and the business **portfolio** (Porac and Thomas, 2002). Here, strategic thinking represents the conceptual glue that holds the organization together in its pursuit of value creation, competitive differentiation, and sustainable competitiveness. The real benefit for the strategist in engaging in strategic thinking is to reflect on industry and competitive assumptions—what Spender (1989) terms the **industry recipe**. Industry recipes can be thought of as the shared view among industry competitors as to the nature of the environment that they collectively face. This involves a common map of knowledge and understanding, and a common consensus of norms as to what works and what does not work in a given context. It is these cognitive structures that give meaning to various environments. In thinking strategically, a critical part of the strategist's focus should be discovering new or different ways in which to challenge industry recipes. In the retail fashion sector, New Look has challenged the industry recipe of selling three collections a year (summer; autumn; winter). It has followed some of the operating principles of the fast-food industry and, in doing so, has increased the frequency of collections and broadened the clothes collection per year. Industry analysts have termed this 'fast fashion'. The next decade may see changes in revenue-generating strategies in the software industry, with users paying annual charges based on licences rather than upfront payment to buy software products outright. IKEA, Dell, Napster, Sky News, Google, eBay, and MTV are examples of organizations that have challenged conventional industry thinking and developed different strategies—which many of their competitors have imitated. This highlights the tension of convergence or divergence that lies at the heart of debates on strategic thinking. The creation and role of cognitive maps are key to our understanding of strategy formation. Indeed, in the most fundamental sense, this is strategy making (Huff, 1990).

Strategic thinking: fact-based or intuition-based?

One of the key points of debate with respect to strategic thinking is whether or not it should it be based on fact or intuition. Traditional perspectives on strategic thinking acknowledge that strategists have 'bounded **rationality**' (Simon, 1991)—that is, they can make rational decisions only within the constraints of the resources and information available to them at the time. For example, early in the banking crisis of 2008–09, many governments had to make rapid decisions, with a limited amount of information, about recapitalization of national banks. Even in such situations, the emphasis is on systematic analysis of data, with strategic thinking encompassing science-based and fact-based analysis. This is sometimes referred to as 'evidence-based planning': the strategist rigorously applies strategic techniques and tools of analysis in addition to undertaking thorough financial analysis to ascertain the commercial value of strategies generated from strategic thinking. By undertaking such analysis, the strategist gains a more intimate understanding of all elements of the competitive environment and his or her own organization, and, based on this, can reduce or minimize some of the risks for the business. Such strategic thinking also forms the basis for transferability of logic and practices. Perkins (1999) illustrates how the supermarket has served repeatedly as the basis for analogical reasoning. For example, Charlie Merrill devised Merrill Lynch's distinctive approach to retail brokerage based on the practices and mode of thinking that he had experienced as a supermarket manager.

An evidence-based, fact-based approach to strategic thinking contrasts markedly with the view that strategic thinking is intuitive, unique, emotional, contextually and personality driven, questioning and contradictory, and socially constructed (Weick, 1995). Here, strategic thinking is said to reflect the creative side of strategists, or what is commonly described as the 'art' side of strategy. As Mintzberg (1991) notes: 'Strategic thinkers see differently from other people; they pick out the precious gems that others miss. They challenge conventional wisdom—the industry recipe, the traditional strategy—and thereby distinguish their organizations.' From this perspective, strategic thinkers think differently from people solving mundane problems (Boar, 1997). Some differences emerge in relation to the terminology used to describe this sort of strategic thinking. Hussey (2001) uses terms such as 'creative thinking' and 'innovative thinking', and argues that without creative thinking and good analysis, companies will not be able to compete effectively. Arguably, some degree of creative thinking is necessary if an organization is to enter a market successfully and sustain success. Indeed, many companies, such as Xerox, have fallen into the trap of getting better without reconfiguring themselves to be different, as strategic thinking might prompt them to do. One can argue that entrepreneurs are intuitive strategic thinkers when they act on or create a market opportunity. This is discussed further in Richard Schroth's practitioner reflection, found at the end of Section 1.

The distinction between an evidence-based and factual view of strategic thinking as opposed to one grounded in intuition and creativity may not always be clear-cut. Some may claim that it was intuitive insight rather than analogical reasoning that led Charlie Merrill to successfully replicate the logic of supermarket thinking in a financial context. Moreover, rather than considering them to be opposite extremes, research finds that rationality is complex and that strategists can be rational in some ways, but not in others (Eishenhardt and Zbaracki, 1992: 22). Accounts of the early days of amazon.com indicate chief executive officer (CEO) Jeff Bezos to be 'a change junkie' who would constantly implement new initiatives balancing intuition and insight (Deutschman, 2004). Indeed perhaps it is through such balanced blending of perspectives that successful strategists find advantages. Likewise, the distinction between levels of strategic thinking is easily blurred in practice. As Susan Docherty, vice president of General Motors captures, 'I can learn twice as much, twice as quickly, if I've got people who think differently than I do around the table' (Bryant, 2011: 7). Overall, there tends to be a consensus that no matter how we see the different ways of achieving competitive advantage, thinking strategically enhances corporate efficiency and effectiveness, especially when this mode of thinking is encouraged in middle managers and is spread throughout the firm (Thakur and Callingo, 1992).

Strategic decision making

Strategic thinking is an integral element of strategic decision making. Strategic decisions are significant and have long-term consequences, ultimately impacting upon the very survival and competitive well-being of the organization. Making the wrong call on the orientation of the organization can be costly. Because of the stakes involved, strategic decisions are typically complex, involving a mass of unstructured information and competing perspectives (see Reading 1.4). Strategic decisions can therefore be contrasted with the routine, mundane decisions that characterize the day-to-day operation of an organization. Not every decision is strategic in terms of determining the future of the business, but operational decisions ultimately do contribute to successful strategy implementation. Strategists in organizations can be involved in both strategic and operational decision making. A new entrant into the market; a competitor adding further functionality to its product offerings; the departure of key talent: these events may make some decisions more strategic in their orientation. Thus the complexity and political context of a decision will determine whether it is strategic or not (Hickson, 1990).

The process of decision making

The purpose of strategic decision making is to harness the ideas generated from strategic thinking and to systematically evaluate these through formal and/or informal processes. It is through this process that ideas, mediated through frames of reference, come closer to having a tangible impact on the strategies implemented by the business. The strategic decision-making process involves information gathering, analysis, and evaluation. As illustrated in Figure 3.2, decision making can be depicted as a sequential, logical process flowing from the recognition of a problem to the implementation of an adequate solution. In reality, given the organizational and environmental complexity, a neat, sequential process is rarely found precisely as depicted. It is nonetheless important to appreciate key elements of the decision-making sequence before we move to explore some of the deeper complexities informing strategic decisions.

The decision-making process typically begins with *problem or opportunity recognition* within an organizational context. This can arise from both internal and external environments: it might be that there are health concerns surrounding the use of a medical product or food produce, or that a company's difficulty with a production line leads to order fulfilment lagging behind or an unacceptable number of product defects, or that a construction material company wishes to explore new growth opportunities in diversifying into renewable energy products for households.

The next stage of the decision-making sequence is focused on *analysis of cause*. Here, the organization seeks to understand the nature of the problem or opportunity through a factual and evidence-based approach (Davenport, 2006). For example, a retailer might use several sources of

Figure 3.2 Decision-making sequence

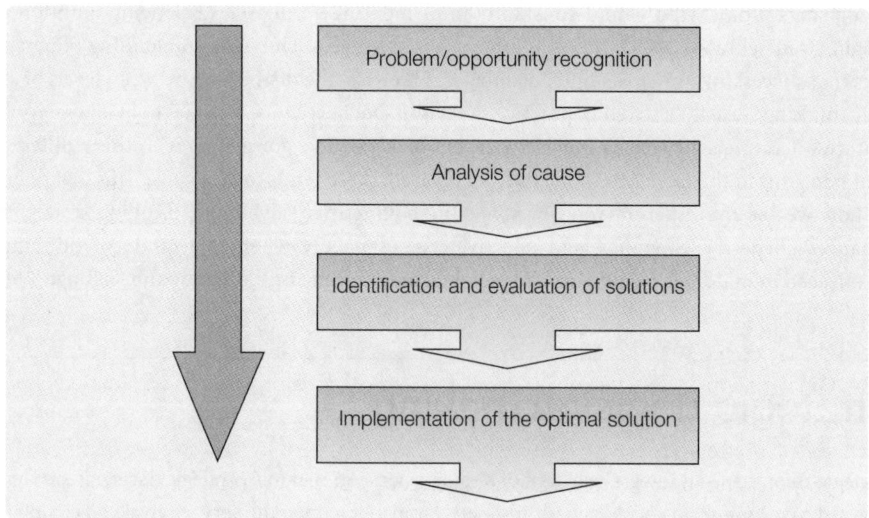

market analysis to identify patterns of shopper behaviour in order to make sense of a consistent decline in sales over a four-month period, and to identify new potential growth categories. Depending on the organizational structure, this analysis will encompass not only many of the functional areas of an organization, but also the competitive and business intelligence capacity drawn from the external environment. Technological advances mean that organizations have ready access to a wealth of information to facilitate analysis. Examples include internal databases of consumer purchases or external analysis of trends on social media such as Twitter and Facebook.

The next stage of the sequence involves *the identification and evaluation of solutions* by the strategist or strategy actors. During the evaluation of solutions, analytical frameworks can be used, which can include scenario analysis, sensitivity analysis, financial analysis (discounted cash flows, etc.), forecasting, and value chain analysis. The analytical frameworks that are used at this stage are dependent on the decision-making architecture that organizations have in place to support strategic decision-making processes. So, in the case of an organization undergoing corporate turnaround, the financial and scenario analysis conducted by the strategist would focus on how to increase the operational efficiency of the business while also evaluating growth opportunities designed to ensure its long-term survival. While a better decision-making infrastructure cannot guarantee better decisions, it can make them more likely (Davenport, 2009: 118).

The final stage in the decision-making sequence is the *implementation* of the solution. For many organizations, this can be the most difficult element in the process. Effective implementation requires buy-in from those tasked to implement, as well as a detailed plan of the desired outcomes that need to be achieved. Arguably, the more inclusive the decision-making sequence in terms of the extent of involvement and type of information sought, the greater the likelihood of buy-in. However, in practice, time pressures, resource constraints, the urgency of the situation, and the nature of leadership style may all impact the feasibility of this approach (Courtney, 2008). Key tensions informing strategic decision making and potentially distorting the sequential approach (Figure 3.2) are explored in the following sections.

Strategic decision making: self-interest, chaos, or structure?

One of the issues within strategic decision making is whether decision makers are biased by self-interest in making decisions or base their decisions on the common (organizational) good. Agency theory suggests that managers will favour decisions that protect their personal interests and promotional opportunities (Lovallo and Sibony, 2006). The human tendency is to develop and sell as positive perspectives and arguments that may never be achievable, in order to secure the strategic decision. Outsourcing to low-cost economies, downsizing, and synergy programmes are some of the situations in which this type of exaggeration and bias can be pervasive. The formal and informal power of proponents from a competing perspective clearly has an impact on the strategic decision-making process (Schoemaker, 1993). As Finkelstein (1992: 531) puts it, 'the ability of a top manager to affect firm strategy depends to a great extent on whether they have the requisite power to be influential'.

Take, for example, the decision in 2002 by Carliona Fiorina, then CEO of Hewlett-Packard (HP), to merge HP with fellow computer giant Compaq. The heirs of the founding members of HP, although they held comparatively few shares, were instrumental in lobbying through informal channels against the proposed deal, arguing that the legacy and future of the company were at stake. Their perspective carried significant clout, although in the end, after what had become a hugely public and personal political battle, Fiorina won by a thin margin, thanks to the support of institutional investors. This case provides a clear example of the power plays and differing interests that surface in the context of strategic decision making.

Another source of tension within strategic decision making is the battle between the extremes of a highly structured or planned strategic decision-making process and a more chaotic process. While rational, evidence-based accounts stress the merits of the former, requirements for organizational responsiveness and agility suggest benefits in the latter. While the former calls for clear lines of decision-making responsibility, the latter sees effectiveness as stemming from strategists skilfully participating and drawing upon the insights of others 'in reflective and imaginative ways' (Stacey, 2010: 4). A hierarchical organization, which requires substantial transparency in decision making, such as a local government planning agency, is likely to be mandated to have a more structured decision-making process. In contrast, to varying degrees, firms in the fast-moving consumer goods industry, high-technology firms, or start-up ventures are more likely to exhibit more flexible and autonomous decision-making procedures. In practice, however, decision making will combine elements of rationality and interactivity. Hence the process can appear complex, chaotic, unstructured, and messy from an outsider's and an insider's perspective. Take the example of UK bank RBS, which was recapitalized and brought into part public ownership by the Labour government's Chancellor of the Exchequer, Alistair Darling. To an outsider, the decision-making process appeared complex, given the terms of recapitalization and the awarding of employee bonuses amounting to £1bn. From an insider's perspective, the decision-making process might have appeared to be structured, based in part on the actual financial need for restructuring. Appreciating the various frames of reference related to decision making can enhance understanding of these issues.

Decision-making frames of reference

Strategists' cognitions and frames of reference have a significant role in strategic decision making. Akin to what Kuhn (1962) famously termed paradigms, in their simplest form these involve the way in which strategists comprehend and conceptualize their competitive landscape and, beyond that, society. Senior management teams in car manufacturing companies in France, the UK, and Japan will have different frames of reference when making strategic decisions about the process of developing a new product category, or about marketing, or about what levels of customer care are appropriate, despite sharing the common goal of delivering shareholder value. Interestingly, Leonard *et al.* (2005) argued that group cognitive style (GCS)—defined as group-level patterns of behaviour in the strategic decision-making process of a group—is critical to understanding the different bases of decision making. This perspective holds that the cultural context within which individuals operate, in addition to organizational past experiences, is reflected in team and organizational cognition; these in turn inform understanding of structure, status, roles, and social interactions. An aggressive new entrant into a market, intent on building market share, such as Asus in the netbook market or Samsung with its Galaxy smartphone, will tend to exhibit a different GCS around the mechanisms of market entry into different geographical territories compared with an incumbent such as Dell or HP, the GCS of which is focused on defending and building existing market share. The UK government, in seeking to change the role of a public service from that of a provider of services to that of a commissioner of services in order to enhance efficiency, is attempting to alter a historically embedded GCS. When Jack Welch was CEO of General Electric (GE), his conceptualization of the GE business was centred on the notion of a shop: subsidiaries had to perform in order to stay on the GE shop shelves, and this formed the nucleus of the GE GSC. Therefore a strategist needs to understand different frames of reference and the organizational GSC in order to embrace more psychological perspectives on strategy and 'go much more deeply into the mental psyche of the strategists and map out their strategic knowledge as to what really constitutes successful strategy making' (Wright, 2006: 289).

To date, efforts to unearth the frames of reference that are held to impinge directly upon decision making have involved perspectives that question the idea of a 'rational man'. Allison's (1971) study of the Cuban missile crisis illustrated the political nature of decision making. The account indicated that deep divisions existed among President Kennedy's advisers regarding an appropriate reaction to the deployment of Russian missiles in Cuba, based on different assumptions and the advisers' places in the hierarchy. Further, Allison's work drew attention to the role of cultural factors and path dependency in ensuring that standard operating procedures applied to strategic decisions. Building on Allison's work, Table 3.1 presents a number of ideal frames of reference that can be said to inform decision making and render a purely rational perspective problematic.

Allison's focus on the military and war helps us to understand the basis of the issues at hand, given the extreme consequences of the type of position held and the decisions made. One could use the ideas presented to explore the debate surrounding the decision by the USA and its allies to carry out military operations in Iraq. Here, a rational frame of reference might suggest that the decision was founded on a clear and concise objective—to rid Iraq of weapons of mass destruction—informed by the logic of the broader US-led 'war on terrorism'. A political frame of reference might refer to 'weapons of mass distraction' and instead highlight that Iraq is a strategic location in terms of global oil production; it might point to debates over UN resolutions and tension in international relations, or the impact of military action in terms of unemployment figures. There is a multitude of ways in which to incorporate various ideas, perhaps even via a creative frame of reference for the most cynically minded. The critical point is that these frames of reference highlight that decision making cannot be abstracted from the series of decisions and actions, and the context, of which it is a part (Pettigrew, 1990).

Strategic decisions are not one-off events that reach a neat end point. This highlights the importance of not only considering the 'go-ahead stage', but also consequential action and implementation processes (as the Iraq example exemplifies). Eisenhardt and Zbaracki (1992: 17) conclude their review of strategic decision making by arguing for an integration of perspectives: 'that strategic makers are at once boundedly rational, that power wins the battle of choice and that chance matters.' However, it is clear that this configuration will vary considerably in terms of the issue at hand and, critically, the organizational context. The ideal frames of reference are therefore useful, facilitating the understanding and interpretation of strategic decision making, but also the frames of reference inherent in research and academic writing; different outcomes or actions will seem plausible within different frames (Schoemaker, 1993: 121). Here, the dominance of the rational model is by no means coincidental—an issue to which we will return again in Chapter 14. For the moment, there are a few further complexities in understanding strategic decision making that warrant consideration.

Complexities in understanding decision making

There can be many dimensions and levels of complexity to decision making. Take President Obama's election promise in 2008 to close Guantanamo Bay by the end of his first year in office. Decision-making complexities around the relocation and release of detainees, legislation, trials, and so on meant that he did not fulfil his promise. As we will explore in the next chapter, Mintzberg (1987—Reading 1.5) argues that strategy is a stream of *actions* as opposed to a stream of *decisions*. For Mintzberg, the process of attempting to track down the precise detail, content, and nature of a decision is a futile exercise. From this perspective, the logical, sequential decision-making process depicted in Figure 3.2 rests on a number of dangerous assumptions, as follows (Mintzberg and Waters, 1990).

- *Decision precedes action.* In fact, action can occur without commitment to act. Consider the professional soccer player who commits a professional foul, or the phenomenon of 'impulse

Table 3.1 Frames of reference informing decision making

	Rational	Political	Cultural	Creative
Objectives	Clear and concise	Contested	Enacted	None or broad
Power base	Organizational position	Formal and informal networks	Experience and historical ties	Dispersed
Focus of decision making	Optimize	Satisfice	Conform	Diverge/ innovate

buying'. These examples may not be too distant from the uneven and complicated ways in which organizations can operate.

- *Commitment to action can be traced to a clear decision/statement of intent.* As the frames of reference indicate, organizations are political and cultural entities from which strategies can emerge inadvertently and informally.

- *When a decision is recorded, that is the time at which a decision is made.* In reality, however, potential options will have been voiced informally. Indeed, the more critical the decision, the more likely it is that political manoeuvring and shuffling have ensured a consensus before the decision ever reached formal consideration. Louis Gerstner (2003) titles the opening chapter of his book on IBM's turnaround 'The courtship'; in it, he documents the informal discussions that he had about the opportunity to become CEO of IBM months before the position even became vacant.

- *Executives have the resources and time to follow a logical process.* The determinants of executive job demands centre around task and performance challenges. These challenges put greater stress on strategists to perform at an optimal level year on year. This stress can impact on strategists' behaviour and how they make decisions; as Hambrick *et al.* (2005) commented, 'we are simply proposing that the heat in the kitchen—executive job demands—is an instrumental factor in shaping executive behaviour, which so far has gone unacknowledged'.

In sum, strategic decision making has implications for the competitiveness of the organization and how it deals with strategic challenges. An integral part of strategic decision making and how a successful balance of self-interest, structure, or chaos can be found are attributable to the strategic leadership of the organization. This is the focus of the final section of this chapter.

Strategic leadership

A criticism historically directed at corporations is that they are over-managed and under-led (Peters, 2001). According to Kotter (1996), leadership involves defining what the future should look like, aligning people with that vision, and inspiring them to make it happen. Thus leadership is the critical vehicle through which the intentions of strategic thinking and decision making can be realized. Strategic leadership is about infusing energy, motivation, and enthusiasm by mapping out the organization's overall strategic intent (Hamel and Prahalad, 1994). The role of leadership is to invest in a perspective and drive others to see this perspective. The quality of CEOs' strategic leadership is inextricably linked to strategic outcomes, or, in other words, the ultimate performance of the business. With the average lifespan of a CEO in a publicly quoted company being three years, the CEO's success is measured by company performance in delivering year-on-year growth and on earnings per share during that compressed period.

It was Chester Barnard (1938) who first contested the view that the primary function of the executive was to design efficient systems. He argued that 'mere' managers could do this, and in contrast argued that the role of the executive was to devise and disseminate moral visions of the organization's mission that would command commitment from participants. This line of argument later found greater currency through the work of Selznick (1957). Early research on leadership focused on the qualities of successful leaders and whether leaders are born or made. Other researchers then focused on behavioural aspects of leadership (Yukl, 1989). However, while these perspectives offered some illumination, they failed to take contextual factors into account.

Unlike traditional leadership theories, which emphasized rational processes, theories of transformational and charismatic leadership emphasize emotions and value the ability to manage meaning and the important symbiotic aspect of visionary leadership. Transformational leadership tends to produce subordinate effort and performance that would go beyond the transactional approach, yet research suggests that successful leaders are both transactional and transformational (Day *et al.*, 2001). Given the broadening of our understanding of leadership, there is consensus that leaders require a broad skill set, encompassing logic, reasoning, and creativity, and have an aggressive performance orientation, as Leithwood *et al.* (1999: 15) note:

> What is important is how leaders respond to the unique organizational circumstances or problems . . . there are wide variations in the contexts for leadership and . . . to be effective, these contexts require different leadership responses . . . individuals providing leadership . . . are capable of mastering a large repertoire of leadership practices.

Managers vs leaders

One source of debate is the nature of core differences between managers and leaders. Sloan (1967) made an early contribution by arguing that managers tend to maintain balance, while leaders create new approaches and imagine new areas to explore. Similar sentiments are argued by other academics, including Kotter (1996), who notes that good management controls complexity, while effective leadership produces useful change, and Yukl (1994: 4), who states that 'managers are oriented toward stability and leaders are oriented toward **innovation**', and 'managers get people to do things more efficiently, whereas leaders get people to agree about what things should be done'. It is clear how both parties may differ in their focus and approach to the task. Abraham Zaleznik (1992) closely examined both parties' orientation towards goals, their workload, their human relations, and their sense of themselves, and concluded that managers and leaders differ fundamentally in their world views, motivations, personal history, and how they think and act. Moreover, managers act as problem solvers who rationally assess situations, systematically select goals, and then formulate responses or strategies to achieve these goals, with particular attention being afforded to organizing, designing, controlling, motivating, and rewarding (Levitt, as cited in Zaleznik, 1992: 68). Kotter (1996) supports this perception when highlighting the planning, budgeting, organizing, staffing, controlling, and problem-solving roles that he associates with managers. Additionally, managers are seen as hard-working individuals and conservative regulators of existing order and institutions, whose goals tend to arise from necessity (Zaleznik, 1992). In sharp contrast to this, leaders are depicted as proactive agents and the shapers of ideas (ibid), and as individuals with an ability to direct, align, and inspire others in the organization (Kotter, 1996). Following this line of thought, the Globe project, which examined leadership across cultures, used the universal definition of leadership as 'the ability to influence, motivate and enable others to contribute toward the effectiveness and success of the organizations of which they are members' (House *et al.*, 2006: 102).

Furthermore, Hambrick and Canella (1989) suggests that leaders, who are fulfilling a more strategic role than their managerial counterparts, need to concern themselves with: both internal operations and external alignment; performing a multifunctional role; prioritizing their ambiguous workloads; and employing intermediaries or managing through others. Table 3.2 presents an overview of some of the key differences between leaders and managers that emerge from the literature.

While the conceptual contrast between managers and leaders appears clear, in practice, it is less so (see Chapter 2). Henry Ford is typically cited as the archetypical manager focusing on internal production, control, efficiencies, and mass production. However, others interpret his success as based on exemplary leadership—as someone who set out to make his own competitive rules and realize a clear vision. Despite the intense research efforts focusing on leadership, there still appears to be a lack of agreement as to a single definition or effective style of leadership (Wheeler *et al.*, 2007). Even within countries, with China being exemplary, there are many subcultures that will directly impact on the appropriate leadership approach (Graen, 2006). In more clearly linking leadership to strategic purpose, authors have usefully identified key characteristics of what constitutes 'strategic leadership'.

Table 3.2 Managers versus leaders

Managers	Leaders
Exploiting key capabilities and strengths	Seek new approaches and avenues
Encourage stability, conservative regulators Controls complexity	Encourage innovation, shape ideas
Seek improvements—do things right	Produces useful change—do the right things
Concern for internal operations	Concerned with internal and external alignment
Rational thinkers and problem solvers	Proactive thinkers who inspire
Plans, organizes, controls, motivates, rewards	Directs and aligns

Source: O'Kane (2008)

Strategic leadership: key characteristics

But how is strategic leadership different? Ireland and Hitt (1999: 63) provide us with an overarching definition: 'Strategic leadership is defined as a person's ability to anticipate, envision, maintain flexibility, think strategically, and work with others to initiate changes that will create a viable future for the organization.' Determining the firm's purpose or vision, exploiting and maintaining core competencies, developing human capital, sustaining an effective organizational culture, emphasizing ethical practices, and establishing balanced organizational controls are the core elements of strategic leadership (Ireland and Hitt, 1999). Table 3.3 outlines the key characteristics of strategic leaders. Getting employees to make decisions voluntarily that enhance the organization's wealth is an important element of strategic leadership (Rowe, 2001) and is one of the elements of effective strategic leadership practices (see Table 3.3). Strategic leaders do not create followers; they create other leaders (Peters, 2001: 124). Furthermore, in the pursuance of strategic leadership, these leaders have to be cognizant of instilling and maintaining an ethical climate (Thomas *et al.*, 2004). Corporate scandals at Enron to News International indicate how apparent failure in this strategic leadership task can have devastating consequences (see Chapter 5).

Strategic leadership involves dealing with the organizational complexity and intensity of competitive environments, and distilling and translating this into simplicity. Success centres upon the identification of a limited number of critical issues, and then communicating a clear intent to energize resources and focus action upon addressing them (Rumelt, 2011). Film audiences are not particularly interested in where a film was shot, its budget, or the problems that occurred on the shoot; their primary interest is in the film itself, and when and where are they going to see it. Applying this analogy to strategic leadership, customers are more interested in the final product and future direction of the organization, and have little interest in the operational specifics of how it will achieve these. Strategic leaders must court different shades of opinion with respect to their performance. They have to deal with organizational politics and cynicism, because it is difficult to get organizations of any size to buy into a common vision and values. To achieve this, strategic leadership consists of the following.

- *Persuasion and conviction* One of the key attributes of a strategic leader is the ability to persuade and communicate the strategy to all levels of the organization. However, this ability to persuade goes beyond the organization boundaries, to include customers, shareholders, and industry competitors. The persuasion is built around a clear universal understanding of the uniqueness and relevance of the organization, and the manner in which it makes itself relevant to its customers. Inevitably, some leaders lack this attribute, but for the organization to buy into the strategy, persuasion and conviction are necessary.

- *Organizational architecture and culture* A key task of a strategic leader is to build an organizational architecture that enables the business to cope no matter what challenges it faces. Achieving

Table 3.3 Characteristics of strategic leaders and strategic leadership practices

Strategic leaders
• Synergistic combination of managerial and visionary leadership • Emphasis on ethical behaviour and value-based decisions • Formulate and implement strategies for immediate impact and preservation of long-term goals to enhance organizational survival, growth, and long-term viability • Have strong, positive expectation of the performance that they expect from their superiors, peers, subordinates, and themselves • Use strategic controls and financial controls, with emphasis on strategic control • Use, and interchange, tacit and explicit knowledge on individual and organizational levels • Use linear and non-linear thinking patterns • Believe in strategic choice—that is, that their choices make a difference in their organizational environments
Strategic leadership practices
• Outcome and process-focused • Confident, but without hubris • Seeks to acquire and leverage knowledge • Seeks to realize and nurture people's creativity • Workflows influenced by relationships • Demonstrates the importance of integrity by actions • Willing to earn respect • Seeks diversity • Acts to anticipate environmental change • Serves as a leader and as a great group member • Views organizational citizens as a critical resource • Operate primarily through a global mindset • Invests significantly in citizens' continuous development

Sources: Adapted from Ireland and Hitt (1999); Rowe (2001)

this is contingent on the flexibility embedded in the organization's culture. It goes beyond the ability to play a strategic game in terms of operational and locational advantages, but instead goes to the heart of how individual employees internalize change. This means developing an organizational culture that promotes flexibility and independence of thought combined with appropriate reward structures. Google is a current exemplar of this flexible organizational architecture and culture, whereby employees can work on their own personal projects. At Proctor and Gamble, chief executive A. G. Lafley undertook the symbolic gesture of removing the oak-panelled executive offices at its headquarters, thereby moving divisional executives closer to their staff and turning the former executive space into an employee learning centre—a clear message of intent and priorities (Wheeler *et al.*, 2007).

• *Performance accountability and emotional connections* Strategic leadership requires leaders to make an emotional connection with employees. For organizations to perform and also to cope with adversity, employees must have an emotional connection to the organization and its values. This instils confidence and achievement orientation, but leaders have to be able to decipher what it is that employees value and hold dear. In a temporal globalizing world, this is becoming more difficult, but the introduction of performance measures and targets with appropriate extrinsic and intrinsic rewards can assist in making this emotional connection. In this sense, employer branding for employees becomes just as important as employer branding for customers (Erickson and Gratton, 2007).

• *Tolerance of difference* Within any team, organization, and even society, there are differences of opinion that can be very divisive and energy sapping. Strategic leadership is about first acknowledging and accepting this, and then putting in place organizational mechanisms through which difference of opinion is treated positively. Moreover, it is about harnessing this difference in a way that challenges the organization's strategy, performance, and future directions.

Finally, as Ciampa (2005) notes, becoming a strategic leader and a CEO 'depends on the situation, the organization culture, the types of people and relationships involved, and the personality and style of the candidate'. In moving to better understand strategic leadership, arguably leaders can learn much from the arts, in which persuasion, conviction, emotional connections, and embracing of difference hold centre stage (Adler, 2006; Flood and Carroll, 2010). Likewise, similarly to art, strategic leadership is about setting tone and creating meaning by using powerful languages and metaphors to provide direction and gain commitment (Smircich and Stubbart, 1985: 730).

Strategic metaphors: conveying thinking and strategic direction

One of the single biggest challenges that strategic leaders face is communicating the company strategy to multiple stakeholders; this is an essential role as figurehead of an organization. In seeking maximum organizational commitment and participation, strategic leaders increasingly rely on strategic metaphors (Cacciaguidi-Fahy and Cunningham, 2007). As Aristotle observed, 'the soul never thinks without a picture'. Metaphors use language to convey information and ideas that can be transferred into tacit knowledge and a way of thinking and viewing the world, but which may not be easily articulated (Andriessen and Gubbins, 2009; Morgan, 2006). Due to the different cognitive abilities of humans, metaphors can create new meanings, which may become very real for people. They have the potential to make the abstract concrete (Tsoukas, 1991). A strategic metaphor is a linguistic construction of carefully chosen words, which conveys the essence of the organization's strategic intent, relevance, uniqueness, and its core values, thereby implicitly encapsulating and articulating organizational thinking and decision making.

For Tesco, 'Every little helps' has multiple meanings for different stakeholders across different countries and socio-economic groups, but a strategic metaphor helps leaders to achieve uniformity of purpose and attempts to develop an emotional link with customers and employees. Due to their different cognitive perspectives, stakeholders in an organization may take the same meaning or different meanings from the strategic metaphor. In Table 3.4, the strategic metaphors used by car companies are outlined; in the case of Toyota, the strategic metaphor is aligned to its core focus on quality. This strategic metaphor is used for advertising and is seen on car stickers on Toyota vehicles throughout the world. The strategic metaphor for Toyota creates a tangible link between the organizational focus and customers. However, Toyota's recall of cars in early 2010 may impact the viability of this strategic metaphor.

Table 3.4 Strategic metaphors: global car manufacturers

Company	Strategic metaphor
Toyota	'The best built cars in the world'
Nissan	'Shift adventure, expectation, conventions, direction and desire'
Honda	'The power of dreams'
Ford	'Designed for living; engineered to last'
GM	'A car company in overdrive'
VW	'Drivers wanted'
Peugeot	'The drive of your life'
Fiat	'A century of success'

Being a strategist requires strategic leadership and the ability to deal with uncertainty and ambiguity, and to have understanding at a deep level of people, context, behaviours, and emotions. Careful attention to strategic metaphor and narratives to describe the strategy of the business to multiple parties can provide a consistent framework within which strategic decisions can be made that will ensure the uniqueness of the business over the long term.

Spotlight In the heat of the moment: wildlife firefighters and suboptimal decision making[1]

The conditions and environmental uncertainty faced by businesses are exacerbated in contexts in which lives are at stake. Here, decisions are clear-cut and the consequences of them immediately and explicitly evident. On the positive side, we observe strategic leadership qualities, such as those exhibited by Mayor Rudy Giuliani in New York after the 9/11 terrorist attacks. Many people took comfort in his strength, energy, compassion, and ability to relate to the people. However, for each positive case that comes to mind, there is a negative one that captures news headlines. Consider the (in)action of the US state departments in the wake of Hurricane Katrina and its devastating impact on New Orleans, or the political wrangling that delayed the deployment of UN forces to prevent genocide in Ruanda and Kosovo. In such times of crisis, the intensity of issues renders previous experience, training, and leadership ability critical to successful intervention.

Nowhere is this more apparent than in the circumstances faced by wildlife firefighters.[1] They are involved in fighting large forest, brush, and grass fires. Firefighters must make quick decisions in a compressed time frame, and these decisions have life-and-death consequences. Fires can rage at 2,700°F, move at over 25 mph, and lethally race forward without warning in a wall of fire equivalent to a hurricane, termed a 'blow-up'. The danger of small-scale fires was shown in the film *Backdraft* (1994), but the scale, environmental conditions, and impact of weather make the fires faced by wildlife firefighters even more severe. While firefighters can monitor and evaluate a fire, ultimately—as with the business environment—the momentum and force of events are beyond their control. Further, given the scale of the challenges that they face, wildlife firefighters typically work as part of larger temporal collaborations of firefighters from different regions or states. This geographical mobility and constant reformulation of firefighting teams leaves little time for induction, socialization, or etiquette. Given these conditions and the stressful environment that firefighters face, it is instructive to consider the decision making, leadership, and actions of wildfire firefighters in the contexts of two major—and eerily similar—disasters some forty-five years apart.

On 5 and 6 July 1994, a group of firefighters comprising three leaders and three crews of firefighters from five states was mobilized to fight a fire on Storm King Mountain, South Canyon, Colorado. While environmental conditions and poor luck played their part, ultimately leadership choices and indecision resulted in the group's entrapment; fourteen firefighters perished. For firefighters, the key criteria for decision making include safety of personnel, the speed at which the fire is tackled, and the best means of repressing the fire. Useem *et al.* (2005) provide an insightful analysis of the circumstances, arguing that the tragedy can be attributed to suboptimal decisions around the above three criteria because of under-preparation, acute stress, and ambiguous authority. Critically, Donald Mackey, who assumed a leadership role overseeing the forty-nine firefighters, was unsure of the legitimacy of his role and failed to command full authority. Useem *et al.*'s analysis suggests that, of the ten key decisions that Mackey made as events unfolded, five were suboptimal. Specifically, there was a failure to coordinate aerial surveillance, a lack of extensive knowledge of the terrain, and a rejection of procedure that warned against downhill fire lines. Nobody obtained a weather bulletin warning of impending winds; this would later be revealed as potentially live-saving information.

Weick (1996), comparing this tragedy with a similar fatal fire at Mann Gulch in Montana some forty-five years previously, found similarities in terms of leadership and decision-making deficiencies. At 16:00 on 5 August 1949, sixteen young men parachuted into the canyon. Two hours later, they were trapped at the bottom of a steep slope; thirteen of

[1] Following the approach taken by Useem *et al.* (2005: 465), in presenting these ideas, we are neither criticizing nor commending the decisions taken, but rather depicting them as a basis for discussion.

them perished as they tried to outrun the fire. Strikingly, records show that at both Mann Gulch in 1949 and at Storm King Mountain in Colorado in 1994, firefighters failed to obey orders to drop their tools as they attempted to outrun the blaze. This would have reduced the weight that they were carrying and thereby heightened their likelihood of escaping. Only the survivors followed these orders. Weick (1996: 304–9) attributes the failure to drop tools to the following factors.

- *Communication* Firefighters may have simply failed to hear the order, given the conditions in which they were operating.
- *Justification* Firefighters may have persisted because they were not given clear reasons for the change in approach. In particular, having more experience of timber than dry grass, firefighters may not have understood the implications of their environmental conditions. Also, they might not have believed that dropping their tools would make a difference to their plight.
- *Ambiguity over leadership* As illustrated by the case of Mackey, there was a lack of established trust or rapport between firefighters and their leaders. This would have been exacerbated by the fact that various multi-team units were attempting to work together.
- *Control* Simple cause-and-effect logic would see the retention of tools as critical to survival.
- *Social factors* For the firefighters, dropping their tools may have been symbolic of failure—or they might have feared the alternatives, to which they were not accustomed.
- *Group think and identity* Because the first person running did not drop his tools, others may simply have followed suit. Also, for a firefighter, his or her tools are linked to his or her very identity and sense of who he or she is; dropping tools might have left that firefighter devoid of identity or social roles.

Ultimately, the pressure of the moment in these cases resulted in poor decisions, a failure in strategic leadership, and inaction. The examples also illustrate that 'thinking strategically depends on making good decisions to acquire and analyse information on the environment, mobilize resources, effective execution' (Useem *et al.*, 2005: 464). The process of strategizing is far from simple and draws on emotion, as well as cognition. The key question is whether businesses make their decisions as if lives depend on them, and, if so, whether they can overcome the deficiencies illustrated so dramatically above.

Implications for strategy practice

In this chapter, we have covered the three interrelated issues of strategic thinking, strategic decision making, and strategic leadership. Thinking and decision making can seem to be abstract concepts—but consider the decisions that we make and the manner in which we think and act in our personal and professional lives. When you go shopping, what do you see? Most of us will see the physical store layout, customers, goods, and cashiers. What we see is framed by our professional experience, personal influences, and biases. The physical attributes of stores are essential to fulfilling customer service. But what is it that we do not see? How do grocery retailers persuade consumers to come into their stores and make informed and/or impulse purchases? Getting the right experience for every customer is a daily challenge. How many times have you experienced an interaction with a company and thought to yourself that it could be significantly improved?

Strategists need to 'buy mirrors' (Miller, 1992: 32) and reflect on current activities from both personal and professional perspectives. Personal reflection can focus on career ambition, contentment with working environment and colleagues, and the appropriateness of skill set. The executive world is filled with regrets: in some cases, managers have not applied rigour to managing their own careers, particularly in the mid-career phase. Understanding who you are as an individual and where your limitations and strengths lie is a significant factor in contributing to career success and fulfillment.

One of the most difficult tasks that any individual undertakes is critical reflection on his or her professional performance, because it tends to be subjective in part, selective, and guarded. Much organizational reflection and thinking is situationally driven (individual performance reviews and turnaround situations), but some professional reflection needs to be focused on the effectiveness of the process by which thought was turned into action. In doing so, teams and individuals improve their individual and collective performances, but also develop a confidence that copes with all manner of adversity and uncertainty. Consequently, learning from effective and ineffective experiences is an important aspect of strategic thinking and decision making. Consider rugby players: the norm is that, after an international rugby match, each player receives a DVD with highlights of his or her performance over the course of the game. The DVD contains passages of play in which individual sporting excellence and shortcomings are highlighted. This then forms the basis of further coaching sessions designed to overcome shortcomings. For strategists, the same challenge exists in terms of finding the organizational time to undertake personal and professional reflection. Success in this task may involve soliciting views of third parties so that strategists can more objectively discover their own blind spots (Miller, 1992: 32). Reflection is integral to understanding the facets of differentiation for the business.

Sometimes, strategists have a tendency to believe their own rhetoric, and always to put a positive spin on their roles and the impact that they have on contributing to success. The issue that should constantly concern strategists when thinking about their organizations and strategic decisions is how the decision makes their organization relevant and unique to the customer: will it ultimately have an impact on the marketplace in a sustainable way? The manner in which strategists think does have a direct impact on how the organization is structured and the manner in which it competes. But how many strategists really challenge the status quo and the core assumptions about the organization and the competitive environment? Strategists would do well to take the mindset of an industry start-up, like that of organizations such as Innocent, Gü, Sage, and Dyson, and challenge the industry status quo by introducing new products or service offerings that are distinctly different from industry standards.

Language and communication mechanisms can facilitate the turning of individual and collective thoughts into action. The ***discourse*** used to achieve a commonality of understanding of 'who we are' and 'what businesses we are in' is critical to providing clarity that aids decision making. If you go into any organization and ask an employee 'who we are' and 'what business we are in', you will get many different replies and probably little commonality around core strategy, purpose, or even values. This is where the ability of the strategic leadership is tested. How effective is the language and communication about the strategy of the organization? How does that language dissect opposing and competing strategy perspectives within the organization? Is that language effective enough in creating an emotional connection with employees?

Strategic decision making turns thinking into potential actions, but the reality for many organizations is that key decisions that have turned out to be very successful can be based on little or no analysis. Intuition—'gut feelings'—still plays a significant role in strategic decision making, as do organizational politics. The momentum generated around implementation, the innate industry knowledge of strategists, and the understanding of customers can contribute to successful strategic decision making. The more experience the strategist obtains, perhaps the greater the likelihood of success in experiential and creative thinking, as 'rule-based thinking as the most important basis for action is replaced by context and intuition' (Flyvberg, 2001: 21). Typically less appreciated, luck and circumstance will also play a role. Where such success occurs, strategists can fall into the replication of the industry/organizational recipe trap: 'It worked for us before; it will work again.' Instead, organizational strategy should be treated as a prototype—something always open for challenge and renewal (Pfeffer and Sutton, 2006).

Strategic thinking brings some real benefits to the organization if harnessed appropriately through internal organizational structures. Company culture, personal bias, and organizational politics and structures can constrain thinking and decision making. Strategic leaders' communication of thought and actions, and the language and narrative used are essential to capturing difference and commonality of organizational purpose simultaneously. The uniqueness of strategic thinking is that strategists do think differently, even though they might have commonalities of experience. Therein lies a real sustainable source of competitive advantage, but also a challenge for how best the organization can harness the diversity of thinking and thereby orientate it towards a specific purpose. Success in this task requires the strategists to at once be a strategic leader generating a sense of purpose, motivating and building culture, but also ensuring that intent is realized via managerial capacity (Bryant, 2011).

Finally, strategic thinking, strategic decision making, and strategic leadership are emotional experiences for the strategist, because elements of his or her personality are imbued in the strategy and in the manner in which he or she conveys this to the organization and its stakeholders. Sometimes, strategists make bad decisions that have long-term costs for organizations, societies, and individuals. The banking crisis that started in 2008 highlights that poor decision making by top management in banks and regulators across the world has had long-term impacts for many economies, businesses, families, and individuals.

Introduction to readings

In Reading 1.4, 'Strategy as strategic decision making' (1999), Kathleen Eisenhardt focuses on four key issues. Eisenhardt has written extensively about decision making and high-velocity environments. In this article, she argues that executives should build collective intuition, simulate quick conflicts, maintain a pace, and defuse politics, and that 'taken together, these approaches direct executive attention toward strategic decision making as the cornerstone of effective strategy'. The article attempts to dispel some myths surrounding strategic decision making in high-velocity environments—but are you convinced that successful management teams meet less often, that it is relatively easy to build organizational intuition, and that organizational politics can be defused through the building of common goals? Certainly, these elements of successful strategic decision making are challenging and thought-provoking for all, but is this true irrespective of context?

In the second reading for the chapter, 'Strategic thinking or strategic planning?' (1998), to which a link is provided on the Online Resource Centre that accompanies this book, Loizos Heracleous attempts to deal with the thorny issue of the inter-relationship between strategic thinking and strategic planning, and the article thereby serves as a useful bridge to issues discussed in Chapter 1. Instead of getting caught up in a simplistic debate, Heracleous draws a link between strategic thinking and double-loop learning, and presents an argument that both strategic-planning and strategic-thinking modes are essential to crafting good strategies. The article raises some interesting questions: does strategic thinking have to be analytical? Can strategic thinking really replace formalized strategic planning? Does strategic thinking really improve strategic planning? Do organizations really learn from successful strategic thinking and strategic planning episodes?

Our final reading for this chapter, also accessible via a link on the Online Resource Centre, is an article by Donald Hambrick, 'Putting top managers back in the strategy picture' (1989). This is a guest editor introduction to a special issue on strategic leaders and leadership. Hambrick outlines the definitional challenges, a framework for mapping strategic leadership research, and illustrative dimensions of strategic leadership. What is interesting is Hambrick's definition of the strategic leader as the person who has the 'management of the overall enterprise, not just a small part'; moreover, he describes the challenges and complexities that strategic leaders have to deal with. Has the focus of these changed much for today's strategic leaders? In the context of post-recession organizations, are new dimensions of strategic leadership necessary both in researching this area and in the development of strategic leaders?

Mini case study Simon Cowell: generating Xtreme reactions

The X Factor, *Pop Idol*, *American Idol*, *America's Got Talent*, *American Inventor*, and guest appearances on *The Simpsons*, *Scary Movie 3*, and *Shrek 2*, have made Simon Cowell an international celebrity and household name. His straight-talking style continues to provoke a myriad of reactions. His comments to contestants are notorious; many critics see them as a key ingredient in the success of such TV series:

> I never want to hear that song again. I cannot stand it. I'm allergic to it ... If lifeguarding duties were as good as your singing, a lot of people would be drowning ... Shave off your beard and wear a dress. You would be a great female impersonator ... Your singing is like ordering a ferocious guard dog for your home and getting delivered a poodle in a leather jacket instead ... Hideous.
>
> (http://celebrities09.com/Rank-1_25/Simon-Cowell/)

With nearly three decades in the music industry, Simon Cowell has experienced the ups and the downs of the industry. In 1979, he started off as a mailroom clerk for EMI Music Publishing, where his father worked as an executive. During the early eighties, he became a record producer for EMI, but left soon afterwards to form E&S Music, which did not find success. Subsequently, he returned to EMI, but left shortly afterwards to set up another independent record label called Fanfare Records, in 1985, with Sinitta as one of the leading signed artists. When Fanfare subsequently went bust, Cowell, aged 30, lost everything and was forced to move back in with his parents. By 1989, he had become a consultant for BMG. Since then, he has signed commercially successful acts to this label including Sonia, 5ive, Robson and Jerome, and Westlife. Working with Pete Waterman of Stock Aitkin Waterman in the 1980s was a significant learning experience for Cowell in terms of becoming a successful record producer. Through his involvement with BMG, he has sold in excess of 150 million records and has had over fifty number-one hits. In the last ten years, he has achieved record sales of over 25 million, seventeen number-one singles, and over seventy top-thirty records. In a creative domain in which success is uncertain, and much is down to timing and taste, Cowell operates on the basis of a clear philosophy; 'I've always treated the music business as a business. Whether I'm making TV shows or signing artists, you have to do it by the head and not the heart—and I run my businesses that way' (Perman, 2006).

The first season of *Pop Idol* was aired on UK television in 2001 and the following year *American Idol* aired on the Fox television network. Cowell's directness as a judge ensured high audience figures, great media attention, and higher audition numbers, with in excess of 10,000 people queuing up. The programme format is based on a singing contest whereby the final pool of selected contestants perform on a weekly basis to live audiences and individual contestants are eliminated based on a combination of voting (telephone, SMS, and online) and judges' comments. Average viewing figures regularly exceed 11 million. In 2002, Cowell set up another record label, S Record, and signed up the two *Pop Idol* finalists, Will Young and Gareth Gates, who subsequently had UK number-one hits.

In 2004, Cowell devised a new programme called *The X Factor*, which was aired on UK television, with Sharon Osbourne and Louis Walsh as judges. The format differed significantly in that Cowell, Osbourne, and Walsh worked with the contestants. The competition between the three made for gripping viewing, increased audience numbers, and ensured that the programme ran for another two seasons. In 2005, the creator of *Pop Idol*, Simon Fuller, sued Cowell because of the similarities between both shows, but later an out-of-court settlement was reached.

The success of *American Idol* has allowed Cowell to produce and develop other programme formats. His interactions with co-judges, Paula Abdul and Randy Jackson, on *American Idol* have become legendary. In 2006, *American Inventor*, co-produced by Cowell's production company Syco, was aired on ABC, in which inventors and entrepreneurs competed to win US$1m to develop their business around their invention. Judges for the show included Ed Evangelisat, Mary Lou Quinlan, Doug Hall, and Peter Jones, the creator of the show.

Cowell is one of the co-creators of *America's Got Talent*, which aired on NBC in June 2006. The show was anchored by the legendary broadcaster Regis Philbin, and the judging panel consisted of Piers Morgan, Brandy, and David Hasselhoff. The show format differs in that it offers a platform to any entertainer in any category, such as dance or comedy, with a top prize of US$1m. Such has been the success of the show that many international television stations have adapted the US show, including Seven Network (Australia), CTV (Canada), and ITV (UK).

By 2008, *The X Factor* had been running for five years, with an expanded judging panel that included debut judge, Cheryl Cole, member of pop band Girls Aloud. The addition of Cheryl Cole, coupled with a strong online presence, *The Xtra Factor* on ITV, and the appearance of Beyonce Knowles with finalist Alexander Burke, ensured another successful season for the show in 2008. The 2009 season surpassed 2008 in terms of viewing numbers, and the addition of new elements to the show on a weekly basis contributed to the success of the season. The inclusion of Jedward in the final line-up of competing artists in 2009 added variety to the show that will be hard to replicate. Cowell epitomizes the philosophy: 'If you got a big mouth and you're controversial, you're going to get attention.'

Overall, Simon Cowell has clearly experienced the lows of failure and highs of success. He has managed to create formats that successfully merge activities in both the music and television industries, thereby creating significant value in both sectors. In addition, Cowell has rediscovered people's love for simple entertainment shows, all while continuously evolving his portfolio of shows. Most recently, Cowell featured on the seventh series of *The X Factor* and the fifth series of *Britain's Got Talent*. In September 2011, he featured as a judge on the first season of the US version of *The X Factor*. Cowell's prescription for continued success? 'Work hard, be patient, and be a sponge while learning your business. Learn how to take criticism. Follow your gut instincts and don't compromise.' There is little doubt that he is one individual who clearly has the X Factor.

Source: Perman (2006)

? Questions

1. How would you assess Simon Cowell's strategic thinking capability?

2. What decision-making frames of reference are most likely to yield success for Cowell as he evaluates new business opportunities and future developments?

3. Would you describe Simon Cowell as a manager or leader?

4. Does Simon Cowell display the characteristics of a strategic leader?

Summary

In this chapter, we began by exploring strategic thinking, including key dimensions and levels. We then considered strategic thinking as the conceptual glue that holds the organization together in its pursuit of value creation and how thinking can coalesce at an industry level to form an 'industry recipe'. We concluded our exploration of strategic thinking by examining whether it is fact-based or intuition-based. We then turned our attention to strategic decision making and explored the potential of self-interest, chaos, or structure to impact on strategic decision making. We concluded our exploration of decision making by considering decision-making frames of reference and complexities in understanding decision making. Finally, we concluded the chapter by examining the distinction between managers and leaders, the key characteristics of strategic leadership, and how strategic metaphors help to convey thinking and strategic direction.

The process of strategizing involves the ability of individuals, teams, and organizations to turn strategic thinking into action via an effective strategic decision-making process. This requires strategic leadership. Softer issues, such as politics and different professional and cultural perspectives, add layers of complexity and can impede the effectiveness of the strategizing process, but paradoxically these can also be the source of ideas that can be harnessed into effective strategies. Moreover, a combination of strategic thinking and leadership can mean that an organization constantly challenges core internal and external paradigms for success. This is one way in which organizations can retain innovative thinking, while also developing their ability to respond to marketplace challenges in an organizational setting that can cope with and harness different perspectives for a common purpose (Bryan and Farrell, 2008). The dangers of 'group think' can be pervasive in organizations; platforms for difference to emerge need to be encouraged through effective strategic leadership practices.

This chapter examined the processes of strategizing that provide the bedrock for dealing with some of the strategic tensions that strategists face, such as the crafting of deliberate and emergent strategy (see Chapter 4), negotiating the purpose of the business (see Chapter 5), and understanding the impact of resources and markets (see Chapter 6). Ultimately, honing strategic thinking, ensuring effective strategic-making processes, and exhibiting characteristics of strategic leadership can position organizations to cope with these tensions and market uncertainties; by contrast, the annals of business history are filled with examples of organizations that failed through not having effective strategizing processes in place. The global financial crisis that began in 2008 provided a painful reminder of the dangers of narrow strategic thinking, poor decision making, and failure in leadership, and how not only can each one be destructive, but they can also be mutually reinforcing.

Discussion questions

1. Choose an organization with which you are familiar. What can you say about the key elements of its strategizing process? (See Figure 3.1.)

a) Do its activities suggest that it converges upon or diverges from convention in the way in which it delivers value?

b) What style is exhibited by its leader?

c) What type of decision-making processes would you say occur in this organization and why?

2. Evaluate the factors informing a recent decision that you made. How, if at all, do they relate to the frames of reference depicted in this chapter?

3. What frames of reference should a strategist use as part of the decision-making processes dealing with strategic management challenges: orientation, trade-off, relevance, or change?

4. Choose a leader with whom you are familiar. Does he or she match the characteristics of a strategic leader as shown in Table 3.3? If not, why not?

5. Are strategic leaders born or made? Discuss.

6. Table 3.3 outlines strategic leadership practices. In your opinion, how attainable and effective are they for CEOs?

7. Taking an industry sector with which you are familiar, draw up a list of strategic metaphors for the leading competitors. How effective are strategic metaphors in communicating the strategy of an organization to a diverse group of stakeholders?

Further reading

A. Bryant (2011) *The Corner Office: How Top CEOs Made It and How You Can Too*, London: Harper Press, is an insightful collection based on interviews with over seventy CEOs from leading companies such as Microsoft, Xerox, Cisco Systems, eBay, Disney, and MasterCard. Full of wisdoms, this book examines the basis for CEO career success, and the interaction of management and leadership required of the CEO role.

N. Adler (2011) *Leadership Insights*, London: Routledge, is a superb resource for fostering deep reflection about leadership practice and current business norms. Drawing on the arts, this text offers tools for reflecting upon strategic thinking and how decisions are made, and ultimately allows strategists to explore their own leadership journeys.

G. P. Hodgkinson and I. Clarke (2007) 'Conceptual note: exploring the cognitive significance of organization strategizing—a dual process framework and research agenda', *Human Relations*, 60(1): 243–255, provides some insights as to what lies behind strategists' actions and how this impacts on cognitive styles.

P. C. Nutt (1998) 'How decision makers evaluate alternatives and the influence of complexity', *Management Science*, 44(8): 1148–1166, provides some interesting insights into the evaluation tactics used by decision makers.

visit the Online Resource Centre that accompanies this book to access more learning resources on this chapter topic at www.oxfordtextbooks.co.uk/orc/cunningham/

References

Adler, N. J. 2006. The arts and leadership: now that we can do anything, what will we do? *Academy of Management Learning and Education*, 5(4): 486–499.

Allison, G. T. 1971. *The Essence of Decision: Explaining the Cuban Missile Crisis*. Boston, MA: Little-Brown.

Andriessen, D. G. and Gubbins, C. 2009. Metaphor analysis as an approach for exploring theoretical concepts: the case of social capital. *Organization Studies*, 30: 845–863.

Barnard, C. 1938. *The Functions of the Executive*. Cambridge, MA: Harvard University Press.

Boar, B. 1997. *Strategic Thinking for Information Technology*. New York: John Wiley and Sons.

Bryan, L. and Farrell, D. 2008. Leading through uncertainty. *McKinsey Quarterly*, Dec: 1–13.

Bryant, A. 2011. *The Corner Office: How Top CEOs Made It and How You Can Too*. London: Harper Press.

Cacciaguidi-Fahy, S. and Cunningham, J. 2007. The use of strategic metaphors in intercultural business communication. *Managing Global Transitions*, 5(2): 133–155.

Ciampa, D. 2005. Almost ready: how leaders move up. *Harvard Business Review*, Jan: 46–53.

Courtney, H. 2008. A fresh look at strategy under uncertainty. *McKinsey Quarterly*, Dec: 1–8.

Davenport, T. 2006. Competing on analytics. *Harvard Business Review*, Jan: 2–10.

Davenport, T. 2009. Make better decisions. *Harvard Business Review*, Nov: 117–125.

Day, C., Harris, A., and Hadfield, M. 2001. Challenging the orthodoxy of effective school leadership, *International Journal of Leadership in Education*, 4(1): 39–56.

Deutschman, A. 2004. Inside the mind of Jeff Bezos. *Fast Company*, Aug(85): 52–58.

Eisenhardt, K. M. and Zbaracki, M. 1992. Strategic decision making. *Strategic Management Journal*, 13: 17–37.

Erickson, T. and Gratton, L. 2007. What it means to work here. *Harvard Business Review*, Mar: 104–112.

Finkelstein, S. 1992. Power in top management teams: dimensions, measurement and validation. *Academy of Management Journal*, 35(3): 505–538.

Flood, P. and Carroll, S. 2010. *The Persuasive Leader: Lessons from the Arts*. New York: John Wiley and Sons.

Flyvbjerg, B. 2001. *Making Social Science Matter: Why Social Inquiry Fails and How It Can Succeed Again*. Cambridge: Cambridge University Press.

Garratt, B. 1991. *Learning to Lead*. London: HarperCollins.

Garratt, B. 1995. *Developing Strategic Thought: Rediscovering the Art of Direction-giving*. London: HarperCollins.

Gavetti, G. and Rivkin, J. 2005. How strategists really think: tapping the power of analogy. *Harvard Business Review*, 58(4): 54–63.

Gerstner, L. 2003. *Who Says Elephants Can't Dance? Inside IBM's Historic Turnaround*. London: HarperCollins.

Graen, G. 2006. In the eye of the beholder: cross-cultural lessons in leadership from Project GLOBE. *Academy of Management Perspectives*, 20(4): 95–101.

Hambrick, D. C. and Cannella, A. 1989. Strategy implementation as substance and selling. *Academy of Management Executive*, 3(4): 278–285.

Hambrick, D. C., Finkelstein, S., and Mooney, A. C. (2005). Executive job demands: new insights for explaining strategic decision and leader behaviors. *Academy of Management Review*, 30(3): 472–491.

Hamel, G. and Prahalad, C. 1994. *Competing for the Future*. Cambridge, MA: Harvard University Press.

Hickson, D. J. 1990. Studying deciding an exchange of views between Mintzberg and Waters, Pettigrew and Butler. *Organization Studies*, 11(1): 1–16.

Hodgkinson, G. and Healey, M. 2012. Psychological foundations of dynamic capabilities: reflexion and reflection in strategic management. *Strategic Management Journal*, Forthcoming.

House, R., Javidon, M., Dorfman, P., and Sully de Luque, M. 2006. A failure of scholarship: response to George Graen's critique of Globe. *Academy of Management Perspectives*, 20(4): 95–114.

Huff, A. S. 1990. *Mapping Strategic Thought*. New York: John Wiley and Sons.

Hussey, D. 2001. Creative strategic thinking and the analytical process: critical factors for strategic success. *Strategic Change*, 10(4): 201–213.

Ireland, R. D. and Hitt, M. A. 1999. Achieving and maintaining strategic competitiveness in the 21st century: the role of strategic leadership. *Academy of Management Executive*, 13(1): 43–57.

Kotter, J. 1996. *Leading Change*. Cambridge, MA: Harvard Business School Press.

Kuhn, T. S. 1962. *The Structure of Scientific Revolutions*. Chicago, IL: University of Chicago Press.

Leithwood, K., Jantzi, D., and Steinbach, R. 1999. *Changing Leadership for Changing Times*. Buckingham, PA: Open University Press.

Leonard, N., Beauvais, L., and Scholl, R. 2005. A multi-level model of group cognitive style in decision making. *Journal of Managerial Issues*, Spring: 119–138.

Lorenz, C. 1995. Design as a strategic management resource. In B. Garratt (ed.) *Developing Strategic Thought*. London: HarperCollins.

Lovallo, D. and Sibony, O. 2006. Distortions and deceptions in strategic decisions. *McKinsey Quarterly*, 1: 18–29.

Miller, D. 1992. Icarus paradox: how exceptional companies bring about their own downfall. *Business Horizons*, Jan/Feb: 24–35.

Mintzberg, H. 1991. Strategic thinking as 'seeing'. In J. Nasi (ed.) *Arenas of Strategic Thinking*, Helsinki: Foundation for Economic Education.

Mintzberg, H. and Waters, J. 1990. Does decision get in the way? *Organization Studies*, 11(1): 6–10.

Mintzberg, H., Ahlstrand, J. L., and Lampel, J. 1998. *Strategy Safari: A Guided Tour through the Wilds of Strategic Management.* New York: The Free Press.

Morgan, G. 2006. *Images of Organization*. Rev'd int'l edn. Thousand Oaks, CA: Sage.

Ohmae, K. 1982. *The Mind of the Strategist*. New York: McGraw-Hill Inc.

O'Kane, C. 2008. Top management leadership in the turnaround process. Unpublished PhD thesis. National University of Ireland, Galway.

Perkins, E. J. 1999. *Wall Street to Main Street*. New York: Cambridge University Press.

Perman, S. 2006. Simon Cowell: from idol to inventor. *Business Week*, 31 Jan.

Peters, T. 2001. Rule #3: leadership is confusing as hell. *Fast Company*, 44: 124–140.

Pettigrew, A. 1990. Studying strategic choice and strategic change. A comment on Mintzberg and Waters 'Does decision get in the way?'. *Organization Studies*, 11(1): 6–11.

Pfeffer, J. and Sutton, R. 2006. *Hard Facts, Dangerous Half Truths, and Total Nonsense*. Boston MA: Harvard Business School Press.

Porac, J. and Thomas, H. 2002. Managing cognition and strategy: issues, trends and future directions. In A. Pettigrew, H. Thomas, and R. Whittington (eds) *Handbook of Management and Strategy*. London: Sage.

Porter, M. 1996. What is strategy? *Harvard Business Review*, Dec: 61–78.

Robert, M. 2005. *The New Strategic Thinking*. New York: McGraw-Hill.

Rowe, W. G. 2001. Creating wealth in organizations: the role of strategic leadership. *Academy of Management Executive*, 15(1): 81–94.

Rumelt, R. 2011. *Good Strategy/Bad Strategy*. London: Profile Books.

Schoemaker, P. 1993. Strategic decisions in organizations: rational and behavioural views. *Journal of Management Studies*, 30(1): 107–129.

Selznick, P. 1957. *Leadership in Administration*. New York: Row, Peterson.

Simon, A. 1967. The business school: a problem in organisational design. *Journal of Management Studies*, 4: 1–16.

Simon, H. 1991. Bounded rationality and organizational learning, *Organization Science*, 2(1): 125–134.

Sloan, A. P. 1967. *My Years with General Motors*. Garden City, NY: Doubleday.

Smircich, L. and Stubbart, C. 1985. Strategic management in an enacted world. *Academy of Management Review*, 10: 724–736.

Spender, J. C. 1989. *Industry Recipes: An Enquiry into the Nature and Sources of Managerial Judgement*. Oxford: Blackwell.

Stacey, R. D. 2010. *Complexity and Organisational Reality: Uncertainty and the Need to Rethink Management after the Collapse of Investment Capitalism*. London: Routledge.

Thakur, M. and Callingo, L. 1992. Strategic thinking is hip, but does it make a difference? *Business Horizons*, Sept/Oct: 47–54.

Thomas, T., Schermerhorn, J., and Dienhart, J. 2004. Strategic leadership of ethical behavior in business. *Academy of Management Executive*, 18(2): 56–66.

Tsoukas, H. 1991. The missing link: a transformational view of metaphors in organization science. *Academy of Management Review*, 16: 566–585.

Useem, M., Cook, J., and Sutton, L. 2005. Developing leaders for decision making under stress: Wildland Firefighters in the South Canyon Fire and its aftermath. *Academy of Management Learning and Education*, 4(4): 461–485.

Weick, K. E. 1995. *Sensemaking in Organisations*. London: Sage.

Weick, K. E. 1996. Drop your tools: an allegory for organization studies. *Administrative Science Quarterly*, 41: 301–313.

Wheeler, S., McFarland, W., and Kleiner, A. 2007. A blueprint for strategic leadership. *Strategy + Business*, 49 (Winter): 2–11.

Wright, R. 2006. Rigor and relevance using repertory grid technique in strategy research. In D. J. Ketchen and D. D. Bergh (eds) *Research Methodology in Strategy and Management, Vol. 3*. Bingley: Emerald Group Publishing.

Yukl, G. A. 1994. *Leadership in Organizations*. 3rd edn. Englewood Cliffs, NJ: Prentice Hall.

Zabbriskie, N. and Huellmantel, A. 1991. Thinking strategically. *Long Range Planning*, 24(6): 25–33.

Zaleznik, A. 1992. Managers and leaders: are they different? *Harvard Business Review Classic*, Mar/Apr: 126–135.

4

Dynamics of strategy formulation

Deliberate and emergent approaches

No strategy survives first contact with the enemy.

(Helmuth von Moltke)

Introduction

In the previous chapter, we explored the process of strategizing. We now turn our attention to the dynamics of strategy formulation, in terms of both deliberate and emergent approaches. Think of how you travel. Travelling provokes many different personal emotions. You may have some areas of certainty: you know your destination, the means by which you hope to get there, and in what time. But high degrees of uncertainty also exist, perhaps depending on the type of transport, the weather conditions, and the time of day. What if the bus or train runs late or you are caught in a traffic jam on the motorway? Instinctively, you will be thinking about or will have worked out alternative routes, or what to say to friends should you arrive late. Something may even cause you to alter your intended destination while en route. Certainty and learning from past experience will help you in thinking about the future. Personal mastery is critical: you know your capability, and you know that you will be able to cope no matter what the context and the situation. Thus, in sports such as rugby or hockey, players are generally aware of and play within the rules of the game—but these rules do not make the game predictable. Actual outcomes will be contingent on factors such as the tactics deployed by the opposing team, the tempo of the game, and the support of the crowd, as well as by individual interactions and temperament.

The same can be said of organizations attempting to formulate their strategies. Organizations have uncertainties in relation to the nature of competition and in terms of future trends, usage patterns, and technological developments. An example is book publishers having to make their products available on new technology platforms such as e-readers and tablets. Strategy formulation can help organizations to become more aware of potential uncertainties and associated risks, and to develop specific strategies to deal with current and future challenges. In large organizations with thousands of employees, multiple product lines, and global presence, the task of formulating strategy is a significant challenge. But it is also a challenge for a high-growth small-to-medium-sized enterprise (SME), which, despite resource constraints, needs to develop its capability to formulate strategy in order to realize prospective opportunities. For Swedish niche car manufacturer Keonigsegg, strategy formulation may be easier because of the small size of the organization—but it is also challenging given its niche market position. Similarly, difficulties of strategy formulation are accentuated for public sector organizations because of multiple stakeholders and the contested nature of the key outcomes that need to be achieved (Bryson, 2004). As the opening quote from military strategist von Moltke identified, a key difficulty is that strategies are only really tested once an attempt is made at implementation.

In this chapter, we examine the approaches that organizations can use for strategy formulation. We begin by revisiting the core strategic issues that strategy formulation should address. These are essential irrespective of organizational size, purpose, or context. Then we move our focus onto one of the key debates in the strategy field: namely, *how* strategy is formulated in organizations. In doing so, we examine the debate from two perspectives: deliberate strategy formulation and emergent strategy formulation. From this, we turn to strategy process and the role that learning can play in ensuring increased effectiveness in the strategy-formulation process. We will see that, despite the centrality of the formulation debate to the strategy literature, the reality is that our knowledge about *how* organizations actually go about conducting this task is still in its infancy (Pretorius and Martitz, 2011). Moreover, while many organizations claim to engage in forms of strategic planning (Whittington and Cailluet, 2008), very few appear to reap the expected benefits from this process (Cheung *et al.*, 2009). While strategy researchers have provided snapshot insights into strategy formulation based on limited contexts, further research and multi-method approaches are needed to deepen our understanding of how organizations actually craft strategy. This remains a key challenge.

Core strategic issues

Practising strategists, as well as academics, have often questioned the true value of strategy formulation. Reasons for this range from the cost involved, the inefficiency and inflexibility of the process (particularly in the context of fast-moving, hyper-competitive environments), political factors such as ensuring ownership of and buy-in to the process, and the notion that formal planning can sap creativity (Taylor, 1997). The question of the value of strategy formulation has received some research attention. Gray's (1986) study of US multi-business companies found that the locus of planning responsibility in the main rested with line managers. Planning occurred first, followed by budgeting. The key sources of frustration were implementation issues, skills of line managers, and adequacy of information. Strategy formulation requires sound data collection, but also informed strategy conversations around insightful questions (Simpson, 1998).

Strategy formulation in different contexts

The fact that strategy-formulation processes and the difficulties that they face differ across organizational contexts has been highlighted by some researchers. A conglomerate's strategy-formulation difficulties centre on different environments, reward systems, attitude to risk, reactions to pressure, and project failure (Berg, 1965). For holding companies with a diverse **portfolio** of businesses, short-term returns to shareholders may be the broad underlying logic around which strategies (for example, asset stripping, turnaround, divestment) are formulated. In an SME context, strategy formulation tends to be less systematized due to the limited number of products/services and resources, inadequate administrative procedures/techniques, and the limited expertise of managers beyond their functional areas (Van Hoorn, 1979). This can pose challenges for SMEs seeking external investment. For regulated **industries**, strategy formulation that addresses political and social strategy in tandem with economic issues increases the likelihood of improved strategic outcomes (Mahon and Murray, 1981). So companies in the chemical, oil exploration, and energy sectors have to be aware of and actively manage stakeholders around the political and social aspects of their activities. Other factors shaping the nature of strategy formulation include the influence of the chief executive officer (CEO), the nature of environmental uncertainty, and industry life cycle stage (Pretorius and Martitz, 2011). For example, as an industry matures, data concerning key trends and customer behaviour will be more readily available; this is likely to result in a more rational and formulaic means of devising strategy (Gavetti and Rivkin, 2007). Nonetheless, irrespective of context and the extent of sophistication of practices, there are a number of fundamental questions that should be addressed as part of the strategy-formulation process.

The strategy-formulation process

The strategy-formulation process, according to Vancil and Lorange (1975), should consist of three cycles: the first is the establishment of corporate objectives; the second is the development of formalized programmes designed around meeting these corporate objectives; and the third involves resource allocation. This may be perceived as simple and straightforward, but the authors warn that:

> Good strategic planning can only take place when qualified managers engage in creative thinking—and creativity, by definition, cannot be produced on a schedule. While formal strategic planning cannot guarantee good ideas, it can increase the odds sufficiently to yield a handsome payoff.
>
> Vancil and Lorange (1975: 90)

Thus strategy-formulation and organizational process can be complex and fraught with difficulties. This brings us to the question of on which issues organizations and strategists should focus when they attempt to formulate strategy. There are five core strategic issues that any strategy formulation should attempt to address. These echo the strategic management challenges outlined in Chapter 1 (see Table 1.4). The real challenge is to develop organizational and individual clarity around them.

- Who are we? (The orientation challenge)
- What business(es) are we in? (The orientation challenge)
- What makes us unique? (The **trade-off** challenge)
- What makes us relevant? (The relevance challenge)
- What is our ability to continuously learn, adapt, and change? (The continuous change challenge)

These questions seem straightforward, but history shows that organizations have often neglected them, have focused on a few questions at the expense of others, or have not had sufficient clarity to diffuse consensus on direction throughout the organization.

The strategist's role is to provide ongoing clarity about these questions, and to communicate them effectively and consistently to internal and external stakeholders, as discussed in Chapter 2. Companies such as Woolworths, Royal Bank of Scotland (RBS), and Northern Rock have failed to develop coherency around these core questions.

'Who are we?' focuses on the core mission of the business and how it defines its purpose in terms of future goals and aspirations. In a public sector context, this continues to be a huge challenge, because there is such a broad spectrum of activities, from criminal justice to health and welfare issues. How does the CEO of the UK's National Health Service (NHS) define, articulate, and answer the question: 'Who are we?' Contrast this with your local corner shop: 'Who are we?' may be easier to answer, and the business itself has less internal complexity compared with the NHS and is subject to different types of external force. Increasing technological and product convergence between industry sectors makes the task of mapping and verbalizing core missions all the more difficult for strategists. So how does Microsoft's **acquisition** of Skype for US$8bn in May 2011 shape the future purpose of Microsoft? Ultimately, the core definition of who we are as an organization is defined by the organization's strategic intent. Sainsbury's strategic intent is informed by its corporate responsibility, focused on 'best for food and health, sourcing with integrity, respect for our environment, making a difference in the community and a great place to work'.

The businesses on which organizations are focused are their core activities, and the scope of these activities may be related or unrelated in nature (we discuss the related and unrelated activities in more detail in Chapter 7). Nokia has broadened its definition of its businesses to reflect its consumer-led approach to new communication media and convergent device trends around music, news, email, and social networking. By contrast, low-price department store group HEMA, with a presence in Holland, Belgium, Germany, Luxembourg, and France, describes itself thus:

> Just like HEMA, a nice easy life does not have to be expensive. Walk to the shops, you'll see right away that nowhere else will you find our remarkable combination of the best products for everyday life, with their own unique design, and at remarkably low prices. Nowhere else can you shop in this way. And our staff are always there for you: proud, committed to their HEMA. These are the things that make HEMA unique.
>
> (http://www.hema.nl/nl-NL/over_hema/HEMA.aspx?navmethod = menu)

We can see from this that HEMA has focused its purpose and its businesses on providing good products, unique design, and low prices, and on having committed employees. This mix ensures that customers remain loyal and are less likely to shop anywhere else.

The issue of uniqueness focuses on competitive advantage and core competences. An organization must have resources to compete in a market segment, but also needs to define its difference from competitors in order to sustain its competitive position. Coffee shops define their differences in their advertising, store layout, product offering and quality, and overall service offering. Starbucks, in defining its uniqueness, focuses on the 'Starbucks experience', captured through the quality of its coffee, its relationships with business partners and customers, and the location and layout of its stores. It is about building a community. Contrast this with Caffè Florian, the famous coffee shop in St Mark's Square in Venice, which opened in 1720. Its uniqueness is built around the art of elegant living that pervades the venue itself and its Florian-branded products.

The issue of relevance focuses on how companies maintain their contemporary attractiveness to both current and prospective end customers. This can be through advertising, a broad range of distribution channels, or product design. Apple, with its iMac, iPod, and iPad, has continued to sustain its relevance with end users. A simple product portfolio with logical product updates has been core to Apple's success. Counter this with the Apple of 1997, months away from bankruptcy with a confusing array of products and a clear lack of relevance, except to a very limited number of specialist and tech-savvy purchasers.

The final question—'What is our ability continuously to learn, adapt, and change?'—focuses on an organization's ability to cope and to formulate strategy in tandem with dealing with increased levels of environmental uncertainty. Here, organizations should learn and constantly seek ways in which to improve their strategy-formulation process. This could range from developing more sophisticated analytical tools to refining stakeholder engagement. As Aristotle noted: 'Excellence is not an act, but a habit.' This will ultimately yield better strategic outcomes for the organization as a whole. Continuous review of these core strategic questions is the basis of strategy formulation, and is critical to gaining and sustaining a successful momentum towards competitive advantage. The strategist has a central role in ensuring that these questions are continuously reviewed in the context of competition and evolving industry structures. The pathway to a good strategy comes from 'honestly acknowledging the challenges being faced and providing an approach to overcoming them' (Rumelt, 2011: 4). Strategists should strive to create an infrastructure for strategy formulation that allows for assumptions to be revisited, enables debates about future options, and respects competing concerns and logic. Deep discussion and debate are inevitable; the very essence of strategy formulation is controversial choices and trade-offs (Karnani, 2009).

We now turn from the core issues at the heart of strategy formulation to the differing perspectives on strategy formulation.

Perspectives on strategy formulation

Different terms have been used in the strategy literature to describe the process that results in a company defining its strategy. These broad terms include 'making strategy', 'long-range planning', 'strategic planning', 'crafting strategy', 'strategy formation', and 'strategy formulation'. Irrespective of the terminology used, the key questions are about how companies formulate their strategies and whether this has an impact on company performance. Global economic uncertainty and dramatic stock market fluctuation means that strategists involved in strategy formulation are facing a profoundly uncertain time in their careers, contemplating disaster scenarios that until recently would have been completely unthinkable (Dye *et al.*, 2009).

Examining strategy formulation means touching upon one of the great debates in the strategy literature: does structure follow strategy (Chandler, 1962), or does strategy follow structure (Bower, 1970)? One school of thought is that organizations should take a very deliberate and rational view of strategy formulation, while the other advocates a more emergent approach to strategy formulation that better allows for learning and change. As outlined in Chapter 1 (see Figure 1.1), the economic landscape has changed significantly, posing greater and more complex challenges for strategists; the two perspectives on strategy formulation are born from these challenges. So we begin by examining strategy formulation from the deliberate and rational perspective.

Deliberate strategy formulation

Before the 1950s, formulating strategy equated to devising the financial objectives of the organization. Organizations undertook their financial forecasts every year, and these also doubled as their strategies. However, from the 1950s to early 1970s, strategy formulation became more sophisticated. Typically, in a large organization, it was conducted formally through a part of the organization, often called a 'corporate planning unit', which oversaw and ran the overall strategic-planning process. This unit's focus was on developing long-range plans, but also on developing strategic programmes for the organization to implement. In large conglomerate organizations, such formal strategy-planning systems proved complex and were fraught with difficulties. The process was viewed as a multi-level activity, and both economic and non-economic issues had to be taken into consideration. Conflicts arose to which there were no ready solutions. As one early corporate planner put it: 'If there were any easy answers to any of this, we would have been doing it that way a long time ago' (Berg, 1965: 80).

The relatively stable economic environment of this time meant that organizations began to develop a process of strategy formulation along three organizational levels: corporate planning and strategy; business planning and strategy; and functional planning and strategy (Vancil and Loranage, 1975). In this process, corporate planning and strategy typically set the overall objective of the company, the resources required for implementation, and the resource allocation system. Business planning and strategy dealt with how business units competed in specific markets in line with the overall corporate objectives. Functional planning and strategy were tasked with implementing business strategy objectives, and in doing so mapped out action plans to achieve these objectives.

In tandem, pioneering strategy thinkers such as Andrews (1971), Ansoff (1965; 1977), and Chandler (1962) wrote in detail on the formal planning process, which was seen to be formal, sequential, and rational. In following the division initially created by Frederick Taylor through scientific management and developed in practice by Henry Ford at his automobile factory, analysis and conceptualization of broad strategic goals and objectives were in every way the task of top management, if not the exclusive remit of the CEO. The strategist was the CEO. Implementation and execution were the core task of line managers and employees. This approach has been labelled the 'traditional', 'classical', 'deliberate', or 'design' approach to strategy formulation (Mintzberg, 1994b; Whittington, 2001). It is based on rational design, and the process yields grand strategies that are ready for implementation. Organizational objectives are set through in-depth analysis of internal and external environments and encapsulate clear goals. From this perspective, the CEO in particular is seen as the heroic figure in strategy formulation (Chandler, 1962). In his critique of the deliberate approach to strategy, Mintzberg (1990) outlined several basic premises that underpin this school.

1. Strategy formation should be a controlled, conscious process of thought.
2. Responsibilities for that control and consciousness must rest with the CEO: that person is *the* strategist.
3. The model of strategy formation must be kept simple.

4. Strategies emerge from this design process fully formulated.
5. These strategies should be explicit and, if possible, articulated, which also favours their being kept simple.
6. Finally, only after these unique, full-blown, explicit, and simple strategies are fully formulated can they then be implemented.

Such basic premises served the strategy field well, providing a template that clearly placed the CEO at the core of all activities and which also explicitly separated the activities of formulation and implementation. However, doubts began to be raised about whether this ideal design school template truly captured what occurred in organizations. Take IKEA, the enormously successful Swedish furniture company, which offers unassembled furniture and gives customers access to the warehouse. IKEA is typically used as an example of a rational, clear, deliberate approach to strategy formulation founded on a clear understanding of competitive positioning and what would make the company unique (see Porter, 1996—Reading 1.1). However, when asked about the genesis of the IKEA strategy, Henry Mintzberg offers a somewhat contradictory explanation:

> One of the workers, frustrated in trying to get a table in his car decided to take the legs off. Insight number one—all customers have the same challenge. IKEA began selling unassembled merchandise. Insight number two: when a large new store in Stockholm became inundated with customers, staff began to allow customers to retrieve product from the warehouse—the go-get-the-stuff-yourself model. Opportunism? I call it learning.
>
> (Allio, 2011: 6)

This issue of a deliberate, as opposed to a more emergent, approach to strategy formulation is one that is a hotly debated topic in the strategy literature. Two of the central contributors to the debate are Igor Ansoff (representing the traditional, design school) and Henry Mintzberg (representing the 'emergent school'). In defending the design approach, Ansoff (1991: 457) argues that deliberate strategy has a number of advantages.

- In cases in which decision making is less time-consuming than trial and error, the rational model saves time by selecting action alternatives that are most likely to produces success. This time saving is of great importance in organizations that find themselves in rapidly changing environments.
- It permits additional savings of time through starting strategic response in anticipation of the need to act—a process called strategic planning.
- It reduces the number of strategy errors and reduces costs by eliminating the probable 'non-starters' from the list of possible strategic moves.

Ansoff also rejects criticisms that the design school and deliberate strategy approach is rigid and thereby prevents change and learning: 'the use of explicit strategy in successful practice is not rigid and does not preclude attention to new opportunities outside the scope of strategy' (ibid: 458).

Despite the advantages of deliberate strategy formulation, some notable issues emerge. These include the lack of accuracy of long-term forecasts and the financial plans associated with strategic plans (Paul *et al.*, 1978). These limitations are captured in the adage: 'It is hard to predict anything in advance, especially the future.' In a similar vein, goals stemming from the formal design school approach were largely quantitative and neglected the qualitative difficulties of implementation; in concentrating solely on the front-end task of strategy conception, the equally important back-end task of implementation was largely neglected. The prescriptions to overcome these problems, as Paul *et al.* (1978) stressed, were primarily focused on improving the accuracy of the process, learning from previous mistakes, getting real top management commitment to the process, and opening the process to ongoing scrutiny. According to Paul *et al.* (1978), adapting planning to reality included the following steps.

- Emphasize the process of planning, not the financial aspects of the plan.
- Differentiate between risks to the balance sheet and risks to the profit-and-loss statement.
- Measure the total market and competitive market shares as accurately as possible.
- Gear the plan to events.
- Plan to expend money step by step.
- Build a second plan based on time.
- Decide in advance the criteria for abandoning a project.
- Set up a monitoring system.
- Make a five-year plan every year.
- Avoid excessive publicity about long-term financial goals.

Other recommendations include avoiding considering strategy with budgets and financials, because reviewing the two together is likely to lead to the dominance of short-term financial issues at the expense of long-term strategic ones (Beinhocker and Kaplan, 2002). Others provide a reminder that a focus on change and emergent scenarios should not obscure relevant long-term trends or devalue important existing strategies (Dye *et al.*, 2009). Nonetheless, while undoubtedly useful, such recommendations still fail to appreciate that the notion that strategy, as intended by top management, may not be necessarily realized in practice. In contrast, this is something that is at the heart of the emergent strategy approach.

Emergent strategy formulation

The deliberate formulation strategy school of thought began to come under criticism in particular because of the oil crisis in the early 1970s, intensified competition led by Japanese companies, and inherent problems with the process, as hinted at above. The overall failure of some corporate planning units to deal with or capture some of these events in the 1970s and 1980s led to discontent among practitioners and strategy researchers with respect to the deliberate approach to strategy formulation. Many US multinational organizations began cutting and removing corporate planning units from their organizational charts. In tandem with these events, another perspective emerged, which is now termed 'emergent strategy formulation'. The emergent approach criticized the deliberate approach on two fronts: namely, the assumption of **rationality** and the separation of formulation from implementation (Mintzberg, 1994a). For Mintzberg, strategy conception and execution were meshed together in a fluid and often messy process of **organizational learning** and adaptation. Indeed, each informed the other. As Mintzberg (1987—Reading 1.5) argues, organizations do not simply think in an abstract, isolated manner and then pursue their activities; they also act, experiment and innovate, and then examine the consequences, incorporating successful elements into their strategies. Thus strategy formulation should be an all-encompassing process and therefore flexible enough to allow for periods during which the organization is reformulating its strategy and for other perspectives to be considered. As part of his ongoing debate with Igor Ansoff, the proponent of the design school, Mintzberg (1990: 465) forcefully argued: 'Come on, Igor. Of course, we need to think. Of course we want to be rational. But it is a complicated world out there. We both know that we shall get nowhere without an emergent learning alongside deliberate planning.'

Mintzberg's critique was not completely novel. Much earlier, Lindblom (1959: 86) had referred to policy making as the 'science of muddling through'—a process of 'successive approximation' during which the end objective itself is always open to constant renewal and alteration. Likewise, Wrapp (1967: 91) referred to managers as 'opportunists' who mesh themselves in operational detail while also considering the big picture; 'rather than produce a full grown decision tree, they start with a twig, help it grow, and ease themselves out on the limbs only after they have tested to see how much weights the limbs can stand' (ibid: 97). For many, the emergent formulation approach was much closer to realities as experienced by strategists. Sony's success with the Walkman in the 1980s stemmed from a perceptive CEO realizing that a unit working on the miniaturization of portable cassette-recorders should come together with another unit working separately on devising better quality headphones. The result was that the Walkman was born. This was not a strategy that was *formulated*, but rather one that *formed* as a result of a CEO keeping close to the action and bringing various capabilities in the organization together to meet latent demand. To this day, organizations are urged to be more agile and flexible with their strategies, thereby staying alert to spot and seize game-changing opportunities (Sull, 2010). Some even claim that the present-day turbulent environment calls for a 'just in time' approach to strategy formulation, risk taking, and resource allocation, with regular 'hands on decks' meetings organized for strategists to exchange information and ideas (Bryan and Farrell, 2008).

Strategy formulation and performance

One of the key questions that remains to be definitively answered by strategy researchers is the precise relationship between types of strategy formulation and company performance. What is the link between strategy processes and strategic outcomes, both quantitatively and qualitatively? A study carried out by Kudla (1980) found no significant difference in shareholder returns between organizations that had formal planning systems and those that did not. A similar study by Leontiades and Tezel (1980) noted: 'our research extends a line of investigation begun in a number of prior studies, but it fails to support the contention that formal planners outperform informal planners.' Further studies by Boyd (1991) and Ramanujam *et al.* (1986) highlight the contradictory nature of the links between planning and performance. However, a study by Miller and Cardinal (1994), even taking account of their noted methodological weaknesses, found that there was some positive link between strategy formulation and performance. A key challenge for strategy researchers is to explore this link. If Miller and Cardinal's positive link is replicated in other studies, this strengthens the argument that companies need to pay particular attention to strategy formulation and strategy processes. Beyond direct linkages to performance, indirectly there is also pressure on organizations to be 'seen to be doing' formal and rational strategic planning. After all, if something as fundamental as strategy formulation is left to whatever methodology takes the CEO's fancy at any given time, how might we expect this to inspire confidence among investors and stakeholders (Wilson, 1998)? The reason why strategy formulation might have to be portrayed as rational and deliberate, even if this does not match how it occurs in practice, is explored more critically in Chapter 14. For the moment, our attention turns to strategy process, which provides a broader understanding of what strategy formulation is.

Strategy process

Strategy process scholars have expanded the concept of strategy formulation to include how strategy is formulated and then implemented, and the changes that this brings to an organization. The change from a narrow planning-orientated view to examining strategy process involves looking more broadly and critically at the environment, both external and internal (Cummings and Daellenbach, 2009: 251). Strategic planning, as traditionally understood, is not designed to accommodate the essence of strategy formation—the messy process of generating insights and moulding them into winning strategy (Campbell and Marcus, 1997). The reality for many organizations is that there are multiple strategy processes at different levels, such as corporate, business, and individual units, which involve a myriad of people with a variety of cultural, educational, and professional attainments. Company-wide involvement in the strategy processes creates clarity of vision and mission, instils greater organizational adaptiveness, and provides a platform for enhanced strategic decisions (Collier *et al.*, 2004). A well-designed strategy process can generate a more cohesive and bonded company culture, which can cope and react quickly and decisively to external competitive events. In outlining what strategy process actually is, Garvin (1998: 45) provides an interesting classification of process in relation to the key managerial processes involved.

1. *Direction-setting processes* These incorporate formal and informal processes of information gathering and processing, managerial learning, agenda setting, and mobilization of structural and processual support for directions.

2. *Negotiation and selling processes* These involve the personal interactions, vertically and horizontally, necessary to implement a direction.

3. *Monitoring and control processes* These are designed to monitor the progress of strategy implementation, involving formal analysis and routine and non-routine action to correct or align behaviour in accordance with direction.

Taking these classifications within the strategy process, we can appreciate the challenges faced by the CEO and board of a local authority compared with those faced by an Internet-based social network business employing only ten people and using offshore resources for its website development.

Strategy process also implicitly applies social interaction between various parties as part of the strategy-formulation process. Strategies exist in cognition—that is, in strategists' minds—and are elaborated, shaped, and legitimized as a result of personal interactions between individuals and teams (see Chapter 3), in addition to being informed and framed by the firms' culture, activities, and routines (Gavetti and Rivkin, 2007). This perspective broadens and complicates our understanding of formulation, as Pettigrew (1992) observes.

1. Social reality is not a steady state, but rather a dynamic process: it occurs rather than exists.

2. The human process is constructed, created by human agents—individuals or collective—through their actions.

3. Social life is a process of structural emergence via actions, and the tension between actions and structures is the ultimate moving force of the process.

4. The interchange of action and structure occurs in time and is cumulative, such that the legacy of the past is always shaping the emerging future. What happens, how it happens, why it happens, what results it brings about are dependent on when it happens, the location in the processual sequence, and the place in the rhythm of events characteristic for a given process.

These observations by Pettigrew are at the core of strategy process. Interaction of people, actions, structures, and the tensions therein means that strategy and its formulation is an inherently social process. The social reality differs significantly in companies in the same industry. The structures and human process may differ significantly and change over time to reflect the current and future challenges that they face.

Hart and Banbury (1994) found that organizations have multiple ways of strategy making that combine into an overall strategy process. They argue that organizations that can combine these various ways of strategy making will have higher performance levels irrespective of size and competitive environment. Their message to managers is clear:

> The process through which strategy is made holds the potential for competitive advantage and requires purposeful design and management attention. To achieve high performance, managers must provide a strong sense of strategic direction and organizational members must be active players in the strategy-making process . . . Purity of process thus appears to be much less the objective than the nurturing of multiple, competing processes of strategy-making deep within the organization.
>
> (Hart and Banbury, 1994: 266)

However, Lumpkin and Dess (1995) found that a simple strategy process had a high impact on performance in the early growth phases of the organization, but that, as organizations matured, the effectiveness of the strategy process lessened and this ultimately impacted upon organizational performance. Critical in all accounts is who is actually involved in the process and the nature of their input. This is explored next.

Involvement of the CEO and top management team

The personality of the CEO can have an influence on the strategy process of organizations (Miller *et al.*, 1982). The role of top management in the strategy process should focus on managing organizational culture and motivating appropriate strategic behaviour (Van Cauewenbergh and Cool, 1982). As Table 4.1 illustrates, this task involves a number of elements. First, top management should animate and motivate behaviour to align with the desired culture of the organization. Here, strategists can manage information flows strategically: making visible requests for certain information, thereby signalling its importance, or by disseminating selected information or purposefully using informal information channels or speculative rumours to gauge the likely acceptance of a strategic decision and/or orientate those at lower levels of an organization. Strategists can also keep options open by formulating broad and imprecise objectives, leaving the means by which these will be achieved open to alteration and emergence. This is akin to what Hamel and Prahalad (1989) call 'strategic intent': an ambitious far-reaching objective that at once provides direction, but also motivates.

A further way in which strategists can communicate intent and areas of importance is by redeploying highly talented individuals to certain tasks or committees, thereby 'signalling preferences in an indirect way to peers and subordinates' (Van Cauewenbergh and Cool, 1982: 257). Finally, non-verbal cues can also be critical in communicating strategic intent, be it in the form of body language, the time that CEOs visibly allocate to tasks, or in their behaviour internally at meetings and towards staff or externally towards stakeholders. Take Richard Branson: in pursuing world records in sailing and attempting to circumnavigate the globe by balloon, he is not merely following an individual pursuit; he is also reinforcing the Virgin Brand as innovative, ground-breaking, ambitious, and determined. Again, this is a message that peers and employees are likely to internalize and so is crucial to creating sufficient coherence in strategic deliberations. In terms of strategy making, CEOs should be risk takers, taking the lead rather than following, and generating more market-led innovations (Miller *et al.*, 1982).

Further elements of managing organizational culture and motivating appropriate strategic behaviour (Table 4.1) include ensuring control over the enterprise by leveraging the power of the top management position and maintaining control over the allocation of resources. This frequently involves utilizing the symbolic management processes discussed above. The final element is recognizing and rewarding talent in order to reinforce strategic values and high performance. This is a vital input not only to strategy formulation, but also, as we will review in Chapters 9 and 10, to realizing advantage. Many CEOs fail to pick the type of diverse top management team (age; personality; gender;

Table 4.1 Top management's tools for managing organizational culture and motivating strategic behaviour

Managing organizational culture	Motivating adequate strategy behaviour
Managing corporate values	Managing symbolic behaviour Strategic gathering and dissemination of information Formulation of broad objectives Assistants and staff members Attention to non-verbal cues
Ensuring full span of control	Leveraging and reinforcing power of position
Recognizing talent	Reinforcing and rewarding desired role behaviours Recognizing high potential talent at lower managerial echelons

Source: Drawing on Van Cauwenbergh and Cool (1982: 256–258)

background) necessitated by their business environment and instead play it safe by picking people with whom they feel comfortable.

Middle management involvement

Middle management's role in the strategy process and in facilitating the articulation of strategy is fundamentally undervalued and misunderstood. Actively involving middle management considerably influences the extent to which companies are successful in effecting a chosen strategic direction (Van Cauewenbergh and Cool, 1982). Middle managers have to develop a broad skill range that interfaces between strategic and operational levels, and thereby gain greater insights into the strategy trade-offs that have to be made within a company. Middle managers contribute more effectively to strategy processes when top management sets the strategic direction and they are given the freedom to assess the range of strategic alternatives. Through this model, the strategy process allows for increased two-way interaction between middle managers and top managers (Wooldridge and Floyd, 1990). Group processes at different levels in the organization, as well as membership of these groups, can have a bearing on the effectiveness of a company's strategy process (Kraut *et al.*, 2005).

Failure to engage middle managers in an effective manner may lead to resistance at this level, because top managers may view them not as partners in the strategy process, but as an opposition taking the view: 'Who has time for strategy when execution is all that matters?' Middle managers need to be involved in strategic-planning processes and associated strategy conversations in order to be effective strategy executors. If they are not convinced of the organizational strategy, they can impede and frustrate implementation efforts. If the strategy-formulation process appears remote and mysterious, complete buy-in and energy behind initiatives is unlikely (Stern, 2007). The issue is not simply one of buy-in to execution activities. Arguably, the root of dramatic changes in the strategy of large, complex firms is frequently the autonomous strategic initiatives taken at middle management and operational levels (Burgelman, 1983: 67; Campbell and Marcus, 1997). Mintzberg (2009) advocates rebuilding organizations as communities, coining the term 'communityship' based on the idea of building organizations from the middle out, with middle managers coming together armed with critical upward communication from employees (Tourish, 2005) and driving key changes in their organizations. Dye and Sibony (2007) go a step further and argue that those who carry out strategy should necessarily also develop it.

Organizational politics

Getting greater organizational involvement in the strategy process can have some negative effects, particularly centred on organizational politics. The political nature of strategy formation is rarely acknowledged in strategic planning literature (Jarzabkowski and Balogun, 2009). Yet organizations are like governments in that all of their activities and decisions are framed by some form of politics (Pfeffer, 1992). We can define 'organizational politics' as competing internal interests for factors such as resources and job opportunities, resulting in the formation of coalitions. This may lead to suboptimal outcomes in choosing a strategic direction. Politics can also mean expending energy in order to overcome internal organizational barriers and achieve a consensus about strategy direction. Such politics can have a negative impact on the organizational culture, may lead to slow decision-making processes, and may feed into an insularity of perspective and inertia about overall company purpose. In times of change, some groups may be particularly reluctant to give up a long-held basis of power. Frequently, political wrangling occurs across organizational departments in which intra-organizational fighting limits the achievement of organization-wide objectives. On an individual basis, managers may not like to admit an error and will rarely recommend suspensions of projects if there is a risk of reputational damage or endangering the livelihoods of their subordinates (Sull, 2010). Rather than be ignored, political conflict should be surfaced, embraced, and debated. Interestingly, Cummings and Daellenbach (2009: 257) have called for more attention on the role of strategist as politician and 'less focus on command and control, more on influencing, steering, nudging, connecting interests and internal marketing'. At the strategy-formulation stage, at which the very essence of what the organization is and does is up for debate, a greater understanding of political behaviour would seem particularly relevant.

The role of organizational learning

Fine-tuning the strategy formulation in any organization is a particular challenge for the CEO and top management teams as the chief architects of the strategy process. In stepping back from the 'Does strategy follow structure or does structure follow strategy?' debate, Burgelman (1983) argues that organizational learning has a role in the strategy process. Organizations can and should learn from their strategy formulation experiences, their successes and failures (Gino and Pisano, 2011). Quinn (1980: 48) terms this a 'logical incrementalism', noting that:

> Strategy deals with the unknowable, not the uncertain. It involves forces of such great numbers, strength, and combinatory powers that one cannot predict events in a probabilistic sense. Hence logic dictates that one proceeds flexibly and experimentally from broad concepts toward specific commitments, making the latter concrete as late as possible in order to narrow the bands of uncertainty and to benefit from the available information. This is the process of 'logical incrementalism'.

Even organizations that today seem to have great clarity in their strategy have progressed via a form of incrementalism. For example, in the case of Starbucks, CEO Howard Schultz initially attempted to directly replicate models of Milan coffee houses in the USA, including by having tables, but no chairs, dressing staff in formal attire, and providing an ambiance by playing opera music. Over time, Schultz amended these features to form the Starbucks experience with which we are familiar today. Thus, through consistent engagement with strategic planning, managers develop and hone their strategic capability and this allows them to cope with uncertainties, but also to learn from their experiences (Christensen, 1997) and to ensure continuing relevance (Lindblom, 1959: 84).

Hence organizations need to be conscious of knowledge-management capabilities and how their experiences of strategy making are communicated to the organization as a whole, with a view to improving the process so that it leads to meaningful outcomes. To meet this requirement effectively, companies need to be cognizant of four important types of business knowledge:

1. what we know we know—emphasis on knowledge sharing;
2. what we know we don't know—emphasis on knowledge seeking and creation;
3. what we don't know we know—uncovering hidden or tacit knowledge; and
4. what we don't know we don't know—discovering key risks, exposures, and opportunities.

In the task of facilitating learning the new, and occasionally unlearning the old, the strategist takes the role of a facilitator, or an architect designing and supporting continuous change (Senge, 1990). A key tool in this task is technology, which allows real-time exploration of data and mining the wisdom of crowds (Davenport, 2009). Also vital is ensuring an adequate pool of reliable, independent information on which to make informed choices. Questions to consider include the following (Kahneman and Klein, 2010).

- Is the information coming from multiple sources, or only one source that is being regurgitated in different ways?
- Is there a possibility of groupthink?
- Does the leader have an opinion that seems to be influencing others?
- Where are key metrics coming from?
- Are there quantitative and qualitative insights? Are they consistent?

According to Rumelt (2011: 253), by definition all businesses have access to 'privileged information' produced in everyday operations; 'all alert business people can know more about their own customers, their own products, and their production technology than anyone else can in the world.' Learning therefore occurs by accumulating and exploiting the insights from such privileged information.

Strategy as practice

In an attempt to gain some real insights into how strategists actually behave and act in strategy formulation, a new domain encompassing learning and knowledge management is taking hold within the strategy field: namely, 'strategy as practice'. Strategy as practice is an attempt to move beyond strategy as either planned or emergent, or the dichotomy between formulation and implementation, to a focus on the 'practical competence' of managers, 'existing structures', and the 'nitty-gritty, often tiresome and repetitive routines of strategy' (Whittington, 1996: 732). Strategy as practice is about understanding the 'actions and interactions within the whole strategy-making process' (ibid). This evolution highlights the potential merits of shifting from dominant macro institutional and resource-based approaches towards an examination of the micro processes and practices of strategy. What the 'producers' of strategy actually do and the activities that they use to achieve this have become a central concern in these practice-based forms of research (Hendry, 2000; Jazabkowski, 2003; Johnson *et al.*, 2003; Whittington, 2007).

The practice movement is sympathetic towards Mintzbergian attempts to move away from calculative and rational depictions of strategy epitomized through notions of 'crafting strategy' (Mintzberg, 1987). The limitations of this strategy process tradition, however, stem from its focus on the organizational (that is, macro) level at the expense of the practical activity of those who actually constitute the process (Johnson *et al.*, 2003). The practice-based approach is therefore seen as 'a necessary corrective' enabling strategy researchers to examine the underlying processes and activities shaping formation (Chia, 2004) through an actual focus on praxis, practitioners, and practices (Whittington, 2007). As Johnson *et al.* (2003: 5) put it:

> If we are to aid management and the managing of organizations we need to achieve a higher degree of reflexivity amongst those actors about what they are doing at that level and its effects. Much of the influential literature on strategy, important as it is, has left the manager bereft of insights, let alone guidelines for action, at this micro level.

The development of the **strategy-as-practice** perspective has provided new insights in understanding strategy at a micro level by bringing theoretical approaches from inside and outside the strategy field. This has the potential to advance our understanding of how strategy lives and is experienced in a variety of contexts, further reinforcing the centrality and importance of strategy.

Spotlight The art and science of crafting strategy

Crafting strategy can involve the science and art sides of strategy, as discussed in Chapter 1. The science side often involves the use of well-recognized analytical tools. The results of research on the extent to which analytical tools were used at company strategy workshops from over 1,300 firms are presented below (see Table 4.2). The most popular tools used are basic in nature, the most used by far being the SWOT analysis (62 per cent), followed by stakeholder analysis (30 per cent). 'SWOT' is an acronym for 'strengths, weaknesses, opportunities, and threats'. Strengths and weaknesses analysis focuses internally, while opportunities and threats analysis has an external focus.

The research by Hodgkinson *et al.* (2006) also found that while strategy workshops are an important vehicle in the process of developing strategy, they are typically attended by senior management only. This suggests the dominance of an elitist approach to strategy development that does not extend to middle management or employees.

Relying solely on the science side of strategy and on limited voices can be fatal, however, because long-term

Table 4.2 Analytical tools applied in strategy workshops

Which of the following analytical tools were applied during the strategy workshop?	
SWOT	62%
Stakeholder analysis	30%
Scenario planning	28.5%
Market segmentation	22.6%
Competence analysis	21.5%
PEST(EL) analysis	17.2%
Value chain analysis	15.1%
BCG Matrix	8.6%
Porter's Five Forces	8.5%
Cultural web	5.5%
McKinsey's 7 'S's	5.3%
Other	12.5%

Source: Hodgkinson *et al.* (2006)

predictions can often be well wide of the mark (see 'Forecasting errors' below). Nevertheless, as discussed in Chapters 2 and 3, the strategist's ability to think differently is fundamental and crucial to crafting strategy. Exploring new market segments, deploying new **business models**, and exploiting convergent technologies rely on the strategist's capability to see differently, with the result that companies gain a clear understanding of who they are and what makes them unique and relevant.

Forecasting errors

Atomic energy might be good as our present-day explosives, but it is unlikely to produce anything more dangerous.

(Winston Churchill, 1939*)

I think there is a world market for about five computers.

(Thomas J. Watson, president of IBM, 1948*)

In 1795, philosopher Immanuel Kant argued that war would become economically impossible.

Not within a thousand years will man ever fly.

(Wilbur Wright, 1901*)

Rail travel at high speeds is not possible because passengers, unable to breathe, would die of asphyxia.

(Dionysius Lardner, Irish scientist, 1823)

Guitar bands are on the way out.

(Dick Rowe, Decca Records, on not signing The Beatles)

No woman in my time will be prime minister.

(Margaret Thatcher, 1969)

For God's sake, go down to reception and get rid of the lunatic who's down there. He says he's got a machine for seeing by wireless! Watch him, he may have a razor!

(Editor, Daily Express, refusing to see John Logie Baird, inventor of television, 1925)

Sources: *Mintzberg *et al.* (1998); *Sunday Times* (2007)

Some of the principles of strategy making, as espoused by Gray (1986), offer useful guidance including gaining clarity about business definition, control and performance measures, the roles of strategic business units, participative strategies, and analytical techniques.

- Strategic planning is a management function for which training in strategic analysis and participative skills is usually necessary.
- Strategic business units need to be defined so that one executive can control the key variables essential to the execution of his or her strategic business plan.

- A unit's concept of the business it is in must above all be formulated from the outside in so that it can most effectively engage with the dynamics of its strategic environment.
- Action plans for achieving business objectives are the key to implementing and monitoring strategy. They require extensive lower-level participation and special leadership skills. Action plans are complete when underlying assumptions, allocation of responsibilities, time and resource requirements, risks, and likely responses have been made explicit.
- Participative strategy development, a prerequisite for successful strategy execution, often requires cultural change at the upper levels of corporations and their business units.
- The strategic planning system and other control systems designed to guide managerial and organizational behaviour must be integrated in a consistent whole if business strategies are to be executed well.
- Well managed organizations must be both centralized and decentralized—centralized so that strategies and control systems can be integrated and decentralized so that units in each strategic environment can act and be treated with appropriate differentiation.
- Over time, good strategic planning, once considered a separate activity, becomes a mindset, a style and a set of techniques for running a business—not something more to do but a better way of doing what had always had to be done.

(Gray, 1986: 92)

But how is strategy *really* crafted in practice? In the case of Jack Welch (then CEO of General Electric), the beginnings of one of GE's major strategy initiatives of the 1990s emerged when he was on honeymoon. This is how he describes it in his autobiography:

> I was sitting on a beach under an umbrella in Barbados in December 1989 on a belated honeymoon with my second wife, Jane. My year-in-advance schedule had kept us from having a typical honeymoon when we were married in April. Now we were having our 'romantic vacation' at last, but as usual I ended up talking about work—not what you'd call pillow talk.
>
> Work-Out has become a huge success. We were kicking bureaucracy's butt with it. Ideas were flowing faster all over the company. I was groping for a way to describe this, something that might capture the whole organization and take idea sharing to the next level.
>
> I was testing out on Jane my idea of focusing the brain power of 300,000-plus people into every person's head. It would be like having a great dinner party with eight bright guests all knowing something different. Think how much better everyone at the table would be if there was a way to transfer the best of their ideas into each guest. That's really what I was after.
>
> Sandy Lane in Barbados was a great place. I'd never experienced a Caribbean Christmas—it was different. Seeing Santa Claus pop out of a submarine while I was lying on the beach may have been the jolt I needed. That day, I got the idea that would obsess me for the next decade.
>
> Poor Jane, I was on a roll. Kept talking about all the boundaries that Work-Out was breaking down. Suddenly, the word boundaryless popped into my head. It really summed up my dream for the company. I couldn't get the word out of my mind.
>
> Silly as it sounds, it felt like a scientific breakthrough.
>
> (Welch, 2001: 185–186)

In this description, it is interesting to note the simplicity of the idea and the manner in which Welch conceptualized it around a regular occurrence—a dinner party—at which many stories are told.

Crafting the initial concepts of the strategy is only the beginning; the designing of strategy process that assimilates these strategy concepts into executable strategies is the real challenge. As Lorange and Vancil (1976: 77) put it: 'to remain effective, the design of the planning process is a continuous task requiring vigilance and insight on the part of management.'

Implications for strategy practice

In reflecting on the issues in this chapter, we can get a real sense of the enormity of the challenges that strategists face in developing strategy. A McKinsey study on the formal strategic planning process carried out in 2006 revealed that fewer than half of the executives who responded stated that they were satisfied with their organization's approach to strategic planning. In addition, the study revealed that it is the CEO and senior managers who make decisions about strategy, whereas the strategy process is key to decision making for only 23 per cent of respondents, with boards approving final strategy in six out of ten organizations surveyed. Organizations expend a significant amount of effort on the dynamics of strategy formulation, but are dubious about the results in terms of overall performance or in generating new ideas.

For many public sector organizations, there is a legal requirement to have a strategy-formulation process that requires them to engage with their stakeholders in order to produce both strategic and operational plans. The low take-up of decisions from the strategy process, as indicated in the McKinsey (2006) study, is reflective of the embryonic nature of the strategy process in organizations and the fact that it is the CEO and senior managers that make the decisions about strategy. How have you experienced the dynamics of strategy formulation in organizations for which you have worked, in sports or leisure clubs, or in voluntary organizations? What were the personal benefits of this experience? Did the process deliver the desired outcomes that you envisaged?

Organizational politics can lead to situations in which the organization pursues a suboptimal strategy that results in poorer competitive outcomes. This can occur for several reasons, but we see organizations attempting to placate interest groups and thereby choosing a strategic direction that is not truly in the long-term sustainable interests of the organizations. This has been the case for many previously owned national airlines, where government policy has blocked significant changes in work practices that would increase efficiencies and improve customer experience in line with competitive market conditions. In public sector organizational contexts, we see how political pressure can influence decisions. Examples include the additional runway at Heathrow, the further development of Stansted airport, increases in public sector worker pension contributions, and additional capital requirements for eurozone banks to ensure a well-functioning banking system.

The real danger with strategy formulation is that it becomes a ritual without any visible outcome to the organization as a whole. As part of the process, you participate in an organization-wide effort, but in reality it might feel like a top-down exercise, with your inputs neither valued nor considered, nor even visible in the finalized strategy. Therefore those responsible for strategy formulation must give careful consideration to the process by which they solicit the engagement of the whole organization. This involves being mindful of the analytical approaches used, the language chosen to describe the process, and its rationale, as well as the anticipated outcomes. The communication process and mechanisms used are critical elements in the strategy-formulation processes.

In practice, perception of the value of strategy formulation is set by the top management team and the CEO, and by the cultural value and importance that they attach to this activity. Perceptions are also created by the organization's belief about whether strategy formulation should be a democratic or top-down process. Some CEOs and top management operate strategy formulation as a top-down process, whereby they predetermine the strategic outcomes and orientate the process in a certain direction, doing so under the guise of a democratic process. Other organizations, by virtue of their contexts, have an open democratic strategy-formulation process that involves, harnesses, and implements good ideas from groups and individuals across all levels of the organization and among key stakeholder groups.

It would be wrong, however, to make the assumption that all organizations have a formal strategy-formulation process; many organizations adjust in a reactive or ad hoc manner. Does your local sports club, local shop, or significant

Table 4.3 Main characteristics of strategy as absence

Absence as failure	Absence as transition	Absence as virtue (constructive ambiguity and symbol)
Key characteristics Stuck-in-the-middle firms Poor strategic position Low profitability Can be equated to failure and suboptimal outcomes	**Key characteristics** Transitional phase in firm's life cycle An emerging, start-up firm with a limited history of decision making An organization focused on survival and viability 'steadying the ship'; common at the early phase of turnaround situations A firm operating in an unpredictable and fast-moving environment may rely more on talent and skill set of workers than it does on visionary thinking	**Key characteristics** Conscious decisions and action/inaction by management 'Deliberate building in of strategic voids' 'Apparent incoherency in decision making as part of its organizational design' Tolerance for ambiguity Generate flexibility

local employer have a formal strategic plan? There tends to be a universal assumption that all organizations have strategies, but the reality is that there may be strategy absence. Inkpen and Choudhury (1995) describe cases of strategy absence—that is, 'where strategy is expected but is not'. The articulation of strategy absence can be in three particular contexts: namely, absence as failure, absence as transition, and absence as virtue (see Table 4.3). In certain organizational contexts, absence as virtue may be a deliberate act by the strategists not to formulate strategy. In the context of the credit crunch, many organizations set aside deliberate strategy formulation activities in favour of emergent strategy, given the intense volatility of their competitive environment.

Finally, in practice, organizations have varying formal and informal strategy processes depending on the organizational setting and their corporate history. As an employee of an organization, you will experience elements of both. For example, management teams of multinational corporations in host countries may put in place informal strategy processes designed to ensure the sustainability and viability of their local operations, while participating in the various strategy processes set out by their corporate headquarters. Critical in all incidences is the nature and sources of information that inform strategy development.

Tourish (2005) argues that upward communication of good and bad information is a critical input to formulating and successfully implementing a viable strategy. Strategists should be strategic in sourcing information, bypassing lines on the organizational chart to seek multiple views when the need arises (Wrapp, 1967). Likewise, strategy workshops and meetings should be managed in order to stimulate debate, confront difficult challenges, and draw upon a broad and inclusive range of voices. This in turn is likely to diminish the impact of cognitive biases and power plays in shaping the outcome of critical decisions (Lovallo and Sibony, 2010: 3).

Introduction to readings

Reading 1.5, 'Crafting strategy' by Mintzberg (1987), is a classic in the strategy field, and is a rich and thought-provoking article with timeless relevance. Using the analogy of a potter and her wheel, Mintzberg argues that crafting is an accurate description of how companies decide on their strategies. He argues that crafting strategy comes with control and learning, and he outlines the needs for organizations to manage stability, to be aware of discontinuities in their external environment, to have real understanding of their business, to manage patterns which shape strategy, and to be able to manage the tension between change and continuity. One of his key messages is: 'There is no best way to make strategy.' But how many organizations relentlessly attempt to benchmark and replicate strategy-formulation processes that yield poor strategic outcomes due to the organizations not considering their own contexts? While descriptively useful, what does Mintzberg's approach offer by way of practical implications for organizations?

Reading 1.6, a classic by Richard Rumelt entitled 'Evaluation of strategy' (1979), provides key principles and a process by which a strategist can evaluate the strategy of the business. The broad criteria devised by Rumelt include consistency, consonance, advantage, and feasibility. These criteria focus on the core issues of strategy and, in particular, the need for fit, focus, and the use of the firm's resources appropriately. Why do organizations consistently fail these tests? Are these criteria difficult to implement in different contexts? Rumelt makes the interesting observation that 'a good strategy does not need constant reformulation'. Does such a hypothesis stand up in a dynamic market? How easy is it for any organization to maintain a dual view of strategy and strategy evaluation?

Our final article for Section 1, Reading 1.7, 'Strategic planning in a turbulent environment: evidence from oil majors' by Robert Grant (2003), provides some telling insights into strategic planning systems. In particular, it is interesting to note that there are differences in the strategy planning cycles, how strategy is actually crafted, and the time parameters used by various players. From content analysis of strategic plans, common trends include shortening time horizons, a shift from detailed planning to strategic direction, and increased emphasis on performance planning. Interestingly, Grant's study reveals that strategic planning processes have become more decentralized, and are used more for coordination and performance purposes than for making strategic decisions. The study reveals a lack of sophistication in terms of analytical tools being used by oil majors and that few strategic innovations were derived from strategy planning cycles. Given these findings, why should organizations have strategy planning cycles and processes?

Mini case study BAA, BA, and the opening of Heathrow Terminal 5: not quite ready for take-off

On 27 March 2008, after some twenty-two years of planning and six years of construction, Terminal 5 (T5) at London Heathrow airport opened on time and within its £4.3bn budget. The largest single construction project of its time in Europe, the design and construction of T5 drew upon the resources of some 60,000 professional and construction workers. Such was the phenomenal success of the T5 cross-functional team and risk-sharing project management model that it formed the best practice template for the London 2012 Olympics project. The operational achievement of the T5 project is evident from the title of Sharon Doherty's book, *Heathrow's Terminal 5: History in the Making*. With a foundation as 'the most successful UK construction project' and passengers promised a 'calmer, smoother, simpler airport experience', T5 was destined to become a national treasure.

Opening to the public

T5 is owned by BAA (British Airport Authority), and used exclusively by British Airways (BA) as a global hub. With all BA passengers departing from the same terminal, the intention for BA was that T5 would enhance punctuality and provide for an enhanced consumer experience—not least by making operations more efficient, integrated, and manageable. With respect to capacity, T5 would increase Heathrow's annual passenger throughout from 67 million to 95 million. Both BAA and BA had spent three years in preparation to ensure that all people, processes, and systems at the terminal would be ready and working from day one. The opening of a new airport terminal is a highly complex task carrying a significant degree of risk. History lists a number of airports that have been impacted by difficulties upon opening, such as Denver airport in 1996, which had major problems with baggage handling, and Hong Kong in 1998, for which it took nearly two years to smooth out problems.

While Queen Elizabeth II had officially opened T5 in a ceremony on the 14 March 2008, it was not until the morning of the 27 March that the terminal opened its doors to the travelling public. The first passenger passed through security at 4.20 a.m.: Paul Walker, a UK ex-pat from Kenya, was presented with a boarding pass by BA CEO, Willie Walsh, for the first departing flight, BA302 to Paris. The first inbound flight was an arrival from Hong Kong at 4.50 a.m. Bright and early, T5 was up and running—but already its operations were experiencing some problems.

Turbulence at T5

BA staff arriving at T5 found parking difficult, having to queue for long periods, thereby delaying them getting to the terminal building. Once inside T5, a shortage of security staff meant further delays getting through the central search area (that is, the security search for staff going from the land-side areas of the terminal to the air side). In addition, a number of both passenger and staff lifts were not operable, there were electrical ground power unit failures resulting in the unplanned towing of mobile ground power units around the apron, and temperature control for the entire building, the largest free-standing structure in the UK, had to be operated manually. On the air side of the terminal, staff accommodation areas and access routes were left incomplete: either not painted, not fitted out, or littered with construction materials. Acting BAA CEO, Colin Mathews, later acknowledged that this 'without question, create[d] a poor impression with BA staff'.

Already-stressed staff found themselves in a location and using technology with which they were less than familiar. Although BA had run an intensive training programme, 'Fit for Five', to engage staff in the benefits of moving to T5, in terms of specifics CEO Willie Walsh acknowledged that 'the training and familiarization was compromised because, in effect, we were familiarizing people in an environment that was not fully complete and, again, having reviewed the operation of T5 in the first few days, that clearly had in an impact on our staff'. BA employee, Mr Iggy Vaid, speaking at a Transport Committee hearing, reiterated that the training received was insufficient:

> People were taken to a hotel and shown some sort of film or slides and told this was what it looked like. They were then given familiarisation training for three days to cover an area as big as Hyde Park. That was not sufficient at all. For that reason people were totally confused. Two days out of the three were devoted to putting them into a coach to show them x, y and z, and where to enter and exit and so on, but what was missing was hands on training as to where the spurs were, where the bags would come in and so on. For baggage in particular it was still a building site.

Passenger chaos

With such problems, it would not be long before passengers were directly impacted. On the first day of operations, 36,584 passengers were frustrated by the 'Heathrow hassle' that T5 had been designed to eliminate. A key problem concerned baggage handlers, who first had difficulty locating their work stations and then were unfamiliar with the new system. As a consequence, the baggage system failed and overloaded; baggage distribution along 18 km of conveyer belts began to pile up at the bottom of the chutes, where they were supposed to be loaded into containers to be transported to the respective aircraft. The pile-up of luggage was so great that bags had to be transported off-site to be sorted manually. The knock on effect for passengers who had already experienced problems with lifts and escalators was immediate. Arriving at check-in desks, they were told that they could either (a) fly, but that their bags would not fly with them, or (b) rebook their flights. Over the following ten days, some 42,000 bags failed to travel with their owners, while 501 flights were cancelled. Such was the commotion around T5 opening that the UK House of Commons ordered the Transport Committee to conduct a hearing to examine the events, the motivation of which was clear:

> We acknowledge the inevitability of 'teething problems' but it is deeply regrettable that so many were allowed to bring the operation of Heathrow's newest terminal to a halt. What should have been an occasion of national pride was in fact an occasion of national embarrassment.

Looking for answers

It is estimated that the disrupted opening cost BA an estimated £18m directly, and further damage by way of reputation. Following interviews with key stakeholders, the House of Commons Transport Committee reported that the problems were most likely caused by insufficient communication between BAA and BA, poor staff training, and deficient systems testing. While BAA and BA had worked together in the construction phase, acting BAA CEO, Colin Matthews, acknowledged to the Committee that 'around about or just prior to the opening of T5 it seems that that togetherness deteriorated. It is that togetherness that allows you to cope with the issues that arise on the day'. With respect to systems testing, extensive trials were conducted, involving 15,000 members of the public acting as trial passengers. That said, Mathews acknowledged that these were of a rather technical nature; 'with the benefit of hindsight, we can clearly say that we were not successful in replicating in a test situation every aspect of the real-life situation.' For Walsh, the catalyst was a concurrence of factors: 'We could have coped with a couple of the problems. But all of the problems hitting us led to a cascade.'

A *Financial Times* (FT) investigation saw the problems as being caused by a mix of 'incompetence and hubris'. Given the turbulent nature of the airline industry itself, coupled with the recognized risk of opening a new terminal, it was surprising that little scenario and contingency planning had been explicitly conducted by management and communicated to staff. Members of the Transport Committee were struck by how much 'hoping for the best' BAA had engaged in prior to the opening of T5. The FT investigation also saw the failure of preparing staff at BA as being compounded by a management culture in which employees were reluctant to surface details of potential problems: 'Willie Walsh expected to be brought solutions rather than problems.' While stakeholder groups, including employees and trade unions, seemed to express concern over issues such as familiarity, these were largely not recognized (Colin Mathews) or acted upon (Willie Walsh). Walsh, in particular, was driven by financial pressure and a desire not to miss the peak summer traffic, holding to the logic that 'the cost to British Airways of delaying would have been significantly greater than the cost ... incurred as a result of the problems that we encountered in the first few days'.

A further factor to consider is the extent to which both BAA and BA had a culture that ensured that they monitored and evaluated their actions, and the extent to which instructions had been carried out as intended. This point comes across in the lessons that BAA indicated that it had learnt from the opening of T5 (as reported to the Transport Committee). Specifically, the Authority had found it necessary:

- to refine the parameters for live monitoring of baggage performance;
- to over-provide for staff search and control posts on the opening day;
- to establish a joint BA–BAA crisis management team at terminal level for critical events and crisis situations; and
- to ensure a direct link between the BAA and BA baggage and logistics teams, with early warning indicators and protocols established for decision making in critical baggage operational scenarios.

All is well that ends well . . .

After a construction that demonstrated exceptional planning and operational prowess, Shadow Home Secretary David Davis termed the subsequent T5 opening 'a dreadful national embarrassment'. While apologetic, BAA and BA

CEOs Colin Mathews and Willie Walsh instead claimed that, relative to other terminal openings, the situation had been dealt with promptly. Both were less vocal in assessing the root causes of the problems. Twelve days after opening, T5 was operating effectively and successfully. As a BA spokesperson noted: 'T5's opening is history. Its present is a great success.'

Questions

1. What were the key difficulties in the opening of T5? Were these issues of strategy formulation or execution?

2. If you were hired as a consultant to devise a strategy for opening a new airport terminal, what key recommendations would you make?

3. Soon after the event, BA's director of operations and director of customer services left the organization. The company declined to comment on whether the two had chosen to depart or were asked to leave. This raises the question of who should take ultimate responsibility for the debacle, or whether the success of T5 after this event outweighs the negative impact?

Sources: Davies *et al.* (2009); BBC News (2008a; 2008b; 2008c); Doherty (2008); House of Commons Transport Committee (2008); Thomson (2008); William and Done (2008)

Summary

We began this chapter by considering the core strategic issues facing strategists when formulating strategy, then turned our attention to the deliberate and emergent approaches to strategy formulation. We explored the strategy process, and the involvement of CEOs, top management teams, middle managers, and other stakeholders. We concluded by focusing on issues such as organizational politics, the role of organizational learning, and strategy as practice.

The reality for most organizations is that the dynamics of strategy formulation involve both deliberate and emergent approaches. While some may have declared strategic planning dead, in practice it has simply evolved to take on new forms (Ocasio and Joseph, 2008). Research on strategy formulation has found this to be true, as organizations integrate emergent strategy stemming from everyday activities of the periphery with deliberate strategy at the core (Regner, 2003: 79). Consequently, Whittington *et al.* (2006: 625) argue that 'formal and deliberate strategy will be the more effective the more craft is accepted rather than suspected'.

Overall, strategy formulation has the potential to be a **dynamic capability** leading to superior organizational performance (Slater *et al.*, 2006: 1221). That said, our knowledge of the dynamics of strategy formulation is minimal. As Gary Hamel (2000: 74) puts it: 'The dirty little secret of the strategy industry is that it doesn't have any theory of strategy creation.' For organizations, the ongoing challenge is to experiment and to learn from strategy-making experiences, but also to have the capacity and maturity to operate multiple and complex layers of strategy-making processes that work effectively in the organizational and competitive contexts. This is the real challenge, whereby the organization accrues real value from strategy processes. The strategy-as-practice perspective, with its micro focus, has the potential to yield rich accounts of how strategy manifests and who is involved. This may sound trivial, but organizational success may be more dependent on micro activities than we think. Strategy-formulation processes should be open to ongoing scrutiny and fresh thinking and ideas. For some organizations, these are neither contemplated nor acceptable. Finally, the level of sophistication of strategy formulation remains poor, raising the question of whether shareholders are getting a good return on their investment. Evidence from the limited studies to date, in terms of tools used, the processes, and the ability to harness good ideas in tandem with control and learning, would indicate that organizations have much work to do. In reality, how many strategy processes really consistently address the five core questions of strategy? How many organizations really provide training for employees to participate effectively in strategy formulation activities? In order to be successful, strategy formulation must not be seen as something that enterprises simply do, it must be something that they live and breathe (Demos *et al.*, 2001).

Discussion questions

1. Write a critique of the emergent approach to strategy for a CEO. Your critique should address the key strengths and weaknesses of this approach. In which contexts is the emergent approach to strategy most appropriate?

2. What are the key limitations of the design school approach? Can you think of contexts in which it might be more or less appropriate?

3. Evaluate Mintzberg's critique of the design school. Do you agree with it? How would you use Mintzberg's argument to guide strategy making?

4. When and how should an organization evaluate the success of its strategy-formulation process?

5. Source a reading from a journal that contributes to the debate in this chapter. Which, if any, perspective does it support? What is its contribution? Does it advance the debate in any way?

6. Review the history of an organization with which you are familiar. What can you find out about how its strategy has developed, the key milestones and challenges that it has faced, and the nature of strategy development process? What are the key lessons for managers and strategy researchers?

Further reading

E. H. Wrapp (1967) 'Good managers don't make policy decisions', ***Harvard Business Review***, Sept/Oct: 91–99, is a classic article from the strategy archives that is well worth revisiting. Wrapp offers valuable insights into the true nature of the managerial role in strategy formulation. In so doing, he pre-empts many of the arguments that would still consume attention some four decades later.

W. Ocasio and J. Joseph (2008) 'Rise and fall—or transformation? The evolution of strategic planning at the General Electric Company, 1940–2006', ***Long Range Planning***, 41(3): 248–272, is a rare and fascinating account of the evolution of strategic-planning practices at General Electric, which indicates that strategic planning is not a fad, but rather an enduring and evolving managerial practice heavily influenced by the influence of the CEO.

H. Mintzberg (1994) ***The Rise and Fall of Strategic Planning***, New York: Free Press, provides an in-depth overview of deliberate and emergent strategy. It charts the emergence, failing, and abandonment of traditional strategic planning, and offers Mintzberg's emergent strategy as a viable alternative.

R. Whittington and L. Cailluet (2008) 'The crafts of strategy: special issue introduction by the guest editors', ***Long Range Planning***, 41(3): 241–247, is an overview of a special issue that reappraises Mintzberg's (1987) emergent strategy argument in light of current and historical practice.

visit the Online Resource Centre that accompanies this book to access more learning resources on this chapter topic at www.oxfordtextbooks.co.uk/orc/cunningham/

References

Allio, R. 2011. Henry Mintzberg: still the zealous skeptic and scold. ***Strategy and Leadership***, 39(2): 4–8.

Andrews, K. 1971. ***The Concept of Corporate Strategy***. Homewood, IL: Dow Jones-Irwin.

Ansoff, I. 1965. ***Corporate Strategy: An Analytical Approach to Business Policy for Growth and Expansion***. New York: McGraw Hill.

Ansoff, I. 1977. The state of practice in planning systems. ***Sloan Management Review***, Winter: 1–24.

Ansoff, I. 1991. Critique of Henry Mintzberg's 'The design school: reconsidering the basic premises of strategic management'. ***Strategic Management Journal***, 12(6): 174–187.

BBC News. 2008a. 28,000 bags caught in T5 foul-up. 31 March. Available online at http://news.bbc.co.uk/2/hi/uk_news/7323198.stm

BBC News. 2008b. T5 was 'national embarrassment'. 3 November. Available online at http://news.bbc.co.uk/2/hi/uk_news/england/london/7704846.stm

BBC News. 2008c. What went wrong at Heathrow's T5? 31 March. Available online at http://news.bbc.co.uk/2/hi/uk_news/7322453.stm

Beinhocker, E. and Kaplan, S. 2002. Tired of strategic planning? ***McKinsey Quarterly***, 2(Special edn): 48–57.

Berg, N. 1965. Strategic planning in conglomerate companies. ***Harvard Business Review***, 43(3): 79–92.

Bower, J. L. 1970. ***Managing the Resource Allocation Process: A Study of Corporate Planning and Investment***. Cambridge, MA: Harvard Business School Press.

Boyd, B. 1991. Strategic planning and financial performance. ***Journal of Management Studies***, 28(4): 353–374.

Bryan, L. and Farrell, D. 2008. Leading through uncertainty. ***McKinsey Quarterly***, Dec: 1–13.

Bryson, J. 2004. What to do when stakeholders matter. ***Public Management Review***, 6(1): 21–53.

Burgelman, R. A. 1983. A model of the interaction of strategic behaviour, corporate context and the concept of strategy. ***Academy of Management Review***, 8(1): 61–70.

Campbell, A. and Marcus, A. 1997. What's wrong with strategy? ***Harvard Business Review***, 75(6): 42–51.

Chandler, A. D. 1962. ***Strategy and Structure***. Cambridge, MA: MIT Press.

Cheung, A., Kutcher, E., and Dilip, W. 2009. Strategic planning in crisis. ***McKinsey Quarterly***, 3: 122–123.

Chia, R. 2004. Strategy-as-practice: reflections on the research agenda. ***European Management Review***, 1: 29–34.

Christensen, C. M. 1997. Making strategy: learning by doing. ***Harvard Business Review***, 75(6): 141–156.

Collier, N., Fishwick, F., and Floyd, S. W. 2004. Managerial involvement and perceptions of strategy process. ***Long Range Planning***, 37(1): 67–83.

Cummings, S. and Daellenbach, U. 2009. A guide to the future of strategy? The history of long range planning. ***Long Range Planning***, 42: 234–263.

Davenport, T. 2009. Make better decisions. ***Harvard Business Review***, Nov: 117–125.

Davies, A., Gann, D., and Douglas, T. 2009. Innovation in megaprojects: systems integration at London Heathrow Terminal 5. ***California Management Review***, 51(2): 101–125.

Demos, N., Chung, S., and Beck, M. 2001. The new strategy and why it's new. ***Strategy and Business***, 25: 1–5.

Doherty, S. 2008. ***Heathrow's Terminal 5: History in the Making***. Chichester: John Wiley and Sons.

Dye, R. and Sibony, O. 2007. How to improve strategic planning, ***McKinsey Quarterly***, 3: 40–49.

Dye, R., Sibony, O., and Viguerie, P. 2009. Strategic planning: three tips for 2009. ***McKinsey Quarterly***, Apr: 1–3.

Garvin, D. 1998. The process of organisation and management. ***Sloan Management Review***, Summer: 33–50.

Gavetti, G. and Rivkin, J. 2007. On the origin of strategy: action and cognition over time. ***Organization Science***, 18(3): 420–439.

Gino, F. and Pisano, G. 2011. What leaders don't learn from success: failures get a post-mortem—why not triumphs? ***Harvard Business Review***, Apr: 68–83.

Grant, R. M. 2003. Strategic planning in a turbulent environment: evidence from the oil majors. ***Strategic Management Journal***, 24(6): 491–517.

Gray, D. H. 1986. Uses and misuses of strategic planning. ***Harvard Business Review***, 64(1): 89–97.

Hamel, G. 2000. Otto Scharmer in conversation with Gary Hamel. ***Reflections***, 1(3): 72–77.

Hamel, G. and Prahalad, C. 1989. Strategic intent. ***Harvard Business Review***, May/June: 63–76.

Hart, S. and Banbury, C. 1994. How strategy-making processes can make a difference. ***Strategic Management Journal***, 15(4): 251–269.

Hendry, J. 2000. Strategic decision making, discourse and strategy as social practice. ***Journal of Management Studies***, 37(3): 955–976.

Hodgkinson, G., Whittington, R., Johnson, G., and Schwarz, M. 2006. The role of strategy workshops in strategy development processes: formality, communication, coordination and inclusion. ***Long Range Planning***, 39: 479–496.

House of Commons Transport Committee. 2008. ***The Opening of Heathrow Terminal 5: Twelfth Report of Session 2007–08***. HC 543, London: HMSO.

Inkpen, A. and Choudbury, N. 1995. The seeking of strategy where it is not: towards a theory of strategy absence. ***Strategic Management Journal***, 16(4): 329–342.

Jarzabkowski, P. 2003. Strategy in practice: recursiveness, adaptation, and practice-in-use. ***Organization Studies***, 24: 529–560.

Jarzabkowski, P. and Balogun, J. 2009. The practice and process of delivering integration through strategic planning. ***Journal of Management Studies***, 46(8): 1255–1288.

Johnson, G., Melin, L., and Whittington, R. 2003. Micro strategy and strategizing: towards an activity-based view. ***Journal of Management Studies***, 40(7): 3–22.

Kahneman, D. and Klein, G. 2010. Strategic decisions: when can you trust your gut? ***McKinsey Quarterly***, Mar: 2–10.

Karnani, A. 2009. Controversy: the essence of strategy. ***Business Strategy Review***, Winter: 29–34.

Kraut, A., Pedigo, P., McKenna, D., and Dunnette, M. 2005. The role of the manager: what's really important in different management jobs. ***Academy of Management Executive***, 19(4): 122–129.

Kudla, R. 1980. The effects of strategic planning on common stock returns. ***Academy of Management Journal***, 23(1): 5–20.

Leontiades, M. and Tezel, A. 1980. Planning perceptions and planning results. ***Strategic Management Journal***, 1(1): 65–75.

Lindblom, C. E. 1959. The science of 'muddling through'. ***Public Administration Review***, 19: 79–88.

Lorange, P. and Vancil, C. R. 1976. How to design a strategic planning system. ***Harvard Business Review***, 54(5): 75–81.

Lovallo, D. and Sibony, O. 2010. The case for behavioral strategy. ***McKinsey Quarterly***, Mar: 1–14.

Lumpkin, G. T. and Dess, G. G. 1995. Simplicity as a strategy-making process: the effects of stage of organizational development. ***Academy of Management Journal***, 38(5): 1386–1407.

Mahon, J. F. and Murray Jr., E. A. 1981. Strategic planning for regulated companies. ***Strategic Management Journal***, 2(3): 251–262.

McKinsey. 2006. Improving strategic planning: a McKinsey survey. Available online at http://www.mckinseyquarterly.com/Improving_strategic_planning_A_McKinsey_Survey_1819

Miller, C. and Cardinal, L. 1994. Strategic planning and firm performance: a synthesis of more than two decades of research. ***Academy of Management Journal***, 37(6): 1649–1665.

Miller, C., Burke, L., and Glick, W. 1998. Cognitive diversity among upper-echelon executives: implications for strategic decision processes. ***Strategic Management Journal***, 19: 39–58.

Miller, D., Kets de Vries, M. F. R., and Toulouse, J.-M. 1982. Top executive locus of control and its relationship to strategy-making, structure, and environment. ***Academy of Management Journal***, 25(2): 237–253.

Mintzberg, H. 1987. Crafting strategy. ***Harvard Business Review***, 65(4): 66–75.

Mintzberg, H. 1990. The design school: reconsidering the basic premises of strategic management. ***Strategic Management Journal***, 11(3): 171–196.

Mintzberg, H. 1991. Learning 1, planning 0. ***Strategic Management Journal***, 12(6): 463–466.

Mintzberg, H. 1994a. Rethinking strategic planning Part II: new roles for planners. ***Long Range Planning***, 27(3): 22–30.

Mintzberg, H. 1994b. The fall and rise of strategic planning. ***Harvard Business Review***, 72(1): 107.

Mintzberg, H. 2009. Rebuilding companies as communities. ***Harvard Business Review***, July/Aug: 140–143.

Mintzberg, H., Ahlstrand, B., and Lampel, J. 1998. ***Strategy Safari: A Guided Tour through the Wilds of Strategic Management***. New York: Free Press.

Nonaka, I. and Takeuchi, H. 1995. ***The Knowledge-creating Company: How Japanese Companies Create the Dynamics of Innovation***. New York: Oxford University Press.

Ocasio, W. and Joseph, J. 2008. Rise and fall—or transformation? The evolution of strategic planning at the General Electric Company, 1940–2006. ***Long Range Planning***, 41(3): 248–272.

Paul, R. N., Donovan, N. B., and Taylor, J. W. 1978. The reality gap in strategic planning. ***Harvard Business Review***, 56(3): 124–130.

Pettigrew, A. M. 1992. The character and significance of strategy process research. ***Strategic Management Journal***, 13(8): 5–16.

Pfeffer, J. 1992. Understanding power in organizations. ***Californian Management Review***, 34(2): 29–50.

Porter, M. 1996. What is strategy? ***Harvard Business Review***, Dec: 61–78.

Pretorius, M. and Martitz, R. 2011. Strategy making: the approach matters. ***Journal of Business Strategy***, 32(4): 25–31.

Quinn, J. B. 1980. ***Strategies for Change: Logical Incrementalism***. Homewood, IL: Richard D. Irwin.

Ramanujam, V., Venkatraman, N., and Camilus, J. 1986. Multi-objective assessment of effectiveness of strategic planning: a discriminate analysis approach. *Academy of Management Journal*, 29(2): 347–372.

Regner, P. 2003. Strategy creation in the periphery: inductive versus deductive strategy making. *Journal of Management Studies*, 40(1): 57–82.

Rumelt, R. 2011. *Good Strategy/Bad Strategy*. London: Profile Books.

Senge, P. 1990. The leader's new work: building learning organisations. *Sloan Management Review*, 32(1): 7–23.

Simpson, D. G. 1998. Why strategic planning is a waste of time and what you can do about it. *Long Range Planning*, 31(3): 476–480.

Slater, S., Olson, E., and Thomas, H. 2006. The moderating influence of strategic orientation on the strategy formation capability-performance relationship. *Strategic Management Journal*, 27: 1221–1231.

Stern, S. 2007. Wanted: more emotion and less rationality about strategy. *Financial Times*: 20 Feb: 9.

Sull, D. 2010. Competing on agility. *McKinsey Quarterly*, Dec: 1–9.

Sunday Times. 2007. Futureology's dismal past: the great minds who got it horribly wrong. 23 December.

Szulanski, G. and Amin, K. 2001. Learning to make strategy: balancing discipline and imagination. *Long Range Planning*, 34(5): 537–556.

Taylor, B. 1997. The return of strategic planning: once more with feeling. *Long Range Planning*, 30(2): 334–344.

Thomson, R. 2008. British Airways reveals what went wrong with Terminal 5. *Computer Weekly*, 14 May. Available online at http://www.computerweekly.com/Articles/2008/05/14/230680/british-airways-reveals-what-went-wrong-with-terminal.htm

Tourish, D. 2005. Critical upward communications: ten commandments for improving strategy and decision making. *Long Range Planning*, 38: 495–503.

Van Cauwenbergh, A. and Cool, K. 1982. Strategic management in a new framework. *Strategic Management Journal*, 3: 245–264.

van Hoorn, T. 1979. Strategic planning in small and medium-sized companies. *Long Range Planning*, 12(2): 84–91.

Vancil, R. F. and Lorange, P. 1975. Strategic planning in diversified companies. *Harvard Business Review*, 53(1): 81–90.

Welch, J. 2001. *Jack: What I've Learned Leading a Great Company and Great People*. London: Warner/Headline.

Whittington, R. 1996. Strategy as practice. *Long Range Planning*, 29(5): 731–735.

Whittington, R. 2001. *What is Strategy and Does it Matter?* London: Routledge.

Whittington, R. 2007. Strategy practice and strategy process: family differences and the sociological eye. *Organization Studies*, 28(10): 1575–1586.

Whittington, R. and Cailluet, L. 2008. The crafts of strategy: special issue introduction by the guest editors. *Long Range Planning*, 41(3): 241–247.

Whittington, R., Molloy, E., Mayer, M., and Smith, A. 2006. Practices of strategising/organizing. *Long Range Planning*, 39: 615–629.

William, J. and Done, K. 2008. BA struggles to escape its T5 twilight zone. *Financial Times*, 5 April.

Wilson, I. 1998. Strategic planning for the millennium: resolving the dilemma. *Long Range Planning*, 31(4): 507–513.

Wooldridge, B. and Floyd, S. W. 1990. The strategy process, middle management involvement, and organizational performance. *Strategic Management Journal*, 11(3): 231–241.

Wrapp, E. H. 1967. Good managers don't make policy decisions. *Harvard Business Review*, Sept/Oct: 91–99.

Section 1 readings

Introduction

In this section, we have considered the meaning of 'strategy' and the people involved in developing strategy, the strategists. The readings that we have selected provide some valuable insights into the rich debate surrounding the very definition of strategy and strategists.

- **Reading 1.1** by Michael E. Porter on 'What is strategy' (1996) explores the nature of strategy and the key issues that strategists need to understand in order to ensure that their organization has a unique way of delivering value.
- **Reading 1.2** by Kathleen Eisenhardt and Donald Sull on 'Strategy as simple rules' (2001) argues that complex strategy can be reduced to a small number of guiding principles.
- **Reading 1.3** by Stephen Cummings on 'The first strategists' (1993) outlines some of the attributes required to be a strategist. This is relevant to organizations seeking to develop strategists or for strategists who are seeking to understand their own role.
- **Reading 1.4** on 'Strategy as strategic decision making' by Kathleen Eisenhardt (1999), explores the nature of both decision making and decision makers in the formulation of strategy.
- **Reading 1.5** is a classic reading by Henry Mintzberg on 'Crafting strategy' (1987), which provides us with a sense of the richness of what strategy is and how it emerges in practice, in particular drawing our attention to the art as well as the science of strategy.
- **Reading 1.6** by Rumelt, 'Evaluation of strategy' (1979), is another classic that explores the key dimensions that can be used in assessing the viability and likely success of proposed strategy.
- Finally, in **Reading 1.7** by Robert M. Grant, 'Strategic planning in a turbulent environment: evidence from the oil majors' (2003), we are given empirical insight into the realities of strategy and strategic planning.

Overall, these readings provide perspectives to sharpen our understanding of the meaning of strategy and the role of strategists in the process of strategizing and strategy formulation.

Reading 1.1 What is strategy? *Michael E. Porter*

First published: (1996) *Harvard Business Review*, November–December: 61–78. Reprinted by permission of *Harvard Business Review*. 'What is Strategy?' by Michael E. Porter, Nov 01, 1996.

I. Operational effectiveness is not strategy

For almost two decades, managers have been learning to play by a new set of rules. Companies must be flexible to respond rapidly to competitive and market changes. They must benchmark continuously to achieve best practice. They must outsource aggressively to gain efficiencies. And they must nurture a few core competencies in the race to stay ahead of rivals.

Positioning – once the heart of strategy – is rejected as too static for today's dynamic markets and changing technologies. According to the new dogma, rivals can quickly copy any market position, and competitive advantage is, at best, temporary.

But those beliefs are dangerous half-truths, and they are leading more and more companies down the path of mutually destructive competition. True, some barriers to competition are falling as regulation eases and markets become global. True, companies have properly invested energy in becoming leaner and more nimble. In many industries, however, what some call *hypercompetition* is a self-inflicted wound, not the inevitable outcome of a changing paradigm of competition.

The root of the problem is the failure to distinguish between operational effectiveness and strategy. The quest for productivity, quality, and speed has spawned a remarkable number of management tools and techniques: total quality management, benchmarking, time-based competition, outsourcing, partnering, reengineering, change management. Although the resulting operational improvements have often been dramatic, many companies have been frustrated by their inability to translate those gains into sustainable profitability. And bit by bit, almost imperceptibly, management tools have taken the place of strategy. As managers push to improve on all fronts, they move farther away from viable competitive positions.

Operational effectiveness: necessary but not sufficient

Operational effectiveness and strategy are both essential to superior performance, which, after all, is the primary goal of any enterprise. But they work in very different ways.

A company can outperform rivals only if it can establish a difference that it can preserve. It must deliver greater value to customers or create comparable value at a lower cost, or do both. The arithmetic of superior profitability then follows: delivering greater value allows a company to charge higher average unit prices, greater efficiency results in lower average unit costs.

Ultimately, all differences between companies in cost or price derive from the hundreds of activities required to create, produce, sell, and deliver their products or services, such as calling on customers, assembling final products, and training employees. Cost is generated by performing activities, and cost advantage arises from performing particular activities more efficiently than competitors. Similarly, differentiation arises from both the choice of activities and how they are performed. Activities, then, are the basic units of competitive advantage. Overall advantage or disadvantage results from all a company's activities, not only a few.

Operational effectiveness (OE) means performing similar activities *better* than rivals perform them. Operational effectiveness includes but is not limited to efficiency. It refers to any number of practices that allow a company to better utilize its inputs by, for example, reducing defects in products or developing *better* products faster. In contrast, strategic positioning means performing *different* activities from rivals' or performing similar activities in *different* ways.

Differences in operational effectiveness among companies are pervasive. Some companies are able to get more out of their inputs than others because they eliminate wasted effort, employ more advanced technology, motivate employees better, or have greater insight into managing particular activities or sets of activities. Such differences in operational effectiveness are an important source of differences in profitability among competitors because they directly affect relative cost positions and levels of differentiation.

Differences in operational effectiveness were at the heart of the Japanese challenge to Western companies in the 1980s. The Japanese were so far ahead of rivals in operational effectiveness that they could offer lower cost and superior quality at the same time. It is worth dwelling on this point, because so much recent thinking about competition depends on it. Imagine for a moment a *productivity frontier* that constitutes the sum of all existing best practices at any given time. Think of it as the maximum value that a company delivering a particular product or service can create at a given cost, using the best available technologies, skills, management techniques, and purchased inputs. The productivity frontier can apply to individual activities, to groups of linked activities such as order processing and manufacturing, and to an entire company's activities. When a company improves its operational effectiveness, it moves toward the frontier. Doing so may require capital investment, different personnel, or simply new ways of managing.

The productivity frontier is constantly shifting outward as new technologies and management approaches are developed and as new inputs become available. Laptop computers, mobile communications, the Internet, and software such as Lotus Notes, for example, have redefined the productivity frontier for sales-force operations and created rich possibilities for linking sales with such activities as order processing and after-sales support. Similarly, lean production,

Figure 1.1.1 Operational effectiveness versus strategic positioning

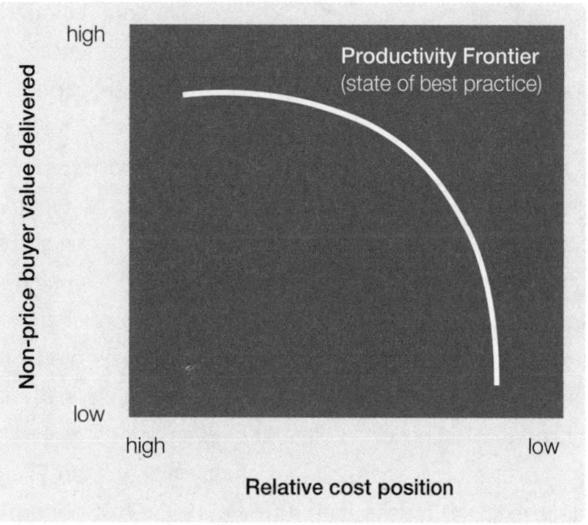

which involves a family of activities, has allowed substantial improvements in manufacturing productivity and asset utilization.

For at least the past decade, managers have been preoccupied with improving operational effectiveness. Through programs such as TQM, time-based competition, and benchmarking, they have changed how they perform activities in order to eliminate inefficiencies, improve customer satisfaction, and achieve best practice. Hoping to keep up with shifts in the productivity frontier, managers have embraced continuous improvement, empowerment, change management, and the so-called learning organization. The popularity of outsourcing and the virtual corporation reflect the growing recognition that it is difficult to perform all activities as productively as specialists.

As companies move to the frontier, they can often improve on multiple dimensions of performance at the same time. For example, manufacturers that adopted the Japanese practice of rapid changeovers in the 1980s were able to lower cost and improve differentiation simultaneously. What were once believed to be real trade-offs – between defects and costs, for example – turned out to be illusions created by poor operational effectiveness. Managers have learned to reject such false trade-offs.

Constant improvement in operational effectiveness is necessary to achieve superior profitability. However, it is not usually sufficient. Few companies have competed successfully on the basis of operational effectiveness over an extended period, and staying ahead of rivals gets harder every day. The most obvious reason for that is the rapid diffusion of best practices. Competitors can quickly imitate management techniques, new technologies, input improvements, and superior ways of meeting customers' needs. The most generic solutions – those that can be used in multiple settings – diffuse the fastest. Witness the proliferation of OE techniques accelerated by support from consultants.

OE competition shifts the productivity frontier outward, effectively raising the bar for everyone. But although such competition produces absolute improvement in operational effectiveness, it leads to relative improvement for no one. Consider the $5 billion-plus U.S. commercial-printing industry. The major players – R. R. Donnelley &. Sons Company, Quebecor, World Color Press, and Big Flower Press – are competing head to head, serving all types of customers, offering the same array of printing technologies (gravure and web offset), investing heavily in the same new equipment, running their presses faster, and reducing crew sizes. But the resulting major productivity gains are being captured by customers and equipment suppliers, not retained in superior profitability. Even industry leader Donnelley's profit margin, consistently higher than 7% in the 1980s, fell to less than 4.6% in 1995. This pattern is playing itself out in industry after industry. Even the Japanese, pioneers of the new competition, suffer from persistently low profits.

The second reason that improved operational effectiveness is insufficient – competitive convergence – is more subtle and insidious. The more benchmarking companies do, the more they look alike. The more that rivals outsource activities to efficient third parties, often the same ones, the more generic those activities become. As rivals imitate one another's improvements in quality, cycle times, or supplier partnerships, strategies converge and competition becomes a series of races down identical paths that no one can win. Competition based on operational effectiveness alone is mutually destructive, leading to wars of attrition that can be arrested only by limiting competition.

The recent wave of industry consolidation through mergers makes sense in the context of OE competition. Driven by performance pressures but lacking strategic vision, company after company has had no better idea than to buy up its rivals. The competitors left standing are often those that outlasted others, not companies with real advantage.

After a decade of impressive gains in operational effectiveness, many companies are facing diminishing returns. Continuous improvement has been etched on managers' brains. But its tools unwittingly draw companies toward imitation and homogeneity. Gradually, managers have let operational effectiveness supplant strategy. The result is zero-sum competition, static or declining prices, and pressures on costs that compromise companies' ability to invest in the business for the long term.

II. Strategy rests on unique activities

Competitive strategy is about being different. It means deliberately choosing a different set of activities to deliver a unique mix of value.

Southwest Airlines Company, for example, offers short-haul, low-cost, point-to-point service between midsize cities and secondary airports in large cities. Southwest avoids large airports and does not fly great distances. Its customers include business travelers, families, and students. Southwest's frequent departures and low fares attract price-sensitive customers who otherwise would travel by bus or car, and convenience-oriented travelers who would choose a full-service airline on other routes.

Most managers describe strategic positioning in terms of their customers. "Southwest Airlines serves price- and convenience-sensitive travelers," for example. But the essence of strategy is in the activities – choosing to perform activities differently or to perform different activities than rivals. Otherwise, a strategy is nothing more than a marketing slogan that will not withstand competition.

A full-service airline is configured to get passengers from almost any point A to any point B. To reach a large number of destinations and serve passengers with connecting flights, full-service airlines employ a hub-and-spoke system centered on major airports. To attract passengers who desire more comfort, they offer first-class or business-class service. To accommodate passengers who must change planes, they coordinate schedules and check and transfer baggage. Because some passengers will be traveling for many hours, full-service airlines serve meals.

Southwest, in contrast, tailors all its activities to deliver low-cost, convenient service on its particular type of route. Through fast turnarounds at the gate of only 15 minutes, Southwest is able to keep planes flying longer hours than rivals and provide frequent departures with fewer aircraft. Southwest does not offer meals, assigned seats, interline baggage checking, or premium classes of service. Automated ticketing at the gate encourages customers to bypass travel agents, allowing Southwest to avoid their commissions. A standardized fleet of 737 aircraft boosts the efficiency of maintenance.

Southwest has staked out a unique and valuable strategic position based on a tailored of activities. On the routes served by Southwest, a full-service airline could never be as convenient or as low cost.

Ikea, the global furniture retailer based in Sweden, also has a clear strategic positioning. Ikea targets young furniture buyers who want style at low cost. What turns this marketing concept into a strategic positioning is the tailored set of activities that make it work. Like Southwest, Ikea has chosen to perform activities differently from its rivals.

Consider the typical furniture store. Showrooms display samples of the merchandise. One area might contain 25 sofas, another will display five dining tables. But those items represent only a fraction of the choices available to customers. Dozens of books displaying fabric swatches or wood samples or alternate styles offer customers thousands of product varieties to choose from. Salespeople often escort customers through the store, answering questions and helping them navigate this maze of choices. Once a customer makes a selection, the order is relayed to a third-party manufacturer. With luck, the furniture will be delivered to the customer's home within six to eight weeks. This is a value chain that maximizes customization and service but does so at high cost.

In contrast, Ikea serves customers who are happy to trade off service for cost. Instead of having a sales associate trail customers around the store, Ikea uses a self-service model based on clear, in-store displays. Rather than rely solely on third-party manufacturers, Ikea designs its own low-cost, modular, ready-to-assemble furniture to fit its positioning. In huge stores, Ikea displays every product it sells in room-like settings, so customers don't need a decorator to help them imagine how to put the pieces together. Adjacent to the furnished showrooms is a warehouse section with the products in boxes on pallets. Customers are expected to do their own pickup and delivery, and Ikea will even sell you a roof rack for your car that you can return for a refund on your next visit.

Although much of its low-cost position comes from having customers "do it themselves," Ikea offers a number of extra services that its competitors do not. In-store child care is one. Extended hours are another. Those services are uniquely aligned with the needs of its customers, who are young, not wealthy, likely to have children (but no nanny), and, because they work for a living, have a need to shop at odd hours.

The origins of strategic positions

Strategic positions emerge from three distract sources, which are not mutually exclusive and often overlap. First, positioning can be based on producing a subset of an industry's products or services. I call this *variety-based positioning* because it is based on the choice of product or service varieties rather than customer segments. Variety-based positioning makes economic sense when a company can best produce particular products or services using distinctive sets of activities.

Jiffy Lube International, for instance, specializes in automotive lubricants and does not offer other car repair or maintenance services. Its value chain produces faster service at a lower cost than broader line repair shops, a combination so attractive that many customers subdivide their purchases, buying oil changes from the focused competitor, Jiffy Lube, and going to rivals for other services.

The Vanguard Group, a leader in the mutual fund industry, is another example of variety-based positioning. Vanguard provides an array of common stock, bond, and money market funds that offer predictable performance and rock-bottom expenses. The company's investment approach deliberately sacrifices the possibility of extraordinary performance in any one year for good relative performance in every year. Vanguard is known, for example, for its index funds. It avoids making bets on interest rates and steers clear of narrow stock groups. Fund managers keep trading levels low, which holds expenses down; in addition, the company discourages customers from rapid buying and selling because doing so drives up costs and can force a fund manager to trade in order to deploy new capital and raise cash for redemptions. Vanguard also takes a consistent low-cost approach to managing distribution, customer service, and marketing. Many investors include one or more Vanguard funds in their portfolio, while buying aggressively managed or specialized funds from competitors.

The people who use Vanguard or Jiffy Lube arc responding to a superior value chain for a particular type of service. A variety-based positioning can serve a wide array of customers, but for most it will meet only a subset of their needs.

A second basis for positioning is that of serving most or all the needs of a particular group of customers. I call this *needs-based positioning*, which comes closer to traditional thinking about targeting a segment of customers. It arises when there are groups of customers with differing needs, and when a tailored set of activities can serve those needs best. Some groups of customers are more price sensitive than others, demand different product features, and need varying amounts of information, support, and services. Ikea's customers are a good example of such a group. Ikea seeks to meet all the home furnishing needs of its target customers, not just a subset of them.

A variant of needs-based positioning arises when the same customer has different needs on different occasions or for different types of transactions. The same person, for example, may have different needs when traveling on business than when traveling for pleasure with the family. Buyers of cans – beverage companies, for example – will likely have different needs from their primary supplier than from their secondary source.

It is intuitive for most managers to conceive of their business in terms of the customers' needs they are meeting. But a critical element of needs-based positioning is not at all intuitive and is often overlooked. Differences in needs will not translate into meaningful positions unless the best set of activities to satisfy them *also* differs. If that were not the case, every competitor could meet those same needs, and there would be nothing unique or valuable about the positioning.

In private banking, for example, Bessemer Trust Company targets families with a minimum of $5 million in investable assets who want capital preservation combined with wealth accumulation. By assigning one sophisticated account officer for every 14 families, Bessemer has configured its activities for personalized service. Meetings, for example, are more likely to be held at a client's ranch or yacht than in the office. Bessemer offers a wide array of customized services, including investment management and estate administration, oversight of oil and gas investments, and accounting for racehorses and aircraft. Loans, a staple of most private banks, are rarely needed by Bessemer's clients and make up a tiny fraction of its client balances and income. Despite the most generous compensation of account officers and the highest personnel cost as a percentage of operating expenses, Bessemer's differentiation with its target families produces a return on equity estimated to be the highest of any private banking competitor.

Citibank's private bank, on the other hand, serves clients with minimum assets of about $250,000 who, in contrast to Bessemer's clients, want convenient access to loans – from jumbo mortgages to deal financing. Citibank's account managers are primarily lenders. When clients need other services, their account manager refers them to other Citibank specialists, each of whom handles prepackaged products. Citibank's system is less customized than Bessemer's and allows it to have a lower manager-to-client ratio of 1:125. Biannual office meetings are offered only for the largest clients. Both Bessemer and Citibank have tailored their activities to meet the needs of a different group of private banking customers. The same value chain cannot profitably meet the needs of both groups.

The third basis for positioning is that of segmenting customers who are accessible in different ways. Although their needs are similar to those of other customers, the best configuration of activities in reach them is different. I call this *access-based positioning*. Access can be a function of customer geography or customer scale – or of anything that requires a different set of activities to reach customers in the best way.

Segmenting by access is less common and less well understood than the other two bases. Carmike Cinemas, for example, operates movie theaters exclusively in cities and towns with populations under 200,000. How does Carmike make money in markets that are not only small but also won't support big-city ticket prices? It dots so through a set of activities that result in a lean cost structure. Carmike's small-town customers can be served through standardized, low-cost theater complexes requiring fewer screens and less sophisticated projection technology than big-city theaters. The company's proprietary information system and management process eliminate the need for local administrative staff beyond a single theater manager. Carmike also reaps advantages from centralized purchasing, lower rent and payroll costs (because of its locations), and rock-bottom corporate overhead of 2% (the industry average is 5%). Operating in small communities also allows Carmike to practice a highly personal form of marketing in which the theater manager knows patrons and promotes attendance through personal contacts. By being the dominant if not the only theater in its markets – the main competition is often the high school football team – Carmike is also able to get its pick of films and negotiate better terms with distributors.

Rural versus urban-based customers are one example of access driving differences in activities. Serving small rather than large customers or densely rather than sparsely situated customers are other examples in which the best way to configure marketing, order processing, logistics, and after-sale service activities to meet the similar needs of distinct groups will often differ.

Positioning is not only about carving out a niche. A position emerging from any of the sources can be broad or narrow. A focused competitor, such as Ikea, targets the special needs of a subset of customers and designs its activities accordingly. Focused competitors thrive on groups of customers who are overserved (and hence overpriced) by more broadly targeted competitors, or underserved (and hence underpriced). A broadly targeted competitor – for example Vanguard or Delta Air Lines – serves a wide array of customers, performing a set of activities designed to meet their common needs. It ignores or meets only partially the more idiosyncratic needs of particular customer groups.

Whatever the basis – variety, needs, access, or some combination of the three – positioning requires a tailored set of activities because it is always a function of differences on the supply side, that is, of differences in activities. However, positioning is not always a function of differences on the demand, or customer, side. Variety and access positionings, in particular, do not rely on *any* customer differences. In practice, however, variety or access differences often accompany needs differences. The tastes – that is, the needs – of Carmike's small-town customers, for instance, run more toward comedies, Westerns, action films, and family entertainment. Carmike does not run any films rated NC-17.

Having defined positioning, we can now begin to answer the question, "What is strategy?" Strategy is the creation of a unique and valuable position, involving a different set of activities. If there were only one ideal position, there would be no need for strategy. Companies would face a simple imperative – win the race to discover and preempt it. The essence of strategic positioning is to choose activities that are different from rivals'. If the same set of activities were best to produce all varieties, meet all needs, and access all customers, companies could easily shift among them and operational effectiveness would determine performance.

III. A sustainable strategic position requires trade-offs

Choosing a unique position, however, is not enough to guarantee a sustainable advantage. A valuable position will attract imitation by incumbents, who are likely to copy it in one of two ways.

First, a competitor can reposition itself to match the superior performer. J.C. Penney, for instance, has been repositioning itself from a Sears clone to a more upscale, fashion-oriented, soft-goods retailer. A second and far more common type of imitation is straddling. The straddler seeks to match the benefits of a successful position while maintaining its existing position. It grafts new features, services, or technologies onto the activities it already performs.

For those who argue that competitors can copy any market position, the airline industry is a perfect test case. It would seem that nearly any competitor could imitate any other airline's activities. Any airline can buy the same planes, lease the gates, and match the menus and ticketing and baggage handling services offered by other airlines.

Continental Airlines saw how well Southwest was doing and decided to straddle. While maintaining its position as a full-service airline, Continental also set out to match Southwest on a number of point-to-point routes. The airline dubbed the new service Continental Lite. It eliminated meals and first-class service, increased departure frequency, lowered fares, and shortened turnaround time at the gate. Because Continental remained a full-service airline on other routes, it continued to use travel agents and its mixed fleet of planes and to provide baggage checking and seat assignments.

But a strategic position is not sustainable unless there are trade-offs with other positions. Trade-offs occur when activities are incompatible. Simply put, a trade-off means that more of one thing necessitates less of another. An airline can choose to serve meals – adding cost and slowing turnaround time at the gate – or it can choose not to, but it cannot do both without bearing major inefficiencies.

Trade-offs create the need for choice and protect against repositioners and straddlers. Consider Neutrogena soap. Neutrogena Corporation's variety-based positioning is built on a "kind to the skin," residue-free soap formulated for pH balance. With a large detail force calling on dermatologists, Neutrogena's marketing strategy looks more like a drug company's than a soap maker's. It advertises in medical journals, sends direct mail to doctors, attends medical conferences, and performs research at its own Skincare Institute. To reinforce its positioning, Neutrogena originally focused its distribution on drugstores and avoided price promotions. Neutrogena uses a slow, more expensive manufacturing process to mold its fragile soap.

In choosing this position, Neutrogena said no to the deodorants and skin softeners that many customers desire in their soap. It gave up the large-volume potential of selling through supermarkets and using price promotions. It sacrificed manufacturing efficiencies to achieve the soap's desired attributes. In its original positioning, Neutrogena made a whole raft of trade-offs like those, trade-offs that protected the company from imitators.

Trade-offs arise for three reasons. The first is inconsistencies in image or reputation. A company known for delivering one kind of value may lack credibility and confuse customers – or even undermine its reputation – if it delivers another kind of value or attempts to deliver two inconsistent things at the same time. For example, Ivory soap, with its position as a basic, inexpensive everyday soap would have a hard time reshaping its image to match Neutrogena's premium "medical" reputation. Efforts to create a new image typically cost tens or even hundreds of millions of dollars in a major industry – a powerful barrier to imitation.

Second, and more important, trade-offs arise from activities themselves. Different positions (with their tailored activities) require different product configurations, different equipment, different employee behavior, different skills, and different management systems. Many trade-offs reflect inflexibilities in machinery, people, or systems. The more Ikea has configured its activities to lower costs by having its customers do their own assembly and delivery, the less able it is to satisfy customers who require higher levels of service.

However, trade-offs can be even more basic. In general, value is destroyed if an activity is overdesigned or underdesigned for its use. For example, even if a given salesperson were capable of providing a high level of assistance to one customer and none to another, the salesperson's talent (and some of his or her cost) would be wasted on the second customer. Moreover, productivity can improve when variation of an activity is limited. By providing a high level of assistance all the time, the salesperson and the entire sales activity can often achieve efficiencies of learning and scale.

Finally, trade-offs arise from limits on internal coordination and control. By clearly choosing to compete in one way and not another, senior management makes organizational priorities clear. Companies that try to be all things to all customers, in contrast, risk confusion in the trenches as employees attempt to make day-to-day operating decisions without a clear framework.

Positioning trade-offs are pervasive in competition and essential to strategy. They create the need for choice and purposefully limit what a company offers. They deter straddling or repositioning, because competitors that engage in those approaches undermine their strategies and degrade the value of their existing activities.

Trade-offs ultimately grounded Continental Lite. The airline lost hundreds of millions of dollars, and the CEO lost his job. Its planes were delayed leaving congested hub cities or slowed at the gate by baggage transfers. Late flights and cancellations generated a thousand complaints a day. Continental Lite could not afford to compete on price and still pay standard travel-agent commissions, but neither could it do without agents for its full-service business. The airline compromised by cutting commissions for all Continental flights across the board. Similarly, it could not afford to offer the same frequent-flier benefits to travelers paying the much lower ticket prices for Lite service. It compromised again by lowering the rewards of Continental's entire frequent-flier program. The results: angry travel agents and full-service customers.

Continental tried to compete in two ways at once. In trying to be low cost on some routes and full service on others, Continental paid an enormous straddling penalty. If there were no trade-offs between the two positions, Continental could have succeeded. But the absence of trade-offs is a dangerous half-truth that managers must unlearn. Quality is not always free. Southwest's convenience, one kind of high quality, happens to be consistent with low costs because its frequent departures are facilitated by a number of low-cost practices – fast gate turnarounds and automated ticketing, for example. However, other dimensions of airline quality – an assigned seat, a meal, or baggage transfer – require costs to provide.

In general, false trade-offs between cost and quality occur primarily when there is redundant or wasted effort, poor control or accuracy, or weak coordination. Simultaneous improvement of cost and differentiation is possible only when a company begins far behind the productivity frontier or when the frontier shifts outward. At the frontier, where companies have achieved current best practice, the trade-off between cost and differentiation is very real indeed.

After a decade of enjoying productivity advantages, Honda Motor Company and Toyota Motor Corporation recently bumped up against the frontier. In 1995, faced with increasing customer resistance to higher automobile prices, Honda found that the only way to produce a less-expensive car was to skimp on features. In the United States, it replaced the rear disk brakes on the Civic with lower-cost drum brakes and used cheaper fabric for the back seat, hoping customers would not notice. Toyota tried to sell a version of its best-selling Corolla in Japan with unpainted bumpers and cheaper seats. In Toyota's case, customers rebelled, and the company quickly dropped the new model.

For the past decade, as managers have improved operational effectiveness greatly, they have internalized the idea that eliminating trade-offs is a good thing. But if there are no trade-offs companies will never achieve a sustainable advantage. They will have to run faster and faster just to stay in place.

As we return to the question, What is strategy? we see that trade-offs add a new dimension to the answer. Strategy is making trade-offs in competing. The essence of strategy is choosing what *not* to do. Without trade-offs, there would be no need for choice and thus no need for strategy. Any good idea could and would be quickly imitated. Again, performance would once again depend wholly on operational effectiveness.

IV. Fit drives both competitive advantage and sustainability

Positioning choices determine not only which activities a company will perform and how it will configure individual activities but also how activities relate to one another. While operational effectiveness is about achieving excellence in individual activities, or functions, strategy is about *combining* activities.

Southwest's rapid gate turnaround, which allows frequent departures and greater use of aircraft, is essential to its high-convenience, low-cost positioning. But how does Southwest achieve it? Part of the answer lies in the company's well-paid gate and ground crews, whose productivity in turnarounds is enhanced by flexible union rules. But the bigger part of the answer lies in how Southwest performs other activities. With no meals, no seat assignment, and no interline baggage transfers, Southwest avoids having to perform activities that slow down other airlines. It selects airports and routes to avoid congestion that introduces delays. Southwest's strict limits on the type and length of routes make standardized aircraft possible: every aircraft Southwest turns is a Boeing 737.

What is Southwest's core competence? Its key success factors? The correct answer is that everything matters. Southwest's strategy involves a whole system of activities, not a collection of parts. Its competitive advantage comes from the way its activities fit and reinforce one another.

Fit locks out imitators by creating a chain that is as strong as its *strongest* link. As in most companies with good strategies, Southwest's activities complement one another in ways that create real economic value. One activity's cost, for example, is lowered because of the way other activities are performed. Similarly, one activity's value to customers can be enhanced by a company's other activities. That is the way strategic fit creates competitive advantage and superior profitability.

Types of fit

The importance of fit among functional policies is one of the oldest ideas in strategy. Gradually, however, it has been supplanted on the management agenda. Rather than seeing the company as a whole, managers have turned to "core" competencies, "critical" resources, and "key" success factors. In fact, fit is a far more central component of competitive advantage than most realize.

Fit is important because discrete activities often affect one another. A sophisticated sales force, for example, confers a greater advantage when the company's product embodies premium technology and its marketing approach emphasizes customer assistance and support. A production line with high levels of model variety is more valuable when combined with an inventory and order processing system that minimizes the need for stocking finished goods, a sales process equipped to explain and encourage customization, and an advertising theme that stresses the benefits of product variations that meet a customer's special needs. Such complementarities are pervasive in strategy. Although some fit among activities is generic and applies to many companies, the most valuable fit is strategy-specific because it enhances a position's uniqueness and amplifies trade-offs.

There are three types of fit, although they are not mutually exclusive. First-order fit is *simple consistency* between each activity (function) and the overall strategy. Vanguard, for example, aligns all activities with its low-cost strategy. It minimizes portfolio turnover and does not need highly compensated money managers. The company distributes its funds directly, avoiding commissions to brokers. It also limits its advertising, relying instead on public relations and word-of-mouth recommendations. Vanguard, ties its employees' bonuses to cost savings.

Consistency ensures that the competitive advantages of activities cumulate and do not erode or cancel themselves out. It makes the strategy easier to communicate to customers, employees, and share-holders, and improves implementation through single-mindedness in the corporation.

Second-order fit occurs when *activities are reinforcing*. Neutrogena, for example, markets to upscale hotels eager to offer their guests a soap recommended by dermatologists. Hotels grant Neutrogena the privilege of using its customary packaging while requiring other soaps to feature the hotel's name. Once guests have tried Neutrogena in a luxury hotel, they are more likely to purchase it at the drugstore or ask their doctor about it. Thus Neutrogena's medical and hotel marketing activities reinforce one another, lowering total marketing costs.

In another example, Bic Corporation sells a narrow line of standard, low-priced pens to virtually all major customer markets (retail, commercial, promotional, and giveaway) through virtually all available channels. As with any variety-based positioning serving a broad group of customers, Bic emphasizes a common need (low price for an acceptable pen) and uses marketing approaches with a broad reach (a large sales force and heavy television advertising). Bic gains the benefits of consistency across nearly all activities, including product design that emphasizes ease of manufacturing, plants configured for low cost, aggressive purchasing to minimize material costs, and in-house parts production whenever the economics dictate.

Yet Bic goes beyond simple consistency because its activities reinforcing. For example, the company uses point-of-sale displays and frequent packaging changes to stimulate impulse buying. To handle point-of-sale tasks, a company needs a large sales force. Bic's is the largest in its industry, and it handles point-of-sale activities better than its rivals do. Moreover, the combination of point-of-sale activity, heavy television advertising, and packaging changes yields far more impulse buying than any activity in isolation could.

Third-order fit goes beyond activity reinforcement to what I call *optimization of effort*. The Gap, a retailer of casual

Figure 1.1.2 Mapping activity systems

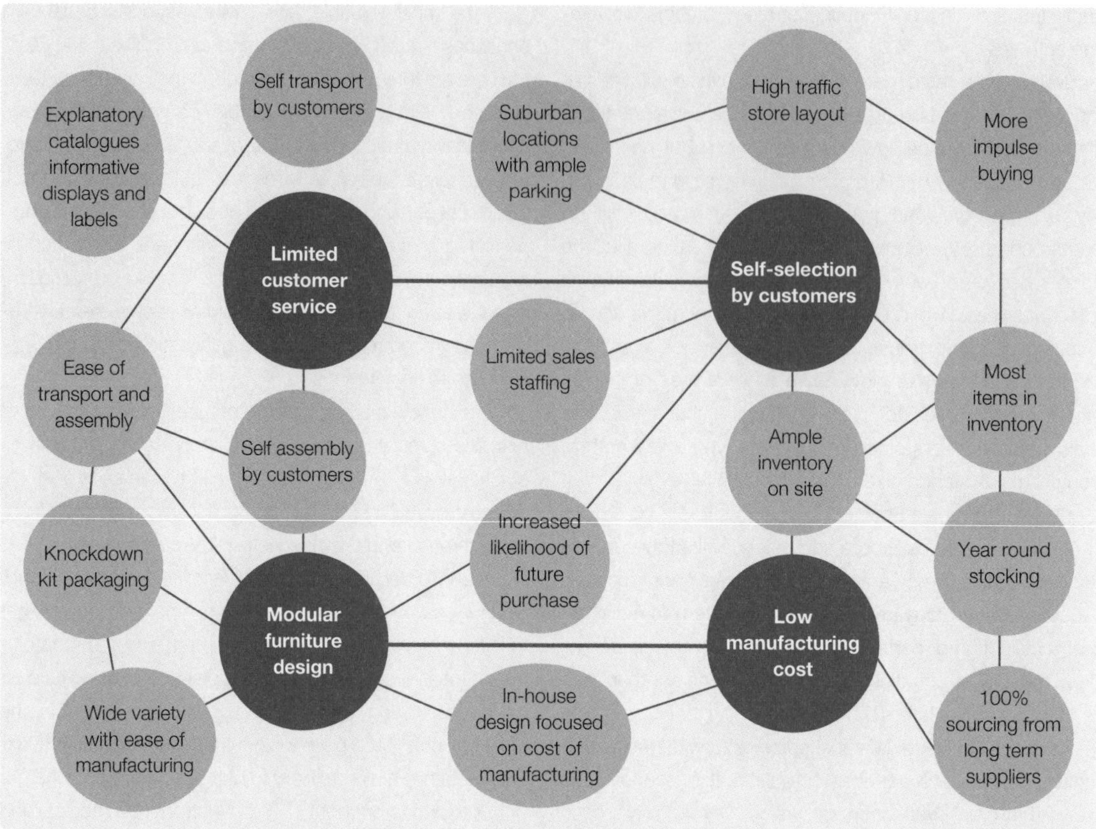

Activity system maps, such as this one for Ikea, show how a company's strategic position is contained in a set of tailored activities designed to deliver it. In companies with a clear strategic position a number of higher-order strategic themes (in darker green) can be identified and implemented through clusters of tightly linked activities (in lighter green)

clothes, considers product availability in its stores a critical element of its strategy. The Gap could keep products either by holding store inventory or by restocking from warehouses. The Gap has optimized its effort across these activities by restocking its selection of basic clothing almost daily out of three warehouses, thereby minimizing the need to carry large in-store inventories. The emphasis is on restocking because the Gap's merchandising strategy sticks to basic items in relatively few colors. While comparable retailers achieve turns of three to four times per year, the Gap turns its inventory seven and a half times per year. Rapid restocking, moreover, reduces the cost of implementing the Gap's short model cycle, which is six to eight weeks long.

Coordination and information exchange across activities to eliminate redundancy and minimize wasted effort are the most basic types of effort optimization. But there are higher levels as well. Product design choices, for example, can eliminate the need for after-sale service or make it possible for customers to perform service activities themselves. Similarly, coordination with suppliers or distribution channels can eliminate the need for some in-house activities, such as end-user training.

In all three types of fit, the whole matters more than any individual part. Competitive advantage grows out of the *entire system* of activities. The fit among activities substantially reduces cost or increases differentiation. Beyond that, the competitive value of individual activities – or the associated skills, competencies, or resources – cannot be decoupled from the system or the strategy. Thus in competitive companies it can be misleading to explain success by specifying individual strengths, core competencies, or critical resources. The list of strengths cuts across many functions, and one strength blends into others. It is more useful to think in terms of themes that pervade many activities, such as low cost, a particular notion of customer service, or a particular conception of the value delivered. These themes are embodied in nests of tightly linked activities.

Fit and sustainability

Strategic fit among many activities is fundamental not only to competitive advantage but also to the sustainability of that advantage. It is harder for a rival to match an array of interlocked activities than it is merely to imitate a particular

Figure 1.1.3 Vanguard's activity system

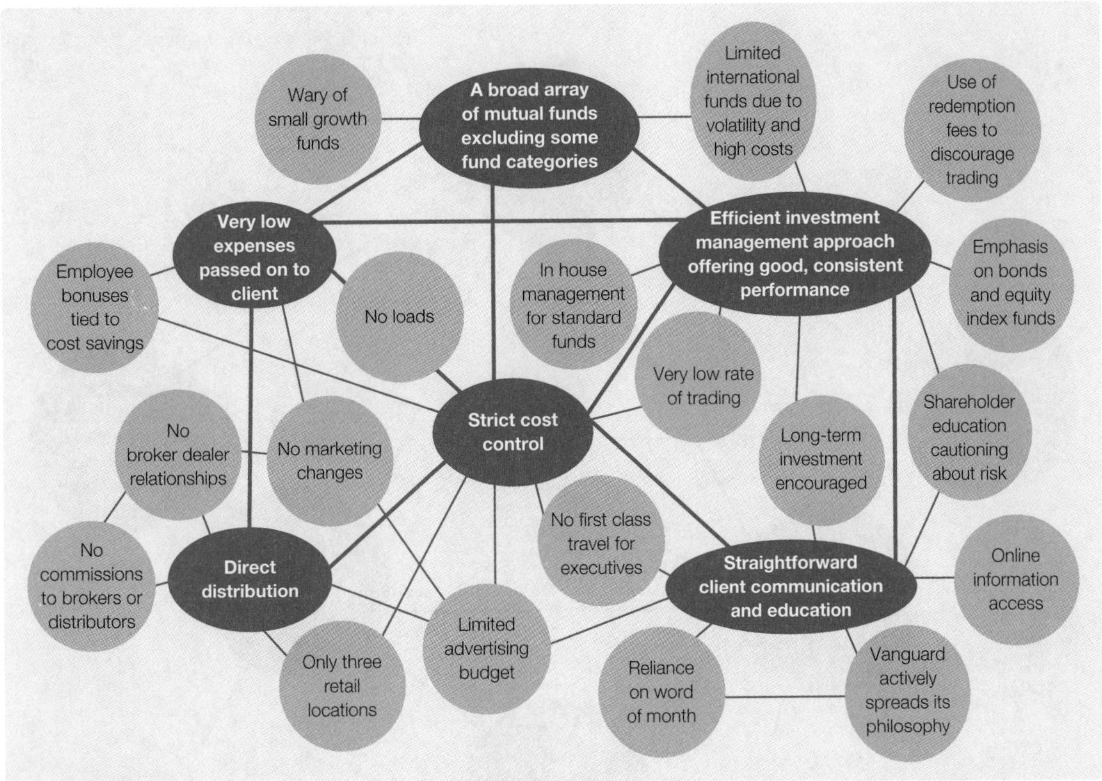

Activity-system maps can be useful for examining and strenghthening strategic fit. A set of basic questions should guide the process First, is each activity consistent with the overall positioning – the varieties produced, the needs served, and the type of customers accessed? Ask those responsible for each activity to identify how other activities within the company improve or detract from their performance. Second, are there ways to strengthen how activities and groups of activities reinforce one another? Finally, could changes in one activity eliminate the need to perform others?

sales-force approach, match a process technology, or replicate a set of product features. Positions built on systems of activities are far more sustainable than those built on individual activities.

Consider this simple exercise. The probability that competitors can match any activity is often less than one. The probabilities then quickly compound to make matching the entire system highly unlikely ($.9 \times .9 = .81$, $.9 \times .9 \times .9 \times .9 = .66$, and so on). Existing companies that try to reposition or straddle will be forced to reconfigure many activities. And even new entrants, though they do not confront the trade-offs facing established rivals, still face formidable barriers to imitation.

The more a company's positioning rests on activity systems with second- and third-order fit, the more sustainable its advantage will be. Such systems, by their very nature, are usually difficult to untangle from outside the company and therefore hard to imitate. And even if rivals can identify the relevant interconnections, they will have difficulty replicating them. Achieving fit is difficult because it requires the integration of decisions and actions across many independent submits.

A competitor seeking to match an activity system gains little by imitating only some activities and not matching the whole. Performance does not improve; it can decline. Recall Continental Lite's disastrous attempt to imitate Southwest.

Finally, fit among a company's activities creates pressures and incentives to improve operational effectiveness, which makes imitation even harder. Fit means that poor performance in one activity will degrade the performance in others, so that weaknesses are exposed and more prone to get attention. Conversely, improvements in one activity will pay dividends in others. Companies with strong fit among their activities are rarely inviting targets. Their superiority in strategy and in execution only compounds their advantages and raises the hurdle for imitators.

When activities complement one another, rivals will get little benefit from imitation unless they successfully match the whole system. Such situations tend to promote winner-take-all competition. The company that builds the best activity system – Toys R Us, for instance – wins, while rivals with similar strategies – Child World and Lionel Leisure – fall behind. Thus finding a new strategic position is often

Figure 1.1.4 Southwest Airlines' activity system

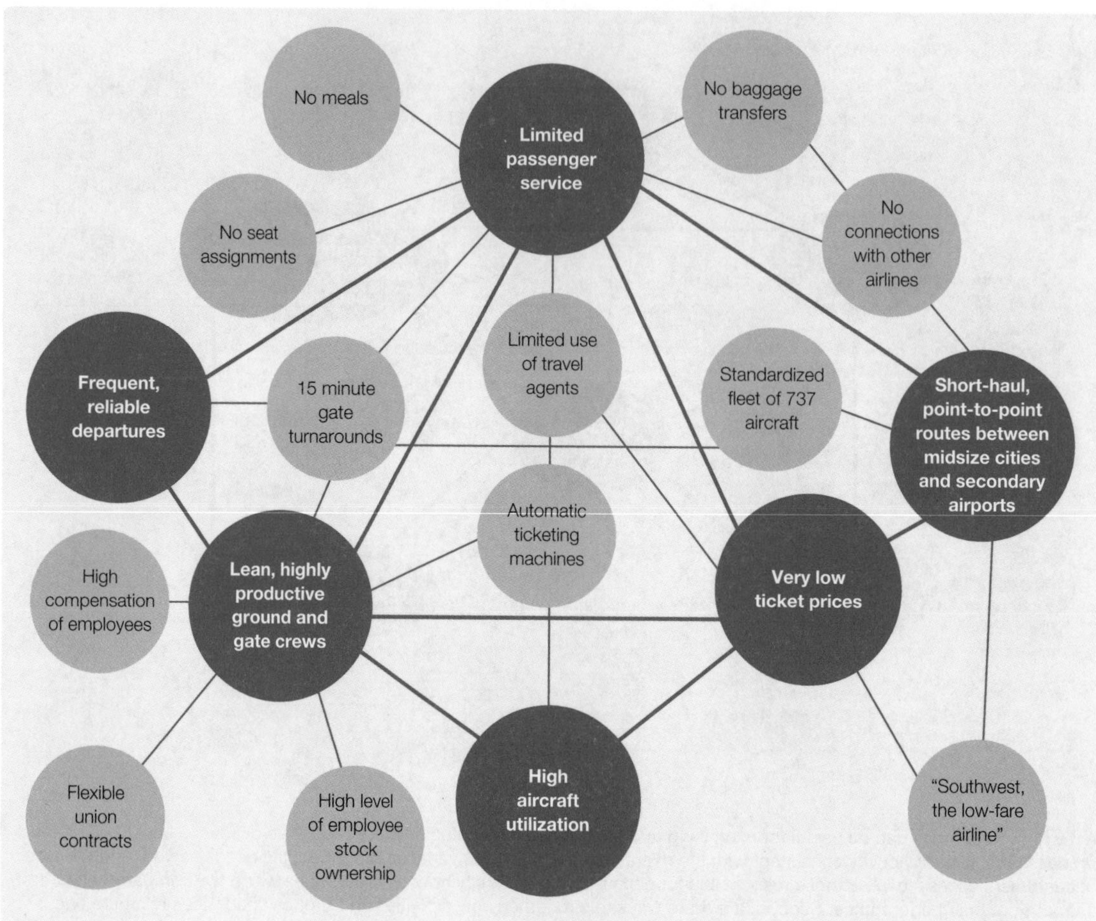

preferable to being the second or third imitator of an occupied position.

The most viable positions are those whose activity systems are incompatible because of trade-offs. Strategic positioning sets the trade-off rules that define how individual activities will be configured and integrated. Seeing strategy in terms of activity systems only makes it clearer why organizational structure, systems, and processes need to be strategy-specific. Tailoring organization to strategy, in turn, makes complementarities more achievable and contributes to sustainability.

One implication is that strategic positions should have a horizon of a decade or more, not of a single planning cycle. Continuity fosters improvements in individual activities and

Table 1.1.1 Alternative views of strategy

The implicit strategy model of the past decade	Sustainable competitive advantage
One ideal competitive position in the industry	Unique competitive position for the company
Benchmarking of all activities and achieving best practice	Activities tailored to strategy
Aggressive outsourcing and partnering to gain efficiencies	Clear trade-offs and choices vis-à-vis competition
Advantages rest on a few key success factors, critical resources, core competencies	Competitive advantage arises from fit across activities
Flexibility and rapid responses to all competitive and market changes	Sustainability comes from the activity system not the parts
	Operational effectiveness a given

the fit across activities, allowing an organization to build unique capabilities and skills tailored to its strategy. Continuity also reinforces a company's identity.

Conversely, frequent shifts in positioning are costly. Not only must a company reconfigure individual activities, but it must also realign entire systems. Some activities may never catch up to the vacillating strategy. The inevitable result of frequent shifts in strategy, or of failure to choose a distinct position in the first place, is "me-too" or hedged activity configurations, inconsistencies across functions, and organizational dissonance.

What is strategy? We can now complete the answer to this question. Strategy is creating fit among a company's activities. The success of a strategy depends on doing many things well – not just a few – and integrating among them. If there is no fit among activities, there is no distinctive strategy and little sustainability. Management reverts to the simpler task of overseeing independent functions, and operational effectiveness determines an organization's relative performance.

V. Rediscovering strategy

The failure to choose

Why do so many companies fail to have a strategy? Why do managers avoid making strategic choices? Or, having made them in the past, why do managers so often let strategies decay and blur?

Commonly, the threats to strategy are seen to emanate from outside a company because of changes in technology or the behavior of competitors. Although external changes can be the problem, the greater threat to strategy often comes from within. A sound strategy is undermined by a misguided view of competition, by organizational failures, and, especially, by the desire to grow.

Managers have become confused about the necessity of making choices. When many companies operate far from the productivity frontier, trade-offs appear unnecessary. It can seem that a well-run company should be able to beat its ineffective rivals on all dimensions simultaneously. Taught by popular management thinkers that they do not have to make trade-offs, managers have acquired a macho sense that to do so is a sign of weakness.

Unnerved by forecasts of hypercompetition, managers increase its likelihood by imitating everything about their competitors. Exhorted to think in terms of revolution, managers chase every new technology for its own sake.

The pursuit of operational effectiveness is seductive because it is concrete and actionable. Over the past decade, managers have been under increasing pressure to deliver tangible, measurable performance improvements. Programs in operational effectiveness produce reassuring progress, although superior profitability may remain elusive. Business publications and consultants flood the market with information about what other companies are doing, reinforcing the best-practice mentality. Caught up in the race for operational effectiveness, many managers simply do not understand the need to have a strategy.

Companies avoid or blur strategic choices for other reasons as well. Conventional wisdom within an industry is often strong, homogenizing competition. Some managers mistake "customer focus" to mean they must serve all customer needs or respond to every request from distribution channels. Others cite the desire to preserve flexibility.

Organizational realities also work against strategy. Trade-offs are frightening, and making no choice is sometimes preferred to risking blame for a bad choice. Companies imitate one another in a type of herd behavior, each assuming rivals know something they do not. Newly empowered employees, who are urged to seek every possible source of improvement, often lack a vision of the whole and the perspective to recognize trade-offs. The failure to choose sometimes comes down to the reluctance to disappoint valued managers or employees.

The growth trap

Among all other influences, the desire to grow has perhaps the most perverse effect on strategy. Trade-offs and limits appear to constrain growth. Serving one group of customers and excluding others, for instance, places a real or imagined limit on revenue growth. Broadly targeted strategies emphasizing low price result in lost sales with customers sensitive to features or service. Differentiators lose sales to price-sensitive customers.

Managers are constantly tempted to take incremental steps that surpass those limits but blur a company's strategic position. Eventually, pressures to grow or apparent saturation of the target market lead managers to broaden the position by extending product lines, adding new features, imitating competitors' popular services, matching processes, and even making acquisitions. For years, Maytag Corporation's success was based on its focus on reliable, durable washers and dryers, later extended to include dishwashers. However, conventional wisdom emerging within the industry supported the notion of selling a full line of products. Concerned with slow industry growth and competition from broad-line appliance makers, Maytag was pressured by dealers and encouraged by customers to extend its line. Maytag expanded into refrigerators and cooking products under the Maytag brand and acquired other brands – Jean-Air, Hardwick Stove, Hoover, Admiral, and Magic Chef – with disparate positions. Maytag has grown substantially from $684 million in 1985 to a peak of $3.4 billion in 1994, but return on sales has declined from 8% to 12% in the 1970s and 1980s to an average of less than 1% between 1989 and 1995. Cost cutting will improve this performance, but laundry and dishwasher products still anchor Maytag's profitability.

Neutrogena may have fallen into the same trap. In the early 1990s, its U.S. distribution broadened to include mass merchandisers such as Wal-Mart Stores. Under the Neutrogena name, the company expanded into a wide variety of products – eye-makeup remover and shampoo, for example – in which it was not unique and which diluted its image and it began turning to price promotions.

Compromises and inconsistencies in the pursuit of growth will erode the competitive advantage a company had with its original varieties or target customers. Attempts to compete in several ways at once create confusion and undermine organizational motivation and focus. Profits fall, but more revenue is seen as the answer. Managers are unable to make choice, so the company embarks on a new round of broadening and compromises. Often, rivals continue to match each other until desperation breaks the cycle, resulting in a merger or downsizing to the original positioning.

Profitable growth

Many companies, after a decade of restructuring and cost-cutting, are turning their attention to growth. Too often, efforts to grow blur uniqueness, create compromises, reduce fit, and ultimately undermine competitive advantage. In fact, the growth imperative is hazardous to strategy.

What approaches to growth preserve and reinforce strategy? Broadly, the prescription is to concentrate on deepening a strategic position rather than broadening and compromising it. One approach is to look for extensions of the strategy that leverage the existing activity system by offering features or services that rivals would find impossible or costly to match on a stand-alone basis. In other words, managers can ask themselves which activities, features, or forms of competition are feasible or less costly to them because of complementary activities that their company performs.

Deepening a position involves making the company's activities more distinctive, strengthening fit, and communicating the strategy better to those customers who should value it. But many companies succumb to the temptation to chase "easy" growth by adding hot features, products, or services without screening them or adapting them to their strategy. Or they target new customers or markets in which the company has little special to offer. A company can often grow faster – and far more profitably – by better penetrating needs and varieties where it is distinctive than by slugging it out in potentially higher growth arenas in which the company lacks uniqueness. Carmike, now the largest theater chain in the United States, owes its rapid growth to its disciplined concentration on small markets. The company quickly sells any big-city theaters that come to it as part of an acquisition.

Globalization often allows growth that is consistent with strategy, opening up larger markets for a focused strategy. Unlike broadening domestically, expanding globally is likely to leverage and reinforce a company's unique position and identity.

Companies seeking growth through broadening within their industry can best contain the risks to strategy by creating stand-alone units, each with its own brand name and tailored activities. Maytag has clearly struggled with this issue. On the one hand, it has organized its premium and value brands into separate units with different strategic positions. On the other, it has created an umbrella appliance company for all its brands to gain critical mass. With shared design, manufacturing, distribution, and customer service, it will be hard to avoid homogenization. If a given business unit attempts to compete with different positions for different products or customers, avoiding compromise is nearly impossible.

The role of leadership

The challenge of developing or reestablishing a clear strategy is often primarily an organizational one and depends on leadership. With so many forces at work against making choices and trade-offs in organizations, a clear intellectual framework to guide strategy is a necessary counterweight. Moreover, strong leaders willing to make choices are essential.

In many companies, leadership has degenerated into orchestrating operational improvements and making deals. But the leader's role is broader and far more important. General management is more than the stewardship of individual functions. Its core is strategy: defining and communicating the company's unique position, making trade-offs, and forging fit among activities. The leader must provide the discipline to decide which industry changes and customer needs the company will respond to, while avoiding organizational distractions and maintaining the company's distinctiveness. Managers at lower levels lack the perspective and the confidence to maintain a strategy. There will be constant pressures to compromise, relax trade-offs, and emulate rivals. One of the leader's jobs is to teach others in the organization about strategy – and to say no.

Strategy renders choices about what not to do as important as choices about what to do. Indeed, setting limits is another function of leadership. Deciding which target group of customers, varieties, and needs the company should serve is fundamental to developing a strategy. But so is deciding not to serve other customers or needs and not to offer certain features or services. Thus strategy requires constant discipline and clear communication. Indeed, one of the most important functions of an explicit, communicated strategy is to guide employees in making choices that arise because of trade-offs in their individual activities and in day-to-day decisions.

Improving operational effectiveness is a necessary part of management, but it is *not strategy.* In confusing the two, managers have unintentionally backed into a way of thinking about competition that is driving many industries toward competitive convergence, which is in no one's best interest and is not inevitable.

Managers must clearly distinguish operational effectiveness from strategy. Both are essential, but the two agendas are different.

The operational agenda involves continual improvement everywhere there are no trade-offs. Failure to do this creates vulnerability even for companies with a good strategy. The operational agenda is the proper place for constant change, flexibility, and relentless efforts to achieve best practice. In contrast, the strategic agenda is the right place for defining a unique position, making clear trade-offs, and tightening fit. It involves the continual search for ways to reinforce and extend the company's position. The strategic agenda demands discipline and continuity; its enemies are distraction and compromise.

Strategic continuity does not imply a static view of competition. A company must continually improve its operational effectiveness and actively try to shift the productivity frontier; at the same time, there needs to be ongoing effort to extend its uniqueness while strengthening the fit among its activities. Strategic continuity, in fact, should make an organization's continual improvement more effective.

A company may have to change its strategy if there are major structural changes in its industry. In fact, new strategic positions often arise because of industry changes, and new entrants unencumbered by history often can exploit them more easily. However, a company's choice of a new position must be driven by the ability to find new trade-offs and leverage a new system of complementary activities into a sustainable advantage.

Reading 1.2 Strategy as simple rules *Kathleen M. Eisenhardt and Donald N. Sull*

First published: (2001) *Harvard Business Review*, January: 107–116. Reprinted by permission of *Harvard Business Review*. 'Strategy as Simple Rules' by Kathleen Eisenhardt and Donald N. Sull, January 2001.

Since its founding in 1994, Yahoo! has emerged as one of the blue chips of the new economy. As the Internet's top portal, Yahoo! generates the astounding numbers we've come to expect from stars of the digital era – more than 100 million visits per day, annual sales growth approaching 200%, and a market capitalization that has exceeded the value of the Walt Disney Company. Yet Yahoo! also provides something we don't generally expect from Internet companies: profits.

Everyone recognizes the unprecedented success of Yahoo!, but it's not easily explained using traditional thinking about competitive strategy. Yahoo!'s rise can't be attributed to an attractive industry structure, for example. In fact, the Internet portal space is a strategist's worst nightmare: it's characterized by intense rivalries, instant imitators, and customers who refuse to pay a cent. Worse yet, there are few barriers to entry. Nor is it possible to attribute Yahoo!'s success to unique or valuable resources – its founders had little more than a computer and a great idea when they started the company. As for strategy, many analysts would say it's not clear that Yahoo! even has one. The company began as a catalog of Web sites, became a content aggregator, and eventually grew into a community of users. Lately it has become a broad network of media, commerce, and communication services. If Yahoo! has a strategy, it would be very hard to pin down using traditional, textbook notions.

While the Yahoo! story is dramatic, it's far from unique. Many other leaders of the new economy, including eBay and America Online, also rose to prominence by pursuing constantly evolving strategies in market spaces that were considered unattractive according to traditional measures. And it's not exclusively a new-economy phenomenon. Companies in even the oldest sectors of the economy have excelled without the advantages of superior resources or strategic positions. Consider Enron and AES in energy, Ispat International in steel, Cemex to cement, and Vodafone and Global Crossing in telecommunications.

The performance of all these companies – despite unattractive industry structures, few apparent resource advantages, and constantly evolving strategies – raises critical questions. How did they succeed? More generally, what art the sources of competitive advantage in high-velocity markets? What does strategy mean in the new economy?

The secret of companies like Yahoo! is *strategy as simple rules.* Managers of such companies know that the greatest opportunities for competitive advantage lie in market confusion, so they jump into chaotic markets, probe for opportunities, build on successful forays, and shift flexibly among opportunities as circumstances dictate. But they recognize the need for a few key strategic processes and a few simple rules to guide them through the chaos. As one Internet executive explained: "I have a thousand opportunities a day; strategy is deciding which 50 to do." In traditional strategy, advantage comes from exploiting resources or stable market positions. In strategy as simple rules, by contrast, advantage comes from successfully seizing fleeting opportunities.

It's not surprising that a young company like Yahoo! should rely on strategy as simple rules. Entrepreneurs have always used that kind of opportunity-grabbing approach because it can help them win against established competitors. What is surprising is that strategy as simple rules makes sense for all kinds of companies – large and small, old and young – in fast-moving markets like those in the new economy. That's because, while information economics and network effects are important, the new economy's most profound strategic implication is that companies must capture unanticipated, fleeting opportunities in order to succeed.

Of course, theory is one thing, but putting it into practice is another. In fact, our recommendations reverse some prescriptions of traditional strategy. Rather than picking a position or leveraging a competence, managers should select a few key strategic processes. Rather than responding to a complicated world with elaborate strategies, they should craft a handful of simple rules. Rather than avoiding uncertainty, they should jump in.

Zeroing in on key processes

Companies that rely on strategy as simple rules are often accused of lacking strategies altogether. Critics have derided AOL as "the cockroach of the Internet" for scurrying from one opportunity to the next. Some analysts accuse Enron of doing same thing. From the outside, companies like these certainly appear to be following an "if it works, anything goes" approach. But that couldn't be further from the truth. Each company follows a disciplined strategy – otherwise, it would be paralyzed by chaos. And, as with all effective strategies, the strategy is unique to the company. But a simple-rules strategy and its underlying logic of pursuing opportunities are harder to see than traditional approaches. ([Table 1.2.1] compares the strategies of position, resources, and simple rules.)

Managers using this strategy pick a small number of strategically significant processes and craft a few simple rules to guide them. The key strategic processes should place the company where the flow of opportunities is swiftest and deepest. The processes might include product innovation, partnering, spinout creation, or new-market entry. For some companies, the choices are obvious – Sun Microsystems' focus on developing new products is a good example. For other companies, the selection of key processes might require some creativity – Akamai, for instance, has developed a focus on customer care. The simple rules provide the guidelines within which managers can pursue opportunities. Strategy, then, consists of the unique set strategically significant processes and the handful of simple rules that guide them.

Autodesk, the global leader in software for design professionals, illustrates strategy as simple rules. In the mid-1990s, Autodesk's markets were mature, and the company

Table 1.2.1 Three approaches to strategy

Managers competing in business can choose among three distinct ways to fight. They can build a fortress and defend it; they can nurture and leverage unique resources; or they can flexibly pursue fleeting opportunities within simple rules. Each approach requires different skill sets and works best under different circumstances.

	Position	Resources	Simple rules
Strategic logic	Establish position	Leverage resources	Pursue opportunities
Strategic steps	Identify an attractive market Locate a defensible position Fortify and defend	Establish a vision Build resources Leverage across markets	Jump into the confusion Keep moving Seize opportunities Finish strong
Strategic question	Where should we be?	What should we be?	How should we proceed?
Source of advantage	Unique, valuable position with tightly integrated activity system	Unique, valuable, inimitable resources	Key processes and unique simple rules
Works best in	Slowly changing, well-structured markets	Moderately changing, well-structured markets	Rapidly changing, ambiguous markets
Duration of advantage	Sustained	Sustained	Unpredictable
Risk	It will be too difficult to alter position as conditions change	Company will be too slow to build new resources as conditions change	Managers will be too tentative in executing on promising opportunities
Performance goal	Profitability	Long-term dominance	Growth

dominated all of them. As a result, growth slowed to single-digit rates. CEO Carol Bartz was sure that her most promising opportunities lay in making of those Autodesk technologies – in areas such as wireless communications, the Internet, imaging, and global positioning – that hadn't yet been exploited. But she wasn't sure which new technologies and related products would be big winners. So she refocused the strategy on the product innovation process and introduced a simple, radical rule: the new-product development schedule would be shortened from a leisurely 18 to 24 months to, in some cases, a hyperkinetic three months. That changed the pace, scale, and strategic logic with which Autodesk tackled technology opportunities.

While a strategy of accelerating product innovation helped identify opportunities more quickly, Bartz lacked the cash to commercialize all of Autodesk's promising technologies. So she added a significant new strategy: spinouts. The first spinout, Buzzaw.com, debuted in 1999. It allowed engineers to purchase construction materials using B2B exchange technology. Buzzsaw.com attracted significant venture capital and benefited from Autodesk's powerful brand and its customer relationships. Autodesk has since created a second spinout, RedSpark, and has developed simple rules for the new key process of spinning of companies.

A company's particular combination of opportunities and constraints often dictates the processes it chooses. Cisco, Autodesk, Lego, and Yahoo! began with strategies in which product innovation was dominant, but their emphases diverged. Cisco's new opportunities lay in the many new networking technologies that were emerging, but the company lacked the time and engineering talent to develop them all. In contrast to technology-rich and stock-price-poor Autodesk, which focused on spinouts, Cisco – with high market capitalization – found that acquisitions was the way to go. Despite its stratospheric market cap, Yahoo! went in. yet another direction. The company wanted to exploit content and commerce opportunities but needed a lot of partners. Many were too big to acquire, so it created partnerships. Lego's best opportunities were in extending its power brand and philosophy into new markets. But since the company faced less competition and operated at a slower pace than Autodesk, Cisco, or Yahoo!, managers could grow organically into new product markets such as children's robotics, clothing, theme parks, and software.

Simple rules for unpredictable markets

Most managers quickly grasp the concept of focusing on key strategic processes that will position their companies where the flow of opportunities is most promising. But because they equate processes with detailed routines, they often miss the notion of simple rules. Yet simple rules are essential. They poise the company on what's termed in complexity theory "the edge of chaos," providing just enough structure to allow it to capture the best opportunities. It may sound counterintuitive, but the complicated improvisational movements that companies like AOL and Enron make as they pursue fleeting opportunities arise from simple rules.

Yahoo!'s managers initially focused their strategy on the branding and product innovation processes and lived by four product innovation rules: know the priority rank of each product in development, ensure that every engineer can work on every project, maintain the Yahoo! look in the user interface, and launch products quietly. As long as they followed the rules, developers could change products in any way they chose, come to work at any hour, wear anything, and bring along their dogs and significant others. One developer decided at midnight to build a new sports page coveting the European soccer championships. Within 48 hours, it became Yahoo!'s most popular page, with more than 100,000 hits per day. Since he knew which lines he had to stay within, he was free to run with a great idea when it occurred to him. A day later, he was back on his primary project. On a bigger scale, the simple rules, in particular the requirement that every engineer be able to work on every project, allowed Yahoo! to change 50% of the code for the enormously successful My Yahoo! service four weeks before launch to adjust to the changing market.

Over the course of studying dozens of companies in turbulent and unpredictable markets, we've discovered that the simple rules fall into five broad categories. (See [Table 1.2.2].)

How-to rules

Yahoo!'s how-to rules kept managers just organized. enough to seize opportunities. Enron provides another how-to example. Its commodities-trading business focuses strategy on the risk management process with two rules: each trade must be offset by another trade that allows the company to hedge its risk, and every trader must complete a daily profit-and-loss statement. Computer giant Dell focuses on the process of rapid reorganization (or patching) around focused customer segments. A key how-to rule for this process is that a business must be split in two when its revenue hits $1 billion.

Boundary rules

Sometimes simple rules delineate boundary conditions that help managers sort through many opportunities quickly. The rules might center on customers, geography, or technologies. For example, when Cisco first moved to an acquisitions-led strategy, its boundary rule was that it could acquire companies with at most 75 employees, 75% of whom were engineers. At a major pharmaceutical company, strategy centers on the drug discovery process

Table 1.2.2 Simple rules, summarized

In turbulent markets, managers should flexibly seize opportunities – but flexibility must be disciplined. Smart companies focus on key processes and simple roles. Different types of rules help executives manage different aspects of seizing opportunities.

Type	Purpose	Example
How-to rules	They spell out key features of how a process is executed–"What makes our process unique?"	Akamai's rules for the customer service process: staff must consist of technical gurus, every question must be answered on the first call or e-mail, and R&D staff must rotate through customer service.
Boundary rules	They focus managers on which opportunities can be pursued and which are outside the pale.	Cisco's early acquisitions rule: companies to be acquired must have no more than 75 employees, 75% of whom are engineers.
Priority rules	They help managers rank the accepted opportunities.	Intel's rule for allocating manufacturing capacity: allocation is based on a product's gross margin.
Timing rules	They synchronize managers with the pace of emerging opportunities and other parts of the company	Nortel's rules for product development: project teams must know when a product has to be delivered to the leading customer to win, and product development time must be less than 18 months.
Exit rules	They help managers decide when to pull out of yesterday's opportunities.	Oticon's rule for pulling the plug on projects in development: if a key team member—manager or not—chooses to leave the project for another within the company, the project is killed.

and several boundary rules: researchers can work on any of ten molecules (no more than four at once) specified by a senior research committee, and a research project must pass a few continuation hurdles related to progress in clinical trials. Within those boundaries, researchers are free to pursue whatever looks promising. The result has been a drug pipeline that's the envy of the industry.

Miramax – well known for artistically innovative movies such as *The Crying Game*, *Life is Beautiful*, and *Pulp Fiction* – has boundary rules that guide the all-important movie-picking process: first, every movie must revolve around a central human condition, such as love (*The Crying Game*) or envy (*The Talented Mr. Ripley*). Second, a movie's main character must be appealing but deeply flawed – the hero of *Shakespeare in love* is gifted and charming but steals ideas from friends and betrays his wife. Third, movies must have a very clear story line with a beginning, middle, and end (although in *Pulp Fiction* the end comes first). Finally, there is a firm cap on production costs. Within the rules, there is flexibility to move quickly when a writer or director shows up with a great script. The result is an enormously creative and even surprising flow of movies and enough discipline to produce superior, consistent financial results. *The English Patient*, for example, cost $27 million to make, grossed more than $200 million, and grabbed nine Oscars.

Lego provides another illustration of boundary rules. At Lego, the product market-entry process is a strategic focus because of the many opportunities to extend the Lego brand and philosophy. But while there is plenty of flexibility, not every market makes the cut. Lego has a checklist of rules. Does the proposed product have the Lego look? Will children learn while having fun? Will parents approve? Does the product maintain high quality standards? Does it stimulate creativity? If an opportunity falls short on one hurdle, the business team can proceed, but ultimately the hurdle must be cleared. Lego children's wear, for example, met all the criteria except one: it didn't stimulate creativity. As a result, the members of the children's wear team worked until they figured out the answer – a line of mix-and-match clothing items that encouraged children to create their own fashion statements.

Priority rules

Simple rules can set priorities for resource allocation among competing opportunities. Intel realized a long time ago that it needed to allocate manufacturing capacity among its products very carefully, given the enormous costs of fabrication facilities. At a time of extreme price volatility in the mid-1980s, when Asian chip manufacturers were disrupting world markets with severe price cuts and accelerated technological improvement, Intel followed a simple rule: allocate manufacturing capacity based on a product's gross margin. Without this rule, the company might have continued to allocate too much capacity to its traditional core memory business rather than seizing the opportunity to dominate the nascent and highly profitable microprocessor niche.

Timing rules

Many companies have timing rules that set the rhythm of key strategic processes. In fact, pacing is one of the important elements that set simple-rules strategies apart from traditional strategies. Timing rules can help synchronize a company with emerging opportunities and coordinate the company's various parts to capture them. Nortel Networks now relies on two timing rules for its strategically important product innovation process: project teams must always know when a product has to be delivered to the leading customer to win, and product development time must be less than 18 months. The first rule keeps Nortel in sync with cutting-edge customers, who represent the best opportunities. The second forces Nortel to move quickly into new opportunities while synchronizing the various parts of the corporation to do so. Together, the rules helped the company shift focus from perfecting its current products to exploiting market openings-to "go from perfection to hitting market windows," as GEO John Roth puts it. At an Internet-based service company where we worked, globalization was the process that put the company squarely in the path of superior opportunities. Managers drove new-country expansion at the rate of one new country every two months, thus maintaining constant movement into new opportunities. Many top Silicon Valley companies set timing rules for the length of the product innovation process. When developers approach a deadline, they drop features to meet the schedule. Such rhythms maintain movement and ensure that the market and various groups within the organization – from manufacturing to marketing to engineering – are on the same beat.

Exit rules

Exit rules help managers pull out from yesterday's opportunities. At the Danish hearing aid company Oticon, executives pull the plug on a product in development if a key team member leaves for another project. Similarly, at a major high-tech multinational where creating new businesses is a key strategic process, senior executives stop new initiatives that don't meet certain sales and profit goals within two years. (For a look at the flip side of simple rules, see the [box] "What Simple Rules Are Not.")

What simple rules are not

It is impossible to dictate exactly what a company's simple rules should be. It is possible, however, to say what they should *not* be.

Broad

Managers often confuse a company's guiding principles with simple rules. The celebrated "HP way" for example, consists of principles like "we focus on a high level of achievement and contribution" and "we encourage flexibility and innovation." The principles are designed to apply to every activity within the company, from purchasing to product innovation. They may create a productive culture, but they provide little concrete guidance for employees trying to evaluate a partner or decide whether to enter a new market. The most effective simple rules, in contrast, are tailored to a single process.

Vague

Some rules cover a single process but are too vague to provide real guidance. One Western bank operating in Russia, for example, provided the following guideline for screening investment proposals: all investments must be currently undervalued and have potential for long-term capital appreciation. Imagine the plight of a newly hired associate who turns to that rule for guidance!

A simple screen can help managers test whether their rules are too vague. Ask: could any reasonable person argue the exact opposite of the rule? In the case of the bank in Russia, it is hard to imagine anyone suggesting that the company target overvalued companies with no potential for long-term capital appreciation. If your rules flunk this test, they are not effective.

Mindless

Companies whose simple rules have remained implicit may find upon examining them that these rules destroy rather than create value. In one company, managers listed their recent partnership relationships and then tried to figure out what rules could have produced the list. To their chagrin, they found that one rule seemed to be: always form partnerships with small, weak companies that we can control. Another was: always form partnerships with companies that are not as successful as they once were. Again, use a simple test – reverse-engineer your processes to determine your implicit simple rules. Throw out the ones that are embarrassing.

Stale

In high-velocity markets, rules can linger beyond their sell-by dates. Consider Banc One. The Columbus, Ohio-based bank grew to be the seventh-largest bank in the United States by acquiring more than 100 regional banks. Banc One's acquisitions followed a set of simple rules that were based on experience: Banc One must never pay so much that earnings are diluted, it must only buy successful banks with established management teams, it must never acquire a bank with assets greater than one-third of Banc One's, and it must allow acquired banks to run as autonomous affiliates. The rules worked well until others in the banking industry consolidated operations to lower their costs substantially. Then Banc One's loose confederation of banks was burdened with redundant operations, and it got clobbered by efficient competitors.

How do you figure out if your rules are stale? Slowing growth is a good indicator. Stock price is even better. Investors obsess about the future, while your own financials report the past. So if your share price is dropping relative to your competitors' share prices, or if your percentage of the industry's market value is declining, or if growth is slipping, your rules may need a refresh.

The number of rules matters

Obviously, it's crucial to write the right rules. But it's also important to have the optimal number of rules. Thick manuals of rules can be paralyzing. They can keep managers from seeing opportunities and moving quickly enough to capture them. We worked with a computer maker, for example, whose minutely structured process for product innovation was highly efficient but left the company no flexibility to respond to market changes. On the other hand, too few rules can also paralyze. Managers chase too many opportunities or become confused about which to pursue and which to ignore. We worked with a biotech company that lagged behind the competition in forming successful partnerships, a key strategic process in that industry. Because the company lacked guidelines, development managers brought in deal after deal, and key scientists were pulled from clinical trials over and over again to perform due diligence. Senior management ended up rejecting most of the proposals. Executives may have had implicit rules, but nobody knew what they were. One business development manager lamented: "It would be so liberating if only I had a few guidelines about what I'm supposed to be looking for."

While creating the right number of rules – it's usually somewhere between two and seven – is central, companies arrive at the optimal number from different directions. On the one hand, young companies usually have too few rules, which prevents them from executing innovative ideas effectively. They need more structure, and they often have to build their simple rules from the ground up. On the other hand, older companies usually have too many rules, which keep them from competing effectively in turbulent markets. They need to throw out massively complex procedures and start over with a few easy-to-follow directives.

The optimal number of rules for a particular company can also shift over time, depending on the nature of the business opportunities. In a period of predictability and focused opportunities, a company should have more rules in order to increase efficiency. When the landscape becomes less predictable and the opportunities more diffuse, it makes sense to have fewer rules in order to increase flexibility. When Cisco started to acquire aggressively, the "75 people, 75% engineers" rule worked extremely well – it ensured a match with Cisco's entrepreneurial culture and left the company with lots of space to maneuver. As the company developed more clarity and focus in its home market, Cisco recognized the need for a few more rules: a target must share Cisco's vision of where the industry is headed, it must have potential for short-term wins with current products, it must have potential for long-term wins with the follow-on product generation, it must have geographic proximity to Cisco, and its culture must be compatible with Cisco's. If a potential acquisition meets all five criteria, it gets a green light. If it meets four, it gets a yellow light – further consideration is required. A candidate that meets fewer than four gets a red light. CEO John Chambers believes that observing these simple rules has helped Cisco resist the temptation to make inappropriate acquisitions. More recently, Cisco has relaxed its rules (especially on proximity) to accommodate new opportunities as the company moves further afield into new technologies and toward new customers.

How rules are created

We're often asked where simple rules come from. While it's appealing to think that they arise from clever thinking, they rarely do. More often, they grow out of experience, especially mistakes. Take Yahoo! and its partnership-creation rules. An exclusive joint venture with a major credit card company proved calamitous. The deal locked Yahoo! into a relationship with a particular firm, thereby limiting e-commerce opportunities. After an expensive exit, Yahoo! developed two simple rules for partnership creation: deals can't be exclusive, and the basic service is always free.

At young companies, where there is no history to learn from, senior executives use experience gained at other companies. CEO George Conrades of Akamai, for example, drew on his decades of marketing experience to focus his company on customer service – a surprising choice of strategy for a high-tech venture. He then declared some simple rules: the company must staff the customer service group with technical gurus, every question must be answered on the first call or e-mail, and R&D people must rotate through customer care. These how-to rules shaped customer service at Akamai but left plenty of room for employees to innovate with individual customers.

Most often, a rough outline of simple rules already exists in some implicit form. It takes an observant manager to make them explicit and then extend them as business opportunities evolve. (It's even possible to trace a young company's evolution by examining how its simple rules have been applied over time.) EBay, for example, started out with two strong values: egalitarianism and community – or, as one user put it, "capitalism for the rest of us." Over time, founder and chairman Pierre Omidyar and CEO Meg Whitman made those values explicit in simple rules that helped managers predict which opportunities would work for eBay. Egalitarianism evolved into two simple how-to rules for running auctions: the number of buyers and sellers must be balanced, and transactions must be as transparent as possible. The first rule equalizes the power of buyers and sellers but does not restrict who can participate, so the eBay site is open to everyone, from individual collectors to corporations (indeed, several major retailers now use eBay as a quiet channel for their merchandise). The second rule gives all participants equal access to as much information as possible. This rule guided eBay managers into a series of moves such as creating feedback ratings on sellers, on-line galleries for expensive items, and authentication services from Lloyd's of London.

The business meaning of community was crystallized into a few simple rules, too: product ads aren't allowed (they compete with the community), prices for basic services must not be raised (increases hurt small members), and eBay must uphold high safety standards (a community needs to feel safe). The rules further clarified which opportunities made sense. For instance, it was okay to launch the Power Sellers program, which offers extra services for community members who sell frequently. It was also okay to allow advertising by financial services companies and to expand into Europe, because neither move broke the rules or threatened the community. On the other hand, it was not okay to have advertising deals with companies such as CDnow whose merchandise competes with the community. Only later did the economic value of the rules become apparent: the strength of the eBay community posed a formidable entry barrier to competitors, while egalitarianism created a high level of trust and transparency among traders that effectively differentiated eBay from its competitors.

It's entirely possible for two companies to focus on the same key process yet develop radically different simple rules to govern it. Consider Ispat International and Cisco. In the last decade, Ispat has gone from running a single steel mill in Indonesia to being the fourth-largest steel company in the world by using a new-economy strategy in an old-economy business. Founder Lakshmi Mittal's strategy centers on the acquisition process. But Ispat's rules for acquisitions look a whole lot different from Cisco's for the same process.

Ispat's rules include buying established, state-owned companies that have problems. Cisco's rules limit its acquisitions to young, well-run, VC-backed companies. Ispat's rules don't include geographic restrictions, so managers search the globe – Mexico, Kazakhstan, Ireland – for ailing companies. At least initially, Cisco's rules required exactly the opposite focus – the company stayed close to home with lots of acquisitions in Silicon Valley. Ispat focuses narrowly on two process technologies – DRI and electric arc furnaces – to drive companywide consistency. At Cisco, the whole point is to acquire new technologies. Ispat's rules center on finding companies in which costs can be cut from current operations. Cisco's rules gauge revenue gains from future products. The bottom line: same strategic process, same entrepreneurial emphasis on seizing fleeting opportunities, same superior wealth creation – but with totally different simple rules.

Knowing when to change

It's important for companies with simple-rules strategies to follow the rules religiously – think Ten Commandments, not optional suggestions – to avoid the temptation to change them too frequently. A consistent strategy helps managers rapidly sort through all kinds of opportunities and gain short-term advantage by exploiting the attractive ones. More subtly, it can lead to patterns that build long-term advantage, such as Lego's powerful brand position and Cisco's interrelated networking technologies.

Although it's unwise to churn the rules, strategies do go stale. Shifting the rules can sometimes rejuvenate strategy, but if the problems are deep, switching strategic processes may be necessary. The ability to switch to new strategic processes has been a success secret of the best new-economy companies. For example, Inktomi, a leader in

Internet infrastructure software, augmented its original strategic focus on the product innovation process with a focus on the market entry process and a few boundary rules: the company must never produce a hardware product, never interface directly with end users, and always develop software for applications with many users and transactions (this exploits Inktomi's basic technology). Company managers did not restrict the business or revenue models. The result was successful new businesses in, for example, search engines, caching, and e-commerce engines. In fact, the company's second business, caching, is now its key growth driver. But CEO Dave Peterschmidt and his team have recently turned their attention to the sales process because corporations – a much bigger customer set than was available in their original portal market – are buying Inktomi software to manage intranets, thus opening a massive stream of new opportunities. Inktomi is turning to this new opportunity flow and crafting fresh simple rules. Inktomi is thus accelerating growth by adding new processes before old ones falter. If managers wait until the opportunity flow dries up before shifting processes, it's already too late . . .

What is strategy?

Like all effective strategies, strategy as simple rules is about being different. But that difference does not arise from tightly linked activity systems or leveraged core competencies, as in traditional strategies. It arises from focusing on key strategic processes and developing simple rules that shape those processes. When a pattern emerges from the processes – a pattern that creates network effects or economies of scale or scope – the result can be a long-term competitive advantage like the ones Intel and Microsoft achieved for over a decade. More often, the competitive advantage is short term.

The more significant point, though, is that no one can predict how long an advantage will last. An executive must manage, therefore, as if it could all end tomorrow. The new economy and other chaotic markets are too uncertain to do otherwise. From newcomers like Yahoo! founder Jerry Yang, who claims, "We live on the edge," to Dell's Michael Dell, who famously said, "The only constant is change," there's almost universal recognition that the most salient feature of competitive advantage in these markets is not sustainability but unpredictability.

In stable markets, managers can rely on complicated strategies built on detailed predictions of the future. But in complicated, fast-moving markets where significant growth and wealth creation can occur, unpredictability reigns. It makes sense to follow the lead of entrepreneurs and underdogs – seize opportunities in the here and now with a handful of rules and a few key processes. In other words, when business becomes complicated, strategy should be simple.

Reading 1.3 The first strategists *Stephen Cummings*

First published: (1993) 'Brief case: the first strategists', *Long Range Planning*, 26(3): 133–135. Reprinted from *Long Range Planning* 'Brief Case: The First Strategists', June 1993 with permission from Elsevier.

Origin of strategy

The word *strategy* derives from the ancient Athenian position of *strategos*. The title was coined in conjunction with the democratic reforms of Kleisthenes (508–7 BC), who developed a new sociopolitical structure in Athens after leading a popular revolution against a Spartan-supported oligarchy. Kleisthenes instituted 10 new tribal divisions, which acted as both military and political subunits of the district of Athens. At the head of each tribe was elected a strategos. Collectively, the 10 incumbent *strategoi* formed the Athenian war council. This council and its individual members, by virtue of the kudos granted them, also largely controlled nonmilitary politics.

Strategos was a compound of *stratos*; which meant 'army,' or more properly an encamped army *spread out* over ground (in this way *stratos* is also allied to *stratum*) and *agein*, 'to lead.' The emergence of the term paralleled increasing military decision-making complexity. Warfare had evolved to a point where winning sides no longer relied on the deeds of heroic individuals, but on the coordination of many units of men each fighting in close formation. Also, the increasing significance of naval forces in this period multiplied the variables a commander must consider in planning action. Consequently, questions of coordination and synergy among the various emergent units of their organizations became imperative considerations for successful commanders.

Of what interest are the origins of strategy to those engaging in strategic activities and decision making in organizations today? In the words of Adlai Stevenson, we can see our future clearly and wisely only when we know the path that leads to the present. Most involved in corporate strategy have little knowledge of where that path began. A great deal of insight into strategy can be gained from examining those from whom we inherit the term. The first strategists, the Greek strategoi, perhaps practiced strategy in its purest sense.

Strategy and strategist as defined by ancient theorists

Aineias the Tactician, who wrote the earliest surviving Western volume on military strategy, *How to Survive under Siege*, in the mid fourth century BC, was primarily concerned with how to deploy available manpower and other resources to best advantage. The term strategy is defined in more detail by Frontinus in the first century AD, as 'everything achieved by a commander, be it characterized by foresight, advantage, enterprise, or resolution.'

Ancient Athenian theorists also had clear ideas about the characteristics that were necessary in an effective strategos. According to Xenophon, a commander 'must be ingenious, energetic, careful, full of stamina and presence of mind, loving and tough, straightforward and crafty, alert and deceptive, ready to gamble everything and wishing to have everything, generous and greedy, trusting and suspicious.' These criteria for identifying an excellent strategist still ring true.

Xenophon goes on to describe the most important attribute for an aspiring strategos/statement as 'knowing the business which you propose to carry out.' The Athenians in this period were very concerned that their leaders had an awareness of how things worked at the 'coal-face.' Strategoi were publicly elected by their fellow members of the Athenian organization; and to be considered a credible candidate, one had to have worked one's way into this position by demonstrating prowess at both individual combat and hands-on military leadership. Wisdom was considered to be a citizen's ability to combine political acumen and practical intelligence, and strategoi should be the wisest of citizens. The organization's future lay in the hands of these men and, ipso facto, the strategic leadership of the Athenian organization was not to consider itself immune from hardship when times were tough: 'No man was fitted to give fair and honest advice in council if he has not, like his fellows, a family at stake in the hour of the city's danger.'

To the ancient Athenians strategy was very much a line of function. The formulation of strategy was a leadership task. The Athenian organization developed by Kleisthenes was extremely recursive. The new tribes, and the local communities that these tribes comprised, formed the units and subunits of the army, and were, in their sociopolitical structures, tantamount to the city-state in microcosm. Decision makers at all levels of the corporation were expected to think strategically, in accordance with the behavior exhibited by those in leadership roles at higher levels of the Athenian system. Strategoi were expected both to direct and take part in the thick of battle, leading their troops into action. For a strategos not to play an active combat role would have resulted in a significant diminution in the morale of those fighting for his tribe.

Practical lessons from the strategoi

If military practice is identified as a metaphor for business competition, the strategic principles of the great strategoi still provide useful guides for those in the business of strategy formulation today. For Pericles, perhaps the greatest of the Athenian strategoi, the goal of military strategies was 'to limit risk while holding fast to essential points and principles.' His often quoted maxims of 'Opportunity waits for no man' and 'Do not make any new conquests during the war' are still applicable advice in a modern business environment.

Epaminondas of Thebes was said to have brought the two arms of his military corporation, infantry and cavalry, together in a 'fruitful organizational blend.' The Theban's strategic principles included economy of force coupled with overwhelming strength at the decisive point; close coordination between units and meticulous staff planning combined with speed of attack; and as the quickest and most economical way of winning a decision, defeat of the competition not at his weakest point but at his strongest. Epaminondas was Philip of Macedon's mentor, and it was largely due to the application of the Theban's innovations that the Macedonian army grew to an extent where it was able to realize Alexander the Great's (Philip's son) vast ambitions. The close integration of all its individual units became the major strength of the Macedonian army organization.

Alexander himself is perhaps the most famous ancient exponent of a contingency approach to strategy. It is often told that as a young man he was asked by his tutor Aristotle what he would do in a given situation. Alexander replied that his answer would depend on the circumstances. Aristotle described a hypothetical set of circumstances and asked his original question again. To this the student answered, 'I cannot tell until the circumstances arise.' In practice Alexander was not often caught without a 'plan B.' An example is related by Frontinus: 'At Arbela, Alexander, fearing the numbers of the enemy, yet confident in the valour of his own troops, drew up a line of battle facing in all directions, in order that the men, if surrounded, might be able to fight from any side.'

Ancient approaches to the learning of strategy

The ancient Greeks took great interest in both the practical and theoretical aspects of strategic leadership. They favored the case method as the best means of passing this knowledge from one generation of strategists to the next.

Frontinus argued that 'in this way commanders will be furnished with specimens of wisdom and foresight, which will serve to foster their own power of conceiving and executing like deeds.' Aineias and Xenophon also used and championed such methods in ways that would please any Harvardophile. The best-crafted exposition of the case method, however, belongs to Plutarch, biographer to the ancient world's greatest leaders:

> It is true, of course, that our outward sense cannot avoid apprehending the various objects it encounters, merely by virtue of their impact and regardless of whether they are useful or not: but a man's conscious intellect is something which he may bring to bear or avert as he chooses, and can very easily transfer . . . to another object as he sees fit. For this reason, we ought to seek out virtue not merely to contemplate it, but to derive benefit from doing so. A colour, for example, is well suited to the eye if its bright and agreeable tones stimulate and refresh the vision, and in the same way we ought to apply our intellectual vision to those models which can inspire it to attain its own proper virtue through the sense of delight they arouse . . . [Such a model is] no sooner seen than it rouses the spectator into action, and yet it does not form his character by mere imitation, but by promoting the understanding of virtuous deeds it provides him with a dominating purpose.

Now, as then, our strategic vision can be refreshed and stimulated through studying the character and deeds of the great strategic leaders of the past.

Reading 1.4 Strategy as strategic decision making *Kathleen M. Eisenhardt*

First published: (1999) *Sloan Management Review,* Spring: 65–72. *MIT Sloan Management Review*, Spring 1999.

Many executives realize that to prosper in the coming decade, they need to turn to the fundamental issue of strategy. What is strategy? To use a simple yet powerful definition from *The Economist*, strategy answers two basic questions: "Where do you want to go?" and "How do you want to get there?[1]

Traditional approaches to strategy focus on the first question. They involve selecting an attractive market, choosing a defensible strategic position, or building core competencies. Only later, if at all, do executives address the second question. Yet in today's high-velocity, hotly competitive markets, these approaches are incomplete. They overemphasize executives ability to analyze and predict which industries, competencies, or strategic positions will be viable and for how long, and they underemphasize the challenge of actually creating effective strategies.

Many managers of successful corporations have adopted a different perspective on strategy that Shone Brown and I call "competing on the edge."[2] At the heart of this approach lies the recognition that strategy combines the questions of "where" and "how" to create a continuing flow of temporary and shifting competitive advantages. Executives from a variety of firms echo this perspective. John Browne, CEO of British Petroleum, stated, "No advantage and no success is ever permanent. The winners are those who keep moving."[3] Michael Dell, CEO of Dell, commented, "The only constant in our business is that everything is changing. We have to be ahead of the game."[4] But creating a series of shifting advantages is challenging. It requires effective strategic decision making at several levels: at the unit level, to improvise business strategy; at the multibusiness level, to create collective strategy and cross-business synergies; and at the corporate level, to articulate major inflection points in strategic direction.

This article describes strategy as strategic decision making, especially in rapidly changing markets. Its underlying assumption is that "bet the company" decisions – those that change the firm's direction and generate new competitive advantages – arise much more often in these markets. Therefore, the ability to make fast, widely supported, and high-quality strategic decisions on a frequent basis is the cornerstone of effective strategy. To use the language of contemporary strategy thinking, strategic decision making is the fundamental dynamic capability in excellent firms.

These ideas come from more than a decade of research on strategy in high-velocity markets. During one phase of that research, Jay Bourgeois and I examined top-management teams and their decisions in twelve entrepreneurial firms in Silicon Valley. Using questionnaires and open-ended interview questions, we studied decision speed, conflict over goals and key decision areas, executive power, and politics. In addition, we traced the multiple strategic decisions and firm and decision performance. During a second phase of research, Shona Brown and I studied six matched pairs of European, Asian, and North American multi-business firms (six dominant and six modestly successful ones) in the broader context of strategy. We gathered data on strategic decision making and other critical processes at multiple levels within these more complex firms.

In both studies, clear differences stood out between the: strategic decision-making processes in the more and less effective firms. Strikingly, these differences counter commonly held beliefs that conflict slows down choice, politicking is typical, and fast decisions are autocratic. In other words, these findings challenge the assumption of trade-offs among speed, quality, and support. Instead, the most effective strategic decision makers made choices that were fast, high quality, and widely supported. How did they do it? Four approaches emerged from this research and my other work with executives. Effective decision makers create strategy by:

- Building collective intuition that enhances the ability of a top-management team to see threats and opportunities sooner and more accurately.
- Stimulating quick conflict to improve the quality of strategic thinking without sacrificing significant time.
- Maintaining a disciplined pace that drives the decision process to a timely conclusion.
- Defusing political behavior that creates unproductive conflict and wastes time.

Build collective intuition

One myth of strategic decision making in high-velocity markets is that there is no time for formal meetings and no place for the careful consideration of extensive information. Executives, the thinking goes, should consider limited, decision-specific data, concentrate on one or two alternatives, and make decisions on the fly.

Effective strategic decision makers do not follow that approach. They use as much as or more information than ineffective executives, and they are far more likely to hold regularly scheduled, "don't miss" meetings. They rely on extensive, real-time information about internal and external operations, which they discuss in intensive meetings. They avoid both accounting-based information because it tends to lag behind the realities of the business and predictions of the future because these are likely to be wrong. From extensive, real-time information, these executives build a collective intuition that allows them to move quickly and accurately as opportunities arise.

A good example is Mercury (all company names in the study are pseudonyms), a highly successful computer venture whose management team is known for its ability to reposition the firm adroitly as opportunities shift. How do they do it? These managers claim to "measure everything." They examine an array of key operating performance metrics that they collectively track monthly, weekly, and sometimes daily: inventory speed, multiple cash-flow measures, average selling price of products, performance against sales goals, manufacturing yields, customer-acquisition costs, and gross margins by product and geographic region. They prefer operating information to more refined, accounting-based numbers. They also pay attention to innovation-related metrics such as sales from new products; time-related metrics such as trends in average sales size per transaction: rales such as number of new product introductions per quarter: and durations such as the time it takes to launch a product globally.

In addition to internal operations information, the managers at Mercury track external information: new product moves by competitors, competition at key accounts, technical developments within the industry, and industry "gossip." Mercury's top-management team members play key roles in gathering and reporting these data. Each has areas of information for which he or she is responsible. For example, the vice president of marketing tracks product introductions and exits by the competition. The vice president of R&D reports the latest information on the "technical pulse" of the industry.

Sharing information at "must attend" meetings is an essential part of building collective intuition. The interplay of ideas during these meetings enhances managers understanding of the data. At Saturn, a global leader in multiple technology-based businesses, the managers of each major business meet every four weeks in a day-long meeting to review the operating basics in their businesses and the state of the industry. Travel is frequent and necessary, but managers do not miss this meeting. As at Mercury, the emphasis is on real-time information, internal and external. In addition, each meeting covers one or two critical strategic issues facing either an individual business or the group of businesses as a whole. The result is a forum for signaling collaborative opportunities across businesses; and for shaping the collective strategy.

In contrast, less successful top-management teams rarely meet with their colleagues in a group. Meetings are infrequent or skipped because of travel commitments. These executives typically make fewer and larger strategic choices. When they do turn their attention to important decisions, they rely on market analyses and future trend projections that are idiosyncratic to the particular decision. The result is groups of strangers who have difficulty engaging with one another productively. While they may each be knowledgeable in their own areas of responsibility, they do not develop collective intuition.

For example, at Aspen, a mediocre computer firm, the managers say they communicate frequently with the CEO but not with each other. One executive sketched herself as an "intelligent observer," detached from her colleagues. Another confided, "I don't really know the rest of the team."

In one decision that involved a reconfiguration of the product mix in several manufacturing plants, the senior executives delegated the analysis to staff and did not return to the topic for four months. During the interim, the staff painstakingly assembled plant performance metrics that were routine at the more successful firms. The executive team then commissioned more analyses while they familiarized themselves with the issues.

Why do real-time information and "must attend" meetings lead to more effective strategic decision making? Intense interaction creates teams of managers who know each other well. Familiarity and friendship make frank conversation easier because people are less constrained by politeness und more willing to express diverse views. The strategic decision process then moves more quickly and benefits from high-quality information. For example, one manager at Mercury described the interactions as "open and direct." Another explained more graphically, "We get it out on the table and yell about it."

In addition, with intense interaction, managers naturally organize antipodal team-member roles, such as short-term versus long-term or status quo versus change.[5] At Mercury, for example, the vice president of marketing was seen as "constantly thinking about the future" whereas the vice president of engineering was considered to be the keeper of the status quo. Describing the interplay of their relationship, the engineering vice president said, "I depend on her to watch out for tomorrow – I look out for today." A range of perspectives improves decision quality by ensuring that managers consider different sides of the issue.

Most important, when intense interaction focuses on the operating metrics of today's businesses, a deep intuition, or "gut feeling," is created, giving managers a superior grasp of changing competitive dynamics. Artificial intelligence research on championship chess players indicates how this intuition is formed. These players, for example, develop their so-called intuition through experience. Through frequent play, they gain the ability to recognize and process information in patterns or blocks that form the basis of intuition. This patterned processing (what we term "intuition") is faster and more accurate than processing single pieces of information. Consistent with this research, many effective decision makers were described by their colleagues as having "an immense instinctive feel," "a high quality of understanding," and "an intuitive sense of the business." This intuition gives managers a head start in recognizing and understanding strategic issues.

Stimulate quick conflict

In high-velocity markets, many executives are tempted to avoid conflict. They assume that conflict will bog down the decision-making process in endless debate and degenerate into personal attacks. They seek to move quickly toward a few alternatives, analyze the best ones, and make a quick choice that beats the competition to the punch.

Reality is different. In dynamic markets, conflict is a natural feature of high-stakes decision making because reasonable managers will often diverge in their views on how the marketplace will unfold. Furthermore, as research demonstrates, conflict stimulates innovative thinking, creates a fuller understanding of options, and improves decision effectiveness. Without conflict, decision makers commonly miss opportunities to question assumptions and overlook key elements of the decision. Given the value of conflict, effective strategic decision makers in rapidly changing markets not only tolerate conflict, they accelerate it.

One way that executives accelerate conflict is by assembling executive teams that are diverse in age, gender, functional background, and corporate experience. At Venus, a high-growth venture in Silicon Valley, the executive team ranges in age from late twenties to mid-fifties. The group includes several Europeans and a woman. Two members hold PhDs in electrical engineering and computer science, respectively. The president has an economics degree, an MBA, and manufacturing experience. The vice president of engineering came from a competitor, while the senior sales executive is a well-traveled industry veteran who had been at a number of firms before settling at Venus several years ago.

Like their counterparts at other successful firms, these executives say that they argue much of the time. The vice president of finance stated, "We all have different opinions." Another executive observed, "The group is very vocal. They all bring their own ideas." Particularly striking are the differences in perspectives across the age groups. The older executives usually rely on their expertise from the industry and from other companies to understand strategic choices. They have strong industry connections that pave the way for valuable collaborations with other firms. The younger executives bring in fresh ideas about how to compete and how to exploit the latest technology.

An alliance decision served to demonstrate the difference in outlook. Several of the experienced managers had been involved with both successful and unsuccessful alliances. They described an alliance as a "marriage between equals." The younger managers framed alliances as a way to gain money and credibility. Their take was that alliance partners were temporary "fellow travelers," not lifetime partners. They saw partners simultaneously as friends and foe. The Venus team engaged in extensive debate about alliances. The result was an innovative, alliance-led growth strategy that synthesized the flexible strategic thinking of the younger team members with the realism of the more mature managers. Describing these interactions, the vice president of marketing commented, "We scream a lot, laugh, and resolve the issues."

Another way that effective strategic decision makers accelerate conflict is by using "frame-breaking" tactics that create alternatives to obvious points of view. One technique is scenario planning: teams systematically consider strategic decisions in the light of several possible future states. Other techniques have executives advocate alternatives that they may or may not favor and perform role-plays of competitors. The details of the techniques are not crucial. Rather, the point is to use and switch among them to prevent stale thinking.

Jupiter, a multibusiness technology firm that has made highly successful acquisitions, provides a good illustration of how the techniques work. One acquisition included a stray business that was not part of the rationale for the purchase. The strategic decision focused on what to do with this business. Managers explored alternatives by creating scenarios of possible futures – such as the Unix operating system prevailing over Microsoft NT or wireless phones becoming more essential then PCs – and then considering how each alternative would play out. They also role-played different competitors to anticipate their responses. In addition, team members used the scenarios to do what is known as "backcasting" to extend their thinking. They envisioned their preferred future (i.e., one in which their firm dominated the market) and then thought backwards about how this ideal future might evolve.

Perhaps the most powerful way to accelerate conflict is by creating multiple alternatives. The idea is to develop alternatives as quickly as possible so that the team can work with an array of possibilities simultaneously. As one executive at Jupiter commented, "We play a larger set of options than most people." It is considered entirely appropriate for executives to advocate options that they may not prefer simply to encourage debate.

The executive team at Jupiter, for example, launched its decision-making process to deal with the stray business by quickly developing several alternatives for that business. One called for the acquired business to operate as a new stand-alone division. The second option was to graft the business onto an existing Jupiter strategic business unit; the two businesses could then leverage a common marketing channel. A third option was to combine the business with an existing one with a complementary technology; this combination of businesses would then have sufficient scale to develop the technologies into a more viable business. The final option was to sell the business. Jupiter's executive team quickly compared options, explored them using the frame-breaking tactics noted above, and chose the third. As one executive observed, "There should be three or four solutions to everything." Added another, "We have a preference for working a multiple array of possibilities instead of just a couple."

Why do diverse teams, frame-breaking techniques, and multiple alternatives lead to faster conflict and ultimately more effective decisions? The rationale for diverse teams is clear: these teams come up with more varied viewpoints than homogeneous teams. The value of frame-breaking techniques is more subtle. In addition to the obvious benefit of generating many different perspectives, these techniques establish the norm that constructive conflict is an expected part of the strategic decision-making process. It is. acceptable and even desirable to engage in conflict. Furthermore, frame-breaking techniques are intellectually engaging and even fun. They can motivate even apathetic executives to participate more actively in expansive strategic thinking.

The power of multiple alternatives comes from several sources. Clearly, pushing for multiple alternatives speeds up conflict by stimulating executives to develop divergent options. It also enables them to rapidly compare alternatives, helping them to better understand their own preferences. Furthermore, multiple alternatives provide executives with the confidence that they have not overlooked a superior option. That confidence is crucial in rapidly changing markets, where the blocks to effective decision making are emotional as much as cognitive. Finally, multiple alternatives defuse the interpersonal tension that can accompany conflict by giving team members room to maneuver and save face when they disagree. One Jupiter manager told us, for example, that he was strongly against selling the business or setting it up as a stand-alone division. But he could "live with" either of the two combination options.

Maintain the pace

Less effective strategic decision makers face a dilemma. On the one hand, they believe that every strategic decision is unique. Each requires its own analytical approach, and each unfolds in its own way. On the other hand, these same decision makers believe that they must decide as quickly as possible. Yet making quick choices conflicts with making one-of-a-kind choices.

Effective strategic decision makers avoid this dilemma by focusing on maintaining decision pace, not pushing decision speed. They launch the decision-making process promptly, keep up the energy surrounding the process, and cut off debate at the appropriate moment. They drive strategic decision-making momentum.

One way that these decision makers maintain decision pace is by following the natural rhythm of strategic choice.[6] They use rules of thumb for how long a major decision should take. Surprisingly, that metric is a fairly constant two to four months. If a decision takes longer, then the management team is trying to decide too big an issue or is procrastinating. If a decision takes less time, then the decision is not strategic enough to warrant management team attention. These decision makers are able to gauge the scale of a decision by recognizing similarities among strategic decisions. That is, each strategic decision is different, but it falls into familiar patterns whose scope and timing are well-known – for example, new product, new technology, or acquisition decisions. They also view a decision as part of a larger web of strategic choices. This allows executives to adjust the scope of a decision to fit the allotted time frame as the process unfolds. Plus, placing strategic decisions in a larger context lowers the emotional stakes of a choice.

The top-management ream at Mars, a leading technology firm, uses a rhythm of three to four months for strategic decisions. Typical strategic decisions include entering or exiting markets, investing in new technology, building manufacturing capacity, or forming strategic partnerships. A decision arose concerning how to enter an emerging Internet-based market in e-commerce tools. Although the team had much to learn about the internet. Mars executives framed the issue as a market-entry decision; as a result, they knew how to begin to gather relevant data. Because they estimated that the decision should take three months, Mars executives could establish milestones and adjust the decision scope as needed to fit the time frame. As the decision-making process progressed. team members realized that the market opportunity fit into a more complex context of e-commerce business than they had originally envisioned. They therefore reconceptualized the immediate strategic choice as part of the larger e-commerce effort and expanded the size of the market under consideration.

In addition, executives maintain pace by prototyping decisions as they analyze them. Instead of merely analyzing options in the abstract, they test them. For example, the Mars executives simultaneously explored relationships with several potential partners to jointly develop e-commerce tools and tested alternative, in-house product designs with several marquee customers. As a result, they were able to hone their understanding of which tools were essential for their e-commerce entry even as they began to implement parts of the final decision.

Effective strategic decision makers skillfully cut off debate, typically using a two-step method called "consensus with qualification" to bring decision making to a close. First, managers conduct the decision process itself with the goal of consensus in mind. If they reach consensus, the choice is made. If consensus does not emerge, they break the deadlock using a decision rule such as voting or, more commonly, allowing the manager with the largest stake in the outcome to make the decision. In the case of the e-commerce entry decision, Mars executives were divided over whether to develop a key product in-house or in partnership with another firm. The CEO and the vice president of engineering finally made the call. Not everyone agreed with the choice, but each team member had a legitimate voice in the process. As one executive told us, "Most of the time we reach consensus, but when we can't, Gary [the CEO] pulls the trigger."

In contrast, less successful strategic decision makers stress the rarity and significance of strategic choices. Because the choice then looms so large, they often procrastinate at the start of the decision-making process. Later, they lack a method for pacing their efforts. They oscillate between letting critical issues languish and making "shot gun" strategic choices against deadlines, as the case of Copper, a modestly successful multibusiness computing firm, illustrates. Managers faced a choice over how to organize a sales channel that was to be shared by several businesses. Sharing the channel offered benefits through cost-sharing and cross-selling of products. Although the opportunity had been apparent for some time, the managers did not get around to doing anything for several months. Everyone was avoiding what appeared to be a big task. Once they did get moving, they attempted to come up with a plan that all the major stakeholders would accept. The decision process stretched out over eight months, with most managers becoming frustrated by the seemingly endless meetings to gain consensus. Several disengaged from the process. Eventually, the head of one major business simply implemented his choice with the field sales force, and the rest of the business heads were left scrambling.

Decision-making rhythm helps managers plan their progress and forces them to recognize the familiar aspects of decision making that make the process more predictable. As significant, it emphasizes that hitting decision liming is more critical than forging consensus or developing massive data analyses. As one manager told us, "The worst decision is no decision at all." Prototyping encourages managers to take concrete actions that remove some of the unpredictability that can trigger procrastination. Furthermore, prototyping keeps managers focused on the goal of executing a choice and even begins the implementation process. The result is momentum that lowers the cognitive and emotional barriers to choice and that spurs managers toward a conclusion.

Consensus with qualification maintains the pace by taking a realistic view of conflict as valuable and inevitable. Therefore, the endless search for consensus emerges as a fruitless goal. At the same time, consensus with qualification allows decision makers to resolve conflict (and so maintain pace) in a way that team members perceive as equitable. Most managers want a strong voice in the decision-making process but do not believe that they must always get their preferred choice. Consensus with qualification lets decision makers drive decision pace by providing an effective way to reach closure without consensus. For example, at Mars, all the key managers contributed to the market-entry discussion. But when it became apparent that they were stuck in two opposing camps, the CEO and VP of engineering made the call. As one manager observed, "Consensus is nice, but we have to keep up with the train."

Defuse politics

Some executives believe that politics are a natural part of strategic choice. They see strategic decision making as involving high stakes that compel managers to lobby one another, manipulate information, and form coalitions. The game quickly becomes a competition among ambitious managers.

More effective strategic decision makers take a negative view of politicking. Since politicking often involves managers using information to their own advantage, it distorts the information base, leading to a poor strategic decision-making process. Furthermore, these executives see political activity as wasting valuable time. Their perspective is collaborative, not competitive, setting limits on politics and, more generally, interpersonal conflict.

One way in which effective executives defuse politics, is by creating common goals. These goals do not imply homogeneous thinking. Rather, they suggest that managers have a shared vision of where they want to be or who their external competitors are. Managers at Neptune, a successful multibusiness computing firm, are highly aware of their external competition. At their monthly meetings, they pay close attention to the moves of the competition and personalize that competition by referring to individual managers in competitor companies, particularly their direct counterparts. They have a clear collective goal for their own ranking and market-share position in the industry. It is to be number one. At Intel, managers typically contend that "only the paranoid survive." Neptune's managers have their own more positive rallying cry: "Let's get rich together!"

A more direct way to defuse politics is through a balanced power structure in which each key decision maker has a clear area of responsibility, but in which the leader is the most powerful decision maker. At Venus, the CEO is described as a "team player." Quantitative ratings and qualitative descriptions reveal that he is the most powerful person on the executive team, but that he directs decision making only in the arena of corporate organization. Other members of the executive team direct other decisions: the vice president of engineering runs the product development portfolio, the vice president of manufacturing makes the key supply-chain choices, and so on. As one manager pointed out, "Kim [the CEO] believes in hiring great people and letting them am their own shows." Paradoxically, the clear delineation of responsibility makes it easier for managers to help one another and share information because each executive operates from a secure power base. As another manager told us, "We just don't worry much about an internal pecking order."

Humor defuses politics. Effective strategic decision makers often relieve tension by making business fun. They emphasize the excitement of fast-paced markets and the "rush" of competing in these settings. Senior executives at Mercury have articulated "fun" as a management goal. Laughter is common, and practical jokes are popular, especially around April Fool's Day and Halloween.

Less effective strategic decision makers usually have an inward, competitive focus. As a result, they lack the sense of teamwork that characterizes more effective teams. The power structure is typically dysfunctional. A good example is Targhee, a modestly successful Internet firm, where the general manager dominates virtually every aspect of the business. As one manager commented, "Chuck runs the entire show." The result is that the managers who work for Chuck concentrate on impressing him rather than on making smart strategic choices. Another manager observed, "We're all trying to maneuver around to look good in front of Chuck." To make matters worse. Chuck constantly blurred the lines of responsibility, leaving managers insecure and jockeying for position. Noted another manager, "It's like a gun about to go off. I just try to stay out of the cross-fire."

Common goals, clear areas of responsibility, and humor defuse politicking and interpersonal conflict. Goals that stress collective success or common enemies give managers a sense of shared fate. They see themselves as players on the same team, not as competitors. A balanced power structure gives managers a sense of security that dispels the assumption that they need to engage in politicking. For example, at Venus, there was little evidence of politicking. As one manager stated, "We don't have time for politics. I barely gel to the meetings. Another said, "We don't have any kind of political stuff. Nobody lobbies behind other people's backs. We just get everything out and talk about it. A third commented, "We're very apolitical." As a result, managers did not hold back information, wasted less time on politics, and made faster, more informed decisions.

Humor strengthens the collaborative outlook. It puts people into a positive mood. Research has shown that people whose frame of mind is positive have more accurate perceptions of each other's arguments and are more optimistic, creative in their problem solving, forgiving, and collaborative. Humor also allows managers to convey negative information in a less-threatening way. Managers can say something as a joke that might otherwise be offensive.[7]

Toward effective strategic decision making

In high-velocity, hotly competitive markets, traditional approaches to strategy give way to "competing on the edge," where strategic decision making is the fundamental capability leading to superior performance. After all, when strategy is a flow of shifting competitive advantages, the choices that shape strategy matter greatly and occur frequently.

The research data corroborate this view, demonstrating that firms with high performance in profitability, growth, and marketplace reputation have superior (i.e., fast, high-quality, and widely supported) strategic decision making processes. These processes support the emergence of effective strategy. Firms that were more modest performers had strategic decision-making processes that were slower and more political. Their strategies were more predictable and less effective. Executives in these firms often recognized that their strategic decision making was flawed, but they did not know how to fix it.

I have described the four keys to strategy as strategic decision making:

- Set the stage by building collective intuition through frequent meetings and real-time metrics that enhance a management team's ability to see threats and opportunities sooner and more accurately.
- Stimulate quick conflict by assembling diverse teams, challenging them through frame-breaking heuristics, and stressing multiple alternatives in order to improve the quality of decision making.
- Discipline the timing of strategic decision making through time pacing, prototyping, and consensus with qualification to sustain the momentum of strategic choice.
- Defuse politics by emphasizing common goals and clear turf, and having fun. These tactics keep decision makers from slipping into destructive interpersonal conflict and time-wasting politics.

Taken together, these approaches direct executive attention toward strategic decision making as the cornerstone of effective strategy.

References

1. "Making Strategy," *The Economist*, 1 March 1997.

2. For a managerial perspective, see: S.L Brown and K.M. Eisenhardt, *Competing on the Edge: Strategy as Structured Chaos* (Boston: Harvard Business School Press, 1998). For an academic perspective, see: S.L. Brown and K.M. Eisenhardt, "The Art of Continuous Change: Linking Complexity and Time-paced Evolution in Relentlessly Shifting Organizations." *Administrative Science Quarterly*, volume 42, March 1997, pp. 1–34.

3. S. Prokesh, "Unleashing the Power of Learning: An Interview with British Petroleum's John Browne," *Harvard Business Review*, volume 75. September–October 1997, p. 166.

4. D. Narayandas, "Dell Computer Corporation" (Boston: Harvard Business School, case 9-596-058, 19961.

5. For ideas on interaction, see: H. Guetzkow, "Differentiation of Roles in Task-oriented Groups." in D. Cartwright and A. Zander, eds., *Group Dynamics: Research and Theory* (New York: Harper & Row, 1968.

6. For more information on time pacing, see: C.J.G. Gersick, "Pacing Strategic Change: The Case of a New Venture," *Academy of Management Journal*, volume 37, February 1995, pp. 9–45.

7. For more information on successful negotiation. see: R. Pinkley and G. Northcraft, "Conflict Frames of Reference: Implications for Dispute Processes and Outcomes." *Academy of Management Journal*, volume 37. February 1994, pp. 193–205: D. Tjosvold, *The Positive-Conflict Organization* (Reading, Massachusetts: Addison-Wesley, 1991): and R. Fisher and W. Ury, *Getting to Yes: Negotiating Agreement without Giving In* (Boston: Houghton Mifflin, 1981).

Reading 1.5 Crafting strategy *Henry Mintzberg*

First published: (1987) *Harvard Business Review*, July–August: 66–75. Reprinted by permission of *Harvard Business Review*. 'Crafting Strategy' by Henry Mintzberg, July 01/1987.

Imagine someone planning strategy. What likely springs to mind is an image of orderly thinking: a senior manager, or a group of them, sitting in an office formulating courses of action that everyone else will implement on schedule. The keynote is reason – rational control, the systematic analysis of competitors and markets, of company strengths and weaknesses, the combination of these analyses producing clear, explicit, full-blown strategies.

Now imagine someone *crafting* strategy. A wholly different image likely results, as different from planning as craft is from mechanization. Craft evokes traditional skill, dedication, perfection through the mastery of detail. What springs to mind is not so much thinking and reason as involvement, a feeling of intimacy and harmony with the materials at hand, developed through long experience and commitment. Formulation and implementation merge into a fluid process of learning through which creative strategies evolve.

My thesis is simple: the crafting image better captures the process by which effective strategies come to be. The planning image, long popular in the literature, distorts these processes and thereby misguides organizations that embrace it unreservedly.

In developing this thesis, I shall draw on the experiences of a single craftsman, a potter, and compare them with the results of a research project that tracked the strategies of a number of corporations across several decades. Because the two contexts are so obviously different, my metaphor, like my assertion, may seem far-fetched at first. Yet if we think of a craftsman as an organization of one, we can see that he or she must also resolve one of the great challenges the corporate strategist faces: knowing the organization's capabilities well enough to think deeply enough about its strategic direction. By considering strategy making from the perspective of one person, free of all the paraphernalia of what has been called the strategy industry, we can learn something about the formation of strategy in the corporation. For much as our potter has to manage her craft, so too managers have to craft their strategy.

At work, the potter sits before a lump of clay on the wheel. Her mind is on the clay, but she is also aware of sitting between her past experiences and her future prospects. She knows exactly what has and has not worked for her in the past. She has an intimate knowledge of her work, her capabilities, and her markets. As a craftsman, she senses rather than analyzes these things; her knowledge is "tacit." All these things are working in her mind as her hands are working the clay. The product that emerges on the wheel is likely to be in the tradition of her past work, but she may break away and embark on a new direction. Even so, the past is no less present, projecting itself into the future.

In my metaphor, managers are craftsmen and strategy is their clay. Like the potter, they sit between a past of corporate capabilities and a future of market opportunities. And if they are truly craftsmen, they bring to their work an equally intimate knowledge of the materials at hand. That is the essence of crafting strategy.

In the pages that follow, we will explore this metaphor by looking at how strategies get made as opposed to how they are supposed to get made. Throughout, I will be drawing on the two sets of experiences I've mentioned. One, described in the insert, is a research project on patterns in strategy formation that has been going on at McGill University under my direction since 1971. The second is the stream of work of a successful potter, my wife, who began her craft in 1967.

Strategies are both plans for the future and patterns from the past

Ask almost anyone what strategy is, and they will define it as a plan of some sort, an explicit guide to future behavior. Then ask them what strategy a competitor or a government or even they themselves have actually pursued. Chances are they will describe consistency in *past* behaviour – a pattern in action over time. Strategy, it turns out, is one of those words that people define in one way and often use in another, without realizing the difference.

The reason for this is simple. Strategy's formal definition and its Greek military origins notwithstanding, we need the word as much to explain past actions as to describe intended behavior. After all, if strategies can be planned and intended, they can also be pursued and realized (or not realized, as the case may be). And pattern in action, or what we call realized strategy, explains that pursuit. Moreover, just as a plan need not produce a pattern (some strategies that are intended are simply not realized), so too a pattern need not result from a plan. An organization can have a pattern (or realized strategy) without knowing it, let alone making it explicit.

Patterns, like beauty, are in the mind of the beholder, of course. But anyone reviewing a chronological lineup of our craftsman's work would have little trouble discerning clear patterns, at least in certain periods. Until 1974, for example, she made small, decorative ceramic animals and objects of various kinds. Then this "knick-knack strategy" stopped abruptly, and eventually new patterns formed around wafer-like sculptures and ceramic bowls, highly textured and unglazed.

Finding equivalent patterns in action for organizations isn't that much more difficult. Indeed, for such large companies as Volkswagenwerk and Air Canada, in our research, it proved simpler! (As well it should. A craftsman, after all, can change what she does in a studio a lot more easily than a Volkswagenwerk can retool its assembly lines.) Mapping the product models at Volkswagenwerk from the late 1940s to the late 1970s, for example, uncovers a clear pattern of concentration on the Beetle, followed in the late 1960s by a frantic search for replacements through acquisitions and internally developed new models, to a strategic reorientation around more stylish, water-cooled, front-wheel-drive vehicles in the mid-1970s.

But what about intended strategies, those formal plans and pronouncements we think of when we use the term *strategy*? Ironically, here we run into all kinds of problems. Even with a single craftsman, how can we know what her intended strategies really were? If we could go back, would we find expressions of intention? And if we could, would we be able to trust them? We often fool ourselves, as well as others, by denying our subconscious motives. And remember that intentions are cheap, at least when compared with realizations.

Reading the organization's mind

If you believe all this has more to do with the Freudian recesses of a craftsman's mind than with the practical realities of producing automobiles, then think again. For who knows what the intended strategies of a Volkswagenwerk really mean, let alone what they are? Can we simply assume in this collective context that the company's intended strategies are represented by its formal plans or by other statements emanating from the executive suite? Might these be just vain hopes or rationalizations or ploys to fool the competition? And even if expressed intentions exist, to what extent do others in the organization share them? How do we read the collective mind? Who is the strategist anyway?

The traditional view of strategic management resolves these problems quite simply, by what organizational theorists call attribution. You see it all the time in the business press. When General Motors acts, it's because Roger Smith has made a strategy. Given realization, there must have been intention, and that is automatically attributed to the chief.

In a short magazine article, this assumption is understandable. Journalists don't have a lot of time to uncover the origins of strategy, and GM is a large, complicated organization. But just consider all the complexity and confusion that gets tucked under this assumption – all the meetings and debates, the many people, the dead ends, the folding and unfolding of ideas. Now imagine trying to build a formal strategy-making system around that assumption. Is it any wonder that formal strategic planning is often such a resounding failure?

To unravel some of the confusion – and move away from the artificial complexity we have piled around the strategy-making process – we need to get back to some basic concepts. The most basic of all is the intimate connection between thought and action. That is the key to craft, and so also to the crafting of strategy.

Strategies need not be deliberate – they can also emerge

Virtually everything that has been written about strategy making depicts it as a deliberate process. First we think, then we act. We formulate, then we implement. The progression seems so perfectly sensible. Why would anybody want to proceed differently?

Our potter is in the studio, rolling the clay to make a waferlike sculpture. The clay sticks to the rolling pin, and a round form appears. Why not make a cylindrical vase? One idea leads to another, until a new pattern forms. Action has driven thinking: a strategy has emerged.

Out in the field, a salesman visits a customer. The product isn't quite right, and together they work out some modifications. The salesman returns to his company and puts the changes through; after two or three more rounds, they finally get it right. A new product emerges, which eventually opens up a new market. The company has changed strategic course.

In fact, most salespeople are less fortunate than this one or than our craftsman. In an organization of one, the implementor is the formulator, so innovations can be incorporated into strategy quickly and easily. In a large organization, the innovator may be ten levels removed from the leader who is supposed to dictate strategy and may also have to sell the idea to dozens of peers doing the same job.

Some salespeople, of course, can proceed on their own, modifying products to suit their customers and convincing skunkworks in the factory to produce them. In effect, they pursue their own strategies. Maybe no one else notices or cares. Sometimes, however, their innovations do get noticed, perhaps years later, when the company's prevalent strategies have broken down and its leaders are groping for something new. Then the salesperson's strategy may be allowed to pervade the system, to become organizational.

Is this story farfetched? Certainly not. We've all heard stories like it. But since we tend to see only what we believe, if we believe that strategies have to be planned, we're unlikely to see the real meaning such stories hold.

Consider how the National Film Board of Canada (NFB) came to adopt a feature-film strategy. The NFB is a federal government agency, famous for its creativity and expert in the production of short documentaries. Some years back, it funded a filmmaker on a project that unexpectedly ran long. To distribute his film, the NFB turned to theaters and so inadvertently gained experience in marketing feature-length films. Other filmmakers caught onto the idea, and eventually the NFB found itself pursuing a feature-film strategy – a pattern of producing such films.

My point is simple, deceptively simple: strategies can *form* as well as be *formulated.* A realized strategy can emerge in response to an evolving situation, or it can be brought about deliberately, through a process of formulation followed by implementation. But when these planned intentions do not produce the desired actions, organizations are left with unrealized strategies.

Today we hear a great deal about unrealized strategies, almost always in concert with the claim that implementation has failed. Management has been lax, controls have been loose, people haven't been committed. Excuses abound. At times, indeed, they may be valid. But often these explanations prove too easy. So some people look beyond implementation to formulation. The strategists haven't been smart enough.

While it is certainly true that many intended strategies are ill conceived, I believe that the problem often lies one step beyond, in the distinction we make between formulation and implementation, the common assumption that thought must be independent of (and precede) action. Sure, people could be smarter – but not only by conceiving more clever strategies. Sometimes they can be smarter by allowing their strategies to develop gradually, through the organization's actions and experiences. Smart strategists appreciate that they cannot always be smart enough to think through everything in advance.

Hands & minds

No craftsman thinks some days and works others. The craftsman's mind is going constantly, in tandem with her hands. Yet large organizations try to separate the work of minds and hands. In so doing, they often sever the vital feedback link between the two. The salesperson who finds a customer with an unmet need may possess the most strategic bit of information in the entire organization. But that information is useless if he or she cannot create a strategy in response to it or else convey the information to someone who can – because the channels are blocked or because the formulators have simply finished formulating. The notion that strategy is something that should happen way up there, far removed from the details of running an organization on a daily basis, is one of the great fallacies of conventional strategic management. And it explains a good many of the most dramatic failures in business and public policy today.

We at McGill call strategies like the NFB's that appear without clear intentions – or in spite of them – emergent strategies. Actions simply converge into patterns. They may become deliberate, of course, if the pattern is recognized and then legitimated by senior management. But that's after the fact.

All this may sound rather strange, I know. Strategies that emerge? Managers who acknowledge strategies already formed? Over the years, our research group at McGill has met with a good deal of resistance from people upset by what they perceive to be our passive definition of a word so bound up with proactive behavior and free will. After all, strategy means control – the ancient Greeks used it to describe the art of the army general.

Strategic learning

But we have persisted in this usage for one reason: learning. Purely deliberate strategy precludes learning once the strategy is formulated; emergent strategy fosters it. People take actions one by one and respond to them, so that patterns eventually form.

Our craftsman tries to make a freestanding sculptural form. It doesn't work, so she rounds it a bit here, flattens it a bit there. The result looks better, but still isn't quite right. She makes another and another and another. Eventually, after days or months or years, she finally has what she wants. She is off on a new strategy

In practice, of course, all strategy making walks on two feet, one deliberate, the other emergent. For just as purely deliberate strategy making precludes learning, so purely emergent strategy making precludes control. Pushed to the limit, neither approach makes much sense. Learning must be coupled with control. That is why the McGill research group uses the word *strategy* for both emergent and deliberate behavior.

Likewise, there is no such thing as a purely deliberate strategy or a purely emergent one. No organization – not even the ones commanded by those ancient Greek generals – knows enough to work everything out in advance, to ignore learning en route. And no one – not even a solitary potter – can be flexible enough to leave everything to happenstance, to give up all control. Craft requires control just as it requires responsiveness to the material at hand. Thus deliberate and emergent strategy form the end points of a continuum along which the strategies that are crafted in the real world may be found. Some strategies may approach either end, but many more fall at intermediate points.

Effective strategies develop in all kinds of strange ways

Effective strategies can show up in the strangest places and develop through the most unexpected means. There is no one best way to make strategy.

The form for a cat collapses on the wheel, and our potter sees a bull taking shape. Clay sticks to a rolling pin, and a line of cylinders results. Wafers come into being because of a shortage of clay and limited kiln space in a studio in France. Thus errors become opportunities, and limitations stimulate creativity. The natural propensity to experiment, even boredom, likewise stimulate strategic change.

Organizations that craft their strategies have similar experiences. Recall the National Film Board with its inadvertently long film. Or consider its experiences with experimental films, which made special use of animation and sound. For 20 years, the NFB produced a bare but steady trickle of such films. In fact, every film but one in that trickle was produced by a single person, Norman McLaren, the NFB's most celebrated filmmaker. McLaren pursued a *personal strategy* of experimentation, deliberate for him perhaps (though who can know whether he had the whole stream in mind or simply planned one film at a time?) but not for the organization. Then 20 years later, others followed his lead and the trickle widened, his personal strategy becoming more broadly organizational.

Conversely, in 1952, when television came to Canada, a *consensus strategy* quickly emerged at the NFB. Senior management was not keen on producing films for the new medium. But while the arguments raged, one filmmaker quietly went off and made a single series for TV. That precedent set, one by one his colleagues leapt in, and within months the NFB – and its management – found themselves committed for several years to a new strategy with an intensity unmatched before or since. This consensus strategy arose spontaneously, as a result of many independent decisions made by the filmmakers about the films they wished to make. Can we call this strategy deliberate? For the filmmakers perhaps; for senior management certainly not. But for the organization? It all depends on your perspective, on how you choose to read the organization's mind.

While the NFB may seem like an extreme case, it highlights behavior that can be found, albeit in muted form, in all organizations. Those who doubt this might read Richard Pascale's account of how Honda stumbled into its enormous success in the American motorcycle market. Brilliant as its strategy may have looked after the fact, Honda's managers made almost every conceivable mistake until the market finally hit them over the head with the right formula. The Honda managers on site in America, driving their products themselves (and thus inadvertently picking up market reaction), did only one thing right: they learned, firsthand.

Grass-roots strategy making

These strategies all reflect, in whole or part, what we like to call a grass-roots approach to strategic management. Strategies grow like weeds in a garden. They take root in all kinds of places, wherever people have the capacity to learn (because they are in touch with the situation) and the resources to support that capacity. These strategies become organizational when they become collective, that is, when they proliferate to guide the behavior of the organization at large.

Of course, this view is overstated. But it is no less extreme than the conventional view of strategic management, which might be labeled the hothouse approach. Neither is right. Reality falls between the two. Some of the most effective strategies we uncovered in our research combined deliberation and control with flexibility and organizational learning.

Consider first what we call the *umbrella strategy.* Here senior management sets out broad guidelines (say, to produce only high-margin products at the cutting edge of technology or to favor products using bonding technology) and leaves the specifics (such as what these products will be) to others lower down in the organization. This strategy is not only deliberate (in its guidelines) and emergent (in its specifics), but it is also deliberately emergent in that the process is consciously managed to allow strategies to emerge en route. IBM used the umbrella strategy in the early 1960s with the impending 360 series, when its senior management approved a set of broad criteria for the design of a family of computers later developed in detail throughout the organization.

Deliberately emergent, too, is what we call the *process strategy*. Here management controls the process of strategy formation – concerning itself with the design of the structure, its staffing, procedures, and so on – while leaving the actual content to others.

Both process and umbrella strategies seem to be especially prevalent in businesses that require great expertise and creativity – a 3M, a Hewlett-Packard, a National Film Board. Such organizations can be effective only if their implementors are allowed to be formulators because it is people way down in the hierarchy who are in touch with the situation at hand and have the requisite technical expertise. In a sense, these are organizations peopled with craftsmen, all of whom must be strategists.

Strategic reorientations happen in brief, quantum leaps

The conventional view of strategic management, especially in the planning literature, claims that change must be continuous: the organization should be adapting all the time. Yet this view proves to be ironic because the very concept of strategy is rooted in stability, not change. As this same literature makes clear, organizations pursue strategies to set direction, to lay out courses of action, and to elicit cooperation from their members around common, established guidelines. By any definition, strategy imposes stability on an organization. No stability means no strategy (no course to the future, no pattern from the past). Indeed, the very fact of having a strategy, and especially of making it explicit (as the conventional literature implores managers to do), creates resistance to strategic change!

What the conventional view fails to come to grips with, then, is how and when to promote change. A fundamental dilemma of strategy making is the need to reconcile the forces for stability and for change – to focus efforts and gain operating efficiencies on the one hand, yet adapt and maintain currency with a changing external environment on the other.

Quantum leaps

Our own research and that of colleagues suggest that organizations resolve these opposing forces by attending first to one and then to the other. Clear periods of stability and change can usually be distinguished in any organization: while it is true that particular strategies may always be changing marginally, it seems equally true that major shifts in strategic orientation occur only rarely.

In our study of Steinberg Inc., a large Quebec supermarket chain headquartered in Montreal, we found only two important reorientations in the 60 years from its founding to the mid-1970s: a shift to self-service in 1933 and the introduction of shopping centers and public financing in 1953. At Volkswagenwerk, we saw only one between the late 1940s and the 1970s, the tumultuous shift from the traditional Beetle to the Audi-type design mentioned earlier. And at Air Canada, we found none over the airline's first four decades, following its initial positioning.

Our colleagues at McGill, Danny Miller and Peter Friesen, found this pattern of change so common in their studies of large numbers of companies (especially the high-performance ones) that they built a theory around it, which they labeled the quantum theory of strategic change. Their basic point is that organizations adopt two distinctly different modes of behavior at different times.

Most of the time they pursue a given strategic orientation. Change may seem continuous, but it occurs in the context of that orientation (perfecting a given retailing formula, for example) and usually amounts to doing more of the same, perhaps better as well. Most organizations favor these periods of stability because they achieve success not by changing strategies but by exploiting the ones they have. They, like craftsmen, seek continuous improvement by using their distinctive competencies in established courses.

While this goes on, however, the world continues to change, sometimes slowly, occasionally in dramatic shifts. Thus gradually or suddenly, the organization's strategic orientation moves out of sync with its environment. Then what Miller and Friesen call a strategic revolution must take place. That long period of evolutionary change is suddenly punctuated by a brief bout of revolutionary turmoil in which the organization quickly alters many of its established patterns. In effect, it tries to leap to a new stability quickly to reestablish an integrated posture among a new set of strategies, structures, arid culture.

But what about all those emergent strategies, growing like weeds around the organization? What the quantum theory suggests is that the really novel ones are generally held in check in some corner of the organization until a strategic revolution becomes necessary. Then as an alternative to having to develop new strategies from scratch or having to import generic strategies from competitors, the organization can turn to its own emerging patterns to find its new orientation. As the old, established strategy disintegrates, the seeds of the new one begin to spread.

This quantum theory of change seems to apply particularly well to large, established, mass-production companies. Because they are especially reliant on standardized procedures, their resistance to strategic reorientation tends to be especially fierce. So we find long periods of stability broken by short disruptive periods of revolutionary change.

Volkswagenwerk is a case in point. Long enamored of the Beetle and armed with a tightly integrated set of strategies, the company ignored fundamental changes in its markets throughout the late 1950s and 1960s. The bureaucratic momentum of its mass-production organization combined with the psychological momentum of its leader, who institutionalized the strategies in the first place. When change finally did come, it was tumultuous: the company groped its way through a hodgepodge of products before it settled on a new set of vehicles championed by a new leader. Strategic reorientations really are cultural revolutions.

Cycles of change

In more creative organizations, we see a somewhat different pattern of change and stability, one that's more balanced. Companies in the business of producing novel outputs apparently need to fly off in all directions from time to time to sustain their creativity. Yet they also need to settle down after such periods to find some order in the resulting chaos.

The National Film Board's tendency to move in and out of focus through remarkably balanced periods of convergence and divergence is a case in point. Concentrated production of films to aid the war effort in the 1940s gave way to great divergence after the war as the organization sought a new raison d'être. Then the advent of television brought back a very sharp focus in the early 1950s, as noted earlier. But in the late 1950s, this dissipated almost as quickly as it began, giving rise to another creative period of exploration. Then the social changes in the early 1960s evoked a new period of convergence around experimental films and social issues.

We use the label "adhocracy" for organizations, like the National Film Board, that produce individual, or custom-made, products (or designs) in an innovative way, on a project basis. Our craftsman is an adhocracy of sorts too, since each of her ceramic sculptures is unique. And her pattern of strategic change was much like that of the NFB's, with evident cycles of convergence and divergence: a focus on knick-knacks from 1967 to 1972; then a period of exploration to about 1976, which resulted in a refocus on ceramic sculptures; that continued to about 1981, to be followed by a period of searching for new directions. More recently, a focus on ceramic murals seems to be emerging.

Whether through quantum revolutions or cycles of convergence and divergence, however, organizations seem to need to separate in time the basic forces for change and stability, reconciling them by attending to each in turn. Many strategic failures can be attributed either to mixing the two or to an obsession with one of these forces at the expense of the other.

The problems are evident in the work of many craftsmen. On the one hand, there are those who seize on the perfection of a single theme and never change. Eventually the creativity disappears from their work and the world passes them by – much as it did Volkswagenwerk until the company was shocked into its strategic revolution. And then there are those who are always changing, who flit from one idea to another and never settle down. Because no theme or strategy ever emerges in their work, they cannot exploit or even develop any distinctive competence. And because their work lacks definition, identity crises are likely to develop, with neither the craftsmen nor their clientele knowing what to make of it. Miller and Friesen found this behavior in conventional business too; they label it "the impulsive firm running blind." How often have we seen it in companies that go on acquisition sprees?

To manage strategy is to craft thought and action, control and learning, stability and change

The popular view sees the strategist as a planner or as a visionary, someone sitting on a pedestal dictating brilliant strategies for everyone else to implement. While recognizing the importance of thinking ahead and especially of the need for creative vision in this pedantic world, I wish to propose an additional view of the strategist – as a pattern recognizer, a learner if you will – who manages a process in which strategies (and visions) can emerge as well as be deliberately conceived. I also wish to redefine that strategist, to extend that someone into the collective entity made up of the many actors whose interplay speaks an organization's mind. This strategist *finds* strategies no less than creates them, often in patterns that form inadvertently in its own behavior.

What, then, does it mean to craft strategy? Let us return to the words associated with craft: dedication, experience, involvement with the material, the personal touch, mastery of detail, a sense of harmony and integration. Managers who craft strategy do not spend much time in executive suites reading MIS reports or industry analyses. They are involved, responsive to their materials, learning about their organizations and industries through personal touch. They are also sensitive to experience, recognizing that while individual vision may be important, other factors must help determine strategy as well.

Manage stability

Managing strategy is mostly managing stability, not change. Indeed, most of the time senior managers should not be formulating strategy at all; they should be getting on with making their organizations as effective as possible in pursuing the strategies they already have. Like distinguished craftsmen, organizations become distinguished because they master the details.

To manage strategy then, at least in the first instance, is not so much to promote change as to know *when* to do so. Advocates of strategic planning often urge managers to plan for perpetual instability in the environment (for example, by rolling over five-year plans annually). But this obsession with change is dysfunctional. Organizations that reassess their strategies continuously are like individuals who reassess their jobs or their marriages continuously – in both cases, people will drive themselves crazy or else reduce themselves to inaction. The formal planning process repeats itself so often and so mechanically that it desensitizes the organization to real change, programs it more and more deeply into set patterns, and thereby encourages it to make only minor adaptations.

So-called strategic planning must be recognized for what it is: a means, not to create strategy but to program a strategy already created – to work out its implications formally. It is essentially analytic in nature, based on decomposition, while strategy creation is essentially a process of synthesis. That is why trying to create strategies through formal planning most often leads to extrapolating existing ones or copying those of competitors.

This is not to say that planners have no role to play in strategy formation. In addition to programming strategies created by other means, they can feed ad hoc analyses into the strategy-making process at the front end to be sure that the hard data are taken into consideration. They can also stimulate others to think strategically. And of course people called planners can be strategists too, so long as they are creative thinkers who are in touch with what is relevant. But that has nothing to do with the technology of formal planning.

Detect discontinuity

Environments do not change on any regular or orderly basis. And they seldom undergo continuous dramatic change, claims about our "age of discontinuity" and environmental "turbulence" notwithstanding. (Go tell people who lived through the Great Depression or survivors of the siege of Leningrad during World War II that ours are turbulent times.) Much of the time, change is minor and even temporary and requires no strategic response. Once in a while there is a truly significant discontinuity or, even less often, a gestalt shift in the environment, where everything important seems to change at once. But these events, while critical, are also easy to recognize.

The real challenge in crafting strategy lies in detecting the subtle discontinuities that may undermine a business in the future. And for that, there is no technique, no program, just a sharp mind in touch with the situation. Such discontinuities are unexpected and irregular, essentially unprecedented. They can be dealt with only by minds that are attuned to existing patterns yet able to perceive important breaks in them. Unfortunately, this form of strategic thinking tends to atrophy during the long periods of stability that most organizations experience (just as it did at Volkswagenwerk during the 1950s and 1960s). So the trick is to manage within a given strategic orientation most of the time yet be able to pick out the occasional discontinuity that really matters.

The Steinberg chain was built and run for more than half a century by a man named Sam Steinberg. For 20 years, the company concentrated on perfecting a self-service retailing formula introduced in 1933. Installing fluorescent lighting and figuring out how to package meat in cellophane wrapping were the "strategic" issues of the day. Then in 1952, with the arrival of the first shopping center in Montreal, Steinberg realized he had to redefine his business almost overnight. He knew he needed to control those shopping centers and that control would require public financing and other major changes. So he reoriented his business. The ability to make that kind of switch in thinking is the essence of strategic management. And it has more to do with vision and involvement than it does with analytic technique.

Know the business

Sam Steinberg was the epitome of the entrepreneur, a man intimately involved with all the details of his business, who spent Saturday mornings visiting his stores. As he told us in discussing his company's competitive advantage:

> "Nobody knew the grocery business like we did. Everything has to do with your knowledge. I knew merchandise, I knew cost, I knew selling, I knew customers. I knew everything, and I passed on all my knowledge; I kept teaching my people. That's the advantage we had. Our competitors couldn't touch us."

Note the kind of knowledge involved: not intellectual knowledge, not analytical reports or abstracted facts and figures (though these can certainly help), but personal knowledge, intimate understanding, equivalent to the craftsman's feel for the clay. Facts are available to anyone; this kind of knowledge is not. Wisdom is the word that captures it best. But wisdom is a word that has been lost in the bureaucracies we have built for ourselves, systems designed to distance leaders from operating details. Show me managers who think they can rely on formal planning to create their strategies, and I'll show you managers who lack intimate knowledge of their businesses or the creativity to do something with it.

Craftsmen have to train themselves to see, to pick up things other people miss. The same holds true for managers of strategy. It is those with a kind of peripheral vision who are best able to detect and take advantage of events as they unfold.

Manage patterns

Whether in an executive suite in Manhattan or a pottery studio in Montreal, a key to managing strategy is the ability to detect emerging patterns and help them take shape. The job of the manager is not just to preconceive specific strategies but also to recognize their emergence elsewhere in the organization and intervene when appropriate.

Like weeds that appear unexpectedly in a garden, some emergent strategies may need to be uprooted immediately. But management cannot be too quick to cut off the unexpected, for tomorrow's vision may grow out of today's aberration. (Europeans, after all, enjoy salads made from the leaves of the dandelion, America's most notorious weed.) Thus some patterns are worth watching until their effects have more clearly manifested themselves. Then those that prove useful can be made deliberate and be incorporated into the formal strategy, even if that means shifting the strategic umbrella to cover them.

To manage in this context, then, is to create the climate within which a wide variety of strategies can grow. In more complex organizations, this may mean building flexible structures, hiring creative people, defining broad umbrella strategies, and watching for the patterns that emerge.

Reconcile change and continuity

Finally, managers considering radical departures need to keep the quantum theory of change in mind. As Ecclesiastes reminds us, there is a time to sow and a time to reap. Some new patterns must be held in check until the organization is ready for a strategic revolution, or at least a period of divergence. Managers who are obsessed with either change or stability are bound eventually to harm their organizations. As pattern recognizer, the manager has to be able to sense when to exploit an established crop of strategies and when to encourage new strains to displace the old.

While strategy is a word that is usually associated with the future, its link to the past is no less central. As Kierkegaard once observed, life is lived forward but understood backward. Managers may have to live strategy in the future, but they must understand it through the past.

Like potters at the wheel, organizations must make sense of the past if they hope to manage the future. Only by coming to understand the patterns that form in their own behavior do they get to know their capabilities and their potential. Thus crafting strategy, like managing craft, requires a natural synthesis of the future, present, and past.

Reading 1.6 Evaluation of strategy: theory and models *Richard P. Rumelt*

First published: (1979) *Strategic Management: A New View of Business Policy and Planning*, Boston, MA: Little, Brown, pp. 196–217.

The formulation of organizational strategy, when it occurs, is problem solving of the most unstructured sort. What little is known about how ill-structured problems are, or should be, dealt with suggests a three-part cycling process among: (1) problem structuring activities, (2) the generation of tentative solutions, and (3) the testing or evaluation of proposed solutions. The creative phases of this process draw heavily on perceptual skills and imagination. Here, pattern recognition and the ability to perceive new meanings amidst complexity play key roles. By contrast, it is the evaluation phase that presents the greatest opportunity to employ rational analysis. The situation is directly analogous to the scientific process wherein hypothesis generation remains a high art; the full power of the scientific method comes into play only after a clear hypothesis has been formulated.

If "evaluation" is the phase of strategy-making that is most amenable to analytic thought, what is the current state of the art? To treat this question, consider the following idealized problem: suppose one is given a reasonably comprehensive description of an organization, its environment and a proposed strategy. What are the legitimate grounds for evaluating the strategy and to what theories, knowledge, or models can one turn for help in making such an evaluation? The purpose of this article is to examine these questions in the light of recent research and conceptual contributions.

The idealized problem posed is somewhat artificial in that descriptions of strategy, organization, and environment are rarely "comprehensive" and strategy evaluation is more often an organizational process than an analytical task. But our interpretation of "state of the art" is that it implies the "best" that can be done rather than what some do, what might be done, or what is most frequently done. Accordingly, the primary concern will be with the limits of rational evaluation – with identifying the cutting edge between what can be said with reasonable surety about general classes of situations and those aspects of evaluation that remain heavily dependent upon intuition, insight, and sharply situational knowledge.

Strategy is a strongly contextual concept. At the core it deals with the adjustment of specific policies to particular situations. In looking at strategy evaluation, therefore, it will be helpful to associate methods of analysis with their appropriate contexts. We will begin with a discussion of the strategy concept itself, establish the functions it is supposed to perform, and identify those evaluation criteria that are context free – that are always valid. Central to this discussion will be the distinction between a solution to *a* problem and solving the *right* problem. We introduce the idea of "frame" as a way of speaking more precisely about this issue and indicate the special characteristics of "frame theories" that are useful in strategy evaluation.

The broadest context in general use is that of "rivalry." In discussing the context of rivalry we will show that many of the traditional tests for evaluating strategy are logical consequences of the nature of the strategy concept and the assumption of rivalry.

Armed with these observations and tools, a variety of models and theories will be discussed. In each case, the relevant context will be identified, the frame content examined, and the specific "tactical" content of the approach noted. After summarizing our analysis we will point out what seem to be the most fruitful directions for further research.

The strategy concept

To evaluate an entity is to determine its utility, truth, or efficacy. This, in turn, requires an appreciation of the function the entity is supposed to perform. Therefore, it will be helpful to examine the special characteristics of the concept of strategy and the role it is supposed to play in the guidance of organizations. Only then can the legitimate grounds for its appraisal be established.

The term "strategy" has a range of related meanings and authors have generally felt quite free to use it quite idiosyncratically. For game theorists, strategies are concrete actions or rules for choosing actions in a conflict situation; for some strategy is "high-level" or "long-term" planning, while others see it as referring only to broad gauge issues of "mission." Still others use it to denote any decision that is "important." The concept of strategy that will be explored here, and that has come to play such an important role in the study of organizational guidance, contains elements of all of the above notions. Its special focus, however, is on the relationship between a whole organization and its external environment.

Policy hierarchies

An observable aspect of organizations is that they develop hierarchies of policy (rules for defining contexts and making choices). While one frequently speaks of policymakers as selecting courses of action, the choices are almost always policies or frameworks for guiding action. Even such a seemingly concrete decision as to "increase plant capacity by twenty-five percent within the next nine months" can also be seen as the precursor to a complex cascade of problem-solving activity. Because policy structures are hierarchical, one can speak of "top-level" policy or organizational "strategy" without meaning the combined totality of *every* policy and rule in the organization.

If each level of an organization supplies structure to the task environment of lower levels, what is the framework for guiding the selection of the top-most level of policy? Unidimensional objectives that call for the maximization of profits, happiness, or the public welfare are quite useless for guiding action. Unless they are expanded into specific rules or policies for their achievement, such objectives can only function as rejection criteria. Thus the postulate of some unidimensional objective does not solve the problem of choosing top-level policy and the assumption of some set of actionable goals as "given" assumes the problem away. Somehow, the organization must maintain and make occasional changes in a set of "local" goals, or policies, that are specific enough to serve as criteria for the selection of other policies. We reserve the term "strategy" for this set of primary goals and policies.

The strategist is thus concerned with at least two levels of objectives. A substantial part of the art of strategy-making lies in discriminating among those objectives which act like values, being fixed and context free, and those which are really tools of administration, changing as strategy changes. In general, fixed objectives serve to constrain the selection of strategy, while operating objectives serve to express a strategy.

While the separation of fixed from operating objectives is a critical part of strategy formulation, it is of little concern in strategy evaluation. In appraising a strategy, the question is whether or not various objectives are consistent with one another, with the chosen context, and with policy. It does not matter where the objectives come from. Therefore, for our purposes, it will be most convenient to simply include all goals and objectives in our definition of strategy.

It is a frequent observation that one person's strategy is another's tactics – that what is strategic depends upon where you sit. One can easily find references to national, political, and industry strategies, to corporate, product, and manufacturing strategies, and even to strategies for conducting an individual interview. Common to all these problem situations is a generic type of poorly structured dilemma: a set of higher-level objectives, frequently flowing from the resolution of a higher-level strategic problem, must be translated into local objectives and the translation depends upon both the objectives, the means at hand, and the detailed content of the situation. Without denying that strategic problems occur on many levels, our primary concern here is with organizational strategy – the problem facing fairly autonomous organizations of selecting domains of activity and ways of coping with those domains.

As a descriptive tool, strategy is the analog of the biologist's method of "explaining" the structure and behavior of organisms by pointing out the functionality of each attribute in a total system (or strategy) designed to cope with or inhabit a particular niche. The normative use of strategy has no counterpart in biology (as yet!), but might be thought of as the problem of designing a living creature (or species) to exist within some environment. The hierarchical nature of policy has its analog in the fact that living systems are not homogeneous but consist of linked subsystems; the "designer," or strategist, can specify the need for "binocular vision" or "integrated production facilities" secure in the knowledge that the problems of creating such entities are solvable.

It is again the hierarchical nature of policy that provides the justification for calling some issues "important" or "critical." Rhenman (1973) notes that most of the problems organizations face are dealt with by standard procedures – they are problems that may be unpleasant, but which the system is designed to cope with. Critical or strategic problems, by contrast, lie outside the limits of the organization's repertoire of coping behavior and may require a redesign of the system. In our biological analogy, strategic issues are ones that lead to extinction unless mutation (or its behavioral equivalent) occurs. Thus, the idea of *critical problems* is not a capricious simplifying assumption, but has firmly grounded analogs in such concepts as "system stability ranges" and "design tolerances."

Problem structuring

The kinds of situations that call for strategic thinking are termed ill-structured. They are characterized by difficulty, ambiguity, and the lack of established methods for moving towards clarification. According to Simon (1958):

> Ill structured problems are difficult because the essential variables are not numerical at all, but symbolic or verbal . . . the goal is vague and nonquantitative . . . Finally, there are many practical problems – it would be accurate to say "most practical problems" – for which computational algorithms simply are not available. Facing facts, we are forced to admit that the majority of decisions that executives face every day – and certainly a majority of the very most important decisions – lie much closer to the ill-structured than to the well structured end of the spectrum.

To this description it is necessary to add two important sources of difficulty. First, ill-structured problems pose very real challenges in simply defining what the problem is. Even the term "ill-structured problem" tends to suggest some type of obstacle to be overcome. In reality, strategists often face situations in which there are many conflicting signs of health and disease, opportunity and risk. Arriving at a formulation of the nature of the situation may well be the principal and most crucial task. Second, the assumption of vague and nonquantitative goals is too strong to be general. In many cases, strategy-making is concerned with the creation of reasonable purposes – with moving from a general awareness of discontent to having identifiable desires.

When confronted by an ill-structured situation an individual or organization may either: (1) classify it and apply standard procedures (the bureaucratic response); or (2) seek some way of structuring the problem that is "meaningful," i.e., that suggests how current knowledge and experience can be brought to bear. The latter, more creative, response requires what Vickers (1965) calls an "appreciation" of the situation and a reduction in ambiguity through the perception of pattern. Little is known about how insight actually operates, but Schon (1963) suggests that metaphor and analogy are the substance of creative thought. New concepts arise, he contends, by the stretching and adapting of old metaphors to meet new situations. The traditional open ended question, "What business are we in?" can be seen as an invitation to metaphor generation. When Timex revolutionized the watch industry with its inexpensive disposable watches, distributed through drug stores, it changed the prevailing metaphor from "a watch is an item of jewelry" to "a watch is a convenience item like a mechanical pencil." Similarly, when diversification away from a traditional area of business induces the senior management group to stop viewing that; area as one in which new markets are "conquered," old ones "defended," distributors "strengthened," and advertising "campaigns" launched, and to see it instead as a "mature field" from which funds are "harvested" for reinvestment in more "fertile fields," a change in metaphor has taken place. The managers are, of course, neither generals nor absentee farmers, but both metaphors, though hardly "models," may provide helpful ways of organizing perceptions.

Whether or not metaphor plays a role, the primary task when facing an ill-structured problem is to reduce ambiguity by structuring the problem. Thus, for our purposes, strategy-making is a response that does not necessarily "solve" the problem, but which redefines it in terms of more familiar subproblems. When, for example, a military commander decides on a strategy of using feints to split the opposing forces into two segments, he is leaving a great many issues unresolved. He is, however, drastically reducing the ambiguity inherent in the original problem and providing a framework for further activity. Unlike rational-analytic problem solving, the function of strategy is not to "solve" a problem, but to so structure a situation that the emergent problems are solvable.

A strategy, then, is a description of what an organization is trying to accomplish and to what ends it is channeling its critical resources and problem-solving energies. As such, it may be regarded as a set of goals and policies, as a way of structuring an ill-structured situation, or as an allocation of resources. None of these views contradicts the others and all are helpful in grasping different aspects of strategy and strategy-making.

Strategy evaluation criteria

Suppose that an analyst is presented with a reasonably comprehensive description of an organization, its environment, and a proposed strategy. What criteria can and should be used in evaluating the strategy?

There may be many features of the proposed strategy that are attractive, insightful, and potentially effective. It takes, however, only one major flaw to invalidate the strategy. Thus, it is helpful to cast the evaluation problem in terms of the negative logic of hypothesis testing: on what grounds may a proposed strategy be "refuted" or rejected?

If the type of organization or environment is not specified, there are four discernible context-free tests, each following directly from the definition and purpose of strategy, that a proposed strategy must pass: (1) the goal consistency test, (2) the frame test, (3) the competence test, and (4) the workability test.

The goal consistency test

In mathematics, conflicting objectives imply a null set of feasible solutions. Similarly, a strategy that contains goals, objectives, and policies that are mutually inconsistent must be rejected. The objective of "growth," for example, is not consistent with that of "maintaining a small informal management team."

Strategies authored by a single individual rarely suffer from such gross inconsistencies, but those that evolve from political processes often do. However, in appraising such strategies, one must realize that publicly announced goals are frequently part of the tactics for implementing an implicit strategy. President Carter's energy program, for example, contains inconsistent goals and policies: "energy conservation, promoting new energy sources, equity of sacrifice, and special taxes and penalties." Yet these statements actually represent political tactics within a larger strategy of relying heavily on legislative, rather than market, mechanisms to reduce U.S. dependence on Arab oil and soften the economic shocks forecasted to occur, when oil production begins to decline.

The frame test

A principal function of strategy is to structure a situation – to separate the important from the unimportant and to define the critical subproblems to be dealt with. An aspect of evaluation must be an appraisal of how well these tasks have been accomplished. Before one can decide whether or not a given strategy will "work," some indication that the right issues are being worked on is needed.

The distinction between problem solving and defining the relevant problems is important in all decision situations, but especially so in strategy-making. It is analogous to Drucker's (1967) distinction between efficiency and effectiveness and the organizational roles of generalist and specialists. In common, parlance, the ability to discriminate the important from the unimportant is usually termed "wisdom." For the sake of discussion we shall call schemes for making this kind of distinction "frame theories" to distinguish them from theories whose purpose is to specify interrelationships among known entities.

To carry out the frame test, an evaluator must have or construct a frame theory that identifies the critical issues within the chosen domain. If the strategy's basic policies and objectives do not address these issues, it must be rejected.

General frame theories, applicable to all situations, do not exist and it is doubtful if such a thing is even possible. There are, however, theories and models of varying power that serve to distinguish the important from the unimportant within specific contexts. For example, as a product/market arena evolves from the early growth to the maturity phase of its life cycle, currently employed models predict that: (1) market share positions become entrenched; (2) cost-based competition becomes ascendant; and (3) the new stability will permit efficiency gains through vertical integration. Such statements are part of *frame models* because they are directed towards revealing the critical *issues* rather than solutions to them. Similarly, assertions that "size is vital in the automobile industry, location in retailing, and image in the liquor business," are pure frame theories (though perhaps untested) in that they indicate what one should have as an objective rather than how to accomplish it.

Many of the complaints concerning the vagueness, incompleteness, and nonoperational nature of such models stem from a basic misunderstanding of their purpose. Frame models need not, and often should not, address the question of exactly how a particular objective or requirement should be achieved. Thus, a frame theory of coal mining might note the pivotal importance of labor productivity while a frame model of oil refining would surely ignore that issue and highlight instead the need for assured sources of supply. In each case, there are various ways in which a strategist might deal with the pivotal issue. One oil refiner might move to integrate back into tanker operations, while another, serving a relatively isolated region, might simply depend on its ability to afford a higher purchase price. Richer and more complex contexts support a greater variety of strategies, but must be framed more abstractly.

Most frame models in current use take the form of rules of thumb: focus your efforts, specialization is vital for the smaller enterprise, segment your market, etc. Some of these are of dubious generality and may apply, if at all, only to special contexts, but others represent the distillation of rather sophisticated theory. In a section that follows we shall discuss an important subset of frame models, masquerading as rules of thumb, that arise under the special context of rivalry.

The competence test

Since a key purpose of a strategy is to structure a situation in a way that creates solvable subproblems, strategies that do not result in solvable subproblems must be rejected. Such strategies simply substitute one ill-structured dilemma for another.

A strategy of competing in the electric typewriter market, for example, by creating a radically cheap yet durable machine defines a subproblem (inventing the machine) that is probably no more amenable to attack than the original strategic problem. The "invention" of such a device is quite unlikely unless some special resources or conditions exist. If the firm in question had a demonstrated competence at similar cost-saving innovations or held a relevant patent, the strategy might be acceptable. Thus, the idea that the subproblems defined by a strategy should be better structured than the original problem has an operational interpretation in the context of organizations – the subproblems should be ones that can be dealt with by existing and demonstrated organizational skills, resources, and competences. While it is not strictly necessary for the strategist, or strategy evaluator, to know "how" such subproblems will be solved, an appreciation for the solvability of various kinds of subproblems is required.

What is particularly interesting about this, observation is that the standard rules of thumb, "build on your strengths" and "first understand your strengths and weaknesses", can be deduced from the basic proposition that strategy is problem structuring and organizational policies are hierarchical. They do not depend on assumptions about the nature of competition or the stressfulness of the environment and, consequently, apply equally to business and not-for-profit organizations. They are simply a convenient way of expressing the idea that the most direct measure of whether a subproblem is solvable, and therefore simpler than the original strategic problem, is to compare it to problems the organization has had to cope with in the past.

The workability test

If a strategy has a consistent goal set, passes the frame test, in that it focuses on the critical issues, and passes the competence test, in that it avoids unreasonable demands oh subsequent policy-making, there still remains the question: "Will it work?" Will the proposed policies and actions work together to produce the results sought?

The issue of workability is what most formal planning documents and procedures address, and there are an enormous variety of tools, theories, and methods for making this evaluation. Most can be placed in one of two rough groups: (1) those that are concerned with the availability and deployment of resources, and (2) those that attempt to predict the outcomes associated with particular actions. The first group contains methods for financial, plant capacity, personnel, logistics, and materials flow planning. Encompassing a great deal of what is taught in formal management education; these methods range in sophistication from simple tables of cash flow to complex computer simulations and linear programming models. Their general intent is to permit proposed actions to be tested for consistency with one another and the available resources.

The second group includes procedures and models for estimating demand, price, future technology, competitive reaction, market share, etc. The best developed methods in this group are those for predicting demand. Macroeconomic models, input-output models, industry models, trend analysis, and other techniques can significantly reduce the uncertainty associated with estimates of future demand. Less well developed are models for predicting which firms, following which strategies, will satisfy this demand. Thus, while reasonably accurate forecasts of the future demand for computer peripherals are available, the rigorous prediction of the market share attainable by a specific set of price, line breadth, technical quality, and support policies is largely beyond the current state of the art. Most practical planning systems rely heavily on judgment, intuition, and debate as means of establishing these estimates. Because, except for the roughest of checks, the workability test usually requires inputs from a variety of specialized viewpoints and disciplines, it is largely carried out by a multilevel process in most organizations. (See, for example, Berg, 1965; Bower, 1970.)

This article is not an appropriate forum for surveying all, or even the most important, of the detailed methods for associating actions with results. Firmly rooted within specific functional disciplines, requiring specialized training for their use, they need to be restructured and adapted to each new problem. There are, however, a growing class of models, or theories that attempt to associate policy with results at high levels of abstraction. These shall be termed "tactical" models to stress the idea that their concern is with the manipulation of policy-type variables *within* a frame, rather than the choice of frame or the explosion of policy into detailed subcomponents. A model giving the direction and approximate magnitude of the associations among profitability, promotional effort, and dealer exclusivity (within, say, Porter's [1976] "nonconvenience" frame) would be classified *tactical*. A method for estimating segment-specific price elasticities of television sets would be classified below the tactical level of abstraction.

In general, most of the current strategy oriented research has both frame and tactical content. The builder of frame models will usually at least offer conjectures about the range of appropriate tactics within a context and the builder of tactical models is, at least implicitly, identifying the chosen parameters as critical within the given frame. Thus, as we turn to an examination of specific theories and models useful in strategy evaluation, no strenuous attempt will be made to discuss frame and tactical models in separate sections. Instead, we shall follow a general path from those approaches that are appropriate in the widest contexts to those that are more narrowly focused. The models and theories covered include: (1) the assumption of rivalry in nonperfect markets, (2) classical evaluation approaches, (3) life cycle models, (4) empirically based frame and tactical models, (5) strategic group models, and (6) experience curve models.

Rivalry and asymmetry: the most general context

The widest context that provides usable theory for strategy-making and evaluation is that provided by the simple assumption of rivalry. Strategy, as a concept, has its roots in the consideration of pure rivalry, so this should not be surprising.

Pure rivalry, as arises in games, military combat, and other interactions in which the stakes are well defined and cooperation unlikely, is a powerful simplifying assumption. Under conditions of pure rivalry, the solution, or outcome, is indeterminate under symmetry. No one can predict which of two identical opposing armies or corporations will prevail. A determinate solution only becomes possible when certain asymmetries exist, such asymmetries being termed "advantages." The winning strategy (as opposed to tactics) is always the same – play only those games in which you have an advantage. Somewhat less mechanistically, one wins games by exploiting asymmetries that make a difference. Thus, in pure rivalry, a frame model is one that tells the strategist which asymmetries constitute advantages.

One interesting consequence of pure rivalry is that the outcomes of balanced confrontations under conditions of full information will necessarily be determined by details not included in current theories of strategy. If all contenders have equal access to the available strategic knowledge, which need not be very good, the only confrontations of interest are those in which, according to the current state of strategic theory, the outcome is indeterminate. Faced with such a situation, the determined strategist will try to discover new sorts of advantages hitherto unrealized. The approach to such discovery would have to be through the study of situational asymmetry rather than the examination of theory. Once the outcome has been determined, the potential store of knowledge will have been increased – a new type of asymmetry will have been tested as to whether or not it constitutes an advantage. Therefore, in a world of pure rivalry, strategists either know in advance the outcome of a confrontation or they are pure situational thinkers. Researchers, in this imaginary world, would have to gain knowledge by the arduous and undignified method of studying a myriad of individual cases, looking for clues as to which asymmetries were critical in each.

Traditional microeconomic theory is based on the assumption of pure rivalry and frames the strategic issues quite simply: the only asymmetry that can constitute an advantage is cost. The theory goes on, of course, to make further assumptions which, in the end, guarantee equilibrium – a condition of complete symmetry. From our perspective, microeconomics is a wide context frame model with this content: (1) Cost asymmetries are critical advantages for business firms. (2) If costs are equal, the nature of advantage is beyond the scope of the theory. Of course, if an economy were in *real* equilibrium, not all variables would be symmetrical, but no advantage would be attainable. In a world in which people learn, in which new insights can occur, and in which every situation contains a universe of complex potential asymmetries, it is doubtful if equilibrium is a conceivable state of affairs for anything but physical systems.

The kind of rivalry characteristic of today's economy is far from "pure rivalry." Perhaps the most important difference is its ecological nature. Not all firms are pitted against one another, protected niches exist, "mutations," in the form of innovations, constantly open up new possibilities and obsolete old sources of advantage. More important still, asymmetries that are not advantages in one arena may be critical advantages in another – we live in a world of multiple contexts. If two firms have identical costs, microeconomic theory predicts a stand-off. Suppose, however, that one firm possesses a particularly rich source of raw materials and the other a special manufacturing process. Each potential advantage reduces cost by the same amount so no cost asymmetry is produced. A strategist, however, might notice that the special process of the first firm gives it an advantage abroad, where it has not yet been introduced. The second firm cannot exploit the cost advantage of its raw material supply at such distances and cannot follow. It may, however, choose to investigate the use of its material advantage in other products. One firm becomes a multinational, and the other diversified. Strategy, in other words, still depends on asymmetry, but under "impure" rivalry advantages other than cost exist, information is far from perfect, and the recognition of asymmetry is as vital as its exploitation.

Rivalrous environments reward the exploitation of asymmetry and the exploitation of asymmetry, in turn, leads to the formation of niches and specialization as a means of adapting to niches. The rivalrous environment, therefore, simplifies the analytical job by usually restricting attention to the immediate niche in question and its close neighbors. Furthermore, in a particular niche, rivalry tends to be on certain key factors. Accumulated histories have given the competing organizations (or organisms) roughly equivalent endowments in the basic functions necessary for survival; factors that formed the center of strategic battles in the past (e.g., coping with labor unions, use of EDP technology) come into balance for the survivors and competition extends to new grounds.

The implications of assuming rivalry for strategy-making and the appropriate focus of strategy analysis are rarely made explicit. We have dwelt on them because statements that are frequently passed off as simply heuristics, or rules of thumb, are often deductions from a model of rivalrous competition. The model lacks the rigor so attractive to those trained in economics or the physical sciences, but is more accurate in its essentials than any available rigorous model. Biologists studying niches, ecologies, and species adaptation realize the enormous variety of solutions to competitive problems that evolving organisms can produce, and employ the same kind of situational functional analysis as do students of organizational strategy in their search for understanding. The assumption of rivalry, in sum, can be seen as a frame model that (1) invites a focus on the comparison of roughly similar entities rather than elaborate models of an entire system, (2) implies that strategic factors are discoverable through the inspection asymmetries rather than common factors, (3) implies that stable solutions to strategic problems take the form of niches and niche maintenance behavior, and (4) implies that the fundamental threats to stability will arise from changes in the climate and innovation (mutation).

The assumption of rivalry, therefore, allows the use of a powerful rejection rule in evaluating strategy: *a strategy that does not either create or exploit an asymmetry constituting an advantage must be rejected*. Which asymmetries produce advantages is determined either from an appropriate frame model or situational analysis. The rule is *powerful* in the same way that the conservation of energy law permits one to reject proposed perpetual motion machines without studying their inner logics.

Classical evaluation approaches

The strategy concept as described here developed out of the contributions of a number of scholars. While Reilley (1955) and Kline (1955) were among the earliest authors to apply the term "strategy" to the idea of a comprehensive business plan, the first well articulated descriptions of strategy as a mechanism for adapting an organization to its environment were those of Selznik (1957), Chandler (1962), Tilles (1963), Learned *et al.* (1965), and Ansoff (1965). While Chandler saw strategy as mediating between environment and organizational structure, and Selznik saw "mission" as the essence of organizational leadership, neither author dwelt on either the formulation or evaluation of strategy. We take, therefore, Tilles's approach to evaluation, which is a distillation of the Harvard Business School concept of strategy later published by Learned *et al.*, and Ansoff's normative prescriptions for strategy formulation and evaluation, as the "classical" approaches.

Identifying strategy as a "set of goals and major policies," Tilles suggested that strategy be evaluated on six criteria: (1) internal consistency, (2) consistency with the environment, (3) appropriateness in the light of available resources, (4) satisfactory degree of risk, (5) appropriate time horizon, and (6) adequacy of results achieved. Tilles's terminology, of course, does not match our own, but his discussion makes it clear that his first criterion corresponds to our test for goal consistency and the resource oriented part of our workability test. By "consistency with the environment" Tilles means a requirement that the strategy address and deal with the critical success factors and problems within the chosen domain – this corresponds to our frame test. The third criterion, Tilles makes clear, is a test of whether certain resources are employed to "advantage" by the strategy. Specifically mentioned are money, competence, and physical facilities. The fourth and fifth criteria are suggested elements or characteristics of the goal set and the sixth refers to *a posteriori* appraisal.

The Tilles approach can be seen as a simple frame model of general business rivalry – it posits the need for some type of workability test and suggests that advantage be sought in the three broad areas of money, competence, and physical facilities. Admittedly general, the model stands in striking contrast to many prior approaches to the guidance of corporations that emphasized such factors as forecasting, superior product quality, and low costs or that suggested that success would be attained by those who possessed "vision," "aggressiveness," or "sound management practice." While the frame model employed by Tilles is quite broad, his article recounts a number of anecdotes which serve to suggest a number of specific issues that may be critical in certain situations. Similarly, the Learned *et al.* text on the evaluation of strategy relies on a series of cases to make explicit the issues that the authors believe to be critical in selected situations.

Ansoff presents a normative approach to strategy formulation that emphasizes the issue of diversification. Paralleling Tilles and the Harvard group in his approach to intra-industry strategy, Ansoff suggests that diversification strategy be framed by consideration of (1) the available funds, (2) the available level of general management skills, (3) the demand/capacity relationship in the area being considered, (4) the barriers to entry, and (5) the potential synergy. The synergy idea is the heart of the matter and, in its raw form, is simply a measure of increased efficiency through combination of activities. Ansoff, however, requires that synergy be compared to the profile of strengths and weaknesses of the firms operating in the area being considered for entry. Thus, it actually becomes a measure of the degree to which a corporate resource is capable of being an advantage in the new area. The synergy argument, therefore, amounts to the proposition that the firm should possess resources that can be used to advantage in the proposed new venture. Where Ansoff differs from Tilles and the Harvard group's approaches is over the issue of whether such advantage is *required* – while Ansoff values its presence highly, he does not reject the idea of diversification if synergy is absent.

In summary, these two "classical" approaches to strategy evaluation provide some very wide context frame models, but no explicit tactical theories for the evaluation process. They do provide the first comprehensive descriptions of the strategy concept, emphasize the importance of deploying resources in ways that produce relative advantage, and suggest a number of areas in which advantage will normally be found. In short, the classical approach is roughly equivalent to our basic frame of rivalry. Drawing its power from its generality, it remains the approach to which one must turn when context-specific theories or models are not available.

Life cycle models

The product/market life cycle concept provides a powerful frame theory that has yet to be fully developed. Originally employed as a tool for marketing specialists, the (product) life cycle concept has been gradually elaborated to include such factors as industry structure and raw material sourcing patterns. Hofer (1975) succinctly summarizes most of the comprehensive life cycle models, including those of Levitt (1965), Fox (1973), and Wasson (1974), and also gives his own synthesis.

Most product/market life cycle models divide the evolution of a product/market area into five contexts: introduction, growth, shakeout, maturity, and decline. Ideally, if formulated as a pure *frame* model, a product/market life cycle model would identify those areas or issues which form the primary basis of rivalry in each context. Such a model would, for example, indicate how rivalry in the maturity phase differs from rivalry in the growth phase, point out the issues that would be considered strategic in each phase, and highlight the areas in each phase in which asymmetry may produce advantage. Most of the product life cycle models that have been put forward, however, are mixtures of descriptions of activities, suggested actions, and frame models. Fox (1973), for example, indicates that during the growth phase rivalry will be among a few firms offering similar products, production should be centralized, and manufacturing efficiency will be the critical focus. The first point is descriptive, providing what is actually a key for identifying the phase, the second is a normative proposition (of questionable generality), and the third a frame-type statement (i.e., that advantages in efficient production will be critical) that may or may not be valid.

In most product/market life cycle models the area of greatest interest is the transition from growth to maturity, with some type of passage through a "shakeout" phase in the process. The basic idea is that the basis of rivalry and the activities of rival firms change as this transition takes place. While much of the information provided by the life cycle theorists describes "normal" or "common" activities that will occur during each phase, there is a consensus frame model, albeit broad, that is useful in strategy formulation and evaluation. Obviously pertaining only to fairly standardized products aimed at a variety of buyers, the consensus frame is approximately as follows:

In the growth phase, demand pull provides margins that may allow relatively inefficient producers to survive. Rivalry focuses on product performance, price, access to distribution channels and the identification of viable market segments and the special product characteristics appropriate to each. Depending on the competences of the rival firms and the nature of the market, strategies will be fashioned to take advantage of asymmetries in cost, product quality, distribution channels, and image in or access to market segments.

Shakeout is signaled by falling margins and a reduction in the rate of demand growth. By this time, market segments have been defined and footholds gained. Those with inferior products, poor distribution, high costs, or indefensible segmentation commitments have either fallen by the wayside or soon will. Rivalry shifts to a new phase – segments are cleared of weaker competitors and strategic advantage is sought in production efficiency, selling efficiency, and distribution intensity *within* segments. While the factors that were important during the growth phase continue to be necessary, rivals with a chance at survival already possess these skills or resources. Efficiency in one's chosen segments, and efficiencies gained by scale economies of linked segments are translated into increased ability to advertise and promote the product.

Once maturity sets in, relative stability reigns. The maturity phase, almost by definition, is one in which the rivals have established defensible territories and the attainment of critical advantage is virtually impossible. Strategy shifts to niche maintenance and the honing of established skills and tactics. Without innovation or a major change in the environment, there is no way of "winning" in a mature market unless rivals commit blunders.

As Hofer (1975) has pointed out, for the product/market life cycle frame to be truly useful in strategy evaluation, more specific contexts must be defined. The variables he suggests as important delimiters of different contexts include product differentiability, purchase frequency, nature of the buyer's needs, rate of technological change, the ratio of distribution costs to value added, price elasticity of demand, marginal plant size, and others. Hofer and other researchers are currently attempting to build a "contingency" theory of strategy by using such variables to predict the emergent winning strategies. Hofer's fundamental frame theory is that the product/market life cycle is the most critical determinant of strategy, followed closely by the nature of buyer needs (economic vs. noneconomic) and the degree of product differentiation. He goes on to specify sets of resources or market characteristics that are most significant in each stage of the life cycle and offers a number of hypotheses concerning the appropriate tactics in quite specific contexts.

The contingency approach is not only a potentially fruitful source of frame and tactical theory, it also permits theory building to be directly tied to case-type data. We do, however, disagree somewhat with the idea that the models can be used to (and be validated by) successfully predict(ing) winning strategies. There is a subtle difference between trying to predict what a firm's strategy should be in a particular context and trying to identify the issues with which it must come to grips. The predictive approach, if successful, amounts to describing the *common* characteristics of all surviving rivals. However, *among* those rivals it is still asymmetry and uniqueness rather than commonality that will govern and structure the nature of current and future rivalry. Our position is that, to be useful in the formulation and evaluation of strategy, a model must not only describe what is necessary for existence in a given context, it must also indicate what the rivalry is about – the areas in which advantage will make a critical difference. How a particular firm uses its unique history and position to attain an advantage is, ultimately, beyond the reach of general theory.

A true frame model that bears a close resemblance to life cycle theories is Abernathy's model (Abernathy and Utterback, 1975; Abernathy and Townsend, 1975) on the ways in which standardization and variety act as conflicting forces to affect relative emphasis on product vs. process innovation. According to this model, the period immediately following the introduction of a complex (composed of many subunits and requiring a wide variety of materials and specialized production steps) innovative product is one in which rival firms jockey for position by testing alternative designs. During this period, constant changes in the design of the product and the wide variety of alternate forms necessary to explore the environment limit the usefulness of highly standardized production or vertical integration. Rivalry is essentially on the basis of product performance, and product innovation is the strategic issue. Eventually, the model holds, product design and the environment come into balance and a "dominant design" appears – the model T Ford, the DC-3, the vinyl LP stereo disc, etc. The consequent stability in product and reduction in variety now permit backward integration, standardization of manufacturing process, and economies of scale in integrated production to become strategic factors. While during the product innovation phase the fluidity of design did not permit a firm to firmly commit to a particular set of subassemblies or production processes, the era of stability allows production efficiency and process innovation to become critical competitive factors.

The Abernathy model also predicts that the advantages gained by standardization will eventually work against the firm if product innovation activity is renewed. Simply stated, the strategies required for success in the stable phase make the firm more and more vulnerable to the next cycle of product innovation. Of course, the reverse may also be possible – the advantage gained by the integrated producer, particularly if significant *process* innovation is involved, may be sufficient to ensure the economic viability of its version of the dominant design for a very long period of time. Nevertheless, the idea that strategy can be too focused, producing barriers to future adaptation in addition to barriers to entry, has direct analogs in biology and provides an intriguing counterpoint to received microeconomic equilibrium models. Some empirical support for these notions comes from the Cooper and Schendel (1976) study of how the dominant producers in seven industries responded to significant technological innovations by "outsiders." Their principal finding was that, over the long run, the traditional firms that tried to participate in the new technology were not successful.

Empirically based frame and tactical models

Cross sectional analyses of policy–performance relationships in various contexts can provide valuable insights into the underlying parameters that influence variation among firms and the range of attainable states. Such studies can produce both frame and tactical theories but remain limited by the fundamental limitation of cross sectional analysis – the observed associations do not imply causality. Two examples of fairly comprehensive cross sectional studies are the PIMS project (see Schoeffler *et al,* 1974; Buzzell *et al.*, 1975) and Rumelt's (1974) study of diversification strategy.

The discovery of policy–performance relationships on a business level has historically been hampered by the unavailability of data on anything but the firm level. The PIMS project is an ongoing study that is continually building a data base of business-level statistics. Administered by the Strategic Planning Institute (SPI), the project's member firms pay a fee in order to add their business-level data to the bank and, in return, gain access to the project's proprietary programs and results. SPI ensures confidentiality and supports research based on the accumulating data.

The central theme of the PIMS results is the association between market share and return on investment (ROI). This association turns out to be quite strong and is enhanced when capital intensity is low, when the product is sold to industrial customers, when product differentiation is increased, purchase frequency decreased, and in a variety of other circumstances. The published two-way contingency tables also indicate positive associations between product quality and ROI and a host of other associations. Thought provoking and suggestive, the two-way displays unfortunately leave unanswered the question of whether or not these associations continue to hold as other conditions are changed.

The PIMS data provide what is perhaps the most potent *general* tactical model that is available for strategy evaluation at the business level. By selecting a subsample which occupies the general context of interest, the analyst can explore, on an ad hoc basis, the historical and cross sectional associations between variations in policy and changes in outcomes. No strong theory lies behind the observed associations, and quantitative theories concerning relationships among variables of this type simply do not exist.

In addition to providing immediate tactical tests of strategy workability, the PIMS data can be a rich source of frame theories. While much attention has been paid to the factors that influence profitability, an important empirical finding is that only a *few* factors explain the preponderance of profitability variance, and that these factors *change* as context changes. For example, while capital Intensity is strongly associated with profitability among firms with moderate to low market shares, it is much less important in explaining profitability variations among firms with high market shares. It is from collections of such observations and their detailed analysis that future frame theories can be constructed.

Rumelt's (1974) study of 273 large industrial corporations focused on the relationship between profitability and diversification strategy. After defining eight patterns of diversification posture, ranging from single business to unrelated portfolio, tests for long-term profitability differentials were performed. It was found that the critical explanatory factor was *not* the absolute degree of diversity, but the way in which businesses had been related to one another. In particular, the highest levels of profitability were associated with firms that were diversified but which related the majority of their activities to some central core skill, competence, or resource. The lowest levels of profitability were displayed by vertically integrated raw material producers and slowly growing conglomerates. Like the PIMS results, Rumelt's findings cannot be interpreted causally – it remains unclear whether the high performing group is profitable because of its strategy or whether the strategy of limited diversity reflects an unwillingness to abandon a highly profitable area. Nevertheless, the study provides this frame content: when diversification is at issue, the degree and type of interrelationships among activities tends to be a more critical decision area than the absolute degree of diversity.

In a more recent study, Rumelt (1977) has found that the high profitability of related-constrained firms is due to their ability to consistently take positions in industries characterized by high levels of return on capital. Furthermore, these "high-profit" industries are themselves largely composed of related-business firms.

The emergent picture is one of a class of high-profit industries existing chiefly as the intersections of related-business firms rather than as separate fields dominated by specialists. It appears that both the industry and firm phenomena are reflections of a more fundamental determinant of profitability: extensible skills together with activity in product/market arenas subject to product differentiation and market segmentation.

In summing up empirical studies on the effectiveness of strategy content, it seems evident that cross-sectional methods can be used to separate the important from the unimportant within a variety of contexts. In addition, with access to sufficient data, strong mutual associations among variables can be used as tactical models. The fact remains, however, that without an underlying theory to explain *why* the observed associations occur, there are distinct limitations on these models' ability to aid one in understanding the detailed forces at work in a particular situation.

Strategic groups models

A branch of strategy research that promises to provide a rich source of both frame and tactical models is concerned with the discovery and understanding of heterogeneous competitive groups within industries. The traditional assumption that has guided economists in the study of industrial organization is homogeneity – that firms within an industry differ only with respect to scale. A dubious assumption at best, this approach has led inexorably to characterizing industries in terms of concentration (relative size being, after all, the only attribute the model allows) or in terms of characteristics possessed collectively by all firms in the industry (e.g., entry barriers). While the roots of an effective challenge to this tradition are many, the significant contributions currently defining the field have been made by Hatten (1974) and Patton (1976) from Purdue, strongly influenced by Schendel, Cooper, and Bass (see Bass, 1969; Hatten and Schendel, 1977; Schendel and Patton, 1976), and Hunt (1972), Newman (1973), and Porter (1976) from Harvard, strongly influenced by Bower and Caves (see Caves and Porter, 1977).

Hatten studied the brewing industry between 1952 and 1971 by building a linear regression model relating observable policy variables (e.g., number of plants, price, number of brands, market share, etc.) to return on equity. Using a clustering algorithm together with a statistical test for homogeneity of regression models, he showed that the industry could actually be broken into subindustries, each with its own distinct policy–performance relationship. The five clusters corresponded to large national brewers, smaller national brewers, strong regional, weak regional, and small regional brewers. Patton used the same data but a different approach – he grouped the firms into three clusters (national, large regional, and small regional) and fitted simultaneous equation regression models to each cluster with the cyclic independent variables being return on equity, market share, and efficiency (price–cost margin).

Perhaps most striking among Patton's findings is that while market share is positively and significantly related to return on equity (ROE) for the industry taken as a whole, the relationship is negative within each cluster. In other words, the national brewers have higher levels of both market share and ROE than do regional brewers, but marginal additions to market share by either group of firms lowers profitability. The regression equations thus reveal the type of niche structure that has long been the mainstay of qualitative strategic analysis.

Taken as a frame model, Patton's results suggest that rivalry among the national brewers has been essentially on efficiency and promotion – exploiting economies of scale and the efficiency of new automated facilities in order to support massive promotional campaigns. The regional firms, by contrast, cannot play this game and, rather than being direct rivals, compete with the national firms by focusing all their efforts on one or two brands in a limited, but heavy beer drinking, region.

The beer industry is one of the most mature industries and one would not expect to find either incompetent firms or hidden winning strategies that have been missed. It is, therefore, somewhat surprising to find the model suggesting that brand proliferation strategies and plant acquisition programs by regional brewers have generally been both unsuccessful and damaging. Of course, the model cannot tell us what would have happened to firms undertaking these programs had they not done so, nor can it reveal whether the relationship is causal or just a reflection of firms in trouble taking such actions as "last ditch" efforts. Still, the general picture presented is that efficiency on a national level is the critical issue for the large brewer, and maintaining some defensible hold on a regional area, and *not* expansion, is the critical issue for the smaller brewer.

Patton's model also provides a tactical model that is useful in strategy formulation and evaluation. The regression equations that have been fitted to the brewing industry are the substance of that model and provide the strategy evaluator with a description of the "strategy possibility," or feasibility, frontier. More simply, the equations provide a check on the consistency of a set of goals and policies.

Intriguing questions remain with regard to the Hatten and Patton studies. How unique is the beer industry? Why have so few beer firms diversified to any extent? Is the observed pattern generalizable or a function of the rather unique characteristics of the beer market (e.g., unusually high resistance to new brands)?

Porter's investigation of bilateral market power provides a new frame model and additional support for the strategic group concept. Focusing on the interaction between manufacturers and retailers, Porter hypothesized that the manufacturer's profits would, other things being equal, decline as retailer bargaining power in creased. That power, he reasoned, depends chiefly on the retailer's ability to help differentiate the product. Splitting retailers (and products) into "convenience" (frequently purchased goods sold through self-service outlets) and "nonconvenience" (shopping goods sold through specialty stores and/or dealers) outlets, the latter would be expected to have a greater impact on product differentiation. Manufacturers' primary weapon in countering retailer power is strongly advertised brands since stores can hardly deny shelf space to items that consumers demand. Using these and other arguments, Porter built a model predicting that manufacturer profit rates would vary strongly with advertising intensity in convenience goods, but that advertising intensity would have a much smaller influence on the profitability of makers of non-convenience goods. The prediction was strongly supported by several tests comparing the form of traditional industry structure models in each of the two contexts.

Porter states quite clearly that his intention was to build and test a frame-type model (1976: 234): "The model identifies what strategic elements are crucial in determining profits and which ones have little effect." His results not only suggest that strong brands are the critical issue in convenience goods, but that *there is little room for strategic variability in convenience goods*. A simple bilateral model explains a great deal of the profitability variance. By contrast, branding and advertising are less critical issues in nonconvenience goods *and* the room for strategic variability is much greater. Thus, while there are only a few viable strategies in the convenience goods arena, nonconvenience goods businesses can seek advantage in many different ways (e.g., branding, service, product quality, geographical specialization; type of outlet, and so on). Porter has not only provided a new model, he has significantly increased our ability to speak clearly about and validate frame-type models.

The BCG experience effect

The Boston Consulting Group (1968) has taken the well-known learning curve effect, generalized it to apply to whole business units, and built a fairly elaborate structure that is essentially a strongly quantitative tactical model. According to BCG, the cost elements of value added tend to drop by 20 to 30% each time *accumulated* production (in units) doubles. In essence, BCG is arguing that the general observable trend of decreasing costs (adjusted for inflation) is due to a special type of scale economy that must be earned by experience rather than purchased. The immediate consequences of this proposition are: (1) of firms following roughly parallel expansion paths, the one with the largest market share will have the lowest unit costs; (2) as long as the product does not change radically, and providing that the market leader commits no blunders, trailing firms will never be able to overtake the market leader; (3) accumulated experience, or its proxy, market share, is a valuable resource and rational strategy-making requires that it be treated as an investment; and (4) eventual market dominance is determined early in the struggle for position.

Economics is supposed to be the "dismal" science; the BCG theory is dismal news indeed for many strategists. It suggests that most market positions currently being worked on are hopeless, that taking high profits in a growth industry is the road to disaster, and that the game, in the end, goes to the swiftest and most efficient.

The basic model's frame content is straightforward. The areas in which advantage occur are in having a good product ready to market earlier than one's rivals and in having the financial and organizational strength to sustain more rapid growth (at perhaps a lower margin!) than one's rivals. Like all frame models, this one is silent on the issues of gaining these advantages in the first place. BCG tends to suggest that a properly managed diversified firm has the best mix of resources to provide these advantages. In theory this may be true, but few diversified firms have been able to solve the problems of getting innovative new products to market early and of supporting division-level strategies of foregoing current profit for future return.

The BCG framework is also a powerful tactical model, especially when combined with some model of price elasticity of demand. The analyst can, by setting a few key parameters, estimate the cash flow accruing to the firm under a variety of pricing and growth policies.

The major stumbling block in using the BCG model is that the contexts in which it is valid are not well established. The electronics industry, among others, appears to be a context which supports the model, but it is not clear to what degree it applies in areas characterized by heavy branding and promotion, highly segmented markets, custom engineered products, etc. In addition, anyone who has tried to tie down the concept of "market share" in any but the simplest industries is aware how vague a concept it really is.

Our conjecture is that the BCG model will continue to be elaborated and the contexts within which it is appropriate will become better defined. In addition, it seems probable that the concept of "shared experience" among different products will ultimately prove to be a more fertile ground for strategic models than the raw experience effect theory. For example, current strategic theories almost invariably imply that persistently profitless business areas be dropped. The idea of shared experience, by contrast, suggests that careful attention must be paid to the possibility of continuing to gain experience in a low profit area in order to lower costs in a related, but more profitable, business.

Summary . . .

Focusing on analytical approaches, we began our examination of strategy evaluation by noting; that the primary function of strategy is to provide a consistent set of objectives and policies that restructures an ambiguous reality into a set of organizationally solvable subproblems. We then argued that this purpose implied four tests that must be passed if a strategy is to be judged acceptable. They were:

1. *The Coal Consistency Test* – a proposed strategy must be rejected if it contains mutually inconsistent goals, objectives, and/or policies.

2. *The Frame Test* – the strategy must be rejected if it does not address those issues on problem areas which are crucially important within the chosen context. Assuming rivalry, the strategy must exploit asymmetries which constitute advantages within the chosen domain.

3. *The Competence Test* – the strategy must be rejected if the subproblems it poses do not lie within the realm of those that are solvable by demonstrated resources or organizational skills and competences.

4. *The Workability Test* – the strategy must be rejected if the combined policies are infeasible from a resource point of view or if available knowledge indicates that the desired objectives will not be obtained by the policy set.

These tests are context free and apply to any organization in any environment. Turning to the problem of making these tests operational, we examined, in progressively narrower contexts, the frame and tactical aspects of a number of recent research efforts and contributions to theory building pertaining to the content of effective strategies.

What, then, is the state of the art? Our survey of approaches was illustrative but necessarily incomplete. Omitted was the vast literature on industrial organization, a goodly number of specific tactical models, many insightful, but as yet untested, normative propositions, the whole political process approach to the strategy formulation/evaluating issue, and many other worthwhile contributions. Nevertheless, even if our survey had been comprehensive, the simple answer would have to be that strategy evaluation is still pretty much of an art. Progress is being made, but that progress is itself an art practiced by individuals with widely varying points of view, employing disparate techniques, and aiming toward different goals. Knowledge is accumulating, but there has not, as yet, appeared a paradigm powerful enough to permit its integration. Strategy continues to be studied because of its importance rather than its tractability.

A more complete answer would have to begin by noting that the approaches examined in this article appear to conform to a pernicious variant of Heisenberg's uncertainty principle: apparently, one can gain concreteness only through a narrowing of scope, and breadth of vision is purchased at the price of essential detail. The classical approach permits the consideration of the broadest range of issues, but provides only the flimsiest structure and no calculus for the manipulation of the constructs it suggests. The BCG model, by contrast, attains a crystal clear inner logic by focusing almost entirely on the single issue of unit cost.

References

Abernathy, William J. and Phillip L. Townsend. 'Technology, Productivity, and Process Change.' *Technological Forecasting and Social Change*, Vol. 7, No. 4,197S.

Abernathy, William J. and James M. Utterback. 'Innovation and the Evolving Structure of the Firm.' Harvard Business School Working Paper 75–18, 1975.

Andrews, Kenneth. *The Concept of Corporate Strategy*. Homewood, Ill.: Dow-Jones-Irwin, 1971.

Ansoff, H. Igor. *Corporate Strategy: An Analytical Approach to Business Policy for Growth and Expansion*. New York: McGraw-Hill, 1965.

Bass, Frank. 'A New Product Growth Model for Consumer Durables.' *Management Science*, January 1969.

Berg, Norman A. 'Strategic Planning in Conglomerate Companies.' *Harvard Business Review*, May–June 1965.

Boston Consulting Group Staff. *Perspectives on Experience*. Boston: The Boston Consulting Group, 1968.

Bower, Joseph L. 'Planning within the Firm.' *American Economic Review*, May 1970.

Braybrooke, David and Charles E. Lindblom. *A Strategy of Decision*. New York: The Free Press, 1963.

Buzzell, Robert D., Bradley T. Gale and Ralph G. M. Sultan. 'Market Share—Key to Profitability.' *Harvard Business Review*. January–February 1975.

Caves, R. E. and M. E. Porter. 'From Entry Barriers to Mobility Barriers: Conjectural Decisions and. Contrived Deterrence to New Competition.' *Quarterly Journal of Economics*, May 1977.

Chandler, Alfred D. *Strategy and Structure: Chapters in the History of the American Industrial Enterprise*. Cambridge, Mass.: M.I.T. Press, 1962.

Christensen, H. Kurt. 'Product, Market, and Company Influences upon the Profitability of Business Unit Research and Development Expenditures.' Doctoral diss., Columbia University, 1977.

Cooper, Arnold C. and Dan Schendel. 'Strategic Responses to Technological Threats.' *Business Horizons*, February 1976.

Dhalla, Nariman K. and Sonia Yuspeh, 'Forget the Product Life Cycle Concept!' *Harvard Business Review*, January–February 1976.

Drucker, Peter F. 'The Effective Decision.' *Harvard Business Review*, January–February 1967.

Fiedler, Fred E. *A Theory of Leadership Effectiveness*. New York: McGraw-Hill, 1967.

Fox, Harold. 'A Framework for Functional Coordination.' *Atlanta Economic Review*, November–December 1973.

Gale, Bradley T. 'Market Share and Rate of Return.' *Review of Economics and Statistics*, November 1972.

Hatten, Kenneth J. 'Strategic Models in the Brewing Industry.' Doctoral diss., Purdue University, 1974.

Hatten, Kenneth J. and Dan E. Schendel. 'Heterogeneity within an Industry: Firm Conduct in the U. S. Brewing Industry 1952-1971.' *Journal of Industrial Economics*, December 1977.

Hofer, Charles W. 'Toward a Contingency Theory of Business Strategy.' *Academy of Management Journal*, December 1975.

Hofer, Charles W. 'Research on Strategic Planning: A Survey of Past Studies and Suggestions for Future Efforts.' *Journal of Economics and Business*, Spring–Summer 1976.

Hofer, Charles W. and Dan Schendel. *Strategy Formulation: Analytical Concepts*. St Paul, Minn.: West Publishing Company, 1978.

Hunt, Michael S. 'Competition in the Major Home Appliance Industry, 1960-1970.' Doctoral diss., Harvard University, 1972.

Kirchhoff, Bruce A. *A Foundation for the Measurement of Management by Objectives*. Salt Lake City, Bureau of Economic and Business Research, University of Utah, 1971.

Kirchhoff, Bruce A. 'Empirical Analysis of Strategic Factors Contributing to Return on Investment.' *Academy of Management Proceedings*, August 10, 1975a.

Kirchhoff, Bruce A. 'A Diagnostic Tool for Management by Objectives.' *Personnel Psychology*, Autumn 1975b.

Kirchhoff, Bruce A. and Dan Schendel. 'Linking Strategy and Operations through MBO.' Presented at the Academy of Management National Meetings, Orlando, Florida, August 1977.

Kline, C. H. 'The Strategy of Product Policy.' *Harvard Business Review*, July–August 1955.

Learned, Edmund P., C. Roland Christensen, Kenneth R. Andrews and William D. Guth. *Business Policy: Text and Cases*. Homewood, Ill.: Richard D. Irwin, 1965.

Levitt, Theodore. 'Exploit the Product Life Cycle.' *Harvard Business Review*, November–December 1965.

Likert, Rensis. *The Human Organization: Its Management and Value*. New York: McGraw-Hill, 1967.

March, James G. and Herbert A. Simon. *Organizations*. New York: Wiley, 1958.

McClelland, David C. *The Achieving Society*. New York: The Free Press, 1967.

McDonald, John. *The Game of Business*. Garden City, N.Y.: Doubleday and Co., 1975.

Mintzberg, Henry. *The Nature of Managerial Work*. New York: Harper and Row, 1973.

Newman, Howard H. 'Strategic Groups and the Structure–Performance Relationship.' Doctoral diss., Harvard University, 1973.

Patton, G. Richard. 'A Simultaneous Equation Model of Corporate Strategy: The Case of the U.S. Brewing Industry.' Doctoral diss., Purdue University, 1976.

Perrow, Charles. 'The Analysis of Goals in Complex Organizations.' *American Sociological Review*, December 1961.

Porter, Michael E. 'Interbrand Choice, Strategy, and Bilateral Market Power.' *Harvard Economic Studies*, Vol. 146. Cambridge, Mass.: Harvard University Press, 1976.

Reilley, E, W. 'Planning the Future Strategy of the Business.' *Advanced Management*, December 1955.

Rhenman, Eric. *Organization Theory for Long Range Planning*. New York: Wiley, 1973.

Rumelt, Richard P. *Strategy, Structure; and Economic Performance*. Boston: Division of Research, Graduate School of Business Administration, Harvard University, 1974.

Rumelt, Richard P. 'Diversity and Profitability.' Managerial Studies Center Working Paper MGL–51, Graduate School of Management, University of California at Los Angeles, 1977.

Schendel, Dan E. and G. Richard Patton. 'A Simultaneous Equation Model of Corporate Strategy.' Institute for Research in the Behavioral, Economic and Management Sciences Paper No. 582. Purdue University, July 1976.

Scherer, Frederic M. *The Economics of Multi-Plant Operation: An International Comparison Study*. Cambridge, Mass.: Harvard University Press, 1975.

Schoeffler, Sidney, Robert D. Buzzell and Donald F. Heany. 'Impact of Strategic Planning on Profit Performance.' *Harvard Business Review*, March–April 1974.

Schon, Donald A. *Displacement of Concepts*. London: Tavistock Publications, 1963.

Selznik, Phillip. *Leadership in Administration*. New York: Harper and Row, 1957.

Simon, Herbert A. 'Decision Rules for Production and Inventory Controls with Probability Forecasts or Sales.' O.N.R. Research Memorandum, Carnegie Institute of Technology, 1958. Quoted in Shull, F. A., A. L. Delbecq and L. L. Cummings. *Organizational Decision Making*. New York: McGraw-Hill, 1970.

Stodgill, Ralph M. *Handbook of Leadership*. New York: The Free Press, 1974.

Tilles, Seymour. 'How to Evaluate Corporate Strategy.' *Harvard Business Review*, July–August 1963.

Van de Ven, Andrew H. *Group Decision Making and Effectiveness: An Experimental Study*. Kent, Ohio: Administrative Research Institute, Kent State University, 1975.

Vickers, Sir Geoffry. *The Art of Judgment: A Study of Policy Making*. New York: Basic Books, 1965.

Wasson, Chester R. *Dynamic Competitive Strategy and Product Life Cycles*. St. Charles, Ill.: Challenge Books, 1974.

Reading 1.7 Strategic planning in a turbulent environment: evidence from the oil majors *Robert M. Grant*

First published: (2003) *Strategic Management Journal*, 24: 491–517. 'Strategy and Society', Michael E. Porter and Mark R. Kramer, *Strategic Management Journal*, Volume 24, Issue 6, June 2003. Reproduced with the kind permission of John Wiley and Sons Ltd.

Introduction

Since the early 1980s, strategic planning—systematic, formalized approaches to strategy formulation—has come under heavy attack from management scholars. Criticisms have addressed the theoretical foundations of strategic planning, particularly the impossibility of forecasting (Mintzberg, 1994b: 110), while empirical evidence—both longitudinal case studies (e.g., Mintzberg and Waters, 1982; Pascale, 1984) and investigations of strategic decision making (e.g., Bower, 1970; Burgelman, 1983)—points to strategies emerging from the weakly coordinated decisions of multiple organizational members.

Increased volatility of the business environment makes systematic strategic planning more difficult. Rapid change requires strategies that are flexible and creative—characteristics which, according to Hamel, are seldom associated with formalized planning: 'In the vast majority of companies, strategic planning is a calendar-driven ritual ... [which assumes] that the future will be more or less like the present' (Hamel, 1996: 70). Eisenhardt's research into 'high velocity environments' points to the advantages of 'semicoherent' strategic decision-making processes that are unpredictable, uncontrolled, inefficient, proactive, continuous, and diverse (Eisenhardt, 1989; Brown and Eisenhardt, 1997). If complexity and uncertainty render decision making impossible, then self-organization may be more conducive to high performance than hierarchical direction (Pascale, 1999).

The goal of this paper is to explore whether and how companies' strategic planning practices have adapted to a world of rapid, unpredictable change. The study identifies the key features of strategic planning systems in an industry that transitioned from stability to turbulence—the world petroleum industry. It explores the changing characteristics of the oil majors' strategic planning processes and the changing role of strategic planning within the companies. The study fills a gap in the literature: despite the intense debate over the merits of strategic planning and continued interest in strategic decision processes within firms, we know little about the formal systems through which companies formulate their strategic plans. The paper contributes to strategic management knowledge in three areas. First, it provides descriptive data on the strategic planning practices of some the world's largest and most complex companies during the late 1990s and how these practices changed in response to increasing environment turbulence. Second, it informs the long-running debate between the 'design' and 'process' schools of strategic management and suggests a possible reconciliation of the two. Third, it sheds light upon the coordination and control in large, complex enterprises operating in fast-changing business environments.

Planning and environmental turbulence: theory and evidence

The literature

Interest in strategy as an area of management study followed the diffusion of strategic planning ('long-range planning') among large companies during the 1950s and 1960s. Articles on long-range planning began appearing in the *Harvard Business Review* during 1956–61 (Ewing, 1956; Wrap, 1957; Payne, 1957; Platt and Maines, 1959; Quinn, 1961) and by 1965 the first systematic, analytically based frameworks for strategy formulation appeared (Ansoff, 1965; Learned *et al.*, 1965).[1] Empirical studies of corporate planning practices included, in the United States, Cleland (1962), Henry (1967), the U.S. House of Representatives Committee on Science and Technology (1976), Ang and Chua (1979), and Capon, Farley, and Hulbert (1987); and in the United Kingdom, Denning and Lehr (1971, 1972) and Grinyer and Norburn (1975).

As strategic management developed as an area of academic study, interest in companies' strategic planning practices waned. By the 1980s empirical research in strategic planning systems focused upon just two areas: the impact of strategic planning on firm performance and the role of strategic planning in strategic decision making. The first area spawned many studies but no robust findings. Ramanujam, Ramanujam, and Camillus (1986: 347) observed: 'The

[1] Professional organizations for corporate planners stimulated the development of strategy ideas and techniques. The North American Society of Corporate Planners was founded in 1961. It merged with the Planning Executives Institute to create the Planning Forum (later renamed the Strategic Leadership Forum). In the United Kingdom, the Long Range Planning Society (later renamed the Strategic Planning Society) was founded in 1966. Both societies launched journals: *Planning Review* (since renamed *Strategy & Leadership*) and *Long Range Planning*.

results of this body of research are fragmented and contra dictory,' while Boyd's (1991) survey concluded: 'The overall effect of planning on performance is very weak.[2]

The second area of research explored the organizational processes of strategy formulation. Longitudinal studies of strategy formation (Mintzberg and Waters, 1982; Mintzberg and McHugh, 1985; Mintzberg, Brunet, and Waters, 1986) and Pascale (1984) identified a process of emergence that bore little resemblance to formal, rational, strategic planning processes. Corporate-level strategic decisions emerged from complex interactions between individuals with different interests and different perceptions (Bower, 1970; Burgelman, 1983). The resulting debate pitted the advocates of systematic, rational analysis (Ansoff, 1991; Goold, 1992) against those who favored the empirical validity and normative merits of emergent processes (Mintzberg, 1991, 1994a).

The contribution of both areas of research has been limited by lack of empirical investigation of the phenomenon itself. Planning–performance studies relied upon largely superficial characterizations of strategic planning practices based mainly upon questionnaire data.[3] The 'design vs. process' debate has centered on a few well-known case examples—notably Honda's entry into the U.S. motorcycle market (Pascale, 1984; Mintzberg *et al.*, 1996); yet the validity of the Honda case remains dubious—its author described it as a 'small foundation of anecdote' arising from a 'quest for amusement rather than scholarly ambition' (Mintzberg *et al.*, 1996: 112).

The impact of environmental turbulence

Changes in the business environment reinforced the case against formal strategic planning. In the last quarter of the twentieth century, macroeconomic disequilibrium, exchange rate volatility, the microelectronics revolution, and the emergence of newly industrializing countries marked the end of postwar economic stability. Since economic and market forecasts provided the foundation for strategic planning, inability to predict demand, prices, exchange rates and interest rates represented a fundamental challenge to companies' ability to plan.

The challenge of making strategy when the future is unknowable encouraged reconsideration of both the processes of strategy formulation and the nature of organizational strategy. Attempts to reconcile systematic strategic planning with turbulent, unpredictable business environments included the following.

Scenario planning

Multiple scenario planning seeks not to predict the future but to envisage alternative views of the future in the form of distinct configurations of key environmental variables (Shoemaker, 1993, 1995). Abandoning single-point forecasts in favor of alternative futures implies forsaking single-point plans in favor of strategy alternatives, emphasizing strategic flexibility that creates option values. However, as recognized by Shell—the foremost exponent of scenario planning within the corporate sector—the primary contribution of scenario planning is not so much the creation of strategic plans as establishing a process for strategic thinking and organizational learning. Shell's former head of planning observed: 'the real purpose of effective planning is not to make to plans but to change the mental models that decision makers carry in their heads' (De Geus, 1988: 73). With scenario analysis, strategic planning is a process where decision-makers share and synthesize their different knowledge sets and surface their implicit assumptions and the mental models.

Strategic intent and the role of vision

If uncertainty precludes planning in any detailed sense, then strategy is primarily concerned with establishing broad parameters for the development of the enterprise with regard to 'domain selection' and 'domain navigation' (Bourgeois, 1980). Uncertainty requires that strategy is concerned less with specific actions and the more with establishing clarity of direction within which short-term flexibility can be reconciled with overall coordination of strategic decisions. This requires that long-term strategic goals are established, articulated through statements of 'vision' and 'mission' (Van Der Heijden, 1993), and committed to through 'strategic intent' (Hamel and Prahalad, 1989).

Strategic innovation

If established companies are to prosper and survive, new external environments require new strategies (Baden-Fuller and Stopford, 1994; Markides, 1998). Strategic planning may be a source of institutional inertia rather than innovation: 'Search all those strategic planning diagrams, all those interconnected boxes that supposedly give you strategies, and nowhere will you find a single one that explains the creative act of synthesizing experiences into a novel strategy' (Mintzberg, 1994b: 109); 'The essential problem in organizations today is a failure to distinguish planning from strategizing' (Hamel, 1996: 71). Yet, systematic approaches to strategy can encouraging managers to explore alternatives beyond the scope of their prior experiences: 'Good

[2] Miller and Cardinal (1994) did find that 'strategic planning positively influences firm performance,' however their 'meta-analysis' of 35 previous studies meant accepting the methodological weaknesses of prior studies.

[3] In some cases questionnaire data were from managers not directly involved in strategic planning. Thus, Brews and Hunt analyzed relationships between strategic planning and 'overall firm performance' using written questionnaires given to 'senior and mid-level executives attending 39 educational programs offered at three business schools' (Brews and Hunt, 1999: 896).

scenarios challenge tunnel vision by instilling a deeper appreciation for the myriad factors that shape the future' (Schoemaker, 1995: 31). Strategic inertia may be more to do with the planners than of planning per se. If top management teams are characterized by lack of genetic diversity and heavy investments of emotional equity in the past, breaking the conservative bias of strategic planning may require involving younger organizational members who are further from the corporate HQ (Hamel, 2000: 148). Strategic innovation can also be enhanced through sensitivity to emerging discontinuities in a company's evolution—these strategy/environment misalignments ('strategic inflection points') offer the potential for radical strategic change (Burgelman and Grove, 1996).

Complexity and self-organization

Mintzberg and Pascale's arguments in favor of strategy making as an organic, unsystematic, informal process have received conceptual reinforcement from complexity theory. Models of complex adaptive systems developed mainly for analyzing biological evolution have also been applied to the evolution of organizations (Anderson, 1999). These models offer interesting implications for organizational strategy. For example, faced with a constantly changing fitness landscape, maximizing survival (reaching high fitness peaks) implies constant exploration, parallel exploration efforts by different organizational members, and the combination of incremental steps ('adaptive walks') with occasional major leaps (Beinhocker, 1999). What kinds of strategy can achieve this adaptation? Brown and Eisenhardt's (1997) study of six computer firms points to the role of 'limited probes into the future' that involve experimentation, strategic alliances, and 'time-based transition processes' that link the present with the future. A key feature of strategic processes is the presence of 'semistructures' that create plans, standards, and responsibilities for certain activities, while allowing freedom elsewhere (Brown and Eisenhardt, 1997: 28–29). One application of the semistructure concept to strategy formulation concerns the use of simple rules that permit adaptation while establishing bounds that can prevent companies from falling off the edge of chaos (Eisenhardt and Sull, 2001). [See Reading 1.2]

Empirical evidence

Empirical evidence points to the coexistence of formal and informal strategic planning processes. Most large companies maintain some form of formal strategic planning. Bain & Company's annual survey of business techniques consistently identifies strategic planning as the most popular and widely utilized of any management tool (Rigby, 1999), while studies by the American Productivity and Quality Center (1996a, 1996b) report features of strategic planning systems among leading-edge U.S. corporations. Yet most strategic decisions appear to be made outside of formal strategic planning systems. Analyzing 1087 decisions by 127 *Fortune 500* companies, Sinha concluded: 'the overall contributions of formal strategic planning systems ... are modest' (Sinha, 1990: 489). In unstructured and fast-moving contexts, strategies tend to emerge: Mintzberg and McHugh (1985) identified a 'grass roots' process of strategy formulation, while Burgelman's study of Intel's exit from DRAM chips (Burgelman, 1994, 1996) pointed to the smooth and timely adaptation to external change that resulted from unplanned decision processes forming an 'internal selection mechanism.'

Evidence of the impact of environmental turbulence upon strategic planning is limited. Cross-sectional studies have produced inconsistent findings.[4] Longitudinal evidence is fragmented, but more consistent: in response to increasing environmental turbulence, strategic planning systems have changed substantially from the highly formalized processes of the 1960s and 1970s. *Business Week's* (1996: 46) proclamation that 'strategic planning is back with a vengeance' acknowledged that 'it's also back with a difference.' Details of how strategic planning systems have been adapted to increasingly unstable, unpredictable business environments are sparse. Descriptions of strategic planning practices are available for some companies, e.g., General Electric (Aguilar, Hamermesh and Brainard, 1993; Slater, 1999), Royal Dutch/Shell (De Geus, 1997), MCI (Simons and Weston, 1990), and PowerGen (Jennings, 2000), while Wilson (1994) provides more general evidence on changes in strategic planning practices. Overall, the evidence points less to a 'decline of strategic planning' (Mintzberg, 1994a), than to fundamental changes in the ways in which companies undertake their strategic planning.

Investigating these changes in companies' strategic planning practices is likely to require richer data than that used in most prior studies. Boyd and Reuning-Elliot (1998) observed that researchers have represented strategic planning—a complex, multidimensional construct—by a few indicators. However, despite their finding that 'strategic planning is a construct that can be reliably measured through seven indicators: mission statement, trend analysis, competitor analysis, long-term goals, annual goals, short-term action plans, and ongoing evaluation' (Boyd and Reuning-Elliot, 1998: 189), even multiple indicators may fail to recognize the characteris-

[4] Lindsay and Rue (1980) and Kukalis (1991) found external uncertainty to be positively associated with completeness of planning processes. Similarly, Grinyer *et al.* (1986) found that the use of specialist planners was associated with the vulnerability of companies' core technology to external threats. However, Javidan (1984) found that increased external uncertainty had not significant impact on the extent of planning.

tics of overall strategic planning configurations and their links with other processes of decision making and control.

Research questions and research method

The approach

To investigate how companies' strategic planning systems had adapted to increased environmental turbulence, I adopted an exploratory methodology in preference to formal hypothesis testing. This was for two reasons. First, a major goal of the research was to gather descriptive data on contemporary strategic planning practices in large corporations and their changes over time. Second, there is little theory relating to the design and functions of strategic planning systems within organizations. Analysis of the impact of organizational and environmental factors on the characteristics of strategic planning processes (e.g., Lindsay and Rue, 1980; Javidan, 1984; Grinyer, Al-Bazzaz, and Yasai-Ardekani, 1986) has been based upon ad hoc hypothesizing rather than any integrated theory of the design and role of strategic planning processes.

This is not to imply that my research was a-theoretic in motivation or conduct. My goal was not simply to generate descriptive data, but to shed light upon wider issues concerning the role of management in strategic decision making and corporate change. Despite the vast literature on organizational adaptation to environmental change,[5] little explicit attention has been given to the role of formal strategic planning. To understand the role of strategic planning systems in companies' processes of decision making and change, the first task is to recognize the characteristics of these systems.

The research questions

The primary questions that the research addressed were:

1. What were the principal features of the strategic planning systems of large, multibusiness, multinational corporations?

2. What has been the impact of increased volatility and unpredictability of the business environment upon companies' strategic planning processes?

3. To what extent do companies' systems of strategic planning correspond to the rational, analytic, formalized, staff-driven processes associated with the 'design school' of strategic management, and to what extent are they consistent with the emergent strategies associated with the 'process school'?

In researching these questions, I was guided by the existing literature. The research cited in the previous section suggested environmental volatility and uncertainty might have the following effects on firms' strategic planning systems:

1. *Redistribution of strategic planning decision-making authority.* Earlier studies pointed to environmental turbulence as encouraging decentralization of strategic decision-making authority from corporate to business level (Lindsay and Rue, 1980; Grinyer *et al.*, 1986) and diminishing role of staff planners relative to that of line managers (Wilson, 1994).

2. *Shorter planning horizons.* If strategic planning requires prediction, greater uncertainty about the future should shorten planning horizons. Empirical evidence is mixed: Lindsay and Rue (1980) and Javidan (1984) found no relationship between planning time spans and external stability; Kukalis (1991) found planning horizons were shorter in unpredictable markets with high levels of innovation and competition.

3. *Less formality of planning processes*. Organizational theory predicts that less stable external environments should be associated with less bureaucratization and more flexible decision making (Burns and Stalker, 1961; Courtright, Fairhurst, and Rogers, 1989). In relation to strategic planning, formality relates to fixed timescales for the planning cycle, reliance upon extensive documentation and written reports, use of standardized methodologies, and deployment of planning specialists. The empirical evidence is mixed. Wilson (1994) found external instability led to greater informality (e.g., less documentation and more flexible schedules) and Kukalis (1991) observed that increased rates of external change (interpreted as 'environmental complexity') increased the flexibility of planning practices. However, this did not necessarily mean less detailed plans: Lindsay and Rue (1980) pointed to firms' attempts to counteract uncertainty with greater planning efforts.

Method

Most studies of strategic planning processes have used questionnaire data with samples of between 48 (Grinyer *et al.*, 1986) and 199 firms (Lindsay and Rue, 1980). The result is quantitative data that can be subjected to statistical analysis, but which fail to capture the richness and complexity of firms' planning practices. As Ramanujam *et al.* (1986: 348) observed: 'Planning systems are multifaceted

[5] Theoretical streams include, *inter alia*, organizations ecology (Hannan and Freeman, 1989), punctuated equilibrium (Romanelli and Tushman, 1994), learning and evolution (e.g., March, 1981; Nelson and Winter, 1982).

management systems that are context embedded. Hence, they cannot be adequately described in terms of one or two characteristics such as "formality".' Not only are questionnaire-based descriptions of strategic planning systems overly 'thin,' they lack consistency (Boyd and Reuning-Elliott, 1998: 182). To gain insight into how the different characteristics of a company's planning system interacted and interrelated both with one another or with the other systems of decision making, coordination, and control, I adopted a comparative case study approach. Because my research did not involve hypothesis testing and because the goal was to identify *commonalities* among companies' strategic planning practices rather than analyze cross-sectional *differences*, the disadvantages of case study research in limiting the research sample were less critical.

The research site

I selected the international oil majors for my research site for four reasons. First, the oil majors were among the world's largest industrial corporations. By 1996, even after a decade of downsizing and depressed oil prices, 10 of the world's 40 largest industrial corporations (ranked by revenues) were oil companies. Second, the companies were unusual in their complexity. They were vertically integrated, diversified, and multinational, and the close linkages between their activities gave rise to complex coordination problems. Third, the companies had traditionally been at the leading edge of strategic planning practices: they had pioneered the creation of corporate planning departments and application of economic forecasting, risk analysis, portfolio planning, and scenario analysis. Finally, they had experienced a radical transformation of their industry environment from one of stability and continuity to one of uncertainty and turbulence. After several decades of stability and growth when they had been masters of their destiny, their competitive environment was thrown into turmoil by the oil shocks of 1973–74 and 1979–80, the nationalization of the reserves, and the growth of competition (Grant and Cibin, 1996).

The 10 leading oil and gas oil majors (as listed in the 1997 *Fortune Global 500*) which formed my study sample included the six surviving 'Seven Sisters'—Exxon, Shell, BP, Mobil, Texaco, and Chevron—together with a four comparative newcomers to the ranks of the international majors—Elf Aquitaine, ENI, Total, and Amoco. They are shown in [Table 1.7.1].

Data collection

The research proceeded as follows:

1. I wrote to the head of corporate planning of each company, typically the vice president, director, or general manager of strategic planning, outlining the purpose of the research and requesting cooperation. Of the 10, eight agreed to participate (these are indicated in [Table 1.7.1]).

2. Interviews were arranged with the head of the corporate planning group and with one or two other strategic planning professionals, where possible, with the manager with responsibility for the administration and support of the strategic planning process. At five of the companies (Shell, BP, ENI, Elf, and Amoco) staff members from finance and/or human resources were also interviewed in order to explore the relationships between strategic planning and the other

Table 1.7.1 The world's 10 biggest oil and gas corporations, 1996

Company	Country	Sales revenue 1996 ($m)	Employees 1996
Royal Dutch/Shell[a]	Netherlands/UK	128,174	101,000
Exxon[a]	US	119,434	79,000
Mobil[a]	US	72,267	43,000
British Petroleum[a]	UK	69,852	53,150
Elf Aquitaine[a]	France	46,818	85,400
Texaco[a]	US	44,561	28,957
ENI[a]	Italy	38,844	83,424
Chevron	US	38,691	40,820
Total	France	34,513	57,555
Amoco[a]	US	32,726	41,723

[a]Included in study sample.

Source: *Fortune Global 500*, 1997.

mechanisms for coordination and control. [Table 1.7.2] lists the interviewees at each company. The interviews were conducted between March 1996 and April 1997. The interviews were semi-structured. Notes were taken during the interviews and full reports of the interviews were written up immediately after each interview. The interviews covered the following areas:

- the planning process, including the annual planning cycle, individuals involved, methodologies employed, and the content and role of meetings and documents;
- the structure and role of the corporate strategic planning department, and of strategic planning specialists at the business level;
- the role of the strategic planning process within the overall management of the corporation;
- the linkages between strategic planning and the other systems of decision making, coordination, and control including: capital budgeting, financial control, and human resource management.

1. Interview data were supplemented with information from case studies, research papers, and company reports and documents. These were particularly useful sources of historical data on the companies' strategic planning processes. For this purpose, some former strategic planning managers were contacted.

2. A case study describing each company's strategic planning process was prepared. Where gaps or inconsistencies were apparent, the interviewees were telephoned to request clarification or additional information. Once written up, the case study was returned to the primary interviewee (typically the head of strategic planning) for comment and amendment.

The amount and quality of the data varied between the companies depending on their degree of cooperation and their concerns over disclosing proprietary information. For example, while Shell was very open about its strategic planning system and methods employed, Exxon was highly secretive. At BP and Shell, data collection was hampered by large-scale organizational changes which meant that these companies' strategic planning systems were in transition phase. Nevertheless, a detailed case study was prepared for each company describing the main features of strategic planning, the changes in these systems over time, and their role within broader management processes.

Table 1.7.2 The interviewees

Company	Position (at the time of interview)
Royal Dutch/Shell	Head of Group Planning Senior Strategist Manager, Group Planning Group Treasurer Head, Management Development
Exxon	General Manager, Corporate Planning Department Former General Manager, Corporate Planning Department Manager, Corporate Strategy Division, Corporate Planning Department Assistant Treasurer
Mobil	Vice President, Strategic Planning Global Industry Analyst, Strategic Planning Vice President, Planning, Downstream Division
British Petroleum	Strategy Coordinator Manager, Upstream Strategy, Former Head of Chairman's Office
Elf Aquitaine	Director, Direction Prospective Economie Strategic Manager, Direction Prospective Economie Strategic
Texaco	Vice President, Corporate Strategy and Planning Director of Planning Manager, Corporate Strategy and Planning Director of Organization and Executive Development
ENI	Director, Planning and Control Department Deputy Director, Planning and Control Department Manager, Planning and Control Department Deputy Director, Personnel and Organization
Amoco	Director, Market Analysis, Strategic Planning Practice Leader, Competency Modeling Organization Effectiveness Consultant

The main features of strategic planning among the oil majors

The strategic planning cycle

All the companies in the sample engaged in a formal, strategic planning process built around an annual planning cycle. Each company's planning cycle (with the exception of BP, which declined to make available its planning framework) is shown in [Figure 1.7.1]. Despite differences between companies in the depiction of their planning processes and the terminology they used to describe it, the similarities were sufficient to identify a 'generic' strategic planning cycle (see [Figure 1.7.2]).

The principal stages of the planning process common to all the companies were the following:

1. *Planning guidelines*. The starting point for the annual planning cycle was an announcement by the corporate headquarters of guidelines and assumptions to be used by the businesses in preparing their business-level strategic plans. These guidelines and assumptions comprised two major elements. First, a view of the external environment: This typically included guidance as to some features of energy markets over the planning period—demand, supply, prices, and margins—which were not so much forecasts as a set of assumptions relating to prices and supply and demand conditions that provided a common basis for strategic planning across the company. Some companies put greater emphasis on scenarios—alternative views of possible developments in the energy sector. Second, corporate management provided overall direction to the planning process through a statement of priorities, guidelines, and expectations. A key aspect of Ibis direction was setting company-wide performance targets (e.g., 'raise return on capital employed to 12%,' 'reduce costs per barrel by 10%,' 'a 110% reserve replacement rate,' 'reduce the ratio of debt to equity ratio to 25% by 2000'). Guidance often related to resource allocation, e.g., 'to shift investment from downstream to upstream,' 'to refocus on core businesses,' 'to take advantage of opportunities in China and East Asia,' 'to increase the proportion of gas in our hydrocarbon reserves.'

2. *Draft business plans.* Strategic plans were formulated bottom-up: the individual businesses took the initiative in formulating their strategic plans.[6]

3. *Discussion with corporate.* The draft business plans were submitted to the corporate headquarters. After some initial analysis by the corporate planning staff, a meeting was held between senior corporate and senior divisional management. These face-to-face meetings lasted between 2 hours and a full day and discussed the rationale for the strategies being pursued, the performance implications of these strategies, and the compatibility of the business strategy with corporate goals.

4. *Revised business plans.* The draft business plans were then revised in the light of the discussions.

5. *Annual capital and operating budgets.* The strategic planning process was closely linked with the annual budgeting process. Although budgeting is coordinated and administered by the controller's department, the first year of the strategic plan typically provided the basis for next year's capital expenditure budget and operating budget.

6. *Corporate plan.* The corporate plan resulted from the aggregation of the business plans, which was undertaken by the corporate planning department.

7. *Board approval.* The final formality of the strategic planning formulation was approval of the corporate and business plans by the board of directors.

8. *Performance targets.* From the corporate and business plans a limited number of key financial and strategic targets were extracted to provide the basis for performance monitoring and appraisal. Targets related to the life of the plan with a more detailed emphasis on performance targets for the coming year.

9. *Performance appraisal.* The performance plans provided the basis for corporate-level appraisal of business level performance. In addition to ongoing performance monitoring, a key event was the annual meeting between the top management team and divisional senior managers to discuss each business's performance during the prior year.

For companies whose financial years corresponded to calendar years, the planning cycle began in the spring, with corporate and business plans finally approved in November or December, and performance reviews occurring around the beginning of the following year (see [Figure 1.7.3]).

The role and organization of corporate planning staffs

All of the companies possessed a corporate staff unit responsible for strategic planning headed by a vice president or a director of corporate planning or strategy (or, in the case of Exxon, a general manager). The functions of these corporate planning departments included:

- Providing technical and administrative support to strategic management activities. In all the companies,

[6] For most companies, strategic planning was a three-stage process: business unit strategy, divisional strategy, and corporate strategy. For simplicity, I treat strategic planning as a two-stage process distinguishing between corporate strategy and business-level strategy that comprised both divisional and business unit strategies.

Figure 1.7.1 The companies' strategic planning cycles

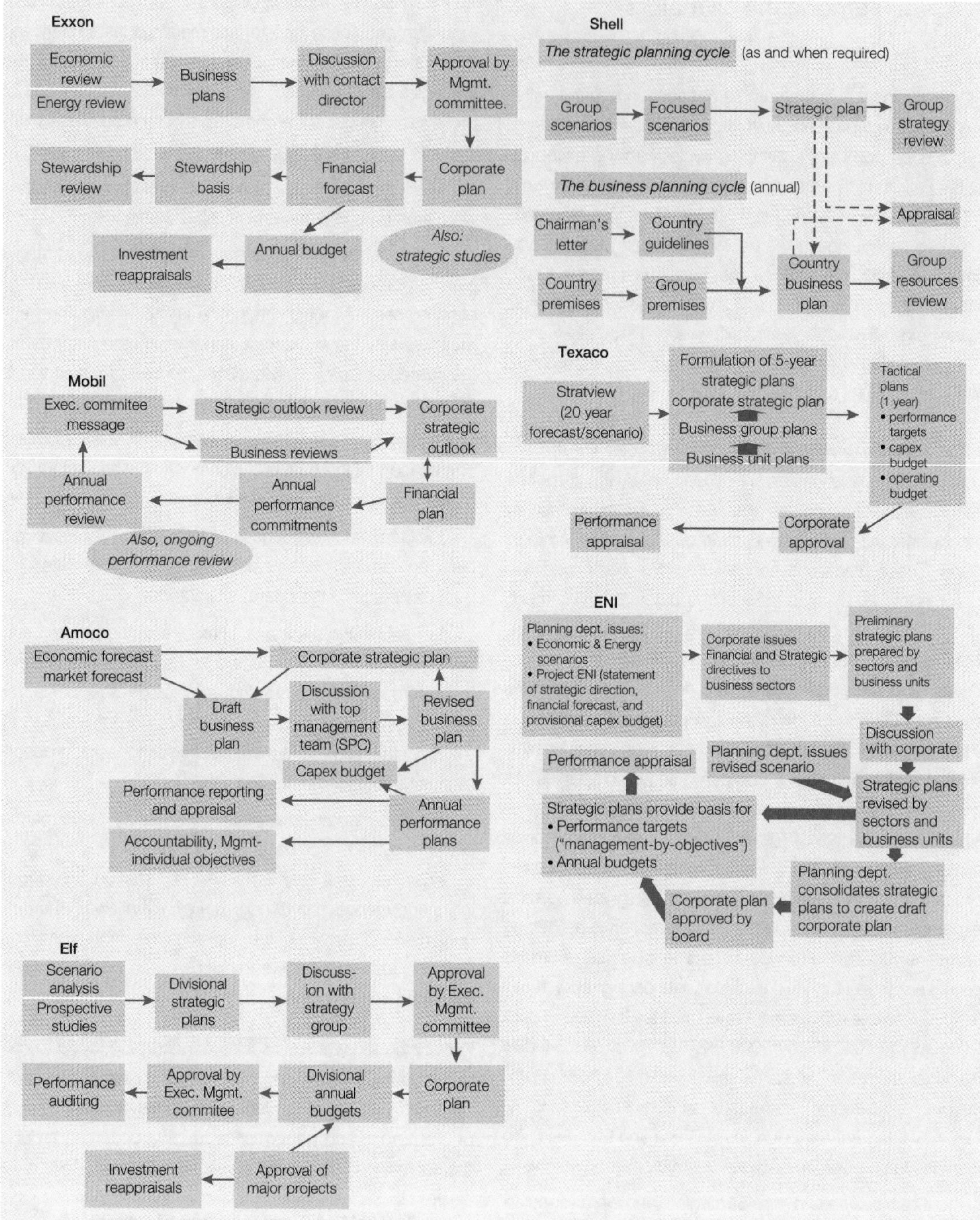

responsibility for corporate strategy lay with the top management team. The corporate planning staff's responsibility was to support the corporate executive team in its strategic management role (for example, in providing information and analysis, and exploring the impacts of alternative assumptions and courses of action) and to administer the planning process.

• Preparing economic, political, and market forecasts, risk analysis, competitor analysis, and other investigations of the business environment to assist strategic planning through the company.

• Fostering communication between corporate and business management. In some of the companies—notably

Figure 1.7.2 The generic strategic planning cycle among the oil majors

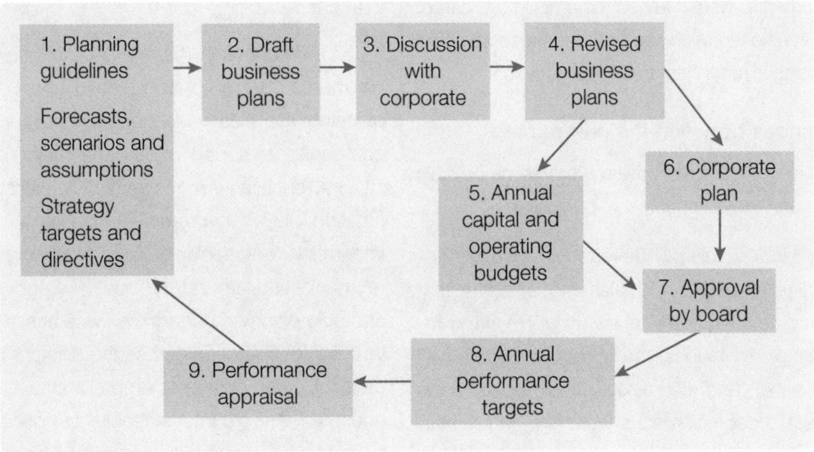

1. Planning guidelines
Forecasts, scenarios and assumptions
Strategy targets and directives
2. Draft business plans
3. Discussion with corporate
4. Revised business plans
5. Annual capital and operating budgets
6. Corporate plan
7. Approval by board
8. Annual performance targets
9. Performance appraisal

Figure 1.7.3 Timing of the planning cycle

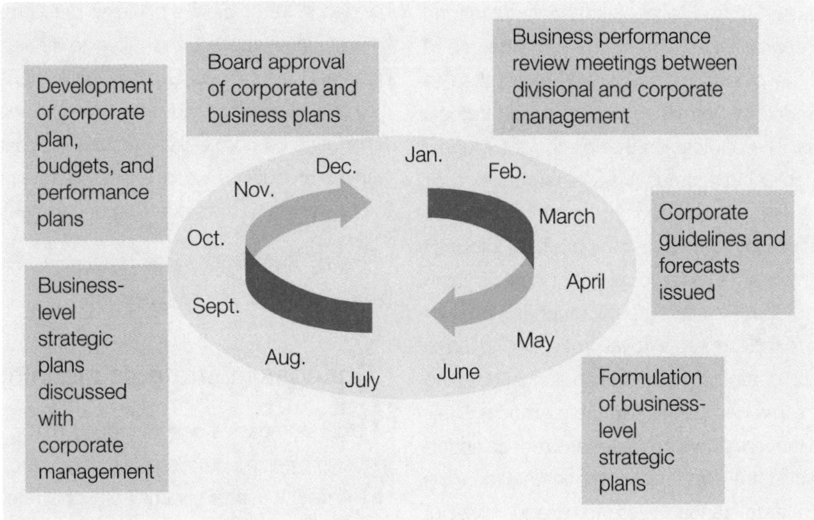

Shell, Mobil, ENI, and Amoco—corporate planners liaised with divisional managers and divisional planners, and fostered dialog through a common format and terminology for strategic plans. In other companies—notably Exxon and BP—high levels of involvement by corporate planning staff was viewed as a barrier to strategy dialog between business-level chief executives and corporate top management.

• Internal consulting. To the extent that corporate planning departments became repositories of expertise about strategy analysis and strategic planning techniques, they tended to develop internal consulting roles in relation to the businesses and other functions.[7]

[7] The activities of corporate planning departments are reflected in the organizational structures. Organization charts for the planning departments are available from the author.

Who are the corporate planners?

Unlike certain other corporate functions (finance, law, and information systems), none of the companies recognized strategic planning as a career track. Corporate planners were drawn from line management positions within the businesses and, in some cases, from other staff functions (e.g., finance and IT). Planners typically spent between 3 and 5 years in corporate planning posts before returning to a line management position. The only examples of career track planners were, first, the few professional economists that resided in corporate planning departments and, second, some corporate planning managers in two companies with significant public ownership, ENI and Elf, who spent 15 years or more within the planning function. Several companies explained that their staffing of corporate planning departments reflected their intention to combine the analytic skills of younger staff with the deep experiential knowledge of longer-serving managers. At all the companies corporate planning assignments were viewed as important career development stages offering corporate-level exposure and a 'big-picture' perspective for 'fast track' executives.

Differences between the companies

Within this common framework, there were some notable differences between the companies. In particular:

1. *Formality and regularity.* Several companies, notably Elf Aquitaine and ENI, had planning systems that were more formal (e.g., greater reliance upon written reports and formal presentations), more regular (in terms of a fixed annual cycle), and less flexible than those of the other companies. These differences were related primarily to differences in overall management styles—Elf and ENI had retained more traditional hierarchical structures and formal administrative styles, in contrast to the other companies (most notably BP and Texaco) that had encouraged a more entrepreneurial management style. The degree of formalization of the planning process was also linked to the emphasis given to performance targets in the strategic planning process. The companies that placed the biggest emphasis on establishing rigorous financial targets for their businesses—BP, Texaco, and Exxon, in particular—also had planning processes that were comparatively informal. Conversely, companies that emphasized strategic control—ENI, Elf, and Shell—placed greater emphasis on written strategic plans and formal approval processes. In terms of regularity, all the companies pursued an annual planning cycle; however, some companies—notably Amoco, Shell, and Mobil—had moved away from standardized, calendar-driven annual cycles; they updated environmental analysis and performance targets annually (or more frequently), but called for revision of business strategies only when circumstances required.

2. *The time horizon of strategic plans.* Strategic plans were typically for 4–5 years, although in upstream planning horizons tended to be longer—up to 15 years in the case of Exxon. Several companies—notably Shell, Texaco and Elf—operated a dual system of planning: long-term planning that extended for 10 years or more and was typically qualitative and scenario based, and medium-term planning that was more detailed and quantitative and involved a greater level of commitment. Shell had the longest horizon for its strategic plans—up to 20 years—however, these long-term strategic plans took the forms of long-term views of the business and the environment where the primary object was to encourage long term-thinking about the business in the light of underlying technological, political, and business trends. Texaco maintained 15- to 20-year strategic views, though, like Shell, Texaco's long-term plans involved no formal resource commitment.

3. *Differences in the role and activities of planning departments.* The emphasis placed upon different strategic planning activities varied across the companies. Among companies that had undergone major internal reorganizations, such as Amoco and ENI, the strategic planning function played a prominent role as a coordinating and integrating mechanism. Thus, following Amoco's 1995 reorganization around 17 business separate groups, the strategic planning department was actively involved in developing cooperation across the different business, e.g., in creating cross-business 'umbrella strategies' for individual countries. A more interventionist role of corporate planning departments was also apparent within those companies whose corporate planners fulfilled an internal consulting role. Although Shell's internal consulting unit was disbanded in 1992, Shell's planning group maintained an active role in promoting and diffusing strategic management ideas and techniques. Similarly, ENI's planning department maintained a strong advisory role and was active in disseminating corporate-level goals and priorities. Companies with the broadest roles for their corporate planners also had the biggest corporate planning departments.

[Table 1.7.3] summarizes key features of the individual companies' strategic planning systems.

Changes in strategic planning systems

All eight companies acknowledged major changes in their strategic planning practices over the previous decade and a half. While the basic framework of strategic planning—in terms of the strategic planning cycle and its key phases—remained little changed, the content of strategic plans, the strategic planning process, and the role of planning within the companies' management systems changed considerably.

The planning heritage of 'Big Oil'

From the interviewees' accounts and prior research (notably, Grayson, 1987), I was able to identify the major features of the companies' strategic planning systems at the beginning of the 1980s. Corporate planning had been adopted by most of the companies during the early 1960s, in response to the increasing difficulties of coordination and control that the companies faced as they expanded their vertical, geographical, and product scope during the postwar period. Strategic planning began within their supply departments, where planning of international flows of oil and refined products had developed expertise in forecasting prices and market trends. By the late 1960s, most

Table 1.7.3 Features of the oil majors' strategic planning systems

	Types and duration of plans	Frequency	Strategic planning goals	Capital expenditure authorization limits	Special features of planning system
Amoco	Each of the 17 business groups and the whole corporation formulate: • 5-year strategic plans • 1-year performance plans that include financial targets, strategic milestones, and capex budgets	Corporate plan annual; business group strategic plans updated when needed	Emphasis on: • improving quality of decision making among the businesses • more effective coordination among businesses • creating emphasis on improved shareholder return	For projects with outline approval within the business strategic plans, business heads could approve capital expenditures up to $50m	Strategic planning central mechanism for system managing Amoco's newly decentralized structure and driving company transformation to becoming a global, high-performance company
BP	5-year strategic plans are formulated for each business and for whole company. In addition a longer-term qualitative view of the development of the company and its environment is created by the corporate planning unit. The 5-year strategic plans are closely linked with annual operating plans that are strongly financially oriented	Annual	Emphasis on: • performance contracts between each business and the corporate center • developing and exploiting distinctive competences	Division-level authorization levels increased from between £5m to £15m in the mid-1980s; by 1996 only proposals involving expenditure above $150m needed board approval	Post-1985, annual strategic planning cycle displaced by annual performance planning cycle and strategic planning became an informal process managed by the businesses with emphasis on continuous dialog between the businesses and the corporate center
Elf Aquitaine	Strategic plans formulated by each business unit, each division, and the Corporation as a whole. Upstream plans for 10 years, downstream and chemicals for 5 years	Annual planning cycle	Emphasis on corporate control of the divisions, together with need for improved corporate performance	Divisional heads could approve up to FF60m (approx. $10m)—higher for E&P, lower for Health and Beauty division)	Heritage of top-down, scenario-driven planning being moderated with increased attention to profitability goals
ENI	4-year strategic plans formulated for each business unit, each sector, and for the group as a whole. The first year of the plan forms the basis for annual capital and operating budgets and annual performance objectives	Annual planning cycle	Emphasis on corporate control over operating company strategy and corporate pressure for efficiency and cost reduction	Up to 50 billion lire (approximately $30m) could be approved by operating company presidents; larger sums required corporate-level approval. Limits increased in 1996	Corporate planning department played central role in 1994–97 privatization forcing financial discipline, cost cutting, and asset divestment upon the operating companies
Exxon	Business units and divisions formulate: • strategic plans (upstream 14 years; downstream and chemicals 4–5 years) • 2-year financial forecasts • annual operating and capital budgets • annual stewardship targets including financial, operational, and environmental goals and strategic mileposts	Annual planning cycle	Planning system primarily a means of setting stretch targets for the divisions and coordinating the division strategies	Divisional presidents could; authorize expenditures up to $15m ($20m for E&P); individual members of the Management Committee; could authorize up to $50m	Since transformations of Exxon's corporate management systems in 1985–90, strategic planning emphasizes close informal collaboration between divisional presidents and the Management Committee

Table 1.7.3 Features of the oil majors' strategic planning systems (Continued)

	Types and duration of plans	Frequency	Strategic planning goals	Capital expenditure authorization limits	Special features of planning system
Mobil	Business units, business groups and the corporation as a whole each formulate 5-year strategic plans. The first year of the plan provides the basis for the Annual Financial Plan and the Annual Performance Commitments	Annual planning cycle	Planning system used to drive entrepreneurship among businesses and improve performance through quantitative targets	Corporate-level approval required for expenditures over $10m	Strategic planning mainly decentralized to the businesses. Major emphasis on performance metrics
RD/Shell	Strategic planning organized around two processes: • 20-year strategic plans that grew out of Shell's scenario planning process • 5- to 10-year business plans that are formulated for sectors, countries, and regions	Strategic plans every 4 or 5 years Business plans annual	Planning system a means of enhancing the quality of operating company strategies and coordinating across sectors and regions	In 1996, operating co. CEOs could approve up to $lm and individual Managing Directors up to $10m. After reorganization 'all discretionary levels were increased greatly to relieve the Committee of Managing Directors from having to approve endless numbers of individual projects'	Traditionally a communication-intensive planning process with coordination around sectors, regions, and functions. Break-up of Shell's matrix structure and increased emphasis on profitability causing Shell's planning system to become more performance oriented
Texaco	Strategic planning involves: • 15- to 20-year scenario-based, qualitative 'strategic views' • 5-year quantitative strategic plans undertaken by the businesses and combined into the corporate strategic plan • 1-year tactical plans comprising budgets and performance targets	Strategic views each 3–5 years Strategic plans annual	Emphasis of strategic planning as a mechanism for 'capturing knowledge' and for driving shareholder return	Capital expenditure authorization limits were not disclosed	Strong bottom-up strategic planning orientation with corporate-level focusing mainly upon performance requirement. Coordination achieved more through open communication than through hierarchical integration of plans

of the oil majors had established corporate planning departments.[8]

The primary task of these corporate planning departments was forecasting trends in energy markets and the general economy. Macroeconomic forecasts provided the basis for predictions of the demand, supply, and prices of oil and refined products upon which outputs, revenues, profits, and capital investment requirements were projected. Hence, all the planning departments included an economics unit typically headed by a professional economist.[9] Diversification during the 1970s expanded the role of the corporate planning departments. By 1980 the corporate planning departments were involved in: forecasting demand, supply, prices, and profit margins; creating scenarios; undertaking country risk

[8] Conoco established its planning department in 1953, Standard Oil (Ohio) in 1961, Atlantic Richfield in 1962, Royal Dutch/Shell and Elf Aquitaine in 1967, British Petroleum and Total in 1968, ENI in 1971, and Chevron in 1974.

[9] The typical functions were to provide 'appraisals of domestic and international political–economic patterns and the potential consequence of these patterns; ... macroeconomic studies and predictions of the U.S. economy; [and] political, economic and energy policy analysis and consultation in support of the development of policies, strategies, and environmental assumptions by the Planning Division, Governmental and Public Affairs Division, and other Company units' (memo by Robert Wycoff, Vice President, Planning, Arco, November 18, 1974).

analysis; building corporate financial models to link economic and market forecasts to company financial performance; administering the annual strategic planning cycle; developing planning methodologies and techniques; advising corporate and divisional management on strategic issues; and providing strategic analysis of major capital investment projects.

In administering the strategic planning process, the corporate planning departments became important intermediaries between corporate and divisional management—communicating corporate goals and priorities to divisional managers, assessing business-level plans presented to top management, and aggregating business-level plans into corporate plans. This pivotal role resulted in them exerting significant influence not just over the process of strategy formulation, but in many instances over its content as well.

Forces for change

The transformation of energy majors' market environment from stability and continuity to uncertainty and turbulence also created a far more hostile environment. The catastrophic fall in the price of oil in 1986 and increased competition at all stages of the companies' value chains put profits under considerable pressure. Simultaneously, a surge in acquisitions and leveraged buyouts created a more active market for corporate control that pressured top management to improve returns to shareholders. This transformation had far-reaching implications for the companies' strategies, structures, and management processes (Cibin and Grant, 1996)—including their strategic planning systems.

The changing foundations of strategic planning

The dangers of using medium-term forecasts as a foundation for business and corporate plans became painfully apparent during the 1980s, when the accuracy of macroeconomic and market forecasts—especially of crude oil prices—declined precipitously. As late as 1992, BP was brought to the brink of catastrophe as the result of a strategy that had assumed an oil price of $20 a barrel. CEO John Browne subsequently remarked:

> We gave up trying to forecast what would happen some time ago—we'd just learned from experience that even the most sophisticated models can't predict the reality of oil prices or any of the other key variables. All you can do is to look at the current reality, and the recent pattern of the economic cycle and from that set yourself some guidelines against which you can judge your own performance.

During the 1980s and 1990s, all the companies reduced their forecasting efforts and downsized or eliminated their economist staff. Exxon's economic forecasting and analysis unit was reduced to a single staff economist. In place of forecasts, the companies' external analysis shifted in two directions. The first was scenario planning. While Shell was the only company to base its entire strategic planning process upon multiple scenario analysis, other companies adopted scenario planning to a more limited extent, for example, to explore particular issues (such as the future of OPEC or strategies for the former Soviet Union). Replacing single-point forecasts with alternative scenarios of the future had important implications for the nature of strategic planning. Instead of a single basis for competitive positioning and resource deployment, scenario analysis was a tool for contingency planning that fostered alertness and responsiveness among decision-makers to changing market circumstances. The reluctance of some companies to use scenarios more widely as a basis for strategy formulation was partly the result of the perceived costs of developing and disseminating scenarios in terms of management time.

The second response was to replace forecasts of key variables with assumptions about these variables. Thus, in relation to the prices of crude oil, natural gas, and refined products and key currency exchange rates, all the companies introduced 'reference prices' which provided a basis for financial projections and performance targets. Again, this shifting basis for planning had far-reaching implications for the nature of strategic planning.[10] The purpose of reference prices and other fixed assumptions about the environment was not to provide a basis for strategic decisions, but to provide a consistent foundation against which financial performance could be targeted and monitored. This shift of planning from 'strategy-as-resource-deployment' to 'strategy-as-aspirations-and-performance-goals' is a key transition that I return to below.

Growing informality of the planning process

The planning systems of the 1970s and 1980s were highly formalized in terms of documentation, formal presentations, emphasis on techniques and quantitative analysis, and the central role of specialist planners. By 1996–97, planning systems were far more informal: there was less emphasis on written documentation, strategic plans were shorter, and there was less emphasis on set-piece presentations and more on open discussion. To encourage discussion and the exchange of ideas: new rules-of-play were adopted: BP discouraged the use of multiple graphs at strategy meetings; Amoco limited the number of slides at strategy presentations. Meetings between business-level and corporate executives became shorter and the balance shifted from presentation to discussion. All the companies

[10] Exxon and several other companies used the term 'reference prices.' BP used the term 'mid-cycle prices' (referring to price assumptions that were averaged across the economic cycle).

reported that the annual meetings between corporate and business executives to discuss business-level strategic plans were increasingly focused around discussion of a few underlying issues. Similarly, at strategy and performance review meetings, discussion became focused around just a smaller set of performance variables. As a result, meetings become shorter:

- At Mobil performance reviews were downsized from 2-day meetings with each division with formal presentations by business managers to shorter, more informal interactions where business group management reported to the Executive Committee on 'How we did. What we did. What we didn't do.'
- At Exxon, the annual 'stewardship reviews' between the divisional president and the Management Committee were cut from 3 or 4 days down to a half-day. These meetings focused upon reports of key performance indicators and 'Things we feel good about, and things we feel bad about.'

Less formality was also evident in a move from a regular, standardized planning cycle to more flexible and ad hoc process. As noted above, Amoco allowed its business groups to develop new strategic plans as and when needed, while the long-term, scenario-based projections by Shell and Texaco became less regular.

Shifting strategic planning responsibilities

Increasing volatility and uncertainty of the external environment was accompanied by two changes in strategic planning responsibilities: first, a shift of decision-making responsibility from corporate to business-level managers; second, a shift of planning responsibilities from planning staff to line managers.

From corporate management to business management

By the late 1990s, strategic planning was primarily a bottom-up process. The content of the strategic plans were determined mainly at the business unit and divisional levels under the principle that business-level chief executives were responsible for their businesses—including their business strategies. This concept of business-level management 'owning' the business and being responsible to shareholders and corporate executives for its management was a particularly strong philosophy at Exxon and BP. The corporate influence was primarily in establishing the context for business strategy formulation and intervening to question, criticize, and cajole business managers. Decentralization of strategic management authority was indicated by the increasing levels of discretion exercised by business unit and divisional managers over capital expenditures. As [Table 1.7.3] shows, during the 1990s all the companies raised authorization levels of individual executives.

This transfer of strategic planning responsibilities from corporate to divisional level was part of a broader shift in the relationship between corporate and divisional management. The key priorities of the 1990s were speedier decision making to respond to fast-changing external circumstances and the increasing returns of shareholders. Strategic planning systems became less about planning the majors' long-run growth and stability, and more about squeezing increased profitability from mature, slow growth businesses. If business-level managers were to take responsibility for strategic decisions, while corporate management was to be responsible for shareholder returns, decentralization of strategic decision making needed to be matched by divisional executives being unambiguously accountable for divisional performance. By 1996, the primary focus of the strategic planning processes of the majors was medium-term performance targets. If the primary responsibility of divisional management was to achieve the levels of performance expected by corporate management, the inevitable corollary was that divisional management must be free to select strategies capable of delivering the required performance. The role of the corporate headquarters in strategic planning focused less on endorsing and approving business-level strategies and more on negotiation with the divisions over expected performance levels and questioning and challenging the thinking behind the proposed strategies in order to improve the quality of divisional strategic decision making.

From staff to line managers

Decentralization of strategic planning from corporate to business levels coincided with a declining role of planning staff as corporate and divisional line managers became increasingly responsible for strategic planning. This diminishing role of strategic planning staff reflected the increasing personal responsibility on executives at all levels. As chief executives became more accountable to shareholders for corporate performance and divisional heads became increasingly responsible to their chief executives for divisional performance, so these executives became individually responsibility for strategy. The shift of responsibility from staff planners to executives is indicated by the shrinking size of corporate planning departments (see [Table 1.7.4]). This downsizing of corporate planning staffs was reinforced by the reduction in economic forecasting activities and the outsourcing of intelligence activities and analysis to consulting companies. In addition, planning staff became increasingly located within the operating divisions. For example, at Mobil in 1996, corporate planning staff numbered only 13; however, each of Mobil's 13 business groups had its own planning units, and throughout the (approximately) 100 'natural businesses' there were some 470 planning staff. Similarly, at ENI, at the beginning of 1995, the 72 corporate planning

Table 1.7.4 Numbers employed in corporate planning departments

	1990	1993	1996
Amoco	90	60	30
BP	48[a]	12	3
Elf	n.a.	15	14
ENI	n.a.	72	65
Exxon	42[a]	20	17
Mobil	38	n.a.	12
Shell	48[b]	23	17
Texaco	40	n.a.	27

[a]Estimated. In 1986 Exxon's corporate planning staff numbered 60.

[b]Estimated. In 1985 Shell's corporate planning staff numbered 54.

staff were outnumbered by the 416 strategic planning staff located in the operating companies.

The content of strategic plans

A detailed analysis of the content of strategic plans was not possible owing to the reluctance of the companies to make available their plans. Only two of the companies made available recent planning documents. Nonetheless, it was clear from the interviews that some significant changes had occurred in the content of strategic plans over the previous decade. Three trends were common to all the companies:

1. *Shortening time horizons.* [Table 1.7.3] shows the periods for which the companies prepared their strategic plans. All the companies reported a shortening of their planning horizons over the previous decade.[11] Among my sample, five out of the eight companies had planning periods of 5 years or less. However, the major contraction of companies' strategy horizons resulted, not from formal changes to their planning periods, but from shifting their emphasis from the long term to the short and medium term. For example, the companies that engaged in both medium-term strategic planning and longer-term scenario planning (Shell, Texaco, and Elf) increased their emphasis on medium-term planning at the expense of longer-term projections. Foreshortened planning horizons were most apparent among companies whose strategic priorities were dominated by restructuring, cost cutting, and the need to boost shareholder return (e.g., ENI's strategic plans period was only 4 years). A second trend was to link planning periods more closely to the lives of investment. Thus, Exxon and Elf each required their upstream sector to plan for 10–15 years as compared to 5 years for their downstream and chemical sectors.

2. *A shift from detailed planning to strategic direction.* Increased environmental instability resulted not only in less formality and rigidity of the planning process, but also in less precision and greater flexibility in the content of strategic plans. Strategic plans became less concerned with detailed programs of action, commitments to particular projects, and resource deployments, and placed greater emphasis upon more broadly defined goals. For example, Amoco's strategic plan of 1995–99 was specified almost entirely in terms of 'strategic themes' and 'specific strategies and goals'. These strategies and goals related to themes that included financial targets ('net income to exceed $3 billion by 1998') and cost reduction ('achieve cost savings of $1–2 billion from restructuring') and international expansion (e.g., 'to develop a global gas business'). This shift to broad strategic direction is also indicated by the adoption by all the companies (with the exception of Exxon and Elf Aquitaine) of statements of 'mission' and/or 'vision' to communicate and guide their strategies. Although these mission and vision statements were partly exercises in image management, the interviewees pointed to their significant role in the strategy-making process in terms of creating a sense of corporate, identity-setting boundaries for corporate scope and establishing long-term strategic intent.

3. *Increased emphasis on performance planning.* In discussing the shifting relationship between corporate and divisional levels in the planning processes, I noted the increasing emphasis placed on performance targets. During the 1990s, the strategic plans of all the companies shifted their focus away from forecasts and specific strategic decisions that specified timetables and resource deployments, and towards targets relating to financial and operational performance targets. Thus, of Amoco's six strategic themes of 1995–99, four were couched entirely in terms of performance outcomes rather than commitments to take specific actions. The growing preoccupation with performance goals was also evident in the increasing emphasis placed upon short and medium performance planning within the strategic planning process. Despite different terminology—'performance plans' (Amoco), 'management by objectives' (ENI), 'stewardship basis' (Exxon), and 'performance commitments' (Mobil)—the elements were similar:

- *Financial targets.* These focused upon total profit (typically net profit and/or operating profit, and in some cases economic profit, e.g. EVA) and profitability ratios (return on capital employed was the most widely used). Several companies set targets for shareholder return (typically defining targets in relation to the sector as a

[11] This was consistent with Grayson (1987), who identified only one oil company with a planning period of less than 8 years.

whole, e.g., 'to achieve a return to shareholders in the top quartile of the industry').

- *Operating targets*. For upstream these might include production, wells drilled, lease agreements signed, reserves added. For downstream these might include throughput, capacity utilization, inventories.
- *Safety and environmental objectives.*
- *Strategic mileposts*—intermediate objectives which were indicators that a strategy was on track. For a division, strategic mileposts might relate to entry into specific countries, specific cost reduction, targets, new product introductions, and divestments of specified assets.
- *Capital expenditure limits.*

Among these different objectives, the overwhelming priority for all the companies was financial targets. This emphasis was evident in the tools and techniques used by the companies' planning departments. Despite all the strategy concepts, tools, and techniques developed during the 1990s—from competitive analysis to the analyses of resources and capabilities—most of the new tools and techniques deployed by the oil majors during the 1990s were financial in nature. These included new measures of profitability (e.g., EVA), techniques of shareholder value analysis, and real options analysis.

The companies were acutely aware of the problems of reconciling short-term (annual) performance targets with longer-term performance goals—while effective performance monitoring required quarterly and annual appraisal, maximization of shareholder value required long-term profit maximization. Hence all the companies sought to combine short-term profit targets with strategic and operational targets that were consistent with building longer-term competitive advantage (e.g., the operating targets and strategic mileposts referred to above). Mobil, Texaco, and Amoco used 'balanced scorecards' for achieving consistency between short-term performance targets and longer-term strategic goals. At Mobil, balanced scorecards played a key role in 'cascading down' corporate and divisional strategies to business units and individual departments.

The essential complements to performance plans were performance reviews. At all the companies, reviews of business performance against performance targets and strategic plan were central elements of the strategic planning process. Most companies had quarterly performance reviews based on the businesses submitting written performance reports with informal discussion between divisional and corporate management. The major business-corporate interactions were at the annual performance reviews that took place in the early part of the calendar year and involved face-to-face meetings between divisional and corporate top management.

The role of strategic planning

Changes in the oil majors' strategic planning practices pointed to a different role for strategic planning within the companies. The strategic planning systems of the 1960s and 1970s were mechanisms for formulating strategy—they planned growth and allocated resources. By the late 1990s, strategy formulation was occurring, for the most part, outside of the companies' strategic planning systems. When interviewees were asked to identify the sources of critical strategic decisions that their companies had made in recent years—acquisitions, divestments, restructuring measures, and cost-cutting initiatives—it was apparent that few had their origins in the plans that emerged from the companies' strategic planning systems. The typical sequence was the other way round: strategic decisions were made in response to the opportunities and threats that appeared, and were subsequently incorporated into strategic plans. If the purpose of the strategic planning system was not primarily to take strategic decisions, what role did it play within the companies' management? The interview data pointed to three key roles.

Strategic planning as a context for strategic decision making

Even if strategic planning systems were no longer the primary decision paths for making strategy, they created contexts that influenced the content and quality of strategic decisions. Even here, the mechanisms through which the corporate center conventionally influenced business-level strategies—providing forecasts and detailed scrutiny—had progressively eroded. This left two key processes through which the corporate planning processes contributed to the quality of business-level strategic management:

1. *Influencing the methodologies and techniques of strategic planning.* Although corporate planning departments continued to act as centers of excellence for strategy methods and strategy techniques, downsizing of planning departments downsized and increased reliance upon outside consultants for analytical expertise constrained this role. Some tools of strategy analysis were widely used, including Porter-type industry analysis, shareholder value analysis, game theory, appraisals of competencies and capabilities, PIMS analysis, and the identification of critical success factors. However, several companies, Exxon in particular, were skeptical of most formal strategy techniques and the jargon associated with them, believing that they created a barrier to deploying experience-based knowledge and hampered

the shift of strategic planning responsibility from planning staff to line managers.[12]

2. *Providing channels and forums for communication and knowledge sharing.* All the companies placed greater emphasis on the communication and knowledge sharing role of planning processes. Indeed, the desire to promote dialog between businesses and the corporate executives on fundamental strategy issues was the main motive for reducing the formality of the planning process. This involved shifting emphasis of strategy meetings from formal presentations to face-to-face discussion where assumptions and beliefs were challenged and critical issues identified. Shell and Exxon provide contrasting examples of this trend:

- Shell has placed particular weight upon strategic planning as a vehicle for organizational learning. Shell's scenario planning process was primarily a process for sharing and integrating multiple knowledge bases from both within and outside the Shell group. Shell's 'scenario-to-strategy' framework involved discussion workshops in which scenarios would provide the foundation for an interactive strategy formulation. To maximize the organizational learning occurring through the strategic planning process, Shell has attempted to make explicit the perceptions and judgments of the various decision makers within the strategy process through techniques such as 'mental mapping.'

- Exxon's emphasis was upon a strategic planning process that was tightly integrated within a management structure that stressed the close bonds of communication and accountability between each divisional president and the corresponding 'contact director' on the corporate management committee. Thus, while Exxon had a well-defined strategic planning system, the formalities relating to the submission, discussion, and approval of divisional strategic plans were inseparable from the regular communication and interaction between the division presidents and the management committee that allowed strategic plans to be informed and guided by the continual integration of divisional and corporate-level knowledge.

Strategic planning as a mechanism for coordination

Increased emphasis on planning as a process of communication and knowledge sharing was intended not only to influence and improve strategic decisions, but also to provide a basis for coordinating decentralized decision making. The interview data suggested that increased environmental turbulence had enhanced the role of the strategic planning system as a coordinating device. As decision making had become increasingly decentralized, there was a growing need for a structured process of dialog, adjustment, and agreement to coordinate these dispersed decisions. This increased emphasis on coordination was evident from a number of the changes already described, notably the transition by the corporate center from detailed control towards more general direction and guidance, and the increased emphasis placed upon business-corporate dialog and consensus building. The priority accorded to this coordinating role of strategic planning varied between the companies. In general, the more decentralized was strategic decision making, the greater the emphasis on strategic planning as a coordinating device. Thus, Shell with its 200 separate operating companies had long regarded its strategic planning process as primarily a vehicle for coordination and consensus within its far-flung business: empire, Similarly, once Amoco reorganized as 17 separate business groups, the corporate planning department became increasingly concerned with providing vertical coordination between corporate and business levels, and developing horizontal coordination, e.g., through involving different business groups in country 'umbrella strategies.' Exxon's emphasis upon strategic planning as a coordinating device was a central rationale for embedding its strategic planning process within ongoing dialog between the divisional presidents and 'contact directors.' Exxon's head of corporate planning described Exxon's strategic planning as having evolved from a 'product-based' to a 'process-based' system.

Strategic planning as a mechanism for control

Hierarchical control in organizations can be exerted through behavioral control which manages the *inputs* into decisions through supervision and approval, and *output* control which manages the performance outcomes of decisions (Ouchi, 1979; Eisenhardt, 1985). Establishing control over increasing large and unwieldy corporate empires was a major motive for the adoption of strategic planning. Corporate planning provided a medium- and long-term control mechanism that complemented the short-term controls provided by budgeting systems. Under the 'old model' corporate management's ability to approve (or reject) business-level strategic and the resource allocations to support these plans represented a form of input control.

By the late 1990s, strategic planning's function as a control system had shifted from one based upon strategy content to one based upon strategy outcomes defined in terms of the performance that the strategy would deliver. This shift was apparent from three types of evidence. First,

[12] This was consistent with the experience of General Electric where simplification of the strategic planning system was accompanied by less reliance upon technical strategic analysis (Aguilar *et al.*, 1993)

the corporate guidelines that shaped business-level strategic planning (stage 1 of the generic strategic planning cycle) places increased emphasis on company-wide financial performance goals. This shift was also evident in the ways in which the companies revised their statements of mission, vision, and business principles. By the late 1990s, pride of place was given to shareholder return and superior profitability. Second, most companies reported that the meetings to discuss business-level strategic plans (stage 3 of the generic planning cycle) had become increasingly focused around performance targets (especially for operating profit and return on capital employed). Third, as attention shifted to the setting and monitoring of performance targets, so the performance planning process (stage 8 of the generic strategic planning cycle) became increasingly prominent.

Preoccupation with shareholder return was translated into rising aspirations for ROCE. Belief in the efficacy of 'stretch goals' also influenced thinking about the role of strategy. Hamel and Prahalad's (1989, 1994) analysis of 'strategic intent' and 'strategy as leverage and stretch' suggests that strategy's biggest contribution to company's performance is not so much through superior strategic decisions as in raising levels of aspiration and commitment through setting challenging goals.

Increasing emphasis on performance and quantification of performance targets was accompanied by less detailed strategic plans. This was most evident among the companies that placed the biggest emphasis on performance planning—BP, Exxon, and Texaco. These companies argued that commitments by divisional presidents to ambitious performance targets required their taking responsibility for divisional strategy. The more corporate was involved in influencing divisional strategies, the greater the erosion of divisional responsibility and accountability. Increasingly the corporate message was: 'Here's the performance we require. You figure out how to deliver it.' This shift from strategic control to performance planning (supported by stronger performance incentives) was typically described by the companies in terms of 'empowerment'—divisional and business unit managers were accorded greater decision-making discretion, while becoming more individually accountable for results.[13]

[13] The principle that tighter controls on performance targets inevitably require weaker controls over strategy is consistent with the tenets of control theory. A system may be controlled either by controlling outputs or inputs, but not both. If corporate controls the strategic decisions being taken at divisional level, it must accept the performance resulting from those decisions; conversely, if it is setting performance targets, then the divisions must be free to make the decisions needed to reach these targets.

Discussion

Implications for design vs. process debate

The evidence on the strategic planning practices of the major oil companies suggests that the long-running debate over the roles of rational design and organizational emergence in strategy formulation has been perpetuated by misconceptions of the reality of strategic planning. The vivid caricatures presented by each side of the other's conceptualization of strategy making bear little resemblance to the realities of strategic planning as pursued by large companies during the late 1990s.

Although hierarchical in structure with decision-making power ultimately vested in the top management team and critical inputs provided by corporate planning staff, the major oil companies' strategic planning systems of the late 1990s had little in common with the highly bureaucratized, top-down processes caricatured by Henry Mintzberg. In particular, strategic planning was primarily a bottom-up process in which corporate management provided direction, but primary inputs came from the business units and operating divisions. However, consistent with the process view of strategy formation, it was clear that the strategies of the oil majors were not created by their strategic planning systems. Strategic planning systems were mechanisms for improving the quality of strategic decisions, for coordinating strategic decision making, and for driving performance improvement. However, the critical strategic decisions that fundamentally affected the business portfolios and direction of development of the companies were, for the most part, taken outside formal systems of strategic planning.

By disbanding aspects of strategic planning conventionally associated with rational, top-down strategy design and embracing adaptive, emergent aspects of strategy making, none of the oil majors appeared to be deluded by Mintzberg's (1994b: 110–112) 'fallacies of strategic planning.' In terms of the 'fallacy of prediction,' none of the strategic planning systems relied upon precise predictions of key external variables. In terms of the 'fallacy of detachment,' all the companies located primary strategy responsibilities with line managers. In terms of 'fallacy of formalization,' all the companies had substantially reduced the formality of their planning procedures.

In short, the strategic planning systems of the international majors could be described as processes of 'planned emergence.' The primary direction of planning was bottom-up—from the business units to the corporate headquarters—and with business managers exhibiting substantial autonomy and flexibility in strategy making. At the same time, the structure of the planning systems allowed corporate management established constraints and guidelines in the form of vision and mission statements, corporate initiatives, and performance expectations. In bringing together these bottom-up and top-down initiatives through dialog, debate, and compromise, the systems displayed aspects of the 'generative planning model' that Liedtka (2000) suggests is conducive to strategic change.

To what extent do these systems of 'both incremental learning and deliberate planning' (Goold, 1992: 169) assist the companies in adapting effectively to the challenges and opportunities of the 1990s? Distinguishing the contribution of strategic planning as distinct from other aspects of the companies' management processes is difficult. What is apparent, however, is that the major oil companies were exceptionally successful in adapting to the challenges of the decade. Key strategic adjustments by the oil majors included: rationalization of downstream and chemical businesses in the face of chronic excess capacity (especially through joint ventures and asset swaps), refocusing upon core energy businesses, upstream expansion into new geographical areas (especially China, the Former Soviet Union and Latin America), the adoption of new technologies (e.g., deep-water exploration, directional drilling, 3D seismic analysis, and environmentally friendlier fuels), adaptation to social and political pressures, and responsiveness to the demands of owners (especially Elf and ENI's transformation from state to shareholder ownership). Perhaps the strongest evidence of the effectiveness of strategic adjustment lies in bottom-line performance: despite the low oil prices that prevailed for most of the 1990s, profitability for most of the companies was higher than during earlier periods when oil prices were significantly higher (see [Table 1.7.5]).

However, as mechanisms for aligning the companies more closely and effectively with their changing environment and guiding their long-term development, the effectiveness of the companies' strategic planning may also have deteriorated in three respects:

1. The foreshortening of planning horizons may reflect a shift in top management priority from long-term development to short- and medium-term performance goals. When investment projects have lives that extended to 40 years, strategic planning horizons of 4 and 5 years limited the potential for companies to relate their current resource allocations with their longer-term vision.

2. The transfer of strategic planning responsibilities from staff planners to line managers, while resolving problems of formalization and detachment, also entailed a loss of analytical capability. One of the ancillary observations of our study was the limited use by the companies of recently developed strategy concepts and techniques. Despite the rapid diffusion of the tools and techniques of strategic management during the 1980s and 1990s, few of these found application in the strategic planning processes of the oil majors. Although performance management tools—shareholder value analysis, EVA, balanced scorecards, and the like—had achieved significant uptake, the same was not apparent for concepts and techniques of strategy analysis. For example, while interviewees frequently referred to 'building competitive advantage,' 'exploiting key strengths,' and 'leveraging core competences,' only one of the companies (Amoco) had introduced any systematic process for assessing and developing organizational capabilities. It is possible that the priority accorded to financial performance targets in strategic planning squeezed out analysis. For example, the reluctance of several of the majors to introduce option valuation into their capital budgeting procedures stemmed from the fear that adding greater complexity might result in losing the discipline associated with unambiguous hurdle rates of return.

3. While breaking down the rigidities of the old formalized planning systems and embracing emergent strategy-making processes, the companies had done little in terms of positive measures to encourage innovation in strategy making. If competitive advantage in changing markets depends critically upon strategic innovation (Hamel, 2000; Baden-Fuller and Stopford, 1994; Markides, 1998), then the sources of strategic innovation need to be considered. While bottom-up, informal strategic planning systems offer the potential for innovative strategies to emerge, the absence of impediments to such innovation is not the same as positive measures to foster such innovation.

Table 1.7.5 The oil majors' return on equity, 1970s, 1980s, and 1990s

	1970–79	1980–89	1990–98
Return on equity			
Shell Group	10.76	13.87	13.82
Exxon	13.63	15.30	16.14
Mobil	11.15	11.57	12.87
BP	9.07	12.08	11.09
ENI	4.83	0.13	10.20
Elf Aquitaine	6.24	11.91	9.37
Texaco	10.30	8.93	12.30
Amoco	11.57	14.56	12.54
Average price of crude Oil (US wellhead purchase price at constant 1996 $ per barrel)	**17.1**	**28.6**	**17.4**

Source: *Fortune Global 500*; WTRG Economics

Implications for the management of complexity

In discussing the literature on the implications of environmental turbulence for strategic planning, I noted the potential contribution of complexity theory in providing a bridge between the opposing views of the strategy-as-design and strategy-as-process camps. Several of the features of the oil majors' strategic planning systems are consistent with the observations of other management scholars regarding the implications of complexity theory for business management. If scaling fitness peaks requires combining incremental steps with occasional major leaps (Anderson, 1999; Beinhocker, 1999), performance-focused strategic planning may facilitate this goal. Bottom-up strategic planning is conducive to incremental adaptation. Yet, as Shell, BP, ENI, and Texaco demonstrated, when realized performance falls far short of targeted level, the natural bias towards incremental-ism is supplanted by pressures for more radical strategic changes.

My characterization of the companies' strategic planning processes as ones of 'planned emergence' corresponds closely to Brown and Eisenhardt's (1997) concept of 'semistructures': the planning systems created an organizational structure, a fixed time schedule, and defined goals and responsibilities, while offering considerable freedom for experimentation, entrepreneurship, and initiative at the business level. Two aspects of this 'semistructure' character of strategic planning systems were particularly apparent. First, the strategy planning processes embodied the concept of simple rules which models of complex adaptive systems suggest can be remarkably effective in predicting and guiding the adaptation of nonhierarchical systems to changing environmental conditions (Gell-Mann, 1994; Eisenhardt and Sull, 2001). The strategy initiatives and guidelines established by corporate management in the form of mission and vision statements and targets for cost reduction, reserve replacement, and debt/equity ratios represented a framework of constraints and objectives that bounded and directed strategic choices. Second, existence of rigid annual planning cycles and the emphasis on breaking down longer-term strategic goals into short-term objectives in the form of strategic milestones, programmed targets, and scorecards corresponded to Brown and Eisenhardt's (1997) concept of time-paced transition from the present to the future.[14]

Implications for the theory of the multidivisional corporation

These observations of the characteristics and nature of strategic planning in large multiproduct, multinational corporations also have implications for the theory of the multidivisional organizations as developed by Williamson (1975, 1985) based upon empirical research of Chandler (1962). The efficiency of the multidivisional form ('M-form') in organizing activities spanning multiple product markets and/or multiple countries rests upon its efficiency both as a coordinating device and alignment, the study shows how the oil majors' strategic planning systems embodied the opportunism-limiting features of the M-form. The linking of strategic planning authority with profit and loss responsibilities has created a management system much more closely aligned with Williamson's principles of 'effective multidivisionalization,' especially in relation to 'monitoring efficient performance,' 'awarding incentives,' and 'allocating cash flows to high yield uses' (Williamson, 1985: 284). In relation to efficiency of coordination, the evidence is only partly consistent with the existing theory of the M-form. Williamson draws upon Ashby's theory of cybernetics and Simon's theory of nearly decomposable systems to argue that the efficiency of the M-form derives from its separation of high-frequency (operating) decisions from low-frequency strategic decisions. Given that the oil majors' strategic planning is located as much (if not more) in the divisions as in corporate headquarters, it appears that the critical distinction between corporate and divisional activities is based more upon realms of knowledge than decision frequency: the divisional managers focus on business strategy and corporate managers focus upon corporate strategy on the simple basis that decisions need to be co-located with the knowledge pertinent to these decisions.

Conclusion

The findings from this study, together with other recent evidence, show that strategic planning continues to play a central role in the management systems of large companies. At the same time, strategic planning practices have changed substantially over the past two decades in response to the challenges of strategy formulation in turbulent and unpredictable environments. Strategic planning processes have become more decentralized, less staff driven, and more informal, while strategic plans themselves have become shorter term, more goal focused, and less specific with regard to actions and resource allocations. The role of strategic planning systems within companies' overall management has also changed. Strategic planning had become less about strategic decision making and more a mechanism for coordination and performance managing. The growing prominence of performance targets within strategic plans has changed the role of strategic planning as a corporate control system, permitting increased decentralization of strategic decision making and greater adaptability and responsiveness to external change.

Despite the apparently successful adaptation of strategic planning systems to unstable, uncertain environments,

[14] Although Brown and Eisenhardt apply the concept to project management, the idea of linking change to a clear time schedule is common to both.

the study pointed to the limited impact of strategic planning processes upon the quality of strategic decisions. Decentralization and informality of strategic planning processes permitted access to a broader range of expertise, but there was limited use of new tools and concepts of strategic analysis and little evidence that the systems of strategic planning were conducive to strategic innovation.

The study has implications for the study of strategic management. The features of strategic planning revealed by the study suggest that much of the debate between the 'strategy-as-rational-design' and 'strategy-as-emergent-process' schools has been based upon a misconception of how strategic planning works in the real world. The process of 'planned emergence' evident in the companies' strategic planning systems is consistent with management principles derived from complexity theory and observations of complex adaptive systems, and offers insights into the design principles of the multidivisional firm.

References

Aguilar FJ, Hamermesh RG, Brainard CE. 1993. General Electric Co.: 1984, Case 385315. Harvard Business School: Boston, MA.

American Productivity and Quality Center. 1996a. *Strategic Planning: Final Report*. APQC's International Benchmarking Clearinghouse: Houston, TX.

American Productivity and Quality Center. 1996b. *Reinventing Strategic Planning for a Dynamic Environment*. APQC's International Benchmarking Clearinghouse: Houston, TX.

Anderson P. 1999. Complexity theory and organizational science. *Organization Science* 10: 216–232.

Ang JS, Chua JH. 1979. Long-range planning in large United States corporations: a survey. *Long Range Planning* 12(April): 99–102.

Ansoff HI. 1965. *Corporate Strategy*. McGraw-Hill: New York.

Ansoff HI. 1991. Critique of Henry Mintzberg's 'The design school: reconsidering the basic premises of strategic management'. *Strategic Management Journal* 12(6): 449–462.

Baden-Fuller C, Stopford JM. 1994. *Rejuvenating the Mature Business: The Competitive Challenge*. Harvard Business School Press: Boston, MA.

Beinhocker ED. 1999. Robust adaptive strategies. *Sloan Management Journal*, Spring: 95–106.

Bourgeois LJ. Strategy and the environment: a conceptual integration. *Academy of Management Review* 5: 25–39.

Bower JL. 1970. *Managing the Resource Allocation Process*. Division of Research, Harvard Business School: Boston, MA.

Boyd BK. 1991. Strategic planning and financial performance: a meta-analysis. *Journal of Management Studies* 28: 353–374.

Boyd BK, Reuning-Elliot E. 1998. A measurement model of strategic planning. *Strategic Management Journal* 19(2): 181–192.

Brews PJ, Hunt M. 1999. Learning to plan and planning to learn: resolving the planning school/learning school debate. *Strategic Management Journal* 20(10): 889–914.

Brown SL, Eisenhardt KM. 1997. The art of continuous change: linking complexity theory and time-based evolution in relentlessly shifting organizations. *Administrative Science Quarterly* 42: 1–34.

Burgelman RA. 1983. A process model of internal corporate venturing in a diversified major firm. *Administrative Science Quarterly* 28: 223–244.

Burgelman RA. 1994. Fading memories: a process theory of strategic business exit in dynamic environments. *Administrative Science Quarterly* 39: 24–36.

Burgelman RA. 1996. A process model of strategic business exit: implications of an evolutionary perspective on strategy. *Strategic Management Journal*, Summer Special Issue 17: 193–214.

Burgelman RA, Grove A. 1996. Strategic dissonance. *California Management Review* 38(2): 8–28.

Burns T, Stalker GM. 1961. *The Management of Innovation*. Tavistock: London.

Business Week. 1996. Strategic planning. 26 August: 45–52.

Capon N, Farley JU, Hulbert JM. 1987. *Corporate Strategic Planning*. Columbia University Press: New York.

Chandler AD. 1962. *Strategy and Structure*. MIT Press: Cambridge, MA.

Cibin R, Grant RM. 1996. Restructuring among the world's leading oil companies. *British Journal of Management* 7: 283–307.

Cleland DI. 1976. *The Origin and Development of a Philosophy of Long-Range Planning in American Business*. Arno Press: New York. (Original PhD thesis submitted Ohio State University, 1962.)

Courtright JA, Fairhurst GT, Rogers LE. 1989. Interaction patterns in organic and mechanistic systems. *Academy of Management Journal* 32: 773–802.

De Geus A. 1988. Planning as learning. *Harvard Business Review* 66(2): 70–74.

De Geus A. 1997. *The Living Company*. Harvard Business School Press: Boston, MA.

Denning BW, Lehr ME. 1971. The extent and nature of long-range planning in the United Kingdom—I. *Journal of Management Studies* 8: 145–161.

Denning BW, Lehr ME. 1972. The extent and nature of long-range planning in the United Kingdom—II. *Journal of Management Studies* 9: 1–18.

Eisenhardt KM. 1985. Control: organizational and economic approaches. *Management Science* 31: 134–149.

Eisenhardt KM. 1989. Making fast strategic decisions in high-velocity environments. *Academy of Management Journal* 32: 543–559.

Eisenhardt KM, Sull DN. 2001. Strategy as simple rules. *Harvard Business Review* 79(1): 107–116.

Ewing DW. 1956. Looking around: long-range business planning. *Harvard Business Review* 56(4): 135–146.

Gell-Mann M. 1994. *The Quark and the Jaguar*. Freeman: New York.

Goold M. 1992. Design, learning and planning: a further observation on the design school debate. *Strategic Management Journal* 13(2): 169–170.

Grant RM, Cibin R. 1996. Strategy, structure and market turbulence: the international oil majors, 1970–91. *Scandinavian Journal of Management* 12: 165–188.

Grayson LE. 1987. *Who and How in Planning for Large Companies: Generalizations from the Experiences of Oil Companies*. St Martin's Press: New York.

Grinyer PH, Norburn D. 1975. Strategic planning in 21 UK companies. *Long Range Planning* 7(August): 80–88.

Grinyer PH, Al-Bazzaz S, Yasai-Ardekani M. 1986. Towards a contingency theory of corporate planning: findings in 48 UK companies. *Strategic Management Journal* 7(1): 3–28.

Hamel G. 1996. Strategy as revolution. *Harvard Business Review* 74(4): 69–76.

Hamel G. 2000. *Leading the Revolution*. Harvard Business School Press: Boston, MA.

Hamel G, Prahalad CK. 1989. Strategic intent. *Harvard Business Review* 67(3): 63–76.

Hamel G, Prahalad CK. 1994. *Competing for the Future*. Harvard Business School Press: Boston, MA.

Hannan MT, Freeman J. 1989. *Organizational Ecology*. Harvard University Press: Cambridge, MA.

Henry HW. 1967. *Long-Range Planning Practices in 45 Industrial Companies*. Prentice Hall: Englewood Cliffs, NJ.

Javidan M. 1984. The impact of environmental uncertainty on long-range planning practices of the U.S. savings and loan industry. *Strategic Management Journal* 5(4): 381–392.

Jennings D. 2000. PowerGen: the development of corporate planning in a privatized utility. *Long Range Planning* 33(2): 201–218.

Kukalis S. 1991. Determinants of strategic planning systems in large organizations: a contingency approach. *Journal of Management Studies* 28: 143–160.

Learned E, Christensen CR, Andrews KR, Guth WD. 1965. *Business Policy: Text and Cases*. Irwin: Homewood, IL.

Liedtka J. 2000. Strategic planning as a contributor to strategic change: a generative model. *European Management Journal* 18(2): 195–206.

Lindsay WM, Rue LW. 1980. Impact of organization environment on the long-range planning process: a contingency view. *Academy of Management Journal* 23: 385–404.

March JG. 1981. Footnotes to organizational change. *Administrative Science Quarterly* 26: 563–577.

Markides C. 1998. Strategic innovation in established companies. *Sloan Management Review* 39(Spring): 27–36.

Miller CC, Cardinal LB. 1994. Strategic planning and firm performance: a synthesis of more than two decades of research. *Academy of Management Journal* 37: 1649–1665.

Mintzberg H. 1991. Learning 1, planning 0: reply to Igor Ansoff. *Strategic Management Journal* 12(6): 463–466.

Mintzberg H. 1994a. *The Rise and Fall of Strategic Planning*. Free Press: New York.

Mintzberg H. 1994b. The fall and rise of strategic planning. *Harvard Business Review* 72(1): 107–114.

Mintzberg H, Brunet P, Waters J. 1986. Does planning impede strategic thinking? Tracking the strategies of Air Canada from l937 to l976. In *Advances in Strategic Management*, Vol. 4, Lamb RB, Shivastava P (eds). JAI Press: Greenwich, CT; 3–41.

Mintzberg H, McHugh A. 1985. Strategy formulation in an adhocracy. *Administrative Science Quarterly* 30: 160–197.

Mintzberg H, Pascale RT, Goold M, Rumelt RP. 1996. The Honda effect revisited. *California Management Review* 38(Summer): 78–117.

Mintzberg H, Waters JA. 1982. Tracking strategy in an entrepreneurial firm. *Academy of Management Journal* 15: 465–499.

Nelson RR, Winter SG. 1982. *An Evolutionary Theory of Economic Change*. Harvard University Press: Cambridge, MA.

Ouchi W. 1979. A conceptual framework for design of organizational control mechanisms. *Management Science* 25: 833–848.

Pascale RT. 1984. Perspective on strategy: the real story behind Honda's success. *California Management Review* 26(Spring): 47–72.

Pascale RT. 1999. Surfing the edge of chaos. *Sloan Management Review*, Spring: 83–94.

Payne B. 1957. Steps in long-range planning. *Harvard Business Review* 35(2): 95–101.

Platt WJ, Maines NR. 1959. Pretest your long-range plans. *Harvard Business Review* 37(1): 119–127.

Quinn JB. 1961. Long-range planning of industrial research. *Harvard Business Review* 39(4): 88–102.

Ramanujam V, Ramanujam N, Camillus JC. 1986. Multiobjective assessment of effectiveness of strategic planning: a discriminant analysis approach. *Academy of Management Journal* 29(2): 347–472.

Rigby D. 1999. *Management Tools and Techniques*. Bain: Boston, MA.

Romanelli E, Tushman ME. 1994. Organizational transformation as punctuated equilibrium. *Academy of Management Journal* 36: 701–732.

Schoemaker PJ. 1993. Multiple scenario development: its conceptual and behavioral basis. *Strategic Management Journal* 14(3): 193–213.

Schoemaker PJ. 1995. Scenario planning: a tool for strategic thinking. *Sloan Management Review* 23(2): 25–34.

Simons RL, Weston HA. 1990. MCI Communications Corp.: planning for the 1990s. Case number 1-90136, Harvard Business School: Boston, MA.

Sinha DK. 1990. The contribution of formal planning to decisions. *Strategic Management Journal* 11(6): 479–492.

Slater R. 1999. *Jack Welch and the GE Way*. McGraw- Hill: New York.

U.S. House of Representatives, Committee on Science and Technology. 1976. *Long Range Planning*. U.S. Government Printing Office: Washington, DC.

Van Der Heijden K. 1993. Strategic vision at work: discussing strategic vision in management teams. In *Strategic Thinking: Leadership and the Management of Change*, Hendry J, Johnson G, Newton J (eds).Wiley: New York; 137–150.

Williamson OE. 1975. *Markets and Hierarchies*. Free Press: New York.

Williamson OE. 1985. *The Economic Institutions of Capitalism*. Free Press: New York.

Wilson I. 1994. Strategic planning isn't dead—it changed. *Long Range Planning* 27(4): 12–24.

Wrap HE. 1957. Organization for long-range planning. *Harvard Business Review* 35(1): 37–47.

Practitioner reflection

Dr Richard Schroth

Discovering strategy and strategists

Reflecting on Chapters 1–4, I noted that the longer one successfully practises engaging in the strategy development process, the more one typically locks into a style and comfort zone. Reading these chapters provides an important opportunity to consider the principles of crafting strategy afresh.

Chapter 2 tackles the difficult job of trying to identify those who constitute critical leadership in the strategy process. There is one principle that I offer to supplement the authors' remarks when it comes to understanding the dark art of strategy: *Strategists should never claim 'ownership' of their creation*. Strategists might share in the credit if the circumstance warrants, but the ownership of the directions and implementations should, nine times out of ten, belong to someone other than the strategist. The goal is to create 'championed' ownership by others. The most successful 'strategists' have champions all over the organization. The exception to this is, of course, that you no longer want to be a strategist and choose to follow your creation into the market. For the most part, a career strategist should always have a new horizon that he or she is waiting to explore, with dreams of attempting the next journey used to energize himself or herself for his or her current work. Once mastered, this state of mind allows release of ownership as a natural and welcomed gesture.

One of the 'down' sides of never claiming ownership, especially in large organizations, is the vulnerability of being associated with entities without profit-and-loss responsibilities, and in which there is only a handful of specialized expensive people. Entities that look like staff and smell like staff are generally ultimately determined to *be* staff—and are subject to more intense budget scrutiny, especially during tough fiscal cycles; ergo, many strategy positions are the first to be considered for release in tight budget times.

Chapters 3 and 4 concern themselves with the process of strategizing: strategic thinking, decision making, leadership, and the dynamics of strategy formulation. I lump these two chapters together because they begin to form the basis of action. For me, the entire process represents the initiation of a form of 'corporate spring cleaning', an event for most corporations that marks a chance to re-examine existing directions and to modify next-stage initiatives. It provides a much-needed pause to step out of the daily grind and a chance to see a bigger picture. One of the greatest lessons that I've learned in my thirty years of conducting and participating in strategy sessions is that there must be executive sponsorship and commitment to the exercises. Without the correct executive sponsorship, most attempts to strategize anything eventually fail. I say 'correct' executive sponsorship, because having the wrong executive sponsor creates new and horrific outcomes such as dissent, deflated morale, and damage to the entire organization's trust system that things can get done. Executives must also be involved in the process of strategizing in order to understand the nuisances that enable the decision making to take place. There is nothing worse than the organization spending time and money to gel a group, sending them through the exercise of suspending their disbelief that the company can actually accomplish a new vision that they are involved in creating, and then have it criticized or rejected by the executive sponsor. While integrating executives into the strategizing process may seem like common sense, you can't imagine how many initiatives fail because of poor executive engagement and endorsement skills.

The other key element of strategizing is the evolution of metrics that can begin to provide new tools for success. With the advent of technologies that are based in wireless monitoring, radio frequency identification (RFID), nanotechnologies, DNA structures, and so on, the opportunity to challenge the traditional metrics used for monitoring business behaviour, transparency, and accountability need to be incorporated in the 'inventive' part of the strategy process. I find it very useful to have an element of any strategy session deal with defining new goals for metrics, using five times (5×), ten times (10×), and fifty times (50×) productivity gains to push the old models away from the table and focus on what new models might eventually be available to the solution. The reality bridge between the known and these unknown states generally starts to broaden the opportunity portfolio.

In summary, as I walk away from these chapters, the following are some observations.

As an interested reader, I would step back from Chapters 1–4 in awe, knowing that executives have operated businesses over decades of time using all of these approaches. Over these periods, they have probably experienced the same success and failure rates as using any of the methods over the life of each of the strategies. In fact, the authors cite references in these chapters that put the odds at about even that strategy translates into profitability and successful operations. As a reader, I'd be highly interested in the relationship between the leadership characteristics of those who lead their companies with passion every morning and those organizations that are led by self-serving and emotionless corporate executives, who profess strategy and strategic initiatives, yet quietly and ignorantly drive their companies into bankruptcy, receivership, and illegal acts. I would clearly have in mind how many strategists must General Motors, Chrysler, Merrill Lynch, and Lehman Brothers have had who, in the end, had no major relevance in the difficulties experienced by these and others during the great economic collapse of the early 2000s. If their strategy represents the best that money can buy, then we clearly must acknowledge that strategy alone is hardly a surrogate for great leadership.

As a student of strategy, I would look at Chapters 1–4 as a guide for understanding the different approaches that one may take to strategy and choose the strategy that reflect my greatest passions, supporting my belief systems that help in the discovery of truth in understanding business. Once I had landed on an approach that felt right, I would place my emphasis in this area, knowing that many others hold my beliefs in contempt *and* that their passions, views, and approaches can defeat me, especially if they don't share my fundamental beliefs. I would then reread the book, the case studies, and the referred readings, and shape an understanding that provided personal clarity and objectivity in how I would ultimately see myself raising the performance of organizations.

If I were a consultant reading this text, I would immediately attempt to understand that, on my next strategy pitch to my client, I must be mindful and conscious that arrogance in believing that my approach is the 'answer' for the client is only as good as the weakness in the lies that my competitor will pitch.

As an executive reading this book, I would endorse 'focus' as the key to my strategic initiatives and I would choose wisely my approach and style for evolving and deploying my strategic beliefs. I would always have a curmudgeon whom I trusted nearby, constantly reminding the strategy teams and me that only a fool would believe that there is only one way in which to plan for success.

Dr Richard Schroth is one of the world's top executive consultants, professional speakers, and private advisers on technology and business for leading corporations around the globe. He is the US State Department's 2008–13 Senior Fulbright Scholar for Information Sciences. In June 2008, Dr Schroth was named one of the top twenty-five consultants in the world by Consulting Magazine. He was the first chief technology officer for the Marriott Corporation, and has served as executive vice president of Computers Sciences Corporation and as senior vice president and chief technology officer for Perot Systems.

Section 2

Foundations of advantage

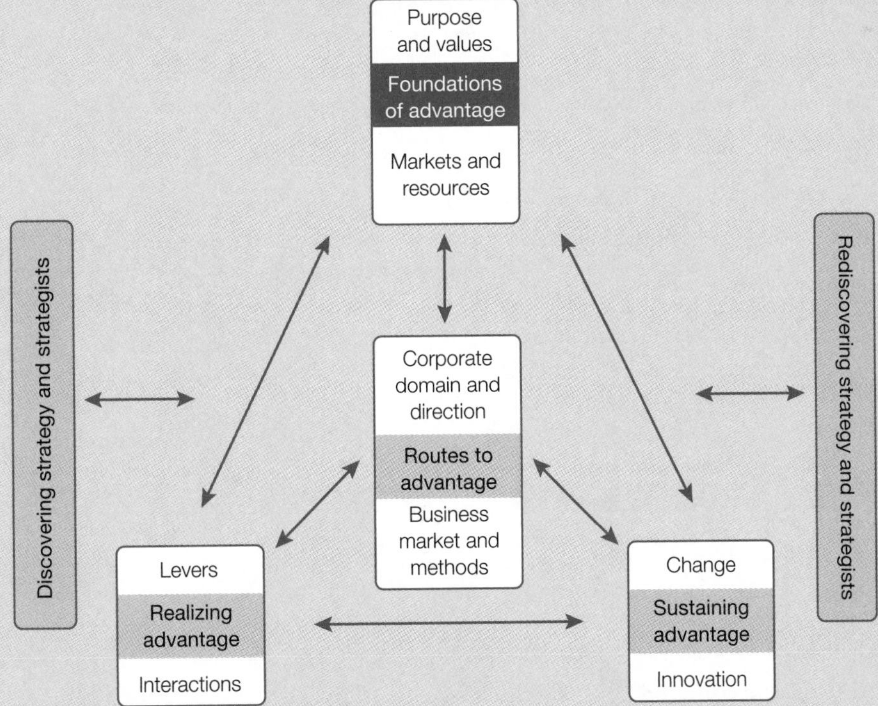

5

Purpose and values

Diverse responsibilities of business

How we behave. Respect: We treat others as we would like to be treated ourselves. Ruthlessness, callousness, and arrogance don't belong here.

(Extract from the values statement of Enron)

Introduction

In the previous chapter, we examined the dynamics of strategy formulation. Now, we turn our attention to the purpose and values of business as one element of the foundations of advantage. A headline in the *Financial Times* of 5 January 2007 read 'Activists seek more scalps at Home Depot', referring to one of America's largest DIY chains. Discontent rose among shareholders because of the US$240m severance package approved by the board of directors for former chief executive officer (CEO) Bob Nardelli. In the context of declining share performance since 2000, the departure of Nardelli as CEO was not enough and shareholders demanded that the majority of the board of directors be replaced. Similar demands have been reported during the international banking crisis in 2008 and 2009 as many major international banks paid bonuses to their management teams and employees that bore no relation to the organizations' declining performance. For example, in 2009, Morgan Stanley, Bank of America, and Goldman Sachs awarded bonuses to employees—albeit some of them lower than other years. Are these examples of executives being overpaid and underperforming? What can shareholders do to force changes? What role do society and regulation play in forcing change? What is the impact on corporate purpose and values of a 600:1 ratio of CEO compensation to average worker wage? As individuals, we are bombarded daily with adverts from organizations providing an array of claims: their products are fat-free; their loans have the lowest interest rates; they provide the best customer service; and their product quality is superior. Organizations claim to value you as a customer, but when products malfunction, customer value is truly tested. Threatening to reveal bad customer experiences to media watchdog programmes or setting up a blog seem the only ways of getting organizations to take notice of customer experiences. This brings us to the core dilemmas in this chapter: which comes first, profit or people? In essence, what are the purpose and values of the organization?

There are numerous examples of organizations marketing their corporate responsibility credentials to society through sponsorship of charities and donation of equipment and resources to improve the quality of life for key stakeholders. For example, most alcoholic drinks companies have the line 'Enjoy alcohol sensibly' inserted as part of their marketing documents, but in practice this advice is not always followed by the consumers purchasing the alcohol. Individual members of society can become sceptical of the motivation of organizations in implementing social impact programmes as part of corporate social responsibility (CSR). As consumers, we demand that organizations behave in an ethical and moral manner—but we also demand that we get value for money for our purchases. Before the banking crisis, customers demanded an array of debt products, from mortgages, to car and holiday loans, to increases in credit card limits. Commentators, consumers, and governments blamed banks for not acting in an ethical and moral manner, for not undertaking sufficiently stringent financial stress testing of customer applications and thereby failing to decline demands for more debt. Is this a sustainable situation for individual businesses and society? It is the economic imperative of business that makes issues of ethics and responsibility more contentious in this arena than in any other (Finlay, 2000).

In this chapter, we begin by exploring what exactly is, or should be, meant by 'the business of business'. We then focus on how organizations respond to the dual demands of increasing shareholder value while being socially responsible. We examine how organizational democracy can assist in developing long-term relationships with key stakeholders. We conclude the chapter by focusing on **mission statements**, which serve as tangible statements of organizational purpose and values, and typically encompass stakeholder, social, and business aspirations. The key questions are whether mission statements actually influence stakeholder behaviour or even make an impact on shareholder value. As we see in the quote at the head of the chapter, Enron had great aspirations and ideals. Commentators often cited its approach as exemplary, but in reality Enron's words proved mere rhetoric without meaning. This highlights the imperative of an appropriate corporate culture in which dilemmas surrounding profit and people are brought to the surface and discussed, to the benefit of all stakeholders. It also highlights the importance of the **strategists** in explicitly addressing such issues and then, in turn, leading by example.

The business of business

Corporate scandals, substantial profits, and remuneration packages for executives have given business in general a somewhat tarnished image and reputation. The names of Enron, Worldcom, and Lehman Brothers have entered the global lexicon of infamy. One root cause of these scandals has been traced to the fact that 'American corporations have been forced in recent years to maximize shareholder value without regard for the effects of their actions on other stakeholders' (Kochan, 2002: 139). Corporate scandals, coupled with the dot.com boom and bust in the 2000s, and followed by concerns over the global financial **industry**, energy consumption, and climate change, have eroded confidence and trust in business and those charged with ensuring that business operates in the best interests of shareholders (Birkinshaw, 2010). The global financial crisis of 2008 and 2009 has further reduced confidence in governance, regulatory controls, and managerial performance and competence. In Chapter 4, we saw how organizations lack sophistication when it comes to strategic planning and the possible implications that this has for shareholder value. A fundamental strategic question for business and society is: 'What is the ultimate purpose of business and whose goals should be prioritized?'

Beyond shareholder value

Milton Friedman argued that the 'business of business is business', meaning that a business should strive to maximize profits through short-term routes. Any activities (except for those required by legislation) that counter this purpose are deemed irrelevant and are accused of diluting return to shareholders. Over the years, this harsh neo-liberal stance has been questioned (Carroll and Shabana, 2010). A McKinsey (2006) survey of 6,000 executives highlights that organizations are now looking beyond shareholder value as a key metric for success and are seeking to measure their companies' contribution to society. Some 84 per cent of respondents believed that the responsibility of organizations is to 'generate high returns to investors but balance this with contributions to the broader public good'. Rigby's (2003) study found high levels of satisfaction with corporate codes of ethics, strategic planning, **core competences**, and customer segmentation as corporate discipline tools. Other corporate discipline tools include customer surveys, benchmarking, pay for performance, **balanced scorecard**, and economic value-added analysis. This evolution of thinking beyond shareholder value means that strategists need to consider the manner in which they engage with stakeholders in a meaningful way and ensure that this is reflected in practice through CSR activities and programmes.

Defining corporate social responsibility (CSR)

It has been difficult to define what is meant by 'corporate social responsibility' (CSR), because different stakeholders take different meanings from the term. The World Business Council for Sustainable Development (1999: 3) defines CSR as 'the continuing commitment by business to behave ethically and contribute to economic development while improving the quality of life of the workforce and their families as well as of the local community and society as a whole'. Lindgreen and Swaen (2010: 3) question what practices really count as responsible CSR behaviour: is it the public intent and **discourse** that an organization espouses or is it the activities that it enacts in practice? Unfortunately, the former perspective seems to dominate. The reality is that CSR is a contestable concept and remains in an embryonic state (Windsor, 2006). Different models have been developed in the attempt to deepen our understanding of CSR, the main four of which are: CSR; corporate social responsiveness; corporate social performance; and corporate citizenship.

The CSR model's emphasis is on the responsibilities of business—particularly economic, legal, ethical, and discretionary—with early models during the 1960s suggesting that these responsibilities were over and above economic and legal obligations (Matten and Crane, 2005). The CSR model developed by Carroll (1978) suggested that economic responsibility was to make a profit and grow the organization; legal responsibility was to ensure compliance with regulations and that the organization behaves accordingly; ethical responsibility focused on following societal norms; and discretionary responsibilities focused on what we now term 'philanthropic activities'.

Corporate social responsiveness focuses on the process and posture that organizations take in dealing with social responsibility issues. These can range from doing nothing to having a proactive response to social responsibility issues (Lotila, 2010). Carroll (1978: 505) describes corporate social responsiveness as 'the action phase of management responding in the social sphere'. The categorization of responsiveness, according to McAdam (1973), includes: 'fight all the way'; 'do only what is required'; and 'be progressive and lead the industry'.

The focus of corporate social performance is on what organizations actually do with respect to their social responsibility issues. Using a broad framework of analysis, the emphasis of this model is to focus on outcomes of organizational action. The assessment of social performance can be either narrow, focusing only on key social performance indicators, or very broad, in which many aspects of the organization's operations can be used to assess organizational actions. Wartick and Cochran (1985) suggest that corporate social performance is assessed along three dimensions, including responsibilities, responsiveness, and social issues. This assessment of social performance at an organizational level encompasses principles, processes, policies, and programmes.

In the final model of CSR, that of corporate citizenship, the focus is on the link between organizations, communities, rights, and responsibilities. This is about organizations being proactively engaged with communities and thereby influencing society and individuals with a common societal purpose. By being proactively engaged, the organization is also meeting its own obligations from economic and societal perspectives. This model also means that the state is not the only guarantor of citizenship (Matten and Crane, 2005).

The CSR debates can be traced back to the debate between capitalism and free markets versus socialism and social markets. Friedman argues that free markets should be allowed to operate and that maximizing shareholder value should be the only concern of the board of directors, CEOs, and managers. Organizations should not get involved in any activities that would diminish shareholder value. Proponents argue that capitalism has meant the efficient deployment of resources, increased levels of entrepreneurship, increased standards of living, and technological progression, which have benefited society as a whole (see Long case 8, 'Reassessing value in strategy'). A contemporary argument against the pure form of capitalism, as advocated by Friedman, is that organizations should develop CSR performance metrics for their organization that go beyond maximizing shareholder value. Shareholder value is only one of many measures that can be used to assess the performance of an organization. These could include, for example, a work environment that enhances employee well-being, that the organization contributes to societal good both within its local environmental and more generally, and that the organization is fair in all of its transactions and dealings. The difficulty that organizations face in pursuing CSR initiatives is the issue of trust. Society has become distrustful of businesses' involvement in CSR activities; the tendency is to focus on the commercial motive for an organization's pursuance of CSR initiatives rather than on CSR outcomes. This is particularly the case with multinational corporations operating in low-cost economies. For example, in the mid-1990s, Nike's reputation was under scrutiny after allegations about the use of sweatshop labour in contract manufacturing of its apparel. In January 2009, Primark, a major low-cost retailer in the UK and Ireland, was the subject of an undercover BBC investigation (see http://news.bbc.co.uk/2/hi/uk_news/7825167.stm) into the alleged employment of illegal workers and the payment of workers below minimum wage within its supply chain network.

To counteract such negativity and in order to build trust between business and society, governments have responded with regulations that enforce minimum standards of behaviour on companies. This is in response to what Adam Smith (1937: 128) described: 'People of the same trade seldom meet together, even for merriment and diversion, but the conversation ends in a conspiracy against the public, or in some contrivance to raise prices.' Another response has been the development of a number of international CSR standards by various agencies (see Long case 4, 'The Ethical Trading Initiative'). For example, the International Standards Organization (ISO) has developed Environmental Management Standard ISO 14000, Social Accountability Standard SA 8000, and a CSR index for stock markets. Del Monte, an international food organization that distributes and markets a wide variety of food products, has been accredited and certified by various international agencies in accordance with standards including ISO 14000 and EurepGAP protocols.

CSR and firm performance

Academic studies reveal some mixed and interesting results about CSR and firm performance. Early CSR studies by Alexander and Buchholz (1978) and Abbott and Monsen (1979) found that there was no clear link between CSR and profitability. McGuire *et al.* (1988: 854) found that a 'firm's prior performance, assessed by both stock-market returns and accounting-based measures, is more closely related to corporate social responsibility than its subsequent performance'. Taking diversity as an indicator of CSR, Singh and Point (2004: 295) found that 'the drivers for diversity management are better performance, enhancing corporate reputation and meeting stakeholder needs'. However, Vogel (2005) argues that:

> CSR is best understood as a business strategy that, like any business strategy, makes sense for a subset of companies under specific circumstances . . . One reason CSR often *seems* to pay is that relatively few companies devote substantial resources to it. Were they to do so, the limits of the business case would rapidly become apparent.

Despite a proliferation of academic studies, there is no definitive link established between CSR, profitability, and firm performance. Differences in measurement criteria have also meant that CSR ratings can be seen as meaningless (Chatterji and Levine, 2006). With no clear link between CSR and firm performance, who decides that an organization should commit to CSR and on what basis? This is the subject of our next section.

CSR leadership and engagement

Ultimately, who is responsible for developing a CSR perspective within organizations and how should companies be orientated in terms of CSR engagements? The McKinsey survey (2006) clearly shows that CEOs or chairpersons of boards should (and do) take the lead. Interestingly, strategy, human resources (HR), and CSR departments were seen to have a very limited role to play in terms of CSR management and leadership (see Table 5.1).

Table 5.1 CSR leadership: who does lead and who should lead?

Position	Percentage of respondents
CEO or chair	Takes the lead 56%
	Should take the lead 74%
Public or corporate affairs department	Takes the lead 14%
	Should take the lead 4%
Other executive members of board	Takes the lead 10%
	Should take the lead 7%
Core business divisions	Takes the lead 5%
	Should take the lead 6%
Department of corporate social responsibility	Takes the lead 5%
	Should take the lead 3%
HR department	Takes the lead 2%
	Should take the lead 1%
Strategy department	Takes the lead 1%
	Should take the lead 3%

Source: Adapted from McKinsey (2006: 7)

The challenge that CEOs face is to ensure that the organization as a whole is following their lead in terms of CSR leadership. In reality, in any organization, there are individuals who will not commit to or abide by CSR guidelines, which may result in a tarnished reputation. For some companies, operational malfunctions or other media controversies around their marketing can cause reputational damage. In the case of Cadbury, an international confectionery manufacturer, a salmonella outbreak allegedly left more than thirty people ill (Herman, 2007) and, in a separate incident, there were some complaints to the UK Advertising Standards Agency (ASA) about its Trident chewing gum advertisement (Advertising Standards Agency, 2007). Cadbury took a proactive approach to CSR and developed a dedicated CSR website, in a bid to enhance its CSR reputation and as a mechanism with which to engage directly with its customers. Such CSR initiatives have been amalgamated into Kraft Foods following its **acquisition** of Cadbury.

Leaders and organizations can be forced into CSR initiatives through public pressure, threats from the regulator, and/or government intervention through legislation. Munilla and Miles (2005) term this 'social blackmail'. Munilla and Miles argue that enforced CSR may result in a loss of **sustainable competitive advantage**, leave long-term reputation damage, and create internal managerial and strategic conflicts. This suggests that organizations might be best taking a proactive stance in relation to such issues.

Engaging and developing CSR initiatives is a complex task for organizations, given the different stakeholders' power and influence over strategy in addition to environmental competitive pressures and societal trends. Three key motivations for CSR engagement have been identified (Swanson, 1995):

- the first focuses on delivering operational excellence in terms of profitability, return on investment, and sales volumes;
- the second is a negative duty motivation, whereby the organization has to conform to stakeholders' expectations; and
- the third is a self-driven motivation internally in the organization that has a CSR orientation and ethos.

Irrespective of the motivational aspects of CSR engagements, Zadek (2004) argues that organizations pass through five stages of **organizational learning** in reaching sustainable levels of CSR: namely, defensive, compliance, managerial, strategic, and civil (see Table 5.2).

Another response by companies to CSR engagement has been to set up an ethics office and hire ethics officers who assist with organizational compliance issues. Such companies include United Health Group USA, Norvatis Corporation, Merick & Co., and Textron (USA). Typically, ethics offices are a by-product of the strategic plan of a company. According to Rasberry (2000: 20), ethics programmes typically consist of:

1. a vision statement;
2. a values statement;
3. a code of ethics;
4. an ethics officer;
5. an ethics committee;
6. an ethics communication strategy;
7. ethics training;
8. an ethics helpline;
9. measurements and rewards;
10. a monitoring and tracking system;
11. periodic evaluation;
12. ethical leadership.

The stance that a company takes regarding CSR is a function of the organization's adherence to **corporate governance** requirements and the power of stakeholders, with which we will deal in the next section.

Table 5.2 Corporate responsibility: five stages of organizational learning

Stage	What organizations do	Why they do it
Defensive	Deny practices, outcomes, or responsibilities	To defend against attacks on their reputation that, in the short term, could affect sales, recruitment, productivity, and the brand
Compliance	Adopt a policy-based compliance approach as a cost of doing business	To mitigate the erosion of economic value in the medium term because of ongoing reputation and litigation risks
Managerial	Embed the societal issues in their core management processes	To mitigate the erosion of economic value in the medium term and to achieve long-term gain by integrating responsible business practices into their daily operations
Strategic	Integrate the societal issue into their core business strategies	To enhance economic value in the long term and to gain first-mover advantage by aligning strategy and process innovations with societal issues
Civil	Promote broad industry participation in corporate responsibility	To enhance long-term economic value by overcoming any first-mover disadvantages and to realize gains through collective action

Source: Zadek (2004)

Corporate governance and stakeholders

The issues of corporate culture, stakeholder involvement, and corporate governance are fundamentally interlinked. Nowhere is this more apparent than in the debates concerning football and, in particular, the Premier League in England. Takeovers and financial investments seem to be the order of the day, but at what expense to the game overall? Who benefits from a club's success on the field: the club as a corporation, or the ordinary football fan? Manchester United, one of the most famous football clubs in the world, is a case in point. When Malcolm Glazier bought the club and delisted it from the UK stock exchange, he generated a great outpouring of anger among season ticket holders and fans. By early 2010, soccer commentators began to question the long-term survival of the club as one of the top four clubs in the UK Premier League given its high level of debt. How could an American investor buy the club with such apparent total disregard for its supporters? Why were the supporters not involved in the decision-making process of what was best for the club's long-term future? What was the role of the board of directors in the takeover? Would the team's performance be affected? Would the club have the resources to buy and retain leading footballers for its Premier League campaigns? Would it have enough resources to fund its football academies for young players? Although all of these issues were well aired in the media at the time of the takeover, protesting fans at Old Trafford bearing banners reading 'Manchester United is not for sale' seemed oblivious to the implications of the club being a public limited company. The takeover is a microcosm of the complex issues faced by organizations in dealing with corporate governance and stakeholder involvement. We begin by looking at what corporate governance is.

Corporate governance

The overall purpose of an organization, including the manner in which it embraces CSR, is a function of the corporate governance structures and processes that it has in place. 'Corporate governance' is defined in the *International Corporate Governance Network Yearbook* (2005: 1) as:

> the meeting of the private interest and the public good: shareholders rely upon effective governance for the investment returns which fund pensions and insurance and protect savings; for companies it underpins both enterprise and accountability; for the wider community transparency and accountability in governance [are] vital for ensuring prosperity and the contribution to the public purse upon which social welfare [depends].

A combination of an effective regulatory environment, coupled with good governance by organizations (appropriate internal processes and practices), and the integrity and independence of professional service providers such as accountants and auditors, all contribute to good governance and efficiency of capital markets; most importantly, they instil confidence and trust in investors. In essence, corporate governance ensures that: organizations are managed well; the risks to the business are managed appropriately; national and international legal obligations are met or even exceeded; processes are monitored by internal control systems and validated by external professional service firms such as accountants and auditors; and the interests of the shareholders are represented by a board of directors. Boards of directors usually include independent appointees. Failures in corporate governance, such as the Enron scandal, AIG, Fannie Mae, Northern Rock, RBS, and HBOS, diminish investor confidence and trust, thereby undermining the efficiency of capital markets. In response, the model of corporate governance is changing, as Halal (2000: 10) describes: 'Corporate governance has evolved from the traditional "profit-centred model" to the "social responsibility model" and now seems to be moving toward collaborative working relations that could be called the "corporate community model"' (see Figure 5.1). These changes have, in part, been fuelled by a range of standards and legislative mechanisms introduced in the light of high-profile scandals.

Figure 5.1 Evolution of corporate governance (Halal, 2000)

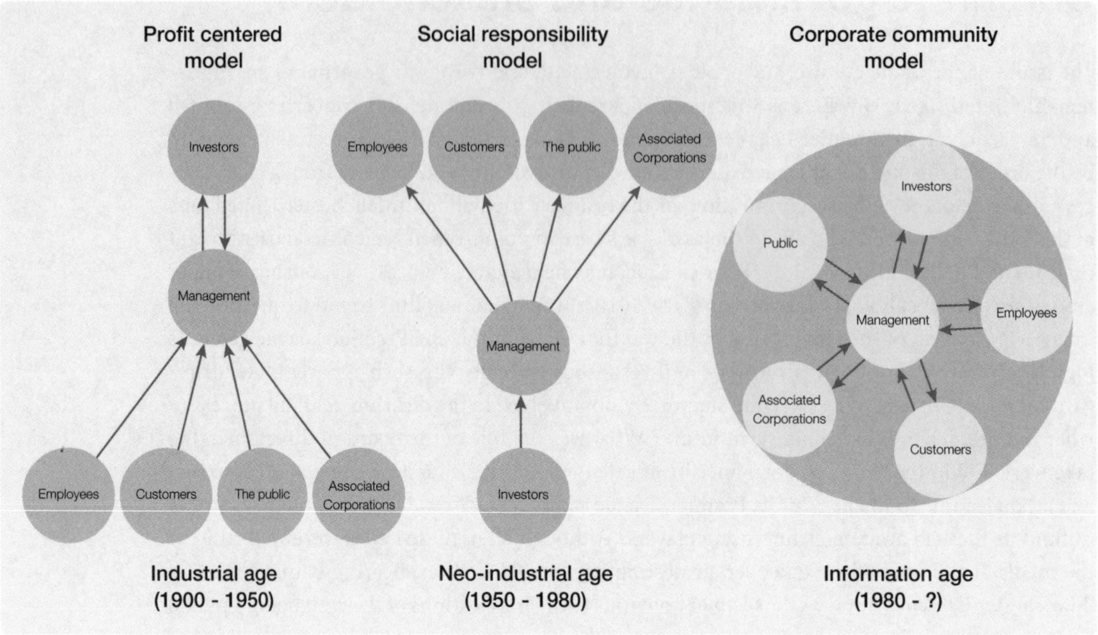

At an organizational level, corporate governance addresses a broad range of issues that affect the organization's interaction with society and other businesses. Corporate governance at company level is concerned with complying with regulatory legal and accounting requirements and standards. Corporate governance also deals with:

- risk management and internal controls;
- corporate culture;
- stewardship and accountability;
- board operations and composition;
- monitoring and evaluation of activities.

(Fahy *et al.*, 2005)

In turning to understand the key players involved in corporate governance, it is important to consider the board of directors.

Board of directors

The CEO and board of directors have legal, fiduciary, and, some would argue, moral responsibilities to deal with conformance to corporate governance issues. Typically, boards of directors consist of executive and non-executive members; these can be internal or external to the organization. In some cases, external members are drawn from different industries. For example, in Table 5.3, we see this in the example of the board of directors of General Motors. Frequently, analysis of the composition, background, experience, and skill set of a board of directors can provide a strong indication of the direction, intent, and culture of an organization.

The role of the board includes ensuring that the right CEO, CFO, and management team are appointed, and that there is oversight in terms of company strategy and the monitoring of firm performance and risk levels, particularly in company strategies. As Glassman (2005), former US Securities and Exchange Commissioner, stated:

Table 5.3 General Motors board of directors

Daniel F. Akerson	Chief executive officer	GM board chairman
Stephen J. Girsky	Vice chairman, corporate strategy, business development, global product planning, and global purchasing and supply chain	GM
Philip A. Laskawy	Chairman and chief executive officer (retired)	Ernst and Young LLP
Carol Stephenson	Dean	Richard Ivey School of Business, University of Western Ontario
David Bonderman	Co-founding partner and managing general partner	TPG
E. Neville Isdell	Chairman and chief executive officer (retired)	The Coca-Cola Company
Kathryn V. Marinello	Chairman and chief executive officer	Stream Global Services Inc.
Dr Cynthia A. Telles	Associate clinical professor	UCLA School of Medicine
Errol B. Davis Jr	Chancellor	University System of Georgia
Robert D. Krebs	Chairman and chief executive officer (retired)	Burlington Northern Santa Fe Corporation
Patricia F. Russo	Chief executive officer	Alcatel-Lucent

Source: http://www.gm.com/corporate/about/board.jsp

> The board must understand the drivers of performance and set the tolerance for risk. This covers oversight of operations, financial performance and reporting as well as regulatory compliance and risk management issues. Again, the overall goal of the governance structure and process is to maximize shareholder value through effective use of the firm's capital.

The main role of non-executive directors (NEDs) is to focus on the strategic aspects of the business by probing and playing devil's advocate, thus ensuring the robustness of the chosen strategy, in addition to monitoring financial performance and ensuring that adequate control measures are in place. Further roles include determining remuneration packages for top management teams, recruitment, and CEO succession issues. As the Higgs Report (2003) outlined, the role of NEDs is 'to create accountability, through challenging, questioning, testing, probing, debating, advising and informing'. The role of NEDs on boards of financial institutions hit by the financial crisis of 2008 and 2009 was called into question by commentators, particularly given the scale of national government support needed to rescue some of these institutions. The ensuing debate in many countries was focused on how companies—in this case, financial institutions—deal with the competing demands of delivering shareholder returns while being fully accountable.

Chairman's independence and responsibilities

The governance models and norms in countries vary extensively. In the UK governance model, the roles of the CEO and chairman of the board are usually separate, whereas in the USA, the CEO is also, in many cases, the chairman of the board. For example, in the UK, the chairman of the board is an independent appointment, with only 20 per cent of FTSE 100 companies failing to disclose whether the chairman was independently appointed (Grant Thornton, 2007: 24). In the USA, 75 per cent of the top 200 companies by revenue have combined CEO and chairman roles (Pearl Meyer & Partner, 2008: 13). The danger for companies is that duality of roles vests a lot of power and decision making in one individual; this raises the issue of whether shareholders are really getting value. According to ICAEW (2006), the many roles that an independent chairman of a board fulfils include:

- providing guidance to the CEO, often with insights from own past experience as a CEO;
- playing a vital role in shaping the board's agenda and facilitating meetings;
- creating an environment in which open and frank discussion is encouraged;
- liaising with external organizations, shareholders, and other stakeholders, who may wish to discuss an issue with someone other than the CEO; and
- overseeing the performance of executive management together with other NEDs or directors.

Effectiveness of boards

The Home Depot case mentioned at the beginning of the chapter highlights the issue of the effectiveness of boards in ensuring that the capital of the business is used to generate shareholder value that is sustainable over the long term. Particular criticism is levelled at the effectiveness of state boards in ensuring value for multiple stakeholders. Boards should have an active commitment to the **strategic decision making** of an organization (Westphal, 1999). In terms of strategy, a study by McNulty and Pettigrew (1999) found that the majority of board members do abdicate their strategy responsibilities. This has serious implications for good governance and the efficient use of capital. In their empirical study of boards, Minichilli *et al.* (2009) found significant predicators on the different board service (advice, networking, and strategic focus) and control tasks (behavioural control, output control, and strategic control). To increase the effectiveness of boards, Finkelstein and Mooney (2003) suggest that boards should: engage in constructive conflict, particularly with the CEO; avoid destructive conflicts; work together as a team; know the appropriate level of strategic involvement; and address decisions comprehensively. Kaufman and Englander (2005: 9) suggest that boards use a team production model of corporate governance, whereby instead of solely representing shareholder interest, they 'should represent those stakeholders that add value, assume unique risk and possess strategic information'. Carpenter and Westphal (2001: 639) found that 'strategic context of social network ties, not simply the number of ties, is an important influence on corporate governance'. Such a perspective raises some interesting points as we now look at the role of stakeholders.

Stakeholders

As companies move towards valuing and measuring their social impacts, understanding the role of stakeholders and how to engage meaningfully with them come to the fore. A moral argument holds that firms ought to engage with stakeholders for moral reasons, while an ethical strategist's approach is more instrumental, suggesting that engagement of stakeholders is integral to a firm's strategy if it is to fully leverage the foundations of advantage (Noland and Philips, 2010: 39). Stakeholders are constituent groups who, through interactions and involvement with business, hold the power to influence the business and its strategy. Stakeholders can be divided into primary and secondary stakeholders (see the example in Table 5.4). In the case of British Airways, the primary stakeholders have a direct interest in the business and hold considerable influence over the strategy of the organization. In contrast, secondary stakeholders, while having an interest in the evolution of British Airways, hold a degree of influence over strategy that varies with the nature of their relationship with the organization.

For strategists, a key challenge is to maintain positive and meaningful relationships with key stakeholders, but also to harness their ideas for the overall betterment of the business. The stakeholder challenge is described by Bill George (2003: 38), former CEO and chair of Medtronic:

Table 5.4 BA primary and secondary stakeholders

Primary stakeholders	Power to influence strategy
Board of directors	High
Employees	Medium to high
Competition regulators	High
Customers	Medium
Shareholders	Medium to high
Trade unions	Medium to high
Secondary stakeholders	**Power to influence strategy**
Subcontracting companies	Low to medium
Affiliated aviation partners	Medium to high
Airport ground transportation	Low to medium
Airport manufacturer	Medium
Other regulatory agencies	Medium to high

> The key to dealing with stakeholder groups is a balanced approach. It rarely serves a leader well to focus on one group to the exclusion of others. All stakeholders have legitimate needs that must be met by the company to the best of its ability. This is the only way to achieve exceptional results over the long term. Yes, there are competing interests among stakeholders. The leader's job is to define them and ensure that all stakeholders are well served.

In today's media world, this is a difficult challenge, with the proliferation of blogs and social networking sites on which stakeholders can freely articulate their views about any aspect of the organization. Nevertheless, organizations need to engage with stakeholders meaningfully. Police authorities have developed an active engagement model with local communities in developing local policing plans and priorities, and the membership of police authorities reflects the diverse nature of the communities that they serve. LG, the Netherlands-based global electronics firm, has identified its key stakeholders, their primary responsibilities, the communication channels that they use, and other details.

Some key questions remain: are all stakeholders really represented on boards and do they (or should they) really have a significant influence in the running of an organization? Evidence from studies such as that by Luoma and Goodstein (1999) indicates that organizations are beginning to take stakeholder interests seriously through board involvement. Luoma and Goodstein found that legal environments and organizational size are associated with the adoption of stakeholder-oriented boards. In many respects, whether stakeholders are involved or have a say in the running of the organization is a function of organizational democracy. This can lead to both positive and negative organizational impacts, categorized by Harrison and Freeman (2004) as follows.

- **Advantages**

  – People like to have a voice, or ability to influence the organizations in which they work. Therefore democracy may foster commitment to organization and purposeful behaviour.

  – Participation in decisions tends to enhance commitment to the final decisions made, which can aid in their implementation.

  – Democracy in organizations helps people to feel more responsible for organizational outcomes. This sense of responsibility could reduce the incidence of behaviours that are inconsistent with the values of the particular society in which the organization exists.

  – Democratic processes help to create a more participatory climate overall, which may enhance innovation and the ability to change.

- Giving more discretion to employees and managers allows them to develop skills and abilities more fully, making them more valuable to their organizations.
- It is the right thing to do, from a moral perspective.

- **Disadvantages**

- To the extent that decision-making power is given to lower levels in organizations, those people may choose a path that is not advantageous for the organization.
- Democratic processes take time, which can hurt efficiency.
- Implementation of democratic processes requires sweeping organizational changes that are difficult and time-consuming to make.
- Resistance to democratic processes can come from middle and upper-level managers due to the new skills that they will be required to develop and their loss of traditional authority.
- Democracy may not fit some situations.
- It may not be the right thing to do, from a moral perspective.

There are some notable examples of successful integration of organization democracy that affected the performance of business. Breman Group, a mid-sized Dutch engineering company, has been operating a model of organizational democracy since the 1970s (de Jong and van Witteloostunijn, 2004). Its model consists of three elements: shared residual claims (shared equity, profit sharing, fixed interest, and priority shares); supportive organizational structures (an employee association; an advisory board); and democratic decision-making rules (election procedures, equal approval, an arbitration safety net, and a decision web).

Another method of engaging organizational democracy has been through appreciative inquiry. This includes four stages: dream—the highest aspiration; discovery—when we are at our best; destiny—implementation, continuous learning, and improvization; and design—organizing principles and action plans (Powley *et al.*, 2004).

The successful implementation of organizational democracy is dependent on the type and work of the organization, existing organizational structures, and the commitment of management (Kerr, 2004). These structural mechanisms are embedded in the legislative and normative values of each country in which a company operates. In Germany, co-determination ensures that employees have an input into key organizational decisions. Likewise, in Asia, informality, long-term contacts, and loyalty play a critical role in shaping organizational decision making and board composition. This long-termism and sharing of decision making are still an exception in the Anglo-Saxon world. European Union (EU) legislation, such as the Information and Consultation Directive, which ensures that organizations consult in advance with employees on key strategic decisions, may go some way to correct this. There is a growing trend by many organizations to partner with non-governmental organizations (NGOs) as a way of demonstrating their broader commitment to society. Adobe Systems has several initiatives to support communities, including a software donation programme in Canada for primary and secondary schools and NGOs. In operating organizational democracy through stakeholder engagement with NGO activists, Deri (2003) suggests that an organization should:

1. act and respond as one global brand;
2. prepare for greater transparency;
3. not be forced into a 'yes or no' public confrontation on any issue;
4. enlist and engage multiple partners and perspectives;
5. not rely solely on industry-wide action or hide behind it;
6. distinguish between an NGO's rhetoric and its actual objectives; and
7. know when to stand its ground.

Ultimately, leaders should do as George (2003: 38) states:

> To create lasting value, I believe the CEO should pay most attention to the long-term stockholders and concentrate on meeting their needs. Otherwise, leaders can get whipsawed by the short-term holders, hedge funds, security analysts and even the short-seller.

The problem with making shareholder value the prime objective and focus of business is that it has the unintended consequence of emphasizing immediate operational and temporary gains to the detriment of the long-term investment and strategic thinking that may be core to a company's future viability (Martin, 2010: 65). Indeed, evidence suggests that shareholders actually do better when firms put stakeholders, such as customers, first (ibid). One way in which leaders can do this is to engage long-term stockholders in passionately living and believing in the mission of the business. Boards have to own and live the mission of the organization, the importance of which is highlighted in the next section.

Mission

If you were to ask yourself what your favourite mission statement is, you would probably struggle to come up with one, including that of your own organization or others with which you have come into contact through work or leisure. When you see a mission statement on office walls, in glossy annual reports, or on an organization's website, what is your reaction? Does it clearly communicate organizational values and purpose? Does it have customer credibility? Alternatively, are you sceptical of its meaning? Is there a gap between the mission and what you experience as a customer?

Purpose of the mission statement

A mission statement is a tangible statement about an organization that typically encapsulates its purpose, activities, and products. Such statements are included in annual reports, as part of promotion and marketing initiatives, and for recruitment purposes. They can also be used in the strategy process to define organization competitive boundaries. In a strategy formulation context, a mission statement provides the basis for defining the business and ultimately its attempts to answer the 'Who are we?' and 'What business(es) are we in?' questions. Mission statements can be used to some effect in clarifying business opportunities against organizational strategy and can assist organizations in providing them with a greater sense of where the **trade-off** points are in their strategy. A study of Canadian companies by Baetz and Bart (1996) confirms this. They found that the main rationales for having mission statements include:

- to guide the strategic planning system;
- to define the organization's scope of business operations/activities;
- to provide a common purpose/direction transcending individual and department needs;
- to promote a sense of shared expectations among all levels of employees, thereby building a corporate culture (that is, shared values); and
- to guide leadership styles.

Their study also found that the least important uses of mission statements included resource allocation and job designs and specifications.

Mission statements can vary in length depending on the context and complexity of the business. They can also be open to interpretation depending on the stakeholder's perspective and position. Theoretically, in terms of crafting a mission statement for an organization, the conventional wisdom is to involve multiple stakeholders in reaching a definitive version. In practice, as Baetz and

Bart (1996) found, the top management team, the CEO, and middle line managers were the key stakeholders involved in developing mission statements. Other external stakeholders, suppliers, and customers were least involved in developing mission statements. The study also found that 55 per cent of respondents regarded the content of the mission statement and the process by which it was crafted as being of equal importance.

Components of the mission statement

The orientation and language of mission statements vary. The tendency is for organizations to focus the mission statement content towards the key stakeholders and, in doing so, highlight the uniqueness of the organizational offering. A mission statement for a private-sector organization is not simply to make a profit, but rather what activities it should conduct to make a profit. Typically, organizations outline in clear and plain terms what their business activity is. This is a critical component of any statement, irrespective of sectoral context (Baetz and Bart, 1996; Morris, 1996). The sample mission statements outlined in the box below highlight the variety of statements and the language used to describe company values and purpose. The mission statement for Avon Products is a comprehensive statement developed around five themes, whereas Chevron presents its vision and the means by which this will be realized with a particular focus on its intention to be a company admired by key stakeholders. Finally, the Alcatel-Lucent Technologies excerpt neatly captures the purposes of a vision as a definition of future success and of the mission statement as a roadmap, or pathway, to realizing this vision. The examples illustrate that while the conceptual distinction between vision, mission, and values is clear, this is not always the case in practice. The ultimate criterion is that the organization uses its vision, values, and mission to present a coherent, consistent sense of its purpose and activities, and of the benefits that these will leverage financially for shareholders and, more broadly, for stakeholders and society.

Avon Products

The Avon Vision

To be the company that best understands and satisfies the product, service, and self-fulfilment needs of women—globally.

Avon's Mission

The global beauty leader. We will build a unique **portfolio** of beauty and related brands, striving to surpass our competitors in quality, innovation and value, and elevating our image to become the beauty company most women turn to worldwide.

The women's choice for buying. We will become the destination store for women, offering the convenience of multiple brands and channels, and providing a personal high touch shopping experience that helps create lifelong customer relationships.

The premier direct seller. We will expand our presence in direct selling and lead the reinvention of the channel, offering an entrepreneurial opportunity that delivers superior earnings, recognition, service and support, making it easy and rewarding to be affiliated with Avon and elevating the image of our industry.

The best place to work. We will be known for our leadership edge, through our passion for high standards, our respect for diversity and our commitment to create exceptional opportunities for professional growth so that associates can fulfil their highest potential.

The largest women's foundation. We will be a committed global champion for the health and well-being of women through philanthropic efforts that eliminate breast cancer from the face of the earth, and that empower women to achieve economic independence.

The most admired company. We will deliver superior returns to our shareholders by tirelessly pursuing new growth opportunities while continually improving our profitability, a socially responsible, ethical company that is watched and emulated as a model of success.

Source: http://www.avoncompany.com/corporatecitizenship/corporateresponsibility/whatwestandfor/visionmission.html

Chevron

At the heart of The Chevron Way is our vision to be the global energy company most admired for its people, partnership and performance. Our vision means we:

- safely provide energy products vital to sustainable economic progress and human development throughout the world;
- are people and an organization with superior capabilities and commitment;
- are the partner of choice;
- earn the admiration of all our stakeholders—investors, customers, host governments, local communities and our employees—not only for the goals we achieve but how we achieve them;
- deliver world-class performance.

Source: http://www.chevron.com/about/chevronway/

Alcatel-Lucent

The Alcatel-Lucent vision, mission and values form the cornerstones of our company. These statements set the tone for the way the company operates.

Our vision—definition of future success

To realize the potential of a connected world.

Our mission—purpose and path to realize the vision

To deliver the innovation our customers need to stay ahead, to evolve, to become radically more efficient, and to move at the speed of ideas.

Our values—a system of shared beliefs that are at the heart of everything we do

- *Customers first*: We exist to serve our customers. Our success will be determined by how well we perform for them.
- *Innovation*: We are intuitive, curious, inventive, practical and bold, which allows us to create new ideas for our customers, our business and employees. New thinking and new ideas are encouraged and nurtured throughout our global operations.
- *Teamwork*: Success requires teamwork. We are collaborative and respect the contributions of each person to the team's success.
- *Respect*: We are a global company with many cultures. We respect and embrace people and perspectives from all over the world.
- *Accountability*: We do what we say we will do. We own a collective responsibility towards customers, colleagues, communities and shareholders.

Source: http://www.aiesec.org/cms/aiesec/AI/partners/Alcatel-Lucent/index.html

A benchmark study of Fortune 500 companies by Pearce *et al.* (1987) demonstrated that higher-performing companies have comprehensive mission statements. The study highlighted eight key components of statements:

1. the specification of target customers and markets;
2. the identification of principal products/services;
3. the specification of geographical domain;
4. the identification of core technologies;
5. the expression of commitments to survival, growth, and profitability;
6. the satisfaction of key elements in the company philosophy;
7. the identification of the company self-concept; and
8. the identification of the firm's desired public image.

In particular, Pearce *et al.* (1987) found that philosophy, self-concept, and public image were the most important elements of mission statements of high-performing companies.

Value of mission statements

How mission statements contribute to value creation is difficult to decipher. Considered in a sceptical light, mission statements would not be seen to make a positive contribution to organizational purpose. Nash (1988: 155) put it thus: 'at their worst, these statements are ponderous or pompous, static summaries of past exploits and future inadequacies. Some are nothing more than a passing fancy or a piece or corporate window dressing.' Nevertheless, the ability of organizations to reach shared understanding through the communication of mission statements is critical to ensuring strategy alignment and sustainable success, and as a means of protecting shareholder value. To increase the daily relevance of mission statements, CEOs and top management teams need to break the mission down into strategies and, ultimately, objectives for business units, departments, and individuals (Crotts *et al.*, 2005). This element of aligning the mission statement is outlined by Crotts *et al.* as follows.

- Define the outcome of the mission in measurable terms (for example, customer satisfaction scores).
- Identify key policies, procedures, and practices that cue employee behaviour (for example, job descriptions, annual plans).
- Create an audit of whether or not the mission is included in each key policy, procedure, and practice.
- Conduct the audit.
- Fix and align any item that is out of alignment.
- Compare the audit results against the mission outcome measurement to affirm value of alignment.

In a non-profit context, this is more critical, because statements containing heroic missions (such as 'Make Poverty History') need to be broken down into specific programmes based on operational missions and strategy platforms (Rangan, 2004; see Chapter 13 for a discussion of context). Ultimately, one of the fundamental values of having a mission statement is that it contributes to shaping organizational culture. In the case of the A.P. Moller–Maersk Group, a Danish-based conglomerate with business activities that include container shipping, tankers, and offshore, terminal activities, oil and gas, retail, and technology, having clearly articulated values is essential given its diverse global operations and more than 115,000 employees.

A.P Moller–Maersk Group values

Our values are a set of fundamental shared beliefs. They are closely linked to our founder, Mr Arnold Peter Møller, and his son, Mr Mærsk Mc-Kinney Møller, and they form our guiding principles for behaviour, decisions and interaction.

Guiding everything we do, our values apply to all our employees—whether in Beijing, Kazakhstan, Honduras or elsewhere—and they play a critical role in how we work and in our continued success.

Our values are:

- Constant Care: Take care of today, actively prepare for tomorrow
- Humbleness: Listen, learn, share, and give space to others
- Uprightness: Our word is our bond
- Our Employees: The right environment for the right people
- Our Name: The sum of our values: passionately striving higher

Source: http://www.maersk.com/AboutMaersk/WhoWeAre/Pages/Values.aspx

Spotlight BP oil spill: Deepwater, deep trouble

The explosion aboard the Deepwater Horizon rig in April 2010 killed eleven workers, and caused 4.9 million barrels of oil to be spewed into the Gulf of Mexico. It was one of the worst spills in history, combining natural destruction, economic damage, and even diplomatic tension between London and Washington, as they rowed about BP's punishment. And, according to the National Oil Spill Commission set up by US President Barack Obama, it was entirely 'avoidable'. After reviewing thousands of pages of documents from government and industry (including company internal documents), and interviewing hundreds of officials, oil-industry employees, and other witnesses, the Commission found that 'most of the mistakes and oversights at Macondo [BP's well] can be traced back to a single overarching failure—a failure of management. Better management by BP, [and its key contractors] Halliburton and Transocean would almost certainly have prevented the blowout'. There will be much argument in coming months and years over what that phrase means, and whether it is true. But the clearest implication is this: the lethal Deepwater blast need never have happened—if only BP and its key contractors, three of the biggest and richest firms in the industry, had done their jobs better.

A chapter released ahead of the full report's publication included only forty-eight pages—but even only these pages conveyed much technical analysis and argument in clear, cool prose, making for a devastating charge sheet. Seasoned BP-watchers mainly agreed that the extract was not as bad for the oil giant as it looked, largely because it spared then chief executive Tony Hayward and his staff from accusations of gross negligence. But that is to miss the point: the Oil Spill Commission was never meant to argue any particular case, but to investigate the blowout, its causes, and its immediate aftermath—not to be the prosecution so much as the investigating detective. Yet if the rest of the report matched up to this chapter, it was to be Exhibit A for the US government in its civil lawsuit against BP.

What the Oil Spill Commission made clear is that drilling the Macondo well was a meticulously planned and well-designed operation—which, in execution, was sometimes rushed to the point of thoughtlessness. Substandard equipment turned up and, rather than wait, the drillers pressed on, with a BP engineer talking about 'the risk/reward equation' and claiming that all would 'probably be fine'. Behind this under-considered haste lay an overwhelming desire to cut costs. As the report remarks: 'Whether purposeful or not, many of the decisions that BP, Halliburton, and Transocean made that increased the risk of the Macondo blowout clearly saved those companies significant time (and money).' The Commission lists nine key decisions that may have contributed to the disaster: seven of them saved the drillers time, and only two were not made by BP.

There is nothing necessarily wrong with companies seeking to do business more efficiently—but there is everything wrong in cutting corners when the risks are so huge and widespread. That must be unarguable after the Deepwater disaster.

Two more sobering points to consider: first, the three companies named and shamed in the Commission report are three of the biggest in the world, and they were operating off the US coastline. Imagine what smaller firms may be up to in less regulated territories. Second, US regulators clearly do not have enough oversight of deep-water drilling. Officials must be called in not only to judge plans for wells, but also to supervise closely how those plans are implemented; otherwise, they are regulators of theory rather than practice. There is a lot more in the Deepwater Horizon saga still to run; on the initial evidence, however, it is not only BP that needs to improve its act, but rather an entire industry and area of government.

Source: © *Guardian News & Media Ltd* (2011)

Implications for strategy practice

The global financial crisis in 2008 and 2009, the failure of major financial institutions, and the closure of many large and small businesses throughout the world have forced governments, regulators, societies, businesses, and individual consumers to rethink and remodel the diverse responsibilities of business. Strong global companies such as AIG, GM, and Ford all secured government assistance—something that could not have been comprehended in the 1990s. These events have shown the impact that business has on society in real ways. This leads to a core question: 'How many organizations really devote significant time and energy to truly balancing the pursuit of profit against societal interests?' For entrepreneurial organizations, the challenge in getting equity or debt investment and generating sales and cash flows in order for the business to survive can take precedence over dealing with CSR issues outside regulatory compliance. As organizations grow in global scale and scope, generating a positive image about the brand and the organization is a threshold requirement. Consequently, the business case for CSR and engaging with influential stakeholders from a strategic perspective becomes more compelling. One significant challenge for all organizations is how they measure their CSR activities and whether they really have a long-term impact on stakeholder groups. Would you use the same CSR measure for organizations competing in nuclear energy production, grocery retailing, and mobile telecommunications? How would you reward best performers? Society after the global financial crisis will become even more suspicious of claims and reassurances made by business. Therefore the values and purpose of an organization need to be credible, tangible, and truly reflective of the organization.

The worrying issue from an academic and a business perspective is that we actually do not have any really clear understanding of, and insights into, what happens at board level in organizations, even though boards are charged with great responsibilities of delivering shareholder and, more recently, societal value. Much of the distrust of business emanates from media coverage of business stories and the fact that most CEOs of publicly quoted companies experience no real penalties for non-performance, having negotiated 'golden parachute' packages that ensure threshold remuneration irrespective of performance. Sir Fred Goodwin's severance and pension package when he stepped down as CEO of RBS has been the subject of much media and political comment, particularly as RBS posted the largest corporate losses in UK history in 2009. When non-performance occurs, shareholder attention focuses on the remuneration levels rather than the strategies that will be deployed by the CEO in turning the situation around. In addition, the role of NEDs comes under increased scrutiny in such circumstances. In coming decades, many organizations will experience increased levels of regulation because of the 2008–09 global financial crisis.

At the core of values and purpose are people. Most organizations would espouse the mantra 'people are our best asset', but many organizations are not as democratic in terms of their activities as they would like external stakeholders to believe, particularly given the performance environment under which they operate to deliver shareholder value. For CEOs, the real challenge is to develop corporate environments that allow for organizational democracy, while keeping ultimate responsibility for shareholder value with CEOs and boards. Employees in many organizations can see the CEO as someone closeted away from organizational life and immune to the ups and downs of its everyday reality. Some CEOs can have several filter layers between them and the organization. Pursuing organizational democracy in such contexts may be a futile exercise for key internal stakeholders. If organizational democracy is to work effectively, employees must have the tools and training that allow them to participate effectively in governance and strategy structures. It also requires high degrees of trust among management and employees.

Deciding which stakeholders really have influence over the organization can be a real challenge for organizations, and external events may force organizations to act, as illustrated in the spotlight piece on BP. We have referred to McDonald's, which was widely criticized for not providing healthy alternatives in its product selection. The company's response was to invest heavily in healthy meal offerings and to provide customers with more information about product ingredients. The message for organizations and strategists is to understand thoroughly what society demands and where the organizational trade-off is in meeting customer and societal demands.

Finally, defining the purpose of an organization allows for organizational values to develop, which is another way of addressing in a formal sense the dual demands that organizations face: those of shareholders and society. Many hardened executives can dismiss the importance of mission statements, but a key element of a leader's role is constantly communicating and reiterating the mission of the organization to all constituent stakeholders. What executives can forget is that human beings crave certainty in terms of values and purpose. The challenge for leaders is presenting a mission that reflects organizational aspirations and ambitions, while having regard for societal issues. This provides a basis for building a strong and responsible corporate culture that attempts to meet both profit and people needs. The challenge for leaders and strategists is to generate the emotional connection of stakeholders to the mission of the business and its strategy. Renault's return to Formula One (F1) motor racing was in line with the renewed purpose and mission captured in its strategic metaphor, '*Createur d'Automobile*'. Success on the F1 racing track has helped Renault to create that emotional connection with its primary and secondary stakeholders. Such an emotional connection can translate into employees going the extra mile for customers and co-workers because they believe in the values and purpose of the business. Too often, strategists can overlook the soft side of strategy that actually has a real impact on operational performance. In an age in which people are bombarded with different messages in multiple formats, getting stakeholders to believe in and commit to a credible and authentic mission statement is a real organizational challenge. It is nonetheless a critical one, because, in future years, values and purpose are likely to matter even more to shareholders and society.

Introduction to readings

Over the course of the chapter, we have seen the complexity involved for organizations in dealing with the multiple issues and often-competing challenges of ensuring sustainable advantage and profit while also attempting to make a positive contribution to society.

Reading 2.1, 'Strategy and society' by Michael Porter and Mark Kramer (2006), attempts to link CSR to competitive advantage. The central tenet of their argument is that organizations should focus on a narrow set of CSR activities; this will produce better results for society than could be achieved by any philanthropic organization. To do this, organizations must understand the inter-relationships that they have with society, choose which social issues to address, and from that process develop a corporate social agenda. Porter and Kramer argue that CSR investments should be viewed similarly to research and development (R&D), thereby implying a long-term perspective that generates meaningful legacy impacts. How many CEOs will take heed of such advice, particularly given the daily realities of competitive and shareholder value pressures? How realistic is it to expect organizations to view CSR investment in the same light as R&D?

Our second reading for this chapter, to which a link is provided on the Online Resource Centre that accompanies this book, Ian Wilson's 'The agenda for redefining corporate purpose: five key executive actions' (2004), was written after the corporate scandals of the early 2000s. Wilson attempts to reflect the changes in attitudes of executives and the business community, but also argues that we need to rethink the role of organizations in society. The reading raises the key question of how realistic and achievable Wilson's agenda for executive action is. How realistic is it for an organization to move from profit to service as its purpose? How realistic is it for a management team to maintain sincerity when shareholder expectations constantly increase? In the examples of George Merck and David Packard, Wilson shows that focusing on customer needs or viewing profit as an enabler rather than an end can lead to sustainable success. How many CEOs and corporate board members of publicly listed companies would buy into this view?

Our final reading, also accessible via a link on the Online Resource Centre, 'The dynamics of the boardroom' by Lorin Letendre (2004), presents a very bleak picture of our understanding of what happens in boardrooms. But is this a bad thing? If we were to find out what really goes on at board level, would we find an absence of sophistication of strategic thought, of preparedness, and of analytical capability to look after the interests of shareholders properly? How many boards would really welcome an in-depth review of their performance? What might explain the lack of research and knowledge about boardroom activities? How might we better understand the behaviour and activities of corporate boards?

Mini case study Fairtrade: making a difference?

The Fairtrade label can be found on an increasing number of product ranges—more than 1,500 products in retail stores and coffee shops (see the box below). According to Fairtrade (2010), by 2008, Fairtrade-certified sales amounted to approximately €3.8bn worldwide, a 22 per cent year-on-year increase and nearly 40 per cent average growth per year since 2003. In terms of producer organizations, there are now 827 Fairtrade-certified producer organizations in fifty-eight producing countries, representing over 1.2 million farmers and workers. In addition to other benefits, approximately €43m was distributed to communities in 2008 for use in community development. Including families and dependants, Fairtrade Labelling Organizations International (FLO), the umbrella organization for the eighteen national Fairtrade organizations, estimates that 6 million people directly benefit from Fairtrade (Fairtrade, 2010). In the UK, between 2003 and 2007, there was a 47 per cent increase in yearly sales of Fairtrade-certified products. The mission of Fairtrade (2011) 'is to connect disadvantaged producers and consumers, promote fairer trading conditions and empower producers to combat poverty, strengthen their position and take more control over their lives'. Independent studies carried out in relation to the impacts of Fairtrade on coffee producers found that the organization financially strengthened them, their families, and communities. The studies also highlight other impacts, such as stable home environments for children, increased opportunities to access education, the preserving of indigenous cultures, and greater political influence for producers through their involvement with the Fairtrade organization. Economists who are critical of this type of assistance argue that Fairtrade is providing producers with subsidies that ultimately impede growth. Critics would argue that the assistance provided by the Fairtrade system undermines natural market forces and that this approach in the long run will not be sustainable from producer or customer perspectives.

Fairtrade-certified products

- Bananas
- Cocoa
- Coffee
- Cotton
- Flowers
- Fresh fruit
- Gold
- Honey
- Juices
- Rice
- Spices and herbs
- Sports balls
- Sugar
- Tea
- Wine

Source: http://www.fairtrade.net/products.html

Fairtrade was founded and launched by Max Havelaar on 15 November 1998 in Holland, and was aimed at developing a new, more sustainable model of aid, driven by consumer awareness and aimed at small coffee producers in developing economies. At the time, small coffee producers had little power and were at the mercy of landowners, moneylenders, and traders. The reality for small producers was that they were being squeezed financially due to higher input costs while receiving less than market value for their end product. Coffee producers in developing countries had to deal with market imperfections on top of financial pressures, which meant that they found it hard to escape the poverty trap. These market imperfections included lack of market access, imperfect information, lack of access to credit, the inability to switch to other sources of income generation, and weak legal systems and enforcement of laws (Nicholls and Opal, 2005).

Previous attempts to sell certified coffee through churches and Third World stores in Holland resulted in only a 0.2 per cent market share. Havelaar knew that getting the brand into retail stores was a must and market research estimated that such a brand could attain approximately 14 per cent market share. Getting coffee roasters to sign up to the Fairtrade certification process was also essential. To this end, the Max Havelaar Foundation became the independent owner of the certification mark. By 1988, Havelaar had signed up fifteen coffee roasters and one retail supermarket. By 1989, he had captured 1.7 per cent market share, and over 65 per cent of the Dutch population had heard of Fairtrade, thanks to the publicity about the concept.

Typically, individual coffee producers form a cooperative. Fairtrade pays the producers more per gram and requires them to comply with a number of standards in order to become certified, including the following.

- The aim of the cooperative organization is the improvement of the position and socio-economic development of the members.
- The majority of members are smallholders—that is, farmers who operate their coffee farms with family labour.
- The organization has a democratic, transparent structure. Members must be able to actively participate and effectively control the organization.
- The organization does not discriminate: anyone must be able to join, regardless of skin colour, race, sex, political, or religious conviction.
- The organization must comply with basic practical requirements.
- A responsible environmental policy is adopted.

Coffee producers have constantly experienced price volatility—particularly from 1997 onwards when coffee consumers switched to soft drinks in key markets such as the USA. This coincided with greater investment in coffee plantations in Vietnam, and increased coffee volumes produced in Brazil. The model developed by Havelaar imposes trade conditions, including direct purchasing, pre-financing, long-term trade relations, a premium on top of market prices, and guaranteed minimum prices.

To ensure that producers adhere to Fairtrade's standards, FLO carries out inspections. Other organizations involved are:

- the World Fair Trade Organization (WFTO), formerly the International Fair Trade Association;
- the Network of European Worldshops (NEWS!), founded in 1994; and

• the European Fair Trade Association (EFTA), founded in 1990 and importing products from 400 economically disadvantaged producer groups in Asia, Africa, and South America.

The collective acronym for the network as a whole is FINE.

Nicholls (2005: 12) summarizes the ongoing challenge that Fairtrade faces:

> Fair trade also makes the free trade system work the way it is supposed to. By providing farmers access to credit and information, it corrects market imperfections. As with any market, the more knowledge one's trading partner has, the more they are likely to gain in a negotiation. Transferring market knowledge to developing-country producers will inevitably make them better off.

The new strategy developed and approved by the governing council in December 2008, entitled 'Making the difference: the global strategy for Fairtrade', aims to continue the growth and increase the global recognition of fair trade. As Fairtrade scales up, this model of market support will be tested further; only time will tell if this approach continues to benefit developing country producers and their customers.

Questions

1. What is the organizational mission of Fairtrade?
2. Describe the CSR approach of Fairtrade. How sustainable is it?
3. What measures should Fairtrade take to engage actively in CSR?
4. What governance structure would you recommend fairtrade should put in place to reflect its growing portfolio of activities? Where are the potential weaknesses in Fairtrade activities that could impact its business?
5. Write a mission statement for Fairtrade that encompasses its values, purpose, activities, and ambitions.

Summary

We began this chapter by exploring the business of business, and by examining corporate social responsibility and CSR leadership and engagement. We then turned our attention to corporate governance and stakeholders, and in particular outlined the role that stakeholders play in shaping values and purpose. We concluded the chapter by discussing the purpose, components, and value of organizational mission statements. We have seen that the values and purpose of business are core issues that strategists need to understand in order to craft strategy and put in place internal strategy-formulation mechanisms that reflect both shareholder value and societal impacts. This is one of the core foundations of advantage for organizations.

Strategists must intuitively understand the values and purpose of their organization, the corporate governance landscape, and stakeholder needs. These will be ingrained in the strategy, strategy process, and performance metrics of organizations. Strategists and strategy departments have to be involved in shaping purpose and missions, but these also require the involvement of everyone in the organization, and of outside stakeholders, to ensure that the values and purpose of the organization become a lived daily reality. This is a significant task and a responsibility for everyone in the organization, not only for the strategists. How organizations behave, with respect to purpose and mission, impacts not only on competing organizations, but also on society as a whole. White-collar crime and organizational corruption illustrate the negative impacts of values and purpose, while also reinforcing that organizations do have diverse responsibilities that are essential to their long-term sustainability. If organizations, CEOs, and strategists do not take these responsibilities seriously, the relationship between business and society could be weakened and undermined. This highlights the importance of understanding values and purpose as a critical foundation of advantage rather than an afterthought.

Discussion questions

1. Outline some of the key issues that should shape an organization's values and purpose.
2. What are the possible advantages and disadvantages of CSR?
3. Review Internet and media material on Enron. What factors account for its fall from grace? What lessons can be learnt?
4. Is it possible to link CSR and performance?

5. What function should corporate governance play in strategy?

6. Do mission statements simply serve as powerful rhetoric or do they inform organizational action in practice?

7. Take a mission statement of an organization with which you are familiar. Using Pearce *et al.*'s (1987) eight components, analyse the statement. Does it convey clear values and purpose? What changes would you recommend?

8. Imagining yourself to be a strategist for A. P. Moller–Maersk, develop a mission statement that reflects its core values.

9. Source a recent journal article that contributes to the issues raised in this chapter. How does its argument differ from or relate to debates in this area?

Further reading

The book *Harvard Business Review on Corporate Governance* (2000), Boston, MA: Harvard Business School Press, gives a comprehensive and practical overview of the key organizational and strategic issues concerning corporate governance.

In *Blueprint for Corporate Governance: A Strategy—Accountability and the Preservation of Shareholder Value* (2003), New York: AMACOM, Fred R. Kaen deals with strategy and shareholder values.

A classic and timeless article on creating a sense of purpose in an organization is A. Campbell and S. Yeung (1991) 'Creating a sense of mission', *Long Range Planning*, 24(4): 10–20.

In his 2010 article 'The age of customer capitalism', *Harvard Business Review*, Jan/Feb: 58–65, Roger Martin presents an insightful overview of the key theories informing how the value of business should be conceptualized, from the separation of ownership and control, through shareholder value, to a new era that he labels 'customer capitalism'. In so doing, he offers a strong critique of the short-termism of stock market valuations.

visit the Online Resource Centre that accompanies this book to access more learning resources on this chapter topic at www.oxfordtextbooks.co.uk/orc/cunningham/

References

Abbott, W. F. and Monsen, R. J. 1979. On the measurement of corporate social responsibility: self-reported disclosures as a method of measuring corporate social involvement. *Academy of Management Journal*, 22(3): 501–515.

Adler, P. S. 2002. Corporate scandals: it's time for reflection in business schools. *Academy of Management Executive*, 16(3): 148–149.

Advertising Standards Agency (ASA). 2007. ASA Adjudication on Cadbury Trebor Bassett Services Ltd. Available online at http://www.asa.org.uk/asa/adjudications/Public/TF_ADJ_42400.htm

Alexander, G. J. and Buchholz, R. A. 1978. Corporate social responsibility and stock market performance. *Academy of Management Journal*, 21(3): 479–486.

Baetz, M. C. and Bart, C. K. 1996. Developing mission statements which work. *Long Range Planning*, 29(4): 526–533.

Birkinshaw, J. 2010. *Reinventing Management: Smarter Choices for Getting Work Done*. Chichester: John Wiley and Sons.

Carpenter, M. and Westpal, J. 2001. A team production model of corporate governance. *Academy of Management Journal*, 4(4): 639–660.

Carroll, A. B. 1978. Setting operational goals for corporate social responsibility. *Long Range Planning*, 11(2): 35–38.

Carroll, A. B. 1979. A three-dimensional conceptual model of corporate performance. *Academy of Management Review*, 4(4): 497–505.

Carroll, A. B. and Shabana, K. 2010. The business case for corporate social responsibility: a review of concepts, research and practice. *International Journal of Management Reviews*, 12(1): 85–105.

Charan, R. 2006a. Conquering a culture of indecision. *Harvard Business Review*, 84(1): 108–117.

Charan, R. 2006b. Home Depot's blueprint for culture change. *Harvard Business Review*, 84(4): 60–70.

Chatteri, A. and Levine, D. 2006. Breaking down the wall of codes: evaluating non-financial performance measurement. *California Management Review*, 48(2): 29–51.

Crotts, J. C., Dickson, D. R., and Ford, R. C. 2005. Aligning organizational processes with mission: the case of service excellence. *Academy of Management Executive*, 19(3): 54–68.

De Jong, G. and Van Witteloostuijn, A. 2004. Successful corporate democracy: sustainable cooperation of capital and labor in the Dutch Breman Group. *Academy of Management Executive*, 18(3): 54–66.

Deri, C. 2003. Make alliances, not war, with crusading external stakeholders. *Strategy and Leadership*, 31(5): 26–33.

Fahy, M., Roche, J., and Weiner, A. 2005. *Beyond Governance: Creating Corporate Value through Performance, Conformance and Responsibility*. Chichester: John Wiley & Sons.

Fairtrade. 2010. Facts and figures. Available online at http://www.fairtrade.net/facts_and_figures.html

Fairtrade. 2011. Our vision. Available online at http://www.fairtrade.net/our_vision.0.html

Finkelstein, S. and Mooney, A. C. 2003. Not the usual suspects: how to use board process to make boards better. *Academy of Management Executive*, 17(2): 101–113.

Finlay, P. 2000. *Strategic Management*. New York: FT Prentice Hall.

George, B. 2003. Managing stakeholders vs responding to shareholders. *Strategy and Leadership*, 31(6): 36–40.

Glassman, C. 2005. Speech by SEC Commissioner: remarks at 'Beyond the Myth of Anglo-American Corporate Governance'. US

Securities and Exchange Commission/Institute of Chartered Accountants in England & Wales, Washington DC, 6 December. Available online at http://www.sec.gov/news/speech/spch120605cag.htm

Grant Thornton. 2007. *Sixth FTSE 350 Corporate Governance Review: Highlighting Trends in Practice*. Available online at http://www.gtuk.com/pdf/CGR-2007.pdf

The Guardian. 2011. BP oil spill: Deepwater, deep trouble. 7 January. Available online at http://www.guardian.co.uk/commentisfree/2011/jan/07/bp-oil-spill

Halal, W. E. 2000. Corporate community: a theory of the firm uniting profitability and responsibility. *Strategy and Leadership*, 28(2): 10–16.

Harrison, J. S. and Freeman, R. E. 2004. Special topic: democracy in and around organizations. *Academy of Management Executive*, 18(3): 49–53.

Herman, M. 2007. Cadbury admits Salmonella charges. *Times Online*, 15 June. Available online at http://business.timesonline.co.uk/tol/business/law/article1936836.ece

Higgs. D. 2003. *Report on the Role and Effectiveness of Non-executive Directors*. London: HMSO.

Hurley, R. F. 2006. The decision to trust. *Harvard Business Review*, 84(9): 55–62.

Institute of Chartered Accountants in England and Wales (ICAEW). 2006. *Business Dialogue, Board Responsibilities and Creating Value: Demonstrating Leadership and Accountability*. London: ICAEW.

International Corporate Governance Network (ICGN). 2005. *International Corporate Governance Yearbook*. Available online at http://www.icgn.org/files/icgn_main/pdfs/year_books/2005_yearbook.pdf

Kaufman, A. and Englander, E. 2005. A team production model of corporate governance. *Academy of Management Executive*, 19(3): 9–22.

Kerr, J. L. 2004. The limits of organizational democracy. *Academy of Management Executive*, 18(3): 81–95.

Kerr, S. 2004. Introduction: bringing practitioners and academics together. *Academy of Management Executive*, 18(1): 94–96.

Kochan, T. A. 2002. Addressing the crisis in confidence in corporations: root causes, victims, and strategies for reform. *Academy of Management Executive*, 16(3): 139–141.

Letendre, L. 2004. The dynamics of the boardroom. *Academy of Management Executive*, 18(1): 101–104.

Lindgreen, A. and Swaen, V. 2010. Corporate social responsibility. *International Journal of Management Reviews*, 12(1): 1–8.

Lotila, P. 2010. Corporate responsiveness to social pressure: an interaction-based model. *Journal of Business Ethics*, 94: 395–409.

Luoma, P. and Goodstein, J. 1999. Stakeholders and corporate boards: institutional influences on board composition and structure. *Academy of Management Journal*, 42(5): 553–563.

Martin, R. 2010. The age of customer capitalism. *Harvard Business Review*, Jan/Feb: 58–65.

Matten, D. and Crane, A. 2005. Corporate citizenship: toward an extended theoretical conceptualization. *Academy of Management Review*, 30(1): 166–179.

McAdam, T. 1973. How to put corporate responsibility into practice. *Business and Society Review*, 973(6): 8–16.

McGuire, J. B., Sundgren, A., and Schneeweis, T. 1988. Corporate social responsibility and firm financial performance. *Academy of Management Journal*, 31(4): 854–872.

McKinsey. 2006. *The McKinsey Global Survey of Business Executives: Business and Society*. Available online at https://www.mckinseyquarterly.com/The_McKinsey_Global_Survey_of_Business_Executives_Business_and_Society_1741

McNulty, T. and Pettigrew, A. 1999. Strategists on the board. *Organization Studies*, 20(1): 47–74.

Minichilli, A., Zattoni, A., and Zona, F. 2009. Making boards effective. *British Journal of Management*, 20(1): 55–74.

Morris, R. L. 1996. Developing a mission for a diversified company. *Long Range Planning*, 29(1): 103–115.

Munilla, L. and Miles, M. 2005. The corporate social responsibility continuum as a component of stakeholder theory. *Business and Society Review*, 110(4): 371–387.

Nash, L. 1988. Mission statements: mirrors and windows. *Harvard Business Review*, 66(2): 155–156.

Nicholls, A. 2005. Survival in a hostile environment: Fairtrade's role as a positive market mechanism for disadvantaged producers. Available online at http://www.universitynetwork.org/sites/universitynetwork.org/files/files/FTF%20Paper%20Survival%20in%20a%20Hostile%20Market.doc

Nicholls, A. and Opal, C. 2005. *Fair Trade: Market-driven Ethical Consumption*. London: Sage.

Noland, J. and Philips, R. 2010. Stakeholder engagement, discourse ethics and strategic management. *International Journal of Management Reviews*, 12(1): 39–49.

Pearce, I., John A., and David, F. 1987. Corporate mission statements: the bottom line. *Academy of Management Executive*, 1(2): 109–115.

Pearl Meyer and Partners. 2008. Director compensation report: study of the top 200 corporations. Available online at http://www.pearlmeyer.com/Pearl/media/PearlMeyer/PDF/2007director.pdf

Powley, E. H., Fry, R. E., Barrett, F. J., and Bright, D. S. 2004. Dialogic democracy meets command and control: transformation through the Appreciative Inquiry Summit. *Academy of Management Executive*, 18(3): 67–80.

Rangan, V. K. 2004. Lofty missions, down-to-earth plans. *Harvard Business Review*, 82(3): 112–119.

Rasberry, R. W. 2000. The conscience of an organization: the ethics office. *Strategy & Leadership*, 3: 17–21.

Rigby, D. 2003. Management tools survey 2003: usage up as companies strive to make headway in tough times. *Strategy and Leadership*, 31(5): 4–11.

Singh, V. and Point, S. B. 2004. Strategic responses by European companies to the diversity challenge: an online comparison. *Long Range Planning*, 37(4): 295–318.

Smith, A. 1937 (1776). *An Enquiry concerning the Causes of the Wealth of Nations*. New York: Modern Library.

Swanson, D. 1995. Addressing a theoretical problem by reorienting the corporate social performance model. *Academy of Management Review*, 20(1): 43–64.

Vogel. D. 2005. The low value of virtue. Harvard Business Review, June. Available online at http://hbr.org/2005/06/the-low-value-of-virtue/ar/1

Wartick, S. and Cochran, P. L. 1985. The evolution of the corporate social performance model. *Academy of Management Review*, 10(4): 758–769.

Whesphal, J. D. 1999. Collaboration in the boardroom: behavioural and performance consequences of CEO–board social ties. *Academy of Management Journal*, 42: 7–24.

Wilson, I. 2004. The agenda for redefining corporate purpose: five key executive actions. *Strategy and Leadership*, 32(1): 21–26.

Windsor, D. 2006. Corporate social responsibility: three key approaches. *Journal of Management Studies*, 23(1): 93–114.

World Council for Sustainable Development. 1999. Meeting changing expectations. Available online at http://www.wbcsd.org/DocRoot/hbdf19Txhmk3kDxBQDWW/CSRmeeting.pdf

Zadek. S. 2004. The path to corporate social responsibility. *Harvard Business Review*, 82(12): 125–132.

6

Market-based and resource-based approaches

Those who fail to understand their environment will fall foul of it.

(Boxall and Purcell, 2008)

Introduction

In the last chapter, our focus was on the nature of values and purpose as one core element of the foundation of advantage. In this chapter, we focus on analysis. Specifically, we explore whether a market-based or resource-based approach is likely to offer a more secure foundation of advantage. Time and again, the business press reports on nimble competitors who beat and overtake the dominant player in a market and, by so doing, change the rules of the game. One of the mostly cited examples is Canon who, at one tenth the size of dominant player Xerox, entered what was deemed an impenetrable photocopier market. Canon had developed optic capabilities in the production of cameras that readily transferred to photocopiers. At the time, Xerox, with its high-speed, high-volume copiers, coupled with its model leasing and repairs service, had already seen off competition from main players IBM and Kodak, who had flirted with the market and left. As well as customer lock-in, Xerox held over 500 patents. For all intents and purposes, the industry had high barriers to entry. In 1970, Canon entered the market through a dealer network deliberately focusing on smaller offices and individual users who might have slipped under Xerox's radar. Canon was able to leverage and integrate its abilities and experience in optics, precision technologies, and microelectronics to provide products that proved superior to Xerox's on quality and price. Within twenty years, Canon was the dominant player in copiers, rewriting rules of competition that had previously seemed set in stone.

The story is now strategy folklore, although interpretations of the foundations of Canon's advantage vary. One version notes that 'it chose a unique and well-defined strategic position in the industry—one with distinctive customers, products and activities' (Markides, 2004: 9). An equally plausible account attributes Canon's success to its unique resources and capabilities, and ability to leverage these as core competences to its advantage (Grant, 1991). Understanding the precise foundations of advantage is never uncontested, but in the main explanations tend to centre on what we will term in this chapter 'market-based' or 'resource-based' approaches. What are the foundations of a firm's advantage? Should it take competitive rules as given, and do what external analysis would prescribe—that is, decipher the rules as best it can and position itself accordingly? Should it try to make its own rules and use internal resources to change the game or create a new way of doing things, as internal analysis might suggest? The strategist has to decipher the foundations of advantage, examining external factors (competitive dynamics, competitors, and customers) and internal resources (competencies and dynamics capabilities) in order to define organizational difference and achieve competitive dominance (see Figure 6.1).

We begin the chapter by outlining the nature of competitive advantage. Our focus then turns to external foundations of advantage—the market-based view of the firm. Here, we examine various analytical tools that can be used to assess the external foundations of advantage and the market perspective, as well as exploring some of their limitations. Failing to understand the environment,

Figure 6.1 Foundations of advantage

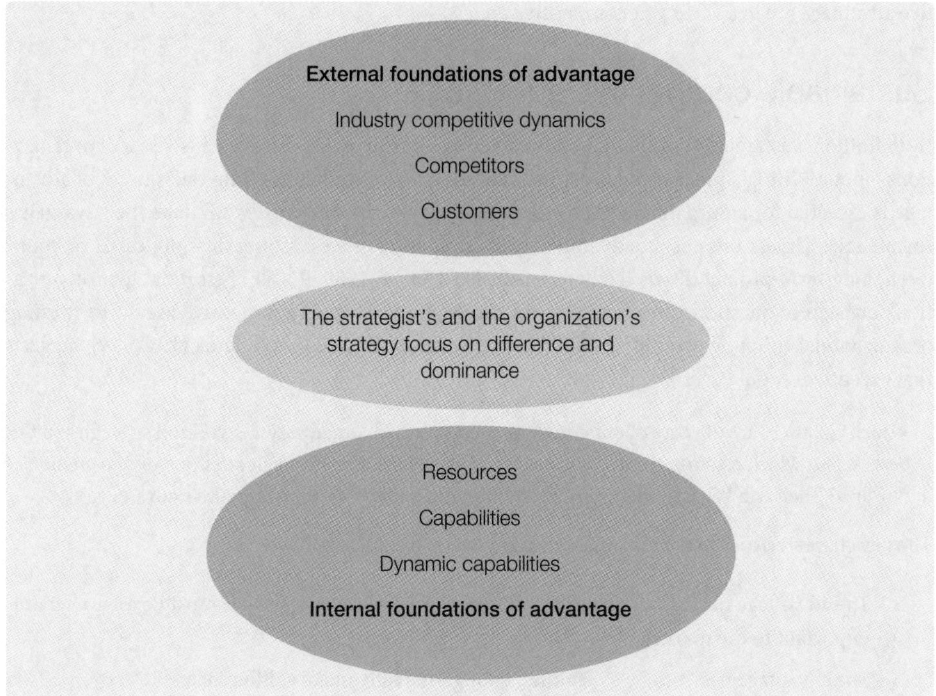

as Boxall and Purcell outline in the opening quote, can cost companies and individuals dearly. Our attention then turns to the internal foundations of advantage: namely, resources, competences, and capabilities. This is a contentious issue and the debate between the two perspectives has swung back and forth (Hoskisson *et al.*, 1999).

The nature of competitive advantage: sustainable or temporal?

What makes a business unique and relevant is relentlessly discussed and tested in a variety of organizational settings. Being different and knowing how to utilize that difference to dominate a competitive space are at the core of strategy. Difference can manifest itself in many forms and be based on a multitude of internal and external foundations. The challenge for today's strategist is:

> to think strategically about their company's position and about the impact of changing conditions. They have to monitor the company's external environment and internal capabilities closely enough to know when to institute strategy changes.
>
> (Thompson and Strickland, 2003: 28)

Organizations are continuously mandated to defeat, exploit, or destroy the competition: for example, Komatsu, a manufacturer of construction equipment, set itself the strategic intent 'to kill Caterpillar'. Strategists know that the key question is how an advantage will be achieved in practice. For example, how would you distinguish the competitive advantage for coffee shops such as Starbucks, Insomnia, or Pret A Manger, or car manufacturers such as Ford, Volkswagen (VW), General Motors (GM), BMW and Volvo? Is it the customer or the organization that makes the distinction? The issue then becomes how temporal or sustainable a business's sources of competitive advantage are in a variety of competitive arenas.

Sustainable competitive advantage

By definition, **sustainable competitive advantage** will be the reserve of an exclusive set of organizations—but reaching a precise and accepted definition proves difficult. Using the sources of advantage is essential for an organization, but the challenge for the strategist is to make the advantages sustainable: 'Unless there is an advantage over competitors that is not easily duplicated or countered, long-term profitability is likely to be elusive' (Aaker, 1989: 91). It is essential that organizations constantly question the workings and assumptions of their competitive arena. In framing organizational thinking around sustainable competitive advantage, Williams (1992: 29) suggests that executives should ask:

> Which resources are the core of our company success (which organization styles and strategies suit us best) versus which resources and routines are peripheral (i.e. non-strategic) to the evolving mission of our firm? Then ask: What does this say about the sustainability of our competitive advantage?

The key characteristics of an advantage that is sustainable are as follows.

1. The advantage needs to involve key success factors of the market—it must be an area that is important to the market.
2. The advantage needs to be substantial enough to really make a difference.
3. Needs to be sustainable in the face of environmental changes and competitor actions.

(Aaker, 1984)

Of course, the reality is that 'the ability to develop a sustained competitive advantage today is increasingly rare. A competitive advantage laboriously achieved can be quickly lost' (Duncan *et al.*, 1998: 7). Some even doubt whether any advantage can ever be fully sustainable and instead claim that we should refer to 'temporal advantage' (D'Aveni *et al.*, 2010).

Sources of competitive advantage

Scholars have identified a bewildering array of competitive advantages, including those based on information technology (Porter and Millar, 1985), on time (Stalk, 1988), on shareholder value analysis (Day and Fahey, 1990), on strategic leadership and practices (Ireland and Hitt, 2005), on people (Pfeffer, 2005), on collaboration (Liedtka, 1996), on organizational capabilities (Ulrich and Lake, 1991), on human resources and information technology (Broderick and Boudreau, 1992), and on technological pioneering (Zahra *et al.*, 1995). In practice, understanding current and future foundations for advantage is best achieved through the systematic assessment of an organization's environment. As Ohmae (1982) commented, 'analysis is the critical starting point of strategic thinking', while it is invariably the case that flawed analysis will yield a flawed strategy.

Within the strategic management field, two competing perspectives of foundations of advantage have emerged. One is a market-based perspective, from which a company takes a competitive position in the marketplace that it can defend. This has come from an industrial organization perspective (Bain, 1956) and involves developing an understanding of the key rules of the game. The other perspective argues that the advantage can be found internally within the firm, through resources, competencies, and **dynamic capabilities**. This is termed the 'resource-based' view of the firm and centres on breaking the rules or making your own rules. We begin by examining the market perspective, which was strongly associated with the planning and positioning perspectives of the industrial era that we reviewed in Chapter 1.

Sources of competitive advantage

Information technology

The importance of the information revolution is not in dispute. The question is whether information technology will have a significant impact on a company's competitive position; rather the question is when and how this impact will strike. Companies that anticipate the power of information technology will be in control of events. Companies that do not respond will be forced to accept changes that others initiate and will find themselves at a competitive disadvantage.

(Porter and Millar, 1985: 149)

People

Achieving competitive success through people involves fundamentally altering how we think about the workforce and the employment relationship. It means achieving success by working with people, not by replacing them or limiting the scope of their activities. It entails seeing the workforce as a source of strategic advantage, not just as a cost to be minimized or avoided. Firms that take this different perspective are often able to successfully outmanoeuvre and outperform their rivals.

(Pfeffer, 1995: 55)

Time

Like competition itself, competitive advantage is a constantly moving target. For any company in any industry, the key is not to get stuck with a single notion of its sources of advantage. The best competitors, the most successful ones, know how to keep moving and always stay on the cutting edge. Today, time on the cutting edge ... In fact, as a strategic weapon, time is the equivalent of money, productivity, quality, even innovation.

(Stalk, 1988: 41)

Organizational capabilities

Building better products or services, pricing goods or services lower than the competition or incorporating technological innovation into research and manufacturing operations must today be supplemented by organizational capability—the firm's ability to manage people to gain competitive advantage ... We believe that building organizational capability from the inside out has become and will continue to be a primary management agenda.

(Ulrich and Lake, 1991: 77)

Shareholder value analysis (SVA)

Used correctly, shareholder value analysis is much more like an examination of strategic fundamentals than a number-crunching exercise. Without a basis in the hard organization and competitive realities, value-based numbers have no meaning. SVA is useful only when it is the last step in a rigorous evaluation of how strategic alternatives are likely to fare in the marketplace. When accompanied by sharp, critical thinking, SVA gives reliable signals about a strategy's potential to create both shareholder value and sustainable competitive advantage.

(Day and Fahey, 1990: 156)

Human resources and information technology

All managers have a stake in exploiting information technology to better manage their human resources . . . HR information technology can improve human resource management and contribute to competitive advantage.

(Broderick and Boudreau, 1992: 7)

Strategic leadership

CEOs who apply practices associated with 21st-century strategic leadership can create sources of competitive advantage for their organizations. The competitive advantages resulting from the work of CEOs as chief leaders and the contributions of great groups as members of organizational communities will allow firms to improve their global competitiveness.

(Ireland and Hitt, 2005: 95)

Technological pioneering

Still, the pioneer's best option lies with ensuring that its technology remains the industry's standard by innovating continuously. Thus, the pioneer's success in creating an advantage from its technology depends on its progress in building capabilities, overcoming inertia, creating an organization that enhances technological development and commercialization, and achieving a position of leadership in the industry.

(Zahra *et al.*, 1995: 289)

External foundations of advantage: deciphering the rules

Much of the research effort and focus has been on the external analysis and foundations of advantage. This is understandable, because external forces have visible impacts and will be similar to those that competitors face. While many external forces are uncontrollable and cannot be prevented, an understanding of them means that likely impact can be considered and key trends can be woven into the strategy **formulation** process. By understanding the competitive arena, strategists can gain insights into understanding the written and unwritten rules of the competitive game, thus providing a view on how the organization should achieve competitive dominance and define its difference. The impact of external change can be dramatic: the sub-prime mortgage market crisis in the USA in late 2007 had ripple effects in all international financial markets, resulted in liquidity problems for interbank borrowings, and caused the near collapse of Northern Rock in the UK. This external event resulted in a world recession in 2009 that impacted organizations, governments, financial institutions, and societies.

Despite the rate and pace of change and multitude of external variables that impinge on his or her organization, the strategist can begin to understand external factors by conceptualizing the various layers of the competitive arena, as illustrated in Figure 6.2. This schematic separation of the external environment into the layers of macro drivers, meso industry, **strategic group**, and more proximate **business ecosystems** facilitates a more complete analysis. The macro-level perspective is focused on broad or global concerns of any business, such as economic factors, and is captured by the PESTEL analysis (that is, analysis of the political, economic, social, technical, environmental, and legal forces). The next level is the meso, at which the strategist will have to answer the key question of what business he or she is in and how he or she will best compete. A key tool for this task, with a long-standing legacy in the strategy field, is Michael Porter's 'five forces' industry analysis (see Reading 2.2). Within an industry, a strategic group map enables the organization to understand the distribution of competition—and, critically, those competitors of closest proximity who can pose the greatest threat. Below this is the ecosystem of the organization, encompassing its network and **innovation** partners and key stakeholders, all of which may impinge on strategic decisions. The final level of analysis focuses on the **key success factors (KSFs)**, differentiating between those that have to be met simply for the organization to compete and remain viable, and those that must be met to yield a competitive advantage.

Macro context

In response to the growing complexity of competitive environments, a number of analytical tools have been developed within the strategic management field to facilitate the strategist's thinking around external foundations of advantage. PEST (or PESTEL) analysis provides the strategist with an overview of macro drivers in their competitive arena (see Figure 6.3 for an example of PEST analysis relevant to the European airline industry). Key factors will differ in importance depending on the competitive arena. For example, in the pharmaceutical industry, regulation of product testing and patents will dramatically impact organizations such as Pfizer and GlaxoSmithKline. Consumer trends and socio-demographic factors will be particularly important for service companies in positioning their value propositions. Economic cycles will influence all businesses, but some—particularly those offering more differentiated products and charging a premium price—will be affected more adversely by a recession. For strategists, this analytical tool provides clear insight into the important macro drivers that will have the greatest impact on their competitive space. So, for example, after the financial crisis, European retail banks such as Santander, which have operations in many European countries, will be playing particular attention to additional

Figure 6.2 Levels of external forces

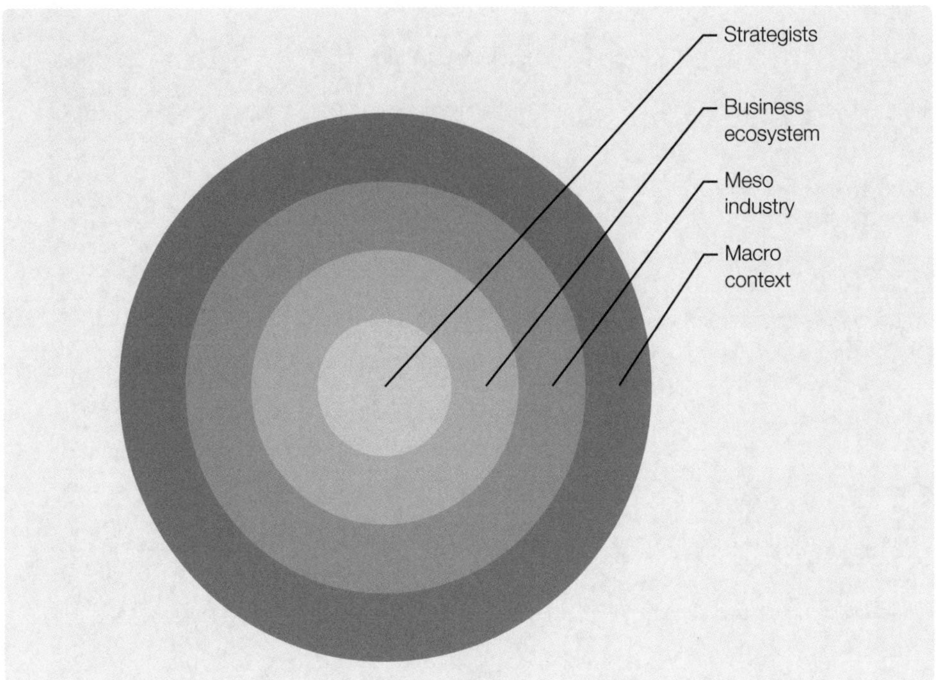

regulatory requirements as well as future national and European Union (EU) legislation that could impact on their operations. These changes could range from changing the 'cooling-off' period for consumer debt products to having increased cash reserves. These are key issues that Santander executives would have noted from a PEST analysis. While it is easy to generate a long list of factors, the critical ones are those that have the greatest implications for the organization in terms of developing and sustaining competitive advantage. This is the broadest macro level of analysis.

Meso industry and competitor-level analysis

Looking at business-unit level, Porter (1979; 2008) developed the 'five forces' framework analysis to understand the competitive structure of an industry. This holds that the ability to gain competitive advantage rests mainly on how well the firm positions and differentiates itself in an industry. A critical starting point is a thorough understanding of the organization's industry or sector, because this will determine the scope of activities and the nature of competitors. For a long time, Kodak defined itself as being in the photography industry, competing with the likes of Fujitsu. Kodak adhered to its definition in spite of the rise of the digital age. When the company finally began to embrace digital photography, it realized that the industry parameters had dramatically altered and it was now in direct competition with the likes of HP, Sony, Samsung, and Dell.

Defining an industry or sector is by no means simple. What are the industry definitions for the National Health Service (NHS), P&O Ferries, or Heineken? Arguably, UK Premier League clubs are as much in the entertainment and hospitality industries as they are in football or sport. The issue is central to understanding the foundations of advantage. Industry definition can be based on traditional industry boundaries, product and customer basis, or the scope of the business (McTavish, 1995). Nokia has revised its definition of its business and industry from being a mobile phone designer and manufacturer to being in the services business.

Figure 6.3 Sample PEST analysis of the European airline industry

Political factors	**Economic factors**
Open skies agreement between the USA and European Union (EU) No national support available within the EU to support national flag carriers EU passenger charter British airport authority was required to sell interests in some UK airports	Global recession in 2009 Low levels of GNP growth High inflation levels Low interest rates and higher levels of taxation Oil price fluctuations Less disposable income per head of population Softening demand for airline travel
Socio-cultural factors	**Technological factors**
Reduction in disposal incomes due to inflation, and increased direct and indirect taxation Reduction in annual foreign holidays and short breaks—more 'staycationing' Reduced migration from Eastern European EU states to UK, Ireland, and France, etc. has led to a decrease in the number of flights from Poland, Bulgaria, Latvia, and the Czech Republic	All European airlines have dedicated web-based reservation and check-in systems Introduction of bag-and-tag systems for airlines at airports Cross-selling of other services, such as travel insurance, accommodation, sightseeing activities, etc. to airline customers through web-based reservation systems Low carbon emissions with newer planes Next-generation airbus planes have expanded services and passenger capacity

Achieving clarity about business definition is a difficult and challenging task for strategists. Porter's 'five forces' framework provides a useful analytical tool for assessing an industry's attractiveness along a structure–conduct–performance paradigm, whereby industry structure determines the conduct of firms, which in turn determines the collective performance of the firm in the marketplace (Porter, 1981: 611). An attractive industry is one in which the five forces—threat of new entrants, buyer power, supplier power, threat of substitutes, and competitive rivalry—can be worked in such a way that a firm can find a stable and defensible position; it thus avoids competition and earns superior rents, thereby sustaining profitability (Porter, 1979; see Reading 2.2 for an elaboration of the five forces).

To illustrate the five forces analysis, we can consider the mobile phone industry. The threat of substitution is high, with the advent of Skype-enabled mobile handsets; the power of the buyer is also high, given low switching costs and an ability to change network easily, with Vodafone, O2, and other operators offering shorter contractual agreements. The threat of new entrants is increasing as convergence accelerates and regulators ease licensing regimes to encourage new market entrants. The bargaining power of suppliers is moderate, with large mobile handset manufacturers, such as HTC and Samsung, holding some sway over marketplace activities. Overall, this makes for intense competitive rivalry, with organizational consolidations and collaborations a likely outcome as market growth opportunities moderate.

Moreover, with the convergence of technology and entrants such as Google and Apple, some may claim that we have witnessed the death of the mobile phone industry as traditionally conceived.

Industrial organizational economists have found that the ability to earn acceptable returns over long periods of time is related to industry structure. This analysis of competitive context provides strategists with a clear sense of the dominant competitive forces at play in their competitive arena and how some of these must be reduced or 'managed' to enhance profitability: the stronger the competitive forces, the lower the profitability of both the industry and individual firms. In responding to strong competitive forces, firms can take a position in the marketplace to defend and ultimately reduce these competitive forces.

Business ecosystem

A number of analytical tools can be applied to understanding the organization's business ecosystem. These include strategic group maps, competitor analysis, scenario analysis, and KSFs. Analytical tools can be used by the strategist to understand the competitive drivers in their environment and in their strategic group. Strategic groups are groups of firms within an industry that compete on a similar basis—that is, they are using similar strategies to pursue customers. These are formed when 'firms within a group make strategic decisions that cannot readily be imitated by firms outside the group without substantial costs, significant elapsed time or uncertainty about the outcome of those decisions' (McGee and Thomas, 1986: 150). By tracking the evolution of strategic group maps over time, strategists can see patterns of similarity emerging, which then in turn challenge their own company's definition of difference. Strategic group maps also provide clarity around performance and the basis of competition. Importantly, competitors that are similar to a specific firm are the most dangerous to it. Take the airline industry: Ryanair will be much more concerned by the decisions and actions of other low-cost carriers than the actions of luxury airlines such as Qatar Airways. Mobility barriers typically prevent firms moving from one strategic group to another. Strategic groups with higher mobility barriers will achieve higher levels of profitability (McGee and Thomas, 1986). Figure 6.4 shows a strategic group map for the European car industry.

Competitor analysis provides the strategist with insights into who the main direct and indirect competitors are; it also provides a rationale of the basis of competition. This analytical tool and its

Figure 6.4 Strategic group map for European car industry

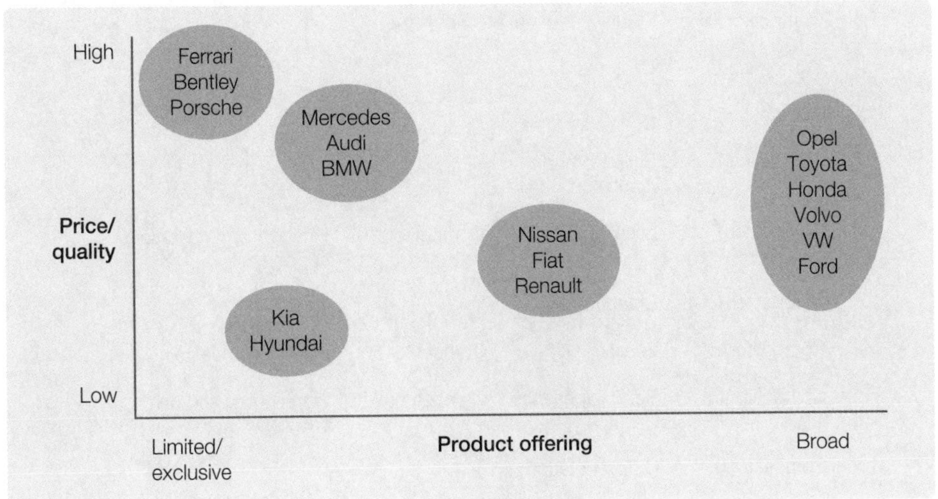

application have received less attention than other tools. With growing trends towards industry, market, and technology convergence, indirect competitors may become direct competitors in a short time period. Figure 6.5, a sample competitor analysis focused on the retail sector, shows competitors in relation to one another, and the differing bases on which they compete. The broad competitor set could include those competing retailers in direct competition in the local area or those who are located in out-of-town locations or even within another town. From that broad set of competitors, the strategist assesses the basis of competition for each retail store. For example, Competitor A is focused on price and quality, whereas Competitor G is focused on brand loyalty. From this analysis, the strategist then evaluates the firm's most relevant competitor and the associated rationale.

Scenario analysis uses 'What if?' scenarios. Strategists analysing the macro and meso industry and business ecosystem develop likely scenarios that would impact on the competitive dynamics within their competitive arena. The analysis focuses on potential areas of uncertainty within the industry; only certain firms would use this analytical technique—in particular, where there is a limited variety of potential impacting factors. Shell, one of the world's leading oil companies, uses this technique as part of its long-term planning. Its current **scenario planning** document forecasts until 2050 and is updated annually (available online at http://www.shell.com/home/content/aboutshell/our_strategy/shell_global_scenarios/shell_energy_scenarios_2050/).

There are six steps to developing scenarios, as follows.

- Decide drivers for change.
- Bring drivers together into a viable framework.
- Produce initial (7–9) mini scenarios.
- Reduce to 2–3 scenarios.
- Write the scenarios.
- Identify issues arising.

(Mercer, 1995: 82)

Figure 6.5 Competitor analysis: retail sector

Broad competitor set	Competitor criteria	Relevant competitors	Rationale
Competitor A	Price and quality	Competitor A	International parent
Competitor B	Quality		
Competitor C	Customer offering		
Competitor D	Financial strength		
Competitor E	Strong brand reputation		
Competitor F	Location	Competitor F	Financial and operational support
Competitor G	Brand loyalty		
Competitor H	Service	Competitor H	Indirect competitor
Competitor I	Retail experience	Competitor I	Using online and offline offerings
Competitor J	CSR reputation		

To assess the basis of differentiation further, strategists can analyse the KSFs that, first, are vital for success and, second, are potential areas of differentiation from competitors. In analysing sustainable competitive advantage, Aaker (1984) suggests that strategists need to identify:

- the industry KSFs and skill assets that competitors need to compete effectively;
- the strengths and weaknesses (assets, liabilities, and distinctive competences) of the business with respect to the KSFs; and
- the competitor strengths and weaknesses with respect to the KSFs.

The examples of KSFs for a mobile telecoms operator in Figure 6.6 highlight the factors that competitors need to have in order to stay competitive in their competitive arena and the factors that could be exploited for differentiation purposes. O2 would have several elements of differentiation, whereas eMobile, in the Irish market, would have a limited product range and compete on limited areas of differentiation.

Criticisms of market foundations of advantage

The market perspective has generated much debate and criticism. The market view of competitive advantage is ascribed to external characteristics rather than to the firm's idiosyncratic competencies and resource-based deployments. Criticism of market foundations of advantage centres on the static nature of the perspective, the challenge of industry definition, and on the core theoretical foundations of the market perspective.

The market perspective provides a here-and-now analysis of a market that is static and not future-orientated. In order to achieve sustainable competitive advantage over rivals, organizational

Figure 6.6 Key success factors in mobile telecoms

Key success factors
• Total population coverage • Roaming agreements—voice and data • Variety of handsets with varied functionality—basic to smart handset • Content—sports; news; gossip • Pay-as-you-go top-up facilities
Potential factors of differentiation
• Price • Offering voice, text, data, video conferencing, and mobile web connectivity • Location of stores • First to market with new mobile handsets • Product offering to appeal to different customer segments • Customer loyalty programmes • Strategic partnerships with content providers such as Sky News, Reuters, etc. • Call quality

perspectives have to be future-oriented—particularly if the organization is attempting to defend a specific position in the marketplace. Advances in competitive arenas such as globalization and digital waves may render the analytical tools of the market view of advantage less valuable. For example, industry analyses and the development of differentiated positions may quickly become obsolete (Jarzabkowski and Wilson, 2006). As Jacobides (2010: 78) notes, 'academics and executives spend so much time studying the landscape, like Botanists who carefully classify and categorize, they forget the importance of understanding evolutionary dynamics before creating strategy'. A second criticism is the real difficulty in defining precisely where an industry boundary begins and ends. Typical tools assume that an industry is well defined and that organizations know exactly who their competitors, suppliers, and customers are. Further, the market perspective assumes that firms within an industry are homogeneous in terms of their strategically relevant resources and that resource heterogeneity development will be short-lived, because the resources that organizations use to execute their strategies are highly mobile—that is, they can easily be bought or sold (Barney, 1991: 100). This is certainly true for financial services, telecommunications, health care, and a variety of other industries, but the question 'What industry are we in?' is becoming harder and harder to answer (Hamel, 1996) as the pace of industry, market, product, and technology convergence increases.

Microsoft's masterful cultivation of Porter's five forces has done little to slow Google's meteoric rise in market capitalization. Google's 2006 acquisition of YouTube for US$1.65bn in stock and Microsoft's acquisition of Skype in 2011 similarly attest to the fact that entry, even when entry barriers are low, can lead to formidable value creation (Chesbrough and Appleyard, 2007: 61). The key challenge for firms is the transformation of resources:

> We have come to expect that the thing to do with resources is to manage them, whereas in the future we will need to embrace the principle that the thing to do with resources is to transform their value. This will stop unnecessary fights for limited resources.
>
> (Patel, 2005: 220)

Consequently, the foundation of advantage is broader and deeper than external analysis or a market-based view might suggest. Research by Rumelt (1991) suggested that neither industry nor corporate ownership could explain the difference in profitability among business units. As Pfeffer and Sutton (2006: 140) capture:

> there is clear evidence that company performance varies widely among firms in the same industry, suggesting that competitive advantage may reside at least partly at the level of the company and its management, not only at the level of industry structure.

This suggests the importance of a more internally orientated consideration of the foundations of advantage, the topic of our next section.

Internal foundations of advantage: breaking and/or making your own rules

The market-based view of the foundations of advantage, as outlined in the previous section, tends to assume that the future is like the past. External foundations of advantage matter to company performance, but internal foundations of advantage can matter even more irrespective of the competitive arena setting. Therefore use of the organization's internal advantages in the form of resources contributes to achieving desired strategic outcomes. A focus on internal analysis, or what is now known as the resource-based view of the firm, is founded upon the basic premise that the essence of competitive advantage resides within the firm (Barney, 1991; Prahalad and Hamel, 1990).

The traditional focus of economists was on issues outside the firm. Few economists thought it necessary to inquire what happened inside an organization. However, some saw the importance of the resource-based view, an internally orientated perspective. Penrose (1959) noted that firms were more than an administrative unit, but also a collection of productive resources. Similarly, early institutionalists posited that organizational values and distinctive competence reflect 'the people who have been in [the organization], the groups it embodies, and the vested interests they have created' (Selznick, 1957: 16). As Stinchcombe (1997: 17–18) puts it, people are the 'guts' of formal organizations. Individuals provide material, cultural, and informational resources; they also make and execute decisions. For these reasons, the forms, activities, effectiveness, and fates of organizations will hinge on the capabilities and actions of their members (Haveman, 2000: 488).

The concepts associated with the resource-based view of the firm are relevant to both corporate-level (Chapter 7) and business-unit strategy (Chapter 8). At the corporate level, resource-based theorists recognize the firm as bundles of resources that can be deployed in different businesses with different end products. At the business-unit level, competitive advantage stems from a firm's unique resources and capabilities, which are difficult for competitors to imitate or acquire. The resource-based view, therefore, was as powerful and important to strategy in the 1990s as industry analysis was in the 1980s.

The resource-based view has four theoretical conditions that underpin competitive advantage (Peteraf, 1993), all of which must be met:

- resource heterogeneity—from which come Ricardian, or monopoly, rents;
- *ex post* limits to competition—necessary to sustain rents;
- imperfect resource mobility—which ensures that rents are bound to the firm and shared by it; and
- *ex ante* limits to competition—to prevent costs from offsetting the rents.

In the last decade, three further theoretical views of the resource-based firm have emerged: dynamic resource-based; the relationship between resources and strategy implementation; and the persistence of sustainable competitive advantage among firms (Armstrong and Shimizu, 2007). These have enabled strategy researchers and executives to view internal resources differently. Consequently, the bases of internal foundations of advantage are resources, competences, and dynamic capabilities. In expanding on these internal foundations of advantage, several studies have been undertaken by strategy scholars using the resource-based view of the firm. Armstrong and Shimizu (2007) identified 125 empirical studies from 1990 to 2007. A study of the Hollywood film studios from 1936 to 1965 by Miller and Shamsie (1996) found that property and knowledge-based resources are difficult to imitate or acquire. Property resources provide advantage in stable competitive arenas and knowledge-based resources provide advantage in more fluid competitive arenas. Russo and Fouts (1997), taking a resource-based perspective, found that environmental and economic performances are positively linked and that this is strengthened as the industry grows. In a study of Dutch accounting firms (1880–1990), Pennings *et al.* (1998) found that human capital is idiosyncratic and difficult to transfer, and so is a key source of competitive advantage. We can consider the resource-based view of advantage by exploring resources, competencies, and dynamic capabilities respectively.

Resources

The first significant contribution to outlining an internal perspective on advantage was made by Wernerfelt (1984: 173), who was interested in exploring 'some simple economic tools for analysing a firm's resource position and to look at some strategic options suggested by this analysis'. In focusing on internal competitive advantage, Wernerfelt concentrates on resources rather than products and suggests identifying resources that lead to higher profits. The strategy of a company requires balancing the exploration and exploitation of resources. Two years later, in a further seminal contribution to the development of the resource-based view, Barney (1986: 1231) argued that:

> firms seeking to obtain above normal returns from implementing product market strategies must have consistently more accurate expectations about the future value of those strategies when acquiring the resources necessary to implement them, although firms can be lucky. While it is usually not possible to obtain these advantages through the analysis of firms' competitive environment, firms can sometimes obtain them when choosing to implement strategies that exploit resources already under their control.

The focus of Barney's contribution has been developing product market strategies that exploit resources over which a firm has control. In the case of, say, Quickstep, a Belgian laminate and parquet floors manufacturer with a strong European market presence, this might mean exploiting existing resources to gain advantage over European and national competitors. Barney (1991) later argued that sustainable competitive advantage based on resources could be achieved by a firm if resources were of value, rare, inimitable, and sustainable. Thus Quickstep might consider developing new flooring products via technology or human capital in a means that cannot be imitated by competitors, thereby enabling the firm to exploit existing resources and secure a sustainable advantage over the medium-to-long term.

Resources are within and under the control of the firm. Barney (1991) describes resources as 'all assets, capabilities, organizational processes, firm attributes, information and knowledge, etc. controlled by the firm that enable the firm to conceive of and implement strategies that improve its efficiency and effectiveness', whereas Miller (2003) defines resources as 'Asymmetries that produce superior economic returns; examples include technical skills, patents, scarce raw materials sources, exclusive alliances and a fine reputation'. In consumer electronics, resources could encompass brand names, distribution channels, production facilities, and patents.

The issue of resources comes down to a question of value, and whether the resources provide the firm with the opportunities for exploitation and an ability to defend the firm against potential threat (Barney, 1986). In this sense, resources must be understood in their competitive context. Peteraf (1993: 189) makes a distinction between fixed and quasi-fixed resources:

> Fixed resources are limited in supply and their supply cannot be expanded (rare by definition). Quasi-fixed resources are resources limited in the short run, but which can be renewed and expanded incrementally within the firm that utilizes them. Utilization of such resources may in fact augment their value, e.g. some skills and knowledge can be expanded through one's experience or training.

In summary, when formulating and implementing strategy, the strategist needs to understand the type of resources that the firm has available to it. The problem of relying exclusively on resources as a foundation of advantage is that they are at risk of being acquired, replicated, or substituted. Consequently, approaches have emerged that suggest that true resource-based advantage comes from the systems and processes that an organization has in place with which to exploit and leverage resources.

Core competences

A further perspective on internal foundations of advantage is what Hamel and Prahalad (1990: 83) term 'core competences', which they define as:

> the collective learning in the organization, especially how to coordinate diverse production skills and integrate multiple streams of technology ... [They are] also about the organization of work and the delivery of value ... Core competence is communication, involvement and a deep commitment to working across organizational boundaries.

In describing the concept of core competence, they use the metaphor of a tree, in which the trunk and limbs are core products, branches are business units, and leaves are end products. The roots of the tree are the core competences that provide sustenance for the core and end products, which in aggregate provide organizations in diversified contexts with a real capability to compete sustainably and effectively in their chosen competitive arena. The classic examples from the strategy literature include Honda's core competence in engine technology or Sony's ability to miniaturize electronic products. In a diversified context, Hamel and Prahalad (1990) argue that core competences do not dissipate with use. Core competences are built and developed over a long period of time throughout the organization, and they are linked to the development of core products. More subtly, Hamel and Prahalad suggest that companies should dominate in core competences, core products, and end products in their competitive arena; this requires competency carriers within organizations and a strategic architecture designed to leverage and build core competences. For the most part, core competences are hidden from the customer (Petts, 1997).

Dynamic capabilities

The final perspective on internal foundations of advantage deals with capabilities (Stalk *et al.*, 1992) and dynamic capabilities (Teece, 2007; Teece *et al.*, 1997). The focus on developing capabilities as a foundation for advantage is linked to organizations having flexible structures that are responsive to changes in the competitive arena (see Reading 2.3). Amit and Schoemaker (1993: 35) state that 'Capabilities . . . refer to a firm's capacity to deploy resource, usually in combination, using organizational processes, to effect a desired end', while Miller (2003: 691) defines capabilities as 'resources [that] can be configured into capabilities—bundles of complementary resources such as tacit knowledge, administrative skills, routines, and physical assets with the flexibility to generate adaptive and valuable outputs'. Some commentators would see Ryanair's ability to turn around an aircraft in 25 minutes as a capability that is transferable to any route on which it flies, in addition to its capability to create additional revenue streams by disaggregating its internal value chain.

There are four principles of capabilities-based competition, outlined by Stalk *et al.* (1992).

Four principles of capabilities-based competition

- The building blocks of corporate strategy are not products and markets but business processes.
- Competitive success depends on transforming a company's key processes into strategic capabilities that consistently provide superior value to the customer.
- Companies create these capabilities by making strategic investments in a support infrastructure that links together and transcends traditional SBUs and functions.
- Because capabilities necessarily cross functions, the champion of a capabilities-based strategy is a CEO.

Source: Stalk *et al.* (1992)

Competing on capabilities means that companies can outperform competitors on speed, consistency, acuity, agility, and innovativeness (Stalk *et al.*, 1992). In addition, management cognition has an important role to play in directing **organizational learning** in developing capabilities and organizational adaptation (Tripsas and Gavetti, 2000). Interestingly, Ray *et al.* (2004: 23) found:

> Intangible and socially complex capabilities—service climate and managerial IT knowledge performance—are positively related to customer service performance. Tangible and non-socially complex resources—technology resources and investment in customer services—do not seem to explain variation in customer service performance.

Dynamic capabilities are another potential form of internal foundation of advantage whereby, through leveraging and constant reconfiguration of resource base, organizational, and strategic routines, managers attempt to create value and competitive advantage (Grant, 1996). Teece *et al.* (1997: 516) describe dynamic capabilities as:

> The firm's processes that use resources—specifically the processes to integrate, reconfigure, gain and release resources—to match and even create market change. Dynamic capabilities thus are the organizational and strategic routine by which to achieve new resource configuration as markets emerge, collide, split and evolve, and die.

Dynamic capabilities can be used to sense and shape opportunities and threats, to seize opportunities, and to maintain competitiveness (Teece, 2007). In contexts in which companies have strong dynamic capabilities, they are highly entrepreneurial and able to adapt to competitive arenas through innovation and collaboration; 'dynamic' connotes change (Winter, 2003). There are many identifiable dynamic capabilities (see Figure 6.7).

From a sociological perspective, Galunic and Eisenhardt (2001) view dynamic capabilities as a collection of capabilities within corporate divisions that can be reconfigured in many ways, thereby creating a new organizational form, termed 'dynamic communities'. The concept of dynamic capabilities has been theoretically extended even further by Helfat and Peteraf (2003) through dynamic resource-based theory, the 'capability life cycle' (CLC), which 'provides a common language and way of thinking about the evolution of capabilities, as well as a more fully dynamic approach to resource-based theory' (ibid: 998). The six branches of the CLC include retirement, retrenchment, replication, renewal, redeployment, or recombination (ibid). Understanding capabilities and dynamic capabilities is essential for strategists to assess the internal foundations of advantage through the use of analytical approaches.

Assessing internal foundations of advantage

One of the key analytical frameworks for assessing internal foundations of advantage is value chain analysis, developed by Porter (1985), which strategists can use to determine where value is created in their firms. Value chain analysis allows the strategist to map out all of the activities that are required to produce the end product or service, through primary activities and support activities. Value is created when there is difference between revenue and costs. Some of the firm's activities may not be generating any value or revenue; therefore the firm might outsource these activities to third parties. Some airlines contract out all of their ground handling, baggage handling, and customer services to companies such as Servair. Firms need to develop their linkages between primary and secondary activities so that they can create further value-creating capacities and a potential basis for differentiation. This linkage is essential; Porter (1985: 48) outlines it as 'the relationship between the way in which value activity is performed and the cost or performance of

Figure 6.7 Identifiable dynamic capabilities (adapted from Eisenhardt and Martin, 2000)

- Product development routines to create products and service (Clark and Fujimoto, 1991; Dougherty, 1992; Helfat and Raubitschek, 2000)
- Superior product development at Toyota (Clark and Fujimoto, 1991)
- Strategic decision making through using the pool of managerial talent (Eisenhardt, 1989; Fredrickson, 1984; Judge and Millar, 1991)
- Transfer processes—routines for replication and brokering (Hansen, 1999; Hargadon and Sutton, 1997; Szulanski, 1996)
- Resource allocation (Burgelan, 1994)
- Constant market segmentation (Magretta, 1998)
- Knowledge-creating routines (Helfat, 1997; Henderson and Cockburn, 1994; Rosenkopf and Nerkar, 1999)
- Alliance and acquisition routines (Capron *et al.*, 1998; Gulati, 1999; Lane and Lubatkin, 1998; Powell *et al.*, 1996)

another activity'. In the Ryanair case, the linkage of the secondary activities of human resources to the primary activities of operations is critical to achieve aircraft turnaround of 25 minutes. To enhance these linkages, firms need to invest time and resource in developing internal coordination mechanisms. Those advocating a market-based foundation of advantage (such as Porter) tend to recommend linking all organizational activities in an interlocking manner to best position the organization in the external environment. On the other hand, those advocating a resource-based foundation of advantage (such as Prahalad and Hamel) claim that organizations should conduct only those activities in which they excel, outsourcing the rest.

Critique of internal foundations of advantage

The resource-based view of the firm as a foundation of competitive advantage has been subject to criticisms along a number of grounds: namely, its tautological nature, inaccurate definitions of resources, lack of prescription for practising managers, lack of analytical rigour, and failure to account for management and leadership approaches. The first major criticism of the resource-based view is that it suffers from tautological reasoning (Connor, 2002; Priem and Butler, 2001). To develop competitive advantage, organizations must have resources that are rare and valuable; organizations that possess such resources will have superior results. Arguably, this is a circular viewpoint stating the obvious. In response, Barney (2001) argues that all strategic management theories could be reduced to tautologies following the logic of Priem and Butler (2001). Secondly, within the resource-based view, there are few clear definitions of key terms—something that is essential to empirical investigations and enhanced analytical understanding. Thirdly, the resource-based view offers little by way of clear prescriptive advice for practising managers (McGuinness and Morgan, 2000) and therefore does not equip strategists with practical competitive advantage-building propositions (Connor, 2002). Fourthly, the resource-based view has not yet reached a solid theoretical foundation, because further conceptual work remains to solidify its position as a theory within the strategy field (Priem and Butler, 2001). Fifthly, the resource-based perspective lacks analytical tools to assess core competences and capabilities that are deeply embedded in the firm. Priem and Butler (2001) contend that the processes through which particular resources provide competitive advantage remain concealed; conceivably, all resources in the firm's control may provide an advantage. Finally, the resource-based view does not take into account management and leadership approaches, given the rationalistic perspective of the theory (Truss, 2001).

Spotlight Reengineering industry rules in the music industry *Grace Walsh, Doctoral Researcher, J. E. Cairnes School of Business and Economics, National University of Ireland, Galway*

The boundaries of doing business in the music industry are constantly shifting as technological advances have caused the industry to evolve at a rapid rate, particularly since the inception of Napster in 1999. Napster began as a platform for the peer-to-peer (P2P) sharing of MP3 files. Traditionally, music acts had to get signed by a record label in order to propel, distribute, and market their talent as a means of driving record sales and filling concert theatres; in return, the record label would receive a percentage of the profits and, in most cases, copyright over the signed artist's work. The creation of Napster signified the beginning of the end for this traditional model and, over a decade later, the industry is still scrambling from the shake-up.

The Recording Industry of America Association (RIAA), a trade group that represented the music industry, resisted the technologically propelled shift that was happening in the trade and claimed that P2P networks enabled users to 'steal and share' files and, as such, to decimate the industry's profits through plummeting CD sales (Mooney *et al.*, 2010). Conversely, proponents of P2P networks argued that file-sharing sites exposed individuals to new artists and allowed them to sample their work, which they may not have otherwise come across, and hence drove CD sales by broadening artists' reach. However, legal actions were taken against Napster by the RIAA, and these were followed by copyright infringement suits from industry heavyweights including Metallica, Dr Dre, Madonna, and finally by A&M Records, which led the company to file for bankruptcy in 2002 (David, 2010).

Napster died an untimely and controversial death, yet it changed the listening habits of a generation. Although the record labels had won the battle, the war was just beginning, and Napster had completely altered consumers' behaviours and perceptions towards music by satisfying the market's desire for instant gratification. The four 'P's of marketing (product, price, promotion, and place) were wiped out in one swift move.

- **Product** CD ⇒ MP3
- **Price** € ⇒ 0
- **Promotion** Press release ⇒ Word-of-mouth (WOM)
- **Place** Retail store ⇒ Website

The already elusive concept of sustainable competitive advantage has become increasingly difficult to attain as the industry's key success factors have shifted from influential connections, talented signings, and strong distribution channels to discovering novelty acts, sourcing overnight sensations, and the ability to tap into outlets for cross-media exposure. The industry has become increasingly fragmented and has left strategists unclear of the most lucrative way in which to harness these components into a viable **business model**. As change has become a reliable constant, being at the frontier and pioneering new technologies has paid dividends for some strategy savvy performers.

Deadmau5, a Canadian, Grammy-nominated electronic artist, embraced the upheaval created by technological advances and demonstrated his dynamic capabilities. In 2009, the DJ used software developed by an Irish company, Future Audio Workshop, to produce a ten-track iPhone application that allows iPhone users to mix and remix every song on the album regardless of their musical capabilities—all at the low price of US$3 (Van Buskirk, 2009). Icelandic artist Björk adopted a similar strategy for the release of her 2011 album *Biophilia*, but she went a step further and has collaborated with 'some of the world's top software designers' to develop ten iPad applications, one for each song, which 'integrate interactive games, musical animations, animated scores, lyrics and academic essays' (Michaels, 2011).

It is important to note the strong presence of the Apple Corporation in shaping the future of digital music. The firm's core competences are its agile nature and dynamic capabilities, which allow it to be a breeding ground for innovation under the strong leadership of Steve Jobs. In the words of Professor Henry Jenkins, an American media scholar, 'our focus should not be on emerging technologies but on emerging cultural practices', but Apple has managed to carve out a dominate role in the market by shaping cultural practices through its clever pioneering of technologies, thus placing it in an incredibly powerful and influential position (Jenkins, 2006).

The business models of the music industry's future are primarily geared towards creating value and user interactivity that cannot be attained through illegal downloads. A novel approach to creating value in an industry rife with creative destruction was heralded by Downtown Music Label's hip hop artist Mos Def when he released his album *The Ecstatic* as a music T-shirt in 2009. The shirt had album artwork on the front and track listings on the back, similar to the traditional album sleeve, but the shirt's tag had a download code that allowed fans to obtain the album legally, online, in digital format (Kogelschatz, 2010). Another act signed to Downtown Music who have striven to enhance their fans' music experience is Cold War Kids. In 'I've Seen Enough', the band's four musicians created an interactive, multi-track music video, with each band member pre-recording four performances that can be mixed and matched by the user to create 256 permutations of the song, from the album version right through to a simple drum solo (http://www.coldwarkids.com/iveseeenenough).

Industry innovator, Google, has also recognized the potential of utilizing music as a means of attracting consumers to its site. Google China uses free and legal music downloads as a means of gaining market share over its competitor Baidu. The move has been called 'a milestone for cooperation between portals and the music industry' (Barboza, 2009). It is expected that advertisers will cover the costs incurred from offering free music in order to gain access to and extract data from the massive consumer market.

Adding value and enhancing user experiences are the key components of successful business models in this revolutionized music scene in which function and form have been replaced by convenience and stimulation. We exist in an age of information overload, in which gaining and maintaining people's attention is a challenge; distribution is merely a default. The convergence of media in recent years has shifted consumers from an ego-system in which ownership is paramount, to an eco-system in which sharing is embraced and expected without reprehension (Leonhard, 2009). Pushing the boundaries and experimenting with new creative outlets, whilst embracing the industry's technological advances and keeping them at the core of strategy, is the only viable way forward.

Sources: Barboza (2009); David (2010); Jenkins (2006); Kogelschatz (2010); Leonhard (2009); Michaels (2011); Mooney *et al.* (2010); Van Buskirk (2009)

Implications for strategy practice

Advantage is the foundation of organization performance and ultimate competitive success. The defining of the competitive arena in which an organization competes is essential, yet problematic, given the increasing convergence of industries, technologies, and markets. This is a fundamental aspect of organizational purpose. The challenge for an organization is conceptualizing the definition and communicating it with clarity, in the form of organizational purpose, vision, and mission (discussed in Chapter 5). How would you define the industry of the Fox Corporation, the BBC, and Independent Newspapers? This could be as narrow as 'broadcast and print media operators', or as broad as 'communications and content providers'. Firm cognition about industry definition is based on collective and individual interpretation, and means that firms see competitive arenas of value and difference differently (see Chapters 2 and 3). The role of the strategist is to help with this definition, but also to consistently and persistently communicate the industry parameters and any changes to these.

The foundations of advantage require an organization to really understand how to create difference that adds value for the firm and, in doing so, dominate competitive arenas. Strategists need to be architects and consistent communicators of difference. Being different will enable the organization to attract and retain customers. Competitive advantage comes in many forms, depending on the competitive context, marketplace competitive dynamics, and the manner in which the firm competes on a position and/or resource perspective. Therefore strategists might view advantage through value creation around differences in their selected competitive arenas rather than from a market-based or a resource-based perspective. The reality is that value is created through assets and resources internal and external to the organization. For example, Procter and Gamble state that 50 per cent of their innovations will come from outside the firm. In many senses, given the competitive dynamics in many industries, value creation has no boundaries and the core challenge for organizations is to produce sustainable value that creates differentiation and dominance. One of the responsibilities of the strategist is to define, articulate, and ensure the organizational structures and resources necessary to enable front-line staff to deliver consistently on the articulated differentiation.

To assess external foundations of advantage, there is a wide variety of useful analytical perspectives. In practice, some of these tools can be subjective rather than provide the independent analytical perspective that is required to make strategic decisions: we see what we want to see. This subjectivity can be driven by the inappropriate use of tools, the selective use of research material to support a particular dominant internal view, flawed market and industry assumptions, a lack of critical reflection within the organization, and the insularity of internal perspective. In using these tools, strategists also have to capture the unwritten rules of competition that exist in most industries. In-depth analytical analysis provides higher levels of clarity that can ensure that resources are being deployed where competitive advantage can be secured and sustained. To build this analytical rigour, strategists need to have primary interactions with actors outside the firm to assess their core assumptions and to understand all of the competitive dynamics in their industry.

With intensity of competition, firms and strategists may not set aside enough time and space to really understand the basis of their internal foundations of advantage in terms of resources, competences, and capabilities. If you were to ask employees what the key resources, competences, and capabilities of their organizations are, you would receive a variety of answers. Strategists need to understand and conceptualize the firm's resources, competences, and capabilities, and analyse what internal mix generates sustainable value and difference for the organization. They must consider what internal mix could provide the firm with sustained competitive dominance in a competitive arena.

Finally, the time frames of advantage can vary depending on competitive context, in addition to the mix and emphasis of internal and external foundation. Will the mixes of asset and skill that Facebook, Pfizer, Cemex, and Coca-Cola currently have be sufficient to sustain value this time next week, next month, next year, and in five years' time? The strategist has to be aware of the temporal nature of foundations of advantage. In this sense, while competitive success may be fleeting, sound market and resource-based analysis offers the prospect of a durable foundation for advantage. All the while, it must be remembered that analysis is not something that simply happens automatically in a rational, sequential manner, but rather a social process that is conducted by strategists. Consequently, echoing the theme of Chapter 2, it can be argued that 'environmental analysis is much less critical than managerial analysis' (Smircich and Stubbart, 1985: 724). This highlights the development of strategists, surfacing assumptions, and strategic conversations about future options as critical processes that will inform the likely success of both external and internal analysis.

Introduction to readings

Reading 2.2, 'The five competitive forces that shape strategy' by Michael Porter (2008), has had a lasting influence and impact on both scholars and practitioners. The article reaffirms and extends Porter's positioning view of advantage set out in his 1979 article in the *Harvard Business Review*. Again, he raises some thought-provoking issues about industry definition. He also highlights that rigorous analysis provides an understanding of the competitive forces that shape strategy and possible 'fruitful possibilities for strategic action' for the firm. How many boards, CEOs, strategic business unit managers, and company strategists really answer with clarity and unanimity? A fundamental question that Porter poses is: 'What is the potential of this business?' Do strategists really understand, from a conceptual and analytical perspective, 'the factors that create true economic value in their firms'? Porter offers a robust defence of his 'five forces' framework even in an era of technological convergence and **hyper-competition**—but what of the limitations of the approach? Has the value of industry analysis passed?

Reading 2.3, 'Dynamic capabilities and strategic management', by David Teece, Gary Pisano, and Amy Sheun (1997), is a seminal theoretical contribution in understanding how competitive advantage is created and sustained. The authors highlight the role of path dependencies, stability of market demands, and processes, and argue that strategizing is less fundamental than 'identifying new opportunities and organizing effectively and efficiently to embrace them'. The real question that this article raises is the usefulness of this theoretical approach to understanding competitive advantage and, more fundamentally, value creation. Are dynamic capabilities truly dynamic in terms of ensuring dominance and creating difference for firms, given the low short-term capacity for strategic orientation? What assumptions are made of managerial behaviour? Does the approach offer clear prescriptions for managers? Is it realistic for firms to identify and manage dynamic capabilities to achieve advantage?

Our final reading for this chapter, accessible via a link on the Online Resource Centre that accompanies this book, Grant's 'The resource-based theory of competitive advantage: implications for strategy formulation' (1991), provides a practical framework for strategy analysis from a resource-based perspective. We see the economic roots of the resource-based perspective in Grant's discussion of the concept of rent-earning potential. This reading links the resource-based perspective to strategy formulation, in which the firm should protect and leverage its 'crown jewels' for advantage. But do organizations consciously assess their resources and capabilities? Do they really protect their resource and capabilities as Grant describes? Are the consequences for not protecting their resources and capabilities really dire? Is the resource-based theory best understood in relation to strategy formulation or implementation?

Mini case study The format war: HD-DVDs vs Blu-ray

For Hollywood studios, the development of DVD technology has provided significant revenue streams; in some cases, over half of their income comes from the DVD sales of movies. Some would see this as a revenue lifeline for the studios. DVD has replaced VHS technology and provided technical capacity for content such as films and music that is five times greater than other formats. By 2004, the DVD format had reached over 50 per cent of homes in the USA. DVD drives became a standard shipped item for computers, both desktop and laptop. The customer faced an array of offerings based on the DVD format, including DVD, DVD + R, and DVD RAM. In short, the DVD has been one of the most successful consumer products in history, given its worldwide proliferation and market penetration.

The format war to secure the next-generation industry standard began to unfold with the developing of two competing technologies and industry consortia. The development of high-definition televisions (HDTVs) and their growing market share left many players with a deficit of product offerings to record and play high-definition (HD) content. One side of this intense format battle is HD-DVD (high-definition DVD—the industry successor to the DVD), led by industry collaborations between Toshiba and NEC. HD-DVD was adopted by the DVD Forum. HD-DVD technology was developed from the same underlying technologies as the DVD; an HD-DVD disc can store significantly more data than a DVD—typically 15 GB single layer and 30 GB dual layer.

The other competing format is the Blu-ray disc, developed by the Blu-ray Disc Association, a consortium comprising Sony, Philips, Matsushita, and Samsung. The consortium has grown to include consumer electronics manufacturers, content providers, media manufacturers, PC and PC peripheral manufacturers, and consumers. Its board of directors includes household names such as Apple, Dell, Hitachi, HP, LG, Mitsubishi Electric, Panasonic, Philips, Pioneer, Samsung, Sharp, Sony, Sun Microsystems, TDK, Thomson, 20th Century Fox, Walt Disney, and Warner Bros. The Blu-ray disc is an optical disc read by a blue laser and with more capacity than the HD-DVD: 25 GB single layer and 50 GB dual layer—nearly six times the capacity of a DVD disc.

Some attempts were made to avoid the format war in early 2005. One of the key issues of contention included physical formats of the disc and the core platforms (the DVD Forum platform was based on Microsoft iHD, while the Blu-ray consortium favoured a Java platform). Despite intense industry efforts, a deal could not be brokered. By early 2006, the first HD-DVD players were brought to market, followed in June by Blu-ray players. A number of HD-DVD movie titles were released, including *The Last Samurai* and *Million Dollar Baby*. By the end of 2006, Toshiba had sold in the region of 300,000 HD-DVD players, and HD-DVD became available for the Xbox 360. HD-DVD players are cheaper to buy and have fully compatible players. Even though Blu-ray was beaten to the player market in 2006, further product launches followed, including Blu-ray rewriting drives for PCs and movies available on 50 GB Blu-ray discs.

For film studios, home movie sales have become a significant revenue stream, but the format battle has provided them with challenges over which format to support. Blu-ray has movie studio backing of about 70 per cent of the home market through its alliances and agreements with Sony Pictures (exclusive), MGM (exclusive), Lionsgate, Disney, 20th Century Fox, and New Line Cinema. Other studios, such as First Look Studios, Magnolia Pictures, Image Entertainment, and the BBC, support both formats.

The current round of the format war may have been won by Blu-ray, with the announcement in January 2008 that Warner Bros, which supported both formats, would discontinue supporting HD-DVDs. The Blu-ray Association Newsletter of 24 January 2008 noted:

> Throughout 2007, Blu-ray disc sales have consistently outsold HD-DVD by a factor of two to one, but during the week of CES 2008 [Consumer Electronics Show], up to January 13 those numbers shifted significantly in favour of Blu-ray disc . . . The 85/15 split between the two rival formats represented the largest guild yet.

The consortium of non-direct collaborators of the DVD Forum may have lost some momentum and may have lost money in being first to the market with their HD-DVD players. The key question remains whether the war continues and whether the DVD Forum will eventually support the Blu-ray format. Or will another technological leap occur in formats? Will Panasonic's 3D recorder, released in 2010, or the Internet (enabling TV content providers to deliver 100 MB per second, as in South Korea) make the format war obsolete?

Sources: Blu-ray Association (http://www.blu-raydisc.com/en/); *Business Week* (2005); DVD Forum (http://www.dvdforum.org/forum.shtml); Waters *et al.* (2008)

Questions

1. Assess the market position of both formats, as outlined in the case. What is the nature of competitive advantage for Blu-ray versus HD-DVD?
2. What are the key success factors needed to succeed in this market in the short term and medium term?
3. Applying Barney's sustainable competitive advantage test, how temporal or sustainable is the advantage of Blu-ray? Is the advantage based predominately on markets or resources?
4. What resources does Blu-ray have that enabled it to prevail in early 2008?
5. What market and resource strategies can the DVD Forum use to beat Blu-ray?
6. What strategies should the DVD Forum put in place to ensure value and differentiation to its customers in the light of new technological threats such as 3D recorders or Internet-enabled TV content providers?

Summary

In this chapter, we began by examining the nature of competitive advantage and its longevity, either temporal or sustainable. We saw how firms have many potential sources of advantage. We then turned our attention to the external foundations of advantage—namely, the market view—and we examined the various analytical perspectives that the strategist can use to understand the rules of the game. The final focus of the chapter was to examine a contending view of advantage that is internal to the firms, termed the resource-based perspective. In outlining the resource-based view, we focused on resources, competences, and capabilities of the firm. The key questions for the strategist are about best fit or unique fit, and how this is best analysed.

The pendulum of the foundations of advantage continues to swing between internal and external resources, with the use of a mix of models. Each successive model seems to ignore the contributions of its predecessor (Hoskisson *et al.*, 1999). More importantly, the strategic challenges addressed by each strategic analysis model have not subsided. For example, Royal Dutch Shell continues to use long-term strategic planning scenarios successfully; Microsoft uses external environmental and competitor analysis models to redirect its Internet strategy; and Komatsu's ascent as a threat to Caterpillar is credited to the company's application of resource-based strategic analysis models (Shay and Rothaermel, 1999: 561). What also remains unchanged is the importance of competitive insight, knowledge, and learning in understanding the foundations of advantage. Arguably, the ability to analyse, forecast, and understand can itself become a key capability for an organization. Overall, having a clear sense of purpose (Chapter 5), coupled with an in-depth appreciation of the basis of advantage (market and/or resources), offers a vital foundation for and critical input into choosing the best route to advantage—the topic of our next two chapters.

Discussion questions

1. What are the key limitations of the market-based approach? Can you think of contexts in which it might be more or less appropriate?

2. What are the key limitations of the resource-based approach? Can you think of contexts in which it might be more or less appropriate?

3. Evaluate the nature of competitive advantage in a particular context of your choice. Which advantages are temporal and which sustainable?

4. How could the analytical perspective of the market-based perspective be shaped to be more future-orientated?

5. Review the history of an organization with which you are familiar. What are its resources, competences, and capabilities? As the strategist in that organization, would you have done things differently?

6. Outline the ways in which organizations can build internal foundations of advantage. Are they temporal or sustainable in nature?

7. Source a reading from an academic journal that contributes to the debate in this chapter. Which, if any, perspective does it support? What is its contribution? Does it advance the debate in any way?

8. What assumptions are made about the strategist's role in both market-based and resource-based analysis?

Further reading

Key contributions from the market-based approach include the classic works of M. Porter (1980) ***Competitive Strategy***, New York: Free Press, and (1985) ***Competitive Advantage***, New York: Free Press.

Seminal books on the resource-based approach include E. Penrose (1959) ***The Theory of the Growth of the Firm***, Oxford: Basil Blackwell, and R. Nelson and S. Winter (1982) ***An Evolutionary Theory of Economic Change***, Cambridge, MA: Harvard University Press. Drawing on this logic and more practical in orientation is work by C. Prahalad and G. Hamel (1990) 'The core competencies of the corporation', ***Harvard Business Review***, May/June(3): 79–91. For a novel perspective on uncertainty and the impact of the improbable, see N. Taleb (2007) ***The Black Swan: The Impact of the Highly Improbable***, New York: Random House.

In this chapter, the strategist has largely been a silent character, in part because it has been assumed that analysis will be rationale and unbiased. For an excellent counter to this argument, which includes key barriers to analysis and also means for their resolution, see S. Zahra and A. Chaples (1993) 'Blind spots in competitive analysis', ***Academy of Management Executive***, 7(2): 7–28. Finally, L. Smircich and C. Stubbart (1985) 'Strategic management in an enacted world', ***Academy of Management Review***, 10: 724–736, offer an insightful, but frequently neglected, view about how environments are not simply perceived, but rather ***enacted*** by strategists. This perspective has dramatic consequences for our understanding of both internal and external analysis.

visit the Online Resource Centre that accompanies this book to access more learning resources on this chapter topic at www.oxfordtextbooks.co.uk/orc/cunningham/

References

Aaker, D. A. 1984. How to select a business strategy. *California Management Review*, 26(3): 167–175.

Aaker, D. A. 1989. Managing assets and skills: the key to a sustainable competitive advantage. *California Management Review*, 31(2): 91–106.

Amit, R. and Schoemaker, P. 1993. Strategic assets and organization rent. *Strategic Management Journal*, 14(1): 33–46.

Armstrong, C. and Shimizu, K. 2007. A review of approaches to empirical research on the resource-based view of the firm. *Journal of Management*, 33(6): 959–986.

Bain, J. S. 1956. *Barriers to New Competition*. Cambridge, MA: Harvard University Press.

Barboza, D. 2009. Google offers links to free music downloads in China. *New York Times*, 30 March. Available online at http://www.nytimes.com/2009/03/31/technology/companies/31music.html

Barney, J. B. 1986. Strategic factor markets: expectations, luck and business strategy. *Management Science*, 32(10): 1231–1241.

Barney, J. B. 1991. Firm resources and sustained competitive advantage. *Journal of Management*, 17(1): 99–120.

Barney, J. B. 1995. Looking inside for competitive advantage. *Academy of Management Executive*, 9(4): 49–61.

Barney, J. B. 2001. Is the resource-based view a useful perspective for strategic management research? Yes. *Academy of Management Review*, 26(1): 41–56.

Barney, J. B. and Zajac, E. J. 1994. Competitive organizational behavior: toward an organizationally based theory of competitive advantage. *Strategic Management Journal*, 15(8): 5–9.

Boxall, P. and Purcell, J. 2008. *Strategy and Human Resource Management*. 2nd edn. London: Palgrave Macmillan.

Broderick, R. and Bounreau, J. W. 1992. Human resource management, information technology, and the competitive edge. *Academy of Management Executive*, 6(2): 7–17.

Burgelman, R. A. 1994. Fading memories: a process theory of strategic business exit in dynamic environments. *Administrative Science Quarterly*, 39(1): 24–56.

Business Week. 2005. Daggers drawn over DVDs. 17 October. Available online at http://www.businessweek.com/magazine/content/05_42/b3955113.htm

Capron, L., Dussauge, P., and Mitchell, W. 1998. Resource redeployment following horizontal acquisitions in Europe and North America, 1988–1992. *Strategic Management Journal*, 19(7): 631–661.

Chesbrough, H. and Appleyard, M. 2007. Open innovation and strategy. *California Management Review*, 50(1): 57–76.

Clark, K. B. and Fujimoto, T. 1991. *Product Development Performance: Strategy, Organization, and Management in the World Auto Industry*. Boston, MA: Harvard Business School Press.

Cockburn, I. M. and Henderson, R. M. 2000. Untangling the origins of competitive advantage. *Strategic Management Journal*, 21(10/11): 1123–1145.

Collis, D. J. 1991. A resource-based analysis of global competition: the case of the bearings industry. *Strategic Management Journal*, 12(4): 49–68.

Collis, D. J. 1994. Research note: how valuable are organizational capabilities? *Strategic Management Journal*, 15(8): 143–152.

Combs, J. G. and Ketchen Jr, D. J. 1999. Explaining inter-firm cooperation and performance: toward a reconciliation of predictions. *Strategic Management Journal*, 20(9): 867–888.

Connor, T. 2002. The resource-based view of strategy and its value to practising managers. *Strategic Change*, 11(Sep/Oct): 307–316.

D'Aveni, R. A., Dagnino, G., and Smith, K. G. 2010. The age of temporary advantage. *Strategic Management Journal*, 31: 1371–1385.

David, M. 2010. *Peer to Peer and the Music Industry: The Criminalization of Sharing*. Thousand Oaks, CA: Sage, in association with *Theory, Culture, and Society*.

Day, G. S. and Fahey, L. 1990. Putting strategy into shareholder value analysis. *Harvard Business Review*, 68(2): 156–162.

Dougherty, D. 1992. Interpretive barriers to successful product innovation in large firms. *Organization Science*, 3: 179–202.

Dowling, G. R. 2004. Corporate reputations: should you compete on yours? *California Management Review*, 46(3): 19–36.

Duncan, W. J., Ginter, P. M., and Swayne, L. E. 1998. Competitive advantage and internal organizational assessment. *Academy of Management Executive*, 12(3): 6–16.

Durand, R. 2002. Competitive advantages exist: a critique of Powell. *Strategic Management Journal*, 23(9): 867–872.

Dutta, S., Zbaracki, M. J., and Bergen, M. 2003. Pricing process as a capability: a resource-based perspective. *Strategic Management Journal*, 24(7): 615–630.

The Economist. 2003. Who gets eaten and who gets to eat. 10 July, pp. 65–67.

Eisenhardt, K. M. 1989. Making fast strategic decisions in high-velocity environments. *Academy of Management Journal*, 32(3): 543–576.

Eisenhardt, K. M. and Martin, J. A. 2000. Dynamic capabilities: what are they? *Strategic Management Journal*, 21(10/11): 1105–1121.

Fredrickson, J. W. 1984. The comprehensiveness of strategic decision processes: extension, observations, future directions. *Academy of Management Journal*, 27(3): 445–467.

Galunic, D. C. and Eisenhardt, K. M. 2001. Architectural innovation and modular corporate forms. *Academy of Management Journal*, 44(6): 1229–1249.

Ghemawat, P. 1991. Sustainable advantage in strategy seeking and securing competitive advantage. In C. A. Montegomery and M. E. Porter (eds) *Strategy: Seeking and Securing Competitive Advantage*. Boston, MA: Harvard Business School Press.

Ginsberg, A. 1994. Minding the competition: from mapping to mastery. *Strategic Management Journal*, 15(8): 153–174.

Gluck, F. W. and Kaufman, S. P. 1980. Strategic management for competitive advantage. *Harvard Business Review*, 58(4): 154–161.

Grant, R. M. 1991. The resource-based theory of competitive advantage: implications for strategy formulation. *California Management Review*, 33(3): 114–135.

Grant, R. M. 1996. Towards a knowledge theory of the firm. *Strategic Management Journal*, 17: 109–122.

Gulati, R. 1999. Network location and learning: the influence of network resources and firm capabilities on alliance formation. *Strategic Management Journal*, 20(5): 397–420.

Hamel, G. 1996. Strategy as revolution. *Harvard Business Review*, July/Aug: 69–82.

Hansen, M. H., Perry, L. T., and Reese, C. S. 2004. A Bayesian operationalization of the resource-based view. *Strategic Management Journal*, 25(13): 1279–1295.

Hansen, M. T. 1999. The search–transfer problem: the role of weak ties in sharing knowledge across organization subunits. *Administrative Science Quarterly*, 44(Mar): 82–111.

Hargadon, A. and Sutton, R. I. 1997. Technology brokering and innovation in a product development firm. *Administrative Science Quarterly*, 42(4): 716–749.

Hatch, N. W. and Dyer, J. H. 2004. Human capital and learning as a source of sustainable competitive advantage. *Strategic Management Journal*, 25(12): 1155–1178.

Haveman, H. 2000. The future of organisational sociology: forging ties among paradigms. *Contemporary Sociology*, 29: 476–486.

Helfat, C. E. 1997. Know-how and asset complementarity and dynamic capability accumulation. *Strategic Management Journal*, 18(5): 339–360.

Helfat, C. E. and Peteraf, M. A. 2003. The dynamic resource-based view: capability lifecycles deconstructed. *Strategic Management Journal*, 24(10): 997–1010.

Helfat, C. E. and Raubitschek, R. S. 2000. Product sequencing: co-evolution of knowledge, capabilities and products. *Strategic Management Journal*, 21(10/11): 961–979.

Henderson, R. and Cockburn, I. 1994. Measuring competence? Exploring firm effects in pharmaceutical research. *Strategic Management Journal*, Winter Special Issue 15: 63–84.

Hill, T. and Westbrook, R. 1997. SWOT analysis: it's time for a product recall. *Long Range Planning*, 30(1): 46–52.

Hitt, M. A., Hoskisson, R. E., and Kim, H. 1997. International diversification: effects on innovation and firm performance in product-diversified. *Academy of Management Journal*, 40(4): 767–798.

Hitt, M. A., Hoskisson, R. E., Johnson, R. A., and Moesel, D. D. 1996. The market for corporate control and firm innovation. *Academy of Management Journal*, 39(5): 1084–1119.

Hitt, M. A., Keats, B. W., and DeMarie, S. M. 1998. Navigating in the new competitive landscape: building strategic flexibility and competitive advantage in the 21st century. *Academy of Management Executive*, 12(4): 22–42.

Hoopes, D. G., Hadsen, T. L., and Walker, G. 2003. Guest editors' introduction to the special issue: why is there a resource-based view? Toward a theory of competitive heterogeneity. *Strategic Management Journal*, 24(10): 889–902.

Hoskisson, R. E., Hitt, M. A., Wan, W. P., and Yiu, D. 1999. Theory and research in strategic management: swings of a pendulum. *Journal of Management*, 25(3): 417–456.

Hult, G. T. M. and Ketchen Jr, D. J. 2001. Does market orientation matter? A test of the relationship between positional advantage and performance. *Strategic Management Journal*, 22(9): 899–906.

Hult, G. T. M., Ketchen Jr, D. J., and Nichols Jr, E. L. 2002. An examination of cultural competitiveness and order fulfillment cycle time within supply chains. *Academy of Management Journal*, 45(3): 577–586.

Hung, S.-C. 2002. Mobilising networks to achieve strategic difference. *Long Range Planning*, 35(6): 591–613.

Hurst, D. K. 1989. Creating competitive advantage: welding imagination to experience. *Academy of Management Executive*, 3: 29–36.

Ireland, R. D. and Hitt, M. A. 2005. Achieving and maintaining strategic competitiveness in the twenty-first century: the role of strategic leadership. *Academy of Management Executive*, 13(1): 95–110.

Jacobides, M. 2010. Strategy tools for a shifting landscape. *Harvard Business Review*, Jan/Feb: 77–84.

Jarzabkowski, P. and Wilson, D. 2006. Actionable strategy knowledge: a practice perspective. *European Management Journal*, 24(5): 348–367.

Jenkins, H. 2006. Eight traits of the new media landscape. 6 November. Available online at http://www.henryjenkins.org/2006/11/eight_traits_of_the_new_media.html

Judge, W. Q. and Miller. A. 1991. Antecedents and outcomes of decision speed in different environments. *Academy of Management Journal*, 34(2): 449–464.

Kaplan, R. S. and Norton, D. P. 2004. Measuring the strategic readiness of intangible assets. *Harvard Business Review*, 82(2): 52–63.

Katz, J. P. 1996. Getting partnering right: how market leaders are creating long-term competitive advantage. *Academy of Management Executive*, 10(3): 70–71.

Ketchen Jr, D. J., Hult, G. T. M., and Slater, S. F. 2007. Toward greater understanding of market orientation and the resource-based view. *Strategic Management Journal*, 28(9): 961–964.

Kettinger, W. J. and Teng, J. T. C. 1998. Aligning BPR to strategy: a framework for analysis. *Long Range Planning*, 31(1): 93–107.

Kiernan, M. J. 1993. The new strategic architecture: learning to compete in the twenty-first century. *Academy of Management Executive*, 7(1): 7–21.

Kim, W. C. and Mauborgne, R. E. 2004. Blue ocean strategy. *Harvard Business Review*, 82(10): 76–84.

King, A. W. and Zeithaml, C. P. 2001. Competencies and firm performance: examining the causal ambiguity paradox. *Strategic Management Journal*, 22(1): 75–99.

Klassen, R. D. and Whybark, D. C. 1999. The impact of environmental technologies on manufacturing performance. *Academy of Management Journal*, 42(6): 599–615.

Knott, A. M. 2003. The organizational routines factor market paradox. *Strategic Management Journal*, 24(10): 929–943.

Kogelschatz, E. 2010. A digital Rolling Stone 2.0. *Shark&Minnow*, 1 July. Available online at http://sharkandminnow.com/tag/bjork/

Kor, Y. Y. and Leblebici, H. 2005. How do interdependencies among human-capital deployment, development, and diversification strategies affect firms' financial performance? *Strategic Management Journal*, 26(10): 967–985.

Lane, P. J. and Lubatkin, M. 1998. Relative absorptive capacity and interorganizational learning. *Strategic Management Journal*, 19(5): 461–477.

Lei, D. and Slocum Jr, J. W. 2005. Strategic and organizational requirements for competitive advantage. *Academy of Management Executive*, 19(1): 31–45.

Leonhard, G. 2009. The road to music 2.0. Presentation at Creative Capital/Future Music Lab, London, 12 May. Available online at http://www.mediafuturist.com/2009/05/the-road-to-music-20-my-presentation-at-creative-capital-future-music-lab-in-london.html

Liedtka, J. M. 1996. Collaborating across lines of business for competitive advantage. *Academy of Management Executive*, 10(2): 20–34.

Linnehan, F. and De Carolis, D. 2005. Strategic frameworks for understanding employer participation in school-to-work programs. *Strategic Management Journal*, 26(6): 523–539.

MacMillan, I. C. 1988. Controlling competitive dynamics by taking strategic initiative. *Academy of Management Executive*, 2(2): 111–118.

Madhok, A. 2002. Reassessing the fundamentals and beyond: Ronald Coase, the transaction cost and resource-based theories of the firm and the institutional structure of production. *Strategic Management Journal*, 23(6): 535–550.

Magretta, J. 1998. The power of virtual integration: an interview with Dell Computer's Michael Dell. *Harvard Business Review*, 76(2): 72–84.

Mahoney, J. T. and Pandian, J. R. 1992. The resource-based view within the conversation of strategic management. *Strategic Management Journal*, 13(5): 363–380.

Makhija, M. 2003. Comparing the resource-based and market-based views of the firm: empirical evidence from Czech privatization. *Strategic Management Journal*, 24(5): 433–451.

Marino, K. E. 1996. Developing consensus on firm competencies and capabilities. *Academy of Management Executive*, 10(3): 40–51.

Markides, C. 2004. What is strategy and how do you know if you have one? *Business Strategy Review*, 15(2): 5–12.

McGahan, A. M. 1994. Industry structure and competitive advantage. *Harvard Business Review*, 72(6): 115–124.

McGee, J. 1998. Commentary on corporate strategies and environmental regulations: an organizing framework. *Strategic Management Journal*, 19(4): 377–387.

McGee, J. and Thomas, H. 1986. Strategic groups: theory, research and taxonomy. *Strategic Management Journal*, 7(2): 141–160.

McGrath, R. G. and MacMillan, I. C. 1995. Discovery-driven planning. *Harvard Business Review*, 73(4): 44–54.

McGuiness, T. and Morgan, R. 2000. Strategy, dynamic capabilities and complex science: management rhetoric vs reality. *Strategic Change*, 9(4): 209–220.

McKiernan, P. 1997. Strategy past; strategy futures. *Long Range Planning*, 30(5): 790–798.

McTavish, R. 1995. One more time: what business are you in? *Long Range Planning*, 28(2): 49–60.

Mercer, D. 1995. Scenarios made easy. *Long Range Planning*, 28(4): 81–86.

Michaels, S. 2011. Bjork plans three-year educational tour for *Biophilia* project. *The Guardian*, 30 June. Available online at http://www.guardian.co.uk/music/2011/jun/30/bjork-tour-biophilia

Miller, D. 2003. An asymmetry-based view of advantage: towards an attainable sustainability. *Strategic Management Journal*, 24(10): 961–976.

Miller, D. and Shamsie, J. 1996. The resource-based view of the firm in two environments: the Hollywood film studios from 1936 to 1965. *Academy of Management Journal*, 39(3): 519–543.

Miller, D., Eisenstat, R., and Foote, N. 2002. Strategy from the inside out: building capability-creating organizations. *California Management Review*, 44(3): 37–54.

Miller, K. D. and Waller, H. G. 2003. Scenarios, real options and integrated risk management. *Long Range Planning*, 36(1): 93–107.

Mishina, Y., Pollock, T. G., and Porac, J. F. 2004. Are more resources always better for growth? Resource stickiness in market and product expansion. *Strategic Management Journal*, 25(12): 1179–1197.

Montgomery, C. A. 2008. Putting leadership back into strategy. *Harvard Business Review*, 86(1): 54–60.

Mooney, P., Samanta, S., and Zadeh, A. H. M. 2010. Napster and its effects on the music industry: an empirical analysis. *Journal of Social Sciences*, 6(3): 303–309.

Navarro, P. 2005. The well-timed strategy: managing the business cycle. *California Management Review*, 48(1): 71–91.

Newbert, S. L. 2007. Empirical research on the resource-based view of the firm: an assessment and suggestions for future research. *Strategic Management Journal*, 28(2): 121–146.

Ohmae, K. 1982. *The Mind of the Strategist*. New York, McGraw-Hill Inc.

Oliver, C. 1997. Sustainable competitive advantage: combining institutional and resource-based views. *Strategic Management Journal*, 18(9): 697–713.

Patel, K. 2005. *The Master Strategist: Power, Purpose and Principle*. London, Arrow Books.

Penrose, E. 1959. *Theory of the Growth of the Firm*. Oxford, Oxford University Press.

Pennings, J. M., Lee, K., and Witteloostuijn, A. V. 1998. Human capital, social capital, and firm dissolution. *Academy of Management Journal*, 41(4): 425–440.

Peteraf, M. A. 1993. The cornerstones of competitive advantage: a resource-based view. *Strategic Management Journal*, 14(3): 179–191.

Petts, N. 1997. Building growth on core competences: a practical approach. *Long Range Planning*, 30(4): 551–561.

Pfeffer, J. 1995. Producing sustainable competitive advantage through the effective management of people. *Academy of Management Executive*, 9(1): 55–69.

Pfeffer, J. 2005. Producing sustainable competitive advantage through the effective management of people. *Academy of Management Executive*, 19(4): 95–106.

Pfeffer, J. and Sutton, R. 2006. *Hard Facts, Dangerous Half Truths, and Total Nonsense*. Boston, MA: Harvard Business School Press.

Pittenger, K. 1996. Networking strategies for minority managers. *Academy of Management Executive*, 10(3): 62–63.

Ployhart, R. E., Weekley, J. A., and Baughman, K. 2006. The structure and function of human capital emergence: a multilevel examination of the attraction–selection–attrition model. *Academy of Management Journal*, 49(4): 661–677.

Pomerleau, D. 1997. Competitive advantage, Hollywood style. *Academy of Management Executive*, 11(1): 116–118.

Porter, M. E. 1979. How competitive forces shape strategy. *Harvard Business Review*, 57(2): 93–101.

Porter, M. E. 1981. The contribution of individual organisation to strategic management. *Academy of Management Review*, 6(4): 609–620.

Porter, M. E. 1985. *Competitive Advantage*. New York: Free Press.

Porter, M. E. 1987. From competitive advantage to corporate strategy. *Harvard Business Review*, 65(3): 43–59.

Porter, M. E. 1990. The competitive advantage of nations. *Harvard Business Review*, 68(2): 73–93.

Porter, M. E. 1995. The competitive advantage of the inner city. *Harvard Business Review*, 73(3): 55–71.

Porter, M. E. 2008. The competitive forces that shape strategy. *Harvard Business Review*, Jan: 78–93.

Porter, M. E. and Kramer, M. R. 2002. The competitive advantage of corporate philanthropy. *Harvard Business Review*, 80(12): 56–69.

Porter, M. E. and Millar, V. E. 1985. How information gives you competitive advantage. *Harvard Business Review*, 63(4): 149–160.

Powell, T. C. 2001. Complete advantage: logical and philosophical considerations. *Strategic Management Journal*, 22(9): 875–888.

Powell, W. W., Koput, K. W., and Smith-Doerr, L. 1996. Interorganizational collaboration and the locus of innovation. *Administrative Science Quarterly*, 41(1): 116–145.

Prahalad, C. and Hamel, G. 1990. The core competencies of the corporation. *Harvard Business Review*, May/June(3): 79–91.

Press, G. 1990. Assessing competitors' business philosophies. *Long Range Planning*, 23(5): 71–75.

Priem, R. and Butler, J. 2001. Tautology in the resource-based view and the implications of externally determined resource value: further comments. *Academy of Management Review*, 26: 57–67.

Ray, G., Barney, J. B., and Muhanna, W. A. 2004. Capabilities, business processes, and competitive advantage: choosing the dependent variable in empirical tests of the resource-based view. *Strategic Management Journal*, 25(1): 23–37.

Richard, O. C. 2000. Racial diversity, business strategy, and firm performance: a resource-based view. *Academy of Management Journal*, 43(2): 164–177.

Rigby, D. and Bilodeau, B. 2007. A growing focus on preparedness. *Harvard Business Review*, 85(7/8): 21–22.

Rindova, V. P. and Kotha, S. 2001. Continuous 'morphing': competing through dynamic capabilities, form, and function. *Academy of Management Journal*, 44(6): 1263–1280.

Rosen, C. M. 2001. Environmental strategy and competitive advantage: an introduction. *California Management Review*, 43(3): 8–15.

Rumelt, R. P. 1991. How much does industry matter? *Strategic Management Journal*, 12(3): 167–185.

Russo, M. V. and Fouts, P. A. 1997. A resource-based perspective on corporate environmental performance and profitability. *Academy of Management Journal*, 40(3): 534–559.

Sarvary, M. 1999. Knowledge management and competition in the consulting industry. *California Management Review*, 41(2): 95–107.

Schreyägg, G. and Kliesch-Eberl, M. 2007. How dynamic can organizational capabilities be? Towards a dual-process model of capability dynamization. *Strategic Management Journal*, 28(9): 913–933.

Schroeder, R. G., Bates, K. A., and Junttila, M. A. 2002. A resource-based view of manufacturing strategy and the relationship to manufacturing performance. *Strategic Management Journal*, 23(2): 105–117.

Selznick, P. 1957. *Leadership in Administration*. Evanston, IL: Row, Peterson.

Shankar, V. and Bayus, B. L. 2003. Network effects and competition: an empirical analysis of the home video game industry. *Strategic Management Journal*, 24(4): 375–384.

Shay, J. and Rothaermel, F. 1999. Dynamic competitive strategy: towards a multi-perspective conceptual framework. *Long Range Planning*, 32(6): 559–572.

Smircich, L. and Stubbart. C. 1985. Strategic management in an enacted world. *Academy of Management Review*, 10: 724–736.

Smith, K. G., Grimm, C. M., Gannon, M. J., and Chen, M.-J. 1991. Organizational information processing, competitive responses, and performance in the U.S. domestic airline industry. *Academy of Management Journal*, 34(1): 60–85.

Spanos, Y. E. and Lioukas, S. 2001. An examination into the causal logic of rent generation: contrasting Porter's competitive strategy framework and the resource-based perspective. *Strategic Management Journal*, 22(10): 907–934.

Stalk Jr, G. 1988. Time: the next source of competitive advantage. *Harvard Business Review*, 66(4): 41–51.

Stalk Jr, G., Evans, P., and Shulman, L. 1992. Competing on capabilities. *Harvard Business Review*, Mar/Apr: 57–69.

Stinchcombe, A. 1997. On the virtues of the old institutionalism. *Annual Review of Sociology*, 23: 1–18.

Strategy Train. 2010. Strategic analysis. Available online at http://www.strategy-train.eu/index.php?id = 8

Szulanski, G. 1996. Exploring internal stickiness: impediments to the transfer of best practice within the firm. *Strategic Management Journal*, Winter Special Issue 17: 27–43.

Teece, D. 2007. Explicating dynamic capabilities: the nature and microfoundations of (sustainable) enterprise performance. *Strategic Management Journal*, 28: 1319–1359.

Teece, D. J., Pisano, G., and Shuen, A. 1997. Dynamic capabilities and strategic management. *Strategic Management Journal*, 18(7): 509–533.

Teng, B.-S. and Cummings, J. L. 2002. Trade-offs in managing resources and capabilities. *Academy of Management Executive*, 16(2): 81–91.

Thomas, H., Pollock, T., and Gorman, P. 1999. Global strategic analyses: frameworks and approaches. *Academy of Management Executive*, 13(1): 70–82.

Thomke, S. and Kuemmerle, W. 2002. Asset accumulation, interdependence and technological change: evidence from pharmaceutical drug discovery. *Strategic Management Journal*, 23(7): 619–635.

Tripsas, M. and Gavetti, G. 2000. Capabilities, cognition, and inertia: evidence from digital imaging. *Strategic Management Journal*. 21: 1147–1161.

Truss, K. 2001. Complexities and controversies in linking HRM with organizational outcomes. *Journal of Management Studies*, 38(8): 1121–1149.

Ulrick, D. and Lake, D. 1991. Organizational capability: creating competitive advantage. *Academy of Management Executive*, 5(1): 77–92.

Van Buskirk, E. 2009. Remixable iPhone album points to future. *Wired*, 13 February. Available online at http://www.wired.com/epicenter/2009/02/remixable-album/

Waters, R., Taylor, P., and Sanchanta, M. 2008. Sony DVD move deals blow to Microsoft. *Financial Times*, 6 January.

Wernerfelt, B. 1984. A resource-based view of the firm. *Strategic Management Journal*, 5: 171–180.

Wernerfelt, B. 1995. The resource-based view of the firm: ten years after. *Strategic Management Journal*, 16(3): 171–174.

Williams, J. R. 1992. How sustainable is your competitive advantage? *California Management Review*, 34(3): 29–51.

Winter, S. 2003. Understanding dynamic capabilities. *Strategic Management Journal*, 24(10): 991–995.

Wright, P., Ferris, S. P., Hiller, J. S., and Kroll, M. 1995. Competitiveness through management of diversity: effects on stock price valuation. *Academy of Management Journal*, 38(1): 272–287.

Zahra, S. 1995. Technology strategy and new venture performance: a study of corporate-sponsored and independent biotechnology ventures. *Journal of Business Venturing*, 11(4): 289–321.

Section 2 readings

Introduction

In this section, we have considered the foundations of advantage, which has been the focus of much theoretical and empirical analysis by strategy researchers. One of the central questions that organizations have to ask themselves is what is their core purpose? The question is even more difficult now, because society, citizens, and customers are more aware of how companies impact and influence local communities and the environment, as well as the economy.

- **Reading 2.1** by Michael Porter and Mark Kramer on 'Strategy and society' (2001) was written long before the economic crisis at the end of the first decade of the twenty-first century, and suggests that companies need to take corporate social responsibility (CSR) as seriously as they do other areas of their operations such as research and development (R&D). Taking a long-term perspective when viewing investments in CSR can have positive benefits for organizations; taking such a perspective can challenge organizational definitions of 'core purpose'.

- **Reading 2.2** by Michael Porter on 'The five competitive forces that shape strategy' (2008) views advantage through a positioning perspective. This perspective remains popular and is utilized by organizations to understand the competitive dynamics in their industry and how they can potentially achieve competitive advantage over rival firms. This can be challenging in traditional industries, but is also difficult in industries that are converging due to technological advances.

- In contrast, in **Reading 2.3**, a seminal article by David Teece, Gary Pisano, and Amy Sheun entitled 'Dynamic capabilities and strategic management' (1997), the authors view advantage through a dynamic capabilities perspective. This raises some interesting issues on how organizations should formulate strategy, view their competitive environment, and attempt to create a robust foundation for advantage.

Reading 2.1 Strategy and society *Michael E. Porter and Mark R. Kramer*

First published: (2006) *Harvard Business Review*, December: 78–92. Reprinted by permission of *Harvard Business Review*. 'Strategy and Society' Michael E. Porter and Mark R. Kramer December 2006.

Governments, activists, and the media have become adept at holding companies to account for the social consequences of their activities. Myriad organizations rank companies on the performance of their corporate social responsibility (CSR), and, despite sometimes questionable methodologies, these rankings attract considerable publicity. As a result, CSR has emerged as an inescapable priority for business leaders in every country.

Many companies have already done much to improve the social and environmental consequences of their activities, yet these efforts have not been nearly as productive as they could be – for two reasons. First, they pit business against society, when clearly the two are interdependent. Second, they pressure companies to think of corporate social responsibility in generic ways instead of in the way most appropriate to each firm's strategy.

The fact is, the prevailing approaches to CSR are so fragmented and so disconnected from business and strategy as to obscure many of the greatest opportunities for companies to benefit society. If, instead, corporations were to analyze their prospects for social responsibility using the same frameworks that guide their core business choices, they would discover that CSR can be much more than a cost, a constraint, or a charitable deed – it can be a source of opportunity, innovation, and competitive advantage.

In this article, we propose a new way to look at the relationship between business and society that does not treat corporate success and social welfare as a zero-sum game. We introduce a framework companies can use to identify all of the effects, both positive and negative, they have on society, determine which ones to address; and suggest effective ways to do so. When looked at strategically, corporate social responsibility can become a source of tremendous social progress, as the business applies its considerable resources, expertise, and insights to activities that benefit society.

The emergence of corporate social responsibility

Heightened corporate attention to CSR has not been entirely voluntary. Many companies awoke to it only after being surprised by public responses to issues they had not previously thought were part of their business responsibilities. Nike, for example, faced an extensive consumer boycott after the *New York Times* and other media outlets reported abusive labor practices at some of its Indonesian suppliers in the early 1990s. Shell Oil's decision to sink the *Brent Spar*, an obsolete oil rig, in the North Sea led to Greenpeace protests in 1995 and to international headlines. Pharmaceutical companies discovered that they were expected to respond to the AIDS pandemic in Africa even though it was far removed from their primary product lines and markets. Fast-food and packaged food companies are now being held responsible for obesity and poor nutrition.

Activist organizations of all kinds, both on the right and the left, have grown much more aggressive and effective in bringing public pressure to bear on corporations. Activists may target the most visible or successful companies merely to draw attention to an issue, even if those corporations actually have had little impact on the problem at hand. Nestlé, for example, the world's largest purveyor of bottled water, has become a major target in the global debate about access to fresh water, despite the fact that Nestlé's bottled water sales consume just 0.0008% of the world's fresh water supply. The inefficiency of agricultural irrigation, which uses 70% of the world's supply annually, is a far more pressing issue, but it offers no equally convenient multinational corporation to target.

Debates about CSR have moved all the way into corporate boardrooms. In 2005, 360 different CSR-related shareholder resolutions were filed on issues ranging from labor conditions to global warming. Government regulation increasingly mandates social responsibility reporting. Pending legislation in the UK, for example, would require every publicly listed company to disclose ethical, social, and environmental risks in its annual report. These pressures clearly demonstrate the extent to which external stakeholders are seeking to hold companies accountable for social issues and highlight the potentially large financial risks for any firm whose conduct is deemed unacceptable.

While businesses have awakened to these risks, they are much less clear on what to do about them. In fact, the most common corporate response has been neither strategic nor operational but cosmetic: public relations and media campaigns, the centerpieces of which are often glossy CSR reports that showcase companies' social and environmental good deeds. Of the 250 largest multinational corporations, 64% published CSR reports in 2005, either within their annual report or, for most, in separate sustainability reports – supporting a new cottage industry of report writers.

Such publications rarely offer a coherent framework for CSR activities, let alone a strategic one. Instead, they aggregate anecdotes about uncoordinated initiatives to demonstrate a company's social sensitivity. What these reports leave out is often as telling as what they include. Reductions in pollution, waste, carbon emissions, or energy use, for example may be documented for specific divisions or regions but not for the company as a whole. Philanthropic initiatives are typically described in terms of dollars or volunteer hours spent but almost never in terms of impact. Forward-looking commitments to reach explicit performance targets are even rarer.

This proliferation of CSR reports has been paralleled by growth in CSR ratings and rankings. While rigorous and reliable ratings might constructively influence corporate behavior, the existing cacophony of self-appointed scorekeepers does little more than add to the confusion. (See the [box] "The ratings game.")

In an effort to move beyond this confusion, corporate leaders have turned for advice to a growing collection of increasingly sophisticated nonprofit organizations, consulting firms, and academic experts. A rich literature on CSR has emerged, though what practical guidance it offers corporate leaders is often unclear. Examining the primary schools of thought about CSR is an essential starting point in understanding why a new approach is needed to integrating social considerations more effectively into core business operations and strategy.

Four prevailing justifications for CSR

Broadly speaking, proponents of CSR have used four arguments to make their case: moral obligation, sustainability, license to operate, and reputation. The moral appeal – arguing that companies have a duty to be good citizens and to "do the right thing" – is prominent in the goal of Business for Social Responsibility, the leading nonprofit CSR business association in the United States. It asks that its members "achieve commercial success in ways that honor ethical values and respect people, communities, and the natural environment." Sustainability emphasizes environmental and community stewardship. An excellent definition was developed in the 1980s by Norwegian Prime Minister Gro Harlem Brundtland and used by the World Business Council for Sustainable Development: "Meeting the needs of the present without compromising the ability of future generations to meet their own needs." The notion of license to operate derives from the fact that every company needs tacit or explicit permission from governments, communities, and numerous other stakeholders to do business. Finally, reputation is used by many companies to justify CSR initiatives on the grounds that they will improve a company's image, strengthen its brand, enliven morale, and even raise the value of its stock. These justifications have advanced thinking in the field, but none offers sufficient guidance for the difficult choices corporate leaders must make. Consider the practical limitations of each approach.

The ratings game

Measuring and publicizing social performance is a potentially powerful way to influence corporate behaviour – assuming that the ratings are consistently measured and accurately reflect corporate social impact. Unfortunately, neither condition holds true in the current profusion of CSR checklists.

The criteria used in the rankings vary widely. The Dow Jones Sustainability Index, for example, includes aspects of economic performance in its evaluation. It weights customer service almost 50% more heavily than corporate citizenship. The equally prominent FTSE4Good Index, by contrast, contains no measures of economic performance or customer service at all. Even when criteria happen to be the same, they are invariably weighted differently in the final scoring.

Beyond the choice of criteria and their weightings lies the even more perplexing question of how to judge whether the criteria have been met. Most media, nonprofits, and investment advisory organizations have too few resources to audit a universe of complicated global corporate activities. As a result, they tend to use measures for which data are readily and inexpensively available, even though they may not be good proxies for the social or environmental effects they are intended to reflect. The Dow Jones Sustainability

Index, for example, uses the size of a company's board as a measure of community involvement, even though size and involvement may be entirely unrelated.

Finally, even if the measures chosen accurately reflect social impact, the data are frequently unreliable. Most ratings rely on surveys whose response rates are statistically insignificant, as well as on self-reported company data that have not been verified externally. Companies with the most to hide are the least likely to respond. The result is a jumble of largely meaningless rankings, allowing almost any company to boast that it meets some measure of social responsibility – and most do.

The CSR field remains strongly imbued with a moral imperative. In some areas, such as honesty in filing financial statements and operating within the law, moral considerations are easy to understand and apply. It is the nature of moral obligations to be absolute mandates, however, while most corporate social choices involve balancing competing values, interests, and costs. Google's recent entry into China, for example, has created an irreconcilable conflict between its U.S. customers' abhorrence of censorship and the legal constraints imposed by the Chinese government. The moral calculus needed to weigh one social benefit against another, or against its financial costs, has yet to be developed. Moral principles do not tell a pharmaceutical company how to allocate its revenues among subsidizing care for the indigent today, developing cures for the future, and providing dividends to its investors.

The principle of sustainability appeals to enlightened self-interest, often invoking the so-called triple bottom line of economic, social, and environmental performance. In other words, companies should operate in ways that secure long-term economic performance by avoiding short-term behavior that is socially detrimental or environmentally wasteful. The principle works best for issues that coincide with a company's economic or regulatory interests. DuPont, for example, has saved over $2 billion from reductions in energy use since 1990. Changes to the materials McDonald's uses to wrap its food have reduced its solid waste by 30%. These were smart business decisions entirely apart from their environmental benefits. In other areas, however, the notion of sustainability can become so vague as to be meaningless. Transparency may be said to be more "sustainable" than corruption. Good employment practices are more "sustainable" than sweatshops. Philanthropy may contribute to the "sustainability" of a society. However true these assertions are, they offer little basis for balancing long-term objectives against the short-term costs they incur. The sustainability school raises questions about these trade-offs without offering a framework to answer them. Managers without a strategic understanding of CSR are prone to postpone these costs, which can lead to far greater costs when the company is later judged to have violated its social obligation.

The license-to-operate approach, by contrast, is far more pragmatic. It offers a concrete way for a business to identify social issues that matter to its stakeholders and make decisions about them. This approach also fosters constructive dialogue with regulators, the local citizenry, and activists – one reason, perhaps, that it is especially prevalent among companies that depend on government consent, such as those in mining and other highly regulated and extractive industries. That is also why the approach is common at companies that rely on the forbearance of their neighbors, such as those, like chemical manufacturing, whose operations are noxious or environmentally hazardous. By seeking to satisfy stakeholders, however, companies cede primary control of their CSR agendas to outsiders. Stakeholders' views are obviously important, but these groups can never fully understand a corporation's capabilities, competitive positioning, or the trade-offs it must make. Nor does the vehemence of a stakeholder group necessarily signify the importance of an issue – either to the company or to the world. A firm that views CSR as a way to placate pressure groups often finds that its approach devolves into a series of short-term defensive reactions – a never-ending public relations palliative with minimal value to society and no strategic benefit for the business.

Finally, the reputation argument seeks that strategic benefit but rarely finds it. Concerns about reputation, like license to operate, focus on satisfying external audiences. In consumer-oriented companies, it often leads to high-profile cause-related marketing campaigns. In stigmatized industries, such as chemicals and energy, a company may instead pursue social responsibility initiatives as a form of insurance, in the hope that its reputation for social consciousness will temper public criticism in the event of a crisis. This rationale once again risks confusing public relations with social and business results.

A few corporations, such as Ben & Jerry's, Newman's Own, Patagonia, and the Body Shop, have distinguished themselves through an extraordinary long-term commitment to social responsibility. But even for these companies, the social impact achieved, much less the business benefit, is hard to determine. Studies of the effect of a company's social reputation on consumer purchasing preferences or on stock market performance have been inconclusive at best. As for the concept of CSR as insurance, the connection between the good deeds and consumer attitudes is so indirect as to be impossible to measure. Having no way to quantify the benefits of these investments puts such CSR programs on shaky ground, liable to be dislodged by a change of management or a swing in the business cycle.

All four schools of thought share the same weakness: They focus on the tension between business and society rather than on their interdependence. Each creates a generic rationale that is not tied to the strategy and operations of any specific company or the places in which it operates. Consequently, none of them is sufficient to help a company identify, prioritize, and address the social issues that matter most or the ones on which it can make the biggest impact. The result is oftentimes a hodgepodge of uncoordinated CSR and philanthropic activities disconnected from the company's strategy that neither make any meaningful social impact nor strengthen the firm's long-term competitiveness. Internally, CSR practices and initiatives are often isolated from operating units – and even separated from corporate philanthropy. Externally, the company's social impact becomes diffused among numerous unrelated efforts, each responding to a different stakeholder group or corporate pressure point.

The consequence of this fragmentation is a tremendous lost opportunity. The power of corporations to create social benefit is dissipated, and so is the potential of companies to take actions that would support both their communities and their business goals.

Integrating business and society

To advance CSR, we must root it in a broad understanding of the interrelationship between a corporation and society while at the same time anchoring it in the strategies and activities of specific companies. To say broadly that business and society need each other might seem like a cliché, but it is also the basic truth that will pull companies out of the muddle that their current corporate-responsibility thinking has created.

Successful corporations need a healthy society. Education, health care, and equal opportunity are essential to a productive workforce. Safe products and working conditions not only attract customers but lower the internal costs of accidents. Efficient utilization of land, water, energy, and other natural resources makes business more productive. Good government, the rule of law, and property rights are essential for efficiency and innovation. Strong regulatory standards protect both consumers and competitive companies from exploitation. Ultimately, a healthy society creates expanding demand for business, as more human needs are met and aspirations grow. Any business that pursues its ends at the expense of the society in which it operates will find its success to be illusory and ultimately temporary.

At the same time, a healthy society needs successful companies. No social program can rival the business sector when it comes to creating the jobs, wealth, and innovation that improve standards of living and social conditions over time. If governments, NGOs, and other participants in civil society weaken the ability of business to operate productively, they may win battles but will lose the war, as corporate and regional competitiveness fade, wages stagnate, jobs disappear, and the wealth that pays taxes and supports nonprofit contributions evaporates.

Leaders in both business and civil society have focused too much on the friction between them and not enough on the points of intersection. The mutual dependence of corporations and society implies that both business decisions and social policies must follow the principle of *shared value*. That is, choices must benefit both sides. If either a business or a society pursues policies that benefit its interests at the expense of the other, it will find itself on a dangerous path. A temporary gain to one will undermine the long-term prosperity of both.

To put these broad principles into practice, a company must integrate a social perspective into the core frameworks it already uses to understand competition and guide its business strategy.

Identifying the points of intersection

The interdependence between a company and society takes two forms. First, a company impinges upon society through its operations in the normal course of business: these are *inside-out linkages*.

Virtually every activity in a company's value chain touches on the communities in which the firm operates, creating either positive or negative social consequences. While companies are increasingly aware of the social impact of their activities (such as hiring practices, emissions, and waste disposal), these impacts can be more subtle and variable than many managers realize. For one thing, they depend on location. The same manufacturing operation will have very different social consequences in China than in the United States.

A company's impact on society also changes over time, as social standards evolve and science progresses. Asbestos, now understood as a serious health risk, was thought to be safe in the early 1900s, given the scientific knowledge then available. Evidence of its risks gradually mounted for more than 50 years before any company was held liable for the harms it can cause. Many firms that failed to anticipate the consequences of this evolving body of research have been bankrupted by the results. No longer can companies be content to monitor only the obvious social impacts of today. Without a careful process for identifying evolving social effects of tomorrow, firms may risk their very survival.

Not only does corporate activity affect society, but external social conditions also influence corporations, for better and for worse. These are *outside-in linkages*.

Every company operates within a competitive context, which significantly affects its ability to carry out its strategy, especially in the long run. Social conditions form a key part of this context. Competitive context garners far less attention than value chain impacts but can have far greater strategic importance for both companies and societies. Ensuring the health of the competitive context benefits both the company and the community.

Competitive context can be divided into four broad areas: first, the quantity and quality of available business inputs – human resources, for example, or transportation infrastructure; second, the rules and incentives that govern competition – such as policies that protect intellectual property, ensure transparency, safeguard against corruption, and encourage investment; third, the size and sophistication of local demand, influenced by such things as standards for product quality and safety, consumer rights, and fairness in government purchasing; fourth, the local availability of supporting industries, such as service providers and machinery producers. Any and all of these aspects of context can be opportunities for CSR initiatives. The ability to recruit appropriate human resources, for example, may depend on a number of social factors that companies can influence, such as the local educational system, the availability of housing, the existence of discrimination (which limits the pool of workers), and the adequacy of the public health infrastructure.

Choosing which social issues to address

No business can solve all of society's problems or bear the cost of doing so. Instead, each company must select issues that intersect with its particular business. Other social agendas are best left to those companies in other industries, NGOs, or government institutions that are better positioned to address them. The essential test that should guide CSR is not whether a cause is worthy but whether it presents an opportunity to create shared value – that is, a meaningful benefit for society that is also valuable to the business.

Our framework suggests that the social issues affecting a company fall into three categories, which distinguish between the many worthy causes and the narrower set of social issues that are both important and strategic for the business.

Generic social issues may be important to society but are neither significantly affected by the company's operations nor influence the company's long-term competitiveness. *Value chain social impacts* are those that are significantly affected by the company's activities in the ordinary course of business. *Social dimensions of competitive context* are factors in the external environment that significantly affect the underlying drivers of competitiveness in those places where the company operates. [See Figure 2.1.1].

Every company will need to sort social issues into these three categories for each of its business units and primary locations, then rank them in terms of potential impact. Into which category a given social issue falls will vary from business unit to business unit, industry to industry, and place to place.

Supporting a dance company may be a generic social issue for a utility like Southern California Edison but an important part of the competitive context for a corporation like American Express, which depends on the high-end entertainment, hospitality, and tourism cluster. Carbon emissions may be a generic social issue for a financial

Figure 2.1.1 Prioritizing social issues

Generic social issues	Value chain social impacts	Social dimensions of competitive context
Social issues that are not significantly affected by a company's operations nor materially affect its long-term competitiveness	Social issues that are significantly affected by a company's activities in the ordinary course of business	Social issues in the external environment that significantly affect the underlying drivers of a company's competitiveness in the locations where it operates

services firm like Bank of America, a negative value chain impact for a transportation-based company like UPS, or both a value chain impact and a competitive context issue for a car manufacturer like Toyota. The AIDS pandemic in Africa may be a generic social issue for a U.S. retailer like Home Depot, a value chain impact for a pharmaceutical company like GlaxoSmithKline, and a competitive context issue for a mining company like Anglo American that depends on local labor in Africa for its operations.

Even issues that apply widely in the economy, such as diversity in hiring or conservation of energy, can have greater significance for some industries than for others. Health care benefits, for example, will present fewer challenges for software development or biotechnology firms, where workforces tend to be small and well compensated, than for companies in a field like retailing, which is heavily dependent on large numbers of lower-wage workers.

Within an industry, a given social issue may cut differently for different companies, owing to differences in competitive positioning. In the auto industry, for example, Volvo has chosen to make safety a central element of its competitive positioning, while Toyota has built a competitive advantage from the environmental benefits of its hybrid technology. For an individual company, some issues will prove to be important for many of its business units and locations, offering opportunities for strategic corporate-wide CSR initiatives.

Where a social issue is salient for many companies across multiple industries, it can often be addressed most effectively through cooperative models. The Extractive Industries Transparency Initiative, for example, includes 19 major oil, gas, and mining companies that have agreed to discourage corruption through full public disclosure and verification of all corporate payments to governments in the countries in which they operate. Collective action by all major corporations in these industries prevents corrupt governments from undermining social benefit by simply choosing not to deal with the firms that disclose their payments.

Creating a corporate social agenda

Categorizing and ranking social issues is just the means to an end, which is to create an explicit and affirmative corporate social agenda. A corporate social agenda looks beyond community expectations to opportunities to achieve social and economic benefits simultaneously. It moves from mitigating harm to finding ways to reinforce corporate strategy by advancing social conditions.

Such a social agenda must be responsive to stakeholders, but it cannot stop there. A substantial portion of corporate resources and attention must migrate to truly strategic CSR [see Figure 2.1.2]. It is through strategic CSR that the company will make the most significant social impact and reap the greatest business benefits.

Responsive CSR

Responsive CSR comprises two elements: acting as a good corporate citizen, attuned to the evolving social concerns of stakeholders, and mitigating existing or anticipated adverse effects from business activities.

Figure 2.1.2 Corporate involvement in society: a strategic approach

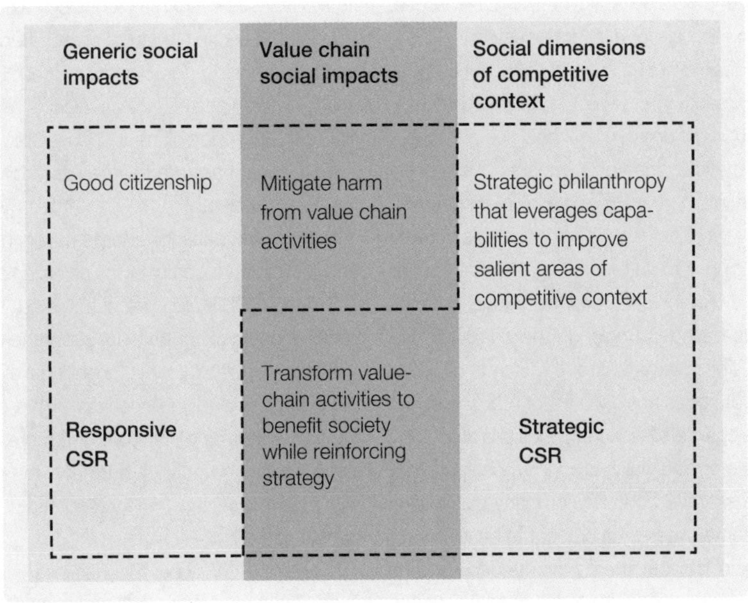

Generic social impacts	**Value chain social impacts**	**Social dimensions of competitive context**
Good citizenship	Mitigate harm from value chain activities	Strategic philanthropy that leverages capabilities to improve salient areas of competitive context
Responsive CSR	Transform value-chain activities to benefit society while reinforcing strategy	**Strategic CSR**

Good citizenship is a sine qua non of CSR, and companies need to do it well. Many worthy local organizations rely on corporate contributions, while employees derive justifiable pride from their company's positive involvement in the community.

The best corporate citizenship initiatives involve far more than writing a check: they specify clear, measurable goals and track results over time. A good example is GE's program to adopt underperforming public high schools near several of its major U.S. facilities. The company contributes between $250,000 and $1 million over a five-year period to each school and makes in-kind donations as well. GE managers and employees take an active role by working with school administrators to assess needs and mentor or tutor students. In an independent study of ten schools in the program between 1989 and 1999, nearly all showed significant improvement, while the graduation rate in four of the five worst-performing schools doubled from an average of 30% to 60%.

Effective corporate citizenship initiatives such as this one create goodwill and improve relations with local governments and other important constituencies. What's more, GE's employees feel great pride in their participation. Their effect is inherently limited, however. No matter how beneficial the program is, it remains incidental to the company's business, and the direct effect on GE's recruiting and retention is modest.

The second part of responsive CSR – mitigating the harm arising from a firm's value chain activities – is essentially an operational challenge. Because there are a myriad of possible value chain impacts for each business unit, many companies have adopted a checklist approach to CSR, using standardized sets of social and environmental risks. The Global Reporting Initiative, which is rapidly becoming a standard for CSR reporting, has enumerated a list of 141 CSR issues, supplemented by auxiliary lists for different industries.

These lists make for an excellent starting point, but companies need a more proactive and tailored internal process. Managers at each business unit can use the value chain as a tool to identify systematically the social impacts of the unit's activities in each location. Here operating management, which is closest to the work actually being done, is particularly helpful. Most challenging is to anticipate impacts that are not yet well recognized. Consider B&Q, an international chain of home supply centers based in England. The company has begun to analyze systematically tens of thousands of products in its hundreds of stores against a list of a dozen social issues – from climate change to working conditions at its suppliers' factories – to determine which products pose potential social responsibility risks and how the company might take action before any external pressure is brought to bear.

For most value chain impacts, there is no need to reinvent the wheel. The company should identify best practices for dealing with each one, with an eye toward how those practices are changing. Some companies will be more proactive and effective in mitigating the wide array of social problems that the value chain can create. These companies will gain an edge, but – just as for procurement and other operational improvements – any advantage is likely to be temporary.

Strategic CSR

For any company, strategy must go beyond best practices. It is about choosing a unique position – doing things differently from competitors in a way that lowers costs or better serves a particular set of customer needs. These principles apply to a company's relationship to society as readily as to its relationship to its customers and rivals.

Strategic CSR moves beyond good corporate citizenship and mitigating harmful value chain impacts to mount a small number of initiatives whose social and business benefits are large and distinctive. Strategic CSR involves both inside-out and outside-in dimensions working in tandem. It is here that the opportunities for shared value truly lie.

Many opportunities to pioneer innovations to benefit both society and a company's own competitiveness can arise in the product offering and the value chain. Toyota's response to concerns over automobile emissions is an example. Toyota's Prius, the hybrid electric/gasoline vehicle, is the first in a series of innovative car models that have produced competitive advantage *and* environmental benefits. Hybrid engines emit as little as 10% of the harmful pollutants conventional vehicles produce while consuming only half as much gas. Voted 2004 Car of the Year by *Motor Trend* magazine, Prius has given Toyota a lead so substantial that Ford and other car companies are licensing the technology. Toyota has created a unique position with customers and is well on its way to establishing its technology as the world standard.

Urbi, a Mexican construction company, has prospered by building housing for disadvantaged buyers using novel financing vehicles such as flexible mortgage payments made through payroll deductions. Crédit Agricole, France's largest bank, has differentiated itself by offering specialized financial products related to the environment, such as financing packages for energy-saving home improvements and for audits to certify farms as organic.

Strategic CSR also unlocks shared value by investing in social aspects of context that strengthen company competitiveness. A symbiotic relationship develops: the success of the company and the success of the community become mutually reinforcing. Typically, the more closely tied a social issue is to the company's business, the greater the opportunity to leverage the firm's resources and capabilities, and benefit society.

Microsoft's Working Connections partnership with the American Association of Community Colleges (AACC) is a good example of a shared-value opportunity arising from investments in context The shortage of information technology workers is a significant constraint on Microsoft's growth; currently, there are more than 450,000 unfilled IT positions in the United States alone. Community colleges, with an enrolment of.11.6 million students, representing 45% of all U.S. undergraduates, could be a major solution. Microsoft recognizes, however, that community colleges face special challenges: IT curricula are not standardized, technology used in classrooms is often outdated, and there are no systematic professional development programs to keep faculty up to date.

Microsoft's $50 million five-year initiative was aimed at all three problems. In addition to contributing money and products, Microsoft sent employee volunteers to colleges to assess needs, contribute to curriculum development, and create faculty development institutes. Note that, in this case, volunteers and assigned staff were able to use their core professional skills to address a social need, a far cry from typical volunteer programs. Microsoft has achieved results that have benefited many communities while having a direct – and potentially significant – impact on the company.

Integrating inside-out and outside-in practices

Pioneering value chain innovations and addressing social constraints to competitiveness are each powerful tools for creating economic and social value. However, as our examples illustrate, the impact is even greater if they work together. Activities in the value chain can be performed in ways that reinforce improvements in the social dimensions of context. At the same time, investments in competitive context have the potential to reduce constraints on a company's value chain activities. Marriott, for example, provides 180 hours of paid classroom and on-the-job training to chronically unemployed job candidates. The company has combined this with support for local community service organizations, which identify, screen, and refer the candidates to Marriott. The net result is both a major benefit to communities and a reduction in Marriott's cost of recruiting entry-level employees. Ninety percent of those in the training program take jobs with Marriott. One year later, more than 65% are still in their jobs, a substantially higher retention rate than the norm.

When value chain practices and investments in competitive context are fully integrated, CSR becomes hard to distinguish from the day-to-day business of the company. Nestlé for example, works directly with small farmers in developing countries to source the basic commodities, such as milk, coffee, and cocoa, on which much of its global business depends. ... The company's investment in local infrastructure and its transfer of world–class knowledge and technology over decades has produced enormous social benefits through improved health care, better education, and economic development, while giving Nestlé direct and reliable access to the commodities it needs to maintain a profitable global business. Nestlé's distinctive strategy is inseparable from its social impact.

Creating a social dimension to the value proposition

At the heart of any strategy is a unique value proposition: a set of needs a company can meet for its chosen customers that others cannot. The most strategic CSR occurs when a company adds a social dimension to its value proposition, making social impact integral to the overall strategy.

Consider Whole Foods Market, whose value proposition is to sell organic, natural, and healthy food products to customers who are passionate about food and the environment. Social issues are fundamental to what makes Whole Foods unique in food retailing and to its ability to command premium prices. The company's sourcing emphasizes purchases from local farmers through each store's procurement process. Buyers screen out foods containing any of nearly 100 common ingredients that the company considers unhealthy or environmentally damaging. The same standards apply to products made internally. Whole Foods' baked goods, for example, use only unbleached and unbromated flour.

Whole Foods' commitment to natural and environmentally friendly operating practices extends well beyond sourcing. Stores are constructed using a minimum of virgin raw materials. Recently, the company purchased renewable wind energy credits equal to 100% of its electricity use in all of its stores and facilities, the only *Fortune* 500 company to offset its electricity consumption entirely. Spoiled produce and biodegradable waste are trucked to regional centers for composting. Whole Foods' vehicles are being converted to run on biofuels. Even the cleaning products used in its stores are environmentally friendly. And through its philanthropy, the company has created the Animal Compassion Foundation to develop more natural and humane ways of raising farm animals. In short, nearly every aspect of the company's value chain reinforces the social dimensions of its value proposition, distinguishing Whole Foods from its competitors.

Not every company can build its entire value proposition around social issues as Whole Foods does, but adding a social dimension to the value proposition offers a new frontier in competitive positioning. Government regulation, exposure to criticism and liability, and consumers' attention to social issues are all persistently increasing. As a result, the number of industries and companies whose competitive advantage can involve social value propositions is constantly growing. Sysco, for example, the largest distributor of food products to restaurants and institutions in North America, has begun an initiative to preserve small, family-owned farms and offer locally grown produce to its customers as a source of competitive differentiation. Even large global multinationals – such as General Electric, with its "ecomagination" initiative that focuses on developing water purification technology and other "green" businesses, and Unilever, through its efforts to pioneer new products, packaging, and distribution systems to meet the needs of the poorest populations – have decided that major business opportunities lie in integrating business and society.

Organizing for CSR

Integrating business and social needs takes more than good intentions and strong leadership. It requires adjustments in organization, reporting relationships, and incentives. Few companies have engaged operating management in processes that identify and prioritize social issues based on their salience to business operations and their importance to the company's competitive context. Even fewer have unified their philanthropy with the management of their CSR efforts, much less sought to embed a social dimension into their core value proposition. Doing these things requires a far different approach to both CSR and philanthropy than the one prevalent today. Companies must shift from a fragmented, defensive posture to an integrated, affirmative approach. The focus must move away from an emphasis on image to an emphasis on substance.

The current preoccupation with measuring stakeholder satisfaction has it backwards. What needs to be measured is social impact. Operating managers must understand the importance of the outside-in influence of competitive context, while people with responsibility for CSR initiatives must have a granular understanding of every activity in the value chain. Value chain and competitive-context investments in CSR need to be incorporated into the performance measures of managers with P&L responsibility. These transformations require more than a broadening of job definition; they require overcoming a number of longstanding prejudices. Many operating managers have developed an ingrained us-versus-them mind-set that responds defensively to the discussion of any social issue, just as many NGOs view askance the pursuit of social value for profit. These attitudes must change if companies want to leverage the social dimension of corporate strategy.

Strategy is always about making choices, and success in corporate social responsibility is no different. It is about choosing which social issues to focus on. The short-term performance pressures companies face rule out indiscriminate investments in social value creation. They suggest, instead, that creating shared value should be viewed like research and development, as a long-term investment in a company's future competitiveness. The billions of dollars already being spent on CSR and corporate philanthropy would generate far more benefit to both business and society if consistently invested using the principles we have outlined.

While responsive CSR depends on being a good corporate citizen and addressing every social harm the business creates, strategic CSR is far more selective. Companies are called on to address hundreds of social issues, but only a few represent opportunities to make a real difference to society or to confer a competitive advantage. Organizations that make the right choices and build focused, proactive, and integrated social initiatives in concert with their core strategies will increasingly distance themselves from the pack.

The moral purpose of business

By providing jobs, investing capital, purchasing goods, and doing business every day, corporations have a profound and positive influence on society. The most important thing a corporation can do for society, and for any community, is contribute to a prosperous economy. Governments and NGOs often forget this basic truth. When developing countries distort rules and incentives for business, for example, they penalize productive companies. Such countries are doomed to poverty, low wages, and selling off their natural resources. Corporations have the know-how and resources to change this state of affairs, not only in the developing world but also in economically disadvantaged communities in advanced economies.

This cannot excuse businesses that seek short-term profits deceptively or shirk the social and environmental consequences of their actions. But CSR should not be only about what businesses have done that is wrong – important as that is. Nor should it be only about making philanthropic contributions to local charities, lending a hand in time of disaster, or providing relief to society's needy – worthy though these contributions may be. Efforts to find shared value in operating practices and in the social dimensions of competitive context have the potential not only to foster economic and social development but to change the way companies and society think about each other. NGOs, governments, and companies must stop thinking in terms of "corporate social responsibility" and start thinking in terms of "corporate social integration."

Perceiving social responsibility as building shared value rather than as damage control or as a PR campaign will require dramatically different thinking in business. We are convinced, however, that CSR will become increasingly important to competitive success.

Corporations are not responsible for all the world's problems, nor do they have the resources to solve them all. Each company can identify the particular set of societal problems that it is best equipped to help resolve and from which it can gain the greatest competitive benefit. Addressing social issues by creating shared value will lead to self-sustaining solutions that do not depend on private or government subsidies. When a well-run business applies its vast resources, expertise, and management talent to problems that it understands and in which it has a stake, it can have a greater impact on social good than any other institution or philanthropic organization.

Reading 2.2 The five competitive forces that shape strategy

Michael E. Porter

First published: (2008) *Harvard Business Review*, January: 79–93. Reprinted by permission of *Harvard Business Review*. 'The five competitive forces that shape strategy', Michael E. Porter, January 01 2008.

In essence, the job of the strategist is to understand and cope with competition. Often, however, managers define competition too narrowly, as if it occurred only among today's direct competitors. Yet competition for profits goes beyond established industry rivals to include four other competitive forces as well: customers, suppliers, potential entrants, and substitute products. The extended rivalry that results from all five forces defines an industry's structure and shapes the nature of competitive interaction within an industry.

As different from one another as industries might appear on the surface, the underlying drivers of profitability are the same. The global auto industry, for instance, appears to have nothing in common with the worldwide market for art masterpieces or the heavily regulated health-care delivery industry in Europe. But to understand industry competition and profitability in each of those three cases, one must analyze the industry's underlying structure in terms of the five forces. (See [Figure 2.2.1].)

If the forces are intense, as they are in such industries as airlines, textiles, and hotels, almost no company earns attractive returns on investment. If the forces are benign, as they are in industries such as software, soft drinks, and toiletries, many companies are profitable. Industry structure drives competition and profitability, not whether an industry produces a product or service, is emerging or mature, high tech or low tech, regulated or unregulated. While a myriad of factors can affect industry profitability in the short run – including the weather and the business cycle – industry structure, manifested in the competitive forces, sets industry profitability in the medium and long run. (See the [box] "Differences in industry profitability.")

Figure 2.2.1 The five forces that shape industry competition

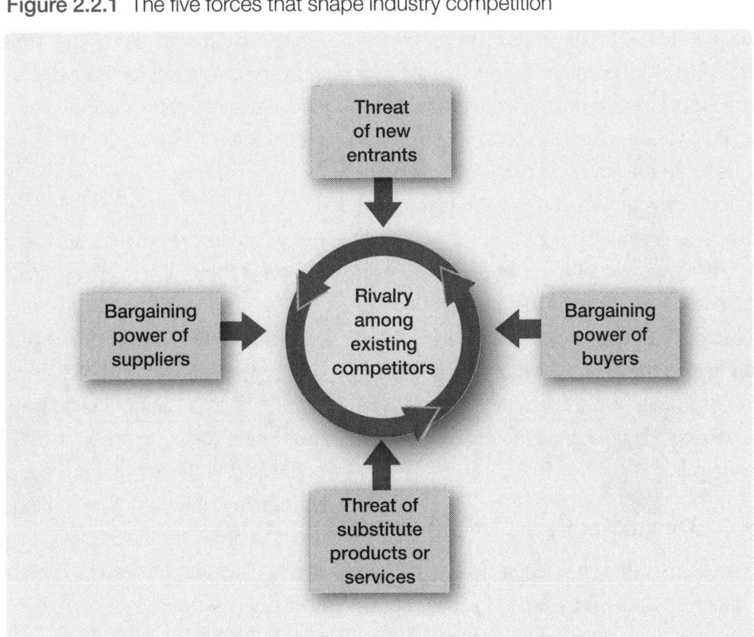

Understanding the competitive forces, and their underlying causes, reveals the roots of an industry's current profitability while providing a framework for anticipating and influencing competition (and profitability) over time. A healthy industry structure should be as much a competitive concern to strategists as their company's own position. Understanding industry structure is also essential to effective strategic positioning. As we will see, defending against the competitive forces and shaping them in a company's favor are crucial to strategy.

Differences in industry profitability

The average return on invested capital varies markedly from industry to industry. Between 1992 and 2006, for example, average return on invested capital in U.S. industries ranged as low as zero or even negative to more than 50%. At the high end are industries like soft drinks and prepackaged software, which have been almost six times more profitable than the airline industry over the period. [See Figures 2.2.2 and 2.2.3]

Forces that shape competition

The configuration of the five forces differs by industry. In the market for commercial aircraft, fierce rivalry between dominant producers Airbus and Boeing and the bargaining power of the airlines that place huge orders for aircraft are strong, while the threat of entry, the threat of substitutes, and the power of suppliers are more benign. In the movie theater industry, the proliferation of substitute forms of entertainment and the power of the movie producers and distributors who supply movies, the critical input, are important.

The strongest competitive force or forces determine the profitability of an industry and become the most important to strategy formulation. The most salient force, however, is not always obvious.

For example, even though rivalry is often fierce in commodity industries, it may not be the factor limiting profitability. Low returns in the photographic film industry, for instance, are the result of a superior substitute product – as Kodak and Fuji, the world's leading producers of photographic film, learned with the advent of digital photography. In such a situation, coping with the substitute product becomes the number one strategic priority.

Industry structure grows out of a set of economic and technical characteristics that determine the strength of each competitive force. We will examine these drivers in the pages that follow, taking the perspective of an incumbent, or a company already present in the industry. The analysis can be readily extended to understand the challenges facing a potential entrant.

Threat of entry

New entrants to an industry bring new capacity and a desire to gain market share that puts pressure on prices, costs, and the rate of investment necessary to compete. Particularly when new entrants are diversifying from other markets, they can leverage existing capabilities and cash flows to shake up competition, as Pepsi did when it entered the bottled water industry, Microsoft did when it began to offer internet browsers, and Apple did when it entered the music distribution business.

The threat of entry, therefore, puts a cap on the profit potential of an industry. When the threat is high, incumbents must hold down their prices or boost investment to deter new competitors. In specialty coffee retailing, for example, relatively low entry barriers mean that Starbucks must invest aggressively in modernizing stores and menus.

The threat of entry in an industry depends on the height of entry barriers that are present and on the reaction entrants can expect from incumbents. If entry barriers are low and newcomers expect little retaliation from the entrenched competitors, the threat of entry is high and industry profitability is moderated. It is the threat of entry, not whether entry actually occurs, that holds down profitability.

Barriers to entry

Entry barriers are advantages that incumbents have relative to new entrants. There are seven major sources:

1. *Supply-side economies of scale.* These economies arise when firms that produce at larger volumes enjoy lower costs per unit because they can spread fixed costs over more units, employ more efficient technology, or command better terms from suppliers. Supply-side scale economies deter entry by forcing the aspiring entrant either to come into the industry on a large scale, which requires dislodging entrenched competitors, or to accept a cost disadvantage.

Scale economies can be found in virtually every activity in the value chain; which ones are most important varies by industry. In microprocessors, incumbents such as Intel are protected by scale economies in research, chip fabrication, and consumer marketing. For lawn care companies like Scotts Miracle-Gro, the most important scale economies are found in the supply chain and media advertising. In small-package delivery, economies of scale arise in national logistical systems and information technology.

2. *Demand-side benefits of scale.* These benefits, also known as network effects, arise in industries where a buyer's willingness to pay for a company's product increases with the number of other buyers who also patronize the company. Buyers may trust larger companies more for a crucial product. Recall the old adage that no one ever got fired for buying from IBM (when it was the dominant computer maker). Buyers may also value being in a "network" with a larger number of fellow customers. For instance, online auction participants are attracted to eBay because it offers the most potential trading partners. Demand-side benefits of scale discourage entry by limiting the willingness of customers to buy from a newcomer and by reducing the price the newcomer can command until it builds up a large base of customers.

3. *Customer switching costs*. Switching costs are fixed costs that buyers face when they change suppliers. Such costs may arise because a buyer who switches vendors must, for example, alter product specifications, retrain employees to use a new product, or modify processes or information systems. The larger the switching costs, the harder it will be for an entrant to gain customers. Enterprise resource planning (ERP) software is an example of a product with very high switching costs. Once a company has installed SAP's ERP system, for example, the costs of moving to a new vendor are astronomical because of embedded data, the fact that internal processes have been adapted to SAP, major retraining needs, and the mission-critical nature of the applications.

4. *Capital requirements.* The need to invest large financial resources in order to compete can deter new entrants. Capital may be necessary not only for fixed facilities but also to extend customer credit, build inventories, and fund start-up losses. The barrier is particularly great if the capital is required for unrecoverable and therefore harder-to-finance expenditures, such as up-front advertising or research and development. While major corporations have the financial resources to invade almost any industry, the huge capital requirements in certain fields limit the pool of likely entrants. Conversely, in such fields as tax preparation services or short-haul trucking, capital requirements are minimal and potential entrants plentiful.

It is important not to overstate the degree to which capital requirements alone deter entry. If industry returns are attractive and are expected to remain so, and if capital markets are efficient, investors will provide entrants with the funds they need. For aspiring air carriers, for instance, financing is available to purchase expensive aircraft because of their high resale value, one reason why there have been numerous new airlines in almost every region.

5. *Incumbency advantages independent of size.* No matter what their size, incumbents may have cost or quality advantages not available to potential rivals. These advantages can stem from such sources as proprietary technology, preferential access to the best raw material sources, preemption of the most favorable geographic locations, established brand identities, or cumulative experience that has allowed incumbents to learn how to produce more efficiently. Entrants try to bypass such advantages. Upstart discounters such as Target and Wal-Mart, for example, have located stores in freestanding sites rather than regional shopping centers where established department stores were well entrenched.

6. *Unequal access to distribution channels*. The new entrant must, of course, secure distribution of its product or service. A new food item, for example, must displace others from the supermarket shelf via price breaks, promotions, intense selling efforts, or some other means. The more limited the wholesale or retail channels are and the more that existing competitors have tied them up, the tougher entry into an industry will be. Sometimes access to distribution is so high a barrier that new entrants must bypass distribution channels altogether or create their own. Thus, upstart low-cost airlines have avoided distribution through travel agents (who tend to favor established higher-fare carriers) and have encouraged passengers to book their own flights on the internet.

7. *Restrictive government policy.* Government policy can hinder or aid new entry directly, as well as amplify (or nullify) the other entry barriers. Government directly limits or even forecloses entry into industries through, for instance, licensing requirements and restrictions on foreign investment. Regulated industries like liquor retailing, taxi services, and airlines are visible examples. Government policy can heighten other entry barriers through such means as expans65ive patenting rules that protect proprietary technology from imitation or environmental or safety regulations that raise scale economies facing newcomers. Of course, government policies may also make entry easier – directly through subsidies, for instance, or indirectly by funding basic research and making it available to all firms, new and old, reducing scale economies.

Entry barriers should be assessed relative to the capabilities of potential entrants, which may be start-ups, foreign firms, or companies in related industries. And, as some of our examples illustrate, the strategist must be mindful of the creative ways newcomers might find to circumvent apparent barriers.

Expected retaliation

How potential entrants believe incumbents may react will also influence their decision to enter or stay out of an industry. If reaction is vigorous and protracted enough, the profit potential of participating in the industry can fall below the cost of capital. Incumbents often use public statements and responses to one entrant to send a message to other prospective entrants about their commitment to defending market share.

Newcomers are likely to fear expected retaliation if:

- Incumbents have previously responded vigorously to new entrants.
- Incumbents possess substantial resources to fight back, including excess cash and unused borrowing power, available productive capacity, or clout with distribution channels and customers.
- Incumbents seem likely to cut prices because they are committed to retaining market share at all costs or because the industry has high fixed costs, which create a strong motivation to drop prices to fill excess capacity.
- Industry growth is slow so newcomers can gain volume only by taking it from incumbents.

An analysis of barriers to entry and expected retaliation is obviously crucial for any company contemplating entry into a new industry. The challenge is to find ways to surmount the entry barriers without nullifying, through heavy investment, the profitability of participating in the industry.

The power of suppliers

Powerful suppliers capture more of the value for themselves by charging higher prices, limiting quality or services, or shifting costs to industry participants. Powerful suppliers, including suppliers of labor, can squeeze profitability out of an industry that is unable to pass on cost increases in its own prices. Microsoft, for instance, has contributed to the erosion of profitability among personal computer makers by raising prices on operating systems. PC makers, competing fiercely for customers who can easily switch among them, have limited freedom to raise their prices accordingly.

Companies depend on a wide range of different supplier groups for inputs. A supplier group is powerful if:

- It is more concentrated than the industry it sells to. Microsoft's near monopoly in operating systems, coupled with the fragmentation of PC assemblers, exemplifies this situation.
- The supplier group does not depend heavily on the industry for its revenues. Suppliers serving many industries will not hesitate to extract maximum profits from each one. If a particular industry accounts for a large portion of a supplier group's volume or profit, however, suppliers will want to protect the industry through reasonable pricing and assist in activities such as R&D and lobbying.
- Industry participants face switching costs in changing suppliers. For example, shifting suppliers is difficult if companies have invested heavily in specialized ancillary equipment or in learning how to operate a supplier's equipment (as with Bloomberg terminals used by financial professionals). Or firms may have located their production lines adjacent to a supplier's manufacturing facilities (as in the case of some beverage companies and container manufacturers). When switching costs are high, industry participants find it hard to play suppliers off against one another. (Note that suppliers may have switching costs as well. This limits their power.)
- Suppliers offer products that are differentiated. Pharmaceutical companies that offer patented drugs with distinctive medical benefits have more power over hospitals, health maintenance organizations, and other drug buyers, for example, than drug companies offering me-too or generic products.
- There is no substitute for what the supplier group provides. Pilots' unions, for example, exercise considerable supplier power over airlines partly because there is no good alternative to a well-trained pilot in the cockpit.
- The supplier group can credibly threaten to integrate forward into the industry. In that case, if industry participants make too much money relative to suppliers, they will induce suppliers to enter the market.

The power of buyers

Powerful customers the flip side of powerful suppliers can capture more value by forcing down prices, demanding better quality or more service (thereby driving up costs), and generally playing industry participants off against one another, all at the expense of industry profitability. Buyers are powerful if they have negotiating leverage relative to industry participants, especially if they are price sensitive, using their clout primarily to pressure price reductions.

Figure 2.2.2 Average return on invested capital in US industries, 1992–2006

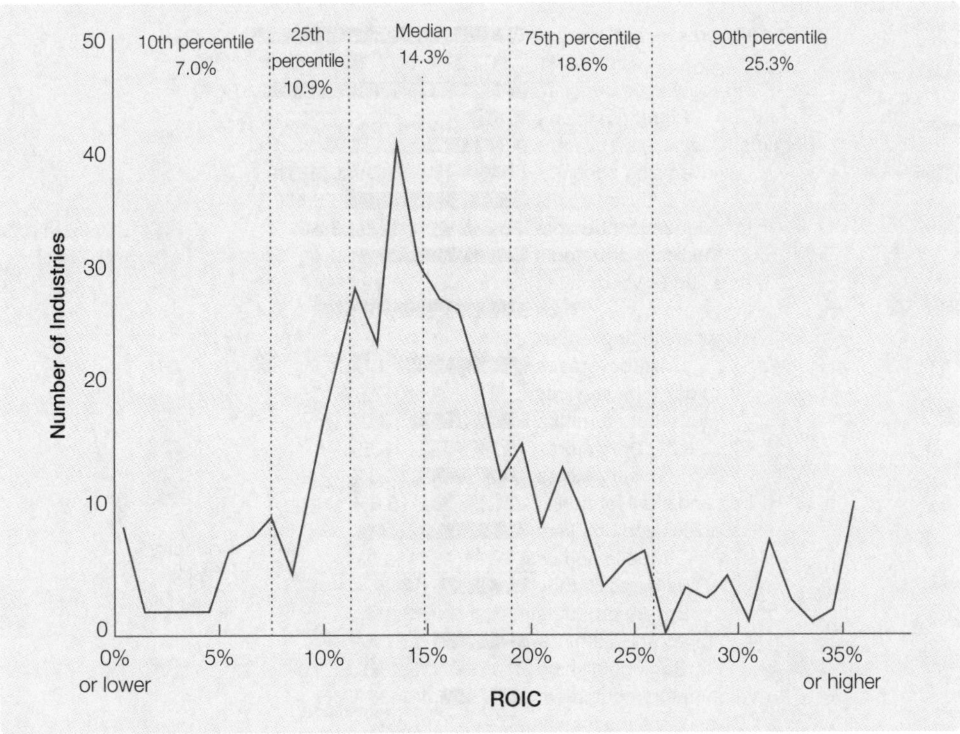

Return on inverted capital (ROIC) is the appropriate measure of profitability for strategy formulation, not to mention for equity investors. Return on sales or the growth rate of profits fail to account for the capital required to compete in the industry. Here, we utilize earnings before interest and taxes divided by average invested capital less excess cash as the measure of ROIC. This measure controls for idiosyncratic differences in capital structure and tax rates across companies and industries.

Source: Standard & Poor's Compustat and author's calculations

As with suppliers, there may be distinct groups of customers who differ in bargaining power. A customer group has negotiating leverage if:

- There are few buyers, or each one purchases in volumes that are large relative to the size of a single vendor. Large-volume buyers are particularly powerful in industries with high fixed costs, such as telecommunications equipment, offshore drilling, and bulk chemicals. High fixed costs and low marginal costs amplify the pressure on rivals to keep capacity filled through discounting.
- The industry's products are standardized or undifferentiated. If buyers believe they can always find an equivalent product, they tend to play one vendor against another.
- Buyers face few switching costs in changing vendors.
- Buyers can credibly threaten to integrate backward and produce the industry's product themselves if vendors are too profitable. Producers of soft drinks and beer have long controlled the power of packaging manufacturers by threatening to make, and at times actually making, packaging materials themselves.

A buyer group is price sensitive if:

- The product it purchases from the industry represents a significant fraction of its cost structure or procurement budget. Here buyers are likely to shop around and bargain hard, as consumers do for home mortgages. Where the product sold by an industry is a small fraction of buyers' costs or expenditures, buyers are usually less price sensitive.
- The buyer group earns low profits, is strapped for cash, or is otherwise under pressure to trim its purchasing costs. Highly profitable or cash-rich customers, in contrast, are generally less price sensitive (that is, of course, if the item does not represent a large fraction of their costs).
- The quality of buyers' products or services is little affected by the industry's product. Where quality is very much affected by the industry's product, buyers are generally less price sensitive. When purchasing or renting

Figure 2.2.3 Profitability of selected US industries

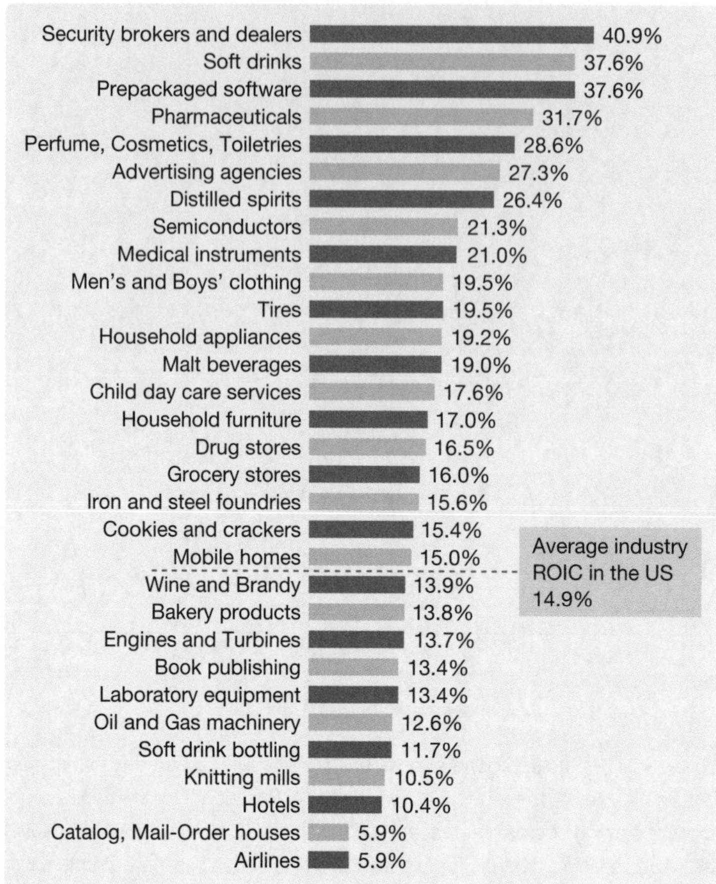

production quality cameras, for instance, makers of major motion pictures opt for highly reliable equipment with the latest features. They pay limited attention to price.

- The industry's product has little effect on the buyer's other costs. Here, buyers focus on price. Conversely, where an industry's product or service can pay for itself many times over by improving performance or reducing labor, material, or other costs, buyers are usually more interested in quality than in price. Examples include products and services like tax accounting or well logging (which measures below-ground conditions of oil wells) that can save or even make the buyer money. Similarly, buyers tend not to be price sensitive in services such as investment banking, where poor performance can be costly and embarrassing.

Most sources of buyer power apply equally to consumers and to business-to-business customers. Like industrial customers, consumers tend to be more price sensitive if they are purchasing products that are undifferentiated, expensive relative to incomes, and of a sort where product performance has limited consequences. The major difference with consumers is that their needs can be more intangible and harder to quantify.

Intermediate customers, or customers who purchase the product but are not the end user (such as assemblers or distribution channels), can be analyzed the same way as other buyers, with one important addition. Intermediate customers gain significant bargaining power when they can influence the purchasing decisions of customers downstream. Consumer electronics retailers, jewelry retailers, and agricultural-equipment distributors are examples of distribution channels that exert a strong influence on end customers.

Producers often attempt to diminish channel clout through exclusive arrangements with particular distributors or retailers or by marketing directly to end users. Component manufacturers seek to develop power over assemblers by creating preferences for their components with downstream customers. Such is the case with bicycle parts and with sweeteners. DuPont has created enormous clout by advertising its Stainmaster brand of carpet fibers not only to the carpet manufacturers that actually buy them but also to downstream consumers. Many consumers request Stainmaster carpet even though DuPont is not a carpet manufacturer.

The threat of substitutes

A substitute performs the same or a similar function as an industry's product by a different means. Videoconferencing is a substitute for travel. Plastic is a substitute for aluminum. E-mail is a substitute for express mail. Sometimes, the threat of substitution is downstream or indirect, when a substitute replaces a buyer industry's product. For example, lawn-care products and services are threatened when multifamily homes in urban areas substitute for single-family homes in the suburbs. Software sold to agents is threatened when airline and travel websites substitute for travel agents.

Substitutes are always present, but they are easy to overlook because they may appear to be very different from the industry's product: To someone searching for a Father's Day gift, neckties and power tools may be substitutes. It is a substitute to do without, to purchase a used product rather than a new one, or to do it yourself (bring the service or product in-house).

When the threat of substitutes is high, industry profitability suffers. Substitute products or services limit an industry's profit potential by placing a ceiling on prices. If an industry does not distance itself from substitutes through product performance, marketing, or other means, it will suffer in terms of profitability – and often growth potential.

Substitutes not only limit profits in normal times, they also reduce the bonanza an industry can reap in good times. In emerging economies, for example, the surge in demand for wired telephone lines has been capped as many consumers opt to make a mobile telephone their first and only phone line.

The threat of a substitute is high if.

- It offers an attractive price-performance trade-off to the industry's product. The better the relative value of the substitute, the tighter is the lid on an industry's profit potential. For example, conventional providers of long-distance telephone service have suffered from the advent of inexpensive internet-based phone services such as Vonage and Skype. Similarly, video rental outlets are struggling with the emergence of cable and satellite video-on-demand services, online video rental services such as Netflix, and the rise of internet video sites like Google's YouTube.

- The buyer's cost of switching to the substitute is low. Switching from a proprietary, branded drug to a generic drug usually involves minimal costs, for example, which is why the shift to generics (and the fall in prices) is so substantial and rapid.

Strategists should be particularly alert to changes in other industries that may make them attractive substitutes when they were not before. Improvements in plastic materials, for example, allowed them to substitute for steel in many automobile components. In this way, technological changes or competitive discontinuities in seemingly unrelated businesses can have major impacts on industry profitability. Of course the substitution threat can also shift in favor of an industry, which bodes well for its future profitability and growth potential.

Rivalry among existing competitors

Rivalry among existing competitors takes many familiar forms, including price discounting, new product introductions, advertising campaigns, and service improvements. High rivalry limits the profitability of an industry. The degree to which rivalry drives down an industry's profit potential depends, first, on the intensity with which companies compete and, second, on the basis on which they compete.

The intensity of rivalry is greatest if:

- Competitors are numerous or are roughly equal in size and power. In such situations, rivals find it hard to avoid poaching business. Without an industry leader, practices desirable for the industry as a whole go unenforced.

- Industry growth is slow. Slow growth precipitates fights for market share.

- Exit barriers are high. Exit barriers, the flip side of entry barriers, arise because of such things as highly specialized assets or management's devotion to a particular business. These barriers keep companies in the market even though they may be earning low or negative returns. Excess capacity remains in use, and the profitability of healthy competitors suffers as the sick ones hang on.

- Rivals are highly committed to the business and have aspirations for leadership, especially if they have goals that go beyond economic performance in the particular industry. High commitment to a business arises for a variety of reasons. For example, state-owned competitors may have goals that include employment or prestige. Units of larger companies may participate in an industry for image reasons or to offer a full line. Clashes of personality and ego have sometimes exaggerated rivalry to the detriment of profitability in fields such as the media and high technology.

- Firms cannot read each other's signals well because of lack of familiarity with one another, diverse approaches to competing, or differing goals.

The strength of rivalry reflects not just the intensity of competition but also the basis of competition. The *dimensions* on which competition takes place, and whether rivals converge to compete on the *same dimensions*, have a major influence on profitability.

Rivalry is especially destructive to profitability if it gravitates solely to price because price competition transfers profits directly from an industry to its customers. Price cuts are usually easy for competitors to see and match, making successive rounds of retaliation likely. Sustained price competition also trains customers to pay less attention to product features and service.

Price competition is most liable to occur if.

- Products or services of rivals are nearly identical and there are few switching costs for buyers. This encourages competitors to cut prices to win new customers. Years of airline price wars reflect these circumstances in that industry.

- Fixed costs are high and marginal costs are low. This creates intense pressure for competitors to cut prices below their average costs, even close to their marginal costs, to steal incremental customers while still making some contribution to covering fixed costs. Many basic-materials businesses, such as paper and aluminum, suffer from this problem, especially if demand is not growing. So do delivery companies with fixed networks of routes that must be served regardless of volume.

- Capacity must be expanded in large increments to be efficient. The need for large capacity expansions, as in the polyvinyl chloride business, disrupts the industry's supply–demand balance and often leads to long and recurring periods of overcapacity and price cutting.

- The product is perishable. Perishability creates a strong temptation to cut prices and sell a product while it still has value. More products and services are perishable than is commonly thought. Just as tomatoes are perishable because they rot, models of computers are perishable because they soon become obsolete, and information may be perishable if it diffuses rapidly or becomes outdated, thereby losing its value. Services such as hotel accommodations are perishable in the sense that unused capacity can never be recovered.

Competition on dimensions other than price – on product features, support services, delivery time, or brand image, for instance – is less likely to erode profitability because it improves customer value and can support higher prices. Also, rivalry focused on such dimensions can improve value relative to substitutes or raise the barriers facing new entrants. While nonprice rivalry sometimes escalates to levels that undermine industry profitability, this is less likely to occur than it is with price rivalry.

As important as the dimensions of rivalry is whether rivals compete on the *same* dimensions. When all or many competitors aim to meet the same heeds or compete on the same attributes, the result is zero-sum competition. Here, one firm's gain is often another's loss, driving down profitability. While price competition runs a stronger risk than nonprice competition of becoming zero sum, this may not happen if companies take care to segment their markets, targeting their low-price offerings to different customers.

Rivalry can be positive sum, or actually increase the average profitability of an industry, when each competitor aims to serve the needs of different customer segments, with different mixes of price, products, services, features, or brand identities. Such competition can not only support higher average profitability but also expand the industry, as the needs of more customer groups are better met. The opportunity for positive-sum competition will be greater in industries serving diverse customer groups. With a clear understanding of the structural underpinnings of rivalry, strategists can sometimes take steps to shift the nature of competition in a more positive direction.

Factors, not forces

Industry structure, as manifested in the strength of the five competitive forces, determines the industry's long-run profit potential because it determines how the economic value created by the industry is divided – how much is retained by companies in the industry versus bargained away by customers and suppliers, limited by substitutes, or constrained by potential new entrants. By considering all five forces, a strategist keeps overall structure in mind instead of gravitating to any one element. In addition, the strategist's attention remains focused on structural conditions rather than on fleeting factors.

It is especially important to avoid the common pitfall of mistaking certain visible attributes of an industry for its underlying structure. Consider the following:

Industry growth rate

A common mistake is to assume that fast-growing industries are always attractive. Growth does tend to mute rivalry, because an expanding pie offers opportunities for all competitors. But fast growth can put suppliers in a powerful position, and high growth with low entry barriers will draw in entrants. Even without new entrants, a high growth rate will not guarantee profitability if customers are powerful or substitutes are attractive. Indeed, some fast-growth businesses, such as personal computers, have been among the least profitable industries in recent years. A narrow focus on growth is one of the major causes of bad strategy decisions.

Technology and innovation

Advanced technology or innovations are not by themselves enough to make an industry structurally attractive (or unattractive). Mundane, low-technology industries with price-insensitive buyers, high switching costs, or high entry barriers arising from scale economies are often far more profitable than sexy industries, such as software and internet technologies, that attract competitors.

Government

Government is not best understood as a sixth force because government involvement is neither inherently good nor bad for industry profitability. The best way to understand the influence of government on competition is to analyze how specific government policies affect the five competitive forces. For instance, patents raise barriers to entry, boosting industry profit potential. Conversely, government policies favoring unions may raise supplier power and diminish profit potential. Bankruptcy rules that allow failing companies to reorganize rather than exit can lead to excess capacity and intense rivalry. Government operates at multiple levels and through many different policies, each of which will affect structure in different ways.

Complementary products and services

Complements are products or services used together with an industry's product. Complements arise when the customer benefit of two products combined is greater than the sum of each product's value in isolation. Computer hardware and software, for instance, are valuable together and worthless when separated.

In recent years, strategy researchers have highlighted the role of complements, especially in high-technology industries where they are most obvious. By no means, however, do complements appear only there. The value of a car, for example, is greater when the driver also has access to gasoline stations, roadside assistance, and auto insurance.

Complements can be important when they affect the overall demand for an industry's product. However, like government policy, complements are not a sixth force determining industry profitability since the presence of strong complements is not necessarily bad (or good) for industry profitability. Complements affect profitability through the way they influence the five forces.

The strategist must trace the positive or negative influence of complements on all five forces to ascertain their impact on profitability. The presence of complements can raise or lower barriers to entry. In application software, for example, barriers to entry were lowered when producers of complementary operating system software, notably Microsoft, provided tool sets making it easier to write applications. Conversely, the need to attract producers of complements can raise barriers to entry, as it does in video game hardware.

The presence of complements can also affect the threat of substitutes. For instance, the need for appropriate fueling stations makes it difficult for cars using alternative fuels to substitute for conventional vehicles. But complements can also make substitution easier. For example, Apple's iTunes hastened the substitution from CDs to digital music.

Complements can factor into industry rivalry either positively (as when they raise switching costs) or negatively (as when they neutralize product differentiation). Similar analyses can be done for buyer and supplier power. Sometimes companies compete by altering conditions in complementary industries in their favor, such as when videocassette-recorder producer JVC persuaded movie studios to favor its standard in issuing prerecorded tapes even though rival Sony's standard was probably superior from a technical standpoint.

Identifying complements is part of the analyst's work. As with government policies or important technologies, the strategic significance of complements will be best understood through the lens of the five forces.

Industry analysis in practice

Good industry analysis looks rigorously at the structural underpinnings of profitability. A first step is to understand the appropriate time horizon. One of the essential tasks in industry analysis is to distinguish temporary or cyclical changes from structural changes. A good guideline for the appropriate time horizon is the full business cycle for the particular industry. For most industries, a three-to-five-year horizon is appropriate, although in some industries with long lead times, such as mining, the appropriate horizon might be a decade or more. It is average profitability over this period, not profitability in any particular year, that should be the focus of analysis.

The point of industry analysis is not to declare the industry attractive or unattractive but to understand the underpinnings of competition and the root causes of profitability. As much as possible, analysts should look at industry structure quantitatively, rather than be satisfied with lists of qualitative factors. Many elements of the five forces can be quantified: the percentage of the buyer's total cost accounted for by the industry's product (to understand buyer price sensitivity); the percentage of industry sales required to fill a plant or operate a logistical network of efficient scale (to help assess barriers to entry); the buyer's switching cost (determining the inducement an entrant or rival must offer customers).

The strength of the competitive forces affects prices, costs, and the investment required to compete; thus the forces are directly tied to the income statements and balance sheets of industry participants. Industry structure defines the gap between revenues and costs. For example, intense rivalry drives down prices or elevates the costs of marketing, R&D, or customer service, reducing margins. How much? Strong suppliers drive up input costs. How much? Buyer power lowers prices or elevates the costs of meeting buyers' demands, such as the requirement to hold more inventory or provide financing. How much? Low barriers to entry or close substitutes limit the level of sustainable prices. How much? It is these economic relationships that sharpen the strategist's understanding of industry competition.

Finally, good industry analysis does not just list pluses and minuses but sees an industry in overall, systemic terms. Which forces are underpinning (or constraining) today's profitability? How might shifts in one competitive force trigger reactions in others? Answering such questions is often the source of true strategic insights.

Changes in industry structure

So far, we have discussed the competitive forces at a single point in time. Industry structure proves to be relatively stable, and industry profitability differences are remarkably persistent over time in practice. However, industry structure is constantly undergoing modest adjustment – and occasionally it can change abruptly.

Shifts in structure may emanate from outside an industry or from within. They can boost the industry's profit potential or reduce it. They may be caused by changes in technology, changes in customer needs, or other events. The five competitive forces provide a framework for identifying the most important industry developments and for anticipating their impact on industry attractiveness.

Shifting threat of new entry

Changes to any of the seven barriers described above can raise or lower the threat of new entry. The expiration of a patent, for instance, may unleash new entrants. On the day that Merck's patents for the cholesterol reducer Zocor expired, three pharmaceutical makers entered the market for the drug. Conversely, the proliferation of products in the ice cream industry has gradually filled up the limited freezer space in grocery stores, making it harder for new ice cream makers to gain access to distribution in North America and Europe.

Strategic decisions of leading competitors often have a major impact on the threat of entry. Starting in the 1970s, for example, retailers such as Wal-Mart, Kmart, and Toys "R" Us began to adopt new procurement, distribution, and inventory control technologies with large fixed costs, including automated distribution centers, bar coding, and point-of-sale terminals. These investments increased the economies of scale and made it more difficult for small retailers to enter the business (and for existing small players to survive).

Changing supplier or buyer power

As the factors underlying the power of suppliers and buyers change with time, their clout rises or declines. In the global appliance industry, for instance, competitors including Electrolux, General Electric, and Whirlpool have been squeezed by the consolidation of retail channels (the decline of appliance specialty stores, for instance, and the rise of big-box retailers like Best Buy and Home Depot in the United States). Another example is travel agents, who depend on airlines as a key supplier. When the internet allowed airlines to sell tickets directly to customers, this significantly increased their power to bargain down agents' commissions.

Shifting threat of substitution

The most common reason substitutes become more or less threatening over time is that advances in technology create new substitutes or shift price–performance comparisons in one direction or the other. The earliest microwave ovens, for example, were large and priced above $2,000, making them poor substitutes for conventional ovens. With technological advances, they became serious substitutes. Flash computer memory has improved enough recently to become a meaningful substitute for low-capacity hard-disk drives. Trends in the availability or performance of complementary producers also shift the threat of substitutes.

New bases of rivalry

Rivalry often intensifies naturally over time. As an industry matures, growth slows. Competitors become more alike as industry conventions emerge, technology diffuses, and consumer tastes converge. Industry profitability falls, and weaker competitors are driven from the business. This story has played out in industry after industry; televisions, snowmobiles, and telecommunications equipment are just a few examples.

A trend toward intensifying price competition and other forms of rivalry, however, is by no means inevitable. For example, there has been enormous competitive activity in the U.S. casino industry in recent decades, but most of it has been positive-sum competition directed toward new niches and geographic segments (such as riverboats, trophy properties, Native American reservations, international expansion, and novel customer groups like families). Head-to-head rivalry that lowers prices or boosts the payouts to winners has been limited.

The nature of rivalry in an industry is altered by mergers and acquisitions that introduce new capabilities and ways of competing. Or, technological innovation can reshape rivalry. In the retail brokerage industry, the advent of the internet lowered marginal costs and reduced differentiation, triggering far more intense competition on commissions and fees than in the past.

In some industries, companies turn to mergers and consolidation not to improve cost and quality but to attempt to stop intense competition. Eliminating rivals is a risky strategy, however. The five competitive forces tell us that a profit windfall from removing today's competitors often attracts new competitors and backlash from customers and suppliers. In New York banking, for example, the 1980s and 1990s saw escalating consolidations of commercial and savings banks, including Manufacturers Hanover, Chemical, Chase, and Dime Savings. But today the retail-banking landscape of Manhattan is as diverse as ever, as new entrants such as Wachovia, Bank of America, and Washington Mutual have entered the market.

Implications for strategy

Understanding the forces that shape industry competition is the starting point for developing strategy. Every company should already know what the average profitability of its industry is and how that has been changing over time. The five forces reveal *why* industry profitability is what it is. Only then can a company incorporate industry conditions into strategy.

The forces reveal the most significant aspects of the competitive environment. They also provide a baseline for sizing up a company's strengths and weaknesses: Where does the company stand versus buyers, suppliers, entrants, rivals, and substitutes? Most importantly, an understanding of industry structure guides managers toward fruitful possibilities for strategic action, which may include any or all of the following: positioning the company to better cope with the current competitive forces; anticipating and exploiting shifts in the forces; and shaping the balance of forces to create a new industry structure that is more favorable to the company. The best strategies exploit more than one of these possibilities.

Positioning the company

Strategy can be viewed as building defenses against the competitive forces or finding a position in the industry where the forces are weakest. Consider, for instance, the position of Paccar in the market for heavy trucks. The heavy-truck industry is structurally challenging. Many buyers operate large fleets or are large leasing companies, with both the leverage and the motivation to drive down the price of one of their largest purchases. Most trucks are built to regulated standards and offer similar features, so price competition is rampant. Capital intensity causes rivalry to be fierce, especially during the recurring cyclical downturns. Unions exercise considerable supplier power. Though there are few direct substitutes for an 18-wheeler, truck buyers face important substitutes for their services, such as cargo delivery by rail.

In this setting, Paccar, a Bellevue, Washington-based company with about 20% of the North American heavy-truck market, has chosen to focus on one group of customers: owner-operators – drivers who own their trucks and contract directly with shippers or serve as subcontractors to larger trucking companies. Such small operators have limited clout as truck buyers. They are also less price sensitive because of their strong emotional ties to and economic dependence on the product. They take great pride in their trucks, in which they spend most of their time.

Paccar has invested heavily to develop an array of features with owner-operators in mind: luxurious sleeper cabins, plush leather seats, noise-insulated cabins, sleek exterior styling, and so on. At the company's extensive network of dealers, prospective buyers use software to select among thousands of options to put their personal signature on their trucks. These customized trucks are built to order, not to stock, and delivered in six to eight weeks. Paccar's trucks also have aerodynamic designs that reduce fuel consumption, and they maintain their resale value better than other trucks. Paccar's roadside assistance program and IT-supported system for distributing spare parts reduce the time a truck is out of service. All these are crucial considerations for an owner-operator. Customers pay Paccar a 10% premium, and its Kenworth and Peterbilt brands are considered status symbols at truck stops.

Paccar illustrates the principles of positioning a company within a given industry structure. The firm has found a portion of its industry where the competitive forces are weaker – where it can avoid buyer power and price-based rivalry. And it has tailored every single part of the value chain to cope well with the forces in its segment. As a result, Paccar has been profitable for 68 years straight and has earned a long-run return on equity above 20%.

In addition to revealing positioning opportunities within an existing industry, the five forces framework allows companies to rigorously analyze entry and exit. Both depend on answering the difficult question: "What is the potential of this business?" Exit is indicated when industry structure is poor or declining and the company has no prospect of a superior positioning. In considering entry into a new industry, creative strategists can use the framework to spot an industry with a good future before this good future is reflected in the prices of acquisition candidates. Five forces analysis may also reveal industries that are not necessarily attractive for the average entrant but in which a company has good reason to believe it can surmount entry barriers at lower cost than most firms or has a unique ability to cope with the industry's competitive forces.

Exploiting industry change

Industry changes bring the opportunity to spot and claim promising new strategic positions if the strategist has a sophisticated understanding of the competitive forces and their underpinnings. Consider, for instance, the evolution of the music industry during the past decade. With the advent of the internet and the digital distribution of music, some analysts predicted the birth of thousands of music labels (that is, record companies that develop artists and bring their music to market). This, the analysts argued, would break a pattern that had held since Edison invented the phonograph: Between three and six major record companies had always dominated the industry. The internet would, they predicted, remove distribution as a barrier to entry, unleashing a flood of new players into the music industry.

A careful analysis, however, would have revealed that physical distribution was not the crucial barrier to entry. Rather, entry was barred by other benefits that large music labels enjoyed. Large labels could pool the risks of developing new artists over many bets, cushioning the impact of inevitable failures. Even more important, they had advantages in breaking through the clutter and getting their new artists heard. To do so, they could promise radio stations and record stores access to well-known artists in exchange for promotion of new artists. New labels would find this nearly impossible to match. The major labels stayed the course, and new music labels have been rare.

This is not to say that the music industry is structurally unchanged by digital distribution. Unauthorized downloading created an illegal but potent substitute. The labels tried for years to develop technical platforms for digital distribution themselves, but major companies hesitated to sell their music through a platform owned by a rival. Into this vacuum stepped Apple with its iTunes music store, launched in 2003 to support its iPod music player. By permitting the creation of a powerful new gatekeeper, the major labels allowed industry structure to shift against them. The number of major record companies has actually declined – from six in 1997 to four today – as companies struggled to cope with the digital phenomenon.

When industry structure is in flux, new and promising competitive positions may appear. Structural changes open up new needs and new ways to serve existing needs. Established leaders may overlook these or be constrained by past strategies from pursuing them. Smaller competitors in the industry can capitalize on such changes, or the void may well be filled by new entrants.

Shaping industry structure

When a company exploits structural change, it is recognizing, and reacting to, the inevitable. However, companies also have the ability to shape industry structure. A firm can lead its industry toward new ways of competing that alter the five forces for the better. In reshaping structure, a company wants its competitors to follow so that the entire industry will be transformed. While many industry participants may benefit in the process, the innovator can benefit most if it can shift competition in directions where it can excel.

An industry's structure can be reshaped in two ways: by redividing profitability in favor of incumbents or by expanding the overall profit pool. Redividing the industry pie aims to increase the share of profits to industry competitors instead of to suppliers, buyers, substitutes, and keeping out potential entrants. Expanding the profit pool involves increasing the overall pool of economic value generated by the industry in which rivals, buyers, and suppliers can all share.

Redividing profitability

To capture more profits for industry rivals, the starting point is to determine which force or forces are currently constraining industry profitability and address them. A company can potentially influence all of the competitive forces. The strategist's goal here is to reduce the share of profits that leak to suppliers, buyers, and substitutes or are sacrificed to deter entrants.

To neutralize supplier power, for example, a firm can standardize specifications for parts to make it easier to switch among suppliers. It can cultivate additional vendors, or alter technology to avoid a powerful supplier group altogether. To counter customer power, companies may expand services that raise buyers' switching costs or find alternative means of reaching customers to neutralize powerful channels. To, temper profit-eroding price rivalry, companies can invest more heavily in unique products, as pharmaceutical firms have done, or expand support services to customers. To scare off entrants, incumbents can elevate the fixed cost of competing – for instance, by escalating their R&D or marketing expenditures. To limit the threat of substitutes, companies can offer better value through new features or wider product accessibility. When soft-drink producers introduced vending machines and convenience store channels, for example, they dramatically improved the availability of soft drinks relative to other beverages.

Sysco, the largest food-service distributor in North America, offers a revealing example of how an industry leader can change the structure of an industry for the better. Food-service distributors purchase food and related items from farmers and food processors. They then warehouse and deliver these items to restaurants, hospitals, employer cafeterias, schools, and other food-service institutions. Given low barriers to entry, the food-service distribution industry has historically been highly fragmented, with numerous local competitors. While rivals try to cultivate customer relationships, buyers are price sensitive because food represents a large share of their costs. Buyers can also choose the substitute approaches of purchasing directly from manufacturers or using retail sources, avoiding distributors altogether. Suppliers wield bargaining power: they are often large companies with strong brand names that food preparers and consumers recognize. Average profitability in the industry has been modest.

Sysco recognized that, given its size and national reach, it might change this state of affairs. It led the move to introduce private-label distributor brands with specifications tailored to the food-service market, moderating supplier power. Sysco emphasized value-added services to buyers such as credit, menu planning, and inventory management to shift the basis of competition away from just price. These moves, together with stepped-up investments in information technology and regional distribution centers, substantially raised the bar for new entrants while making the substitutes less attractive. Not surprisingly, the industry has been consolidating, and industry profitability appears to be rising.

Industry leaders have a special responsibility for improving industry structure. Doing so often requires resources that only large players possess. Moreover, an improved industry structure is a public good because it benefits every firm in the industry, not just the company that initiated the improvement. Often, it is more in the interests of an industry leader than any other participant to invest for the common good because leaders will usually benefit the most. Indeed, improving the industry may be a leader's most profitable strategic opportunity, in part because attempts to gain further market share can trigger strong reactions from rivals, customers, and even suppliers.

There is a dark side to shaping industry structure that is equally important to understand. Ill-advised changes in competitive positioning and operating practices can undermine industry structure. Faced with pressures to gain market share or enamored with innovation for its own sake, managers may trigger new kinds of competition that no incumbent can win. When taking actions to improve their own company's competitive advantage, then, strategists should ask whether they are setting in motion dynamics that will undermine industry structure in the long run. In the early days of the personal computer industry, for instance, IBM tried to make up for its late entry by offering an open architecture that would set industry standards and attract complementary makers of application software and peripherals. In the process, it ceded ownership of the critical components of the PC the operating system and the microprocessor – to Microsoft and Intel. By standardizing PCs, it encouraged price-based rivalry and shifted power to suppliers. Consequently, IBM became the temporarily dominant firm in an industry with an enduringly unattractive structure.

Expanding the profit pool

When overall demand grows, the industry's quality level rises, intrinsic costs are reduced, or waste is eliminated, the pie expands. The total pool of value available to competitors, suppliers, and buyers grows. The total profit pool expands, for example, when channels become more competitive or when an industry discovers latent buyers for its product that are not currently being served. When soft-drink producers rationalized their independent bottler networks to make them more efficient and effective, both the soft-drink companies and the bottlers benefited. Overall value can also expand when firms work collaboratively with suppliers to improve coordination and limit unnecessary costs incurred in the supply chain. This lowers the inherent cost structure of the industry, allowing higher profit, greater demand through lower prices, or both. Or, agreeing on quality standards can bring up industry wide quality and service levels, and hence prices, benefiting rivals, suppliers, and customers.

Expanding the overall profit pool creates win–win opportunities for multiple industry participants. It can also reduce the risk of destructive rivalry that arises when incumbents attempt to shift bargaining power or capture more market share. However, expanding the pie does not reduce the importance of industry structure. How the expanded pie is divided will ultimately be determined by the five forces. The most successful companies are those that expand the industry profit pool in ways that allow them to share disproportionately in the benefits.

Defining the industry

The five competitive forces also hold the key to defining the relevant industry (or industries) in which a company competes. Drawing industry boundaries correctly, around the arena in which competition actually takes place, will clarify the causes of profitability and the appropriate unit for setting strategy. A company needs a separate strategy for each distinct industry. Mistakes in industry definition made by competitors present opportunities for staking out superior strategic positions. (See the [box] "Defining the relevant industry.")

Defining the relevant industry

Defining the industry in which competition actually takes place is important for good industry analysis, not to mention for developing strategy and setting business unit boundaries. Many strategy errors emanate from mistaking the relevant industry, defining it too broadly or too narrowly. Defining the industry too broadly obscures differences among products, customers, or geographic regions that are important to competition, strategic positioning, and profitability. Defining the industry too narrowly overlooks commonalities and linkages across related products or geographic markets that are crucial to competitive advantage. Also, strategists must be sensitive to the possibility that industry boundaries can shift. The boundaries of an industry consist of two primary dimensions. First is the *scope of products or services.* For example, is motor oil used in cars part of the same industry as motor oil used in heavy trucks and stationary engines, or are these different industries? The second dimension is *geographic scope.* Most industries are present in many parts of the world. However, is competition contained within each state, or is it national? Does competition take place within regions such as Europe or North America, or is there a single global industry? The five forces are the basic tool to resolve these questions. If industry structure for two products is the same or very similar (that is, if they have the same buyers, suppliers, barriers to entry, and so forth), then the products are best treated as being part of the same industry. If industry structure differs markedly, however, the two products may be best understood as separate industries.

In lubricants, the oil used in cars is similar or even identical to the oil used in trucks, but the similarity largely ends there. Automotive motor oil is sold to fragmented, generally unsophisticated customers through numerous and often powerful channels, using extensive advertising. Products are packaged in small containers and logistical costs are high, necessitating local production. Truck and power generation lubricants are sold to entirely different buyers in entirely different ways using a separate supply chain. Industry structure (buyer power, barriers to entry, and so forth) is substantially different. Automotive oil is thus a distinct industry from oil for truck and stationary engine uses. Industry profitability will differ in these two cases, and a lubricant company will need a separate strategy for competing in each area.

Differences in the five competitive forces also reveal the geographic scope of competition. If an industry has a similar structure in every country (rivals, buyers, and so on), the presumption is that competition is global, and the five forces analyzed from a global perspective will set average profitability. A single global strategy is needed. If an industry has quite different structures in different geographic regions, however, each region may well be a distinct industry. Otherwise, competition would have leveled the differences. The five forces analyzed for each region will set profitability there.

The extent of differences in the five forces for related products or across geographic areas is a matter of degree, making industry definition often a matter of judgment. A rule of thumb is that where the differences in any one force are large, and where the differences involve more than one force, distinct industries may well be present.

Fortunately, however, even if industry boundaries are drawn incorrectly, careful five forces analysis should reveal important competitive threats. A closely related product omitted from the industry definition will show up as a substitute, for example, or competitors overlooked as rivals will be recognized as potential entrants. At the same time, the five forces analysis should reveal major differences within overly broad industries that will indicate the need to adjust industry boundaries or strategies.

Typical steps in industry analysis

Define the relevant industry:

- What products are in it? Which ones are part of another distinct industry?
- What is the geographic scope of competition?

Identify the participants and segment them into groups, if appropriate:

Who are

- the buyers and buyer groups?
- the suppliers and supplier groups?
- the competitors?
- the substitutes?
- the potential entrants?

Assess the underlying drivers of each competitive force to determine which forces are strong and which are weak and why.

Determine overall industry structure, and test the analysis for consistency:

- *Why* is the level of profitability what it is?
- Which are the *controlling* forces for profitability?
- Is the industry analysis consistent with actual long-run profitability?
- Are more-profitable players better positioned in relation to the five forces?

Analyze recent and likely future changes in each force, both positive and negative.

Identify aspects of industry structure that might be influenced by competitors, by new entrants, or by your company.

Common pitfalls

In conducting the analysis avoid the following common mistakes:

- Defining the industry too broadly or too narrowly.
- Making lists instead of engaging in rigorous analysis.
- Paying equal attention to all of the forces rather than digging deeply into the most important ones.
- Confusing effect (price sensitivity) with cause (buyer economics).
- Using static analysis that ignores industry trends.
- Confusing cyclical or transient changes with true structural changes.
- Using the framework to declare an industry attractive or unattractive rather than using it to guide strategic choices.

Competition and value

The competitive forces reveal the drivers of industry competition. A company strategist who understands that competition extends well beyond existing rivals will detect wider competitive threats and be better equipped to address them. At the same time, thinking comprehensively about an industry's structure can uncover opportunities: differences in customers, suppliers, substitutes, potential entrants, and rivals that can become the basis for distinct strategies yielding superior performance. In a world of more open competition and relentless change, it is more important than ever to think structurally about competition.

Understanding industry structure is equally important for investors as for managers. The five competitive forces reveal whether an industry is truly attractive, and they help investors anticipate positive or negative shifts in industry structure before they are obvious. The five forces distinguish short-term blips from structural changes and allow investors to take advantage of undue pessimism or optimism. Those companies whose strategies have industry-transforming potential become far clearer. This deeper thinking about competition is a more powerful way to achieve genuine investment success than the financial projections and trend extrapolation that dominate today's investment analysis.

If both executives and investors looked at competition this way, capital markets would be a far more effective force for company success and economic prosperity. Executives and investors would both be focused on the same fundamentals that drive sustained profitability. The conversation between investors and executives would focus on the structural, not the transient. Imagine the improvement in company performance – and in the economy as a whole – if all the energy expended in "pleasing the Street" were redirected toward the factors that create true economic value.

Reading 2.3 Dynamic capabilities and strategic management

David J. Teece, Gary Pisano, and Amy Shuen

First published: (1997) *Strategic Management Journal*, 18(7): 509–533. 'Dynamic Capabilities and Strategic Management', David Teece, Gary Pisano and Amy Shuen, *Strategic Management Journal*, Vol.18:7, 1997. Reproduced with the kind permission of John Wiley and Sons Ltd.

Introduction

The fundamental question in the field of strategic management is how firms achieve and sustain competitive advantage.[1] We confront this question here by developing the dynamic capabilities approach, which endeavors to analyze the sources of wealth creation and capture by firms. The development of this framework flows from a recognition by the authors that strategic theory is replete with analyses of firm-level strategies for sustaining and safeguarding extant competitive advantage, but has performed less well with respect to assisting in the understanding of how and why certain firms build competitive advantage in regimes of rapid change. Our approach is especially relevant in a Schumpeterian world of innovation-based competition, price/performance rivalry, increasing returns, and the 'creative destruction' of existing competences. The approach endeavors to explain firm-level success and failure. We are interested in both building a better theory of firm performance, as well as informing managerial practice.

In order to position our analysis in a manner that displays similarities and differences with existing approaches, we begin by briefly reviewing accepted frameworks for strategic management. We endeavor to expose implicit assumptions, and identify competitive circumstances where each paradigm might display some relative advantage as both a useful descriptive and normative theory of competitive strategy. While numerous theories have been advanced over the past two decades about the sources of competitive advantage, many cluster around just a few loosely structured frameworks or paradigms. In this paper we attempt to identify three existing paradigms and describe aspects of an emerging new paradigm that we label dynamic capabilities.

The dominant paradigm in the field during the 1980s was the competitive forces approach developed by Porter (1980). This approach, rooted in the structure–conduct–performance paradigm of industrial organization (Mason, 1949; Bain, 1959), emphasizes the actions a firm can take to create defensible positions against competitive forces. A second approach, referred to as a strategic conflict approach (e.g., Shapiro, 1989), is closely related to the first in its focus on product market imperfections, entry deterrence, and strategic interaction. The strategic conflict approach uses the tools of game theory and thus implicitly views competitive outcomes as a function of the effectiveness with which firms keep their rivals off balance through strategic investments, pricing strategies, signaling, and the control of information. Both the competitive forces and the strategic conflict approaches appear to share the view that rents flow from privileged product market positions.

Another distinct class of approaches emphasizes building competitive advantage through capturing entrepreneurial rents stemming from fundamental firm-level efficiency advantages. These approaches have their roots in a much older discussion of corporate strengths and weaknesses; they have taken on new life as evidence suggests that firms build enduring advantages only through efficiency and effectiveness, and as developments in organizational economics and the study of technological and organizational change become applied to strategy questions. One strand of this literature, often referred to as the 'resource-based perspective,' emphasizes firm-specific capabilities and assets and the existence of isolating mechanisms as the fundamental determinants of firm performance (Penrose, 1959; Rumelt, 1984; Teece, 1984; Wernerfelt, 1984).[2] This perspective recognizes but does not attempt to explain the nature of the isolating mechanisms that enable entrepreneurial rents and competitive advantage to be sustained.

Another component of the efficiency-based approach is developed in this paper. Rudimentary efforts are made to identify the dimensions of firm-specific capabilities that can be sources of advantage, and to explain how combinations of competences and resources can be developed, deployed, and protected. We refer to this as the 'dynamic capabilities' approach in order to stress exploiting existing internal and external firm-specific competences to address changing environments. Elements of the approach can be found in Schumpeter (1942), Penrose (1959), Nelson and Winter (1982), Prahalad and Hamel (1990), Teece (1976, 1986a, 1986b, 1988) and in Hayes, Wheelwright, and Clark (1988): Because this approach emphasizes the development of management capabilities, and difficult-to-imitate combinations of organizational, functional and technological skills, it integrates and draws upon research in such areas as the management of R&D, product and process development, technology transfer, intellectual property, manufacturing, human resources, and organizational learning. Because these fields are often viewed as outside the traditional boundaries of strategy, much of this research has not been incorporated into existing economic approaches to strategy issues. As a result, dynamic capabilities can be seen as an emerging

[1] For a review of the fundamental questions in the field of strategy, see Rumelt, Schendal, and Teece (1994).

[2] Of these authors, Rumelt may have been the first to self consciously apply a resource perspective to the field of strategy. Rumelt (1984: 561) notes that the strategic firm 'is characterized by a bundle of linked and idiosyncratic resources and resource conversion activities.' Similarly, Teece (1984: 95) notes: 'Successful firms possess one or more forms of intangible assets, such as technological or managerial know-how. Over time, these assets may expand beyond the point of profitable reinvestment in a firm's traditional market. Accordingly, the firm may consider deploying its intangible assets in different product or geographical markets, where the expected returns are higher, if efficient transfer modes exist.' Wernerfelt (1984) was early to recognize that this approach was at odds with product market approaches and might constitute a distinct paradigm of strategy.

and potentially integrative approach to understanding the newer sources of competitive advantage.

We suggest that the dynamic capabilities approach is promising both in terms of future research potential and as an aid to management endeavoring to gain competitive advantage in increasingly demanding environments. To illustrate the essential elements of the dynamic capabilities approach, the sections that follow compare and contrast this approach to other models of strategy. Each section highlights the strategic insights provided by each approach as well as the different competitive circumstances in which it might be most appropriate. Needless to say, these approaches are in many ways complementary and a full understanding of firm-level, competitive advantage requires an appreciation of all four approaches and more.

Models of strategy emphasizing the exploitation of market power

Competitive forces

The dominant paradigm in strategy at least during the 1980s was the competitive forces approach. Pioneered by Porter (1980), the competitive forces approach views the essence of competitive strategy formulation as 'relating a company to its environment . . . [T]he key aspect of the firm's environment is the industry or industries in which it competes.' Industry structure strongly influences the competitive rules of the game as well as the strategies potentially available to firms.

In the competitive forces model, five industry-level forces—entry barriers, threat of substitution, bargaining power of buyers, bargaining power of suppliers, and rivalry among industry incumbents—determine the inherent profit potential of an industry or subsegment of an industry. The approach can be used to help the firm find a position in an industry from which it can best defend itself against competitive forces or influence them in its favor (Porter, 1980: 4).

This 'five-forces' framework provides a systematic way of thinking about how competitive forces work at the industry level and how these forces determine the profitability of different industries and industry segments. The competitive forces framework also contains a number of underlying assumptions about the sources of competition and the nature of the strategy process. To facilitate comparisons with other approaches, we highlight several distinctive characteristics of the framework.

Economic rents in the competitive forces framework are monopoly rents (Teece, 1984). Firms in an industry earn rents when they are somehow able to impede the competitive forces (in either factor markets or product markets) which tend to drive economic returns to zero. Available strategies are described in Porter (1980). Competitive strategies are often aimed at altering the firm's position in the industry vis-à-vis competitors and suppliers. Industry structure plays a central role in determining and limiting strategic action.

Some industries or subsectors of industries become more 'attractive' because they have structural impediments to competitive forces (e.g., entry barriers) that allow firms better opportunities for creating sustainable competitive advantages. Rents are created largely at the industry or subsector level rather than at the firm level. While there is some recognition given to firm-specific assets, differences among firms relate primarily to scale. This approach to strategy reflects its incubation inside the field of industrial organization and in particular the industrial structure school of Mason and Bain[3] (Teece, 1984).

Strategic conflict

The publication of Carl Shapiro's 1989 article, confidently titled 'The Theory of Business Strategy,' announced the emergence of a new approach to business strategy, if not strategic management. This approach utilizes the tools of game theory to analyze the nature of competitive interaction between rival firms. The main thrust of work in this tradition is to reveal how a firm can influence the behavior and actions of rival firms and thus the market environment.[4] Examples of such moves are investment in capacity (Dixit, 1980), R&D (Gilbert and Newberry, 1982), and advertising (Schmalensee, 1983). To be effective, these strategic moves require irreversible commitments.[5] The moves in question will have no effect if they can be costlessly undone. A key idea is that by manipulating the market environment, a firm may be able to increase its profits.

This literature, together with the contestability literature (Baumol, Panzar, and Willig, 1982), has led to a greater appreciation of the role of sunk costs, as opposed to fixed costs, in determining competitive outcomes. Strategic moves can also be designed to influence rivals' behavior through signaling. Strategic signaling has been examined in a number of contexts, including predatory pricing (Kreps and Wilson, 1982a, 1982b) and limit pricing (Milgrom and Roberts, 1982a, 1982b). More recent treatments have emphasized the role of

[3] In competitive environments characterized by sustainable and stable mobility and structural barriers, these forces may become the determinants of industry-level profitability. However, competitive advantage is more complex to ascertain in environments of rapid technological change where specific assets owned by heterogeneous firms can be expected to play a larger role in explaining rents.

[4] The market environment is all factors that influence market outcomes (prices, quantities, profits) including the beliefs of customers and of rivals, the number of potential technologies employed, and the costs or speed with which a rival can enter the industry.

[5] For an excellent discussion of committed competition in multiple contexts, see Ghemawat (1991).

commitment and reputation (e.g., Ghemawat, 1991) and the benefits of firms simultaneously pursuing competition[6] and cooperation (Brandenburger and Nalebnff, 1995, 1996).

In many instances, game theory formalizes long-standing intuitive arguments about various types of business behavior (e.g., predatory pricing, patent races), though in some instances it has induced a substantial change in the conventional wisdom. But by rationalizing observed behavior by reference to suitably designed games, in explaining everything these models also explain nothing, as they do not generate testable predictions (Sutton, 1992). Many specific game-theoretic models admit multiple equilibrium, and a wide range of choice exists as to the design of the appropriate game form to be used. Unfortunately, the results often depend on the precise specification chosen. The equilibrium in models of strategic behavior crucially depends on what one rival believes another rival will do in a particular situation. Thus the qualitative features of the results may depend on the way price competition is modeled (e.g., Bertrand or Cournot) or on the presence or absence of strategic asymmetries such as first-mover advantages. The analysis of strategic moves using game theory can be thought of as 'dynamic' in the sense that multiperiod analyses can be pursued both intuitively and formally. However, we use the term 'dynamic' in this paper in a different sense, referring to situations where there is rapid change in technology and market forces, and 'feedback' effects on firms.[7]

We have a particular view of the contexts in which the strategic conflict literature is relevant to strategic management. Firms that have a tremendous cost or other competitive advantage *vis-à-vis* their rivals ought not be transfixed by the moves and countermoves of their rivals. Their competitive fortunes will swing more on total demand conditions, not on how competitors deploy and redeploy their competitive assets. Put differently, when there are gross asymmetries in competitive advantage between firms, the results of game-theoretic analysis are likely to be obvious and uninteresting. The stronger competitor will generally advance, even if disadvantaged by certain information asymmetries. To be sure, incumbent firms can be undone by new entrants with a dramatic cost advantage, but no 'gaming' will overturn that outcome. On the other hand, if firms' competitive positions are more delicately balanced, as with Coke and Pepsi, and United Airlines and American Airlines, then strategic conflict is of interest to competitive outcomes. Needless to say, there are many such circumstances, but they are rare in industries where there is rapid technological change and fast-shifting market circumstances.

In short, where competitors do not have deep-seated competitive advantages, the moves and countermoves of competitors can often be usefully formulated in game-theoretic terms. However, we doubt that game theory can comprehensively illuminate how Chrysler should compete against Toyota and Honda, or how United Airlines can best respond to Southwest Airlines since Southwest's advantage is built on organizational attributes which United cannot readily replicate.[8] Indeed, the entrepreneurial side of strategy—how significant new rent streams are created and protected—is largely ignored by the game-theoretic approach.[9] Accordingly, we find that the approach, while important, is most relevant when competitors are closely matched[10] and the population of relevant competitors and the identity of their strategic alternatives can be readily ascertained. Nevertheless, coupled with other approaches it can sometimes yield powerful insights.

However, this research has an orientation that we are concerned about in terms of the implicit framing of strategic issues. Rents, from a game-theoretic perspective, are ultimately a result of managers' intellectual ability to 'play the game.' The adage of the strategist steeped in this approach is 'do unto others before they do unto you.' We worry that fascination with strategic moves and Machiavellian tricks will distract managers from seeking to build more enduring sources of competitive advantage. The approach unfortunately ignores competition as a process involving the development, accumulation, combination, and protection of unique skills and capabilities. Since strategic interactions are what receive focal attention, the impression one might receive from this literature is that success in the marketplace is the result of sophisticated plays and counterplays, when this is generally not the case at all.[11]

[6] Competition and cooperation have also been analyzed outside of this tradition. See, for example, Teece (1992) and Link, Teece and Finan (1996).

[7] Accordingly, both approaches are dynamic, but in very different senses.

[8] Thus even in the air transport industry game-theoretic formulations by no means capture all the relevant dimensions of competitive rivalry. United Airlines' and United Express's difficulties in competing with Southwest Airlines because of United's inability to fully replicate Southwest's operation capabilities is documented in Oittel (1995).

[9] Important exceptions can be found in Brandenburger and Nalebuff (1996) such as their emphasis on the role of complements. However, these insights do not flow uniquely from game theory and can be found in the organizational economics literature (e.g., Teece, 1986a, 1986b; de Figueiredo and Teece, 1996).

[10] When closely matched in an aggregate sense, they may nevertheless display asymmetries which game theorists can analyze.

[11] The strategic conflict literature also tends to focus practitioners on product market positioning rather than on developing the unique assets which make possible superior product market positions (Dierickx and Cool, 1989).

In what follows, we suggest that building a dynamic view of the business enterprise—something missing from the two approaches we have so far identified—enhances the probability of establishing an acceptable descriptive theory of strategy that can assist practitioners in the building of long-run advantage and competitive flexibility. Below, we discuss first the resource-based perspective and then an extension we call the dynamic capabilities approach.

Models of strategy emphasizing efficiency

Resource-based perspective

The resource-based approach sees firms with superior systems and structures being profitable not because they engage in strategic investments that may deter entry and raise prices above long-run costs, but because they have markedly lower costs, or offer markedly higher quality or product performance. This approach focuses on the rents accruing to the owners of scarce firm-specific resources rather than the economic profits from product market positioning.[12] Competitive advantage lies 'upstream' of product markets and rests on the firm's idiosyncratic and difficult-to-imitate resources.[13]

One can find the resources approach suggested by the earlier preanalytic strategy literature. A leading text of the 1960s (Learned *et al.*, 1969) noted that the capability of an organization is its demonstrated and potential ability to accomplish against the opposition of circumstance or competition, whatever it sets out to do. Every organization has actual and potential strengths and weaknesses; it is important to try to determine what they are and to distinguish one from the other. Thus what a firm can do is not just a function of the opportunities it confronts; it also depends on what resources the organization can muster.

Learned *et al.* proposed that the real key to a company's success or even to its future development lies in its ability to find or create 'a competence that is truly distinctive.'[14] This literature also recognized the constraints on firm behavior and, in particular, noted that one should not assume that management 'can rise to any occasion.' These insights do appear to keenly anticipate the resource-based approach that has since emerged, but they did not provide a theory or systematic framework for analyzing business strategies. Indeed, Andrews (1987: 46) noted that 'much of what is intuitive in this process is yet to be identified.' Unfortunately, the academic literature on capabilities stalled for a couple of decades.

New impetus has been given to the resource-based approach by recent theoretical developments in organizational economics and in the theory of strategy, as well as by a growing body of anecdotal and empirical literature[15] that highlights the importance of firm-specific factors in explaining firm performance. Cool and Schendel (1988) have shown that there are systematic and significant performance differences among firms which belong to the same strategic group within the U.S. pharmaceutical industry. Rumelt (1991) has shown that intraindustry differences in profits are greater than inter-industry differences in profits, strongly suggesting the importance of firm-specific factors and the relative unimportance of industry effects.[16] Jacobsen (1988) and Hansen and Wernerfelt (1989) made similar findings.

A comparison of the resource by based approach and the competitive forces approach (discussed earlier in the paper) in terms of their implications for the strategy process is revealing. From the first perspective, an entry decision looks roughly as follows: (1) pick an industry (based on its 'structural attractiveness'); (2) choose an entry strategy based on conjectures about competitors' rational strategies; (3) if not already possessed, acquire or otherwise obtain the requisite assets to compete in the market. From this perspective, the process of identifying and developing the requisite assets is not particularly problematic. The process involves nothing more than choosing rationally among a well-defined set of investment alternatives. If assets are not already owned, they can be bought. The resource-based perspective is strongly at odds with this conceptualization.

From the resource-based perspective, firms are heterogeneous with respect to their resources/ capabilities/ endowments. Further, resource endowments are 'sticky:' at least in the short run, firms are to some degree stuck with what they have and may have to live with what they lack.[17] This stickiness arises for three reasons. First, business development is viewed as an extremely complex process.[18]

[12] In the language of economics, rents flow from unique firm-specific assets that cannot readily be replicated, rather than from tactics which deter entry and keep competitors off balance. In short, rents are Ricardian.

[13] Teece (1982: 46) saw the firm as having 'a variety of end products which it can produce with its organizational technology.'

[14] Elsewhere Andrews (1987: 47) defined a distinctive competence as what an organization can do particularly well.

[15] Studies of the automobile and other industries displayed differences in organization which often underlay differences amongst firms. See, for example, Womack, Jones, and Roos, 1991; Hayes and Clark, 1985; Barney, Spender and Reve, 1994; Clark and Fujimoto, 1991; Henderson and Cockburn, 1994; Nelson, 1991; Levinthal and Myatt, 1994.

[16] Using FTC line of business data, Rumelt showed that stable industry effects account for only 8 percent of the variance in business unit returns. Furthermore, only about 40 percent of the dispersion in industry returns is due to stable industry effects.

[17] In this regard, this approach has much in common with recent work on organizational ecology (e.g., Freeman and Boeker, 1984) and also on commitment (Ghemawat, 1991: 17–25).

[18] Capability development, however, is not really analyzed.

Quite simply, firms lack the organizational capacity to develop new competences quickly (Dierickx and Cool, 1989). Secondly, some assets are simply not readily tradeable, for example, tacit know-how (Teece, 1976, 1980) and reputation (Dierickx and Cool, 1989). Thus, resource endowments cannot equilibrate through factor input markets. Finally, even when an asset can be purchased, firms may stand to gain little by doing so. As Barney (1986) points out, unless a firm is lucky, possesses superior information, or both, the price it pays in a competitive factor market will fully capitalize the rents from the asset.

Given that in the resources perspective firms possess heterogeneous and sticky resource bundles, the entry decision process suggested by this approach is as follows: (1) identify your firm's unique resources; (2) decide in which markets those resources can earn the highest rents; and (3) decide whether the rents from those assets are most effectively utilized by (a) integrating into related market(s), (b) selling the relevant intermediate output to related firms, or (c) selling the assets themselves to a firm in related businesses (Teece, 1980, 1982).

The resource-based perspective puts both vertical integration and diversification into a new strategic light. Both can be viewed as ways of capturing rents on scarce, firm-specific assets whose services are difficult to sell in intermediate markets (Penrose, 1959; Williamson, 1975; Teece, 1980, 1982, 1986a, 1986b; Wernerfelt, 1984). Empirical work on the relationship between performance and diversification by Wernerfelt and Montgomery (1988) provides evidence for this proposition. It is evident that the resource-based perspective focuses on strategies for exploiting existing firm-specific assets.

However, the resource-based perspective also invites consideration of managerial strategies for developing new capabilities (Wernerfelt, 1984). Indeed, if control over scarce resources is the source of economic profits, then it follows that such issues as skill acquisition, the management of knowledge and know-how (Shuen, 1994), and learning become fundamental strategic issues. It is in this second dimension, encompassing skill acquisition, learning, and accumulation of organizational and intangible or 'invisible' assets (Itami and Roehl, 1987), that we believe lies the greatest potential for contributions to strategy.

The dynamic capabilities approach: overview

The global competitive battles in high-technology industries such as semiconductors, information services, and software have demonstrated the need for an expanded paradigm to understand how competitive advantage is achieved. Well-known companies like IBM, Texas Instruments, Philips, and others appear to have followed a 'resource-based strategy' of accumulating valuable technology assets, often guarded by an aggressive intellectual property stance. However, this strategy is often not enough to support a significant competitive advantage. Winners in the global marketplace have been firms that can demonstrate timely responsiveness and rapid and flexible product innovation, coupled with the management capability to effectively coordinate and redeploy internal and external competences. Not surprisingly, industry observers have remarked that companies can accumulate a large stock of valuable technology assets and still not have many useful capabilities.

We refer to this ability to achieve new forms of competitive advantage as 'dynamic capabilities' to emphasize two key aspects that were not the main focus of attention in previous strategy perspectives. The term 'dynamic' refers to the capacity to renew competences so as to achieve congruence with the changing business environment; certain innovative responses are required when time-to-market and timing are critical, the rate of technological change is rapid, and the nature of future competition and markets difficult to determine. The term 'capabilities' emphasizes the key role of strategic management in appropriately adapting, integrating, and reconfiguring internal and external organizational skills, resources, and functional competences to match the requirements of a changing environment.

One aspect of the strategic problem facing an innovating firm in a world of Schumpeterian competition is to identify difficult-to-imitate internal and external competences most likely to support valuable products and services. Thus, as argued by Dierickx and Cool (1989), choices about how much to spend (invest) on different possible areas are central to the firm's strategy. However, choices about domains of competence are influenced by past choices. At any given point in time, firms must follow a certain trajectory or path of competence development. This path not only defines what choices are open to the firm today, but it also puts bounds around what its internal repertoire is likely to be in the future. Thus, firms, at various points in time, make long-term, quasi-irreversible commitments to certain domains of competence.[19]

The notion that competitive advantage requires both the exploitation of existing internal and external firm-specific capabilities, and developing new ones is partially developed in Penrose (1959), Teece (1982), and Wernerfelt (1984). However, only recently have researchers begun to focus on the specifics of how some organizations first develop firm-specific capabilities and how they renew competences to

[19] Deciding, under significant uncertainty about future states of the world, which long-term paths to commit to and when to change paths is the central strategic problem confronting the firm. In this regard, the work of Ghemawat (1991) is highly germane to the dynamic capabilities approach to strategy.

respond to shifts in the business environment.[20] These issues are intimately tied to the firm's business processes, market positions, and expansion paths. Several writers have recently offered insights and evidence on how firms can develop their capability to adapt and even capitalize on rapidly changing environments.[21] The dynamic capabilities approach seeks to provide a coherent framework which can both integrate existing conceptual and empirical knowledge, and facilitate prescription. In doing so, it builds upon the theoretical foundations provided by Schumpeter (1934), Penrose (1959), Williamson (1975, 1985), Barney (1986), Nelson and Winter (1982), Teece (1988), and Teece *et al.* (1994).

Toward a dynamic capabilities framework

Terminology

In order to facilitate theory development and intellectual dialogue, some acceptable definitions are desirable. We propose the following.

Factors of production

These are 'undifferentiated' inputs available in disaggregate form in factor markets. By undifferentiated we mean that they lack a firm-specific component. Land, unskilled labor, and capital are typical examples. Some factors may be available for the taking, such as public knowledge. In the language of Arrow, such resources must be 'non-fugitive.'[22] Property rights are usually well defined for factors of roduction.

Resources[23]

Resources are firm-specific assets that are difficult if not impossible to imitate. Trade secrets and certain specialized production facilities and engineering experience are examples. Such assets are difficult to transfer among firms because of transactions costs and transfer costs, and because the assets may contain tacit knowledge.

Organizational routines/competences

When firm-specific assets are assembled in integrated clusters spanning individuals and groups so that they enable distinctive activities to be performed, these activities constitute organizational routines and processes. Examples include quality, miniaturization, and systems integration. Such competences are typically viable across multiple product lines, and may extend outside the firm to embrace alliance partners.

Core competences

We define those competences that define a firm's fundamental business as core. Core competences must accordingly be derived by looking across the range of a firm's (and its competitors) products and services.[24] The value of core competences can be enhanced by combination with the appropriate complementary assets. The degree to which a core competence is distinctive depends on how well endowed the firm is relative to its competitors, and on how difficult it is for competitors to replicate its competences.

Dynamic capabilities

We define dynamic capabilities as the firm's ability to integrate, build, and reconfigure internal and external competences to address rapidly changing environments. Dynamic capabilities thus reflect an organization's ability to achieve new and innovative forms of competitive advantage given path dependencies and market positions (Leonard-Barton, 1992).

Products

End products are the final goods and services produced by the firm based on utilizing the competences that it possesses. The performance (price, quality, etc.) of a firm's products relative to its competitors at any point in time will depend upon its competences (which over time depend on its capabilities).

Markets and strategic capabilities

Different approaches to strategy view sources of wealth creation and the essence of the strategic problem faced by firms differently. The competitive forces framework sees the strategic problem in terms of industry structure, entry deterrence, and positioning; game-theoretic models view the strategic problem as one of interaction between rivals with certain, expectations about how each other will behave;[25] resource-based perspectives have focused on the exploitation of firm-specific assets. Each approach asks different, often complementary questions. A key step in building a conceptual framework related to dynamic capabilities is to identify the foundations upon which distinctive and difficult-

[20] See, for example, Iansiti and Clark (1994) and Henderson (1994).

[21] See Hayes *et al.* (1988), Prahalad and Hamel (1990), Dierickx and Coot (1989), Chandler (1990), and Teece (1993).

[22] Arrow (1996) defines fugitive resources as once that can move cheaply amongst individuals and firms.

[23] *We do not like the term 'resource' and believe it is misleading. We prefer to use the term firm-spccific asset. We use it here to try and maintain links to the literature on the resource-based approach which we believe is important.*

[24] Thus Eastman Kodak's core competence might be considered imaging, IBM's might be considered integrated data processing and service, and Motorola's untethered communications.

[25] In sequential move games, each player looks ahead and anticipates his rival's future responses in order to reason back and decide action, i.e., look forward, reason backward.

to-replicate advantages can be built, maintained, and enhanced.

A useful way to vector in on the strategic elements of the business enterprise is first to identify what is not strategic. To be strategic, a capability must be honed to a user need[26] (so there is a source of revenues), unique (so that the products/services produced can be priced without too much regard to competition) and difficult to replicate (so profits will not be competed away). Accordingly, any assets or entity which are homogeneous and can be bought and sold at an established price cannot be all that strategic (Barney, 1986). What is it, then, about firms which undergirds competitive advantage?

To answer this, one must first make some fundamental distinctions between markets and internal organization (firms). The essence of the firm, as Coase (1937) pointed out, is that it displaces market organization. It does so in the main because inside the firms one can organize certain types of economic activity in ways one cannot using markets. This is not only because of transaction costs, as Williamson (1975, 1985) emphasized, but also because there are many types of arrangements where injecting high-powered (market like) incentives might well be quite destructive of cooperative activity and learning.[27] Inside an organization, exchange cannot take place in the same manner that it can outside an organization, not just because it might be destructive to provide high-powered individual incentives, but because it is difficult if not impossible to tightly calibrate individual contribution to a joint effort. Hence, contrary to Arrow's (1969) view of firms as quasi markets, and the task of management to inject markets into firms, we recognize the inherent limits and possible counterproductive results of attempting to fashion firms into simply clusters of internal markets. In particular, learning and internal technology transfer may well be jeopardized.

Indeed, what is distinctive about firms is that they are domains for organizing activity in a nonmarket-like fashion. Accordingly, as we discuss what is distinctive about firms, we stress competences/capabilities which are ways of organizing and getting things done which cannot be accomplished merely by using the price system to coordinate activity.[28] The very essence of most capabilities/competences is that they cannot be readily assembled through markets (Teece, 1982, 1986a; Zander and Kogut, 1995). If the ability to assemble competences using markets is what is meant by the firm as a nexus of contracts (Fama, 1980), then we unequivocally state that the firm about which we theorize cannot be usefully modeled as a nexus of contracts. By 'contract' we are referring to a transaction undergirded by a legal agreement, or some other arrangement which clearly spells out rights, rewards, and responsibilities. Moreover, the firm as a nexus of contracts suggests a series of bilateral contracts orchestrated by a coordinator. Our view of the firm is that the organization takes place in a more multilateral fashion, with patterns of behavior and learning being orchestrated in a much more decentralized fashion, but with a viable headquarters operation.

The key point, however, is that the properties of internal organization cannot be replicated by a portfolio of business units amalgamated just through formal contracts as many distinctive elements of internal organization simply cannot be replicated in the market.[29] That is, entrepreneurial activity cannot lead to the immediate replication of unique organizational skills through simply entering a market and piecing the parts together overnight. Replication takes time, and the replication of best practice may be illusive. Indeed, firm capabilities need to be understood not in terms of balance sheet items, but mainly in terms of the organizational structures and managerial processes which support productive activity. By construction, the firm's balance sheet contains items that can be valued, at least at original market prices (cost). It is necessarily the case, therefore, that the balance sheet is a poor shadow of a firm's distinctive competences.[30] That which is distinctive cannot be bought and sold short of buying the firm itself, or one or more of its subunits.

There are many dimensions of the business firm that must be understood if one is to grasp firm-level distinctive competences/capabilities. In this paper we merely identify several classes of factors that will help determine a firm's distinctive competence and dynamic capabilities. We organize these in three categories: processes, positions, and paths. The essence of competences and capabilities is embedded in organizational processes of one kind or another. But the content of these processes and the opportunities they afford for developing competitive advantage at any point in time are shaped significantly by the assets the firm possesses

[26] Needless to say, users need not be the current customers of the enterprise. Thus a capability can be the basis for diversification into new product markets.

[27] Indeed, the essence of internal organization is that it is a domain of unleveraged or low-powered incentives. By unleveraged we mean that rewards are determined at the group or organization level, not primarily at the individual level, in an effort to encourage team behavior, not individual behavior.

[28] We see the problem of market contracting as a matter of coordination as much as we see it a problem of opportunism in the fact of contractual hazards. In this sense, we are consonant with both Richardson (1960) and Williamson (1975. 1985).

[29] As we note in Teece *et al.* (1994), the conglomerate offers few if any efficiencies because there is little provided by the conglomerate form that shareholders cannot obtain for themselves simply by holding a diversified portfolio of stocks.

[30] Owners' equity may reflect, in part, certain historic capabilities. Recently, some scholars have begun to attempt to measure organizational capability using financial statement data. See Baldwin and Clark (1991) and Lev and Sougiannis (1992).

(internal and market) and by the evolutionary path it has adopted/inherited. Hence organizational processes, shaped by the firm's asset positions and molded by its evolutionary and co-evolutionary paths, explain the essence of the firm's dynamic capabilities and its competitive advantage.

Processes, positions, and paths

We thus advance the argument that the competitive advantage of firms lies with its managerial and organizational processes, shaped by its (specific) asset position, and the paths available to it.[31] By managerial and organizational processes, we refer to the way things are done in the firm, or what might be referred to as its routines, or patterns of current practice and learning. By position we refer to its current specific endowments of technology, intellectual property, complementary assets, customer base, and its external relations with suppliers and complementors. By paths we refer to the strategic alternatives available to the firm, and the presence or absence of increasing returns and attendant path dependencies.

Our focus throughout is on asset structures for which no ready market exists, as these are the only assets of strategic interest. A final section focuses on replication and imitation, as it is these phenomena which determine how readily a competence or capability can be cloned by competitors, and therefore distinctiveness of its competences and the durability of its advantage.

The firm's processes and positions collectively encompass its competences and capabilities. A hierarchy of competences/capabilities ought to be recognized, as some competences may be on the factory floor, some in the R&D labs, some in the executive suites, and some in the way everything is integrated. A difficult-to-replicate or difficult-to-imitate competence was defined earlier as a distinctive competence. As indicated, the key feature of distinctive competence is that there is not a market for it, except possibly through the market for business units. Hence competences and capabilities are intriguing assets as they typically must be built because they cannot be bought.

Organizational and managerial processes

Organizational processes have three roles: coordination/integration (a static concept); learning (a dynamic concept); and reconfiguration (a transformational concept). We discuss each in turn.

Coordination/integration While the price system supposedly coordinates the economy,[32] managers coordinate or integrate activity inside the firm. How efficiently and effectively internal coordination or integration is achieved is very important (Aoki, 1990).[33] Likewise for external coordination.[34] Increasingly, strategic advantage requires the integration of external activities and technologies. The growing literature on strategic alliances, the virtual corporation, and buyer–supplier relations and technology collaboration evidences the importance of external integration and sourcing.

There is some field-based empirical research that provides support for the notion that the way production is organized by management inside the firm is the source of differences in firms' competence in various domains. For example, Garvin's (1988) study of 18 room air-conditioning plants reveals that quality performance was not related to either capital investment or the degree of automation of the facilities. Instead, quality performance was driven by special organizational routines. These included routines for gathering and processing information, for linking customer experiences with engineering design choices, and for coordinating factories and component suppliers.[35] The work of Clark and Fujimoto (1991) on project development in the automobile industry also illustrates the role played by coordinative routines. Their study reveals a significant degree of variation in how different firms coordinate the various activities required to bring a new model from concept to market. These differences in coordinative routines and capabilities seem to have a significant impact on such performance variables as development cost, development lead times, and quality. Furthermore, Clark and Fujimoto tended to find significant firm-level differences in coordination routines and these differences seemed to have persisted for a long time. This suggests that routines related to coordination are firm-specific in nature.

Also, the notion that competence/capability is embedded in distinct ways of coordinating and combining helps to

[31] We are implicitly saying that fixed assets, like plant and equipment which can be purchased off-the-shelf by all industry participants, cannot be the source of a firm's competitive advantage. In as much as financial balance sheets typically reflect such assets, we point out that the assets that matter for competitive advantage are rarely reflected in the balance sheet, while those that do not are.

[32] The coordinative properties of markets depend on prices being 'sufficient' upon which to base resource allocation decisions.

[33] Indeed, Ronald Coase, author of the pathbreaking 1937 article 'The nature of the firm,' which focused on the costs of organizational coordination inside the firm as compared to across the market, half a century later has identified as critical the understanding of 'why the costs of organizing particular activities differs among firms' (Coase, 1988: 47). We argue that a firm's distinctive ability needs to be understood as a reflection of distinctive organizational or coordinative capabilities. This form of integration (i.e., inside business units) is different from the integration between business units; they could be viable on a stand-alone basis (external integration). For a useful taxonomy, see Iansiti and Clark (1994).

[34] Shuen (1994) examines the gains and hazards of the technology make-vs.-buy decision and supplier codevelopment.

[35] Garvin (1994) provides a typology of organizational processes.

explain how and why seemingly minor technological changes can have devastating impacts on incumbent firms' abilities to compete in a market. Henderson and Clark (1990), for example, have shown that incumbments in the photolithographic equipment industry were sequentially devastated by seemingly minor innovations that, nevertheless, had major impacts on how systems had to be configured. They attribute these difficulties to the fact that systems-level or 'architectural' innovations often require new routines to integrate and coordinate engineering tasks. These findings and others suggest that productive systems display high interdependency, and that it may not be possible to change one level without changing others. This appears to be true with respect to the 'lean production' model (Womack *et al.*, 1991) which has now transformed the Taylor or Ford model of manufacturing organization in the automobile industry.[36] Lean production requires distinctive shop floor practices and processes as well as distinctive higher-order managerial processes. Put differently, organizational processes often display high levels of coherence, and when they do, replication may be difficult because it requires systemic changes throughout the organization and also among inter-organizational linkages, which might be very hard to effectuate. Put differently, partial imitation or replication of a successful model may yield zero benefits.[37]

The notion that there is a certain rationality or coherence to processes and systems is not quite the same concept as corporate culture, as we understand the latter. Corporate culture refers to the values and beliefs that employees hold; culture can be a *de facto* governance system as it mediates the behavior of individuals and economizes on more formal administrative methods. Rationality or coherence notions are more akin to the Nelson and Winter (1982) notion of organizational routines. However, the routines concept is a little too amorphous to properly capture the congruence amongst processes and between processes and incentives that we have in mind. Consider a professional service organization like an accounting firm. If it is to have relatively high-powered incentives that reward individual performance, then it must build organizational processes that channel individual behavior; if it has weak or low-powered incentives, it must find symbolic ways to recognize the high performers, and it must use alternative methods to build effort and enthusiasm. What one may think of as styles of organization in fact contain necessary, not discretionary, elements to achieve performance.

Recognizing the congruences and complementarities among processes, and between processes and incentives, is critical to the understanding of organizational capabilities. In particular, they can help us explain why architectural and radical innovations are so often introduced into an industry by new entrants. The incumbents develop distinctive organizational processes that cannot support the new technology, despite certain overt similarities between the old and the new. The frequent failure of incumbents to introduce new technologies can thus be seen as a consequence of the mismatch that so often exists between the set of organizational processes needed to support the conventional product/service and the requirements of the new. Radical organizational reengineering will usually be required to support the new product, which may well do better embedded in a separate subsidiary where a new set of coherent organizational processes can be fashioned.[38]

Learning Perhaps even more important than integration is learning. Learning is a process by which repetition and experimentation enable tasks to be performed better and quicker. It also enables new production opportunities to be

[36] Fujimoto (1994: 18-20) describes key elements as they existed in the Japanese auto industry as follows: 'The typical volume production system of effective Japanese makers of the 1980s (e.g., Toyota) consists of various intertwined elements that might lead to competitive advantages. Just-in-Time (JIT), Jidoka (automatic defect detection and machine stop), Total Quality Control (TQC), and continuous improvement (Kaizen) are often pointed out as its core subsystems. The elements of such a system include inventory reduction mechanisms by Kanban system; levelization of production volume and product mix (heijunka); reduction of "muda" (non-value adding activities), "mura" (uneven pace of production) and "muri" (excessive workload); production plans based on dealers' order volume (genyo seisan); reduction of die set-up time and lot size in stamping operation; mixed model assembly; piece-by-piece transfer of parts between machines (ikko-nagashi); flexible task assignment for volume changes and productivity improvement (shojinka); multi-task job assignment along the process flow (takotei-mochi); U-shape machine layout that facilitates flexible and multiple task assignment, on-the-spot inspection by direct workers (tsukurikomi); fool-proof prevention of defects (poka-yoke); real-time feedback of production troubles (andon); assembly line stop cord; emphasis on cleanliness, order and discipline on the shop floor (5-S); frequent revision of standard operating procedures by supervisors; quality control circles; standardized tools for quality improvement (e.g., 7 tools for QC. QC story); worker involvement in preventive maintenance (Total Productive Maintenance); low cost automation or semi-automation with just-enough functions); reduction of process steps for saving of tools and dies, and so on. The human-resource management factors that back up the above elements include stable employment of core workers (with temporary workers in the periphery); long-term training of multi-skilled (multitask) workers; wage system based in part on skill accumulation; internal promotion to shop floor supervisors; cooperative relationships with labor unions; inclusion of production supervisors in union members; generally egalitarian policies for corporate welfare, communication and worker motivation. Parts procurement policies are also painted out often as a source of the competitive advantage.'

[37] For a theoretical argument along these lines, see Milgrom and Roberts (1990).

[38] See Abernathy and Clark (1985).

identified.[39] In the context of the firm, if not more generally, learning has several key characteristics. First, learning involves organizational as well as individual skills.[40] While individual skills are of relevance, their value depends upon their employment, in particular organizational settings. Learning processes are intrinsically social and collective and occur not only through the imitation and emulation of individuals, as with teacher–student or master–apprentice, but also because of joint contributions to the understanding of complex problems.[41] Learning requires common codes of communication and coordinated search procedures. Second, the organizational knowledge generated by such activity resides in new patterns of activity, in 'routines,' or a new logic of organization. As indicated earlier, routines are patterns of interactions that represent successful solutions to particular problems. These patterns of interaction are resident in group behavior, though certain subroutines may be resident in individual behavior. The concept of dynamic capabilities as a coordinative management process opens the door to the potential for inter-organizational learning. Researchers (Doz and Shuen, 1990; Mody, 1993) have pointed out that collaborations and partnerships can be a vehicle for new organizational learning, helping firms to recognize dysfunctional routines, and preventing strategic blind-spots.

Reconfiguration and transformation In rapidly changing environments, there is obviously value in the ability to sense the need to reconfigure the firm's asset structure, and to accomplish the necessary internal and external transformation (Amit and Schoemaker, 1993; Langlois, 1994). This requires constant surveillance of markets and technologies and the willingness to adopt best practice. In this regard, benchmarking is of considerable value as an organized process for accomplishing such ends (Camp, 1989). In dynamic environments, narcissistic organizations are likely to be impaired. The capacity to reconfigure and transform is itself a learned organizational skill. The more frequently practiced, the easier accomplished.

Change is costly and so firms must develop processes to minimize low pay-off change. The ability to calibrate the requirements for change and to effectuate the necessary adjustments would appear to depend on the ability to scan the environment, to evaluate markets and competitors, and to quickly accomplish reconfiguration and transformation ahead of competition. Decentralization and local autonomy assist these processes. Firms that have honed these capabilities are sometimes referred to as 'high-flex'.

Positions

The strategic posture of a firm is determined not only by its learning processes and by the coherence of its internal and external processes and incentives, but also by its specific assets. By specific assets we mean for example its specialized plant and equipment. These include its difficult-to-trade knowledge assets and assets complementary to them, as well as its reputational and relational assets. Such assets determine its competitive advantage at any point in time. We identify several illustrative classes.

Technological assets While there is an emerging market for know-how (Teece, 1981), much technology does not enter it. This is either because the firm is unwilling to sell it[42] or because of difficulties in transacting in the market for know-how (Teece, 1980). A firm's technological assets may or may not be protected by the standard instruments of intellectual property law. Either way, the ownership protection and utilization of technological assets are clearly key differentiators among firms. Likewise for complementary assets.

Complementary assets Technological innovations require the use of certain related assets to produce and deliver new products and services. Prior commercialization activities require and enable firms to build such complementarities (Teece, 1986b). Such capabilities and assets, while necessary for the firm's established activities, may have other uses as well. These assets typically lie downstream. New products and processes either can enhance or destroy the value of such assets (Tushman, Newman, and Romanelli, 1986). Thus the development of computers enhanced the value of IBM's direct sales force in office products, while disk brakes rendered useless much of the auto industry's investment in drum brakes.

Financial assets In the short run, a firm's cash position and degree of leverage may have strategic implications. While there is nothing more fungible than cash, it cannot always be raised from external markets without the dissemination of considerable information to potential investors. Accordingly, what a firm can do in short order is often a function of its balance sheet. In the longer run, that ought not be so, as cash flow ought be more determinative.

[39] For a useful review and contribution, see Levitt and March (1988).

[40] Levinthal and March, 1993. Mahooey (1992) and Mahoney and Pandian (1995) suggest that both resources and mental models are intertwined in firm-level teaming.

[41] There is a large literature on learning, although only a small fraction of it deals with organizational learning. Relevant contributors include Levitt and March (1988), Argyris and Schon (1978), Levinthal and March (1981), Nelson and Winter (1982), and Leonard-Barton (1995).

[42] Managers often evoke the 'crown jewels' metaphor. That is, if the technology is released, the kingdom will be lost.

Reputational assets Firms, like individuals, have reputations. Reputations often summarize a good deal of information about firms and shape the responses of customers, suppliers, and competitors. It is sometimes difficult to disentangle reputation from the firm's current asset and market position. However, in our view, reputational assets are best viewed as an intangible asset that enables firms to achieve various goals in the market. Its main value is external, since what is critical about reputation is that it is a kind of summary statistic about the firm's current assets and position, and its likely future behavior. Because there is generally a strong asymmetry between what is known inside the firm and what is known externally, reputations may sometimes be more salient than the true state of affairs, in the sense that external actors must respond to what they know rather than what is knowable.

Structural assets The formal and informal structure of organizations and their external linkages have an important bearing on the rate and direction of innovation, and how competences and capabilities co-evolve (Argyres, 1995; Teece, 1996). The degree of hierarchy and the level of vertical and lateral integration are elements of firm-specific structure. Distinctive governance modes can be recognized (e.g., multiproduct, integrated firms; high 'flex' firms; virtual corporations; conglomerates), and these modes support different types of innovation to a greater or lesser degree. For instance, virtual structures work well when innovation is autonomous; integrated structures work better for systemic innovations.

Institutional assets Environments cannot be defined in terms of markets alone. While public policies are usually recognized as important in constraining what firms can do, there is a tendency particularly by economists, to see these as acting through markets or through incentives. However, institutions themselves are a critical element of the business environment. Regulatory systems, as well as intellectual property regimes, tort laws, and antitrust laws, are also part of the environment. So is the system of higher education and national culture. There are significant national differences here, which is just one of the reasons geographic location matters (Nelson, 1994). Such assets may not be entirely firm specific; firms of different national and regional origin may have quite different institutional assets to call upon because their institutional/policy settings are so different.

Market structure assets Product market position matters, but it is often not at all determinative of the fundamental position of the enterprise in its external environment. Part of the problem lies in defining the market in which a firm competes in a way that gives economic meaning. More importantly, market position in regimes of rapid technological change is often extremely fragile. This is in part because time moves on a different clock in such environments.[43] Moreover, the link between market share and innovation has long been broken, if it ever existed (Teece, 1996). All of this is to suggest that product market position, while important, is too often overplayed. Strategy should be formulated with regard to the more fundamental aspects of firm performance, which we believe are rooted in competences and capabilities and shaped by positions and paths.

Organizational boundaries An important dimension of 'position' is the location of a firm's boundaries. Put differently, the degree of integration (vertical, lateral, and horizontal) is of quite some significance. Boundaries are not only significant with respect to the technological and complementary assets contained within, but also with respect to the nature of the coordination that can be achieved internally as compared to through markets. When specific assets or poorly protected intellectual capital are at issue, pure market arrangements expose the parties to recontracting hazards or appropriability hazards. In such circumstances, hierarchical control structures may work better than pure arms-length contracts.[44]

Paths

Path dependencies Where a firm can go is a function of its current position and the paths ahead. Its current position is often shaped by the path it has traveled. In standard economics textbooks, firms have an infinite range of technologies from which they can choose and markets they can occupy. Changes in product or factor prices will be responded to instantaneously, with technologies moving in and out according to value maximization criteria. Only in the short run are irreversibilities recognized. Fixed costs—such

[43] For instance, an Internet year might well be thought of as equivalent to 10 years on many industry clocks, because as much change occurs in the Internet business in a year that occurs in say the auto industry in a decade.

[44] Williamson (1996: 102–103) has observed, failures of coordination may arise because 'parties that bear a long term bilateral dependency relationship to one another must recognize that incomplete contracts require gap filling and sometimes get out of alignment. Although it is always in the collective interest of autonomous parties to fill gaps, correct errors, and affect efficient realignments, it is also the case that the distribution of the resulting gains is indeterminate. Self-interested bargaining predictably obtains. Such bargaining is itself costly. The main costs, however, are that transactions are maladapted to the environment during the bargaining interval. Also, the prospect of ex post bargaining invites ex ante prepositioning of an inefficient kind.'

as equipment and overheads—cause firms to price below fully amortized costs but never constrain future investment choices. 'Bygones are bygones.' Path dependencies are simply not recognized. This is a major limitation of microeconomic theory.

The notion of path dependencies recognizes that 'history matters.' Bygones are rarely bygones, despite the predictions of rational actor theory. Thus a firm's previous investments and its repertoire of routines (its 'history') constrain its future behavior.[45] This follows because learning tends to be local. That is, opportunities for learning will be 'close in' to previous activities and thus will be transaction and production specific (Teece, 1988). This is because learning is often a process of trial, feedback, and evaluation. If too many parameters are changed simultaneously, the ability of firms to conduct meaningful natural quasi experiments is attenuated. If many aspects of a firm's learning environment change simultaneously, the ability to ascertain cause–effect relationships is confounded because cognitive structures will not be formed and rates of learning diminish as a result. One implication is that many investments are much longer term than is commonly thought.

The importance of path dependencies is amplified where conditions of increasing returns to adoption exist. This is a demand-side phenomenon, and it tends to make technologies and products embodying those technologies more attractive the more they are adopted. Attractiveness flows from the greater adoption of the product amongst users, which in turn enables them to become more developed and hence more useful. Increasing returns to adoption has many sources including network externalities (Katz and Shapiro, 1985), the presence of complementary assets (Teece, 1986b) and supporting infrastructure (Nelson, 1996), learning by using (Rosenberg, 1982), and scale economies in production and distribution. Competition between and amongst technologies is shaped by increasing returns. Early leads won by good luck or special circumstances (Arthur, 1983) can become amplified by increasing returns. This is not to suggest that first movers necessarily win. Because increasing returns have multiple sources, the prior positioning of firms can affect their capacity to exploit increasing returns. Thus, in Mitchell's (1989) study of medical diagnostic imaging, firms already controlling the relevant complementary assets could in theory start last and finish first.

In the presence of increasing returns, firms can compete passively, or they may compete strategically through technology-sponsoring activities.[46] The first type of competition is not unlike biological competition amongst species, although it can be sharpened by managerial activities that enhance the performance of products and processes. The reality is that companies with the best products will not always win, as chance events may cause 'lock-in' on inferior technologies (Arthur, 1983) and may even in special cases generate switching costs for consumers. However, while switching costs may favor the incumbent, in regimes of rapid technological change switching costs can become quickly swamped by switching benefits. Put differently, new products employing different standards often appear with alacrity in market environments experiencing rapid technological change, and incumbents can be readily challenged by superior products and services that yield switching benefits. Thus the degree to which switching costs cause 'lock-in' is a function of factors such as user learning, rapidity of technological change, and the amount of ferment in the competitive environment.

Technological opportunities The concept of path dependencies is given forward meaning through the consideration of an industry's technological opportunities. It is well recognized that how far and how fast a particular area of industrial activity can proceed is in part due to the technological opportunities that lie before it such opportunities are usually a lagged function of foment and diversity in basic science, and the rapidity with which new scientific breakthroughs are being made.

However, technological opportunities may not be completely exogenous to industry, not only because some firms have the capacity to engage in or at least support basic research, but also because technological opportunities are often fed by innovative activity itself. Moreover, the recognition of such opportunities is affected by the organizational structures that link the institutions engaging in basic research (primarily the university) to the business enterprise. Hence, the existence of technological opportunities can be quite firm specific.

Important for our purposes is the rate and direction in which relevant scientific frontiers are being rolled back. Firms engaging in R&D may find the path dead ahead

[45] For further development, see Bercovitz, de Figueiredo, and Teece, 1996.

[46] Because of huge uncertainties, it may be extremely difficult to determine viable strategies early on. Since the rules of the game and the identity of the players will be revealed only after the market has begun to evolve, the pay-off is likely to lie with building and maintaining organizational capabilities that support flexibility. For example, Microsoft's recent about-face and vigorous pursuit of Internet business once the NetScape phenomenon became apparent is impressive, not so much because it perceived the need to change strategy, but because of its organizational capacity to effectuate a strategic shift.

closed off, though breakthroughs in related areas may be sufficiently close to be attractive. Likewise, if the path dead ahead is extremely attractive, there may be no incentive for firms to shift the allocation of resources away from traditional pursuits. The depth and width of technological opportunities in the neighborhood of a firm's prior research activities thus are likely to impact a firm's options with respect to both the amount and level of R&D activity that it can justify. In addition, a firm's past experience conditions the alternatives management is able to perceive. Thus, not only do firms in the same industry face 'menus' with different costs associated with particular technological choices, they also are looking at menus containing different choices.[47]

Assessment

The essence of a firm's competence and dynamic capabilities is presented here as being resident in the firm's organizational processes, that are in turn shaped by the firm's assets (positions) and its evolutionary path. Its evolutionary path, despite managerial hubris that might suggest otherwise, is often rather narrow.[48] What the firm can do and where it can go are thus rather constrained by its positions and paths. Its competitors are likewise constrained. Rents (profits) thus tend to flow not just from the asset structure of the firm and, as we shall see, the degree of its instability, but also by the firm's ability to reconfigure and transform.

The parameters we have identified for determining performance are quite different from those in the standard textbook theory of the firm, and in the competitive forces and strategic conflict approaches to the firm and to strategy.[49] Moreover, the agency theoretic view of the firm as a nexus of contracts would put no weight on processes, positions, and paths. While agency approaches to the firm may recognize that opportunism and shirking may limit what a firm can do, they do not recognize the opportunities and constraints imposed by processes, positions, and paths.

Moreover, the firm in our conceptualization is much more than the sum of its parts—or a team tied together by contracts.[50] Indeed, to some extent individuals can be moved in and out of organizations and, so long as the internal processes and structures remain in place, performance will not necessarily be impaired. A shift in the environment is a far more serious threat to the firm than is the loss of key individuals, as individuals can be replaced more readily than organizations can be transformed. Furthermore, the dynamic capabilities view of the firm would suggest that the behavior and performance of particular firms may be quite hard to replicate, even if its coherence and rationality are observable. This matter and related issues involving replication and imitation are taken up in the section that follows.

Replicability and imitatability of organizational processes and positions

Thus far, we have argued that the competences and capabilities (and hence competitive advantage) of a firm rest fundamentally on processes, shaped by positions and paths. However, competences can provide competitive advantage and generate rents only if they are based on a collection of routines, skills, and complementary assets that are difficult to imitate.[51] A particular set of routines can lose their value if they support a competence which no longer matters in the marketplace, or if they can be readily replicated or emulated by competitors. Imitation occurs when firms discover and simply copy a firm's organizational routines and procedures. Emulation occurs when firms discover alternative ways of achieving the same functionality.[52]

Replication

To understand imitation, one must first understand replication. Replication involves transferring or redeploying competences from one concrete economic setting to another. Since productive knowledge is embodied, this cannot be accomplished by simply transmitting information. Only in those instances where all relevant knowledge is fully codified and understood can replication be collapsed into a simple problem of information transfer. Too often, the contextual dependence of original performance is poorly appreciated, so unless firms have replicated their systems of productive knowledge on many prior occasions, the act of replication is likely to be difficult (Teece, 1976). Indeed, replication and transfer are often impossible absent the transfer of people, though this can be minimized if investments are made to convert tacit knowledge to codified knowledge. Often, however, this is simply not possible.

In short, competences and capabilities, and the routines upon which they rest, are normally rather difficult to

[47] This is a critical element in Nelson and Winter's (1982) view of firms and technical change.

[48] We also recognize that the processes, positions, and paths of customers also matter. See our discussion above on increasing returns, including customer learning and network externalities.

[49] In both the firm is still largely a black box. Certainly, little or no attention is given to processes, positions, and paths.

[50] See Alchian and Demsetz (1972).

[51] We call such competences distinctive. See also Dierickx and Cool (1989) for a discussion of the characteristics of assets which make them a source of rents.

[52] There is ample evidence that a given type of competence (e.g., quality) can be supported by different routines and combinations of skills. For example, the Garvin (1988) and Clark and Fujimoto (1991) studies both indicate that there was no one 'formula' for achieving either high quality or high product development performance.

replicate.[53] Even understanding what all the relevant routines are that support a particular competence may not be transparent. Indeed, Lippman and Rumelt (1992) have argued that some sources of competitive advantage are so complex that the firm itself, let alone its competitors, does not understand them.[54] As Nelson and Winter (1982) and Teece (1982) have explained, many organizational routines are quite tacit in nature. Imitation can also be hindered by the fact few routines are 'stand-alone;' coherence may require that a change in one set of routines in one part of the firm (e.g., production) requires changes in some other part (e.g., R & D).

Some routines and competences seem to be attributable to local or regional forces that shape firms' capabilities at early stages in their lives. Porter (1990), for example, shows that differences in local product markets, local factor markets, and institutions play an important role in shaping competitive capabilities. Differences also exist within populations of firms from the same country. Various studies of the automobile industry, for example, show that not all Japanese automobile companies are top performers in terms of quality, productivity, or product development (see, for example, Clark and Fujimoto, 1991). The role of firm-specific history has been highlighted as a critical factor explaining such firm-level (as opposed to regional or national-level) differences (Nelson and Winter, 1982). Replication in a different context may thus be rather difficult.

At least two types of strategic value flow from replication. One is the ability to support geographic and product line expansion. To the extent that the capabilities in question are relevant to customer needs elsewhere, replication can confer value.[55] Another is that the ability to replicate also indicates that the firm has the foundations in place for learning and improvement. Considerable empirical evidence supports the notion that the understanding of processes, both in production and in management, is the key to process improvement. In short, an organization cannot improve that which it does not understand. Deep process understanding is often required to accomplish codification. Indeed, if knowledge is highly tacit, it indicates that underlying structures are not well understood, which limits learning because scientific and engineering principles cannot be as systematically applied.[56] Instead, learning is confined to proceeding through trial and error, and the leverage that might otherwise come from the application of scientific theory is denied.

Imitation

Imitation is simply replication performed by a competitor. If self-replication is difficult, imitation is likely to be harder. In competitive markets, it is the ease of imitation that determines the sustainability of competitive advantage. Easy imitation implies the rapid dissipation of rents.

Factors that make replication difficult also make imitation difficult. Thus, the more tacit the firm's productive knowledge, the harder it is to replicate by the firm itself or its competitors. When the tacit component is high, imitation may well be impossible, absent the hiring away of key individuals and the transfers of key organization processes.

However, another set of barriers impedes imitation of certain capabilities in advanced industrial countries. This is the system of intellectual property rights, such as patents, trade secrets, and trademarks, and even trade dress.[57] Intellectual property protection is of increasing importance in the United States, as since 1982 the legal system has adopted a more pro-patent posture. Similar trends are evident outside the United States. Besides the patent system, several other factors cause there to be a difference between replication costs and imitation costs. The observability of the technology or the organization is one such important factor. Whereas vistas into product technology can be obtained through strategies such as reverse engineering, this is not the case for process technology, as a firm need not expose its process technology to the outside in order to benefit from it.[58] Firms with product technology, on the other hand, confront the unfortunate circumstances that they must expose what they have got in order to profit from the

[53] See Szulanski's (1995) discussion of the intrafirm transfer of best practice. He quotes a senior vice president of Xerox as saying 'you can see a high performance factory or office, but it just doesn't spread. I don't know why.' Szulanski also discusses the role of benchmarking in facilitating the transfer of best practice.

[54] If so, it is our belief that the firm's advantage is likely to fade, as luck does run out.

[55] Needless to say, there are many examples of firms replicating their capabilities inappropriately by applying extant routines to circumstances where they may not be applicable, e.g., Nestlé's transfer of developed-country marketing methods for infant formula to the Third World (Hartley, 1989). A key strategic need is for firms to screen capabilities for their applicability to new environments.

[56] Different approaches to learning are required depending on the depth of knowledge. Where knowledge is less articulated and structured, trial and error and learning-by-doing are necessary, whereas in mature environments where the underlying engineering science is better understood, organizations can undertake more deductive approaches or what Pisano (1994) refers to as 'learning-before-doing.'

[57] Trade dress refers to the 'look and feel' of a retail establishment, e.g., the distinctive marketing and presentation style of The Nature Company.

[58] An interesting but important exception to this can be found in second sourcing. In the microprocessor business, until the introduction of the 386 chip, Intel and most other merchant semi producers were encouraged by large customers like IBM to provide second sources, i.e., to license and share their proprietary process technology with competitors like AMD and NEC. The microprocessor developers did so to assure customers that they had sufficient manufacturing capability to meet demand at all times

technology. Secrets are thus more protectable if there is no need to expose them in contexts where competitors can learn about them.

One should not, however, overestimate the overall importance of intellectual property protection; yet it presents a formidable imitation barrier in certain particular contexts. Intellectual property protection is not uniform across products, processes, and technologies, and is best thought of as islands in a sea of open competition. If one is not able to place the fruits of one's investment, ingenuity, or creativity on one or more of the islands, then one indeed is at sea.

We use the term appropriability regimes to describe the ease of imitation. Appropriability is a function both of the ease of replication and the efficacy of intellectual property rights as a barrier to imitation. Appropriability is strong when a technology is both inherently difficult to replicate and the intellectual property system provides legal barriers to imitation. When it is inherently easy to replicate and intellectual property protection is either unavailable or ineffectual, then appropriability is weak. Intermediate conditions also exist.

Conclusion

The four paradigms discussed above are quite different, though the first two have much in common with each other (strategizing) as do the last two (economizing). But are these paradigms complementary or competitive? According to some authors, 'the resource perspective complements the industry analysis framework' (Amit and Schoemaker, 1993: 35). While this is undoubtedly true, we think that in several important respects the perspectives are also competitive. While this should be recognized, it is not to suggest that there is only one framework that has value. Indeed, complex problems are likely to benefit from insights obtained from all of the paradigms we have identified plus more. The trick is to work out which frameworks are appropriate for the problem at hand. Slavish adherence to one class to the neglect of all others is likely to generate strategic blind-spots. The tools themselves then generate strategic vulnerability. We now explore these issues further. Table [2.3.1] summarizes some similarities and differences.

Efficiency vs. market power

The competitive forces and strategic conflict approaches generally see profits as stemming from strategizing—that is, from limitations on competition which firms achieve through raising rivals' costs and exclusionary behavior (Teece, 1984). The competitive forces approach in particular leads one to see concentrated industries as being attractive—market positions can be shielded behind entry barriers, and

Table 2.3.1 Paradigms of strategy: salient characteristics

Paradigm	Intellectual roots	Representative authors addressing strategic management questions	Nature of rents	Rationality assumptions of managers	Fundamental units of analysis	Short-run capacity for strategic reorientation	Role of industrial structure	Focal concern
(1) Attenuating competitive forces	Mason, Bain	Porter (1980)	Chamberlinean	Rational	Industries, firms, products	High	Exogenous	Structural conditions and competitor positioning
(2) Strategic conflict	Machiavelli, Schelling, Cournot, Nash, Harsanyi, Shapiro	Ghemawat (1986); Shapiro (1989); Brandenburger and Nalebuff (1995)	Chamberlinean	Hyper-rational	Firms, products	Often infinite	Endogenous	Strategic interactions
(3) Resource-based perspectives	Penrose, Selznick, Christensen, Andrews	Rumelt (1984); Chandler (1966); Wernerfelt (1984); Teece (1980, 1982)	Ricardian	Rational	Resources	Low	Endogenous	Asset fungibility
(4) Dynamic capabilities perspective	Schumpeter, Nelson, Winter, Teece	Dosi, Teece, and Winter (1989); Prahalad and Hamel (1990) Hayes and Wheelwright (1984); Dierickx and Cool (1989) Porter (1990)	Schumpeterian	Rational	Processes, positions, paths	Low	Endogenous	Asset accumulation, replicability and inimitability

rivals costs can be raised. It also suggests that the sources of competitive advantage lie at the level of the industry, of possibly groups within an industry. In text book presentations, there is almost no attention at all devoted to discovering, creating, and commercializing new sources of value.

The dynamic capabilities and resources approaches clearly have a different orientation. They see competitive advantage stemming from high-performance routines operating 'inside the firm,' shaped by processes and positions. Path dependencies (including increasing returns) and technological opportunities mark the road ahead. Because of imperfect factor markets, or more precisely the nontradability of 'soft' assets like values, culture, and organizational experience, distinctive competences and capabilities generally cannot be acquired; they must be built. This sometimes takes years—possibly decades. In some cases, as when the competence is protected by patents, replication by a competitor is ineffectual as a means to access the technology. The capabilities approach accordingly sees definite limits on strategic options, at least in the short run. Competitive success occurs in part because of policies pursued and experience and efficiency obtained in earlier periods.

Competitive success can undoubtedly flow from both strategizing and economizing,[59] but along with Williamson (1991) we believe that 'economizing is more fundamental than strategizing or put differently, that economy is the best strategy.'[60] Indeed, we suggest that, except in special circumstances, too much 'strategizing' can lead firms to underinvest in core competences and neglect dynamic capabilities, and thus harm long-term competitiveness.

Normative implications

The field of strategic management is avowedly normative. It seeks to guide those aspects of general management that have material effects on the survival and success of the business enterprise. Unless these various approaches differ in terms of the framework and heuristics they offer management, then the discourse we have gone through is of limited immediate value. In this paper, we have already alluded to the fact that the capabilities approach tends to steer managers toward creating distinctive and difficult-to-imitate advantages and avoiding games with customers and competitors. We now survey possible differences, recognizing that the paradigms are still in their infancy and cannot confidently support strong normative conclusions.

Unit of analysis and analytic focus

Because in the capabilities and the resources framework business opportunities flow from a firm's unique processes, strategy analysis must be situational.[61] This is also true with the strategic conflict approach. There is no algorithm for creating wealth for the entire industry. Prescriptions they apply to industries or groups of firms at best suggest overall direction, and may indicate errors to be avoided. In contrast, the competitive forces approach is not particularly firm specific; it is industry and group specific.

Strategic change

The competitive forces and the strategic conflict approach, since they pay little attention to skills, know-how, and path dependency, tend to see strategic choice occurring with relative facility. The capabilities approach sees value augmenting strategic change as being difficult and costly. Moreover, it can generally only occur incrementally. Capabilities cannot easily be bought; they must be built. From the capabilities perspective, strategy involves choosing among and committing to long-term paths or trajectories of competence development.

In this regard, we speculate that the dominance of competitive forces and the strategic conflict approaches in the United States may have something to do with observed differences in strategic approaches adopted by some U.S. and some foreign firms. Hayes (1985) has noted that American companies tend to favor 'strategic leaps' while, in contrast, Japanese and German companies tend to favor incremental, but rapid, improvements.

Entry strategies

Here the resources and the capabilities approaches suggest that entry decisions must be made with reference to the competences and capabilities which new entrants have, relative to the competition. Whereas the other approaches tell you little about where to look to find likely entrants, the capabilities approach identifies likely entrants. Relatedly, whereas the entry deterrence approach suggests an unconstrained search for new business opportunities, the capabilities approach suggests that such opportunities lie close in to

[59] Phillips (1971) and Demsetz (1974) also made the case that market concentration resulted from the competitive success of more efficient firms, and not from entry barriers and restrictive practices.

[60] We concur with Williamson that economizing and strategizing are not mutually exclusive. Strategic ploys can be used to disguise inefficiencies and to promote economizing outcomes, as with pricing with reference to learning curve costs. Our view of economizing is perhaps more expansive than Williamson's as it embraces more than efficient contract design and the minimization of transactions costs. We also address production and organizational economies, and the distinctive ways that things are accomplished inside the business enterprise.

[61] On this point, the strategic conflict and the resources and capabilities are congruent. However, the aspects of 'situation' that matter are dramatically different, as described earlier in this paper.

one's existing business. As Richard Rumelt has explained it in conversation, 'the capabilities approach suggests that if a firm looks inside itself, and at its market environment, sooner or later it will find a business opportunity.'

Entry timing

Whereas the strategic conflict approach tells little abut where to look to find likely entrants, the resources and the capabilities approach identifies likely entrants and their timing of entry. Brittain and Freeman (1980) using population ecology methodologies argued that an organization is quick to expand when there is a significant overlap between its core capabilities and those needed to survive in a new market. Recent research (Mitchell, 1989) showed that the more industry-specialized assets or capabilities a firm possesses, the more likely it is to enter an emerging technical subfield in its industry, following a technological discontinuity. Additionally, the interaction between specialized assets such as firm-specific capabilities and rivalry had the greatest influence on entry timing.

Diversification

Related diversification—that is, diversification that builds upon or extends existing capabilities—is about the only form of diversification that a resources/capabilities framework is likely to view as meritorious (Rumelt, 1974; Teece, 1980, 1982; Teece *et al.*, 1994). Such diversification will be justifiable when the firms' traditional markets decline.[62] The strategic conflict approach is likely to be a little more permissive; acquisitions that raise rivals' costs or enable firms to effectuate exclusive arrangements are likely to be seen as efficacious in certain circumstances.

Focus and specialization

Focus needs to be defined in terms of distinctive competences or capability, not products. Products are the manifestation of competences, as competences can be molded into a variety of products. Product market specialization and decentalization configured around product markets may cause firms to neglect the development of core competences and dynamic capabilities, to the extent to which competences require accessing assets across divisions.

The capabilities approach places emphasis on the internal processes that a firm utilizes, as well as how they are deployed and how they will evolve. The approach has the benefit of indicating that competitive advantage is not just a function of how one plays the game; it is also a function of the 'assets' one has to play with, and how these assets can be deployed and redeployed in a changing market.

Future directions

We have merely sketched an outline for a dynamic capabilities approach. Further theoretical work is needed to tighten the framework, and empirical research is critical to helping us understand how firms get to be good, how they sometimes stay that way, why and how they improve, and why they sometimes decline.[63] Researchers in the field of strategy need to join forces with researchers in the fields of innovation, manufacturing, and organizational behavior and business history if they are to unlock the riddles that lie behind corporate as well as national competitive advantage. There could hardly be a more ambitious research agenda in the social sciences today.

References

Abernathy, W. J. and K. Clark (1985). 'Innovation: Mapping the winds of creative destruction', ***Research Policy***, 14, pp. 3–22.

Alchian, A. A. and H. Demsetz (1972). 'Production, information costs, and economic organization', ***American Economic Review***, 62, pp. 777–795.

Amit, R. and P. Schoemaker (1993). 'Strategic assets and organizational rent', ***Strategic Management Journal*** 14(1), pp. 33–46.

Andrews, K. (1987). ***The Concept of Corporate Strategy*** (3rd ed.). Dow Jories-Irwin, Homewood, IL.

Aoki, M. (1990). 'The participatory generation of information rents and the theory of the firm'. In M. Aoki, B. Gustafsson and O. E Williamson (eds.), ***The Firm as a Nexus of Treaties***. Sage, London, pp. 26–52.

Argyres, N. (1995). 'Technology strategy, governance structure and interdivisional coordination', ***Journal of Economic Behavior and Organization***, 28, pp. 337–358.

Argyris, C. and D. Schon (1978). ***Organizational Learning***. Addison-Wesley, Reading, MA.

Arrow, K. (1969). 'The organization of economic activity: Issues pertinent to the choice of market vs. nonmarket allocation'. In ***The Analysis and Evaluation of Public Expenditures: The PPB System***, I.U.S. Joint Economic Committee, 91st Session. U.S. Government Printing Office, Washington, DC, pp. 59–73.

Arrow, K. (1996) 'Technical information and industrial structure', ***Industrial and Corporate Change***, 5(2), pp. 645–652.

Arthur, W. B. (1983). 'Competing technologies and lock-in by historical events: The dynamics of allocation under increasing

[62] Cantwell shows that the technological competence of firms persists over time, gradually evolving through firm-specific learning. He shows that technological diversification has been greater for chemicals and pharmaceuticals than for electrical and electronic-related fields, and he offers as an explanation the greater straight-ahead opportunities in electrical and electronic fields than in chemicals and pharmaceuticals. See Cantwell (1993).

[63] For a gallant start, see Miyazaki (1995) and McGrath *et al.* (1996). Chandler's (1990) work on scale and scope, summarized in Teece (1993), provides some historical support for the capabilities approach. Other relevant studies can be found in a special issue of *Industrial and Corporate Change* 3(3), 1994, that was devoted to dynamic capabilities.

returns', working paper WP-83-90, International Institute for Applied Systems Analysis, Laxenburg, Austria.

Bain, J. S. (1959). ***Industrial Organization***. Wiley, New York.

Baldwin, C. and K. Clark (1991). 'Capabilities and capital investment: New perspectives on capital budgeting', Harvard Business School working paper #92–004.

Barney, J. B. (1986). 'Strategic factor markets: Expectations, luck, and business strategy', ***Management Science*** 32(10), pp. 1231–1241.

Barney, J. B., J.-C. Spender and T. Reve (1994). ***Crafoord Lectures***, Vol. 6. Chartwell-Bratt, Bromley, U.K. and Lund University Press, Lund, Sweden.

Baumol, W., J. Panzar and R. Willing (1982). ***Contestable Markets and the Theory of Industry Structure***. Harcourt Brace Jovanovich, New York.

Bercovitz, J. E. L., J. M. de Figueiredo and D. J. Teece (1996). 'Firm capabilities and managerial decisionmaking: A theory of innovation biases'. In R. Garud, P. Nayyar and Z. Shapira (eds), ***Innovation: Oversights and Foresights***. Cambridge University Press, Cambridge, U.K. pp. 233–259.

Brandenburger, A. M. and B. J. Nalebuff (1996). ***Co-opetition***. Doubleday, New York.

Brandenburger, A. M. and B. J. Nalebuff (1995). 'The right game: Use game theory to shape strategy', ***Harvard Business Review***, 73(4), pp. 57–71.

Brittain, J. and J. Freeman (1980). 'Organizational proliferation and density-dependent selection'. In J. R. Kimberly and R. Miles (eds.). ***The Organizational Life Cycle***. Jossey-Bass, San Francisco, CA, pp. 291–338.

Camp, R. (1989). ***Benchmarking: The Search for Industry Best practices that Lead to Superior Performance***. Quality Press, Milwaukee, WL.

Cantwell, J. (1993). 'Corporate technological specialization in international industries'. In M. Casson and J. Creedy (eds.), ***Industrial Concentration and Economic Inequality***. Edward Elgar, Aldershot, pp. 216–232.

Chandler, A.D., Jr. (1966). ***Strategy and Structure***, Doubleday, Anchor Books Edition, New York.

Chandler, A. D., Jr. (1990). ***Scale and Scope: The Dynamics of Industrial Competition***. Harvard University Press, Cambridge, MA.

Clark, K. and T. Fujimoto (1991). ***Product Development Performance: Strategy, Organization and Management in the World Auto Industries***. Harvard Business School Press, Cambridge, MA.

Coase, R. (1937). 'The nature of the firm', ***Economica***, 4, pp. 386–405.

Coase, R. (1988). 'Lecture on the Nature of the Firm, III', ***Journal of Law, Economics and Organization***, 4, pp. 33–47.

Cool, K. and D. Schendel (1988). 'Performance differences among strategic group members', ***Strategic Management Journal***, 9(3), pp. 207–223.

de Figueiredo, J. M. and D. J. Teece (1996). 'Mitigating procurement hazards in the context of innovation', ***Industrial and Corporate Change***, 5(2), pp. 537–559.

Demsetz, H. (1974). 'Two systems of belief about monopoly'. In H. Goldschmid, M. Mann and J. F. Weston (eds.), ***Industrial Concentration: The New Learning***. Little, Brown, Boston, MA, pp. 161–184.

Dierickx, I. and K. Cool (1989). 'Asset stock accumulation and sustainability of competitive advantage', ***Management Science***, 35(12), pp. 1504–1511.

Dixit, A. (1980). 'The role of investment in entry deterrence', ***Economic Journal***, 90, pp. 95–106.

Dosi, G., D. J. Teece and S. Winter (1989). 'Toward a theory of corporate coherence: Preliminary remarks', unpublished paper, Center for Research in Management, University of California at Berkeley.

Doz, Y. and A. Shuen (1990). 'From intent to outcome: A process framework for partnerships', INSEAD working paper.

Fama, E. F. (1980). 'Agency problems and the theory of the firm', ***Journal of Political Economy***, 88, pp. 288–307.

Freeman, J. and W. Boeker (1984). 'The ecological analysis of business strategy'. In G. Carroll and D. Vogel (eds.), ***Strategy and Organization***. Pitman, Boston, MA, pp. 64–77.

Fujimoto, T. (1994). 'Reinterpreting the resource-capability view of the firm: A case of the development-production systems of the Japanese automakers', draft working paper, Faculty of Economics, University of Tokyo.

Garvin, D. (1988). ***Managing Quality***. Free Press, New York.

Garvin, D. (1994). 'The processes of organization and management', Harvard Business School working paper #94–084.

Ghemawat, P. (1986). 'Sustainable advantage', ***Harvard Business Review***, 64(5), pp. 53–58.

Ghemawat, P. (1991). ***Commitment: The Dynamics of Strategy***. Free Press, New York.

Gilbert, R. J. and D. M. G. Newberry (1982). 'Preemptive patenting and the persistence of monopoly', ***American Economic Review***, 72, pp. 514–526.

Gittell, J. H. (1995). 'Cross-functional coordination, control and human resource systems: Evidence from the airline industry', unpublished Ph.D. thesis, Massachusetts Institute of Technology.

Hansen, G. S. and B. Wernerfelt (1989). 'Determinants of firm performance: The relative importance of economic and organizational factors', ***Strategic Management Journal***, 10(5), pp. 399–411.

Hartley, R. F. (1989). ***Marketing Mistakes***. Wiley, New York.

Hayes, R. (1985). 'Strategic planning: Forward in reverse', ***Harvard Business Review***, 63(6), pp. 111–119.

Hayes, R. and K. Clark (1985). 'Exploring the sources of productivity differences at the factory level'. In K. Clark, R. M, Hayes and C. Lorenz (eds.), ***The Uneasy Alliance: Managing the Productivity–Technology Dilemma***. Harvard Business School Press, Boston, MA, pp. 151–188.

Hayes, R. and S. Wheelwright (1984). ***Restoring our Competitive Edge: Competing Through Manufacturing***. Wiley, New York.

Hayes, R., S. Wheelwright and K. Clark (1988). ***Dynamic Manufacturing: Creating the Learning Organization***. Free Press, New York.

Henderson, R. M. (1994). 'The evolution of integrative capability: Innovation in cardiovascular drug discovery', ***Industrial and Corporate Change***, 3(3), pp. 607–630.

Henderson, R. M. and K. B. Clark (1990). 'Architectural innovation: The reconfiguration of existing product technologies and the failure of established firms', ***Administrative Science Quarterly***, 35, pp. 9–30.

Henderson, R. M. and I. Cockbum (1994). 'Measuring competence? Exploring firm effects in pharmaceutical research. ***Strategic Management Journal***, Summer Special Issue, 15, pp. 63–84.

Iansiti, M. and K. B. Clark (1994). 'Integration and dynamic capability: Evidence from product development in automobiles and mainframe computers', ***Industrial and Corporate Change***, 3(3), pp. 557–605.

Itami, H. and T. W. Roehl (1987). ***Mobilizing Invisible Assets***. Harvard University Press, Cambridge, MA.

Jacobsen, R. (1988). 'The persistence of abnormal returns', *Strategic Management Journal*, 9(5), pp. 415–430.

Katz, M. and C. Shapiro (1985). 'Network externalities, competition and compatibility', *American Economic Review*, 75, pp. 424–440.

Kreps, D. M. and R. Wilson (1982a). 'Sequential equilibria', *Econometrica*, 50, pp. 863–894.

Kreps, D. M. and R. Wilson (1982b). 'Reputation and imperfect information', *Journal of Economic Theory*, 27, pp. 253–279.

Langlois, R. (1994). 'Cognition and capabilities: Opportunities seized and missed in the history of the computer industry', working paper, University of Connecticut. Presented at the conference on Technological Oversights and Foresights, Stern School of Business, New York University, 11–12 March 1994.

Learned, E., C. Christensen, K. Andrews and W. Guth (1969). *Business Policy: Text and Cases*. Irwin, Homewood, IL.

Leonard-Barton, D. (1992). 'Core capabilities and core rigidities: A paradox in managing new product development', *Strategic Management Journal*, Summer Special Issue, 13, pp. 111–125.

Leonard-Barton, D. (1995). *Wellsprings of Knowledge*. Harvard Business School Press, Boston, MA.

Lev, B. and T. Sougiannis (1992). 'The capitalization, amortization and value-relevance of R&D', unpublished manuscript, University of California, Berkeley, and University of Illinois, Urbana–Champaign.

Levinthal, D. and J. March (1981). 'A model of adaptive organizational search', *Journal of Economic Behavior and Organization*, 2, pp. 307–333.

Levinthal, D. A. and J. G. March (1993). 'The myopia of learning', *Strategic Management Journal*, Winter Special Issue, 14, pp. 95–112.

Levinthal, D. and J. Myatt (1994). 'Co-evolution of capabilities and industry: The evolution of mutual fund processing', *Strategic Management Journal*, Winter Special Issue, 15, pp. 45–62.

Levitt, B. and J. March (1988). 'Organizational learning', *Annual Review of Sociology*, 14, pp. 319–340.

Link, A. N., D. J. Teece and W. F. Finan (October 1996). 'Estimating the benefits from collaboration: The Case of SEMATECH', *Review of Industrial Organization*, 11, pp. 737–751.

Lippman, S. A. and R. P. Rumelt (1992) 'Demand uncertainty and investment in industry-specific capital', *Industrial and Corporate Change*, 1(1), pp. 235–262.

Mahoney, J. (1995). 'The management of resources and the resources of management', *Journal of Business Research*, 33(2), pp. 91–101.

Mahoney, J. T. and J. R. Pandian (1992). 'The resource-based view within the conversation of strategic management', *Strategic Management Journal*, 13(5), pp. 363–380.

Mason, E. (1949). 'The current state of the monopoly problem in the U.S.', *Harvard Law Review*, 62, pp. 1265–1285.

McGrath, R. G., M-H. Tsai, S. Venkataraman and I. C. MacMillan (1996). 'Innovation, competitive advantage and rent: A model and test', *Management Science*, 42(3), pp. 389–403.

Milgrom, P. and J. Roberts (1982a). 'Limit pricing and entry under incomplete information: An equilibrium analysis', *Econometrica*, 50, pp. 443–459.

Milgrom, P. and J. Roberts (1982b). 'Predation, reputation and entry deterrence', *Journal of Economic Theory*, 27, pp. 280–312.

Milgrom, P. and J. Roberts (1990). 'The economics of modern manufacturing: Technology, strategy, and organization', *American Economic Review*, 80(3), pp. 511–528.

Mitchell, W. (1989). 'Whether and when? Probability and timing of incumbents' entry into emerging industrial subfields', *Administrative Science Quarterly*, 34, pp. 208–230.

Miyazaki, K. (1995). *Building Competences in the Firm: Lessons from Japanese and European Optoelectronics*. St. Martins Press, New York.

Mody, A. (1993). 'Learning through alliances', *Journal of Economic Behavior and Organization*, 20(2), pp. 151–170.

Nelson, R. R. (1991). 'Why do firms differ, and how does it matter?' *Strategic Management Journal*, Winter Special Issue, 12, pp. 61–74.

Nelson, R. R. (1994). 'The co-evolution of technology, industrial structure, and supporting institutions', *Industrial and Corporate Change*, 3(1), pp. 47–63.

Nelson. R. (1996). 'The evolution of competitive or comparative advantage: A preliminary report on a study', WP-96-21, International Institute for Applied Systems Analysis, Laxenburg, Austria.

Nelson, R. and S. Winter (1982). *An Evolutionary Theory of Economic Change*. Harvard University Press, Cambridge, MA.

Penrose, E. (1959). *The Theory of the Growth of the Firm*. Basil Blackwell, London.

Phillips, A. C. (1971). *Technology and Market Structure*. Lexington Books, Toronto.

Pisano, G. (1994). 'Knowledge integration and the locus of learning: An empirical analysis of process development', *Strategic Management Journal*, Winter Special Issue, 15, pp. 85–100.

Porter, M. E. (1980). *Competitive Strategy*. Free Press, New York.

Porter, M. E. (1990). *The Competitive Advantage of Nations*. Free Press, New York.

Prahalad, C. K. and G. Hamel (1990). 'The core competence of the corporation', *Harvard Business Review*, 68(3), pp. 79–91.

Richardson, G. B. H. (1960, 1990). *Information and Investment*. Oxford University Press, New York.

Rosenberg, N. (1982). *Inside the Black Box: Technology and Economics*. Cambridge University Press, Cambridge, MA.

Rumelt, R. P. (1974). *Strategy, Structure and Economic Performance*. Harvard University Press, Cambridge, MA.

Rumelt, R. P. (1984). 'Towards a strategic theory of the firm'. In R. B. Lamb (ed.), *Competitive Strategic Management*. Prentice-Hall, Englewood Cliffs, NJ, pp. 556–570.

Rumelt, R. P. (1991). 'How much does industry matter?', *Strategic Management Journal*, 12(3), pp. 167–185.

Rumelt, R. P., D. Schendel and D. Teece (1994). *Fundamental Issues in Strategy*. Harvard Business School Press, Cambridge, MA.

Schmalensee, R. (1983). 'Advertising and entry deterrence: An exploratory model', *Journal of Political Economy*, 91(4), pp. 636–653.

Schumpeter, J. A. (1934). *Theory of Economic Development*. Harvard University Press, Cambridge, MA.

Schumpeter, J. A. (1942). *Capitalism, Socialism, and Democracy*. Harper, New York.

Shapiro, C. (1989). 'The theory of business strategy', *RAND Journal of Economics*, 20(1), pp. 125–137.

Shuen, A. (1994). 'Technology sourcing and learning strategies in the semiconductor industry', unpublished Ph.D. dissertation. University of California, Berkeley.

Sutton, J. (1992). 'Implementing game theoretical models in industrial economies', In A. Del Monte (ed.), *Recent Developments in the Theory of Industrial Organization*. University of Michigan Press, Ann Arbor, MI, pp. 19–33.

Szulanski, G. (1995). 'Unpacking stickiness: An empirical investigation of the barriers to transfer best practice inside the firm', *Academy of Management Journal*, Best Papers Proceedings, pp. 437–441.

Teece, D. J. (1976). *The Multinational Corporation and the Resource Cost of International Technology Transfer*. Ballinger, Cambridge, MA.

Teece, D. J. (1980). 'Economics of scope and the scope of the enterprise', *Journal of Economic Behavior and Organization*, 1, pp. 223–247.

Teece, D. J. (1981). 'The market for know-how and the efficient international transfer of technology', *Annals of the Academy of Political and Social Science*, 458, pp. 81–96.

Teece, D. J. (1982). 'Towards an economic theory of the multiproduct firm', *Journal of Economic Behavior and Organization*, 3, pp. 39–63

Teece, D. J. (1984). 'Economic analysis and strategic management', *California Management Review*, 26(3), pp. 87–110.

Teece, D. J. (1986a). 'Transactions cost economics and the multinational enterprise', *Journal of Economic Behavior and Organization*, 7, pp. 21–45.

Teece, D. J. (1986b). 'Profiting from technological innovation', *Research Policy*, 15(6), pp. 285–305.

Teece, D. J. 1988. 'Technological change and the nature of the firm'. In G. Dosi, C. Freeman, R. Nelson, G. Silverberg and L. Soete (eds.), *Technical Change and Economic Theory*. Pinter Publishers, New York, pp. 256–281.

Teece, D. J. (1992). 'Competition, cooperation, and innovation: Organizational arrangements for regimes of rapid technological progress', *Journal of Economic Behavior and Organization*, 18(1), pp. 1–25.

Teece, D. J. (1993). 'The dynamics of industrial capitalism: Perspectives on Alfred Chandler's Scale and Scope (1990)', *Journal of Economic Literature*, 31(1), pp. 199–225.

Teece, D. J.(1996) 'Firm organization, industrial structure, and technological innovation', *Journal of Economic Behavior and Organization*, 31, pp. 193–224.

Teece, D. J. and G. Pisano (1994). 'The dynamic capabilities of firms: An introduction', *Industrial and Corporate Change*, 3(3), pp. 537–556.

Teece, D. J., R. Rumelt, G. Dosi and S. Winter (1994). 'Understanding corporate coherence: Theory and evidence', *Journal of Economic Behavior and Organization*, 23, pp. 1–30.

Tushman, M. L., W. H. Newman and E. Romanelli (1986). 'Convergence and upheaval: Managing the unsteady pace of organizational evolution', *California Management Review*, 29(1), pp. 29–44.

Wernerfelt, B. (1984). 'A resource-based view of the firm', *Strategic Management Journal*, 5(2), pp. 171–180.

Wernerfelt, B. and C. Montgomery (1988). 'Tobin's Q and the importance of focus in firm performance', *American Economic Review*, 78(1), pp. 246–250.

Williamson, O. E. (1975). *Markets and Hierarchies*. Free Press, New York.

Williamson, O. E. (1985). *The Economic Institutions of Capitalism*. Free Press, New York.

Williamson, O. E. (1991). 'Strategizing, economizing, and economic organization', *Strategic Management Journal*, Winter Special Issue, 12, pp. 75–94.

Williamson, O. E. (1996) *The Mechanisms of Governance*. Oxford University Press, New York.

Womack, J., D. Jones and D. Roos (1991). *The Machine that Changed the World*. Harper-Perennial, New York.

Zander, U. and B. Kogut (1995). 'Knowledge and the speed of the transfer and imitation of organizational capabilities: An empirical test', *Organization Science*, 6(1), pp. 76–92.

Section 3

Routes to advantage

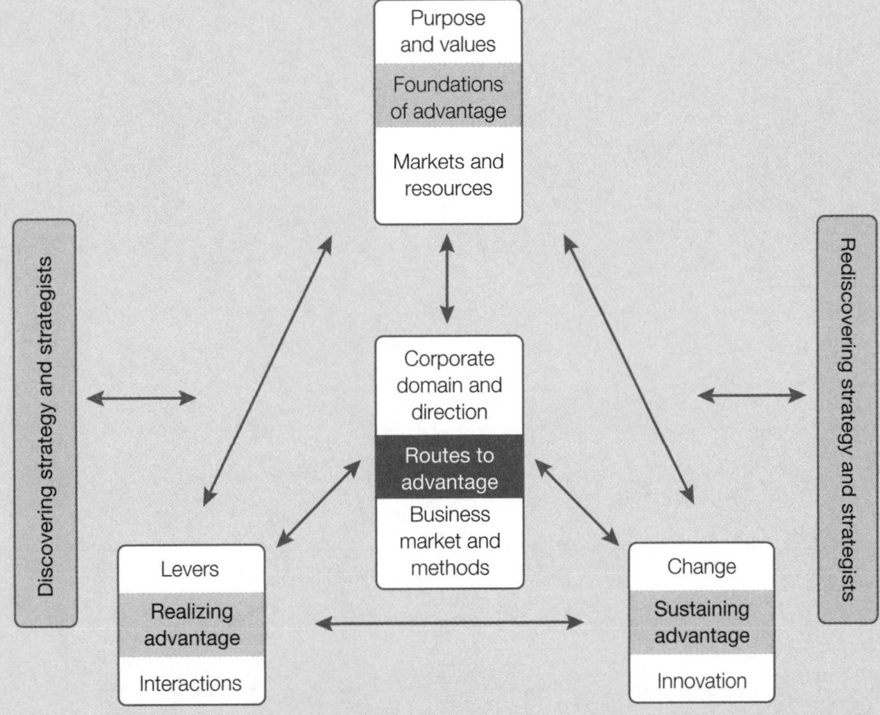

7

Corporate and global strategy

Domain and direction

To succeed in the global bazaar requires a global mindset.

(Narayana Murthy, chairman and chief mentor, Infosys)

Introduction

In the previous two chapters, we focused on the foundations of advantage. We now turn our attention to the routes of advantage, examining domain and direction in the context of corporate and global strategy: specifically, what businesses the corporation should be in and how should the configuration of these businesses be managed (Porter, 1987)? When we travel to other countries, we take great comfort in seeing global brands such as McDonald's, Burger King, Starbucks, KFC, Coca-Cola, and Unilever products. These provide us with a certain degree of comfort given the universal consistency of their product offerings. The differences between high streets in major worldwide cities are being reduced dramatically with the growth of global brands and organizations. The scale of global companies can be staggering. How do such organizations develop a global mindset, as Narayana Murthy of Infosys describes in the opening quote of the chapter? China Mobile had over 611 million subscribers by June 2011, which was half that of Vodafone globally. It adds between 4 million and 5 million subscribers every month to its network. Tesco has built a business outside the UK that is nearly twice the size of its UK operations; in the UK market, £1 in every £6 spent in retailing is spent in Tesco. How do companies achieve such scale and dominance in global marketplaces?

The focus in this chapter is to examine corporate-level routes to advantage and, in particular, the nature, scope, and configuration of businesses in which the organization should operate (see Figure 7.1). We begin by focusing on domain-related questions, including fit, corporate parenting styles, type of corporate parenting, and how value is created and destroyed. We then focus on direction, examining the diversification debate, in terms of both related and unrelated diversification. For the latter part of the chapter, we turn our attention to global strategy. In particular, we examine the rationale behind global strategy and the drivers of globalization. The rewards and dangers of pursuing global strategy are considered, as well as the standardization and culture issues with which corporate managers have to contend. We conclude the section on global strategies by outlining other international strategies: namely, multi-domestic, international, and transnational strategies.

While few organizations pursue a truly global strategy, the reality for most is that they must look beyond national borders to survive. Competitive pressures, consumer trends, and technological developments do not respect organizational or national boundaries. The strategic challenge and paradox for strategists charged with pursuing a global strategy is the matter of how far the firm goes in localizing or globalizing its products and services: local versus global, or, as Ohmae (1990) articulated it, 'thinking local, acting global'. The issue at corporate level is to determine the most appropriate way in which to structure fit between business units and how to create value that will benefit the business as a whole (the domain question), and then to consider direction with respect to the reach of the organization.

Figure 7.1 Overview of corporate and global strategy

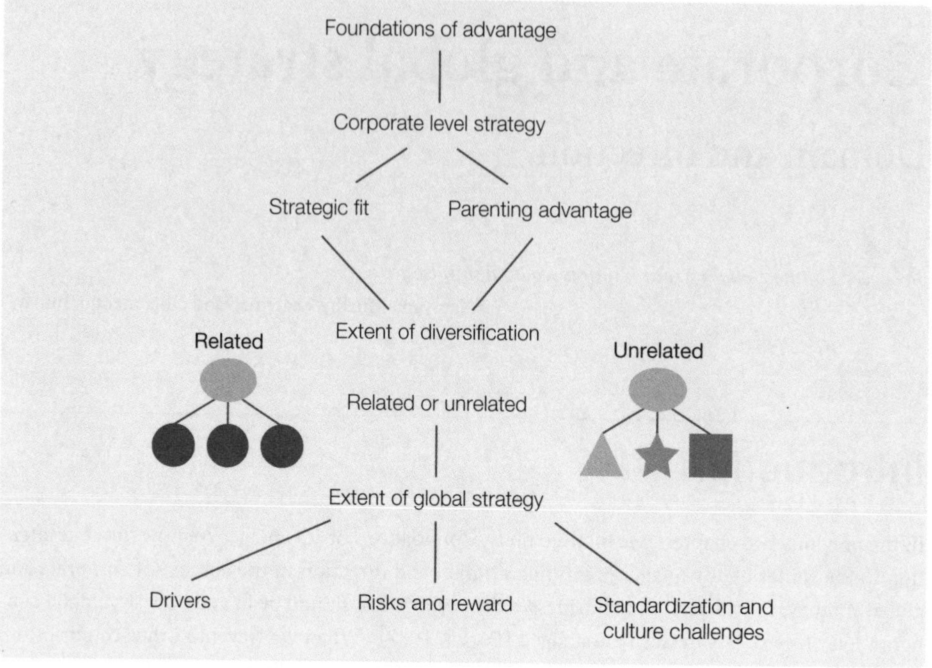

Routes to advantage

There are various routes to advantage (see Table 7.1). The focus of corporate-level strategy is on setting the overall domain and direction of the company, dealing with how best to organize the firm and how to leverage its foundations of advantage for competitive success. The key questions of who we are and what business(es) we are in are the remit of corporate-level strategy. Issues of corporate parenting style, synergy, **resource** allocation, and cross-cultural management are also the remit of corporate-level strategy. We can use Vodafone as an example of **corporate strategy**. In 2009, it had 323 million customers, with ownership interests in thirty countries across five continents and a partner network in a further forty countries. Vittorio Coloa, group chief executive officer (CEO),

Table 7.1 Levels of strategy

Levels of strategy	Strategic management challenge	Focus	Some key issues	Whose responsibility/ strategist's role
Corporate-level strategy	Orientation challenge	Who we are What businesses are we in?	Value creation Industry definition Resource allocation Organizational design Synergy Cross-cultural issues	CEO Board of directors Chairman of the board Top management team
Business-level strategy	Relevance and trade-off challenge	What makes us unique and relevant?	Cost and/or quality focus Consumer relevance	SBU managers or Heads of function
Operational-level strategy		How sustainable is our business model?	Delivering objectives Systems and procedures management	Operational managers

has responsibility for setting the overall strategy direction for Vodafone. The task for the CEO, top management, and the strategist is to make corporate-level strategic objectives a lived reality for everyone in the organization, while at the same time ensuring alignment and value creation.

Business-level strategy (the focus of Chapter 8) is the means by which organizations crystallize advantage into various aspects of their business operations and activities. Specifically, it deals with markets and with methods of delivering business-level strategy. Here, the focus is on how the organization should compete in a given business and the best methods or bridging strategies to facilitate this (Child, 2005), such as organic growth, **joint venture**, and strategic **alliances**. Business-level strategy tends to focus on building uniqueness and competitive dominance, and attempts to use the foundations of advantage to ensure that the firm achieves or exceeds a threshold level of competitiveness in its chosen competitive arena. In the case of Vodafone, in 2008, Michel Combes, CEO of Europe, and Paul Donovan, CEO Central Europe, Middle East, Asia Pacific, and Affiliates, were tasked with implementing and delivering Vodafone corporate strategies at business-unit level.

Operational-level strategy is tasked with ensuring that, from a day-to-day perspective, the strategy of the business is being implemented. For Vodafone, in 2010, Guy Laurence, CEO UK, and Jeroen Hoencamp, CEO Ireland (appointed July 2010), were tasked with ensuring that business-level strategy became a reality in the UK and Ireland, respectively. At business level, a decision might be made to undertake joint ventures, merge, or acquire. The task of operational-level strategy is to ensure that these initiatives are implemented successfully. Operational-level strategy can be very messy, unstructured, and seem pointless to those people tasked with implementing this level of strategy. Consequently, the support of business-level and corporate-level strategy is necessary, through organizational design, resource allocation, and communication channels. Mintzberg (1994: 74) sums up the various routes to advantage:

> the strategy hierarchy is conventionally described to flow from corporate strategies (intentions concerning the portfolio of businesses), to business strategies (intended positions on specific product markets), to functional strategies (intentions concerning marketing, production, sourcing, etc.).

Arguably, within small firms and single business organizations, the distinction between corporate-level and business-level strategy becomes blurred.

Corporate-level strategy

Definitions of corporate-level strategy vary. Vance (1970: 5) notes that 'Corporate strategy fundamentally is about the deployment of resources', while Grant (1995, cited in Bowman and Helfat, 2001: 1) argues that 'corporate strategy deals with the ways in which a corporate manages a set of businesses together'. The key focus of corporate-level strategy is how best to generate value from resources, based on the domain and direction set for the firm. In Figure 7.2, we see that Vodafone's corporate strategy is designed to achieve further scope and an increased level of returns. This was revamped in 2006 to reflect growing market pressures and again in 2008 in response to the global recession. This exemplifies the fact that assumptions and routes of advantage should be systematically reconsidered and altered where appropriate (what we termed the 'continuous change challenge' in Chapter 1).

For Vodafone, this means attempting to develop structures and processes at corporate level that will support business and operation strategies across its network, in a way that is seamless to customers, but which will ultimately achieve the stated objective of delighting them. What is interesting to note is that the key focus remains on delivering shareholder value, as well as on responding to both market and technological changes.

Corporate-level strategy should focus on the composition of business, resource allocation, control of business-unit performance, coordination of business units, and the creation of company cohesiveness and direction (Grant, 1995: 396–397). According to Vance (1970), corporate-level strategy should meet three criteria.

Figure 7.2 Vodafone's corporate-level strategy

Post-2006

Our strategy is founded on five core strategic objectives:

- Revenue stimulation and cost reduction in Europe
- Innovate and deliver on our customers' total communications needs
- Deliver strong growth in emerging markets
- Actively manage our portfolio to maximise returns
- Align capital structure and shareholder returns policy to strategy

Post-2008

We will pursue a growth strategy focused particularly on Europe, Africa and India

1. Mobile data
2. Enterprise
3. Emerging markets
4. Total communications
5. New services-to-machine services and financial mobile services

We will continue to drive benefits from the Group's scale advantage and cost focus.
We will seek to generate free cash flow or liquidity from non-controlled assets and investments.
We will continue to apply capital discipline to our approach to investment.

Source: http://www.vodafone.com/content/index/investors/company_information/strategy.html

1. It recognizes and understands how the forces of the past have affected the organization.
2. It is responsive to the current forces of change.
3. It is capable of implementing programmes based on the first two considerations.

At corporate level, companies such as Imperial Tobacco, Whitbread, and Cable and Wireless must find a balance between understanding the domain of the organization (what business(es) it should be in) and navigating the direction of development. Our next section considers the domain questions of appropriate fit, parenting styles, and creating value.

The issue of fit

For corporate-level strategy, the fit between the corporate parent and the characteristics of its businesses is one aspect of achieving some form of parenting advantage: a business unit that is part of a larger corporation can be conferred with competitive advantages through the corporate parent. The other aspect is a fit across the decisions that the parent makes about each of its businesses (Campbell *et al.*, 1995). Having a fit between corporate-level strategy and business-unit strategy is essential in creating and adding shareholder value and to ensure that the company, as a whole, maintains its competitiveness in the markets in which it competes. The role of corporate-level strategists is to define the purpose, embed corporate ambition, and instill organizational values. Barlett and Ghoshal (1994: 88) put this succinctly: 'Purpose, not strategy, is the reason an organization exists. Its definition and articulation must be top management's first responsibility.'

The fit issue for corporate parents also encompasses management of risk, investment perspective (long term versus short term), and having the appropriate organizational structure that supports the achievement of strategic objectives. This ties into having an appropriate balance and configuration of businesses. Achieving fit requires an alignment between resources, organizations, and businesses, as Collis and Montegomery (1998: 72) describe:

> An outstanding corporate strategy is not a random collection of individual building blocks but a carefully constructed system of interdependent parts ... all elements are aligned with one another. The alignment is driven by the nature of the firm's resources—its special assets, skills and capabilities. The firm's resources are the unifying thread, the element that ultimately determines the others.

The role of corporate parent

One of the questions often posed by managers at lower levels of an organization is what value the corporate parent adds to the day-to-day operations of the organization. Does it provide the organization with an advantage? The role of the corporate centre includes: business planning, through which the corporate shapes the plans, domain, and direction for the business units; the evaluation of investment plans; the selection of key managerial talent for business units; the rotation of key talent throughout the business units; motivation by providing career incentives; coordination and support; and resource allocation (Ginsberg, 1990; van Oijen and Douma, 2000). The approach that a corporate parent takes to managing its business units is manifest in its corporate parenting style.

Corporate parenting style

Parenting style falls into two categories: minimum corporate parenting and value-adding parenting (Goold and Campbell, 2002). Minimum corporate parenting centres around ensuring the survival of the firm. This includes ensuring that constraints such as legal, governance, regulatory, tax compliance, and health and safety issues are complied with by the organization in different jurisdictions. Other minimum roles of the corporate parent might include raising capital, dealing with shareholders, appointing senior managers, and developing an appropriate firm structure to allow these tasks to be fulfilled. This minimalist approach might be found in large conglomerates.

Value-adding parenting involves the clear articulation of the parenting propositions and a parent with a clear view of how it influences the adding of value to the business. Hanson in the UK, once owned and run by Lord Hanson and Lord White of Hull, who set up the Hanson Trust in 1964, added value to ailing businesses through its management teams' turnaround capability (Imperial Tobacco, the Energy Group, and Millennium Chemicals). Virgin's corporate branding parenting proposition can be deployed in a variety of unrelated competitive arenas. Goold and Campbell (2002) note that the nature of corporate parenting is dependent on complex interdependent structures, which include:

- retaining, or sharing with other units, more responsibilities;
- being more involved in guiding coordination between units;
- being less able to exercise control through unit-specific, objective output-based measures of performance; and
- needing to pay more attention to the design and working of the organization.

From this list, it is evident that significant interdependencies are necessary to achieve the coordination and value-adding aspects of corporate parents. Achieving some degree of uniformity in an organization might be difficult in practice.

Parenting fit assessment

At the core of corporate parenting is the fit between the parent at corporate level and the business units in order to create value. Assessing this parenting style requires an assessment of the following, according to Campbell *et al.* (1995):

- the parent's mental map—values, aspirations, rules of thumb, biases, and success formulas that guide parent managers as they deal with businesses;
- parenting structures, systems, and processes—how parents create value through human resources, resource allocation, decision making, transfer pricing system, coordination and linkage mechanisms;
- central functions and resource—how the corporate parent provides support to front-line management, in terms of corporate brand, financial assets, etc.;
- experience and skills of corporate parent management—having managers whose expertise creates, nurtures, and supports business units and their relationship with the corporate parent; and
- decentralized contract between corporate parent and business unit—how does the corporate parent influence the behaviour of business units? Corporate parent contributions should be directed towards issue that concern the business unit and not those that could cause harm.

Campbell *et al.*'s (1995) assessment spans individuals, structures, processes, experience, and behaviour, and in doing so poses some fundamental questions about parenting styles at corporate level. In using this type of assessment, the strategist can see whether there is a natural fit between corporate parenting characteristics, styles, opportunities, and the capability of the business unit to leverage benefit from them. Opportunities can come from external sources or from parenting. Parenting opportunities can arise from size and age, management, business definition, predictable errors, linkages, common capabilities, special expertise, external relations, major decisions, and changes (Campbell *et al.*, 1995).

In their parenting fit matrix, Campbell *et al.* (1995) identified four quadrants, with implications for corporate strategy based upon the positive or negative impact of corporate parenting fit. These positions focused on the nature of the relationship between the corporate parent and the business unit, with the relationships including 'heartland businesses', 'edge-of-heartland businesses', 'ballast businesses', 'alien territory businesses', and 'value-trap businesses'. The heartland position is that in which the corporate parent has real understanding of how to add value to its business through parenting advantage, in addition to being able to capitalize on opportunities through parent characteristics that enhance business positions. Businesses at the edge of heartland are those to which the corporate parent can add value in some aspects of the businesses, but not in all. Businesses at the edge of heartland may move, over time, to become core heartland businesses.

The ballast position consists of businesses that fit with the corporate parent, but which may not create significant value, because they may have been part of the corporate family for a number of years. Ballast businesses may support corporate parents by providing significant cash flows that are consistent and reliable. The real danger for corporate parents is that businesses in the ballast position move to the alien territory business, in which the fit, corporate parenting advantage, and value creation have passed. In that context, corporate parents have to give careful consideration to divesting themselves of alien territory businesses. This can cause difficulty if the businesses in question have a historical association with the brand.

The final position is that of value-trap businesses, for which there is no fit or parenting advantage between a corporate parent and its businesses. Having value-trap businesses can have a significant negative impact on parenting advantage and lead to myopic thinking among corporate managers about value creation and opportunities, rather than their being cognizant about the real risk and dangers of having such businesses as part of the corporate family. Using the parenting fit matrix highlights the impact of the corporate parent. For example, EDF, one of the world's leading energy companies, could use the parenting fit matrix to understand the advantage it provides in areas such as biomass, geothermal, energy efficiency, and wind and solar energy.

Creating or destroying value

The core role of any corporate parent is to add and create value for the overall organization. The key test for any corporate parent is whether the business unit or function area would be better off as part of the parent's corporate entity or on its own. Saab, owned by General Motors (GM) in early 2009, was under pressure given the financial losses that its parent had suffered. This meant that GM had to consider the fit between itself and the rest of its business units in the context of declining global demand for cars. Fit between corporate parent and the business units is essential; as Campbell *et al.* (1995: 122) put it, 'Whether a parent and its businesses fit is a tough question that few managers address.' The disturbing reality for many organizations is that corporate parents can actually destroy value rather than creating it. Van Oijen and Douma (2000: 568) put it more bluntly: 'It is not diversification but fit that appears to determine performance.'

Corporate parents can destroy value through heavy policing and monitoring of performance targets, and when the parent fails to create synergy or coordination within the firm. Companies such as Shell have rolled out SAP systems to improve organizational efficiency and coordination, and other companies such as Philips use shared service centres for back-office functions in an attempt to create value. Essentially, where corporate parents do not add value through organizational platforms such as SAP or shared service centres, they risk hindering the functioning of business unit managers in their day-to-day activity.

Corporate parents can also destroy value in central functions and services roles if these activities are not properly aligned with the business units and managers they are meant to support, or are a costly overhead and so eat into the scarce resources of the firm. In terms of corporate development, parents can also destroy value by misjudging the value of corporate development activities or, as Campbell *et al.* (1996: 380) note, 'The weight of the research evidence indicates that the majority of corporately sponsored **acquisitions**, alliances, new ventures and business redefinitions fail to create value.'

Value creation can occur only if parenting opportunities exist, if the parent possesses characteristics that are the 'engine of value creation', and if the parent understands the critical success factors. Value creation also comes from corporate parents who are simply good at creating value (Campbell *et al.*, 1995). In a study of a diverse range of firms, Campbell *et al.* (1995) found that it takes time to develop and refine appropriate value creation insights.

Creating value: portfolio management

Corporate strategists must decide how best to organize their businesses to leverage parenting advantage and create value that will lead to dominance in their competitive arenas. Value creation can be based on **portfolio** management if the corporate parent owns, or has a majority interest in, a number of businesses across a number of **industries** and/or geographical territories. This issue concerns the scope and configuration of businesses in which a firm operates. The aim of the corporate parent is to maximize the aggregated return on the investment through the allocation of resources to businesses within the portfolio:

> Portfolio planning recognizes that diversified companies are a collection of businesses, each of which makes a distinct contribution to the overall corporate performance and which should be managed accordingly ... the approach helps build a framework for allocating resources directly and selectively and for differentiating strategic influence.
>
> (Haspeslagh, 1982: 73)

Using a portfolio approach to value creation, a corporate parent can divest non-performing businesses or add new businesses to the portfolio with relative ease. The analogy sometimes offered for portfolio management is that the corporate parent is like a banker who allocates resources to clients

Products and services of General Electric

- Appliances
- Aviation
- Consumer electronics
- Electrical distribution
- Energy
- Finance—business
- Finance—consumer
- Health care
- Lighting
- Oil and gas
- Rail
- Software and services
- Water

Source: http://www.ge.com/products_services/index.html

that are profitable and within a certain risk profile. The position of the business within the portfolio will determine the general characteristic of the strategy for the business (Bettis and Hall, 1983). The classic exemplar of portfolio management is General Electric (GE), which owns a diverse range of businesses across many industries. To stay in the GE portfolio, businesses have to be in the top three in their industry and reach certain threshold levels of financial performance.

The portfolio approach is not without its flaws. Hamermesh (1986: 117) argues: 'Portfolio planning can have some serious, unintended effects on the organization. The most important involve the mismanagement of mature businesses, the planning staff's role and the generation of growth opportunities.' Labelling businesses in the portfolio can have negative effects on business management teams. What team wants to run a business categorized as a poor performer? How many managers of 'cash cow' businesses are content to pass their operation's surplus cash to the corporate parent for it to allocate rather than to retain the surplus for their own purposes? The portfolio approach is very transactional in its approach to considering business units and can focus exclusively on short-term, narrow criteria such as growth and market share. While the approach may be appropriate in some domains, it lacks an appreciation of synergy and the inter-relationships between business units and the corporate parent (Campbell *et al.*, 1995, see Reading 3.1).

The definition of a market causes problems for corporate planners, which can lead to fewer new business proposals, thereby limiting the thinking capacity of the corporate parent. Thus the tendency when defining market share is to narrow the definition of the market, which may turn out to be a niche market rather than one in which the business could dominate the whole competitive arena. Consequently, a business unit could be categorized inappropriately using the portfolio management approach and, as a result, not receive the level of support from the corporate parent that would maximize market opportunities. A further danger is that businesses in the corporate portfolio could be small players in a large market rather than the other way around. In addition, there is debate over what the most appropriate performance metric is—for example, market share or profitability—and the most relevant time frame. Thus it is clear that there are a number of potential problems with the portfolio approach. To overcome them, Hamermesh (1986) recommends the following.

1. Do not confuse resource allocation with strategy.
2. Pay close attention to business-level strategies.
3. Avoid a home-run mentality.
4. Involve line managers in planning.
5. Add approaches that encourage growth.
6. Tailor planning to the situation.
7. Articulate a vision to formulate and institutionalize strategy.
8. Do not confuse strategic thinking with strategic planning.

The real danger in the portfolio management approach is that resource allocation is vague and does not consider the business-level strategy of each business unit.

Hamel and Prahalad (1990: 86) offer some additional words of caution about the portfolio concept:

> The new competitive engagement cannot be understood using analytical tools devised to manage the diversified corporation of 20 years ago, when competition was primarily domestic (GE versus Westinghouse, General Motors versus Ford) and all the key players were speaking the language of the same business schools and consultancies. Old prescriptions have potentially toxic side effects. The need for new principles is most obvious in companies organized exclusively according to the logic of SBUs.

Such debate led to large corporations thinking in new ways about how they create value: namely, through a synergistic approach.

Creating value: a synergistic approach

Achieving synergy is a holy grail for corporate managers. Synergy is 'the ability of two or more units or companies to generate greater value working together than they could working apart' (Goold and Campbell, 1998: 133). Synergy is often expressed as 'two plus two equals five'. Synergy can take a number of forms, such as shared know-how, coordinated strategies, shared tangible resources, vertical integration, pooled negotiating power, and combined business creation (Goold and Campbell, 1998). The simple representation of synergy is very convincing and easily understood (Teece, 1982), but synergistic benefits are difficult to achieve—and sometimes never materialize. Synergy aspirations can be used as a key driver behind mergers, acquisitions, and alliances (Gruca *et al.*, 1997).

European retailers such as Netto, Asda, and Carrefour attempt to achieve synergy through having common store layouts, sophisticated IT systems, and efficient and centralized distribution centres (warehouses to which suppliers deliver goods rather than delivering them to individual shops). An absolute focus on synergy can lead to managerial bias (Goold and Campbell, 1998). This, in theory, should force corporate managers to really understand and assess the real benefits and costs of each synergy opportunity. In practice, envisaged synergy benefits may not materialize. Consider how some UK insurance companies offshored their call centres to low-cost locations, only to reverse this because of unforeseen costs and cross-cultural problems with customer interactions. On paper, the synergies looked attractive, but the reality of implementation and customer concerns negated any potential synergistic benefits.

To ensure that synergy benefits do materialize, careful consideration has to be given to where synergy opportunities actually exist. For car manufacturers, real synergy opportunities lie in developing car platform strategies. This means sharing parts, engines, and the actual platform of the car. In the case of the VAG auto group, headquartered in Germany, Volkswagen (VW), Skoda, and Seat all share parts and engines even though they have different market positions. Renault–Nissan has a similar synergy approach, which has led to the development of the Note car, which is common to both brands. For car manufacturers, such synergies present significant opportunities if implemented and executed well. This hinges on the approach adopted by the corporate parent in terms of philosophy, attitudes, and beliefs, but also more practically on the internal processes and systems that support synergy (Goold and Campbell, 2002). Some corporate parents will also carefully manage and empower their business units. In some cases, subsidiary managers will be active in taking strategic initiatives, and these in turn will be diffused back and incorporated into the corporate parent philosophy, strategy, and mode of operation (Delany, 2000).

A core role of a corporate parent is to assess the domain routes to advantage by defining, and refining the purpose of the organization and the scope of the businesses in which it operates. A corporate parent must also determine the direction of the organization by assessing the potential growth opportunities, including related and unrelated diversification strategies. This focus on direction is the topic of our next section.

Direction

The strategists in any organization need to have a clear understanding of the role that they play in formulating strategy (Westphal and Fredrickson, 2001). Given the large-scale nature of many organizations, the role of corporate-level strategy is to define the purpose of the organization (as discussed in Chapter 5). It is the responsibility of top management to define, crystallize, and communicate this sense of purpose. This means capturing employees' attention and interest, engaging the organization, creating momentum, and instilling core values throughout the firm (Barlett and Ghoshal, 1994). IBM traditionally invested significant organizational effort in developing the 'Big Blue' culture and ethos throughout the organization. The CEO has a clear role in setting the organizational purpose at corporate level, as Montgomery (2008: 58) outlines: 'Guiding this never-ending process, bringing perspective to the midst of action and purpose to the flow—not solving the strategy puzzle once—is the crowning responsibility of the CEO.' To do this, CEOs must really understand the value creation capability within their organizations and have a clear idea about the direction of growth over the short, medium, and long terms.

Direction and growth strategies

Setting the direction for the growth of the business is dependent on factors such as **core competences** and capabilities, resources, appropriate organizational structures, and clarity around acceptable levels of risk, as well as external environmental conditions. The allure of double-digit growth may dazzle some corporate managers, but it may risk destabilizing the whole business. An important role of corporate parents is to assess and set sustainable levels of growth for each single business unit and the business as a whole. Ansoff (1965) provides us with an analytical framework within which companies can assess the appropriate directions of growth. The different growth strategies include market penetration, market development, product development, and diversification.

A market penetration strategy is one in which a company seeks to increase its market share in existing markets using existing products or services. For the strategist, this means configuring the firm's offerings in such a manner that they attract new customers or provide existing customers with the opportunity to use the existing products more. Through offers of free minutes, Internet access, or texts, mobile telecoms operators attempt to retain and increase the usage levels of existing customers. They subsidize the cost of handsets for new customers so that they can purchase phones at low cost or for free.

Market development strategies are focused on entering new markets with existing products. Little or no product modification may be necessary to do this. An example is car manufacturers such as Chevrolet, Jeep Cherokee, and Chrysler entering the UK market with their existing models.

Product development strategies are focused on developing new products to sell into existing markets. This enables firms to monetize further a cohort of users, again with a proliferation of new-generation products or services. In some industries, the product life cycle can be relatively short, such as in consumer goods; in others, the life cycle can be very long, such as medical devices and pharmaceuticals. Examples of product development strategies include Sony's PlayStations and Nintendo's Wii, Wii Fit, and DS Lite.

It may be the case that organizations pursue multiple options. McDonald's focused very much on market penetration before expanding its product into global markets. At the same time, it has innovated in product development, from the Egg McMuffin, through to a range of salads and wraps, while also diversifying into children's clothing with its McKids range. Diversification is perhaps the most risky strategy, but if successful it can yield great growth opportunities. At a corporate level, strategists need to decide the diversification strategy and the extent to which it aligns with the overall purpose of the organization.

Diversification

Diversification is a fundamental issue for corporate-level managers, CEOs, chief strategy officers (CSOs), and boards of directors. Should the business 'stick to its knitting' in terms of the business and industries that it knows (known as 'related diversification', which can be backward, forward, or horizontal), or should it enter new industries and new competitive arenas (known as 'unrelated diversification')? The evolution of diversification thinking has gone from general management skills in the 1950s and 1960s that were externally focused, to internally orientated thinking and synergy values in the 2000s (see Figure 7.3). The approaches to diversification adopted by companies has reflected the different ways corporate managers have dealt with the complexity of managing large multi-businesses. In many ways, corporate strategy management thinking has been learning by doing, given competitive threats and the nimbleness required to compete in many arenas on a global scale. For example, through studying US firms between 1987 and 1999, Wierseman and Bowen (2008: 129) found that 'a firm whose core business industry is characterized by increased market openness and greater global market linkages is likely to have both a higher degree and a greater scope of international diversifications'. The experience of developing global linkages creates opportunities for **organizational learning** and an intensity of international efforts. However, pursuing both product and geographical diversification may lead to suboptimal outcomes, because managerial attention can be spread too thinly (Delios and Beamish, 1999). The strategist has to determine how to manage the balance.

To reduce some of the risks associated with diversification, Markides (1997) recommends that corporate managers ask themselves the following questions.

- What can our company do better than any of its competitors in its current market?
- What strategic assets do we need in order to succeed in the new market?
- Can we catch up with or leapfrog competitors at their own game?
- Will diversification break up strategic assets that need to be kept together?
- Will we be simply a player in the new market or will we emerge as a winner?
- What can our company learn by diversifying, and are we sufficiently organized to learn it?

Related diversification: backward, forward, or horizontal

Related diversification occurs when the company, through the exploitation of its competence or capabilities, develops its scope beyond its current product or market arena into other activities and

Figure 7.3 The evolution of diversification (adapted from Goold and Luchs, 1993)

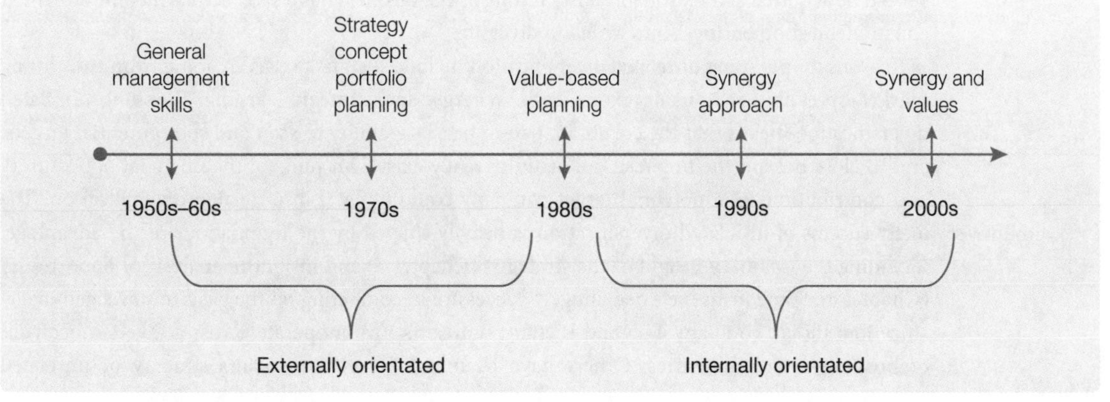

competitive arenas of an industry in which it already competes. Related diversification can encompass three directions: backward, forward, and horizontal.

Backward integration occurs when the corporate parent extends its scope of activities into the inputs of its operations, which could include raw materials, machinery, labour, and finance. A brewing company might integrate backward by purchasing cereal production farms, or a building contractor might buy a quarry to control some raw material costs.

Forward integration arises when the corporate parent extends the range of its activities to the output side of the business operations, which includes after-sales services, distribution, and marketing channels. Examples include brewing companies buying pubs in the UK, or Clarks, the shoe manufacturer, with its retail network in the UK and Ireland.

Horizontal integration occurs when the corporate parent develops the scope of its activities into areas that are in competition with, or directly complementary to, its current activities. For the brewing company, horizontal integration might involve developing a product offering in a new beverage arena. Another example would be mobile telecoms operators entering the fixed line market, such as Vodafone in Ireland and Horizon Wireless in the USA.

The advantages of related diversification over unrelated diversification include control over inputs, market controls, access to information, reduced costs, increased use of resources, and lower levels of risk. One of the central issues that corporate strategists face is what the nature of the corporate fit will be and how the corporate parent will achieve some unity in its activities. This could lead to the development of **sustainable competitive advantages** that competitors find difficult to imitate. Many financial institutions, such as HSBC, have opted for related diversification, offering, in partnership with car manufacturers and retail outlets, financial products designed to increase their competitive dominance and market share. Pursuing related diversification can make it easier for firms to promote a clear sense of their identity and purpose, and therefore to have clear brand identification with customers. In contrast, unrelated diversification risks diluting the purpose of the organization and can require substantial investment in shared services in order for synergies to be realized.

Unrelated diversification

Unrelated diversification occurs when the corporate parent diversifies into opportunities that hold the promise of attractive financial gain outside its current range of activities and operations. United Technologies Corporation (UTC), with more than 208,000 employees, has an unrelated diversified portfolio including air conditioning, aerospace and industrial products, elevators, aircraft engines, helicopters, fuel cells, and fire and security systems. Well-known organizations such as Pratt and Whitney, Sikorsky, and Otis are part of UTC. The strategic fit between corporate parent and the potential opportunity are of secondary concern. This is because the corporate parent has developed a capability for screening potential opportunities and investing only in financially attractive ones. The central tenet of acquiring businesses to achieve unrelated diversification is that the business should be acquired at a reasonable cost; as long as the business has a satisfactory income stream, it constitutes a good business into which to diversify.

Reasons for pursuing unrelated diversification include such factors as escaping from a declining market, spreading risk, using excess cash, synergy, and strategic learning. Pursuing unrelated diversification means that the corporate parent has a capability to scan and spot potential targets, and to close deals if the financial opportunity really exists. Misjudging the financial opportunity and contributions of a potential target company could be fatal in unrelated diversification. The likely success of unrelated diversification is heavily shaped by the foundations of the advantage, including the visionary insight of the strategist (Chapter 5) and insightful analysis of opportunity (Chapter 6). Some firms have been hugely successful in competing on the basis of unrelated diversification: Indian company Tata and Richard Branson's Virgin operate across a diverse spectrum of businesses and industries. Others have been much less so: Kodak's strategy of unrelated

strategy. So for example, the Brazilian economy has been experiencing strong economic growth despite the global recession, resulting in many international companies seeking to access or enter various Brazilian markets. However, two distinct changes have driven global strategy. First is the increase in the number and reach of subsidiaries of multinational corporations and their associated product offerings. For example, the consumer electronics market comprises a dizzying array of companies and products, particularly HD, LCD, and 3D televisions, DVD players, and personal communication devices.

Secondly, the difference between countries and markets is reducing (Vernon, 1979). Increasingly, the same main international retail brands are located in the major shopping districts of European capital cities. Further drivers include the 'Californization' of need (the convergence of customers' preferences and needs), the dispersion of technology, and local exploitation of advantage by corporate parents in their pursuance of global strategies (Dunning, 1980; Ohmae, 1989; Porter, 1986). It is possible, as Porter (1986: 37) describes, that:

> the global competitor can locate activities wherever comparative advantage lies, decoupling comparative advantage from its home base or country of ownership ... Comparative advantage is specific to the activity and not the location of the value chain as a whole. One of the potent advantages of the global firm is that it can spread activities among locations to reflect different preferred locations for different activities, something a domestic or country-centred competitor does not do.

We can see manifestations of this in every country: global companies have manufacturing and R&D facilities in different country locations; national governments use location incentives to attract foreign direct investment, fuelling the global strategy ambitions of many organizations. Strategists must create a competitive advantage through a superior configuration of internal organizational integration, responsiveness to local market conditions, and a strong administrative and organizational core that supports the global strategy.

Local versus global

The key dilemma in pursuing a global strategy is localization versus globalization of the product or service offering. A food manufacturer pursuing a global strategy must develop standardized products that can be rolled out in a number of countries, thereby gaining economies of scale. The level of localization might be limited to information about the product in a number of languages on packaging. We see this with many Unilever household products. Standardization of products and offerings has an attractive allure for organizations, particularly as there can be significant economies of scale and cost benefits. On the other hand, local market competitive conditions may demand significant localization of the food product in terms of taste, packaging, and distribution. McDonald's, IKEA, Unilever, and Nestlé have successfully standardized and customized their product offerings and operations to overcome this local versus global dilemma.

Cultural challenges

Another significant challenge in pursuing a global strategy is culture. Different countries and regions have distinct cultures, which global companies must understand and to which they must adapt in order to compete in a sustainable manner. Diageo, selling beers and spirits globally, has to take account of local tastes and preferences in developing new products and rolling out existing products into new markets.

Functions such as finance, marketing, and operations can differ from one country to another. Global organizations need to achieve greater degrees of operating standardization while fitting in with local cultures. Therefore global companies and managers need to understand the different cultural underpinnings of the markets that they serve—particularly national variables (laws, government, economy, and technology), societal variables (language, ethnic origin, and religion), societal/national culture, and individual values and behaviours of individuals. Global managers must consider how to respond to these issues of cultural diversity.

Hofstede (1983; 1993) identified four dimensions in which cultures differ: namely, power and distance, uncertainty avoidance, individualism, and masculinity. In dealing with these, Kanter and Dretler (1998), reflecting on their study of Gillette Singapore, advocated the need for integration across functions and divisions, the need to manage change, and the need to respect local cultures and understand a corporation's culture. They sum up the cultural issue for global companies thus:

> The key to success in the global economy is for companies to behave in a more integrated fashion—to tap the collaborative advantage that comes from being able to use all their resources and being able to work across boundaries. That means becoming knowledgeable about local needs, skilful at managing local changes, and expert at forging cross-boundary relationships—and doing this in many places at the same time with a global, or holistic, strategy in mind.
>
> (Kanter and Dretler, 1998: 66)

Competitive rewards and drawbacks of going global

The competitive rewards and drawbacks of pursuing a global strategy reflect the key issue faced by strategists: namely, the local versus global debate. The competitive rewards include cost reductions, improved quality of products and programmes, enhanced customer preference, and increased competitive leverage (Yip, 1989), as well as leveraging sources of competitive advantage such as national differences, scale economies, and scope economies (Ghoshal, 1987). For the Intercontinental Hotel group, having a presence in many markets means economies of scale in customer programmes, marketing, sales, and operations.

However, there are inherent dangers in pursuing a global strategy, particularly if product standardization cannot be achieved and if it is difficult to be responsive to customers given the distance between locations and the cross-cultural issues and sensitivities (Yip, 1989). Coca-Cola had to withdraw 2 litre bottles in Japan because they were too large to fit in limited kitchen spaces. In addition, economies of scale may not always work in the organization's favour, because they may be negated by internal standard operating procedures. For example, centralized warehousing means that products are shipped needlessly from country of origin to another country, consolidated there, and shipped back again to the country of origin. This creates additional cost in business operations.

Other international strategies

Irrespective of which international strategy is pursued by an organization, three conditions must be met: namely, location-specific advantages, the development of distinct strategic competence in order to cope with the uncertainties and nuances of new markets, and organizational capabilities that the firm can leverage for competitive advantage over and above other 'market mechanisms such as contacts or licenses' (Barlett and Ghoshal, 1995: 10–11).

Companies pursuing a multi-domestic strategy are focused on delivering a product or service to a number of national markets typically surrounding their home countries, in which national markets strategists clearly see local opportunities. In terms of configuration of structures and strategy, these tend to be decentralized, nationally self-reliant, with each unit having control over the formulation of its own business strategy. Kingspan, which competes in various markets in the construction sector, is pursuing a multi-domestic strategy, with operations in the UK, Ireland, and other European countries.

An international strategy is one in which companies have configured an offering that is aligned with their core competences and can be deployed in several markets, so that individual country operations can leverage these core competences for competitive success. The organization develops the core competences and these are then transferred to all of the units within the corporate portfolio. There have to be high levels of absorptive capacity in all units in order to leverage these core competences in each competitive territory. Economic and technological considerations are seen as the main driving force behind the adoption of international strategies (Barlett and Ghoshal, 1995: 8). Examples of companies that have pursued international strategies using different approaches are Nike, with core competences around branding and marketing, Honda, with core competence around engine technology, and Philips, with core competence in miniaturization.

The final international strategy is that of transnational company strategy. According to Barlett and Ghoshal (1989: 68), this is where a company:

> seeks efficiency not for its own sake, but as a means to achieve global competitiveness. It acknowledges the importance of local responsiveness but as a tool for achieving flexibility in international operations. Innovations are regarded as an outcome of a larger process of organizational learning that encompasses every member of the company. This redefinition of the issues allows managers of the transnational company to develop a broader perspective and leads to very different criteria for making choices.

This means that companies pursuing a global strategy need to balance overall efficiencies and synergies with ensuring that they have the skills for local adaptation in countries in which they have a market presence. So, in transnational contexts, the development and diffusion of knowledge are effected jointly and shared worldwide, and there is organizational flexibility through differentiated and specialized subsidiary roles.

The diamond of competitive advantage

Porter argues that, to achieve competitive success at an international and global level, firms have to hone their competitive capabilities and instincts in highly competitive national markets. The experience of this intense national competition provides the necessary competitive foundations to succeed in international marketplaces.

Achieving sustained global success can be difficult. Four attributes of national markets need to be considered if companies are to achieve global success: factor conditions; demand conditions; firm strategy, structure, and rivalry; and related and supporting industries (Porter, 1990). Factor conditions include factors of production such as land, labour, and capital. Efficient use and deployment of these may lead to comparative advantage at firm level and at national level. Factor conditions make the US state of Michigan one of the leading locations in the world for biotechnology research and product development.

Demand conditions are focused on the sophistication of the customer in terms of his or her expectation levels. More sophisticated customer expectations force competitors into being more innovative with offerings. This focus on continuous improvement and innovation increases the competitive rivalry in home markets, which in turn endows firms with significant competitive advantages in international markets. The Japanese consumer electronics market is a classic example of demand conditions.

Related and supporting industries are the ancillary organizations and services that provide inputs to support individual firms in a cost-effective manner. Organizations develop long-term relationships with a whole ecosystem of suppliers that not only offer cost advantage to the firms, but are also a source of innovation. If the relationships are managed well, both parties benefit; the firm competing on a global scale obtains flexibility and nimbleness of response to competitive demands.

Firm strategy, structure, and rivalry may provide advantages at firm and industry levels in national markets, enabling competitive success in global markets. Porter (1990) also argues that change and the role of government are further elements in determining national competitive advantage. This perspective is not without its critics, who argue that it is a simplistic representation of home country and foreign country advantage (Rugman and Verbeke, 1993).

Spotlight Corporate-level strategy

Organizations have adopted a wide variety of approaches in corporate-level and global-level strategy. The purpose, structure, and culture vary depending on the context in which companies operate.

eBay

eBay describes itself as 'The World's Online Marketplace®', with a global customer base of 233 million. Founded by Pierre Omidyar in 1995, it has created a powerful marketplace for the sale of goods and services by a passionate community of individuals and small businesses. eBay now has a global presence in thirty-seven markets, including the USA. The core of its corporate strategy is the provision of a platform to buy and sell goods electronically. It now owns a number of companies that enable it to create and sustain this platform, such as PayPal, Shopping.com, Rent.com, and online classifieds such as Kijiji, Gumtree.com, LoQUo.com, Intoko, Markplaats.nl, and mobile.de (see Figure 7.5).

General Electric

General Electric (GE) has a proud corporate history and has pursued an unrelated diversification strategy. With the tag line 'Imagination at work', GE is headquartered in Fairfield, USA, operates in over a hundred countries with more than 304,000 employees, and has an R&D budget of US$5.2bn. In 2009, GE filed 2,370 patents. In 2010, it was ranked in *Business Week*'s list of the world's twenty-five most inventive organizations. The GE portfolio of activities spans several different industry sectors, including commercial finance, health care, industrial, infrastructure, TV, and leisure (see Figure 7.6).

Google

Google's product range and approach differ from GE's. According to co-founder Larry Page, Google's mission is to develop the 'perfect search engine' based on ten truths (http://www.google.com/corporate/history.html):

1. Focus on the user and all else will follow.
2. It's best to do one thing really, really well.
3. Fast is better than slow.
4. Democracy on the web works.
5. You don't need to be at your desk to need an answer.
6. You can make money without doing evil.
7. There's always more information out there.
8. The need for information crosses all borders.
9. You can be serious without a suit.
10. Great just isn't good enough.

To achieve the perfect search engine, Google has a broad product range, as outlined in Figure 7.7, designed to achieve its mission.

European Union Directorate for Research

In a contrasting context, that of public administration, the European Union Directorate for Research has seven directors reporting to its Director General, with fifteen directorates. This appears to be a complex and bureaucratic structure, but reflects the nature of the organization's core tasks.

Europol

Europol is charged with handling criminal intelligence in the European Union (EU) by improving coordination and cooperation between member states. It commenced activities in July 1999 and supports police forces in EU member states, particularly in dealing with drug trafficking, terrorism, money laundering, and human trafficking, as well as cybercrime. Each EU member state seconds liaison officers to Europol, which facilitates information exchange and other forms of cooperation with other member state police forces. By 2007, more than 105 liaison officers worked for Europol out of a total headcount of 610 employees. Given its focus, the organizational structure is based around three key areas: serious crime; information technology (for analysis and threat assessment purposes); and corporate governance.

Summary

In these examples, we see organizations that have taken different approaches to corporate and global strategy with respect to domain and direction:

- eBay has focused on approaches that enhance the buying and selling of goods online;
- GE operates an unrelated diversification approach to its portfolio of activities;
- Google seems to have flexibility regarding its domain, but also a clear focus on developing the 'perfect search engine'; and

Figure 7.5 Overview of eBay's business activities

E-Commerce

- StubHub
- Shopping.com
- Half.com
- ProStores
- Rent.com
- brands4friends
- GSI Commerce

Payments

- PayPal
- Billmelater.com

Selected partnerships and investments

- MercadoLibre
- China (EachNet)
- Taiwan (Ruten)
- Craigslist
- ChannelAdvisor
- mFoundry
- Union Mobile Pay

Sustainability

- eBay Green Team
- WorldofGood.com
- eBay Giving Works
- MicroPlace
- PayPal Nonprofits
- eBay Foundation

Source: http://www.ebayinc.com/who

Figure 7.6 General Electric businesses

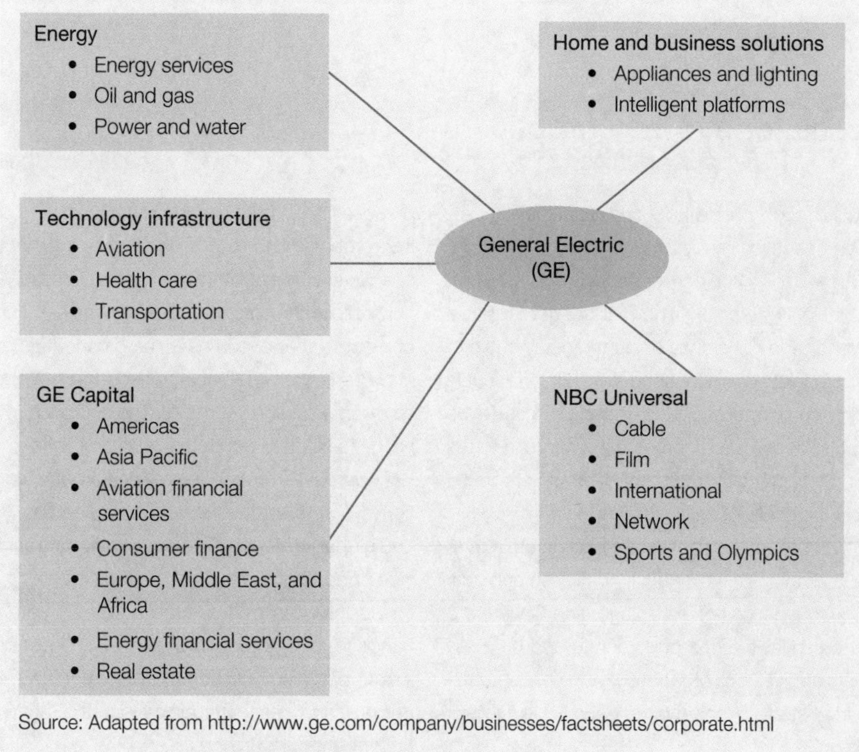

Source: Adapted from http://www.ge.com/company/businesses/factsheets/corporate.html

Figure 7.7 Google's product offerings

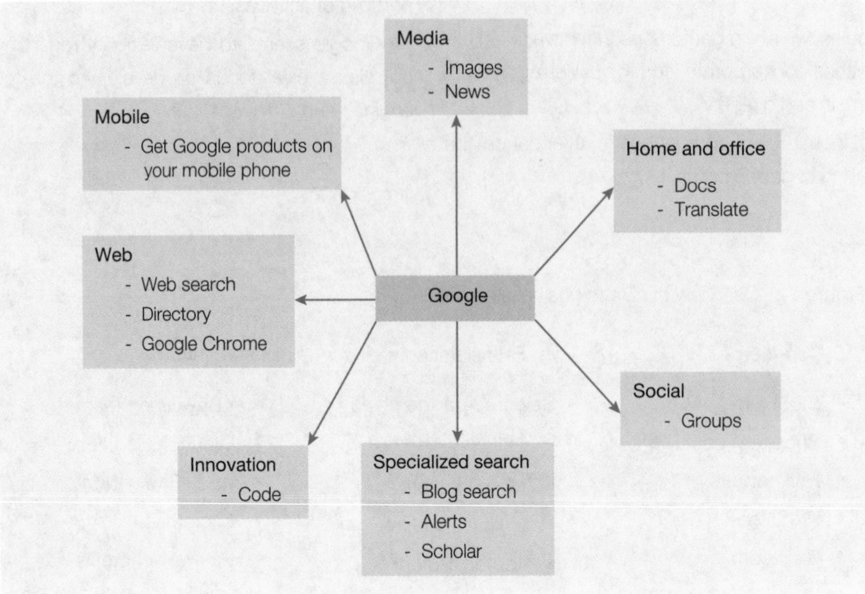

- Europol's domain is focused on its nature, and its entire corporate structures are based around the three key areas necessary to deliver its core mission.

What is not in doubt is that the appropriateness of organizational structures, reporting relationships, and their link to corporate level strategy, particularly parenting advantage, continue to be a contentious issue within corporate-level strategy, and that the context, purpose, and **stakeholder** influences shape the organization's domain and direction.

Implications for strategy practice

Aggressive pursuit of corporate-level and global-level strategies continues apace by many organizations throughout the world, but the reality for corporate strategists is that their practice is highly complex. The real danger is that a lack of consistency and coherency of strategy may begin to pervade the organization. Consequently, the rationale behind pursuing corporate and global strategy has to be clear; if it is not, suboptimal outcomes will emerge in terms of poor decision making, abandonment of global products, and paying over the odds for opportunities.

A real test for global companies and their corporate strategists is conceptualization of their industry definition and their purpose (that is, foundations of advantage; see Chapters 5 and 6). This is essential in terms of corporate and business unit fit, in order to add value to organizations. In conceptualizing corporate-level strategy, some organizations devise their purpose from a pure economic perspective and/or a capabilities, process, and resources perspective that can be developed over time in different competitive arenas. Another way of conceptualizing corporate strategy is to see it as communities of practice that encompass the organization and stakeholders. But corporate strategy needs to be aligned to external environmental and internal fit. The approach to value creation needs to be clear, consistent, and sustainable.

Appropriate organizational design and resource allocation systems are essential for succeeding with corporate and global strategies. The organizational design should provide opportunities for parenting advantages to emerge, and for business units to differentiate and create market dominance in their competitive arenas. Without coherent alignment between corporate-level strategy, organizational design, and resource allocation, the corporate parent's value-creation investments may dissipate and not achieve the desired competitive outcomes. Therefore the role of the corporate parent evolves according to the diversification and global strategy pursued. The services, management styles, and resource mix at the centre have to be responsive to the needs of business units, but also attuned to external environmental changes.

Value creation is a rhetoric used at corporate level as a rationale that underpins growth and synergy approaches. In reality, there is often a significant performance gap between value creation, forecasted growth, and synergy approaches. Portfolio approaches to value creation can also prove disappointing. This is a consequence of over-exuberance in terms of stated value creation prospects and underestimation of what is really involved to achieve value creation in practice. This underestimation can also extend to the type of diversification and international strategy that companies pursue.

Finally, the real opportunity for corporate strategists is to create a mindshare in the organization about the core values, purpose, and ambition of the organization, irrespective of cultural and geographic differences. This means investing time and effort in building an organizational culture around clear core values. This mindshare is essential in getting the best from employees, attracting the best talent, and dominating arenas in which the organization has chosen to compete. In today's world, this is probably one of the most significant hurdles that corporate strategists face. It has become even more challenging since the global recession in 2009.

Introduction to readings

Reading 3.1, 'Portfolio matrices' by David Faulkner (1998), provides an overview of the different approaches used to assess the attractiveness of a corporate portfolio and outlines a new approach that Faulkner terms 'the portfolio cube'. This reading raises a number of interesting questions. First, if a corporate parent were to apply all of the analytical frameworks to assess its corporate portfolio, would it generate similar analytical insights? Secondly, does such analysis improve decision making by the corporate parent? Thirdly, is market attractiveness in the eye of the beholder?

Reading 3.2, 'Global strategy: an organizing framework', by Sumantra Ghoshal (1987), provides a comprehensive overview of global strategy, particularly in terms of purpose and ends. The strategic objectives of global strategy are to achieve efficiency in current operations, to manage risk, and to innovate, learn, and adapt: strategy choice or strategic adaptation. Are these strategic objectives still relevant in today's global strategy context? Do the structures of the industry influence corporate strategy or does corporate strategy influence industry structure?

The final reading for this chapter, accessible via a link on the Online Resource Centre that accompanies this book, 'Parenting in complex structures' by Michael Goold and Andrew Campbell (2002), explores the nuances and complexity of corporate parenting. The authors argue that the role of the corporate parent has become even more complex, and that the issue of parenting advantage is a key driver of corporate-level strategy and structure. If that is the case, why do so many organizations frequently change their corporate-level strategies and structures? Have such companies not grasped the core definition of their businesses, or is their redefinition of business purpose too radical for both corporate-level strategy and associated organizational structures? Should it be a corporate-level role to add value and to ensure coherent collaboration between business units and employees?

Mini case study Coca-Cola: 'Making every drop count'

Coca-Cola is probably one of the most recognized, valuable, and well-known global brands, with a market presence in North America, Latin America, South Pacific, Europe, Africa, and Asia. Developed in 1886, the product was originally intended as a medicine, based on an invention by John Pemberton. The business was bought by Asa Griggs Candler, a marketer who created the foundation for this global brand. Its global recognition is based on the fact it owns four out of the top five non-alcoholic sparkling beverage brands in the world (Coke, Diet Coke, Fanta, and Sprite), has over 71,000 associates worldwide, has an operational reach of 200-plus countries, and has over 3,500 products with 1.7 billion beverage servings each day.

Product proliferation

The company has launched several products from the Coke platform, including Cherry Coke (1985), Coca-Cola Lemon (2001), Coca-Cola Vanilla (2002), Coca-Cola C2 (2003), Coca-Cola Lime (2005), Coca-Cola Raspberry (2005), Coca-Cola M5 (2005), Coca-Cola Black Cherry Vanilla (2006), Coca-Cola Citra (2006), and Coca-Cola Orange (2007). Alongside this product proliferation, Coca-Cola has been at the forefront of packaging varieties, ranging from the original contour glass bottle to 2 litre plastic bottles and aluminium cans. The combination of product and packaging is an attempt to have superior segment execution in diversified distribution contexts—to have the 'right pack, right price, right channel'.

The decline

The death of CEO Roberto Goizueta in 1997 marked a change of fortunes for Coca-Cola. Goizueta had presided over double-digit growth during his seven-year period as CEO by focusing the business on the development of core carbonated products, such as Coke, through its franchise system. At the turn of the present century, Coca-Cola continued to struggle to maintain global competitiveness and regain some of its previous glory. Since the launch of New Coke in 1985, several structural changes had begun to emerge in the beverage market as new beverages began to threaten Coca-Cola's dominant market share and core products. The years after the death of Goizueta saw two further CEO appointments, Douglas Ivester and Douglas Daft, whose tenures were dogged by setbacks in the form of failed products, takeovers, and scandals. The appointment of Irishman Neville Isdell, former head of Coca-Cola's operations in the Philippines in the 1980s, marked a change in direction for the company. Isdell (2005: 24) describes the task that he faced:

> When I returned to the Coca-Cola Company, I knew we had three important things going for us . . . We have some of the world's greatest brands . . . We have the beverage industry's most extensive selling and distribution system. And we have got many strong, value-creating customer relationships. Those three assets are the key to our future. Building on all of them, though, takes execution.

Isdell's transformational focus was to re-energize the Coca-Cola system, but also to refocus its business beyond core carbonated products, extending into such beverages as water, tea, coffee, and energy drinks.

The scale of the change challenge

In the European market alone, by 2005 there were over 2,000 different non-alcoholic beverage brands, over 10,000 products with different flavours, and over 100,000 different combinations of packaging materials and sizes. Globally, consumer tastes and preferences had changed, favouring non-carbonated drinks, and there was an increased emphasis on health benefits, driven by concern over global obesity levels, particularly in the US market in which 50 per cent of the population is categorized as obese (there are now more obese people in the world than starving people).

A further obstacle for Isdell was that the company needed to invest significant levels of cash into broadening its product range beyond the traditional carbonated beverage product ranges. The core business model needed to change significantly in order to pursue new market opportunities. In 2005, the 8 per cent shareholding of Warren Buffet, through Berkshire Hathaway, was seen by some financial analysts as a stumbling block to transformation and a broadening of direction, given the fact that, in 2000, Coca-Cola's board turned down Ivester's proposal to acquire the Quaker Oats and Gatorade brands due to their high acquisition price of US$16bn. Coca-Cola's rival Pepsi acquired both brands, which turned out to be core products and revenue earners for them. Broadening beyond core products would require significant levels of cash investment for new product development, acquisitions, strategic alliances, and for organic growth.

Isdell begins to put the fizz back

Isdell's transformational task between 2004 and 2007 was huge, but redefining the traditional core business was a critical element during his tenure as CEO. One of his first decisions was to invest US$400m a year in innovation and marketing; he was explicit that he would lead the board in his role as chairman and CEO to do whatever it would take to halt the decline in the company. The transformation that he devised had four key dimensions: namely, growing core global brands, capturing emerging need-state platforms, increasing customer value, and providing franchise leadership. This pushed the business definition for Coca-Cola to capture growth opportunities in beverages that include health, beauty, and nutrition, active replenishment, and energy stimulation—what Coca-Cola termed 'wellness platforms'. Isdell (2006: 24) describes the process as:

> The need maps work at a fundamental level, across diverse cultures, by identifying and understanding the functional or

> emotional reason any beverage—from tap water to yoghurt drinks to beer—is consumed in a 24-hour period. Consumption events are then segmented into need states based on this underlying motivation. From 19 foundational needs, we've identified 10 overarching global need states, each one associated with a meaning, an occasion and a beverage. Because each need state can also be quantified by volume and value, the need-state maps allow us to make comparisons across categories, brands, occasions and demographics in order to identify regional or global scalable opportunities.

This redefinition of focus has meant that Coca-Cola now has between 20 and 25 per cent market share. This can be compared with its old beverage industry definition, in which it held 80 per cent of a market with limited growth opportunities. The change in focus is also evident in its mission and value statements.

'Making every drop count'

This transformation of Coca-Cola has coincided with the company's first integrated corporate identity campaign of 'Making every drop count' and a cross-media marketing campaign on the theme of 'The Coke side of life'. The latter marked a re-engagement with customers and reaffirmed Coca-Cola's market position, as Esther Lee (2006), chief creative officer, described:

> Because Coca-Cola is a global brand with local connections and meaning, the Coke side of life offers each country an opportunity to interpret their own moments of happiness and the brand's role in those. Working with markets around the world, we have collaboratively co-authored an integrated creative platform that can be adapted to fit different market needs. And we are inviting countries to add to the effort through joint global initiatives.

Coca-Cola has been active in executing along its redefined core business. In March 2006, Dasani launched a further brand extension in the US market, Dasani Sensation, a hybrid of water and carbonated soft drink. Four months later, in June 2006, the tea-based Nesta brand was re-energized, with a product makeover and extensions such as green tea. The following month, Coca-Cola relaunched Gold Peak, a premium iced tea product in five flavours: sweetened, unsweetened, lemon, diet, and green tea. In the European market, Coca-Cola entered a partnership with Apple in August 2006. It gave away 70 million songs from iTunes Music Stores, with key market focus on the UK, Germany, Austria, and Switzerland. During 2007, Coca-Cola became even more active with integrated marketing campaigns around such television shows as *American Idol*, and after nine years returned to advertising for the Superbowl final broadcasts. In addition to rolling out marketing campaigns in key markets, Coca-Cola launched Enviga, a green tea that burns calories, Diet Coke Plus, a calorie-free and vitamin-enhanced beverage. It also acquired vitamin water business Glacéau for US$4.1bn and signed an agreement for distribution of Campbell's beverage portfolio.

At the end of 2007, Muhtar Kent was appointed CEO, the company's fourth since 1997. Kent continued the implementation of the company redirection set by Isdell, reinvigorating the Coca-Cola system again to meet the new market opportunities.

By 2009, Coca-Cola had forty-eight consecutive years of increased dividends, with 3,300-plus beverage offerings. The company's mission, as part of its 'Vision 2020', is to prepare for a future that 'serves as the standard against which we weigh our actions and decisions'. The mission is (Coca-Cola, 2010):

- 'to refresh the world . . .';
- 'to inspire moments of optimism and happiness . . .'; and
- 'to create value and make a difference'.

Only time will tell whether the 139,600 employees led by Muhtar Kent will deliver on this and succeed in 'making every drop count'.

Sources: Coca-Cola (2010); Isdell (2005; 2006); Ignatius (2011)

? Questions

1. How would you describe the corporate strategy of Coca-Cola? Does it pass Vance's (1970) three criteria?
2. What is the parenting style adopted by Coca-Cola? What is the basis of fit within the Coca-Cola corporation?
3. Does the parenting style of Coca-Cola create or destroy value?
4. Describe the growth strategy of Coca-Cola. What is its diversification strategy and is it consistent with the company's stated mission and values?
5. What is the logic of the global strategy pursued by Coca-Cola? Has the strategy managed to reduce differences between markets?
6. Discuss the future challenges that Coca-Cola will face as it rolls out its current global strategy.

Summary

The strategic question that we addressed in this chapter is how best to develop the strategic scope of an organization through its corporate and global strategies.

We began the chapter by examining corporate-level strategy. The issues of fit between the corporate parent and the rest of its businesses and activities, and parenting advantage, are two essential elements of corporate-level strategy. We saw that corporate parents can really create and add value, but can also destroy it if there is no fit, or an inappropriate fit. In terms of creating value, there are typically two approaches that corporate strategists take: portfolio management and the synergy approach. Each approach is useful, but each also has limitations. We focused on the diversification debate, related or unrelated. In the latter part of the chapter, our attention focused on global strategy—particularly the rationale behind it, key drivers, and the rewards and downsides of going global. Finally, we considered two of the key challenges that strategists face—those of standardization and cultural factors—but the most significant and underlying task faced by global companies is that of creating a global mindset. This overview of domain and direction gives us a broad sense of the routes to advantage available at a corporate level. The next chapter explores markets and methods, examining the specific routes available to organizations for competing in a given market.

Review questions

1. Source a reading from a journal that contributes to the debate in this chapter. Which, if any, perspective does it support? What is its contribution? Does it advance the debate in any way?

2. What are the key limitations of the portfolio approach? Can you think of contexts in which it might be more or less appropriate?

3. What are the key limitations of the synergy approach? Can you think of contexts in which it might be more or less appropriate?

4. Consider the various forces that may shape an organization's strategy. Do the readings in this chapter adequately address these?

5. Apply the diversification test to the examples in the Spotlight box. Is there coherence of purpose and direction behind the diversification strategy pursued by these organizations? As the strategist for one of these organizations, what would you consider the best way in which it can realize strategic scope?

6. Is it really possible for companies to 'behave in a more integrated fashion', as argued by Kanter and Dretler (1998)? If so, how?

7. Identify the drivers of global strategy in an industry with which you are familiar and consider if there is logic about pursuing a global strategy among the industry players.

8. What recommendation do you have for a corporate strategist in dealing with the local versus global dilemma?

Further reading

In his 1982 article 'Portfolio planning: uses and limits', *Harvard Business Review*, Jan/Feb: 58–73, Philippe Haspeslagh provides a good overview of the mechanics of portfolio planning, in addition to providing some valuable advice to practising managers.

Charles Hampden-Turner and Fons Trompenaars (2000) *Building Cross-Cultural Competence*, Chichester: John Wiley and Sons, provides real insights as well as practical advice in dealing with cross-cultural management.

Steve Tappin and Andre Cave (2008) *The Secret of CEOs*, London: Nicholas Brealey Publishing, provides a fascinating insight into CEO thinking about globalization, sustainability, and leadership.

visit the Online Resource Centre that accompanies this book to access more learning resources on this chapter topic at www.oxfordtextbooks.co.uk/orc/cunningham/

References

Ansoff, I. 1965. *Corporate Strategy: An Analytical Approach to Business Policy for Growth and Expansion*. London: Penguin Books.

Bartlett, C. and Ghoshal, S. 1989. *Managing across Borders: The Transnational Solution*. Boston, MA: Harvard Business School Press.

Bartlett, C. and Ghoshal, S. 1994. Changing the role of top management: beyond strategy to purpose. *Harvard Business Review*, 72(6): 79–88.

Bettis, R. and Hall, W. 1983. The business portfolio approach: where it falls down in practice. *Long Range Planning*, Apr: 95–104.

Bowman, E. H. and Helfat, C. E. 2001. Does corporate strategy matter? *Strategic Management Journal*, 22: 1–23.

Burgelman, R. A. 1983. A model of the interaction of strategic behavior, corporate context, and the concept of strategy. *Academy Of Management Review*, 8: 61–70.

Burgelman, R. A. and Grove, A. S. 1996. Strategic dissonance. *California Management Review*, 38: 8–28.

Campbell, A. 1995. Vertical integration synergy or seduction? *Long Range Planning*, 28: 126–128.

Campbell, A., Goold, M., and Alexander, M. 1995. Corporate strategy: the quest for parenting advantage. *Harvard Business Review*, 73: 120–132.

Campbell, A., Goold, M., and Alexander, M. 1996. The value of the parent company. In M. Goold and K. Luchs (eds) *Managing the Multibusiness Company: Strategic Issues for Diversified Groups*. Andover: Cengage Learning.

Carroll, A. B. 2004. Managing ethically with global stakeholders: a present and future challenge. *Academy Of Management Executive*, 18: 114–120.

Chakrabarti, A., Singh, K., and Mahmood, I. 2007. Diversification and performance: evidence from east Asian firms. *Strategic Management Journal*, 28: 101–120.

Chatterjee, S. 1986. Types Of synergy and economic value: the impact of acquisitions on merging and rival firms. *Strategic Management Journal*, 7: 119–139.

Child, J. 2005. *Organization*. Malden, MA: Blackwell.

Coca-Cola. 2010. Mission, vision and values. Available online at http://www.thecoca-colacompany.com/ourcompany/mission_vision_values.html

Collis, D. and Montgomery, C. 1998. Creating corporate advantage. *Harvard Business Review*, May/June: 71–83.

Delany, E. 2000. Strategic development of the multi-national subsidiary through subsidiary initiative taking. *Long Range Planning*, 33: 220–244.

Delios, A. and Beamish, P. 1999. Geographic scope, product diversification and the corporate performance of Japanese firms. *Strategic Management Journal*, 20(8): 711–727.

Dubofsky, P. and Varadarahan, P. 1987. Diversification and measures of performance: additional empirical evidence. *Academy Of Management Journal*, 30: 597–608.

Dunning, J. H. 1980. Toward an eclectic theory of international production: some empirical tests. *Journal of International Business Studies*, 11(1): 9–31.

Eccles, R. G., Lanes, K. L. and Wilson, T. C. 1999. Are you paying too much for that acquisition? *Harvard Business Review*, 77: 136–146.

Eisenhardt, K. M. and Brown, S. L. 1999. Patching. *Harvard Business Review*, 77: 72–82.

Gates, S. and Very, P. 2003. Measuring performance during M&A integration. *Long Range Planning*, 36: 167–185.

Ghemawat, P. 2007. Managing difference: the central challenge of global strategy. *Harvard Business Review*, 85(3): 58–68.

Ghoshal, S. 1987. Global strategy: an organizing framework. *Strategic Management Journal*, 8: 425–440.

Ginsberg, A. 1990. Connecting diversification to performance: a sociocognitive approach. *Academy Of Management Review*, 15: 514–535.

Goold, M. 1996. Parenting strategies for multibusiness companies. *Long Range Planning*, 29: 419–421.

Goold, M. and Campbell, A. 1998. Desperately seeking synergy. *Harvard Business Review*, 76: 131–143.

Goold, M. and Campbell, A. 2000. Taking stock of synergy: a framework for assessing linkages between business. *Long Range Planning*, 33: 72–96.

Goold, M. and Campbell, A. 2002. Parenting In complex structures. *Long Range Planning*, 35: 219–243.

Goold, M. and Luchs, K. S. 1993. Why diversify? Four decades of management thinking. *Academy Of Management Executive*, 7: 7–25.

Grant, R. M. 1995. *Contemporary Strategy Analysis*. 2nd edn. Oxford: Basil Blackwell.

Gruca, T. S., Nath, D., and Mehra, A. 1997. Exploiting synergy for competitive advantage. *Long Range Planning*, 30: 605–611.

Hall, J. 2001. The end of globalization: why global strategy is a myth and how to profit from the realities of regional markets. *Academy Of Management Executive*, 15: 140–142.

Hamel, G. and Prahalad, C. K. 1985. Do you really have a global strategy? *Harvard Business Review*, 63: 139–148.

Hamermesh, R. G. 1986. Making planning strategic. *Harvard Business Review*, 64: 115–120.

Harzing, A.-W. 2002. Acquisitions versus greenfield investments: international strategy and management of entry modes. *Strategic Management Journal*, 23: 211–227.

Haspeslagph., D. 1982. Portfolio planning: uses and limits. *Harvard Business Review*, 60(1): 58–73.

Hill, C. W. L. and Hoskisson, R. E. 1987. Strategy and structure in the multiproduct firm. *Academy Of Management Review*, 12: 331–341.

Hitt, M. A., Dacin, M. T., Levitas, E., Arregle, J.-L., and Borza, A. 2000. Partner selection in emerging and developed market contexts: resource-based and organizational learning perspectives. *Academy Of Management Journal*, 43: 449–467.

Hitt, M. A., Hoskisson, R. E., and Kim, H. 1997. International diversification: effects on innovation and firm performance in product-diversified firms. *Academy Of Management Journal*, 40: 767–798.

Hofstede, G. 1983. *Culture's Consequences: International Differences in Work-related Values*. Palo Alto, CA: Sage.

Hofstede, G. 1993. Cultural constraints in management theories. *Academy of Management Executive*, 7(1): 81–94.

Ignatius, A. 2011. Shaking things up at Coca-Cola. *Harvard Business Review*, Oct: 22–30.

Inkpen, A. C. 1998. Learning and knowledge acquisition through international strategic alliances. *Academy Of Management Executive*, 12: 69–80.

Isdell, N. 2005. Remarks made at the Food Marketing Institute Mid Winter Conference, Boca Raton, FL, 24 January.

Isdell, N. 2006. Leadership and transforming an organization. Speech delivered at the CEIS–The Food Business Forum, World Food Business Summit, *Flying High in the Face of Competition*, Paris, 22 June.

Jensen, M. and Zajac, E. J. 2004. Corporate elites and corporate strategy: how demographic preferences and structural position shape the scope of the firm. *Strategic Management Journal*, 25: 507–524.

Johansson, J. K. and Yip, G. S. 1994. Exploiting globalization potential: U.S. and Japanese strategies. *Strategic Management Journal*, 15: 579–601.

Kanter, R. M. and Dretler, T. D. 1998. 'Global strategy' and its impact on local operations: lessons from Gillette Singapore. *Academy Of Management Executive*, 12: 60–68.

Kim, B. and Lee, Y. 2001. Global capacity expansion strategies: lessons learned from two Korean carmakers. *Long Range Planning*, 34: 309–333.

Kim, W. C. and Mauborgne, R. E. A. 1991. Implementing global strategies: the role of procedural justice. *Strategic Management Journal*, 12: 125–143.

Kogut, B. 1985. Designing global strategies: comparative and competitive value added chains. *Sloan Management Review*, 26(4): 15–28.

Lee, E. 2006. The Coke side of life. Available online at http://www.thecoca-colacompany.com/investors/annualandotherreports/2006/pdf/koar_06_complete.pdf

Leknes, H. M. and Carr, C. 2004. Globalisation, international configurations and strategic implications: the case of retailing. *Long Range Planning*, 37: 29–49.

Levitt, T. 1983. The globalization of markets. *Harvard Business Review*, May/June: 92–102.

Lovallo, D., Viguerie, P., Uhlaner, R., and Horn, J. 2007. Deals without delusions. *Harvard Business Review*, 85: 92–99.

Lovelock, C. H. and Yip, G. S. 1996. Developing global strategies for service businesses. *California Management Review*, 38(2): 64–86.

Luo, Y. 1996. Evaluating the performance of strategic alliances In China. *Long Range Planning*, 29: 534–542.

Markides, C. C. 1997. To diversify or not to diversify. *Harvard Business Review*, 75: 93–99.

Marks, M. L. and Mirvis, P. H. 2001. Making mergers and acquisitions work: strategic and psychological preparation. *Academy Of Management Executive*, 15: 80–92.

McGahan, A. M. and Porter, M. E. 1997. How much does industry matter, really? *Strategic Management Journal*, 18: 15–30.

McGrath, R. G., Ming-Jer, C., and Macmillan, I. C. 1998. Multimarket maneuvering in uncertain spheres of influence: resource diversion strategies. *Academy Of Management Review*, 23: 724–740.

McKendrick, D. G. 2001. Global strategy and population-level learning: the case of hard disk drives. *Strategic Management Journal*, 22(4): 307–334.

Midoro, R. and Pitto, A. 2000. A critical evaluation of strategic alliances in liner shipping. *Maritime Policy and Management*, 27: 31–40.

Mintzberg, H. 1994. *The Rise and Fall Of Strategic Planning*. New York: Free Press.

Montgomery, C. A. 2008. Putting leadership back into strategy. *Harvard Business Review*, 86: 54–60.

Murtha, T. P., Lenway, S. A., and Bagozzi, R. P. 1998. Global mind-sets and cognitive shift in a complex multinational corporation. *Strategic Management Journal*, 19: 97–114.

Ohmae, K. 1989. The global logic of strategic alliances. *Harvard Business Review*, 67(2): 143–154.

Ohmae, K. 1990. *The Borderless World: Power and Strategy in the Interlinked Economy*. New York: Harper Business.

Ojah, K. 2007. Costs, valuation, and long-term operating effects of global strategic alliances. *Review Of Financial Economics*, 16: 69–90.

Parkhe, A. 1991. Interfirm diversity, organizational learnings, and longevity in global strategic alliances. *Journal Of International Business Studies*, 22: 579–601.

Porter, M.E. (ed.) 1986. *Competition in Global Industries*. Boston, MA: Harvard Business School Press.

Porter, M. E. 1987. From competitive advantage to corporate strategy. *Harvard Business Review*, 653: 43–60.

Porter, M.E. 1990. *The Competitive Advantage of Nations*. New York: The Free Press.

Raynor, M. E. and Bower, J. L. 2001. Lead from the center. *Harvard Business Review*, 79: 92–100.

Reuer, J. J. and Leiblein, M. J. 2000. Downside risk implications of multinationality and international joint ventures. *Academy Of Management Journal*, 43: 203–214.

Rugman, A. M. and Verbeke, A. 1993. Foreign subsidiaries and multinational strategic management: an extension of Porter's single diamond framework. *Management International Review*, 33(2): 71–84.

Rumelt, R. P. 1991. How much does industry matter? *Strategic Management Journal*, 12: 167–185.

Schendel, D. 1991. Introduction to the special issue on global strategy. *Strategic Management Journal*, 12: 1–3.

Shaver, J. M. 2006. A paradox of synergy: contagion and capacity effects in mergers and acquisitions. *Academy Of Management Review*, 31: 962–976.

Shayne Gary, M. 2005. Implementation strategy and performance outcomes in related diversification. *Strategic Management Journal*, 26: 643–664.

Shimizu, K., Hitt, M. A., Vaidyanath, D., and Pisano, V. 2004. Theoretical foundations of cross-border mergers and acquisitions: a review of current research and recommendations for the future. *Journal Of International Management*, 10: 307–353.

Sleuwaegen, L., Schep, K., Den Hartog, G., and Commandeur, H. 2003. Value creation and the alliance experiences Of Dutch companies. *Long Range Planning*, 36: 533–542.

Stalk, G., Evans, P., and Shulman, L. E. 1992. Competing on capabilities: the new rules of corporate strategy. *Harvard Business Review*, 70: 54–66.

Stan Xiao, L. and Greenwood, R. 2004. The effect of within-industry diversification on firm performance: synergy creation, multi-market contact and market structuration. *Strategic Management Journal*, 25: 1131–1153.

Teece, D. J. 1982. Towards an economic theory of the multiproduct firm. *Journal of Economic Behavior and Organization*, 3: 39–63.

Thomas, D. A. 2004. Diversity as strategy. *Harvard Business Review*, 82: 98–108.

Tihanyi, L., Johnson, R. A., Hoskisson, R. E., and Hitt, M. A. 2003. Institutional ownership differences and international diversification: the effects of boards of directors and technological opportunity. *Academy Of Management Journal*, 46: 195–211.

Trent, R. J. and Monczka, R. M. 2002. Pursuing competitive advantage through integrated global sourcing. *Academy Of Management Executive*, 16: 66–80.

Van Oijen, A. and Douma, S. 2000. Diversification strategy and the roles of the centre. *Long Range Planning*, 33: 560–578.

Vance, J. O. 1970. The anatomy of a corporate strategy. *California Management Review*, 13: 5–12.

Vernon, R. 1979. The product cycle hypothesis in a new international environment. *Oxford Bulletin of Economics and Statistics*, 41(4): 255–326.

Villalonga, B. N. and McGahan, A. M. 2005. The choice among acquisitions, alliances, and divestitures. *Strategic Management Journal*, 26: 1183–1208.

Westphal, J. D. and Fredrickson, J. W. 2001. Who directs strategic change? Director experience, the selection of new CEOs, and change in corporate strategy. *Strategic Management Journal*, 22: 1113–1137.

Wiersema, M. and Bowen, H. 2007. Corporate diversification: the impact of foreign competition, industry globalization, and product diversification. *Strategic Management Journal*, 29(2): 115–132.

Wolf, J. and Egelhoff, W. G. 2002. A reexamination and extension of international strategy-structure theory. *Strategic Management Journal*, 23: 181–189.

Yip, G.S. 1989. Global strategy ... in a world of nations? *Sloan Management Review*, Autumn: 29–41.

Zollo, M. and Singh, H. 2004. Deliberate learning in corporate acquisitions: post-acquisition strategies and integration capability in U.S. bank mergers. *Strategic Management Journal*, 25: 1233–1256.

Business and network strategies

Market and methods

The fundamental question in the strategic management field is how firms achieve and sustain competitive advantage.

(Teece *et al.*, 1997)

Introduction

In the previous chapter, we examined domain and direction routes to advantage in the form of corporate and global strategies. The fundamental questions concerned the nature, scope, and configuration of businesses in which the organization should operate. In the current chapter, we turn our attention towards how organizations should compete in these given businesses. Specifically, we address the market and methods routes to advantage by considering business and network strategies.

The business world is littered with organizations that have developed cutting-edge products or services, but ultimately failed to take advantage of such developments because they had ill-defined business strategies of how to compete in their market. Another common occurrence is once-successful organizations that have been unable to successfully reposition themselves in light of a new or changing environment. Consider Polaroid, dominant for decades in instant photography until the digital revolution of the 1990s and 2000s, which meant that consumers could take pictures instantly and easily using mobile phones, PDAs, and digital cameras. Competitors such as Fuji and Kodak responded to this technology trend by reconfiguring their value proposition to reflect the digital photography revolution. Polaroid, on the other hand, failed to respond, resulting in a company world-renowned for instant photography going bankrupt in 2005. As the opening quote by Teece *et al.* (1997) and the case of Polaroid illustrate, the challenge facing organizations lies not only in achieving competitive advantage, but also in ensuring that this advantage is sustainable over time.

In the quest to develop a **sustainable competitive advantage**, organizations need to address key issues covering both the market and methods routes to advantage (see Figure 8.1). With respect to **business-level strategy**, key questions concern the nature of strategic choice open to firms and how they can best compete and deliver value in their chosen business. In considering this, we examine business-level strategy from three perspectives—strategy types, generic strategies, and strategic positions—in addition to examining strategic fit and **business models**.

In terms of methods for competing, **strategists** must navigate the core tension of competition versus collaboration. This is complex to manage, particularly as organizations may be collaborating with businesses in one area while competing against the same business in others. Network-level strategy involves deciding whether the firm has the competencies to deliver value as a stand-alone unit (Chapter 6) or should work with other firms to optimize its value proposition. This issue is further complicated by the array of network strategy forms available—strategic **alliances**, **joint ventures**, **mergers**, and **acquisitions**; this is the focus of the latter part of the chapter.

The quest for competitive advantage is an arduous one: by definition, competitive advantage is the exception rather than the rule. Firms can have strong foundations for advantage in the form of **resources** and value sets (Chapters 5 and 6), but these in turn need to be leveraged and directed into a coherent value proposition. Exploring possible routes for advantage at both a corporate

Figure 8.1 Overview of business and network strategies

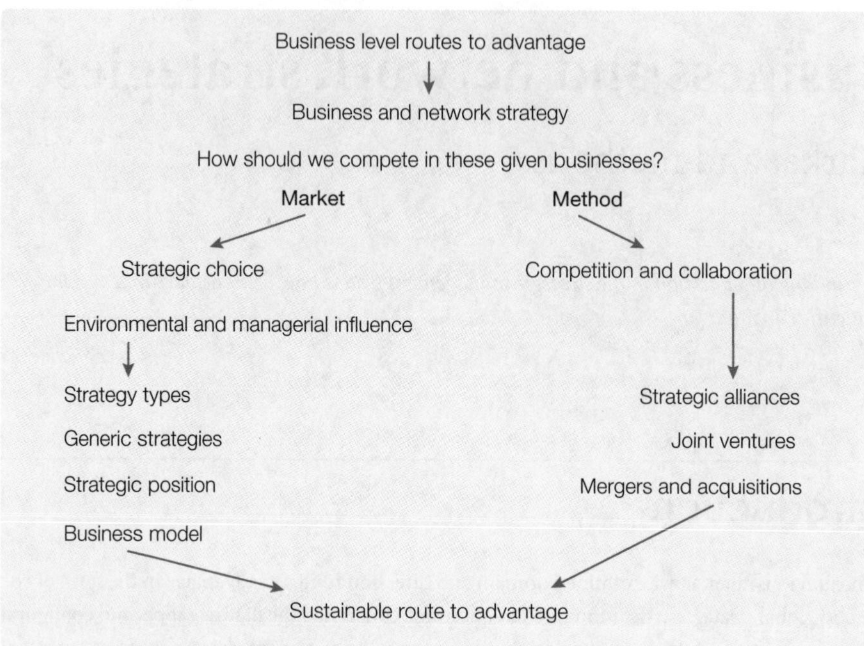

level, via domain and direction (Chapter 7), and business-unit level, via markets and methods, is one means of achieving this task. We begin the chapter by examining market routes to advantage in the form of strategic choice and business-level strategy.

Strategic choice

One of the central debates within the strategic management field concerns how an organization should align itself to its competitive environment (Bourgeois, 1984; Miles *et al.*, 1978). This strategic choice is centred on whether the external environment or managerial influence is the more significant determinant of firm performance. On one side of the debate are those who argue that the external environment is the more significant factor impacting the performance of an organization, so that the organization has to respond to environmental forces by introducing appropriate organizational structures (Di Maggio and Powell, 1983; Pfeffer and Salancik, 1978). This view is known as 'external determinism'. The general argument, as Child (1972: 8) puts it, is: 'if organizational structure is not adapted to context, then opportunities are lost, costs rise, and the maintenance of the organization is threatened.'

The counter perspective argues that top managers have greater influence on organizational performance than other factors. This is because top managers have significant power, which can be used to set the direction of the firm (Thomas, 1988). The power that a top management team possesses can mediate strategy, structure, and the external environment. This can be achieved through evaluating the characteristics and constraints of the environment before selecting appropriate technology, structure, and human resources. This is subsequently reflected in the firm's strategic activity and levels of performance (Child, 1997). Strategic choice, from the perspective of managerial influence, is focused on organizational actors and views the evolution of organizations as a product of these actors' decisions rather than only a passive environmental selection process whereby a firm's existence is solely determined by its external business environment (Child, 1972). Our debate in Chapters 4 and 6 similarly illustrated how strategists can shape, rather than be shaped by, the external environment.

While these competing perspectives are useful, caution must be exercised in exploring strategic choice. As an example, one may consider that Marc Bolland, chief executive officer (CEO) of Marks and Spencer (M&S), and his top management team have the capacity to influence the strategic choices of M&S; their influence outweighs other factors, because they have a clear understanding of strategy, structure, and the external environment. However, this view must be accompanied by an acknowledgement that the activities of M&S will be heavily informed by key legislation as it relates to retail (for example, caps on store size, Competition Acts), the activities of the competition (for example, new strategies, new entrants), and the demands of key stakeholders, while all the while having to please the markets and shareholders. Appreciating that, for organizations, pure, unabated choice is unlikely, the concept of the 'zones of manoeuvre' available to a firm (Clark, 2000: 52) acknowledges the environmental and political constraints that are likely frame decision making. As we move to consider business-level strategy, this is an important point: too often, the routes to advantage are understood in isolation, as a complete menu of options from which organizations can simply pick and choose; in practice, viable options for firms will be somewhat limited, while choices may be contested.

Business-level strategy

Against the backdrop of the strategic choice debate, the focus of business-level strategy is to ensure that the company is able to compete as effectively as possible in its chosen business. For the strategist, achieving alignment between environmental conditions and the appropriate business-level strategy is critical to achieving and sustaining a competitive advantage. Business-level strategy is the remit of the business unit. An organization with diversified portfolio of businesses may have a vast spectrum of business units competing via a diverse range of business strategies. One business unit may compete as a low-cost provider in a commodity-based industry (such as Tata Steel), while another may operate at the frontier of innovation in a high-tech, research and development (R&D) based domain (Tata Technologies). In outlining a theory of business strategy, Shapiro (1989: 127) notes:

> we should distinguish strategic decisions, which involve long-lasting commitments, from tactical decisions, which are short-term responses to the current environment. In the language of game theory, the strategic decisions determine the evolution of state variables that provide a setting in which current tactics are played out.

These state variables include investment in physical capital, intangible assets, horizontal measures, network competition, product standardization, and contracting. Business-level strategy at firm level can be viewed from a number of perspectives, including strategy types (Miles *et al.*, 1978), generic strategies (Porter, 1985), and strategic position (Porter, 1996); at its core is ensuring organizational competitiveness within competitive arenas. In many respects, these perspectives can be viewed as means by which organizations attempt to take control of the environment and, in doing so, to achieve and sustain competitive advantage. Making a clear decision on the business strategy to be pursued further enables this by mobilizing resources, activities, and people to form a coherent value proposition.

Strategy types: types of organizational adaptation

Researchers of business-level strategy disagree on how organizations can achieve a competitive advantage at business level. The earliest academics to address this thorny issue were Miles *et al.* (1978), who outlined four basic strategy types that pervade the business environment. In doing so, they introduced the concept of the 'adaptive cycle', consisting of the entrepreneurial problem (choice of product–market domain), the administrative problem (roles, relationships, and organizational processes), and the engineering problem (choice of technologies for production and distribution). According to Miles and Snow (2003: 27), 'although organizational adaptation is a complex and dynamic process, it can be broadly conceptualized as a cycle of adjustment potentially requiring the simultaneous solution of three major problems'. Key features of the model include the following.

1. The adaptive cycle is a general physiology of organizational behaviour.
2. The three adaptive problems—entrepreneurial, engineering, and administrative—are intricately interwoven.
3. Adaptation frequently occurs by moving sequentially through the entrepreneurial, engineering, and administrative phases, but the cycle can be triggered at any one of these points.
4. Adaptive decisions today tend to harden and become aspects of tomorrow's structure.

In tandem with their conceptual development of an adaptive cycle, the four business-level strategy/organization types outlined by Miles *et al.* (1978) are 'defenders', 'prospectors', 'analysers', and 'reactors'.

Defenders

Organizations that are defenders typically have a narrow product–market focus, with top managers being experts in a limited functional or market range. This type of strategy is evident in the hotel market. With the boom of the 1990s, there was a proliferation of new hotels. Well-established hotels have attempted to defend their market share by spending resources in redeveloping bedrooms, and adding spas and leisure facilities. This narrow product–market focus means that defender firms rarely seek new market opportunities, instead devoting their main organizational effort to improving the effectiveness and efficiency of their existing operations. In terms of growing, the defender organizations attempt to develop greater market share incrementally—what Miles *et al.* (1978) describe as 'sealing off'—with the planning process following the classic sequence of planning and evaluating. The real danger for firms pursuing a defender strategy is their over-reliance and, ultimately, dependence on a narrow product–market focus. Because of this, they may be incapable of responding to new competitive opportunities.

Prospectors

Prospectors are those organizations that continually seek out new market opportunities and consequently experiment with new products and services in the marketplace. Software companies such as Sage are constantly seeking new market opportunities and products. Prospector organizations can change the competitive dynamics within an industry with their new products and services; this, in turn, may cause competitive problems for competitors. The danger for prospector organizations is that they may not achieve the efficiency levels required to compete, given that their focus is on seeking and creating new market opportunities (Miller, 1992). Growth for prospector organizations is achieved by product and market exploration, and by having flexibility with their technological commitments. The approach to planning takes a broader perspective, focused on problem solving and 'contingent upon feedback from experimental action' (Miles and Snow, 2003: 61). Some real risks exist for prospectors in terms of over-proliferation of products and markets, technological inefficiency, and lack of exploitation of administrative systems due to inefficiencies.

Analysers: the avid followers

Analysers are those organizations that attempt to have a dual product–market presence. One part of the business operates in a product–market domain that is relatively stable, thereby affording the organization the capacity to become as lean and efficient as possible in serving these product–market domains. In consumer electronics, a number of manufacturers enter a market once the technology and products have been established, such as HD TVs. The second element of this dual product–market presence involves the organization competing in product–market domains that are competitively fluid. The analyser firms in these domains keep track of new developments. Organizations will imitate, implement, and deploy those developments that are likely to make an impact. An analyser's growth emanates from a number of sources, including market penetration and product and market development. The planning process for an analyser follows the process of evaluation, planning, and action, and the organization places significant emphasis on intensive market and industry surveillance. The potential shortcomings of analyser organizations centre on their dual focus, which never yields total efficiency and responsiveness in stable and growing markets; their management teams must also deal with the delicate balance between the dual product–market domains. The idea of balancing exploitation of existing markets with exploring new opportunities is one that has much influence in thinking about organizations (March, 1991; Thompson, 1967).

Reactors

In examining the routes to advantage, it is easy to fall into the trap of considering only those routes that successfully leverage advantage. Miles and Snow (2003) offer a useful reminder that not all organizations are successful or follow a clear strategic route. For them, reactor organizations are those that will only respond to product and market changes when they are forced to do so by environmental conditions. Reactors have an inability to respond swiftly to environmental changes, even though their management may be attuned to movements in the external environment. According to the authors:

> This inconsistency potentially may stem from at least three sources: (1) management fails to articulate a viable organizational strategy; (2) a strategy is articulated by technology [but] structure and processes are not linked to it in an appropriate manner; or (3) management adheres to a particular strategy–structure relation even though it is no longer relevant to environmental conditions.
>
> (Miles and Snow, 2003: 84)

In depicting different modes of strategy and organizational adaptation, successful or otherwise, Miles and Snow offered a clear language with which to consider the strategic options available to firms. However, building upon the logic of his 'five forces' framework (see Reading 2.2), Michael Porter offered not only labels for strategies, but also a means for understanding why certain strategies were likely to be more viable than others as a result of industry conditions.

Generic competitive strategies

The next perspective of business strategy that we consider is Porter's three generic competitive strategies. This is one of the universally used perspectives with which to conceptualize and understand the interactions between business-level strategy and the environment. Generic competitive strategies can be adopted by organizations to achieve competitive advantage over rivals in the marketplace; in doing so, they build a position that they can defend. In implementing a generic strategy, an organization can generate superior returns that can be used to defend, develop, and grow its market position, ultimately beating rivals and outperforming key financial industry averages, such as return on capital employed and return on investment. As a result of existing conditions within industry, Porter identified three generic competitive strategies on the basis of which to compete: cost leadership, differentiation, and focus (see Figure 8.2). Porter argued that the strategies could be applied to a large variety of situations and contexts.

Low-cost leadership

In pursuing a cost leadership strategy, organizations seek to make their product or service available to the largest possible number of potential customers, because volume and scale are important

Figure 8.2 Examples of generic strategies

Business level routes to advantage

Low-cost leadership

A firm pursuing a cost-leadership strategy seeks to be the lowest-cost producer of a good or service in the industry in which it competes,while ensuring that it also maintains the quality and other standards necessary to compete.

Examples: easyJet; Aldi; Ibis Hotels

Differentiation strategy

Firms compete on points of uniqueness and value for their products or services, which allow the firms to seek and ultimately receive a premium price in the market.

Examples: BMW (differentiating on the ultimate driving experience); M&S (on quality and value of offerings)

Focus strategy

The company competes in a certain segment of the market, based on a costor a differentiation strategy.

Examples: Rolex; Lexus

elements to successful pursuit of a low-cost strategy. The organization needs to achieve a consistent cost advantage through its value chain, which should be the lowest cost in the industry. It achieves this by reconfiguring the value chain to reduce or cut out expensive or unnecessary activities, by managing all costs within the value chain, and by remaining consistently focused on driving costs down. This also means ensuring that there are efficient coordination and interaction between all activities within the firm's value chain (Porter, 1980: 97). In reality, this is consistently difficult for firms to achieve given organizational complexities around processes and cultures.

Successful cost leadership requires an organization to gain economies of scale and ensure that the benefits of the experience curve effects accrue to it. Learning and experience curve effects are the combination of the cost of production and the accumulated experience that an organization acquires from competing in an industry. A company that has been manufacturing yogurt products for fifteen years has significant learning and experience curve effects compared with a new market entrant or rival firm that has been competing in the industry for only two years. Cumulative wealth of experience means that the established firm may have automated the manufacturing process, streamlined the supplier network, enhanced the product's packaging, developed new products, and created a flexible distribution system, all of which yield a lower cost of production and place it at a distinct cost advantage over rivals. Other ways of controlling costs include better internal linkages of activities, sharing resources and opportunities with other business units or firms, vertical integration, and increased capacity utilization (Porter, 1980: 70–107).

One of the significant dangers in pursuing a low-cost strategy is that customer tastes and preferences can change significantly, which then impacts on scale and scope advantages. Other dangers include an exclusive focus on cost reduction to the neglect of other factors, imitation by competitive rivals, and the development of new technologies that erode any cost advantage achieved by the firm. Therefore the organization has to ensure that it has sufficient flexibility in product or service features to meet any changes in customer tastes and preferences.

Differentiation

A critical element of a successful differentiation strategy is ensuring that the customer attributes a value to the product or service and is willing to pay a premium price. This means developing points of differentiation that may be difficult to imitate, can be defended, and provide a platform of growth for the organization. If executed well, a differentiation strategy can yield higher margins for the firm, increase its scale and market scope, and develop an emotional connection with customers that can be monetized further.

Points of differentiation extend to a range of attributes in a single product or service, or across a suite, and can include, for example, brand, features, product design, purchasing experience, after-sales services, flexible processes, and reliability. In reality, organizations potentially have several points of differentiation, some subjective and some tangible, but customers have to perceive that the differentiation is worth a premium price. Customers have to *feel* the differentiated experience. Some organizations fail to communicate and signal to the customer their differentiation strategy, which is subjective and/or intangible. It is therefore essential for firms to signal effectively their differentiation strategy at pre-purchase and post-purchase stages. For example, it could be argued that there is a lot of wastage in the advertising of marques such as BMW and Mercedes, but the counter-argument is that these organizations are communicating consistently their points of differentiation to potential buyers, as well as to existing owners, thereby continually reassuring them of differentiation attributes.

Differentiation strategies succeed in competitive contexts in which a product or service can be differentiated in a variety of ways—that is, it is not a commodity product—when other competitors are not pursuing differentiation strategies effectively, and when the usage and needs of customers are varied. It is important to ensure that, irrespective of the points of differentiation, the cost base of the organization is in line with, or lower than, the industry average. Without this, the organization's ability to achieve sustained high margins lessens, as does the economic rationale. However, the real danger in pursuing a differentiation strategy is that a customer does not perceive the subjective and/or actual differentiation and will not pay the premium for the product or service. Other dangers include imitation and substitution, a decline in the value that the market attributes to points of differentiation, failure to signal differentiation, and a shrinkage in the potential customer pool that reduces the economic returns on extensive points of differentiation. In addition, new technology or an alternative business model may enable new entrants or existing competitors to offer a similar value proposition from a lower cost base.

Focus

The key difference between focus strategy based on cost or differentiation and the other generic strategies is that, with a focus strategy, the organization competes only in a particular market segment or territory rather than in the whole range of market segments. A focused strategy means that an organization chooses a segment that it can enter and, more importantly, defend successfully from rivals. If a firm uses a cost-focused strategy, it seeks the cost leadership position within that market segment. If it pursues a differentiation strategy, the subjective and/or actual basis of differentiation is targeted at a specific market segment that it can defend. Rivals may deem the economic value of such market segments too small to justify competing on the basis of differentiation or cost leadership.

One of the key dangers of a focused strategy is that the size of the market segment might decline, reducing the economic value of serving it. Other dangers include changes in customer preferences, blurring of market segment boundaries, and the segment becoming attractive to other industry competitors who then enter it with differentiation. According to Porter (1980: 41), the overriding danger for any firm in the context of generic strategies is a failure to pursue a single strategy clearly and thereby risk being 'stuck in the middle'. This is likely to lead to a value proposition that is confusing for customers and the internal operations of the organization being stretched in competing directions.

Criticisms of generic strategies

Several criticisms have been levelled at Porter's generic strategies, such as the observation that organizations can pursue all of them in a single industry; it is not a case of choosing one strategic position or another. Porter's generic strategies can appear to offer rational solutions to business without these solutions being undermined by their application. In short, the universality of Porter's analysis of strategy remains plausible only if it is adequate either in its construction or application (Knights, 1992: 526). VAG in Germany pursues cost leadership through the Seat and Skoda brands, differentiation through the Volkswagen (VW) brand, and focus through the Porsche and Audi brands. In other words, VAG pursues all of the generic strategies within the same industry. This gives VAG the ability to respond effectively over the external environment. Successful execution of strategy in Porter's model is assumed rather than designed for (Akan *et al.*, 2006). We make a distinction between choosing routes to advantage and realizing advantage for the very reason that what a firm intends cannot be equated to what it actually achieves in practice. In fact, there is very frequently a disconnect between the two.

Another criticism questions the relevance and limitations of the generic strategies in a world that is becoming more network-centric. Venkatraman and Subramaniam (2002: 472) argue that 'the path ahead is open for us to collectively recognize the limitations of current approaches to theorizing—not because they were wrong but because they have outlived their usefulness'. How would the generic strategies of Facebook and Skype be defined? Is viewing their business strategy through generic strategies the most appropriate perspective to take?

A further criticism is that Porter ignored socio-political relations both inside and outside any particular organization—that his 'concept of strategy based on positioning did not adequately address cross-business synergies and hence the value added of a corporation' (Venkatraman and Subramaniam, 2002: 464). Returning to VAG as an example, it has achieved savings and efficiencies by pursuing a platform strategy and through sharing of parts in the manufacturing process across a number of its brands.

One of the most forceful criticisms directed at Porter's work is that organizations are not necessarily stuck in the middle when they compete on the basis of quality and cost. Arguably, organizations such as Dell and IKEA have illustrated that competing on this basis can be a very viable and successful strategy. Porter also offers little guidance about how organizations cope with change or may go about moving from one generic strategy to another.

While largely interpreted as implying that organizations can control their environment, the theoretical underpinning of Porter's work, in the guise of the industry structure–firm conduct–performance (SCP) **paradigm**, suggests otherwise (Porter, 2008). SCP deliberately commences with the conditions of the external environment and works backward to explore the implications for firm strategy. Arguably, this is a form of environmental determinism that leaves little scope for firm choice. In fact, in this model, and given the three limited generic options available, the strategist plays a very limited role.

Despite these criticisms, generic strategies still occupy a central place in the strategic management field. Campbell-Hunt (2000: 151) notes:

> Although this study [Campbell-Hunt's] has affirmed that cost and differentiation do play a high-level role in discriminating between competitive strategy designs, its accumulation of the empirical record has uncovered a richer and more fine-grained descriptive system than that originally proposed and has focused attention on the need for a more complete, and possibly different, specification of line between competitive strategy and firm performance.

Therefore it is conceivable that, over time, generic strategies may not be the most appropriate means by which to understand or analyse business-level strategy. The real task for strategy researchers and strategists alike is to reach an even deeper understanding of business-level strategy and to build on the existing theoretical contributions. In response to some of the criticism of his work by those suggesting a resource-based foundation for advantage (Barney, 1991; Prahalad and Hamel, 1990; see Chapter 6), Porter himself elaborated and refined his own ideas via a positioning-based argument.

Strategy positioning

In 1996, the *Harvard Business Review* published 'What is strategy?' (Porter, 1996—Reading 1.1). This was Porter's robust defence of his external positioning-based perspective. In this piece, Porter argued that focusing attention on successful Japanese firms was misguided, because in attempting to compete on cost and quality, such firms were 'stuck in the middle' and hence 'rarely have strategies' (ibid: 62). Porter also used the opportunity to expand upon his strategic positioning perspective, categorizing three strategic positions as 'variety-based positioning', 'needs-based positioning', and 'access-based positioning'. With variety-based positioning, an organization offers a variety of products and services, which provide choice to many customer segments, not only to one. Organizations can pursue this strategy if they have distinctive activities that enhance the economic case of this positioning strategy. The major difficulty with a variety-based positioning is that, given the spread of products and services over many customer segments, organizations may serve only some of the customer needs.

Needs-based positioning occurs when a business's products and services are centred on a segment of customers who have differing needs. Through the organization of its activities, the business meets the differing needs of these segments of customers who have competing preferences and demands. Porter (1996: 66) argues that:

> A variant of needs-based positioning arises when the same customer has different needs on different occasions or for different types of transactions ... Differences in needs will not translate into meaningful positions unless the best set of activities to satisfy them *also* differs. If it were not the case, every competitor could meet those same needs, and there would be nothing unique or valuable about the positioning.

In needs-based positioning, firms must organize systems and processes by which customers can experience a difference that meets their individual tastes and preferences.

Access-based positioning focuses on 'segmenting customers who are accessible in different ways. Although their needs are similar to those of other customers, the best configuration of activities to reach them is different' (Porter, 1996: 67). In the UK, Unilever's distribution channels mean that its products are available in major grocery retailing outlets, petrol stations, and corner shops. In India, Unilever depends on individual door-to-door salesmen to sell and distribute its washing powder. Both customer segments have the same needs, to wash clothes, but the manner in which Unilever meets these needs differs.

In summing up strategic positioning, Porter (1996: 64) argues: 'Strategy is the creation of a unique and valuable position, involving a different set of activities ... The essence of strategic positioning is to choose activities that are different to rivals'.' But strategic positioning is also about the conceptualization of difference, value, and uniqueness in the customer's mind.

Overall, the concept of fit is common to all of the business-strategy approaches that we have reviewed, with the exception of reactors, who struggle to obtain fit. The role of fit between the organization and its competitive environment goes to the heart of the strategic choice issue. Also important, as the work of Porter (1996) demonstrates, is the fit between internal activities along the value chain. Hence Chorn (1991: 21) describes fit as the 'degree of alignment that exists between competitive situation, strategy, organization culture and leadership styles. In this sense it is the "appropriateness" of the various elements to one another'. Another perspective that captures the dynamics of fit underpinning a business strategy value proposition is that of business models.

Business models

The concept of business models developed momentum during the dot.com boom at the end of the 1990s, when many Internet businesses used this terminology to describe their offering and revenue models (Yip, 2004). Skarzynski and Gibson (2008: 112) define a business model as 'a conceptual framework that describes how a company creates, delivers, and extracts value'. There are two critical tests for business models: the narrative test, examining the coherence and logic of the story, and the numbers test, examining the profit-and-loss impact of the story. As Magretta (2002: 90) points out: 'Business modelling is the managerial equivalent of the scientific method—you start with a hypothesis, which you then test in action and revise when necessary.' Business models are not business-level strategies, because models focus on systems, whereas strategy, as Magretta (2002: 92) puts it, is 'how you are going to do better by being different'. Business models are a way in which to better capture the alignment of activities that underpin your strategy.

Business model innovation involves creating new business models that potentially disrupt the industry. In attempting to build new business models, a firm needs to address the following elements, according to Yip (2004: 20):

- the value proposition;
- the nature of inputs;
- how to transform inputs;
- the nature of outputs;
- the nature of customers; and
- how to organize.

Thus while an organization such easyGroup competes on the basis of a defender or a no-frill, low-cost leadership strategy in domains such as airlines (easyJet) and car rental (easyCar), we can further understand this proposition by disaggregating the key elements of its business model. Drawing on Yip (2004: 20–21) there is a clear value proposition. The 'easy' concept captures the idea of bringing cheap, affordable services to a mass market in an efficient manner. Inputs tend to be standardized: one type of aircraft; one type of car. The common pervasive technology is the Internet, allowing for online booking and a dominant online presence and a prominent brand. Outputs are the minimal, no-frills services. Target customers are young, urban, and cost-conscious customers. Finally, the organization is lean in its structure and activities.

We can see why business models became so popular and important for Internet-based companies, because they served as tangible outlines and demonstrations illustrating how an otherwise intangible online entity would deliver value. However, they are also important for all organizations; 'they are at heart, stories—stories that explain how enterprises work' (Magretta, 2002: 87). Recent new business models are heavily associated with emerging markets (Baden-Fuller, 2010). Not only a neat way of capturing activities, a successful business model will represent a better way of operating or better 'story' than the alternatives available. Assumptions about customer behaviour are a critical cornerstone on which business models are built. This again reinforces the importance of robust foundations of advantage (Chapters 5 and 6) as stepping stones to choosing the optimal route to advantage. Clarity around business models is also likely to facilitate the realization of advantage, because if the business model tells a good story, 'it can be used to get everyone in the organization aligned around the kind of value the company wants to create' (Magretta, 2002: 92). Business models are likely to have increasing significance as system-level units of analysis, depicting how firms' activities create and capture advantage (Zott *et al.*, 2011).

As we have seen, there are different ways of conceptualizing business-level strategy and its application should give the strategist a real sense of how to compete appropriately in his or her chosen markets. What is clearly evident from examining business-level strategy is the real need for organizations to differentiate themselves from their competitors; otherwise, there is a danger that they become 'me too' operations. Business-level strategy provides some interesting perspectives that the strategist can use in determining how that differentiation should manifest itself in the competitive marketplace. Strategists should always monitor and continually devise appropriate levels of strategic fit in order to achieve and sustain competitive advantage. So far, our consideration of business strategy has assumed the business unit to be operating as a stand-alone entity in competition with rival firms (Dyer and Singh, 1998). Traditional understanding, such as the resource-based view of the firm, holds that advantage must come from activities and processes *within* the firm (Lavie, 2006: 640). However, the pace of change, requirement for innovation, and need to operate across regions, networks, and consumer bases has opened up the suggestion that collaboration rather than competition may form the essence of competitive advantage. Consequently, in the next section, we explore *methods* of collaboration in the form of a diverse range of network strategies as potential routes to advantage.

Network strategies

Network strategy is focused on the methods that an organization uses to achieve advantage in a competitive market. Strategists have to find a pragmatic balance between collaborating and competing. Organizations with scope and scale use various forms of collaboration to maintain their competitive positions and dominance. Collaboration provides sources of new ideas and a means of extracting further value from protected intellectual property. Microsoft registers several thousand patents annually. Collaboration with a range of universities (Carayannis and Alexander, 1999) and other industry players is essential to develop and enhance its product and service offering, and to maintain its competitive dominance. Through its venture group, it has the ability to license software products that are non-core to its businesses, thereby extracting further value from its activities.

The challenge that the strategist faces in network strategy is best summed up by Brandenburger and Nalebuff (1997), who coined the term 'coopetition'. In this, 'a company has to keep its eye on both balls, creating and capturing at the same time . . . it combines competition and cooperation' (ibid: 28). Coopetition is in direct conflict with the fundamental nature of competition, as Porter (1990: 122) views it, arguing that 'Direct cooperation among competitors . . . undermines competitive advantage unless it takes some limited and specific forms. It eliminates diversity, saps incentives, and slows the rate of industry improvement'. However, for many, the military idea of competition focused on rivalry, clear divisions, and one single winner is outdated; instead, conceptions of viable routes to advantage should evolve to encompass inclusion, synergy, and common goals across firms (Patel, 2005). In sum, network strategies can create competitive advantage for organizations in terms of economies of scale, economies of scope, and economies of expertise (Venkatraman and Subramaniam, 2002).

Competition

The adage goes that competition is the lifeblood of any industry. There are multiple perspectives on how competition should be encouraged and regulated from both business executives and economists. The dichotomy of perspectives on competition is captured by Dean (1954: 64): 'To the businessman, generally speaking, competition is whatever he has to do to get sales away from his rivals and whatever they do to take sales away from him'. To the economist, competition is:

> the welfare of the consumer. And this welfare is fostered primarily by (a) a wide range of choice for buyers—assuming adequate know-how to exercise this choice—and (b) compulsions to efficiency for sellers—that is, rivalry that tends to push prices down toward the costs of the most efficient producer.
>
> (Dean, 1954: 68)

The nature of competition during the life cycle of an industry varies. A typical industry life cycle goes through four main phases: the pioneering or early stage; the growth phase; maturity; and decline. Understanding the nature of competition provides the strategist with insights into how a company should adapt and respond to the competitive pressures.

In the pioneering or early stage of an industry, there may be limited competition, because the focus is on developing the product or service and getting it to market. Companies tend to experiment with their business models in terms of getting their offering into the marketplace. For example, Asus was one of the first firms into the market with netbooks, a miniaturized version of a laptop used for emails and web browsing. Other companies, such as HP, Sony, Advent, and Dell, responded with their own netbooks.

During the growth phase, the level of competition intensifies as more competitors enter the competitive arena, attracted by the market opportunity and the growth prospects. During this period, the basis of competition intensifies, with organizations differentiating and positioning their offerings. In the case of e-book readers, Sony launched its e-reader and Amazon launched its Kindle.

The next stage in the industry life cycle is when an industry goes through a maturity phase, in which the market opportunities and growth prospects are low. At this stage, there is likely to be much emphasis on low prices and value for money propositions. This results in organizations devoting more organizational effort to maximizing operational efficiency and focusing on customer retention initiatives. This stage also sees some companies beginning to exit the market. During the credit crunch in 2008, several small airline carriers exited the industry and further consolidation occurred.

The final stage in the industry life cycle model is decline, in which market growth prospects are poor, if not non-existent. At this stage, several competitors tend to leave the market in search of new growth opportunities. Consequently, some consolidation can take place within an industry sector and the intensity of competition may lessen as a result. Some analysts suggest that segments of the car industry have reached maturity, along with sectors of the natural minerals industry as global sources begin to decline.

Taking an ecological view of competition, the evolutionary stages of a **business ecosystem** include birth, expansion, leadership, and self-renewal. The competitive requirement at birth is to protect the idea. During expansion, the need is to compete with other ideas in the marketplace to ensure that the firm's idea prevails in terms of product or service. During the leadership phase, the competitive requirement is to keep a strong bargaining position with other stakeholders in the ecosystem. During the self-renewal period, it is to keep other firms out by creating high barriers to entry, as well as by serving the customers (Moore, 1993). While useful for understanding how the nature and intensity of competition is likely to vary, such life cycle models still largely view the firm as exclusively operating in competition with other firms and evolving in a linear fashion. However, it is frequently the case that collaborative capability is a necessity to maintaining a competitive advantage.

Collaboration

The rationale and promise of collaboration is best summarized by Simonin (1997: 1150), who states that 'collaborations have become important, if not critical, means of supplementing corporate strengths and covering weaknesses'. At the same time, Simonin also notes the reality that many collaborations often do not achieve their original goals, and that many fail. Taking a transaction-cost economics perspective, collaboration can be viewed as an extension of the make-or-buy decision (Hennart, 1988). Collaboration also means that organizations collectively and individually are in a better position to compete with, withstand, and deal with competitive pressures, while also having opportunities to learn and absorb from other entities.

One of the central motivations of organizations using collaboration is its deployment as a strategic weapon, as Stiles (1995: 110) illustrates:

> the business environment becomes increasingly hostile, the strategy of the firm needs to be able to provide it with the means with which to defend its position and to tackle the opposition . . . the organization's strategy of developing a variety of focused collaborative partnership is providing the company with the ability to invest in a wider variety of R&D projects, thus reducing the considerable costs and risks associated with this form of operation.

In the airline industry, it is common practice for competitors to enter collaborative arrangements to complement and expand their route offerings to customers, which combine short-haul and long-haul options and are presented seamlessly to the customer. The Star Alliance is an example of this form of collaboration. Another motivation for collaboration, particularly in international settings, is so that a firm can recoup some of its R&D expenditure in foreign markets and different industry sectors (Oviatt and McDougall, 1994). An organization may achieve a technological advantage and may also reduce risks associated with technological obsolescence through collaboration.

Successful collaboration

Key issues around any collaborative arrangement centre on the strategic rationale, trust between parties, associated collective and individual benefits, the operational arrangement, and organizational infrastructure. MacCormack and Forbath (2008) also note that people (with a particular focus on soft skills), processes, platforms (infrastructure), and programmes are crucial to the collaborative innovation. There is a myth that effective collaboration means teaming; an effective incentive system will ensure successful alignment and execution (Weiss and Hughes, 2005). However, the process of collaboration from activities related to inception, through partnership, to evaluation of outcomes is extremely complex. Collaboration typically goes through the collaborative cycle as follows (Simonin, 1997):

- identifying and selecting potential collaborators;
- negotiating the terms and structure of a collaborative arrangement;
- monitoring and managing an ongoing collaboration;
- terminating a collaboration.

As a result of this cycle, the collaborators can gain know-how and experience that can be shared and used to improve the outcome of future collaborations.

Empirical evidence has demonstrated the impact of collaboration at firm level (Ritala, 2011). After studies of over 1,000 firms and 378 collaborations, Ang (2008: 1057) concludes: 'Collaboration leads to higher growth for firms facing lower levels of competitive intensity than for firms facing higher levels of competitive intensity only in more technology-intensive industries.' Sampson's (2005) study of 464 R&D alliances in the telecom equipment industry found that 'While collaborative benefits are enhanced with prior alliance experiences, more extensive experience does not appear to improve outcomes over more limited experience . . . the benefits of prior alliance experience depreciate rapidly over time' (ibid: 1027). These empirical studies highlight the benefits of collaboration and the need for parties to continue to devote time and effort in ensuring that collaborative efforts succeed over time and do not dissipate after the initial period of enthusiasm. This also suggests that collaboration is more likely to work in certain contexts and under certain conditions (Ritala, 2011).

Open and closed collaboration

Increasingly, levels of inter-firm collaboration will focus on innovation, particularly around convergent technology opportunities. As an example, information communication technology (ICT) and biotechnology companies are collaborating to develop new products and services for business and customers in the health sector. These collaborative arrangements can fall into two categories: open collaboration, in which all stakeholders' expertise are used, and closed collaboration, in which 'the players are equal partners in the process and share the power to decide key issues' (Pisano and Verganit, 2008: 80). The four modes of collaborative innovation identified by Pisano and Verganit (2008) are as follows.

- *Elite circles* One company selects the participants, defines the problem, and chooses the solutions.
- *Innovation mall* One company posts a problem, anyone can propose solutions, and the company chooses the solutions that it likes best.

- *Innovation community* Anybody can propose problems, offer solutions, and decide which solutions to use.
- *Consortium* Operates like a private club, with participants jointly selecting problems, deciding how to conduct work, and choosing solutions.

Challenges inherent in collaboration

There are specific challenges for organizations in creating any form of collaborative arrangement: namely, designing incentives that attract external collaborators. This issue within collaborative arrangements is linked to the need to balance governance and uncertainty, particularly in relation to administrative control and commitment. Within any collaborative arrangement, one party may seek to have dominant control. Consequently, it might invest considerable time and effort to ensure this. In other collaborative arrangements, competitive and technological uncertainties may be so great at a particular time that collaboration makes strategic sense and there are clear benefits. Sometimes, the cost of collaboration might not make financial sense as these uncertainties increase or even decrease. Folta (1998: 1007) found that 'the cost of commitment in the face of technological uncertainty may offset the administrative benefits of hierarchical governance'.

Another key challenge is dealing with the reality that conflict and tension are an integral part of any collaborative arrangement. As in any human relationship, there will be periods of tension and conflict. In managing such conflict in collaborative contexts, Weiss and Hughes (2005) suggest several approaches, including:

- devise and implement a common method for resolving conflict;
- provide people with criteria for making **trade-offs**;
- use the escalation of conflict as an opportunity for coaching;
- establish and enforce a requirement of joint escalation;
- ensure that managers resolve escalated conflicts directly with their counterparts; and
- make the process for escalated conflict resolution transparent.

The potential for conflict and mechanisms for its resolution will not be universal across all types of collaborative arrangement. Intensity of relations, power dynamics, and trust issues will inevitably vary, depending on the network form in question and the range, type, and culture of the organizations involved.

Network forms

There are various methods by which an organization can align itself with other organizations in an effort to find a more secure and sustainable route to advantage. Key networking strategies include strategic alliances, joint ventures, and mergers and acquisitions (M&As). In considering the nature of network strategies, an organization must explore the potential impact in terms of its brand and customer base, in addition to how the culture of the organization may help or hinder such arrangements. Likewise, when there is an international dimension to the network strategy, national culture and customs will also form part of considerations. Moreover, what will key stakeholders and shareholder make of the arrangement? Is it likely to be interpreted as a sign that the organization is progressive and ambitious, or as an admission that the organization has key weaknesses?

At the core of any network strategy is the issue of inter-organizational trust. This can be difficult to establish and complex to manage, particularly if the network form extends across a number of geographical boundaries and cultures.

Strategic alliances

In industries as diverse as steel, travel, and car manufacturing, strategic alliances are becoming a key network form for many firms as they attempt to gain competitive dominance and control, and to shape some of the competitive forces that they face. Ohmae (1989: 143) summarizes the need for strategic alliance: 'To compete in the global arena, you have to incur and defray immense fixed costs. You need partners ... With enough time, money and luck, you can do everything yourself. But who has enough?' In practical terms, the growth of alliances can be accounted for in part by the fact that they have been found to outperform other forms of networking strategies (Medcof, 1997).

Strategic alliance forms can range from basic agreement to equity ownership and shared managerial control over activities. The rationale behind strategic alliances can be based on three distinct purposes (Doz and Hamel, 1998: 4–5): co-option, co-specialization, and learning and internationalization (Lei and Slocum, 1992). Co-option allows firms to enter strategic alliances with competitors, rendering them less of a competitive threat. It can also provide a competitive platform to build new products and services. With co-specialization, the firms enter alliances with strengths in different activities such as marketing, R&D, operations, and supply chain management, which, when combined, are more valuable. Alliances can also be an opportunity for learning new skills. Strategic alliances provide opportunities for learning, which can be used to make future and even current strategic alliances operate more effectively and achieve the envisioned objectives for all parties. Petrofac, founded in Tyler, Texas, is an international provider of facilities solutions to the oil and gas production and processing industries. In November 2010, it entered a strategic alliance with Seven Energy International Limited, a Nigerian production and development company. In making this move, Petrofac demonstrated the distinct purposes of alliances, as outlined by Doz and Hamel (1998: 4–5).

Selecting alliance partners

An important task for a firm is choosing the appropriate strategic alliance partners that will benefit its activities. Many studies have indicated that alliance partners can be disappointed with the outcomes of their alliances (Contractor and Lorange, 1998; Mathews and Harvey, 1988), with many alliances ending up in failure and break-up. If strategic alliances include partners with previous alliance experiences or if the alliance has an equity element to it, there is a higher probability of alliance survival over a longer period of time (Pangarkar, 2003). Brouthers *et al.* (1995) suggest that, in selecting an appropriate strategic alliance partner, companies should give consideration to:

- the complementary skills offered by partners;
- the cooperative cultures that exist between the firms;
- the compatible goals between all firms; and
- the commensurate levels of risk, if alliance partners share risk.

The issue of fit is a key strategic question that organizations need to address when seeking and selecting potential alliance partners. Preconditions for strategic fit include shared vision, compatibility of strategies, strategic importance, mutual dependency, added value for partners and/or their customers, and market acceptance. Drivers of organizational fit in an alliance context include addressing organizational differences, providing strategic and organizational flexibility, enabling effective management control for both partners, and addressing potential strategic conflicts (Douma *et al.*, 2000). In a strategic alliance context, questions that need to be addressed, according to Medcof (1997: 720), are: 'Does the alliance have a good business strategy rationale? Is the prospective partner a good strategic fit?' Doz and Hamel (1998: 265) suggest that when firms are selecting and considering alliance partners, they also need to consider the following.

1. What will each partner gain from the alliance?
2. What are the various ways in which the alliance will create value?
3. Is the alliance to provide value primarily in one way or in several ways?

The selection of a suitable alliance partner should also encompass the absorptive capacity assessment of the firm to learn and extract knowledge and capability from outside itself (Koza and Lewin, 1998). Essentially, this involves considering whether the firm is able to learn from the expertise of the partner and reapply this knowledge to enhance its own operations.

Value creation and trust

Two further significant issues that are central to strategic alliance success are value creation and trust. Value creation for each partner in the alliance can ultimately determine its level of commitment and willingness to invest and cooperate effectively, and affects whether the alliance achieves the envisaged goals. In evaluating value creation in any alliance, organizations should focus on 'how much further value is likely to be created; whether value is being shared equitably between partners and given uncertainties and change whether partners are able and willing to make needed adjustments in the way they work together' (Doz and Hamel, 1998: 281–282). In measuring value creation outcomes, Chan *et al.* (1997: 199) concluded:

> We find that strategic alliances can provide an effective alternative to the integrated corporation. Our principal findings are: (1) strategic alliances produce a positive wealth effect for the combined partner firms with no evidence of wealth transfers between partners; (2) horizontal alliances, which involve partner firms in the same three-digit SIC code industry, and non-horizontal alliances are both valuable; (3) horizontal alliances add more value when the alliance involves the transfer and/or pooling of technical knowledge, compared with marketing alliances; and (4) firms that enter into strategic alliances exhibit superior operating performance relative to their industry peers.

Alliances also create opportunities to access partner **core competences**, strategic direction, and technologies (Lei and Slocum, 1992).

The other significant issue in any strategic alliance is trust among all partners, defined by Cook and Wall (1980: 39) as 'the extent to which one is willing to ascribe good intentions to and have confidence in the works and actions of other people'. Ellis (1996: 8) notes:

> To make a strategic alliance succeed, its manager must be able to create an environment of trust, maintain broad strategic vision, feel genuine empathy for others, even those who are still competitors in other areas ... successful strategic alliance managers are much like diplomats ... creating an environment of trust is critical and it requires enormous effort and careful attention.

Trust capabilities have to be nurtured and developed, particularly as competitive environments become more dynamic. While a strategic alliance is a form of partnership, a more formal and legalistic mode of network strategy between firms is the creation of a joint venture.

Joint ventures

A joint venture is a legal partnership between two (or more) companies in which they both create a new (third) entity in an effort to achieve competitive advantage over a finite time period. Joint ventures, like strategic alliances, have received significant research attention. Kogut (1988: 320) states:

> Narrowly defined, a joint venture occurs when two or more firms pool a portion of their resources within a common legal organization. Conceptually, a joint venture is selecting among alternative modes by which two or more firms can transact. Thus, a theory of joint ventures must explain why this particular mode of transacting is chosen over such alternatives as acquisition, supply contract, licensing or spot market purchases.

Doz and Hamel (1998) distinguish between what they term 'new alliances' and old joint ventures, arguing that:

> Typically, joint ventures were formed to exploit specific opportunities that were somewhat peripheral to the strategic priorities of the firm ... Also, joint ventures were rarely used by leading companies in

> the pursuit of fundamentally new markets and technologies. Their main purpose was most often to obtain economies of scale and scope in marginal but well-known market segments.
>
> (Doz and Hamel, 1998: 6–7)

In practice, this might mean a bookstore chain conducting a joint venture with a coffee company to provide in-store coffee to customers. For the bookstore chain, the joint venture is about providing an additional service to its customers, but not opening up any new markets; for the coffee company, it means additional market reach.

The motivations for firms pursuing joint ventures are based on the 'evasion of small-number bargaining, enhancement of competitive positioning (or market power) and mechanisms to transfer organizational knowledge' (Kogut, 1988: 322). Other motivations for pursuing joint ventures include reducing risk, sharing costs, pooling resources, securing access to global marketplaces, enhancing technology transfer, market entry purposes, **diversification** of operations, and overcoming regulatory controls (Kukalis and Jungemann, 1995). Several international examples exist of joint ventures, including Ford and Mazda, Sony and Ericsson, LG and Philips, Microsoft and NBC Universal.

Mergers and acquisitions (M&As)

M&As are a common occurrence within industries as individual firms execute their strategic plans and avail themselves of opportunities that arise in the marketplace. With the banking crisis in the latter half of 2008, a number of forced mergers and acquisitions occurred, such as Lloyds and HBOS.

A merger arises when two firms agree to combine their activities and operations, which, given the combined entity, create competitive capability and power over market conditions. In the cases of Daimler-Benz and Chrysler, it was a merger of equals and the name of the combined entity symbolized this: 'DaimlerChrysler'. With mergers, firms seek to gain synergy, scale, scope, and risk advantages that place the merged firm in a strong financial, as well as competitive, position. In the pharmaceutical industry, mega-mergers have occurred, such as Glaxo and SmithKline Beecham. Mergers can take several forms, including: horizontal mergers, in which firms have the same product or service in the same industry; vertical mergers, in which firms at different stages of the industry value chain combine; and conglomerate mergers, in which two firms competing in different industries combine. In November 2010, the merger between British Airways and Iberia was approved; it provides greater operational synergies, as well as opportunities for route expansion and consolidation. Referring back to our understanding of industry life cycles, M&As are more likely to occur as the industry matures and consolidation is the norm.

Acquisitions can be hostile and involve one firm taking over the assets, activities, and operations of another firm at a fair market price. The source of tension and hostility in an acquisition can focus on what is deemed a fair market price and the motivations of the acquirer post-acquisition, particularly to do with employment and activity levels. In 2008, Ryanair, Europe's largest low-cost airline carrier, launched its second takeover bid in a two-year period for Aer Lingus, based in Dublin. The previous bid was rejected by the Aer Lingus board; the second bid also failed, but Ryanair became a minority shareholder. In an acquisition, the acquiring firm will attempt to buy shares in the target company and, once sufficient shares have been obtained, take ownership control of the firm. The real issue for top managers in post-M&A integration is that value can be easily created or destroyed. Firms that are successful in M&A activities may use the network form as a means of completing their competitive intent as a tool rather than a specific strategy (Palter and Srinivasan, 2006). Building materials group, CRH, is one organization that has been hugely successfully in growing globally via acquisition. Its track record means that the ability to integrate acquisitions is clearly a core competency of the organization.

The rationale for pursing M&A activities can be based on a variety of factors, including achieving economies of scale, diversification (related and unrelated—see Chapter 7), taxation and regulatory affairs, the exploitation of resources, synergy, resource transfer, and shareholder value. Acquisition can also be a means to enter a market quickly when the firm is a late entrant. Typically, motivations for acquirers include adding capabilities, geographical expansion, buying growth, consolidation, increasing sales, diversity portfolio, and innovation (Goedhart *et al.*, 2010; Palter and Srinivasan, 2006). The overarching core rationale is centred around value creation, as Seth (1990: 99) describes: 'The empirical results indicate that value creation in related acquisitions is associated with economic efficiencies hypothesized to arise both from economies of scale and scope and from operating efficiencies, and with market power.'

For M&A activities to yield their envisaged benefits, the role of the management team and the process that supports M&A are critical. This was highlighted some time ago by Mace and Montgomery (1962: 75) in their study of acquisitions, in which they found 'that in every company in which there was a successful acquisition program, the chief operating executive was personally involved. There were no exceptions'. Lack of direction and focus within the organization can mean that the top management team acquires companies that do not have any relevance or fit with their operations, as the authors point out:

> The failure to define objectives seems to result in a sense of top management dissatisfaction, a feeling that something needs to be done. Under the circumstances top executives may become overanxious to buy something that looks good to them without defining what is good, and too often they embark on purchase programs later to be regretted. They think of defining objectives as an academic exercise without realizing its elemental importance.
>
> (Mace and Montgomery, 1962: 65)

The alignment between top management teams and the merged entity is of critical importance, as explained by Fubini *et al.* (2006a: 2):

> Our research shows that when top teams turn their attention to the external environment, they often experience a catalytic effect, which carries them past the usual internal frictions much more quickly. Compared with the pressing need to thrive in the marketplace, these frictions simply do not matter very much ... Establishing the top team poses a critical and immediate priority for merging companies. The new company's leaders must appoint the best possible top team for achieving its goals, and the top teams must be aligned around them.

This highlights the role and importance of strategists in the process (Chapter 2), an appreciation that is largely absent in the business and network strategy literature. Frequently, however, methods of collaborating will be made possible as a result of the network, competence, and personality of key strategists. A factor rarely mentioned is 'likeability', not only of the business idea, but also of the key people involved in promoting it (Casciaro and Lobo, 2005).

In conclusion, irrespective of the network form that organizations adopt, the strategic purpose is to ensure organizational competitiveness in the short, medium, and long terms. Network forms provide significant opportunities for firms to learn and to manage risk in a more controlled way. Strategic alliance and joint venture network forms provide real opportunities to manage risk and to learn. Many companies underestimate the organizational effort and cost required to successfully manage a network form, yet effective use of network strategies can offer firms a robust method of securing a route to advantage.

Spotlight Woolworths: losing a national institution

After ninety-nine years in business, Woolworths Group plc, one of the UK's major retail chains, saw its shares suspended on 26 November 2008. At its peak, the business had 815 stores in the UK, employed 27,000 people, and owned 40 per cent of publisher 2 Entertain and Entertainment UK, which supplied DVDs to supermarket groups. For many generations, in the UK, it had been a national institution.

'Woolies', as it was affectionately referred to by many customers, was founded by Frank Woolworth, an American, in Liverpool on 5 November 1909. The expansion of Woolworths was funded exclusively through internal earnings. In 1930, the 400th branch was opened in Southport, Lancashire; in 1953, the 800th was opened in Victoria, London. In 2001, the company began trading on the London Stock Exchange after a demerger with Kingfisher.

In describing the charm of Woolworths, Geoghegan (2008) notes:

> It's a love born out of childhood visits to the pick'n' mix, or a few years later for the seven-inch single storming the charts. Or to the only photo booths in town, found in the corner next to the ironing boards and bean bags. Or that last frantic, last-minute Christmas Eve shopping dash to bag a Daniel O'Donnell calendar, a car scratch remover and a Ronco CD player that resembles a football.

The period between 2007 and 2008 saw a 90 per cent drop in share value and debts rising to £385m. In August 2008, the company rejected a £50m takeover bid by Iceland, one of the UK's largest frozen food chains. In September of that year, it reported a half-year pre-tax loss of £90.8m, leading to the suspension of payment of dividends to shareholders (BBC News, 2008).

Why did Woolworths end up in administration? There are a number of reasons. During the height of the credit crunch in 2008, many suppliers changed credit terms, meaning that they required cash on delivery. From the 1980s, other major retailers including Tesco and Asda expanded their product range into non-food items such as CDs, DVDs, and household products, cutting into a market that Woolworths had created. Online retailers such as Amazon provide credible alternatives to Woolworths for customers whose preferences and tastes had changed with economic prosperity. From a customer's perspective, there was a lack of clarity about the brand and it was trying to do too many things, creating further confusion among its customer base. What did Woolies stand for? Customers associated other retailers with specific value propositions and particular positions in the marketplace. Store layouts in Woolworths were not optimized to generate further sales and the quality of product offering was inferior to those of competitors. The shopping experience had moved on, but Woolworths had not kept pace, as Hodge (quoted in Geoghegan, 2008) describes:

> They brought everything under one roof and you could go to a place that sold everything. Now that charm has worn off . . . As a shopping composition, it's not clear what it is. You could say it has an identity crisis . . . The British have an empathy [for] and an emotional attachment to it but if you talk to consumers they don't know when they last bought anything of value.

Given the competition in the market, customers demanded a high-quality and sophisticated shopping experience. As Baker (quoted in Geoghegan, 2008) describes matters: 'Going into Primark, the whole atmosphere says "It's fine, this is cheap" but you feel good about yourself. But you feel a loser going into Woolworths.' For those who worked for many decades in Woolworths stores, their employment was more than just a job; it was about serving a community and being part of the high street retail fabric of the nation. James (quoted in Barkham, 2009) reported a former employee's words: 'I couldn't imagine life not coming here. It wasn't just losing our jobs, it was losing our family.'

Sources: Barkham (2009); BBC News (2008); Geoghegan (2008)

Implications for strategy practice

In practice, the strategic choice debate about whether the environment or managerial influence matters is moot for strategists who are tasked by shareholders to deliver sustained returns. Bottom-line business strategy targets have to be met. Many industries have experienced periods during which external environmental forces have engulfed managerial influence. The global financial crisis that began in 2008 saw the exit from the industry of giants such as Lehman Brothers, forced M&As, and increased levels of regulatory oversight in the banking sector. The size and scale of the crisis meant that managerial influence in the sector waned, and most industry competitors had no control over events for a number of months. This contrasts with the influence that management of the Tata Motor Group has attempted to have on the car industry with the 2009 launch of the Nano, the cheapest car in the world.

The rapid pace of change in many industries is altering industry and competitive dynamics. In dealing with this, fit and alignment of business-level strategy, corporate-level strategy, and competitive environment are consistent issues for a strategist. Appropriate levels of fit are necessary to enable the firm to achieve competitive dominance. Sales of newspapers have declined worldwide. Newspaper companies must reorientate their fit to reflect the change in the distribution channels used by consumers of news if they are to achieve competitive dominance. This means developing content for mobile applications and other opportunities, such as Apple's tablet PC, the iPad.

The core of any business-level and network-level strategy has to be anchored and aligned with the purpose of the business. The real danger is that where this alignment is not strong, business-level and network-level strategies do not deliver the envisaged outcomes and, in time, will ultimately lessen the competitive strength of the firm in the marketplace, as in the case of Woolworths. This alignment is critically important to competitive success, given the complexity and sheer size of many organizations that employ thousands of people and have multiple processes, products, and services. Non-alignment and strategists not thinking through the long-term implications of various network forms can have a detrimental impact on the growth prospects of the organization, which may ultimately lead to decline and failure. Many industries are littered with examples of non-alignment.

Business models have crept into the business lexicon as a means of competing more aggressively and sustainably. Business models are likely to grow in importance and receive more research attention from academics. With the blurring of industry boundaries and growth prospects around convergent technologies, products, and services, business models provide the freedom and flexibility necessary to explore beyond the constraints of strategy types, generic strategies, or strategic positioning, moving beyond value capture to explore how value is actually created. Business models give organizations the organizational flexibility needed to respond to change, and also to anticipate where the firm needs to build future strategic capability both in business and network strategies. Business models also provide organizations with the ability to change the rules of competition and to sustain value-creation capacity. We see examples of new business models in the music, fashion, and financial services industries. Every strategist should be able to articulate the story of his or her organization and the basis of its value proposition. In this sense, the concept of business models offers strategists a key **discourse** and toolkit for assessing their contribution.

Irrespective of size or scale, organizations cannot escape the reality that network strategies are a necessary part of the response to the competitive environment. Effective network strategies provide an organization with the capability of extending scale and scope, but can also assist in building towards competitive dominance in a competitive arena. In developing economies such as India, China, and Vietnam, network strategies within country firms are essential in order to gain a foothold in these markets. In pursuing network strategies, many firms fail to align the organizational structures and processes that support their network strategies. Each network form—alliance, joint venture, and M&A—requires distinct skill sets and processes that support effective execution. The lure and excitement associated with doing a deal around these network forms can blind management teams to the reality of implementation and integration post-deal.

Overall, there is a need for strategists to have finely honed skills built around collaboration both internally and externally. This key skill is often overlooked in practice and by academic researchers. The collaborative skills of strategists enable effective execution of business and network strategies, but these skills have to be developed and nurtured. Organizational culture and rewards have a role to play in incentivizing the development of collaborative skill sets.

Finally, network strategies and forms can contribute immensely to an organization's knowledge and capability base. The strategist must harness these benefits to really improve organizational competitiveness in a sustainable manner, while also reflecting on the process of learning and absorption itself. For everyone in an organization, this requires introspection that feeds into a collective view of competitive success and how this should be evaluated. For organizations with origins in Asia, the criteria used to evaluate and acquire knowledge and capability extend over many decades; for Western-based firms, the time horizon tends to be a lot shorter. In time, this view may change too.

Introduction to readings

Our first reading, accessible via a link on the Online Resource Centre that accompanies this book, 'Critical tactics for implementing Porter's generic strategies' by Akan *et al.* (2006), focuses on what pursuing a given generic strategy actually means for an organization. Drawing on key examples such as Proctor and Gamble, the authors provide an approach that enables strategists to better tailor their strategy implementation to more effectively implement whatever generic strategy they are attempting to pursue. However, in drawing upon Porter's work, do the authors not simply reproduce its core limitations? Which implementation tactics are likely to be most appropriate for an organization competing on quality and cost? What of changes to generic strategies, organizational adaptation, innovation, and flexibility? Is success likely to come from pursuing a given generic strategy via associated implementation tactics or from drawing upon organizational learning and experience? What assumptions do the authors make about successful implementation?

Our second reading, also accessible via the Online Resource Centre, 'Creating strategic alliances which endure', by Robert Spekman, Lynn Isabella, Thomas C. MacAcoy, and Theodore Forbes (1996), focuses on the business and interpersonal relationships within alliances over their life cycle. The authors outline the stages within an alliance life cycle in addition to the key relationship activities, the role of the alliance manager, and the alliance structure. What is interesting is the importance of voice in communicating a compelling vision to both parties. The article highlights the complexity of relationships that evolve as alliances develop and the central role that the alliance manager plays in developing these relationships. A key question for managers is whether the unteachable competences are teachable in a culturally specific sense. In reality, how many alliance managers really reflect the differing perspectives, given the competing demands that they face daily?

Reading 3.3 is an award-winning contribution in the *MIT Sloan Management Review*, 'How to build collaborative advantage', by Morten Hansen and Nitin Nohria (2004). It deals with the issues of collaboration, alignment, adaptability, and innovation in a firm's quest for competitive advantage. One interesting point raised by the authors that is often overlooked in practice is the collaborative skill set that firms should possess to compete effectively, which must be honed and developed within the firm. How many executives really accept that their main focus is on fostering collaboration within their firms? Does the argument hold across all contexts?

Mini case study Zara

Dr Conor O'Kane, Otago Business School, University of Otago, New Zealand

The Inditex Group's Zara chain, a leading player in today's fashion industry, was founded by Amancio Ortega in 1975 in Arteixo, a small town in the north of Spain. After growing at a moderate pace until the late 1980s, Zara underwent rapid international expansion, including store openings in Porto, New York, France, Mexico, Greece, Belgium, Sweden, and Italy. Interestingly, however, as the expansion drive continues, the heart of Inditex continues to be in Arteixo, where the company has fourteen factories connected by tunnels to a giant distribution centre. From here, clothes are shipped out twice a week directly to individual shops, with most stores never having to wait more than seventy-two hours to receive any new order. Indeed, such is the unique and efficient nature of the entire chain of activities that Zara's merchandise reaches the stores fifteen days after being designed.

The highly successful fashion chain follows a relatively simple concept: namely, taking the lead from high-end and cutting-edge fashions, mass producing similar designs, and selling them at mid-market prices to the fashion-conscious young. The level of success enjoyed with this concept led Zara to be described as 'possibly the most innovative and devastating retailer in the world', by LVMH fashion director Daniel Piette. The principal components of Zara's 'winning' strategy or formula revolve around: short lead times—to satisfy emerging customer tastes; lower quantities—to compensate for the risk of some trends proving unpopular with the market; and more styles—which abolishes the traditional concept of seasons, offers customers a wider variety of clothing, and allows each store to freshen up its look and displays more frequently.

Methods that enable the company to continuously adapt and integrate each of its departments and to stay ahead of the fashion curve include extensive market research, tight corporate control of strategically located businesses, and extensive use of communication and IT processes. Remarkably, however, Zara has never resorted to grandiose advertising through traditional media, preferring instead to market itself through store openings, shop refurbishments, and new window displays. Before entering any market, Zara analyses the tastes and trends of local customers, and then adapts the basics of its style to each country. Key information is also provided by regular shop manager and customer communications, which offer an insight into those products that are popular and those that need to be altered or recreated. As well as designing, making, distributing, and selling its own clothes, Zara coordinates and controls every part of the business. Controlling the entire process from factory to shop floor helps Zara to react quickly and to adjust its offerings, based on changing fashion trends and customers' tastes. Interestingly, while demonstrating how speed, flexibility, and low inventories are important in keeping expenses down, Ortega prefers to position Zara's production close to its markets and produces up to 80 per cent of its merchandise in Europe. In contrast to its Third-World-employing competitors, Zara designs, picks, and cuts the cloth before sending it to workshops and cooperatives in northern Portugal and the surrounding area of Galicia for sewing, before the clothes are finally finished off in La Coruna, a municipality of Galicia. Indeed, only Zara's most elaborately prepared garments are manufactured in workshops in Peru, Morocco, Cambodia, or Thailand—and even then, in following a code of ethics drawn up in 2001 (announced in its annual report), each of its foreign workshops is investigated to ensure that no exploitation of the workforce takes place.

There is little question that Zara went very much against the grain of the apparel industry, which is often characterized by the outsourcing of production and by hefty advertising budgets. As indicated by one of Spain's leading management consultants, Dr Pedro Nueno, Zara had become a market leader not by imitating the business practices of other successful retailers, but by 'being contrarian' to apparel industry norms. Indeed, by inciting change rather than embracing it or succumbing to it, Zara has been a resounding success, with a number of competitors, including Mango, H&M, and Topshop, now emulating the Zara-pioneered business model. The question now for others in the industry, including the once-dominant mass-market competitors, is whether they can ever catch up.

Sources: CNN (2001); juststyle.com (2004); Ryan (2001)

Questions

1. How would you define Zara's strategy?
2. Apply Yip's (2004) core elements of a business model to examine how Zara creates value.
3. Does Zara have a sustainable competitive advantage? What key challenges is it likely to face in the future?

Summary

We began the chapter by examining business-level strategy and, in terms of strategic choice, considering whether environmental or managerial influences have more significant influence over firm business-level strategy. We then examined the types of business-level strategy: strategy types, generic strategy, and strategic positioning. We concluded this section by examining business models. For strategists, the key requirement of business-level strategy is achieving appropriate and unique levels of fit and, in doing so, achieving a competitive advantage.

Increasingly, an exclusive focus on competition is seen as a narrow form of analysis (Patel, 2005). Consequently, in the latter part of the chapter, we focused on the issues of competition and collaboration. In our examination of competition, we focused on industry life cycle and how firms respond to competitive threats. In dealing with collaboration, issues such as collaborative motivation were explored. We concluded by focusing on key network forms: strategic alliances, joint ventures, and M&As. While deciding upon an appropriate route to advantage via business and network strategies is clearly necessary, on its own, it is not sufficient. Many organizations will make the decision to compete on low cost or to expand their competencies via strategic alliance, but only a few will succeed. As our next two chapters highlight, sound execution is critical if chosen routes are to be exploited and true advantage realized.

Discussion questions

1. Why is it important for businesses that managers have influence over competitive environments? Do you believe that managers have influence over their competitive environment?

2. Apply the strategy types, generic strategy, and strategic positioning to an organization with which you are familiar. What strategic insights do you gain from applying these perspectives? How useful are these perspectives to a strategist? What are the limitations of the perspectives?

3. Take a business model of a company with which you are familiar and discuss how the business model expands our understanding of the business strategy.

4. Take a firm with which you are familiar and identify the network forms with which it is currently involved. Examine the strategic rationale for these network forms. Is there a clear alignment between network forms and the business strategy being pursued?

5. From your understanding of routes to advantage, discuss whether you believe sustainable competitive advantage to be achievable through business and network strategies.

Further reading

For an overview of work by Michael Porter related to the key themes of this chapter, read 2008's *On Competition* (Updated and expanded edn, Boston, MA: Harvard Business School Press).

Business models are receiving increased attention in the media. However, the term itself is typically ill-defined, lacks a clear theoretical underpinning, and by consequence is often used interchangeably with strategy. A special issue of *Long Range Planning* does a good job in bring clarity to these issues and highlighting the potential utility of the term: C. Baden-Fuller (2010) 'Special issue on business models', *Long Range Planning*, 43: 143–145.

For further insights into the challenges of competition and collaboration, read A. Brandenburger and B. J. Nalebuff (1997) *Co-opetition Currency*, New York: Doubleday.

A good overview of research contributing to the debate about whether M&A is value adding or value destroying is J. Haleblian, C. Devers, D. McNamara, M. Carpenter, and R. Davison (2009) 'Taking stock of what we know about mergers and acquisitions: a review and research agenda', *Journal of Management*, 35: 469–502.

For an overview of competitive advantage, competition, and cooperation, read Bruce Greenwald and Judd Kahn (2007) *Competition Demystified: A Radically Simplified Approach to Business Strategy*, New York: Portfolio Trade.

In K. Patel (2005) *The Master Strategist: Power, Purpose and Principle*, London: Arrow Books, the author provides some interesting views on the nature of competition and dealing with competitive rivals. In particular, he challenges the military basis of strategy and the associated 'I win–you lose' natural order of things. Patel also focuses on the importance of adaptability, paying particular attention to the skills required of strategists to achieve ultimate success and personal meaning.

visit the Online Resource Centre that accompanies this book to access more learning resources on this chapter topic at www.oxfordtextbooks.co.uk/orc/cunningham/

References

Akan, O., Allen, R., Helms, M., and Spralls, S. 2006. Critical tactics for implementing Porter's generic strategies. *Long Range Planning*, 271: 43–53.

Ang, S. H. 2008. Competitive intensity and collaboration: impact on firm growth across technological environments. *Strategic Management Journal*, 29(10): 1057–1075.

Baden-Fuller, C. 2010. Special issue on business models. *Long Range Planning*, 43: 143–145.

Barkham, P. 2009. Welcome to Wellworths! *The Guardian*, 20 February. Available online at http://www.guardian.co.uk/business/2009/feb/20/woolworths-retail

Barney, J. 1991. Firm resources and sustained competitive advantage. *Journal of Management*, 17(1): 99–120.

BBC News. 2008. Woolworths shares are suspended. 26 November, Available online at http://news.bbc.co.uk/go/pr/fr/-/2/hi/business/7749530.stm

Bourgeois, L. J. I. 1984. Strategic management and determinism. *Academy of Management Review*, 9(4): 586–596.

Brandenburger A. and Nalebuff, B. J. 1997. Co-opetition: competitive and cooperative business strategies for the digital economy. *Strategy and Leadership*, 25(6): 28–35.

Brouthers, K. D., Brouthers, L. E., and Wilkinson, T. J. 1995. Strategic alliances: choose your partners. *Long Range Planning*, 28(3): 18–25.

Campbell-Hunt, C. 2000. What have we learned about generic competitive strategy? A meta-analysis. *Strategic Management Journal*, 21: 127–154.

Capron, L. 1999. The long-term performance of horizontal acquisitions. *Strategic Management Journal*, 20(11): 987–1018.

Carayannis, E. and Alexander, J. 1999. Winning by co-opeting in strategic government-industry-university R&D partnerships: the power of complex, dynamic knowledge networks. *Journal of Technology Transfer*, 24(2): 197–210.

Casciaro, T. and Lobo, M. S. 2005. Competent jerks, lovable fools and the formation of social networks. *Harvard Business Review*, 83(6): 92–100.

Chan, S., Kensinger, J., Keown, A., and Martin, J. 1997. Do strategic alliances create value? *Journal of Financial Economics*, 46(2): 199–221.

Child, J. 1972. Organizational structure, environment and performance: the role of strategic choice. *Sociology*, 6: 1–22.

Child, J. 1997. Strategic choice in the analysis of action, structure, organizations and environment: retrospect and prospect. *Organization Studies*, 18(1): 43–76.

Child, J. 2005. *Organization*. Malden, MA: Blackwell.

Chorn, N. 1991. The 'alignment' theory: creating strategic fit. *Management Decision*, 29(1): 20–24.

Clark, P. 2000. *Organizations in Action: Competition between Contexts*. London: Routledge.

CNN. 2001. Zara: a Spanish success story. 15 June. Available online at http://edition.cnn.com/BUSINESS/programs/yourbusiness/stories2001/zara/

Contractor F. J. and Lorange, P. 1988. *Cooperative Strategies in International Business*. Lexington, MA: Lexington Books.

Cook. J. and Wall. T. 1980. New work attitude measures of trust, organizational commitment and personal need non-fulfillment. *Journal of Occupational Psychology*, 53: 39–52.

Dean, J. 1954. Competition: inside and out. *Harvard Business Review*, 32(6): 63–71.

Di Maggio, P. J. and Powell, W. W. 1983. The iron cage revisited: institutional isomorphism and collective rationality in organizational fields. *American Sociological Review*, 23: 111–136.

Douma, M. U., Bilderbeek, J., Idenburg, P. J., and Looise, J. K. 2000. Strategic alliances: managing the dynamics of fit. *Long Range Planning*, 33(4): 579–598.

Doz, Y. L. and Hamel. G. 1998. *Alliance Advantage*. Boston, MA: Harvard Business School Press.

Dyer, J. H., and Singh, H. 1998. The relational view: cooperative strategy and sources of interorganisational competitive advantage. *Academy of Management Review*, 23: 660–679.

Ellis, C. 1996. Making strategic alliances succeed. *Harvard Business Review*, 74(4): 8–9.

Folta, T. 1998. Governance and uncertainty: the trade-off between administrative control and commitment. *Strategic Management Journal*, 19(11): 1007–1028.

Fubini, D. G., Price, C., and Zollo, M. 2006a. Successful mergers start at the top, *McKinsey Quarterly*, Nov: 2–7.

Goedhart, M., Koller, T., and Wessels, D. 2010. The five types of successful acquisition. *McKinsey Quarterly*, 36: 2–7.

Geoghegan, T. 2008. What is the point of Woolworths? *BBC News Magazine*, 26 November. Available online at http://news.bbc.co.uk/go/pr/fr/-/2/hi/uk_news/magazine/7741199.stm

Hennart, J.-F. 1988. A transaction costs theory of equity joint ventures. *Strategic Management Journal*, 9(4): 361–374.

Hennart, J.-F. and Reddy, S. 1997. The choice between mergers/acquisitions and joint ventures: the case of Japanese investors in the United States. *Strategic Management Journal*, 18(1): 1–12.

juststyle.com. 2004. Zara: success on its own terms. 9 July. Available online at http://www.just-style.com/article.aspx?id = 92368

Knights, D. 1992. Changing spaces: the disruptive impact of a new epistemological location for the study of management. *Academy of Management Review*, 17: 514–536.

Kogut, B. 1988. Joint ventures: theoretical and empirical perspectives. *Strategic Management Journal*, 9(4): 319–332.

Koza, M. P. and Lewin, A. Y. 1999. The co-evolution of network alliances: a longitudinal analysis of an international professional service network. *Organization Science*, 10(5): 638–653.

Krishnan, R. A., Joshi, S., and Krishnan, H. 2004. The influence of mergers on firms' product-mix strategies. *Strategic Management Journal*, 25(6): 587–611.

Kukalis, S. and Jungemann, M. 1995. Strategic planning for a joint venture. *Long Range Planning*, 28(3): 4–5.

Lavie, D. 2006. The competitive advantage of interconnected firms: an extension of the resource-based view. *Academy of Management Review*, 31(3): 638–658.

Lei, D. and Slocum, J. W. 1992. Global strategy, competence-building and strategic alliances. *California Management Review*, 31(1): 81–97.

MacCormack, A. and Forbath, T. 2008. Learning the fine art of global collaboration. *Harvard Business Review*, 86(1): 24–26.

Mace, M. L. and Montgomery, G. G. 1962. *Management Problems of Corporate Acquisitions*. Boston, MA: Harvard University Press.

Magretta, J. 2002. Why business models matter. *Harvard Business Review*, May: 86–92.

March, J. G. 1991. Exploration and exploitation in organisational learning. *Organization Science*, 2(1): 71–87.

Mathews, H. L. and Harvey, T. W. 1988. The sugar baby gamit: funding strategic alliances with venture capital. *Planning Review*, Nov/Dec: 36–41.

Medcof, J. W. 1997. Why do so many alliances end in divorce? *Long Range Planning*, 30(5): 718–732.

Miles, R. and Snow, C. 2003. *Organisational Strategy, Structure and Process*. Stanford, CA: Stanford University Press.

Miles, R., Snow, C., Meyer, A., and Coleman, H. 1978. Organisation strategy, structure and process. *Academy of Management Review*, 3: 546–662.

Miller, D. 1992. Icarus paradox: how exceptional companies bring about their own downfall. *Business Horizons*, Jan/Feb: 24–35.

Moore, J. F. 1993. Predators and prey: a new ecology of competition. *Harvard Business Review*, 71(3): 75–86.

Ohmae, K. 1989. The global logic of strategic alliances. *Harvard Business Review*, 67(2): 143–154.

Oviatt, B. M. and McDougall, P. P. 1994. Towards a theory of international new ventures. *Journal of International Business Studies*, 25: 45–64.

Palter, R. N. and Srinivasan, D. 2006. Habits of the busiest acquirers. *McKinsey Quarterly*, July: 8–13.

Pangarkar, N. 2003. Determinants of alliance duration in uncertain environments: the case of the biotechnology sector. *Long Range Planning*, 36(3): 269–284.

Patel, K. 2005. *The Master Strategist: Power, Purpose and Principle*. London: Arrow Books.

Pfeffer, J. and Salanick, G. R. 1978. *The External Control of Organisations: A Resource Dependence Perspective*. New York: Harper and Row.

Pisano, G. P. and Verganti, R. 2008. Which kind of collaboration is right for you? *Harvard Business Review*, 86(12): 78–86.

Porter, M. 1980. *Competitive Strategy*. New York: Free Press.

Porter, M. 1985. *Competitive Advantage*. New York: Free Press.

Porter, M. 1990. *Competitive Advantage of Nations*. New York: Free Press.

Porter, M. 1996. What is strategy? *Harvard Business Review*, Dec: 61–78.

Porter, M. 2008. The competitive forces that shape strategy. *Harvard Business Review*, Jan: 78–93.

Porter, M. and Teisberg, E. O. 2004. Redefining competition in health care. *Harvard Business Review*, 82(6): 64–76.

Prahalad, C. and Hamel, G. 1990. The core competencies of the corporation. *Harvard Business Review*, May/June(3): 79–91.

Ritala, P. 2011. Coopetition strategy: when is it successful? Empirical evidence on innovation and market performance. *Journal of Management*, DOI: 10.1111/j.1467-8551.2011.00741.x

Ryan, O. 2001. Spain's retail success story. BBC News, 23 May. Available online at http://news.bbc.co.uk/2/hi/business/1346473.stm

Sampson, R. C. 2005. Experience effects and collaborative returns in R&D alliances. *Strategic Management Journal*, 26(11): 1009–1031.

Seth, A. 1990. Value creation in acquisitions: a re-examination of performance issues. *Strategic Management Journal*, 11(2): 99–115.

Shapiro, C. 1989. The theory of business strategy. *RAND Journal of Economics*, 20(1): 125–137.

Silhan, P. A. and Thomas, H. 1986. Using simulated mergers to evaluate corporate diversification strategies. *Strategic Management Journal*, 7(6): 523–534.

Simonin, B.L. 1997. The importance of collaborative know-how: an empirical test of the learning organization. *Academy of Management Journal*, 40(5): 1150–1174.

Skarzynski, P. and Gibson, R. 2008. *Innovation to the Core.* Boston, MA: Harvard Business School Press.

Stiles, J. 1995. Collaboration for competitive advantage: the changing world of alliances and partnerships. *Long Range Planning*, 28(5): 109–112.

Teece, D., Pisano, G., and Shuen, A. 1997. Dynamic capabilities and strategic management. *Strategic Management Journal*, 18: 509–533.

Thomas, A. B. 1988. Does leadership make a difference to organizational performance? *Administrative Science Quarterly*, 33: 388–400.

Thompson, J. D. 2005. *Organizations in Action: Social Science Bases of Administrative Theory*. New Brunswick, NJ: Transaction Publications.

Trautwein, F. 1990. Merger motives and prescriptions. *Strategic Management Journal*, 11(4): 283–295.

Venkatraman, N. and Camillus, J. 1984. Exploring the concept of 'fit' in strategic management. *Academy of Management Review*, 9(3): 513–525.

Venkatraman, N. and Subramaniam, M. 2002. Theorizing the future of strategy: questions for shaping strategy research in the knowledge economy. In A. Pettigrew, H. Thomas, and R. Whittington (eds) *Handbook of Strategy and Management*. London: Sage.

Weiss, J. and Hughes, J. 2005. Want collaboration? *Harvard Business Review*, 83(3): 93–101.

Yip, G. 2004. Using strategy to change your business model. *Business Strategy Review*, 15(2): 17–24.

Zott, C., Amit, R., and Massa, L. 2011. The business model: recent developments and future research. *Journal of Management*, 37(4): 1019–1042.

Section 3 readings

Introduction

In this section, our focus has been on the routes to advantage and we have considered the ways in which an organization can achieve competitive advantage. In doing so, we focused on corporate and global strategy.

- **Reading 3.1** by David Faulkner, on 'Portfolio matrices' (1998), is focused on corporate-level strategy and provides a framework that strategists can use to assess the attractiveness of their corporate portfolios to identify new routes to advantage.
- **Reading 3.2** on 'Global strategy: an organizing framework', by Sumantra Ghoshal (1987), focuses on global strategy—particularly on purpose and ends. In focusing on global strategy, Ghoshal addresses relevant themes for strategists, such as efficiency. Pursuing corporate and global-level strategies can potentially provide advantages to organizations in terms of synergy and efficiency, but these can be difficult to translate into practice.
- Finally, in **Reading 3.3** on 'How to build collaborative advantage' (2004), Morten Hansen and Nitin Nohria suggest that organizations need to better hone their collaborative skills. Doing so can lead to improved collaborative outcomes, particularly because many on the routes to advantage increasingly require external partners. Fostering a collaborative environment can be significantly challenging for an organization and is a fundamental question relevant to the heart of the core purpose of the business.

Reading 3.1 Portfolio matrices *David Faulkner*

First published: (1998) in Véronique Ambrosini, Gerry Johnson, and Kevan Scholes (eds) *Exploring Techniques of Analysis and Evaluation in Strategic Management*, London/New York: Prentice Hall, pp. 205–218. Faulkner, D. (1998). 'Portfolio Matrices', in V. Ambrosini, G. Johnson and K. Scholes (eds.) 'Exploring Techniques of Analysis and Evaluation in Strategic Management', *Financial Times*: Prentice Hall, pp. 205–218. Reproduced with the kind permission of David Faulkner.

Introduction

What businesses to be in is a fundamental issue for the corporate board. Traditionally, or at least since the early 1970s, the issue has been addressed by employing one or more of the strategic consultancy company portfolio matrices, the 'box' of the Boston Consulting Group, the directional policy matrix of McKinsey or the life-cycle matrix of Arthur D. Little. However, none of these matrices explicitly takes into account the resource-based theory of the firm or makes any rigorous attempt to determine the firm's key or core competences (1) in order to discover the area in which the company is most likely to succeed. This chapter briefly describes the three most common portfolio matrices and identifies their respective limitations. It then suggests how the addition of a third axis for 'mesh' can take account of the weakness referred to above.

The Boston box

The Boston box (2) was the earliest of the matrices to hit the market, and being perhaps the easiest to understand is probably still the most popular in the business world. As shown in [Figure 3.1.1], it has four quadrants and two axes: market growth and relative market share.

The Boston box has the attraction of its simplicity, but it suffers from a number of problems and weaknesses and should be used with caution. The two axes attempt to relate the attractiveness of a market to the inherent strength of the business unit. However, market growth rate is only a very approximate surrogate for market attractiveness. The five forces competitive intensity model (3) illustrates the complexity of the

Figure 3.1.1 The Boston box

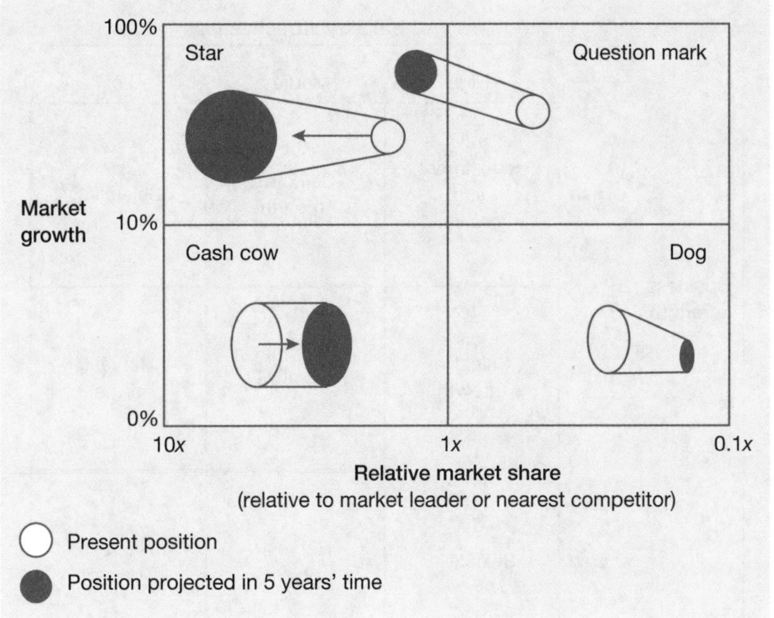

attractiveness concept in which market growth has only one part to play in one of the five identified key forces determining attractiveness. Whether growth is important also depends on whether the business unit concerned has strategic advantage in the key competences that enable the growth to lead to improved results for the company.

Relative market share is also an uncertain surrogate for company strength. Market share can be bought easily by pricing below cost without the possession of any real internal strength. It also refers to the past, not the future and could be said to be more the result than the cause of business unit strength. Economic research almost unfailingly correlates high market share with high profitability (hence strength) but correlations do not of course indicate the direction of causality. Does business strength lead to high market share, does high market share lead to high business strength, or does some third factor cause them both?

The Boston box does not allow for declining markets, applies mostly to fast-moving consumer goods companies and certainly does not apply easily to industrial goods companies, to fragmented industries or to industries in which the experience curve and scale economies give small unit cost advantages. It is also not evident why companies in slow-growth industries who are not market leaders should be divested. Many may still make good profits without requiring large investment funds. Indeed, in many industries it would not be difficult to find examples for the concept of the 'cash dog'. Furthermore, even slow-growth industries exhibit investment opportunities in particular segments or niches, and many well-focused companies in this box may well be acceptably profitable, e.g. Imperial Tobacco. This company is not the market leader, and its industry is in decline. Since it joined the Hanson Group, however, it has shown ever-increasing profitability year on year.

The McKinsey directional policy matrix

The McKinsey matrix (2) attempts to overcome some of the weaknesses of the Boston box by selecting more realistic multidimensional axes to represent industry attractiveness and business strength, as shown in [Figure 3.1.2].

McKinsey are careful not to be over-prescriptive regarding the dimensions of industry attractiveness or of internal business strength. Indeed, they emphasise that the relevant factors will vary from industry to industry. However, if the matrix had been developed after the publication of Porter's *Competitive Strategy* (3) and *Competitive Advantage* (4), it may well be that the five forces industry attractiveness model would be recommended as a means of assessing one axis, and the value chain the other.

This matrix has its axes in reverse to those of the Boston box. They are, however, conceptually similar in that the box where high industry attractiveness meets high business strength leads to a recommendation of investment with the objective of growth, similar to that of the 'star'. Correspondingly, low attractiveness/low strength as with Boston's 'dog' leads to the recommendation 'harvest/divest'. The other boxes follow a similar logic. Although the McKinsey matrix purports to be an investment matrix in contrast to Boston's cash matrix, the distinction is more a formal than a real difference.

Figure 3.1.2 The directional policy matrix

Business strength ↑ / Industry attractiveness ←	High	Medium	Low
High	Investment and growth	Selective growth	Selectivity
Medium	Selective growth	Selectivity	Harvest/ divest
Low	Selectivity	Harvest/ divest	Harvest/ divest

The major weakness of the McKinsey matrix is that there is no easily applied means of establishing the appropriate weightings for the many dimensions of attractiveness and business strength, and this enables practitioners to bias weightings to meet their already established ideas if they are so inclined. Therefore, in the wrong hands, it can be more of a demonstration tool than an analytical model capable of giving surprising insights. This same criticism can, however, also be levied against the Porter five forces model.

The Arthur D. Little life-cycle matrix

A third variant of the portfolio matrix is the Arthur D. Little life-cycle matrix (ADL) (2). Following the customary internal axis, it chooses competitive position as its measure of the firm's strength, not a far cry from McKinsey's business strength axis although measured somewhat differently. Its other axis is quite different, however. It selects market maturity as its external measure (see [Figure 3.1.3]).

This requires it to aver that there are appropriate strategies for any maturity, and therefore that no particular maturity is 'good' or 'bad'; indeed, diversified groups such as Hanson or Tompkins seem to prefer that their acquisitions be in mature rather than growth markets, since this often means greater stability and lower demand for investment funds.

Very deterministic rules are applied to this matrix for the calculation of competitive position and market maturity, leading to a positioning on the matrix which, in turn, leads to the recommendation of a very limited range of 'natural' strategic thrusts. A problem here exists in that if every business unit in a particular matrix position adopts the same strategic thrust in a given market, it is difficult to see how competitive advantage will be gained. In business, as in life generally, the winner is often the competitor who does something unusual, rather than the one who applies rigorously a formula known and available to all.

There are other problems attached to this matrix. It is possible through the use of the ADL methodology to determine the maturity of the market concerned. It is not possible, however to determine how quickly the maturing process will take place, or indeed whether it will take place at all. Some products/markets mature very rapidly, e.g. personal computers; others don't seem to mature at all, e.g. houses, staple foods or non-fashion clothing; while others, due to fashion, technology breakthroughs or strong marketing activity, reverse maturity, e.g. watches or sports shoes. As a predictor of the ageing of markets, the matrix is of little use. Its value for strategy guidance must be similarly limited for the same reasons.

Other problems

All three matrices have basic flaws that attach to each of them individually. They also have some limitations that apply to them all collectively. All assume that each business unit has not a synergistic achieved relationship with any other. Indeed, if this were not the case it would not be possible to regard the positioning of a strategic business unit (SBU) on a matrix as implying any particular strategic implications,

Figure 3.1.3 The life-cycle portfolio matrix

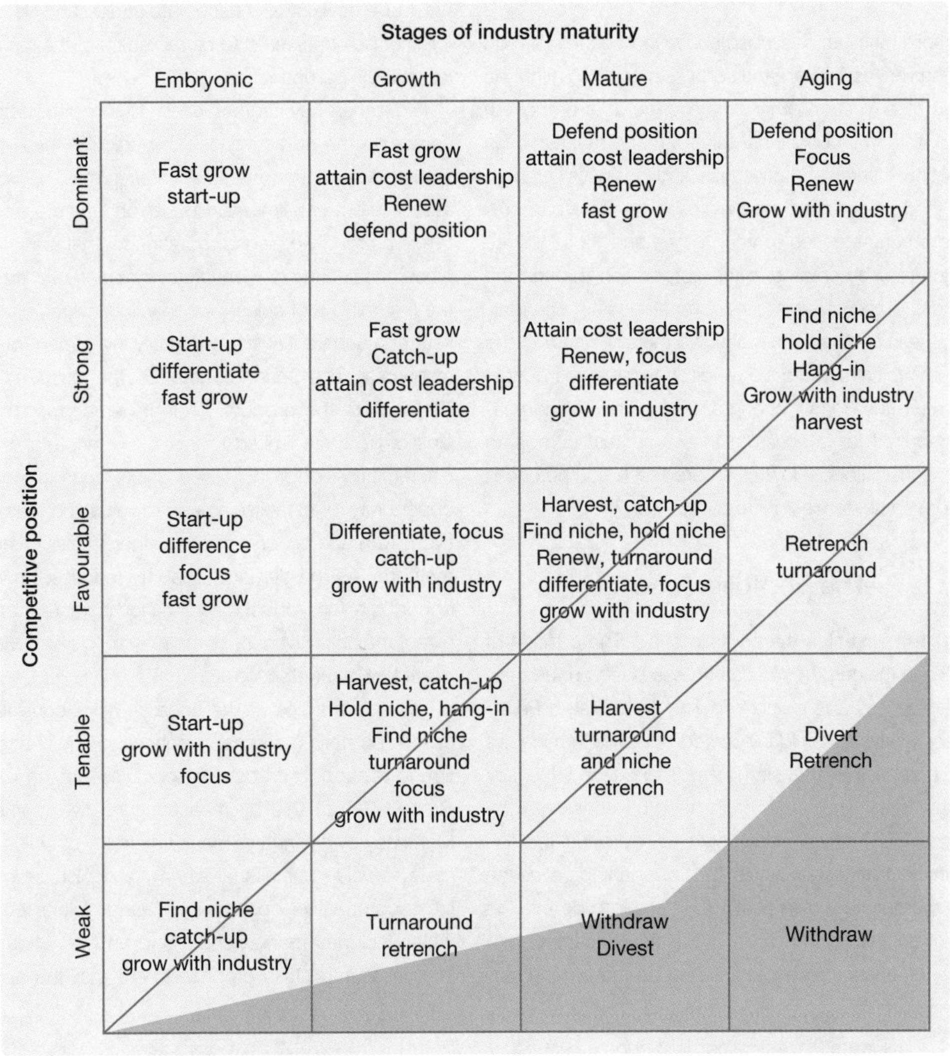

Stages of industry maturity

Competitive position	Embryonic	Growth	Mature	Aging
Dominant	Fast grow start-up	Fast grow attain cost leadership Renew defend position	Defend position attain cost leadership Renew fast grow	Defend position Focus Renew Grow with industry
Strong	Start-up differentiate fast grow	Fast grow Catch-up attain cost leadership differentiate	Attain cost leadership Renew, focus differentiate grow in industry	Find niche hold niche Hang-in Grow with industry harvest
Favourable	Start-up difference focus fast grow	Differentiate, focus catch-up grow with industry	Harvest, catch-up Find niche, hold niche Renew, turnaround differentiate, focus grow with industry	Retrench turnaround
Tenable	Start-up grow with industry focus	Harvest, catch-up Hold niche, hang-in Find niche turnaround focus grow with industry	Harvest turnaround and niche retrench	Divert Retrench
Weak	Find niche catch-up grow with industry	Turnaround retrench	Withdraw Divest	Withdraw

without considering carefully any relationship one SBU might have with any other, be it supplier, distributor, joint economy of scope achiever, or whatever. Strictly speaking, therefore, the portfolio matrix approach to corporate resource allocation can only be used effectively where no synergies are sought between the units. Yet one of the major justifications for the existence of a corporation over and above that of SBUs is the belief that such synergies can be realised and thereby give competitive advantage.

Such matrices are also, by their nature, an example of comparative statics and do not enable accurate insights necessarily to be gained into enduring future trends, but perhaps this is to expect too much. Other criticisms of the portfolio matrices are that they assume that corporations have to be self-sufficient in capital, and must find a use for all internally generated cash, and are incapable of raising more finance for attractive projects. The matrices are also silent on the question of the competitive advantage a business received from being owned by a corporation compared with the costs of owning it.

However, a more fundamental criticism is that, in purporting to provide an aid to the corporate chief executive in his difficult resource allocation decisions involving the product/markets on which to concentrate, they play little if any attention to the growth of risk with increasing unfamiliarity, and of the wisdom of getting involved only in new businesses whose key factors for success relate closely to the corporation's already demonstrated competences. Indeed all three matrices can be used to justify totally unrelated acquisitions based on no clearly existing competences within the corporation whatsoever. As Collis and Montgomery (5) point out:

> 'The problem with the portfolio matrix was that it did not address how value was being created across the divisions ... The only relation between them was cash. As we have come to learn, the relatedness of businesses is at the heart of value creation in diversified companies.'

A new approach to resource allocation

The portfolio matrices described above ignore the question of how the various SBUs in the corporate portfolio might be expected to help each other create value. It is proposed, therefore, to add an additional axis to the normal two axes representing market attractiveness and business strength (1). The third axis will illustrate the closeness of the corporation's core competences to each other, and thus indicate how value may be created in the corporation through the relatedness of the corporation's competences in one market to those in another. The matrix will therefore answer the questions: Which markets are we or should we be in? How attractive are they? How strong are we in the key competences required for success in these markets compared with our competitors? How close are these competences to the core competences of the corporation?

The portfolio cube

[Figure 3.1.4] illustrates the portfolio cube. The position of each SBU in the corporation can be assessed on the market attractiveness axis in the following way. First, a Porter five forces analysis should be carried out to determine the level of competitive intensity in the market and the key structural forces. The future might then be considered by applying a PEST factor checklist, and reviewing the five forces analysis in the light of this. It is important to define the market appropriate to this analysis. In order to do this the degree of substitutability of the products concerned with their nearest needs neighbours should be the guiding factor. Thus a Mini is only substitutable for a Rolls Royce if the would-be traveller is in desperate straits, and should therefore not be considered to be members of the same market for analysis purposes.

Two other key factors need to be considered when assessing the attractiveness of particular markets. Firstly, market size is important. A market may be structurally attractive but very limited in its size and therefore not attractive to a broadly based corporation for that reason. Indeed, when considering new markets, their potential size is often the first thing a businessperson will consider, as only markets of a substantial size will justify investment of time and resources. The second factor is the price elasticity of demand for the product. Thus if demand is totally price elastic, firms are limited to the role of price takers and no differentiation of product is possible, thus eliminating the opportunity for establishing added value and thus competitive advantage by branding or other similar differentiating methods. As the demand elasticity reduces, however, the opportunity for product differentiation increases, and to that extent the attractiveness of the market to a firm with appropriate key competences.

The second axis of the cube is, as is consistently the case in portfolio matrices, a measure of the strength of the firm in relation to its competitors. The Boston Consulting Group attempt this by measuring relative market share, McKinsey by a range of measures many of which approximate to value chain analysis (4), and ADL estimates the firm's competitive position by means of their own rubric, which includes market share and an evaluation of many internal factors. It is proposed here that the appropriate

Figure 3.1.4 The portfolio cube

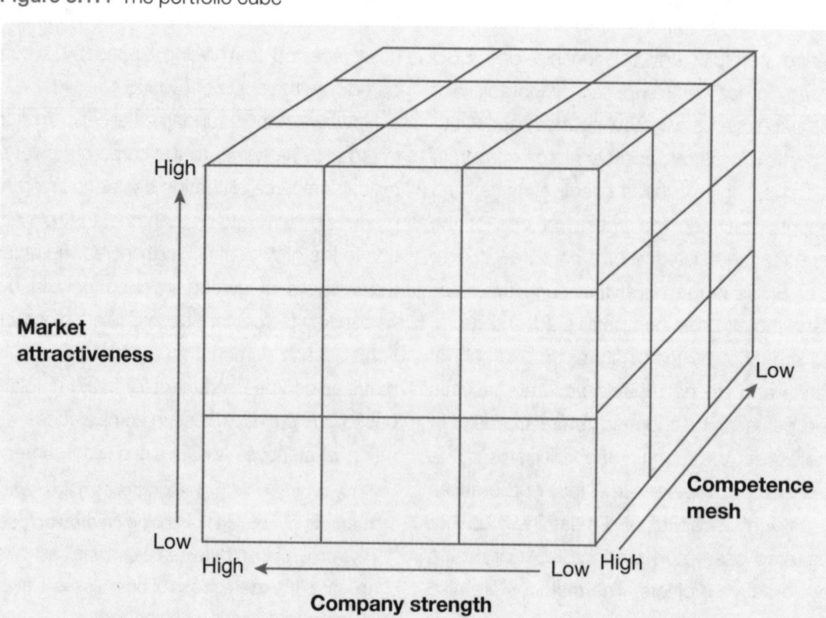

measure of a firm's competitive strength lies in the level of its possession of the key competences required for success in each particular in market. Key competences are those capabilities in a firm measurable in terms of effectiveness (value adding) and efficiency (unit cost reducing) required to succeed in a particular market. They may be contrasted or related to a firm's core competences which are capabilities similarly measured but defined purely as, the functions in which the firm is most proficient. Thus, for example, Burroughs might have had excellent core competences in mechanical engineering, which might also have been some of the key competences to succeed in the mechanical adding machine market. They ceased to be key competences, however, with the onset of the electronic age, and core competences that were closely aligned with the required key competences suddenly ceased to be so, and the firm found itself needing to develop new and sometimes alien competences if it was to survive.

The position on the company strength axis of the cube can be determined by constructing a producer matrix, as described in Chapter 2 of *Exploring Corporate Strategy* (1997) (or in Bowman and Faulkner (1)). This will position the firm in terms of its key competences relative to its competitors in each market in which it operates.

The third axis is necessary in order to develop a view on the degree to which the portfolio of SBUs' in the corporation's ownership are able to add value to each other by the relatedness of their competences, and thus justify their existence within the same corporation, according to the dictates of the resource-based view (RBV) of the firm. This view suggests that firms are unique bundles of physical and intangible assets, capabilities, and organisational cultures. The configuration of the factors determines how well a company performs its activities, and it is best positioned to succeed where these internal factors are the most appropriate ones for particular markets. The RBV therefore combines both the external and the internal aspects of competitive strategy.

It also suggests that investing in resources that are valuable because they are in high demand in particular markets, are scarce and are difficult to imitate is a good route to corporate success. Some competences may be specific to markets and hence to competitive strategy. Many corporation competences are, however, likely to apply across the board and thus be linchpins of corporate strategy. Thus Disney's brand name, and its skills in characterisation and in animation, apply across more than one potential product/market SBU. The corporation's core competences therefore represent the basic high-level capabilities that should guide it in determining the businesses in which it is most likely to succeed. Some core competences are extremely wide in their application, e.g. Hanson's ability to identify undervalued mature businesses and increase their profitability through tight financial control and strong motivation of SBU managers. Others are much narrower, e.g. when Xerox tried to use its strong brand name to diversify into a complete range of 'office of the future' products, it discovered that the market saw it principally as a photocopier company. By building outwards from limited core competences the corporation can, however, deliberately extend its range of capabilities in an incremental fashion. It is this aspect of the portfolio matrix that the third axis aims to capture.

Xerox and the portfolio cube

The Xerox Group portfolio as at 1982 provides a good example of how the portfolio cube works. During the period prior to that date Xerox had been conscious that its pre-eminence in the plain paper photocopier market was coming to an end. Its patents were running out and the Japanese, with Canon in the lead, were eating away at its market share. In order to combat this assault, Xerox decided to diversify its product range and attempt to become the leading office automation company. As the 'office of the future' took longer to become translated from concepts into actual sales volume, Xerox then decided that they were credible as a major diversified corporation with a wide and varied industry portfolio, and bought into the financial services industry through the acquisition of Crum & Forster, the insurance company. Later in the 1980s, having discovered that such diversification did not lead to high corporate performance, Xerox divested themselves of most of their acquisitions unrelated to xerography, and concentrated on fighting the competition in the areas of their competitive strength, i.e. reprographics. In this they were successful, but only after billions of dollars of shareholders' funds had been lost on unrelated diversification.

In three-dimensional form the Xerox portfolio looked something like [Figure 3.1.5]. Xerox's core competences lay in the skills associated with designing, manufacturing, selling and servicing photocopiers. In more detail they could be said to be understanding and operating with electrostatic processes, particularly the process of xerography, providing all the necessary services in relation to photocopiers from design through manufacture to after-sales support services, research and development skills concentrating in this and related areas, and the marketing and distribution of photocopiers and related paper and chemicals. More general competences, or at least strengths, were to be found in the financial strength of the company and its strong brand name, although this latter factor proved problematic, since

Figure 3.1.5 The Xerox portfolio cube

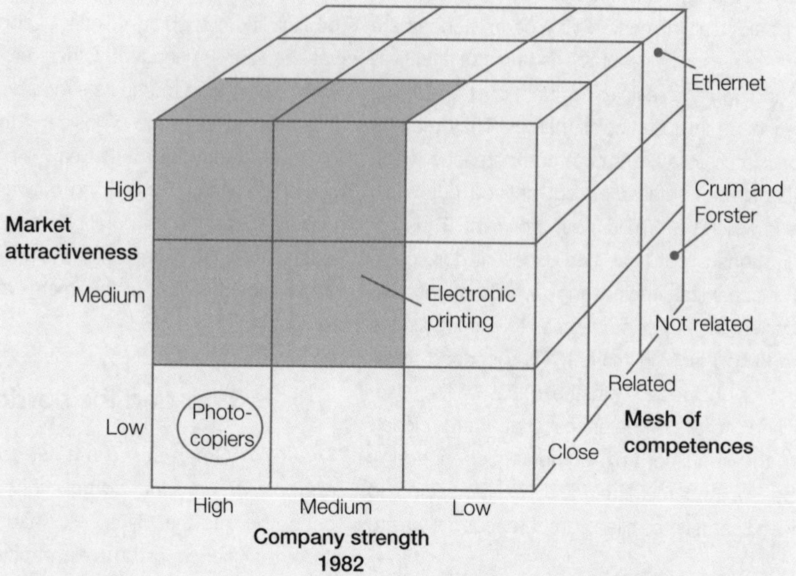

Portfolio

- Photocopiers – reprographics
- Paper
- Electric typewriters
- Word processors
- Small computers – Shugart (floppy disk drives) Diabio systems (daisy wheel printers)
- Fax machines
- Toner and other supplies
- Publicity educational material
- Electronic printing, combining computer technology and xerography
- Ethernet

the company believed its name to be instantly transferable to other products, whereas the market identified it only with photocopiers.

The Xerox portfolio cube attempts to measure on the vertical axis the attractiveness of the market for each of Xerox's products. Along the horizontal axis it measures company strength as in the product matrix by measuring each SBU's competitive strength in the key competences required for success in each segment, and adds to this its market share in order to determine the degree to which the SBU's competences have been successfully translated into success in the marketplace. The third axis assesses the mesh between an individual SBU's core competences and the core competences of the corporation, in this case the competences associated with the xerography business. Using the resource-based view of an appropriate portfolio for a corporation, the shaded area of the cube represents the sub-cube within which it would be recommended that the majority of the portfolio should fall. It can be seen from the figure that only electronic printers (that use electrostatic technology) join the core reprographics business within that sub-cube. Ethernet, while in an attractive market, is not closely related to reprographic technologies, and Xerox are not strong in it. Crum & Forster are neither in an attractive market nor particularly strong, and they are quite unrelated to Xerox's known competences. It is, perhaps, not surprising that the stock market marked Xerox shares drastically down when news of the intended purchase reached it.

[Figure 3.1.6] breaks the cube out into its three planes to project a better view of the individual SBUs of the portfolio. It can be seen that only the Versatic product range of electrostatic printers and plotters are closely meshed to Xerox technology, and the company is not strong in this market, nor is the market particularly attractive. Electronic printing comes within the related mesh plane, but the vast majority of the acquisitions and developments fall within the unrelated plane and suggest, therefore, on the basis of the RBV a poorly constructed portfolio, with few synergies between the SBUs and an excess of products in areas in which Xerox cannot demonstrate high degrees of core competence.

Despite the disapproval of Wall Street of its acquisition of the insurance company Crum & Forster against all RBV logic, Xerox went further and acquired Furman Selz, an investment bank, and Van Kampen Merritt, a mutual fund

Figure 3.1.6 Xerox's portfolio

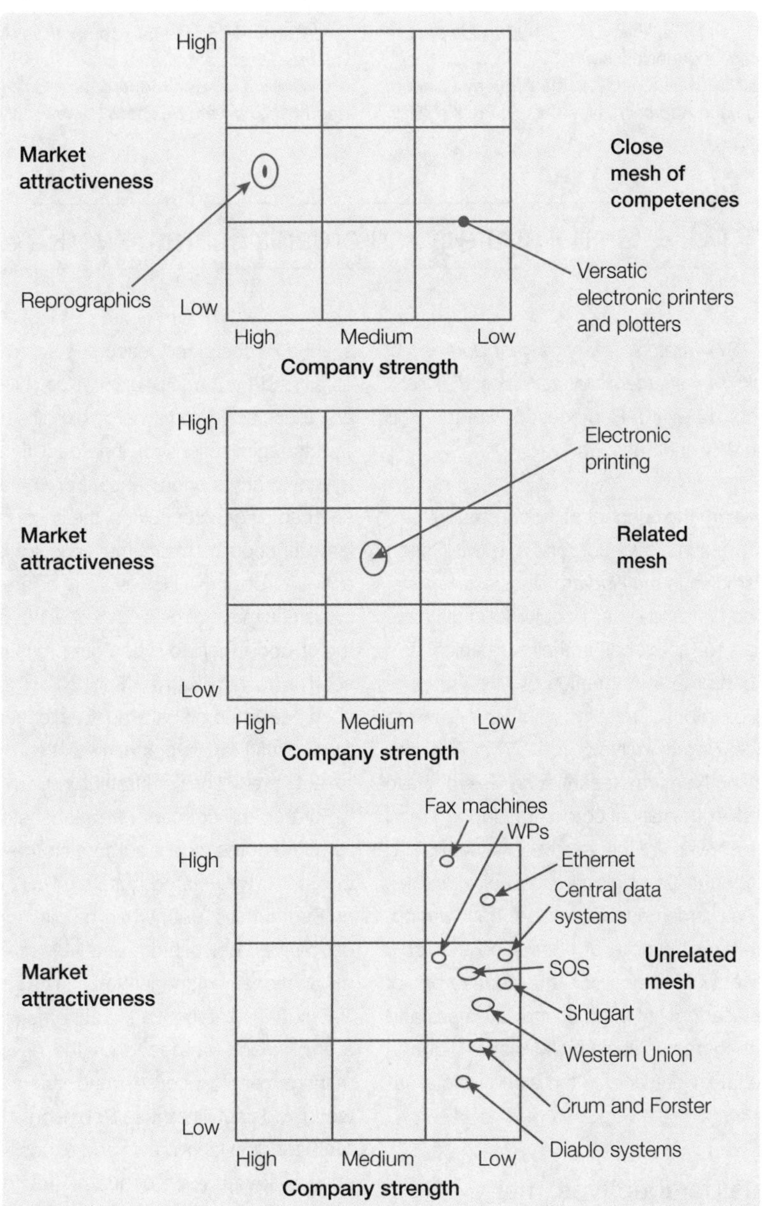

business. The remainder of the 1980s saw Xerox working hard to improve the performance of its traditional core business, with some success, and devoting an increasing level of resources to its new love, financial services. Indeed, by 1991 financial services operations contributed one-third of Xerox's revenues, but only 3 per cent of its profits. In 1991, under a new chairman, Xerox decided to divest itself entirely of its financial services arm. Xerox shareholders have thus had to pay a heavy price for Xerox's directors' decision to ignore the dictates of RBV theory and develop a corporate portfolio without reference to the corporation's core competences.

Summary

The three traditional portfolio matrices show, in their different ways, how business strength and market attractiveness can be combined in relation to a portfolio of SBUs to give a picture of the balance and potential of a corporation's businesses. They do not, however, give any indication of how the SBUs relate, in terms of their contributions, to each other and to the corporation as a whole. The addition of a third axis labelled 'mesh' attempts to address this question and makes portfolio matrices usable for advocates of the development of strategy through the resource-based view of the firm.

References

1. Bowman, C.C. and Faulkner, D.O. (1996). ***Competitive and Corporate Strategy***, London: Irwin.

2. Hax, A.C. and Majluf, N.S. (1991). ***The Strategy Concept and Process: A Pragmatic Approach***, New Jersey: Prentice Hall.

3. Porter, M.E. (1980). ***Competitive Strategy***, New York: The Free Press.

4. Porter, M.E. (1985). ***Competitive Advantage***, New York: The Free Press.

5. Collis, D.K. and Montgomery, C.A. (1995). 'Competing on resources', ***Harvard Business Review***, July/August, 118–128.

Reading 3.2 Global strategy: an organizing framework *Sumantra Ghoshal*

First published: (1987) *Strategic Management Journal*, 8: 425–440. *Strategic Management Journal*, Vol. 8, No. 5 (Sep–Oct 1987), pp. 425–440. Reproduced with the kind permission of John Wily and Sons Ltd.

Over the past few years the concept of global strategy has taken the world of multinational corporations (MNCs) by storm. Scores of articles in the *Harvard Business Review, Fortune*, *The Economist* and other popular journals have urged multinationals to 'go global' in their strategies. The topic has clearly captured the attention of MNC managers. Conferences on global strategy, whether organized by the Conference Board in New York, *The Financial Times* in London, or Nomura Securities in Tokyo, have invariably attracted enthusiastic corporate support and sizeable audiences. Even in the relatively slow-moving world of academe the issue of globalization of industries and companies has emerged as a new bandwagon, as manifest in the large number of papers on the topic presented at recent meetings of the Academy of Management, the Academy of International Business and the Strategic Management Society. 'Manage globally' appears to be the latest battlecry in the world of international business.

Multiple perspectives, many prescriptions

This enthusiasm notwithstanding, there is a great deal of conceptual ambiguity about what a 'global' strategy really means. As pointed out by Hamel and Prahalad (1985), the distinction among a global industry, a global firm, and a global strategy is somewhat blurred in the literature. According to Hout, Porter and Rudden (1982), a global strategy is appropriate for global industries which are defined as those in which a firm's competitive position in one national market is significantly affected by its competitive position in other national markets. Such interactions between a firm's positions in different markets may arise from scale benefits or from the potential of synergies or sharing of costs and resources across markets. However, as argued by Bartlett (1985), Kogut (1984) and many others, those scale and synergy benefits may often be created by strategic actions of individual firms and may not be 'given' in any *a priori* sense. For some industries, such as aeroframes or aeroengines, the economies of scale may be large enough to make the need for global integration of activities obvious. However, in a large number of cases industries may not be born global but may have globalness thrust upon them by the entrepreneurship of a company such as Yoshida Kagyo KK (YKK) or Procter and Gamble. In such cases the global industry-global strategy link may be more useful for ex-post explanation of outcomes than for ex-ante predictions or strategizing.

Further, the concept of a global strategy is not as new as some of the recent authors on the topic have assumed it to be. It was stated quite explicitly about 20 years ago by Perlmutter (1969) when he distinguished between the geocentric, polycentric, and ethnocentric approaches to multinational management. The starting point for Perlmutter's categorization scheme was the world view of a firm, which was seen as the driving force behind its management processes and the way it structured its world-wide activities (see Robinson, 1978 and Rutenberg, 1982 for detailed reviews and expositions). In much of the current literature, in contrast, the focus has been narrowed and the concept of global strategy has been linked almost exclusively with how the firm structures the flow of tasks within its world-wide value-adding system. The more integrated and rationalized the flow of tasks appears to be, the more global the firm's strategy is assumed to be (e.g. Leontiades, 1984). On the one hand, this focus has led to improved understanding of the fact that different tasks offer different degrees of advantages from global integration and national differentiation and that, optimally, a firm must configure its value chain to obtain the best possible advantages from both (Porter, 1984). But, on the other hand, it has also led to certain dysfunctional simplifications. The complexities of managing large, world-wide organizations have been obscured by creating polar alternatives between centralization and decentralization, or between global and multidomestic strategies (e.g. Hout *et al.*, 1982). Complex management tasks have been seen as composites of simple global and local components. By emphasizing the importance of rationalizing the flow of components and final products within a multinational system, the importance of internal flows of people, technology, information, and values has been de-emphasized.

Differences among authors writing on the topic of global strategy are not limited to concepts and perspectives. Their prescriptions on how to manage globally have also been very different, and often contradictory.

1. Levitt (1983) has argued that effective global strategy is not a bag of many tricks but the successful practice of just one: product standardization. According to him, the core of a global strategy lies in developing a standardized product to be produced and sold the same way throughout the world.

2. According to Haut, et al. (1982), on the other hand, effective global strategy requires the approach not of a hedgehog, who knows only one trick, but that of a fox, who knows many. Exploiting economies of scale through global volume, taking pre-emptive positions through quick and large investments, and managing interdependently to achieve synergies across different activities are, according to these authors, some of the more important moves that a winning global strategist must muster.

3. Hamel and Prahalad's (1985) prescription for a global strategy contradicts that of Levitt (1983) even more sharply. Instead of a single standardized product, they recommend a broad product portfolio, with many product varieties, so that investments on technologies and distribution channels can be shared. Cross- subsidization across products and markets, and the development of a strong world-wide distribution system, are the two moves that find the pride of place in these authors' views on how to succeed in the game of global chess.

4. If Hout, et al.'s (1982) global strategist is the heavyweight champion who knocks out opponents with scale and pre-emptive investments, Kogut's (1985b) global strategist is the nimble-footed athlete who wins through flexibility and arbitrage. He creates options so as to turn the uncertainties of an increasingly volatile global economy to his own advantage. Multiple sourcing, production shifting to benefit from changing factor costs and exchange rates, and arbitrage to exploit imperfections in financial and information markets are, according to Kogut, some of the hallmarks of a superior global strategy.

These are only a few of the many prescriptions available to MNC managers about how to build a global strategy for their firms. All these suggestions have been derived from rich and insightful analyses of real-life situations. They are all reasonable and intuitively appealing, but their managerial implications are not easy to reconcile.

The need for an organizing framework

The difficulty for both practitioners and researchers in dealing with the small but rich literature on global strategies is that there is no organizing framework within which the different perspectives and prescriptions can be assimilated. An unfortunate fact of corporate life is that any particular strategic action is rarely an unmixed blessing. Corporate objectives are multidimensional, and often mutually contradictory. Contrary to received wisdom, it is also usually difficult to prioritize them. Actions to achieve a particular objective often impede another equally important objective. Each of these prescriptions is aimed at achieving certain objectives of a global strategy. An overall framework can be particularly useful in identifying the trade-offs between those objectives and therefore in understanding not only the benefits but also the potential costs associated with the different strategic alternatives.

The objective of this paper is to suggest such an organizing framework which may help managers and academics in formulating the various issues that arise in global strategic management. The underlying premise is that simple categorization schemes such as the distinction between global and multidomestic strategies are not very helpful in understanding the complexities of corporate-level strategy in large multinational corporations. Instead, what may be more useful is to understand what the key strategic objectives of an MNC are, and the tools that it possesses for achieving them. An integrated analysis of the different means and the different ends can help both managers and researchers in formulating, describing, classifying and analyzing the content of global strategies. Besides, such a framework can relate academic research, that is often partial, to the totality of real life that managers must deal with.

The framework: mapping means and ends

The proposed framework is shown in Table [3.2.1]. While the specific construct may be new, the conceptual foundation on which it is built is derived from a synthesis of existing literature.

The basic argument is simple. The goals of a multinational—as indeed of any organization—can be classified into three broad categories. The firm must achieve efficiency in

Table 3.2.1 Global strategy: an organizing framework

Sources of competitive advantage			
Strategic objectives	**National differences**	**Scale economies**	**Scope economies**
Achieving efficiency in current operations	Benefiting from differences in factor costs—wages and cost of capital	Expanding and exploiting potential scale economies in each activity	Sharing of investments and costs across products, markets and businesses
Managing risks	Managing different kinds of risks arising from market or policy-induced changes in comparative advantages of different countries	Balancing scale with strategic and operational flexibility	Portfolio diversification of risks and creation of options and side-bets
Innovation learning and adaptation	Learning from societal differences in organizational and managerial processes and systems	Benefiting from experience—cost reduction and innovation	Shared learning across organizational components in different products markets or businesses

its current activities; it must manage the risks that it assumes in carrying out those activities; and it must develop internal learning capabilities so as to be able to innovate and adapt to future changes. Competitive advantage is developed by taking strategic actions that optimize the firm's achievement of these different and, at times, conflicting goals.

A multinational has three sets of tools for developing such competitive advantage. It can exploit the differences in input and output markets among the many countries in which it operates. It can benefit from scale economies in its different activities. It can also exploit synergies or economies of scope that may be available because of the diversity of its activities and organization.

The strategic task of managing globally is to use all three sources of competitive advantage to optimize efficiency, risk and learning simultaneously in a world-wide business. The key to a successful global strategy is to manage the interactions between these different goals and means. That, in essence, is the organizing framework. Viewing the tasks of global strategy this way can be helpful to both managers and academics in a number of ways. For example, it can help managers in generating a comprehensive checklist of factors and issues that must be considered in reviewing different strategic alternatives. Such a checklist can serve as a basis for mapping the overall strategies of their own companies and those of their competitors so as to understand the comparative strengths and vulnerabilities of both. Table [3.2.1] shows some illustrative examples of factors that must be considered while carrying out such comprehensive strategic audits. Another practical utility of the framework is that it can highlight the contradictions between the different goals and between the different means, and thereby make salient the strategic dilemmas that may otherwise get resolved through omission.

In the next two sections the framework is explained more fully by describing the two dimensions of its construct, viz. the strategic objectives of the firm and the sources of competitive advantage available to a multinational corporation. Subsequent sections show how selected articles contribute to the literature and fit within the overall framework. The paper concludes with a brief discussion of the trade-offs that are implicit in some of the more recent prescriptions on global strategic management.

The goals: strategic objectives

Achieving efficiency

A general premise in the literature on strategic management is that the concept of strategy is relevant only when the actions of one firm can affect the actions or performance of another. Firms competing in imperfect markets earn different efficiency rents' from the use of their resources (Caves, 1980). The objective of strategy, given this perspective, is to enhance such efficiency rents.

Viewing a firm broadly as an input–output system, the overall efficiency of the firm can be defined as the ratio of the value of its outputs to the costs of all its inputs. It is by maximizing this ratio that the firm obtains the surplus resources required to secure its own future. Thus it differentiates its products to enhance the exchange value of its outputs, and seeks low cost factors to minimize the costs of its inputs. It also tries to enhance the efficiency of its throughput processes by achieving higher scale economies or by finding more efficient production processes.

The field of strategic management is currently dominated by this efficiency perspective. The generic strategies of Porter (1980), different versions of the portfolio model, as well as overall strategic management frameworks such as those proposed by Hofer and Schendel (1978) and Hax and Majluf (1984) are all based on the underlying notion of maximizing efficiency rents of the different resources available to the firm.

In the field of global strategy this efficiency perspective has been reflected in the widespread use of the

Figure 3.2.1 The integration-responsiveness framework

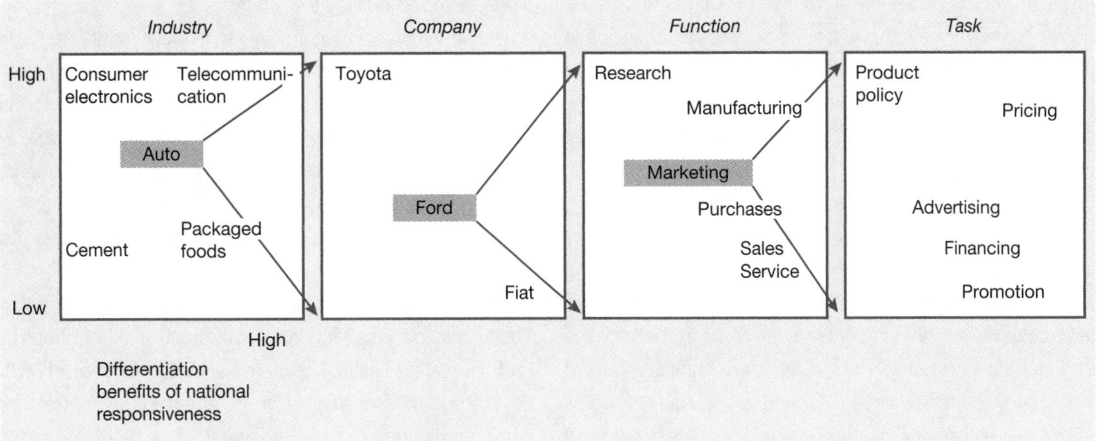

integration-responsiveness framework originally proposed by Prahalad (1975) and subsequently developed and applied by a number of authors including Doz, Bartlett and Prahalad (1981) and Porter (1984). In essence, the framework is a conceptual lens for visualizing the cost advantages of global integration of certain tasks vis-à-vis the differentiation benefits of responding to national differences in tastes, industry structures, distribution systems, and government regulations. As suggested by Bartlett (1985), the same framework can be used to understand differences in the benefits of integration and responsiveness at the aggregate level of industries, at the level of individual companies within an industry, or even, at the level of different functions within a company. Thus the consumer electronics industry may be characterized by low differentiation benefits and high integration advantages, while the position of the packaged foods industry may be quite the opposite. In the telecommunications switching industry, in contrast, both local and global forces may be strong, while in the automobile industry both may be of moderate and comparable importance.

Within an industry (say, automobile), the strategy of one firm (such as Toyota) may be based on exploiting the advantages of global integration through centralized production and decision-making, while that of another (such as Fiat) may aim at exploiting the benefits of national differentiation by creating integrated and autonomous subsidiaries which can exploit strong links with local stakeholders to defend themselves against more efficient global competitors. Within a firm, research may offer greater efficiency benefits of integration, while sales and service may provide greater differentiation advantages. As illustrated in figure 3.2.1, one can apply the framework to even lower levels of analysis, right down to the level of individual tasks. Based on such analysis, a multinational firm can determine the optimum way to configure its value chain so as to achieve the highest overall efficiency in the use of its resources (Porter, 1984).

However, while efficiency is clearly an important strategic objective, it is not the only one. As argued recently by a number of authors, the broader objective of strategic management is to create value which is determined not only by the returns that specific assets are expected to generate, but also by the risks that are assumed in the process (see Woo and Cool (1985) for a review). This leads to the second strategic objective of firms—that of managing risks.[1]

Managing risks

A multinational corporation faces many different kinds of risks, some of which are endemic to all firms and some others are unique to organizations operating across national boundaries. For analytical simplicity these different kinds of risks may be collapsed into four broad categories.

First, an MNC faces certain *macroeconomic risks* which are completely outside its control. These include cataclysmic events such as wars and natural calamities, and also equilibrium-seeking or even random movements in wage rates, interest rates, exchange rates, commodity prices, and so on.

Second, the MNC faces what is usually referred to in the literature as political risks but may be more appropriately called *policy risks* to emphasize that they arise from policy actions of national governments and not from either long-term equilibrium-seeking forces of global markets, nor from short-term random fluctuations in economic variables arising out of stickiness or unpredictability of market

[1] In the interest of simplicity the distinction between risk and uncertainty is ignored, as is the distinction between systematic and unsystematic risks.

mechanisms. The net effect of such policy actions may often be indistinguishable from the effect of macroeconomic forces; for example, both may lead to changes in the exchange rate of a particular currency. But from a management perspective the two must be distinguished, since the former is uncontrollable but the latter is at least partially controllable.

Third, a firm also faces certain *competitive risks* arising from the uncertainties of competitors' responses to its own strategies (including the strategy of doing nothing and trying to maintain the status quo). While all companies face such risks to varying extents (since both monopolies and perfect competition are rare), their implications are particularly complex in the context of global strategies since the responses of competitors may take place in many different forms and in many different markets. Further, technological risk can also be considered as a part of competitive risk since a new technology can adversely affect a firm only when it is adopted by a competitor, and not otherwise.[2]

Finally, a firm also faces what may be called *resource risks*. This is the risk that the adopted strategy will require resources that the firm does not have, cannot acquire, or cannot spare. A key scarce resource for most firms is managerial talent. But resource risks can also arise from lack of appropriate technology, or even capital (if managers, for reasons of control, do not want to use capital markets, or if the market is less efficient than finance theorists would have us believe).

One important issue with regard to risks is that they change over time. Vernon (1977) has highlighted this issue in the context of policy risks, but the same is true of the others. Consider resource risks as an example. Often the strategy of a multinational will assume that appropriate resources will be acquired as the strategy unfolds. Yet the initial conditions on which the plans for ongoing resource acquisition and development have been based may change over time. Nissan, for instance, based its aggressive internationalization strategy on the expectation of developing technological, financial, and managerial resources out of its home base. Changing competitive positions among local car manufacturers in Japan have affected these resource development plans of the company, and its internationalizing strategy has been threatened significantly. A more careful analysis of alternative competitive scenarios, and of their effects on the resource allocation plans of the company, may have led Nissan to either a slower pace of internationalization, or to a more aggressive process of resource acquisition at an earlier stage of implementing its strategy.

The strategic task, with regard to management of risks, is to consider these different kinds of risks *jointly* in the context of particular strategic decisions. However, not all forms of risk are strategic since some risks can be easily diversified, shifted, or shared through routine market transactions. It is only those risks which cannot be diversified through a readily available external market that are of concern at the strategic level.

As an example, consider the case of currency risks. These can be classified as contractual, semi-contractual and operating risks (Lessard and Lightstone, 1983). Contractual risks arise when a firm enters into a contract for which costs and revenues are expected to be generated in different currencies: for example a Japanese firm entering into a contract for supplying an item to be made in Japan to an American customer at a price fixed in dollars. Semi-contractual risks are assumed when a firm offers an option denominated in foreign currencies, such as a British company quoting a firm rate in guilders. Operating risks, on the other hand, refer to exchange rate-related changes in the firm's competitiveness arising out of long-term commitments of revenues or costs in different currencies. For example, to compete with a Korean firm, an American firm may set up production facilities in Singapore for supplying its customers in the United States and Europe. A gradual strengthening of the Singapore dollar, in comparison with the Korean won, can erode the overall competitiveness of the Singapore plant.

Both contractual and semi-contractual currency risks can be easily shifted or diversified, at relatively low cost, through various hedging mechanisms. If a firm does not so hedge these risks, it is essentially operating as a currency speculator and the risks must be associated with the speculation business and not to its product-market operations. Operating risks, on the other hand, cannot be hedged so easily,[3] and must be considered at the strategic rather than the operational level.

Analysis of strategic risks will have significant implications for a firm's decisions regarding the structures and locations of its cost and revenue streams. It will lead to more explicit analysis of the effects of environmental uncertainties on the configuration of its value chain. There may be a shift from ownership to rental of resources; from fixed to variable costs. Output and activity distributions may be broadened to achieve the benefits of diversification. Incrementalism and opportunism may be given greater emphasis in its

[2] This assumes that the firm has defined its business correctly and has identified as competitors all the firms whose offerings are aimed at meeting the same set of market needs that the firm meets.

[3] Some market mechanisms such as long-term currency swaps are now available which can allow at least partial hedging of operating risks.

strategy in comparison to pre-emptive resource commitments and long-term planning. Overall strategies may be formulated in more general and flexible terms, so as to be robust to different environmental scenarios. In addition, side-bets may be laid to cover contingencies and to create strategic options which may or may not be exercised in the future (see Kogut, 1985b; Aaker and Mascarenhas, 1984; and Mascarenhas, 1982).

Innovation, learning and adaptation

Most existing theories of the multinational corporation view it as an instrument to extract additional rents from capabilities internalized by the firm (see Calvet, 1981, for a review). A firm goes abroad to make more profits by exploiting its technology, or brand name, or management capabilities in different countries around the world. It is assumed that the key competencies of the multinational always reside at the center.

While the search for additional profits or the desire to protect existing revenues may explain why multinationals comes to exist, they may not provide an equally complete explanation of why some of them continue to grow and flourish. An alternative view may well be that a key asset of the multinational is the diversity of environments in which it operates. This diversity exposes it to multiple stimuli, allows it to develop diverse capabilities, and provides it with a broader learning opportunity than is available to a purely domestic firm. The enhanced organizational learning that results from the diversity internalized by the multinational may be a key explanator of its ongoing success, while its initial stock of knowledge may well be the strength that allows it to create such organizational diversity in the first place (Bartlett and Ghoshal, 1985).

Internal diversity may lead to strategic advantages for a firm in many different ways. In an unpredictable environment it may not be possible, ex ante, to predict the competencies that will be required in the future Diversity of internal capabilities, following the logic of population ecologists (e.g. Hannan and Freeman, 1977; Aldrich, 1979), will enhance the probability of the firm's survival by enhancing the chances that it will be in possession of the capabilities required to cope with an uncertain future state. Similarly, diversity of resources and competencies may also enhance the firm's ability to create joint innovations, and to exploit them in multiple locations. One example of such benefits of diversity was recently described in the *Wall Street Journal* (April 29, 1985):

> P&G [Procter and Gamble Co.] recently introduced its new Liquid Tide, but the product has a distinctly international heritage. A new ingredient that helps suspend dirt in wash water came from the company's research center near P&G's Cincinnati headquarters. But the formula for Liquid Tide's surfactants, or cleaning agents, was developed by P&G technicians in Japan. The ingredients that fight mineral salts present in hard water came from P&G's scientists in Brussels.

As discussed in the same WSJ article, P&G's research center in Brussels has developed a special capability in water softening technology due, in part, to the fact that water in Europe contains more than twice the level of mineral content compared to wash water available in the United States. Similarly, surfactant technology is particularly advanced in Japan because Japanese consumers wash their clothes in colder waters compared to consumers in the US or Europe, and this makes greater demands on the cleaning ability of the surfactants. The advantage of P&G as a multinational is that it is exposed to these different operating environments and has learned, in each environment, the skills and knowledge that coping with that environment specially requires. Liquid Tide is an example of the strategic advantages that accrue from such diverse learning.

The mere existence of diversity, however, does not enhance learning. It only creates the potential for learning. To exploit this potential, the organization must consider learning as an explicit objective, and must create mechanisms and systems for such learning to take place. In the absence of explicit intention and appropriate mechanisms, the learning potential may be lost. In some companies, where all organizational resources are centralized and where the national subsidiaries are seen as mere delivery pipelines to supply the organization's value-added to different countries, diverse learning may not take place either because the subsidiaries may not possess appropriate sensing, analyzing, and responding capabilities to learn from their local environments, or because the centralized decision processes may be insensitive to knowledge accumulated outside the corporate headquarters. Other companies, in which the subsidiaries may enjoy very high levels of local resources and autonomy, may similarly fail to exploit global learning benefits because of their inability to transfer and synthesize knowledge and expertise developed in different organizational components. Local loyalties, turf protection, and the 'not invented' here' (NIH) syndrome—the three handmaidens of decentralization—may restrict internal flow of information across national boundaries which is essential for global learning to occur. In other words, both centralization and decentralization may impede learning.

The means: sources of competitive advantage

Most recent articles on global strategy have been aimed at identifying generic strategies (such as global cost leadership, focus or niche) and advocating particular strategic moves (such as cross-subsidy or pre-emptive investments).

Underlying these concepts, however, are three fundamental tools for building global competitive advantage: exploiting differences in input and output markets in different countries, exploiting economies of scale, and exploiting economies of scope (Porter, 1985).

National differences

The comparative advantage of locations in terms of differences in factor costs is perhaps the most discussed, and also the best understood, source of competitive advantage in international business.

Different nations have different factor endowments, and in the absence of efficient markets this leads to inter-country differences in factor costs. Different activities of the firm, such as R&D, production, marketing, etc., have different factor intensities. A firm can therefore gain cost advantages by configuring its value-chain so that each activity is located in the country which has the least cost for the factor that the activity uses most intensely. This is the core concept of comparative advantage-based competitive advantage—a concept for which highly developed analytical tools are available from the discipline of international economics. Kogut (1985a) provides an excellent managerial overview of this concept.

National differences may also exist in output markets. Customer tastes and preferences may be different in different countries, as may be distribution systems, government regulations applicable to the concerned product-markets, or the effectiveness of different promotion strategies and other marketing techniques. A firm can augment the exchange value of its output by tailoring its offerings to fit the unique requirements in each national market. This, in essence, is the strategy of national differentiation, and it lies at the core of what has come to be referred to as the multidomestic approach in multinational management (Hout *et al.*, 1982).

From a strategic perspective, however, this static and purely economic view of national differences may not be adequate. What may be more useful is to take a dynamic view of comparative advantage and to broaden the concept to include both societal and economic factors.

In the traditional economics view, comparative advantages of countries are determined by their relative factor endowments and they do not change. However, in reality one lesson of the past four decades is that comparative advantages change and a prime objective of the industrial policies of many nations is to effect such changes. Thus, for any nation, the availability and cost of capital change, as do the availability of technical manpower and the wages of skilled and unskilled labor. Such changes take place, in the long run, to accommodate different levels of economic and social performance of nations, and in the short run they occur in response to specific policies and regulations of governments.

This dynamic aspect of comparative advantages adds considerable complexity to the strategic considerations of the firm. There is a first-order effect of such changes—such as possible increases in wage rates, interest rates or currency exchange rates for particular countries that can affect future viability of a strategy that has been based on the current levels of these economic variables. There can also be a more intriguing second-order effect. If an activity is located in an economically inefficient environment, and if the firm is able to achieve a higher level of efficiency in its own operations compared to the rest of the local economy, its competitive advantage may actually increase as the local economy slips lower and lower. This is because the macroeconomic variables such as wage or exchange rates may change to reflect the overall performance of the economy relative to the rest of the world and, to the extent that the firm's performance is better than this national aggregate, it may benefit from these macro-level changes (Kiechel, 1981).

Consistent with the discipline that gave birth to the concept, the usual view of comparative advantage is limited to factors that an economist admits into the production function, such as the costs of labor and capital. However, from a managerial perspective it may be more appropriate to take a broader view of societal comparative advantages to include 'all the relative advantages conferred on a society by the quality, quantity and configuration of its material, human and institutional resources, including "soft" resources such as inter-organizational linkages, the nature of its educational system, and organizational and managerial know-how' (Westney, 1985: 4). As argued by Westney, these 'soft' societal factors, if absorbed in the overall organizational system, can provide benefits as real to a multinational as those provided by such economic factors as cheap labor or low-cost capital.

While the concept of comparative advantage is quite clear, available evidence on its actual effect on the overall competitiveness of firms is weak and conflicting. For example, it has often been claimed that one source of competitive advantage for Japanese firms is the lower cost of capital in Japan (Hatsopoulos, 1983). However, more systematic studies have shown that there is practically no difference in the risk-adjusted cost of capital in the United States and Japan, and that capital cost advantages of Japanese firms, if any, arise from complex interactions between government subsidies and corporate ownership structures (Flaherty and Itami, 1984). Similarly, relatively low wage rates in Japan have been suggested by some authors as the primary reason for the success of Japanese companies in. the US market (Itami, 1978). However, recently, companies such as Honda and Nissan have commissioned plants in the USA and have been able to retain practically the same levels of cost advantages over US manufacturers as they had for their production in Japan (Allen, 1985). Overall, there is increasing evidence that while comparative advantages of countries can provide competitive advantages to firms, the realization of such benefits is not automatic but depends on complex organizational factors and processes.

Scale economies

Scale economies, again, is a fairly well established concept, and its implications for competitive advantage are quite well understood. Microeconomic theory provides a strong theoretical and empirical basis for evaluating the effect of scale on cost reduction, and the use of scale as a competitive tool is common in practice. Its primary implication for strategy is that a firm must expand the volume of its output so as to achieve available scale benefits. Otherwise a competitor who can achieve such volume can build cost advantages, and this can lead to a vicious cycle in which the low-volume firm can progressively lose its competitive viability.

While scale, by itself, is a static concept, there may be dynamic benefits of scale through what has been variously described as the experience or learning effect. The higher volume that helps a firm to exploit scale benefits also allows it to accumulate learning, and this leads to progressive cost reduction as the firm moves down its learning curve.

The concept of the value-added chain recently popularized by Porter (1985) adds considerable richness to the analysis of scale as a source of competitive advantage. This conceptual apparatus allows a disaggregated analysis of scale benefits in different value-creating activities of the firm. The efficient scale may vary widely by activity— being higher for component production, say than for assembly. In contrast to a unitary view of scale, this disaggregated view permits the firm to configure different elements of its value chain to attain optimum scale economies in each.

Traditionally, scale has been seen as an unmixed blessing—something that always helps and never hurts. Recently, however, many researchers have argued otherwise (e.g. Evans, 1982). It has been suggested that scale efficiencies are obtained through increased specialization and through creation of dedicated assets and systems. The same processes cause inflexibilities and limit the firm's ability to cope with change. As environmental turbulence has increased, so has the need for strategic and operational flexibility (Mascarenhas, 1982). At the extreme, this line of argument has led to predictions of a re-emergence of the craft form of production to replace the scale-dominated assembly form (Piore and Sabel, 1984). A more typical argument has been to emphasize the need to balance scale and flexibility, through the use of modern technologies such as CAD/CAM and flexible manufacturing Systems (Gold, 1982).

Scope economies

Relatively speaking the concept of scope economies is both new and not very well understood. It is based on the notion that certain economies arise from the fact that the cost of the joint production of two or more products can be less than the cost of producing them separately. Such cost reductions can take place due to many reasons—for example resources such as information or technologies, once acquired for use in producing one item, may be available costlessly for production of other items (Baumol, Panzer, and Willig, 1982).

The strategic importance of scope economies arise from a diversified firm's ability to share investments and costs across the same or different value chains that competitors, not possessing such internal and external diversity, cannot. Such sharing can take place across segments, products, or markets (Porter, 1985) and may involve joint use of different kinds of assets (see Table [3.2.2]).

A diversified firm may share physical assets such as production equipment, cash or brand names across different businesses and markets. Flexible manufacturing systems using robots, which can be used for production of different items, is one example of how a firm can exploit such scope benefits. Cross-subsidization of markets and exploitation of a global brand name are other examples of sharing a tangible asset across different components of a firm's product and market portfolios.

A second important source of scope economies is shared external relations: with customers, suppliers, distributors, governments, and other institutions. A multinational bank like Citibank can provide relatively more effective service to a multinational customer than can a bank that

Table 3.2.2 Scope economies in product and market diversification

Sources of scope economies		
	Product diversification	**Market diversification**
Shared physical assets	Factory automation with flexibility to produce multiple products (Ford)	Global brand name (Coca-Cola)
Shared external relations	Using common distribution channel for multiple products (Matsushita)	Servicing multinational customers worldwide (Citibank)
Shared learning	Sharing R&D in computer and communications businesses (NEC)	Pooling knowledge developed in different markets (Procter and Gamble)

operates in a single country (see Terpstra, 1982). Similarly, as argued by Hamel and Prahalad (1985), companies such as Matsushita have benefited considerably from their ability to market a diverse range of products through the same distribution channel. In another variation, Japanese trading companies have expanded into new businesses to meet different requirements of their existing customers.

Finally, shared knowledge is the third important component of scope economies. The fundamental thrust of NEC's global strategy is 'C&C'—computers and communication. The company firmly believes that its even strengths in the two technologies and resulting capabilities of merging them in-house to create new products gives it a competitive edge over global giants such as IBM and AT&T, who have technological strength in only one of these two areas. Another example of the scope advantages of shared learning is the case of Liquid Tide described earlier in this paper.

Even scope economies, however, may not be costless. Different segments, products or markets of a diversified company face different environmental demands. To succeed, a firm needs to differentiate its management systems and processes so that each of its activities can develop *external consistency* with the requirements of its own environment. The search for scope economies, on the other hand, is a search for *internal consistencies* within the firm and across its different activities. The effort to create such synergies may invariably result in some compromise with the objective of external consistency in each activity.

Further, the search for internal synergies also enhances the complexities in a firm's management processes. In the extreme, such complexities can overwhelm the organization, as it did in the case of EMI, the UK-based music, electronics, and leisure products company which attempted to manage its new CT scanner business within the framework of its existing organizational structure and processes (see EMI and the CT scanner, ICCH case 9-383-194). Certain parts of a company's portfolio of businesses or markets may be inherently very different from some others, and it may be best not to look for economies of scope across them. For example, in the soft drinks industry, bottling and distribution are intensely local in scope, while the tasks of creating and maintaining a brand image, or that of designing efficient bottling plants, may offer significant benefits from global integration. Carrying out both these sets of functions in-house would clearly lead to internalizing enormous differences within the company with regard to the organizing, coordinating, and controlling tasks. Instead of trying to cope with these complexities. Coca-Cola has externalized those functions which are purely local in scope (in all but some key strategic markets). In a variation of the same theme, IBM has 'externalized' the PC business by setting up an almost stand-alone organization, instead of trying to exploit scope benefits by integrating this business within the structure of its existing organization (for a more detailed discussion on multinational scope economies and on the conflicts between internal and external consistencies, see Lorange, Scott Morton and Ghoshal. 1986).

Prescriptions in perspective

Existing literature on global strategy offers analytical insights and helpful prescriptions for almost all the different issues indicated in Table [3.2.1]. Table [3.2.3] shows a selective list of relevant publications, categorized on the basis of issues that, according to this author's interpretations, the pieces primarily focus on.

From an academic point of view, strategy of the multinational corporation is a specialized and highly applied field of study. It is built on the broader field of business policy and strategy which, in turn, rests on the foundation of a number of academic disciplines such as economics, organization theory, finance theory, operations research, etc. A number of publications in those underlying disciplines, and a significant body of research carried out in the field of strategy, in general, provide interesting insights

Table 3.2.3 Selected references for further reading

	Sources of competitive advantage		
Strategic objectives	**National differences**	**Scale economies**	**Scope economies**
Achieving efficiency in current operations	Kogut (1985a); Itami (1978); Okimoto, Sugano and Weinstein (1984)	Hout, Porter and Rudden (1982); Levitt (1983); Doz (1978); Leontiades (1984); Gluck (1983)	Hamel and Prahalad (1985); Hout, Porter and Rudden (1982); Porter(1985); Obmae (1985)
Managing risks	Kiechel (1981); Kobrin (1982); Poynter (1985); Lessard and Lightstone (1983); Srinivasulu (1981); Herring (1983)	Evans (1982); Piore and Sabel (1984); Gold (1982); Aaker and Mascarenhas (1984)	Kogut (1985b); Lorange, Scott Morton and Ghoshal (1986)
Innovation, learning and adaptation	Westney (1985); Terpstra (1977); Ronstadt and Krammer (1982)	BCG (1982); Rapp (1973)	Bartlett and Ghoshal (1985)

on the different issues highlighted in Table [3.2.1]. However, given the objective of suggesting a limited list of further readings that *managers* may find useful, such publications have not been included in Table [3.2.3]. Further, even for the more applied and prescriptive literature on global strategy, the list is only illustrative and not exhaustive.

Pigeon-holing academic contributions into different parts of a conceptual framework tends to be unfair to their authors. In highlighting what the authors focus on, such categorization often amounts to an implicit criticism for what they did not write. Besides, most publications cover a broader range of issues and ideas than can be reflected in any such categorization scheme. Table [3.2.3] suffers from all these deficiencies. At the same time, however, it suggests how the proposed framework can be helpful in integrating the literature and in relating the individual pieces to each other.

From parts to the whole

For managers, the advantage of such synthesis is that it allows them to combine a set of insightful but often partial analyses to address the totality of a multidimensional and complex phenomenon. Consider, for example, a topic that has been the staple for academics interested in international management: explaining and drawing normative conclusions from the global successes of many Japanese companies. Based on detailed comparisons across a set of matched pairs of US and Japanese firms, Itami concludes that the relative successes of the Japanese firms can be wholly explained as due to the advantages of lower wage rates and higher labor productivity. In the context of a specific industry, on the other hand, Toder (1978) shows that manufacturing scale is the single most important source of the Japanese competitive advantage. In the small car business, for example, the minimum efficient scale requires an annual production level of about 400,000 units. In the late 1970s no US auto manufacturer produced even 200,000 units of any subcompact configuration vehicle, while Toyota produced around 500,000 Corollas and Nissan produced between 300,000 and 400,000 B210s per year. Toder estimates that US manufacturers suffered a cost disadvantage of between 9 and 17 percent on account of inefficient scale alone. Add to it the effects of wage rate differentials and exchange rate movements, and Japanese success in the US auto market may not require any further explanation. Yet process-orientated scholars such as Hamel and Prahalad suggest a much more complex explanation of the Japanese tidal wave. They see it as arising out of a dynamic process of strategic evolution that exploits scope economies as a crucial weapon in the final stages. All these authors provide compelling arguments to support their own explanations, but do not consider or refute each other's hypotheses.

This multiplicity of explanations only shows the complexity of global strategic management. However, though different, these explanations and prescriptions are not always mutually exclusive. The manager's task is to find how these insights can be combined to build a multidimensional and flexible strategy that is robust to the different assumptions and explanations.

The strategic trade-offs

This, however, is not always possible because there are certain inherent contradictions between the different strategic objectives and between the different sources of competitive advantage. Consider, for instance, the popular distinction between a global and a multidomestic strategy described by Hout *et al.* (1982). A global strategy requires that the firm should carefully separate different value elements, and should locate each activity at the most efficient level of scale in the location where the activity can be carried out at the cheapest cost. Each activity should then be integrated and managed interdependently so as to exploit available scope economies. In essence, it is a strategy to maximize efficiency of current operations.

Such a strategy may, however, increase both endogenous and exogenous risks for the firm. Global scale of certain activities such as R&D and manufacturing may result in the firm's costs being concentrated in a few countries, while its revenues accrue globally, from sales in many different countries. This increases the operating exposure of the firm to the vicissitudes of exchange rate movements because of the mismatch between the currencies in which revenues are obtained and those in which costs are incurred. Similarly, the search for efficiency in a global business may lead to greater amounts of intra-company, but inter-country, flows of goods, capital, information and other resources. These flows are visible, salient and tend to attract policy interventions from different host governments. Organizationally, such an integrated system requires a high degree of coordination, which enhances the risks of management failures. These are lessons that many Japanese companies have learned well recently.

Similarly, consideration of the learning objective will again contradict some of the proclaimed benefits of a global strategy. The implementation of a global strategy tends to enhance the forces of centralization and to shift organizational power from the subsidiaries to the headquarters. This may result in demotivation of subsidiary managers and may erode one key asset of the MNC—the potential for learning from its many environments. The experiences of Caterpillar is a case in point. An exemplary practitioner of global strategy, Cat has recently spilled a lot of red ink on its balance sheet and has lost ground steadily to its archrival, Komatsu. Many factors contributed to Caterpillar's woes, not the least of which was the inability of its centralized management processes to benefit from the experiences of its foreign subsidiaries.

On the flipside of the coin, strategies aimed at optimizing risk or learning may compromise current efficiency. Poynter (1985) has recommended 'upgrade', i.e. increasing commitment of technology and resources in subsidiaries, as a way to overcome risk of policy interventions by host governments. Kogut (1985b), Mascarenhas (1982) and many others have suggested creating strategic and operational flexibility as a mechanism for coping with macroenvironmental risks. Bartlett and Ghoshal (1985) have proposed the differentiated network model of multinational organizations as a way to operationalize the benefits of global learning. All these recommendations carry certain efficiency penalties, which the authors have ignored.

Similar trade-offs exist between the different sources of competitive advantages. Trying to make the most of factor cost economies may prevent scale efficiency, and may impede benefiting from synergies across products or functions. Trying to benefit from scope through product diversification may affect scale, and so on. In effect these contradictions between the different strategic objectives, and between the different means for achieving them, lead to trade-offs between each cell in the framework and practically all others.

These trade-offs imply that to formulate and implement a global strategy, MNC managers must consider all the issues suggested in Table [3.2.1], and must evaluate the implications of different strategic alternatives on each of these issues. Under a particular set of circumstances a particular strategic objective may dominate and a particular source of competitive advantage may play a more important role than the others (Fayerweather, 1981). The complexity of global strategic management arises from the need to understand those situational contingencies, and to adopt a strategy after evaluating the trade-offs it implies. Existing prescriptions can sensitize MNC managers to the different factors they must consider, but cannot provide ready-made and standardized solutions for them to adopt.

Conclusion

This paper has proposed a framework that can help MNC managers in reviewing and analyzing the strategies of their firms. It is not a blueprint for formulating strategies; it is a road map for reviewing them. Irrespective of whether strategies are analytically formulated or organizationally formed (Mintzberg, 1978), every firm has a realized strategy. To the extent that the realized strategy may differ from the intended one, managers need to review what the strategies of their firms really are. The paper suggests a scheme for such a review which can be an effective instrument for exercising strategic control.

Three arguments underlie the construct of the framework. First, in the global strategy literature, a kind of industry determinism has come to prevail not unlike the technological determinism that dominated management literature in the 1960s. The structures of industries may often have important influences on the appropriateness of corporate strategy, but they are only one of many such influences. Besides, corporate strategy may influence industry structure just as much as be influenced by it.

Second, simple schemes for categorizing strategies of firms under different labels tend to hide more than they reveal. A map for more detailed comparison of the content of strategies can be more helpful to managers in understanding and improving the competitive positions of their companies.

Third, the issues of risk and learning have not been given adequate importance in the strategy literature in general, and in the area of global strategies in particular. Both these are important strategic objectives and must be explicitly considered while evaluating or reviewing the strategic positions of companies.

The proposed framework is not a replacement of existing analytical tools but an enhancement that incorporates these beliefs. It does not present any new concepts or solutions, but only a synthesis of existing ideas and techniques. The benefit of such synthesis is that it can help managers in integrating an array of strategic moves into an overall strategic thrust by revealing the consistencies and contradictions among those moves.

For academics this brief view of the existing literature on global strategy will clearly reveal the need for more empirically grounded and systematic research to test and validate the hypotheses which currently appear in the literature as prescriptions and research conclusions. For partial analyses to lead to valid conclusions, excluded variables must be controlled for, and rival hypotheses must be considered and eliminated. The existing body of descriptive and normative research is rich enough to allow future researchers to adopt a more rigorous and systematic approach to enhance the reliability and validity of their findings and suggestions. The proposed framework, it is hoped, may be of value to some researchers in thinking about appropriate research issues and designs for furthering the field of global strategic management.

Acknowledgements

The ideas presented in this paper emerged in the course of discussions with many friends and colleagues. Don Lessard, Eleanor Westney, Bruce Kogut, Chris Bartlett and Nitin Nohria were particularly helpful. I also benefited greatly from the comments and suggestions of the two anonymous referees from the *Strategic Management Journal*.

References

Aaker, D. A. and B. Mascarenhas. 'The need for strategic flexibility'. *Journal of Business Strategy*, 5(2), Fall 1984, pp. 74–82.

Aldrich, H. E. *Organizations and Environment.* Prentice-Hall, Englewood Cliffs, NJ, 1979.

Allen, M. K. 'Japanese companies in the United States: the success of Nissan and Honda'. Unpublished manuscript, Sloan School of Management, MIT, November 1985.

Bartlett, C. A. 'Global competition and MNC managers', ICCH Note No. 0-385-287, Harvard Business School, Boston. 1985.

Bartlett, C. A. and S. Ghosbal. 'The new global organization differentiated roles and dispersed responsibilities', Working Paper No. 9-786-013, Harare Business School, Boston, October 1985.

Baumol W. J., J. C. Panzer and R. D. Willing. *Contestable Markets and the Theory of Industry Structure.* Harcourt, Brace, Jovanovich, New York, 1982.

Boston Consulting Group, *Perspectives on Experience.* BCG, Boston, MA, 1982.

Calvet, A. L. A synthesis of foreign direct investment theories and theories of the multinational firm', *Journal of International Business Studies*. Spring–Summer 1981, pp. 43–60.

Caves, R. E. 'Industrial organization, corporate strategy and structure', *Journal of Economic Literature*. XVIII, March 1980, pp. 64–92.

Doz, Y. L. 'Managing manufacturing rationalization within multinational companies', *Columbia Journal of World Business*, Fall 1978, pp. 82–94.

Doz, Y. L., C. A. Bartlett and C. K. Prahalad. 'Global competitive pressures and host country demands: managing tensions in MNCs', *California Management Review*, Spring 1981, pp. 63–74.

Evans, J. S. *Strategic Flexibility in Business.* Report No. 678, SRI International, December 1982.

Fayerweather, J. 'Four winning strategies for the international corporation', *Journal of Business Strategy*, Fall 1981, pp. 23–36.

Flaherty, M. T. and H. Itami. 'Finance', in Okimoto, D.I., T. Sugano and F. B. Weinstein (eds) *Competitive Edge.* Stanford University Press, Stanford, CA, 1984.

Gluck, F. 'Global competition in the l980s'. *Journal of Business Strategy*, Spring 1983, pp. 22–27.

Gold, B. 'Robotics, programmable automation, and international competitiveness', *IEEE Transactions on Engineering Management*, November 1982.

Hamel, G. and C. K. Prahalad. 'Do you really have a global strategy?', *Harvard Business Review*, July–August 1985, pp. 139–148.

Hannan, M. T. and J. Freeman. 'The population ecology of organizations', *American Journal of Sociology*, 82, 1977, pp. 929–964.

Hatsopoulos, G.N. 'High cost of capital: handicap of American industry', Report Sponsored by the American Business Conference and Thermo-Electron Corporation. April 1983.

Hax, A, C. and N. S. *Majluf Strategic Management: An Integrative Perspective*. Prentice-Hall Englewood Cliffs, NJ, 1984.

Herring R. J, (ed.), *Managing International Risk*. Cambridge University Press, Cambridge, 1983.

Hofer, C. W. and D. Schendel. *Strategy Formulation: Analytical Concepts*. West Publishing Co., St Paul, MN, T978.

Hout, T., M. E. Porter and E. Rudden. 'How global 'companies win out', *Harvard Business Review*, September–October 1982, pp. 98–108.

Itami, H. "Japanese-U.S. comparison of managerial productivity', *Japanese Economic Studies*, Fall 1978.

Kiechel, W. 'Playing the global game', *Fortune*, November 16, 1981, pp. 111–126.

Kobrin, S. J. *Managing Political Risk Assessment.* University of California Press, Los Angeles, CA, 1982.

Kogut, B. 'Normative observations on the international value-added chain and strategic groups', *Journal of International Business Studies*, Fall 1984, pp. 151–167.

Kogut, B. 'Designing global strategies: comparative and competitive value added chains', *Sloan Management Review*, 26(4): Summer 1985a, pp. 15–28.

Kogut, B. 'Designing global strategies: profiting from operational flexibility', *Sloan Management Review*, Fall 1985b, pp. 27–38.

Leontiades, J. 'Market share and corporate strategy in international industries', *Journal of Business Strategy*, 5(1), Summer 1984, pp. 30–37.

Lessard, D. and J. Lightstone. 'The impact of exchange rates on operating profits: new business and financial responses', mimeo, Lightstone-Lessard Associates, 1983.

Levitt, T. "The globalization of markets', *Harvard Business Review*, May–June 1983, pp. 92–102.

Lorange, P., M. S. Scott Morton and S. Ghoshal. *Strategic Control*. West Publishing Co., St Paul, MN, 1986.

Mascarenhas, B. 'Coping with uncertainty in international business', *Journal of International Business Studies*, Fall 1982, pp. 87–98.

Mintzberg, H. 'Patterns in strategic formation', *Management Science*, 24, 1978, pp. 934–948.

Ohmae, K. *Triad Power: The Coming Shape of Global Competition.* Free Press, New York, 1985,

Okimoto, D. L, T. Sugano and F. B. Weinstein (eds). *Competitive Edge*. Stanford University Press, Stanford, CA, 1984.

Perlmutter, H. V. 'The tortuous evolution of the multinational corporation', *Columbia Journal of World Business*, January–February 1969, pp. 9–18.

Piore, M. J. and C. Sabel. *The Second Industrial Divide: Possibilities and Prospects.* Basic Books, New York, 1984.

Porter, M. E. *Competitive Strategy.* Basic Books, New York, 1980.

Porter, M. E. 'Competition in global industries: a conceptual framework', paper presented to the Colloquium on Competition in Global Industries, Harvard Business School, 1984.

Porter, M. E. *Competitive Advantage*. Free Press, New York, 1985.

Poynter, T. A. *International Enterprises and Government Intervention*. Croom Helm, London, 1985.

Prahalad, C. K. 'The strategic process in a multinational corporation'. Unpublished doctoral dissertation Graduate School of Business Administration, Harvard University, 1975.

Rapp, W. V. 'Strategy formulation and international competition', *Columbia Journal of World Business*, Summer 1983, pp. 98–112.

Robinson, R. D. *International Business Management: A Guide to Decision Making*. Dryden Press, Illinois, 1978.

Ronstadt, R. and R. J. Krammer. 'Getting the most out of innovation abroad', *Harvard Business Review*, March–April 1982, pp. 94–99.

Rutenberg, D. P. *Multinational Management*. Little, Brown, Boston, MA, 1982.

Srinivasula S. 'Strategic response to foreign exchange risks', *Columbia Journal of World Business*, Spring 1981, pp. 13–23.

Terpstra, V. 'International product policy: the role of foreign R&D', *Columbia Journal of World Business*, Winter 1977, pp. 24–32.

Terpstra, V. *International Dimension of Marketing*. Kent, Boston, MA, 1982.

Toder, E. J. *Trade Policy and the U.S. Automobile Industry*. Praeger Special Studies, New York, 1978.

Vernon, R. *Storm over the Multinationals*. Harvard University Press, Cambridge, MA, 1977.

The Wall Street Journal, April 29, 1985, p. 1.

Westney, D. E. 'International dimensions of information and communications technology'. Unpublished manuscript, Sloan School of Management, MIT, 1985.

Woo, C. Y. and K. O. Cool. 'The impact of strategic management of systematic risk', mimeo, Krannert Graduate School of Management, Purdue University, 1985.

Reading 3.3 How to build collaborative advantage *Morten T. Hansen and Nitin Nohria*

First published: (2004) *Sloan Management Review*, 46(1): 4–12. *MIT Sloan Management Review*, Fall 2004.

For many years, multinational corporations could compete successfully by exploiting scale and scope economies or by taking advantage of imperfections in the world's goods, labor and capital markets. But these ways of competing are no longer as profitable as they once were. In most industries, multinationals no longer compete primarily with companies whose boundaries are confined to a single nation. Rather, they go head-to-head with a handful of other giants that are comparable in size, in their access to international resources and in worldwide market position. Against such global competitors, it is hard to sustain an advantage based on traditional economies of scale and scope.

Consider the oil industry. The industry is dominated by a handful of global players such as Exxon Mobil, BP, Shell and ChevronTexaco. They each have global exploration, refining and distribution operations, leaving little room for any company to gain competitive advantage with economies of scale. Similarly, they each have brands that are more or less equally well recognized the world over, reducing opportunities for a company to seize competitive advantage with an economy of scope based on its brand power. Such relative parity among multinational corporations can also be observed in consumer electronics, information technology, pharmaceuticals, banking, professional services and even retailing.

Under these circumstances, MNCs must seek new sources of competitive advantage. While multinationals in the past realized economies of scope principally by utilizing physical assets (such as distribution systems) and exploiting a companywide brand, the new economies of scope are based on the ability of business units, subsidiaries and functional departments within the company to collaborate successfully by sharing knowledge and jointly developing new products and services.[1] Multinationals that can stimulate and support collaboration will be better able to leverage their dispersed resources and capabilities in subsidiaries and divisions around the globe.

Collaboration can be an MNC's source of competitive advantage because it does not occur automatically – far from it. Indeed, several barriers impede collaboration within complex multiunit organizations. And in order to overcome those barriers, companies will have to develop distinct organizing capabilities that cannot be easily imitated.

Interunit collaboration is not only difficult to achieve but also poorly understood. However, a framework that links managerial action, barriers to interunit collaboration, and value creation in MNCs can help managers "unpack" the concept. The framework conceptualizes collaboration as a set of management levers that reduce four specific barriers to collaboration, leading in turn to several types of value creation. (See [Figure 3.3.1].) It makes most sense to explain the three elements of the framework in reverse order, beginning with value creation.

Value creation from interunit collaboration

A company should not collaborate across units for collaboration's sake alone, of course, but only if it can reap economic benefits by doing so. The potential varies by company; for instance, a firm with many related businesses or country subsidiaries stands to benefit more than a loose conglomerate of businesses. And the type of benefits will vary, too, from among five major categories:

- Cost savings through the transfer of best practices;
- Better decision making as a result of advice obtained from colleagues in other subsidiaries;
- Increased revenue through the sharing of expertise and products among subsidiaries;
- Innovation through the combination and cross-pollination of ideas; and
- Enhanced capacity for collective action that involves dispersed units.

Figure 3.3.1 A framework for creating value through interunit collaboration

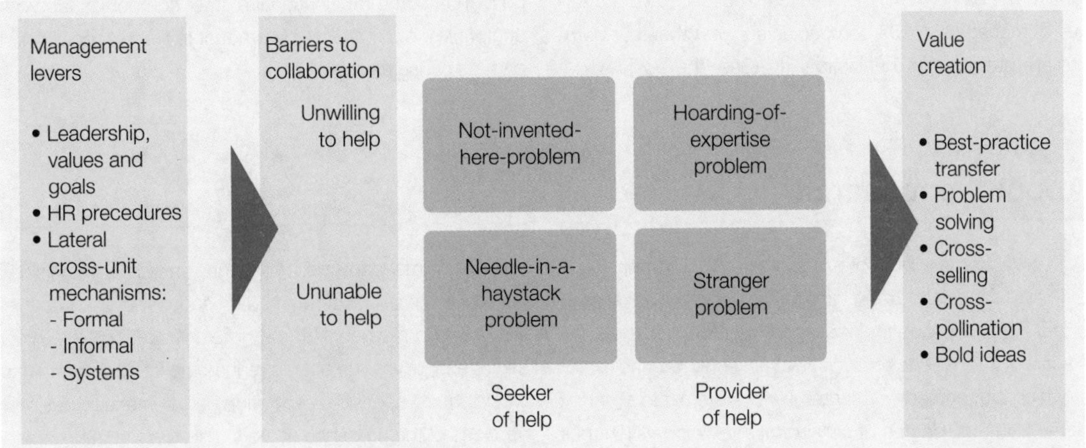

To concretely grasp the notion of collaboration in a multinational company, consider the case of BP Plc, which has operations in more than 100 countries.[2] Over the last decade, senior executives of this oil and gas giant have transformed the company from a collection of individual fiefdoms into a vast collaborative organization with significant improvements in costs, efficiency and revenues as a result.

Several major initiatives were implemented to foster collaboration between business units and country operations. Responsibility for resource allocation, for example, was taken away from individual units and handed to groups of peers – business-unit heads running similar businesses. This approach effectively forced the peers to work together to optimize the allocations for the group as a whole rather than for individual units. The company also developed "peer assist" and "peer challenge" processes, whereby managers and engineers in one unit can ask for technical and help from other units, including technical expertise and problem-solving advice. Engineers in a typical business unit spend about 5% of their time on peer assists. Peer assists are supported by several electronic knowledge-management systems as well as videoconferencing technology. And strong personal relationships also have developed as a result of the frequent rotation of managers among units and country operations.

BP also changed its promotion and reward systems. Managers undergo a 360-degree feedback process that includes reviews from peers, and managers who do not collaborate effectively throughout the organization suffer when they are being considered for promotion. In addition, 30% to 50% of bonuses for senior managers are contingent on the performance of the firm as a whole. Naturally, BP's executives continue to change these practices as the company evolves, but the fundamental idea of creating additional value through interunit collaboration remains at the center of the company's organizational model.

These changes have produced real, measurable results at BP. For example, there have been cost savings through the transfer of best practices: A business-unit head in the United States sought to improve the inventory turns of service stations. Tapping the expertise of her peer group, she obtained knowledge of best practices from operations in the United Kingdom and the Netherlands, leading to a 20% decrease in working capital needed by U.S. service stations. Better decision making was a second result: Another unit head used a peer assist to receive input from six people in other units who had expertise in ordering oil tankers. After several meetings in which the peers advised the unit head's team, the unit bought three tankers and took options on another three. Revenue also grew: During the development of an acetic acid plant in Western China, more than 75 people from various units flew to China to assist the core project team, enabling BP to finish the project on time and to realize revenues from the plant earlier than planned. There was cross-pollination of ideas: Managers from 15 units met to brainstorm e-commerce initiatives, and 150 new ideas were implemented. Finally, BP benefited from collective action: The company used peer groups to integrate ahead of schedule its acquisitions of Amoco Corp. and later Atlantic Richfield Co.

To obtain these important benefits, BP had to overcome barriers to collaboration between units, as all companies must do to realize similar creation of value.

Four barriers to interunit collaboration

Although recent research on basic drivers of human action suggests that cooperation may be a natural human tendency, collaboration at multinationals does not just happen on its own.[3] Companies often erect barriers that prevent individuals from engaging in collaborative activities that they might otherwise have undertaken. The first task, then, is to identify the barriers and their causes. The results from a survey of managers in 107 companies suggest that four barriers are prevalent in multinationals.[4] (See [the box] "About the research.") While all four barriers to collaboration may be high in some multinationals, other companies face only one or two. It is therefore paramount to first diagnose which barriers cause a problem.

About the research

We conducted a survey of executives in 107 companies in the manufacturing, retail, consumer-goods, health-care, professional-services, financial and high-tech industries. On a scale of 1 to 100, executives were asked to rate the extent to which they agreed or disagreed with statements aimed at determining the degree of collaboration existing within their firms and to what extent they were using management levers to encourage collaboration. On the basis of a factor analysis of the survey data, management levers that can reduce any of the barriers to collaboration were found to fall into three broad categories: leadership behaviors, shared values and goals; human resources procedures; and lateral cross-unit mechanisms. Although based on subjective assessments of benefits, the data suggest that companies enjoy economic benefits from interunit collaboration when senior executives are able to reduce the four barriers. There was a strong negative association between executives' perceptions of the presence of the four barriers in their companies and their perceptions of the benefits from the five sources of value – the higher the perceived barriers, the lower the perceived value creation. In addition, we interviewed managers from more than 30 companies and conducted several in-depth case studies in companies such as BP Pic and Intuit Inc.

First barrier: unwillingness to seek input and learn from others

For several reasons, employees in one unit may close themselves off to help from those in others. Sometimes it is the norm in a unit that people are expected to fix their own problems. In other cases, formal and informal reward systems may give more credit for heroic individual efforts than for collaborative efforts. Some employees may simply believe that others have nothing to teach them. They may have developed what social psychologists call an in-group bias, in which they overvalue their own group and undervalue nonmembers.[5] As in-group members spend time with one another to the exclusion of outsiders, they necessarily restrict the influx of new viewpoints and reinforce their own commonly held beliefs.[6] As a result, they become prone to the not-invented-here syndrome, in which ideas, knowledge and inventions developed outside their own group are rejected.[7]

Consider this experience in Hewlett-Packard Co.'s European operations a few years ago. HP executives had created a new internal benchmarking system that compared the times to process computer orders at factories in various countries. Although the system revealed several underperforming country operations, the managers with worse processing times were not willing to contact and visit the best performers, partly because they did not believe that others could teach them useful practices and partly because they viewed their problems as unique (they were not). Only when senior managers intervened did the necessary collaboration between country operations take place.

Short of such after-the-fact intervention, management can use several levers to attenuate this problem. At BP, senior executives keep a close eye on the extent to which business-unit managers ask for peer assists and will intervene if someone is not seeking enough help.[8] More direct help comes through peer challenges, in which peers lend on-the-scene support to help a unit improve in specific areas. Another fundamental lever is recruitment – hiring people who have a natural inclination and the confidence to ask for help. At an international chain of up-market restaurants in the United States, prospective staff members are asked, "What obstacles have you faced in a previous job that prevented you from doing a quality job, and how did you overcome those obstacles?" The company is looking for people who asked for help, communicated a problem to others and didn't try to be a hero by fixing it alone.

Second barrier: inability to seek and find expertise

Even when employees are willing to seek help in other business units or country subsidiaries, they may not be able to find it or to search efficiently so that the benefits outweigh the costs of searching.[9] In large and dispersed MNCs, this needle-in-a-haystack problem can become a significant barrier to collaboration: Somewhere in the company someone often knows the answer to a problem, but it is nearly impossible to connect the person who has the expertise with the person who needs it.

Databases and electronic search engines can help. In most management-consulting companies, for instance, consultants upload sanitized documents containing their finished work into databases; others in the firm can then access the documents and contact the consultants who did the original work.[10] Another way to help people find expertise is to create transparent benchmarking systems. Netherlands-based Ispat International N.V., one of the largest steel companies in the world, has a system that performs costing at the plant level and allows managers to compare all their operating units in the world on many dimensions. For instance, one manager found that his furnace maintenance costs were higher than those of other plants, prompting him to contact the most cost-efficient plants in this area for help.

Technology has its limits, however. Expert directories go out of date and do not fully capture what each person knows. More important, they do not allow for creative combinations of ideas and individuals. Companies may therefore need to cultivate "connectors;" that is, people who know where experts and ideas reside and who can connect people who do not know each other. Connectors tend to be long-tenured employees who have worked in many different areas in the company and hence have an extensive personal network.

A manager in GlaxoSmithKline Plc, for example, created substantial value for his company by connecting two country managers who did not know each other. A few years ago, an area director in Singapore received a phone call from the company's managing director in the Philippines, who was looking for new product opportunities that could be introduced in his country. Acting on a hunch that there might be an opportunity in India, the area director set up a meeting with the managing director in Bombay. During his visit, the managing director from the Philippines saw that the Indian product developers were creating line extensions in the area of tuberculosis medication – not a major field in the company worldwide but one that is highly relevant in developing countries. The visit to the lab sparked a joint effort between the teams in India and Philippines, resulting in a modified TB medication and several other line extensions for the Philippine market. The area director, acting as a connector, was in effect an entrepreneur who saw an opportunity for value creation based on the combination of talent, ideas and expertise from two country subsidiaries.

Third barrier: unwillingness to help

In some cases, the problem lies with the potential provider of help, not the seeker. Some employees are reluctant to share what they know – or refuse to help outright – leading to a hoarding-of-expertise problem.[11] Competition between subsidiaries can undermine people's motivation to cooperate.[12] When two subsidiaries are selling products to the same markets and seeking to develop similar technologies, employees will hesitate to help people in the competing unit. Paradoxically, the emphasis on performance management over the past decade has also fueled this problem. As employees are pressured to perform, they feel that they don't have the time to help others or they just don't care; all that matters is delivering their own numbers. While this focus on individual performance is clearly important, executives also need to create a counterbalancing force by developing incentives aimed at fostering cooperation and a shared identity among employees.

Unwillingness to help is a significant problem in many investment banks, where bankers chase their own opportunities. When John Mack took over Morgan Stanley Group Inc. in the early 1990s, he set out to create a more collaborative culture and changed the promotion criteria.[13] "Lone stars" – those who delivered great results but did not assist others – would not be promoted. To attain the coveted position of managing director, Morgan Stanley's bankers had to demonstrate both individual performance and their contributions to others. To measure this, executives put in place a 360-degree review procedure in which peers and subordinates were asked to evaluate a person's contributions beyond his or her department. Not surprisingly, behavior changed; cooperation within the company became much more prevalent. This system also helped break down some of the barriers to collaboration across geographic boundaries. Bankers from Europe, Asia and the United States became more willing to serve global clients collectively rather than chasing the local business of such clients in each country.

Fourth barrier: inability to work together and transfer knowledge

Finally, sometimes people are willing to work together but can't easily transfer what they know to others because of the "stranger" problem. In this case, the nature of the knowledge in question requires that people already have relationships in order to understand each other. For example, when knowledge is tacit, it is difficult to explain its content and nuances to others, who in turn may find it hard to understand, thereby making the tasks of modifying and incorporating it into their own local conditions difficult, too. The same problem crops up with knowledge that is viewed as specific to a context or a culture.[14] Because of these difficulties, transferring tacit or specific knowledge is likely to be more cumbersome, take longer and thus be more costly than transferring explicit or general knowledge.

These problems can be alleviated if the two parties to a transfer have developed a strong professional relationship. In that case, they are likely to have developed a shared communication frame in which each party understands how the other uses subtle phrases and explains difficult concepts. In the absence of such relations, strangers are likely to find it difficult to work together effectively. For example, in a study of time-to-market performance of new product-development projects in a global high-tech company, it was discovered that project engineers who worked with counterparts from other

A road map to building collaborative advantage in your company

The tools below can help a manager identify the mix of barriers to collaboration present in a company and the appropriate choice of levers for that specific situation. Any organizational unit of analysis (the entire company, a business unit, a country subsidiary, a functional department) can be selected and the extent of the barriers within that unit assessed.

1. **Which barriers to collaboration are present in our organizational unit?**

Assess your unit from 1 (not at all) to 100 (to a large extent).

First barrier: unwillingness to seek input and learn from others	Enter 1–100
1. Even when they need help, our employees are not willing to seek input from outside their organizational unit.	
2. When faced with problems, employees in our unit strive to solve them by themselves without asking for help from outsiders.	
3. There is a prevailing attitude in our unit that people ought to fix their own problems and not rely on help from others outside the unit.	
Total of responses to questions 1 to 3	
Second barrier: inability to seek and find expertise	
4 Our employees often complain about the difficulty they have locating colleagues who possess the information and expertise they need.	
5. Experts in our company are very difficult to locate.	
6. Our employees have great difficulties finding the documents and information they need in the company's databases and knowledge management systems.	
Total of responses to questions 4 to 6	
Third barrier: unwillingness to help	
7. Our people keep their expertise and information to themselves and do not want to share it across organizational units.	
8. Our employees do not share their expertise and information for fear of becoming less valuable.	
9. Our employees seldom return phone calls and e-mails when asked for help.	
Total of responses to questions 7 to 9	
Fourth barrier: inability to work together to transfer knowledge	
10. Our employees have not learned to work together effectively across organizational units to transfer tacit knowledge.	
11. Employees from different organizational units are not used to working together and find it hard to do so.	
12. Our employees find it difficult to work across units to transfer complex technologies and best practices.	
Total of responses to questions 10 to 12	

Check the categories that best correlate to your sum of responses for each of the barriers. The table benchmarks the level of barriers in your organizational unit against a sample of 107 companies.

	Lowest quartile (lowest barriers) *Implication: Barrier is not a problem*	Second lowest quartile *Implication: Barrier might cause some problems*	Median *Implication: Barrier might cause some problems*	Second highest quartile *Implication: Barrier is a problem*	Highest quartile (highest barriers) *Implication: Barrier is a big problem*
First Barrier: Unwillingness to seek input and learn from others	Scores between 3 and 105	106–159	160	161–200	201–300

Second Barrier: Inability to seek and find expertise	3–90	91–134	135	136–180	181–300
Third Barrier: Unwillingness to help	3–60	61–99	100	101–140	141–300
Fourth Barrier: Inability to work together to transfer knowledge	3–110	111–167	168	169–210	211–300

2. **Which management levers should you use to reduce barriers to collaboration?**

Your scores above indicate which barrier(s) need to be reduced in your organizational unit. This table shows the management levers that are most appropriate for each of the barriers (marked with a ✓).

	First barrier: unwilling to seek input	Second barrier: unable to find expertise	Third barrier: unwilling to help	Fourth barrier: unable to transfer knowledge
Demonstration of leadership behaviors	✓		✓	
Articulation of shared value related to teamwork	✓		✓	
Development of unifying goal	✓		✓	
HR procedures				
• Recruitment	✓		✓	
• Promotion	✓		✓	
• Compensation	✓		✓	
Informal networks		✓		
• Connectors				
• Strong professional relationships				✓
Formal lateral mechanisms (for example, cross-unit groups)				✓
Information systems				
• Knowledge-management databases		✓		
• Benchmark system		✓		

divisions or subsidiaries took 20% to 30% longer to complete their projects when close personal relationships between them did not exist beforehand. The engineers found it hard to articulate, understand and absorb complex technologies that were transferred between organizational units. Even though they were motivated to cooperate, they were slowed down by the need to learn to work together during the project.

To alleviate the stranger problem, executives can work to establish relationships between employees from different subsidiaries – but they must do so before specific collaborative events are launched. One of the most effective mechanisms is to rotate people through jobs at different units and subsidiaries. Employees who move to other places temporarily to work on assignments often develop strong bonds with colleagues in those locations. When people are back working in their original sites, those bonds are especially important to the success of cross-unit projects.

Management levers to promote collaboration

Potential management levers that can reduce the barriers fall into three broad categories: leadership, values and goals; human resources procedures; and lateral cross-unit mechanisms. The latter category can in turn be divided into information systems, informal networks and formalized lateral mechanisms. Each mix of barriers in a company requires a specific mix of management levers to foster collaboration across business units, subsidiaries and departments. (See [the box] "A road map to building collaborative advantage in your company.") It's important to carefully choose and implement a management lever or levers that will reduce a specific barrier.

Leadership, values and goals

These levers reduce people's unwillingness to seek and provide help. As leaders signal the importance of collaboration by working together among themselves, articulating the shared values related to teamwork and developing unifying goals, employees are more likely to be motivated to seek and provide help.

Some companies have been particularly good at articulating powerful goals that stop myopic unit-focused behaviors and motivate people to work across company units to realize them. In 1990, Sam Walton said that Wal-Mart Stores Inc. should reach $125 billion in sales by 2000, up from $32 billion at the time. Nike Inc. wanted to "Crush Adidas," its main rival in the athletic shoes industry in the 1960s. Over the past few years employees at Airbus S.A.S. have informally aspired to beating Boeing Co. In the late 1990s, Starbucks Corp. articulated the very ambitious goal of establishing itself as "the most recognized and respected brand in the world."[15] Such goals both stretch and unify an organization's employees; they cannot be reached unless everyone stops pursuing self-promoting, narrow-minded goals and becomes motivated to pull together by seeking and providing help across units.

Levers involving leadership, values and goals, however, do not affect the people's ability to find help and work together. A leader who preaches collaboration may motivate the troops but cannot by words alone help them locate experts or enable employees to work well together. Leadership behaviors and the articulation of shared values and goals are necessary but not sufficient conditions for effective collaboration in MNCs.

Human resources procedures

Recruitment and promotion criteria also reduce unwillingness to seek or provide help. By selecting job candidates who have an inclination to search for and offer help, an organization will over time be populated with people who thrive on cooperative work. Likewise, making demonstrated collaborative behavviors a criterion for promotion to senior positions in a company ensures that the top team will, over time, be composed of leaders who exhibit collaborative behaviors. In addition, having such a promotion criterion sends a powerful signal to employees vying for leadership positions; those who do not have the inclination to collaborate are likely to leave a company that enforces the rule consistently. Finally, compensating employees based on their collaborative behaviors is also a useful lever.

To make the promotion and compensation levers work, a company needs to change its annual performance criteria. Intuit Inc., the financial-software company, has implemented an annual performance system in which employees are evaluated on two questions: "What was accomplished?" and "How were the goals accomplished?"[16] The "how" part evaluates an employee's collaborative efforts across functions and business units in reaching those goals. An employee who did not collaborate enough will receive a lower mark for the year, even if he reached the individual goals.

Lateral cross-unit mechanisms

If the problem is the inability to find help, then the most effective levers tend to be these three: the cultivation of connectors; the development of electronic yellow pages that list experts by area; and the development of benchmark systems that allow employees to identify best practices in the company. If the problem is the inability to work together to transfer knowledge, an effective lever is the cultivation of strong professional relationships between employees from different units and the development of formal cross-unit groups and committees that structure regularly occurring interactions. These provide a forum for people to get to know one another and develop personal bonds that facilitate sharing.

While all four barriers to collaboration may be high in some MNCs, other companies face only one or two. It is therefore paramount to first diagnose which barriers cause a problem. For example, if the problem is an inability to find help, putting in a knowledge-management or benchmarking system would be appropriate, but changing HR procedures would not – if people cannot find experts, it makes no sense to make promotion contingent on doing so. In contrast, if the problem is a widespread not-invented-here syndrome, changing the HR procedures should help, but a new knowledge-management system is unlikely to have any effect on employees who will not seek help or who hoard what they know.

Potential downsides of collaboration

While collaboration can create substantial value, it also has a downside that executives need to manage. One pitfall is that it can easily be overdone. Prompted by collaboration initiatives, employees may begin to participate in all kinds of meetings in which nothing of substance is accomplished. Such unproductive collaboration will undermine overall company performance. For example, when executives were just beginning to develop collaborative behaviors within BP, employees started to form an unforeseen number of cross-unit networks. An audit within the oil exploration business alone identified several hundred of these networks, including one on helicopter utilization. According to John Leggate, who ran several business units during that time, "People always had a good reason to meet, but increasingly we found that people were flying around the world and simply sharing ideas without always having a strong focus on the bottom line." BP's executives had to reduce the number of networks and limit interunit meetings to those focused on getting specific results.

Management levers to create a collaborative organization must be counterbalanced with performance management of each individual and business unit, including a clear specification of who's responsible for what. At BP, each manager has an individual performance contract that is coupled with clear expectations for participating across the organization. These managers have a "T-shaped" role – while their primary responsibility is to deliver results for their own business unit or country subsidiary (the vertical part of the T), their other responsibility is to seek help and to aid others (the horizontal part of the T). This dual role is difficult to carry out well and is a source of stress. Effective T-shaped managers tend to be good at prioritizing and delegating to subordinates. While those are attributes of any good manager, they are especially important in MNCs that require their managers to be effective along both dimensions of the T.

The central role of collaboration

How one views the importance of collaboration relates directly to ideas about the purpose of any corporation and the reason for its existence. In the standard economic argument, firms arise when markets fail.[17] In consonance with that view, market failures in the exchange of goods, people and knowledge across geographic boundaries have long occupied center stage in economic theories of the multinational enterprise.[18] When global markets were relatively underdeveloped and prone to failure, this view made a legitimate contribution to our understanding. But now that global markets have become much more developed and relatively more efficient, it is time to consider an equally long-standing conception of why firms exist.[19]

In the alternative view, firms come into being in order to enable human beings to achieve collaboratively what they could not achieve alone. If one accepts this as the true purpose of any organization, then the main focus of executives' attention should be on how to foster collaboration within their companies. Especially in an era when advantages based on traditional economies of scale and scope are rapidly diminishing, the successful exploitation of collaborative possibilities may hold the key for multinationals seeking to gain or maintain leads over their rivals.

References

1. See B. Kogut and U. Zander, "Knowledge of the Firm, Combinative Capabilities, and the Replication of Technology," ***Organization Science*** 3, no. 3 (1992): 383–397; C. Hill, "Diversification and Economic Performance: Bringing Structure and Corporate Management Back Into the Picture," in ***Fundamental Issues in Strategy***, eds. R. Rumelt, D. Schendel and D. Teece (Boston: Harvard Business School Press, 1995), 297–322; and J. Nahapiet and S. Ghoshal, "Social Capital, Intellectual Capital and the Organizational Advantage," ***Academy of Management Review*** 23, no. 2 (April 1998): 242–266.

2. For an in-depth look at BP on this issue, see S.E. Prokesch, "Unleashing the Power of Learning: An Interview With British Petroleum's John Browne," ***Harvard Business Review*** 75, no. 5 (September–October 1997): 146–168; and M.T. Hansen and B. Von Oetinger, "Introducing T-Shaped Managers: Knowledge Management's Next Generation," ***Harvard Business Review*** 79, no. 3. (March 2001): 106–116. The section on BP in the text draws on the latter article.

3. See P.R. Lawrence and N. Nohria, ***Driven: How Human Nature Shapes Our Choices*** (San Francisco: Jossey-Bass, 2002).

4. This section draws on M. Hansen, "Turning the Lone Star into a Real Team Player," ***Financial Times***, Aug. 7, 2002, 11–13.

5. See, for example, M.B. Brewer, "Ingroup Bias in the Minimal Inter-group Situation: A Cognitive Motivational Analysis," ***Psychological Bulletin*** 86 (1979): 307–324; and H. Tajfel and J.C. Turner, "The Social Identity Theory of Intergroup Behavior," in ***Psychology of Intergroup Relations***, 2nd ed., eds. S. Worchel and W.G. Austin (Chicago: Nelson Hall Publishers, 1986), 7–24.

6. See P.J. Oakes, S.A. Haslam, B. Morrison and D. Grace, "Becoming an In-Group: Reexamining the Impact of Familiarity on Perceptions of Group Homogeneity," ***Social Psychology Quarterly*** 58, no. 1 (March 1995): 52–60; and D.A. Wilder, "Reduction of Intergroup Discrimination Through Individuation of the Out-Group," ***Journal of Personality & Social Psychology*** 36 (1978): 1361–1374.

7. See R.H. Hayes and K.B. Clark, "Exploring the Sources of Productivity Differences at the Factory Level" (New York: Wiley, 1985); and R. Katz and T.J. Allen, "Investigating the Not Invented Here (NIH) Syndrome: A Look at the Performance, Tenure and Communication Patterns of 50 R&D Project Groups," in ***Readings in the Management of Innovation***, 2nd ed., M.L. Tushman and W.L. Moore, eds. (New York: HarperCollins Publishers, 1988), 293–309.

8. See also S. Ghoshal and L. Gratton, "Integrating the Enterprise," ***MIT Sloan Management Review*** 44, no. 1 (fall 2002): 31–38.

9. See M.T. Hansen, "The Search–Transfer Problem: The Role of Weak Ties in Sharing Knowledge Across Organization Subunits," ***Administrative Science Quarterly*** 44, no. 1 (March 1999): 82–111; and M.T. Hansen and B. Lovas, "How Do Multinational Companies Leverage Technological Competencies? Moving From Single to Interdependent Explanations," ***Strategic Management Journal***, in press.

10. For more details on knowledge management in management-consulting companies, see M.T. Hansen, N. Nohria and T. Tierney, "What's Your Strategy for Managing Knowledge?" ***Harvard Business Review*** 77, no. 2 (March–April, 1999): 106–116.

11. See A.K. Gupta and V. Govindarajan, "Knowledge Flows Within Multinational Corporations," ***Strategic Management Journal*** 21 (April 2000): 473–496.

12. See W. Tsai, "Social Structure of 'Coopetition' Within a Multiunit Organization: Coordination, Competition and

Intraorganizational Knowledge Sharing," *Organization Science* 13, no. 2 (March–April 2002): 179–190.

13. For a detailed description of these changes at Morgan Stanley, see M.D. Burton, T.J. DeLong and K. Lawrence, "Morgan Stanley: Becoming a 'One-Firm' Firm," Harvard Business School case no. 9-400-043 (Boston: Harvard Business School Publishing, 1999); and M.D. Burton, "The Firmwide 360-Degree Performance Evaluation Process at Morgan Stanley," Harvard Business School case no. 9-498-053 (Boston: Harvard Business School Publishing, 1998).

14. See M. Haas, "Acting on What Others Know: Distributed Knowledge and Team Performance" (unpublished Ph.D. diss., Harvard University, 2002).

15. For an in-depth look at inspiring common goals, see J. Collins and J. Porras, "Building Your Company's Vision," *Harvard Business Review* 74, no. 5 (September–October 1996): 65–77.

16. See M.T. Hansen and C. Darwall, 2003, "Intuit Inc.: Transforming an Entrepreneurial Company Into a Collaborative Organization," Harvard Business School case 9-403-064 (Boston: Harvard Business School Publishing, 2003).

17. See R.H. Coase, "The Nature of the Firm," *Econometrica* 4 (1937): 386–405.

18. See R.E. Caves, *Multinational Enterprise and Economic Analysis* (Cambridge, United Kingdom: Cambridge University Press, 1982).

19. See C. Barnard, *The Functions of the Executive* (Cambridge, Massachusetts: Harvard University Press, 1939).

Practitioner reflection

Michael Devane

Foundations to advantage/Routes to advantage

When reading this book and being specifically mindful of the importance of Sections 2 and 3, I am keenly aware that this subject area is evolving quickly. For future strategic thinkers, it is important to understand the concepts and theories, what we have tried, and what has worked as much as what has not worked.

This textbook quite rightly raises many important corporate challenges and dilemmas, including that of placing a lot of power with chief executive officers (CEOs) and, particularly in the USA, compounding that by allowing the dual responsibility of CEO and chair to remain with the one individual, while at the same time not really being able to hold that person to account or having 'no real penalties for non-performance'. It points to many of the dangers in formulating and implementing strategy, and in particular examines the reality that change creates for enterprise. Frankly, some of the current debate—particularly in relation to subjects such as corporate social responsibility and organizational democracy, which have been a feature of good organizations for a very long time—is overly hyped. In my experience, it requires no more than the pragmatic engagement of stakeholders and keeping a longer-term view. 'Greening' is becoming another hype topic, which again is only about balance between an enterprise and its environment—putting back what you take out. The common-sense approach suggested influences policy in the best interest of society, the environment, and the company, and encourages flexibility and resolution through collaboration.

The role of the board of directors as the primary instrument of governance is raised and poses key questions that must be discussed by the next generation of leaders and strategists. The discussion points to the difficulties that arise between a board and the executive leadership when setting direction within a company, including conflicting strategic thinking. In my view, a board 'should represent those stakeholders that add value, assume risk, and possess strategic information', and should be active in the development of corporate strategy, rather than have a benign existence solely concerned with compliance and mediocre shareholder value. The role of the board as a positive challenger to the CEO and executive is simple, and a concept that carries within it all of the responsibilities of oversight, compliance, good judgement, and sound business acumen that are part of that role.

Of course, the critical focus of leadership must be sustainable shareholder value and ensuring this in an ever-changing environment. I absolutely agree that maintaining alignment of purpose, objectives, and goals as basic organizational housekeeping is essential in the mobilization of the enterprise. Creating mindshare is crucial to getting value from employees, and in a more knowledge-based economy, this is even more critical. Keeping all stakeholders on board is also central to the progress and success of any company. It highlights the importance of communications and the value of a good mission statement in communicating inside and outside the organization. The authors make a critical connection when they rightly identify the need for leaders and strategists to emotionally connect stakeholders to the business and its strategy. When focusing on organization alignment and communication and their positive effect on organization performance, I have always found that the strategic planning process itself is an excellent mechanism for engaging the organization at all levels. Keeping employees and stakeholders on board is more easily done when leaders are prepared to discuss and debate the purpose, mission, and strategy as a means of engaging people and ensuring their understanding. This is a form of buy-in that is invaluable when the company is changing and encountering difficulties. Buy-in is the most important factor when trying to energize an organization and reconfigure it to respond to the future challenge.

The debate on a market-based or resource-based approach as a foundation of corporate advantage is about balance and appraising both the external and internal factors correctly before formulating a response or strategy. Doing so allows us to appraise external factors and to understand/identify the target objectives. It also allows us to appraise the internal factors, assess resources and capability, consider the organizational (human assets) alternatives, and determine the 'do-ability' of any strategy. Not taking the time to assess both internal and external factors and not taking soundings from a more widely informed base will lead to an inappropriate formulation and/or execution of a strategy. I have witnessed excellent appraisal of the external landscape and sound strategic thinking that have led to ambitious long-term strategic plans, resulting in failure because the internal capability to execute was not there. Sometimes, failure is a result of not engaging the organization; other times, it is a lack of knowledge or competence; mostly, it is a lack of management resolve at the most senior level. In other situations, I have seen the danger of a strategy being overly influenced by a single perspective, and have seen the classic case of strong and successful leaders dismissing a new technology or emerging market reality, while dismissing internal or external perspectives that are counter to their own—hence failing spectacularly later.

The process of creating value or destroying it is well covered within these chapters. I believe that understanding the strategy at each level of the corporation and its effect on the organization and business is important in the comprehensive engagement of the organization. Personally, I am a great enthusiast of scenario planning. This method of strategic planning engages the wider organization and has, in my opinion, a better opportunity to build a consensus view about the future. It is a process that can be innovative and encourage lateral thinking, and it concentrates on the end game of building value. It has, most importantly, the best chance to seek out the lone voice in an organization that may have the best insight. The notion of having strategic fit between corporate and business is, of course, also important, but the means by which this is achieved is what presents the greatest challenge. In my experience, good leaders keep corporate strategy simple and afford the rest of the organization the opportunity to align with and respond to it. This allows for autonomy and initiative within the organization. Maximizing contribution and creating value in a synergistic way across organizations yields a '2 + 2 = 5' effect. The top-down strategy prescription does not work, not only because it is an old prescription, but also because *talking* about it is not *doing* it—engagement is required to do it.

'Do-ability', in my opinion, is the harder assessment to make when setting out a strategy. It is, of course, down to good leadership and a high-performing organization. It is also dependent on having an organizational culture that is well developed and sound. Spreading resources thinly or not having the right resources is the biggest risk when implementing a strategy. Often, this results from a senior management failure to assess the do-ability or—much worse—knowing that it was not do-able, but not having the courage to address this with the CEO. Do-ability is an assessment not only of internal capability, but also of related external capability. The concept of an enterprises eco-system develops the idea that there are other related entities that can synergistically enhance the capability of implementing a strategy. It is my opinion that this becomes even more critical in a knowledge-based environment.

Diversification, often the solution to a corporate problem of falling revenue or a need to acquire a technology path to the future, is often sound from a strategic perspective. It is, however, often a path that may fail or, in many cases, disappoint from a shareholder perspective. Some of those strategic initiatives, particularly in related diversification, run into trouble when an existing executive—with no experience of the new business domain—heads the new activity and expects to learn while executing on a strategic mission. Unrelated diversification is even more prone to poor leadership judgement. While the leader of the new venture may be external and hold the requisite skill and experience, his or her time in the role may often be short-lived. Following an acquisition, it is common for the newly acquired company to see its CEO quickly replaced by an internal candidate.

In addressing the critical question of 'What business are we in?', the company will often need to re-establish the purpose of the organization, which can change—albeit in a slow and subtle way. I am always sceptical when I see a product company announcing a major strategic shift—for example, that it is becoming a service company—with commentators and analysts describing it as a 'bold strategic move'. I often think that this is more about not knowing what the business is about as markets change than about a true strategic switch. A concise understanding of business industry definition to determine market boundary and nature of competition is essential in formulating a strategy. As rightly pointed out by the authors, convergence of technologies will increasingly blur traditional market–industry boundaries; thus it will be interesting for the many students and practitioners who use this book to study the strategic response of today's successful companies to this new reality.

Michael Devane is a partner at Quilly, a business consulting company based in Dublin, Ireland, where he is a business and industry consultant focused on the development of enterprise and the promotion of new ventures. He is active in the brokering and leveraging of diverse capability, and the development of collaborative initiative. He contributes in both executive and non-executive roles in an advisory or leadership capacity. Mike is a member of the Board of American Chambers of Commerce and is the chairman of the American Chamber Research and Development Working Group. He has chaired the Nano-Ireland Taskforce set up to advise on strategy for the adoption of and investment in nanotechnology.

Section 4

Realizing advantage

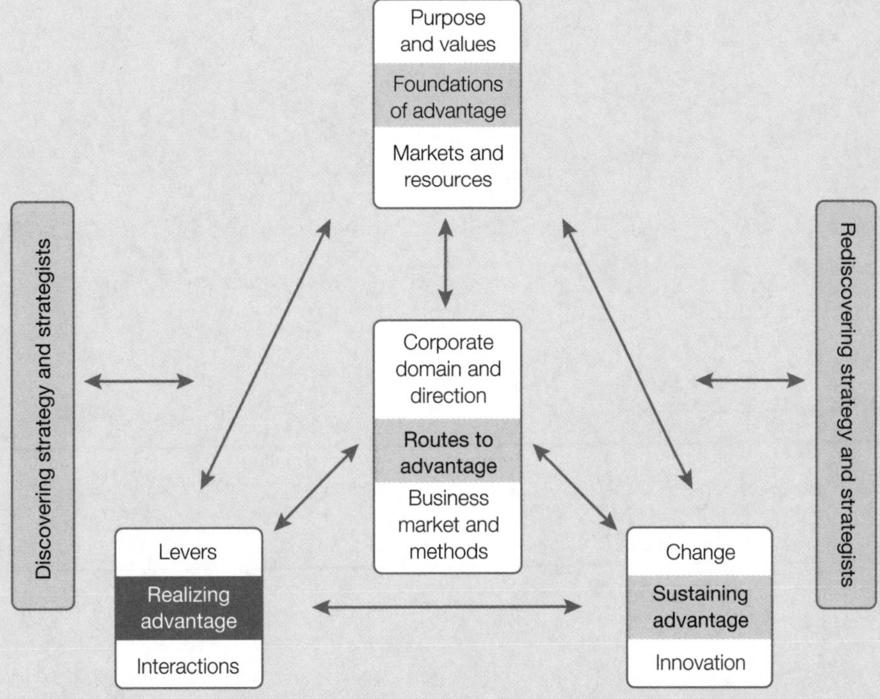

9

Levers for implementing strategy

Strategic control and empowerment

The art of war is simple: everything is a matter of execution.

(Napoleon)

Introduction

The routes to advantage were the focus of our previous two chapters. Now, we turn our attention to realizing advantage through strategic control and **empowerment** (this chapter) and the interactions in implementing strategy (Chapter 10). Bridging the gap between aspiration and action is perhaps the most difficult, complex, and neglected task in strategy and for **strategists**. For example, when organizations suffer a decline in growth or reduced profitability, media commentators typically call for the organization to revisit its strategy. If this is not forthcoming, they may eventually call for new leadership. Rarely is it considered that it may be equally important to ensure that the organization is performing to the best of its abilities. As Pfeffer and Sutton (2006: 146) note, 'competence and capability are important for corporate success. Too much attention to getting the strategy right can divert attention away from building the capability to operate effectively'. Given that there are only a limited number of strategic routes available to compete, ranging from low cost, as seen in Aldi/Lidl, to differentiation, as in Marks and Spencer (see Chapter 8), one might wonder if the scope for obtaining **sustainable competitive advantage** purely on the basis of choosing a certain route is rather limited. Instead, a more promising focus might be to consider the processes and levers that shape *how* organizations actually implement and enact their intentions. While this question is still challenging to many strategists, a focus on strategy execution may offer insight into a more sustainable basis of advantage. As noted by Hambrick (2004: 95), 'grand strategic initiatives may be the glamorous, exciting part of the executive's job; but it is in the mundane task of execution, more often than not, that organizational success is won or lost'—or, as Napoleon captures in our opening quote, 'everything is a matter of execution'.

Even when organizations have appropriate foundations for advantage (Chapters 5 and 6) and have chosen a clear route to advantage that leverages these (Chapters 7 and 8), failure can still occur. Indeed, most organizations realize only a fraction of the financial performance promised in their strategic plans (Kaplan and Norton, 2008a). The disconnection between strategic intent and strategic achievement is one of the most common reasons why strategies fail. Realizing advantage through effective levers for implementing strategy is therefore critical (see Figure 9.1). However, the reality is that we know very little about the strategy of achieving strategy. Typical definitions of strategy (see Chapter 1) help us to chart the direction and map the territory, but say little about the actual process of navigating the route. Environment analysis and detailing values really only lead to expressions of intent; the processes involved are fundamental to strategy, but unless they progress from words, ideas, and experiences to actual action, they will remain as intent (Hambrick and Cannella, 1989). Hence our attention in this chapter focuses on ensuring coordination between thinking (strategy **formulation**) and doing (strategy implementation): the domain of realizing advantage. Specifically, we focus on control and empowerment as levers for implementing strategy, and the role of organizational culture, rewards, and performance evaluation as underpinning processes supporting them. The levers of control and empowerment form the bedrock of high

Figure 9.1 Realizing advantage: bridging intent and action

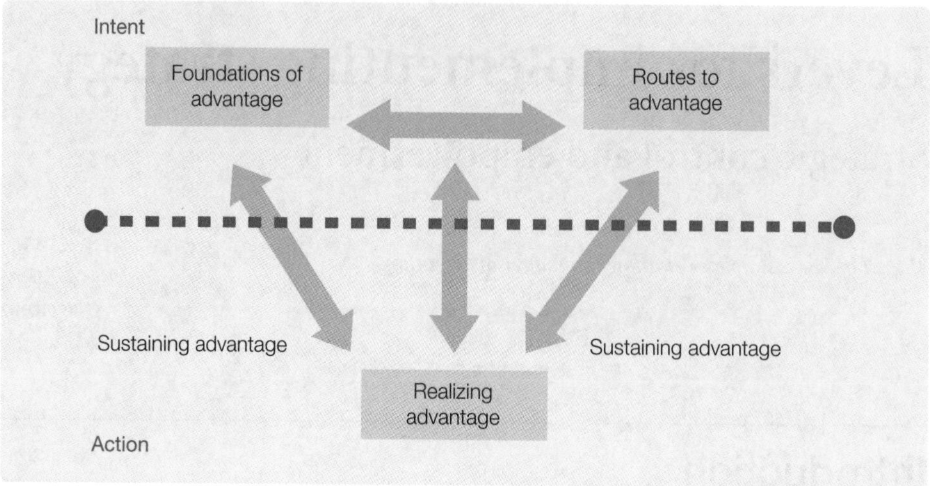

performance, shaping the extent to which people in an organization act in line with strategists' intentions, and how much freedom they have to take independent action (Bungay, 2011).

Organizations that stand apart from their competitors do not simply do so on the basis of their strategic stance or **business model**. Ahold, the Dutch-headquartered international group of supermarkets in Europe and the USA, is not successful simply because of its retailing models or customer focus; nor is IKEA merely successful because of its focus on cost and quality. What makes these organizations unique is the way in which they excel in realizing advantage in their chosen strategic route. At the heart of their success are consistency of strategy implementation and having in place appropriate levers, culture, rewards, and performance evaluation that enable and ensure that the desired strategy is enacted. The key sentiment and values of such organizations are diffused through the actions and gestures of leaders, and through their corporate culture. In November 2009, Ahold announced a restructuring of its global activities. Ahold's chief executive officer (CEO), John Rishton (2009), noted: 'The changes we have announced today build a strong platform for future growth. We are further simplifying and streamlining our businesses and will be able to provide even greater focus on our customers.' The founder of IKEA put each of his sons in charge of a business unit and assessed their performance in order to decide which one would replace him—thus establishing a competitive mindset across the organization. Effective strategy implementation becomes all the more important in conditions of change or competitive intensity. With the advent of the Internet and a shift to cheaper ground shipping, Fedex faced a threat to its core business. However, by leveraging its seemingly remote Alaskan base, which enabled it to reach 90 per cent of destinations in less than ten hours, Fedex is still on top and renowned for its logistics, combining a smart strategy with superb execution (Boyle and Chester, 2004). In these examples, the role of an organization's culture, rewards, incentives, and performance evaluation play a critical role in reinforcing levers for strategy implementation.

The traditional focus of strategy can be somewhat misdirected as a fixation on strategic content and can obscure as much as illuminate, causing leaders, as Pfeffer and Sutton (2006: 136) note, 'to overlook other, even more crucial and more sustainable avenues for success.' Reaching a decision is not the end product of strategy: strategists get things done, act, and induce others to act (Brunsson, 1982: 32). Strategy is not only positioning or execution; it is both. Thus the decision to take a certain strategic route should be the beginning and not the end of analysis (Fuchs *et al.*, 2000: 122). The task of implementation is where strategists direct much of their time and energy; more often than not, change and **innovation** occur not from continuously shifting strategy, but in terms of how a given strategy is delivered (Argyres and McGahan, 2002). This attention to detail and focus on strategy implementation may easily be a distinctive competency of an organization and one that differentiates its performance from competitors.

In this chapter, we examine how strategists can use strategic control and empowerment as levers for strategy implementation. Carrefour, the French retail group, has a very simple strategy of 'making Carrefour the preferred retailer where it operates'. To achieve this, Carrefour needs to balance the appropriate control systems with ensuring that all employees can contribute effectively to this strategy. Central to this is an organizational culture, rewards, and performance evaluation system that both supports effective control and empowers individual employees. In simple terms, this means that the manager of the Carrefour store in Alicante in Spain needs to have the necessary control systems in place to monitor and ensure that his or her store can actively contribute to the implementation of the overall group strategy. Do section heads and individual employees within the store have the freedom to make, suggest, and implement changes that will increase sales and improve the customer experience in a way that aligns to the overall group strategy? How can the store manager reward and incentivize his or her staff? How effective is the performance evaluation system in aligning the levers for strategy implementation with desired employee behaviour and at store level? When we bear in mind that this delicate balance needs to be replicated throughout the Carrefour group in every country in which it operates, we appreciate the scale of the strategy implementation challenge. Achieving this delicate balance between control and empowerment is of critical importance if true advantage is to be realized.

We begin this chapter by focusing on strategic control as a lever for implementation and reviewing closed systems approaches to monitoring performance. In sharp contrast, we then consider the lever of empowerment and explore its associated open systems thinking. The chapter then reviews interactive control systems, before exploring how the culture, rewards, and performance evaluation system can support the levers for strategy implementation in realizing advantage. We start by considering control.

Levers for implementation: control

Control, as traditionally perceived, is a key mechanism of strategy implementation (Hatch, 1997). Strategists must achieve cooperation among the diverse constituents of the organization and must balance functions that have competing claims for **resources**. Control systems at corporate level are critical in enabling multinational corporations to keep track of and monitor the performance of subsidiary organizations. BASF, the German-headquartered chemical company, has 105,000 employees, 385 production sites, and customers and partners all over the world. Strategic control and empowerment challenges are significant compared with a business start-up or small and entrepreneurial organizations in which operations and the actions of implementation are more visible, making their coordination task somewhat easier. In Chapter 7, we outlined the different management styles that may be applied by a corporate parent, ranging from purely financial control (the corporate centre acting as an institutional investor and making decisions based on which subsidiaries offer the greatest return on investments rather than concern over the content of their strategies), to approaches that stress strategic control and how subsidiaries link together in creating a value proposition. The latter approach typically affords a greater time horizon and flexibility in the delivery of results, appreciating the long-term benefits of a focused course of action (Goold *et al.*, 1994). Similarly, such large organizations will often grow through **acquisition** or **joint ventures**, particularly when entering new territories. This means that the task of integration can be critical for success (Burgelman and McKinney, 2006).

Purpose of strategic control

Control is a fundamental task for the strategist and a key lever in implementing strategy. Strategists are dependent upon other organizational members to act in ways that are consistent with strategic objectives. To help to ensure that these actions occur, organizations and management teams set up control systems to monitor and make adjustments along the way to realizing their strategy (Hatch, 1997: 329). While its importance is uncontested, precisely *how* strategists best control their organizations, evaluate performance, and know whether their plans and intentions are being realized is a much more uncertain (Daft and MacIntosh, 1984). The term 'control' invokes a sense of rigidity and prescription, and is suggestive of a single strategist or group of strategists at the top of the organization dictating operations to those on the factory floor. As detailed in the following section, this interpretation reflects a traditional approach to strategic control.

Traditional strategic control approach: closed system

The traditional strategic control approach, or the 'closed system' perspective of strategic control, was developed in an era of less external environmental volatility and change. The strategic control system was clearly targeted at defined outputs that were specific and fixed. Cause and effect were mechanical in orientation and there was clarity around each operational activity.

In a sense, the closed system approach reflects early strategic thinking of the industrial era whereby there was a limited focus on the dynamics of implementation. Strategists set the broad guidelines and objectives, which were then in turn broken down into detailed plans and objectives for each function, such as marketing, finance, and operations. So, for example, using a closed systems approach, an organization's two-year objective could be to increase market share by 7 per cent in a given market. Each functional head would develop detailed plans for his or her functions in order to achieve this objective. The nature of these objectives is framed by functional budgets that make managers aware of the resources available to meet fixed goals for a fixed time period. Feedback on realized performance was then compared with the predetermined standard. In the era of strategic planning, these implementation methods linked neatly with the structure of organizations. Communication was one-way and top-down; the military metaphor of 'command and control' was thus readily applied to understand the nature and functioning of organizations. Within this overarching framework of control, successful strategy implementation was associated with generating scale and scope, and with sweating assets to the maximum of their ability. Key lessons in strategy at this time were derived from companies such as GM and Du Pont (Chandler, 1962).

This process was facilitated by the fact that, in the industrial era, operations were built on tangible entities and visible productive processes and so could be readily monitored, assessed, and altered as appropriate. The scientific management approach introduced by Frederick Taylor and made popular by Henry Ford at his automobile manufacturing plant in the early twentieth century illustrated how the management of operations could be precisely calculated and measured. The purpose of control was largely to ensure that implementation ran according to a detailed plan, aligning organizational capabilities, activities, and performance with the original intent. The physical nature of activities made it easy to link work tasks with output; thus the piece-rate system of paying for each individual contribution became popular. The emergence of management theory in the wake of mass industrialization has led to an obsession with measurement and control, and attempts to impose order and structure (Delbridge *et al.*, 2006: 107). From Figure 9.2, we see the traditional strategic control uses in a functional organization. This is a top-down approach with limited input from employees. Key activities are clearly measured and monitored, and any discrepancies between predicted and realized outcomes are fed back to top management.

Organizations that use controls as an implementation lever need to fully understand all aspects of their business operations and culture in order to put in place effective controls by which activities and performance can be assessed. Understanding how control impacts both positively and negatively on human behaviour is also essential to ensuring successful implementation of strategic objectives (Micheli and Manzoni, 2010). The liquid limits on passenger airlines and the banning of certain types of item for hand luggage caused considerable delays in many airports throughout the world when first implemented. Now, is it is an accepted part of travelling, and passengers are conditioned to these limits and requirements. Many commentators thought that the indoor smoking ban in pubs and nightclubs in the UK and Ireland would fail, but it proved hugely successful. The ban was one element of national governments' public health strategies to reduce the effects of smoking

Figure 9.2 Traditional strategic control in the functional organization

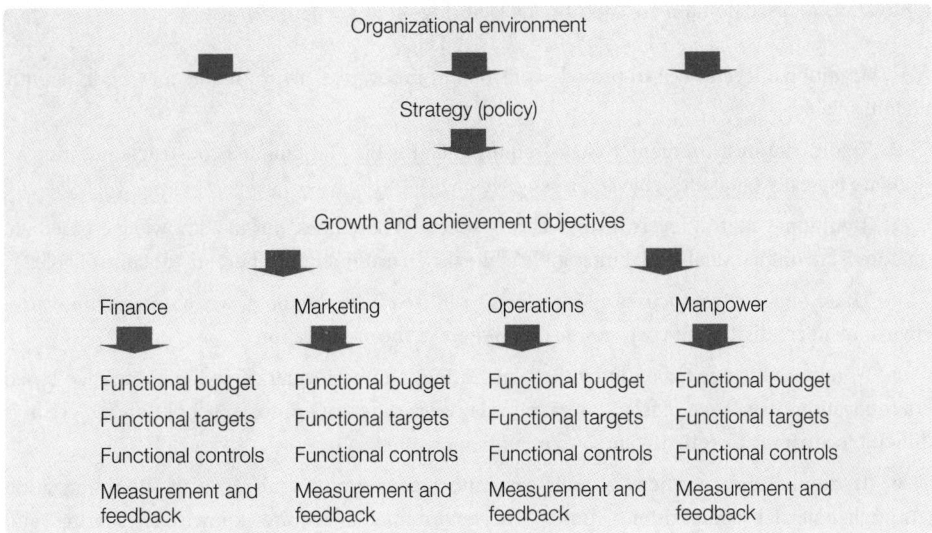

and passive smoking, and has been adopted by other countries such as France and some US states. The implementation of a plastic bag shopping tax in Ireland reduced the number of plastic bags shoppers used. It achieved both individual and societal impacts. That said, a focus on exclusively measuring one area can lead to an overzealous concentration on meeting targets to the neglect of innovation and more difficult to measure, but nonetheless critical, processes. Using a pure command-and-control approach can have negative impacts on culture, performance management, and learning.

Many organizations across different industries operate elements of a closed system, particularly where there is a significant fixed cost base to their operations. Industries such as paper and cardboard manufacturers, airlines, hotels, cars, and health care, use strategic control as a lever for strategy implementation. Such systems can also facilitate important dialogue between multinational headquarters and subsidiaries (Delaney, 2000). It is also true that rigid systems can serve to enhance legitimacy of certain groups by giving the appearance that the organization is rationally managed and efficient. In practice, however, tensions will frequently exist between functions such as marketing and production, with each attempting to push the resources of the organization in differing directions. Moreover, control and measurement issues will hold different meanings for different groups: top management may be consumed by issues of institutional control, while supervisors will be more concerned with more immediate operational control issues. A successful control system will bridge and integrate various platforms and units of analysis to ensure that the organization moves in tandem. Nonetheless, an exclusive focus on levers of control may not be appropriate in all contexts and especially if desired outcomes are more uncertain. This brings us to the levers of empowerment.

Levers for implementation: empowerment

In terms of strategy implementation, rather than relying entirely on levers focused on control, an alternative approach taken by strategists is to offer greater empowerment to employees. The essence of this approach is promoting 'communities of actors who get on with things naturally' (Mintzberg, 2009: 9). The arrival of the knowledge and innovation era, with its focus on intangible processes and knowledge as the keys to competitive advantage (Grant, 1996), has led many commentators to question the traditional basis of organizational control that we examined above. The tensions resulting from the application of traditional levers of control in a knowledge-focused and innovation-focused domain are captured by Delbridge *et al.* (2006: 119):

1. Traditional levers seek to provide control, but innovative environments may be inherently uncontrollable.
2. Traditional measurement systems require quantifiable and tangible constructs but innovations are typically unquantifiable and intangible.
3. Traditional control levers involve clearly specified outcomes, but in a knowledge-based era outcomes are unquantifiable and intangible while the environment is inherently uncontrollable.
4. Traditional control focuses on ideas being diffused from the top down, but in an innovative environment creativity is likely to reside everywhere in the organization.
5. As opposed to a focus on individual suggestions and performance, in the knowledge-based era innovations usually arise from interactions between different groups of people, and so credit is difficult to attribute directly to one source.
6. Traditional measurement systems can hinder cooperation and result in suboptimization (through internal competition); innovative environments require knowledge sharing and cooperation.

In dealing with environmental challenges, organizations need to organize strategic control systems that align to the appropriate strategy, focus on broader outcomes, and have a behavioural focus. The tensions outlined by Delbridge *et al.* (2006: 119) highlight the need for flexibility and adaptiveness within an organization (as will be discussed in Chapter 11) in order to achieve consistency in strategy implementation. Innovations in biotechnology, pharmaceutical breakthroughs, and technological enhancement through open innovation (see Chapter 12) all point to processes that are emergent, often unanticipated, and sometimes even unintended. The rigid framework of the levers of control discussed above can stifle such processes and actually attempt to take human discretion and discovery out of the equation. Taking an open systems view focused on empowerment may therefore be a more appropriate lever for strategy implementation.

An open systems view

A focus on empowerment directs attention towards information flows, interaction between groups, and effort and risk undertaken on behalf of the organization (Neilson *et al.*, 2008: 61). It is not possible simply to mandate people to be creative, while 'years of study have produced little progress toward the control of creativity and innovation' (Hatch, 1997: 332). Instead, the emphasis is on broad goals and strategic intent, while leaving the processes by which this is realized flexible and open (see Reading 1.2). From this perspective, a more open systems understanding of how organizations operate is more appropriate. This contrasts with the discussion around the levers of control, which assumed that organizations were largely closed systems, retaining a mechanical orientation and assuming that all implementation mechanisms are transparent and easy to alter. These differences between closed and open systems are illustrated in Table 9.1.

From an open systems view, using the lever of empowerment suggests a focus on encouraging behaviours, whereas in the closed system, control mechanisms are targeted at outputs. Likewise, from a closed system perspective, outcomes are fixed; from an open system perspective, goals and the means to achieve them are broad, flexible, and open to revision. This means that professional norms take on great importance in shaping the way in which tasks are conducted and the expectations that individuals hold. With this more normative orientation, an organization's culture plays an important role from an open system perspective.

In attempting to develop a more open, rather than closed, system, many organizations have attempted to create their own internal Silicon Valley, founded on energy, innovation, and a

Table 9.1 Closed and open systems as implementation levers

	Closed system view	Open systems view
Implementation lever	Control	Empowerment
Appropriate era	Industrial	Knowledge-based
Model	Clockwork/engineering	Organic
Cause and effect	Mechanical and transparent	Multi-layered and complex
Targeted at	Outputs	Behaviours
Goals and means	Fixed and specific	Broad and flexible

dedicated commitment to shifting the rules of the game. In doing so, they are attempting to engage readily with employees to encourage discretionary effort. Semco was famed for allowing people to choose their own activities and stretch the organization into any area that they wished once there was a potential for returns. Employees could even choose how they got paid, ranging from a fixed salary to commission on gross margins. As CEO Ricardo Semler (2000: 58) noted:

> You can build a great company without fixed plans, you can have an efficient organization without rules and controls. You can be unbuttoned and creative without sacrificing profit. You can lead without wielding power. All it takes is faith in people.

This is an extreme example of how empowerment can improve innovation and customer responsiveness—but, as we will see in Chapter 12, such an approach may be essential if organizations are to exploit innovation and advantage is to be sustained.

This emphasis on the soft side of strategy places less emphasis on control, but is subject to its own dilemmas, such as how to build an infrastructure that empowers and yet captures value, and how to reward knowledge-based activities when their connections to outcomes may not be transparent. Just as implementation levers of control have unintended consequences, so too empowerment is not a universal path to successful outcomes. Empowerment is successful only in the context of individuals willing and motivated to act of their own accord. This means that the success of empowerment is intertwined with the operation of organizational rewards and incentives that encourage desired role behaviours. Once such behaviour is encouraged, it is important that its returns are recognized within the organization and make their way to the market as a value-based proposition. Xerox was famous for its inventions, but many of its initiatives were not developed further. Taken to its extreme, unbridled behaviour can also have serious consequences. Tyco International, a leading provider of security products and services, fire protection and detection, and other industrial products, pursued a strategy of unrelated **diversification**, operating under the broad unifying objective of maximizing profit. Much of its operations were textbook prescriptions, but they led to a focus on ends at all costs, to the ignorance of the best and appropriate means with which to achieve these ends. The result is activities that destroy rather than create value. This means that companies may have a short-term period of profitability and success that is not sustainable in the long term. The banking sector in Europe was very buoyant for over a decade, but with the global recession beginning in 2008, many banks have been brought into public ownership or received liquidity support. Many banks empowered retail branch staff to sell a variety of debt products with maximized performance. However, this would appear to have been unsustainable and very susceptible to external global economic influences. The problem of constant encouragement to think outside the box, as Gladwell notes (2009: 374), is that it fosters risk taking and creativity, which may mean that problems within the box, such as lack of risk management, go unnoticed.

At a more individual level, professionals may be reluctant to subordinate themselves to others, or to support organizational goals not completely congruent with their particular viewpoint. To overcome this, organizations cultivate the necessary behaviour by multiple means. Working with peers diffuses professionalism, contact or knowledge of customer preferences ensures relevance, while enterprise norms limit the bias induced by professional orientation (Quinn *et al.*, 1996: 82). An extension of the open systems approach is for an organization to develop an interactive control system that places greater emphasis on learning, thereby providing a better balance of control and empowerment.

Interactive control systems

One means of allowing for business dynamics and learning is to conceive of control as an interactive system. The competitive imperative of learning dictates that 'organisations that adapt an execution as learning model don't focus on getting things done more efficiently than competitors do. Instead they focus on learning faster' (Edmondson, 2008: 65). For this type of control system, the organization uses a more experimental approach in which it tests assumptions, makes some minor changes and from that learns, observes and analyses the results. If the outcomes are positive, then it could be introduced across the organization. Interactive control systems support innovation and new ideas. In the case of new leaders, for example, they may use a combination of systems to overcome organizational inertia, to communicate the substance of their new agenda, to structure implementation timetables and targets, to ensure continuing attention through incentives, and to focus **organizational learning** on the strategic uncertainties associated with their new visions of the future (Simons, 1994: 186) Used in this way, control systems are not simply tools of strategy implementation; they can also be catalysts for new strategic initiatives (Simons, 1991, see Reading 4.1). Systems that direct attention towards strategy formulation *and* implementation have been termed 'strategic performance measurement systems' (Kolehmainen, 2010). Overall, having learning as the primary focus for employees as opposed to a focus purely on measurement can 'help the reflective manager to square the circle, supporting rather than hindering innovation at the same time as yielding a more supple, less constricting form of control' (Delbridge *et al.*, 2006: 108). This also draws attention to the role of culture, rewards, and mechanisms for performance evaluation in underpinning and supporting the levers of implementation.

Culture, rewards, and performance evaluation

While hard strategic control systems are the most visible and obvious manifestation of realizing advantage, in practice they are complemented by the equally powerful emphasis of belief systems and rewards: in other words, culture, rewards, incentives, and 'the way we do business around here'. Hard levers are not sufficient for success; organizations need also to pay attention to their behavioural context—the motivation, values, and commitments of the organization's employees. Bartlett and Ghoshal (2002) suggested that most successful international organizations devote much of their attention to such 'soft aspects' and the demanding task of cultivating the right employee attitudes, assumptions, and behaviours. The belief systems that permeate the organization and shape its thinking provide a sense of identity, facilitate commitment, and may help to channel behaviour towards desired ends (Barney, 1986). The box below illustrates how E.ON, a DAX-listed utility company focused on power and gas, with over 88,000 employees in thirty countries, has identified key behaviours that shape its corporate culture, including customer orientation, drive for performance, change initiation, teamwork, leadership, diversity and development.

Often, when implementation is discussed, it is described as if its activities were being introduced on a blank canvas. All organizations have organizational histories that may facilitate or hinder initiatives. Organizations can have significant difficulties with transformational and incremental change (see Chapter 11). International organizations such as Accenture or the Marriot International hotel chain face the additional tension of nurturing a corporation-wide mindset, while at the same time

E.ON's 'Our behaviours'

Guided by our values, these key behaviours are essential to achieve our mission:

Customer orientation

We strive to satisfy the needs of our customers and add value creating solutions to homes and businesses. Our customer orientation is reflected in our business processes, systems, organizational structures and procedures. In dealing with our suppliers we aim at long-term relationships which create lasting value for both parties. Our suppliers are essential contributors to quality customer service.

Drive for performance

We focus our strategies on the individual markets in which we operate. We seek profitable growth to achieve sustainable success. We set ambitious performance targets to produce superior returns for those who have entrusted us with their capital. We constantly search for best practice and rigorously pursue efficiency and excellence in our operations. We are reliable and results-oriented. We work with a long-term view, focusing as much on the future as the present. We are passionate in the pursuit of our vision and mission.

Change initiation

We are never satisfied with the status quo. We look to the future and the opportunities it brings. We promote constructive change and we readily accept such change when it comes. Innovation is the key to improvement and we will constantly seek ways to improve what we do. We value creativity and seek ways to build solutions ahead of crisis.

Teamwork

We accomplish more by working together. We value one another's insight and cooperation. We trust one another's good intentions. The group optimum is 'a win for all is a win for each of us.' Good teamwork requires our active participation, sharing of our talents and resources and sensitivity for how our actions may impact others.

Leadership

We are at our best when we have strong, capable leadership throughout our company. Working within their own area of responsibility, each leader serves the broader strategies and interests of the entire organization. We strive to grow our leadership skills and to reward effective leaders. Our leaders provide the motivation, guidance, coaching and creativity to inspire the best from our teams. They recognize and reward superior knowledge, competence and performance. Every leader shares the obligation to model our values and behaviours.

Diversity and development

Our people are our most important resource. We serve a diverse world and we seek to reflect that diversity and inclusiveness in the approach we take to all our tasks. Our company and our colleagues thrive when exposed to different perspectives and methods. We seek equality but difference. We invest in our people with consistent coaching and meaningful development to help them reach their potential.

Source: http://www.eon.com/en/corporate/2105.jsp

successfully adapting practices to diverse local economic and cultural conditions (Bellin and Chi, 2007). In addition, answers to implementation problems are not necessarily obvious. Examining Southwest Airlines, Gittell (2000) found that, contrary to popular belief, which might assume that more direct supervision should be replaced with systems of accountability and performance measurement (that is, traditional control or closed systems), coordination across the organization actually benefited from strengthening the role of supervisors while weakening the role of accountability and performance measurement. This was underpinned by a view of corporate headquarters as supportive and a willingness to solve problems rather than to allocate blame for flight delays. Supervision was more than monitoring, and also included coaching and feedback to front-line employees. The meaning and not only the operation of hard levers of control therefore varies. The culture of the organization plays a significant role in strategy implementation.

The impact of cultures also helps in gaining an understanding of the discrepancy between having structures in place and people actually using them or behaving according to them. The traditional approach of structural change within organizations is the most visible and obvious fix, but not always the most effective. Old ways of working may remain latent behind the lines on an organizational chart (Cardinal *et al.*, 2004: 427). Culture may also serve as a filter to restrict the alternative options available to organizations. Aligning levers for implementation with a supportive culture is therefore an important, if difficult, task for the strategist. Andrew Witty, boss of GlaxoSmithKline, likened the firm's culture in 2008 to a police state, arguing that he wanted to take it away from its excessively regimented, rule-based culture to a more value-based culture with a more open style of management (*The Economist*, 2008). Overall, culture can be said to consist of 'such symbolic vehicles of meaning, including beliefs, ritual practices, art forms and ceremonies as well as cultural practices such as language, gossip, stories and rituals of everyday life' (Swidler, 1986: 273) (see Chapter 11). The culture of an organization is heavily shaped by the rewards and incentives that are offered to employees tasked with leading and implementing strategy. Rewards and incentives are used to reinforce and support strategic control and empowerment levers for implementing strategy.

Rewards

A further indication of the nature of an organization's culture is the system it has in place to foster desired behaviours and reward performance. The impact of such incentives and rewards is often overlooked in strategy implementation. This is a substantial oversight, since they are a major basis for redirecting the efforts of individuals (Hambrick and Cannella, 1989: 282). Nohria *et al.*'s (2003: 48) study of top-performing organizations found that nearly 90 per cent of the winning organizations linked pay tightly to performance, while only 15 per cent of the losers did the same: 'the winners were scrupulous in setting specific goals, raising the bar every year, and enforcing those benchmarks. No bonuses, stock options, or other rewards were given when targets were missed. And the pay-for-performance commitment extended to the very top of the organization.' According to agency theory, such rewards may serve to align the behaviour of agents with the desire of principals (those who own the organization). Agency theory predicts that, without such alignment, strategists may act in their own self-interest rather than for the broader benefit of the organization (Davis *et al.*, 1997: 20). The connection between performance and reward and its link to implementation of strategy should therefore be transparent and obvious for managers and employees alike (Neilson *et al.*, 2008: 62).

Rewards and incentives place boundaries on what is perceived as desirable behaviour and so draw a perimeter around organizational activities. At a personal level, such incentives can be an important motivator for strategists and for every member of an organization. Incentives are seen as the primary tool for aligning individual behaviour with organizational objectives (Pfeffer and Sutton, 2006: 110). The Linde Group, a leading supplier of industrial process and speciality gases throughout the world, has an explicit performance management and employee development programme.

The Linde Group: performance management and employee development

Adequate performance measurement is indispensable to appreciate each employee's individual success and to identify those employees whose initiative and ideas contribute to making The Linde Group the number one in gases and engineering.

We understand Performance Management as a business-critical leadership responsibility because it provides the fundamental way to execute business strategy and align the efforts of everyone around a common goal. Therefore we

- Provide strategic orientation to all employees,
- Connect employee motivation, behaviors and contribution to the results the organisation needs to achieve
- Challenge employees to uphold Linde's values and principles
- Build a high-performance culture where people take responsibility for continuously improving business processes, and their own skills and contribution

Performance management and employee development

Superiors and employees together define objectives and development measures. In regular intervals, they review the progress together and decide on the expertise and skills which the employee needs to acquire in the respective phases of development.

Source: http://www.the-linde-group.com/en/careers/linde_talent_suite/performance/index.html

However, as with the levers of control and empowerment discussed previously, rewards can have unintended consequences. Taken to extremes, such individual incentives can lead to behaviours that place the whole organization at risk. The banking crisis of 2009 highlighted this, necessitating attempts by many national governments to cap the bonuses of bankers to ensure that such individual risk-and-reward behaviour could never again undermine the whole banking systems or individual banks. More generally, according to Henry Mintzberg (cited in Allio, 2011: 5), 'anyone who accepts excessive rewards is not a leader. Almost every CEO of a Fortune 500 company is therefore corrupt. Although they're not breaking any law, they are allowing the bonus system to disconnect them from their organization'.

In some instances, strategists' rewards may be linked to something distant from them over which they have limited control. In this instance, the incentive may even serve as a demotivator. The same is likely if other systems and processes are not coordinated so that an appropriate infrastructure is available for achieving tasks. Explicit pay for performance practices may also lead to individuals working to enhance their own returns and attempting to look good rather than thinking of the organization as a whole. Even the process of considering the organization as a whole is unlikely to be smooth. A cash cow business unit is unlikely to be completely enthusiastic about the fruits of its success being transferred to a less well-performing unit. Others criticize rewards on the basis that they are simple bribes, which may be successful in securing temporary compliance, but do not fundamentally alter attitudes and behaviour; as Kohn (1993: 55) notes, 'they do not create an enduring commitment to any value or action'. The challenge for the strategist is to put in place a performance system that rewards and incentivizes individual behaviours that support, are consistent with, and align to the levers of implementation: strategic controls and empowerment. In order to reward behaviour, the strategist needs to have in place a performance evaluation system that acts as a further support for realizing advantage.

Performance evaluation

Most organizations can state where they are going and how they will get there—but there is limited evidence of companies defining strategic milestones so that they can judge if they are making progress (Goold and Quinn, 1990: 47). If you do not measure progress toward an objective, you cannot manage and improve it (Kaplan and Norton, 2008b: 68). No matter how the empowerment-based and knowledge-based era may have challenged the traditional conception of control, the arguments cannot eradicate the organizational reality that, however flawed, 'measurement is inevitable' (Delbridge *et al.*, 2006: 121). The challenge of measuring performance can be demonstrated with the example of a national health system in which the wide variety of clinical settings and service providers, different medical and professional administrators, and a growing array of diagnostic tests and drugs used in patient treatment make measuring performance particularly challenging. Measuring organizational performance plays an important part in translating **corporate strategy** into results (Pun and White, 2005). Performance evaluation ensures that orientation goals are in place, and have been appropriately documented and mapped out. This may seem obvious, but at organizational, project, or individual level, such clarity is often absent. As a starting point, strategists must be clear about their key strategic objectives and communicate them in a manner intended to motivate their achievement—but they must also be clear about measurement criteria and the performance management system needed to support levers for strategy implementation. Complementing long-term goals with stepping stones or milestone achievements that indicate progress en route can be important. Milestones must include both financial and non-financial elements (Goold and Quinn, 1990: 50).

Goold and Quinn (1990: 50) set out some criteria for strategic objectives for motivating managers including setting specific goals that are stretching and involve feedback and incentives that have a results orientation. They also suggest that these strategic objectives should be few in number, involve prioritization, and balance long-term objectives and short-term milestones with financial and non-financial objectives, as well as include some element of benchmarking.

Measurement is equally important for contexts beyond the private sector. As we explore in Chapter 13, having some measurement of the impact of progress towards common aims is increasingly important for organizations in the public sector, such as the UK Border Control Agency, and for **not-for-profit organizations** such as Oxfam. Measurement not only acts as a barometer for assessing progress, but is also a mechanism to ensure that the activities of the organization have more transparency. It is therefore important in conferring legitimacy upon the organization. This becomes all the more important in an era in which institutional investors and the markets are consistently focused on short-term performance metrics. Performance evaluation provides a template and common language with which to interpret action and discuss decisions. This role of providing a language for understanding organizations is often neglected, but is central to contributing to organizational effectiveness A company's performance measurement system, as Eccles and Nohria (1992: 149) describe, 'furnishes a language game. It provides conventions by which people act, helps determine how they interpret these actions, and becomes a major component of how they understand their identity within the firm'. We return to this role of language again in Chapter 14. We now focus on some of the mechanisms by which organizations can actually evaluate performance, namely benchmarking and the use of the **balanced scorecard**.

Benchmarking

One clear way of assessing and evaluating performance is to examine activities and performance along key metrics relative to competitors. This process is typically called 'benchmarking' and became popular as part of the total quality movement in the 1980s. It enables performance to be located in context and can provide a clear motivator to increase productivity. Benchmarking has also become important in assessing public sector performance, although here it becomes difficult to find a directly comparable source. Many public utility regulators for energy, telecoms, etc. benchmark the performance of all operators in a national market against key operational criteria and make such information available to the public. Ofgem regulates the gas and electricity markets in the UK and, like other public utility regulators, it reports on the performance of different operators. Table 9.2 illustrates the performance of regulated operators across two different dimensions for 2007–08. This performance information is used by operators themselves, new and existing customers, and investors in the industry.

How equitable is it to compare the performance of two hospitals along the metrics of mortalities per year? Some governments have also attempted to benchmark pay and productivity of staff against equivalent jobs in the private sector, but again the source of comparison can become problematic. What is the private sector equivalent of a fireman or a nurse? Overall, a key problem with benchmarking is that it encourages similarity rather than difference. This is the basis of Porter's (1996) critique of the strategy literature (see Chapter 1). He noted that a focus on benchmarking to achieve best practice using management tools leads 'more and more companies down the path of

Table 9.2 UK electricity regulator Ofgem: reported and revised 2007–08 customer interruptions (CIs) and customer minutes lost (CMLs)

Distribution network operator (DNO)	Reported 2007–08 CIs	Reported 2007–08 CMLs
CN West	123.24	121.69
CN East	83.58	79.74
ENW	52.46	52.14
CE NEDL	76.10	85.36
CE YEDL	92.50	131.56
WPD S Wales	80.66	46.32
WPD S West	85.21	60.69
EDFE LPN	31.95	43.46
EDFE SPN	94.25	108.57
EDFE EPN	77.58	84.00
SP Distribution	69.50	71.72
SP Manweb	46.86	63.62
SSE Hydro	94.04	105.89
SSE Southern	69.74	92.47
Great Britain		

Source: Ofgem (2008: 40)

mutually destructive competition' (ibid: 61). Yet other firms have been more innovative in their approach to benchmarking than simply benchmarking what their competitors are doing. The argument of **core competencies** (Prahalad and Hamel, 1990) suggests that firms should be creative and look beyond their industry as they try to utilize their resources to create the maximum value proposition. Hence when British Airways wished to improve their turnaround times, it looked at the techniques used in Formula One motor racing where this process is critical.

Balanced scorecard

Another evaluation of performance beyond benchmarking is the balanced scorecard introduced by Kaplan and Norton (1992). This provides for a more rounded assessment of implementation activities than mere accounting measures. In particular, the balanced scorecard focuses on the following perspectives.

- *Customer perspective* How do customers see us? (This includes, for example, time to delivery, quality, performance and service, and cost.)
- *Internal business perspective* At what must we excel? (Managers need to focus on those critical internal operations that enable them to satisfy customer needs.)
- *Innovation and learning perspective* Can we continue to improve and create value? (Targets for success keep changing.)
- *Financial perspective* How do we look to shareholders? (Traditional measures include cash flow, operating income, and return on equity.)

The balanced scorecard is widely used by organizations such as Mobil and Skandia, the Swedish insurance company. It functions as a key way of understanding and checking what you have to do throughout the organization to make your strategy work (Kaplan and Norton, 1996: 76). It is subject to some limitations, however, in that there is no clear focus on human resources, which would be a critical assessment factor in knowledge-intensive industries. Similarly, environmental or ecological features do not receive adequate attention, while the quality of relations with suppliers is also not included. Another inherent risk with such approaches is that they operate on the assumption that what is measurable is necessarily the most important thing on which to focus. However, the argument of the resource-based view directs attention to complex social processes, which are difficult to disentangle, and organizational path dependencies. By definition, these will not feature as performance evaluation metrics. Even Kaplan and Norton (2001: 88) note that 'by the end of the 20th century, intangible assets became the major source for competitive advantage'. One way around this is the extension of the logic of the balanced scorecard to a management system (see Reading 4.2); another is to explore the other key elements of Simons' focus on dynamics and interactive control systems (see Reading 4.1). Ultimately, no measure by itself will suffice as an adequate snapshot of an organization's performance (Eccles and Nohira, 1992: 146).

Performance evaluation and unintended consequences

Increasingly, in light of decentralized structures, organizations are evaluating business units as separate profit centres. This is linked to financial control at the corporate centre. Business units and their managers are assessed on short-term financial measurements such as return on investment. The structural distance between those entrusted with exploiting actual competitive opportunities and those who must judge the quality of their works makes reliance on objectively quantifiable short-term criteria all the more important and likely (Hayes and Abernathy, 1980: 70). One result is that risk taking is avoided and there is no room for not meeting immediate returns or for learning from failure. This emphasis also encourages business units and functions to become silos that perform well on their local measures, but fail to contribute to divisional and corporate synergies (Kaplan and Norton, 2006: 104).

Evaluating performance can foster negative and unintended consequences—most notably, the short-termism encouraged by reporting earnings per share on a quarterly basis. Such accounting measures can direct attention away from the content of strategy and its longer-term prospects, while leading to a focus on cost reduction as opposed to the long-term development of, for example, technological competence. As noted by Martin (2010: 60), 'the harder a CEO is pushed to increase shareholder value, the more the CEO will be tempted to make moves that actually hurt the shareholders'. The key to long-term success—even survival—in business is what it has always been: to invest; to innovate; to lead; to create value where none existed before. Such determination, such striving to excel, requires leaders, not only controllers. In our preoccupation with the exterior trim of our corporations—their superficial aspects—and external factors such as banking systems, we may have neglected drive trains of corporation (Hayes and Abernathy, 1980: 77). For a long time, it has been noted that 'profitability as a measure of success led to a reduction in experimental work and de-emphasized the importance of production quantity, quality, and assortment' (Ridgway, 1956: 243). Managers may have become motivated to make results appear more positive—for example, reducing long-term beneficial investment has the short-term effect of making the immediate level of return more impressive—but this may have detrimental long-term consequences. As Clegg (1990: 197) notes:

> a profit center manager can achieve quicker, surer and easier results by delaying replacement of old worn-out equipment, replacing equipment eventually with technologically dated or inferior substitutes and skimping in maintenance, research and development and personnel development.

Ironically, success can also lead to blind spots and partial evaluation of performance. As Gino and Pisano (2011: 72) explain, 'when we succeed, we just focus on applying what we already know to solving our problems. We don't revise our theories or expand our knowledge of how the business works'.

Spotlight Google: 'Great just isn't good enough'

The core mission of Google is 'to organize the world's information and make it universally accessible and useful'. Some would say that this is an impossible task. Iyer and Davenport (2008) calculate that it would take Google at least 300 years to achieve its core mission. Google has entered everyday language, has developed a significant global organization based on a web search engine that enables a proliferation of activities across a number of technology applications, and has created revenue streams from online advertising. At the cutting edge of technology, Google needs to attract and retain the best people. In this, it has done things differently. As Sullivan (2010) describes:

> What they have done better than anyone else is to develop the world's first recruiting culture ... As a result of this culture, not only does Google fund recruiting to the point where the function is in a league by itself, but they have also gone to the extraordinary step of changing the way employees work in order to attract and retain the very best.
>
> (Sullivan, 2010)

Google has articulated clear core principles that reinforce a culture that supports ensuring market relevance, performance, control and empowerment, and, most importantly, marketplace ubiquity. This core philosophy includes:

> focus on the user and all else will follow; it is best to do one thing really, really well; fast is better than slow; democracy on the web works; you don't need to be at your desk to need an answer; you can make money without doing evil; there's always more information out there; the need for information crosses all borders; you can be serious without a suit; great just isn't good enough.
>
> (Google, 2011)

So how does Google translate these core philosophies into everyday realities?

It has created fun working environments that do not conform to a typical office layout. This is an attempt to create simulating, dynamic, and interesting work environments. In some locations, employees have the freedom to bring pets to work. The provision of different types of work and recreation spaces in one location is designed to 'foster collaboration, creativity, health and happiness' (Google, 2010a). Some of the benefits for employees include free food, an on-site doctor, shuttle services depending on location, financial planning classes, and on-site facilities such as oil change and car wash services, dry cleaning, gym, hair stylist, fitness classes, and bike repair (Google, 2010b).

In recruiting new staff, Google is explicit about the key reasons to work for Google. The recruitment process is intense. Key tools include ad words, contests, brain teasers, and 'friends of Google' as key means with which to attract the best talent. Work is apportioned for technical staff into 80 per cent core projects and 20 per cent own projects of individual choice. For managers, the time allocation is 70 per cent on core business, 20 per cent on related projects, and 10 per cent on new product and business opportunities. Personal-interest-orientated activities, in addition to a dynamic work environment, build innovation capacity. Employees are empowered to act, as the following quote illustrates:

> In my first month at Google I complained to a friend on the Gmail team about a couple of small things that I disliked about Gmail. But he told me to fix it myself, pointing me to a document on how to bring up the Gmail development environment on my work station. The next day my code was reviewed by Gmail engineers, and then I submitted it. A week later my change was live. I was amazed by the freedom to work across teams, the ability to check in code to another project, the trust in engineers to work on the right thing, and the excitement and speed of getting things done for our users ... I didn't have to ask for anyone's permission to work on this.
>
> (Iyer and Davenport, 2008: 65)

In creating such a work environment, Google is using a variety of levers of implementation that span from traditional control to empowerment, and it is explicitly using organizational culture to enable strategy implementation. But for all of this, as Iyer and Davenport (2008: 68) conclude: 'Google expect hard, almost obsessive, work ... Few organizations are both so paternalistic and so highly analytical in evaluating performance ... At the moment, Google sets the standard for twenty-first-century productivity and growth.'

Sources: Google (2010a; 2010b); Iyer and Davenport (2008); Sullivan (2010)

Implications for strategy practice

From a strategist's perspectives, turning strategic intent, objectives, and goals into action is one of the most challenging aspects of strategy. Achieving focus on the foundations of advantage (see Chapters 5 and 6) and the routes of advantage (Chapters 7 and 8) can be difficult for any organization, but bringing this to reality every day is even a more significant challenge for management teams, strategists, and the whole organization. Careful consideration has to be given to developing an appropriate balance between strategic control and empowerment. These levers for implementing strategy can be powerful if harnessed and deployed appropriately in securing the desired strategic objectives of an organization. If strategic control is used appropriately and aligned to individuals and teams, it ensures progression along the route to advantage, and facilitates conversations about the viability of the route in the long term. Its value to an organization is not only for these tasks, but it can also help in conferring legitimacy and communicating expectations to key stakeholders, including external investors, government legislators, suppliers, and customers.

In many competitive environments, or where there is increasing and intense interest from stakeholders about the activities and performance of the organization, the strategist has to consider the purpose, meaning, and effects of control on individuals, team, departments, and units. To function effectively, organizations need control, but a strategist needs to be aware of the impact that controls can have at an individual level—particularly when organizations need to be adaptable, flexible, and responsive to external factors. Having in place a strategic control framework that is not aligned to or reflective of overall strategic objectives is a fundamental flaw and weakness in strategy implementation.

Learning is a critical, but often overlooked, aspect of strategic control and empowerment. Organizations and individuals can learn more from instances in which performance does not reach intended levels or occasions on which there has been a failure to implement aspects of the organization's strategy. In designing levers for implementing strategy, organizations therefore need to put in place formal and informal mechanisms around learning from successes and failures, as Google does. Far too often, performance evaluation is focused on the indicators or metrics, with little attention paid to understanding how that performance will actually be achieved by individuals and units, and how it will be achieved consistently quarter by quarter and year by year. To this end, the strategist needs to engage in an active way with units and individuals around developing quantifiable targets, but in doing so empower and enable them to achieve these targets consistently and in ways that develop and embed the values and purpose of the business (see Chapter 5).

Finally, strategic controls can assist with maximizing output, be cathartic, provide identity and motivation, be symbolic and provide legitimacy, provide validation and justification for action (strategic controls as post hoc rationalization), and evaluate performance and be a benchmark for any and all actors within an organization. In the end, successful strategies come down to consistent— even flawless— implementation and the appropriate use of levers that are aligned to the organization's structure, needs, focus, and mission.

Introduction to readings

Reading 4.1, 'Strategic orientation and top management attention to control systems' by Simons (1991), is a rare empirical study of strategy implementation and levers of control. This paper focuses on the way in which top management uses specific control systems to focus organizational attention on strategic uncertainties and thereby guide the development of strategic initiatives. This helps to get to the heart of the potential of implementation levers. But the findings are from one context in which innovation is important; will control systems have the same value elsewhere? Are managers likely to consciously use reward systems in this manner?

In Reading 4.2, 'Transforming the balanced scorecard from performance measurement to strategic management: Part 1' (2001), Kaplan and Norton explore their balanced scorecard contribution, as introduced in this chapter. Specifically, they place its emergence in a historical context and then move to extend the argument beyond simple performance measurement to mapping the organization as a strategy system. Their argument is compelling as always—but does this ambitious attempt add value to the balanced scorecard and is it really distinct from other approaches, such as stakeholder mapping? Does it make unrealistic assumptions about the organization's ability to rationally map its operations? What of culture and context? Does the process presuppose that a correct strategy is in place? Will emphasis on measures vary between entrepreneurial firms and a mature organization experiencing a turnaround?

Reading 4.3, 'Turning great strategy into great performance' by Mankins and Steele (2005), looks at the barriers and impediments to successful strategy execution, or what they term the 'strategy-to-performance gap'. This difficulty is often mentioned, but how well do the seven prescriptive steps suggested address the key issues? Will they provide guidance to strategists in realizing advantage, or are they too broad and likely to be contested? How well are the assumptions underpinning the strategy questioned? Will the advice be new to strategists?

Mini case study Toyota: 'The best built cars in the world'?

Since its foundation in 1937, Toyota has become one the world's largest car manufacturers. In doing so, as Leithead (2010) notes, it became 'a bastion of quality, attention to detail, efficiency and trustworthiness. It has always been more than just a brand name or just a car maker'. Toyota pioneered a lean production system, influenced by Edward Deming, which involved just-in-time assembly of vehicles. In addition, it involved individual employees on the manufacturing line taking active control over quality, whereby they could stop an assembly line to fix a problem. Such production approaches were unheard of in other car manufacturers or even in other manufacturing environments. Consequently, Toyota's lean production system was used by many companies as the benchmark in developing an efficient production system based on continuous quality improvement and providing individual autonomy to employees to rectify problems on a real-time basis. It encouraged and developed a strong team and collaborative environment within the company, but also with its external partners.

Over the decades, Toyota has spent considerable organizational effort developing people and a strong corporate culture. This includes a number of guiding principles:

- Honour the language and spirit of the law of every nation and undertake open and fair corporate activities to be a good corporate citizen around the world.
- Respect the culture and customs of every nation and contribute to economic and social development through corporate activities in local communities.
- Dedicate ourselves to providing clean and safe products and to enhancing the quality of life everywhere through our activities.
- Create and develop advanced technologies and provide outstanding products and services that fulfil the needs of customers worldwide.
- Foster a corporate culture that enhances individual creativity and teamwork, while honouring mutual trust and respect between labour and management.
- Pursue growth in harmony with the global community through innovative management.
- Work with business partners in research and creation to achieve stable, long-term growth and mutual benefits, while keeping ourselves open to new partnerships.

Such an approach helped to shape a long-term perspective rather than a short-term one, an organization that was continuously problem solving, learning, and reflecting, and one that respected and valued the contribution of every member of the organization. The combination of developing a strong organization culture and lean production systems has enabled Toyota to develop new technologies, particularly electric technology in pioneering hybrid cars such as the Prius. Toyota is also testing plug-in electric hybrids with potentially lower emissions than the current Prius.

Product recalls

Recently, complaints about sudden acceleration problems have led to the recall of millions of Toyotas. The scale of product recalls is unprecedented in Toyota's history: by the first quarter of 2010, over sixty countries were affected. In 2009, Toyota recalled 4.2 million cars in the US market because of floor mats that allegedly interfered with accelerator pedals. By February 2010, over 8.5 million vehicles worldwide were recalled due to sticky accelerators, a braking glitch in hybrid models, and the floor mats issue. The scale of the recall and the perceived slow response from Toyota in communicating with customers and regulators led to Toyota's president, Akio Toyoda, grandson of Toyota's founder, testifying before the US House Oversight and Government Reform Committee on 24 February 2010.

Given the lack of initial communication from Toyota, some customers set up blogs and websites, such as toyotarecall.org, to share experiences, provide consumer forums, and disseminate latest news. In April 2010, in the USA, Toyota announced the establishment of the Swift Market Analysis Response Team (SMART), consisting of product engineers, field specialists, and specially trained technicians to deal with customer issues for Toyota, Lexus, and Scion vehicles. These SMART teams:

> will attempt to contact customers within 24 hours of receiving a complaint of unintended acceleration to arrange for comprehensive on-site vehicle analysis ... As part of the SMART program, dealerships will utilize structured business processes and materials to address owners' concerns or reported experiences with unintended acceleration.
>
> (Toyota, 2010)

Steve St Angelo, chief of quality for the US market, stated:

> As Toyota's president, Akio Toyoda, told Congress in February, we are committed to listening to our customers even more intently and addressing their concerns even more promptly. Our multi-tier SMART approach is just one of the many steps we are taking to make sure that Toyota sets an even higher standard.
>
> (Burney, 2010)

For some commentators, it reflected a more deep-rooted management and cultural issue, as Holt (2010) reflects:

> When I read that Toyota was recalling vehicles in Japan and abroad, my response was a combination of mild surprise and a sense of complete inevitability. I was surprised because, in my experience, Japanese engineers and craftsmen are meticulous in their attention to detail—which is probably why we take the quality of their products for granted and why an everyday event such as a car recall has somehow become newsworthy. The feeling of inevitability, however, came from what I know of management practices in many Japanese companies, which leave employees exhausted, sleep deprived and unable to perform at their best ... Nobody would respond better to progressive management practices than Japanese workers, because they possess an overabundance of goodwill and determination.

Recall fallout

Despite the publicity, sales for Toyota in the US market in March 2010 increased by 41 per cent from 2009 figures, which was significant since year-on-year sales were down 16 per cent in January and 20 per cent in February 2010. The increases were due to offering customers special deals including discounts and interest-free loans. Such incentives, particularly government-backed ones, meant that Toyota sales in March 2010 were up 51 per cent in Japan and 33 per cent in China.

Toyota appointed chief quality officers for Japan, the USA, China, and Europe, as well as other key markets, to investigate customer complaints and ensure that an even more robust quality process pervaded the organization. The company has also been considering making English its in-house language and appointing outsiders to assist the company review its practices.

By 19 April 2010, Toyota announced that it had agreed with US regulators to pay a US$16.4m fine for safety violations. But, as Wearden (2010) described:

> This is the largest fine to have been levied against a carmaker in America. Toyota still faces a series of legal challenges from consumers who claim they have been affected by the crisis. As well as wrongful death and injury lawsuits, there are class actions from owners upset that the value of their cars has fallen.

The impact on Toyota's workers can be summarized by one worker's comment to Leithead (2010): 'There will be some damage, but Toyota is strong and could even become stronger from this experience.'

Toyota was further challenged by the devastating effects of the earthquake in Japan in March 2011. The earthquake had a significant impact on new products' key markets and also disrupted production. The next few years will tell if becoming stronger through such experiences is a reality for the makers of 'the best built cars in the world'.

Sources: Holt (2010); Leithead (2010); St Angelo (2010); Toyota (2010); Wearden (2010)

Questions

1. What levers for implementation has Toyota used in becoming a major competitive force?
2. Discuss the unintended consequences of levers for implementation in Toyota. Could these have been avoided?
3. Did culture play a role in leading to the product recall?
4. Are the levers for implementation to blame for the global recall? Could Toyota have used different levels and created a different culture and rewards and performance evaluation, and still have become a major competitive force in the car industry?

Summary

The effective implementation of strategy is essential to realizing advantage. Implementation is not simply the creation of an appropriate structure, as was traditionally assumed, but rather involves managing a system of levers that operate in an ongoing process (Galbraith and Nathanson, 1978). It requires a consistency of effort by everyone in the organization to work together to realize the strategic intent. This is difficult and challenging if the organization has a broad scope of products or services over many geographical territories. This is why the foundations of advantage (Chapters 5 and 6) and the routes to advantage (Chapters 7 and 8) need to be clearly articulated and understood by all in an organization. The strategist has a central role in this articulation process and also in ensuring that the appropriate levers for implementing strategy are used to support the realization of organizational strategy.

In this chapter, we have directed attention towards two contrasting levers for implementing strategy—strategic control and empowerment—which can be used to realize advantage. In doing so, we explored how organizational culture, rewards, incentives, and performance systems have a critical role in supporting the levers of strategy implementation. As the discussion evolved from traditional control and empowerment to interactive control systems, the nature of strategy execution has emphasized the importance of the words of Alfred Sloan (1967: 22) that 'there is no resting place for an enterprise in a competitive economy'. It is important that strategy evaluation mechanisms also track the assumptions underpinning the strategy rather than simply the results achieved. Organizations need to be ambidextrous, simultaneously executing today's strategy while developing that of tomorrow (Birkinshaw and Gibson, 2004). Indeed, it is unlikely that the initial trajectory of the organization will be accurate, as could perhaps be more safely assumed in the industrial era by writers such as Ansoff and Andrews.

In the knowledge-based era, strategy is best viewed as akin to the guided missile, the trajectory of which is rarely correct, but is in a constant state of being corrected (Cardinal *et al.*, 2004). Treating strategy as an unfinished prototype unleashes energy and enthusiasm, or else complacency sinks in. In this era, the scope for prediction becomes limited, and success cannot be collapsed into one issue, method, or measure. Each is contingent on a context and the appropriate infrastructure that will facilitate their achievement. One common denominator for successful strategy implementation, however, is that strategy is embedded so forcefully that the organization thinks it, lives it, and breathes it. There is no substitute for passion, desire, cohesiveness, and a winning mentality (Gratton and Truss, 2003). After all, it is people, not organizations, that make strategy in the sense of both formulation and realization (Walker, 1992). This means that successful strategy cannot be taught or prescribed; it can only emerge from the momentum of action and experience. Using the levers of strategy implementation, supported by organizational culture, rewards, and performance evaluation, can ensure a consistency of strategy implementation because, as Iyer and Davenport (2008: 59), in describing Google's strategic capability, state: 'Every piece of the business plays a part, every past is indispensable, every failure breeds success, and every success demands improvements.' The metaphor of levers of implementation is useful because situations have levers that enable the situation to be 'controlled'. However the complexity of situations means that no set of levers will ever be complete. Consequently, it is important to remind ourselves that 'poor strategy often results from the delusion that we have found the ultimate set of levers' (Patel, 2005: 142).

Discussion questions

1. Take an organization with which you are familiar and assess the levers the organization uses for control and empowerment.

2. What are key levers that can be used to implement strategy? Are empowerment and control incompatible?

3. Develop criteria for strategic objectives for your local fire service, using Table 9.2. How will it motivate the performance of fire officers and the overall service?

4. As a strategist for a large-scale semiconductor organization that is seeking to expand via unrelated diversification (see Chapter 7), discuss the control and empowerment challenges that will be part of this future growth strategy.

5. 'Performance evaluation varies by context and has a temporal dimension.' Discuss.

6. With reference to the Google Spotlight, discuss whether Google's levers of strategy implementation can be replicable in other contexts. Will Google need to change its levers of strategy implementation as other organizations replicate its approach?

7. From your reading of this chapter, explain why so many organizations fail in implementing strategy.

8. Outline how culture and rewards impact on control and empowerment in realizing advantage.

Further reading

Kaplan and Norton are the most cited authors in this domain, and present an interesting and readable account of strategy implementation using a broad spectrum of organizations as examples. See R. Kaplan and D. Norton (2008) *Execution Premium: Linking Strategy to Operations for Competitive Advantage*, Boston, MA: Harvard Business School Press.

That said, there has been a lack of detailed material in this area, and so one of the foundational texts still holds much relevance and insight: J. Galbraith and D. Nathanson (1978) *Strategy Implementation: The Role of Structure and Process*, St Paul, MN: West Publishing.

Likewise, Walton's classic article still has much value and its imprint can be found in many of the distinctions made between empowerment and control: R. E. Walton (1985) 'From control to commitment on the workplace', *Harvard Business Review*, 63: 77–84.

visit the Online Resource Centre that accompanies this book to access more learning resources on this chapter topic at www.oxfordtextbooks.co.uk/orc/cunningham/

References

Allio, R. 2011. Henry Mintzberg: still the zealous skeptic and scold. *Strategy & Leadership*, 39(2): 4–8.

Argyres, N. and McGahan, A. 2002. Michael Porter on competitive strategy. *Academy of Management Executive*, 16(May): 41–53.

Barney, J. 1986. Organisational culture: can it be a source of competitive advantage? *Academy of Management Review*, 11(3): 556–565.

Bartlett, C. and Ghoshal, S. 2002. *Managing across Borders: The Transnational Solution*. Boston, MA: Harvard Business School Press.

Bellin, J. and Chi, P. 2007. Global expansion: balancing a uniform performance culture with local conditions. *Strategy and Leadership*, 35(6): 44–50.

Birkinshaw, J. and Gibson, C. 2004. Building ambidexterity into organizations. *Sloan Management Review*, 45(4): 47–55.

Boyle, M. and Chester, C. 2004. Why Fedex is flying high. *Fortune*, 150(9): 145–150.

Brunsson, N. 1982. The irrationality of action and action rationality: decision, ideologies and organizational actions. *Journal of Management Studies*, 19: 29–44.

Bungay, S. 2011. How to make the most of your company's strategy. *Harvard Business Review*, Jan/Feb: 132–140.

Burgelman, R. A. and McKinney, W. 2006. Managing the strategic dynamics of acquisition integration: lessons from HP and Compaq *California Management Review*, 48(3): 6–27.

Burney, J. 2010. Toyota gets SMARTer. Available online at http://www.toyotainthenews.com/toyota-gets-smarter/

Cardinal, L., Sitkin, S., and Long, C. 2004. Balancing and rebalancing in the creation and evolution of organizational control. *Organization Science*, 15(4): 411–431.

Chandler, A. D. 1962. *Strategy and Structure*. Cambridge, MA: MIT Press.

Child, J. 1997. Strategic choice in the analysis of action, structure, organizations and environment: retrospect and Prospect. *Organization Studies*, 18(1): 43–76.

Clegg, S. 1990. *Modern Organizations*. London: Sage.

Daft, R. and Macintosh, N. 1984. The nature and use of formal control systems for management control and strategy implementation. *Journal of Management*, 10(1): 43–66.

Davis, J. H., Schoorman, F. D., and Donaldson, L. 1997. Toward a stewardship theory of management. *Academy of Management Review*, 22(1): 20–47.

Delany, E. 2000. Strategic development of the multi-national subsidiary through subsidiary initiative taking. *Long Range Planning*, 33: 220–244.

Delbridge, R., Gratton, L., and Johnson, G. 2006. *The Exceptional Manager: Making the Difference*. Oxford: Oxford University Press.

Eccles, R. and Nohria, N. 1992. *Beyond the Hype: Rediscovering the Essence of Management*. Boston, MA: Harvard Business School Press.

The Economist. 2008. Face value: triple therapy. 14 August, 57.

Edmondson, A. 2008. The competitive imperative of learning. *Harvard Business Review*, July/Aug: 60–67.

Fuchs, P., Mifflin, K., Miller, D., and Whitney, J. 2000. Strategic integration: competing in the age of capabilities. *California Management Review*, 42(3): 118–147.

Galbraith, J. and Nathanson, D. 1978. *Strategy Implementation: The Role of Structure and Process*. St Paul, MN: West Publishing.

Gino, F. and Pisano, G. 2011. What leaders don't learn from success: failures get a post-mortem—why not triumphs? *Harvard Business Review*, Apr: 68–83.

Gittel, J. 2000. The paradox of coordination and control. *California Management Review*, 42(3): 101–117.

Gladwell, M. 2009. *What the Dog Saw and Other Adventures*. New York: Little, Brown and Co.

Google. 2010a. Let's work together: US jobs. Available online at http://www.google.com/intl/en/jobs/index.html

Google. 2010b. US jobs: benefits. Available online at http://www.google.com/intl/en/jobs/lifeatgoogle/benefits/

Google. 2011. Our philosophy: ten things we know to be true. Available online at http://www.google.com/about/corporate/company/tenthings.html

Goold, M. and Quinn, J. B. 1990. The paradox of strategic controls. *Strategic Management Journal*, 11: 43–57.

Goold, M., Campbell, A., and Alexander, M. 1994. *Corporate Level Strategy*. Chichester: John Wiley and Sons.

Grant, R. M. 1996. Towards a knowledge theory of the firm. *Strategic Management Journal*, 17: 109–122.

Gratton, L. and Truss, C. 2003. The three-dimensional people strategy: putting human resources policies into action. *Academy of Management Executive*, 17(3): 74–86.

Hambrick, D. 2004. The disintegration of strategic management: it's time to consolidate our gains. *Strategic Organization*, 2(1): 91–98.

Hambrick, D. and Cannella, A. 1989. Strategy implementation as substance and selling. *Academy of Management Executive*, 3(4): 278–285.

Handy, C. 1985. *Understanding Organizations.* 3rd edn. London: Penguin.

Hatch, M. J. 1997. *Organization Theory: Modern Symbolic and Postmodern Perspectives*. Oxford: Oxford University Press.

Hayes, R. H. and Abernathy, W. 1980. Managing our way to economic decline. *Harvard Business Review*, July/Aug: 67–77.

Holt, J. 2010. Toyota undone by Japan's work ethic? *The Guardian*, 11 February. Available online at http://www.guardian.co.uk/commentisfree/2010/feb/11/toyota-japan-work-ethic

Iyer, B. and Davenport, T. 2008. Reverse engineering Google's innovation machine. *Harvard Business Review*, Apr: 59–68.

Kaplan, R. and Norton, D. 1992. The balanced scorecard: measures that drive performance. *Harvard Business Review*, Jan/Feb: 71–79.

Kaplan, R. and Norton, D. 1996. Using the balanced scorecard as a strategic management system. *Harvard Business Review*, 74(1): 75–85.

Kaplan, R. S. and Norton, D. P. 2001. Transforming the balanced scorecard from performance measurement to strategic management. *Accounting Horizons*, 15(1): 87–104.

Kaplan, R. and Norton, D. 2006. How to implement a strategy without disrupting your organization. *Harvard Business Review*, 84(3): 100–109.

Kaplan, R. and Norton, D. 2008a. *Execution Premium: Linking Strategy to Operations for Competitive Advantage*. Boston, MA: Harvard Business School Press.

Kaplan, R. and Norton, D. 2008b. Mastering the management system. *Harvard Business Review*, Jan: 63–77.

Kohn, A. 1993. Why incentive plans cannot work. *Harvard Business Review*, Sept/Oct: 54–62.

Kolehmainen, K. 2010. Dynamic strategic performance measurement systems: balancing empowerment and alignment. *Long Range Planning*, 43(4): 527–554.

Leithead, A. 2010. Hitting home: recall dulls Toyota's image. *BBC News*, 6 February. Available online at http://news.bbc.co.uk/2/hi/8501832.stm

Martin, R. 2010. The age of customer capitalism. *Harvard Business Review*, Jan/Feb: 58–65.

Micheli, P. and Manzoni, J.-F. 2010. Strategic performance measurement: benefits, limitations and paradoxes. *Long Range Planning*, 43(4): 465–476.

Mintzberg, H. 2009. *Managing*. London: FT Prentice Hall.

Neilson, G., Martin, K., and Powers, E. 2008. The secrets to successful strategy execution. *Harvard Business Review*, June: 61–70.

Nohria, N., Joyce, W., and Robertson, B. 2003. What really works. *Harvard Business Review*, 81(7): 12–26

Ofgem. 2008. ***2007/2008 Electricity distribution quality of service report,*** Available online at http://www.probeinternational.org/files/2007-08%20Electricity%20Distribution%20Quality%20of%20Service%20Report.pdf

Patel, K. 2005. *The Master Strategist: Power, Purpose and Principle*. London: Arrow Books.

Pfeffer, J. 1977. The ambiguity of leadership. *Academy of Management Review*, 2: 104–112.

Pfeffer, J. and Sutton, R. 2006. *Hard Facts, Dangerous Half Truths, and Total Nonsense*. Boston, MA: Harvard Business School Press.

Porter, M. 1996. What is strategy? *Harvard Business Review*, Dec: 61–78.

Prahalad, C. and Hamel, G. 1990. The core competencies of the corporation. *Harvard Business Review*, May/June(3): 79–91.

Preble, J. F. 1992. Towards a comprehensive theory of strategic control. *Journal of Management Studies*, 29: 391–409.

Pun, K. and White, A. 2005. A performance measurement paradigm for integrating strategy formulation: a review of systems and frameworks. *International Journal of Management Reviews*, 7(1): 49–71.

Quinn, J. B., Anderson, P., and Finkelstein, S. 1996. Leveraging intellect. *Academy of Management Executive*, 19(4): 78–94.

Ridgway, V. F. 1956. Dysfunctional consequences of performance measurement. *Administrative Science Quarterly*, 1(2): 240–247.

Rishton, J. 2009. Ahold's strategy for profitable growth. Available online at http://www.ahold.com/node/3321

Semler, R. 2000. How we went digital without a strategy. *Harvard Business Review*, Sept/Oct: 51–58.

Simons, R. 1991. Strategic orientation and top management attention to control systems. *Strategic Management Journal*, 12: 49–62.

Simons, R. 1994. How new top managers use control systems as levers of strategic renewal. *Strategic Management Journal*, 15: 169–189.

Sloan, A. P. 1967. *My Years with General Motors*. Garden City, NY: Doubleday.

Snow, C., Raymond, M., and Miles, G. 2005. A configurational approach to the integration of strategy and organization research. *Strategic Organization*, 3(4): 431–439.

Sullivan, J. 2006. A look inside the Google talent machine. *HR Management*, 29 April. Available online at http://www.hcamag.com/resources/hr-strategy/a-look-inside-the-google-talent-machine/112999/

Swidler, A. 1986. Culture in action: symbols and strategies. *American Sociological Review*, 51(2): 273–286.

Toyota. 2010. Toyota announces 'SMART' business process for quick evaluation of unintended acceleration report. Toyota USA Newsroom press release. Available online at http://pressroom.toyota.com/pr/tms/toyota-announces-smart-business-156380.aspx

Walker, J. W. 1992. *Human Resource Strategy*. New York: McGraw-Hill International Editions.

Wearden, G. 2010. Toyota to pay record $16.4m fine. *The Guardian*, 19 April. Available online at http://www.guardian.co.uk/business/2010/apr/19/toyota-pay-record-fine-safety

10

Interactions in executing strategy

Structure, knowledge, people, and customers

It is good to have an end to journey toward, but it is the journey that matters in the end.

(Ursula K. Le Guin)

Introduction

Research suggests that even the most cunning strategy will fail to realize its potential unless it is supported by an appropriate organizational infrastructure (Worley and Lawler, 2010). In our last chapter, we explored the role of the strategic levers of control and **empowerment** in realizing advantage. In this chapter, we turn our focus to interactions in executing strategy and, in particular, structure, knowledge, people, and customers. In the 1990s, firms such as ABB, Proctor and Gamble, and Xerox all experienced success and subsequent downfalls as a result of poor organization design, weakness of reporting and authority structures, and an inability to recognize and adapt to key trends (Bryan and Joyce, 2007). Executing strategy is a complex activity: it requires consistent interactions between structures, information, employees, and the customer, as well as appropriate strategic control and empowerment. Through these interactions, strategy moves from an abstract intent to one that is alive for those charged with enacting it within the organization. In October 2010, the UK government announced its intention to cut 480,000 public sector jobs. On what information did the government base the announcement? What would be the appropriate organizational structure to deliver services to the public? What impact will the government's intention have on public sector workers? Will such a cut diminish the customer experience and level of service that the UK citizen receives from public agencies?

These types of question, common in times of crisis, indicate how strategy **formulation** and execution comprise two sides of the same coin. As the opening quote by American author Ursula Le Guin suggests, an organization's strategy constitutes not only an articulated purpose, but also the means by which it is achieved (Snow *et al.*, 2005). The levers of control and empowerment discussed in the previous chapter are broad orientations that organizations may use in pursuit of their stated objectives. However, in addition to nurturing and guiding behaviour through these levers, the ability of an organization to realize advantage will hinge upon how it manages its structure, leverages its knowledge infrastructure, nurtures talent, and incorporates customer insights. This is the focus of this chapter. These elements not only interact with each other, but also critically need to interact with strategy if advantage is to be realized. While identification of these key dimensions may well be easy (Nohria *et al.*, 2003), understanding key tensions inherent to them and how they can be managed is far from it, as the next section illustrates.

Dimensions of the strategy infrastructure

In this chapter, we explore the dimensions of building organizational structure, having an appropriate knowledge infrastructure, leveraging organizational talent, and understanding customers. At the heart of each discussion is the tension between traditional structures and policies akin to those of the industrial era, and more recent emphasis on the processes, broad architectures, and complex networks of a knowledge-based era (see Figure 1.1 in Chapter 1). While the structures of the industrial era provide for control and stability, those of the knowledge era enable flexibility and change, such as is evident in the information and communications technology (ICT) sector, in which agility is essential in responding to market demands. Similarly, while the industrial era facilitates evaluation and control, the knowledge era emphasizes empowerment and **innovation**. Whereas traditional approaches focus on efficiency and reducing uncertainty, some argue that this focus is now redundant:

> today's economy thrives by leveraging uncertainty. Competitive advantage may no longer be a function of a 'fit' between uncertainty and information-processing capacities as we have traditionally understood—but a function of an organization's ability to continually navigate its way into realms of the unknown and concurrently develop new expertise.
>
> (Venkatraman and Subramaniam, 2002: 471)

Others argue that an organization that exclusively thrives on innovation risks undermining the long-term orientation and structures that are required to sustain it (Lawlor, 2008). Such tensions are not easily resolved, but one can gain an appreciation of key elements of the strategy infrastructure that should at least form part of the debate. These are introduced in Table 10.1 and discussed further below.

In exploring organizational structure, this chapter confronts the long-standing contrast between hierarchical and more organic forms of organizing. This is the contrast between traditional hierarchical structures, such as those found in **public sector organizations**, and experimental organizational forms, such as Blade.org, an online community initiated by IBM. Is one of these forms more appropriate than the other? Has the time of the bureaucratic organization passed? In terms of knowledge infrastructure, we explore the distinction between 'hard' and 'soft' data, and in particular whether knowledge can be extracted and shared like any other **resource**—or does knowledge remain deeply embedded within business units, within specialized areas such as software engineering, or within individuals? In terms of leveraging talent, a key question is whether strategy is the reserve of an elite within an organization or an organization-wide phenomenon; on either basis, what are the implications for motivation and reward? Finally, we consider whether depicting a clear boundary between the customer and the organization is a redundant model in a Web 2.0 era of open innovation.

Having an appropriate infrastructure in place is the essence of realizing advantage. Nonetheless, interactions and integration are the key capabilities that remain unexplored and underexploited (Chan *et al.*, 2007; Fuchs *et al.*, 2000: 118). Telefónica, the Spanish mobile telephony and communications firm, is one organization that has invested heavily in its organizational infrastructure to support its international expansion. In highlighting the four dimensions of structure, information, people, and customers, we move away from viewing them as functional tasks that are the remit of specific units and exclusively associated with implementation. Instead, we consider how each links with strategy to form a critical part of the strategy infrastructure—what Kaplan and Norton (2008) term the 'management system' (see Reading 4.2). Here, the **strategist**'s role is critical. In calling for

Table 10.1 Strategy interactions in the industrial and knowledge-based eras

	Industrial era	Knowledge-based era
Structure	Hierarchy Formal Structure follows strategy	Organic Informal Strategy follows structure
Knowledge	Hard, explicit knowledge Universal processes Economies of scale	Soft, tacit knowledge Idiosyncratic processes Communities of experience
People	Command and control Focus on elite few	Empowerment Focus on 'the many'
Customers	Diagnostic understanding Firm-driven relations	Interactive understanding Customer-driven relations

the reinvention of management, Birkinshaw (2010: 34) emphasizes the importance of understanding *how* management is carried out in organizations. Central to this is an appreciation of how activities are coordinated (structure), how people are managed (motivation), and how key decisions are made (customers and knowledge). In discussing each of the dimensions, this chapter will illustrate that there are tensions common to each. Surfacing and exploring such tensions are vital. Strategists who pursue detailed formulation without consideration of the complexities of realizing advantage can be likened to the inventor who has a great idea, but is unable to bring it to market. Instead, strategists must bridge conception and realization as the 'entrepreneurs of advantage'. The first issue to be explored is organizational structure.

Structuring organizations and organizing structure

Organizational structure is acknowledged to be a key strategic variable and problem-solving device in meeting contemporary management challenges (Palmer and Hardy, 2000: 11). Formal structure is the most visible manifestation of an organization, the easiest to capture on paper, and the easiest to communicate. It follows that when strategy execution is not being realized as intended, changing the structure is often one of the first fixes considered (Neilson *et al.*, 2008). However, even when the simplest of organizations, such as a small retail store, is reduced to its bare essentials, it is still complex (Lawlor, 2008: 36). Organizations face social pressures in the form of media hype insisting that they implement what is perceived as the new 'best' and most effective way of doing things. Industrial and organizational entities in Europe, such as banks, insurance companies, financial regulators, police and defence forces, and medical providers, face pressure from many quarters to implement new ways of organizing core activities. In order to retain legitimacy in the eyes of key stakeholders and customers, strategists in these organizational settings feel that they have to respond to such pressure (Suchman, 1995). Yet without detailed consideration of how a certain structural change may operate and its specific benefits, organizations can fall all too easily into the trap of assuming that structural change will solve all of their strategic and operational problems.

An *appropriate* organizational structure is therefore critical in ensuring that processes and effort can be directed and guided in a direction that will realize advantage for an organization. An effective organizational structure can help to ensure consistency and accountability in all organizational actions. An *inappropriate* structure can hinder execution, create inefficiencies, suffocate innovation, and, at worst, destroy advantage. All organizations need formal and informal structures in order to carry out their daily activities. As Mintzberg (1979: 3) notes, 'every organized activity, from putting a man on the moon to making pots, gives rise to two fundamental and opposing requirements: the division of labour into various tasks to be performed, and the coordination of these tasks to accomplish the activity'. The structure of an organization can be defined simply as the sum total of the ways in which it divides its labour into distinct tasks and then achieves coordination among them. In a hospital setting, there are clear divisions of labour between clinicians, nursing staff, and the diagnostic support provided to patients; in a small retail store, there might be a less rigid division of labour.

Structure follows strategy or strategy follows structure

A focus on the relationship between structure and strategy emerged in the 1960s through the work of Alfred Chandler (1962), who argued that structure followed strategy, observing that growth strategies were normally accompanied by decentralization through a divisional structure. Since then, the extent to which structure is a tool of strategy execution or informs strategy development has been the subject of long-standing debate. The traditional approach is captured in the dictum 'Structure follows strategy'. Its key central argument is that 'unless structure follows strategy, inefficiency results' (Chandler, 1962: 150). The 'structure follows strategy' approach retains the classic conception of formulation and then implementation: the environment determines the strategic and operating resources of the firm, and these in turn determine the structure of authority, responsibility, work flows, and information flows within the firm (Ansoff, 1987: 25). In contrast, according to Mintzberg's (1994) logic, 'strategy follows structure'. This argument notes that strategy is complex and messy, with strategy implementation informing formulation rather than the other way around. Organizations select their situations in accordance with their structural designs just as much as they can select their designs in accordance with their situations. This argument holds that decisions in relation to structure will inevitably be a function of path dependency and organizational history. As Hall and Saias (1980: 149) noted, while strategists 'may build the structure of an organization, in practice it is this very structure which later constrains the strategic choices that they make'. From this perspective, structure and strategy will naturally inform each other.

The difference in perspectives may involve organizations' specific focus, as noted by Burgelman (1983). While it is certainly the case that **corporate strategy** will *induce* strategic behaviour and structures, at the same time more radical changes are likely to emerge from autonomous strategic initiatives at the lower level of the organization (see Chapter 4). These only subsequently become bound into formal strategy; thus strategy follows autonomous strategic initiatives (Burgelman, 1983: 67). This two-sided function of structure is important, because the organization can become short-sighted or blind. Miles *et al.* (1974: 261) noted: 'The organization whose managerial talent is fully employed in the operation of the existing technology and process is unlikely to perceive new environmental threats or opportunities.' An organization needs a structure that focuses on effective execution, and which also has capacity to act upon external opportunities and competitive threats.

Organizational structures

Irrespective of the 'structure follows strategy' debate, a strategist has to consider what organizational structure is most appropriate given the competitive environment in which he or she operates, the strategic objectives of the organization, and available resources. In further exploring the differences between organizational structures, Mintzberg (2003) notes that an organization founded on stability, standardization, and efficiency is likely to seek a more stable environment (for example, Wal-mart in retailing), while an innovative, risk-taking organization is likely to seek an environment that enables these characteristics (Samsung). Over time, and reflecting the changing environment since Chandler's work, a range of possible organizational forms has emerged. In particular, the focus has turned to organizational forms founded upon knowledge and enterprise rather than capital and scale (Bartlett and Ghoshal, 1993). A summary of key organizational forms, coupled with their strengths and weaknesses, is provided in Table 10.2.

Hierarchal and multidivisional structures characterize the industrial era. Here, organizational designs emphasized size, clarity, formalization, specialization, and control in the service of efficiency and economies of scale (Beckman, 2009; Palmer and Hardy, 2000: 13). In contrast, matrix and networked organizations have emerged to deal with issues of globalization and the intensified competition of the knowledge-based era. While traditional structures are claimed to be resource-centric aimed at physical production, structures associated with the knowledge era are said to be customer-centric focused on knowledge exploitation and exploration (Strikwerda and Stoelhorst, 2009). Swedish international publisher, Metro, has a network-based organization, the operations of which, in contrast to traditional media organizations, involve few reporters. Instead, as a network orchestrator, Metro buys in all media content and outsources printing. Such organizations have realized that if they are not the best in the world at a certain activity, then they '[give] up competitive edge by performing that activity in-house' (Quinn *et al.*, 1996: 82). Other organizations or team-based projects are more like 'Velcro organizations', or the 'innovation' or 'I-form' organization (Miles *et al.*, 2009), continuously being pulled apart and reassembled. The shift to network organizations has not

Table 10.2 Ideal organizational structures: strengths and weaknesses

Label	Functional	Multidivisional	Matrix	Networked organization
Strengths	Clear authority Well-defined roles Greater control over activities Specialisms—avoid duplication	Global view of strategy Facilitate strategic evaluation and control by division Flexible Value creating corporate parent Easier for growth	Integrate separate areas of knowledge Cooperation Varied work experience Flexibility Leverage available knowledge Enhance global policy and local responsiveness	Focus on core competencies Leverage resources of others Facilitate flexibility, quick reaction Network, cluster effects Transfer of best practice Dynamic learning opportunities
Weaknesses	Limited cross-communication Isolationism Conflict among functions Top management time consumed by operational matters Slow to change Distance from market Distorted information flows Difficult to motivate lower levels	Isolated from market pressures Costly Risk of transfer pricing Duplication among divisions Competition among divisions	Longer decision making Costly Confusion over responsibility/accountability Role conflict	Coordination costs Power effects, knock-on effects of closure, relocation Ability to guarantee quality rests on partners operating in good faith Control over cost

been confined to the private sector, but is also found within public sector organizations, with the National Health Service (NHS) frequently contracting out aspects of service delivery and having to develop capabilities in managing partnerships and diverse networks (Ferlie and Pettigrew, 1996).

Assuming a sweeping progression from the rigid hierarchy to a flatter and more flexible structure characteristic of the knowledge-based era is somewhat flawed (Bahrami, 1992). The death of traditional organizational structures in the form of hierarchies, bureaucracy, and command-and-control management has been predicted for some time. The Hawthorne studies in the 1930s indicated that attention to individuals and their well-being was more likely to enhance productivity than rigid structures and control mechanisms. Fifty years later, in the 1980s, Piore and Sabel (1984) noted the rise of a craft-based era based on small, flexible, and networked enterprises, which would be the seedbed for innovation and competitive advantage. Their thesis of a 'second industrial divide' highlighted the merits of regional specialization. Later, Western business would try to replicate the lean production principles that emanated from Japan. Again, the model was very different from the bureaucratic principles of old, focusing on teamwork, just-in-time production, and flat and flexible organizations. In all cases, the universalistic alternative never came to pass. Still, a range of traditional structures remain. Task-focused organizations, such as Premier Hotels and McDonald's, have managed to be innovative while delivering a standardized product in a standardized way (Stace and Dunphy, 1991), while organizations with a completely novel structure and approach, such as the innovative culture of online retail store Zappo or the flexible policies at Netflix, remain the exception. A browse through company websites and annual reports indicates that despite the rhetoric of shamrock, spherical, 'plug and play' organizational structures, traditional forms are alive and well.

As Table 10.2 makes clear, each approach has its own merits and limitations. Procedures and protocols are necessary for any organization to function well. Adler (1993: 104) refers to the 'learning bureaucracy' and argues that 'standardization and specialization properly understood and organized can be a tremendous stimulus to learning'. But it is also the case that too much red tape can impede progress, dampen employees' enthusiasm, and consume their energy (Nohria *et al.*, 2003: 49). The utility of a given structure will also alter over time. Thus, while General Motors' (GM's) divisional structure of separate brands initially helped to distinguish the organization, over time it led to duplicated functions, proliferating products, and rising costs as divisions acted as independent units (Kanter, 2009: 67), ultimately serving organizational rather than market demands (Birkinshaw, 2010: 25).

A 'working' organizational structure

Although the frequency with which it is discussed may suggest otherwise, changing organizational structure is not like changing clothes. Existing ways of working tend to become deeply institutionalized and therefore difficult to alter. If an organization employs thousands of people in many locations throughout the world, the challenge is even greater. Consequently, many organizations do not really make a substantial effort to change their organizational structure unless they are forced by inefficiency or competitive intensity to do so. The focus can be more on initiating organization-wide projects or initiatives designed to deliver value rather than addressing fundamental organizational structural issues. In the case of **mergers** and **acquisitions** (M&As), the introduction and embedding of new structures can prove difficult and take years to get right. Goold and Campbell (2002) offer some useful questions that can help in developing a 'working' organizational structure.

- *Market advantage test* Does the organizational design direct sufficient attention towards your sources of competitive advantage in each market?
- *Parenting advantage test* Does your design help the corporate parent to add value to the organization?
- *People test* Does your design reflect the strengths, weaknesses, and motivations of your people?
- *Feasibility test* Have you taken account of all of the constraints that may impede the implementation of your design?
- *Specialist cultures test* Does your design protect units that need distinct cultures?
- *Difficult link test* Does your design provide coordinated solutions for the unit-to-unit links that are likely to be problematic?
- *Redundant-hierarchy test* Does your design have too many parent levels and units?
- *Accountability test* Does your design support effective controls?
- Does your design facilitate the development of new strategies and provide the flexibility required to adapt to change?

The areas on which Goold and Campbell (2002) focus are the critical aspects of an effective organizational structure; without these, a firm will not be able to serve its customers effectively or profitably. The people test reflects the key issues raised in the previous chapter—those of strategic control and empowerment—and the feasibility test should capture the many seen and unforeseen issues and costs associated with organization design. Given the costs and difficulties involved in using structure to unlock value, some commentators have questioned whether structure is *the* vital tool in strategy execution. A study of 26,000 people from thirty-two organizations concluded that 'structural change can and should be part of the path to improved execution, but it's best to think of it as the capstone, not the cornerstone, of any organizational transformation' (Neilson *et al.*, 2008: 62). Kaplan and Norton (2006: 102) suggest that organizations do not need to find 'the' perfect structure for their strategy; rather, the task is to find an optimal structure that 'works without major conflicts and then design a customized strategic system to align that structure with the strategy'. In this sense, 'the importance of structure is that it should not get in the way' (Miller *et al.*, 2004: 210). Nohira *et al.* (2003: 49) found that it made little difference whether organizations were organized by function, geography, or product; what mattered was whether the organization structure simplified the work. Thus all structural solutions will have their merits and limitations, while how a structure operates in practice will be inextricably bound up with organizational processes. This highlights that specific structures cannot be judged as having a predetermined impact, nor can structures be understood in isolation from factors such as the nature of talent employed, information systems, and the desired customer interface that inform their success as part of an integrated strategy infrastructure (Christensen and Raynor, 2003; Laseter, 2009). Strategists therefore need to develop a workable organizational structure that supports strategy implementation and enables the individuals tasked to deliver strategic objectives.

In an early contribution, Galbraith and Nathanson (1978) recognized the danger of focusing exclusively on the formal aspects of structure and the associated organizational chart to the neglect of other elements of the design. Therefore strategists need to develop a workable organizational structure that supports strategy implementation and enables the individuals tasked to deliver strategic objectives. Inherent to this is a consideration of the knowledge infrastructures and knowledge flows within an organization.

Knowledge infrastructure

In many ways, the ability to organize effectively, to leverage appropriate talent, and to build customer relationships stems from having appropriate and up-to-date information. This is the domain of the knowledge infrastructure of an organization and how successfully it functions. Organizations have the capacity to collate data from sources inside and outside the firm every day. Small online retailers can use Google Analytics to assess the effectiveness of their web presence and how the usage pattern translates into purchases. Larger corporations use SAP systems to capture key internal data necessary to control their activities and to undertake monthly and annual financial reporting. In the knowledge-based era, capabilities in managing and deploying information have taken on much greater significance, because knowledge is said to be a significant factor contributing to economic growth (Drucker, 1988). Additionally, as organizations compete on a global basis, knowledge must be transferred to enhance competition in diverse locations. It is therefore important for organizations to have the capability to adequately share knowledge.

In capturing this trend, some have advocated a knowledge-based view of the firm (Grant, 1996), which holds that competitive advantage resides in an organization's ability to 'create, transfer, assemble, integrate, and exploit knowledge assets' (Soo *et al.*, 2002: 130). For strategists, this means developing a skill set that can leverage the intellect and knowledge base of individuals and groups to an aggregate level so that it is embodied in organizational output (Quinn, 2005). Davenport (2006; 2009) stresses the huge potential that organizations can leverage from being more systematic in how information is exploited across multiple domains. For example, they can use information from supply chains, customers, and research and development (for example, Acer, Sony), pricing (Marriott Hotels), and quality (Motorola and Intel) to inform strategy. Therefore, while decision making has typically been viewed as the prerogative of key individuals, in practice it can also stem from rigorous analysis of collective facts within the firm. However, just because many organizations gather massive amounts of data, this does not mean that the data are sifted and systematically exploited to generate positive outcomes (Davenport, 2009). Ultimately, data must be processed to generate information and information then analysed to create knowledge that is of strategic value to the firm.

Sharing information and collaborative communities

Organizations and strategists need to decide how best to share available information and how it is used in decision making. How information is shared and the integrity of the data-collection process are key elements to consider. While it can be relatively easy to transfer hard data about finances or market penetration, some question whether the same is true of the intimate knowledge that employees have of processes and activities. 'Tacit knowledge' is knowledge gained through actual practice and experience, in contrast to more formal and explicit knowledge, which is codified in company documentation and policies. Nonoka and Takeuchi (1995) argue that the tacit knowledge that is embedded in organizational routines and activities can be shared through informal interactions, socialization activities, informal social events, and working in cross-functional teams. In addition, tacit knowledge can be externalized through stories that celebrate past successes or key organizational values. Yet, for some, the idea of a simple transfer of knowledge from the individual level to the aggregate organizational level is difficult. Davenport (1994) notes that there has been a tendency to glorify the role of information technology and ignore human psychology.

Essentially, assuming that people will willingly share information may be a flawed starting point. Profit motivation, the desire for recognition, and the career aspirations of strategists can mean that information and knowledge repositories within organizations become battlegrounds for internal power struggles rather than platforms for generating organizational advantage (Pfeffer, 1992). The old adage that 'knowledge is power' holds much relevance. Managers will rarely recommend killing projects when this might damage their reputations or endanger the livelihoods of their subordinates (Sull, 2010). This can become particularly detrimental when critical information about the realities of competitive conditions fails to reach the top of the organization (Neilson *et al.*, 2008: 65). It is important therefore for leaders to identify the key information flows within organizations and attempt to remove any barriers or blockages. This means that they may need to act as 'human sponges', absorbing news about value creation at different levels of the business (Nohria *et al.*, 2003). Key tasks may include shadowing key managers and processes, and working with front-line employees—as practised by Ray Kroc, founder of McDonald's, or as represented by Bill Hewlett and Dave Packard's management by walking about (MBWA) at HP—or ensuring that employees are well versed on the financial and operational objectives of the firm.

New ways of sharing information have been developed that foster working relations conducive to both knowledge creation and sharing in the form of 'collaborative communities/communities of practice' (Adler *et al.*, 2008; Brown and Duguid, 1991). This links with the idea that a firm should 'be understood as a social community specializing in speed and efficiency in the creation and transfer of knowledge' (Kogut and Zander, 1996: 503). Central notions here are interdependence and engagement with individuals, both committed to their key tasks and working together towards a common, but frequently ambiguous, goal (Mintzberg, 2009). Collaborative communities rely heavily on trust and, more widely, on the structure and quality of social relations among their members to create, share, combine, and integrate knowledge (Adler *et al.*, 2008). Perhaps unsurprisingly, this mode of organizing and knowledge sharing is common among scientific research teams and among professionals. Increasingly, however, it is cited as a useful template for fostering the type of innovative activity required of the knowledge-based era.

There are also some useful historical precedents concerning the benefits of disseminating knowledge. McGrath (2005), for example, explored the historical commonalities between the operation of early Irish monastic communities and knowledge-intensive firms, arguing that both required an open community and supportive infrastructure, pursued organic growth, and cultivated a unique sense of identity. Relying on autonomous units and communities also links to the idea of 'collective wisdom', whereby it is understood that 'a large group of individuals with diverse points of view will often reach a better final decision than a single expert' (Birkinshaw, 2010: 86). Of course, this mode of knowledge generation and sharing may not sit easily with command-and-control structures, or with an exclusive focus on generating hard data for a specific purpose. Clearly, knowledge management is not about managing knowledge, but about creating a culture conducive to knowledge sharing (Korac-Kakabadse *et al.*, 2002). However, a focus on communities of practice does help to communicate that what constitutes knowledge is always evolving and subject to change, while capturing the reality that it is also likely to be a key power resource for particular groups within organizations (Brown and Duguid, 1991; Nelson and Winter, 1982). It follows that the success of any structure or knowledge-sharing infrastructure will be contingent on the people to whom it is applied—that is, on their level of talent and their motivation to engage with strategy. This highlights the critical role of nurturing and enabling the appropriate talent in the quest for realizing advantage.

People: nurturing and enabling talent

Human capital is placed centre stage as the embodiment of organizational competencies (Wright and Snell, 1991). According to Barney (1991), an advantage's sustainability is based on the extent to which the resources are valuable, inimitable, rare, and exploited. This approach should mean that managing people and leveraging talent are central to strategy not only in terms of implementation, but also in terms of developing strategic capability and improving the long-term resilience of the firm (Boxall, 1996). According to Cappelli and Crocker-Hefter (1996), the fact that employment practices can become so embedded helps to reinforce the notion that core competencies should drive business strategy and not vice versa. They go as far as to argue that 'it may be easier to find a new business strategy to go with one's existing practices and competencies than to develop new practices and competencies to go with a new strategy' (ibid: 366).

Nonetheless, while it is commonplace to hear organizations claim that 'people are our greatest asset', the reality, as Jim Collins (2001: 13) put it, is that 'people are not your most important asset. The *right* people are'. Ultimately, the type of people an organization has in place will determine the success or otherwise of a given strategy. Consequently, talent management cannot be judged as an end in and of itself; it exists to support the organization's objectives (Cappelli, 2008: 3). Organizations know how to learn and adjust because people know how to learn and adjust (Jaffee, 2001). This is best captured by Hambrick (2004: 94):

> we need to reintroduce the human element to our research. During the last two decades, human beings have been largely discarded from a great part of strategic management research, as scholars have sought to anthropomorphize organizations, treating them as wilful, purposive entities.

Strategy and talent

This leads to the question of the relationship between strategy and talent. How should considerations of talent be best incorporated into strategy? Should strategy be the reserve of an exclusive elite within an organization, or should the linkages between strategy and talent stretch across the entire population of the organization? Consequently, what policies are most appropriate in motivating and incentivizing?

McKinsey coined the notion of a 'war for talent' in 1998 when it noted that demographic changes, globalization, and the rise of the knowledge-based worker were, at one and the same time, altering the expectations of executives and creating a shortage of talent pipelines in and through organizations. A huge underexploited resource within firms was dealing with underperformers (Chambers and Foulton, 1998: 57). The result was a call for organizations to conduct a talent audit of their organizations, to distinguish between top, middle, and low performers, and to use the organizations' brands in order to attract the best talent. The rigid allocation of performers into categories echoed the approach that Jack Welch had used at General Electric (GE). The result, reinforced by tight labour markets for executive talent, was that managing talent increasingly became seen as a top priority for organizations. At the same time, a supporting stream of research was emerging in human resource management (HRM) that directly linked investment in sophisticated human capital management practices to improved financial performance of the firm (for example, Huselid, 1995).

In order to ensure that talent pools are integrated with business strategy, organizations are encouraged to conceive of themselves as 'talent factories', so that they 'marry functionality, rigorous talent processes that support strategic and cultural objectives, and vitality' (Ready and Cogner, 2007: 70). This involves identifying high performers and creating routes for their promotion. Some sample questions developed by Ready and Conger (2007: 74) include the following.

- Do you know what skills your company needs to execute its growth objectives?
- Does your company have a process for identifying, assessing, and developing its next generation of leaders in all of its businesses and regions?

- Do you have a diverse and plentiful pool of leaders who are capable of moving into your organization's most senior executive roles?
- Do you hold your managers and leaders accountable for identifying and developing talent in their businesses, functions, and regions?

For each question, strategists are also asked to consider: 'What will you do to strengthen your company's capability in this area?' Nonetheless, despite the rhetoric and perceived importance of a focus on talent and talent management processes as a durable basis for advantage, recent research indicates that only 15 per cent of companies in North America and Asia, and 30 per cent of companies in Europe, believe that they have enough qualified successors for key positions (Fernández-Aráoz *et al.*, 2011).

Problems with talent management

There are problems with some of the approaches to talent management. For a start, fixed categories mean that only a few individuals can be classed as top performers—but what if the whole organization is performing well? A focus on individual performance seems to counter an emphasis on teamwork and collective contributions of the type discussed in relation to collaborative communities. Indeed, some organizations, such as Aviva, recognize the 'vital many' B players rather than focus on a select few A players (Delong and Vijayaraghavan, 2003). Equally critical, while the focus was originally very much centred on executive talent, it was increasingly recognized, including by McKinsey, that 'organisations can't afford to neglect the contributions of other employees' (Guthridge *et al.*, 2008: 56). This highlights some of the complexities in aligning strategy and talent management policies, even before one considers how talent is actually measured and the most appropriate time frame within which it might be assessed.

Nurturing talent

It is critical that an organization has a people proposition that motivates those working for the company to execute its strategy (Kim and Mauborgne, 2009: 75). There are different ways in which organizations can achieve such an alignment. The world's largest cement manufacturer, Cemex, gives prospective employees a two-month period in which to find a role in the company that will add value to their operations. Other organizations, such as the innovative company Semco, employ a long recruitment process to ensure adequate fit with the organization. Subsequently, hired talent gets to choose on what projects they should work and to which they can add most value (termed 'Let talent find its place'; Semler, 2001). Film-rental company Netflix is attempting to create a 'freedom and responsibility culture' by letting employees take as much annual leave as they like. However, at both Semco and Netflix, there is a clear performance agenda whereby employees who do not perform to the required standard are removed from their jobs (*The Economist*, 2011). Other organizations deploy rigorous recruitment testing to ensure cultural fit with the values of the organization (for example, Google), or use incentives to direct desired employee role behaviours (for example, Intel).

However, a focus on nurturing and developing individual talent in isolation may be problematic. Instead, some commentators have pointed to the importance of capabilities in evolving the appropriate infrastructure to develop and enable talent to excel (Ready and Conger, 2007: 69). A narrow focus on a few key individuals identified as high potential might be seen as a riskier strategy than a broader focus on organization-wide systems, culture, and processes for managing talent. Human resource knowledge management activities should function as the firm's strategic infrastructure in terms of generating and leveraging the entrepreneurial knowledge needed to sustain a firm's competitive advantages over time (Chadwick and Dabu, 2009: 264). Other commentators suggest that if strategy is stretched to include employees and organizational arrangements, it becomes virtually everything that a company does and of which it consists; by so doing, it loses focus and thereby meaning (Porter, 1997). Developing and nurturing talent within an organization are critical to the long-term sustainable development of an organization. However, it is also increasingly recognized that organizations can leverage the talent and knowledge of individuals beyond organizational boundaries, in particular through better understanding and interacting with customers.

Customer insights

Understanding and meeting your customer expectations on a consistent basis are at the core of successful execution. The primary purpose of a business is to acquire and keep customers (Kanter, 2009). The essence of strategy involves understanding who your key customers are and what they want. Success in strategy hinges on the development and alignment of value propositions that attract buyers (Kim and Mauborgne, 2009). Febo, the Dutch fast-food company, has to ensure consistency of product offering in terms of a 'perfect product, produced and presented and prepared'. This idea has been core to the development of strategy (Chapter 1), and forms the basis for organizational analysis (Chapter 6). At the same time, it is the key compass in capturing the routes of advantage available to organizations (Chapter 8). Nonetheless, despite this importance, traditional models of strategy generally treat customers as relatively passive, having predetermined impulses and demographics that can be easily documented and segmented. Customers have been subject *to*, rather than subjects *of*, strategy.

The customer experience

Quality and authentic customer experiences are an integral element of the value proposition in services industries. This approach has been adopted by other industries given the intense nature of competition, resulting in heightened awareness of the importance of having an appropriate infrastructure in place to support the desired customer experience (Lovelock, 1992). The importance of consumer interactions overlaps with structure and talent management, particularly in the context of service industries in which employees form the face of the organization. In such instances, providing employees with the appropriate knowledge, infrastructure, and empowerment to deal with customers' demands can be critical to the service encounter. In retail banking, the teller has all of the information about the customer readily available, including effective product awareness, and can reinforce the customer experience. In domains such as retail, exceeding customer expectations in customer service counters can serve as a critical differentiator, such as has been achieved by Waitrose in the UK. In a clinical setting, the products, dialysis services, and new treatment concepts provided by Fresenius Medical Care can improve the quality of life for patients.

Many organizations outsource or automate their more standardized interactions, such as ordering and checking bank balances. Most Fortune 500 companies have at least one call centre or contact centre. According to Quinn *et al.* (1996), organizations should retain their focus and concentrate on the limited few activities most desired by customers, in which they can excel by performing at top-class level. Some suggest that this is best done no longer by distinguishing between products and services, but instead by focusing on value as defined by the customer (Michel *et al.*, 2008). This comes from an understanding that any innovation in product or process requires changes to customer thinking, participation, and capabilities to create and realize value (Michel *et al.*, 2008: 50).

Customer empowerment

During the 1980s, the focus was on quality and customer service, but the advance of web and mobile technology has empowered customers even more. In turn, this has meant that organizations must have multiple customer platforms and product and service categories. In some competitive arenas, organizations need the ability to customize their offering for customers. The logic of mass production was turned on its head with organizations such as Dell developing the capability to customize products with the help of flexible technology and online ordering (England and Newton, 2001). In the knowledge-based era, the balance of power has shifted in favour of the customer compared to the traditional industrial era. Womack and Jones (2005) coined the term 'lean consumption', stressing the benefits of minimizing the customer's time and effort and delivering exactly what consumers want, when they want it. So, for example, traditional means of segmenting markets have altered, with organizations such as Tesco seemingly able to offer a full complement of formats to deal with a multitude of customer needs. These can range from local convenience stores (Tesco Express), to mid-size stores in town centres (Tesco Metro), to standard-size supermarkets in the suburbs (Tesco Superstore), to hypermarkets on the periphery (Tesco Extra), to web-based shopping (Tesco.com) (Womack and Jones, 2005).

Engaging with customers

Customer empowerment simply highlights the importance of having adequate contact with consumers and knowledge of what they value. In fact, Martin (2010) claims that, while recently executives may have made maximizing shareholder value their top priority, evidence from organizations such as Proctor and Gamble suggests that shareholders do better when firms put the customer first. This point is perhaps even more relevant given the ability of consumers to operate and communicate together through the forum of online blogs, social media, and social networking sites. These provide consumers with greater power, making it more important for corporations to pay attention to their needs, concerns, and complaints. A failure to have a web detection strategy that acts as a barometer for customer opinion can mean that negative attention and opinions quickly escalate, with damaging effects for the reputation of the organization. At the same time, focusing exclusively on existing consumers can limit the horizons and opportunities open to the organization. Bower and Christensen (1995) argue that organizations that pay too much attention to their existing customers in times of technological change will fail. Customers may well know what their needs are, but will often define those needs in terms of existing products, processes, prices, and markets (Hayes and Abernathy, 1980: 71). Consequently, Harrington and Tjan (2008: 70) argue that:

> front-end customer strategies must be continually re-evaluated and refined, because markets and competition can change so quickly. To execute an evolving strategy, we needed to have a flexible go-to-market plan and a well considered approach for rolling the strategy out across segments and businesses.

Of course, it is also important to remember that while customer satisfaction and accommodation are critical, their accomplishment must be underpinned by a sound strategy and not one that leads to unnecessary product proliferation, inflated costs, unfocused **diversification**, and a lagging commitment to investment in new capabilities (Hayes and Abernathy, 1980: 71). Clearly, in domains such as open software, the boundaries between customer and producer have become significantly blurred so that customers are integral to strategy formulation and development. Others caution that this is more the exception than the rule, and instead favour more traditional segmentations.

Harnessing the customer in the production process

Many organizations have developed sophisticated and complex e-commerce strategies designed to meet a variety of internal and external customer needs. The marketplace has become the 'marketspace' (Rayport and Svioka, 1994), with Hamel and Sampler (1998: 59) arguing that the Internet is a catalyst to 'break every business free of geographical mooring', thus leading to intensified competition and greater price transparency that would be to the benefit of the consumer. Evans and

Wurster (1997) draw attention to the increasingly 'sophisticated consumer' who uses online resources and information to inform his or her purchase decision. While the dot.com boom in the mid-1990s reduced the expectations of a total revolution, there can be little doubt that these developments have altered the way in which organizations interact with consumers (see also Chapter 12). This can entail managing customers, who are not simply consumers of a service, but can also be integral to its production (Frei, 2008). Many airlines have invested in self-service kiosks at airports, where the customer checks in, chooses his or her seat, and drops his or her luggage at a bag-and-tag point. Many also offer the facility for customers to check in online and arrive at the airport with a printed ticket. In doing this, the customer is involved in part of the production process that Frei (2008) describes.

Organizations and even whole industries (such as software) are experimenting with novel **business models** based on harnessing collective creativity through open innovation (Chesbrough and Appleyard, 2007: 57). One emerging online business model sees the majority of content given away free in order to gain an audience, for example Adobe. Here, the majority of revenue is sourced by the limited number of customers who pay for the premium version: 'after all, 1% of a big number can also be a big number' (Anderson, 2007: 129). Business models increasingly involve more devolution of tasks and empowerment of choice to consumers (Womack and Jones, 2005). In this context, increased emphasis is placed on cultivating relationships with customers and prospective customers rather than focusing on the marketing of a specific product or service (Rust *et al.*, 2010). The *process* of relationship building has supplanted a focus on the *content* of products/services.

Spotlight Client and company charters

In this chapter, we have seen the importance of effective engagement with customers in the execution of strategy. More and more organizations have developed customer charters to connect with customers, to reassure them, and to persuade customers of their commitment to them. In this spotlight piece, we look at two types of charter. The first is from NatWest and is a client-focused charter outlining the organization's commitments to the customer. It is designed to reassure customers about service levels, security, community support, and engagement with customers. Behind this charter lies a complex interaction between people, knowledge, and structures. NatWest publishes its performance as 'Customer Charter Results' based on these fourteen commitments (see http://www.natwest.com/global/customer-charter/g1/2010/jul-dec/results.ashx).

Our commitment to our customers

We want to become Britain's most helpful bank and our Customer Charter is key to achieving that goal. It continues to be our long-standing commitment to you, our customers, as we provide the services you want and need. Everything in it is based on the things that you have told us are important and we are committed to acting on them.

We don't expect to achieve everything immediately and we will be open about our progress. We also understand that over time, the things that are most important to you may change. So our Customer Charter commitments will be regularly reviewed by a representative panel of customers to make sure that everything we are doing stays relevant.

1. We will extend our opening hours in our busiest branches. During 2011 more than 650 branches will be open on Saturdays, while our 160 busiest branches will continue to open either early in the morning, or late in the evening. We will regularly review customer demand for longer opening hours.

2. We will serve the majority of customers within 5 minutes in our branches. This year we will serve 80% of customers within 5 minutes in our busiest branches.

3. We will provide you with friendly, helpful service whenever you deal with us. We are aiming for 9 out of 10 customers to rate our service as friendly and helpful.

4. We will help you to make the right choices for you and your money, providing a clear product range with simply explained features and charges In line with customer feedback, all of our branch literature, standard letters and key

web pages will be rewritten to make them simpler and easier to understand.

5. We will provide a 24/7 telephone banking service from our UK based call centres. All of our call centres will continue to be based in the UK and you will always have the option to speak to a real person.

6. We will work with you to keep you safe when you bank online and on your mobile device with us. We will provide free market-leading enhanced security software for all online banking users.

If you become a victim of fraud when banking with us online, or on your mobile phone, we promise to refund any money taken from your account in full, in accordance with our security promise published online.

7. We will help you quickly if your debit card is lost or stolen and you need access to cash. We will despatch all lost and stolen replacement debit cards the next working day by first class post. We will also offer a free emergency cash service through our ATMs to customers whose debit card is lost or stolen.

8. We will continue to be a responsible lender and are committed to finding new ways to help. We will send text messages when you register for our Act Now Alerts, helping you take action to avoid current account charges. We will not provide credit limit increases if we know you are struggling to meet payments on your credit card.

We will support first time buyers by always having mortgages available for up to 90% of the property value.

9. We pledge to stay open for business if we are the last bank in town and will consider a range of options to ensure a local banking service is available. We will continue to provide a local banking service wherever we are the last bank in town and will continue to serve more than 45 communities with our mobile banks.

10. We will provide young people with financial education through our independently accredited MoneySense programme. In 2011 we will deliver 19,000 MoneySense lessons in schools.

11. We will actively support the local communities in which we live and work. We are launching CommunityForce, a new initiative to support local communities, by donating time, expertise and £1.9m in funding. We will also offer all our employees a day of paid leave for local voluntary work and provide 7,000 days of community volunteering in 2011.

12. We will resolve customer complaints fairly, consistently, and promptly so that 75% of customers will be satisfied with the way their complaints have been handled.

13. Twice a year we will publish the most common complaints. And we will strive to address the causes.

14. We will actively seek your thoughts and suggestions on how we can become more helpful. We will continue our Customer Listening Programme to ensure our staff, including executives, hear first hand about the needs and frustrations of our customers.

(http://www.natwest.com/global/customer-charter.ashx)

The second charter is from Novo Group, a Danish multinational and a world leader in diabetes care. Its other product areas include haemostasis management (the treatment of haemophilia patients), growth hormone therapy, and hormone replacement therapy. Novo Group operates in seventy-four countries and employs 31,300 staff. Its charter takes a different approach by outlining the company characteristics, values, and commitments that are necessary for strategy execution in a organization operating in seventy-four countries. Given Novo Group's business areas and its scope of activities, articulating clearly the fundamentals of its activities is essential.

Charter for companies in the Novo Group

Present as well as future companies in the Novo Group must demonstrate willingness, ability and resolve to meet the following criteria:

- Company products and services make a significant difference in improving the way people live and work.
- The company is perceived to be the innovator—in technology, in products, in services and/or in market approach.
- The company is among the best in its business and a challenging place to work.
- The company delivers competitive financial performance.

Companies in the Novo Group commit to:

- Value-based management
- Open and honest dialogue with its stakeholders
- Continuous improvement of:
- Financial performance
- Environmental performance
- Social performance
- Reporting in accordance with relevant, internationally approved, conventions

(http://www.novo.dk/composite-646.htm)

Implications for strategy practice

One of the most fundamental issues of successful strategy execution is having an appropriate organizational structure that enables the organization to succeed. This is easy to say, but hard for a strategist and organization to do. Far too often, we see organizations that have articulated a strategy, but the structures of which are not aligned to deliver it. Strategists have to understand the limitations of different organizational structures and be aware of the broad strategic outcomes that can be achieved through adopting a certain organizational structure. In considering what structure to adopt, strategists have to consider the appropriate division of labour and how different groups will collaborate across the organization on the delivery of common objectives. Organizational structures have to be developed that enable smooth and effective interactions of people, knowledge, and customers. Strategists must also appreciate that deciding upon and designing an organizational structure is only the beginning rather than the end of execution activities.

In order to realize and maintain advantage, it is important to be continuously open to change. This involves taking on board employee voice, consumer wants, and stakeholder concerns. So how can this be done? By continuously collecting and assessing this information, the organization might be in a better position to deal with competitive threats and to seize on market opportunities. Pragmatically, this may involve ensuring that the talent flows within the organization do not become culturally homogeneous, which would risk fostering cloning and a similar outlook in assessing risks and markets. If organizations wish to avoid cultural homogeneity, they must attempt to have in place senior management teams composed of executives who are sensitive to multiple needs and different types of business. O'Reilly and Tushman (2004: 81) term this requirement as one of being 'consistently inconsistent'. This means that strategists must be open to different channels of knowledge and interact with a wide set of industry and organizational stakeholders.

In terms of specific skill sets, listening, adaptation, and a tolerance for critical questioning can be vital tools for strategists and essential resources to inform strategy execution. Strategists need to distil significant amounts of information and data, but should consider interactions in the context of delivering the best product or service to customers. Therefore the strategist has to continually assess whether the current alignment of structure, knowledge, and people with customers is making a sustained difference in the marketplace. More importantly, is there consistency in this alignment such that the customer experience has uniformity about it irrespective of where or in what form it is delivered? Technological and societal progress suggests that potential resources for this task can increasingly be found beyond as well as within the organization, in the form of online communities, networks, and by better integrating end users into strategy formulation and execution. A proficient strategist has an ability to integrate intuition with logical, analytical decision making; what distinguishes true strategic expertise is deliberation that is founded upon critical reflection (Flyvbjerg, 2001: 17). In part, this means being sensitive to the limitations of purely hard data. There is also a danger that strategists may not have access to timely data and may have to make decisions based on old data that is not context-specific. The intuition of the strategist will always influence interactions in implementing strategy.

Introduction to readings

Our first reading for this chapter, accessible via a link on the Online Resource Centre that accompanies this book, is by Jeffrey Pfeffer (1995) and represents a key statement in the evolution of HRM to an area of strategic significance. With typical force, Pfeffer notes how the source of competitive advantage has shifted over time to stress human resources over industry positioning and traditional economies of scale. In strategy terms, Pfeffer presents a somewhat different reading of the success of Southwest Airlines from that presented by Michael Porter in Reading 1.1. This leads to a key question: are the two accounts compatible or do they offer alternative accounts of the essence of competitive advantage? In terms of people management, Pfeffer depicts thirteen policies and practices that are said to characterize companies that are effective in achieving competitive success through how they manage people. Pfeffer makes the case for each practice by reference to examples from well-established, successful companies. But how well does his emphasis on how the practices fit together in a system come across in his analysis? He seems to suggest that these practices need not necessarily depend on the organization's particular competitive strategy; are there contradictions to this argument or does the logic of best practice in people management hold? Do environmental and cultural factors jeopardize job security, high wages, and internal promotion, or is it precisely because implementation of all of these practices remains rare that they offer the potential for advantage? In many ways, this a thought-provoking piece; at a minimum, it serves its purpose of bringing the idea of effective people management as a possible basis for advantage to centre stage in strategy conversations.

Reading 4.4, 'Configurations of strategy and structure: towards a synthesis' by Danny Miller (1986), takes on the strategy and structure debate in order to provide a more thorough treatment of this association. This overview starts off by arguing that the concepts 'strategy' and 'structure' have themselves been used in a very simplistic fashion. Critical of the methods and approach of previous work, Miller argues that strategy and organization often join in mutually reinforcing ways into new types. He then presents some ideal models of strategy building on classic studies. But what is the general utility of Miller's configurational approach? Does it advance previous efforts and what relevance will it hold for practice? Miller is very thorough in his analysis, but the text was written some twenty years ago, prior to the enhancement of technology, the development of the Internet, and the rise of networking and cooperative relationships: how well can Miller's ideal types deal with these new complexities? Miller suggests that change is rare unless forced or mandated by the extent of advantage that can be leveraged; is this quantum-leap understanding of change realistic in today's environment, or does it adequately depict the embedded nature and path dependency of existing structures?

Finally, Reading 4.5, 'The co-creation connection' by Prahalad and Ramaswamy (2002), which focuses on the role of the customer in value creation, depicts a paradigm shift from managing efficiencies to managing experiences. The authors argue that the consumer now has potential scope for inputting into all aspects of value chain activities rather than merely being the end point. But is this image of a paradigm shift too dramatic? Does it hold in all contexts and does it place too much power in the hands of consumers? Should consumers equally directly input into strategy making? If we follow Prahalad and Ramaswamy's consumer-centric logic, should it be the organization or its customers who define what industry a business is in? How do we decide which customers should exert the most influence and will this affect the eventual outcome? What are the key developments not incorporated in this article? Do they diminish or strengthen the argument proposed?

Mini case study The British Broadcasting Corporation's (BBC) Strategic Review: doing more with less?

In 2009, BBC director general Mark Thompson announced a cut in the numbers of senior managers and a suspension of bonuses. As Sweeney (2009) describes:

> More than 100 BBC managers are to be culled and the pay of the corporation's executive board, including director general Mark Thompson, frozen for a further three years as part of moves to reduce the corporation's £79 million executive remuneration budget by 25%. The measures come after sustained criticism of its executive pay policy from across the political spectrum ... The restructuring will see the number of senior managers at the BBC cut by 114 of the current 634.

In addition, pay freezes and suspension of bonuses were put in place. This announcement followed a previous one by Mark Thompson in October 2007, in which he announced plans to downsize the corporation through 1,800 redundancies, consolidation in news and programming output, and focusing more on quality output.

As the largest broadcasting corporation in the world, the BBC has developed an international reputation for its quality of journalism and news reportage. With its vision—'to be the most creative organization in the world'—its main responsibility is to provide public service broadcasting supported through a licence fee to the UK, Channel Islands, and the Isle of Man. The BBC has eight national television channels, BBC Red Button Interactive TV, BBC HD, ten national radio stations, forty-plus local radio stations for England, BBC Online, BBC iPlayer, BBC Mobile, a BBC channel on YouTube, and community channel TV. The BBC's World Service is broadcast worldwide in over thirty-two different languages and is funded by the UK Foreign and Commonwealth Office (BBC, 2010a). The BBC also has a significant online presence, with over 400 websites, but in line with the cutback in the corporation, the number of websites will be halved by 2012. Huggers (2010), director of BBC future media and technology, defended this cut in online presence:

> I know some have questioned the importance of this number ... however, tackling the symptom of a problem does provide a real incentive to change, and in meeting the

> tld [top level domain] challenge we are reviewing the entire site from top to bottom. As a result, we will be making some tough decisions about what we want to commit to in future, and what not to.

The BBC has a separate commercial ventures division, with public services such as BBC America and BBC World News.

During the summer of 2009, Mark Thompson announced that the BBC was undertaking a strategic review of its operations and activities, to position the corporation to respond to technological changes, changes in the media industry, and changes in resourcing. This was in response to the following questions posed by the BBC Trust (2010: iv–v).

1. How can the BBC best maintain quality and distinctiveness?
2. Where, if necessary, could the BBC's focus be narrow and its scale reduced?
3. What will a fully digital BBC look like?
4. Can the BBC better define the 'public space' that it provides?
5. How can the BBC create most value from its scale?

The four themes of the strategic review were focus, quality, efficiency, and market impact. In March 2010, as part of this strategic review, the BBC published *Putting Quality First: The BBC and Public Space*, in which it restated its core mission 'to enrich people's lives with programmes and services that inform, educate and entertain'. The objective of the strategy is to 'direct the BBC to put quality first; do fewer things better; guarantee access to all; make the licence fee work harder; and set new boundaries for itself'. In practice, this means moving to higher-quality content by reprioritizing over £600m a year, investing £50m to increase quality and originality, and from 2013 onwards to spend no less than 90p per £1 on quality content and its dissemination to audiences.

Not everyone agrees with the direction in which the BBC is heading. John Simpson, one of the BBC's top correspondents and its world affairs editor, expressed his fear for the future of the corporation for which he has worked for forty years:

> I'm very pessimistic about the future of the BBC. This is something that I really disagree about with Mark Thompson. When I saw him recently I argued it out. He's very upbeat about the future of the BBC, not just for public consumption but also in private, but I'm not, because I think it's an anomaly in today's world and the licence fee is under such an intense amount of pressure. I don't think British people understand what a huge voice the BBC gives this country in the world. That lays it open to endless attacks, usually on this ideological basis that it's a tax, plus all the usual nonsense about how it's left-wing, or indeed right-wing if you listen to other voices. It all seems quite childish to me, but nevertheless those voices are louder than they've been in my life, and I've watched these things for 44 years.
>
> (Quoted in Moss, 2010)

He is not alone: forty of the UK's best-known performers signed a public letter in April 2010 denouncing plans to cut what they describe as a 'cherished part of our national life'. Mark Thompson hopes, however, that there will be strong support from the BBC Trust and through public consultation for 'a BBC focused on high-quality content and enduring values, keeping open a public space for all' (BBC, 2010b: 3).

Sources: BBC Trust (2010); BBC (2010a; 2010b); Huggers (2010); Moss (2010); Sweney (2009)

Questions

1. Using Goold and Campbell's (2002) questions presented in this chapter, what organizational structure should the BBC adopt in order to create more value from its scale? What are the potential benefits to the organization and the public?

2. With the multiplicity of data that BBC collates on a daily basis, how should it share this information in building collaborative communities and, in doing so, maintain its quality and distinctiveness?

3. Will the cull of senior managers have an impact on the ability of the BBC to nurture and enable talent within the corporation?

4. 'A BBC focused on high-quality content and enduring values, keeping open a public space for all': how should the BBC engage its customers as both customers and potential producers?

Summary

This chapter has explored some of the key influences and subsequent complexities involved in both framing a strategic idea and seeing it through to execution. While many debates emerge, at its core the chapter highlights the importance of understanding key aspects of the strategy infrastructure and their interaction. Home Depot, for example, has excelled in the low-cost provision of do-it-yourself (DIY) merchandise. Its ability to realize advantage is attributable to its renowned customer service, and its policy of attracting and retaining the best talent, coupled with technological resources, such as electronic data interchange with vendors, rapid order replenishment, and an information infrastructure that includes a critical communication network linking stores and head office. The result is what Woiceshyn and Falkenberg (2008: 85) refer to as 'a value-creating alignment of strategy, resources and activities'. Unless organizations develop a similar complementary set of value propositions across key dimensions of the strategy infrastructure, they are 'unlikely to produce a high-performing sustainable strategy' (Kim and Mauborgne, 2009: 75). Such mutually reinforcing interactions are why Kaplan and Norton (2008: 64) stress that frequently underperformance comes from a breakdown of the 'management system' rather than a lack of ability or effort by strategists. This idea is neatly captured by the metaphor of an orchestra:

> an orchestra demands at least three things to render a fine performance: a comprehensive complement of talented musicians, an ability to play as a perfectly aligned unit, and an emphasis on the right musicians for the right compositions. In the corporate context, strategic integration—and the outstanding performance that accompanies it—demands all of these same qualities of comprehensiveness, alignment, and thematic emphasis.
>
> (Fuchs *et al.*, 2000: 119)

The notion of interactions helps to capture some of the key dynamics in realizing value, although how these play out in practice will be contingent on organizational circumstances and shaped by the power and influence of the key actors involved. Understanding key tensions is a critical part of the process, enabling strategists to become more conscious of the guiding principles used to run their organizations, particularly in cases in which such choices have not been made explicit (Birkinshaw, 2010: 21, 25). While strategists may see themselves as being on top in terms of an organizational structure, this does not necessarily mean that they are on top in terms of what takes place there (Mintzberg and Van der Heyden, 1999: 93). Matters are further complicated by the reality that it is increasingly difficult to isolate the precise boundary between value-creating activities conducted solely by and within the organization, and the value appropriated from the more general business ecosystem. This is particularly true where organizations operate as part of a dense network, where innovation is conducted openly across multiple actors, and where end customer influence extends the length of the value chain (Chesborough and Appleyard, 2007). It is also true when it comes to the management of critical strategists, staff, and those who may be linked to the organization through a variety of arrangements from partnerships, consultant roles, right down to contract employment through intermediaries (Marchington *et al.*, 2004). The emergence and accentuation of these trends have made the job of the strategist more complex, but equally have enhanced his or her palette of options. While machine-like arrangements characteristic of the past served to 'stifle initiative, creativity and diversity', in many ways 'that is their point' (Ghoshal *et al.*, 1999: 11). In moving the focus from efficiency and economies of scale to effectiveness and economies of experience, in the knowledge-based era, autonomy and innovation become the key weapons of competitive advantage, so that organizations need to embrace ambiguity by experimenting and adapting (Kanter, 2009: 67).

Overall, understanding how to best manage various interactions, balancing the need for exploitation of current competencies and exploration of future opportunities, is one of the key challenges facing strategists (Venkatraman and Subramaniam, 2002: 471). In essence, this means combining the merits of both: for example, having exploratory units separated from more traditional functions and allowing these units to operate by means of different structures, processes, and cultures. Here, strategists play a key role as the integrative function linking units at the top of the organization. Separation is managed through a tightly integrated senior management team, with the implication that 'an organization does not have to escape its past to renew itself for the future' (O'Reilly and Tushman, 2004: 76).

This helps bring us to an understanding that execution and the realization of value are an ongoing and continuous process, as opposed to series of one-off interventions. As Patel (2005: 69) notes, 'there is no such thing as an outcome in an absolute sense. Outcome is a transitory state and, as such, is simply a milestone in a flow of events. Master strategists see the flow of events and influence the flow'. Too often, the emphasis is on the content rather than the process of managing. This is why success for the strategist is as much about having a reflective mindset as a specific mode of being or fixed set of solutions (Burgelman and Grove, 1996). Indeed, this is one of the key reasons why paying due attention to interactions in realizing advantage may provide for a solid and non-imitable basis of advantage.

Discussion questions

1. A newly appointed CEO of a healthcare multinational wants advice on the importance of organizational structure in realizing advantage. Outline some key points that you would make and discuss potential challenges.

2. Review Goold and Campbell's (2002) nine criteria for assessing organizational structures. How easy would it be for an organization to answer these questions? What factors may facilitate/hinder such an evaluation?

3. Is talent critical to strategy? What can organizations do to ensure that they attract and retain the correct people?

4. Why might organizations find it so difficult to share information?

5. To what extent should customers be directly incorporated into the strategy formulation process?

6. Are each of the dimensions reviewed in this chapter simply operational tasks or do they have strategic significance? In what way can/should they inform strategy?

7. What role does the strategist play in ensuring that the interactions of structure, knowledge, people, and customers work in an effective manner?

Further reading

As an account of organizational structure, H. Mintzberg (1979) *The Structuring of Organizations*, Englewood Cliffs, NJ: Prentice Hall, still remains a classic and comprehensive overview of the forms, types, and configurations, while some twenty years later, in H. Mintzberg and V. D. Heyden (1999) 'Organigraphs: drawing how organizations really work', *Harvard Business Review*, 77: 87–94, he provides a fascinating and different account of how we conceive of organizations.

Many of the issues surfaced here resonate with those discussed in Julian Birkinshaw's (2010) *Reinventing Management*, Chichester: John Wiley and Sons. This is an excellent text, which uses the context of the financial crisis to rebuild a sense of what the purpose of management should be and the key dimensions that should be used to shape its key activities.

For a short, prescriptive, but yet insightful template for organizational success, based on an extensive and longitudinal research project examining the relationship between best practice and performance, see N. Nohria, W. Joyce, and B. Robertson (2003) 'What really works', *Harvard Business Review*, 81(7): 12–26.

For a comprehensive overview of the linkages between talent and strategy, see E. E. Lawler (2008) *Talent: Making People Your Competitive Advantage*, San Francisco, CA: Jossey-Bass.

visit the Online Resource Centre that accompanies this book to access more learning resources on this chapter topic at www.oxfordtextbooks.co.uk/orc/cunningham/

References

Adler, P. 1993. Time and motion regained. ***Harvard Business Review***, Jan/Feb: 97–108.

Adler, P., Kwon, S., and Heckscher, C. 2008. Professional work: the emergence of collaborative community. ***Organization Science***, 19(2): 359–376.

Anderson, C. 2007. Freeconomics. ***The Economist***. Special edn: 129–130.

Ansoff, I. 1987. ***Corporate Strategy: An Analytical Approach to Business Policy for Growth and Expansion.*** Rev'd edn. London: Penguin Books.

Bahrami, H. 1992. The emerging flexible organization: perspectives from Silicon Valley. ***California Management Review***, 34(4): 33–48.

Barney, J. 1991. Firm resources and sustained competitive advantage. ***Journal of Management***, 17(1): 99–120.

Bartlett, C. and Ghoshal, S. 1993. Beyond the M-form: towards a managerial theory of the firm. ***Strategic Management Journal***, 14: 23–46.

BBC Trust. 2010. BBC Strategy Review. Available online at http://downloads.bbc.co.uk/aboutthebbc/reports/pdf/strategy_review.pdf

Beckman, S. 2009. Introduction to a symposium on organizational design. ***California Management Review***, 51(4): 6–10.

Bernoff, J. and Schadler, T. 2010. Empowered. ***Harvard Business Review***, July/Aug: 95–101.

Birkinshaw, J. 2010. ***Reinventing Management***. Chichester: John Wiley and Sons.

Bower, J. and Christensen, C. 1995. Disruptive technologies: catching the wave. ***Harvard Business Review***, Jan/Feb: 43–53.

Boxall, P. 1996. The strategic HRM debate and the resource based view of the firm. ***Human Resource Management Journal***, 6(3): 59–75.

British Broadcasting Corporation (BBC). 2010a. About the BBC: mission and values. Available online at http://www.bbc.co.uk/aboutthebbc/purpose

British Broadcasting Corporation (BBC). 2010b. Putting quality first: the BBC and public space—proposal to the BBC Trust. Available online at http://www.bbc.co.uk/aboutthebbc/future/strategy_review.shtml

Brown, J. S. and Duguid, P. 1991. Organizational learning and communities of practice: toward a unified view of working, learning and innovation. ***Organization Science***, 2(1): 40–57.

Bryan, L. L. and Joyce, C. L. 2007. ***Mobilizing Minds: Creating Wealth from Talent in the 21st Century.*** New York: McGraw-Hill.

Burgelman, R. A. 1983. A model of the interaction of strategic behaviour, corporate context and the concept of strategy. ***Academy of Management Review***, 8(1): 61–70.

Burgelman, R. A. and Grove, A. 1996. Strategic dissonance. ***California Management Review***, 38(2): 8–28.

Cappelli, P. 2008. Talent management for the twenty first century. ***Harvard Business Review***, Mar: 1–8.

Cappelli, P. and Crocker-Hefter, A. 1996. Distinctive human resources as a firms' core competencies. ***Organizational Dynamics***, 24(3): 7–22.

Chadwick, C. and Dabu, A. 2009. Human resources, human resource management, and the competitive advantage of firms: toward a more comprehensive model of causal linkages. *Organization Science*, 20(1): 253–272.

Chambers, E. and Foulon, M. 1998. The war for talent. *McKinsey Quarterly*, 3: 44–57.

Chan, J., Beckman, S. L., and Lawrence, P. G. 2007. Workplace design: a new managerial imperative. *California Management Review*, 49(2): 6–22.

Chandler, A. D. 1962. *Strategy and Structure*. Cambridge, MA: MIT Press.

Chesbrough, H. and Appleyard, M. 2007. Open innovation and strategy. *California Management Review*, 50(1): 57–76.

Christensen, C. and Raynor, M. 2003. Why hard-nosed executives should care about management theory. *Harvard Business Review*, 81(9): 66–74.

Collins, J. 2001. *Good to Great: Why Some Companies Make the Leap—and Others Don't*. New York: Harper Business.

Davenport, T. 1994. Saving IT's soul: human centered information management. *Harvard Business Review*, 72(2): 119–141.

Davenport, T. 2006. Competing on analytics. *Harvard Business Review*, Jan: 2–10.

Davenport, T. 2009. Make better decisions. *Harvard Business Review*, Nov: 117–125.

Delong, T. and Vijayaraghavan, V. 2003. Let's hear it for B players. *Harvard Business Review*, 81(6): 96–101.

Drucker, P. F. 1988. The coming of the new organization. *Harvard Business Review*, Jan/Feb: 45–53.

The Economist. 2011. Special report on the future of jobs: got talent. 10 September, p. 12.

England, S. and Newton, I. 2001. Special report: mass customisation—a long march. *The Economist*. 12 July.

Evans, P. and Wurster, T. S. 1997. Strategy and the new economics of information. *Harvard Business Review*, Sept/Oct: 70–82.

Ferlie, E. and Pettigrew, A. 1996. Managing through networks. *British Journal of Management*, 7: 581–599.

Fernández-Aráoz, C. Groysberg, B., and Nohria, N. 2011. How to hang on to your high potentials. *Harvard Business Review*, 89(10): 76–83.

Flyvbjerg, B. 2001. *Making Social Science Matter: Why Social Inquiry Fails and How It Can Succeed Again*. Cambridge: Cambridge University Press.

Frei, F. X. 2008. The four things a service business must get right. *Harvard Business Review*, Apr: 70–80.

Fuchs, P., Mifflin, K., Miller, D., and Whitney, J. 2000. Strategic integration: competing in the age of capabilities. *California Management Review*, 42(3): 118–147.

Galbraith, J. and Nathanson, D. 1978. *Strategy Implementation: The Role of Structure and Process*. St Paul, MN: West Publishing.

Ghoshal, S., Bartlett, C., and Moran, P. 1999. A new manifesto for management. *Sloan Management Review*, 40(3): 9–20.

Goold, M. and Campbell, A. 2002. Do you have a well designed organization? *Harvard Business Review*, 80(3): 117–24.

Grant, R. M. 1996. Towards a knowledge theory of the firm. *Strategic Management Journal*, 17: 109–122.

Gregen, K. 1992. Organization theory in the postmodern era. In M. Reed and M. Hughes (eds) *Rethinking Organization: New Directions in Organization Theory and Analysis*. London: Sage.

Guthridge, M., Komm, A., and Lawson, E. 2008. Making talent a strategic priority. *McKinsey Quarterly*, 1: 48–59.

Hall, D. and Saias, M. 1980. Strategy follows structure! *Strategic Management Journal*, 1(2): 149–163.

Hambrick, D. 2004. The disintegration of strategic management: it's time to consolidate our gains. *Strategic Organization*, 2(1): 91–98.

Hamel, G. 2000. *Leading the Revolution*. Boston, MA: Harvard Business School Press.

Hamel, G. and Sampler, J. 1998. The e-corporation. *Fortune*, 7: 52–63.

Harrington, R. and Tjan, A. 2008. Transforming strategy: one customer at a time. *Harvard Business Review*, Mar: 62–72.

Hayes, R. H. and Abernathy, W. 1980. Managing our way to economic decline. *Harvard Business Review*, July/Aug: 67–77.

Huggers, M. 2010. Erik Higger: the BBC's 400 websites. *The Guardian*, 29 March.

Huselid, M. A. 1995. The impact of human resource practices on turnover, productivity, and corporate financial performance. *Academy of Management Journal*, 38(3): 635–672.

Jaffee, D. 2001. *Organization Theory: Tension and Change*. Boston, MA: McGraw-Hill.

Kanter, E. M. 2009. What would Peter say? *Harvard Business Review*, Nov: 65–70.

Kaplan, R. and Norton, D. 2006. How to implement a strategy without disrupting your organization. *Harvard Business Review*, 84(3): 100–109.

Kaplan, R. and Norton, D. 2008. Mastering the management system. *Harvard Business Review*, Jan: 63–77.

Katzenbach, J. and Khan, Z. 2010. Leading outside the lines. *Strategy + Business*, 59: 1–10.

Kim, C. and Mauborgne, R. 2009. How strategy shapes structure. *Harvard Business Review*, Sept: 73–80.

Kogut, B. and Zander, U. 1996. What do firms do? Coordination, identity, and learning. *Organization Science*, 7: 502–518.

Korac-Kakabadse, N., Kouzmin, A., and Kakabadse, A. 2002. Knowledge management: strategic change capacity or the attempted routinization of professionals? *Strategic Change*, 11: 59–69.

Laseter, T. 2009. An essential step for corporate strategy. *Strategy + Business*, 57: 16–24.

Lawlor, E. E. 2008. *Talent: Making People Your Competitive Advantage*. San Francisco, CA: Jossey-Bass.

Lovelock, J. 1992. *Managing Services: Marketing, Operations, and Human Resources*. Upper Saddle River, NJ: Prentice Hall.

Marchington, M., Grimshaw, D., Rubery, J., and Wilmott, H. 2004. *Fragmenting Work: Blurring Organizational Boundaries and Disordering Hierarchies*. Oxford: Oxford University Press.

Martin, R. 2010. The age of customer capitalism. *Harvard Business Review*, Jan/Feb: 58–65.

McGrath, P. 2005. Thinking differently about knowledge intensive firms: insights from early medieval Irish monasticism. *Organization*, 12(4): 549–566.

Michel, S., Brown, S., and Gallan, A. 2008. Service-logic innovations: how to innovate customers, not products. *California Management Review*, 50(3): 49–65.

Miles, R., Miles, G., Snow, C., Blomqvist, K., and Rocha, H. 2009. The I-form organization. *California Management Review*, 51(4): 61–76.

Miles, R., Snow, C., and Pfeffer, J. 1974. Organisation-environment: concepts and issues. *Industrial Relations*, 13(Oct): 244–264.

Miller, S., Wilson, D., and Hickson, D. J. 2004. Beyond planning: strategies for successfully implementing strategic decisions. *Long Range Planning*, 37(3): 201–218.

Mintzberg, H. 1979. *The Structuring of Organizations*. Englewood Cliffs, NJ: Prentice Hall.

Mintzberg, H. 1994. *The Rise and Fall of Strategic Planning*. New York: Free Press.

Mintzberg, H. 2003. The structuring of organizations. In H. Mintzberg, J. Lampel, J. B. Quinn, and S. Ghoshal (eds) *The Strategy Process: Concepts, Contexts, Cases*. Harlow: Pearson Education.

Mintzberg, H. 2009. Rebuilding companies as communities. *Harvard Business Review*, July/Aug: 140–143.

Mintzberg, H. and Van der Heyden, L. 1999. Organigraphs: drawing how organizations really work. *Harvard Business Review*, 77: 87–94.

Moss, S. 2010. John Simpson: 'I'm very pessimistic about the future of the BBC'. *The Guardian*, 15 March. Available online at http://www.guardian.co.uk/media/2010/mar/15/john-simpson-bbc-murdoch-journalism

Neilson, G., Martin, K., and Powers, E. 2008. The secrets to successful strategy execution. *Harvard Business Review*, June: 61–70.

Nelson, R. and S. Winter. 1982. *An Evolutionary Theory of Economic Change*. Cambridge, MA: The Belknap Press of Harvard University.

Nohria, N., Joyce, W., and Robertson, B. 2003. What really works. *Harvard Business Review*, 81(7): 12–26.

Nonaka, I. 1991. The knowledge creating company. *Harvard Business Review*, 69(6): 96–104.

Nonaka, I. and Takeuchi, H. 1995. *The Knowledge-Creating Company: How Japanese Companies Create the Dynamics of Innovation*. New York: Oxford University Press.

O'Reilly III, C. and Tushman, M. L. 2004. The ambidextrous organization. *Harvard Business Review*, 82(4): 74–81.

Palmer, I. and Hardy, C. 2000. *Thinking about Management*. London: Sage.

Patel, K. 2005. *The Master Strategist: Power, Purpose and Principle*. London: Arrow Books.

Pfeffer, J. 1992. Understanding power in organizations. *Californian Management Review*, 34(2): 29–50.

Piore, M. J. and Sabel, C. F. 1984. *The Second Industrial Divide: Possibilities for Prosperity*. New York: Basic Books.

Porter, M. 1997. Letters to the editor: Michael Porter replies. *Harvard Business Review*, Mar/Apr: 162–163.

Powell, T. C. 1997. Information technology as competitive advantage: the role of human, business, and technology resources. *Strategic Management Journal*, 18(5): 375–405.

Quinn, J. B. 2005. The intelligent enterprise: a new paradigm. *Academy of Management Perspectives*, 19(4): 109–121.

Quinn, J. B., Anderson, P., and Finkelstein, S. 1996. Leveraging intellect. *Academy of Management Executive*, 19(4): 78–94.

Rayport, J. F. and Svioka, J. 1994. Managing in the marketspace *Harvard Business Review*, Nov/Dec: 141–150.

Ready, D. and Cogner, J. 2007. Make your company a talent management factory. *Harvard Business Review*, June: 68–77.

Rosenzweig, P. 2007. *The Halo Effect ... and the Eight Other Business Decisions that Deceive Managers.* New York: Free Press.

Rucci, A., Kirn, S., and Quinn, R. 1998. The employee customer profit chain as Sears. *Harvard Business Review*, Jan/Feb: 82–97.

Rust, R., Moorman, C., and Bhalla, G. 2010. Rethinking marketing. *Harvard Business Review*, Jan/Feb: 94–101.

Semler, R. 2001. How we went digital without a strategy. *Harvard Business Review*, Sept/Oct: 51–98.

Shrivastava, P. 1986. Is strategic management ideological? *Journal of Management*, 12(3): 363–377.

Snow, C., Raymond, M., and Miles, G. 2005. A configurational approach to the integration of strategy and organization research. *Strategic Organization*, 3(4): 431–439.

Soo, C., Devinney, T., Midgley, D., and Deering, A. 2002. Knowledge management: philosophy, processes and pitfalls. *California Management Review*, 44(4): 129–150.

Stace, D. and Dunphy, D. 1991. Beyond traditional paternalistic and developmental approaches to organizational change and human resource strategies. *International Journal of Human Resource Management*, 22(3): 263–284.

Strikwerda, J. and Stoelhorst, J. 2009. The emergence and evolution of the multidimensional organization. *California Management Review*, 51(4): 11–31.

Suchman, M. 1995. Managing legitimacy: strategic and institutional approaches. *Academy of Management Review*, 20(3): 571–610.

Sull, D. 2010. Competing on agility. *McKinsey Quarterly*, Dec: 1–9.

Sweney, M. 2009. BBC to sack 114 bosses and freeze board's pay. *The Guardian*, 29 October. Available online at http://www.guardian.co.uk/media/2009/oct/29/bbc-senior-managers-pay-freeze

Venkatraman, N. and Subramaniam, M. 2002. Theorizing the future of strategy: questions for shaping strategy research in the knowledge economy. In A. Pettigrew, H. Thomas, and R. Whittington (eds) *Handbook of Strategy and Management*. London: Sage.

Walker, J. W. 1992. *Human Resource Strategy.* New York: McGraw-Hill International Editions.

Waterman, R. H., Peters, T. J., and Philips, J. 1980. Structure is not organization. *Business Horizons*, June: 14–26.

Woiceshyn, J. and Falkenberg, L. 2008. Value creation in knowledge-based firms: aligning problems and resources. *Academy of Management Perspectives*, 22(2): 85–99.

Womack, J. P. and Jones, D. 2005. Lean consumption. *Harvard Business Review*, Mar: 59–68.

Worley, C. and Lawler, E. E. 2010. Agility and organization design: a diagnostic framework. *Organizational Dynamics*, 39(2): 194–204.

Wright, P. M. and Snell, S. 1991. Towards an integrative view of strategic human resource management. *Human Resource Management Review*, 1(3): 203–205.

Section 4 readings

Introduction

In this section, we focused on the critical task of how organizations attempt to realize advantage.

- **Reading 4.1** by Robert Simons, on 'Strategic orientation and top management attention to control systems' (1991), offers a valuable perspective on the levers of implementation and the dynamic role that control systems can play in directing attention to key areas of strategic significance, both in terms of strategy formulation and implementation.
- The balanced scorecard is used by many organizations in their attempts to reach higher levels of competitive performance. In **Reading 4.2** by Robert Kaplan and David Norton, on 'Transforming the balanced scorecard from performance measurement to strategic management' (2001), the authors highlight the importance of viewing the organization as a strategy system, and of devising measures of strategy implementation that can be both retrospective and forward-looking.
- In **Reading 4.3** on 'Turning great strategy into great performance' (2005), Michael Mankins and Richard Steele outline some common barriers that can prevent successful strategy execution.

These readings serve to highlight the vital, yet complex, realities of strategy implementation.

- In **Reading 4.4** on 'Configurations of strategy and structure: towards a synthesis' (1986), Danny Miller deals with an important issue in strategy: strategy and structure. This interaction between strategy and structure impacts on strategy execution. This is an ongoing debate in strategy; in practice, the organizational structure is often not designed to deliver the intended strategy.
- Finally, **Reading 4.5** on 'The co-creation connection', by C. K. Prahalad and Venkatram Ramaswamy (2002), highlights the importance of leveraging knowledge outside of the organization as a route to developing strategy that is more likely to realize advantage.

While often neglected, the readings in this section highlight that a focus on realizing advantage should be a central and ongoing concern for strategists.

Reading 4.1 Strategic orientation and top management attention to control systems *Robert Simons*

First published: (1991) *Strategic Management Journal*, 12(1): 49–62. 'Strategic Orientation and Top Management Attention to Control Systems', Robert Simons, *Strategic Management Journal*, Volume 12, Issue 1, 1991. Reproduced with the kind permission of John Wiley and Sons Ltd.

Introduction

Management control systems are viewed typically as tools of strategy implementation. The research reported in this paper departs from this perspective by exploring the circumstances under which managers use control systems as catalysts for new strategic initiatives. An empirical study of 30 businesses in one U.S. industry is used to model and illustrate how top managers use formal systems *interactively* in different strategic settings to focus organizational attention and learning, and thereby shape the formation of new strategies.

In this study, management control systems are defined broadly as the *formalized routines and procedures that use information to maintain or alter patterns in organizational activity* (Simons, 1987a). These systems include formalized information-based processes for planning, budgeting, cost control, environmental scanning, competitor analysis, performance evaluation, resource allocation, and employee rewards.

Management control systems are usually described as information feedback systems (Green and Welsh, 1988; Giglioni and Bedeian. 1974). Goals are set in advance, outcomes are compared with preset objectives, and significant variances are reported to managers for remedial action and follow-up (Anthony, Dearden, and Bedford, 1989: Chapter 1). In this description of the management control process, strategy is a constraint: strategies are approved (if not developed) by top managers, plans are communicated downward through the organization, and formal systems are used to inform top managers if actions or outcomes are not in accordance with intended plans. Since control systems are a primary tool for management-by-exception, systems of this type may be labeled *diagnostic control systems*.

Recent research has indicated, however, that control systems are not always used to manage by exception. In certain circumstances, top managers use control systems far more actively on a day-to-day basis to intervene in organizational decision-making. Based on the amount of top management attention directed to a control system, a management control system can be labeled as *interactive* when top managers use that system to *personally and regularly involve themselves in the decisions of subordinates*.

When systems are used interactively, four conditions are typically present (Simons. 1987b: 351–352):

1. information generated by the management control system is an important and recurring agenda addressed by the *highest levels of management*;

2. the process demands *frequent and regular attention* from *operating managers* at all levels of the organization;

3. data are interpreted and discussed in face-to-face *meetings of superiors, subordinates, and peers*; and

4. the process relies on the *continual challenge and debate* of underlying data, assumptions, and action plans.

Through intensive and focused top-management attention on a specific control system, signals are provided to the entire organization to guide information gathering and the search for understanding. As participants throughout the organization respond to the interactive management control process to set agendas to challenge and assess new information and action plans, new strategic initiatives are likely to emerge. Thus, by using a control system interactively, top managers can guide organizational learning and thereby unobtrusively influence the process of strategy-making throughout the firm (Figure [4.1.1]).

In a pilot study that preceded the current research, a model was developed to illustrate that the choice of systems to be used interactively depends on an assessment of *strategic uncertainties* by top managers (Simons, 1990). Strategic uncertainties do not relate typically to what the firm already knows how to do well, i.e. its critical success factors (Daniel, 1966); rather, strategic uncertainties refer to contingencies that could provide throats or opportunities as circumstances change (Daft *et al.* 1988). Top managers focus their attention on strategic uncertainties that could derail their vision for the future and use selected systems interactively to focus the attention of the entire organization on these uncertainties.

Most of today's medium and large businesses have similar control systems: planning systems, budgeting systems, project management systems, human resource systems, and cost accounting systems are commonplace. Recent research suggests that top managers choose from this array to make a very limited number of control systems interactive and use the remaining control systems diagnostically (and thereby limit top-level involvement to periodic or exception-based reviews) (Simons, 1990). Moreover, top managers in different strategic settings appear to make different choices as to which systems to use interactively and which to use diagnostically.

The question pursued in this study, therefore, is whether systematic forces cause, top managers to focus their attention on certain control systems in specific strategic settings.

The current study

Objectives and sample selection

The concept of top managers choosing to use a limited subset of systems interactively and using the remaining systems diagnostically was developed during an intensive field study at Johnson & Johnson, a large company in the health care products industry (Simons, 1987b). With the objective of obtaining a comprehensive industry sample to identify how top managers in competing firms use management control systems, Johnson & Johnson's (top managers provided a list of nineteen companies considered to be significant competitors.

The nineteen companies are all large, publicly held, and profitable; all compete in the health care products industry with varying degrees of focus on consumer products (e.g. personal health care and beauty products), professional products (e.g. equipment for health care professionals and hospitals), and over-the-counter and prescription drugs.

Figure 4.1.1 Process model of relationship between business strategy and management control systems

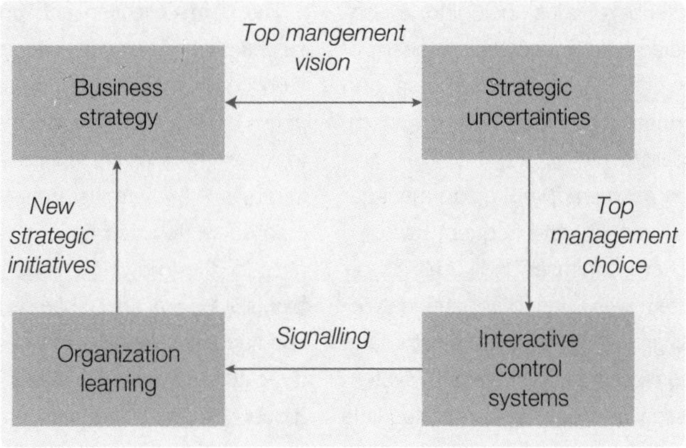

While these firms are direct competitors, each has chosen to compete in different ways: some by low price, some by product innovation, some by brand marketing, and some by seeking protected niches. Since these firms are followed closely by investment analysts and the business press, it was possible to obtain independent analyses of company history, strategy, and performance spanning many years.

Based on the model presented in Figure [4.1.1], the research was designed to gather data from each of these firms to assess (1) each firm's current strategy, (2) top management's sense of future direction for the business and related strategic uncertainties, (3) how their control systems were configured, and (4) the extent to which any control system received a disproportionate amount of top management attention. Of the nineteen firms contacted, sixteen agreed to participate in the research (Table [4.1.1]).

Data gathering and analysis procedures

The unit of analysis for the study is the business unit where the responsibility for strategy rests. In highly focused companies the entire firm is one business and the responsibility for strategy rests with the topmost level of management. In more diversified companies, several business units are included in the sample since responsibility for business strategy was located in individual business units. Thus, the sixteen companies yielded data on thirty business units (hereafter referred to as businesses).

Interviews were scheduled with top, policy-making managers (e.g. president and top business unit managers) in the companies that agreed to participate. On average, five interviews with top managers and their direct subordinates were conducted in each company. Other data used in the analysis included investment analyst reports, business press articles, annual reports, internal company documents supplied by interviewees, and, in some cases, personal observation while attending company meetings.

Interviews, which averaged two hours in length, were based on an interview schedule intended to gather information on company history, background of the interviewee, current strategy of the business, business strengths and weaknesses, direction for the future, major uncertainties relating to continuing success, and the interviewee's use of management control systems. During discussions of management control systems, particular

Table 4.1.1 Participating companies

American Home Products Corporation
Baxter Travenol Laboratories, Inc.
Becton-Dickinson and Company
Bristol-Myers Company
Chesebrough-Pond's Company
Colgate-Palmolive Company
Johnson & Johnson
Kimberly-Clark Corporation
Eli Lilly and Company
Marion Laboratories, Inc.
Merck & Co., Inc.
Pfizer Inc.
Smith Kline Beecham Corporation
Squibb Corporation
Tambrands Inc.
The Upjohn Company
Warner-Lambert Company

emphasis was placed on the individual's perception of the importance of specific management control systems to himself, his superior, and subordinates, including: allocation of time to various systems; frequency and intensity of data review; participation of superiors, subordinates, and peers in discussing information provided by the system; and the role of staff specialists.

A system was *classified as interactive* if a top manager reported that his personal, regular, and frequent use of a system was a top priority both for himself and for his subordinates, and that this system was used to set agendas for regular interlocking meetings with direct subordinates and others to review data) and resulting action plans. A system was *classified as diagnostic* if a top manager reported little personal involvement with it, delegated the operation of the system to staff groups or lower-level managers, and relied on others to inform him when his attention to the system was required. During follow-up interviews, subordinates independently confirmed the importance that superiors attached to certain systems. Similarly, they also confirmed when their superiors paid minimal attention to most other systems.

Although this research design treats systems as either interactive or diagnostic, these labels represent two extremes of a continuum of top management attention. Nevertheless, ascertaining which systems were interactive in each firm was relatively straightforward. Top managers described the high priority and personal attention that they attached to specific systems. In many cases, agendas were produced to illustrate the frequency with which meetings were scheduled throughout the organization to discuss the information provided by these systems. Illustrative reports were close at hand and were brought out often during discussions. When prompted, these managers responded that they personally involved themselves very little in the non-interactive, diagnostic systems.

Recognizing that the same system may be classified as interactive in one business and diagnostic in other businesses is important in understanding the results of this study. Profit planning, for example, was highly interactive at Johnson & Johnson and several other businesses in the sample; the revision and re-estimation of profit plans by operating managers throughout the year was intense and continuous.[1] In most other businesses in the sample, however, profit planning was clearly diagnostic. After the annual budget was approved by top management it was not revised during the ensuing year, and was used instead as a performance target to be monitored by staff groups and reported to top management on an exception, diagnostic basis.

The data collection and analysis proceeded in several stages. After field work was completed in eighteen of the thirty businesses the data were summarized into nine categories developed by adding two additional categories (strategic uncertainties and success) to the well-known 'seven S' framework (Waterman, Peters, and Phillips, 1980). Thus, detailed written descriptions were prepared for each business for the following categories: systems, strategy, structure, skills, style, staff, shared values, strategic uncertainties, and success. Next, businesses that used similar interactive management control systems (the 'systems' variable) were grouped together and the attributes of each group were studied to identify commonalities among the remaining eight variables. This analysis led to preliminary configurations that were then tested and refined during data collection and analysis of the remaining twelve businesses in the study.

Finally, after the field work was complete, the total data set for all thirty businesses was reanalyzed using the '9-S' framework. A draft research report was prepared and sent to managers in each of the thirty businesses for comment. Responses were received from top managers in seventeen of the businesses and evaluated to ensure that the reported theory and configurations were in line with their experiences.

Results

What types of systems are used interactively?

Data analysis reveals that top managers of thirty businesses in the health care products industry choose among five different types of control systems to use interactively. The five systems are:

1. *Program management systems*. This type of management control system monitors discrete blocks of organizational activity, typically on a project basis. New programs or projects focus on ways of improving product attributes, on ways of improving workflow processes, and on various types of basic and applied research programs. Critical path analyses, Gantt charts, and other types of milestone planning and analysis are typical in these systems.

2. *Profit planning systems*. These management control systems focus on individual business units and encompass annual profit plans or budgets, second-year forecasts, strategic operating and financial plans, and long-range plans. Stated in financial terms, and supported by analysis and action plane, these systems report planned and actual revenues and expenses for each major business by revenue and cost-category.

[1] Johnson & Johnson's interactive profit planning systems are described in detail in Simons (1987b) and (1987c).

3. *Brand revenue budgets*. These systems report in detail on a subset of the information contained in profit plans described above. Brand revenue budgets focus exclusively on revenue by brand. Brand revenue data are decomposed into unit volume and price by market segment, type of packaging, and promotion campaign. Market share data and shipment data by brand are also typically included in these systems.

4. *Intelligence systems*. These management control systems gather information about the social, political, and technical environments of the business. Industry data are purchased: legislative groups based in key policy-making capitals file weekly intelligence and lobbying reports; top managers solicit briefs and position papers in advance of industry meetings. This information—as well as information from political speeches, scientific and trade journals, and annual reports of competitors—is compiled in data bases, disseminated, and monitored regularly throughout the organization.

5. *Human development systems.* These management control systems include long-range strategic manpower systems, management-by-objectives systems, career planning and counselling systems, and succession planning systems. These systems establish an inventory of skills and management potential, and monitor the development plans of selected employees.

When do top managers use specific control systems interactively?

The detailed results of the study are described below by reference to three propositions. Figure [4.1.2] presents an overview of the analysis.

Proposition 1. Top managers with a clear sense of strategic vision choose one management control system to use interactively

Top managers in seventeen businesses in the sample used only one of the five different types of management control systems interactively; all other management control systems in each business were used diagnostically. Top managers of these businesses were able to articulate a clear sense of how they believed their businesses would compete and evolve in the future; in each case the top manager's choice of which system to use interactively related to strategic uncertainties that he attached to the business's future, i.e. to perceived competitive attributes of envisioned product markets. The strategic orientation of the firms that used each type of interactive system are described below.

Interactive program management systems (three businesses or 10 percent of total sample)

The three businesses in this cluster were currently, or aspired to be, low-cost producers in their industry. Two of these businesses competed in high-volume, low-price, disposable products categories—what managers referred to as 'tonnage' businesses. The third business was a consumer business with considerable marketing skill and a long-standing orientation to low-cost production. Over the years, however, the low-cost position had been achieved by failing to respond to product quality innovations of competitors. The current top manager was determined to maintain the business's low-cost position while, at the same time, improving the performance features of its well-known consumer products.

New programs and related information systems were developed in these businesses to analyze the cost and features of competitor products, to assess product performance and customer needs, and to investigate the potential impact of emerging technologies on existing product lines and production processes. Top managers made program management systems interactive by their continual personal involvement in helping to establish new programs and milestones, weekly or bi-monthly reviews of progress and action plans, and regular follow-up of new information.

The strategic uncertainties perceived by top managers in these businesses related to the ability to deliver product feature advantages to customers. A continuing concern for these managers was ensuring that their organizations maintained the capabilities to pre-empt a technological end-run by competitors. They worried about missing changes in customer needs caused by fundamental technological innovations that could undermine their current or future ability to deliver cost-effective products to customers.

These managers used program management systems interactively to challenge the organization to develop new products and process improvements that would enable their businesses to achieve or maintain low-cost advantages. As one top manager explained:

> One of my key jobs is to identify which should be the key programs—to emphasize these and de-emphasize everything else. I really work those programs and everyone understands that. People get frustrated with me because I am the world's worst planner, but they don't realize that the real plans are laid into those programs.

Each of these three businesses was functionally organized, yet programs bridged functional boundaries to involve people in all parts of the organization. The time horizon for programs tended to be fairly long, i.e. a year or more since changes in one product often affected other integrated

Figure 4.1.2 A framework for choosing interactive management control systems in the US healthcare products industry

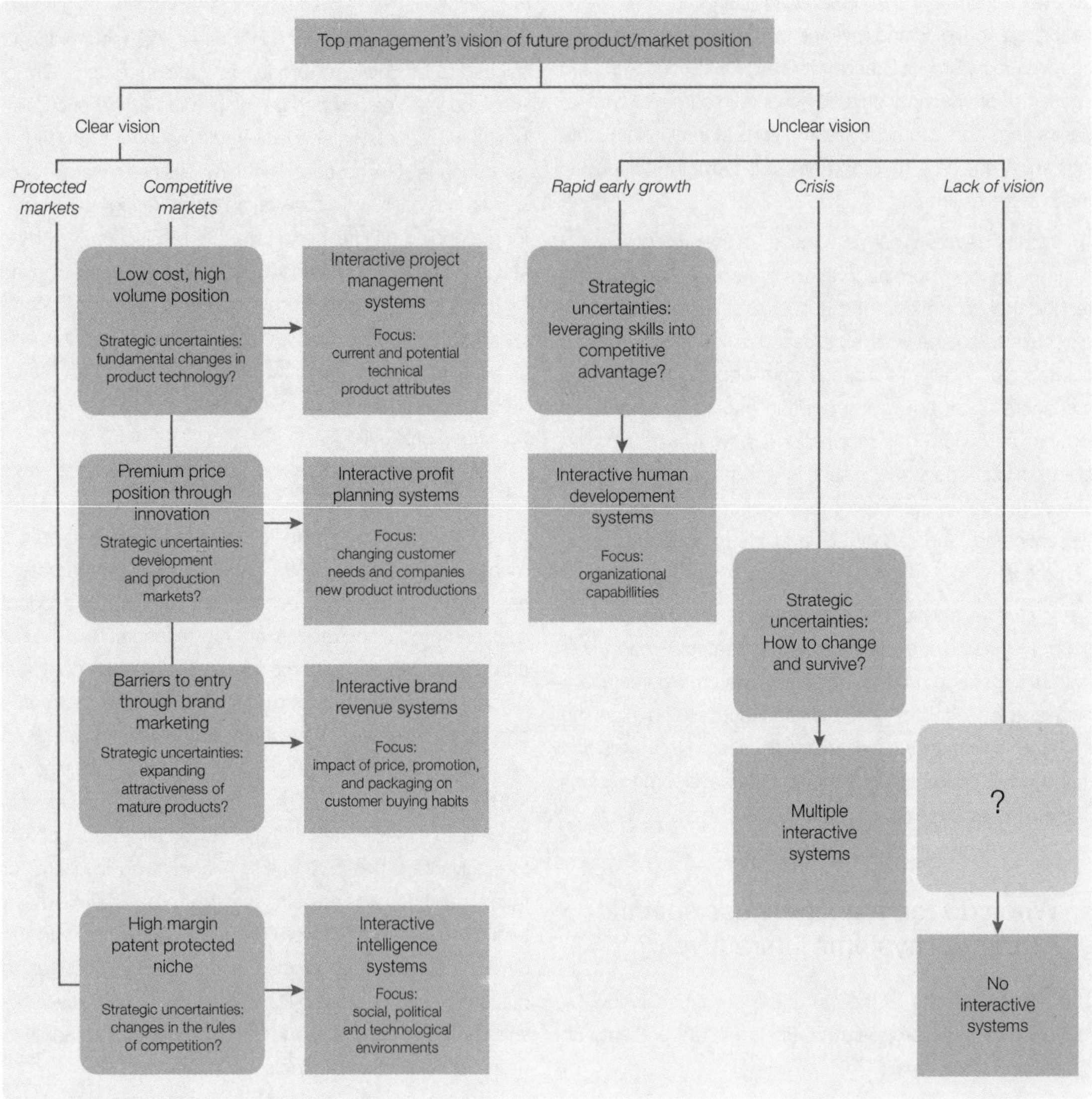

product lines. The competitive environment of these businesses was relatively stable, with a limited number of large competitors and product technologies that were relatively easy to understand.

Interactive profit planning systems (five businesses or 16.7 percent of total sample)

The common denominator for these five businesses was the desire to compete through product and market innovations. Four of the businesses already had reputations for product innovation: two supplied health care products to professional users; two competed primarily in consumer markets. All four had strong capabilities in marketing and in product development. At the fifth business, a consumer business that was not perceived in the industry as innovative, top managers were making a concerted effort to reorient the business to emphasize new product development.

The competitive environment for these businesses changes rapidly and is often difficult to comprehend because of complex product technologies and a diversity of competitors attempting to erode market leadership positions. Time horizons for new product and market introductions are relatively short (6–12 months) as new products and marketing programs are rolled out to pre-empt or to react to the offensive moves of competitors. Because of rapidly changing markets the relevant horizon for long-range plans is typically quite short (e.g. 3 years).

The strategic uncertainty for top managers that use interactive profit planning is: how can we develop proactive tactics to establish and maintain positions of market leadership through high-price/high-value products? For these managers a primary concern is to stimulate the organization to be an innovation leader and thereby forestall the advance of diverse and hostile competitors. Ongoing product development is essential since barriers to entry are often low and start-up businesses, with new technologies and low overheads, are often able to compete effectively.

Managers of these businesses spend a great deal of time debating and adjusting profit plans during the year. Top managers are continually revising and discussing profit commitments with subordinates. Although financial planning and budget data are used to frame the discussion, the debate centers on the effects of competitor actions, the timing and success of new product roll-outs and withdrawals, changing customer needs, and consideration of appropriate responses to new market opportunities and threats. Driven by the recurring profit planning cycle with its bottom-up revisions of revenue and expense estimates, managers throughout the organization use profit plans as a regular forum to develop and present now action plans and strategies.

Businesses that use interactive profit planning are decentralized to allow close Working relationships with their rapidly changing markets. The interactive profit planning systems, therefore, often play an important integrating role in these decentralized organizations. The role of the corporate controller's office in profit planning is limited, and operating managers assume personal responsibility for using and overseeing the profit planning system data.

Interactive brand revenue budgeting (six businesses or 20 percent of total sample)

> Every week, month, and quarter, I review each brand's sales in units and dollars. I look for downward trends and, equally important, for signs of unusual vitality. If a brand starts doing something, I get interested. What have we done that's new? Have we changed the packaging to say something new to the consumer?

Interactive brand revenue budgets focus organizational attention on unit volume and price for each brand category. Top managers in those businesses are intensely interested in following information related to volume in units and dollars, and total sales. Any trends or unanticipated changes animate a search for understanding.

The businesses that employed interactive brand revenue budgeting compete by selling mature products and brands. These managers are expert at exploiting strong brand franchises and extending product life cycles for seemingly indefinite periods. Four of the six businesses are consumer-oriented. Their strategy is to maintain brand loyalty at all costs: the main levers are price, promotion, and packaging. These businesses do very little product innovation, although they can be highly effective in marketing extensions of existing product lines.

The other two businesses in this group are successful research-based, ethical pharmaceutical businesses in difficult positions. The problem facing top managers in these businesses was that no major new products would reach market until the next decade.[2] Accordingly, the strategy of top managers was to focus on aggressive marketing of existing brands to hold up earnings until new products arrive in the 1990s.

For top managers who have chosen to use brand revenue budgets interactively, strategic uncertainties focus on new ways of exploiting brand franchises and extending the life cycle of mature products. Because, of high barriers to entry created by strong brand franchises, these businesses tend to face only a few major competitors. Competitor actions, however, cause relative market share positions to change rapidly.

Information provided by the brand revenue budgets frames the discussion agendas for top managers, brand managers, and other subordinates who interact regularly throughout the organization. Market share and shipment data are critical real-time indicators of tactical threats and opportunities. Decision horizons are extremely short—typically 1 or 2 months. These businesses can mount advertising and promotion campaigns, modify product packaging, and change pricing strategies quickly to defend their market share against competitor attacks. Because product/market decisions are reactive and rapid, top managers reported little interest in planning more than 2 years into the future.

The businesses in this category are organized on a brand structure basis with each brand having its own marketing capabilities and sharing manufacturing and administrative functions. These businesses have very strong, powerful, and centralized finance and control functions. These staff functions ensure tight expenditure control to maximize cash flows and allow reinvestment in promotion and advertising. This tight, diagnostic control by staff groups compensates for top management's singular, interactive focus on brand revenues and relative inattention to elements of cost.

[2] The position of these businesses is not unusual in a market segment where competitors can go a decade or more without a new product 'hit'. One pharmaceutical business reported being in a similar situation in the 1970s and employing similar strategies and management control procedures until new products came to market.

Table 4.1.2 Factors affecting design of interactive management control systems in competing firms in the US healthcare products industry

Interactive system design variable	Determinant		
		High	Low
System focus	Technological dependence of business	Focus on emerging new technologies	Focus on changing customer needs
	Regulation and market protection	Focus on socio-political threats and opportunities	Focus on competitive threats and opportunities
Measurement	Value chain complexity	Use of accounting-based measures	Use of input/output unit-based measures
Time horizon	Ease of tactical response by competitors	Short planning horizon	Long planning horizon

Discussion

How do top managers in competitive markets decide which of their various control systems to use interactively? How, for example, do managers choose among program management systems, profit planning systems, and brand revenue systems?

From analysis of the fourteen businesses described above, three interrelated factors appear to influence the design and choice of interactive control systems in competitive markets: technological dependence within product markets, complexity of the value chain, and the ability of competitors to respond to product market initiatives, These factors affect the focus of the interactive System, the types of measures used interactively, and the time horizon for decision-making (Table [4.1.2]).

Systems focus Some markets are highly dependent on a given set of technologies. Businesses competing in these markets are forced to follow technological developments in the field carefully (e.g., hospital equipment). The more dependent a business or industry segment is on a given technological base, the more imperative it becomes for managers to protect competitive advantage (or disrupt the advantage of competitors) by focusing attention on potential new ways of applying technology (e.g., Interactive Program Management Systems). On the other hand, where technological dependence is low or diversified across products, customers tend not to be locked to any one product concept; top managers can focus attention instead on finding unique ways of responding to customer needs through new products or new ways of marketing existing products (e.g., through Interactive Brand Revenue Systems or Interactive Profit Planning Systems).

Measurement Managers of businesses with complex value chains (e.g., those with ongoing product innovation in multiple markets) must monitor many trade-offs across product lines and markets: inputs, production, distribution, and sales and marketing tend to be linked in complex and dynamic ways. For these businesses, control systems that use accounting-based measures (e.g., Interactive Profit Planning Systems) provide. essential indicators of threats and opportunities since these systems highlight the effects on the overall business of changing combinations of variables. By contrast, managers of businesses with stable, well-understood value chains (e.g., mature consumer brands) have far fewer complex trade-offs to manage. They can, therefore, reduce the level of complexity by focusing organizational attention on simpler input and output measures such as brand volume and share (e.g., Brand Revenue Budget Systems).

Time horizon The final factor that appears to influence how systems are used interactively in competitive markets is the ability of competitors to respond quickly to a firm's product market initiatives. If copying a competitor's tactics is easy, the planning horizon will be extremely short. Tactical responsiveness, rather than planning, becomes the key to winning (e.g., interactive brand revenue budgeting systems). If emulating the strategic initiatives of competitors is difficult due to technological or market constraints. Planning horizons can be longer (e.g. interactive program management systems; interactive profit planning systems).

The above discussion focused on businesses operating in competitive markets. A different set of factors appears to influence the choice of interactive systems in businesses that are positioned in protected markets. These are considered next.

Interactive intelligence systems (3 businesses or 10 percent of total sample)

The firms in this group comprise highly focused, research-based pharmaceutical businesses. These businesses engage in a niche strategy by identifying potentially profitable therapeutic drug classes and focusing research and development resources exclusively in these areas. Since public and governmental goodwill is essential for these businesses to maintain credibility in the regulatory and political process and with customers, top managers in these businesses spend more than half their time monitoring and discussing social and environmental issues.

Managers worry less about competitors and more about government legislation, regulators, changes in health-care technology, and shifts in social sentiment. The strategic uncertainties for these top managers relate to changes in the 'rules of the game'. These businesses typically enjoy high margins derived from patent-protected products, and have a great deal to lose if the rules of competition change. Long lead times make significant changes in strategy and product development emphasis difficult and costly.

Interactive intelligence systems gather and disseminate data to help managers understand and, when possible, influence the complex social, political, and technical environments of their businesses. Industry data are purchased, analyzed, and discussed; legislative groups based in Washington and other key policy-making capitals file weekly intelligence and lobbying reports; computerized data bases are used to compile information from political speeches, scientific journals, trade journals, and annual reports of competitors; and top managers seek leadership positions in industry associations and require employees to prepare briefs, tactics, and positions papers in advance of industry meetings.

The formal systems that support these activities are used actively by top managers to motivate participants throughout the organization to scan the environment for emerging trends, to identify and assess new technologies, and to gather intelligence to attempt to influence political discourse.

The time horizon for product market decisions in these businesses is extremely long—typically 5–10 years—as potential new products go through exhaustive clinical tests and regulatory examination. Environments, while complex and difficult to understand because of sophisticated technologies, are relatively stable with new competitors in each market niche. Therefore, these businesses are able to do sophisticated, diagnostic, long-range planning based on the timing of regulatory milestones for new products.

Since control of research is fundamental to the long-term success of these high-margin businesses, the research and finance staff groups in these businesses are large and powerful. The strong and heavily-funded research units, which assume primary responsibility for allocating basic research funds, are centralized and report directly to top managers. Accountants and auditors in the finance group are given responsibility to monitor the diagnostic program management and budgeting systems to ensure that subunits are operating within predetermined resource allocation limits.

Discussion

The seventeen firms described above all used one control system interactively. Managers of these businesses had a clear sense of how they believed their businesses would evolve in the future: some in competitive markets and some in protected markets.

Top managers in two additional businesses (6.7 percent of total sample) also used one control system interactively. In these cases, however, visions for the future were emerging rather than clear. Top managers of these businesses were using their human resource systems to generate a dialog about how their businesses should evolve as they expanded rapidly into new and unknown markets. In one business, sales and head count had increased dramatically over the past several years and the trend was expected to continue. The other business had made a strategic decision to enter international markets. Based on a new worldwide strategy, this business was hiring foreign nationals around the world to manage these new, geographically based business units.

Long-range strategic manpower systems, management-by-objectives systems, career planning and counseling systems, and succession planning systems were a principal concern for these managers and absorbed a disproportionate amount of their time. Because these human development systems were used interactively to promote a dialog throughout the organization, participants were continually discussing what kind of people should be identified for greater responsibility. Indirectly, and perhaps more importantly, these discussions were really about how the organization should evolve in the future. The annual report of one of these businesses had as its theme 'The Management of Change.' The top manager of this business confided, 'we really don't know what the business will look like in fifteen years.' Top managers had a sense of urgency and were counting on new ideas, strategies, and visions to emerge from the introspective debate that was framed by the interactive human development systems. As one manager stated:

> Our success depends on the evolution of those businesses and getting the right people; therefore, management of human resources is a primary focus. I spend a lot of time trying to transfer our philosophy through evaluations and counselling interviews. My primary concern is to get more and more people under our culture. I have to be less concerned about product development and financial results.

> These things will take care of themselves if the organization is working well. The only thing that I bring is attention to process. At the moment, human resources are my most critical concern.

Proposition 2. Top managers use multiple control systems interactively only during short periods of crisis

While top managers of the businesses described above used only one control system interactively, top managers in another six businesses (20 percent of total sample) were using *all* categories of control systems interactively. These were businesses in transition—undergoing revolutionary change as contrasted to the evolutionary changes discussed in the previous group.

Three of these businesses faced crises due to failed strategies and resultant losses. The strategic focus for top managers of these businesses was survival and the strategic uncertainty was: how do we change?

Top managers in each of these businesses focused their attention on formal management control processes to activate organization learning and new strategies. One business developed a highly interactive management control system called 'Back on track.' Meeting weekly, key managers and their subordinates throughout the organization developed ideas, goals, action plans, and evaluated results that focused on new products and processes, ways to boost revenue or cut costs, changes in the competitive environment, and the need to reduce, head counts while at the same time hiring new types of expertise. The short-term result of this effort was a 20 percent staff reduction, a 25 percent overhead reduction, a 12 percent productivity gain, and a 6 percent increase in volume. A similar approach was taken by one of the other two businesses in crisis: in this case the interactive management control system was termed '(Company name) on the move.' The process and results of the exercise for this business were similar.

A new top manager was hired to run the third business in crisis. In an attempt to focus the organization on change, the new manager's approach was to make all management control systems interactive. Existing management control systems that had previously been used diagnostically were made interactive to create a sense of urgency in the organization. At the same time, these systems allowed the new top manager to learn the critical aspects of the business and to form impressions about the strengths and weaknesses of the people around him. A similar response was observed in firms four and five—two successful businesses where new top managers had recently taken over responsibility for the business.

In the final business within this category, top managers used multiple interactive management control systems to stimulate thinking throughout the organization about how to rationalize a major merger that had just been completed. Again, the issue was: how to change? Top managers in this business were using all their formal control systems interactively for the period necessary to figure out what to do. Because of the merger, performance benchmarks had been lost, shared values disintegrated, and choices had to be made as to which employees and systems to retain and which 10 let go. Suddenly, performance-objective systems, budgets, executive-development systems, planning, and program-management systems all became highly interactive. As one of the top managers described:

> We have had these systems for a long time. What is new is that we're really paying attention to them. Our managers are being asked to simultaneously change a lot and do it all well—consolidate operations; cut head count; improve quality; boost sales and earnings; develop new products. Right after the merger, we started taking management objectives very seriously.

For the six businesses in transition, the use of multiple interactive systems lasted for 8–12 months. Once crises began to subside, top managers removed themselves from active involvement in multiple interactive control processes. Instead, top managers began concentrating on pulling their vision for the future in place, and chose one control system to use interactively and began to use other systems on a diagnostic, management-by-exception basis.

Discussion

Why do top managers not use all management control systems interactively? Organizations in transition—where all systems are interactive—report incredible stress as employees are pushed to their limits to respond to the short-term information and action demands of superiors. Top managers begin monitoring and asking questions about information that many subordinates do not fully understand. Managers throughout the organization are forced to divert attention from other tasks to respond to the new information requests. Attempting to focus intensively on all management control systems for extended periods risks information overload, superficial analysis, a lack of perspective, and potential paralysis. Not only is there a limit to the organization's energy and attention, intensive focus on all systems does not allow top managers to send clear signals throughout the organization as to what they consider to be the strategic uncertainties inherent in their vision for the future—the main purpose of using a system interactively.

Proposition 3. Top managers without a strategic vision (or an urgency to create a strategic vision) do not use control systems interactively

In five businesses (16.7 percent of total sample), top managers did not use any control system interactively; all systems were used in a traditional diagnostic basis. Each had a different story. One business was small and the top manager was able to manage by interpersonal contacts with colleagues. A second business was a commodity producer that sold most of its output to a sister subsidiary; this business was effectively sheltered from the competitive marketplace. In the third business the top manager said that he did not have, an overall strategy or sense of the future for his organization, stating that strategies must come from the bottom of the organization and it was not his job to manage too closely.

The top manager of the fourth business worried that the business did not have a clear sense of direction. He had recently announced a strategic-growth-initiative program that was intended to provide strategic focus through better strategic planning, a new system of monthly budget reviews for newly formed strategic business units, and more emphasis on management development and succession planning. Before these system changes could be put in place, however, the corporate parent of this business announced that the business would be sold.

The fifth business was experimenting with state-of-the-art management systems, but none of these systems were used interactively. Powerful staff groups were installing the latest strategic management systems including portfolio management techniques, PIMS data bases, and integrated strategic planning systems. The top manager, however, declined to involve himself in either these systems or related committees. Managers in the organization expressed frustration:

> In theory, the planning is pretty good; the problem is that the planners don't understand the mechanics of the operations. There are books and books to be filled out—it is just unbelievable. Many people in this business are confused as to who is the boss. Sometimes we send memos to the Strategic Review Committee or to the Operating Review Committee and I don't think they understand who is giving orders in this business. We are drifting—giving power to committees. Direction should come from the top.

Discussion

Why are management control systems not interactive in some businesses? Generalizing from these five cases is difficult, but when organizations are small or shielded from the need to develop market strategies, there is probably little benefit in making selected systems interactive. More generally, when top managers of large businesses do not have a vision for the future or a sense of urgency about creating such a vision—they do not appear to make control systems interactive.

Conclusion

The relationship between strategy and management control systems has been depicted consistently in the research literature for many years: management control systems are used to implement the strategies developed by top managers. Questions about this relationship arise, however, when strategy is viewed as an incremental and emergent process (Mintzberg, 1978; Quinn, 1980). How do top managers direct subordinates to develop, champion, and implement sound strategies (Bourgeois and Brodwin, 1984)? How do top managers 'control' a grassroots, bottom-up strategy process (Mintzberg and McHugh, 1985)? How do top managers shape the strategic context in which autonomous strategic behavior can flourish (Burgelman, l983a,b)?

While control systems may appear to be similar across settings (budget documents are remarkably similar in different companies), this study suggests that there are fundamental differences in the way that policy-making managers use control systems. It appears that top managers do not spend a lot of time monitoring the critical success factors associated with current strategies. Contrary to accepted theory, top managers of low-cost, high-volume businesses, for example, do not pay a great deal of attention to efficiency-related controls, such as cost accounting systems (e.g. Miles and Snow, 1978: 48). The parameters for these critical success factors are well understood throughout the organization, and can be monitored effectively by periodic attention to goal-setting and diagnostic, exception-based reporting. Instead, top managers focus on systems that produce and monitor information on the strategic uncertainties that are associated with their visions of the future.

The choice of interactive systems by top managers sometimes appears counterintuitive. Why, for example, do top managers of businesses competing through product innovation choose to use profit planning interactively? Why do managers of low-cost firms focus on program management systems? In each case the chosen system gathers data on strategic uncertainties, is simple to understand, and cascades throughout the organization. The interactive control system is used to stimulate face-to-face dialog and build information bridges among hierarchical levels, functional departments, and profit centers. In the literature, budgeting is often associated with bureaucracy, research inflexibility, and stable product markets. This study suggests that profit planning, when used interactively, can be a proactive and dynamic tool to gather information and stimulate discussion in decentralized businesses about the effects of demographic market changes, competitor actions, and new product roll-outs. Similarly, program management systems can be effective dynamic tools to build information bridges in functionally organized, low-cost firms where top managers worry about the impact of technology changes on customer product needs.

The choice by top managers to use a control system interactively instead of diagnostically represents an element of strategic choice (Child. 1972) not previously recognized in the research literature. Since organization attention is limited (Simon, 1976: 294), top managers must decide what to emphasize and what to de-emphasize. By using selected control systems interactively and others diagnostically, top managers can signal where organizational attention and learning should be focused; this systematic focusing allows top managers to guide the emergence of action plans and new strategic initiatives. Thus, top managers are engaged in a second-order process—a process of choosing among organizational processes.

Traditional diagnostic systems, which top managers monitor on an exception basis, are oriented to implementing past and present strategies. These controls are designed to tell top managers when things are wrong, when actions are not in accordance, with plans. But this is the easy part. The trick is sensing when conditions are right for seizing new opportunities and shifting direction—this is the purpose of using selective control systems interactively.

The results of this study suggest that top management vision is the essential ingredient for interactive, management control systems. It is top managers, after all, who decide which formal processes to use interactively and which to use diagnostically, based on their sense of purpose for the organization and their personal assessment of associated strategic uncertainties. Although it is outside the scope of this paper, it was evident from the data gathered during this study that top management's assessment of strategic uncertainties may change as businesses mature, move into new markets, or react to changes in their environment. Crises may develop. A new top manager may bring a new vision to the organization. With each of these changes, systems that were previously interactive may be de-emphasized and used diagnostically, and other system made newly interactive.

Top managers understand that formal process is often essential to foster dialog from which new ideas and action plans can emerge. Interactive control systems are used by top managers to guide the informal strategy-making process by forcing personal involvement, intimacy with the issues, and commitment (Mintzberg, 1987). Using selective control systems interactively is a way of organizing attention, as distinct from a way of organizing people; as such, it is a powerful tool in guiding and energizing the competitive evolution of the firm.

References

Anthony, Robert N., John Dearden and Norton M. Bedford. *Management Control Systems*, 6th edn, Irwin, Homewood, IL, 1989.

Bourgeois, L.J., III and David R. Brodwin. 'Strategic implementation: Five approaches to an elusive phenomenon', Strategic *Management Journal*, 5(3), 1984, pp. 241–264.

Burgelman, Robert A. 'A process model of internal corporate venturing in the diversified firm', *Administrative Science Quarterly*, June 1983a, pp. 223–244.

Burgelman, Robert A. 'Corporate entrepreneurship and strategic management: Insights from a process study', *Management Science*, December 1983b, pp. 1349–1364.

Child, John. 'Organizational structure, environment and performance: The role of strategic choice', *Sociology*, January 1972, pp. 1–22.

Daft, Richard L., Juhani Sormunen and Don Parks. 'Chief executive scanning, environmental characteristics, and company performance: An empirical study', *Strategic Management Journal*, 9(2), 1988, pp. 123–139.

Daniel. D. Ronald. 'Reorganizing for results', *Harvard Business Review*, November–December 1966, pp. 96–104.

Giglioni, Giovanni B. and Arthur G. Bedeian. 'A conspectus of management control theory: 1900–1972', *Academy of Management Journal*, 17(2), 1974, pp. 292–305.

Green, Stephen G. and M. Ann Welsh. 'Cybernetics and dependence: Reframing the control concept', *Academy of Management Review*, 13(2), 1988, pp. 287–301.

Miles, Raymond E. and Charles C. Snow. *Organizational Strategy, Structure, and Process*, McGraw-Hill, New York, 1978.

Mintzberg, Henry. 'Patterns in strategy formation', *Management Science*, 24(9), 1978, pp. 934–948.

Mintzberg, Henry. 'Crafting strategy', *Harvard Business Review*, July–August 1987, pp. 66–75.

Mintzberg, Henry and Alexandra McHugh. 'Strategy formation in an adhocracy', *Administrative Science Quarterly*, June 1985, pp. 160–197.

Quinn, James B. *Strategies for Change: Logical Incrementalism*, Irwin. Homewood, IL, 1980.

Simon, Herbert A. *Administrative Behavior*, 3rd edn, Free Press, New York, 1976.

Simons, Robert. 'Accounting control systems and business strategy: An empirical analysis', *Accounting, Organizations and Society*, 12(4), 1987a, pp. 357–374.

Simons, Robert. 'Planning, control, and uncertainty: A process view', In W. J. Bruns and R. S. Kaplan (eds). *Accounting and Management: Field Study Perspectives*, Harvard Business School Press, Boston, MA, 1987b.

Simons, Robert. 'Codman & Shurtleff: Planning and control system', Harvard Business School Case Clearing #9-187-081 with teaching note #5-188-029, 1987c.

Simons, Robert. 'The role of management control systems in creating competitive advantage: New perspectives', *Accounting, Organizations and Society*, 15(1/2), 1990, pp. 127–143.

Waterman, Robert H., Jr, Thomas J. Peters and Julien R. Phillips. 'Structure is not organization', *Business Horizons*, June 1980, pp. 14–26.

Reading 4.2 Transforming the balanced scorecard from performance measurement to strategic management: part I *Robert S. Kaplan and David P. Norton*

First published: (2001) *Accounting Horizons*, 15(1): 87–104. Reproduced with the kind permission of American Accounting Association.

Several years ago we introduced the Balanced Scorecard (Kaplan and Norton 1992); we began with the premise that an exclusive reliance on financial measures in a management system is insufficient. Financial measures are lag indicators that report on the outcomes from past actions. Exclusive reliance on financial indicators could promote behavior that sacrifices long-term value creation for short-term performance (Porter 1992; AICPA 1994). The Balanced Scorecard approach retains measures of financial performance—the lagging outcome indicators—but supplements these with measures on the drivers, the lead indicators, of future financial performance.

The balanced scorecard emerges

The limitations of managing of solely with financial measures, however, have been known for decades.[1] What is different now? Why has the Balanced Scorecard concept been so widely adopted by manufacturing and service companies, nonprofit organizations, and government entities around the world since its introduction in 1992?

First, previous systems that incorporated nonfinancial measurements used *ad hoc* collections of such measures, more like checklists of measures for managers to keep track of and improve than a comprehensive system of linked measurements. The Balanced Scorecard emphasizes the linkage of measurements to strategy (Kaplan and Norton 1993) and the cause-and-effect linkages that describe the hypotheses of the strategy (Kaplan and Norton 1996b). The tighter connection between the measurements system and strategy elevates the role for nonfinancial measures from an operational checklist to a comprehensive system for strategy implementation (Kaplan and Norton 1996a).

Second, the Balanced Scorecard reflects the changing nature of technology and competitive advantages in the latter decades of the 20th century. In the industrial-age competition of the 19th and much of the 20th centuries, companies achieved competitive advantages from their investment in and management of tangible assets such as inventory, property, plant, and equipment (Chandler 1990). In an economy dominated by tangible assets, financial measurements were adequate to record investments on companies' balance sheets. Income statements could also capture the expenses associated with the use of these tangible assets to produce and profits. But by the end of the 20th century, intangible assets became the major source for competitive advantages. In 1982, tangible book values represented 62 percent of industrial organizations' market values; ten years later, the ratio had plummeted to 38 percent (Blair 1995). By the end of 20th century, the book value of tangible assets accounted for less than 20 percent of companies' market values (Webber 2000, quoting research by Baruch Lev).

Clearly, strategies for creating value shifted from managing tangible assets to knowledge-based strategies that create and deploy an organization's intangible assets. These include customer relationships, innovative products and services, high-quality and responsive operating processes, skills and knowledge of the workforce, the information technology that supports the work force and links the firms to its customers and suppliers, and the organizational climate that encourages innovation, problem-solving, and improvement. But companies were unable to adequately measure their intangible assets (Johnson and Kaplan 1987, 201–202). Anecdotal data from management publications indicated that many companies could not implement their new strategies in this environment (Kiechel 1982; Charan and Colvin 1999). They could not manage what they could not describe or measure.

Intangible assets: valuation vs. value creation

Some call for accountants to make an organization's intangible assets more visible to managers and investors by placing them on a company's balance sheet. But several factors prevent valid valuation of intangible assets on balance sheets.

First, the value from intangible assets is indirect. Assets such knowledge and technology seldom have a direct impact on revenue and profit. Improvements in intangible assets affect financial outcomes through chains of cause-and-effect relationships involving two or three intermediate stages (Huselid 1995; Becker and Huselid 1998). For example, consider the linkages in the service management profit chain (Heskett et al. 1994):

- investments in employee training lead to improvements in service quality

[1] For example, General Electric attempted a system of nonfinancial measurements in the 1950s (Greenwood 1974), and the French developed the Tableaux de Bord decades ago (Lebas 1994; Epstein and Manzoni 1998).

- better service quality leads to higher customer satisfaction
- higher customer satisfaction leads to increased customer loyalty
- increased customer loyalty generates increase revenues and margins

Financial outcomes are separated causally and temporally from improving employees' capabilities. The complex linkages make it difficult, if not impossible, to place a financial value on an asset such as workforce capabilities or employee morale, much less to measure period-to-period changes in that financial value.

Second, the value from intangible assets depends on organizational context and strategy. This value cannot be separated from the organizational processes that transform intangibles into customer and financial outcomes. The balance sheet is a linear, additive model. It records each class of asset separately and calculates the total by adding up each asset's corded value. The value created from investing in individual intangible assets, however, is neither linear nor additive.

Senior investment bankers in a firm such as Goldman Sachs are immensely valuable because of their knowledge about complex financial products and their capabilities for managing relationships and developing trust with sophisticated customers. People with the same knowledge, experience, and capabilities, however, are nearly worthless to a financial services company such as etrade.com that emphasizes operational efficiency, low-cost, and technology-based trading. The value of an intangible asset depends critically on the context—the organization, the strategy, and other complementary assets—in which the intangible asset is deployed.

Intangible assets seldom have value by themselves.[2] Generally, they must be bundled with other intangible and tangible assets to create value. For example, a new growth-oriented sales strategy could require new knowledge about customers, new training for sales employees, new databases, new information systems, as new organization structure, and a new incentive compensation program. Investing in just one of these capabilities, or in all of them but one, could cause the new sales strategy to fail. The value does not reside in any individual intangible asset. It arises from creating the entire set of assets along with a strategy that links them together. The value-creation process is multiplicative, not additive.

The balanced scorecard supplements conventional financial reporting

Companies' balance sheets report separately on tangible assets, such raw material, land, and equipment, based on their historic cost—the traditional financial counting method. This was adequate for industrial-age companies, which succeeded by combining and transforming their tangible resources into products whose value exceeded their acquisition and production costs. Financial accounting conventions relating to depreciation and cost of goods sold enabled an income statement measure how much value was created beyond the costs incurred to acquire and transform tangible assets into finished products and services.

Some argue that companies should follow the same cost-based convention for their intangible assets—capitalize and subsequently amortize the expenditures on training, employees, conducting research and development, purchasing and developing databases, and advertising that creates brand awareness. But such costs are poor approximations of the realizable value created by investing in these intangible assets. Intangible assets can create value for organizations, but that does not imply that they have separable market values. Many internal and linked organizational processes, such as design, delivery, and service, are required to transform the potential value of intangible assets into products and services that have tangible value.

We introduced the Balanced Scorecard to provide a new framework for describing value-creating strategies that link intangible and tangible assets. The scorecard does not attempt to "value" an organization's intangible assets, but it does measure these assets in units other than currency. The Balanced Scorecard describes how intangible assets get mobilized and combined with intangible and tangible assets to create differentiating customer-value propositions and superior financial outcomes.

Strategy maps

Since introducing the Balanced Scorecard in 1992, we have helped over 200 executive teams design their scorecard programs. Initially we started with a clean sheets of paper, asking, "what is the strategy", and allowed the strategy and the Balanced Scorecard to emerge from interviews and discussions with the senior executives. The scorecard provided a framework for organizing strategic objectives into the four perspectives displayed in Figure [4.2.1]):

1. *Financial*—the strategy for growth, profitability, and risk viewed from the perspective of the shareholder.

2. *Customer*—the strategy for creating value and differentiation from the perspective of the customer.

3. *Internal Business Processes*—the strategic priorities for various business processes that create customer and shareholder satisfaction.

[2] Brand names, which can be sold, are an exception.

Figure 4.2.1 The balanced scorecard defines a strategy's cause-and-effect relationships

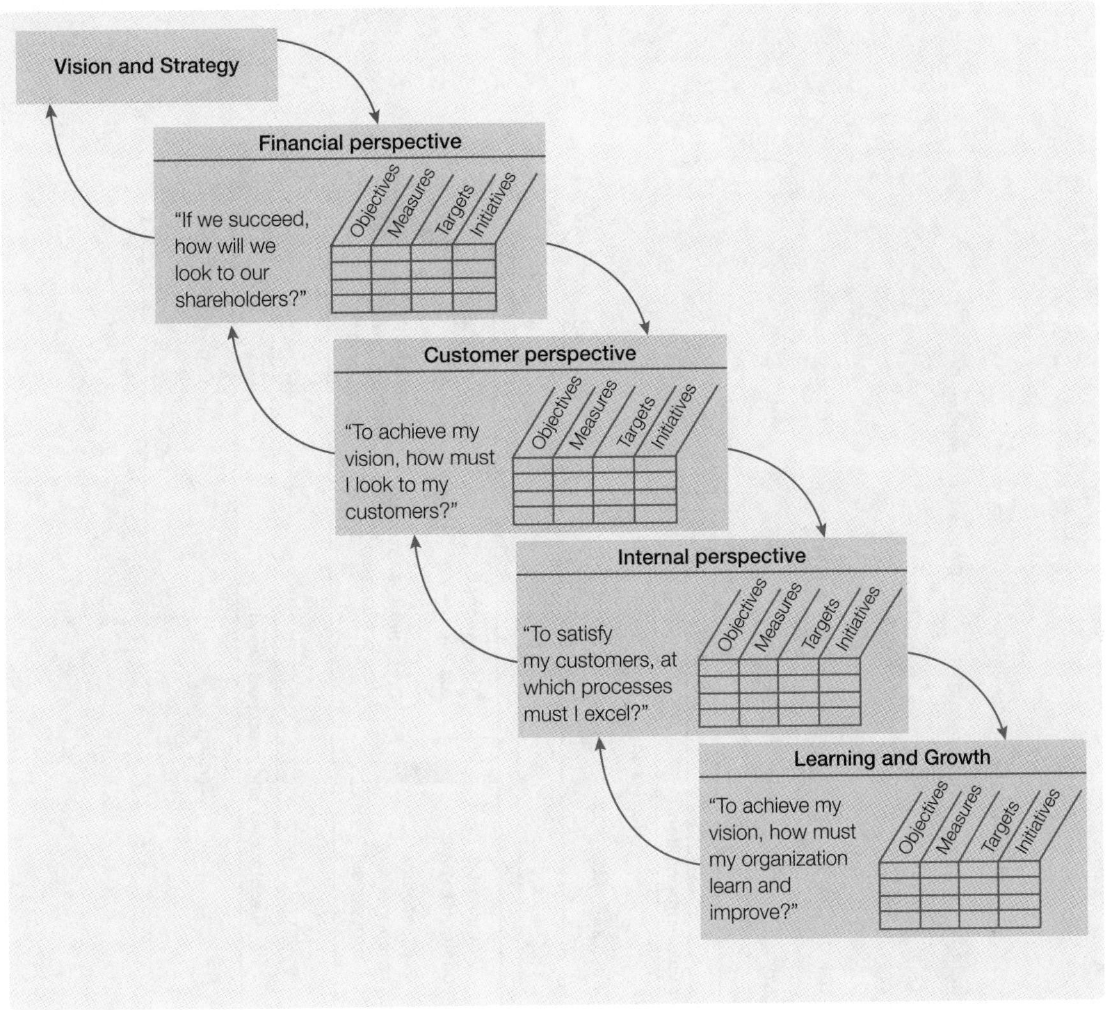

4. *Learning and Growth*—the priorities to create a climate that supports organizational change, innovation, and growth.

From this initial base of experience, we subsequently developed a general framework for describing and implementing strategy that we believe can be as useful as the traditional framework of income statement, balance sheet, and statement of cash flows for financial planning and reporting. The new framework, which we call a "Strategy Map," is a logical and comprehensive architecture for describing strategy, as illustrated in Figure [4.2.2]. A strategy map specifies the critical elements and their linkages for an organization's strategy.

- Objectives for growth and productivity to enhance shareholder value.
- Market and account share, acquisition, and retention of targeted customers where profitable growth will occur.
- Value propositions that would lead customers to do more higher-margin business with the company.
- Innovation and excellence in products, services, and processes that deliver the value proposition to targeted customer segments, promote operational improvements and meet community expectations and regulatory requirements.
- Investments required in people and systems to generate and sustain growth.

By translating their strategy into the logical architecture of a strategy map and Balanced Scorecard, organizations create a common and understandable point of reference for all organizational units and employees.

Organizations build strategy maps from the top down, starting with the destination and then charting the routes that lead there. Corporate executives first review their mission statement, why their company exists, and core values, what their company believes in. From that information, they develop

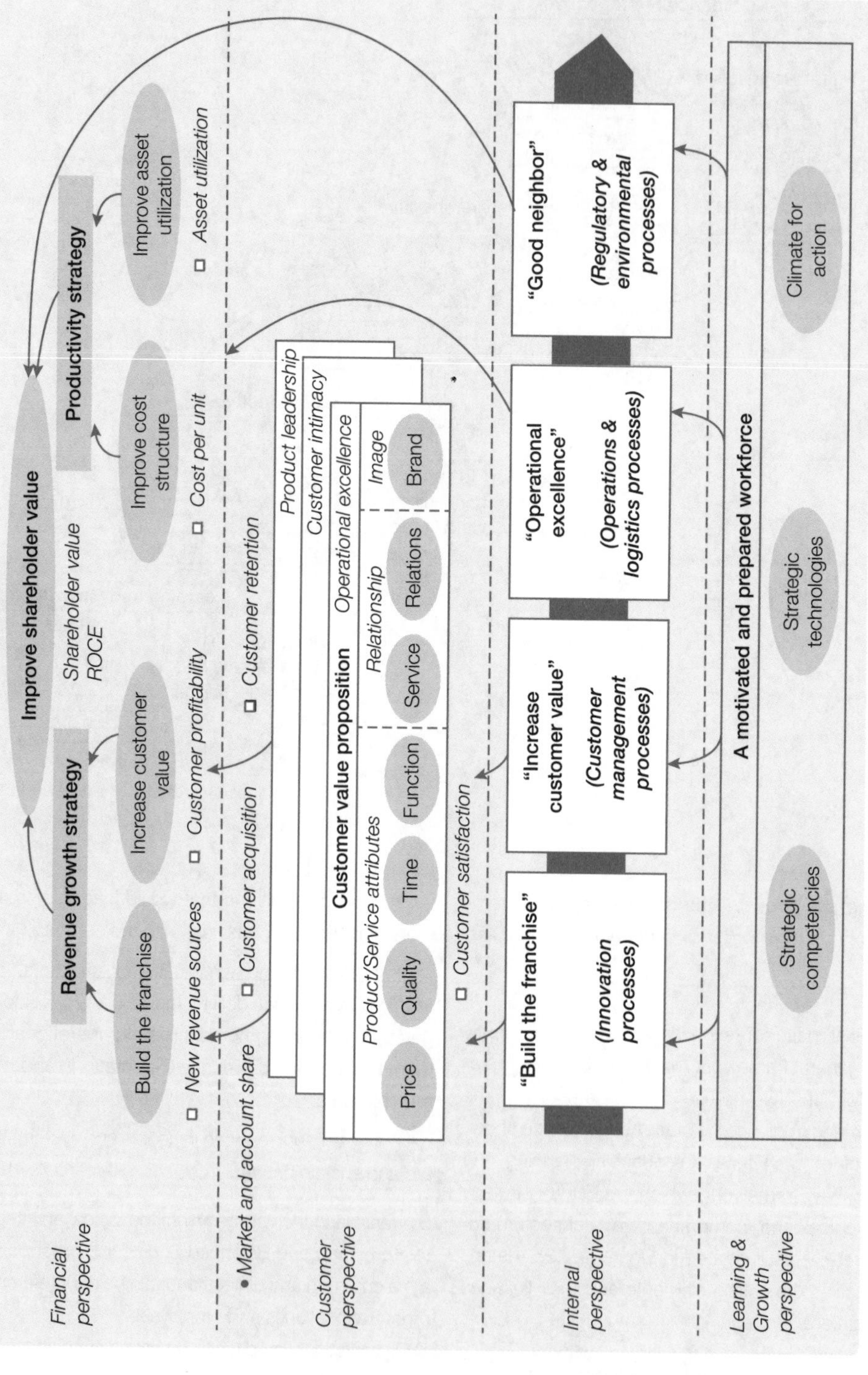

Figure 4.2.2 The balanced scorecard strategy map

their strategic vision, what their company wants to become. This vision creates a clear picture of the company's overall goal, which could be to become a top-quartile performer. The strategy identifies the path intended to reach that destination.

Financial perspective

The typical destination for profit-seeking enterprises is a significant increases in shareholder value (we will discuss the modifications for nonprofit and government organizations later in the paper). Companies increase economic value through two basic approaches—*revenue growth and productivity.*[3] A revenue growth strategy generally has two components: build the franchise with revenue from new markets, new products, and new customers and increase sales to existing customers by deepening relationships with them, including cross-selling multiple products and services, and offering complete solutions. A productivity strategy also generally has two components: improve the cost structure by lowering direct and indirect expenses; and utilize assets more efficiently by reducing the working and fixed capital needed to support a given level of business.

Customer perspective

The core of any business strategy is the *customer-value proposition*, which describes the unique mix of product, price, service, relationship, and image that a company offers. It defines how the organization differentiates itself from competitors to attract, retain, and deepen relationships with targeted customers. The value proposition is crucial because it helps an organization connect its internal processes to improved outcomes with its customers.

Companies differentiate their value proposition by selecting among *operational excellence* (for example, McDonalds and Dell Computer), *customer intimacy* (Home Depot and IBM in the 1960s and 1970s), and *product leadership* (Intel and Sony) (Treacy and Wiersema 1997, 31–45). Sustainable strategies are based on excelling at one of the three while maintaining threshold standards with the other two. After identifying its value proposition, a company knows which classes and types of customers to target.

Specifically, companies that pursue a strategy of operational excellence need to excel at competitive pricing, product quality, product selection, lead time, and on-time delivery. For costumer intimacy, an organization must stress the quality of its relationship with costumers, including exceptional service, and the completeness and suitability of the solution it offers individual customers. Companies that pursue a product leadership strategy must concentrate on the functionality, features, and performance of their, products and services.

The customer perspective also identifies the intended outcomes from delivering a differentiated value proposition. These would include market share in targeted customer segments, account share with targeted customers, acquisition and retention of customers in the targeted segments, and customer profitability.[4]

Internal process perspective

Once an organization has a clear picture of its customer and financial perspectives, it can determine the means by which it will achieve the differentiated value proposition for customers and the productivity improvements for the financial objectives. The internal business perspective captures these critical organizational activities, which fall into four high-level processes:

1. *Build the franchise* by spurring innovation to develop new products and services and to penetrate new markets and customer segments.
2. *Increase customer value* by expanding and deepening relationships with existing customers.
3. *Achieve operational excellence* by improving supply-chain management, internal processes, asset utilization, resource-capability management, and other processes.
4. *Become a good corporate citizen* by establishing effective relationships with the external stakeholders.

Many companies that espouse a strategy calling for innovation or for developing value-adding customer relationships mistakenly choose to measure their internal business processes by focusing only on the cost and quality of their operations. These companies have a complete disconnect between their strategy and how they measure it. Not surprisingly, organizations encounter great difficulty implementing growth strategies when their primary internal measurements emphasize process improvements, not innovation or enhanced customer relationships.

The financial benefits from improvements to the different business processes typically occur in stages. Cost savings from increases in *operational efficiencies* and process improvements deliver short-term benefits. Revenue growth from enhancing *customer relationships* accrues in the intermediate term. Increased *innovation* generally produces long-term revenue and margin improvements. Thus, a

[3] Shareholder value can also be increased through managing the right-hand side of the balance sheet, such as by repurchasing shares and choosing the low-cost mix among debt and equity instruments to lower the cost of capital. In this paper, we focus only on improved management of the organization's assets (tangible and intangible).

[4] Measurement of customer profitability (Kaplan and Cooper 1998, 181–201) provides one of the connections between the Balanced Scorecard and activity-based costing

complete strategy should generate returns from a three high-level internal processes.

Learning and growth perspective

The final region of a strategy map is the learning and growth perspective, which is the foundation of any strategy. In the learning and growth perspective, managers define the employee capabilities and kills, technology, and corporate climates needed to support a strategy. These objectives enable a company to align its human resources and information technology with the strategic requirements from its critical interval business processes, differentiated value proposition, and customer relationships. After addressing the learning and growth perspective, companies have a complete strategy map with linkages across the four major perspectives.

Strategy maps, beyond providing a common framework for describing and building strategies, also are powerful diagnostic tools, capable of detecting flaws in organizations' Balanced Scorecards. For example, Figure [4.2.3] shows the strategy map for the Revenue Growth theme of Mobil North America Marketing & Refining. When senior management compared the scorecards being used by its business units to this template, it found one unit with no objective or measure for dealers, an omission immediately obvious from looking at its strategy map. Had this unit discovered how to bypass dealers and gasoline directly to end-use consumers? Were dealer relationships no longer strategic for this unit? The business unit shown in the lower right comer of Figure [4.2.3] did not mention quality on its scoreboard. Again, had this unit already achieved six sigma

Figure 4.2.3 Mobil uses reverse engineering of a strategy map as a strategy diagnostic

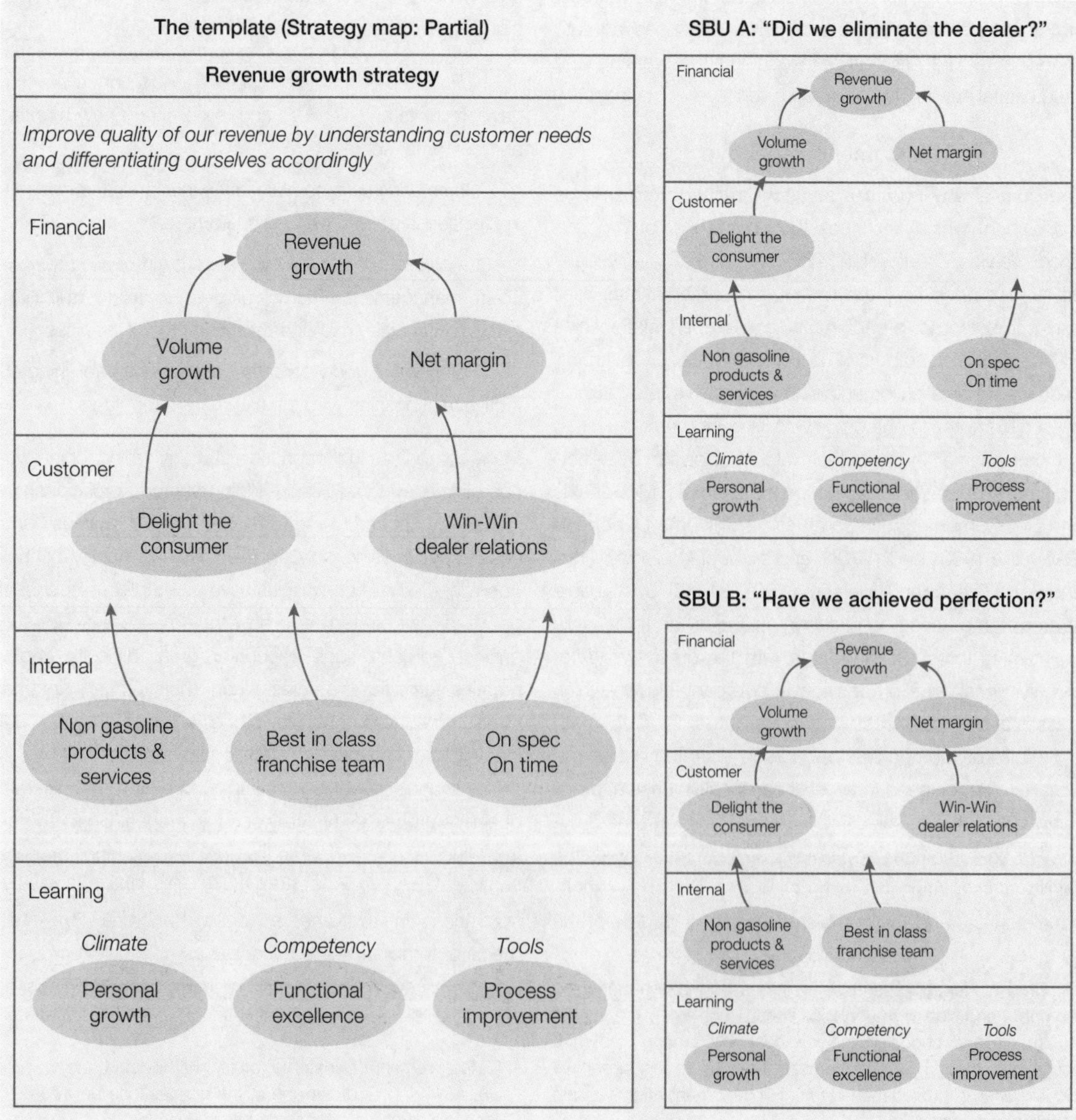

quality levels so quality was no longer a strategic priority? Mobil's executive team used its divisional strategy map to identify and remedy gaps in the strategies being implemented at lower level of the organization.

Stakeholder and key performance indicator scorecards

Many organizations claim to have a Balanced Scorecard because they use a mixture of financial and nonfinancial measures. Such measurement systems are certainly more "balanced" them ones that use financial measures alone. Yet, the assumptions and philosophies underlying these scorecards are quite different from those underlying the strategy scorecards and maps described above. We observe two other scorecard types frequently used in practice: the *stakeholder scorecard* and the *key performance indicator* scorecard.

Stakeholder scorecards

The *stakeholder scorecard* identifies the major constituents of the organization—shareholders, customers, and employees—and frequently other constituents such as suppliers and the community. The scorecard defines the organization's goals for these different constituents, or stakeholders, and develops an appropriate scorecard of measures and targets for them (Atkinson and Waterhouse 1997). For example, Sears built its initial scorecard around three themes:

- "a compelling place to shop"
- "a compelling place to work"
- "a compelling place to invest"

Citicorp used a similar structure for its initial scorecard—"a good place to work, to bank, and to invest." AT&T developed an elaborate internal measurement system based on financial value-added, customer value-added, and people value-added.

All these companies built their measurements around their three dominant constituents—customers, shareholders, and employees—emphasizing satisfaction measures for customers and employees, to ensure that these constituents felt well served by the company. In this sense, they were apparently *balanced*. Comparing these scorecards to the strategy map template in Figure [4.2.2] we can easily detect what is missing from such scorecards; no objectives or measures for *how* these balanced goals are to be achieved. A vision describes as desired outcome; a strategy, however, must describe *how* the outcome will be achieved, how employees, customers, and shareholders will be satisfied. Thus, a stakeholder scorecard is not adequate to describe the strategy of an organization and, therefore, is not an adequate foundation on which to build a management system.

Missing from the stakeholder card are the drivers to achieve the goals. Such drivers include an explicit value proposition such as innovation that generates new products and services or enhanced customer management processes, the deployment of technology, and the specific skills and competencies of employees required to implement the strategy. In a well-constructed *strategy scorecard*, the value proposition in the customer perspective, all the processes in the internal perspective, and the learning and growth, perspective components of the scorecard define the "how" that is as fundamental to strategy as the outcomes that the strategy is expected to achieve.

Stakeholder scorecards are often a first step on the road to a strategy scorecard. But as organizations begin to work with stakeholder cards, they inevitably confront the question of "how." This leads to the next level of strategic thinking and scorecard design. Both Sears and Citicorp quickly moved beyond their stakeholder scorecards, developing an insightful set of internal process objectives to complete the description of their strategy and, ultimately, achieving a strategy Balanced Scorecard. The stakeholder scorecard can also be useful in organizations that do not have internal synergies across business units. Since each unit has a different set of internal drivers, its "corporate" scorecard need only focus on the desired outcomes for the corporation's constituencies, including the community and suppliers. Each business until then defines how it will achieve those goals with its business unit strategy scorecard and strategy map.

Key performance indicator scorecards

Key Performance Indicator (KPI) scorecards are common. The total quality management approach and variants such as the Malcolm Baldrige and European Foundation for Quality Management (EFQM) awards generate many measures to monitor internal process. When migrating to a "Balanced Scorecard," organizations often build on the base already established by classifying their existing measurements into the four BSC categories. KPI scorecards also emerge when the organization's information technology group, which likes to put the company database at the heart of any changes program, triggers the scorecard design. Consulting organizations that sell and install large systems, especially so-called executive information systems, also offer KPI scorecards.

As a simple example of a KPI scorecard, a financial service organization articulated the 4Ps for its "balanced scorecard:"

1. Profits
2. Portfolio (size of loan volume)

3. Process (percent processes ISO certified)
4. People (meeting diversity goals in hiring)

Although this scorecard is more balanced than one using financial measures alone, comparing the 4P measures to a strategy map like that in Figure [4.2.2] reveals the major gaps in the measurement set. The company has no customer measures and only a single internal-process measure, which focuses on an initiative not an outcome. This KPI scorecard has no role for information technology (strange for a financial service organization), no linkages from the internal measure (ISO process certification) to a customer value proposition or to a customer outcome, and no linkage from the learning and growth measure (diverse workforce) to improving an internal process, a customer outcome, or financial outcome.

KPI scorecards are most helpful for departments and teams when a strategic program already exists at a higher level. In this way, the diverse indicators enable individuals and teams to define what they must do well to contribute to higher level goals. Unless, however, the link to strategy is clearly established, the KPI scorecard will lead to local but not global or strategic improvements.

Balanced Scorecards should not just be collections of financial and nonfinancial measures, organized into three to five perspectives. The best Balanced Scorecards reflect the strategy of the organization. A good test is whether you can understand the strategy by looking only at the scorecard and its strategy map. Many organizations fail this test, especially those that create stakeholder scorecards or key performance indicator scorecards.

Strategy scorecards along with their graphical representations on strategy maps provide a logical and comprehensive way to describe strategy. They communicate clearly the organization's desired outcomes and its hypotheses about how these outcomes can be achieved. For example, *if* we improve on-time delivery, *then* customer satisfaction will improve, *if* customer satisfaction improves, *then* customers will purchase, more. The scorecards enable all organizational units and employees to understand the strategy and identify how they can contribute by becoming aligned to the strategy.

Applying the BSC to nonprofits and government organizations

During the past five years, the Balanced Scorecard has also been supplied by nonprofit and government organizations (NPGOs). One of the barriers to applying the scorecard to these sectors is the considerable difficulty NPGOs have in clearly defining their strategy. We reviewed. "strategy" documents of more than 50 pages. Most of the documents, once the mission and vision are articulated, consist of lists of programs initiatives, not the outcomes the organization is trying to achieve. These organizations must understand Porter's (1996, 77) admonition that strategy is not only what the organization intends to do, but also what it decides *not* to do. A message that is particularly relevant for NPGOs.

Most of the initial scorecards of NPGOs feature an operational excellence strategy. The organizations take their current mission as a given and try to do their work more efficiently—at lower cost, with fewer defects, and faster. Often the project builds off of a recently introduced quality initiative that emphasizes process improvements. It is unusual to find nonprofit organizations focusing on a strategy that can be thought of as product leadership or customer intimacy. As a consequence, their scorecards tend to be closer to the KPI scorecards than true strategy scorecards.

The City of Charlotte, North Carolina, however, followed a customer-based strategy by selecting an interrelated set of strategic themes to create distinct value for its citizens (Kaplan 1998). United Way of Southeastern New England also articulated a customer (donor) intimacy strategy (Kaplan and Kaplan 1996). Other nonprofits—the May Institute and New Profit Inc.—selected a clear product-leadership position (Kaplan and Elias 1999). The May Institute uses partnerships with universities and researchers to deliver the best behavioral and rehabilitation care delivery. New Profit Inc. introduces a new selection, monitoring, and governing process unique among nonprofit organizations. Montefiore Hospital uses a combination of product leadership in its centers of excellence, and excellent customer relationships—through its new patient-oriented care centers—to build market share in its local area (Kaplan 2001). These examples demonstrate that NPGOs can be strategic and build competitive advantage in ways other than pure operational excellence. But it takes vision and leadership to move from continuous improvement of existing process to thinking strategically about which processes and activities are most important for fulfilling the organization's mission.

Modifying the architecture of the balanced scorecard

Most NPGOs had difficulty with the original architecture of the Balanced Scorecard that placed the financial perspective at the top of the hierarchy. Given that achieving financial success is not the primary objective for most of these organizations, many rearrange the scorecard to place customers or constituents at the top of the hierarchy.

In a private-sector transaction, the customer plays two distinct roles—paying for the service and receiving the service—that are so complementary most people don't even think about them separately. But in a nonprofit organization, donors provide the financial resources they pay for the service—while another group, the constituents, receives the service. Who is the customer—the one paying or the one receiving? Rather than have to make such a Solomonic decision, organizations place both the donor perspective and the recipient perspective, in parallel, at the top of their Balanced Scorecards. They develop objectives for both donors and recipients, and then identify the internal processes that deliver desired value propositions for both groups of "customers."

In fact, nonprofit and government agencies should consider placing an over-arching objective at the top of their scorecard that represents their long-term objective such as a reduction in poverty or illiteracy, or improvements in the environment. Then the objectives within the scorecard can be oriented toward improving such a high-level objective. High-level financial measures provide private sector companies with an accountability measure to their owners, the shareholders. For a nonprofit or government agency, however, the financial measures are not the relevant indicators of whether the agency is delivering on its mission. The agency's mission should be featured and measured at the highest level of its scorecard. Placing an over-arching objective on the BSC for a nonprofit or government agency communicates clearly the long-term mission of the organization as portrayed in Figure [4.2.4].

Even the financial and customer objectives, however, may need to be re-examined for governmental organizations. Take the case of regulatory and enforcement agencies that monitor and punish violations of environmental, safety and health regulations. These agencies, which detect transgressions, and fine or arrest those who violate the laws and regulations, cannot look to their "immediate customers" for satisfaction and loyalty measures. Clearly not; the true "customers" for such organizations are the citizens at large who benefit from effective but not harsh or idiosyncratic enforcement of laws and regulations. Figure [4.2.5] shows a modified framework in which a government agency has three high-level perspectives:

1. *Cost Incurred*: This perspective emphasizes the importance of operational efficiency. The measured cost should include both the expenses of the agency and the social cost it imposes on citizens and other organizations through its operations. For example, an environmental agency imposes remediation costs on private-sector organizations. These are part of the costs of having the agency carry out its mission. The agency should minimize the direct and social costs required to achieve the benefits called for by its mission.

2. *Value Created*: This perspective identifies the benefits being created by the agency to citizens and is the most problematic and difficult to measure. It is usually difficult to financially quantify the benefits from improved education, reduced pollution, better health, less congestion, and safer neighborhoods. But the balanced scorecard still

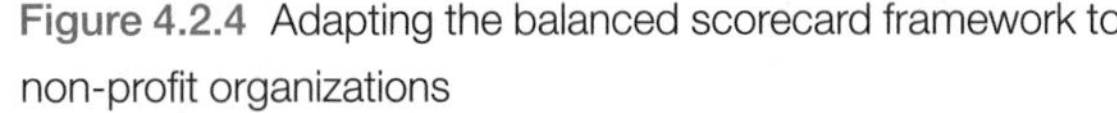

Figure 4.2.4 Adapting the balanced scorecard framework to non-profit organizations

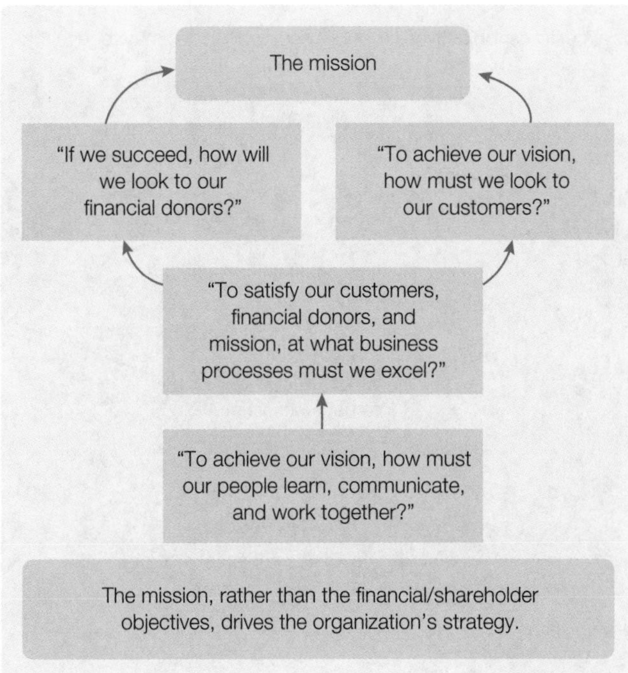

enables organizations to identify the outputs, if not the outcomes, from its activities, and to measure these outputs. Surrogates for value created could include percentage of students acquiring specific skills and knowledge; density of pollutants in water, air, or land; improved morbidity and mortality in targeted populations; crime rates and perception of public safety; and transportation times. In general, public-sector organizations may find they use more output than outcome measures. The citizens and their representatives—elected officials and legislators—will eventually make the judgments about the benefits from these outputs vs. their costs.

3. *Legitimizing Support*: An important "customer" for any government agency will be its "donor," the organization—typically the legislature—that provides the funding for the agency. In order to assure continued funding for its activities, the agency must strive to meet the objectives of its funding source—the legislature and, ultimately, citizens and taxpayers.

After defining these three high-level perspectives, a public-sector agency can identify its objectives for internal processes, learning, and growth that enable objectives in the three high level perspectives to be achieved.

Beyond measurement to management

Originally, we thought the Balanced Scorecard was about performance measurement (Kaplan and Norton 1992). Once organizations developed their basic system for measuring strategy, however, we quickly learned that *measurement* has consequences far beyond reporting on the past. Measurement creates focus for the future. The measures chosen by managers communicate important messages to all organizational units and employees. To take full advantage of this power, companies soon integrated their new measures into a *management system*. Thus the Balanced Scorecard concept evolved from a performance measurement system to become the organizing framework, the operating system, for a new strategic management system (Kaplan and Norton 1996c, Part. II) The academic literature, rooted in the original performance measurement aspects of the scorecard, focuses on the BSC as a measurement system (Ittner et al. 1997; Ittner and Larcker 1998; Banker et at. 2000; Lipe and Salterio 2000) but has yet to examine its role as a management system.

Using this new strategic management system, we observed several organizations achieving performance breakthroughs within two to three years of implementation (Kaplan and Norton 2001a, 4–6, 17–22). The magnitude of the results achieved by the early adopters reveals the power of the Balanced Scorecard management system to focus the entire organization on strategy. The speed with which the new strategies deliver results indicates that the companies' successes are not due to a major new product or service launch, major new capital investments' or even the development of new intangible or "intellectual" assets. The companies, of course, develop new products and services, and invest in both hard, intangible assets, as well as softer, intangible assets. But they cannot benefit much in two

Figure 4.2.5 The financial/customer objectives for public sector agencies may require three different perspectives

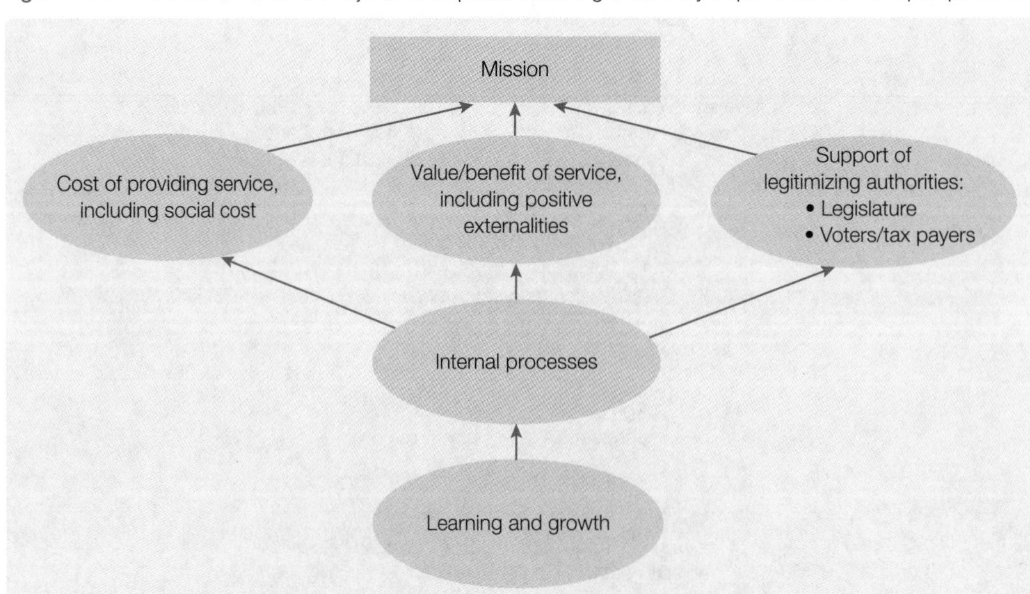

Professor Dutch Leonard, School of Government, Harvard University, collaborated to develop this diagram.

years from such investments. To achieve their breakthrough performance, the companies capitalize on capabilities and assets—both tangible and intangible—that already exist within their organizations.[5] The companies, new strategies and the Balanced Scorecard unleash the capabilities and assets previously hidden (or frozen) within the old organization. In effect, the Balanced Scorecard provides the "recipe" that enables ingredients already existing in the organization to be combined for long-term value creation.

Part II our commentary on the Balanced Scorecard (Kaplan and Norton 2001b) will describe how organizations use Balanced Scorecards and strategy maps to accomplish comprehensive and integrated transformations. These organizations redefine their relationships with customers, reengineer fundamental business processes, re-skill the workforce, and deploy new technology infrastructures. A new culture emerges, centered not on traditional functional silos, but on the team effort required to implement the strategy. By clearly defining the strategy, communicating it consistently, and linking it to the drivers of change, a performance-based culture emerges to link everyone and every unit to the unique features of the strategy. The simple act of describing strategy via strategy maps and scorecards makes a major contribution to the success of the transformation program.

References

American Institute of Certified Public Accountants (AICPA), Special Committee on Financial Reporting. 1994. ***Improving Business Reporting—A Customer Focus: Meeting the Information Needs of Investors and Creditors***. New York, NY: A1CPA.

Atkinson, A. A., and J. H. Waterhouse. 1997. A stakeholder approach to strategic performance measurement. ***Sloan Management Review*** (Spring).

Banker, R., G. Potter, and D. Srinivasan. 2000. An empirical investigation of an incentive plan that includes nonfinancial performance measures. ***The Accounting Review*** (January): 65–92.

Becker, B., and M. Huselid. 1998. High performance work systems and firm performance: A synthesis of research and managerial implications. In ***Research in Personnel and Human Resources Management***, 53:–101. Greenwich, CT: JAI Press.

Blair, M.B. 1995. ***Ownership and Control: Rethinking Corporate Governance for the Twenty-First Century***. Washington, D.C.: Brookings Institution.

Chandler, A. D. 1990. ***Scale and Scope: The Dynamics of Industrial Capitalism***. Cambridge, MA: Harvard University Press.

Charan, R., and G. Colvin. 1999. Why CEOs fail. ***Fortune*** (June 21).

[5] These observations indicate why attempts to "value" individual intangible assets almost surely is a quixotic search. The companies achieved breakthrough performance with essentially the same people, services, and technology that previously delivered dismal performance. The value creation came not from any individual asset—tangible or intangible. It came from the coherent combination and the alignment of existing organizational resources.

Epstein, M., and J. F. Manzoni. 1998. Implementing corporate strategy: From Tableaux de Bord to Balanced Scorecards. ***European Management Journal*** (April).

Greenwood, R. G. 1974. ***Managerial Decentralization: A Study of the General Electric Philosophy***. Lexington, MA: D. C. Heath.

Heskett, J., T. Jones, G. Loveman, E. Sasser, and L. Schlesinger. 1994. Putting the service profit chain to work. ***Harvard Business Review*** (March–April):164–174.

Huselid, M. A. 1995. The impact of human resource management practices on turnover, productivity, and corporate financial performance. ***Academy of Management Journal***: 635–672.

Ittner, C., D. Larcker, and M. Meyer. 1997. Performance, compensation, and the Balanced Scorecard. Working paper, University of Pennsylvania.

——, D. Larcker, and M. Rajan. 1997. The choice of performance measures in annual bonus contracts. ***The Accounting Review*** (April): 231–255.

——, and D. Larcker. 1998. Innovations in performance measurement: Trends and research implications. ***Journal of Management Accounting Research***: 205–238.

Johnson, H. T., and R. S. Kaplan. 1987. ***Relevance Lost: The Rise and Fall of Management Accounting***. Boston, MA: Harvard Business School Press.

Kaplan, R. S., and D. P. Norton. 1992. The Balanced Scorecard: Measures that drive performance. ***Harvard Business Review*** (January–February): 71–79.

– – –, and – – –. 1993. Putting the Balanced Scorecard to work. ***Harvard Business Review*** (September–October) 134–147.

——, and E. L. Kaplan. 1996 United Way of Southeastern New England. Harvard Business School Case 197-036. Boston, MA.

——, and D. P. Norton. 1996a. Using the Balanced Scorecard as a strategic management system. ***Harvard Business Review*** (January–February): 75–85.

——, and ——. 1996b. Linking the Balanced Scorecard to strategy. ***California Management Review*** (Fall): 53–79.

——, and ——. 1996c. ***The Balanced Scorecard: Translating Strategy Into Action***. Boston, MA: Harvard Business School Publishing.

——. 1998. City of Charlotte (A). Harvard Business School Case 199-036. Boston, MA.

——, and R. Cooper. 1998. ***Cost and Effect: Using Integrated Cost Systems to Drive Profitability and Performance***. Boston, MA: Harvard Business School Press.

——, and J. Elias. 1999. New Profit, Inc.: Governing the nonprofit enterprise. Harvard Business School Case 100-052. Boston, M.A.

——. 2001. Montefiore Medical Center. Harvard Business School Case 101-067. Boston, MA.

——, and D. P. Norton. 2000. Having trouble with your strategy? Then map it. ***Harvard Business Review*** (September–October): 167–176.

——, and ——. 2001a. ***The Strategy-Focused Organization: How Balanced Scorecard Companies Thrive in the New Business Environment***. Boston, MA: Harvard Business School Press.

——, and ——. 2001b. Transforming the Balanced Scorecard from performance measurement to strategic management, Part II. ***Accounting Horizon*** (forthcoming).

Kiechel, W. 1982. Corporate strategists under fire. ***Fortune*** (December 27): 88.

Lebas, M. 1994. Managerial accounting in France: Overview of past tradition and current practice. ***European Accounting Review*** 3 (3): 471–487.

Lipe, M., and S. Salterio. 2000. The Balanced Scorecard Judgmental effects of common and unique performance measures. *The Accounting Review* (July): 289–298.

Porter, M. E. 1992. Capital disadvantage: America's failing capital investment system. *Harvard Business Review* (September–October).

——. 1996. What is strategy? *Harvard Business Review* (November–December).

Treacy. F., and M. Wierserma. 1997. *The Wisdom of Market Leaders*. New York, NY: Perseus Books.

Webber, A. M. 2000. New math for a new economy. *Fast Company* (January–February).

Reading 4.3 Turning great strategy into great performance *Michael C. Mankins and Richard Steele*

First published: (2005) *Harvard Business Review*, July–August: 65–72. Reprinted by permission of *Harvard Business Review*. 'Turning Great Strategy into Great Performance' by Michael C. Mankins and Richard Steele, January 01 2005.

Three years ago, the leadership team at a major manufacturer spent months developing a new strategy for its European business. Over the prior half-decade, six new competitors had entered the market, each deploying the latest in low-cost manufacturing technology and slashing prices to gain market share. The performance of the European unit – once the crown, jewel of the company's portfolio – had deteriorated to the point that top management was seriously considering divesting it.

To turn around the operation, the unit's leadership team had recommended a bold new "solutions strategy" – one that would leverage the business's installed base to fuel growth is after-market services and equipment financing. The financial forecasts were exciting – the strategy promised to restore the business's industry-leading returns and growth. Impressed, top management quickly approved the plan, agreeing to provide the unit with all the resources it needed to make the turnaround a reality.

Today, however, the unit's performance is nowhere near what its management team had projected. Returns, while better than before, remain well below the company's cost of capital. The revenues and profits that managers had expected from services and financing have not materialized, and the business's cost position still lags behind that of its major competitors.

At the conclusion of a recent half-day review of the business's strategy and performance, the unit's general manager remained steadfast and vowed to press on. "It's all about execution," she declared. "The strategy we're pursuing is the right one. We're just not delivering the numbers. All we need to do is work harder, work smarter."

The parent company's CEO was not so sure. He wondered: Could the unit's lackluster performance have more to do with a mistaken strategy than poor execution? More important, what should he do to get better performance out of the unit? Should he do as the general manager insisted and stay the course – focusing the organization more intensely on execution – or should he encourage the leadership team to investigate new strategy options? If execution was the issue, what should he do to help the business improve its game? Or should he just cut his losses and sell the business? He left the operating review frustrated and confused – not at all confident that the business would ever deliver the performance its managers had forecast in its strategic plan.

Talk to almost any CEO, and you're likely to hear similar frustrations. For despite the enormous time and energy that goes into strategy development at most companies, many have little to show for the effort. Our research suggests that companies on average deliver only 63% of the financial performance their strategies promise. Even worse, the causes of this strategy-to-performance gap are all but invisible to top management. Leaders then pull the wrong levers in their attempts to turn around performance – pressing for better execution when they actually need a better strategy, or opting to change direction when they really should focus the organization on execution. The result: wasted energy, lost time, and continued underperformance.

But, as our research also shows, a select group of high-performing companies have managed to close the strategy-to-performance gap through better planning *and* execution. These companies – Barclays, Cisco Systems, Dow Chemical, 3M, and Roche, to name a few – develop realistic plans that are solidly grounded in the underlying economics of their markets and then use the plans to drive execution. Their disciplined planning and execution processes make it far less likely that they will race a shortfall in actual performance. And, if they do fall short, their processes enable them to discern the cause quickly and take corrective action. While these companies' practices are broad in scope – ranging from unique forms of planning to integrated processes for deploying and tracking resources – our experience suggests that they can be applied by any business to help craft great plans and turn them into great performance.

The strategy-to-performance gap

In the fall of 2004, our firm, Marakon Associates, in collaboration with the Economist Intelligence Unit, surveyed senior executives from 197 companies worldwide with sales exceeding $500 million. We wanted to see how successful companies are at translating their strategies into performance. Specifically, how effective are they at meeting the financial projections set forth in their strategic plans? And when they fall short, what are the most common causes, and what actions are most effective in closing the strategy-to-performance gap? Our findings were revealing – and troubling.

While the executives we surveyed compete in very different product markets and geographies, they share many concerns about planning and execution. Virtually all of them struggle to produce the financial performance forecasts in their long-range plans. Furthermore, the processes they use to develop plans and monitor performance make it difficult to discern whether the strategy-to-performance gap stems from poor planning, poor execution, both, or neither. Specifically, we discovered:

Companies rarely track performance against long-term plans

In our experience, less than 15% of companies make it a regular practice to go back and compare the business's results with the performance forecast for each unit in its prior years' strategic plans. As a result, top managers can't easily know whether the projections that underlie their capital-investment and portfolio-strategy decisions are in any way predictive of actual performance. More important, they risk embedding the same disconnect between results and forecasts in their future investment decisions. Indeed, the fact that so few companies routinely monitor actual versus planned performance may help explain why so many companies seem to pour good money after bad – continuing to fund losing strategies rather than searching for new and better options.

Multiyear results rarely meet projections

When companies do track performance relative to projections over a number of years, what commonly emerges is a picture one of our clients recently described as a series of "diagonal venetian blinds," where each year's performance projections, when viewed side by side, resemble venetian blinds hung diagonally. (See [Figure 4.3.1].) If things are going reasonably well, the starting point for each year's new "blind" may be a bit higher than the prior year's starting point, but rarely does performance match the prior year's projection. The obvious implication: year after year of under-performance relative to plan.

The venetian blinds phenomenon creates a number of related problems. First, because the plan's financial forecasts are unreliable, senior management cannot confidently tie capital approval to strategic planning. Consequently, strategy development and resource allocation become decoupled, and the annual operating plan (or budget) ends up driving the company's long-term investments and strategy. Second, portfolio management gets derailed. Without credible financial forecasts, top management cannot know whether a particular business is worth more to the company and its shareholders than to potential buyers. As a result, businesses that destroy shareholder value stay in the portfolio too long (in the hope that their performance will eventually turn around), and value-creating businesses are starved for capital and other resources. Third, poor financial forecasts complicate communications with the investment community. Indeed, to avoid coming up short at the end of the quarter, the CFO and head of investor relations frequently impose a "contingency" or "safety margin" on top of the forecast produced by consolidating the business-unit plans. Because this top-down contingency is wrong just as often as it is right, poor financial forecasts run the risk of damaging a company's reputation with analysts and investors.

A lot of value is lost in translation

Given the poor quality of financial forecasts in most strategic plans, it is probably not surprising that most companies fail to realize their strategies' potential value. As we've mentioned, our survey indicates that, on average, most strategies deliver only 63% of their potential financial performance. And more than one-third of the executives surveyed placed the figure at less than 50%. Put differently, if management were to realize the full potential of its current strategy, the increase in value could be as much as 60% to 100%!

As illustrated in [Figure 4.3.2], the strategy-to-performance gap can be attributed to a combination of factors, such as poorly formulated plans, misapplied resources, breakdowns in communication, and limited accountability for results. To elaborate, management starts with a strategy it believes will generate a certain level of financial performance and value over time (100%, as noted in the figure). But, according to the executives we surveyed, the failure to have the right resources in the right place at the right time strips away some 7.5% of the strategy's potential value. Some 5.2% is lost to poor communications, 4.5% to poor action planning, 4.1% to blurred accountabilities, and so on. Of course, these estimates reflect the average experience of the executives we surveyed and may not be representative of every company or

Figure 4.3.1 The Venetian blinds of business

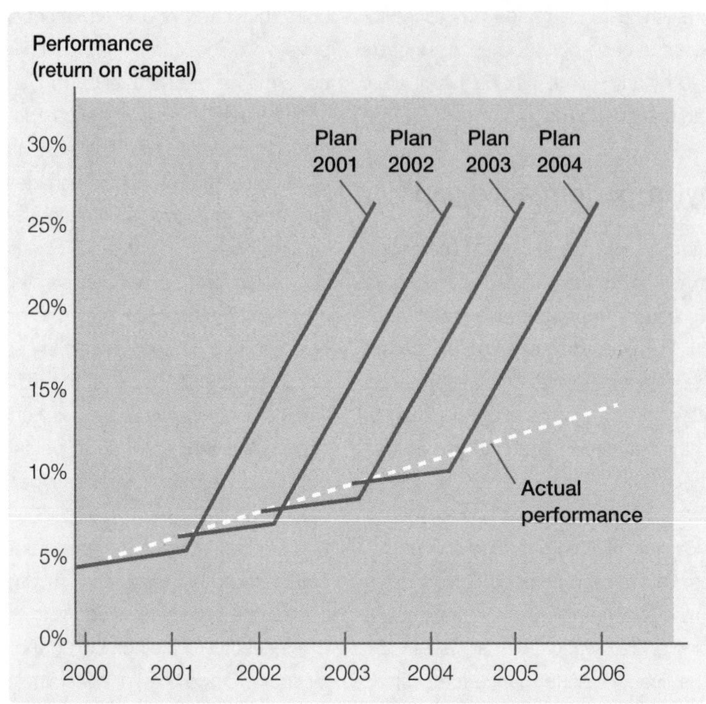

Source: This graphic illustrates a dynamic common to many companies. In January 2001, management approves a strategic plan (Plan 2001) that projects modest performance for the first year and a high rate of performance thereafter, as shown in the first solid line. For beating the first year's projection, the unit management is both commended and handsomely rewarded. A new plan is then prepared, projecting uninspiring results for the first year and once again promising a fast rate of performance improvement thereafter, as shown by the second solid line (Plan 2002). This, too, succeeds only partially, so another plan is drawn up, and so on. The actual rate of performance improvement can be seen by joining the start points of each plan (the dotted line).

every strategy. Nonetheless, they do highlight the issues managers need to focus on as they review their companies' processes for planning and executing strategies.

What emerges from our survey results is a sequence of events that goes something like this: Strategies are approved but poorly communicated. This, in turn, makes the translation of strategy into specific actions and resource plans all but impossible. Lower levels in the organization don't know what they need to do, when they need to do it, or what resources will be required to deliver the performance senior management expects. Consequently, the expected results never materialize. And because no one is held responsible for the shortfall, the cycle of underperformance gets repeated, often for many years.

Performance bottlenecks are frequently invisible to top management

The processes most companies use to develop plans, allocate resources, and track performance make it difficult for top management to discern whether the strategy-to-performance gap stems from poor planning, poor execution, both, or neither. Because so many plans incorporate overly ambitious projections, companies frequently write off performance shortfalls as "just another hockey-stick forecast." And when plans are realistic and performance falls short, executives have few early-warning signals. They often have no way of knowing whether critical actions were carried out as expected, resources were deployed on schedule, competitors responded as anticipated, and so on. Unfortunately, without clear information on how and why performance is falling short, it is virtually impossible for top management to take appropriate corrective action.

The strategy-to-performance gap fosters a culture of underperformance. In many companies, planning and execution breakdowns are reinforced – even magnified – by an insidious shift in culture, in our experience, this change occurs subtly but quickly, and once it has taken root it is very hard to reverse. First, unrealistic plans create the expectation throughout the organization that plans simply will not be fulfilled. Then, as the expectation becomes experience, it

Figure 4.3.2 Where the performance goes

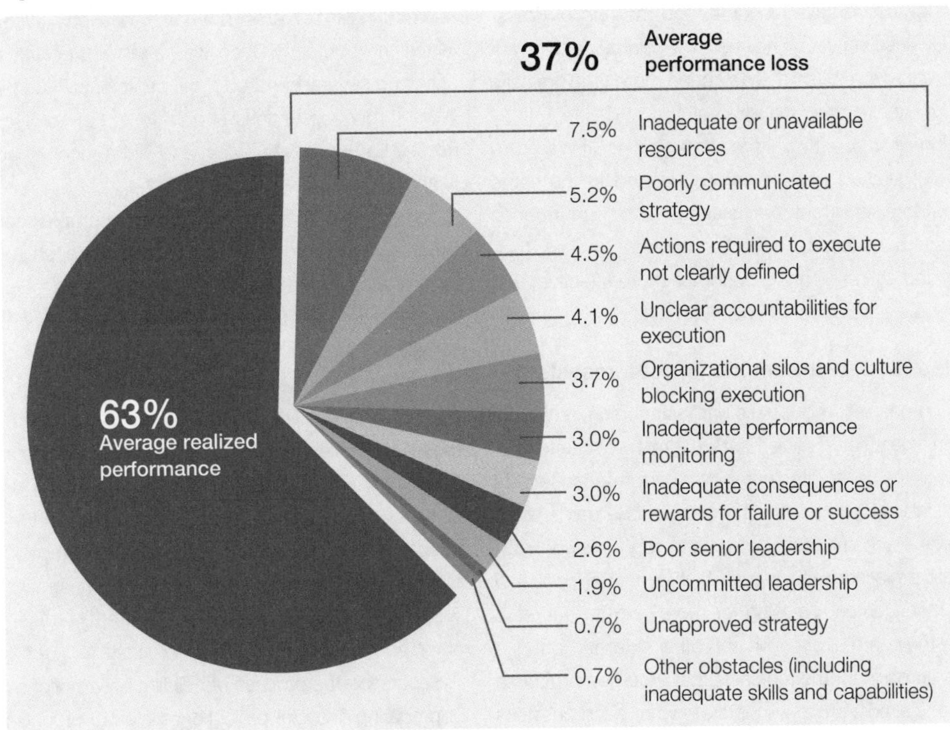

Source: This chart shows the average performance loss implied by the performance ratings that managers in our survey gave to specific breakdowns in the planning and execution process.

becomes the norm that performance commitments won't be kept. So commitments cease to be binding promises with real consequences. Rather than stretching to ensure that commitments are kept, managers, ejecting failure, seek to protect themselves from the eventual fallout. They spend time covering their tracks rather than identifying actions to enhance performance. The organization becomes less self-critical and less intellectually honest about its shortcomings. Consequently, it loses its capacity to perform.

Closing the strategy-to-performance gap

As significant as the strategy-to-performance gap is at most companies, management can close it. A number of high-performing companies have found ways to realize more of their strategies' potential. Rather than focus on improving their planning and execution processes separately to close the gap, these companies work both sides of the equation, raising standards for both planning and execution simultaneously and creating clear links between them.

Our research and experience in working with many of these companies suggests they follow seven rules that apply to planning and execution. Living by these rules enables them to objectively assess any performance shortfall and determine whether it stems from the strategy, the plan, the execution, or employees' capabilities. And the same rules that allow them to spot problems early also help them prevent performance shortfalls in the first place. These rules may seem simple – even obvious – but when strictly and collectively observed, they can transform both, the quality of a company's strategy and its ability to deliver results.

Rule 1: Keep it simple, make it concrete

At most companies, strategy is a highly abstract concept – often confused with vision or aspiration – and is not something that can be easily communicated or translated into action. But without a clear sense of where the company is headed and why, lower levels to the organization cannot put in place executable plans. In short, the link between strategy and performance can't be drawn because the strategy itself is not sufficiently concrete.

To start off the planning and execution process on the right track, high-performing companies avoid long, drawn-out descriptions of lofty goals and instead stick to clear language describing their course of action. Bob Diamond, CEO of Barclays Capital, one of the fastest-growing and best-performing investment banking operations in Europe, puts it this way: "We've been very clear about what we will and will not do. We knew we weren't going to go head-to-head with U.S. bulge bracket firms. We communicated that we wouldn't compete in this way and that we wouldn't play in unprofitable segments within the equity markets but instead would invest to position ourselves for the euro, the burgeoning need for fixed income, and the end of Glass-Steigel. By ensuring everyone knew the strategy and how it was different, we've been able to spend more time on tasks that are key to executing this strategy."

By being clear about what the strategy is and isn't, companies like Barclays keep everyone headed in the same direction. More important, they safeguard the performance their counterparts lose to ineffective communications; their resource and action planning becomes more effective; and accountabilities are easier to specify.

Rule 2: Debate assumptions, not forecasts

At many companies, a business unit's strategic plan is little more than a negotiated settlement – the result of careful bargaining with the corporate center over performance targets and financial forecasts. Planning, therefore, is largely a political process – with unit management arguing for lower near-term profit projections (to secure higher annual bonuses) and top management pressing for more long-term stretch (to satisfy the board of direction and other external constituents) Not surprisingly, the forecasts that emerge from these negotiations almost always understate what each business unit can deliver in the near term and overstate what can reallstically be expected in the long-term – the hockey-stick charts with which CEOs are all too familiar.

Even at companies where the planning process is isolated from the political concerns of performance evaluation and compensation, the approach used to generate financial projections often has built-in biases. Indeed, financial forecasting frequently takes place in complete isolation from the marketing or strategy functions. A business unit's finance function prepares a highly detailed line-item forecast whose short-term assumptions may be realistic, if conservative, but whose long-term assumptions are largely uninformed. For example, revenue forecasts are typically based on crude estimates about average pricing, market growth, and market share. Projections of long-term costs and working capital requirements are based on an assumption about annual productivity gains – expediently tied, perhaps, to some companywide efficiency program. These forecasts ate difficult for top management to pick apart. Each line item may be completely defensible, but the overall plan and projections embed a clear upward bias – rendering them useless for driving strategy execution.

High-performing companies view planning altogether differently. They want their forecasts to drive the work they actually do. To make this possible, they have to ensure that the assumptions underlying their long-term plans reflect both the real economics of their markets and the performance experience of the company relative to competitors. Tyco CEO Ed Breen, brought in to turn the company around in July 2002, credits a revamped plan-building process for contributing to Tyco's dramatic recovery. When Breen joined the company, Tyco was a labyrinth of 42 business units and several hundred profit centers, built up over many years through countless acquisitions. Few of Tyco's businesses had complete plans, and virtually none had reliable financial forecasts.

To get a grip on the conglomerate's complex operations, Breen assigned cross-functional teams at each unit, drawn from strategy, marketing, and finance, to develop detailed information on the profitability of' Tyco's primary markets – as well as the product or service offerings, costs, and price positioning relative to the competition. The teams met with corporate executives bi-weekly during Breen's first six months to review and discuss the findings. These discussions focused on the assumptions that would drive each unit's long-term financial performance, not on the financial forecasts themselves. In fact, once assumptions about market trends were agreed on, it was relatively easy for Tyco's central finance function to prepare externally oriented and internally consistent forecasts for each unit.

Separating the process of building assumptions from that of preparing financial projections helps to ground the business unit–corporate center dialogue in economic reality. Units can't hide behind specious details, and corporate center executives can't push for unrealistic goals. What's more, the fact-based discussion resulting from this kind of approach builds trust between the top team and each unit and removes barriers to fast and effective execution. "When you understand the fundamentals and performance drivers in a detailed way" says Bob Diamond "you can then step back, and you don't have to manage the details. The team knows which issues it can get on with which it needs to flag to me, and which issues we really need to work out together."

Rule 3: Use a rigorous framework, speak a common language

To be productive, the dialogue between the corporate center and the business unite about market trends and assumptions must be conducted within a rigorous framework. Many of the companies we advise use the concept of profit pools, which draws on the competition theories of Michael Porter and others. In this framework, a business's long-term financial performance is tied to the total profit pool available in each of the markets it serves and its share of each profit pool – which, in turn, is tied to the business's market share and relative profitability versus competitors in each market.

In this approach, the first step is for the corporate center and the unit team to agree on the size and growth of each profit pool. Fiercely competitive markets, such as pulp and paper or commercial airlines, have small (or negative) total profit pools. Less competitive markets, like soft drinks or pharmaceuticals, have large total profit pools. We find it helpful to estimate the size of each profit pool directly – through detailed benchmarking – and then forecast changes in the pool's size and growth. Each business unit then assesses what share of the total profit pool it can realistically capture over time, given its business model and positioning. Competitively advantaged businesses can capture a large share of the profit pool – by gaining or sustaining a high market share, generating above-average profitability, or both. Competitively disadvantaged businesses, by contrast, typically capture a negligible share of the profit pool. Once the unit and the corporate center agree on the likely share of the pool the business will capture over time, the corporate center can easily create the financial projections that will serve as the unit's s road map.

In our view, the specific framework a company uses to ground its strategic plans isn't all that important. What is critical is that the framework establish a common language for the dialogue between the corporate center and the units – one that the strategy, marketing, and finance teams all understand and use. Without a rigorous framework to link a business's performance in the product markets with its financial performance over time, it is very difficult for top management to ascertain whether the financial projections that accompany a business unit's strategic plan are reasonable and realistically achievable. As a result, management can't know with confidence whether a performance shortfall stems from poor execution or an unrealistic and ungrounded plan.

Rule 4: Discuss resource deployments early

Companies can create more realistic forecasts and more executable plans if they discuss up front the level and timing of critical resource deployments. At Cisco Systems, for example, a cross-functional team reviews the level and timing of resource deployments early in the planning stage. These teams regularly meet with John Chambers (CEO), Dennis Powell (CFO), Randy Pond (VP of operations), and the other members of Cisco's executive team to discuss their findings and make recommendations. Once agreement is reached on resource allocation and timing at the unit level, those elements are factored into the company's two-year plan. Cisco then monitors each unit's actual resource deployments on a monthly basis (as well as its performance) to make sure things are going according to plan and that the plan is generating the expected results.

Challenging business units about when new resources need to be in place focuses the planning dialogue on what actually needs to happen across the company in order to execute each unit's strategy. Critical questions invariably surface, such as: How long will it take us to change customers' purchase patterns? How fast can we deploy our new sales force? How quickly will competitors respond? These are tough questions. But answering them makes the forecasts and the plans they accompany more feasible.

What's more, an early assessment of resource needs also informs discussions about market trends and drivers, improving the quality of rise strategic plan and making it far more executable. In the course of talking about the resources needed to expand in the rapidly growing cable market for example, Cisco came to realize that additional growth would require more trained engineers to improve existing products and develop new features. So, rather than relying on the functions to provide these resources from the bottom up, corporate management earmarked a specific number of trained engineers to support growth, in cable. Cisco's financial-planning organization carefully monitors the engineering head count, the pace of feature development, and revenues generated by the business to make sure the strategy stays on track.

Rule 5: Clearly identify priorities

To deliver any strategy successfully, managers must make thousands of tactical decisions and put them into action. But not all tactics are equally important. In most instances, a few key steps must be taken – at the right time and in the right way – to meet planned performance. Leading companies make these priorities explicit so that each executive has a clear sense of where to direct his or her efforts.

At Textron, a $10 billion multi-industrial conglomerate, each business unit identifies "improvement priorities" that it must act upon to realize the performance outlined in its strategic plan. Each improvement priority is translated into action items with clearly defined accountabilities, timetables, and key performance indicators (KPIs) that allow executives to tell how a unit is delivering on a priority. Improvement priorities and action items cascade to every level at the company from the management committee (consisting of Textron's top five executives) down to the lowest levels in each of the company's ten business units. Lewis Campbell, Textron's CEO, summarizes the company's approach this way: "Everyone needs to know; 'If I have only one hour to work, here's what I'm going to focus on.' Our goal deployment process makes each individual's accountabilities and priorities clear."

The Swiss pharmaceutical giant Roche goes as far as to turn its badness plans into detailed performance contracts that clearly specify the steps needed and the risks that must be managed to achieve the plans. These contracts all include a "delivery agenda" that lists the five to ten critical priorities with the greatest impact on performance. By maintaining a delivery agenda at each level of the company, Chairman and CEO Franz Humer and his leadership team make sure "everyone at Roche understands exactly what we have agreed to do at a strategic level and that our strategy gets translated into clear execution priorities. Our delivery agenda helps us stay the course with the strategy decisions we have made so that execution is actually allowed to happen. We cannot control implementation from HQ, but we can agree on the priorities, communicate relentlessly, and hold managers accountable for executing against their commitments."

Rule 6: Continuously monitor performance

Seasoned executives know almost instinctively whether a business has asked for too much, too little, or just enough resources to deliver the goods. They develop this capability over time – essentially through trial and error. High-performing companies use real-time performance tracking to help accelerate this trial-and-error process. They continuously monitor their resource deployment patterns and their results against plan, using continuous feedback to reset planning assumptions and reallocate resources. This real-time information allows management to spot and remedy flaws in the plan and shortfalls in execution – and to avoid confusing one with the other.

At Textron, for example, each KPI is carefully monitored, and regular operating reviews percolate performance shortfalls – or "red light" events – up through the management ranks. This provides CEO Lewis Campbell, CFO Ted French, and the other members of Textron's management committee with the information they need to spot and fix breakdowns to execution.

A similar approach has played an important role in the dramatic revival of Dow Chemical's fortunes. In December 2001, with performance in a free fall, Dow's board of directors asked Bill Stavropoulos (Dow's CEO from 1993 to 1999) to return to the helm. Stavropoulos and Andrew Liveris (the current CEO, then COO) immediately focused Dow's entire top leadership team on execution through a project they called the Performance Improvement Drive. They began by defining clear performance metrics for each of Dow's 79 business units. Performance on these key metrics was tracked against plans on a weekly basis, and the entire leadership team discussed any serious discrepancies first thing every Monday morning. As Liveris told us, the weekly monitoring sessions "forced everyone to live the details of execution" and let "the entire organization know how we were performing."

Continuous monitoring of performance is particularly important in highly volatile industries, where events outside anyone's control can render a plan irrelevant Under CEO Alan Mulally, Boeing Commercial Airplanes leadership team holds weekly business performance reviews to track the division's results against its multiyear plan. By tracking the deployment of resources as a leading indicator of whether a plan is being executed effectively, BCA's leadership team can make course corrections each week rather than waiting for quarterly results to roll in.

Furthermore, by proactively monitoring the primary drivers of performance (such as passenger traffic patterns, airline yields and load factors, and new aircraft orders), BCA is better able to develop and deploy effective countermeasures when events throw its plans off course. During the SARS epidemic in late 2002, for example, BCA's leadership team took action to mitigate the adverse consequences of the illness on the business' operating plan within a week of the initial outbreak. The abrupt declare to air traffic to Hong Kong, Singapore, and other Asian business centers signaled that the number of future aircraft deliveries to the region would fall – perhaps precipitously. Accordingly, BCA scaled back its medium-term production plans (delaying the scheduled ramp-up of some programs and accelerating the shutdown of others) and adjusted its multiyear operating plan to reflect the anticipated financial impact.

Rule 7: Reward and develop execution capabilities

No list of rules on this topic would be complete without a reminder that companies have to motivate and develop their staffs; at the end of the day, no process *can* be better than the people who have to make it work. Unsurprisingly, therefore, nearly all of the companies we studied insisted that the selection and development of management was an essential ingredient in their success. And while improving the capabilities of a company's workforce is no easy task – often taking many years – these capabilities, once built, can drive superior planning and execution for decades.

For Barclays' Bob Diamond, nothing is more important than "ensuring that [the company] hires only A players." In his view, "the hidden costs of bad hiring decisions are enormous, so despite the fact that we are doubling in size, we insist that as a top team we take responsibility for all hiring. The jury of your peers is the toughest judgment, so we vet each others' potential hires and challenge each other to keep raising the bar." it's equally important to make sure that talented hires are rewarded for superior execution. To reinforce its core values of "client, "meritocracy," "team," and "integrity" Barclays Capital has innovative pay schemes that "ring fence" rewards. Stars don't lose out just because the business is entering new markets with lower returns during the growth phase. Says Diamond: "It's so bad for the culture if you don't deliver what you promised to people who have delivered ... You've got to make sure you are consistent and fair, unless you want to lose your most productive people."

Companies that are strong on execution also emphasize development. Soon after he became CEO of 3M, Jim McNemey and his top team spent 18 months hashing out a new leadership model for the company. Challenging debates among members of the top team led to agreement on six "leadership attributes" – namely, the ability to "chart the course," "energize and inspire others," "demonstrate ethics, integrity and compliance," "deliver results," "raise the bar and "innovate resourcefully." 3M's leadership greed that these six attributes were essential for the company to become skilled at execution and known for accountability. Today, the leaders credit this model with helping 3M to sustain and even improve its consistently strong performance.

The prize for closing the strategy-to-performance gap is huge – an increase in performance of anywhere from 60% to 100% for most companies. But this almost certainly understates the true benefits. Companies that create tight links between their strategies, their plans, and, ultimately, their performance often experience a cultural multiplier effect. Over time, as they turn their strategies into great performance, leaders in these organizations become much more confident in their own capabilities and much more willing to make the stretch commitments that inspire and transform large companies. In turn, individual managers who keep their commitments are rewarded – with faster progression and fatter paychecks – reinforcing the behaviors needed to drive any company forward.

Eventually, a culture of overperformance emerges, investors start giving management the benefit of the doubt when it comes to bold moves and performance delivery. The result is a performance premium on the company's stock – one that further rewards stretch commitments and performance delivery. Before long, the company's reputation among potential recruits rises, and a virtuous circle is created in which talent begets performance, performance begets rewards, and rewards beget even more talent. In short, closing the strategy-to-performance gap is not only a source of immediate performance improvement but also an important driver of cultural change with a large and lasting impact on the organization's capabilities, strategies, and competitiveness.

Reading 4.4 Configurations of strategy and structure: towards a synthesis *Danny Miller*

First published: (1986) *Strategic Management Journal*, 7: 233–249. 'Configurations of Strategy and Structure', Danny Miller, *Strategic Management Journal*, Volume 7, Issue 3, 1986. Reproduced with the kind permission of John Wiley and Sons Ltd.

This paper examines the relationships and tries to effect a synthesis between several very common configurations of strategy and structure. First, the gaps in the traditional literature are reviewed and a more thorough treatment of the association between strategy and structure is proposed. An attempt is then made to show that a useful methodological approach is to identify and interrelate common configurations of strategy and structure rather than linking a myriad of individual variables in the two respective categories. The prevalence and predictive utility of such configurations is highlighted. The literature is then examined to tentatively isolate some key dimensions of strategy and show how these combine to produce common strategic configurations. These are finally related to various common structural types to elicit potential complementarities and conflicts. It must be stressed at the outset that the proposed configurations and their relationships are illustrative—not final or exhaustive.

The title of this paper is so suggestive. How frequently have we seen the words 'strategy' and 'structure' paired in empirical and conceptual works in the field of policy. Alfred Chandler (1962) in his classic study showed how changes in strategy—namely product–market diversification, required subsequent alterations in structure—particularly divisionalization. A legion of replicators followed with their own empirical studies largely confirming Chandler's conclusions. The thesis that structure followed strategy was so popular that it was tested and confirmed in Britain (Channon, 1973), France (Pooley-Dias, 1972) and Germany (Thanheiser, 1972). Then Richard Rumelt (1974) came along to show how the match between strategy and structure influences performance.

These were important studies; yet they merely scratched the surface. Strategy was characterized mainly in terms of breadth of market: diversified versus undiversified. Structure was largely viewed according to its divisionalized or departmentalized form and the nature of its control systems. Clearly there is so much more to the concepts of both strategy and structure.

Enter Mintzberg (1973), who identified entrepreneurial planning and adaptive modes of strategy-making and related these to the organizational and environmental contexts in which they occur. But here the emphasis was on the way strategic decisions are made, rather than on the content of strategies. Again structure was described along only two or three simple dimensions such as size, age, and power distribution.

The work by Miles and Snow (1978) and Miller and Friesen (1977, 1978) represented attempts to look at strategy and structure from a more multidimensional point of view. Miles and Snow (1978) showed how their prospectors, defenders, reactors and analyzers chose unique strategies to adapt to their environments, and then indicated how this might influence the organization's technology and its structure. Although Miles and Snow's (1978) scheme is based on an *a priori* framework which they later validated empirically, Miller and Friesen's (1977, 1978) types or 'archetypes' were derived from an empirical taxonomy of organizations. They too examined common adaptive strategies and their structural and environmental correlates. In the Miller and Friesen (1978) approach the concentration is once again on the process of strategy-making more than its actual content. This is less true of the Miles and Snow (1978) study, which does indeed discuss strategic content but focuses mostly on innovation and product line breadth. There are relatively few details given about marketing, production, R&D, vertical integration and asset management strategies.

In recent years the field of business strategy/policy has made some very significant advances. The conceptual work of Porter (1980) and the empirical studies of the PIMS data by Hambrick and his collaborators (1983, 1983a) are among the most interesting. These authors have derived extremely suggestive conceptual typologies and empirical taxonomies of strategy, focusing on variables that have enjoyed much attention from industrial economists—variables that were shown repeatedly to influence performance; those that can often be manipulated by managers. These include *differentiation* (e.g. innovation, advertising, product quality); *cost leadership* (capacity utilization, relative direct costs); *focus* (breadth of product lines, heterogeneity of clientele); and *asset parsimony* (fixed assets to revenue). Dimensions of market power are also considered (market share rank, barriers to entry, dependence on suppliers and customers), as are performance variables (ROI, earnings variability, growth in market share). The importance of some of these dimensions had already been suggested by Hofer and Schendel (1978) and Henderson (1979).

A central gap in the literature to date is that the rich content of strategies has never been related to structure. It may be, for example, that strategies of differentiation through innovation would not be easy to implement within a bureaucratic or mechanistic structure (Burns and Stalker, 1961). It also seems incongruous that bureaucratic structures could give rise to differentiation through innovation. By the same token, organizations that have embraced a cost leadership strategy pursue extremely efficient, low cost production to lower prices. They might then require bureaucratic, 'mechanistic' structures that place a great deal of emphasis on sophisticated cost controls; standard, repetitive procedures; cost information systems, etc. Organic structures could be too flexible and inefficient to appropriately serve cost leaders. These conjectures are worthy of further study as the match between strategy and structure may vitally influence performance.

The theme we wish to pursue here is that there are ties that unite strategy and structure; that given a particular strategy there are only a limited number of suitable structures and vice versa. The theme is, of course, anything but novel. But it seems to require development in its particulars. Specifically, it would be useful to relate the rather sophisticated conceptions of recent strategic theorists—particularly those of Porter (1980), Hambrick (1983a,b), and Miles and Snow (1978—to those of the major structural theorists—notably Lawrence and Lorsch (1967), Burns and Stalker (1961), Woodward (1965), Thompson (1967), Galbraith (1973) and Mintzberg (1979). A guiding philosophy that motivates the integration is that all of these authors, whose works have been so very well received, have identified extremely crucial slices of organizational reality. Also, most have tended to do so in terms of ideal or common types. That is, they have isolated frequently occurring configurations of organizational elements. The elements seem to form common gestalts such that each can best be understood in relation to the other elements in the configuration. It is the very fact that we conceive of such configurations that makes it possible for us to order our world of organizations in a rich and holistic way.

Two ways of studying organizations

In order to demonstrate the last point, it may be useful to simplify things by contrasting two modes of relating strategy to structure. One alternative would be to take one or two elements of strategy at a time (e.g. innovation, or salespersons to total employees, or relative product quality) and relate them to individual organizational variables (centralization of decision-making power, organizational differentiation, etc.). A problem with this approach is that we would be in a position of having to formulate a myriad of bivariate or circumscribed multivariate hypotheses. These would be extremely numerous and perhaps conceptually intractable. Any coherent theme might be obscured by the mist of atomistic speculation. An even more serious shortcoming of this approach is that reality usually cannot be expressed in terms of linear bivariate or even multivariate relationships. Statistical and real associations among variables are largely a function of the context in which they occur. For example, the centralization of power may correlate positively with organizational innovation in small organizations pursuing a stable task, while the same relationship could be negative in high-technology organic firms, where experts must be given the power to innovate (Miller, 1983). Relationships cannot, then, be divorced from their context. So the 'few variables at a time' alternative of relating strategy to structure would seem to be not only rather cumbersome and conceptually inelegant, but downright misleading as well.

However we have a second alternative. We believe that elements of structure cohere within common configurations, as do those of strategy. Furthermore, these configurations are themselves interlinked in that there are natural congruences between particular strategic, structural, and indeed environmental configurations. If there is any truth to this thesis, the task of relating the details of strategy to the details of structure will be much simpler. We need only argue for the most functional, and thus possibly the most common, matches between configurations—referring to individual attributes merely to more richly reflect the theme of the global configurations, and to show the most salient specific interdependencies uniting configurations of strategy to those of structure.

The case for configuration

Before we proceed with the second alternative we must argue for the accuracy of its prime assumption: namely, that elements of strategy, structure and environment often coalesce or configure into a manageable number of common, predictively useful types that describe a large proportion of high-performing organizations. The configurations (or 'gestalts', or 'archetypes', or 'generic types') are said to be predictively useful in that they are composed of tight constellations of mutually supportive elements. The presence of certain elements can thus lead to the reliable prediction of the remaining elements (Miller and Mintzberg, 1984).

There are three interrelated arguments for configuration. Recent literature on the population ecology of organizations (Hannan and Freeman, 1977; Aldrich, 1979; McKelvey, 1981) contends that the environment selects out various common organizational forms. There are only a rather limited number of possible strategies and structures feasible in any type of environment. A few favored strategies and structures cause the organizations pursuing them to thrive at the expense of competing organizations. Competitors must therefore either begin to move toward the superior strategies, or perish. In either event the repertoire of viable strategic and structural configurations is reduced. Miller (1982), Astley (1983), Tushman and Romanelli, (1983) and Hinings *et al.*, 1984 argue that this convergence upon viable configurations will tend to happen relatively quickly—in short bursts—and that, once reached, a fairly stable set of configurations will exist over a long period.

A second, related argument for the existence of configurations is that organizational features are interrelated in complex and integral ways. In other words the organization may be driven toward a common configuration to achieve internal harmony among its elements of strategy, structure and context. A central theme is pursued which marshals and orders the individual elements. Consider Miller and Mintzberg's (1984:21) description of the machine bureaucracy:

> The organization has highly specialized, routine operating tasks, very formalized procedures, and large units in its operations. The basis for grouping tasks ... is by function and coordination is effected by rules and hierarchy. Power for decision making is quite centralized, and there exists an elaborate administrative structure with a clear hierarchy of line authority.

Here standardization, rules and regulations, formal communications, and tight controls are emphasized. These large organizations can only function in stable and simple environments in which their inflexibility is not overly limiting.

Clearly many of these attributes are complementary and mutually reinforcing. The stable environment enables the operating procedures to be routinized and formalized, but the procedures in turn cause the organization to seek out a stable environment. Large size encourages standardization since procedures repeat and controls must be impersonal—but standardization in turn encourages growth to boost economies of scale. Cost leadership strategies (Porter, 1980) come to be favored. Large size causes inflexibility which then prompts the search for stability in the environment. But the reverse causal direction may also apply since stability encourages growth to a scale that can optimally exploit opportunities. Thus each element makes sense in terms of the whole—and together they form a cohesive system (Miller and Friesen, 1984b:22). Cohesive configurations reduce the number of possible ways in which the elements combine. They make it that much more likely that common configurations will account for a sizeable proportion of organizations.

This brings us to our third argument for the prevalence of common configurations: that organizations tend to change their elements in a manner that either extends a given configuration, or moves it quickly to a new configuration that is preserved for a very long time. Piecemeal changes will often destroy the complementarities among many elements of configuration and will thus be avoided. Only when change is absolutely necessary or extremely advantageous will organizations be tempted to move concertedly and rapidly (to shorten the disruptive interval of transition) from one configuration to another that is broadly different. Such changes, because they are so expensive, will not be undertaken very frequently. Consequently organizations will adhere to their configurations for fairly long periods. Astley (1983), Miller (1982), Miller and Friesen (1984b) and Tushman and Romanelli (1983), have given more detailed arguments for this quantum view of change. Miller and Friesen (1980, 1982) have found corroborating empirical evidence.

So much for the conceptual arguments in favor of configurations. But there is also strong empirical evidence to support the existence of configurations. This is to be found in the well-known works by Woodward (1965), Lawrence and Lorsch (1967), Burns and Stalker (1961) and others, all of whom found integral structural configurations in their data. Hambrick (1983b) and Miller and Friesen (1984a) have also found configurations among elements of strategy in the PIMS data—largely corresponding to Porter's (1980) strategies and appearing in different environments. Dess and Davis (1984) and Miller and Friesen (1984a) showed that firms pursuing Porter's three generic strategies are quite common, and also that they outperform firms that are 'stuck in the middle'.

One of the most heartening developments is that there is considerable overlap between the structural and strategic typologies and taxonomies. Even though the authors were looking at different parts of the proverbial elephant, their work seems to converge considerably so that it is becoming increasingly possible to construct pictures of the whole beast. For example, our bureaucracy described earlier seems to be reflected by Lawrence and Lorsch's (1967) container firms, Burns and Stalker's (1961) mechanistic organizations, Woodward's (1965) mass producers, Perrow's (1971) routine manufacturers, and Mintzberg's (1979) machine bureaucracy. The adhocracy of Mintzberg (1979) recalls Lawrence and Lorsch's (1967) plastics firms, Burns and Stalker's (1961) organic organizations, Perrow's (1971) nonroutine manufacturers, and so on.

Turning to the literature on strategic types there are notable similarities among Porter's (1980) differentiators, Miller and Friesen's (1978) adaptive firms, and Miles and Snow's (1978) prospectors. By the same token, Porter's (1980) cost leaders roughly recall Miles and Snow's (1978) defenders and Miller and Friesen's (1978) giants under fire.

We do not wish to argue that these typologies are substitutes for one another. They do indeed have different emphases. But there seem to be important areas of commonality that suggest some natural links between types of structures and types of strategies.

Selection of strategic configurations

The concepts of strategy, structure and environment are so broad that we can only select a representative set of categories or configurations for characterizing each of them. We do so very tentatively and in the light of previous literature. Our concern in this section is strategy.

Our criteria for the selection of strategic dimensions were, of necessity, somewhat arbitrary. First, dimensions had to pertain to the content of strategy rather than the process of strategy-making. Second, the dimensions had to be sufficiently specific to be both identifiable and controllable by managers, and general enough to apply to most industries. Third, the dimensions had to exhibit broad coverage in two respects: they had collectively to exhaust a considerable range of possible strategies; and they had to encompass many specific elements that could richly characterize the strategies of most businesses. Although most of our discussion will be confined to strategies at the business rather than the corporate level, we shall address one exception in the case of the Divisionalized Conglomerate. Finally, to boost the relevance of the discussion the dimensions must already have generated considerable interest in both the empirical and theoretical literature on policy.

The conceptual work by Porter (1980), Scherer (1980), Miles and Snow (1978) and MacMillan and Hambrick (1983) suggests four broad categories of variables or 'dimensions' that reflect important competitive strategies. They are *differentiation*, *cost leadership*, *focus* and *asset parsimony.* These dimensions can be used to compare firms' competitive advantages within and across industries. Table [4.4.1] shows some of the many representative variables that are subsumed by each dimension. The empirical work by Hambrick (1983b), Miller and Friesen (1984a) and Dess and Davis (1984) shows how reliably the individual variables cluster together to form the fundamental dimensions. The dimensions do not exhaust the concept of strategy—but they do reflect many of its important elements. We shall discuss each dimension in turn.

Differentiation aims to create a product that is perceived as uniquely attractive. It emphasizes strong marketing abilities, creative, well-designed products, a reputation for quality, a good corporate image, and strong cooperation from marketing channels.

Notwithstanding Porter's (1980) discussion, there appear to be at least two varieties of differentiators—each, as we shall see, with different structural and environmental co-requisites. The *innovating* differentiators are really much like Miles and Snow's (1978) Prospectors, and Miller and Friesen's (1984b) S_B adaptive firms. They differentiate by coming out with new products and new technologies. They lead their competitors in innovation and can charge fairly high prices. There is a strong emphasis on R&D and pioneering. In contrast, the marketing differentiators are more like Miller and Friesen's (1984b) S_A firms which offer an attractive package, good service, convenient locations, and good product/service reliability. These firms are very forceful marketers—spending large sums on advertising, salesmen, promotion, and distribution. They are rarely the first out with new products.

Cost leadership is a strategy that strives to produce goods or services more cheaply than competitors. It stresses

Table 4.4.1 Representative strategic variables within each dimension

Differentiation:
Innovation:
Percentage of sales from products introduced over last 2 or 3 years
R&D as a percentage of sales
Average age of products
Frequency of major product changes
Marketing:
Product quality
Product image
Marketing expenses
Advertising and promotion
Sales force
Services quality
Focus:
Product line breadth
Breadth of customer types
Geographic coverage
Cost leadership:
Relative directive costs/unit
Newness of plant and equipment
Product pricing
Capacity utilization
Backward vertical integration
Process R&D
Asset parsimony:
Fixed asset intensity (gross book value of plant and equipment revenues)
Current asset intensity (current assets/revenues)

efficient scale facilities, the pursuit of cost reductions in manufacture, and the minimization of expenses of product R&D, services, selling and advertising. Cost leaders try to supply a standard, no-frills, high-volume product at the most competitive possible price. They do very little product innovation since this is disruptive of efficiency. The innovations of competitors will only be imitated after a considerable risk-reducing lag. Process R&D, backward vertical integration, and production automation may be pursued to reduce costs. Variants of the cost leadership strategy have been discussed by Buzzell, Gale and Sultan (1975), Henderson (1979), Miles an Snow (1978) and Miller and Friesen (1984b). Porter (1980) claims that differentiation and cost leadership do not usually go well together—that their joint pursuit could lead to a 'stuck-in-the-middle position' which fails to realize the advantages of either strategy.

Focus has been used by Porter (1980) to designate a niche strategy that concentrates the firm's attention on a specific type of customer, product or geographic locale. The firm uses either a differentiation or a cost leadership strategy (or some combination of the two) within a specialized part of the industry. We believe that focus can best be treated as a dimension with both ends of the continuum—very highly focused and very unfocused—having rather different implications. The highly focused firms pursue Miller and Friesen's (1978) niche strategy. The highly diversified firms recall Miller and Friesen's (1984b) conglomerate strategy, and Rumelt's (1974) unrelated diversification strategy. In all cases focus complements, but does not substitute for, differentiation and cost leadership.

It is worthwhile noting that the focus dimension can refer to a business-level strategy or a corporate-level strategy. In the first instance focus measures the degree to which a firm covers one specific industry. At the corporate level, however, focus describes the extent to which the firm has diversified into different industries. In fact, the same firm may employ highly focused business strategies in two very different industries. It could then be said to have an unfocused (diversified) corporate strategy and two focused business strategies. Although our typology will deal with strategy at the business level, we shall make a single exception in the case of the discussion of Divisionalized Conglomerates that pursue an unfocused corporate strategy. This common corporate strategy has important implications both for structure and for business-level strategies, and this warrants some discussion.

Asset parsimony is our final strategic category. It refers to the fewness of assets per unit output (MacMillan and Hambrick, 1983). Initially, the literature on strategy showed that capital intensity seemed to impede performance in

Figure 4.4.1 Five successful configurations of strategy

BUSINESS FOCUS	*DIFFERENTIATION and ASSET PARSIMONY*	*COST LEADERSHIP and ASSET INTENSITY*	
High	A_1 *Niche marketers* (see for example, Miller and Friesen's (1984b) S_{1A} and S_5 strategies, Miller's (1983) entrepreneurial firms)		BUSINESS LEVEL STRATEGY
Moderate to low	A_2 *Innovators* (Miles and Snow's (1978) prospectors, Miller and Freisen's (1984b) S_{1B} firms, Hambrick's (1983b) prospectors) A_3 *Marketers* (Porter's (1980) differentiators)	B *Cost leaders* (Porter's (1980) cost leaders; Hambrick's (1983b) disciplined makers of capital goods)	BUSINESS LEVEL STRATEGY
CORPORATE FOCUS Low	C *Conglomerates* (Miller and Friesen's (1984b) conglomerates; Rumelt's (1974) unrelated diversifiers		CORPORATE LEVEL STRATEGY

many different industries (Schoeffler, Buzzell and Heany, 1974; Gale, 1980; MacMillan, Hambrick and Day, 1982). It tends to reduce flexibility and increase competition when an industry reaches overcapacity. But MacMillan and Hambrick (1983) discovered that asset intensity, because it can provide for greater efficiency, may be quite suitable for cost leaders operating in stable environments. In contrast, where the organization must be flexible, as is often the case with differentiators, asset parsimony is most necessary (MacMillan and Hambrick, 1983).

How do these four strategic dimensions interact to produce effective strategic types or configurations? There are probably many ways, so just a few important ones will be isolated. Three rules of thumb were used as guides in deriving five common strategic configurations. The first rule has already been referred to. It is that successful firms tend to pursue either cost leadership or differentiation strategies, but usually not both (Porter, 1980). The second rule is that asset parsimony is desirable for differentiators who must remain flexible, but less suitable for cost leaders who must pursue efficiency (MacMillan and Hambrick, 1983). The third rule is that most strategies can have various degrees of focus, subject of course, to a few constraints: most cost leaders cannot be too narrowly focused because of their need for economies of scale (Scherer, 1980); innovators cannot be too broadly focused or they will deplete their resources trying to lead in too many markets; but they also should not be too narrowly focused as their innovations can take them into new and profitable markets (Miles and Snow, 1978); conglomerates that are completely unfocused at the *corporate* level can have divisions that pursue most other business-level strategies—but our subsequent analysis will indicate that they will often do best with marketing differentiation and cost leadership strategies.

In light of the above, our five strategic configurations are presented in Figure [4.4.1].

The reader may feel that we have been unduly presumptuous in at least two respects. First, only four dimensions and five strategic types have been chosen. Second, we have constituted the dimensions and types rather broadly so that it is not obvious that the elements or variables within them cohere. The first objection cannot be countered decisively since there are indeed other variables and strategic types that are not included (e.g. financial strategy variables, niche innovator types). It is not that these are not important. But the *variables* do not relate in any very obvious ways to the others discussed and thus it is too early to integrate them into our framework. Moreover, the remaining strategic *types* are not well developed in the literature and therefore would be difficult to relate to any structural context.

The second objection can be addressed more satisfactorily. Previous empirical taxonomies by Hambrick (1983a,b), Miller and Friesen (1984a), MacMillan and Hambrick (1983) and Dess and Davis (1984) have shown how the variables and dimensions of Table [4.4.1] have often cohered to produce the successful strategic types of Figure [4.4.1]. These studies give not only empirical confirmation of the three rules used to generate the types, but also show that these tend to apply only to successful configurations. For example, using cluster analysis, Miller and Friesen (1984a) and Hambrick (1983b) showed four of the five strategy types to be among those that appeared with remarkable regularity in successful businesses (conglomerates were excluded in the PIMS data).

Having identified some common strategic types we shall proceed to examine the structures which can adequately support them, and the environments in which they may thrive.

Bridging strategy and structure

The literature has shown that there are very many types of organization structures and environments. There are also many elements or variables that can be used to characterize them. So we shall again concentrate on only a selection of elements that has already been shown to be important in its possible consequences for strategy. We shall, using the literature, synthesize these elements into common types, and relate each to our five strategic configurations. We must stress at the outset that we do not by any means believe that there are only five successful matches between strategy and structure. These are to be taken as representative, not exhaustive.

Mintzberg's (1979) five structural types provide an excellent synthesis of the literature on structure. While his professional bureaucracies are usually not business firms and therefore are beyond our scope, his other types are quite

Table 4.4.2 Structures, environments, and strategies

Structural dimensions	Simple structure	Machine bureaucracy	Organic	Divisionalized
Power centralization	All at the top	CEO and designers of workflow	Scientists, technocrats and middle managers	Divisional executives
Bureaucratization	Low-informal	Many formal rules, policies and procedures	Organic	Bureaucratic
Specialization	Low	Extensive	Extensive	Extensive
Differentiation	Minimal	Moderate	Very high	High
Integration and coordination of effort	By CEO via direct supervision	By technocrats via formal procedures	By integrating personnel, task forces via mutual adjustment	By formal committees via plan and budgets
Information systems	Crude, informal	Cost controls and budgets	Informal scanning, open communications	Management information systems and profit centers
Environmental dimensions				
Technology	Simple, custom	Mass production, large batch/line	Sophisticated product, automated or custom	Varies
Competition	Extreme	High	Moderate	Varies
Dynamism/uncertainty	Moderate	Very low	Very high	Varies
Growth	Varies	Slow	Rapid	Varies
Concentration ratio	Very low	High	Varies	Varies
Barriers to entry	None	Scales barriers	Knowledge barriers	Varies
	Business-level strategies			Corporate-level strategy
Favored strategy	Niche differentiation	Cost leadership	Innovative differentiation	Conglomeration
Marketing emphasis	Quality, service, convenience	Low price	New products, high quality	Image
Production emphasis	Economy	Efficiency	Flexibility	Vertical integration
Asset management	Parsimony	Intensity	Parsimony	Varies
Innovation and R&D	Little	Almost none	Very high	Low to moderate
Product–market scope	Very narrow	Average	Average	Very broad

relevant: they are the simple structure, the machine bureaucracy, the divisionalized form and the adhocracy. We shall adapt and extend Mintzberg's framework somewhat to make it more easy to relate it to the common strategies. The dimensions of each type are summarized in Table [4.4.2].

Simple niche marketers

Simple structure

The simple structure is used by small firms run by a dominating chief executive, often an owner–manager. The structure is highly informal with coordination of tasks accomplished via direct supervision, and all strategies made at the top. There is little specialization of tasks, a low degree of bureaucratization and formalization (few programs, rules or regulations) (Pugh, Hickson and Hinings, 1969), and information systems are extremely primitive. Because there is a low level of differentiation in the goals, interpersonal orientations, methods and time horizons of the various departments, there is little need for sophisticated integrative or 'liaison' devices (Lawrence and Lorsch, 1967). Power is centralized at the top. Technology is often of Perrow's (1971) engineering or nonroutine manufacturing, or Woodward's (1965) custom variety.

Clearly, simple structures cannot be appropriate in all environments and industries. They typically exist where the industry is fragmented (low concentration) and comprised of small highly competitive firms. Competitive rivalry restricts

Table 4.4.3 Matching strategy and structure

Structure and rationale	Match/conflict	Strategy
Simple structure Can offer quality, convenience, and better service since this will not tax the structure	M	Marketing differentiation
Avoids some competition in hostile environment; reduces liability of being small	M	Niche differentiation
Complex innovation impossible in centralized, monolithic structure	C	Innovative differentiation
Insufficient scale; overly primitive structure	C	Conglomeration
Insufficient scale	C	Cost leadership
Machine bureaucracy Substantial scale economies possible Emphasis on efficiency good in stable setting	M	Cost leadership
Suitable only if differentiation does not upset production regularity and efficiency (e.g. advertising, good service)	M	Marketing differentiation
Structure too inflexible	C	Innovative differentiation
Functional–departmental structure inappropriate	C	Conglomeration
Inflexibility, capital intensity	C	Niche differentiation
Organic structure Flexible, innovative structure	M	Innovative differentiation
May be suitable if niche wide enough to make use of innovation potential; need for caution	M	Niche differentiation
Should not squander resources on selling since state-of-art product is already highly desirable to customers	C	Marketing differentiation
Structure is too inefficient	C	Cost leadership
Would spread innovative efforts too thinly; also, structure is not divisionalized	C	Conglomeration
Divisionalized structure Divisions, profit centers, head office controls, formal plans, etc. suitable for diversification	M	Cost leadership
Consistent with bureaucratic tendency; scale economies and vertical integration if divisions use related inputs	M	Cost leadership
Where cost leadership contraindicated marketing differentiation may be suitable for intermediate level of bureaucracy	M	Marketing differentiation
Generally, divisions are forced by head office to be too bureaucratic to be innovative	C	Innovative differentiation

the munificence of the environment and boosts firms' vulnerability. Because simple technologies are often used to produce products, barriers to entry are very low. Market share instability and cost–price squeezes can therefore be major threats. Firms usually have very little bargaining power over their customers in such a competitive setting (see Table [4.4.2]). Indeed, the environment recalls Hambrick's (1983a) 'unruly mob'.

Niche marketing strategy

Given the simple structure and the competitive environment, which of our five strategic types would be most suitable? Typically, simple firms must pursue some sort of differentiation strategy in order to succeed. They are too small and vulnerable to become fixed asset intensive. This would be extremely risky in the light of the substantial industry instability (MacMillan and Hambrick, 1983). Also, simple technologies and small size generally do not allow for cost leadership. Finally, structures are too primitive, too undifferentiated, and too centralized to support *complex* innovation (although very simple, CEO-driven innovations can be common). Thus firms with simple structures must generally pursue a niche or a marketing differentiation strategy. They may flourish by producing a somewhat distinctive product for a niche of the market that is the least competitive. This minimizes some of the disadvantages of smallness. To defend their niche these firms may differentiate their offerings by providing greater convenience, more reliable service, or a more appealing—higher visibility or better quality—product to a select group of customers (strategies A or A_3 on Figure [4.4.1]). None of these competitive strengths require much structural complexity. To conclude, niche or marketing differentiation strategies and simple structures should probably go together (see Table [4.4.2]). Table [4.4.3] summarizes some of the reasons for the matches and mismatches between the simple structure, its setting, and the five strategic types.

Mechanistic cost leaders

Machine bureaucracy structure

The mechanistic (Burns and Stalker, 1961) or machine bureaucracy structure has been alluded to earlier. It is a very rigid structure in which the coordination of tasks is done via standardization of work. A key part of the organization is the technostructure (Mintzberg, 1979) which designs the production system. The technology is somewhat automated and integrated and is normally of the line or large batch variety (Woodward, 1965). The firm is highly specialized as tasks are finely broken down. As its name implies, the structure is exceedingly bureaucratic and hierarchical with its many formal rules, programs and procedures (Burns and Stalker, 1961; Pugh, Hickson and Hinings, 1969). The information systems are quite well developed—but mainly for reporting cost and output rather than market information. The departmental, functionally organized structure is only moderately differentiated as the emphasis throughout is on following programs and plans. Integration is effected mainly through these programs (Lawrence and Lorsch, 1967). Power rests in the hands of the top executives and the designers of workflow processes. Very little authority resides at lower or middle management levels.

The environments of these firms are quite different from those of the niche marketers. Mechanistic firms can thrive only in stable settings. Industries are often highly concentrated and mature, and all the firms are quite large. There is relatively little uncertainty since competitor and customer behavior is fairly predictable. Demand is quite stable, as are market shares. Hambrick's (1983a) 'orderly producers' environments are recalled (see Table [4.4.2]).

Cost leadership strategy

Clearly the strategic options open to these firms are quite limited. The structures are extremely inflexible and geared to efficiency; so strategies of innovation are out of the question. Also, because markets are not growing much (due to maturity) and because firms are large, it is unwise to focus on too small a segment of the industry. This would increase the risk of declines in demand and underutilization of facilities. There are thus only two possible strategies that remain promising—marketing differentiation and cost leadership. The second is very natural since it requires the least flexibility and the greatest production efficiency—characteristics which inhere in these structures. Some firms are able to make excellent use of their machine-like structures. They cut costs to the bone and either earn margins superior to the competition or else build up market share by selling very cheaply. Although it is less likely that mechanistic structures can support a marketing differentiation strategy, this is not totally out of the question. This might happen when the firm sells a fairly standard product in high volume but offers services, convenience or quality that exceed the competition's. It is important that this firm not be placed in a position of having to react quickly to competitors. It must therefore differentiate in a way that does not interfere with efficient and mechanical operations, and is not easy to imitate. For example, a poor differentiation tactic would be to fragment the product line by customizing products. This would immediately boost costs and invite retaliation. Better alternatives might be to integrate forward (perhaps by buying distributorships), to improve quality, or to boost brand image through advertising. None of these tactics requires structural flexibility and all are facilitated by large size. The theme is clear: these structures and settings favor cost leadership. Only under special conditions can they support a strategy of marketing differentiation (see Table [4.4.3]).

Innovating adhocracies

Organic structure

The organic form (Burns and Stalker, 1961) or adhocracy (Mintzberg, 1979) is a structure that is extremely different from—one might almost say opposite to—the machine bureaucracy. It is ideal for performing unusual and complex tasks which tend to change continually. Such tasks confront Perrow's (1971) R&D firms where there are 'many exceptions' in production and no obvious way of accomplishing the job. Typically, groups of highly trained specialists from a variety of areas work together intensively to design and produce complex and rapidly changing products. Representatives from R&D, marketing and production departments, collaborate face-to-face, via mutual adjustment (Thompson, 1967) in order to coordinate their contributions. A high degree of differentiation prevails as people with different skills, goals and time horizons work together (Lawrence and Lorsch, 1967). Frequent meetings, integrating personnel, committees, and other liaison devices are used to ensure effective collaboration (Galbraith, 1973). Power is decentralized as much of it resides with the technocrats and scientists responsible for innovation. Authority is thus situational and based on expertise (Burns and Stalker, 1961). There are few bureaucratic rules or standard procedures since these are too confining and would in any event rapidly become obsolete. Sensitive information gathering systems are developed for analyzing the environment, and vertical and horizontal communications are open and frequent. Production technology varies both in its degree of automation and its complexity. It is, for example, highly automated and complex in the semiconductor industry, but of a job shop, custom nature in some aerospace firms.

The environment tends to be very complex and dynamic. Technologies change rapidly, as do product designs and customer needs. A high percentage of production may be exported. Advanced industry capabilities create 'knowledge barriers' to entry (Scherer, 1980). As a result, competitive rivalry is usually not quite as intensive as for the simple structures. Competition is further reduced by a fairly brisk rate of demand growth. But market share instability may arise as firms leapfrog one another with their new creative advances. Product sophistication is often substantial. To summarize, the environment is dynamic, uncertain and moderately competitive (see Table [4.4.3]).

Innovative differentiation strategy

One of our strategies immediately comes to mind as a fine match for this structure and environment. It is differentiation through innovation (A_2). The structure is flexible and allows for the collaboration among specialists so necessary to create new products. Burns and Stalker (1961), Lawrence and Lorsch (1967) and Mintzberg (1979), have already stressed this theme. The information and scanning systems keep managers and technocrats up to date with scientific and competitive developments. Intensive collaboration and liaison devices, open communications, and decentralization of power (in fact, the reliance on expertise-based power) facilitate complex and continual innovation. Rapid adaptation to the dynamic environment is essential, and this can only be accomplished with a strategy of innovation. Asset parsimony may be useful as high capital intensity dramatically reduces flexibility (MacMillan and Hambrick, 1983). (The cost leadership strategy is clearly inappropriate since it impedes innovation and inhibits adaptiveness. See Table [4.4.3].)

Innovating adhocracies would do well not to focus too broadly or too narrowly in their selection of markets. While geographic expansion and exporting may be advisable because of barriers to entry and product sophistication, other types of broadening should probably be restricted. For example, if the firm enters too many markets which have different competitive conditions and customer requirements, it may find its efforts spread too thin to do very well in any one of them. Recall that market dynamism places a premium on flexibility, innovation and product sophistication. This entails a large administrative and structural burden even in a limited market. On the other hand, firms probably should not focus as narrowly as the simple niche marketers. This might increase their dependence on a small cyclical market and prevent them from commercializing their discoveries in a new and growing domain. Diversification could allow firms to more easily shift into safer niches when attacked.

We have discussed only the innovation aspects of differentiation as these can best be exploited by adhocracies. The marketing differentiation variables generally should play a smaller role. Customers want state-of-the-art, sophisticated products. If these are not supplied, no amount of advertising or promotion will help. In fact, firms may benefit from holding down their marketing expenses to conserve the resources necessary for innovation. One marketing differentiation strategy that might succeed here stresses high quality. Some customers might be willing to trade off novelty for reliability.

Divisionalized conglomerates

Divisional structure

An organization may be split into divisions that are responsible for producing and marketing a discrete type of product. Usually these divisions are self-contained profit centers run by an executive whose responsibilities are similar to those of the chief executives of most independent enterprises. The individual divisions may in fact be quite different from one another—a few employing organic structure, many more using bureaucratic structures. Therefore we must shift our focus from business-level structures and strategies to those that apply at the corporate level.

Mintzberg (1979) argues that most divisions in his 'divisionalized form' are driven to become somewhat bureaucratic and formalized. The head office standardizes procedures and methods wherever possible to improve control over the divisions (Chandler, 1962; Channon, 1973). It emphasizes performance control through sophisticated management information systems, cost centers, and profit centers. However, a good deal of decision-making power remains in the hands of the divisional managers who know the most about their markets. The divisions tend to operate fairly independently of one another, with company-wide issues being handled by interdivisional committees and head office staff departments (see Table [4.4.2]).

Environments vary from one division to the next. Mintzberg (1979) believes that the bureaucratic orientations of the divisions require that the environment be stable and simple. Clearly, however, there are exceptions as some divisionalized firms operate in rather turbulent sectors of the economy.

Conglomeration and diversification strategy

The literature agrees overwhelmingly that corporate-level conglomerate strategies that embrace very different industries require divisionalized structures. The administrative complexity caused by diversification gets divided up so that each significant market is dealt with by its own specialist and generalist managers. The head office is concerned only with controlling and appraising the divisions, allocating capital, and scouting out new diversification ventures.

This relationship between diversification and divisionalization has given rise to Chandler's (1962) famous dictum that 'structure follows strategy'. We are not at all sure, however, that this is always true. A corporate strategy of conglomeration and a divisional structure may well be part of the same gestalt—diversification creates the need for divisionalization; but divisionalized structures, with their head office venture groups and planning departments, seek out new acquisitions. Often, then, strategy may follow structure. One thing, however, is certain: divisionalized structures tend to be matched by corporate strategies that are the least focused—irrespective of the source of the match (see Table [4.4.3]).

We mentioned earlier that the divisions experience pressures of control from the head office, which often induce bureaucratization, formalization, and a loss of flexibility. This precludes business-level strategies of differentiation through innovation. But marketing differentiation strategies and cost leadership business strategies may be quite useful. Their appropriateness will be a function of the degree of stability in the environment, the prospects of economies of scale, and, of course, the degree of bureaucratization in the divisions. The more prevalent these qualities, the greater the appropriateness of cost leadership. The less prevalent the qualities (all other things being equal) the more suitable the strategy of marketing or even niche differentiation. Of course different divisions may pursue different business strategies.

One element of cost leadership—backward vertical integration at the corporate level—may be quite appropriate for some conglomerates. In cases where divisions use similar raw material inputs, their collective demand for supplies may warrant backward integration. This can allow economies of manufacture for the total organization without reducing the possibilities of differentiation for the division. The same argument might hold for integration forward.

Conclusion

Our arguments throughout have been somewhat crude, the principal aim having been to propose a new method of relating strategy to structure and to suggest some illustrative configurations and linkages. No doubt there are many effective matches between strategies and structures other than the ones we have discussed. Also, the appropriateness of a strategy in general, as well as the relative effectiveness of its various elements, will be a function of much more than structure. It will depend on economic, competitive and customer factors, as well as conditions in international markets. Our arguments, therefore, must be viewed as tentative because we still know so little about the subject. We very much hope that this does not alienate readers but rather spurs them on to more thoroughly investigate the relationships between common structural and strategic configurations and their implications for performance in different environments. More encompassing empirical taxonomies should be of considerable help in this quest.

References

Aguilar, F. *Scanning the Business Environment*. MacMillan, New York, 1967.

Aldrich, H. E. *Organizations and Environments*. Prentice-Hall, Englewood Cliffs, NJ, 1979.

Ansoff, H. I. *Corporate Strategy*. McGraw-Hill, New York, 1965.

Astley, W. G. 'The dynamics of organizational evolution: critical reflections on the variation-selection-retention model'. Working Paper, The Wharton School, Philadelphia, 1983.

Burns, T. and G. Stalker. *The Management of Innovation*. Tavistock, London, 196 1.

Buzzell, R. D., B. Gale and R. Sultan. 'Market share: a key to profitability', *Harvard Business Review*, 51(1), 1975, pp. 97–106.

Chandler, A. *Strategy and Structure*. MIT Press, Cambridge, MA, 1962.

Channon, D. *Strategy and Structure in British Enterprise*. Harvard University Press, Boston, MA, 1973.

Crozier, M. *The Bureaucratic Phenomenon*. University of Chicago Press, Chicago, IL, 1964.

Dess, G. and P. Davis. 'Porter's generic strategies as determinants of strategic group membership and organizational performance', *Academy of Management Journal*, 27, 1984, pp. 467–488.

Galbraith, J. *Designing Complex Organizations*. Addison-Wesley, Reading, MA, 1973.

Gale, B. 'Can more capital buy higher productivity?', *Harvard Business Review*, 58(4), 1980, pp. 67–77.

Hambrick, D. C. 'An empirical typology of mature industrial product environments', *Academy of Management Journal*, 26, 1983a, pp. 213–230.

Hambrick, D. C. 'High profit strategies in mature capital goods industries: a contingency approach', *Academy of Management Journal*, 26, 1983b, pp. 687–707.

Hambrick, D. and S. Schecter. 'Turnaround strategies for mature industrial-product business units', *Academy of Management Journal*, 26, 1983, pp. 231–248.

Hannan, M. and J. Freeman. 'The population ecology of organizations', *American Journal of Sociology*, 83, 1977, pp. 929–964.

[omitted text in original] organization', *Administrative Science Quarterly*, 21, 1976, pp. 41-65.

Henderson, B. *Henderson on Corporate Strategy*. Abt Books, Cambridge, MA, 1979.

Hinings, C. R., R. Greenwood, S. Ranson and K. Walsh. 'Reform reorientation and change: the designing of organizational change'. Unpublished manuscript, Department of Commerce, University of Alberta, Edmonton, 1984.

Hofer, C. and D. Schendel. *Strategy Formulation: Analytical Concepts*. West, St Paul, MN, 1978.

Lawrence, P. R. and J. W. Lorsch. *Organization and Environment*. Harvard University Press, Boston, MA, 1967.

MacMillan, I. C. and D. Hambrick. 'Capital intensity, market share instability and profits: the case for asset parsimony'. Working Paper, Columbia University Strategy Research Center, New York, 1983.

MacMillan, I. C., D. C. Hambrick and D. Day. 'The product portfolio and profitability: a PIMS-based analysis of industrial-product businesses', *Academy of Management Journal*, 25, 1982, pp. 733–755.

McKelvey, W. *Organizational Systematics*. University of California Press, Los Angeles, CA, 1981.

Miles, R. and C. Snow. *Organizational Strategy, Structure and Process*. McGraw-Hill, New York, 1978.

Miller, D. 'Evolution and revolution: a quantum view of structural change in organizations', *Journal of Management Studies*, 19, 1982, pp. 131–151.

Miller, D. 'The correlates of entrepreneurship in three types of firms', *Management Science*, 29, 1983, pp. 770–791.

Miller, D. and P. H. Friesen. 'Strategy making in context: ten empirical archetypes', *Journal of Management Studies*, 14, 1977, pp. 259–280.

Miller, D. and P. H. Friesen. 'Archetypes of strategy formulation', *Management Science*, 24, 1978, pp. 921–933.

Miller, D. and P. H. Friesen. 'Momentum and revolution in organizational adaptation', *Academy of Management Journal*, 23, 1980, pp. 591–614.

Miller, D. and P. H. Friesen. 'Structural change and performance: quantum vs. piecemeal-incremental approaches', *Academy of Management Journal*, 25, 1982, pp. 867–892.

Miller, D. and P. H. Friesen. 'Porter's generic strategies and performance'. Working Paper, McGill University, Montreal, 1984a.

Miller, D. and P. H. Friesen. *Organizations: A Quantum View*. Prentice Hall, Englewood Cliffs, NJ, 1984b.

Miller, D. and H. Mintzberg. 'The case for configuration'. In Miller, D. and P. Friesen (eds), *Organizations: A Quantum View*. Prentice Hall, Englewood Cliffs, NJ, 1984, pp. 10–30.

Mintzberg, H. 'Strategy making in three modes', *California Management Review*, 16, 1973, pp. 44–58.

Mintzberg, H. *The Structuring of Organizations*. Prentice Hall, Englewood Cliffs, NJ, 1979.

Perrow, C. *Organizational Analysis: A Sociological View*. Wadsworth, Belmont, CA, 1971.

Pooley-Dias, G. 'The strategy and structure of French industrial enterprise'. Doctoral dissertation; Harvard Business School, Boston, MA, 1972.

Porter, M. *Competitive Strategy*. Free Press, New York, 1980.

Pugh, D. S., D. J. Hickson and C. R. Hinings. 'An empirical taxonomy of structures of work organizations', *Administrative Science Quarterly*, 14, 1969, pp. 115–126.

Quinn, J. B. *Strategies for Change: Logical Incrementalism*. Irwin, Homewood, IL, 1980.

Rumelt, R. P. *Strategy, Structure, and Economic Performance*. Division of Research, Graduate School of Business Administration, Harvard University, Cambridge, MA, 1974.

Scherer, F. *Industrial Market Structure and Economic Performance*. Rand McNally, Chicago, IL, 1980.

Schoeffler, S., R. D. Buzzell and D. F. Heany. 'Impact of strategic planning on profit performance', *Harvard Business Review*, 52(2), 1974, pp. 137–145.

Starbuck, W., A. Greve and B. Hedberg. 'Responding to crises', *Journal of Business Administration*, 9, 1978, pp. 111–137.

Thanheiser, H. T. 'Strategy and structure in German industrial enterprise'. Doctoral dissertation, Harvard Business School, Boston, MA, 1972.

Thompson, J. *Organizations in Action*. McGraw-Hill, New York, 1967.

Tushman, M. L. and E. Romanelli. 'Organizational evolution: a metamorphosis model of convergence and reorientation'. Working Paper, Columbia University Center for Strategy Research, New York, 1983.

Woodward, J. *Industrial Organization: Theory and Practice*. Oxford University Press, London, 1965.

Reading 4.5 The co-creation connection *C. K. Prahalad and Venkatram Ramaswamy*

First published: (2002) *Strategy + Business*, 27: 1–12. Reprinted with permission from the Second Quarter 2002 issue of *strategy + business magazine*, published by Booz & Company.

For more than 100 years, a company-centric, efficiency-driven view of value creation has shaped our industrial infrastructure and the entire business system. Although this perspective often conflicts with what consumers value—the quality of their experiences with goods and services—companies see value creation as a process of cost-effectively producing goods and services. Now information and communications technology, the Internet in particular, is forcing companies to think differently about value creation and to be more responsive to consumer experiences. In fact, the balance of power in value creation is tipping in favor of consumers.

The disconnect between what companies and consumers value traces back to the early-20th-century industrial principles. Frederick Winslow Taylor's scientific management focused on lowering unit costs of production. The value chain, a concept introduced by Michael Porter in the 1980s, gave managers an integrated framework to identify and manage costs of designing, producing, marketing, delivering, and supporting goods or services. And Michael Hammer and James Champy's business process reengineering was widely interpreted as implicitly linking cost reduction and internal efficiencies to value creation.

During the 1990s, notions of the extended enterprise and the boundaryless organization encouraged managers to broaden their search for efficiencies and discover ways of creating value from their supplier network and beyond. Starting in 1995, the Internet further invigorated the corporate pursuit of efficiency, this time expanding it to include all the activities directly involving or affecting the company–customer relationship. Still, throughout this evolution, the assumption that internal cost efficiency is the source of value creation has remained unchallenged.

Consumers appreciate and expect efficiency when it improves their experience with a product or service. But most of the time, managers are so preoccupied with operating efficiently that they don't even think about value in terms of the consumer's experience. (See [Figure 4.5.1].) Ask yourself: Do you as a consumer of a digital camera think about the complex sourcing patterns and logistics that the manufacturer has to deal with, or are you thinking about the fun you will have when you bring the camera to the beach to record your children's first ocean swim?

Because companies have historically controlled all business activities involved in the creation of the things they sell, it is their view of value that is dominant. Indeed, the consumer typically has little or no influence on value created

Figure 4.5.1 Value creation: how companies and consumers think

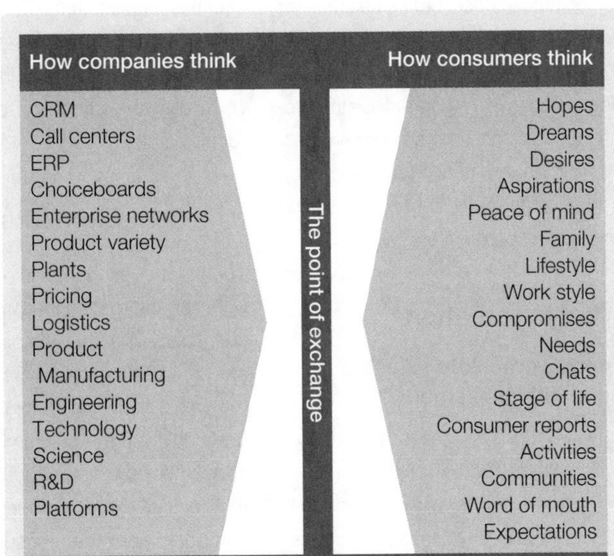

until the point of exchange when ownership of the product is typically transferred to the consumer from the firm. This is true whether the consumer is a company or an individual.

Now consumers are challenging this corporate logic of value creation. Spurred by the consumer-centric culture of the Internet—with its emphasis on interactivity, speed, individuality, and openness—the consumer's influence on value creation has never been greater, and it is spreading to all points in the value chain. . . .

And therein lies a fundamental challenge for business. Companies have grown used to viewing consumers as passive target markets for what they create. But, interestingly, markets are not passive; they are now becoming more like forums, largely because of the Internet. In the "market as a forum," consumers actively define value the way *they* see value—as experiences—and push companies to see it the same way. Today's companies know just how dramatically 40 million consumers networking with each other and challenging the status quo online, in categories as different as music and mortgages, are shaking up the business world.

In this environment, we believe companies need to embrace a new approach to value creation, one in which the basis for value shifts from products to experiences; consumer influence is spread across the value chain (in research and development, design, manufacturing, logistics, service, and points in between); conflicts between companies and consumers are more visible and resolved more productively; and companies don't dictate how value is created.

In short, companies must learn to *co-create* value with their customers.

Although it is only human to feel threatened by a loss of control, it makes little sense for companies not to be open and engaged with consumers. By partnering with them in the value creation process, companies can better balance the objectives of value creation, managing the bottom line (cost and investments) and the top line (growth and revenues). Furthermore, co-creation is becoming a competitive imperative. Information illuminating what consumers value is voluminous, and it flows freely in information networks. If your company does not capture this intelligence to create more fulfilling experiences for consumers, your competitors will.

The art of co-creation

How do companies co-create valuable experiences with consumers?

The traditional company-centric view says: (1) the consumer is outside the domain of the value chain; (2) the enterprise controls where, when, and how value is added in the value chain; (3) value is created in a series of activities controlled by the enterprise before the point of purchase; (4) there is a single point of exchange where value is extracted from the customer for the enterprise.

The consumer-centric view says: (1) the consumer is an integral part of the system for value creation; (2) the consumer can influence where, when, and how value is generated; (3) the consumer need not respect industry boundaries in the search for value; (4) the consumer can compete with companies for value extraction; (5) there are multiple points of exchange where the consumer and the company can co-create value.

In the customer-centric mass production and marketing of automobiles, for example, suppliers provide raw materials, components, subcomponents, and systems to manufacturers, who create value by assembling these inputs into vehicles. Consumers actively decide what vehicle to buy, but companies decide what their choices will be. Cars are sold by dealers acting as intermediaries for the automakers. For companies reliant on this scenario, value creation is defined solely by extracting profit from end consumers.

The Saturn Corporation, billing itself as "a different kind of Car Company," has spurned the industry's traditional ways. In 1985, when the General Motors Corporation launched Saturn, it didn't just start a new car company, it created a "community." Saturn works with its customers in the design, manufacturing, and sales processes, and it engages Saturn owners to help continuously innovate and improve its cars.

Consumers think about the place of a car in their life—how it fits their budget, their desire for comfort, their need for peace of mind, their aesthetics. Companies think about their competitive strategy and their operations— engineering, differentiation, logistics, pricing, and, above all, revenue and profit. Although these views of value do clash, they're not irreconcilable. Saturn is a company trying to merge these two ways of looking at value.

In the pages that follow, we present a framework—a new value creation paradigm—to suggest how companies can better understand the consumer's view of value and productively work with them to co-create more satisfying value for both sides.

Elements of exchange

The point of exchange is often the place where the conflict between the traditional company view of value and the consumer view of value is most exposed. Although companies are not inclined to interact with consumers at all points in the value chain, opportunities for exchanges between the company and the consumer neither begin nor end when a consumer purchases something from a company. Indeed, the point of exchange need not be restricted to where the company and the consumer trade money for finished goods or services.

If experience is the critical source of value for consumers, we need to identify the factors that determine experience. We call these the elements of exchange, and they are:

- How *transactions* are managed.
- How *choices* are determined.
- How the *consumption experience* is staged.
- How *price* and *performance* relate.

By examining the four basic elements that constitute an exchange, companies can explore how current management approaches may positively or negatively affect customer experiences, and discover better ways to create value.

Transactions

Companies have been quick to spot emerging technologies that reduce transaction costs by having consumers perform functions formerly handled by employees (i.e., customer self-service). Gas stations' transitioning from full-service to self-service was an easy win for gasoline retailers and consumers. Companies asked customers to fill their own tanks and pay through devices on the pump. And what drivers lost in attendant service they happily traded for the convenience of self-service and, sometimes, better prices.

But most customer self-service scenarios aren't this smooth. Managers are usually so preoccupied with the cost advantages of self-service that they misjudge its consequences on the customer experience. Or worse, they don't consider the consequences at all. Anyone who has been foiled by automated multiple-choice customer service over the phone, or who has been left on hold listening to bad music, knows the limitations of call centers. When hospitals, laboratories, and pharmacies put health records, diagnoses, and prescription information online to cut costs, are they taking into account consumer concern about privacy?

On the Web—the ultimate self-service technology—corporate indifference to the consumer experience occurs constantly. Witness the number of abandoned "shopping carts"; perhaps shoppers who stop short of purchasing find the interfaces confusing or don't feel secure using a credit card online. For the consumer who doesn't believe a company will not sell his or her personal data to someone else, giving profile information in exchange for the convenience of "one-click" purchasing or instant recognition on a password-protected Web site may not be worth the risk. Companies also have greatly underestimated how differently older and younger people view issues like privacy and security online.

The key issue in automating transactions is consumer heterogeneity. Customers differ in their skills, their propensity for problem solving, and their willingness to spend time to learn a new system, as well as their willingness to trust it. This is true whether it involves the Web or any other system that is unfamiliar.

Self-service works best when it's applied by companies that manage their costs and the customer experience with equal care. Southwest Airlines Company works hard to make sure its standards for being prompt, accurate, and friendly are the same whether the customer exchange is made through an automated channel or handled by an employee. Similarly, Lands' End Inc. has invested in self-service technology and superior agent training so that the consumer experience on its Web site is as good as its catalog operation consumer experience.

Choice

Elaborately structured distribution and communications channels allow companies to control a consumer's choices. But when companies don't offer the same choices across channels, they risk antagonizing the customer. One clothing retailer trying to optimize inventory management and pricing by channel charged $48 for a shirt online and marked the same shirt down to $24.99 in a retail store. Over time, consumers will recognize such differences, and they might accept them, but only if an explicit policy exists that says online and in-store pricing (or styles and colors) may differ.

Information technology has opened a whole new opportunity for manufacturers to cost-effectively offer customized products faster and cheaper. In the computer industry, companies like the Dell Computer Corporation have an impressive competitive advantage in build-to-order PCs. Now BMW is offering a "custom" car, delivered in 12 days. For the Z3 roadster, the automaker offers a choice of 26 wheel designs and 123 console options.

Mass customization allows companies like Dell and BMW to offer variety, but who decides what can be customized? Customization ultimately is a matter of what can be built and delivered to suit the efficient operation of a company's value chain. Even in the most sophisticated mass-customization schemes, the customer chooses from a menu dictated by the company.

Thanks to the Web, companies can become much more astute about what consumers like and don't like, and that knowledge will greatly improve companies' ability to be innovative and to anticipate consumer needs. On the Web, consumer-to-consumer recommendations, new ideas, critiques, musings, and more are having a powerful influence on choice. About.com (owned by Primedia Inc.), one of the most popular consumer word-of-mouth sites, is host to discussions about more than 50,000 subjects, from allergies to zebras. Content, organized by topic, is kept fresh and credible with a thorough oversight system run jointly by About.com and its community members. Sites like About.com are trying to establish businesses promoting

The five powers of the connected consumer

Before the Internet liberated information, companies could do everything—choose materials used in products, design production processes, craft marketing messages, control sales channels—with no interference. Now, consumers exercise their influence in every part of the business system. Nevertheless, companies should welcome, not resist, the consumer powers detailed below.

1. Information access

With access to unprecedented of information, consumers have knowledge to make much more informed amounts decisions. This is causing companies across industries to cede control over value creation and develop new ways of doing business. Consider health care. More than 70 million Americans have reportedly used the internet to learn about diseases and treatment options and investigate how to get involved in clinical drug trials. Consumers now question their physicians more aggressively and participate more fully in choosing treatments. This is dramatically altering traditional pharmaceutical sales practices. In the U.S., it is driving consumer-centric "defined-contribution" health-care reform wherein companies give employees information and ask them to assume more responsibility for selecting and managing their own health-care benefits.

2. Global view

The internet is the first single source of information that gives consumers the ability, 24 hours a day, to see what is happening around the world. That is changing the rules for how companies compete. For example, multinationals are more exposed to consumer scrutiny of product price and performance across geographies, which means those businesses have less latitude to vary the price or quality of products sold in multiple regions. But it also means companies have more information to sharpen global strategies. New competitors and potential partners for large companies are also emerging in the global marketplace. Even poor artisans in Rajasthan, India, can sell high-quality table linen on the Web for $10 and deliver it to buyers in the U.S. in about a week, and for one-tenth the cost of comparable linen in the United States.

3. Networking

Consumers naturally coalesce around common skills, internets, and experiences. The internet amplifies this by encouraging an unparalleled ease and openness of communication among perfect strangers indeed "communities of interest," where individuals confabulate and commiserate without geographic constraints and with few social barriers, exist all over the Web. People participating in a chat area may know nothing more about those they're chatting with than the interest they share. The power of consumer networks is that they're independent and based on real consumer experiences, not what the company tells them they will experience.

Such networking among consumers turns traditional company-controlled marketing and advertising upside down. For example, rather than attempt to shut down unofficial Hobbit fan sites, New line Cinema co-opted them, to help spread word of mouth and create buzz about its movie The *Lord of the Rings*. Gordon Paddison, senior vice president of worldwide interactive marketing reached out to the more than 400 fan sites before the movie was released to communicate with the early influencers and give them insider lips.

Consumer education and feedback sites are struggling to prove themselves as viable business. But this does not diminish their utility as places where consumer can compare and share information, and places where companies can learn what consumer are thinking.

4. Experimentation

Consumers use the Internet to experiment with and develop products, especially digital ones. The German research company Fraunhofer Institute for Experimental Software Engineering released MP3 as a freely available compression standard that accelerated the transmission of digital audio.

The collective competence of software users has enabled the codevelopment of popular products, such as the Apache Web server software and the Linux operating system.

The ability of consumers to experiment with each other goes beyond software and digital products. Cooks can share recipes. Gardening enthusiasts can share tips on growing organic vegetables. Homeowners can share stories about their home improvement projects. The list goes on. Companies that choose the path of co-creation can tap into consumers creativity for the development of products and services.

5. Activism

As people learn, they become more discriminating in their choices about what they buy, and as they network, they become emboldened to speak out. Now consumers provide unsolicited feedback to companies and to each other. There are hundreds of "sounding-off sites" on the Web that target specific companies and brands. AOL Watch, for example, publishes complaints from former and current AOL customers. The Web has also become an influential tool for social groups focused on such issues as child labor and environmental protection to get corporate attention and promote reform. Although activism might seem menacing to companies, it also opens the door to competitive opportunity.

consumer-to-consumer communication, but thousands of Web sites exist that buzz with conversations about what consumers value and don't value. Companies need to listen, learn, and absorb this valuable intelligence.

Even in the world of drugs for treating life-threatening diseases, consumer advocacy in online support groups seems to be as influential as company marketing. For example, when Novartis AG began clinical trials of a promising leukemia drug, word spread so fast that the company was overwhelmed with demand from patients seeking participation.

Consumption experience

Companies like the Starbucks Corporation and Walt Disney Company are highly attuned to human behaviors, preferences, and tastes because experiences are the essence of what they sell. But the fact is companies that manufacture products bear just as much responsibility as restaurants and entertainment companies for enhancing or diminishing the value of consumer experience. For example, most antibiotics are prescribed to be taken several times a day for two to three weeks. If you forget to take the pills, the medicine is ineffective, and many people don't remember to complete the full cycle. The pharmaceutical company Pfizer Inc. saw this behavior as an opportunity to make it easier for people to take medicine the way it was prescribed. It introduced an antibiotic called Zithromax that typically requires an initial dosage of two pills followed by a daily single pill for only four days. Then Pfizer marketed Zithromax in a blister pack called the Z-pak, which clearly reminds users of their daily dosage requirement and how much they have left to take. Pfizer effectively became the patient's partner in making it as easy as possible for the medicine to do its curative work.

Zithromax now dominates its market. Consumers like Zithromax's shorter cycle and the convenient reminders to take their pill. Doctors, too, applaud these features, because they make the drug more effective. With the Z-pak, Pfizer has creatively incorporated the consumption variable into the manufacture and design of the product to increase its value.

Price-performance

The traditional psychology of price setting, largely based on cost structures, is becoming increasingly irrelevant. Further, the relationship between price and performance is no longer implicit and controlled by companies; it is explicit and debated by consumers.

Independent consumer-feedback Web sites, such as Epinions.com, PlanetFeedback.com, and BizRate.com, allow people to share price information recommendations, reviews, and comparative price information for thousands of products. Search engines like Google are also powerful tools consumers can use to collect and compare price and performance data.

Global television and the Internet make it easier for people to see the kinds of products companies sell in different regions and countries and compare them to what's offered in their own market. That is altering consumer desires and raising consumer expectations, especially in developing countries. Consumers in emerging-market countries (e.g., India, Brazil, and Indonesia) with annual incomes sufficient to purchase cars, refrigerators, branded clothing, and other mainstays of comfortable living expect these products to be affordably priced and to meet global quality standards and local cultural requirements.

The new challenge for companies accustomed to producing lower-priced, and often inferior, goods for these markets is to raise the consumer experience bar and make a profit. For example, Hyundai in India is successfully selling its Santro sedan for the equivalent of about $8,000. The Santro's driving performance is comparable to that of a compact car sold in the U.S. for about $11,000, and it has comfort features, such as spacious seating and headroom, that are highly valued by consumers in India.

Even the world's 4 billion poorest consumers, who earn less than $1,500 a year, are aspiring to a better life and demanding more goods and services. This situation represents a huge opportunity for companies to change their mind-sets and their business models (e.g., "the poor can't afford or have no use for consumer products," or "we can't make money in this market"). In 1995, Unilever PLC's subsidiary in India, Hindustan Lever Ltd. (HLL), drastically altered the management of its value chain so it could sell a detergent, called Wheel, to the poor. HLL decentralized its production, marketing, and distribution and quickly established sales channels through thousands of small storefronts. HLL adjusted the cost structure of its detergent business so it could sell Wheel at a very low price point and still make money. Today, Wheel has gross margins and a return on capital as good as, or better than, HLL's higher-end cleaning products, and Unilever has used this business model to create a new detergent market in Brazil.

Patients at India's Aravind Eye Hospital, the world's largest eye-care facility, pay about $10 for cataract surgery, compared to $1,600 for equivalent care in the United States. The hospital, which operates on more than 200,000 patients per year, gives 60 percent of its care at no cost and still is highly profitable. Between 1998 and 1999, Aravind's total income was Rs. 230.6 million (about $5.2 million), with a profit of Rs. 110.1 million (about $2.5 million), and return on capital of more than 200 percent on surgery and its lens manufacturing arm. Like Unilever, Aravind is testing this business model in other regions.

Building blocks for co-creation

Businesses operate in a networked environment in which it is possible both to learn continuously about what people want and need, and to interact with them in ongoing exchanges of value. But companies need to be much more aware of where these opportunities to interact with consumers exist.

We suggest there are four building blocks for co-creating value. *Dialogue* at every stage of the value chain encourages not just knowledge sharing, but, even more importantly, understanding between companies and customers. It also gives consumers more opportunity to interject their view of value into the creation process. In short, *access* challenges the notion that ownership is the only way for the consumer to experience value. By focusing on access to value at multiple points of exchange, as opposed to simply ownership of products, companies can broaden their view of the business opportunities creating good experiences. *Risk reduction* assumes that if consumers become co-creators of value with companies, they will demand more information about potential risks of goods and services; but they may also have to bear more responsibility for handling those risks. *Transparency* of information is required to create the trust between institutions and individuals.

1. Dialogue

Dialogue is creating shared meaning. In dialogues, people listen and learn from each other; in the most productive dialogues, people communicate and debate as equals. Dialogue helps companies to understand the emotional, social, and cultural contexts that shape consumer experiences and provides knowledge companies can use to innovate. Dialogue with consumers is central to Harley-Davidson Inc.'s being able to co-create a multigenerational "way of life." Building a forum for dialogue was how, early on, America Online Inc. created a community—a group of enthusiasts whose shared interests bonded them to the service at the same time that it gave the company insights into service improvements. Dialogue was what kept a loyal community of Macintosh users together when Apple Computer Inc's product development began to wane. And it is dialogue that is helping the personal-computer manufacturer to recover with the introduction of the new iMac.

Dialogue involves more than listening and reacting. It requires deep engagement, lively interactivity, empathetic understanding, and a willingness by both parties to act, especially when they're at odds. What is happening in the music industry today is the antithesis of dialogue. If the record labels were listening, they would hear that consumers don't object to paying for music. They just want to create their own musical experiences once they've paid for it. People have been packaging their own music for years (in the 1970s, parents of Napster and MP3 player fans made custom cassette tapes by copying songs from long-playing records). Why, with even better technology available today to duplicate and mix their own music, would consumers want anything else?

While recording companies fight the battle against "illegal downloading" and resist changing their business models, music sales are declining and sales of blank CDs are soaring. "If the industry doesn't change the way we do business, we're going to be bankrupt," Val Azzoli, cochairman of Atlantic Records, told the *New York Times* in February 2002. The Sony Corporation shows just what's at stake. Its music sales are currently about *$4.6* billion, compared to about $40 billion in sales from consumer electronics, including CD burners and MP3 players.

2. Access

Ownership is the traditional way to look at the transfer of value from the company to the customer. But you don't need to own something to experience its value. Indeed, access without ownership is desirable for consumers and can be very profitable for businesses. Thinking in terms of access expands a company's view of potential markets.

Over the past decade, numerous companies serving European and U.S. cities have begun to offer a novel service for people who want more than just a rental car; they want the convenience of having a car they don't own at their disposal all the time. For example, in Switzerland, people who join Mobility CarSharing receive a personal access device that unlocks a dedicated pool of cars, which are rented on a pay-as-you-drive basis, making the service ideal for running short errands, visiting friends in the suburbs in the evening, and the like. What do Mobility CarSharing and similar companies sell? A new urban lifestyle that is not only economical and convenient, but also reduces pollution and parking problems.

In the music industry, consumers are not fighting for all music to be free; they just want more freedom to choose how they access music once they've paid a fair price. This is a classic instance of the consumer being shut out of the value creation process.

The successful coupling of access with dialogue in the computer community's Open Source movement has had a significant influence on traditional players in the industry as they see its benefits. For example, to promote the use of Linux, the open source operating system, IBM is putting $40 million of its software tools in the public domain. More important, in 2001, IBM made the largest commitment of any computer maker—about 20 percent of its R&D budget ($1 billion)—to Linux and Apache Web servers.

3. Risk reduction

The obligations and responsibilities of the firm and consumers for risk management will always be debated. But it is safe to assume that as consumers become more involved in co-creating experiences with companies, they may be willing to take on more responsibility for managing risk exposures, if companies are willing to reveal more information about the risks associated with the products and services they produce. One key issue in the Firestone–Ford tire case centered on the amount of knowledge Ford and Firestone had about risks associated with the combination of vehicle, tire pressure, and driving conditions. How much should Firestone and Ford have shared with consumers?

In a world where good information is widely available, consumers, within the limits of their technical knowledge, should be able to make more informed choices about risks. Companies can be a part of that process by being both forthcoming in the discussions of risk with the general public, and by disseminating appropriate methods for assessing personal risk and societal risk. Labeling is one way of explicitly passing on to the consumer more responsibility for risk. But that is not enough. Companies will need to be more willing to engage in open dialogues with concerned people. Companies should not approach their communications defensively. On the contrary, proactive risk communication and management offers new opportunities for firms to differentiate themselves.

4. Transparency

In the wake of the Enron debacle, shareholders are demanding more transparent, or thorough, financial disclosure; but transparency is also necessary for consumers of goods and services to become co-creators of value. When companies make vital business-process information visible to consumers, companies, in effect, relinquish control of the value creation process before the traditional point of exchange.

The Federal Express Corporation has high levels of transparency in its logistics system. Customers can log on to its Web site and check the progress of packages in real time using the same information that FedEx employees use; large corporate customers can also reroute packages themselves. Individuals have choices they wouldn't have if FedEx controlled all the information, and that improves the customer experience.

This same type of information transparency has created a revolution in the trading of securities. Global agency brokers like Instinet Group Inc. build transparency into their trading systems so that customers can monitor in real time how much the fund manager's trading is costing them.

In June 2001, Eli Lilly and Company launched a new e-business research venture called InnoCentive LLC. It brings together, via its Web site, companies and researchers from around the world seeking solutions to scientific problems. Significant cash incentives are awarded to researchers who offer the solution judged "best" by the company that posted the problem. InnoCentive represents a bold open source approach to innovation for industries that in the past have been closed and private.

Sumerset Houseboats, the world's largest houseboat manufacturer, based in rural Kentucky, shows how all the pieces of a co-creation model—dialogue, access, risk reduction, and transparency—can fit together. Imagine interactively codesigning the layout and configuration of your dream boat, negotiating specs and prices, connecting with the factory to participate in your boat's construction, and monitoring its progress in real time. Now imagine a personal Web page where you can review drawings; access architectural, aesthetic, and structural expertise; and consult a customer representative. You can see pictures and read the biographies of the people who are crafting your boat. You can critique design elements and fully furnish your boat before it is delivered. You can have dialogues with other Sumerset customers and a wider community of avid sailors.

What is co-created in this process is not just a boat, a physical artifact, but also experiences. Even before owners set sail, they begin to form an emotional attachment to their boat while building their stake in the outcome of the value creation process.

The company also benefits. Sumerset and its suppliers learn more about the end consumer and access new ideas for design, engineering, and manufacturing. Everyone from design engineers to carpenters gains a deeper understanding of consumer desires and the potential value trade-offs. This reduces investment risk for the company as well as the risk the consumer won't be satisfied.

A quiet revolution

As the noise from debates about the old economy and the New Economy dies down, it is easier to detect a quieter revolution—fomented by a shift in how value is perceived and created. Movement toward a market environment in which companies and consumers co-create experiences is gaining momentum, but as with any change in deep-seated assumptions about competition and strategy, the adjustments for companies will be complicated and trying.

First, companies must embrace the notion that consumers can become partners in the co-creation of experiences. Only by letting go of the company-centric view of value creation, once and for all, can companies proceed with the difficult and long-term work of making lasting reforms to the business system. Managers must make a major transformation in the way they conceive of the tasks of value creation, and therefore change how firms are organized. Management disciplines and the relationships between disciplines need to be re-examined—market research, product development, logistics, branding, pricing, and accounting, among others.

Companies are getting more used to competing on the basis of their adaptability and how fast they innovate and apply knowledge, and they are rising to the challenge of keeping down the costs of experimentation as they test new ideas. But business competition is a lot more unpredictable when innovation and flexibility, rather than efficiency, are the main drivers of value.

Firms also need new and different IT strategies and applications that incorporate the principles of a more balanced system of value creation, and a system more sensitive to the consumer's perception of value. A new information architecture that allows a company to maintain a consistent brand identity and quality of customer experience across channels, for example, is an essential strategic asset. Likewise, IT vendors need to work with companies to come up with replacements for today's company-centric business software systems.

Companies can and will make the adjustments to thrive in a world where value is co-created in experiences. But it will take time, courage, and stamina to compete in a different value creation space. If companies rise to the challenge, they are sure to discover an exciting new era of business creativity and opportunity.

Resources

J. Philip Lathrop, Gary D. Ahlquist, and David G. Knott, "Health Care's New Electronic Marketplace," *s + b*, Second Quarter 2000 www.strategy-business.com/press/article/?art = 19291 &pg = 0

C.K. Prahalad and Stuart L. Hart, "The Fortune at the Bottom of the Pyramid," *s + b*, First Quarter 2002 www.strategy-business.com/press/article/?art = 229761&pg = 0

C.K. Prahalad and Venkatram Ramaswamy, "Co-Opting Customer Competence," ***Harvard Business Review***, January–February 2000 www.hbsp.harvard.edu/hbsp

Neil Strauss, "Behind the Grammys, Revolt in the Industry," *New York Times*, February 24, 2002

Section 5

Sustaining advantage

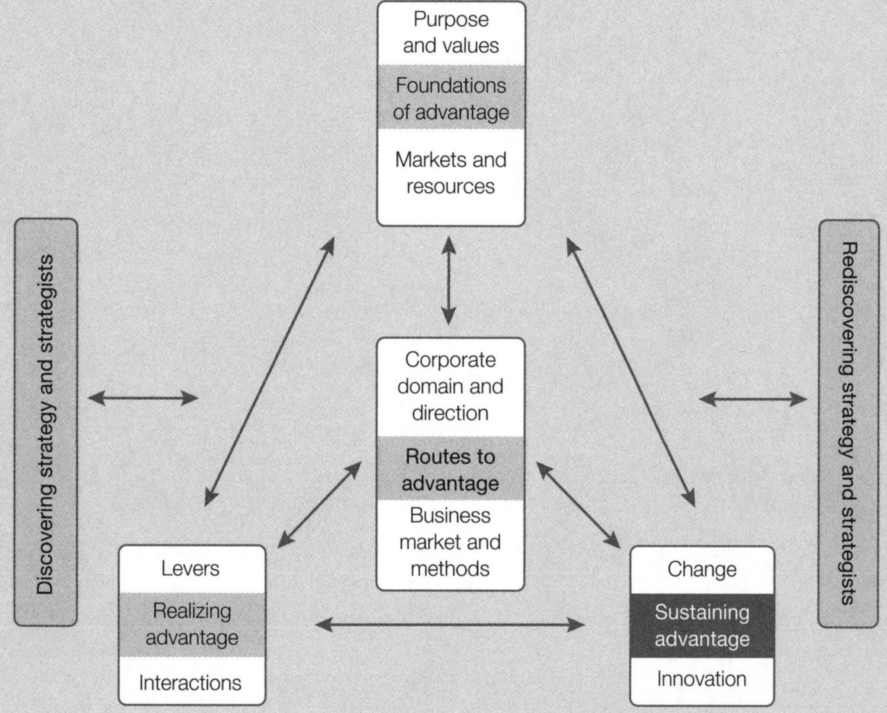

11

Strategic change

Adapting while retaining focus

It is not the strongest of the species that survive, nor the most intelligent, but the ones most responsive to change.

(Charles Darwin)

Introduction

In this chapter, we turn our focus to how organizations sustain advantage. We do this through exploring strategic change, while, to complement this in Chapter 12, we examine strategic innovation and corporate entrepreneurship. Strategic change is about ensuring that the organization is consistently relevant in its market arenas and, as the opening quote from Darwin illustrates, about the need to be responsive to change. Back in 1865, the seeds of the company that we know today as Nokia were sown when Frederik Ideastam set up a paper mill on the banks of the Nokianvirta river in Finland. From this base, over the next hundred years, the company evolved to become a Nordic industrial conglomerate operating in paper, rubber, and cables, and from there to a European player in consumer electronics in the 1970s and 1980s. In 1996, a decision was made to divest all of its other businesses in order to concentrate on becoming a global giant in telecommunications. This is the position that Nokia is attempting to retain as it continues to ride the technological wave of change, focusing on technological convergence in mobile phones, multimedia, and enterprise solutions. Although the reorientation of Nokia over time did not come without its difficulties in integrating acquisitions and developing a strong corporate culture to unite objectives, and the company acknowledges that significant challenges lie ahead, it is clearly the story of a dramatic and successful corporate evolution. Corporate pressure is relentless, however, and in February 2011 Nokia announced a change in strategy, a new leadership team, and a renewed organizational and operational structure. According to chief executive officer (CEO) Stephen Elop, this is designed to accelerate change 'through a new path, aimed at regaining our smartphone leadership, reinforcing our mobile platform and realizing our investment in the future' (Nokia Corporation, 2011). Sustaining advantage is clearly a difficult task.

If history is a guide, in the next twenty-five years, no more than a third of today's major corporations will survive in an economically important way (Foster and Kaplan, 2001). If the very essence of strategy involves exploiting change before your competitors do, why are so many organizations found wanting (Rumelt, 2009)? One reason is that organizations, like human beings, tend to crave stability and certainty—but in order to exploit or respond to competitive market conditions, strategists need to enable their organizations to adapt. This is an extremely difficult task for large global organizations. Irrespective of the size of the strategic change, it is difficult, emotional, and time-consuming for all involved. Simply revisiting product and service offerings may be only a minor part of strategic change. The strategist has to ensure that the organization has the capacity to reconfigure strategy, structure, and processes, and to develop a supportive corporate culture. Organizations such as Walt Disney, Motorola, Ford, Nordstrom, and Merck have struggled to adapt to change, while retaining focus and ensuring an alignment between strategy, structure, and processes. The one ability an organization may have with which to accrue advantage is its capabilities to exploit change faster than its competitors (Howard, 1993: xiv).

Figure 11.1 The dynamic nature of change

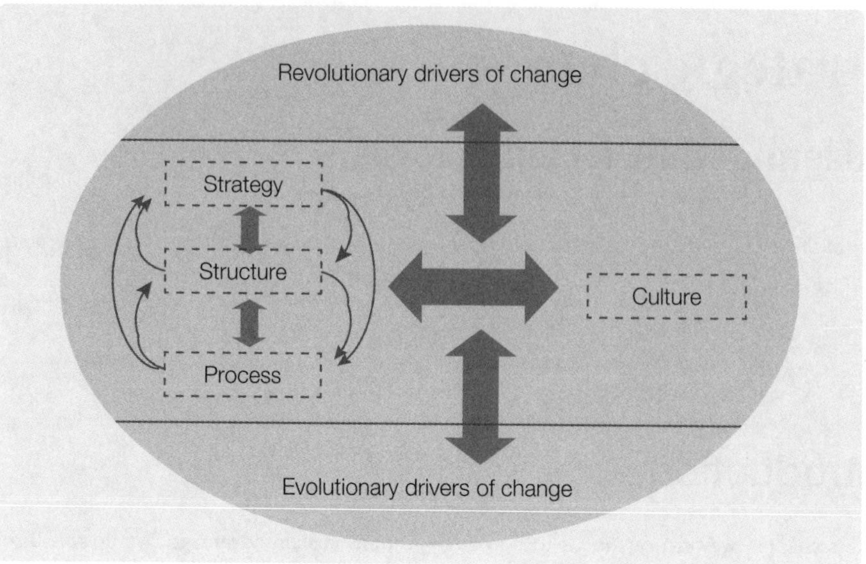

The dynamic nature of change and intricacies of reconfiguration are captured in Figure 11.1. The strategy that an organization intends on pursuing, and the supporting structures and processes selected, can impede or accommodate the drivers of change. The culture of the organization will also serve as a filter determining the nature and eventual impact of change. The figure also helps to illustrate that organizations will frequently be subject to multiple pressures for change from multiple constituents at the same time. Managing such pressures, while also ensuring alignment in activities, is one of the key challenges facing strategists. In this chapter, we seek to understand how organizations adapt to and focus on strategic change, whether this is change of a revolutionary or evolutionary nature. We also explore different perspectives on change, from more rational step-by-step approaches to the extreme chaos of complexity theory. First of all, it is necessary to explore pressures for change in the form of the 'change imperative'; while some may claim that 'change is the only constant', others are more sceptical, observing that 'the fact is that we only notice what is changing. And most things are not' (Mintzberg, 2009: 14).

The change imperative

Since the global financial crisis, the change imperative has come to the fore for many organizations and has been the focus of many boardroom, senior management, and strategists' meetings and discussions. No **industry** sector, **public sector organization**, or government department has escaped the change imperative. Strategic change can be defined as a difference in the form, quality, or state over time in an organization's alignment with its external environment (Van de Ven and Poole, 1995). Misalignment with the external environment can be caused by strategic drift or inertia, which means that the impact of external changes are misconstrued, downplayed, or simply ignored (Johnson, 1988). The banking sector is an example of this misalignment between levels of risk and return on investment. During the early to mid-2000s, many banks continued to lend money, which meant that their operating performances kept growing. Banks kept borrowing money at relatively low interests rates on wholesale markets, as well as from other sources of syndicated debt, and used this money to support retail and commercial operational growth. When the global financial crisis began in 2008, many banks did not have sufficient reserves and experienced increases in loan impairment among their customers. For some banks, this was so great that it required national government support or

Figure 11.2 External and internal drives of change

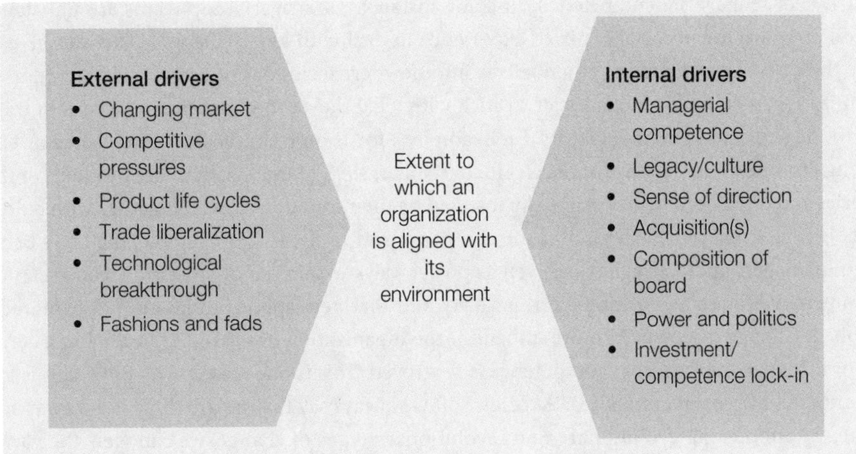

resulted in the orderly wind-down of some banks. The external and internal drivers that can shape and impact an organization's overall alignment with its environment are illustrated in Figure 11.2. External drivers include the following.

- *Changing market conditions* The price of oil is inherently unpredictable and subject to dramatic shifts, which can exert huge pressures on organizations both in the short term to change their pricing structure, hedge their bets, and enhance productivity, and in the longer term to consider alternative fuels.
- *Competitive pressures* US automobile companies in the 1980s suddenly had to direct their attention simultaneously to quality and efficiency concerns in light of the rise of Japanese giants such as Toyota.
- *Product life cycles* Nike transformed the footwear industry, which, until the advent of sportswear, was in a mature and fixed state with little differentiation and an emphasis on cost-cutting.
- *Trade liberalization* This is evident in the impact of privatization on airlines such as British Airways, as well as deregulation, which opened the way for low-cost carriers such as Ryanair and easyJet.
- *Technological breakthroughs* Witness the dramatic power of the Internet to change the rules of the game and create whole new opportunities for **business models**, exploited by companies such as Amazon and eBay.
- *Fashion and fads* Consider the pressure on managers to follow the 'strategy de jour' (see Chapter 14).
- *Structures or procedures being introduced by competitors* These might include delayering, downsizing, outsourcing, or relocation.

Whether an organization pre-empts, predicts, or reacts to external drivers will largely be conditioned by the nature of its internal drivers. Even the most successful organizations can fall foul of complacency as they become victims of their own success (Miller, 1992). The once-powerful sources of success can very easily become sources of rigidity. Sony, which wowed the world for years by linking its competencies in miniaturization to external trends in sport and fitness, exemplified in cutting-edge technology such as the Walkman, fell victim to complacency and watched as the Internet and organizations such as Apple changed the rules of the game. More recently, Japanese giant Samsung's focus on memory chips used in digital cameras and music players has brought immediate revenues, but means that it has lost its longer-term focus on technological breakthroughs.

One key reason for misalignment and a failure to diagnose external change relates to the internal driver of managerial competence. In some instances, managerial top teams are unbalanced and do not have the necessary mix of experience to deal with key challenges. This can be especially the case as an organization globalizes into new territories or enters new product markets. Organizations also find it much easier to stick with what they know, focusing on a certain trajectory to the neglect of external factors: for example, a focus on technological proficiency or engineering prowess at the expense of market focus (Miller, 1992). Organizations are products of their histories and often hold values originally instilled by their founders. These, together with cultural symbols (the visual representation of the company) and routines (for example, the daily behaviour of managers and colleagues), as well as power plays within the organization, can mean that the imperative for change is not a core priority and that new opportunities are not explored or exploited. Change can be even more difficult if the organization has invested heavily in a certain area or if change means a core competence is destroyed. This is one reason why Bill Gates is fond of reminding Microsoft employees: 'At Microsoft we always say that we are three years away from failure.' By contrasting evolutionary and revolutionary types of change, we can view the various dynamics of alignment and misalignment that can impact on organizations and the implications that result for the strategist.

The change dilemma: evolutionary versus revolutionary approaches

The type of change that an organization introduces can be placed along a spectrum from evolutionary to revolutionary. *Evolutionary*, or *continuous*, change involves constantly adapting or readjusting the organization so that it evolves in tandem with changes in its environment. Here, organizations are emergent and self-organizing, and change is constant, evolving, and cumulative, with redirection already under way (Weick and Quinn, 1999: 366). This is often guided by one big idea, or strategic intent, outlining broadly where the organization wants to be and allowing for much learning en route. Evolutionary change can be introduced as a result of proactive learning or attempts to improve performance, or it can be introduced in a reactive manner in order to deal with competitor moves or environmental trends. Barclays Bank has evolved to become a global player focusing on faster growth and developing capabilities shared across disparate operations, from mortgages and Internet banking to Barclay's Capital, with the objective of forming a unified global enterprise. Such a continuous approach to change is not universally advocated. Hamel (1996: 69) argues that 'pursuing incremental improvements while rivals reinvent the industry is like fiddling while Rome burns', while Tushman and O'Reilly (1996: 15) contend that 'slow evolutionary change in a fast-changing world is, as it was for the dinosaurs, a path to the boneyard'. An evolutionary approach to change is contrasted with revolutionary change in Figure 11.3.

Revolutionary, or *discontinuous*, change is transformative in its effects, often changing the organization's business model and involving simultaneous shifts in strategy, structure, processes, and culture (Tushman and O'Reilly, 1996: 15). Reactive revolutionary change can be triggered by a crisis situation such as dramatic performance deficits, or past mistakes that have left the organization seriously misaligned with environmental trends. A typical example would be a turnaround strategy when organizational performance has declined and the very future of the organization is at stake. This involves harsh, yet necessary, top-down direction, imposing on employees new ways of doing things in order to rescue the situation. This type of change is intentional and clearly associated with leadership qualities at the top of the organization. Apple Computers undertook a series of discontinuous changes in strategy, structure, and culture as it moved from the leadership of Steve Jobs through that of John Sculley, Michael Sprindler, Gil Amelio, and back to Jobs (Tushman and O'Reilly, 1996). It is often said that revolutionary change is best led by a new CEO who is external to the organization, because he or she can offer fresh insight and perspective that might have been lacking. According to Slatter (1984), aspects of a successful recovery strategy include change of management, strong financial control, new product focus, improved marketing costs, and cost

Figure 11.3 The change continuum

←——————————→	
Evolution	**Revolution**
Slow-paced	Fast-paced
Mix top-down and bottom-up	Top-down
Consultative/collaborative	Directive/coercive
Build consensus/minimize resistance	Impose order/overcome resistance
Broad idea	Precise blueprint
Freeze–rebalance–unfreeze	Unfreeze–transition–refreeze

reductions. Revolutionary change signals an often abrupt break with the status quo and often involves a transformation of the organization's business model. This type of change necessitates a bias for action, and so tends to be directive and implemented more forcibly as a blueprint.

Because of its dramatic nature, revolutionary change is infrequent, and is often referred to as 'episodic change', or viewed as occurring as punctuated equilibrium following sustained periods of stability (Tushman and Romanelli, 1985; Weick and Quinn, 1999: 365). Revolutionary change, however, does not have to be of the negative sort that is typically suggested, driven by poor performance. Using examples of 'rule-breaking' companies such as Dell, IKEA, and The Body Shop, Hamel (1996) speaks of the revolutionary change brought about by their ability to be shackled by neither convention nor respect for precedent. For Rumelt (2009), this predatory approach of leaping through the window of opportunity and staying focused on big wins rather than on maintenance activities is what distinguishes a real entrepreneurial strategy. For Hamel (1996), the essence of real strategic activity is such revolutionary activity, understanding that the future will not be like the past, listening to those at all levels of the organization, and viewing threats as opportunities. These are lessons exemplified by Nokia in its transition from traditional maturing industries to the dynamic and rapidly growing telecommunications and electronics industries that would create its future. Indeed, at its extreme, revolutionary strategy has the ability to create the future and inform culture. A key distinction between revolutionary and evolutionary change can be further defined by the scope of the change initiative, as discussed in the next section (Nadler and Tushman, 1989).

Scope of evolutionary and revolutionary change

Strategic change is organization-wide and impacts on the content of strategy—that is, what we do. As well as distinguishing between revolutionary change as being intentional, deliberate, and led top-down, and evolutionary change as being more ad hoc and emergent, we can distinguish on the basis of the scope of evolutionary or revolutionary change as being either strategic or subsystem/operational.

Strategic change is guided by the ability to solve new problems and to develop new business models. Strategic change can be revolutionary in the sense discussed above, focusing on organizational transformation either involving a reactive re-energizing, or a change in belief and awareness of what is possible and a 'leap of faith' (Jick and Peiperl, 2003). Alternatively, it can be more evolutionary, involving slower learning by doing and an incremental approach to change, focusing on organizational transition over time from one state to another (as in reorganization, mergers, new products) (Jick and

Peiperl, 2003). However, this is not where the change agenda rests; change can also influence the subsystem or operational level of an organization.

Business process re-engineering in a revolutionary manner at the subsystem/operational level, as promoted by Michael Hammer (1990), involves not simply automating existing processes, but rather dramatically starting afresh: in his terms, 'Don't automate, obliterate'. Thus, rather than leave existing processes intact and use computers simply to speed up an operation, the entire process should be reconfigured. Hammer provides the example of MBL, an insurance company. Instead of an application having to go through discrete steps spanning numerous departments involving nineteen people, the process was overhauled so that one case manager had total responsibility for the application from the time at which it was received until the time at which a policy was issued. This vastly reduced the speed of processing applications and made queries much easier to deal with in a timely fashion. The key to business process re-engineering is to look at the fundamentals in a cross-functional way. The dramatic overhauling of key processes as advocated by business process re-engineering is not without its critics.

A less radical and more evolutionary perspective on change at the operational level is the notion of developmental change or continuous improvement, associated with terms such as 'Kaizen', 'total quality manufacturing', or 'zero defects'. Originating in Japan, Kaizen is a process-orientated way of seeing and a way of life concerning continuous improvement. This perspective highlights organizational fine-tuning, usually manifested at a departmental or divisional level of the organization. Dunphy and Stace (1993) note that organizational fine-tuning facilitates the development of employee skills with which to deliver strategy. Fine-tuning should foster both individual and group commitment to the excellence of departments and the organization's mission, clarify established roles, and promote confidence in accepted beliefs, norms, and myths (Dunphy and Stace, 1993). Spanish retail giant Zara is an expert in continuously getting better, deploying top-of-the-range technology that communicates from stores to manufacturing bases on key purchasing trends. The ability to hone in and improve its ability to stay close to consumer desires allows Zara to stay ahead of the game by constantly changing its displays. Contrast this with traditional high-street outlets, which traditionally only change their stock on a seasonal basis (see Chapter 6).

Overall, the type and scope of change are interrelated and organizations may well pursue many combinations at once. Chapters 7 and 8 highlight the different levels of strategy and how they may be inter-related. An organization may have a **portfolio** of business units, each experiencing a different type of environment and type of change. This indicates how complex and messy the process of managing change can actually be. Tushman and O'Reilly (1996) urge organizations to be ambidextrous—that is, able to implement both incremental and revolutionary change—while Stace and Dunphy (1990) argue that hard levers typically associated with revolutionary change are not necessarily incompatible with the soft levers linked to developmental and incremental change. Given the extent of change, it is probably also likely that if businesses are to be successful over the long term, 'it is the management of strategic transformation that is the prime challenge' (Delbridge *et al.*, 2006: 44). Of course, as the next section shows, a lot depends on the lenses that are brought to bear through which to understand the nature of change and how it evolves, each one emphasizing a different aspect of organizational realities.

Perspectives on change and implementing change

So far in this chapter, we have considered the internal and external drivers that shape change, as well as different types of change and their scope. We have said very little about how change actually comes about—that is, the process of change (Pettigrew, 1987). In order to understand this more fully, we can adopt a number of different perspectives, or 'lenses'. Each provides a different way of looking to the future, and affords different roles to the strategist and our understanding of the implementation of change. How strategic change is understood will reflect differences in the perspective of the observer. We begin by focusing on the rationalistic/mechanistic lens, then the incremental/emergent lens, then the cultural/political lens, and finally the lens of chaos theory.

Rational/mechanistic lens

The rational/mechanistic lens is the typical lens through which change is viewed. From this perspective, change is viewed as a rational, mechanistic, step-by-step sequential process. This coherency facilitates communication to internal and external **stakeholders**, and places key responsibility for the design and implementation of change squarely with the top management team and the CEO. This is a top-down, vision-inspired change, of the kind that features in books and media accounts of transformational leadership. Most of the prescriptive accounts that use this lens find their roots in Lewin's (1951) classic metaphor of change involving unfreezing current attitudes, values, and beliefs, moving these to a new focus or level, and then refreezing and institutionalizing these newer values and beliefs (see Table 11.1). When using the different approaches as outlined in Table 11.1, the strategist has to have a deep understanding of the need for change supported by analytical evidence, multiple and consistent communications including formal and informal, and the support of the top management team, as well as the ability to map out different implementation plans so that the organization can see the tangible signs of change. Lewin has three approaches for change, whereas Jicks (2003) and Kotter (1995) have ten and eight steps, respectively. Nonetheless, all of these approaches suggested an ordered, logical progression to recognizing the need for change, leveraging action, and embedding solutions. Change initiatives in organizations such as Newell Rubbermaid, Reebok, and Lockheed Martin Aeronautical have largely been interpreted as reflecting this rational/mechanistic approach.

The limitations of this perspective are that it can understate the complexities involved—that is, it is founded on the notion that everyone will agree on the vision and that all stakeholders are willing and interested in implementing it (Bamford and Forrester, 2003). The presumption is that conflict and politics can easily be resolved. This approach is built on the assumption that change is a one-off initiative rather than a continuous process. A reliance on past trends as the basis for projecting the future leaves little scope for unexpected trends, ideas, or disruptive technologies that the organization might have to embrace or to which it might have to adapt (Bower and Christensen, 1995). The language of efficiency and optimization associated with the mechanistic perspective assumes that everything can be planned and predicted, and that 'never is a plain old mistake made' (Nelson and

Table 11.1 Rational, mechanistic lens of change management

Lewin's classical approach	Jick (2003): Steps for implementation change	Kotter: Eight stages of transformational change
Unfreeze	1. Analyse the organization and its need for change	1. Establish a sense of urgency
	2. Create a shared vision and a common direction	2. Form a powerful coalition
	3. Separate from the past	3. Create a vision
Move	4. Create a sense of urgency	4. Communicate the vision: change
	5. Support a strong leader role	5. Empower others to act/remove obstacles
	6. Line up political sponsorship	6. Plan for and create short-term wins
Refreeze	7. Craft an implementation plan	7. Consolidate improvements and produce still more change
	8. Develop enabling structures	8. Embed change/institutionalize new approaches
	9. Communicate, involve people, and be honest	
	10. Reinforce and institutionalize change	

Winter, 1982: 8). Imposition of change from top management, even in spite of efforts at moving and institutionalizing by refreezing, may not sit well and appropriately motivate workforces. Nonetheless, explicit step-by-step approaches and decision-making processes communicate a sense of legitimacy about the organization's intentions and so can be valuable in their own right regardless of any consequences for decision outcomes (March, 1996: 286). This idea is explored further in Chapter 14.

Emergent learning lens

In contrast, the emergent learning approach emphasizes a systems view of the organization, which allows for the interactions of its interdependent parts that makes rational, sequential progress less assured. This approach is often associated with bottom-up input. In the words of one key proponent, 'ultimately change is too risky as a deliberate strategy; change is about learning' (Beer *et al.*, 1990: 161). This lens offers an understanding of adaptability, unintended outcomes, and outcomes that may not have been realized as intended. Change is viewed as a complex and messy process. As Jick (2003:176) states, 'only rarely does a company know exactly where it is going or how it should get there'. In a similar vein, in relation to the activities of strategists Mintzberg (1987) argues that the smartest strategists are those who appreciate that they cannot know everything in advance.

From this perspective, change is a continuous process. While the organization may be guided broadly by some notion of strategic intent, this may be a deliberately ambitious, if not unobtainable, end state—stretching the organization in its general direction, yet using its limited reach ability as a motivator (Hamel and Prahalad, 1990). In some cases, the process of the journey in terms of the enhancement of skills and the development of capabilities can be as important as the destination (Allport, 1955). Incremental change in a variety of organizational subsystems in tandem can herald revolutionary output. This mode of development has been likened to a jazz band understanding the general structures, but innovating at the periphery, as opposed to the rigidity dictated by fixed music played by an orchestra. According to Michael Beer, one-size-fits-all change programmes take energy away from efforts to solve key business problems (Beer *et al.*, 1990). Beer argues that attempting to change employee behaviour by altering a company's formal structure and systems is flawed; instead, he contends that managers should first focus on the behaviour required. This bottom-up process of effective change involves six steps.

1. Mobilize commitment through joint diagnosis of business problems.
2. Develop a shared vision of how to organize and manage competitiveness.
3. Foster consensus for the new vision.
4. Spread revitalization to all departments without pushing it from the top.
5. Institutionalize revitalization through formal policies and systems.
6. Monitor and adjust strategies in response to problems in the revitalization process.

Critics of this approach to change might say that it has little value in a crisis, while there is no assurance that the organization is learning about the right things: Polaroid continued to focus efforts on learning and improving the instant camera, while failing to address the development of digital technology. Critically, this approach still views change and the management of change as a process that can be rationalized.

Contrasting the rational/mechanistic lens with that of emergent learning, Mintzberg *et al.* (2005: 225) offer an amusing additional insight:

> John Kotter and Michael Beer taught at the Harvard Business School; their offices were steps apart. They each published an article in the *Harvard Business Review* on steps to effective change, eight in one, six in the other. That is where the similarity ends. One encourages top-down change, the other bottom-up change. If experts can't agree, what are the practitioners to do?

Cultural/political lens

The cultural/political lens has its tradition in critical theory, which recognizes that organizations are made up of powerful coalitions and interest groups that attempt to impose their ways of viewing the world on others. Here, change and the development of visions and plans are best seen as the outcome of political manoeuvring and power plays, rather than simply as optimal efficiency-enhancing outcomes (Nord, 1978). Change often brings with it proposals that threaten managerial power or security, involving the reallocation of resources or the restructuring of relationships. This helps us to understand why change initiatives might be met with resistance. In public, managers may stress the desirability of change, but in private resent and resist it (Pech, 2001). Likewise, dealing with the powers and interests of various stakeholder groups is likely to be a difficult process. To view change as incremental adjustments and performance-enhancing developments, as in the learning/emergent approach, may be to gloss over the issue of organizational power and control. Change can come about as a result of political and cultural factors, just as much as through rational, incremental leaps towards a given purpose. Pettigrew (1987: 649) notes the importance of recognizing 'the theoretical and analytical complexities of the easy use of words such as purpose, intention, and effectiveness in linking behaviour to the processes and outcomes of transformation'.

Similarly, a cultural perspective focuses on how environmental factors are refracted through the cultural paradigm, which can put a different slant on realities, typically tied up with the political processes discussed above (Johnson, 1992). Environmental factors are not understood objectively, but rather are socially constructed and given meaning by actors within organizations (Berger and Luckmann, 1966). Rituals and symbols can have a huge impact on orchestrating and determining outcomes. From this perspective, the focus is very much on whose change agenda is likely to dominate and whose interests the proposed change favours. Caulkin (2011) provides a timely reminder that discussions of power rarely feature in explanations of strategy—in part because the powerful get to make or influence the rules. It is also the case that key players may block proposed changes: in light of a US$2bn trading scandal, UBS CEO Oswald Grubel proposed a radical overhaul of the bank's strategy and corporate governance structures, including the removal of some board members. However, Grubel's plans for change failed to get the backing of the board, resulting in him resigning from his position as CEO (Jenkins and Murphy, 2011). Similar corporate battles over proposed changes are commonplace, but in the main they get played out behind boardroom doors rather than in the public arena.

Lens of complexity/chaos theory

The lens of complexity/chaos theory conflicts with many of the assumptions underlying change programmes. According to Stacey (2010), control of change is highly unlikely—unless hugely conservative and repetitive: 'in all other circumstances the belief in intentional long-term control must be a fantasy defense to protect managers against the anxiety that uncertainty and ambiguity generate' (Stacey, 1995: 140). Faulty assumptions characterizing typical accounts of change are that organizations operate in a stable equilibrium, in which they progress in a linear fashion, either repeating past behaviours or selecting from a limited range of behaviours with foreseeable outcomes. According to chaos theory, that which is truly new is not already in the past or the present and so cannot be predicted; instead, creativity and change stem from the endless variety of behaviours arising from spontaneity that typifies complex systems (ibid: 483). Even small changes can escalate into major qualitative changes in outcomes. Research by Plowman *et al.* (2007) indicated how a relatively small decision by a church to offer Sunday morning breakfast to homeless people ultimately led to a radical change in the church and its rejuvenation, with a focus on 'justice in action'. The radical change was unintended, emergent and slow, facilitated by destabilizing conditions, interdependence between diverse and previously unrelated stakeholders, and positive, reinforcing feedback loops. Complexity theory holds that disorder is not simply a consequence of inertia, incompetence, or ignorance; instead, it is a fundamental property of creative systems and plays a vital role in that creativity (Stacey, 1995: 484). Disregarding clear cause and effect renders sequential intervention futile, because it is not possible to develop meaningful pictures of an end state. Instead, organizations should operate at the 'edge of chaos', where there is experimentation, but within a framework. This approach is said to be most conducive to emergent cultural change, since the people most affected by change are the ones most likely to introduce it. Its non-prescriptive and non-interventionist assumptions, however, do not sit so easily with managers, and there may be ethical implications around simply *letting go*.

Spotlight Rural Payments Agency change programme

The European Union's (EU) Common Agricultural Policy (CAP) provides direct support to farmers within the Union. In 2003, the EU streamlined these payments to into a Single Payment Scheme (SPS), to be administrated by the member states. This was a significant change for member states and in how they administered this new SPS. This payment is important to farmers, because those with smaller holdings rely on it to keep them financially afloat. Delays in receiving this single payment results in considerable hardship for some farmers and can threaten their livelihoods. Also, member states can be fined if they do not administer these payments on time under the CAP. In the UK, in March 2006, the administrative system and the agency charged with making the payments, the Rural Payments Agency (RPA), failed to deliver on time £1.5bn worth of payments to 116,000 farmers, despite having been through a change programme since 2001.

So what happened that resulted in this failure to deliver? The business and IT system that was in place could not cope with the demands and the requirements of this new payment system. It also required additional recruitment of temporary staff to support the processing of claims by farmers. What were required were a system and processes in place that allowed for the timely payment to farmers and realized other benefits associated with change.

In 2001, the RPA had been created to improve the system for paying subsidies to farmers in England under the CAP and to reduce overheads. The creation of the new agency came as a result of a PricewaterhouseCoopers (PwC) report in January 2001 that highlighted the need for change to create a more effective agency that would gain the benefits from of standardizing activities and processes, and having in place an IT system that would support a customer-orientated organization. The vision of the RPA was to be 'A customer-focused paying agency, respected as the European leader in efficient and effective administration and as an authoritative source of advice to policy makers'. The RPA was a merging of the activities of the (then) Ministry of Agriculture, Fisheries and Food (MAFF), and Intervention Board.

In creating the RPA, a change programme was initiated, with a number of objectives in mind.

- The programme was expected to streamline corporate support functions (HR and finance), to reduce staff levels from 3,300 to 1,950, and to reduce regional centres from twelve to five.
- Other objectives included improving levels of staff and customer satisfaction, and reducing the average time that it took farmers to complete a claim for CAP payment.

In the initial phase of the change programme, work was focused on reducing the number of regional offices, the streamlining of activities and key managerial roles, and putting in place a governance structure that reflected the merging of existing activities and key stakeholder interests. However, problems began to emerge in the prioritization of resources and activities. The creation of a single robust IT system was a key objective for the RPA to support its operations and its customers using a single platform. In October 2003, this resulted in Accenture signing a contract with the RPA to deliver a single payment system.

However, the change programme did not go according to plan and numerous difficulties were encountered. Key obstacles included policy issues and time restraints. There were also a large number of systemic problems and gradually the programme drifted away from the original vision. One of the key factors that affected the programme was a significant and radical change in the CAP payment system. This created new business risks, changed the IT requirements, and added a further 46,000 customers with limited experience of claiming under this support programme. It also resulted in a 1,000 per cent increase in land registration volumes. A further issue that undermined the change programme was a lack of alignment of interests between the RPA and the (new) Department for Environment, Food and Rural Affairs (Defra), which was not managed well. The schedule slipped and this led to widespread customer dissatisfaction when, in June 2006, 116,000 customers did not receive their payments.

By looking at the events and factors that impacted the change programme, a number of lessons can be learnt about effective change (both in terms of the process of change and its implementation), overall responsibility for execution of SPS was not clear and the RPA did not provide the intense support required to make its contractual relationship with Accenture work in delivering the IT platform. RPA took some time to define its requirements. From a risk management perspective, some fundamental business risks were underestimated, including customer behaviour and the operational impact on the Accenture-developed IT system. Furthermore, during the testing phase, no provision was made for farmers using the system to test it out in a safe and secure manner. Despite the challenges, successes were found around communication and it was felt that there was a hands-on management presence that resulted in high levels of staff morale.

So what are the lessons to be learnt from this change programme? First, there is a need to have a clear vision of what is required among all stakeholders. This was lacking in the case of the RPA. Secondly, during the change process, the overall levels of responsibility should have been clearly defined and communicated to all stakeholders. Thirdly, change should not focus on internal aspects alone, but should be responsive to radical changes in the external environment. In the case of the RPA, a radical change in policy fundamentally changed the requirements and the associated risks. Fourthly, the RPA case highlights the need for constant and intense communication within the organization during the change process. Finally, having a clear execution and implementation plan is necessary in any change programme.

Source: http://webarchive.nationalarchives.gov.uk/20100503135839/http://www.ogc.gov.uk/index.asp

Implications for strategy practice

Change within business or personal life can be extremely challenging and stressful, invoking emotions of anxiety and loss. For change to be effective, a starting point can be at the level of the individual and understanding the requirement for, impact of, and reasons for change. The strategist needs to understand change at the level of the individual employee in a variety of backgrounds, ranging through marketing, operations, finance, etc. The employee may ask: 'Why should I change my activities and what will be the outcomes/impacts?' Strategists also need to be able to have a deep analytical understanding of the business case and the reasons why change is required. In understanding the case for strategic change, the strategist has to be able to articulate this clearly, offering supporting hard facts to a variety of stakeholders. Only from a personal understanding of the change drivers will the strategist see the rationale for change clearly enough to invest his or her energy behind it and to persuade others with credibility.

Change agents should inspire dissatisfaction with the present order of things and promote the promise offered by alternatives. In outlining alternatives, the strategist has to ground these in reality, because it is easy to be carried away by looking at the positives of alternatives rather than the negatives. Information and communication mechanisms become critical; change agents can build a momentum for change by sharing competitive information, pointing to shortcomings, and providing notions of strategic intent that indicate how far the organization is from its desired state (Spector, 1989). Staying close to the ground facilitates accurate information flows, while agents should ensure that they 'walk the talk' and 'talk the walk' of change. If those who are mandating change are not exhibiting the desired employee role behaviours, others cannot be expected to do so.

Strategists need to be aware that, rather than focusing on change as an isolated event and something that happens on a temporal basis, organizations would do well to encourage proactive change. How this is achieved is very much dependent on the culture of the organization. Fostering a culture that promotes questioning and risk taking is an ongoing task for management. Strategists and organizations require their employees to take some risks, to experiment, and to continually change the conventional thinking about the organization, the competitive environment, and competitors. Such risk taking and experimentation should not put the organization at overall risk, but the levers of change implementation—reward, recognition, and structures—must support and facilitate the values and behaviours expected and required.

The nature of change and the process of building consensus and enacting change will vary depending on the type of organization: what works in a public sector organization might not work in another organization in the same, or a different, country. Equally, there is difference between a highly contentious and political decision to decentralize a government department and the resistance that this might engender, and the decision by a software organization to use agile and lean methods to develop new products. Some communication channels are more appropriate than others in certain contexts. It may be fine to inform staff of a new snack machine in the canteen via text message or email, but this method will not suffice for announcing a new strategy—or, indeed, for informing staff of major organizational changes, such as downsizing or outsourcing. Change also does not have to be introduced in one clean sweep; where time allows, strategists should support various initiatives through pilot schemes or innovations in certain departments, which, if successful, can later be rolled out on a broader scale.

Finally, it is extremely difficult to gauge the extent to which organizational members, departments, and even CEOs are willing to embrace change. Central to all change initiatives seems to be the idea of a consistency in approach through visible actions, in communication, and in the range and type of supporting levers deployed. Change cannot be introduced only for the sake of change; it must have some underlying rationale and be followed through with behaviour that is consistent with this. Ultimately, change agents must recognize that they are in it for the long haul. Organizations are always uncompleted artefacts requiring tinkering and experimentation. To manage strategic change successfully, strategists need to have the prerequisites of belief, desire, and energy—but these must be wrapped in the virtues of patience and perseverance.

Introduction to readings

Reading 5.1, 'Managing radical change' by Ann Todd (1999), focuses on managing radical change, and why this process is so difficult and so often characterized by failure. It presents a model that appreciates the far-reaching and interactive elements of change, including strategy, politics, people, and processes. As opposed to the more prescriptive models presented in this chapter, consideration of these elements helps us to understand dimensions of the key elements of radical change. According to Todd, managing radical change involves understanding the nature of the contracts that employees have with the organization, as well as facing the inevitabilities of uncertainty, fear, and loss. Finally, Todd considers often-neglected issues of how change is resourced and the role of change agents such as consultants. We are left wondering whether the well-designed radical change advocated is always feasible, while the link between recognition of political realities and actually dealing with them might not be so straightforward.

The second reading for this chapter, 'Managing strategic change' by Gerry Johnson (1992), accessible via the Online Resource Centre that accompanies this book, serves to inject a sense of both realism and precision into the discussion of strategic change and its relationship with culture. Moving from the common prescriptive focus (the way things should be), Johnson favours a descriptive lens (the way things actually are). He takes issue with the overly rational perspectives that plague current accounts of organizational change, and instead argues that organizational actions are shaped and formed by the underlying, taken-for-granted assumptions of the organization's cultural paradigm. This means that actions are best judged as 'internally constructed responses' shaped by past experience and managerial cognitive frames of reference rather than objectively understood. Johnson provides an example of a cultural audit in a menswear clothing retailer, a consultancy partnership, and a regional newspaper to illustrate the constitutive elements and embeddedness of cultural paradigms. In turn, this provides an explanation of why evolutionary change might be favoured and revolutionary change may be so difficult. But what does this mean for the feasibility of revolutionary change? What mechanisms can be used for strategic cultural change? While the notion of the cultural paradigm clearly advances our understanding of the role of organizational elements such as symbols and routines, is it possible to conduct an accurate cultural audit? And who is in the best position to conduct it: an insider or an outsider to the organization?

The final reading, by Hambrick and Cannella (1989), also accessed via the Online Resource Centre, provides us with a timely reminder that 'any strategy without successful implementation is but a fantasy'. Focusing on the much-neglected implementation process, they use a case study of change at the Bondall division of Globus Management to indicate how an organization 'gets from here to there'. A three-pronged approach of 'astute preliminary groundwork, prompt broad-gauged substantive initiatives and a lot of selling' is deemed central to implementable strategy and change, with Bondall management serving as an archetypical example. At its heart, this article attempts to make strategists more sensitive to the nature of impacts necessary for successive change—in particular by considering multilayered information flows, symbolic gestures, dealing with negative aspects of change, and capturing the longevity of the process. In advocating initial broad-gauged bursts of change levers, followed by plenty of reinforcing and fine-tuning, Hambrick and Cannella attempt to locate themselves between comprehensive 'all at once schools of change', on the one hand, and 'incremental schools', on the other—but to what extent do they succeed in doing so? Do they make reasonable assumptions about enabling conditions such as time, politics, and leadership? Will this approach work in all contexts?

Mini case study Hard-wired: Kleisterlee is reinventing the inventive Dutch firm Philips

Gerard Kleisterlee followed his father into the electronics firm Philips and has spent nine years at the helm turning it around.

The year that Gerard Kleisterlee took over as CEO of Philips, the company abruptly sank into the largest loss in its history.

The Dutch firm, still best known for consumer electronics, had skirted around bankruptcy in the mid-1990s after a series of strategic blunders, but recovered ground later in the decade. Then, the dotcom bubble burst and the business, which was a leading player in semiconductors, went back into a downwards spiral.

> From a number of dimensions, 2000 had been a record year ... 2001 and 2002 were also record years but in reverse order ... Then of course with the impairments and the write-downs on acquisitions we had done, we reported two years in a row the biggest net income loss in the history of the company. That was my start. But from there on, it can only get better.

Philips, which began as a lightbulb manufacturer in Eindhoven in 1891, has an illustrious past and has been behind some of the most significant advances in consumer technology. It brought to market the first rotary-head shaver in the 1930s and is still widely known for its Philishave brand. It introduced the first cassette tape; in 1972, launched the first video recorder; and in 1982, introduced the compact disc (CD) with Sony. The firm also played a pivotal role in developing the DVD, and still gets a royalty for each disc and DVD player sold.

But, in recent decades, the unwieldy company has struggled to increase its revenues, along the way exiting markets including computers and recorded music with the sale of Polygram. It has also often failed to translate its world-beating technology into a commanding position in the market.

> We initially had a good share of the CD market, but then we moved down the path of CD interactive for example, which was basically a precursor to CD rewriteable or Playstation ... Great technology, maybe too early, or not well positioned. So CD interactive never really made it into the marketplace as a successful application, even if the interactivity was a breakthrough in technology. That is an example of where we had the greatest technology but we were not able necessarily to turn it into the greatest market success.

When Kleisterlee, who trained as an engineer, began running the business, he embarked on the latest of many overhauls. Investors had become so used to Philips reshaping itself that it had become a 'restructuring play', he says.

In a phrase that might ring familiar to workers at the BBC, he told the management board in his first big meeting as chief executive that they were 'too old, too male, too Dutch'. Today, he says: 'I am the only Dutchman on the management board. I have a French chief financial officer, a German who does innovation and countries for me, an Italian is running lifestyle, an American is running healthcare and a Belgian is running lighting.'

The most significant decision was to sell the semiconductors business. The disposal met two aims. Kleisterlee, aged 63, wanted to unlock Philips from the highly cyclical semiconductors business and also to move further from components to finished products. He also quickly got out of making mobile phones, a disastrous foray by his predecessor, and now licenses the brand.

Battles

At the time, Kleisterlee says the business still regarded itself as a high-volume consumer electronics company. But much of that space has now been ceded to manufacturers from Asia and emerging markets, while margins have shrunk: 'We are picking our battles more and more.' The company, he says, had hardly made a profit in televisions in the USA for fifty years, and now licenses its brand there, focusing instead on Europe and Latin America.

The company has been refocused around three areas: consumer lifestyle, which includes televisions, shavers and electric toothbrushes; lighting, in which it remains a world leader and sees growth in LED energy-saving bulbs; and health care, in which it makes products such as CT scanners and home defibrillators. After nearly a decade of restructuring, the company has gone from 189,000 people and sales of €32bn, to 116,000 and sales of €23bn.

Consumer remains the biggest part of the business, but is also the part of the group that has struggled the most during the recession. It is health care, competing against Siemens and General Electric, in which the company clearly sees the biggest potential for growth, with an ageing population in most developed markets and relatively high margins. Philips has spent €10bn on acquisitions in the past few years, many in health care, including its largest to date, the US$5bn takeover of Respironics in 2007, a firm that treats sleep apnoea (a condition that causes people to stop breathing during the night).

Kleisterlee struggles to make sense of the three divisions, talking broadly about how they all touch the consumer, and about health and well-being, before admitting that one can spend too much in 'intellectual rationalization', and that he might be happy with what is 'just a nice portfolio'. Among other changes, he also placed a stronger emphasis on marketing, appointing a chief marketing officer, in the hope that the business might strengthen its branding and better translate its technology into market share. The slogan—'sense and simplicity', which surely owes something to Jane Austen—was introduced in 2005.

Kleisterlee, an imposing business-like presence with ice-blue eyes, has much invested in making a success of the company. Not only did he join straight from national service, but his father had spent his entire career at Philips before him. Working for a large corporation, he says, gives you ample opportunities: he has worked in manufacturing, sales and run the business in Taiwan and China. But in interviews, he also points out that, in post-war Europe, the emphasis was on getting a steady job for life.

Doubling profits

The headquarters of the business moved from Eindhoven in 2001 and remains in a small cluster of towers in Amstel, a quiet suburb of Amsterdam.

It is not yet clear whether the latest reinvention of Philips has paid off. After getting the portfolio into the shape he wanted, Kleisterlee set targets to get the business growing again. Then came the global recession and the target of doubling profits by 2010 was abandoned. In 2009, sales were down 11 per cent year on year: its lighting division depends heavily on the construction market, while consumer electronics was hit by the slump in consumer demand.

Kleisterlee talks perhaps less with exasperation than as someone used to things not going as planned: 'We set a few goals for ourselves, and then comes the crisis, and we said, God, we were getting in shape and now comes the crisis and we can't show [the improvement].' The share price in the past year has risen from €15.59 to €25.33, but still trades below the level when he started.

But he compares Philips' performance in this recession with the years after he joined and finds grounds for optimism. While Philips plunged into the red after the tech bubble burst, it still achieved profit of €424m last year in a far harsher environment. Could the firm be ready to grow after decades of stagnation?

> I definitely have that feeling; of course, the proof of the pudding is in the eating. You have to unlearn a lot of things in a company that has been focused on risk containment, because so many things went wrong over past decades that almost the institutional instinct, the Pavlovian reaction, is always to focus on the downside. You have to create a culture where people are motivated to go for the upside. But I am hopeful we are getting there.

The CV

- **Born** 1946, Germany
- **Education** Eindhoven Technical University, electronic engineering
- **Career** 1974–81, Philips Medical Systems, manufacturing management; 1981–86, Philips Professional Audio, general manager; 1986–94, Philips Components, industrial director; 1994–96, Philips Display Components, managing director; 1996–98, Philips Taiwan & China, president; 1999–2000, Philips Components, chief executive; 2000–01, Philips, chief operations officer; 2001–, Philips, chief executive
- **Family** Married with three children
- **Other posts** Daimler supervisory board

Source: Teather (2010)

? Questions

1. Using Figure 11.2, identify the change drivers for Philips.

2. What type of change approach did Philips use: revolutionary or evolutionary?

3. What perspective on change is most useful in helping us to understand the change at Philips?

4. What initiatives and approaches should Gerard Kleisterlee use to change the culture at Philips so that its employees focus on the upside of new opportunities?

Summary

No change, no matter how small, is ever simple. Balogun *et al.* (2004) report a failure rate of around 70 per cent of all change programmes initiated. Very few organizations have been able to ride the waves of change in their industry without falling off the surfboard. In this chapter, we have explored the change imperative, the change dilemma (evolutionary versus revolutionary), and the different perspectives on change. The strategic questions associated with change are how to change and why we need to change. In order to study and understand change, it is easier to treat it as an episodic event, but in practice, change never starts because it never stops (Weick and Quinn, 1999: 381). There is no doubt that managing change is a messy and tricky process. For every achievement, there is a counter-balancing force that can result in stagnation or destruction (Patel, 2005: 55). The problem with organizational change is that 'the only thing more dangerous than doing one [change] is never doing any' (Pfeffer and Sutton, 2006: 161).

Organizations are composed of complex interrelated parts, so that a change in one aspect will have a domino effect. While this cannot be prevented, at least some elements may be anticipated. Knowing the type of change, using the lenses of differing perspectives, and understanding barriers and levers of implementation can only help this process. Success is shaped by an organization's ability to forget selectively and learn new tricks (Hamel, 1996). The quest to build a capacity for change requires a culture that moves forward, has an appetite for critical inquisition, and is willing to examine the underlying assumptions that are brought to bear upon each situation (Pfeffer and Sutton, 2006). Perhaps our understanding of change has also been limited by the perceptual apparatus that we bring. Insights in relation to the spiralling and open-ended nature of change are perhaps more likely if we embrace a focus on *changing* rather than change (Pettigrew, 1990: 9; Weick and Quinn, 1999), while perhaps to speak of **sustainable competitive advantages** is to invite complacency (Rumelt, 2009). We need to better understand causes of failure and why it has been so difficult for organizations to manage change and grapple with their external environment (Edmondson, 2011). While we have a few broad signposts to facilitate change management, we must recognize that detailed road maps are futile. That change is the only constant may be obvious; how organizations deal with this is clearly not. The late Peter Drucker (2002: 295) offered one potential solution when he suggested that 'every organization will have to turn itself into a change agent. The best way to manage change is to create it'. The task for every strategist is to build a strong organizational infrastructure that has clarity of focus and purpose, but also has the ability to adapt to opportunities and challenges.

Discussion questions

1. Research an organization with which you are familiar and examine the possible 'change imperatives' that it faces.
2. Consider the rational/mechanistic perspective on organizational change (see Table 11.1). What are the benefits and limitations of considering change in this manner?
3. In reviewing the perspectives of organizational change, which do you feel holds most practical value in offering prescriptions for strategists? Which do you feel most accurately captures how real change is likely to occur? Is there a difference between these two? Why?
4. What role should strategists play in managing change?
5. Source a peer-reviewed research article that examines the issue of strategic change. What type of change is involved and what perspective is applied to understanding this change? How does the article contribute to the issues discussed in this chapter?
6. Why do most organizations find managing change so difficult?

Further reading

A seminal article on strategic change is that by James Brian Quinn (1978) 'Strategic change logical incrementalism', *Sloan Management Review*, 20(1): 7–19.

An excellent article examining the implementation of strategic change is A. Franken, C. Edwards, and R. Lambert (2009) 'Executing strategic change: understanding the critical management elements that lead to success', *California Management Review*, 51(3): 49–73.

For an examination of barriers in implementing change, see M. Beer, R. Eisenhardt, and B. Spector (1990) 'Why change programs don't produce change', *Harvard Business Review*, Nov/Dec: 158–166.

For a perspective executing change drawing on the mental models of strategists, see A. Van de Ven and S. Kangyong (2011) 'Breakdowns in implementing models of organization change', *Academy of Management Perspectives*, 23(3): 58–74.

Julia Balogun, Veronica Hope Hailey, and Gerry Johnson's 2008 book *Exploring Corporate Strategy*, 3rd edn, Harlow: Pearson Education, provides a useful frameworks and case studies on change management.

John P. Kotter's 1996 book *Leading Change*, Boston, MA: Harvard Business Press, provides some interesting insights into leading change, highlighting some of the key mistakes that leaders can make.

visit the Online Resource Centre that accompanies this book to access more learning resources on this chapter topic at www.oxfordtextbooks.co.uk/orc/cunningham/

References

Abrahamson, E. 2004. *Change without Pain: How Managers Can Overcome Initiative Overload, Organizational Chaos, and Employee Burnout*. Boston, MA: Harvard Business School Press.

Allport, G. 1955. *Becoming*. New Haven, CT: Yale University Press.

Balogun, J., Hope-Hailey, V., Johnson, G., and Scholes, K. 2004. *Exploring Corporate Change*. Harlow: FT/Prentice Hall.

Bamford, D. and Forrester, P. 2003. Managing planned and emergent change within an operations management environment. *International Journal of Operations & Production Management*, 23(5): 546–556.

Battelle, J. 2006. *The Search: How Google and its Rivals Rewrote the Rules of Business and Transformed Our Culture*. London: Nicholas Publishing.

Beatty, R. and Ulrich, D. 1991. Re-energizing the mature organization. *Organizational Dynamics*, 20(1): 16–30.

Beer, M., Eisenhardt, R., and Spector, B. 1990. Why change programs don't produce change. *Harvard Business Review*, Nov/Dec: 158–166.

Berger, P. and Luckmann, T. 1966. *The Social Construction of Reality*. Harmondsworth: Penguin.

Bower, J. and Christensen, C. 1995. Disruptive technologies: catching the wave. *Harvard Business Review*, 73(1): 43–53.

Caulkin, S. 2011. On management: the winning combination of wealth and power. *Financial Times*, 19 September.

Delbridge, R., Gratton, L., and Johnson, G. 2006. *The Exceptional Manager*. Oxford: Oxford University Press.

Drucker, P. F. 2002. *Managing in the Next Society*. New York: Truman Tally Books.

Dunphy, D. and Stace, D. 1988. Transformational and coercive strategies for planned organizational change: beyond the O.D. model. *Organization Studies*, 9(3): 317–334.

Dunphy, D. and Stace, D. 1993. The strategic management of corporate change. *Human Relations*, 46(8): 905–920.

Edmondson, A. 2011. Strategies for learning from failure. *Harvard Business Review*, Apr: 49–56.

Foster, R. and Kaplan, S. 2001. *Creative Destruction: Why Companies that are Built to Last Underperform the Market—and How to Successfully Transform Them*. New York: Doubleday.

Hamel, G. 1996. Strategy as revolution. *Harvard Business Review*, July/Aug: 69–82.

Hamel, G. and Prahalad, C. 1990. The core competence of the corporation. *Harvard Business Review*, 68(3): 79–91.

Hammer, M. 1990. Re-engineering work: Don't automate, obliterate. *Harvard Business Review*, 68(4): 104–111.

Howard, R. 1993. Foreword; introduction. In R. Howard (ed.) *The Learning Imperative*. Boston, MA: Harvard Business Review Press.

Jenkins, P. and Murphy, M. 2011. Clash on strategy prompted UBS chief to quit. *Financial Times*, 26 September.

Jick, T. 2003. Implementing change. In T. Jick and M. Peiperl (eds) *Managing Change: Cases and Concepts*. London: McGraw-Hill.

Jick, T. and Peiperl, M. 2003. *Managing Change: Concepts and Cases*. 2nd edn. New York: McGraw-Hill.

Johnson, G. 1988. Rethinking incrementalism. *Strategic Management Journal*, 9(1): 75–91.

Johnson, G. 1992. Managing strategic change: strategy, culture and action. *Long Range Planning*, 25(1): 28–36.

Johnson-Cramer, M., Parise, S., and Cross, R. 2007. Managing change through networks and values. *California Management Review*, 49(3): 85–109.

Kotter, J. P. 1995. An eight-stage process of creating major change. *Harvard Business Review*, Mar/Apr: 61–69.

Kotter, J. P. 1996. *Leading Change*. Boston, MA: Harvard Business School Press.

Lewin, K. 1951. *Field Theory in Social Science*. New York: Harper and Row.

March, J. G. 1996. Continuity and change in theories of organizational action. *Administrative Science Quarterly*, 41: 278–287.

Miller, D. 1992. Icarus paradox: how exceptional companies bring about their own downfall. *Business Horizons*, Jan/Feb: 24–35.

Mintzberg, H. 1987. Crafting strategy. *Harvard Business Review*, July/Aug: 66–75.

Mintzberg, H. 2009. *Managing*. London: FT/Prentice Hall.

Mintzberg, H., Ahlstrand, B., and Lampel, J. (eds) 2005. *Strategy Bites Back*. Harlow: FT/Prentice Hall.

Nadler, D. and Tushman, M. 1989. Organizational frame bending: principles for managing re-orientation. *Academy of Management Executive*, 3(3): 194–204.

Nadler, D. and Tushman, M. 1990. Beyond the charismatic leader: leadership and organizational change. *California Management Review*, 32: 66–79.

Nelson, R. and Winter, S. 1982. *An Evolutionary Theory of Economic Change*. Cambridge, MA: The Belknap Press of Harvard University.

Nokia Corporation. 2011. Nokia outlines new strategy, introduces new leadership, operational structure. Stock exchange press release, 11 February. Available online at http://press.nokia.com/2011/02/11/nokia-outlines-new-strategy-introduces-new-leadership-operational-structure/

Nonaka, I. 1988. Creating organizational order out of chaos: self-renewal in Japanese firms. *California Management Review*, Spring: 57–73.

Nord, W. R. 1978. Dreams of humanization and realities of power. *Academy of Management Review*, July: 674–679.

Patel, K. 2005. *The Master Strategist: Power, Purpose and Principle*. London: Arrow Books.

Pech, R. 2001. Reflections: termites, group behaviour, and the loss of innovation—conformity rules! *Journal of Managerial Psychology*, 16(7): 559–574.

Pettigrew, A. 1987. Context and action in the transformation of the firm. *Journal of Management Studies*, 24(6): 649–669.

Pettigrew, A. 1990. Studying strategic choice and strategic change: a comment on Mintzberg and Waters, 'Does decision get in the way?'. *Organization Studies*, 11(1): 6–10.

Pfeffer, J. 1998. *The Human Equation*. Boston, MA: Harvard Business School Press.

Pfeffer, J. and Sutton, R. 2006. *Hard Facts, Dangerous Half Truths, and Total Nonsense*. Boston, MA: Harvard Business School Press.

Plowman, D., Baker, L., Beck, T., Kulkarni, M., Solansky, S., and Travis, D. 2007. Radical change accidentally: the emergence and amplification of small change. *Academy of Management Journal*, 50(3): 515–543.

Rumelt, R. 2009. Strategy in a 'structural break'. *McKinsey Quarterly*, 1: 35–42.

Senge, P. 1992. *The Fifth Discipline: The Art and Practice of the Learning Organization*. London: Century Business.

Slatter, S. 1984. *Corporate Recovery: A Guide to Turnaround Management.* Harmondsworth: Penguin Books.

Spector, B. 1989. From bogged down to fired up: inspiring organizational change. *Sloan Management Review*, Summer: 29–34.

Stace, D. and Dunphy, D. 1991. Beyond traditional paternalistic and developmental approaches to organisational change and human resource strategies. *International Journal of Human Resource Management*, 22(3): 263–284.

Stacey, R. D. 1995. The science of complexity: an alternative perspective for strategic change process. *Strategic Management Journal*, 12: 477–95.

Stacey, R. D. 2010. *Complexity and Organisational Reality: Uncertainty and the Need to Rethink Management after the Collapse of Investment Capitalism*. London: Routledge.

Stalk, G., Evans, P., and Schuman, L. 1992. Competing on capabilities: new rules in corporate strategy. *Harvard Business Review*, 70(2): 54–66.

Teather, D. 2010. Hard-wired: Kleisterlee is reinventing the inventive Dutch firm Philips. *The Guardian*, 2 April. Available online at http://www.guardian.co.uk/business/2010/apr/02/philips-chief-executive-kleisterlee-interview

Teece, D., Pisano, G., and Shuen, A. 1997. Dynamic capabilities and strategic management. *Strategic Management Journal*, 18: 509–533.

Tushman, M. L. and O'Reilly III, C. A. 1996. The ambidextrous organization: managing evolutionary and revolutionary change. *California Management Review*, 38: 1–23.

Tushman, M. L. and Romanelli, E. 1985. Organizational revolution: a metamorphosis model of convergence and reorientation. *Research in Organizational Behaviour*, 7: 171–222.

Van de Ven, A. and Poole, M. 1995. Explaining development and change in organizations. *Academy of Management Review*, 20(3): 510–540.

Weick, K. E. and Quinn, R. 1999. Organizational change and development. *American Review of Psychology*, 50: 361–386.

12

Innovation and corporate entrepreneurship

We will fight our battles not on the low road to commodization, but on the high road of innovation.

(Howard Stringer, chairman and CEO, Sony)

Introduction

Our previous chapter focused on sustaining advantage via strategic change. In this chapter, we continue with the theme of sustaining advantage by exploring **innovation** and **corporate entrepreneurship**. Every day, we hear organizations announcing how innovative and revolutionary they are. These traits have become central to how they define and portray themselves through advertising and media campaigns. Organizations are at pains to highlight the uniqueness of their product offering or customer experience. Volvo's brand image is built around the concept of 'Volvo for life', BMW's is the 'Ultimate driving experience', while Ford's is 'Feel the difference'. We live in societies in which advantages are short-lived; the pursuit of innovation is a competitive imperative, and a challenging objective for **strategists** and their organizations. Innovation and corporate entrepreneurship, as Howard Stringer articulates in our opening quote, are a crucial part of strategy. Without them, organizations would stagnate, lose competitiveness and customers—and ultimately fail. At the heart of innovation are novelty and uniqueness; how to deliver them is a key question that strategists must address when formulating and evaluating their organizational strategies. The simplicity of the question of what makes an organization unique and relevant masks the complex reality of what it takes for an organization to innovate every day of its existence.

Chief executive officers (CEOs) and strategists hear the 'innovate or die' mantra all of the time, but the reality is that organizations can innovate *and* die—or at least have suboptimal outcomes. Audi is part of the VAG group. For its model, the A6, Audi claimed to have developed more patents than the US National Aeronautics and Space Administration (NASA), a key element substantiating its brand claim of '*Vorsprung durch Technik*' ('progress through technology'). Audi's success in the marketplace would seem to signal that its innovations are well recognized and rewarded. Volkswagen (VW), also part of VAG, sought to capitalize on the success of its Mark III Golf and revitalized Passat range by developing the Phaeton, aimed at the same market segment as the A6. It was a clear attempt to demonstrate VW's technical prowess and design capability. However, the impact was minimal. The Phaeton failed the ultimate test of the marketplace, with modest sales in the UK and Europe, and was withdrawn from sale in the USA in 2006. There was no doubting the innovation credentials of the car in terms of design, functionality, and other capabilities, but it did not align with VW customer expectations or those of other potential customers in its market segment.

The top six of *Business Week*'s most innovative companies in 2010 include Apple, Google, Microsoft, IBM, Toyota, and Amazon. These global organizations have built capabilities through innovation and corporate entrepreneurship that are the envy of corporations across the globe. Achieving single-digit growth rates year on year for a large global organization such as ThyssenKrupp, an integrated materials and technology group headquartered in Germany, is a mammoth task requiring creativity and innovation. The focus of this chapter is how such

Figure 12.1 An overview of innovation and corporate entrepreneurship (CE)

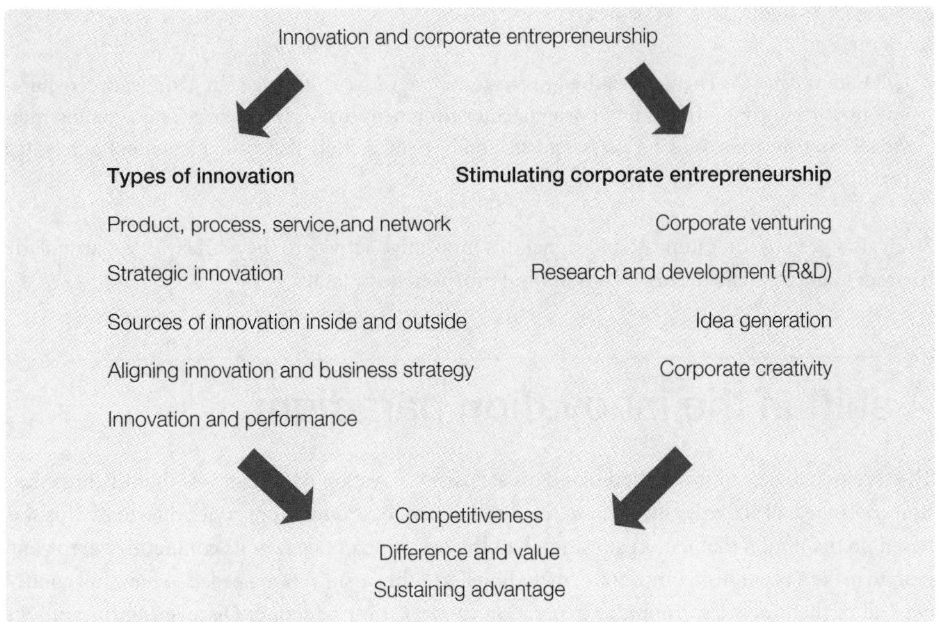

organizations can maintain or exceed threshold levels of advantage through innovation and corporate entrepreneurship.

We begin by examining the shift in the innovation **paradigm** from a closed innovation model to an open innovation model. We then focus on the differing perspectives on innovation: whether to be an innovation leader or follower; the sources of innovation; and innovation implementation issues and obstacles. Our attention then moves to examining the relationship between innovation and performance, and how organizations align their business strategy with their innovation strategy. We close the chapter with a focus on corporate entrepreneurship and how organizations can stimulate corporate entrepreneurship through corporate venturing and research and development (R&D). Figure 12.1 offers an overview of the chapter.

Innovation

The term 'innovation' is as misused as 'strategy'. Organizations, individuals, and economies are constantly being encouraged to become innovative. In our everyday lives, we see the fruits of innovative activity in the products and services that we consume. New **industries** are being created through various types of innovation, resulting in more flexible organization structures. The pursuit of innovation is an ongoing activity for the strategist and the organization. As Klas Kleinfield, president and CEO of Siemens AG, puts it: 'You can only win the "war" with ideas, not with spending cuts.' But why does innovation matter and what is its purpose? Innovation goes to the heart of uniqueness, the difference of an organization's product offerings, and the articulation of specified value propositions. In the marketplace, it means higher margins, increased sales, and reinforcement of branding and marketing activities.

In Chapter 2, we saw that one of the key questions for a strategist is what makes an organization unique, different, and relevant. Innovation enables organizations to refine their uniqueness and relevance to their customers, thereby increasing revenues and profits (Tushman, 1997). Strategists must put in place an organizational structure and culture that supports innovation from multiple sources, and balance this against ensuring a return in the marketplace. An IBM Global Business Services CEO study (2006: 34) states:

> CEOs must drive the changes required to create an innovative culture. Leading innovation requires an unwavering commitment to an orientated environment that also recognizes outstanding individual contributions, and business and technology integration that is implemented across the organization.

Strategists need to communicate and signal this innovative activity to the marketplace, particularly in order to differentiate the organization from prospective imitators.

A shift in the innovation paradigm

The traditional view of innovation based on a closed innovation paradigm was that the organization controlled all activities involved in the development of products or service offerings. This was based on the notion that the organization had the best human talent in its competitive arena and that, to make a profit from innovation, including R&D, the organization needed to have full control over all of the processes, from idea generation to market introduction. Discovering innovations first would mean getting to the market first, and if organizations had the best ideas in their competitive arena, they would win in the marketplace. Control and protection of the intellectual property of the organization meant that competitors did not gain from the organization's innovations. The closed innovation paradigm is based on hiring the best talent in the organization's competitive arena, providing them with special conditions, and freeing them from market conditions; this increases the run rate from ideas to the marketplace in new product and service offerings. An example of a closed innovation paradigm is the pharmaceutical industry, in which it can take up to ten years from product inception to manufacturing and distributing the drugs to patients. Protection of intellectual property is essential in this type of industry.

The closed innovation paradigm began to evolve to an open innovation paradigm due to the increased risks associated with R&D costs, the proliferation of new ideas, the advancing rate of technological and scientific breakthroughs, and the real market opportunities around convergent technologies. The go-it-alone strategy of closed innovation became obsolete in many industries. The principle of the open innovation paradigm is based on harnessing external and internal sources of innovation (Chesborough, 2003). Effective open innovation requires external cooperative partners, be these competitors, universities, etc., and the use of external sources to support innovation. Proctor and Gamble (P&G) is exemplary of this. Its CEO, A. G. Laffey, committed P&G to acquiring 50 per cent of its innovations outside the organization. A further extension of the open innovation paradigm is the creation of collaborative communities for innovation purposes; this is termed 'collaborative entrepreneurship' (Miles *et al.*, 2006). Blade.org, a not-for-profit organization created by IBM to collaborate on next-generation blade technologies, is an example of such a collaborative community.

Perspectives on innovation

There are many different perspectives on and definitions of 'innovation'. Drucker (1985: 17) states: 'Innovation is the specific tool of entrepreneurs, the means by which they exploit change as an opportunity for a different business or a different service. It is capable of being practised.' Moss Kanter (2006: 83) simply describes innovation as involving 'ideas that create the future'. Pfeffer (1994: 345) provides a useful reminder that 'Innovation and change in almost any arena requires the skill to develop power, and the willingness to employ it to get things accomplished'.

Organizations pursuing innovation can fall into traps, including strategy mistakes (hurdles too high; scope too narrow), process mistakes (control too tight), structure mistakes (connections too loose; separations too sharp), and skill mistakes (leadership too weak; communication too poor) (Moss Kanter, 2006). Organizations can overcome these traps by: widening innovation searches and broadening their scope; adding flexibility to planning and control systems; facilitating close connections between innovators and mainstream businesses; selecting leadership with appropriate interpersonal skills; and surrounding innovators with a supportive culture of collaboration. The remedies require organizations to explore and exploit innovation in equal measure, which requires a focus on relationship building and flexibility within organization structures (ibid).

One way of understanding different perspectives on innovation is to consider four innovation forms: namely, product innovation, process innovation, service innovation, and horizontal innovation.

- *Product innovation* arises when the organization makes changes to the product or service that it offers. These changes can include developing a totally new product, increasing the functionality of an existing product, or, in the case of a services business, improving the customer experience. Examples of product innovation include Dyson vacuum cleaners and hand dryers, the hybrid Toyota Prius, and Vista and Windows 7 from Microsoft. The scale of effort and focus on innovation, particularly product innovation, is staggering, with over US$700bn a year spent on R&D in Organization for Economic Co-operation and Development (OECD) countries; approximately twenty-five companies in the USA have R&D budgets in excess of US$1bn each. However, product innovation is actually one of the least successful forms of innovation in terms of returns compared with other forms of innovation.
- *Process innovation* occurs when the organization makes changes to how the product is developed or how a service is delivered. This form of innovation is usually internally driven and is linked to the particular business model that the organization is pursuing. For example, Dell changed the process and business model of the PC industry by building PCs to order and pursuing direct sales with all customers, enterprises, small-to-medium-sized enterprises (SMEs), and government and personal buyers. This process innovation changed the competitive rules in the PC industry and gave Dell a significant competitive advantage. Other notable examples of process innovation include Starbucks, which has started a music label and partnered with book and movie producers to enhance its overall product delivery experience; Samsung Electronics has invested heavily in new production facilities to respond to convergent device opportunities.
- *Service innovation* focuses on the product performance, customer service, and product suite to enhance the customer experience and/or use of the organization's product or service. Examples include the car industry, with typical vehicle service intervals increasing from 5,000 miles to 10,000 miles, or even 20,000 miles, or with breakdown cover provided for the lifetime of the car.
- *Horizontal innovation* can involve: first, a different competitive context in which the organization places its offering; secondly, how the organization uses and leverages multiple stakeholders to ensure dominance of its product and service offering; and thirdly, the reuse of product or service innovation in other context or marketplaces. Honda uses its product innovation with respect to engine technology in markets ranging from cars to lawnmowers. Its current R&D efforts are focused on what Honda describes as 'sustainable mobility', which means, according to Mr Tomohiko Kawanabe (2011), CEO of Honda:

> In the short term our approach is to improve the efficiency of the internal combustion engine –both petrol and diesel engines—but this is not enough to really talk about sustainability. For that we need to think about renewable energies and also renewable energy carriers such as electricity or hydrogen to ensure that we can provide the most appropriate energy source for different requirements.

- Newbridge Cutlery in Ireland, once a traditional maker of silver tableware such as knives, forks, and spoons, has pursued both product and horizontal innovation by expanding its product range to include men's and women's jewellery and other forms of tableware through branded outlets. The collaboration between Nike and Apple in the cross-marketing of iPods and Nike Wear specially designed for iPods is another example of horizontal innovation.

Value and strategic innovation

Other forms of innovation include value and strategic innovation, which is focused on the strategy issues around innovation. The focus of value innovation, according to Kim and Mauborgne (1999; 2005), is to beat competitors by making them irrelevant. The authors argue that conventional logic and value innovation differ along five key dimensions: industry assumptions; strategic logic; customers; assets and capabilities; product and service offerings. Value innovators see opportunities and their associated risks differently. These innovators ask the following questions.

1. Which of the factors that our industry takes for granted can be eliminated?
2. Which factors should be reduced well below the industry's standard?
3. Which factors should be raised well above the industry's standard?
4. Which factors should be created that the industry has never offered?

The focus of strategic innovation is to pursue a strategy that is significantly different from competitors' strategies, thereby avoiding head-to-head competition. Effective strategic innovation means that companies can change the competitive rules to their advantage, as Markides (1997: 9) notes:

> By breaking the rules of the game and thinking of new ways to compete, a company can strategically redefine its business and catch its bigger competitors off guard. The trick is not to play the game better than the competition but to develop and play an altogether different game.

Markides argues that strategic innovation sources come from companies deciding on three basic issues at the strategic level: 'Who is going to be our customer? What products or services should we offer the chosen customers? How should we offer these products or services cost efficiently?' The question for strategists is whether to be at the forefront of new innovations or a follower of innovation within their competitive arena. These conceptions of innovation focus on creating value that is unique, having a unique strategy, and/or delivering value in unique ways. A further question for strategists to consider is whether they should take the lead in such initiatives or follow suit only once an approach is proven to be successful. This is an ongoing dilemma in the domain of managing innovation.

Being an innovation leader or follower

The strategist must find ways of being different and creating value around that difference. From an innovation perspective, this includes the question of whether to be an innovation leader or follower. The aim of innovation leaders is to be first to the market based on their technological leadership, and in so doing gain as much market share as possible. This is termed 'radical innovation'. To pursue innovation leadership effectively, organizations need commitment to creativity, risk taking, and have an appropriate organization structure (see Chapter 10), while also developing very close links with major sources of innovation. They require a resource allocation system that mirrors and supports being an innovation leader. AstraZeneca is an innovation leader in integrated biopharmaceuticals, investing US$4bn in R&D annually and with over 11,000 people working in R&D.

The other option is to be an innovation follower. Here, a wait-and-see approach is adopted. To some degree, follower organizations imitate pioneering innovators. This is termed 'incremental innovation'. Followers learn from the experience of innovation pioneers; they have effective business intelligence and possess the capability to replicate existing offerings already in the marketplace (known as 'reverse engineering').

The choice between being an innovation leader or follower becomes increasingly difficult for most organizations as the technology frontier in their competitive context moves faster, particularly with the advent of convergent technology and convergent market opportunities. Many competitive environments face technology disruption, which potentially threatens their core competitiveness and even their existence. Examples of this include the growth in the online travel industry, which has reduced the travel agent distribution channel, and the advent of social networking, which has changed the way in which music artists and bands interact with their fan base. Christensen (1997: xiii–xiv) summarizes the innovator's dilemma as 'how executives can simultaneously do what is right for the near-term health of their established businesses, while focusing adequate resources on the disruptive technologies that ultimately could lead to their downfall'. To this end, Christensen (1997: 207–210) suggests that, in examining the potential for disruptive technologies, strategists should consider the following issues.

1. The pace of progress that markets demand or can absorb may be different from the progress offered by technology.
2. Managing innovation mirrors the resource allocation process.
3. Just as there is a resource allocation side to every innovation problem, matching the market to the technology is another.
4. The capabilities of most organizations are far more specialized and context-specific than most managers are inclined to believe.
5. In many instances, the information required to make large and decisive investments in the face of disruptive technology simply does not exist.
6. It is not wise to adopt a blanket technology strategy to be always a leader or always a follower.

Being an innovation leader or follower is dependent on a number of issues, including the competitive space in which the organization is operating, and the likelihood of positive lock-in and increasing turns (Arthur, 1996). In emerging technological domains, it is also difficult to predict what will become the dominant standard. Nonetheless, a necessary prerequisite to success is ensuring that the organization has strategic knowledge of both the sources of and key obstacles to innovation.

Sources of innovation

For any organization, there are multiple sources of innovation both inside and outside the organization. Strategists must channel these sources of innovation into organizational structures, processes, and culture so that the novelty and difference generated ultimately lead to positive outcomes, including market share gains and increases in sales and revenue. On any given day, an organization has multiple transactions with different stakeholders, which can lead to new ideas or approaches; if adopted by the organization, these may have an impact on its business.

The IBM Global Business Services CEO study (2006) highlighted that external sources constituted the main source of ideas, particularly for the outperformers in their study. It identified the three most significant sources of innovative ideas as employees, business partners, and customers, while Cohen *et al.*'s (2002) study of information sources for new R&D projects found that customers, own manufacturing operations, and cooperative ventures were the three main information sources.

Drucker (2003) categorized the four internal sources of innovation as unexpected occurrences, incongruities, process needs, and industry and market changes, and the outside sources of innovation as demographic changes, changes in perception, and new knowledge. He suggested (ibid: 54): 'There are of course innovations that spring from a flash of genius. Most innovations, however, especially the successful ones, result from a conscious, purposeful search for innovation opportunities, which are found only in a few situations.' Overall, these studies substantiate that sources of innovation outside the organization are more significant than those inside, with customers and collaborative arrangement with external parties likely to be the really key sources (see Reading 5.2).

Innovation obstacles

According to IBM's study (2006), the most significant obstacles to innovation internally are an unsupportive culture and climate, limited funding for investment, and workforce issues. Externally, the significant obstacles include government and other legal restrictions, economic uncertainty, inadequate enabling technologies, and workforce issues arising externally. A team-orientated environment with an individual reward system is seen as key to driving innovation performance. Google operates a networked model in which ideas, data, and dialogue are encouraged and supported by a flatter organizational structure that empowers employees (ibid: 30–31). To drive this connectivity, instead of having disconnected employees, managers should strive to use mechanisms that tie employees to various knowledge sources. This is important for innovation performance (Rodan and Galunic, 2004).

The challenges of innovation implementation

To be successful, innovations must have an impact on the marketplace. There must be appropriate organizational support and risks must be managed. Often, the outcomes of innovation efforts by organizations can fall short of expectations. To implement innovation, the strategist must resolve three issues: first, where best to source innovation; secondly, how to increase the innovative capacity of the organization from idea generation to diffusion; and thirdly, the issue of risk. In sourcing innovation, the innovation paradigm is moving towards a more open model of innovation, in which organizations source a growing number of ideas from outside. These can come in the form of raw ideas, market-ready ideas, or market-ready products. In using them, the company is seeking to become an 'innovation capitalist' (Nambisan and Sawhney, 2007).

Getting all types of innovation to the marketplace, from idea generation to ultimate diffusion, is a real implementation issue for companies. Some, like Rubbermaid in the USA, claim to implement one innovation a day; for other organizations, making such achievements a daily reality can seem beyond their capability. Hansen and Birkinshaw (2007: 121) note: 'There is no universal solution for organizations wanting to improve their ability to generate, develop and disseminate new ideas. Every firm faces its own challenge in this regard.' The reality is that there is no one solution to dealing with issues of innovation implementation. Hansen and Birkinshaw (2007) argue that organizations should view innovation as an end-to-end process encompassing idea generation, conversion, and diffusion. Where organizations are poor at developing ideas, the authors suggest that companies develop external networks and build internal cross-unit networks. Where deficits occur at the conversion stage, they recommend that companies focus on multi-channel funding and on developing organizational safe havens so that concepts can emerge. In dealing with diffusion deficiencies, they suggest that companies use a variety of catalysts to roll out the developed ideas. Key performance indicators of innovation include the following.

- **Idea generation**
  - Number of high-quality ideas generated within a unit
  - Number of high-quality ideas generated across units
  - Number of high-quality ideas generated from outside the firm
- **Conversion**
  - Percentage of all ideas generated that end up being selected and funded
  - Percentage of funded ideas that lead to revenues
  - Number of months to first sale

- **Diffusion**
  - Percentage of penetration in desired markets, channels, customer groups
  - Number of months to full diffusion

This final issue in innovation implementation is risk. Focusing solely on one form of innovation can be high risk for an organization. Attempting to deploy innovations in markets that the organization does not know well can also raise risk levels. Organizations can reduce risk by focusing innovation activity in the same offering and market arenas with which they are familiar. The probability of failure increases as an organization attempts to deploy innovations into adjacent offerings and markets or new-to-company markets and offerings (Day, 2007).

Innovation and performance

One of the key questions that any CEO, board member, or strategist would ask is: 'What returns does a business gain from investing in innovation?' The IBM Global Business Services CEO study (2006) highlights a broad range of benefits, particularly in the context of collaborative and partnering contexts. Not surprisingly, the top benefit reported was reduced costs, followed by higher quality/customer satisfaction, and access to skills/products. Day (2007: 112) notes: 'Minor innovations make up 85% to 90% of companies' development portfolio, but they rarely generate the growth that companies seek.' While there are no landmark empirical studies demonstrating the direct impact on innovation spending on bottom-line revenues, some empirical studies have examined different aspects of innovation and performance. A survey carried out by the Industrial Research Institute in 2007 (SCINTA, 2007), highlighted that R&D expenditure on new projects was up 5 per cent on previous years, while expenditure on basic research slumped over a seven-year period. Basic research is an essential element in developing new innovations aligned to the strategic goals of the organization. Consequently, this evidence would indicate that organizations were focusing more on short-term goals rather than long-term, innovation-led growth through increased investment in basic research. The Industrial Research Institute annual survey of members in 2010, however, noted a degree of change:

> The primary focus of this investment is on new-business development projects. Aggressively pursuing innovation and balancing innovation in the overall R&D portfolio continue to be management challenges for the leaders who responded to the survey. They are also concerned about acquisition of, and access to, talent.

The relationship between innovativeness, quality, growth, profitability, and market value was empirically tested by Cho and Pucik (2005). They found that organizations should balance quality and innovation as part of their overall corporate strategy and noted:

> Since neither 'profitability without growth' nor 'growth without profitability' guarantees superior market performance, we believe that the capability to balance innovation with quality is indispensable for companies to sustain profitable growth in a fast-moving global economic environment.
>
> (Cho and Pucik, 2005: 573)

When it comes to innovation and performance in a single business unit, Tsai (2001) found that if single business units occupy a central network position, they are likely to have access to useful knowledge from other business units, which provides them with opportunities to share ideas, information, and learning, coupled with higher absorptive capacity levels. Tsai comments that 'internal social processes within organizations affect innovation at the organizational unit level' (ibid: 1002). The improvement of innovation performance by social processes is reinforced by Taylor and Greve (2006), whose study of the comic-book industry revealed that 'multimember teams and teams with experience working together produced innovations with greater variation in value, but individuals were able to combine knowledge diversity more effectively than teams' (ibid: 723). Organizations that are open to external sources of innovation or search channels can have higher levels of innovation performance. This is particularly the case with radical innovation in the early stages of product life cycles; when the technology matures, increased searching activities take place in order to improve and broaden the product or service appeal (Laursen and Salter, 2006). However, the danger is that organizations can search too much, which can impede innovation performance (Katila and Ahuja, 2002).

Looking at innovation and performance in collaborative contexts, Stuart (2000) found that older and larger organizations benefited less from large and innovative strategic **alliance** partners than did smaller, younger organizations. Interestingly, innovation performance is greater in situations in which alliance partners have an equity **joint venture**, when technological diversity between partners is higher, and the organizational form incentivizes and shapes activities such as information sharing, which ultimately affect innovative performance. Some tension between partners can also be positive, because this can encourage further inter-**organizational learning** (Sampson, 2007). In a collaborative context, organizations should actively manage the sharing of knowledge in their own innovation systems, and global firms should actively develop strategies to participate in global innovation systems (Spencer, 2003). Spencer's study of the flat-panel-display industry found that 'firms that shared relevant knowledge with their innovation system earned higher innovative performance than firms that did not share knowledge' (ibid: 217).

Aligning innovation and strategy

As outlined in the opening section of the chapter, the alignment between innovation and strategy is an important element of an organizations' competitiveness in the marketplace. Organizations cannot afford to waste resources on activities that will not enhance its competitive advantage. Ensuring alignment between business and innovation strategies requires organizations to put in place organizational conditions for effective innovation. Businesses such as HTC, Lenovo, and 3M have developed an organization culture around innovation. Creating this over time may mean hiring the best technical and managerial talent available, and creating an organizational context that is comfortable with learning and adapting to new approaches. The cultural context that is created to support innovation needs to encourage continual improvement across the organization in an integrated, rather than partial, manner. In tandem with effective conditions, innovation needs clear top management leadership and an organization's ongoing capacity to leverage the knowledge and capabilities of internal and external stakeholders (Bessant and Tidd, 2007).

Alignment of innovation and strategy also requires a change in mindset that embraces technological aspects alongside understanding societal trends. Driving the innovation imperative in a manufacturing context, leaders with manufacturing experience are more likely to innovate by testing new methods and equipment, will recruit new technical talent internally or externally, will undertake technological forecasting, and will make customers aware of the benefits of any changes (Ettlie, 1990). This means that customers can benefit through product choice, functionality, durability, and price. Effective alignment can occur only when an organization has clarity about its strategy, value propositions, and **core competences**.

Embracing innovation opens up new market opportunities for companies. One of the major inhibiting factors that strategists have to take into account in aligning innovation and strategy is the company's ability to adapt and implement new ideas, knowledge, and know-how that enhances the competitive position of the company. For example, an SME might purchase new software that allows it to undertake several core administrative functions more effectively, such as payroll, timesheets, and customer invoices; for a manufacturing company, purchasing new equipment may improve product efficiency and quality. In both cases, enhancing the competitive position requires acquiring new expertise and knowledge, and internal adaptation. This ability to internalize and retain knowledge is described by Cohen and Levinthal (1990: 128) as 'absorptive capacity':

> The ability to exploit external knowledge is thus a critical component of innovative capabilities. We argue that the ability to evaluate and utilize outside knowledge is largely a function of the level of prior knowledge ... prior knowledge confers an ability to recognize the value of new information,

> assimilate it, and apply it to commercial ends. These abilities collectively constitute what we call a firm's absorptive capacity.

In essence, absorptive capacity is intangible.

Cohen and Levinthal highlighted that absorptive capacity is an issue in resource allocation for innovation purposes, that organizations are sensitive to the context characteristics of their learning environments, and that high levels of absorptive capacity in an R&D investment context can increase innovation and facilitate learning. If a life science company is continuously investing in R&D, bringing in new ideas and knowledge from outside the organization, and combining this with an organizational culture of continuous learning, it means that the organization has high levels of absorptive capacity. It also means that the organization can respond quickly to change. The absorptive capacity for SMEs is less, given their size and scale; however, larger firms, with their multiple products, do have difficulty maximizing their absorptive capacity organization-wide and with outside partners.

These are the complexities and difficulties encountered in making innovation a lived reality for everyone in an organization. Different organizations approach the dilemmas posed by innovation in different ways. However, one fact is constant: the focus of innovation remains steadfastly on organizational differentiation, uniqueness, and competitiveness. We now turn to corporate entrepreneurship as another element in sustaining advantage.

Corporate entrepreneurship

Corporate entrepreneurship, like innovation, is centred on ensuring that organizations maintain threshold competitiveness, particularly around differentiation. In many ways, this is a more tangible response by organizations to the innovation imperative. Traditional entrepreneurship builds on the notion of opportunity recognition and exploitation through configuring the appropriate resources; corporate entrepreneurship is about developing and configuring organizational resources, requiring, as Stopford and Baden Fuller (1994: 522) describe, 'changes in the pattern of resource deployment and the creation of new capabilities to add new possibilities for positioning markets'. Sharp Corporation, headquartered in Osaka, Japan, has a history of corporate entrepreneurship since its foundation in 1912. In the 1960s, Sharp developed the first transistor calculator; in the early 1970s, it developed LCD technology, which is now a common feature in consumer goods. In the mid-1990s, Sharp produced the first commercial camera phone.

Barringer and Bluedorn (1999) found that the links between tangible corporate entrepreneurship and strategic management can be along a number of dimensions, including scanning intensity, planning flexibility, planning horizon (the number of years for which an organization is planning), the locus of planning (the number of employees involved in the planning), and control attributes (strategic and financial). The authors concluded that 'a firm's entrepreneurial intensity is influenced by the nature of its strategic management practices' (ibid: 433) and that having employee involvement facilitates firm-level entrepreneurial behaviour.

Typically, corporate entrepreneurship initiatives within organizations focus on two key areas: creation and pursuit of new venture opportunities, and strategic/organizational renewal (Guth and Ginsberg, 1990; Sathe, 1989). In Sharp Corporation, or Samsung, the senior management teams are focused on getting the balance between creating new technologies and opportunities, and ensuring that both organizations maintain and grow their market positions. It also encompasses the areas of leadership, culture, innovation, risk taking, and the pursuit of new venture opportunities, which Dess and Lumpkin (2005) describe as 'entrepreneurial orientation'. Entrepreneurial orientation includes five key dimensions: autonomy; innovativeness; proactiveness; competitive aggressiveness; and risk taking. This is illustrated in the case of Intel. It has a group called 'Intel Capital', the vision of which 'is to be the preeminent global investing organization in the world. Our mission is to make and manage financially attractive investments in support of Intel's strategic objectives' (http://www.intel.com/about/companyinfo/capital/index.htm). In July 2011, there were 260 companies support by Intel Capital in its portfolio.

Other constituents of corporate entrepreneurship can be learning capabilities, team orientation, experimentation, and ambition; corporate entrepreneurship can be an important influencer in post-acquisition success (Thomson and McNamara, 2001). Garvin and Levesque (2006) suggest that the pursuit of corporate entrepreneurship requires three kinds of balancing act: namely, balancing trial-and-error strategy formulation with rigour and discipline; balancing operational experience with invention; and balancing business identity with integration. They conclude that 'For companies that wish to succeed with corporate entrepreneurship, the lesson is simple. Success is not an either–or proposition' (ibid: 112).

Stimulating corporate entrepreneurship: corporate venturing

Stimulating corporate entrepreneurship is dependent on organizational size, familiarity with business concept, and the length of the planning periods. For organizations to pursue effective corporate entrepreneurship, due consideration has to be given to resources, the perceived costs of innovation, and the associated dangers of fixating on competitive space (companies may lose out on new opportunities if they focus only on their competitive space) (Westfall, 1969). Clarity around entrepreneurial vision, the creation of new venture teams, and the development of appropriate remuneration packages have been key factors in delivering entrepreneurial orientation performance (Kurato *et al.*, 2001).

Creating dedicated corporate venturing activities is one response that some organizations take in nurturing corporate entrepreneurship. Von Hippel (1977: 163) describes corporate venturing as 'an activity which seeks to generate new business for the corporation in which it resides through the establishment of external or internal corporate ventures'. The typical remit of corporate venturing teams is to seek out new market and product opportunities inside and outside the firm. According to Burgleman (1983: 241), for corporate ventures to be led to success, they:

> depend on the availability of autonomous entrepreneurial activity on the part of operational-level participants, on the ability of middle-level managers to conceptualize the strategic implications of these initiatives in more general system terms, and on the capacity of top management to allow viable entrepreneurial initiatives to change the corporate strategy.

The dimensions of internal corporate venturing include structural autonomy, degree of relatedness, extent of innovation, and the nature of sponsorship. The internal dimensions vary according to each organization. Consider Microsoft: it has structured the internal and external dimensions of internal corporate venturing through its Intellectual Property Licensing Group, and has developed specific pathways to encourage corporate venturing and to help it to engage effectively with external parties. This includes technology licensing programmes, intellectual property ventures programmes, and open specification licensing programmes. Microsoft also has an opportunity management centre (OMC), which allows businesses to submit business proposals. External corporate venturing can encompass such activities as joint ventures, spin-offs, and venture capital initiatives (Sharma and Chrisman, 1999).

Baden Fuller (1995: 14) suggests that 'the costs of building corporate entrepreneurship are thetrue costs of undertaking innovations. Organizations which do not have the appropriate level of corporate entrepreneurship will find that they have to build this capability inside the firms before they can innovate'. The danger is that organizations can fall into the familiarity and maturity traps that prevent the development of breakthrough inventions. Organizations can overcome these by experimenting with novel, emerging, and pioneering technologies (Ahuja and Lampert, 2001).

Stimulating corporate venturing: research and development

Creating a dedicated corporate R&D function within the organization is another means to develop corporate entrepreneurship. The annual Booz & Company Global Innovation 1000 R&D study (Jaruzelski and Dehoff, 2010) shows that North America, Europe, and Japan account for the majority of R&D spend among headquartered companies. Roche Holding, Microsoft, Nokia, Toyota, and Pfizer are the top five corporate R&D spending companies, and Apple, Google, 3M, General Electric (GE), and Toyota were classified as the most innovative companies. In reflecting on the changes in the study, the authors note:

> Our annual Global Innovation 1000 study has shown time and time again that there is no statistically significant relationship between financial performance and innovation spending, in terms of either total R&D dollars or R&D as a percentage of revenues. What matter instead is the particular combination of talent, knowledge, team structures, tools, and processes—*the capabilities*...
>
> (Jaruzelski and Dehoff, 2010: 12)

The rationale for investing in R&D is to provide the organization with the opportunity and strategic position to increase profitability in meeting customer demands. R&D commitment is necessary for knowledge building, strategy positioning, and business investments (Mitchell and Hamilton, 1988). In industries such as biotechnology, R&D cooperation and partnership has intensified between firms large and small (Hagedoorn and Roijakkers, 2002: 223–254). The real decision for many organizations is whether to have a central/corporate R&D function or to have R&D units for each business unit. A further choice is whether to organize R&D functions around science or products and markets. In terms of organizational design, for R&D to create value, De Sanctis *et al.* (2002) recommend strategic mechanism, executive-level attention, an entrepreneurial, communications-oriented culture, putting sharing where it matters, externally oriented R&D, and a willingness to mix and match structures. Selden and MacMillian (2006) argue that the R&D effort of organizations should be customer-centric, whereby front-line employees are at the centre of the customer R&D process. This means that organizations need to actively understand the activities and changes in the markets that they serve, and to have a flexible R&D response both internally and externally. G4S Technologies provides integrated security products and services to a variety of public and private sector clients in over eighty countries. Close collaboration with these clients and an understanding of their needs are essential in developing new security solutions (see Reading 5.2).

Idea generation

At the heart of corporate entrepreneurship is the organization's ability to generate new ideas and be creative. These are both difficult activities in which to excel, because most organizations tend to limit creativity and idea generation through archaic organizational structures and processes. Being able to think differently is one of the core skills of a strategist and is critical to defining the uniqueness and difference of the firm. When The Weather Channel was launched in the USA in the early 1980s, it was met with scepticism both within and outside its parent company, Landmark Communications. The general perception was that it would be a non-starter. By 2007, it had become a respected and trusted brand, attracting in excess of 4 billion views per year to its website, weather.com. In describing his experience of launching the channel, Batten (2002: 114) notes:

> The Weather Channel embodies our ambition. It's a business we started in the face of almost universal scepticism, even ridicule. A business that weathered a nearly fatal crisis. A business whose services are now welcomed in the homes and offices of millions of people every day.

Idea generation and creativity form the early stages of innovation. Idea generation can begin with a germ of a proposal for a product, improving a process, a new service offering, or for reconfiguring current organizational offerings. The traditional model of idea generation begins with an idea, then goes through some form of evaluative process that encompasses both market and commercial validation, after which it may then be implemented by the organization.

Corporate creativity

Creativity involves the ability to develop new ideas and explore novel ways of looking at problems and opportunities. This corporate capability is particularly essential because organizations will experience difficulties in implementing their strategies or new opportunities may arise in their competitive environment. In developing the Nano, the world's smallest car, Tata Motors had to use corporate creativity, in terms of its design, functionality, features, and ensuring the lowest price point possible of between US$2,000 and US$3,000. Amabile *et al.*'s (2005) large study of creativity found that creativity can be located anywhere in the organization, but is dependent on the experience and intrinsic motivation of people. Money was not a creativity motivator; time pressure stifles creativity; creativity is positively associated with joy; creativity through collaboration comes when groups have confidence to share ideas; and creativity suffers when an organization is downsized. Amabile suggests that, to develop more creative environments, managers should do the following.

- When time pressure is high, clear out the distractions.
- React to problems with understanding and help.
- Celebrate a good performance in public.
- When times are tough, keep team members informed.

According to Leonard and Swap (1999: 9–13), innovation is the end result of a creative process that involves preparation, opportunity, divergence (generating options), incubation, and convergence (selecting options). The authors argue that 'Creative people can be important to an organization, but group creativity depends more on managing the creative process than on a few "creatives"' (ibid: 16). In assessing Apple's creativity, Anderson (1992: 42) argues that the late Steve Jobs' 'genius' was 'the ability to dream dreams then connive and cajole others into cooperation ... Apple hasn't really "created" anything. But it's been brilliant at synthesis and modification'.

Spotlight Innovation leaders and approaches: Proctor and Gamble

As we have seen, innovation is about more than mindset; it is about the processes, structures, and cultures orientated around innovation activities and practices. Proctor and Gamble (P&G), headquartered in the USA, has twenty-seven R&D facilities worldwide, has 300-plus brands worldwide, and is at the forefront of developing an open innovation model through its P&G Connect and Develop programme. This programme is focused on:

> collaborating with you—with our IP, yours or both—on packaging, design, distribution, business models, marketing models, consumer research methods, trademark licensing, technology research (our R&D efforts are focused on 150 areas of science) and more. We also are interested in commercial innovation opportunities—new ways to increase the sales of our existing brands/products.
>
> (https://secure3.verticali.net/pg-connection-portal/ctx/noauth/0_0_1_4_83_4_5.do)

This has resulted in technology development in and out of P&G, new product developments, trademark know-how, packaging and design, joint ventures, and university collaborations, as outlined in Table 12.1.

P&G also has an activity called FutureWorks. This is designed to support entrepreneurial businesses that are related to the P&G brands and activities.

Table 12.1 P&G Connect and Develop open innovation initiative: some examples

Web submissions	Synothpoix—joint technology development agreement
Bring in technology	Olay Regenerist—new peptide and ongoing collaboration in other P&G projects with a French company Oral B Pulsonic Toothbrush—accelerated product development with a Japanese company
Taking technology out	ConAgra Food Inc—licencing and capabilities agreement Nodax—technology acquisition
Bring products in	Febreze Candles—air care technology and partnership expertise Pringles Stix—new product to US market
Taking products out	Bounce Lint and Freshness Roller—oneCare Toothbrushes—licensing tope kids characters
Know-how	Reliability Technology—manufacturing and capital productivity Tremor—word-of-mouth programme for teenagers
Packaging and design	Olay Definity—new channel packaging Olay Regenerist Eye Derma-Pods—product extentsion Deodorant Packaging—unique packaging solutions
Joint venture	Inverness Medical Innovation, Inc.—health-care management
University collaboration	University of Cincinnati Live Well Collaborative—products for customers over 50.

Source: Proctor and Gamble (2010) https://secure3.verticali.net/pg-connection-portal/ctx/noauth/0_0_1_4_83_4_10.do Accessed 3rd December 2010

What we are seeking ...

• FutureWorks is seeking products and service business opportunities and especially new business models that capitalize on emerging consumer needs in creative ways.

• Disruptive technologies or business models in our strategic areas of interest including Health & Well-Being (products, diagnostics, and services), Franchising, and Information-Based Services that improve the lives of the world's consumers. We are particularly interested in service models that can leverage the power of a P&G Brand or a strong external Brand. Current businesses we are scaling or partnered with include Mr. Clean Car Wash®, Tide Dry Cleaners®, Navigenics®, and MDVIP™.

• Platform technologies that would bring disruptive cost, capability, and/or speed advantage to our current CPG business model and/or retail partners, including but not limited to supply chain, media/marketing, and packaging/prototyping innovations. An excellent example of this type of innovation is our partnership with Shopkick®.

(http://futureworks.pg.com/)

Implications for strategy practice

We have referred to 'innovate or die' as the corporate mantra for CEOs and corporate entrepreneurs alike. In practice, for strategists and organizations, being innovative is difficult, complex, and challenging. Irrespective of organizational or industry context, in order to maintain threshold levels of competitiveness and to grow shareholder value over the long term, organizations have to develop an innovative capacity. Innovation and corporate entrepreneurship provide the organizational glue for business and innovation strategy, uniqueness, value propositions, and customers. Ultimately, innovation and corporate entrepreneurship are about competitiveness and survival.

Being a leader or follower in terms of innovation is dependent on resources and shareholder ownership, but also on whether strategists really believe in the innovation imperative. For innovation to pay off in terms of hard and soft metrics, there needs to be top management commitment to innovation; this has to be seen in the organization in terms of processes and resources. Strategists have to match rhetoric with group support. Allowing the organization too much freedom around innovation and corporate entrepreneurship can border on organizational anarchy. Therefore organizational design and structure that balances individual innovation freedom with appropriate control systems designed to exploit corporate creativity is important for ultimate marketplace application (see Chapter 9). The balance between centralized and decentralized levels of innovation and corporate entrepreneurship also matters, in terms of organizational performance and how the organization views itself and positions itself. In this respect, the strategist can have a central role in shaping the positioning for innovation and corporate entrepreneurship, and the organizational structures and processes that support its collective position and ambitions.

The type of innovation that organizations pursue is a function of marketplace realities and whether the organizational capabilities lie with innovation. The reality is that product innovation is the most difficult and risky form of innovation. Product, process, and service innovation, if managed well, can improve both short-term and long-term performance. Horizontal innovation, if managed well, can provide the organization with the capability to respond to competitive threats. In recent years, significant organizational and industry resources have been focused on altering business models and improving value and strategic innovations. Some of these changes have been brought about by market conditions (such as iPods and other MP3 players in the music industry); others have been driven by industry participants. Intertwined in these new emerging business models are new managerial practices and paradigms that are beginning to shape managerial thinking, such as 'crowdsourcing', which will pervade many industries in the coming years. Organizations are seeking new ways of engaging with key stakeholders internally and externally in order to sustain innovation and corporate entrepreneurship. In the coming years, management innovation will move to centre stage both in practice and among academic researchers.

Pursuing innovation and corporate entrepreneurship also requires the right mix of human capital. Human capital is the critical raw material that organizations need to drive corporate creativity. In their training and development of employees, many organizations dissipate individual creativity; this is at odds with the empirical evidence that employees are a key source of internal innovation and creativity. Harnessing this innovative capacity in a controlled way within an organization is an essential ingredient of innovation and corporate entrepreneurship.

Finally, simply being innovative is not enough; organizations also have to develop a real capability of communicating their innovative capacity to the marketplace. This ultimately differentiates one organizational offering over another. In addition, organizations need clarity about their business strategies in order to execute an innovation strategy effectively and pursue corporate entrepreneurship. The strategist has to enable a clear strategic focus, simplicity of concept, consistency of effort, and an understanding of where the market opportunities will really lie.

Introduction to readings

Reading 5.2, 'The discipline of innovation' by Peter Drucker (1985), is a classic from the innovation literature and one that also addresses the issues of entrepreneurship. Drucker argues that innovation comes from seven sources, four of which emanate from unexpected occurrences (incongruities, process needs, and industry and market changes), and three of which are present outside the organization in its social and intellectual environment (demographic changes, changes in perception, and new knowledge). His approach to using these seven sources of innovation is systematic. One of his key messages in this article is that innovation is a combination of activities and capabilities that require absolute and resolute organizational focus, which harnesses the right and left side of the collective organizational brain. Without this resolute focus, innovation and entrepreneurial efforts will fall short in terms of outcomes. Many organizations, CEOs, strategists, and managers fail to heed this advice. How many really believe Drucker when he argues that 'innovation is work rather than genius. It requires knowledge. It often requires ingenuity'?

Reading 5.3, 'Building bridges: the social structure of interdependent innovation' by Adam Kleinbaum and Michael Tushman (2007), focuses on the failure of multidivisional firms to combine key resources from across divisions within the same organization. The authors argue that inter-divisional innovations are primarily driven by social networks. The social network approach to understanding innovation within large corporations provides a rich research platform in understanding the role that corporate-level executives play in encouraging innovation throughout the organization. This reading raises some interesting questions in terms of the appropriate organizational structures necessary to facilitate the development of social structures—informal and formal—to pursue real innovation. Are social networks important in creating the optimal internal conditions for innovation? Given the complexities of divisions and competing divisional agendas, is it really possible to create coherent social networks against this backdrop?

Finally, Reading 5.4, 'A dynamic view of strategy' by Constantinos Markides (1999), argues that companies should simultaneously exploit their own market position and new opportunities, as well as the innovations of others. He argues that uniqueness is transitory and that companies should be ready for technology innovation—but how many companies really have an early monitoring system to identify turning points before a crisis, or to actively prevent cultural and structural inertia, or even to allow the organization to experiment with new ideas?

Mini case study Innovation in the blood: the story of Siemens

Damien Organ, National University of Ireland Galway

Innovation as a way of life

Siemens is a company used to doing things first. From historic breakthroughs, such as the first electric railway, to modern-day milestones, such as the world's first serial hybrid electric aircraft, Siemens has a proud tradition of working at the boundaries of human capability. Since its foundation in 1847, the company has been at the heart of landmark shifts across several technological paradigms, firmly establishing itself as one of the world's most innovative organizations. Its electronics and electrical engineering expertise now powers operations across ten hugely competitive and rapidly advancing industry sectors, including burgeoning health care and green energy portfolios. Yet Siemens is also a paradox. Its organizational structure is a complex maze of divisions and business units, R&D hubs, subsidiaries, and product groups, all spread across 190 countries and a staggering 1,640 locations (http://www.siemens.com). As illustrated by Cui *et al.* (2011: 8), Siemens 'complements its in-house R&D efforts by collaborating with hundreds of external innovation partners … it thus offers all the ingredients of a complex innovation outsourcing environment'. Controlling and coordinating such a vast network of relationships and activities does not readily lend itself to a culture of flexibility, entrepreneurship, and game-changing ideas.

How, then, has Siemens managed to keep itself to the forefront of so many emerging fields—and, indeed, as the foremost pioneer in many of them? The answer lies not so much in serendipity or in technological ingenuity, but rather in strategy and, in particular, a strategic recognition of the intertwined nature of growth, productivity, and synergy-driven innovation in hi-tech markets. At the frontiers of human knowledge, being the first to venture into the unknown is fraught with danger, and mis-steps carry very serious consequences regardless of the organizational muscle behind you. In this respect, Siemens shares the same risk of sudden catastrophe as the university spinout or the father-and-son engineering firm. In the face of overwhelming complexity, strategic vision becomes the primary instrument of survival.

A child of revolution

> Only when it is closely associated with solutions to the problems of the day does innovative research become useful and assured of success.
>
> Werner von Siemens, 1886 (http://www.siemens.com)

The Siemens organization came into being as an innovator. Its founder, Werner von Siemens, was born the son of a tenant farmer in Hanover, with fourteen brothers and sisters. Despite his fierce intelligence, his family's precarious economic conditions denied Werner the opportunity to pursue his ambitions thorough expensive formal education. In a time when the Industrial Revolution was changing the world, it was the Prussian military that offered young men like Werner an opportunity to study the new sciences. Werner's three years at artillery and engineering school provided him with the necessary foundation to play an active part in an age of relentless technological advance, and would ultimately lead him to found a company that would rapidly become a powerhouse of German engineering.

The breakthrough upon which the firm was founded came in 1847, when Werner turned his attention to an exciting new invention known as the electric telegraph. The electric telegraph had caught the imagination of the public in 1845 when it was used in the capture of British murderer John Tawell, who became widely known as 'the man who was hanged by the electric telegraph'. Just two years later, Werner von Siemens had invented the pointer telegraph, revolutionizing telegraphy and simplifying its utilization by having a needle point to letters (as opposed to Morse code), so that lower-trained technicians could operate it.

This simple, but ingenuous, innovation caught the attention of the authorities and, in 1848, the company founded by Werner and his friend Johann Halske less than a year earlier was given the contract to build Europe's first long-distance telegraph line. This triumph was swiftly followed by a crisis in the relationship between the firm and the Prussian state; in 1851, the company consequently took the bold move of expanding beyond the boundaries of Germanic central Europe, and undertook a contract to build the Russian state telegraph network. Deciding to explore foreign markets further, a British office was established in 1858, and by 1870 the company had established a telegraph line between London and Calcutta. Four years later, it had connected Ireland and the USA. By the time of Werner's retirement in 1890, the company employed more than 6,000 people and, through its major construction projects, had already left an indelible mark on the pages of history.

The scientific entrepreneurs

However, as significant as these landmarks were, it is illustrative to look at the company's R&D output throughout this same period of groundbreaking, large-scale engineering feats. In 1866, the invention of the first battery-free telegraph, in the same year as the discovery of the dynamo-electric principle, helped to pave the way for widespread electrification. In 1878, came the differential arc streetlamp, followed three years later by the world's first electric street-lighting system—powered by a Siemens alternator—and in the same year the first electric streetcar. Innovations were not limited to technology: by 1891, profit-sharing schemes, pension funds, and the 8.5-hour workday had also been introduced for employees (http://www.siemens.com).

This enduring focus on pioneering scientific application and rewarding personnel ensured that many renowned scientists, such as Werner von Bolton, Walter Schottky, Gustav Hertz, Ernst Ruska, and Heinrich Welker, passed through its gates. These men, and others, helped to drive many more technological breakthroughs throughout the twentieth century, including significant advances in semiconductor technology and the world's first cardiac pacemaker in 1958. These latter innovations were a further demonstration of the increasingly diverse application of Siemens' electronic and electrical engineering core competencies. Indeed, this increasing diversity of operations, coupled with the steadily increasing complexity of each new area of application, imposed upon Siemens a need to meet the rapidly changing technological environment of the later twentieth century with a strategy for continuous innovation and for innovation management.

Chasing storms

Understanding this strategy first necessitates an understanding of Siemens' modern-day business-level configuration. From its initial reorganization in 1969 into six operating groups, the company today is organized along three major divisions: industry; health care; and energy. These divisions are in turn supported by ten key product groups: automation; building technologies; communication networks; consumer products; drive technology; medical technology; financial solutions; IT solutions and services; power and energy; and lighting. Naturally, such a range of markets brings a large array of external factors to bear on the company's business interests. In identifying future trends and formulating its 'Pictures of the Future', Siemens actively considers the individual, societal, political, economic, environmental, technological, customer, and competitive shifts in its environment that will dictate its circumstances five, ten, and twenty years from now (Weyrich, 2003).

This analysis enables Siemens to identify the potential scientific and technological trajectories of the respective product groups. Such trends include the replacement of hardware with software, ever-increasing complexity, decentralization of intelligence, technological integration, miniaturization, virtualization, individualization, modularization, standardization, and the increasing importance of sustainability. These developments point the company towards the technological competences that will prove critical in the years ahead, and towards which R&D must gravitate. They include nanomaterials, intelligent sensors, and the semantic web. Such an intimidating list serves to emphasize the extent to which a strategically guided and integrated approach to managing innovation is so essential for Siemens. As argued by head of corporate technology, Claus Weyrich, the future rarely looks how we expect it to look, but the process of creating visions for the future develops the agility, both cognitive and operational, which enables an organization to respond to the demands of the marketplace. The value comes from the exercise itself, as much as it does from the projections that emerge.

Synergy is not a free lunch

If a company is to thrive as a technological leader, then the creation of multiple impact competences and the exploitation of internal synergies are essential. For a company with over 30,000 R&D personal, however, this is easier said than done. Complicating the matter is the company's insistence on having R&D activity close to its markets (and its customers), ensuring a wide geographical spread of R&D centres, as well as introducing multicultural and multilingual diversity into the equation.

Siemens has confronted this challenge in a number of ways. One highly pragmatic solution has been to establish 'idea competitions'. These competitions bring together networks of people from a variety of research and functional backgrounds, matching R&D, manufacturing, and marketing personnel to collective interests and, in so doing, bridging the divide between ideas and the market. The ideas are judged by panels of experts, who send a selection of ideas forward for presentation to R&D management, with the winning ideas in turn awarded seed capital for feasibility analysis and implementation. Many more of the ideas are sent to business group management for further development (Schepers *et al.*, 1999). As with the process of establishing 'Pictures of the Future', the value of idea competitions is not limited to the ideas emerging from the contest itself. Many of the networks established will persist long after the competition has ended, establishing an intricate system of communication that spans functions, research interests, cultures, and languages, creating a culture for joint competence solutions that the complex environment demands.

Pipeline management

As crucial as effective people management is, however, it is not enough. Siemens multibillion-euro annual investment in R&D creates waves of ideas (the total number of patents granted stood at 58,000 by December 2010), which demand rationalization, selection, and application. Innovation ends not with the emergence of an idea, but only when that idea has been successfully brought to market and applied to a problem. This means hard choices and confronting a number of troubling dilemmas. Chief among these is the timing of product introduction. One must delicately balance the urge to be first to market with the need to anticipate customer needs correctly. Another dilemma is the cannibalization of established and successful businesses with the introduction of new technology, and the harsh market reality that old technologies will stir into a determined fight back. The philosophy at Siemens has been that new technology should attack the market via new applications, avoiding head-on confrontation with the incumbent platforms. Fundamentally, this requires integration of innovation and business strategy, with the alignment of the two ultimately determining the consistency and stability of both.

> The early bird catches the worm, and the second mouse gets the cheese, but when you control the holes and the traps you get the worms and the cheese.

Dr Claus Weyrich, Siemens head of corporate technology, 1996–2006

Facing the future

> Predicting the future works best when you create and shape it yourself.
>
> Dr Heinrich von Pierer, CEO Siemens AG, 1992–2005

Over its 164-year history, Siemens has amassed scientific, operational, and financial capacity that could easily lead one to assume that it can survive any shift in the tides of industry. The company's obsession with its own processes of renewal tells a different story. Since Werner von Siemens built his first pointer telegraph, many industrial giants have risen only to be swept away by radical technological change that rendered their strengths obsolete. Yet Siemens has persisted, despite being once regarded as the company that could make anything except a profit (*The Economist*, 2010). Five years ago, had you read a newspaper article about Siemens, you would have read about a company dogged by scandal; today, you read about wind farms, acquisitions in emerging markets, promoting the merits of environmental sustainability, and engagement with the scientific community on a wide range of key issues (Peacock, 2011; Schiller, 2011). Where once the organization paved the way in telecommunications, today it sets new standards in underwater turbines, solar technology, and energy-efficient water treatment (Sibun, 2010).

Indeed, the challenges posed by global concerns such as demographic shifts, energy resources, healthcare costs, and pollution seem only to embolden its research leaders. Others point to more sensitive problems, including not only the mismanagement uncovered by bribery scandals, but also the overwhelmingly German and male concentration of directorships in such a global firm (Schäfer, 2010). Certainly, this calls into question the capacity of the organization to truly represent and utilize its stunningly diverse corporate citizenship. Where others have faded, however, Siemens has stood the test of time. This old-fashioned company's love of 'engineering for engineering's sake' may grate with those who favour the sleek and fashionable outfits that capture the imagination of the business press today. Perhaps Siemens has shown that your own imagination outweighs your ability to capture the imagination of others. Klaus Weyrich is fond of quoting Thomas Edison's inspiration–perspiration ratio. As long as Siemens continues to value that philosophy, Werner's legacy may ride out a few more waves yet.

Questions

1. 'Innovation enables organizations to refine their uniqueness and relevance to their customers, thereby increasing revenues and profits.' Discuss this statement with respect to Siemens. How has it attempted to establish its uniqueness?

2. What form of innovation was Werner von Siemens' pointer telegraph? Given the markets in which Siemens operates, what opportunities exist for exploiting other forms of innovation?

3. Is Siemens better suited to a being an innovation leader or follower?

4. What are Siemens' major sources of innovation? Are there potential sources of innovation that the company might access that are not mentioned in the case above?

5. Evaluate Siemens' efforts to integrate innovation and performance.

6. 'Entrepreneurial orientation includes five key dimensions: autonomy; innovativeness; proactiveness; competitive aggressiveness; and risk taking.' Assume the role of Siemens CEO, Peter Löscher, and outline your strategic vision for the company along these five crucial dimensions.

Sources: Cui *et al.* (2011); *The Economist* (2010); Peacock (2011); Schäfer (2010); Schepers *et al.* (1999); Schiller (2011); Sibun (2010); Siemans (2005; 2007; 2010; 2011); Weyrich (2004); http://www.siemens.com

Summary

In this chapter, our focus was on how and why an organization innovates. We began by exploring the shifts in the innovation paradigm (closed versus open innovation), the different perspectives on innovation, value and strategic innovation, being an innovation leader or follower, sources of innovation, some innovation obstacles, and the challenges of innovation implementation. We then considered links between innovation and performance and how to align innovation and strategy, before concluding the chapter with our focus on corporate entrepreneurship. Pursuing the innovation imperative requires organizations to have an innovation capability that extends to multiple forms of innovations—product, process, service, and horizontal—and also includes strategic and value innovations. Over the coming decade, we will see organizations placing more emphasis on management innovation. Organizations have to search for innovation internally and externally. Innovation requires a combination of consistency of effort and focus set against a background of clearly defined strategy. Top management commitment is an absolute necessity.

Corporate entrepreneurship helps organizations to accelerate their growth potential through corporate venturing and R&D. At its heart are corporate creativity, idea generation, and the ability of organizations to integrate both old and new activities. Being innovative and pursuing corporate entrepreneurship also means that organizations need to be able to differentiate this capability in a very distinctive manner in the marketplace through increased market penetration or the creation of new markets. Finally, innovation and corporate entrepreneurship, like strategy, are a social process based on building and maintaining relationships within and outside organizational boundaries; they are about ensuring that the organization maintains or exceeds threshold levels of competitiveness in chosen competitive arenas. This is a significant, complex, and underestimated challenge for organizations and strategists, but one that is necessary to secure the long-term survival of the organization and to sustain advantage.

Discussion questions

1. Discuss the strategy implications of being an innovation follower. What are the impacts on firm-level competitiveness and uniqueness?

2. In groups, discuss why innovation is so important for contemporary organizations.

3. Critique Drucker's (1985—Reading 5.2) perspective on innovation. How would you use his arguments to guide an organization in being innovative?

4. Source a reading from a journal that contributes to the debate in this chapter. Which perspective, if any, does it

support? What is its contribution? Does it advance the debate in any way?

5. Consider the various sources of innovation that can shape an organization's innovative capability. Do the readings for this chapter adequately accommodate these?

6. Choose an industry sector with which you are familiar and identify what types of innovation the sector has pursued. Discuss how these have shaped and influenced the strategy direction of companies within the industry sector.

7. What is the difference between entrepreneurship and corporate entrepreneurship?

8. 'Time pressure stifles creativity.' Discuss how an organization can overcome this obstacle to corporate creativity.

9. On the basis of the three readings for this chapter, prepare a short presentation on innovation and corporate entrepreneurship to a fictional top-level team of a global information and communication technology (ICT) company, highlighting the practical implications for its managers.

Further reading

For an insight into R&D and innovation in the semiconductor sector, see A. Abbey and J. W. Dickson (1983) 'R&D work climate and innovation in semiconductors', *Academy of Management Journal*, 26(2): 362–368.

For interesting insights into strategy and innovation linkages, see R. Adner (2006) 'Match your innovation strategy to your innovation ecosystem', *Harvard Business Review*, 84(4): 98–107.

For a contextually rich setting about creativity, see K. D. Elsbach and R. M. Kramer (2003) 'Assessing creativity in Hollywood pitch meetings: evidence for a dual-process model of creativity judgments', *Academy of Management Journal*, 46(3): 283–301.

For understanding openness for innovation purposes, see K. Laursen and A. Salter (2006) 'Open for innovation: the role of openness in explaining innovation performance among UK manufacturing firms', *Strategic Management Journal*, 27(2): 131–150.

To understand the role of radical innovation in mature organizations, see R. Leifer, G. C. O'Connor, and M. Rice (2001) 'Implementing radical innovation in mature firms: the role of hubs', *Academy of Management Executive*, 15(3): 102–113.

Given the knowledge-based drive in increasing numbers of economies and organizations, see B. Simpson and M. Powell (1999) 'Designing research organizations for science innovation', *Long Range Planning*, 32(4): 441–451.

visit the Online Resource Centre that accompanies this book to access more learning resources on this chapter topic at www.oxfordtextbooks.co.uk/orc/cunningham/

References

Amabile, T., Barsade, S., Muleller, J.. and Staw. B. M. 2005. Affect and creativity at work. *Administrative Science Quarterly*, 50: 367–403.

Anderson, J. V. 1992. Weirder than fiction: the reality and myths of creativity. *Academy of Management Executive*, 6(4): 40–47.

Anthony, S. D., Eyring, M., and Gibson, L. 2006. Mapping your innovation strategy. *Harvard Business Review*, 84(5): 104–113.

Arthur, B. 1996. Increasing returns and the new world of business. *Harvard Business Review*, 74(4): 100–110.

Ashforth, B. K. and Saks, A. M. 1996. Socialization tactics: longitudinal effects on newcomer adjustment. *Academy of Management Journal*, 39(1): 149–178.

Baba, Y. 1989. The dynamics of continuous innovation in scale-intensive industries. *Strategic Management Journal*, 10(1): 89–100.

Baden-Fuller, C. 1995. Strategic innovation, corporate entrepreneurship and matching outside-in to inside-out approaches to strategy research. *British Journal of Management*, 6: 3–16.

Balkin, D. B., Markman, G. D., and Gomez-Mejia, L. R. 2000. Is CEO pay in high-technology firms related to innovation? *Academy of Management Journal*, 43(6): 1118–1129.

Barkema, H. G. and Shvyrkov, O. 2007. Does top management team diversity promote or hamper foreign expansion? *Strategic Management Journal*, 28(7): 663–680.

Barringer, B. and Bluedorn, A. 1999. The relationship between corporate entrepreneurship and strategic management. *Strategic Management Journal*, 20: 421–444.

Basadur, M. 1992. Managing creativity: a Japanese model. *Academy of Management Executive*, 6(2): 29–42.

Batten, F. 2002. Out of the blue and into the black. *Harvard Business Review*, 80(4): 112–119.

Bell, G. G. 2005. Clusters, networks, and firm innovativeness. *Strategic Management Journal*, 26(3): 287–295.

Berggren, E. and Nacher, T. 2001. Introducing new products can be hazardous to your company: use the right new-solutions delivery tools. *Academy of Management Executive*, 15(3): 92–101.

Bessant, J. and Tidd, J. 2007. *Innovation and Entrepreneurship*. Chichester: John Wiley and Sons.

Buggie, F. D. 1982. Strategies for new product development. *Long Range Planning*, 15(2): 22–31.

Burgelman, R. A. 1983. A process model of internal corporate venturing in the diversified major firm. *Administrative Science Quarterly*, 28(2): 223–244.

Butler, J. E. 1988. Theories of technological innovation as useful tools for corporate strategy. *Strategic Management Journal*, 9(1): 15–29.

Butler, R. J., Price, D. H. R., Coates, P. D., and Pike, B. H. 1998. Organizing for innovation: loose or tight control? *Long Range Planning*, 31(5): 775–782.

Calthrop, P. 2007. Higher net price—or bust. *Harvard Business Review*, 85(5): 30–37.

Carini, G. and Townsend, B. 2007. $152,000 for your thoughts. *Harvard Business Review*, 85(4): 23–31.

Caruso, D. 2006. Staying connected. *Harvard Business Review*, 84: 38–48.

Cascio, W. F. 2005. Strategies for responsible restructuring. *Academy of Management Executive*, 19(4): 39–50.

Chesbrough, H. W. 2003. *Open Innovation: The New Imperative for Creating and Profiting from Technology*. Boston, MA: Harvard Business School Press.

Chesbrough, H. W. and Teece, D. J. 2002. Organizing for innovation: when is virtual virtuous? *Harvard Business Review*, 80(8): 127–135.

Cho, H.-J. and Pucik, V. 2005. Relationship between innovativeness, quality, growth, profitability, and market value. *Strategic Management Journal*, 26(6): 555–575.

Christensen, C. M. 1997. *The Innovator's Dilemma*. Boston, MA: Harvard Business School Press.

Christensen, C. M. and Bower, J. L. 1996. Customer power, strategic investment, and the failure of leading firms. *Strategic Management Journal*, 17(3): 197–218.

Christensen, C. M., Baumann, H., Ruggles, R., and Sadtler, T. M. 2006. Disruptive innovation for social change. *Harvard Business Review*, 84(12): 94–101.

Clapham, M. M. 2000. Employee creativity: the role of leadership. *Academy of Management Executive*, 14(3): 138–139.

Cohen, W. M. and Levinthal, D. 1990. Absorptive capacity: a new perspective on learning and innovation. *Administrative Science Quarterly*, 35(1): 129–152.

Cohen, W. M., Nelson, R. R., and Walsh, J. P. 2002. Links and impacts: the influence public research on industrial R&D. *Management Science*, 48: 1–23.

Cui, Z., Loch, C., Grossmann, B., and He, R. 2011. How the selection and management of providers contribute to successful innovation outsourcing. *Production and Operations Management*, forthcoming.

Daniels, J. D. 1973. A profile of local subsidiary managers. *Academy of Management Journal*, 16(4): 695–700.

Davis, S. and Botkin, J. 1994. The coming of knowledge-based business. *Harvard Business Review*, 72(5): 165–170.

Day, G. 2007. Is it real? Can we win? Is it worth doing? Managing risk and reward in an innovation portfolio. *Harvard Business Review*, 85(12): 110–120.

De Lisi, P. S. 2006. The why, what, and how of management innovation. *Harvard Business Review*, 84: 139–140.

Demarest, M. 1997. Understanding knowledge management. *Long Range Planning*, 30(3): 374–384.

De Sanctis, G., Glass, J. T., and Ensing, I. M. 2002. Organizational designs for R&D. *Academy of Management Executive*, 16(3): 55–66.

Dess, G., Lumpkin, G. T., and Eisner, A. B. 2005. *Strategic Management: Creating Competitive Advantage*. New York: McGraw-Hill.

Dickson, J. W. and Slevin, D. P. 1975. The use of semantic differential scales in studying the innovation boundary. *Academy of Management Journal*, 18(2): 381–388.

Drew, S. A. W. 1997. From knowledge to action: the impact of benchmarking on organizational performance. *Long Range Planning*, 30(3): 427–441.

Drucker, P. F. 1992. The new society of organizations. *Harvard Business Review*, 70(5): 95–105.

Drucker, P. F. 1998. The discipline of innovation. *Harvard Business Review*, 76(6): 149–157.

Drucker, P. F. 2002. The discipline of innovation. *Harvard Business Review*, 80(8): 95–103.

Drucker, P. F. 2003. *On the Profession of Management*. Boston, MA: Harvard Business School Press.

The Economist. 2010. A giant awakens. 9 September. Available online at http://www.economist.com/node/16990709

Economy, E. and Lieberthal, K. 2007. Scorched earth. *Harvard Business Review*, 85(6): 88–96.

Ettlie, J. E. 1990. What makes a manufacturing firm innovative? *Academy of Management Executive*, 4(4): 7–20.

Evink, J. R. 1998. Corporate creativity: how innovation and improvement actually happen. *Academy of Management Executive*, 12(1): 92–93.

Franke, R. H., Hofstede, G., and Bond, M. H. 1991. Cultural roots of economic performance: a research note. *Strategic Management Journal*, 12(4): 165–173.

Frost, T. S. 2001. The geographic sources of foreign subsidiaries' innovations. *Strategic Management Journal*, 22(2): 101–123.

Garg, V. K., Walters, B. A., and Priem, R. L. 2003. Chief executive scanning emphases, environmental dynamism, and manufacturing firm performance. *Strategic Management Journal*, 24(8): 725–744.

Garvin, D. A. and Levesque, L. C. 2006. Meeting the challenge of corporate entrepreneurship. *Harvard Business Review*, 84(10): 102–112.

Gnamm, J. and Neuhaus, K. 2005. Leading from the factory floor. *Harvard Business Review*, 83(11): 22–27.

Gottfredson, M. and Aspinall, K. 2005. Innovation vs complexity. *Harvard Business Review*, 83(11): 62–71.

Grant, R. M. 2003. Strategic planning in a turbulent environment: evidence from the oil majors. *Strategic Management Journal*, 24(6): 491–517.

Greve, H. R. 2003. A behavioral theory of R&D expenditures and innovations: evidence from shipbuilding. *Academy of Management Journal*, 46(6): 685–702.

Guth, W. D. and Ginsberg, A. 1990. Corporate entrepreneurship. *Strategic Management Journal*, 11: 5–15.

Hagedoorn, J. and Roijakkers, N. 2002. Small entrepreneurial firms and large companies in inter-firms R&D networks: the international biotechnology industry. In M. Hitt, R. D. Ireland, M. Camp, and D. Sexton (eds) *Strategy Entrepreneurship: Creating a New Mindset*. Oxford: Blackwell Publishing.

Hamel, G. 2006. The why, what, and how of management innovation. *Harvard Business Review*, 84(2): 72–84.

Hansen, M. T. and Birkinshaw, J. 2007. The innovation value chain. *Harvard Business Review*, 85(6): 121–130.

Harrison, J. S. and Freeman, R. E. 2004. Special topic: democracy in and around organizations. *Academy of Management Executive*, 18(3): 49–53.

Harryson, S. and Lorange, P. 2005. Bringing the college inside. *Harvard Business Review*, 83(12): 30–32.

Hayes, R. H., Abernathy, W. J., and Hayes, R. H. 2007. Managing our way to economic decline. *Harvard Business Review*, 85(7/8): 138–149.

Heracleous, L. 1998. Better than the rest: making Europe the leader in the next wave of innovation and performance. *Long Range Planning*, 31(1): 154–158.

Herzlinger, R. E. 2006. Why innovation in health care is so hard. *Harvard Business Review*, 84(5): 58–66.

Hicks, H. G. and Goronzy, F. 1966. Notes on the nature of standards. *Academy of Management Journal*, 9(4): 281–293.

Hitt, M. A. and Ireland, R. D. 1987. Peters and Waterman revisited: the unended quest for excellence. *Academy of Management Executive*, 1(2): 91–98.

Hitt, M. A., Hoskisson, R. E., and Kim, H. 1997. International diversification: effects on innovation and firm performance in product-diversified firms. *Academy of Management Journal*, 40(4): 767–798.

Howe, N. and Strauss, W. 2007. The next 20 years: how customer and workforce attitudes will evolve. *Harvard Business Review*, 85(7/8): 41–52.

Howell, J. M. 2005. The right stuff: identifying and developing effective champions of innovation. *Academy of Management Executive*, 19(2): 108–119.

IBM Global Services. 2006. Expanding the innovation horizon: Global CEO Study 2006. Available online at http://www-935.ibm.com/services/au/bcs/html/bcs_ceostudy2006.html

Industrial Research Institute. 2011. Industrial Research Institute's R&D trends forecast for 2011, research—technology management. Available online at http://www.iriweb.org/Main/Library/Other_Publications/Trends_Report/Public_Site/RTM/Volume_54_Year_2011/Jan-Feb2011/Industrial_Research_Institute_s_R_D_Trends_Forecast_for_2011.aspx?hkey = 2e5d6936-9902-4518-9ba9-33aaa1f734a6

Ireland, R. D., Hitt, M. A., Camp, S. M., and Sexton, D. L. 2001. Integrating entrepreneurship and strategic management actions to create firm wealth. *Academy of Management Executive*, 15(1): 49–63.

Jaruzelski, B. and Dehoff, K. 2010. The global innovation 1000: how the top innovators keep winning, *Strategy and Business*, 61(Winter): 1–14.

Jassawalla, A. R. and Sashittal, H. C. 2002. Cultures that support product-innovation processes. *Academy of Management Executive*, 16(3): 42–54.

Kanter, R. M. 2006. Innovation: the classic traps. *Harvard Business Review*, 84(11): 72–83.

Karim, S. and Mitchell, W. 2004. Innovating through acquisition and internal development: a quarter-century of boundary evolution at Johnson and Johnson. *Long Range Planning*, 37(6): 525–547.

Katila, R. and Ahuja, G. 2002. Something old, something new: a longitudinal study of search behavior and new product introductions. *Academy of Management Journal*, 45(6): 1183–1194.

Kaufman, A., Wood, C. H., and Theyel, G. 2000. Collaboration and technology linkages: a strategic supplier typology. *Strategic Management Journal*, 21(6): 649.

Kawanabe, T. 2011. Honda's R&D strategy. Available online at http://www.hondanews.eu/en/news/index.pmode/modul,detail,0,1737-DEFAULT,21,text,1/index.pmode

Kazanjian, R., Drazin, R., and Glynn, M. A. 2002. *Implementing Strategies for Corporate Entrepreneurship: A Knowledge-Based Perspective*. Oxford: Blackwell Publishing.

Kim, C. and Mauborgne, R. 1999. Strategy, value innovation and the knowledge economy. *Sloan Management Review*, Spring: 41–54.

Kim, C. and Mauborgne, R. 2005. Blue ocean strategy: from theory to practice. *California Management Review*, 47(3): 105–121.

Klapmeier, A. 2007. Passion. *Harvard Business Review*, 85(1): 22–23.

Klepper, S. and Simons, K. L. 2000. Dominance by birthright: entry of prior radio producers and competitive ramifications in the U.S. Television Receiver Industry. *Strategic Management Journal*, 21(10/11): 997–1016.

Kodama, M. 2002. Transforming an old economy company through strategic communities. *Long Range Planning*, 35(4): 349–365.

Kurato, D., Ireland, D., and Honnsby, J. 2001. Improving firm performance through entrepreneurial actions: Acordia's corporate entrepreneurship strategy. *Academy of Management Executive*, 12(4): 62–71.

Landry, J. T. 2005. The ten faces of innovation: IDEO's strategies for beating the devil's advocate and driving creativity throughout your organization. *Harvard Business Review*, 83(11): 34–44.

Lang, M. 2006. Mapping your innovation strategy., *Harvard Business Review*, 84: 147–148.

Laurie, D. L., Doz, Y. L., and Sheer, C. P. 2006. Creating new growth platforms. *Harvard Business Review*, 84(5): 80–90.

Leonard, D. and Swap, W. 1999. *When Sparks Fly: Igniting Creativity in Groups*. Boston, MA: Harvard Business School Press.

Leonard-Barton, D. 1995. Managing creative abrasion in the workplace. *Harvard Business Review*, 73(4): 2–3.

Levitt, T. 2002. Creativity is not enough. *Harvard Business Review*, 80(8): 137–145.

Lewis, M. W., Welsh, M. A., Dehler, G. E., and Green, S. G. 2002. Product development tensions: exploring contrasting styles of project management. *Academy of Management Journal*, 45(3): 546–564.

Li, H. and Atuahene-Gima, K. 2001. Product innovation strategy and the performance of new technology ventures in China. *Academy of Management Journal*, 44(6): 1123–1134.

Li, H. and Atuahene-Gima, K. 2002. The adoption of agency business activity, product innovation, and performance in Chinese technology ventures. *Strategic Management Journal*, 23(6): 469–490.

Lovelace, K., Shapiro, D. L., and Weingart, L. R. 2001. Maximizing cross-functional new product teams' innovativeness and constraint adherence: a conflict communications perspective. *Academy of Management Journal*, 44(4): 779–793.

Mainiero, L. A. 1994. Corporate renewal: evolutionary or leader driven? *Academy of Management Executive*, 8(1): 83–84.

Makri, M., Lane, P. J., and Gomez-Mejia, L. R. 2006. CEO incentives, innovation, and performance in technology-intensive firms: a reconciliation of outcome and behavior-based incentive schemes. *Strategic Management Journal*, 27(11): 1057–1080.

Marcus, A. A. 1988. Responses to externally induced innovation: their effects on organizational performance. *Strategic Management Journal*, 9(4): 387–402.

Markides, C. 1997. Strategic innovation. *Sloan Management Review*, Spring: 9–23.

Mauborgne, R. E. and Chan Kim, W. 1997. Fair process: managing in the knowledge economy. *Harvard Business Review*, 75(4): 65–75.

McCann, J. E. 1991. Design principles for an innovating company. *Academy of Management Executive*, 5(2): 76–93.

McEvily, S. K. and Chakravarthy, B. 2002. The persistence of knowledge-based advantage: an empirical test for product performance and technological knowledge. *Strategic Management Journal*, 23(4): 285–305.

McGrath, R. G. and Keil, T. 2007. The value captor's process. *Harvard Business Review*, 85(5): 128–136.

Merton, R. C. 2005. You have more capital than you think. *Harvard Business Review*, 83(11): 84–94.

Mezias, S. J. and Glynn, M. A. 1993. The three faces of corporate renewal: institution, revolution, and evolution. *Strategic Management Journal*, 14(2): 77–101.

Miles, R. E., Miles, G., and Snow, C. 2006. Collaborative entrepreneurship: a business model for continuous innovation. *Organization Dynamics*, 35(1): 1–11.

Miles, R. E., Snow, C. S., Mathews, J. A., Miles, G., and Coleman Jr, H. J. 1997. Organizing in the knowledge age: anticipating the cellular form. *Academy of Management Executive*, 11(4): 7–20.

Miller, A. 1988. A taxonomy of technological settings, with related strategies and performance levels. *Strategic Management Journal*, 9(3): 239–254.

Mitchell, G. and Hamilton, W. 1988, Managing R&D as a strategic option. *Research Technology Management*, 31: 15–22.

Moore, G. A. 2007. To succeed in the long term, focus on the middle term. *Harvard Business Review*, 85(7/8): 84–90.

Moran, P. 2005. Structural vs. relational embeddedness: social capital and managerial performance. *Strategic Management Journal*, 26(12): 1129–1151.

Morrison, A. J. and Roth, K. 1992. A taxonomy of business-level strategies in global industries. *Strategic Management Journal*, 13(6): 399–417.

Morse, G. 2006. Connecting maverick minds. *Harvard Business Review*, 84: 23–28.

Nambisan, S. and Sawhney, M. 2007. Meet the innovation capitalist. *Harvard Business Review*, 85(3): 24–31.

Nonaka, I. 2007. The knowledge-creating company. *Harvard Business Review*, 85(7/8): 162–171.

Peacock, L. 2011. From Siemens to Sellafield: how to get young people interested in engineering. *The Telegraph*, 10 March. Available online at http://www.telegraph.co.uk/finance/jobs/hr-news/8371958/From-Siemens-to-Sellafield-How-to-get-young-people-interested-in-engineering.html

Pfeffer, J. 1994. *Managing with Power: Politics and Influence in Organizations*. Boston, MA: Harvard Business School Press.

Quinn, J. B., Anderson, P., and Finkelstein, S. 2005. Leveraging intellect. *Academy of Management Executive*, 19(4): 78–94.

Roberts, P. W. 1999. Product innovation, product-market competition and persistent profitability in the U.S. pharmaceutical industry. *Strategic Management Journal*, 20(7): 655–670.

Robinson Jr, R. B. and Pearce II, J. A. 1988. Planned patterns of strategic behavior and their relationship to business-unit performance. *Strategic Management Journal*, 9(1): 43–60.

Rodan, S. and Galunic, C. 2004. More than network structure: how knowledge heterogeneity influences managerial performance and innovativeness. *Strategic Management Journal*, 25(6): 541–562.

Rothaermel, F. T., Hitt, M. A., and Jobe, L. A. 2006. Balancing vertical integration and strategic outsourcing: effects on product portfolio, product success, and firm performance. *Strategic Management Journal*, 27(11): 1033–1056.

Rudma, S. T. 2001. Are successful innovators high performers? Insights from Israel's largest companies. *Academy of Management Executive*, 15(1): 149–150.

Sampson, R. C. 2007. R&D alliances and firm performance: the impact of technological diversity and alliance organization on innovation. *Academy of Management Journal*, 50(2): 364–386.

Sathe, V. 1989. Fostering entrepreneurship in a large diversified firm. *Organization Dynamics*, 18(1): 20–32.

Schäfer, D. 2010. Out-of-the-box executive search. *Financial Times*, 28 June. Available online at http://www.ft.com/intl/cms/s/0/1cec2116-82fc-11df-8b15-00144feabdc0.html#axzz1UA0i7M2O

Schepers, J., Schnell, R., and Vroom, P. 1999. From idea to business: how Siemens bridges the innovation gap. *Research Technology Management*, 42: 26–31.

Schiller, S. 2011. Siemens will highlight energy-efficient R&D projects at Singapore International Water Week. *Innovations Report*, 8 June. Available online at http://www.innovations-report.com/html/reports/trade_fair_news/siemens_highlight_energy_efficient_r_d_projects_176639.html

Scinta, J. 2007. Where more R&D dollars should go. *Harvard Business Review*, 85(7/8): 26.

Selden, L. and MacMillan, I. C. 2006. Manage customer-centric innovation—systematically. *Harvard Business Review*, 84(4): 108–116.

Sharma, P. and Chrisman, J. J. 1999. Reconciling the definitional issues in the field of corporate entrepreneurship. *Entrepreneurship Theory and Practice*, 23(3): 11–27.

Shortell, S. M. and Zajac, E. J. 1988. Internal corporate joint ventures: development processes and performance outcomes. *Strategic Management Journal*, 9(6): 527–542.

Sibun, J. 2010. Peter Loscher believes green technology is key to Siemens' future. *The Telegraph*, 20 June. Available online at http://www.telegraph.co.uk/finance/newsbysector/energy/7841977/Peter-Loscher-believes-green-technology-is-key-to-Siemens-future.html

Siemans. 2005. Corporate technology: 100 years of corporate research at Siemens—Interview with Claus Weyrich. Available online at http://www.siemens.com/innovation/en/publikationen/publications_pof/pof_fall_2005/corporate_technology/interview_with_claus_weyrich.htm

Siemans. 2007. 160 years of Siemens. Available online at http://www.siemens.com/history/pool/en/history/1847-1865_beginnings_and_initial_expansion/160j_e.pdf

Siemans. 2010. Siemens at a glance. Available online at http://www.siemens.com/investor/pool/en/investor_relations/financial_publications/annual_reports/2010/siemens_ar2010_at-a-glance.pdf

Siemans. 2011. Travel back through the history of Siemens. Available online at http://www.siemens.com/history/en/history/index.htm

Siggelkow, N. and Rivkin, J. W. 2006. When exploration backfires: unintended consequences of multilevel organizational search. *Academy of Management Journal*, 49(4): 779–795.

Spencer, J. W. 2003. Firms' knowledge-sharing strategies in the global innovation system: empirical evidence from the flat panel display industry. *Strategic Management Journal*, 24(3): 217–233.

Stewart, T. A. and Raman, A. P. 2007. Lessons from Toyota's long drive. *Harvard Business Review*, 85: 74–83.

Stopford, J. and Badden-Fuller, C. 1994. Creating corporate entrepreneurship. *Strategic Management Journal*, 15(7): 521–536.

Stuart, T. E. 2000. Inter-organizational alliances and the performance of firms: a study of growth and innovation rates in a high-technology industry. *Strategic Management Journal*, 21(8): 791–811.

Subramanian, R. 1999. Do crowding and prestige explain why organizations collaborate? *Academy of Management Executive*, 13(2): 90–91.

Tabak, F. 1997. Employee creative performance: what makes it happen? *Academy of Management Executive*, 11(1): 119–120.

Taylor, A. and Greve. H. 2006. Superman or the fantastic four? Knowledge combination and experience in innovative teams. *Academy of Management Journal*, 49(4): 723–740.

Taylor, W. 1990. The business of innovation: an interview with Paul Cook. *Harvard Business Review*, 68: 97–106.

Thompson, L. and Brajkovich, L. F. 2003. Improving the creativity of organizational work groups. *Academy of Management Executive*, 17(1): 96–109.

Thomson, N. and McNamara, P. 2001. Achieving post-acquisition success: the role of corporate entrepreneurship. *Long Range Planning*, 34(6): 669–697.

Thuriaux, B. 2006. The why, what, and how of management innovation. *Harvard Business Review*, 84(6): 139–140.

Tsai, W. 2001. Knowledge transfer in intra-organizational networks: effects of network position and absorptive capacity on business unit innovation and performance. *Academy of Management Journal*, 44(5): 996–1004.

Tushman, M. 1997. Winning through innovation. *Strategy & Leadership*, 25(4): 14–20.

Ulrich, D. and Lake, D. 1991. Organization capability: creating competitive advantage. *Academy of Management Executive*, 5(1): 77–92.

Verganti, R. 2006. Innovating through design. *Harvard Business Review*, 84(12): 114–122.

von Krogh, G. 2006. Customers demand their slice of IP. *Harvard Business Review*, 84(2): 45–46.

von Krogh, G. and Haefliger, S. 2007. Nurturing respect for IP in China. *Harvard Business Review*, 85(4): 23–24.

Wadhwa, A. and Kotha, S. 2006. Knowledge creation through external venturing: evidence from the telecommunications equipment manufacturing industry. *Academy of Management Journal*, 49(4): 819–835.

Westfall, S. L. 1969. Simulating corporate entrepreneurship in US industry. *Academy of Management Journal*, 12(2): 235–246.

Weyrich, K. 2004. Innovation management at Siemens AG. Presentation at Massachusetts Institute of Technology, Boston, MA, 24 February 24. Available online at http://mitworld.mit.edu/video/187

Young, G. J., Charns, M. P., and Heeren, T. C. 2004. Product-line management in professional organizations: an empirical test of competing theoretical perspectives. *Academy of Management Journal*, 47(5): 723–734.

Zahra, S. A. 1996. Governance, ownership, and corporate entrepreneurship: the moderating impact of industry technological opportunities. *Academy of Management Journal*, 39(6): 1713–1735.

Section 5 readings

Introduction

Sustaining advantage has been the focus of this section, in which we have considered how organizations use culture and strategic change to ensure competitiveness. We have also explored strategic innovation and corporate entrepreneurship.

- Strategic change has been the focus of much multidisciplinary research and in **Reading 5.1**, Ann Todd's article on 'Managing radical change' (1999), we see how the process is difficult to achieve and often results in failure. This article highlights the complex nature of change in that it involves more than a narrow focus on strategy; it is also about people, processes, and politics. It is about understanding radical change from an employee perspective and the concerns that those employees have in dealing with change.
- In focusing on innovation and corporate entrepreneurship, **Reading 5.2**, 'The discipline of innovation' by Peter Drucker (1985), outlines seven sources of innovation, some of which are highly relevant to those who are persuaded by the dynamic capabilities perspective (see Reading 5.4 below).
- **Reading 5.3** by Adam Kleinbaum and Michael Tushman, 'Building bridges: the social structure of interdependent innovation' (2007), explores the difficulties in capturing new ideas for innovation highlighting the critical role played by social networks and top management in this task.
- Finally, in **Reading 5.4**, 'A dynamic view of strategy' (1999), Constantinos Markides' view of innovation suggests that organizations exploit the innovations of competitors and their own market positions simultaneously.

Overall, these readings offer rich and valuable insights through which strategists can reflect on how they should strive to sustain advantage.

Reading 5.1 Managing radical change *Ann Todd*

First published: (1999) *Long Range Planning*, 32(2): 237–244. Reprinted from *Long Range Planning*, Vol. 32, No. 2, pp. 237–244, copyright 1999 with permission from Elsevier.

A client contacted us over the problems they were experiencing with their change programme. They had intended the turnaround of a problem department, introducing more client focused and commercial behavior. Twelve months after the programme had started it was apparent to them that it had failed. Far from improving performance it had succeeded in increasing overheads, demoralizing staff, and removing the last vestiges of credibility for that particular activity within their customer base, producing devastating client feedback. And yet they had put together what had seemed a reasonable plan; they had identified the problems, they had employed a competent interim manager who had worked with them before, they had used stringent project management and they had funded the project well.

This sort of difficulty is common in many organizations. Investments that sometimes reach millions of pounds in new technologies, managed with the latest in project management techniques, fail to achieve their foreseen benefits. The infamous difficulties with IT projects are a simple example of the improvements that seem so easy to introduce in theory and yet are so difficult to achieve in practice. So frequently new technologies are bought, companies restructured, new managers appointed, but still the organizations do not perform to the levels anticipated. Why?

This article provides some practical guidance for the manager facing change. It is based on the author's practical expertise combined with relevant theory. Rather than detailing a generic 'how to' approach to change it highlights key issues that will block or aid progress. It starts by defining change management, then considers why change is so difficult, before introducing a conceptual framework for understanding change, finishing with a discussion of the practicalities of managing change.

The change management challenge

We define change management as a structured and systemic approach to achieving a *sustainable* change in human behaviour within an organization. It is concerned with moving the majority of the employees of an existing organization into new behaviours whilst retaining key competitive advantages particularly competencies and customer relationships.

We will start with a definition of types of change programme as each make different demands on management. The author has identified three categories described in detail in Table [5.1.1]: Radical Change, Incremental Change and Continuous Improvement. Of these Continuous Improvement is the simplest and well within the skills of the manager and indeed should be part of normal management activities. Incremental Change is more complicated and will require the manager to possess good political skills. Radical Change is the most challenging, and it is the type that this article discusses.

Change is the greatest of management challenges. In addition to any practical difficulties associated with the introduction of new technologies, it requires managers to lead a critical mass of the existing workforce through a period of intense uncertainty, and to do so in such a way that the organization is able to continue operating in its existing markets and relationships whilst learning new behaviours. As in any complex endeavour preparation is the key to success. It requires a holistic vision and approach and calls on the gamut of management skills.

We have developed a conceptual framework for approaching change programmes. This approach 'Strategy, Politics, People and Process' (Table [5.1.2]), many elements of which overlap, provides a structured approach to considering the elements of a radical change programme.

Strategy

Before embarking on a programme of radical change the organization must be sure that it has reviewed and rejected other options. As we shall see radical change is not easy as it concerns personal growth, group dynamics and uncertainty. It is particularly challenging for management and those who have initiated the change.

There are occasions when the appropriate decision is not to initiate a radical change programme but to close a facility down and to start again at a 'green field' site, or to withdraw from a market. This may be the case when the business unit is failing, when the market demands change within a very short period of time,[1] or when the organization does not contain any of the right sets of competencies.

Once decided that the reasons for the change are overwhelming and sure that the funds are available to finance it, and certain that they are prepared to go through the emotional pain involved, management may then proceed to considering how to progress the change.

Senior management commitment is a requirement for programme success.

Politics

Politics are a fact of human life, they are a method of negotiating the allocation of resources in pursuit of conflicting goals. As we will see in a later section, in addition to the usual organizational politics around territory and reward, change programmes increase the volume of politics due to the accompanying levels of uncertainty and fear.

Table 5.1.1 Defining types of change

Radical change	A substantial change that is often forced on the organization by an interaction with its environment. It requires a change in the basic values of the organization. *The organization is required to move from known and established behavior patterns to new behaviors, of which the organization has no real experience.* It is frequently time critical as managers respond to a market window of opportunity or a regulatory target. It is particularly demanding on managers, as it must be combined with the exigencies of daily management as the management team continues the income earning activities of the organization. Because it requires achieving sustainable changes in human behavior its outcome is not guaranteed. Examples of radical change include privatizations, the moving to agency status by state/bureaucratic bodies; company turnarounds; company acquisitions. It should be clearly differentiated from the challenges of incremental change and continuous improvement.
Incremental change	The task of achieving changes in line with the existing culture and objectives of the organization. It will usually be generated from within the company as part of competitive improvement. It will frequently involve more than a single department, often driven by performance improvements.
Continuous improvement	The task of achieving incremental improvements to an existing process.

Table 5.1.2 Framework for change

Strategy	The framework for the change: • Why the change is necessary • What are the parameters of the change • Who will be involved • How will we measure success • The new organizational structures required to support service/product delivery
Politics	The combination of power, influence and authority required to achieve the change
People	The identification and attainment of the combination of skills, attitudes and experience required within the workforce for the new organization (selection, training, hiring, exit packages) The programmes to engage the critical mass of employees to consent to the change and to persuade them to learn and adopt new behaviors
Process	The improvements/changes to service and product delivery process, often technical

The change process may be described as the 'colonization' of an organization by a new set of values. In these circumstances political conflict is inevitable as the new values vie to replace the old. Any challenge to the status quo, unless properly framed, will be vigorously rebuffed. Then we enter the realm of realpolitik and change management becomes a high risk activity for both initiators and implementors.

In Company A the Managing Director was a recent internal appointment. He had spent a number of years working for his predecessor, who had been promoted to a new corporate role with responsibility for the organization. This predecessor had put in place a major programme of change which had resulted in the current company structures. The Managing Director knew that the company was in urgent need of further change. His predecessor also had a directive personal style at odds with the Managing Director's naturally open and consensual approach. Consequently his senior colleagues did not understand the Managing Director's style and thought him weak in comparison. One of their number had considered himself the natural heir and was unsupportive of his new boss. Our advice in this complicated scenario, was that before even proceeding to considering the extent of the change required, the Managing Director had to put in place a strategy that would recognize the political realities and so allow the change to take place.

Change management requires a combination of persuasion and enforcement. The change initiators must have sufficient power, influence and authority to cajole and drive the change through. And yet participation cannot be forced, as sustainable change is self-motivated. In other words the individual working within the organization must want to change. In essence this requires the gaining and maintaining of the consent of the workforce of the organization to the change process. Without this agreement there will only be mechanistic compliance and old behaviours will reassert themselves within three to six months. The disrupting and disabling potential of organizational politics is magnified when there is no accepted imperative for change and when individuals are not rewarded for delivery of service or product. Judging the correct balance of persuasion and enforcement is a matter of expertise and experience and depends upon the specific circumstances of each programme.

People

Once having navigated the strategy and politics, the well designed radical change programme should consider people, specifically how to move the targeted personnel towards the new behaviours. It is at this point that the Change process must explicitly address the emotional as well as the competency concerns of personnel. Thus the change process moves more obviously into the realms of emotional intelligence. Consideration should specifically be given to the following:

- organizational culture,
- implicit and explicit contracts of employment,
- people—competencies and personality,
- dealing with uncertainty, fear and loss,
- managing the change process.

Organizational culture

Culture may be defined as how a group of people agree to interpret their physical environment and how they agree to behave in response to that environment.[2] At its core are a set of agreed beliefs and values.[3] Its literal expression may be seen in a society's dress and decorative codes, attitudes to sex, the use of religion, gender roles and so on. This agreed behaviour—Culture—is how human tribes control the behaviour of individuals. It has been an important element in the success of the human species over millennia. Once the rules are established it is self-policed and extremely powerful.

> Culture is an autonomous entity that carries out a desire to perpetuate itself by setting up expectations and assigning roles, which can vary arbitrarily from society to society.[4]

In the organizational world culture develops as a result of the interplay between the organizations' environment (market and societal/political inputs), the personalities and neuroses of its leaders, and the reward and recruitment structures in place.[5] It is an effective mechanism for management control.

One of the most striking aspects of culture is how set it often becomes over time. Those who succeed in gaining promotions within the organization will necessarily be good at fitting the culture. They then are naturally interested in maintaining the system within which they are so comfortable, in effect maintaining the status quo. Those within the culture will recruit newcomers who 'fit' the team, usually from people and job specifications developed from within the existing organizations. Over time those who do not 'fit' the culture (and have enough authority to disturb the status quo), will either become frustrated and leave of their own accord or will be ejected by the group. These group tendencies are re-enforced in a group that has little real interaction with the wider world. In this circumstance it tends to become an inwardly focused, self-maintaining, closed system.

Some companies sustain cultures which actively and arbitrarily sanction individuals for behaving in ways that are considered inappropriate by the culture. These are often described as 'Blaming' cultures. These are cultures within which mistakes can lead to loss of a job and/or severe curtailment of career prospects. Within this type of environment it is extremely difficult to persuade people to learn new behaviours. Indeed the individual's refusal to engage with the learning process is sensible as to do so would be extremely high risk as part of the process of learning is making mistakes.

Implicit and explicit contracts

Employee behaviour within an organization is bounded by implicit and explicit contract, both of which have logical and emotional components. The explicit contract may be more or less formally expressed through contracts of employment and performance appraisal but may usually be summarized as '*X* behaviour leads to *Y* reward'. As we have seen in the discussion under culture, established organizations will have many systems in place to reinforce the contract. This explicit contract will require review and renegotiation in line with the changed objectives of the organization, before change may be initiated.

The implicit contract is in effect a 'followership'[5] contract. Every leader (or manager) requires 'followers' to lead (or people to manage). The idea of the implicit contract, developed over human experience of living in groups, provides a logical explanation of why, apart from simple monetary reasons, people chose to follow a leader. 'Followers' become part of the group because they believe that the leaders have the interests of the majority of followers at heart. Thus over time followers, have been able to achieve more as a follower in the tribe/association/team/organization than they could on their own. At the simplest level the benefit may be the survival of the tribe in hard times.

Within the business context it is then apparent that an individual's decision to join and stay with an organization is both logical and emotional.[6] This is most apparent within privatizations where employees often joined what was a public service because they wanted to serve the public. Many chose to forsake the risks and rewards of commercial enterprises in return for greater certainty and long-term benefits such as index linked pensions, parental leave and long-term career progressions. Many will have spent their entire working life within the same type of organization. The arbitrary and politically motivated demand that these public servants suddenly become business managers may not, at the individual and personal level, be acceptable.

It should be remembered that even in times of constrained employment opportunities the best employees—usually those you want to keep within the organization—always have other options. The objective of the change process is to maintain the competitive advantages of the organization which mainly rest in personnel. Thus managers must be aware of the implicit contract in their treatment of the change. Attempts to unilaterally change the existing contract will probably be seen by employees as management reneging on the original 'deal'. In these circumstances it should not occasion surprise if employees choose to renege on theirs.

In Company B, the manager had introduced new technology to modernize the service delivery system. The specifications were right, the equipment had been bought at an excellent price, delivery and installation had proceeded well. He was surprised when customer service performance fell away, morale plummeted and the company began to face a number of grievance cases. He had forgotten about the implicit and emotional contract with the people who were to use the equipment. It took several months to rebuild the trust and confidence of that team in their manager.

Managers must be aware of their own management style and tread carefully to ensure that they are deemed to have the interest of their followers at heart. Bullying, arbitrary decisions, and decisions that are seen to lack respect for the followers will backfire. This often presents quite a personal challenge for those who consider a directive, confrontational style to be the apogee of the strong management required in difficult times.

In Company C the manager announced how the change would be, impressing his board of Directors by his strength and vision. Within the company he publicly rebuked and then removed those who opposed the change. He asserted that no one was irreplaceable and replaced employees with contract staff when the opportunity arose. Consequently the highly qualified staff took advantage of the many opportunities available in the wider IT environment including amongst competitors. Core knowledge haemorrhaged from the organization and with it competitive advantage. Levels of both mechanical compliance and passive resistance were high. The covering up of real operational problems became endemic. It was no surprise that after 18 months of this regime, the manager's view of company performance was somewhat at odds of that of his customer base, setting up a vicious circle of decline.

Competency

The change programme will not succeed if the organization does not contain the correct competencies required for successful operation within the new environment. This is not just a question of technical skills, successful leaders are competent in their interaction with the firm's market environment[7] in addition to their technical and people skills.

Our earlier definitions of radical change include the words "to move from known and established behaviour patterns to new behaviours, of which the organization has no real experience". The question for the organization is how to introduce those new behaviours. Training is of course part of this process, and every change programme usually involves company-wide and specific courses. However, short courses do not compensate for practical experience and the resultant applied expertise. The organization must be clear as to the level of competency it requires in the various new behaviours and for which roles. It may require third-party assurance so that it is capable of recognizing the true level of competence that an individual has, rather than accepting individuals who may be available in the job market because they are not skilled enough for current sector conditions.

In Company D, with the growth of sales activity the Managing Director appointed several engineers to the new roles of Account Manager, promising that the company would support them properly. Accordingly they were sent on numerous training courses. Within three years they had all been replaced. Despite the hours and genuine effort they had put in, none had met the challenge and they all quit the company disillusioned at their 'shabby' treatment. In addition one suffered a heart attack brought on by the stress of meeting his new role.

Proficiency in the 'new' skills is particularly important for senior managers who will be required to lead and model the new behaviour and for those required to interact with new market places. Whilst an individual in a key post may be willing to learn new skills (although this very much depends on the individual and their life stage), the organization must be realistic about the likelihood of success. This is particularly so when the new demands are combined with the daily demands of business performance, and the impact of personality.

Change requires leadership throughout all levels of the organization. Leadership is a different behaviour to that of the style of management usually practised within bureaucratic organizations. The organization may lack the leadership resources required.

Personality

Personality type impacts an individual's interaction with the wider world and therefore, their effectiveness as managers. Using the basic Introversion–Extroversion measures as described by Dorothy Rowe, we understand that individuals who are in post and who were chosen for their technical skills with a tendency to introversion may not be the right people to lead change within the organization.

Dealing with uncertainty, fear and loss

For the organization, change is a voyage into the unknown. The majority of the employees, including management, will have had no experience of the type of organization that the change may require. They are in effect being asked to trust the management that the change is the best interests of the organization and themselves, even though the change may have been occasioned by previous management failure. They are also being asked to learn and practice new behaviours whilst in post and whilst their performance is being measured via the appraisal system.

Managers face an additional challenge, that of dealing with their own emotions about the change whilst they are attempting to lead their staff through the change process. When personnel are intelligent it is usually impossible for their managers to hide their own mixed feelings. Their emotional response will include:

- anger—about the long hours and effort they have put into the organization that seem to have been wasted,
- grief—about the loss of status and the disappearance of the known organization and,
- fear—about the unknown future and their part in that future.

The first step to successfully managing these emotions is to acknowledge that they exist. Denial, often the emotional coping strategy of choice in organizations, will not work for this particular issue. Once the emotions are admitted the organization will then be able to find a way of managing them appropriately, which may include the provision of confidential counselling as well as coaching. Senior management must also acknowledge the likelihood, both to themselves but also most particularly to their personnel that not all staff will either wish to continue in the organization or be able to continue, and to provide a dignified exit route.

Managing radical change—the view from within the corporation

Each organization will take their own decision about resourcing change, however, the following comments are offered from practical experience.

Resourcing the change

Managing radical change from within the organization is likely to prove unsuccessful.

- It requires an objectivity of view about the organizations past, present and future that is unlikely to prevail if the programme manager's salary, pension and promotion prospects are within the organization.
- It requires the ability to understand and manage the individual and group emotional response to the proposed change implementation.
- It requires sufficient authority to challenge the vested interests of the status quo.

Success is more likely to result from a partnership between the organization and a third-party Change Manager. Depending on the size of the programme the Change Manager could be an individual or a company (and is used to indicate both in this article).

Interim management

Interim management may well provide an individual with experience of the new market environment, but there are some significant problems associated with its use.

- The difficulty of the individual maintaining objectivity when the natural tendency is to emotionally 'join' the available group—that is, the local management team.
- Interim managers are usually taken on as part of a management team. In order to be able to be effective, the individual must have the co-operation of people who are colleagues. It is difficult to gain and maintain co-operation with colleagues when one is changing the status quo.
- The difficulty of assessing the real level of competence that the interim manager has as a Change Manager or as an expert in the new behaviours. This is particularly so as the organization often has no experience of either managing major change or an understanding of the new behaviours.

In Company E they appointed an Interim Manager as the Change Manager. He was a charming individual and the Managing Director had known him for many years. He had done sterling work for the company as a temporary Marketing Manager and when there was widespread customer dissatisfaction. The senior management team believed that he would work with the departmental Director to achieve the required change without ruffling too many feathers. When we met this manager some months later he was distraught and in response to a sympathetic enquiry of 'how are things going?', he produced a long complaint about how the team would not let him do anything despite his strenuous efforts on their behalf. The end result was a failed project and soured relationships.

The consultancy company

Change management is a distinct area of competence, therefore, the organization is best advised to choose a change specialist. In assessing potential partners, management should be aware that radical change requires emotional intelligence as well as intellectual ability. 'Rocket Scientists' do not necessarily make good Change Managers.

Change requires not just the appropriate lead consultant/director but a good team. Due to the complexity of the change process all of the consulting team will be challenged as no other programme does. The areas of expertise that are called on, on a day-to-day basis, are those of emotional and influencing skills and the contact with client personnel is such that it is not possible to hide behind intellect. Employees are unlikely to respect or be prepared to work with consultants who do not seem credible.

Nor should the company be seduced by technologies or methodologies. Different management models and methodologies are applicable in various situation, they form part of the consultant's tool kit, and should be applied according to need. Unless the consultants are already familiar with your business they are unlikely to be able to predict the particular barriers to change that your organization is confronting. It is therefore unlikely that they will be able to suggest the appropriate approach without some initial work to define the problem. Similarly for this reason it is not advisable to trust 'off the shelf' change packages.

Identifying the effective change manager

The acid test of a Change Manager is the ability to influence the organization whilst remaining objective. In effect the effective Change Manager must be able to enter into an empathic emotional contract with the company personnel. The ability to remain objective is greatly helped by the individual having a group of others who are not part of the company status quo to refer to for support. An example of this is the process within Todd Consulting where colleagues who are not working on the project are invited to challenge the senior consultant concerned on a regular basis.

The key element of the relationship between the organization and the Change Manager is trust. The Change Manager has a dual role, acting as an objective manager of the change, and leading the organization into a future that is not yet known and indeed may not be attained. The role may well require communicating facts and failures that the management team find difficult to accept and hear. There is clearly plenty of scope either for projecting fears about the future onto the Change Manager, or for blaming the messenger for delivering the 'bad' news.

The Change Manager does not need to understand the detail of your business process, you are not after all hiring them as technical or process specialists. It is rather more useful that they should have an understanding of the competitive principles of your business, be it service industry or manufacturing. And for Radical change it not usually advisable to select consultants who have been employees within your industry/organization. This is because they are likely to share your view of 'how the world is'. Change requires an objectivity of view.

We might also mention qualities such as tenacity, the ability to manage high levels of uncertainty, excellent analytical, political and influencing skills and last but certainly not least, a good sense of the absurd!

Managing the change manager

The relationship between Change Manager and organization requires both sides to be sure of their boundaries. This is not easy for the organization as it must sponsor the change at a sufficient level of authority so that the natural resistance of the status quo may be overcome and yet must be able to let go of elements of the process. The organization must achieve ownership of the change—by which is meant ensuring sufficient involvement from organization personnel so that they learn and understand new processes and are willing to take responsibility for them. Letting go does not mean abdication, but it does require allowing a certain level of dependency to develop. What it does mean is the temporary letting go of those parts of the change process that the organization cannot manage by itself, which are likely to be the political and people elements, whilst retaining the process/technical change elements. Both the organization and the Change Manager must be able to manage their respective boundaries.

Project management and measuring success

As the extent of the management challenge is revealed it becomes apparent that measurement and programme/project control are important to the success of the project.

Project and programme management

It is very difficult to manage a change project via a project management methodology that has been developed, say, for IT projects where outcomes and work methodologies are known. In the initial stages of a change project it is often not possible to see ahead in detail more that a couple of months and the project may itself involve the design of a solution which is not known at the outset. There are many project management methodologies, the key to selecting the most suitable is to understand when the project is a change project rather than a technical project.

Measuring success

The choice of measures depends upon the project. Nonetheless every change project addresses emotional, cultural and behavioural issues which are all measurable, given that base line measurements are obtained at project commencement or shortly thereafter. Similarly the market place will tell you when behaviour has changed. Measurement is important both to reassure a management team that is not sure of outcome, and to gauge real progress as changes in project strategy may be required.

The process of agreeing how success is to be measured is an essential first step part of the scoping/initiation phase. It should serve both to build the organizations' confidence that the Change Manager understands the change process and to give the Change Manager the opportunity to ensure that the clients expectations are in line with their own. It not acceptable that the organization should discover some twelve months after the start of the project and after significant expenditure that the projet is failing. Difficulties should be flagged as early as possible and positively confronted.

Conclusion: managing radical change

We have seen the successful radical change project is complex and requires a holistic approach that calls on the full range of management skills and disciplines. It should not be attempted lightly and senior management should be sure that they have considered and rejected the other possibilities. Once the decision has been taken to proceed there must be one hundred percent commitment to the success of the process, this includes being prepared to listen to 'bad' news. A lot of attention must be given to the planning of the change and also to the emotional consequences for individuals within the organization. The more time that is spent on planning, the more likely the programme is to succeed. Care must be taken with the selection of the Change Manager, and the organization should beware too formulaic approaches. Measurement is an integral part of the process.

We know that we have succeeded when the personnel of an organization start taking ownership of the change and become impatient for us to leave. Behaviours that were considered alien just a few months previously become 'normalized', customers notice the improvement, but best of all we see a group of people becoming empowered and with renewed confidence as they step forward to meet the new challenges of their market places. That 'buzz' of seeing a company with an enhanced future is what makes the challenging process of managing radical change worthwhile.

References

1. Todd and Taylor, The babysharks—Britain's supergrowth companies, *Long Range Planning* April (1993).
2. D. Rowe, *The Successful Self*, Harper Collins, London (1988).
3. G. Hofstede, Cultural constraints in management theories, *Academy of Management Executive* 7(1), 81–94 (1993).
4. S. Pinker, *How The Mind Works*, Penguin, Oxford (1998).
5. K. de Vries et al, *Organizations on the Couch*, Jossey-Bass, New York (1991).
6. Fineman, *Emotion in Organizations*, Sage, New York (1993).
7. Spender, *Industry Recipes*, Blackwell, Oxford (1989).

Reading 5.2 The discipline of innovation *Peter F. Drucker*

First published: (1985) *Harvard Business Review*, May–June: 67–72. Reprinted by permission of *Harvard Business Review*. 'The Disciple of Innovation', Peter F. Drucker, August 2002.

Despite much discussion these days of the "entrepreneurial personality," few of the entrepreneurs with whom I have worked during the last 30 years had such personalities. But I have known many people – salespeople, surgeons, journalists, scholars, even musicians – who did have them without being the least bit "entrepreneurial." What all the successful entrepreneurs I have met have in common is not a certain kind of personality but a commitment to the systematic practice of innovation.

Innovation is the specific function of entrepreneurship, whether in an existing business, a public service institution, or a new venture started by a lone individual the family kitchen. It is the means by which the entrepreneur either creates new wealthproducing resources or endows existing resources with enhanced potential for creating wealth.

Today, much confusion exists about the proper definition of entrepreneurship. Some observers use the term to refer to all small businesses, others, to all new businesses. In practice, however, great many well-established businesses engage in highly successful entrepreneurship. The term, them, refers not to an enterprise's size or age, but to a certain kind of activity. At the heart of that activity is innovation: the effort to create purposeful, focused change in an enterprise's economic or social potential.

Sources of innovation

There are, of course, innovations that spring from a flash of genius. Most innovations, however, especially the successful ones, result from a conscious, purposeful search for innovation opportunities, which are found only in a few situations.

Four such areas of opportunity exist *within* a company or industry:

- Unexpected occurrences.
- Incongruities.
- Process needs.
- Industry and market changes.

Three additional sources of opportunity exist *outside* a company in its social and intellectual environment:

- Demographic changes.
- Changes in perception.
- New knowledge.

True, these sources overlap, different as they may be in the nature of their risk, difficulty, and complexity, and the potential for innovation may well lie in more than one area at a time. But among them, they account for the great majority of all innovation opportunities.

Unexpected occurrences

Consider, first, the easiest and simplest source of innovation opportunity: the unexpected. In the early 1930s, IBM developed the first modern accounting machine, which was designed for banks, but banks in 1933 did not buy equipment. What saved the company – according to a story that Thomas Watson, Sr., the company's founder and long-term CEO, often told – was its exploitation of an unexpected success: the New York Public Library wanted to buy a machine. Unlike the banks, libraries in those early New Deal days had money, and Watson sold more than a hundred of his otherwise unsalable machines to libraries.

Fifteen years later, when everyone believed that computers were designed for advanced scientific work, business unexpectedly showed an interest in a machine that could do payroll. Univac, which had the most advanced machine, spurned business applications. But IBM immediately realized it faced a possible unexpected success, redesigned what was basically Univac's machine for such mundane applications as payroll, and within five years became the leader in the computer industry, a position it has maintained to this day.

The unexpected failure may be an equally important innovation opportunity source. Everyone knows about the Ford Motor Company's Edsel as the biggest new car failure in automotive history. What very few people seem to know, however, is that the Edsel's failure was the foundation for much of the company's later success. Ford planned the Edsel, the most carefully designed car to that point in American automotive history, to give the company a full product line with which to compete with GM. When it bombed, despite all the planning, market research, and design that had gone into it, Ford realized that something was happening in the automobile market that ran counter to the basic assumptions on which GM and everyone else had been designing and marketing cars. No longer did the market segment primarily by income groups; suddenly, the new principle of segmentation was what we now call "lifestyles." Ford's immediate responses were the Mustang and the Thunderbird – the cars that gave the company a distinct personality and reestablished it as an industry leader.

Unexpected successes and failures are such productive sources of innovation opportunities because most businesses dismiss them, disregard them, and even resent them. The German scientist who around 1906 synthesized novocaine, the first non-addictive narcotyic, had intended it to be used in major surgical procedures like amputation. Surgeons, however, preferred total anesthesia for such procedures, they still do. Instead, novocaine found a ready appeal among dentists. Its inventor spent the remaining years of his life traveling from dental school to dental school making speeches that forbade dentists to "misuse" his noble invention in applications for which he had not intended it.

This is a caricature, to be sure, but it illustrates the attitude managers often take to the unexpected. "It should not have happened." Corporate reporting systems further ingrain this reaction, for they draw attention away from unanticipated possibilities. The typical monthly or quarterly report has on its first page a list of problems, that is, the areas where results fall short of expectations. Such information is needed, of course, it helps prevent deterioration of performance.

But it also suppresses the recognition of new opportunities. The first acknowledgment of a possible opportunity usually applies to an area in which a company does better than budgeted. Thus genuinely entrepreneurial businesses have two "first pages" – a problem page and an opportunity page – and managers spend equal time on both.

Incongruities

Alcon Industries was one of the great success stories of the 1960s because Bill Connor, the company's founder, exploited an incongruity in medical technology. The cataract operation is the world's third or fourth most common surgical procedure. During the last 300 years, doctors systematized it to the point that the only "old-fashioned" step left was the cutting of a ligament. Eye surgeons had learned to cut the ligament with complete success, but it was so different a procedure from the rest of the operation and so incompatible with it that they often dreaded it. It was incongruous.

Doctors had known for 50 years about an enzyme that could dissolve the ligament without cutting. All Connor did was to add a preservative to this enzyme that gave it a few months' shelf life. Eye surgeons immediately accepted the new compound, and Alcon found itself with a worldwide, monopoly. Fifteen years later, Nestlé bought the company for a fancy price.

Such an incongruity within the logic or rhythm of a process is only one possibility out of which innovation opportunities may arise. Another source is incongruity between economic realities. For instance, whenever an industry has a steadily growing market but falling profit margins – as, say, in the steel industries of developed countries between 1950 and 1970 – an incongruity exists. The innovative response: minimills.

An incongruity between expectations and results can also open up possibilities for innovation. For 50 years after the turn of the century, shipbuilders and shipping companies worked hard both to makes ships faster and to lower their fuel consumption. Even so, the more successful they were in boosting speed and trimming fuel needs, the worse ocean freighter's economics became. By 1950 or so, the ocean freighter was dying, if not already dead.

All that was wrong, however, was an incongruity between the industry's assumptions and its realities. The real costs did not come from doing work (that is, being at sea) but from not doing work (that is, sitting idle in port). Once managers understood where costs truly lay, the innovations were obvious: the roll-on and roll-off ship and the container ship. These solutions, which involved old technology, simply applied to the ocean freighter what railroads and truckers had been using for 30 years. A shift in viewpoint, not in technology, totally changed the economics of ocean shipping and turned it into one of the major growth industries of the last 20 to 30 years.

Process needs

Anyone who has ever driven in Japan knows that the country has no modern highway system. Its roads still follow the paths laid down for – or by – oxcarts in the tenth century. What makes the system work for automobiles and trucks is an adaptation of the reflector used on American highways since the early 1930s. This reflector shows each car, which other cars are approaching, from any one of a half-dozen directions. This minor invention, which enables traffic to move smoothly and with a minimum of accidents, exploited a process need.

Around 1909, a statistician at the American Telephone & Telegraph Company projected two curves 15 years out: telephone traffic and American, population. Viewed together, they showed that by 1920 or so every single female in the United Stated would have to work as a switchboard operator. The process need was obvious, and within two years, AT&T had developed and installed the automatic switchboard.

What we now call "media" also had their origin in two process need-based innovations around 1890. One was Mergenthaler's Linotype, which made it possible to produce a newspaper quickly and in large volume, the other was a social innovation, modern advertising, invented by the first true newspaper publishers, Adolph Ochs of the *New York Times*, Joseph Pulitzer of the *New York World*, and William Randolph Hearst. Advertising made it possible for them to distribute news practically free of charge, with the profit coming from marketing.

Industry & market changes

Managers may believe that industry structures are ordained by the Good Lord, but they can – and often do – change overnight. Such change creates tremendous opportunity for innovation.

One of American business's great success stories in recent decades is the brokerage firm of Donaldson, Lufkin & Jenrette, recently acquired by the Equitable Life Assurance Society. DL&J was founded in1961 by three young men, all graduates of the Harvard Business School, who realized that the structure of the financial industry was changing as institutional investors became dominant. These young men had practically no capital and no connections. Still, within a few years, their firm had become a leader in the move to negotiated commissions and one of Wall Street's stellar performers. It was the first to be incorporated and go public.

In a similar fashion, changes in industry structure have created massive innovation opportunities for American health care providers. During the last 10 or 15 years, independent surgical and psychiatric clinics, emergency centers, and HMOs have opened throughout the country. Comparable opportunities in telecommunications followed industry upheavals – both in equipment (with the emergence of such companies as ROLM in the manufacturing of private branch exchanges) and in transmission (with the emergence of MCI and Sprint in long-distance service).

When an industry grows quickly – the critical figure seems to be in the neighborhood of a 40% growth rate over ten years or less – its structure changes. Established companies, concentrating on defending what they already have, tend not to counter attack when a newcomer challenges them. Indeed, when market or industry structures change, traditional industry leaders again and again neglect the fastest growing market segments. New opportunities rarely fit the way the industry has always approached the market, defined it, or organized to serve it. Innovators therefore have a good chance of being left alone for a long time.

Demographic changes

Of the outside sources of innovation opportunity, demographics are the most reliable. Demographic events have known lead times; for instance, every person who will be in the American labor force by the year 2000 has already been born. Yet, because policymakers often neglect demographics, those who watch them and exploit them can reap great rewards.

The Japanese are ahead in robotics because they paid attention to demographics. Everyone in the developed countries around 1970 or so knew that there was both a baby and an education explosion going on; half or more of the young people were now staying in school beyond high school. Consequently, the number of people available for traditional bluecollar work in manufacturing was bound to decrease and become inadequate by 1990. Everyone knew this, but only the Japanese acted on it and they now have a ten-year lead in robotics.

Much the same is true of Club Mediterranee's success in the travel and resort business. By 1970, thoughtful observers could have seen the emergence of large numbers of affluent and educated young adults in Europe and the United States. Not comfortable with the kind of vacations their working-class parents had enjoyed – the summer weeks at Brighton or Atlantic City – these young people were ideal customers for a new and exotic version of the "hangout" of their teen years.

Managers have known for a long time that demographics matter, but they have always believed that population statistics change slowly. In this century, however, they don't. Indeed, the innovation opportunities that changes in the numbers of people, and their age distribution, education, occupations, and geographic location make possible are among the most rewarding and least risky of entrepreneurial pursuits.

Changes in perception

"The glass is half full" and "the glass is half-empty" are descriptions of the same phenomenon but have vastly different meanings. Changing a manager's perception of a glass from half-full to half-empty opens up big innovation opportunities.

All factual evidence indicates, for instance, that in the last 20 years, Americans' health has improved at unprecedented speed – whether measured by mortality rates for the newborn, survival rates for the very old, the incidence of cancers (other than lung cancer), cancer cure rates, or other factors. Even so, collective hypochondria grips the nation. Never before has there been so much concern with health or so much fear about health. Suddenly everything seems to cause cancer or degenerative heart disease or premature loss of memory. The glass is clearly half-empty.

Rather than rejoicing in great improvements in health, Americans seem to be emphasizing how far away they still are from immortality. This view of things has created many opportunities for innovations: markets for new health care magazines, for all kinds of health foods, and for exercise classes and jogging equipment. The fastest growing new U.S. business in 1983 was a company that makes indoor exercise equipment.

A change in perception does not alter facts. It changes their meaning, though – and very quickly. It took less than two years for the computer to change from being perceived as a threat and as something only big businesses would use to something one buys for doing income tax. Economics do not necessarily dictate such a change; in fact, they may be irrelevant. What determines whether people see a glass as half-full or half-empty is mood rather than fact, and change in mood often defies quantification. But it is not exotic or intangible. It is concrete. It can be defined. It can be tested. And it can be exploited for innovation opportunity.

New knowledge

Among history-making innovations, those based on new knowledge – whether scientific, technical, or social – rank high. They are the superstars of entrepreneurship; they get the publicity and the money. They are what people usually mean when they of innovation, though not all innovations based on knowledge are important. Some are trivial.

Knowledge-based innovations differ from all others in the time they take, in their casualty rates, and in their predictability, as well as in the challenges they pose to entrepreneurs. Like most superstars, they can be temperamental, capricious, and hard to direct. They have, for instance, the longest lead time of all innovations. There is a protracted span between the emergence of new knowledge and its distillation into usable technology. Then, there is another long period before this new technology appears in the marketplace in products, processes, or services. Overall, the lead time involved is something like 50 years, a figure that has not shortened appreciably throughout history.

To become effective, innovation of this sort usually demands not one kind of knowledge but many. Consider one of the most potent knowledge passed innovations: modern banking. The theory of the entrepreneurial bank – that is, of the purposeful use of capital to generate economic development – was formulated by the Comte de Saint-Simon during the era of Napoleon. Despite Saint-Simon's extraordinary prominence, it was not until 30 years after his death in 1826 that two of his disciples, the brothers Jacob and Isaac Pereire, established the first entrepreneurial bank, the Credit Mobilier, and ushered in what we now call "*finance capitalism*."

The Pereires, however, did not know modern commercial banking, which developed at about the same time across the channel in England. The Credit Mobilier failed ignominiously. Ten years later, two young men – one an American, J.P. Morgan, and one a German, Georg Siemens – put together the French theory of entrepreneurial banking and the English theory of commercial banking to create the first successful modern banks, J.P. Morgan & Company in New York and the Deutsche Bank in Berlin. Another ten years later, a young Japanese, Shibusawa Eiichi, adopted Siemens' concept to his country and thereby laid the foundation of Japan's modern economy. This is how knowledge-based innovation always works.

The computer, to cite another example, required no fewer than six separate strands of knowledge: Binary arithmetic; Charles Babbage's conception of a calculating machine in the first half of the nineteenth century; the punch card, invented by Herman Hollerith for the U.S. census of 1890; the audion tube, an electronic switch invented in 1906, symbolic logic, which was created between 1910 and 1913 by Bertrand Russell and Alfred North Whitehead; and the concepts of programming and feedback that came out of abortive attempts during World War I to develop effective anti-aircraft guns. Although all the necessary knowledge was available by 1918, the first operational computer did not appear until 1946.

Long lead times and the need for convergence among different kinds of knowledge explain the peculiar rhythm of knowledge-based innovation, its attractions, and its dangers. During a long gestation period, there is a lot of talk and little action. Then, when all the elements suddenly converge, there is tremendous excitement and activity and an enormous amount of speculation. Between 1880 and 1890, for example, almost 1,000 electrical apparatus companies were founded in developed countries. Then, as always, there was a crash and a shakeout. By 1914, only 25 of these companies were still alive. In the early 1920s, 300 to 500 automobile companies existed in the United States; by 1960, only 4 remained.

It may be difficult, but knowledge-based innovation can be managed. Success requires careful analysis of the various kinds of knowledge needed to make an innovation possible. Both J.P. Morgan and Georg Siemens did this when they established their banking ventures. The Wright brothers did this when they developed the first operational airplane.

Careful analysis of the needs and, above all, the capabilities of the intended user is also essential. It may seem paradoxical, but knowledge-based innovation is more market dependent than any other kind of innovation.

De Havilland, a British company, designed and built the first passenger jet airplane, but it did not analyze what the market needed and therefore did not identify two key factors. One was configuration – that is, the right size with the right payload for the routes on which a jet would give an airline the greatest advantage. The other was equally mundane: how the airlines could finance the purchase of such an expensive plane. Because De Havilland failed to do an adequate user analysis, two American companies, Boeing and Douglas, took over the commercial jet aircraft industry.

Principles of innovation

Purposeful, systematic innovation begins with the analysis of the sources of new opportunities. Depending on the context, sources will have different importance at different times. Demographics, for instance, may be of little concern to innovators in fundamental industrial processes like steel making, although Mergenthaler's Linotype machine became successful primarily because there were not enough skilled typesetters available to satisfy a mass market. By the same token, new knowledge may be of little relevance to someone innovating a social instrument to satisfy a need that changing demographics or tax laws have created. But – whatever the situation – innovators must analyze all opportunity sources.

Because innovation is both conceptual and perceptual, would be innovators must also go out and look, ask, and listen. Successful innovators use both the right and left sides of their brains. They look at figures. They look at people. They work out analytically what the innovation has to be to satisfy an opportunity. Then they go out and look at potential users to study their expectations, their values, and their needs.

To be effective, an innovation has to be simple and it has to be focused. It should do only one thing, otherwise it confuses people. Indeed, the greatest praise an innovation can receive is for people to say. "This is obvious! Why didn't I think of it? It's so simple!" Even the innovation that creates new users and new markets should be directed toward a specific, clear, and carefully designed application.

Effective innovations start small. They are not grandiose. They try to do one specific thing. It may be to enable a moving vehicle to draw electric power while it runs along rails, the innovation that made possible the electric streetcar. Or it may be the elementary idea of putting the same number of matches into a matchbox (it used to be 50). This simple notion made possible the automatic filling of matchboxes and gave the Swedes a world monopoly on matches for half a century. By contrast, grandiose ideas for things that will "revolutionize an industry" are unlikely to work.

In fact, no one can foretell whether a given innovation will end up a big business or a modest achievement. But even if the results are modest, the successful innovation aims from the beginning to become the standard setter, to determine the direction of a new technology or a new industry, to create the business that is – and remains – ahead of the pack. If an innovation does not aim at leadership from the beginning, it is unlikely to be innovative enough.

Above all, innovation is work rather than genius. It requires knowledge. It often requires ingenuity. And it requires focus. There are clearly people who are more talented as innovators than others but their talents lie in well-defined areas. Indeed, innovators rarely work in more than one area. For all his systematic innovative accomplishments, Edison worked only in the electrical field. An innovator in financial areas, Citibank for example, is not likely to embark on innovations in health care.

In innovation as in any other endeavor, there is talent, there is ingenuity, and there is knowledge. But when all is said and done, what innovation requires is hard, focused, purposeful work. If diligence, persistence, and commitment are lacking, talent, ingenuity, and knowledge are of no avail.

There is, of course, far more to entrepreneurship than systematic innovation: distinct entrepreneurial strategies, for example, and the principles of entrepreneurial management, which are needed equally in the established enterprise, the public service organization, and the new venture. But the very foundation of entrepreneurship – as a practice and a discipline – is the practice of systematic innovation.

Reading 5.3 Building bridges: the social structure of interdependent innovation *Adam M. Kleinbaum and Michael L. Tushman*

First published: (2007) *Strategic Entrepreneurship Journal*, 1: 1.3–122. *Strategic Entrepreneurship Journal*, 1: 103–122 (2007). Reproduced with the kind permission of Jon Wiley and Sons.

Multidivisional firms often fail to take advantage of innovations that involve combining resources from distinct divisions. This failure of cross-line-of-business innovation is a consequence of design choices employed to execute the firm's strategy: in organizing around its core businesses, the firm renders interdependence between divisions residual to the formal structure. As a result, those innovations which involve cross-line-of-business interdependence are trumped by the firm's articulated strategy and structure. Social structures could, potentially, fill this coordination gap. But social structures associated with the initiation of interdependent innovation are inversely associated with their execution. We build a dynamic, corporate-level, evolutionary model in which individuals autonomously initiate cross-line-of-business projects not through the formal structure of the firm, but using contacts from their own social networks. Some of these projects are selected and actively supported by senior executives; this support sends clear signals about what collaboration is valued by the firm, which gives other actors powerful, albeit informal, incentives to connect with others across the interunit boundary. As a result, the sparse interunit social structure that was conducive to initiation changes, becoming much more cohesive (at least locally) and is able to support execution and retain these interdependent innovations. Thus, where intradivisional innovations are primarily driven by organizational structure, we suggest that interdivisional innovations are driven primarily by social networks.

Introduction

In spite of the dismay of industry observers such as Cohen, most large firms fail to take advantage of the opportunity to create new businesses that combine resources from disparate parts of the firm. Instead, divisions tend to 'stay in their own lanes,' developing new products for their existing customers (Christensen, 1997), adopting technologies that enhance the value of their existing skills (Tushman and Anderson, 1986) and generally paying little attention to one another. Even when firms use collaborative incentives or cross-divisional teams, they rarely succeed in recombining their portfolios of skills, resources and businesses to bring new products to light (Campbell and Goold, 1999). This inability of multidivisional firms to leverage existing assets is an important lost growth opportunity.

Over the past two decades, scholars have identified many reasons why firms are inertial and resist change, even when change bears new growth opportunities (e.g., Barnett and Carroll, 1995; Benner, 2004; Gavetti and Levinthal, 2000; Henderson, 1993; Leonard-Barton, 1992; Tripsas and Gavetti, 2000). When change requires building bridges across business unit boundaries, the challenge seems to be even greater. We argue that when firms design their internal architecture to minimize coordination costs by organizing around the most strategic interdependencies (Thompson, 1967), they render other possible interdependencies residual to the formal organizational structure. And yet, in firms whose divisions make products that are related, these residual interdependencies offer unique opportunities for growth and strategic renewal; indeed, it has often been argued that the intersection of different disciplines and their respective thought worlds (Dougherty, 1992) is a potential hotbed for innovation (e.g., Johansson, 2004).

Because interdependent innovation—defined as the joint development and implementation of a new product or service by two or more product divisions of a multibusiness firm—is characterized by inconsistency with formal structure, social structure is paramount. We highlight two important roles played by social structure that, absent senior leadership agency, collude to undermine interdependent innovation: emergence and execution. Intraorganizational social networks provide a medium for individuals from disparate parts of the organization to discover and initiate creative new ideas for collaboration across divisional boundaries; they also facilitate the interdivisional coordination necessary to take these ideas and bring them into reality. However, the very network structures that support the discovery and initiation of interdependent innovation undermine their implementation.

Given these self-limiting informal dynamics, we propose an evolutionary approach to interdependent innovation (see Burgelman's, 1991 use of this metaphor for strategic change). In the context of the senior team's overarching aspiration (Bower, 1970; Rotemberg and Saloner, 2000; Siggelkow and Rivkin, 2006), a variety of interdependent innovation initiatives are generated autonomously through the creative initiative of boundary spanning individuals. From this pool of variation, corporate executives proactively select a few innovations as strategic and support their implementation not via formal structural reorganization but rather through hybrid social networks and sustained senior management attention. These hybrid social structures consist of both cross-divisional information brokerage, needed to identify possible collaborations, and pockets of cross-divisional cohesion, needed to implement them.

Where business unit innovation is driven primarily by formal structural changes, we suggest that interunit innovations are driven primarily via social networks. We argue that interdependent innovation is an important form of corporate-level exploration that takes place in the context of the firm's simultaneously exploiting the stand-alone strategies of its existing lines of business. We conclude with the observation that interdependent innovation is a potentially valuable, but underutilized, source of growth and strategic renewal and with a discussion of the implications of this observation for theory and research on top management teams, organizational design, intraorganizational social networks, and diversification.

Interdependent innovation as corporate-level exploration

Sustained organizational performance depends not only on short-term growth, but also on a firm's ability to explore new possibilities (March, 1991). Exploitation involves learning that strengthens and extends the core business by improving efficiency, reinforcing execution, and refining the existing business model. In contrast, exploration of new domains of knowledge is critical to innovation and organizational adaptation, but is inherently more uncertain and the benefits more distant (March, 1991). A firm's ability to balance exploration with exploitation is vital to its long-term survival and growth in the face of changing environments and technologies (Benner and Tushman, 2003; March, 1991; Tushman and Smith, 2002) and is a source of dynamic capabilities (Teece, Pisano, and Shuen, 1997). Collaboration across divisional boundaries to develop new products or services jointly—what we term interdependent innovation—provides multibusiness firms with unique opportunities for exploration.

A range of formal structural solutions has been proposed to attend to the challenges associated with the explore/exploit dilemma (Dunbar and Starbuck, 2006). Scholars have hypothesized (Tushman and O'Reilly, 1996) and found empirical support for (He and Wong, 2004; Tushman *et al.*, 2005) the existence of ambidextrous organizations that successfully manage both exploration and exploitation. Ambidextrous organizations are marked by sharp structural differentiation of exploratory and exploitative units with targeted integration at the top management level (O'Reilly and Tushman, 2004). Others have argued for organization designs that switch between contrasting designs (e.g., Brown and Eisenhardt, 1997; Duncan, 1976; Siggelkow and Levinthal, 2003), while still others have suggested that matrix designs or other formal structural overlays might enable exploratory innovation (e.g., Clark and Wheelwright, 1992; Miles and Snow, 1978; Nadler and Tushman, 1997).

The literature has resulted in important insights into the dynamics of exploration and exploitation, but there remain important unresolved issues. First, the existing literature has focused primarily on managing the tension between exploration and exploitation at the function, project, or business unit levels of analysis (for a recent review, see Dunbar and Starbuck, 2006). For example, in the ambidextrous organizational form, exploratory and exploitative products are developed within a single business unit, leveraging the existing skills and resources at the disposal of its general manager (Tushman *et al.*, 2005); little research has explored streams of innovation at the corporate level. Although some scholars have argued that a benefit of the multidivision corporation is its recombinant potential (Galunic and Eisenhardt, 2001; Helfat and Eisenhardt, 2004), few have directly examined the dynamics of recombining the corporation's diverse resources for cross-line-of-business innovation (cf. Martin and Eisenhardt, 2003).

Second, the existing search literature has implicitly focused on search for new technologies (Katila and Ahuja, 2002), strategies (Tripsas and Gavetti, 2000) or organizational configurations (Levinthal, 1997) outside the scope of

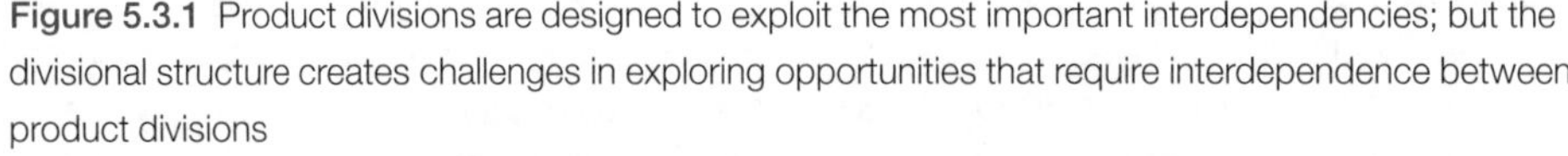

Figure 5.3.1 Product divisions are designed to exploit the most important interdependencies; but the divisional structure creates challenges in exploring opportunities that require interdependence between product divisions

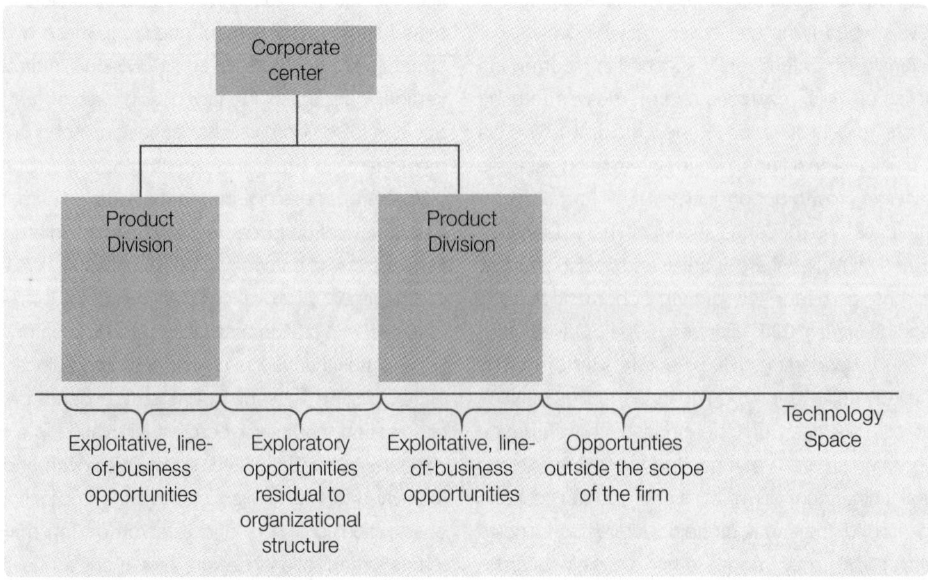

the current organization (see Figure [5.3.1]). The tradition dates back to seminal work at the Carnegie school (Cyert and March, 1963; Simon, 1945), which argued that problemistic search, triggered and perpetuated by failure to achieve goals, should begin locally and expand outward. For managers trying to solve the problem of continual growth, this heuristic focuses managerial attention at, or beyond, the boundaries of the firm. Indeed, most of the strategic management research on diversification assumes that new businesses will be outside the scope of the existing businesses (e.g., Montgomery and Wernerfelt, 1988). By contrast, innovation that occurs through recombination of resources already resident in the firm—what we refer to as interdependent innovation—receives scant attention in the extant literature.

Third, the literature on coordination has focused almost exclusively on the roles of formal organizational structure (e.g., Galbraith, 1973, 1994; Nadler and Tushman, 1988) and incentives (e.g., Kaplan and Henderson, 2005; Prendergast, 1999). Scholars of organization theory and organizational economics have developed a substantial body of theory and empirical evidence about—and firms have become increasingly sophisticated practitioners of—horizontal structures and collaborative incentives. Nevertheless, firms continue to struggle to create new products that recombine knowledge from disparate parts of the firm. Although both formal structure and incentives are indeed important, this literature is undersocialized; it has both underemphasized the role of informal social structure in enabling cross-divisional innovation and underspecified the role of corporate leaders in creating the context for interdependent innovation.

Multidivisional organization design: the inevitability of residual interdependence

Ever since Barnard (1938) distinguished between formal and informal structures, the organization design literature has focused primarily on formal organizational structure. In the pre-Chandlerian world of the early 20th century, firms tended to be formally organized according to function (McCann and Galbraith, 1980), with managers of sales, marketing and R&D departments all reporting to the chief executive. The multidivisional form, by contrast, is characterized by departmentalization according to purpose[1] (McCann and Galbraith, 1980), with the chief executive ceding operational authority to a series of semiautonomous divisional heads, each fully responsible for achieving her own division's purpose, and accordingly, accountable for its profit and loss (Friesen and Mills, 1989). Corporate managers play an important role in monitoring and providing incentives for operating divisions (Jensen and Meckling, 1976); prioritizing resource allocation decisions (Bower, 1970), performing strategic planning (Ansoff, 1965), and managing corporate culture (Schein, 1985) but cannot interfere with divisions' operations without 'thoroughly corrupting' the multidivisional form (Williamson, 1975:148). Thus, in contrast with the interdependence inherent in the functional organization, the multidivisional form explicitly makes divisions conditionally autonomous (Thompson, 1967).

The benefits of the multidivisional form have been well-documented in both the industrial organization economics and organization theory literatures: it reduces the cognitive load on boundedly rational general managers in complex environments and thus helps to solve the information processing problem in large, complex firms (Chandler, 1962, 1990). Separation of operational authority from strategy-making offers benefits for both divisional managers and the corporate parent. For operating managers, the multidivision form 'favors goal pursuit and least-cost behavior,' (Williamson, 1975) increasing their accountability by measuring profitability at a more disaggregated level (Simons, 2005). For corporate managers, the multidivision form reduces the cognitive load and acts as a 'miniature capital market,' increasing the efficiency with which scarce resources are allocated (Williamson, 1975). But the multidivisional form is hardly a panacea for performance and growth in large firms. While recognizing its benefits, some scholars have also critiqued the M-form, arguing that as a result of decentralization, corporate managers lose their intimate familiarity with the operations of the firm's various businesses (Hill and Hoskisson, 1987). As a result, they measure and evaluate divisional performance based primarily on financial objectives, which promote risk-aversion and a short-term orientation that undermine innovation and long-term performance (Hoskisson and Hitt, 1988).

While the economics and strategic management literatures have focused largely on what benefits and problems the multidivisional form offers, the organization theory literature has asked how managers in multidivision firms should divide the work of a firm, establish roles, and create the firm's formal structure. Decades of organization design research suggest that firms should design their organizational structures to minimize coordination costs between actors whose tasks are interdependent. Task interdependence was implicit in the literature as long ago as Adam Smith's (1776) work on the division of labor in a pin factory; Durkheim (1893) was perhaps the first to study it directly, suggesting that task interdependence resulting from the division of labor in society creates organic solidarity among workers. But March and Simon (1958) were among the earliest scholars to identify task interdependence as a critical

[1] A division's 'purpose' may be defined by the type of product it sells or by its geographic focus.

challenge of organization design. Building on the notion that task interdependence emerges as actors divide work through specialization, March and Simon argue that interdependence is problematic—and requires costly coordination devices—due to the ubiquitous presence of variability. Thompson deepened our understanding of the nature of task interdependence by discerning a spectrum of complexity—from pooled, to sequential and reciprocal—and suggesting that each type requires successively more complex coordination devices (Thompson, 1967).

Based on the foundation laid by Thompson (1967) and elaborated by Van de Ven, Delbecq and Koenig (1976), organization theorists have argued that managers choose organizational structure to minimize the costs of coordinating across interdependent units. Grouping decisions are based on a logic of maximizing the interdependencies within units and minimizing the interdependence between units, placing the most highly interdependent units, who have the greatest need to coordinate, into common divisions (Nadler and Tushman, 1997).[2] Residual interdependencies—those left over after the firm has organized around its most strategic interdependencies—are handled through lateral linking mechanisms that overlay the formal hierarchy (Galbraith, 1973).

Such an approach is highly effective at promoting exploitation of core divisional strategies, but squanders combinative innovation opportunities; cross-line-of-business innovations are either not seen or not well-executed. Conversely, organizations that are able to proactively enact interdependence between conditionally autonomous product divisions stand to gain both short-term benefits, in the form of new revenue streams, and long-term benefits, in the form of greater adaptability. By recombining resources from multiple divisions, interdependent innovation takes strategic advantage of residual interdependence that exists between autonomous business units to explore new opportunities, one way of enacting the cooperative M-form organization (Hill, Hitt, and Hoskisson, 1992).

In response to the challenge of coordinating the actions of autonomous product divisions, scholars have emphasized the importance of two primary factors: formal structure and incentives. Organization theorists have argued that when higher-priority coordination requirements prevent the joining of interdependent groups, organizations create either rules to regulate boundary-spanning relations or formal linking structures (Thompson, 1967); numerous formal organizational structures such as heavyweight teams (Clark and Wheelwright, 1992) or matrix designs (Galbraith, 1994) seek to build bridges across divisional boundaries and enable the management of residual interdependence. Organizational economists, on the other hand, have emphasized the role of incentives. Indeed, theory and empirical evidence show that incentives exert a powerful influence on the behavior of organizational actors. Firms' choice of incentive programs impact organizational outcomes at multiple levels of analysis, including individual productivity and motivation (Alchian and Demsetz, 1972; Roy, 1952), the ability of teams to work together effectively (Wageman, 1995), and the realization of cross-divisional collaboration (Kretschmer and Puranam, 2004). While scholars working within each of these literatures have made important steps toward explaining coordination, organizations are still largely unable to successfully execute innovations that cross business unit boundaries. These domains of inquiry can be complemented and extended with research on the social structure of intraorganizational collaboration (Galbraith, 2006; Kleinbaum and Tushman, 2005).

Indeed, formal structures and incentives are not independent of social structures and recent field research argues for an integration of these formal and informal mechanisms of coordination. In her inductive theory of relational coordination, Gittell (2005) argues that coordination requires not only shared goals, which can be achieved through alignment of formal structures and incentives, but also shared knowledge and mutual respect, achievement of which requires social relations. As we focus our theory on social structure, we nevertheless assume that all three levers—incentives, formal structures, and social structures—are important in achieving interdivisional coordination and, indeed, can be mutually reinforcing.

Although the multidivision organizational form offers substantial benefits associated with line of business focus, these benefits also bring unintended consequences associated with cross-line-of-business innovation. As Simon (1962) argued, hierarchical systems are marked by dense interactions within subunits and weaker linkages between subunits. In the context of the multidivision organizational form, we term these linkages that cross divisional boundaries as residual interdependence because, by construction, they take a lower priority in the design of the formal organizational structure. Residual interdependence is, in a very real sense, the residue of organization design.

Intraorganizational social networks and strategic interdependence

A central conclusion of the social networks literature is that networks of relationships are an important source of information and power to actors in organizations, as well as in market and interorganizational settings. Most research on

[2] This logic is also seen in the literature on product design (Ulrich and Eppinger, 1995) and the link between product design and organizational architecture (Baldwin and Clark, 2000; Henderson and Clark, 1990).

intraorganizational networks has focused on the benefits and constraints conferred upon individuals by their position within the network. For example, intraorganizational networks provide individuals with informal sponsorship (Kanter, 1977) and task-based support (Kotter, 1982); social support and instrumental access (Ibarra, 1992); career mobility (Higgins, 2005), and political information about important organizational dynamics (Krackhardt and Porter, 1986). Managers with networks rich in structural holes—which arise when individuals tied to a focal actor are not tied to each other—have been shown to advance in their careers more rapidly (Burt, 1992), to receive better variable compensation (Burt, 2000) due to greater access to the information and control benefits of the intraorganizational social network, and to be more adaptable to changes in their task environments (Gargiulo and Benassi, 2000). Additionally, a 'behavioral orientation toward connecting people in one's social network,' makes individuals more likely to be involved in innovative activity, though it may or may not increase the innovative output of the firm (Obstfeld, 2005). In short, the structural holes perspective emphasizes intraorganizational networks as the 'pipes' through which information and control flow in organizations (see Podolny, 2001 for the use of that metaphor to describe the role of networks in markets).

Another school of thought within the social networks literature suggests that the primary benefit of intraorganizational networks lies in their role in enforcement of organizational norms and practices (Coleman, 1988). Developing a notion of social capital, Coleman argues that network closure—the degree to which a group of people is densely interconnected by a web of strong ties—provides a mechanism for the monitoring and control of individual behavior by the network, thereby enforcing expectations and norms and reducing variability and uncertainty. In theorizing about social capital, Coleman's school of thought aims to bridge the gap between economists' under-socialized view and sociologists' over-socialized view of individual choice. And indeed, empirical research confirms that under some conditions, network closure contributes to the productivity of teams (Reagans and Zuckerman, 2001).

The network closure perspective is rooted in socio-metric work on the social dynamics among triads of actors. This research begins with the observation that when two people share a common contact, they are likely, through that mutual contact, to come into contact with one another. From the perspective of the focal actor, our contacts tend to become increasingly interconnected (Homans, 1951; Simmel, 1902). Theory (Davis and Leinhardt, 1972) and evidence (Khurana, 2002; Obstfeld, 2005) suggest that social structures tend to become increasingly connected over time (Figure [5.3.3]).

The network closure perspective on social capital offers a different view from the structural holes perspective and recent scholarship has tried to reconcile these divergent views to determine which network structure optimizes individual performance. Burt argues that structural holes are the source of network benefits while network closure can help to '[realize] the value buried in the holes' (Burt, 2000:410). Podolny and Baron (1997) argue that the network structure that will be most advantageous is contingent on the content of network ties; when ties convey resources, brokerage is advantageous, but when ties convey normative expectations or social identity, closure is advantageous. Gargiulo and Benassi (2000) suggest that cohesive networks may be more useful when the task structure is constant, but that brokerage structure may be more adaptable to changes in task structure. All of these researchers take some measure of individual performance as their dependent variable, so whatever their differences, adherents to both perspectives share a common focus on the network advantages conferred upon individuals by their positions in the social structure.

Relatively few scholars have directly studied the benefits that intraorganizational social networks bring to the organization itself. Nohria and Ghoshal suggest that underlying the literature's focus on individual-level outcomes, there may be an assumption that 'the social capital of its members aggregates to the social capital of the entire organization' (Nohria and Ghoshal, 1997:154). Early work on the organizational benefits of intraorganizational networks developed within the research and development management literature. Allen (1977) studied the role of intraorganizational communication networks in a research and development department, showing that increased communication between R&D groups increases R&D effectiveness. In a series of follow-on studies, Tushman and colleagues (Tushman, 1977, 1979; Tushman and Katz, 1980; Tushman and Scanlan, 1981) developed a more fine-grained understanding of the network structure needed to increase R&D effectiveness, finding that individuals tend to specialize in spanning particular organizational boundaries (i.e., boundaries between labs within the R&D division; between the R&D division and the rest of the organization; or between the organization and its environment) and that the degree of interunit communication needed and the structure of the communication network are contingent on the nature of the laboratory's tasks. More recent research has shown that intraorganizational social networks benefit organizations by moderating intergroup conflict (Labianca, Brass, and Gray, 1998; Nelson, 1989); by promoting positive relations and task coordination between groups (Ancona and Caldwell, 1992); by providing timely access to information about prospective exchange partners (Mizruchi and Steams, 2001); and by increasing the quality of ideas (Burt, 2004).

Since the early research in the R&D management literature, relatively few scholars have studied the ability of social networks to coordinate interdependence between formally defined organizational sub-units. Even Galbraith, who cites direct communication as the simplest and most effective form of lateral relation, generally focuses on more formal approaches, such as designated liaison positions or cross-divisional teams, only recently recognizing the importance of informal structure (Galbraith, 1973, 1994, 2006). The focus on formal structure is not without reason: the social network often emerges to correspond closely with the formal structure of the organization. Particularly in large organizations, individuals tend to develop network ties with those others with whom they have work-related contact. Formal organizational structure has been shown to both seed and constrain the formation of social ties by organizational members (Han, 1996; Henderson and Clark, 1990; Ibarra, 1995). Burt argues that 'opinion and behavior are more homogeneous within than between groups' (Burt, 2004:349). Nelson puts it more forcefully: 'strong ties between groups do not occur naturally,' (Nelson, 1989:397–398); the social networks in many organizations tend to be strongly correlated with the formal organizational structure (Krackhardt and Stern, 1988). Burt referred to this phenomenon as 'institutional holes' and argued that individuals can broker relations across institutional holes: 'The manager's network is a social construction laid on top of the firm's bureaucratic structure, and there are holes in the bureaucratic structure that can be advantageous' (Burt, 1992:148–9).

A few researchers have explicitly studied the ability of informal structure to manage residual interdependence by examining the consequences of cross-divisional social networks for various organizational outcomes. The work on R&D labs (Tushman, 1977; Tushman and Scanlan, 1981) highlighted the importance of boundary-spanning individuals in gathering information from outside the group, division or organization for innovation. Gould and Fernandez (1989) identified and formally measured several distinct boundary-spanning roles, including the gatekeeper (who collects information from outside and transmits it throughout her unit), the representative (who collects information from her unit and transmits it to the outside) and the liaison (who gathers information from one unit and transmits it to another without being a member of either). In a study of product development in an electronics firm, Hansen (1999) found that network ties serve as conduits for knowledge and, contingent on the degree of fit between tie strength and the type of knowledge being transferred, can speed the product development process.

Joining the organizational literature with the strategic management literature, Tsai (2000) suggests that inter-unit ties seem to be particularly valuable when units are strategically related and have the potential for fruitful collaboration—consistent with research on the collaborative M-form (Hill *et al.*, 1992). Further research suggests that as managers search their organizations for valuable information, such as information about potential collaborations, they tend to rely first on networks of informal relations, even more than relatedness of competences (Casciaro and Lobo, 2006; Hansen and Løvås, 2004). Tsai and Ghoshal (1998) showed that network ties across divisional boundaries in a large, multinational electronics company were positively associated with interdivisional resource exchange and product innovation by the participating division. Similarly, in the context of multinational corporations, Nohria and Ghoshal (1997) suggest that firms perform better when the various national subsidiaries are tightly integrated by a network of boundary-spanning individuals. As managers strive for growth, social networks that span divisional boundaries can provide timely information about potentially beneficial interunit collaborations; can provide referrals for actors to access that information; and can promote interunit coordination and cooperation to better implement those collaborations.

Shaping residual interdependence: an evolutionary model of interdependent innovation

Strategy scholars have distinguished between planned and emergent strategy, suggesting that strategy formulation is conceptually distinct from its implementation. They suggest that planned strategies are those that are developed analytically and realized as intended (Mintzberg and Waters, 1985) and argue that organizational structure is a tool for the implementation of strategy (Chandler, 1962). Indeed, differentiated multidivisional firms often decentralize strategy formulation, with each major product division responsible for developing and implementing its own strategy. As such, coordinated strategic actions are difficult for multidivisional firms to achieve (Eisenmann and Bower, 2000; Quinn, 1978). In the context of decentralized strategies, the exploratory, collaborative opportunities of interdependent innovation are trumped by exploitative actions in autonomous business units.

We suggest that the lost opportunity of interdependent innovation can be captured by activist corporate executives. Far from acting single-handedly (cf. Eisenmann and Bower, 2000), these senior leaders create the context for autonomous interdependent innovation and, in turn, proactively select a few as strategic. Their action reduces the set of possible residual interdependencies into a subset of strategic interdependencies. These senior leaders then proactively shape interdivisional social networks and structural overlays in order to give those selected interdependent innovations a chance to survive. We suggest, then, an evolutionary approach to interdependent innovation where variation, selection, and retention processes are shaped by senior leaders in the context of strong line of business designs (for a summary of the model, see Figure [5.3.2]).

In the evolution of interdependent innovation, variation occurs through decentralized agency, as actors throughout the organization use their social networks to explore possible collaborations. This exploration requires search processes that identify capabilities or resources in another division that could fruitfully be combined with capabilities or resources resident in the focal division. Exploration may take the form of problemistic search (Hansen, 1999; March and Simon, 1958); may arise serendipitously through normal work or casual interactions (Perry-Smith and Shalley, 2003); may be the result of timely referrals by third party information brokers (Burt, 1992, 2000); or may arise in response to the senior team's strategic aspirations (Rotemberg and Saloner, 2000). Whatever the form, this variation phase is marked by autonomous strategic activity by decentralized actors working together with individuals from other divisions of the organization to develop new products or to better serve customer needs (Burgelman, 1991). This period of variation is influenced by actors' perceptions about what kinds of projects are most likely to appeal to corporate managers (Bower, 1970). This autonomous search, if left unchecked, is also associated with partisan actors, self-serving political behaviors, conflicting agendas, and political deadlocks (Hargrave and Van de Ven, 2006; Siggelkow and Rivkin, 2006).

Once particular ideas emerge, agency shifts from a decentralized mode, in which autonomous actors use their social networks as means to pursue ends of their choosing, to a more centralized mode, as corporate management actively decides which opportunities are most promising and are most consistent with the firm's overall corporate strategy. It is through this selection process that some opportunities that were residual to the organization's design are enacted as strategic. In making these selection decisions, corporate management must consider not only the market potential and technical feasibility of the opportunity, but also the degree to which the potential collaborators are likely to work together effectively, given their respective structures as well as the possibility and potential costs associated with the interdependent innovation becoming a distraction from the core exploitative business (Smith and Tushman, 2007).

Implementation of interdependent innovation involves jointly developing and marketing the innovation based on the resources of multiple divisions with a minimum of disruptive interdivisional conflict. A variety of mechanisms may be used to promote retention. Formal structures and incentives are often used; but because implementation of these innovations is, by construction, residual to the organization's design, social structures are critical in assuring the continued collaboration and sharing of information across divisional boundaries. We develop a set of ideas on the social network conditions under which interdependent innovation can be shaped for the development of new products or services that combine knowledge, skills or resources from multiple divisions of a large firm, allowing firms to explore at the corporate level in the context of business unit exploitation.

Effects of social networks on initiating and executing interdependent innovation

Consistent with the literature on brokerage and closure, our theory focuses on two attributes of social structure that bridges formal structural gaps between business units: the strength of interunit ties and the amount of interunit brokerage. Interunit tie strength refers to the average strength of the interpersonal relations that link actors in one unit with actors in another. Strong ties offer the benefits of fine-grained information transfer (Uzzi, 1997) and enforcement of organizational norms and practices, thus reducing the uncertainty that inheres in exchange (Coleman, 1988;

Figure 5.3.2 Overall evolutionary model of interdependent innovation

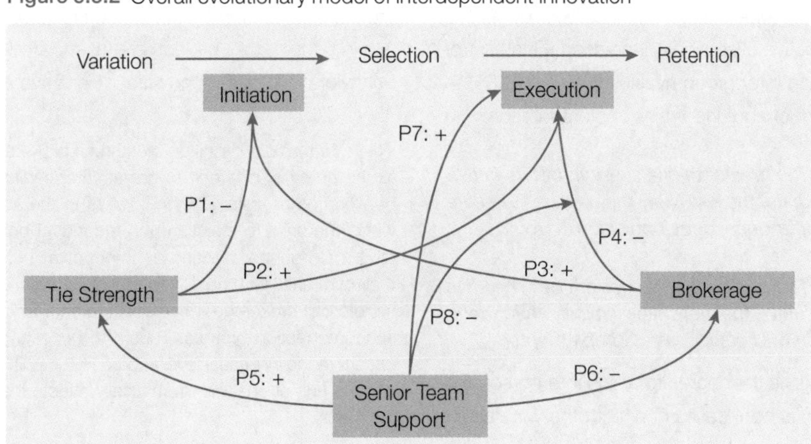

Hansen, Podolny, and Pfeffer, 2001). But strong ties can also lead to problems of over-embeddedness because they are associated with excessive trust and reliance on local partners (Gulati, 1995); over-embeddedness reduces the scope of search and 'insulate[s] actors from information that exists beyond their network' (Uzzi, 1997). Additionally, because maintaining ties is costly (Burt, 1992) and strong ties are more costly to maintain than weak ties (Hansen, 1999; Hansen *et al.*, 2001), weak ties are a more efficient means of search.

In predicting the emergence of interdependent innovation, the benefits of tacit and fine-grained information transfer are relatively unimportant. Conversely, as divisions search for opportunities for interdependent innovation, efficiency of search and broad access to information will be of substantial benefit in discovering novel and useful ideas (Burt, 2004). For this reason, we propose that strong interunit ties will be detrimental to the search process.

Strong lies between two units reduce the efficiency of search for interdependent innovation; but conditioning on the decision to engage in interdependent innovation, strong interunit ties offer substantial benefits for implementation. First, when implementing interdependent innovation, the benefits of fine-grained and tacit information transfer more than compensate for the additional cost of maintaining strong ties (Hansen, 1999; Uzzi, 1997). Strong ties are particularly helpful as organizational actors struggle to navigate the unfamiliar formal structure of their partner division and identify the people whose cooperation is necessary for the interdependent innovation; that knowledge of organizational structure and politics is more likely to traverse the interdivisional boundary through a strong tie than through a weak one. Second, high interunit tie strength is associated with pockets of cohesion in the interunit social networks. This cohesion enables the behavior of individuals to be monitored by the social structure, reinforcing expectations and norms and increasing trust that others will honor their obligations (Coleman, 1988). To the extent that high interunit tie strength increases interunit trust, the uncertainty inherent in interdependent innovation is reduced and the probability of effective execution is increased. Finally, strong ties help to reduce inter-group rivalries (Nelson, 1989) that could lead to conflict and undermine implementation.

Proposition 1: The greater the tie strength between two organizational units, the less likely they will be to initiate interdependent innovation

Proposition 2: The greater the tie strength between two organizational units, the more likely an interdependent innovation will be successfully implemented

Interunit brokerage is the degree to which interpersonal ties that cross divisional boundaries connect otherwise disconnected actors, providing the focal unit with access to nonredundant information that originates in the other unit.[3] The network literature on brokerage traces its roots to the work of Burt (1992), who defines brokerage as the degree to which an individual's contacts are disconnected from one another in the social structure, conferring upon the broker both information and control. In the context of the initiation of interdependent innovation, interunit brokers are particularly important for conveying information across the firm's formal boundaries (Tushman, 1977); indeed, access to novel information is almost definitional of brokerage relations. Just as individuals obtain information that is more diverse and less redundant when they engage in brokerage relationships (Burt, 1992), divisions also obtain more diverse, less redundant information about another division when brokerage relations span the interdivisional boundary. When a high degree of interunit brokerage exists, each unit will have access to a broad range of information about what capabilities reside in the other division; the greater the awareness of what capabilities reside in another division, the more likely it is that opportunities for collaboration will be discovered. In contrast, when interunit brokerage is low, ties will tend to offer access to redundant information; even if there are many ties that provide extensive search, multiple searchers will discover the same capabilities in the other division and, therefore, will discover fewer of the collaborative opportunities that may exist.

While brokerage relations increase each division's ability to access information from another division, and thereby increase the likelihood that the divisions will discover opportunities to collaborate, a social structure of extensive interunit brokerage also accentuates intraorganizational politics as multiple innovation champions, cliques and coalitions vie for scarce human and financial resources even as they compete for limited executive attention (Pfeffer, 1992; Siggelkow and Rivkin, 2006). Such information brokers may enact that brokerage divisively, by seeking to divide actors for one's own benefit, or by playing a more cooperative, linking role (Burt, 1992; Obstfeld, 2005). Whether the actions of brokers are duplicitous or integrative, numerous actors each championing their own project are associated with coalitional behaviors that stunt innovation (Hargrave and Van de Ven,

[3] Note that our definition of interunit brokerage does not refer to the ability of one unit to act as intermediary in the relations between other units. Rather, it refers to the ability of individuals within the units to maintain non-redundant contacts across the divisional boundary, acting as information brokers that provide their own units with novel information. A focal unit with substantial interunit brokerage with respect to an alter unit will have many such information brokers. Thus, the benefits of brokerage that occurs at the individual level accrue to the unit. This subtle difference in unit of analysis dramatically affects the interpretation of the theory.

2006). Such brokerage behaviors may be effective ways to enhance individual careers, but they generate coalitional behaviors that erode the interpersonal trust needed to achieve effective interunit collaboration (Gulati, 1995).

Proposition 3: The greater the degree of brokerage between two organizational units, the more likely they will be to initiate interdependent innovation

Proposition 4: The greater the degree of brokerage between two organizational units, the less likely an interdependent innovation will be successfully implemented

These propositions suggest that high interunit tie strength will be detrimental to the emergence of varied interdependent innovations, but that once an innovation gets selected, high interunit tie strength becomes a substantial asset. Conversely, interunit brokerage is beneficial to search processes that lead to variation, but become a liability following selection. Taken together, these hypotheses suggest an explanation for the dilemma about why firms are generally so unsuccessful at developing interdependent innovation: the social structure needed to generate innovation variants is different from the social structure needed to implement them. The paradox is evident: even when cross-divisional initiatives are supported by appropriate formal organizational structures and collaborative incentives, the initiatives that emerge may lack the informal social structure they need to succeed.

The role of corporate leadership: selection and support of interdependent innovation

The existence of multiple interdependent innovation attempts is associated with heightened potential for cross-unit coalitions, cliques, and interunit politics. In this political context, corporate executives can exert strategic choice (Child, 1972), selecting from the varied interdependent innovation options those opportunities that deserve strategic attention. Once the focus of senior management attention and oversight, those selected innovations—and their associated residual interdependencies—are more sharply attended to and become more sensible (Dutton and Ashford, 1993; Gilbert, 2005; Weick, Sutcliffe, and Obstfeld, 2005). Senior leadership support and attention focuses social activity around boundary spanning individuals, reshaping the firm's social structure to provide the information and political support to implement interdependent innovation. It is through this reshaping that an organization whose social structure previously enabled the initiation of interdependent innovations can come to enable their execution as well.

In particular, once an interdependent innovation receives the backing of senior managers—a clear signal that they consider the interdependence between those divisions to be important—actors in each participating division will feel a strong, albeit informal, incentive to connect with actors in partner divisions (Pfeffer and Salancik, 1978). This motivation may stem from innate curiosity or loyalty to the organization, but is also rooted in career concerns and hopes for future advancement (Gibbons and Murphy, 1992). This incentive may lead to the creation of new ties spanning the boundary between divisions. But more likely, it will lead actors to seek to expand contact with the partner division by taking advantage of already-existing ties. Those actors who play boundary-spanning roles will become increasingly important, as their colleagues will turn to them for help in connecting with actors in the partner division. This demand for cross-unit contact will result in triadic closure (Davis and Leinhardt, 1972; Homans, 1951; Simmel, 1902), as information brokers introduce their local contacts to their primary contacts in the partner division and, conversely, as they meet the contacts of their primary contacts (Figure [5.3.3]). In this way, the support and attention of senior managers leads to an iterative process of triadic closures that enables direct interunit contact to radiate outward from the original boundary-spanning relation, creating a more cohesive social structure across the divisional boundary. This more cohesive social structure, in contrast to the social structure marked by weak brokerage relations, enables the successful implementation of interdependent innovation.

Proposition 5: Senior team selection of and support for an interdependent innovation will strengthen the weak ties that join partner units, increasing the likelihood of successful implementation (see Proposition 2)

Proposition 6: Senior team selection of and support for an interdependent innovation will decrease the degree of brokerage between partner units, increasing the likelihood of successful implementation (see Proposition 4)

In addition to their informal influence on the search and interaction decisions of actors throughout the organization, senior management holds one important formal responsibility: appointment of actors to linking roles. Which actors get appointed to key linking roles is important in both a symbolic and a practical sense (Pfeffer, 1981). Research on product development focuses on the importance of selecting 'heavyweight' actors to occupy formal linking roles across interdependent units (Clark and Wheelwright, 1992; Galbraith, 1973).

The product innovation literature emphasizes structure and process in determining whether a given actor provides sufficient gravity for a role. We suggest that the 'weight' of an actor must be considered in the context of the particular task; actors who are well-connected in the focal divisions—rather than actors who have the most authority in a more

Figure 5.3.3 Triadic closure makes brokerage networks more cohesive

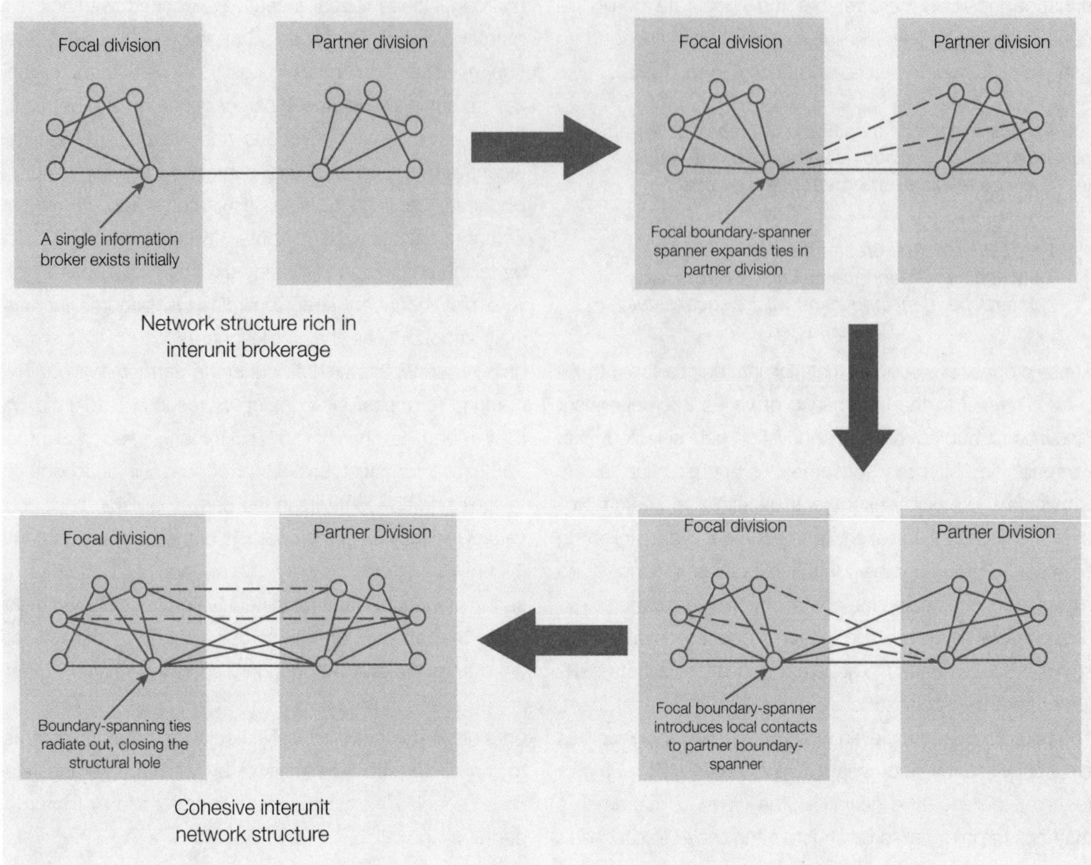

global sense—may be best-suited to occupy formal boundary-spanning roles because they are best able to promote effective contact between actors in both divisions. Thus, by deliberately choosing actors based, in part, on their network structures, the senior team can explicitly 'seed' the closure of the interunit social structure for successful implementation.

Proposition 7: Senior team appointment of actors who are well-connected in both collaborating divisions to formal linking roles will increase the likelihood of successful implementation

The senior leadership team's support for particular interdependent innovations also moderates the relationship between social structure and execution. Whereas the uncertainty that marks the preselection period tends to result in unadjudicated political behavior, as various actors promote their own interdependent innovations, senior team selection of particular innovations eliminates this uncertainty, resulting in dramatically reduced politics and greater cooperation. Senior management's attention to these selected interdependent innovations and to their associated interdependencies creates the strategic focus and political context where boundary-spanning activities take on a collective, integrative character (Allen, 1969; Obstfeld, 2005) as opposed to a careerist, self-interested character (Burt, 1992).

Proposition 8: In the context of strong senior team support, the negative effect of interunit brokerage on the likelihood of successful implementation of interdependent innovation will be attenuated

Corporate executives play a pivotal role in creating contexts that balance induced, exploitative, line of business behaviors with emergent, exploratory behaviors of autonomous internal product champions (Burgelman, 2002; Gilbert, 2005). Where multiple champions trigger political stalemates, the selection by senior leaders of a few interdependent innovations reduces uncertainty and associated political behaviors. These actions by senior leaders reduce the number of interdependent innovation options through selection, sending clear signals to the organization about which initiatives are strategically important and which are not. This more strategically and politically clear context creates the conditions for social networks to reshape in favor of the execution of targeted interdependent innovations.

Finally, whereas these social dynamics are complex among members of two product divisions, as our theory has implicitly assumed, large, multi-divisional firms often have many product divisions. When interdependent innovation requires collaboration from multiple product divisions, or when divisions are particularly dissimilar in their core technologies, these dynamics will be exacerbated.

Conclusion

Growth is a central challenge for firms (e.g., Gulati, 2004), one that only gets accentuated as firms get larger (Christensen, 1997) and older (Hannan and Freeman, 1984; Sørensen and Stuart, 2000). Exploitation crowds out exploration (Benner and Tushman, 2003; March, 1991) such that further growth is often achieved through crisis, strategic renewal, alliances, and/or acquisition (e.g., Gulati, 1995; Hurst, 1995; Tushman and Romanelli, 1985). We argue that large, established firms need not necessarily look outside their boundaries for new opportunities to grow and explore. In related diversified firms, an alternate source of growth and exploration exists in interdependent innovation that relies on the recombination of disparate technologies, skills and resources already resident inside the firm in service of new products. However, interdependent innovation is extremely difficult to manage precisely because the structure of the multidivisional organization—both formal and informal—is designed to manage the primary interdependence within divisions, not the residual interdependence between divisions. Although collaborative incentives and formal organizational structures are useful and well-studied ways to manage interdependent innovation, they can be complemented by corporate leadership actions to shape and leverage interdivisional social networks.

We suggest that among the central roles of corporate executives is to shape the firm's context to facilitate the emergence of autonomous interdependent innovations and to then select from these a few strategic interdependent innovations. Once these residual interdependencies are transformed into strategic interdependencies, the leadership team can, in turn, reshape the social structure to build bridges across divisional boundaries. In this fashion, a crucial role of corporate executives is to balance line of business exploitative behaviors with exploratory cross-line-of-business experimentation. Ironically, then, the context most antithetical to extant theories of organization design—managing strategic interdependence across divisional boundaries—appears to be the most tenable approach to shaping interdependent innovation in service of proactive corporate growth and strategic renewal.

The corporate leadership team's role is particularly central in shaping interdependent innovation. The corporate team both shapes and drives business unit exploitative action even as it creates the conditions to advance exploratory interdependent innovation. Our evolutionary approach to growth through interdependent innovation involves several domains of executive action. Corporate executives stimulate variation by setting an emotionally engaging, broad strategic aspiration that stimulates autonomous, entrepreneurial actions of independent boundary spanning individuals. This source of innovative variation is not induced by corporate fiat, but rather it is generated through autonomous action of individual information brokers across independent business units.

But effective variation is also associated with power, politics, cliques, and coalitional behavior. Thus a critical role of the corporate team is to select from these interdependent innovation variants those few strategic opportunities. This selection action by senior leaders takes multiple instances of residual interdependence and enacts a few instances of strategic interdependence. Once a few strategic interdependent innovations are selected, the senior management team then shapes a fundamentally different set of social networks—cross-line-of-business networks exhibiting elements of both brokerage and cohesion—to execute the selected cross-line-of-business opportunities. In the absence of senior management selection, by contrast, the self-defeating dynamics of brokerage-based search, followed by coalitional behavior without the benefits of pockets of trust that result from cohesion in the social network, are allowed to undermine interdependent innovation. Thus, this evolutionary model of interdependent innovation puts a premium on the senior team's ability to create the conditions for interdependent innovation variants to arise, to be able to exert strategic choice from these variants, and to, in turn, shape social networks to execute the selected interdependent innovations.

These actions to shape interdependent innovation take place in the context of simultaneously managing the business units to execute their existing line of business strategies. These dual and inconsistent roles of business unit exploitation as well as cross-unit exploration put a premium on the corporate team's ability to attend to and deal with fundamentally inconsistent strategic agendas. These contrasting strategic agendas require that the team have sufficiently complex cognitive models that they are able to attend to and deal with contradictory strategic objectives (Hambrick, 1994; Smith and Tushman, 2005). To the extent that informal interactions between organizationally disparate actors become a distraction that undermines performance in core businesses, interdependent innovations will succeed only at tremendous cost for the firm as a whole.

Further, this point of view puts a premium on conceptualizing several distinct types of strategic interdependencies and organizational designs to execute those interdependencies. Senior teams must be able to attend to strategic interdependencies associated with exploiting line of business outcomes as well as exploratory interdependencies associated with cross-line-of-business innovation. In the context of these distinct types of strategic interdependencies, senior teams link strategic interdependencies to the fundamental form of their organization (Henderson and Clark, 1990) even as they influence social networks to execute strategic interdependencies across autonomous business units. Although Thompson focused on task interdependence among organizational units—such as the branch offices of a firm or the operations and maintenance units of an airline (Thompson, 1967:54–55)—in the last decade, few scholars have studied task interdependence at such a macro level (cf. Casciaro, 2003). Research has focused almost exclusively on interpersonal task interdependence or interdependence within teams, across functions, or with alliance partners outside the firm (e.g., Stewart and Barrick, 2000; Wageman, 1995; Wageman and Gordon, 2005). This review suggests a return of the notion of task interdependence at the corporate level of analysis.

This review also suggests that more attention could be fruitfully paid to cross-line-of-business design and the role of senior leaders in creating growth opportunities through cross-line-of-business innovation. We suggest that this source of exploratory growth takes place in the context of line of business exploitation and as such is shaped by senior leaders shaping those contrasting social networks and informal bridge building associated with creating versus executing interdependent innovations. Most fundamentally, it is the primary role of senior leaders to not get caught in what Burgelman (2002) calls strategic vectors rooted in line of business blinders, but rather, to maintain a balance between line of business exploitation and cross-line-of-business exploration. Maintaining such a balance cannot be done by senior executives alone; rather, this theory implies an important role for organizational culture in encouraging managers at all levels to value the dual agendas of exploitation within existing lines of business and cross-line-of-business exploration. Such a culture can help line of business managers to balance these sometimes conflicting agendas by situating them in the context of the long-term performance of the organization and the long-term interests of their own careers (Holmstrom, 1999).

If this evolutionary model of interdependent innovation has merit, then it has implications for at least four areas of theory and research. First, it suggests that the current design work on structures and incentives be complemented with research that explores the role of senior teams in shaping social contexts for interdivisional exploration. These contexts involve shaping contrasting social networks to both explore and, in turn, exploit strategic interdependent innovations. Our evolutionary model of interdependent innovation suggests that senior teams must both select those innovations that are strategic but also proactively reshape social networks as firms move from generating innovation variants to executing a given set of interdependent innovations. But reshaping the social networks to implement an interdependent innovation requires a delicate touch; our theory suggests that wholesale commitment to cohesive networks across divisional boundaries is not only impractical, but potentially perilous to an organization. Cross-divisional ties, when not targeted toward specific interdependent innovations, risk becoming a distraction from core divisional activities. Furthermore, cohesive interunit ties can undermine the information brokerage needed to develop a variety of interdependent innovations to choose from in the future. Rather, the critical task of senior leadership in reshaping the social network is to be highly targeted, involving all those—and only those—people whose formal roles or informal, social structures make them essential to the success of the interdependent innovation. Doing so requires an attention to social dynamics (Krackhardt, 1990) that is seldom demanded of managers, but that is critical to promote the successful implementation of the interdependent innovation, while also maintaining the organization's focus on exploiting core divisional resources and enabling the initiation of new interdependent innovations in the future.

Second, and more generally, our approach suggests that the larger issue of organizational design could be better informed by research on social networks at the corporate level of analysis. This research might focus on the selection and shaping of boundary spanning individuals and the structures that link these key individuals. Who are these individuals, how do they evolve, and do they create networks of gatekeepers in service of interdependent innovation? Are these social networks different for interdependent innovations that differ in terms of the boundaries spanned (i.e., divisional boundaries versus firm boundaries), the number of boundaries spanned, or the complexity of task interdependence?

Third, these ideas on interdependent innovation might also inform the work on diversification (e.g., Ansoff, 1957; Hill and Hoskisson, 1987; Montgomery and Wernerfelt, 1988; Rumelt, 1974; Villalonga, 2004). Scholars have rarely drawn an explicit link between the challenge of successful diversification and the structure of the multidivisional form itself. The multidivision form requires the strategic prioritization of some interdependencies over others, with the high-priority interdependencies contained within divisions; interdependent innovation between divisions is, by construction, the lowest priority. In intensely competitive, highly dynamic environments, these lowest-priority residual interdependencies can be a source of great diversification opportunities. These diversification attempts are extremely difficult to manage precisely because they are the residue of organizational design. The notion of residual interdependence and associated social structures helps inform this diversification work.

The diversification literature examines the sources of benefit that inhere in different types of diversification. Theory suggests that unrelated diversification offers financial benefits (if any benefits at all; see Villalonga, 2004) and should be implemented with a structure of high decentralization and accountability. Related diversification, by contrast, offers benefits of economies of scope, and should be implemented with a structure that is more centralized, allowing corporate managers to play some role in coordinating the actions of autonomous divisions (Hill and Hoskisson, 1987). We suggest that this perspective can be complemeted with greater attention to social structure: in addition to a certain amount of formal centralization, related diversified firms can achieve economies of scope through interdivisional social networks. These networks will, to a limited extent, occur naturally, but must also be proactively managed by corporate leadership.

This theory also contributes to research on the relationship between diversification and innovation. Critics of the multidivisional form have demonstrated a negative relationship between diversification and innovation, with functional form firms and dominant-diversified firms investing substantially more in R&D than related and unrelated diversifiers (Hoskisson and Hitt, 1988). The mechanism they posit for this relationship is based on financial controls and incentives, which promote risk-aversion and short-term orientation in divisional managers (Stonich, 1981). Our theory suggests another possible explanation: as firms become increasingly diversified into a broader range of less-related businesses, divisions have less commonality and, as a result, the number of boundary-spanning social relations lessens, reducing the potential for interdependent innovation.

And fourth, an important direction for research involves the interaction between formal structure and informal structure. The traditional organization design perspective on interdependent innovation involves the creation of formal lateral linking structures, such as cross-divisional teams or liaison roles or the use of matrix structures (Galbraith, 1973). This paper has highlighted the important role of network structure, but, as Barnard (1938) pointed out so long ago, formal structure and network structure are not independent. Future research should empirically examine the endogeneity of formal and social structure, looking at the network structures of individuals involved in such formal lateral structures to determine what kinds of structural positions are most suitable for playing boundary-spanning roles. Additionally, future research should examine the degree to which, and the contingencies under which, formal structure and social structure may be mutually supportive. Theory suggests that formal work relations tend to expand in multiplexity, evolving to incorporate elements of trust, advice, support, or even friendship (McPherson, Smith-Lovin, and Cook, 2001), and furthermore that formal lateral structures, such as task forces, will coalesce into well-functioning teams more quickly and more completely in the context of social relations high in trust (Hackman, 1987). This might be the mechanism to explain why team effectiveness tends to increase over time, at least initially (Allen, 1977). Yet these ideas haven't yet been explored empirically in the context of interdependent innovation.

References

Alchian AA, Demsetz H. 1972. Production, information costs, and economic organization. *American Economic Review* 62(5): 777–795.

Allen TJ. 1969. *Roles in Technical Communication Networks*. MIT Press: Cambridge, MA.

Allen TJ. 1977. *Managing the Flow of Technology: Technology Transfer and the Dissemination of Technological Information within the R&D Organization*. MIT Press: Cambridge, MA.

Ancona DG, Caldwell DF. 1992. Bridging the boundary: external activity and performance in organizational teams. *Administrative Science Quarterly* 37(4): 634–665.

Ansoff HI. 1957. Strategies for diversification. *Harvard Business Review* 35(5): 113–124.

Ansoff HI. 1965. *Corporate Strategy: an Analytic Approach to Business Policy for Growth and Expansion*. McGraw-Hill: New York.

Baldwin CY, Clark KB. 2000. *Design Rules*. MIT Press: Cambridge, MA.

Barnard CI. 1938. *The Functions of the Executive* (30th Anniversary edn). Harvard University Press: Cambridge, MA.

Barnett WP, Carroll GR. 1995. Modeling internal organizational change. *Annual Review of Sociology* 21: 217–236.

Benner MJ. 2004. The incumbent discount: financial institutions and incumbent response to technological change, Wharton working paper: Philadelphia, PA.

Benner MJ, Tushman ML. 2003. Exploitation, exploration, and process management: the productivity dilemma revisited. *Academy of Management Review* 28(2): 238–256.

Bower JL. 1970. *Managing the Resource Allocation Process: A Study of Corporate Planning and Investment* (2nd edn). Graduate School of Business Administration, Harvard University: Boston, MA.

Brown SL, Eisenhardt KM. 1997. The art of continuous change: linking complexity theory and time-paced evolution in relentlessly shifting organizations. *Administrative Science Quarterly* 42(1): 1–34.

Burgelman RA. 1991. Intraorganizational ecology of strategy making and organizational adaptation: theory and field research. *Organization Science* 2(3): 239–262.

Burgelman RA. 2002. Strategy as vector and the inertia of coevolutionary lock-in. *Administrative Science Quarterly* 47(2): 325–357.

Burt RS. 1992. ***Structural Holes: The Social Structure of Competition***. Harvard University Press: Cambridge, MA.

Burt RS. 2000. The network structure of social capital. In ***Research in Organizational Behavior***, Vol. 22, Staw BM, Sutton RI (eds). JAI Press: Greenwich, CT; 345–423.

Burt RS. 2004. Structural holes and good ideas. ***American Journal of Sociology*** 110(2): 349–399.

Campbell A, Goold M. 1999. ***The Collaborative Enterprise: Why Links across the Corporation Often Fail and How to Make Them Work***. Perseus Books: Reading, MA.

Casciaro T. 2003. Determinants of governance structure in alliances: the role of strategic, task and partner uncertainties. ***Industrial and Corporate Change*** 12(6): 1223–1251.

Casciaro T, Lobo MS. 2006. Affective microfoundations of instrumental ties in organizations, Harvard Business School working paper: Boston, MA.

Chandler AD. 1962. ***Strategy and Structure: Chapters in the History of the Industrial Enterprise***. MIT Press: Cambridge, MA.

Chandler AD. 1990. ***Scale and Scope: The Dynamics of Industrial Capitalism***. Belknap Press of Harvard University Press: Cambridge, MA.

Child J. 1972. Organizational structure, environment and performance: the role of strategic choice. ***Sociology*** 6(1): 1–22.

Christensen CM. 1997. ***The Innovator's Dilemma: When New Technologies Cause Great Firms to Fail***. Harvard Business School Press: Boston, MA.

Clark KB, Wheelwright SC. 1992. Organizing and leading 'heavyweight' development teams. ***California Management Review*** 34(3): 9–28.

Coleman JS. 1988. Social capital in the creation of human capital. ***American Journal of Sociology*** 94 (Supplement: Organizations and Institutions: Sociological and Economic Approaches to the Analysis of Social Structure): S95–S120.

Cyert RM, March JG. 1963. ***A Behavioral Theory of the Firm***. Prentice-Hall: Englewood Cliffs, NJ.

Davis JA, Leinhardt S. 1972. The structure of positive interpersonal relations in small groups. In ***Sociological Theories in Progress***, Vol. 2, Berger J, Zelditch M, Anderson B (eds). Houghton Miffl in: Boston, MA; 218–251.

Dougherty D. 1992. Interpretive barriers to successful product innovation in large firms. ***Organization Science*** 3(2): 179–202.

Dunbar RLM, Starbuck WH. 2006. Learning to design organizations and learning from designing them. ***Organization Science*** 17(2): 171–178.

Duncan RB. 1976. The ambidextrous organization: designing dual structures for innovation. ***Management of Organization: Strategy and Implementation*** 1: 167–188.

Durkheim E. 1893. ***The Division of Labor in Society*** (Halls WD, Trans.) (1984 edn). Free Press: New York.

Dutton JE, Ashford SJ. 1993. Selling issues to top management. ***Academy of Management Review*** 18(3): 397–428.

Eisenmann TR, Bower J. 2000. The entrepreneurial M-form: strategic integration in global media firms. ***Organization Science*** 11(3): 348–355.

Friesen GB, Mills DQ. 1989. Note on how organizations can be structured, Case #9-490-040. Harvard Business School Publishing: Boston, MA.

Galbraith JR. 1973. ***Designing Complex Organizations***. Addison-Wesley: Reading, MA.

Galbraith JR. 1994. ***Competing with Flexible Lateral Organizations*** (2nd edn). Addison-Wesley: Reading, MA.

Galbraith JR. 2006. Mastering the law of requisite variety with differentiated networks. In ***The Firm as a Collaborative Community: The Reconstruction of Trust in the Knowledge Economy***, Heckscher C, Adler PS (eds). Oxford University Press: New York; 179–197.

Galunic DC, Eisenhardt KM. 2001. Architectural innovation and modular corporate forms. ***Academy of Management Journal*** 44(6): 1229–1249.

Gargiulo M, Benassi M. 2000. Trapped in your own net? Network cohesion, structural holes, and the adaptation of social capital. ***Organization Science*** 11(2): 183–196.

Gavetti G, Levinthal DA. 2000. Looking forward and looking backward: cognitive and experiential search. ***Administrative Science Quarterly*** 45(1): 113–137.

Gibbons R, Murphy KJ. 1992. Optimal incentive contracts in the presence of career concerns: theory and evidence. ***Journal of Political Economy*** 100(3): 468–505.

Gilbert C. 2005. Unbundling the structure of inertia: resource versus routine rigidity. ***Academy of Management Journal*** 48(5): 741–763.

Gittell JH. 2005. Relational coordination: coordinating work through relationships of shared knowledge, shared goals and mutual respect. In ***Relational Perspectives in Organization Studies***, Kyriakidou O, Özbilgin M (eds). Edward Elgar: Northampton, MA.

Gould RV, Fernandez RM. 1989. Structures of mediation: a formal approach to brokerage in transaction networks. ***Sociological Methodology*** 19: 89–126.

Gulati R. 1995. Does familiarity breed trust? The implications of repeated ties for contractual choice in alliances. ***Academy of Management Journal*** 38(1): 85–112.

Gulati R. 2004. How CEOs manage growth agendas. ***Harvard Business Review*** 82(7/8): 124–126.

Hackman JR. 1987. The design of work teams. In ***Handbook of Organizational Behavior***, Lorsch JW (ed). Prentice-Hall: Englewood Cliffs, NJ; 315–342.

Hambrick DC. 1994. Top management groups: a conceptual integration and reconsideration of the 'team' label. In ***Research in Organizational Behavior***, Staw BM, Cummings LL (eds). JAI Press: Greenwich, CT; 171–214.

Han S-K. 1996. Structuring relations in on-the-job networks. ***Social Networks*** 18(1): 47–67.

Hannan MT, Freeman J. 1984. Structural inertia and organizational change. ***American Sociological Review*** 49(2): 149–164.

Hansen MT. 1999. The search-transfer problem: the role of weak ties in sharing knowledge across organization subunits. ***Administrative Science Quarterly*** 44(1): 82–111.

Hansen MT, Løvås B. 2004. How do multinational companies leverage technological competencies? Moving from single to interdependent explanations. ***Strategic Management Journal*** 25(8–9): 801–822.

Hansen MT, Podolny JM, Pfeffer J. 2001. So many ties, so little time: a task contingency perspective on the value of social capital in organizations. In ***Social Capital of Organizations***, Vol. 18, Gabbay SM, Leenders RTAJ (eds). JAI Press: New York; 21–58.

Hargrave TJ, Van de Ven AH. 2006. A collective action model of institutional innovation. ***Academy of Management Review*** 31(4): 864–888.

He Z-L, Wong P-K. 2004. Exploration vs. exploitation: an empirical test of the ambidexterity hypothesis. ***Organization Science*** 15(4): 481–494.

Helfat CE, Eisenhardt KM. 2004. Inter-temporal economies of scope, organizational modularity, and the dynamics of diversification. ***Strategic Management Journal*** 25(13): 1217–1232.

Henderson RM. 1993. Underinvestment and incompetence as responses to radical innovation: evidence from the photolithographic alignment equipment industry. ***Rand Journal of Economics*** 24(2): 248–270.

Henderson RM, Clark KB. 1990. Architectural innovation: the reconfiguration of existing product technologies and the failure of established firms. *Administrative Science Quarterly* 35(1): 9–30.

Higgins MC. 2005. *Career Imprints: Creating Leaders across an Industry* (1st edn). Jossey-Bass: San Francisco, CA.

Hill CWL, Hitt MA, Hoskisson RE. 1992. Cooperative versus competitive structures in related and unrelated diversified firms. *Organization Science* 3(4): 501–521.

Hill CWL, Hoskisson RE. 1987. Strategy and structure in the multiproduct firm. *Academy of Management Review* 12(2): 331–341.

Holmstrom B. 1999. Managerial incentive problems: a dynamic perspective. *Review of Economic Studies* 66(1): 169–182.

Homans GC. 1951. *The Human Group*. Harcourt Brace: New York.

Hoskisson RE, Hitt MA. 1988. Strategic control systems and relative R&D investment in large multiproduct firms. *Strategic Management Journal* 9(6): 605–621.

Hurst DK. 1995. *Crisis and Renewal: Meeting the Challenge of Organizational Change*. Harvard Business School Press: Boston, MA.

Ibarra H. 1992. Homophily and differential returns: sex differences in network structure and access in an advertising firm. *Administrative Science Quarterly* 37(3): 422–447.

Ibarra H. 1995. Race, opportunity, and diversity of social circles in managerial networks. *Academy of Management Journal* 38(3): 673–703.

Jensen MC, Meckling WH. 1976. Theory of the firm: managerial behavior, agency costs and ownership structure. *Journal of Financial Economics* 3(4): 305–360.

Johansson F. 2004. *The Medici Effect: Breakthrough Insights at the Intersection of Ideas, Concepts, and Cultures*. Harvard Business School Press: Boston, MA.

Kanter RM. 1977. *Men and Women of the Corporation*. Basic Books: New York.

Kaplan S, Henderson R. 2005. Inertia and incentives: bridging organizational economics and organizational theory. *Organization Science* 16(5): 509–521.

Katila R, Ahuja G. 2002. Something old, something new: a longitudinal study of search behavior and new product introduction. *Academy of Management Journal* 45(6): 1183–1194.

Khurana R. 2002. Market triads: a theoretical and empirical analysis of market intermediation. *Journal for the Theory of Social Behaviour* 32(2): 239–262.

Kleinbaum AM, Tushman ML. 2005. Interdependence and innovation: management of exploration and exploitation at the corporate level. Paper presented at Academy of Management Annual Meeting: Honolulu, HI.

Kotter JP. 1982. *The General Managers*. Free Press: New York.

Krackhardt D. 1990. Assessing the political landscape: structure, cognition, and power in organizations. *Administrative Science Quarterly* 35(2): 342–369.

Krackhardt D, Porter LW. 1986. The snowball effect: turnover embedded in communication networks. *Journal of Applied Psychology* 71(1): 50–55.

Krackhardt D, Stern RN. 1988. Informal networks and organizational crises: an experimental simulation. *Social Psychology Quarterly* 51(2): 123–140.

Kretschmer T, Puranam P. 2004. Realizing synergies in complex organizations: when are collaborative incentives useful? London School of Economics working paper.

Labianca G, Brass DJ, Gray B. 1998. Social networks and perceptions of intergroup conflict: the role of negative relationships and third parties. *Academy of Management Journal* 41(1): 55–67.

Leonard-Barton D. 1992. Core capabilities and core rigidities: a paradox in managing new product development. *Strategic Management Journal* 13(Summer Special Issue): 111–125.

Levinthal DA. 1997. Adaptation on rugged landscapes. *Management Science* 43(7): 934–950.

March JG. 1991. Exploration and exploitation in organizational learning. *Organization Science* 2(1): 71–87.

March JG, Simon HA. 1958. *Organizations* (1993 edn). Blackwell: Cambridge, MA.

Martin JA, Eisenhardt KM. 2003. Cross-business synergy: recombination, modularity and the multi-business team, *Best Paper Proceedings*. Academy of Management: Seattle, WA.

McCann J, Galbraith JR. 1980. Interdepartmental relations. In *Handbook of Organizational Design*, Vol. 2, Nystrom PC, Starbuck WH (eds). Oxford University Press: New York; 60–84.

McPherson M, Smith-Lovin L, Cook JM. 2001. Birds of a feather: homophily in social networks. *Annual Review of Sociology* 27(1): 415–444.

Mehta SN, Burke D. 2005. Will Wall Street ever trust Time Warner? *Fortune* 151: 76–84.

Miles RE, Snow CC. 1978. *Organizational Strategy, Structure, and Process*. McGraw-Hill: New York.

Mintzberg H, Waters JA. 1985. Of strategies, deliberate and emergent. *Strategic Management Journal* 6(3): 257–272.

Mizruchi MS, Stearns LB. 2001. Getting deals done: the use of social networks in bank decision-making. *American Sociological Review* 66(5): 647–671.

Montgomery CA, Wernerfelt B. 1988. Diversification, Ricardian rents, and Tobin's q. *Rand Journal of Economics* 19(4): 623–632.

Nadler D, Tushman M. 1997. *Competing by Design: The Power of Organizational Architecture*. Oxford University Press: New York.

Nadler DA, Tushman ML. 1988. Strategic linking: designing formal coordination mechanisms. In *Readings in the Management of Innovation* (2nd edn), Tushman ML, Moore WL (eds). Ballinger: Cambridge, MA; 469–486.

Nelson RE. 1989. The strength of strong ties: social networks and intergroup conflict in organizations. *Academy of Management Journal* 32(2): 377–401.

Nohria N, Ghoshal S. 1997. *The Differentiated Network: Organizing Multinational Corporations for Value Creation*. Jossey-Bass: San Francisco, CA.

O'Reilly CA, Tushman ML. 2004. The ambidextrous organization. *Harvard Business Review* 82(4): 74–81.

Obstfeld D. 2005. Social networks, the *Tertius Iungens* orientation, and involvement in innovation. *Administrative Science Quarterly* 50(1): 100–130.

Perry-Smith JE, Shalley CE. 2003. The social side of creativity: a static and dynamic social network perspective. *Academy of Management Review* 28(1): 89–106.

Pfeffer J. 1981. Management as symbolic action: the creation and maintenance of organizational paradigms. In *Research in Organizational Behavior*, Vol. 3, Staw BM, Cummings LL (eds). JAI Press: Greenwich, CT; 1–52.

Pfeffer J. 1992. *Managing with Power: Politics and Influence in Organizations*. Harvard Business School Press: Boston, MA.

Pfeffer J, Salancik GR. 1978. *The External Control of Organizations: A Resource Dependence Perspective* (2003 edn). Stanford Business Classics: Stanford, CA.

Podolny JM. 2001. Networks as the pipes and prisms of the market. *American Journal of Sociology* 107(1): 33–60.

Podolny JM, Baron JN. 1997. Resources and relationships: social networks and mobility in the workplace. *American Sociological Review* 62(5): 673–693.

Prendergast C. 1999. The provision of incentives in firms. *Journal of Economic Literature* 37(1): 7–63.

Quinn JB. 1978. Strategic change: 'logical incrementalism.' *Sloan Management Review* 20(1): 7–21.

Reagans R, Zuckerman EW. 2001. Networks, diversity, and productivity: the social capital of corporate R&D teams. *Organization Science* 12(4): 502–517.

Rotemberg JJ, Saloner G. 2000. Visionaries, managers, and strategic direction. *Rand Journal of Economics* 31(4): 693–716.

Roy D. 1952. Quota restriction and goldbricking in a machine shop. *American Journal of Sociology* 57(5): 427–442.

Rumelt RP. 1974. *Strategy, Structure, and Economic Performance*. Division of Research, Harvard Business School: Boston, MA.

Schein EH. 1985. *Organizational Culture and Leadership* (2nd edn). Jossey-Bass: San Francisco, CA.

Siggelkow N, Levinthal DA. 2003. Temporarily divide to conquer: centralized, decentralized, and reintegrated organizational approaches to exploration and adaptation. *Organization Science* 14(6): 650–669.

Siggelkow N, Rivkin JW. 2006. When exploration backfires: unintended consequences of multilevel organizational search. *Academy of Management Journal* 49(4): 779–795.

Simmel G. 1902. *The Sociology of Georg Simmel* (Wolff KH, Trans.) (1950 edn). Free Press: Glencoe, IL.

Simon HA. 1945. *Administrative Behavior: A Study of Decision-Making Processes in Administrative Organization* (3rd edn). Free Press: Boston, MA.

Simon HA. 1962. The architecture of complexity. *Proceedings of the American Philosophical Society* 106: 467–482.

Simons R. 2005. *Levers of Organization Design: How Managers Use Accountability Systems for Greater Performance and Commitment*. Harvard Business School Press: Boston.

Smith A. 1776. *An Inquiry into the Nature and Causes of the Wealth of Nations* (1976 edn).

Norman S. Berg: Dunwoody, GA. Smith WK, Tushman ML. 2005. Managing strategic contradictions: a top management model for managing innovation streams. *Organization Science* 16(5): 522–536.

Smith WK, Tushman ML. 2007. Senior teams and strategic contradictions: how top management teams exploit and explore simultaneously. Harvard Business School working paper. Boston, MA.

Sørensen JB, Stuart TE. 2000. Aging, obsolescence, and organizational innovation. *Administrative Science Quarterly* 45(1): 81–112.

Stewart GL, Barrick MR. 2000. Team structure and performance: assessing the mediating role of intrateam process and the moderating role of task type. *Academy of Management Journal* 43(2): 135–148.

Stonich PJ. 1981. Using rewards in implementing strategy. *Strategic Management Journal* 2(4): 345–352.

Teece DJ, Pisano GP, Shuen A. 1997. Dynamic capabilities and strategic management. *Strategic Management Journal* 18(7): 509–533.

Thompson JD. 1967. *Organizations in Action; Social Science Bases of Administrative Theory* (2nd edn). Transaction Publishers: New Brunswick, NJ.

Tripsas M, Gavetti G. 2000. Capabilities, cognition, and inertia: evidence from digital imaging. *Strategic Management Journal* 21(10–11): 1147–1161.

Tsai W. 2000. Social capital, strategic relatedness and the formation of intraorganizational linkages. *Strategic Management Journal* 21(9): 925–939.

Tsai W, Ghoshal S. 1998. Social capital and value creation: the role of intrafirm networks. *Academy of Management Journal* 41(4): 464–476.

Tushman ML. 1977. Special boundary roles in the innovation process. *Administrative Science Quarterly* 22(4): 587–605.

Tushman ML. 1979. Work characteristics and subunit communication structure: a contingency analysis. *Administrative Science Quarterly* 24(1): 82–98.

Tushman ML, Anderson P. 1986. Technological discontinuities and organizational environments. *Administrative Science Quarterly* 31(3): 439–465.

Tushman ML, Katz R. 1980. External communication and project performance: an investigation into the role of gatekeepers. *Management Science* 26(11): 1071–1085.

Tushman ML, O'Reilly CA. 1996. Ambidextrous organizations: managing evolutionary and revolutionary change. *California Management Review* 38(4): 8–31.

Tushman ML, Romanelli E. 1985. Organizational evolution: a metamorphosis model of convergence and reorientation. In *Research in Organizational Behavior*, Vol. 7, Cummings LL, Staw BM (eds). JAI Press: Greenwich, CT; 171–222.

Tushman ML, Scanlan TJ. 1981. Characteristics and external orientations of boundary spanning individuals. *Academy of Management Journal* 24(1): 83–98.

Tushman ML, Smith W. 2002. Organizational technology. In *Blackwell Companion to Organizations*, Baum JAC (ed). Blackwell: London; 386–414.

Tushman ML, Smith W, Wood R, Westerman G, O'Reilly CA. 2005. Innovation streams and ambidextrous organizational designs: on building dynamic capabilities, Harvard Business School working paper. Boston, MA.

Ulrich KT, Eppinger SD. 1995. *Product Design and Development*. McGraw-Hill: New York.

Uzzi B. 1997. Social structure and competition in interfirm networks: the paradox of embeddedness. *Administrative Science Quarterly* 42(1): 35–67.

Van de Ven AH, Delbecq AL, Koenig R, Jr. 1976. Determinants of coordination modes within organizations. *American Sociological Review* 41(2): 322–338.

Villalonga B. 2004. Diversification discount or premium? New evidence from the business information Tracking Series. *Journal of Finance* 59(2): 479–506.

Wageman R. 1995. Interdependence and group effectiveness. *Administrative Science Quarterly* 40(1): 145–180.

Wageman R, Gordon FM. 2005. As the twig is bent: how group values shape emergent task interdependence in groups. *Organization Science* 16(6): 687–700.

Weick KE, Sutcliffe KM, Obstfeld D. 2005. Organizing and the process of sensemaking. *Organization Science* 16(4): 409–421.

Williamson OE. 1975. *Markets and Hierarchies, Analysis and Antitrust Implications: A Study in the Economics of Internal Organization*. Free Press: New York.

Reading 5.4 A dynamic view of strategy *Constantinos C. Markides*

First published: (1999) *Sloan Management Review*, Spring: 55–63. MIT Sloan Management Review, Spring 1999.

In late 1988, the newly appointed CEO of the Nestlé subsidiary, Nespresso, was trying to decide how to rejuvenate his subsidiary's financial fortunes. Jean-Paul Gaillard had just taken over a subsidiary that, despite selling one of Nestlé's most innovative new products, was facing serious financial problems.

The Nespresso product was a system that allowed the consumer to produce a fresh cup of espresso coffee at home. Though simple in appearance and use, it took Nestlé more than ten years to develop it. The system consisted of two parts: a coffee capsule and a machine. The coffee capsule was hermetically sealed in aluminum and contained five grams of ground roast coffee. The machine consisted of a handle, a water container, a pump, and an electrical heating system. These four parts were cast into a body to form the machine.

The use of the Nespresso system was straightforward. The coffee capsule was placed in the handle, which was then inserted into the machine. The act of inserting the handle into the machine pierced the coffee capsule at the top. At the press of a button, pressurized hot water passed through the capsule. The result was a creamy, foamy, high-quality, cup of espresso.

The new product was introduced in 1986. Nestlé's original strategy was to set up a joint venture with a Swiss-based distributor, called Sobal, to sell the new product. This joint venture (named Sobal–Nespresso) would purchase the machines from another Swiss company (called Turmix) and the coffee capsules from Nestlé, after which it would distribute and self everything as a system—one product, one price. Offices and restaurants were targeted as the customers and a separate unit called Nespresso S.A. was set up within Nestlé to support the joint venture and to service and maintain the machines.

By 1988, it was clear that the new product was not living up to its promise. Sales were well below budget, and costs were escalating due to quality problems. Nestlé executives were considering halting the operation when Jean-Paul Gaillard was chosen to decide whether and how to strategically reposition the subsidiary. At the top of Gaillard's list were questions such as:

- Should Nespresso continue targeting offices and restaurants as customers or focus on upper-income households and individuals?
- Should Nespresso continue focusing activities in Switzerland or expand into other espresso-friendly countries?
- Should Nespresso adhere to its strategy of selling the coffee and machines as a system or concentrate solely on coffee?
- Did Nespresso's distribution policy make sense or should the company choose an alternative distribution method, such as mail order?

The heart and soul of strategy

The answers to these questions were not immediately obvious and several possible alternatives were put forward. Debates and disagreements ensued. Yet, out of this debate and uncertainty, specific choices were made and specific decisions implemented. In fact, this process of asking questions, generating alternatives, and making choices that may prove to be the wrong ones is what strategy is all about.

This is because, in every industry, there are several viable positions that companies can occupy. Therefore, the essence of strategy is selecting *one* position that a company can claim as its own. A strategic position is simply the sum of a company's answers to the following questions:

- *Who* should the company target as customers?
- *What* products or services should the company offer the targeted customers?
- *How* can the company do this efficiently [1]?

Strategy involves making tough choices on three dimensions: which customers to focus on, which products to offer, and which activities to perform. Strategy entails *choosing* , and a company will be successful if it chooses a *distinctive* strategic position that differs from those of its competitors. The most common source of strategic failure is the inability to make clear and explicit choices on these three dimensions.

As it turned out, Jean-Paul Gaillard chose correctly for Nespresso—whether by luck or foresight, Nespresso targeted high-income households as its main customer and chose mail order (the "Nespresso Club") for distributing the coffee capsules. As a result of these choices and other strategic decisions, Nespresso grew tremendously during the next five years. The main point of the Nespresso story is simple: the heart and soul of strategy is asking the "who–what–how" questions, developing alternatives, and selecting specific goals and actions.

To substantiate this point further, consider the example of Edward Jones. With 1997 revenues of $1.1 billion, the St. Louis, Missouri-based partnership of Edward Jones is the thirty-fourth largest brokerage firm in the United States. However, the firm is one of the most profitable in the volatile securities industry and is growing rapidly. Since 1981, it has expanded its broker force 15 percent annually without making any acquisitions. It now boasts more than 2,500 partners—up from a 1981 count of eight.

As described by many outside observers including management guru Peter Drucker, the firm is a federation of highly autonomous entrepreneurial units bound by a strong set of values and beliefs. The entrepreneurial units are Edward Jones brokers, who are scattered across the United States. They operate out of one-person offices located in small communities, selling selected financial products to people living in their communities. They are united by the strong cultural belief that their job is to offer sound, long-term financial advice to their customers, even if that does not generate short-term fees. The "customer-first" value is ingrained in every broker working in the Jones system.

It wasn't always like this. During the past fifty years, the firm passed through three evolutionary stages. It was originally set up by Edward Jones, Sr., to be a financial department store able to satisfy all the financial needs of a customer. In the 1960s, the department store concept slowly evolved into a "delivery system" for the rural areas of the United States, as a result of Ted Jones (the owner's son) setting up small offices in rural communities and expanding the firm into a network of 200 offices. At that time, Edward Jones began assigning brokers to small towns (instead of sending them there every week or two). The idea was to convert Edward Jones into a distribution network to sell mutual funds in rural areas.

The third stage in the evolution of Edward Jones took place in 1970 after the firm's managing principal, John Bachmann, arrived. In what he describes as a "defining moment" for the firm, he began to convert Jones into a "merchant"—an informed buyer for the end customer. According to Bachmann, the distinction between a distributor and a merchant is crucial:

> A distributor is structured around the product and tries to sell only profitable products. A merchant, on the other hand, is structured around the end consumer. He acts as an informed buyer for the investor, selecting only the products that are good for the investor, as opposed to products that generate fees for the brokers. Most investment firms look at brokers as their customers. We don't. For us, the customer is the individual investor that signs the checks.

This vision of being a merchant for the individual investor has guided every move of Edward Jones since 1980. It also has shaped the company's currently successful strategy, the main elements of which are as follows (see Table [5.4.1]):

- Edward Jones targets and sells its products only to individual investors, never to institutional investors.
- The firm sells only selected products—often transparent, long-term products such as large-cap equities and highly rated bonds. It avoids selling risky initial public offerings, options, or commodity futures.
- Edward Jones does not manufacture the products it sells, unlike its major competitors (e.g., Merrill Lynch, Smith Barney) that sell their own in-house mutual funds. Jones acts only as a distributor for the products of a few selected manufacturers, such as Capital Research, Putnam, and Morgan Stanley.
- The firm sets up one-person offices in selected areas—usually small communities or specific areas within cities where there is a "sense of community [2]."
- Edward Jones remains a partnership so that individual brokers feel and think like owners, not employees.
- The company behaves like a family whose mission is to help ordinary people invest their money wisely. The glue that holds everything together is Jones's strong culture.

These are the main elements of the successful Jones strategy. John Bachmann likes to point out that each clement involved some kind of trade-off for the company: "We target individual investors not institutional ones. We buy good securities and keep them a long time instead of trying to maximize transaction fees. Rather than have big offices in large cities, our offices are small and are placed in small communities to be convenient to the customer. Our offices are one-person operations not multiperson ones. We do not manufacture our products, and we showcase the products of a limited number of leading houses. We do not sell all products—we select transparent and safe products to promote. We remain a partnership rather than cry to go public."

The company has remained faithful to these judicious choices for more than twenty years. As John Bachmann phrases it; "These principles are cast in stone. We don't debate these things."

Uniqueness is transitory

Edward Jones built its success on finding and exploiting a singular strategic position in its industry. It did not try to

Table 5.4.1 Strategic choices of Edward Jones

Who are the company's faceted customers?	• Individual investors rather than institutional investors Individuals living in areas that have a 'sense of community'
What products or services should the company offer?	• Transparent, long-term products, such as large-cap equities and highly rated bonds No risky initial public offerings or commodity futures
How can the company efficiently conduct business?	• Never manufacture products. Act only as a distributor. • Buy only from a few reputable suppliers, such as Capital Research and Morgan Stanley. • Establish one-person operations in community-based offices. • Remain a partnership. • Focus on the end customer, not the brokers.

imitate the strategic position of other competitors or try to beat its competitors at their specialties. Instead, Jones's unique position allowed it to play an entirely different game. Although no position is truly unique, the idea is to create as much differentiation as possible.

Unquestionably, success stems from exploiting an unparalleled strategic position. Unfortunately, a position's uniqueness will not last forever! Aggressive competitors will not only imitate attractive positions but, perhaps more importantly, new strategic positions will be emerging continually. A novel strategic position is simply another viable who–what–how combination—perhaps a new customer segment (a new "who"), a new value proposition (a new "what"), or a new way of distributing or maufacturing a product (a new "how"). Gradually, such new positions may challenge the domination of existing positions.

This happens in industry after industry: once formidable companies with seemingly unassailable strategic positions find themselves humbled by relatively unknown companies that base their attacks on creating and exploiting *new* strategic positions in the industry. The rise and fall of Xerox from 1960 to 1990 highlights this simple but powerful point.

In the 1960s, Xerox dominated the copier market by following a well-defined and successful strategy. Having segmented the market by volume, Xerox decided to win the corporate reproduction market by concentrating on copiers designed for high-speed, high-volume needs. This, inevitably defined Xerox's customers as big corporations, which in turn determined its distribution method: a direct sales force. Xerox also decided to lease rather than sell its machines, a strategic choice that had worked well in the company's earlier battles with 3M.

The Xerox strategy was clear and precise with sharp boundaries. Undoubtedly, lively debates and disagreements within Xerox preceded the firm's discerning strategic choices. Yet, difficult decisions were made and actions taken. The company prospered because of its distinctive strategic position with well-defined customers, products, and activities. Throughout the 1960s and early 1970s, Xerox maintained a return on equity of around 20 percent.

In fact, Xerox's strategy was so successful that several new competitors, including IBM and Kodak, tried to enter this huge market by adopting the same or similar strategies. Fundamentally, their strategy was to grab market share by being better than Xerox. For example, IBM entered the maket in 1970 with the IBM Copier I, which the IBM sales force marketed on a rental basis to the medium- and high-volume segments. In 1975, Kodak entered the market with the Ektaprint 100 copier/duplicator, a high-quality, low-price substitute for Xerox machines that was aimed at the high-volume end of the market.

Neither of these corporate giants made substantial inroads into the copier business. They failed for many reasons, but their inability to create a distinctive position was undoubtedly one of them. Unlike Xerox, both IBM and Kodak failed to identify or create a distinctive strategic position in the industry. Instead, they tried to colonize Xerox's position and fought for market share by trying to outdo Xerox. Given Xerox's first-mover advantage, it is not surprising that IBM and Kodak failed.

In contrast, Canon chose to play the game differently. After diversifying in the 1960s beyond cameras into copiers, Canon segmented the market by end user, targeting small- and medium-sized businesses while producing personal copiers for the individual as well. Canon also decided to sell its machines through a dealer network rather than lease them. Whereas Xerox emphasized the speed of its machines, Canon elected to concentrate on quality and price as its differentiating features. Unlike IBM and Kodak, Canon successfully penetrated the copier market, emerging as the market leader in terms of volume within twenty years. Canon succeeded for many reasons, but particularly because it established a distinctive, well-defined strategic position rather than trying to beat Xerox as its own game.

Continually emerging new positions

Canon challenged Xerox by creating a new strategic position in the copier business that undermined Xerox's position and destroyed its basis of profitability. Such attacks are common (see Table [5.4.2]). The "dominant" competitors establish unique strategic positions in their respective industries. Over time, "traditional" competitors imitate their predecessors in an attempt to wrest market share from them. Increasingly, though, "strategic innovators" emerge that run away with huge chunks of the market—often a new market that they helped to create.

Incursions into established markets by strategic innovators have resulted in the following notable outcomes:

- Canon's market share in the copier business jumped from zero to 35 percent in about twenty years.
- Komatsu increased its market share in the earth-moving equipment business from 10 percent to 25 percent in less than fifteen years.
- Launched in 1982, *USA Today* had become the top-selling U.S. newspaper by 1993, selling more than 5 million copies per day.
- Dell Computer Corporation emerged from its college-dorm beginnings in the mid-1980s to capture more than 10 percent of the global personal computer market in less than ten years.
- Started in 1989 as the United Kingdom's first dedicated telephone bank, First Direct, had nearly 700,000 customers within seven years—an achievement that the business press described as a miraculous cure for the stagnant banking industry [3].
- Starbucks Coffee grew from a chain of eleven stores and sales of $1.3 million in 1987 to 280 stores and sales of $163.5 million in five years. The store total now tops 1,600.
- Direct Line was launched in 1985 and, within ten years, became one of Britain's biggest motor insurers (2.2 million policyholders).

These companies achieved their hard-earned successes in a similar way, namely, by proactively breaking the rules of the game in their industries. The hallmark of their success was strategic innovation; proactively establishing distinctive strategic positions that were critical to shifting market share or creating new markets.

As industries change, new strategic positions arise to challenge existing positions. Changes in industry conditions, customer needs or preferences, demographics, technology, government policies, competition, and a company's own competencies generate new opportunities and the potential for new ground rules. Existing niches expand while others die, new niches appear, mass markets fragment into new segments (or niches), "old" niches merge to form larger markets, and so on. This dynamic occurs in every industry.

Now, imagine your company as it tries to compete in its industry. Let's say that your company has carved out a nice position in the mass market. It has several competitors in the mass market, and several niche players exist on the

Table 5.4.2 Undermining established strategic positions

Industry	Dominant Competitor	Traditional Competitor	Strategic Innovator
US airline	American	Delta, United, Northwest	Southwest
Car rental	Hertz	Avis, European, National	Enterprise-rent-a-car
US television broadcasting	NBC	CBS, ABC	CNN
UK banking	Northwest	Lloyds, Barclays	First Direct
Earth-moving equipment	Caterpillar	International Harvester, John Deere, J.I. Case	Komatsu
Steel	U.S. Steel	Bethlehem, Inland, National	Nucor
UK supermarket	Sainsbury's	Tesco, Asda, Waitrose	Flanagen's
Coffee	General Foods (Maxwell House)	Procter & Gamble (Folger's), Nestlé (Nescafé), Sara Lee (Douwe Egberts)	Starbucks
UK Insurance	Norwich Union	Prudential, Royal Sun Alliance	Direct Line
Photocopier	Xerox	IBM, Kodak, Ricoh	Canon
UK airline	British Airways	Virgin Atlantic, British Midlands, other European carriers	easyJet
Securities	Merrill Lynch	Smith Barney, Dean Witter, Palne Webber	Edward Jones
Computer	IBM	NCR, Control Data	Microsoft

periphery. While you are competing with your primary competitors, you know that new niches are developing, and you want to ensure that your company does not miss these new opportunities. But, from among hundreds of new niches, identifying a productive one is difficult: so is predicting its growth rate and eventual size. Meanwhile, though your company's sales are increasing, a winning niche arises—its growth resulting from the creation of art entirely new market. Such developments complicate your ability to understand the magnitude of the problem confronting your company. What can you do in this situation?

After a niche becomes a huge market, hindsight confirms that you should have done something earlier. But, it is hard to know which threat to respond to and when! For example, it is only with hindsight that we can say IBM should have responded to the Dell threat long ago. But, in the early 1980s, even if IBM had spotted this new entrant should it have worried about a tiny niche player with 1 percent of the market? How about when Dell's market share grew to 5 percent? Or 10 percent? When did Dell really become a major worry for IBM? Even If IBM wanted to respond to the Dell challenge now, what could it do? Can it play two games simultaneously?

Preparing for the unknown

No company has perfect foresight in predicting emerging strategic innovations. However, lack of certainty is no excuse for inactivity. A company can face up to all this uncertainty by adopting one or both of the following generic options.

Option one: become the innovator

Established competitors can proactively develop the next strategic innovation in an industry. Just as cannibalizing existing products when creating next-generation products is acceptable, companies should not hestitate to cannibalize an existing strategic position to create the "next generation" position. This is difficult, but not impossible [4].

Practically speaking, a company must cultivate the "right" attitude, but also organize itself to compete effectively in its existing business while simultaneously experimenting with new technologies and ideas. How can the old and the new coexist harmoniously [5]? This calls for creating an ambidextrous organization, which is a formidable task. As Tushman and O'Reilly point out: "This requires organizational and management skills to compete in a mature market (where cost, efficiency, and incremental innvoation are key) *and* to develop new products and services (where radical innovation, speed, and flexibility are critical) [6]."

Utterback also forcefully makes this point:

> Firms owe it to themselves to improve and extend the lives of profitable product lines. These represent important cash flows to the firm and links to existing customers. They provide the funds that will finance future products. At the same time, managers must not neglect pleas that advocate major commitments to new initiatives. Typically, top management is pulled by two opposing, responsible forces; those that demand commitment to the old and those that advocate for the future. Unfortunately, advocacy tends to overstate the market potential of new product lines and understate their costs. Management, then, must find the right balance between support for incremental improvements and commitments to new and unproven innovations. Understanding and managing this tension perceptively may well separate the ultimate winners from the losers. [7]

Option two: exploit someone else's innovation

Chances are that an established company will not be the source of the next new strategic innovation. For every established competitor, hundreds of new entrants or entrepreneurs are trying to concoct the next "great" innovation, and it is likely that one will succeed. Nevertheless, an established competitor should be poised and ready to take advantage of emerging innovations. But what does "being ready" imply?

Being ready

Research shows that most established companies fail when a technological innovation invades their market—even when they actually adopt a new technology. Several reasons for this have been identified:

- They lack the necessary core competencies to take advantage of the innovation.
- They are late adopters and abandon an innovation at the first sign of trouble.
- They are trapped in their customary ways of competing, their core competencies having become core rigidities.
- They do not effectively manage the organizational transition from the old to the new when adopting a new technology [8].

This implies that to prepare for the inevitable strategic innovation that will disrupt a company's market, an organization should:

1. *Build an early monitoring system to identify turning points before a crisis occurs.* Firms must develop the capability to recognize early whether a new strategic position is

emerging that will unsettle their markets. The most effective way to do so is to regularly monitor indicators of *strategic* rather than *financial* health—that is, leading indicators of a company's performance such as employee morale, customer satisfaction, and distributor feedback. Also track and benchmark maverick competitors that operate in small niches or appear to be breaking the rules of the game in the industry. In addition, encourage people close to the market to actively monitor and proactively report changes in the market to the appropriate decision makers. Alternatively, build a strong sense of direction, establish the parameters within which people can maneover, and then empower them to take action. In short, develop the capability to identify changes early.

2. *Prevent cultural and structural inertia.* Cultivate a culture that welcomes change and is ready to accept a new strategic innovation even if it disrupts the status quo. Established companies often wait too long to adopt an innovation. Reasons for this are many—not the least of which is the uncertainty of whether the innovation will be a winner. By developing a culture that welcomes change and encourages experimentation and learning, obstacles to innovation may be overcome. Such a culture may be further enhanced if top management uses "shocks to the system" to acclimate employees to change.

For example, cultural inertia at Raychem is challenged every day. Company founder Paul Cook says:

> Raychem is working to make its own products obsolete every day. Right now, we are in the process of making one of our best products obsolete, a system for sealing splices in telephone cables. Now, we could have kept on improving that product for years to come. Instead, we've developed a radically new splice-closure technology that improves performance tremendously, and we're working very hard to cannibalize the earlier generation. Our old product wasn't running out of steam. Our customers had virtually no complaints about it. But because we knew the product and its applications even better than our customers did, we were able to upgrade its performance significantly by using a new technology. Why are we doing it? Because we understand that if we don't make ourselves obsolete, the world will become more competitive [9]."

3. *Develop processes that allow experimenting with new ideas*. New innovations are not adopted quickly because they are not recognized to be winners. If experimentation were to reveal the potential of a new innovation, a company would be more likely to adopt it. Experimentation is the process that Intel's Andrew Grove terms "let chaos reign"—when people explore novel ideas until enough information is collected to allow the firm to make a decision.

Grove further describes the process:

> When danger comes, the adrenaline starts flowing and you want to null the reins in and take control. But the opposite is what is needed. The reason you need to do the opposite is that, in this phase of the curve, you do not know enough to take charge. The fragmented information will come with fragmented suggested directions. You let things develop, and the way you let things develop is to relinquish control and let people—division heads, geography heads, engineers—pull in various directions ... This is the only way to get enough information to really build up a basis on which to decide whether to go for one option or the other [10]."

4. *Be prepared with the required competencies.* Prepare to exploit the company's new position by building the appropriate competencies and skills. Unfortunately, this is easier said than done.

Utterback makes the point succinctly:

> There is no easy answer as to how firms should choose the core competencies that will assure their progress and survival. Certainly, it is essentially to anticipate discontinuities and to try to act in advance of their full impact. Doing so requires constant monitoring of the firm's external environment to notice forerunners of significant change. We have seen that most firms look in exactly the wrong places for vital signs of technological change: namely, their universe of traditional rivals ... Looking toward more obscure new entrants and unconventional sources of competition is more fruitful, although these sources are more diffuse and difficult to monitor. Technological and market uncertainty, however, implies that no one can act with clear anticipation or forecasts. Among equally capable generals, the one with the best contingency plans will usually win the battle. Unexpected departures from the anticipated plan are almost certain to arise and in the best of cases, they will open the way to greater opportunities than at first imagined. This is crucial in the choice of capabilities to foster [11]."

In the face of uncertainty, the best a firm can do is build internal variety (even at the expense of efficiency), and let the market mechanism determine what wins. By nurturing variety, a company also builds the competencies needed in the future. Creating and managing internal variety is intrinsically difficult—but it is achievable if learning is allowed to flourish in the organization.

5. *Manage the transition.* Finally, a firm must manage the transition to the new strategic position. Two issues are involved.

First, the organization must clearly decide whether to adopt the new position. As Grove puts it:

> At last, you have got through the strategic inflection point. In this second phase, it is time to rein in chaos. The phase for experimentation is over. Now is the moment to pull the reins in and to take charge again. At this point, you

must be completely explicit in stating the direction of the new business. When you get out of pursuing multiple architectures, you must be completely explicit that the experiment is stopping, that all resources are being put into one option. No ifs or buts: explicit clarity [12]."

Second, the company must ensure that the "old" and the "new" coexist harmoniously: Any innovation, by virtue of being small in scone relative to the existing company, will receive little attention and limited resources unless it is protected. The solution is to develop a separate organizational unit for the new position to prevent its suffocation. Dedicated people who consider it "their baby" will fight for it.

To summarize the general approach, a company can prepare to take advantage of a strategic change by developing the ability to recognize an innovation early, by promoting a corporate culture that welcomes change, by developing processes that allow experimenting with new ideas, and by developing skills that allow exploitation of the new position. After introducing an innovation, the company must protect it in a separate organizational unit and nurture it by means of consistent investments.

Elements of a dynamic strategy

Given the analysis so far, we can now begin to view strategy in a more dynamic way (see Figure [5.4.1]). In thinking about its strategy, a company must first identify and colonize a *distinctive* strategic position in its industry. It should then excel at playing the game in this position, thus making it the most attractive position in the industry. While competing in its current position, a company also must search continuously for new strategic positions. After identifying another viable strategic position in its industry, the company then must attempt to manage both positions simultaneously—no easy task. As the old position matures and declines, the company must slowly make a transition to the new, at which point, it must start the cycle again: while fighting it out in the new position, it must again search to discover another viable strategic position to colonize.

Of course, at any time during this dynamic process, a company could opt to jump into a new technology or industry. This could happen while the company is still competing in its first strategic position, later while the company is striving to balance the demands of two strategic positions, or at any time during the evolution of a firm's strategy. Notice, however, that after jumping into another industry, the firm must go through the same dynamic process as in its original industry. Moving into another industry does not alter the strategic tasks that a company must undertake in *each* business—it just makes management more complicated in that the firm faces additional challenges, such as how to manage a diversified portfolio and how to exploit synergies among is businesses.

Figure 5.4.1 Elements of a dynamic strategy

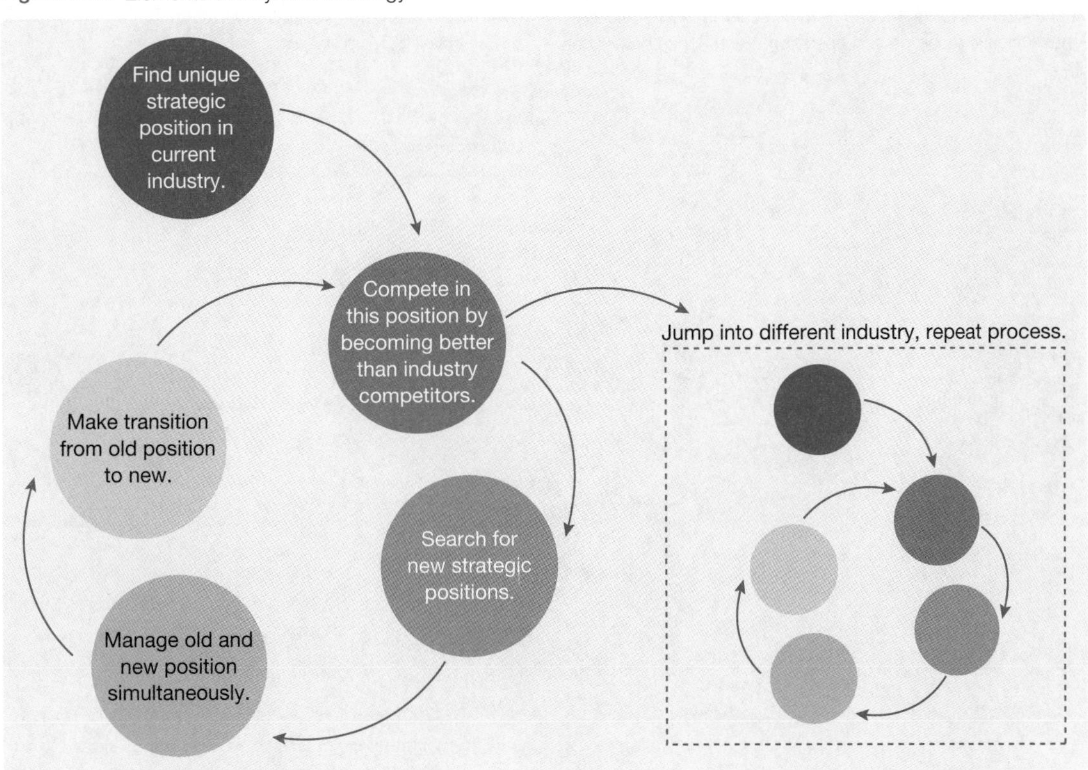

Thus, designing a successful strategy is never-ending. A company needs to continuously revisit and challenge its answers to the who–what–how questions in order to remain flexible and ready to adjust its strategy if feedback from the market is unfavorable. Changing industry conditions and customer needs or preferences, countermoves by competitors, and a company's evolving competencies give rise to new opportunities and the potential for new ways to play the game. A strategy adopted a decade ago on the basis of prevailing industry conditions is certainly not a guaranteed game plan for the future.

Even (or perhaps, especially) successful companies must continuously question the basis of their business and the assumptions behind their successful formulas. Because new who–what–how positions spring forth from the mass market almost ceaselessly, established companies must be on the lookout for these new positions. Like modern-day pioneers, corporate executives must set out to explore the evolving terrain of their industries in search of unexploited strategic positions. Only the intrepid who abandon the safety of the familiar to venture into the unknown will have a future worth discussing.

References

1. The 'who–what–how' framework was introduced in: D. Abell, *Defining the Business: The Starting Point of Strategic Planning* (Englewood Cliffs, New Jersey: Prentice-Hall, 1980), Chapter 2.

2. In nearly all cases and contrary to traditional wisdom that emphasizes exploiting economics of scale in such offices, a Jones Office is a one-person operation. Each Jones broker has extraordinary autonomy in managing his or her office, and every branch is a profit center. A satellite communications network that broadcasts 'home-grown' TV programming tiles brokers to the home office.

3. P. Weever, 'Growing Call of Telephone Banks,' *Sunday Telegraph* (London), 22 December 1996, p. 2; and A. Balley, 'Telephone Banking—It's for You: The Service Has Scope for Great Popularity,' *Financial Times*, 3 April 1996, p. 18.

4. See C. Markides, 'Strategic Innovation,' *Sloan Management Review*, Volume 38, Spring 1997, pp. 9–23; and C. Marklales, 'Strategic Innovation in Established Companies,' *Sloan Management Review*, Volume 29, Spring 1998, pp. 31–42.

5. This same point is also discussed in: M. Tushman and C. O'Reilly, 'The Ambidextrous Organization: Managing Evolutionary and Revolutionary Change,' *California Management Review*, Volume 32, Summer 1996, pp. 8–30; and R. Burogelman and A. Crove, 'Strategic Dissorroding,' *California Management Review*, Volume 38, Winter 1996, pp. 8–28.

6. Tushman and O'Reilly (1996), p. 11.

7. J. M. Utterback, *Mastering the Dynamics of Innovation* (Boston: Harvard Business School Press, 1994), p. 21.

8. A. Cooper and C. Smith, 'How Established Firms Respond to Threatening Technologies,' *Academy of Management Executive*, Volume 16, May 1992, pp. 92–120; R. Foster, *Innovation: The Attacker's Advantage* (New York: Summit Books, 1986), Chapter 6, pp. 139–154; A. Cooper and D. Schendel, 'Strategic Responses to Technological Threats,' *Business Horizons*, Volume 19, February 1976, pp. 61–69; and Utterback (1994), Chapter 9, pp. 189–213.

9. W. Taylor, 'The Business of Innovation: An Interview with Paul Cook,' *Harvara Business Review*, March–April 1990, pp. 96–106.

10. A. S. Grove, 'Navigating Strategic Inflection Points,' *Business Strategy Review*, Volume 8, Number 3, 1997, pp. 11–18.

11. Utterback (1994), p. 220.

12. Grove (1997), p. 17.

Practitioner reflection

Dr Chris Coughlan

Realizing and sustaining advantage

In reading Chapters 9–12 of *Strategy and Strategists*, I see three distinctive economic ages, or waves: agricultural, industrial, and digital. However, as we move from one wave to the next, they do not disappear; they are all still present, and begin to overlap and interact with each other. Therefore the economic and business characteristics of previous ages are not necessarily replaced by the characteristics of the next age. Some characteristics may disappear; others remain; others become modified; new additional characteristics emerge, all of which interact with each other. The implication of this is that in thinking strategically about developing a valid business model for your company to compete successfully in the digital age, you need a mindset of operating in three main economies and six hybrid economies. It is the characteristics from all of these that then define the true characteristics of the digital age and it is only then, based on these, that you can begin to construct a valid and real business model that realizes a competitive advantage. The challenge then is to sustain this over a long period of time; this is even more difficult in the digital age.

In recent years, it was the lack of this mindset that caused the dot.com bubble to burst. Dot.com companies simply created their own rules without considering or taking into account the previous age's influences, interactions, and rules. The dot.com era was, in fact, a *pseudo digital age*, because it operated mainly upon invalid assumptions, such as the lack of return on investment. However, all was not wasted during this period, because there were many lessons that helped to form the basis of the true digital age in which we are now, albeit at a very early stage. In my experience, many companies currently trying to evolve into this age must first operate in a transition mode between the industrial and digital ages—a 'hybrid economy'. In reality, it is a stage of discovery or exercise in fitness to explore whether, over time, they can develop the *crossover protocols* to become a true digital economy-based company or if they can continue to operate only either in the industrial age or in a hybrid industrial-digital age, which is still a very valid and powerful business model. Therefore a key strategic planning decision for any company is to decide in which of the nine economies it is currently operating, and whether it can move to the next to increase competitive advantage and growth opportunities. In many cases, this is becoming more dependent on how a company can innovatively apply or use current or emerging technologies. In fact, technologies—particularly information and digital technologies—have become critical strategic drivers that enable companies to create and build business environments in which to operate and compete in today's and tomorrow's world.

Business environments and organizations are becoming more complex as a result of operating within a potential multitude of economies, and by the increasing use and application of technology. This is further complicated by the rate of change of technology, as defined by Moore's Law,[1] and increasing global connectivity, as defined by Metcalf's Law.[2] This increasing complexity gives rise to a further consideration: the chaos effect, explained by the popular summary, 'A butterfly flaps its wings on one side of the Atlantic and a storm rises on the other side'. In a business context, such as a value or supply chain, a small action at one end can cause an unravelling that leads to major consequences internally and externally as it works its way through to an end result. In other words, as business environments grow more complex and connected, they become more volatile, with a greater propensity for things to go wrong or for unpredictable outcomes to emerge. Managers have to look at this from a strategic and an operational perspective, and have to plan to protect themselves and their competitive environment from potential chaos effects that may arise internally, but equally can arise externally without their making or control. This 'business chaos effect' that we see in markets today, especially in the financial sector, has become a virulent phenomenon similar in its effects to a computer virus bringing down global networks.

When introducing strategic technology change, within a company and to customers, other effects that have to be considered and understood are technology lead and organization and economic lag. There is always a lag effect between technology change and its acceptance within the marketplace. The strategic challenge is correct timing, because implementing technology change too early or too late can have devastating effects for a company. This is dependent on careful preparation and on knowing when the lag–lead gap value reaches a critical alignment point in the context of readiness of the organization, its customers, and the marketplace in general. There are also different customer lags. These are between the different generations in your customer set: the current generation; the generation that is beginning to enter the marketplace; and future generations that you want to attract. Remember that the Wii and PlayStation young consumers of today are the buyers and sellers of tomorrow who will determine the shape of the marketplace in the future. Understanding the subculture in which you operate today will give insight into the mainstream marketplace of tomorrow. In doing so, you will have a basis from which you can plan the strategic application of technology not only for the current generation, but also for future generations.

In my experience, communication and championship, both within and outside organizational boundaries, remain fundamental and paramount factors in driving strategy formulation and implementation, and are essential in getting high levels of participation, understanding, and buy-in from all stakeholders. This requires clear articulation of the vision, the mission, the goals, the objectives, and the metrics involved in measuring ongoing successful performance. This is important if you are leading people, business units, the organization, or customers along a changed path or new marketplace business model. The stakeholders have to understand where they are contributing and gaining, at both a big-picture and individual level, and how they will be measured and rewarded for their contribution and acceptance. It is also essential to celebrate milestones of success along the journey, not only within the organization, but also externally with customers and other key stakeholders. In Chapters 9 and 10, the authors highlight some of the key challenges facing strategists and managers as they attempt to achieve what they refer to as 'realizing advantage'.

In my professional career, I have seen control moving from the centre to the periphery of organizations and back again. Control is typically over people, processes, systems, and technologies. It can become organizationally destructive if it remains locked in either a centralized or decentralized extreme. Therefore the balance or movement of control is necessary, as it keeps the internal dynamics of an organization in constant synergy or change and prevents stagnation. Too much central control, in my experience, can have a negative impact on creativity and innovation, because it prevents people's talents developing. I believe that innovation begins with the request and freedom to contribute at an individual level, which then pervades the organization and beyond. Equally, too much decentralized control gives rise to an uncoordinated organization with a lack of focus. This is one of the core tensions explored in Chapter 9. Tight control is necessary for fiscal, CSR, ethical, legal, and governance perspectives, and should be hardwired into an organization, while loose control is necessary for innovation and corporate entrepreneurship, and should be softwired, or reconfigurable, within an organization. Therefore, besides the other considerations already outlined, a successful strategy is also dependent on an organization achieving a proper balance between decentralized and centralized control. This requires, as the authors rightly highlight, maintaining some degree of agility and flexibility, while maintaining a core focus that challenges all parts of the company.

Dr Chris Coughlan is a recognized futurologist in the area of technology. He has advised governments and corporates on what technology can do, how to apply it, and what (or where) it might bring us. Chris has worked with some of the world's leading technology giants and currently works as a Senior Manager for Hewlett Packard.

Endnotes

1 The performance of semiconductor chip technology in speed and density, as measured against its price, doubles every eighteen months.

2 The value of a network is proportional to the number of users squared.

Section 6

Rediscovering strategy and strategists

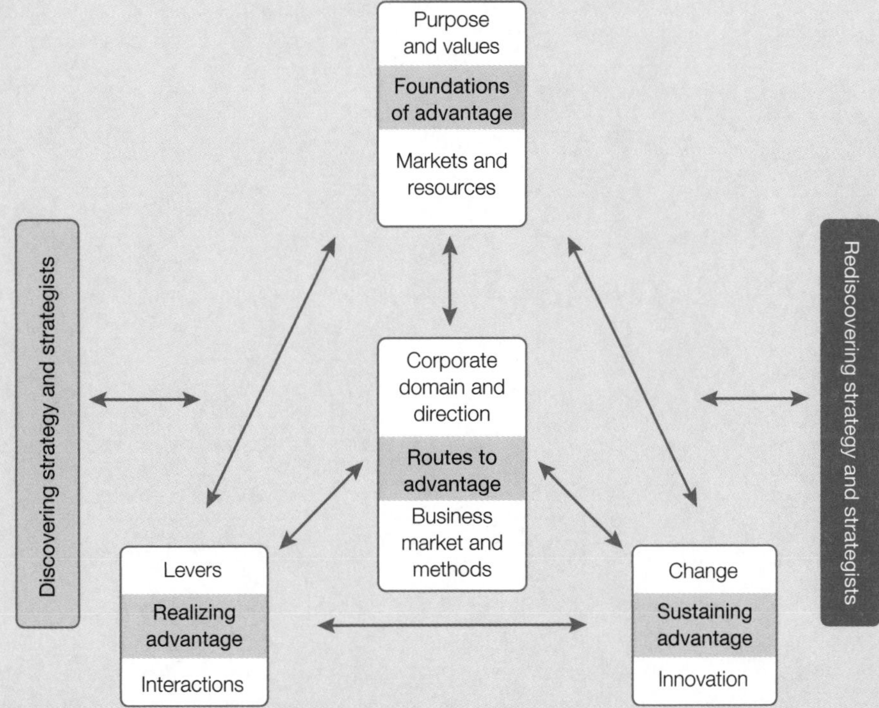

13

Managing strategy in context

Public sector, non-profit, and small firms

Running the Red Cross is not exactly like running IBM.

(Sharon Oster, 1995: 3)

Introduction

The largest organizations in the world are not only the agents of the private sector, but also include the public service agencies of governments and international **not-for-profit organizations** (Kelman, 2007). International charities such as the International Red Cross and Red Crescent movement have millions of volunteers worldwide. This reality is often overlooked in discussions of strategy, which tend to be grounded in the assumptions of private sector corporations. Yet as Oster (1995) notes in the opening quote of the chapter, there is likely to be a notable distinction between management of for-profit and other organizations. In our daily lives, we encounter and rely upon a vast range of organizations pursuing a diverse range of goals—from educational institutions, to religious orders, to charities. Coupled with this, we experience a range of service provisions, from public transport and medical care, to protection from the police. Given that the successful functioning of these organizations directly affects us as individuals and communities, we should be equally interested in what these firms do and the role of strategy and strategic thinking in facilitating them with the realization of their key objectives.

In this chapter, we take a different approach from that of previous chapters as we explore key situational opportunities and constraints that affect the occurrence and meaning of strategy in differing contexts (Johns, 2006). Specifically, we examine not-for-profit organizations (NPOs), **public sector organizations** (PSOs), and small firms. For each context, we explore the main characteristics that shape and inform strategy, discuss the key strategic tensions, and consider some issues of strategy **formulation** and execution. We conclude by exploring the nature and relevance of the four strategic challenges that we identified in Chapter 1 and their specific implications in each context. We begin by focusing on NPOs.

Not-for-profit organizations (NPOs)

NPOs encompass a diverse range of organizations, from those addressing local concerns (for example, providing shelter for the homeless) right up to global organizations that alleviate poverty, provide humanitarian aid, address human rights violations (such as Oxfam, Amnesty International), or highlight ecologically damaging activities (Greenpeace) and animal protection (WWF). Traditionally, NPOs have been heavily involved in the provision of services in the areas of health and education. The most basic definition of the sector is that it comprises all of those self-governing organizations that are left when we exclude for-profit business and government (Harris, 2001; Paton, 1992: 4). In this 'middle way' between the market and state control, NPOs often deal with unmet demand for public goods, provide an independent viewpoint, give a voice to a minority, or act in a watchdog function. At the same time, NPOs are outlets through which people can channel their efforts voluntarily for a cause that affects them or about which they have a strong belief. The voluntary sector therefore encompasses a mixed group of organizations: charities; self-help groups; community groups; not-for-profit service providers; membership associations; faith-based organizations; campaigning groups; philanthropic trusts (Harris, 2001). There are also foundations that use the wealth of specific individuals to provide services to those in need or to undertake research (for example, The Bill and Melinda Gates Foundation, Atlantic Philanthropies, and Wellcome Trust). While a few NPOs are well known, the vast majority are smaller organizations that carry out their activities under the public radar. In a context in which public resources are decreasing, NPOs are facing increasing pressure from donors and funding bodies to be more accountable and professional in their activities—that is, 'to do well while doing good'. To assess how this tension is managed, we need to explore the key characteristics of NPOs.

Contextual features and characteristics that shape and influence strategy

While we can debate whether the not-for-profit sector demands an entirely new array of strategic management tools and concepts (Kong, 2008), there can be little doubt that it is, in many ways, distinct. Even though a diverse range of organizations make up the sector, they do share common features and problems, which include the following.

- **Non-profit distribution constraint**

  By definition, NPOs cannot distribute profits to those in control of the organization. This is probably their most distinguishing characteristic. Typically, such firms are accorded a special tax and regulatory status that specifies limits on how their revenues can be deployed. This enables NPOs to conduct a range of activities that would be difficult to sustain under more typical constraints (Oster, 1995). A further benefit is that because those running the organization are constrained in their ability to personally benefit from activities, they are much less likely to eschew their responsibilities or to apply a low-quality service, because there is no benefit from such opportunism (Hansmann, 1987). However, this status can mean that NPOs have more difficulty in raising capital or absorbing risk.

- **Mission and values**

  NPOs are mission-driven organizations, founded on an ideological concern or desire to meet certain social needs. The mission and its associated values are their overarching and differentiating factor (Tillet, 1970). The mission of the World Wide Fund for Nature (WWF) is 'the conservation of nature'. This provides a clear focus for the strategist and is essential to strategy formulation. However, the centrality of such missions can place limits on the flexibility of actions available to NPOs (Kanter and Summers, 1987).

- **Social and multidimensional goals**

  While the mission and values of NPOs may be obvious, the means of measuring their obtainment are far from straightforward. In contrast to the transparency and obvious measure of profit in the private sector, NPOs address social goals; this makes it more difficult to determine priorities and evaluate performance (Paton, 1992). Social goals can be vague and hard to quantify, while service provision is often intangible and hard to measure, making it difficult to justify activities to funding bodies and donors.

- **Organizational personnel and characteristics**

  Their expressive character and the way in which NPOs enable people to demonstrate commitment to social ends and values are what differentiate NPOs (Frumkin and Andre-Clark, 2000:

142). Aligning social ends and values in a strategic plan is difficult, but it is this that makes NPOs unique. This is not only about what NPOs do; it is also about the way in which they do it. NPOs often have a distinctive culture that is couched in ideology, and which is informal and mission-driven. In addition, the activities of NPOs are typically labour-intensive and involve the management of both paid staff and volunteer workers.

- **Resource acquisition and dependency**
  For other commentators, the fundamental differences between NPOs and for-profit firms rest not so much on organizational criteria as they do 'on the differences in the availability of resources and the constraints associated with their acquisition' (Powell and Friedkin, 1987: 181). NPOs experience a different pattern of resource acquisition, because they must rely on funding from a range of external constituents to maintain operations. This creates uncertainty for NPOs, making long-term planning difficult, and can limit their strategic options.

- **Board and stakeholder management**
  One direct consequence of having to both source funds and deliver services is that the importance of networking, stakeholder management, and legitimacy is dramatically enhanced (Middleton, 1987). The boards of NPOs play a critical 'boundary spanning function', navigating the external environment to obtain funds and contacts. Having reputable and well-connected people on the board can help an NPO 'to establish legitimacy and power in the community' (Middleton, 1987: 142). Internally, the board also plays a critical role in decision making and can take an active operational role, especially in younger and smaller NPOs (Oster, 1995).

Table13.1 summarizes the unique features and characteristics of NPOs that shape and influence strategy, and details some key strategic tensions that emerge as a result. We discuss these in more detail in the next section.

Key strategic tensions

Key strategic tensions can impede or undermine the core purposes of NPOs. Table 13.1 identifies strategic tensions at organizational, managerial, and environmental levels; strategists have to be aware of these in formulating and implementing strategy. At the organizational level, NPOs have a clear sense of orientation or purpose, but it can be difficult to measure the impact of their activities. For a heart disease charity, the focus of which is on educational awareness, quantification of the numbers of people with whom it engages is one high-level measure, but it would be more difficult

Table 13.1 Key distinguishing features and characteristics of NPOs: resulting strategic tensions at different levels

Level	Features	Strategic tensions
Organizational	Non-profit distribution constraint Mission-driven Social goals Informality and volunteers	Clear orientation, yet difficult to measure impact Informality can conflict with pressures for professionalism
Managerial	Boundary-spanning activities Volunteers and management	Getting the right balance and type of people to serve on boards Tensions between paid staff and unpaid volunteers
Environmental	Dependency on funding agencies and government Stakeholder management	Have to 'face both ways' dealing with funders and clients Multiple stakeholders with multiple expectations

to measure the preventative value of these educational programmes. The second organizational tension is in balancing informality of organizational structure with a professional approach to structure and management. Chapter 11 shows that this is a tension for many commercial organizations, because they deal with regulatory and governance requirements while needing to have an adaptive organizational structure. At the same time, informality may be critical to the culture and day-to-day running of the NPO.

At a managerial level, the strategist has to ensure that there are the right balance and type of people to serve on boards. This can be difficult to achieve, but it is necessary if the NPO is to have real clarity about its core purpose and in the execution of its strategy. Some board members are appointed through funder requirements, and can have both positive and negative influences in ensuring the sustainability of the NPO. This can also be the case for the founder of the NPO. A second managerial tension is around the management of paid and unpaid volunteers. A key question for the strategist is whether unpaid volunteers should be involved in the strategy development process, particularly in light of the need for everyone in an organization to have ownership of strategy, as we outlined in Chapter 5.

In terms of environmental influences, NPOs must deal with the sometimes conflicting demands of funders and clients. In many cases, an understanding of client needs by the NPO leads to the development of new services, but funders may not be willing to support such expansion or do not appreciate its value. NPOs can be faced with stark choices, and the issues of resources and how to be innovative and entrepreneurial (see Chapters 6 and 12) come to the fore for the strategist. This is coupled with dealing with the high multiple-level expectations of stakeholders. Most NPOs have multiple funding sources, ranging from state agencies to small individual donations. Some stakeholders provide real credibility for the NPO, some provide financial support, whereas other stakeholders provide expertise that is vital to the long-term sustainability of the NPO. Getting the optimal balance of support is a relentless activity for NPOs.

Formulation and implementation issues

NPO strategists face many issues in the formulation and implementation of strategy that tie in with strategic tensions discussed in the previous section. The first issue is about crafting strategy. It has two dimensions: having an effective management system in place, and needing to focus on appropriate strategies (Oz and Toker, 2008). A good management structure is essential in enabling operational effectiveness and the process of crafting strategy, because it strengthens the identity of the NPO, creating ownership and a sense of consensus among stakeholders.

The second issue—that of strategic positioning, on which we focused in Chapter 8—presents difficulties for NPOs in formulating strategy. How does a strategist conceptualize and bring into effect a strategic position for an NPO? Key considerations involve the scope of activities that the NPO will conduct. For example, although a local support group for sufferers of a rare disease might wish to provide support and education to sufferers, raise public awareness of the disease, and fund research in search of a prevention/cure, all of these activities may not be feasible for such a small-scale organization or may not reap the maximum benefit. In this case, instead of asking how they will compete in each market, NPOs consider the specific ways in which their activities may add value. NPOs therefore need to carefully consider the activities at which they will be most effective and will deliver the most social value (MacMillan, 1983). Having a clearly defined strategy is a must-have rather than a nice-to-have for NPOs if they are to survive in economies in which there are fewer resources available from public and private sources to support their core purposes.

Thirdly, the boards and organizational structures of NPOs and their influence on shaping strategic styles can be a significant factor in affecting the formulation of strategy. One of the key roles of boards is to assist in improving the operational performance of the organization and reinforce the organizational purpose. In some cases, NPOs deliberately select boards and put in place organizational structures that reflect their core philosophies; some NPOs use **mission statements** to ensure consistency and stability (Brown and Iverson, 2004). However, as Cornford (2001: 225) argues, board members 'are not just recruited because they are enthusiastic but because they have the right skills and experience, and the time necessary to do the job'. Board members with experience of strategy formulation and implementation will shape strategy development within an NPO, and help the NPO to adopt new processes and structures that will support strategy.

Strategy in public sector organizations (PSOs)

In October 2007, two computer disks from the UK Child Benefit database were lost while on transit from HM Revenue and Customs (HMRC) in the north-east of England to the National Audit Office (NAO) in London. The disks, which were both unregistered and unencrypted, contained the personal details of 25 million people, including their addresses, bank account details, and National Insurance numbers. The information was valued at nearly £1.5bn should it fall into criminal hands. Then Prime Minister Gordon Brown claimed that the loss was the result of an 'operational error', stemming from a failure to pay due attention to official procedures. Opposition parties, however, claimed that it was further evidence of 'systemic failure' in the government's provision of services to the public.

PSOs constitute some of the largest and most influential organizations that we encounter, from global institutions such as the World Bank, United Nations (UN), and North Atlantic Treaty Organization (NATO), through to national and local government. The public sector produces core goods and services in the areas of health care, education, social security, justice, defence, and criminal justice, all of critical significance in the functioning of society as a whole (Ferlie, 1992). Indeed, the public sector provides 'the very foundation for civilized life through providing individual security and the ground rules for operation of the market' (Kelman, 2007: 226). It usually takes events such as that outlined above to remind us of the importance of well-run government organizations (Feldman, 2005: 958).

As a result of being inseparable from politics, the nature and form of public sector provision is always an area of constant debate among policymakers and media commentators. The 1980s witnessed a wave of reforms under the banner of 'New Public Management' (see Reading 6.1). Prime Minister David Cameron has emphasized a similar logic with his idea of the 'Big Society'. The goal of such initiatives is to promote efficiency, introduce a customer focus, and readily promote the adoption of models and ideas from the private sector. Overall, in the wake of New Public Management, governments have sought to increase the accountability and responsiveness of public service providers by collecting, auditing, and publishing data on their performance (Rhys *et al.*, 2008: 325).

Contextual features and characteristics that shape and influence strategy

Although concepts from strategic management may yield benefits in the PSO context, it is also important to appreciate that PSOs face 'special challenges' (Feldman, 2005). The key distinguishing features and characteristics that shape and impact strategy in PSOs are as follows.

- **Provision of public goods**

  PSO provision centres around goods with unique characteristics, often labelled 'public goods'. These are goods that cost no more to provide to many people than to one individual, and which it is difficult to prevent others consuming (Hansmann, 1987). It is easy to charge someone for a sandwich—once they have eaten it, no one else can eat it; the same cannot be said for national defence forces or public street lighting. The PSOs concern is for the collective impact of their activities on society as a whole.

- **Provision of public value**

  Like NPOs, PSOs do not operate by a profit-maximizing logic, but instead focus on maximizing net public welfare (Collier *et al.*, 2001). The aim of managerial work in this context is the creation of public value (Moore, 1995). 'Public value' is value that is delivered for, and consumed by, the public collectively (Alford, 2001).

- **Monopoly providers**

  In many cases, PSOs are monopoly providers and suppliers producing non-traded goods and services; they lack the incentive to improve productivity and efficiency that is typically induced by market mechanisms. As a result, some commentators question the applicability of private sector models, because these assume that competition in the marketplace will act as a constant incentive for managers to maximize their performance (Alford, 2001). Operational effectiveness is a real issue for PSO strategists.

- **Multiple influential stakeholders**

  PSOs face the dilemma of having to manage a diverse range of stakeholders, all of whom can influence the organization's activities (Bryson, 2004). Most notably, PSOs are subject to the preferences and influence of politically elected representatives charged with their efficient running. These issues impact not only policy formulation, but also implementation, because PSOs cannot be assured of commitment of resources or that politicians will not intervene and decide how activities should be conducted (Alford, 2001).

- **Ambiguous goals and outcomes**

  A direct consequence of the features and characteristics listed are that PSOs face ambiguous, often conflicting, goals, as well as producing outcomes that, in the absence of market-based price mechanisms, are very difficult to assess in terms of efficiency and effectiveness. In the public sector, the quest for ultimate performance is contested, with national policy as the main driver rather than being 'better' than other providers (Francis and Holloway, 2007: 183). Delivering public value may stem from the provision of legislation, the remedy of market failure, and the promotion of equity. The fact that pressure to perform comes from the political system and the media—not the marketplace—makes the appropriate outcomes less than obvious (Kelman, 2007). Public citizens place greater expectation and demand on PSOs than was evident in the past. Goals must be politically acceptable, while outcomes must be operationally feasible (Alford, 2001: 10).

- **Political**

  The public sector is the central administrative apparatus of the government and so is inevitably bound up with associated politics. Different parties will have different views on the extent to which the state should intervene and deliver certain services. At one extreme, a neo-liberal approach would tend to favour less state intervention, desiring the roll-back of the state in favour of market mechanisms. In contrast, left-wing governments and those inclining towards a more socialist approach would favour state intervention and stress the state's role in providing for a more equitable society. Thus the boundaries and domains of PSOs are politically contested. Politics does not only influence the formulation of PSO strategy; it also shapes its implementation as various departments compete for limited resources, and government changes policies and interferes in implementation (Mintzberg, 1996).

- **Bureaucratic**

  As a result of their sheer size, the necessity of record keeping, and the requirement to be accountable, PSOs typically operate as bureaucracies (see Chapter 10). An effective bureaucracy can provide the necessary alignment and support in executing strategy: for example, the swine flu vaccination programme was rolled out effectively to vulnerable groups. PSOs are rule-driven organizations with a clear hierarchy of staff and responsibilities. This can give rise to criticisms of inflexibility and red tape, as well as the accusation that PSOs are not delivering value for taxpayers' money. For example, the National Health Service (NHS) project of creating one single IT system for all patient records started in 2003 and had cost close to £7bn by mid-2011; some members of Parliament (MPs) have consequently called for this project to be abandoned given its spiralling costs.

Table 13.2 summarizes the factors that shape and impact strategy in PSOs at organizational, managerial, and environmental levels. It is interesting to note the contrast between these factors and those facing NPOs. One of the key differences relates to how focused the organizations are in their missions. In the case of NPOs, missions are clear; for PSOs, political and other stakeholder influences can undermine organizational efforts and deflect them from their core missions. For PSOs, being a monopoly provider is in sharp contrast to the dependency environment in which many NPOs exist: in some cases, NPOs rely on PSOs for vital financial support to maintain their services and activities. Defining outcomes is a common challenge for both NPOs and PSOs given that the nature of their activities is under constant external scrutiny—by taxpayers in the case of PSOs and by donors in the case of NPOs. Similarly, NPOs and PSOs also share challenges around the allocation and long-term sustainability of resources to deliver their services. In the case of PSOs, political change and a decline in tax revenue can dramatically impact on resource allocation.

Key strategic tensions in PSOs

A key strategic tension of PSOs is identifying who the strategists actually are. Who is charged with running a government department: the minister or the head of the civil service? This issue can have a real impact on strategy formulation and implementation: at an organizational level, it can hinder or make long-term planning difficult. Tension arises between political change necessary for the sustainability of a democracy and taking long-term decisions around issues of national importance such as energy security. The second organizational tension is about consistency in the provision of facilities and the delivery of collective public value. In the case of healthcare services, significant expenditure is focused on service delivery, which can vary depending on budgetary constraints, while typically less expenditure is made on preventative and educational programmes, which have a collective public value.

Table 13.2 PSOs' key distinguishing features and characteristics: resulting strategic tensions at different levels

Level	Features	Strategic tensions
Organizational	Bureaucratic Public goods and value Ambiguous goals and outcomes	Political change and interference makes long-term planning difficult Consistency in provision of facilities and the delivery of collective public value
Managerial	Influential stakeholders Internal politics	Diverse range of expectations In-house resource battles and politics expend much energy and effort
Environmental	Monopoly provider Public value	Lack of market mechanisms to assess productivity outcomes Public service provision outcomes are fundamental to the functioning of society

Key strategic tensions with which PSOs have to deal at a managerial level include a diverse range of expectations. Some stakeholders can have a poor understanding of the core purpose of the PSO. For example, is the purpose of HM Prison Service to imprison or rehabilitate prisoners? Lack of clarity, coupled with the potential for political influence, can lessen the impact of strategy in this context. A further managerial tension is the competition between PSOs for resources. This is accentuated in the run-up to government budgets and can disadvantage long-term planning for the sake of short-term outcomes.

At the environmental level, the key strategic tensions are focused on productivity and measurement of outcomes that are fundamental to the functioning of society. In productivity, the key strategic tension is how to measure activity in the absence of market mechanisms. How do we assess the productivity outcomes of our local authority or police force? A further tension is around public service provision outcomes: how should the strategist in a PSO define, implement, and communicate these to both internal and external stakeholders? Given the complexity involved in PSOs, defining high-level provision outcomes can be a major challenge, not always comparable to that in other settings.

Strategy formulation and implementation issues

There are some elements of strategy formulation and implementation that PSOs face in a more acute way than other contexts. The most obvious is the need to adopt a strategic management approach. As Poister and Streib (1999: 323) argue, in public agencies of any size and complexity:

> it is impossible to manage for results in the long or short run without a well-developed capacity for strategic management. Indeed, on a macro level, strategic management, with its emphasis on developing and implementing a strategic agenda, is synonymous with managing for results.

Strategic management is necessary for public administration, and PSOs need to develop a strategic management capacity within their organizations. Many PSOs are required by legislation to have a strategic plan, but that does not necessarily equate to the adoption of strategic management approaches.

Related to this need is understanding the purpose of having a strategy. Once a strategy is in place, what purpose does it really serve? Defining strategic aims and outcomes to the public is now a necessity, given the transparency required. A strategic document fulfils this necessary public role, but the strategy itself is subject to political and funding changes. The purpose of strategy is to garner some legitimacy, as well as resources, and PSO strategy documents reaffirm the legitimacy and core purpose of a PSO.

Finally, with respect to strategy formulation and implementation, particularly around high-profile change programmes, some measure of realism needs to be conveyed to supporters of change, because there is no guarantee of success (Ferlie *et al.*, 2003). Some transformation programmes can promise a lot, but when it comes to implementation the envisaged outcomes may not materialize for a variety of internal and external reasons, including those frequently beyond the direct control of the PSO in question.

The smaller firm context

No matter what definition is employed, the reality is that, in most countries, the industrial landscape is dominated by smaller firms conducting a diverse range of activities, from hairdressing to software development (Storey, 1994). As the field of strategy emerged during the planning era of the 1960s and 1970s, the focus was very much on large multidivisional organizations: the likes of General Motors (GM), Du Pont, and General Electric (GE). For much of this time, 'bigger' was seen to be 'better', with the best path to competitive success said to be economies of scale and increasing market share. However, as the positioning perspective of Michael Porter (1980; 1985) and the work of Miles *et al.* (1978) came to the fore, the potential role that could be played by smaller firms—in particular through niche and prospector strategies—gained increasing recognition. Smaller firms possessed the very qualities that were often found lacking in larger firms, such as **innovation**, flexibility, and proximity to the end consumer (Dean *et al.*, 1998).

It is still the case that we lack an understanding of how the language and ideas of strategy—which, after all, were founded and developed in larger firms—may transfer to this context (McKiernan and Morris, 1994: 532). Is strategy simply a large-firm concept? Can we afford to ignore the diversity and prominence of smaller firms—which typically account for 99 per cent of firms in most industrialized countries? Do the language and formal tools of strategy help or hinder small-firm competitiveness? A useful starting point is to consider the distinct characteristics and features that shape and impact on strategy for smaller firms.

Contextual features and characteristics that shape and influence strategy

Research has shown repeatedly that small firms are much less likely to use, or even have knowledge of, key strategic management tools (such as SWOT, PESTEL, or Porter's five forces). This raises the question of whether small firms are in some way deficient or whether there is something unique about the small firm context, which means that they practise strategy in a different way. Key features that shape and impact on strategy in smaller firms include the following.

- **The liability of smallness**

  Small firms suffer from resource poverty (Welsh and White, 1981), meaning that they typically lack time, managerial know-how, and human and financial resources. These deficiencies can be self-perpetuating, leading to difficulty in raising capital and securing labour, and leaving small firms vulnerable to the bargaining power of larger firm suppliers or customers (Dean *et al.*, 1998: 724).

- **The liability of newness**

  Not all small firms are entrepreneurial. Entrepreneurial firms are those that are typically motivated by profitability and growth, and are characterized by innovative strategic practices (Carland *et al.*, 1984: 358). In contrast, many small-firm owners simply inherit or replace an existing, proven form of small business (Curran and Burrows, 1986: 270). While both types of venture operate under conditions of risk, the entrepreneurial venture will experience substantially more uncertainty, because the market for its product or service is unknown (Alvarez and Barney, 2005: 788). It is these types of entrepreneurial firm, struggling to gain legitimacy and a market and reputation for their businesses, that are more likely to suffer from the liability of newness. For growth-orientated entrepreneurial firms, mortality rates are said to decline with increases in organizational size (Melahi and Wilkinson, 2004). The likelihood of failure will also vary by firm type.

- **Informality**

  As a result of their size and flat structure, operations and decision making in smaller firms are typically more informal. This engenders flexibility, meaning that smaller firms are able to react and respond more quickly. This may also mean that ad hoc informal strategic planning is more prominent and can lead to reluctance to invest in formal planning systems, which may be viewed as sources of constraint and rigidity (Garengo *et al.*, 2005: 41).

- **Concentrated ownership and control**

  One of the most significant structural characteristics of small businesses is the centrality of the entrepreneur/owner-manager (Scase and Goffee, 1987). Smaller firms are typically led by an owner manager/entrepreneur, who, like a one-person orchestra, attends at once to the issues of strategy and operations, with little, if any, distinction made between policy formulation and implementation.

- **Environmental uncertainty**

  Small firms are less likely to have the resources to influence or withstand external shocks or market downturns in the way that large firms can (for example, by transferring resources across areas or departments). Small firms tend to work in concentrated activities and markets, which makes this much more difficult. Consequently, smaller firms have greater vulnerability to changes in the external environment (Storey, 1994). The result can be reactive, flexible strategic manoeuvring as smaller firms 'spend more time adjusting to environmental turbulence rather than trying to predict or control it' (D'Amboise and Muldowney, 1988: 227). However, within the external environment and specific industries, there may be certain routes to advantage that are more suitable and profitable for smaller firms to seek out (Dean *et al.*, 1998).

Table 13.3 summarizes the unique features of smaller firms at their various levels and the resultant strategic tensions, which we discuss in more detail in the next section. From this, we see that NPOs and small firms share and face different types of environmental uncertainty, risk, and informality around the running of their activities. Dynamic and charismatic leaders in both NPOs and smaller firms can have a real impact on direction and stakeholder perceptions. Decision making in small firms can be agile and nimble, whereas in PSOs this can be slow and unwieldy because of organizational bureaucracy. Given the scale and size of many NPOs and smaller firms, both face a constant sustainability and resource struggle, which can lead to short-term thinking and action at the expense of long-term direction setting. In small firms, the strategist can be equated to the owner-manager or the NPO founder, while, as we have mentioned, defining who the strategist is in a PSO is not clear-cut.

Key strategic tensions

At an organizational level, the key strategic tensions that we have identified focus on strategic planning and flexibility. In terms of strategic management techniques and planning, the tension is focused on the deliberate and emergent nature of the strategy of the small firm and is one that we explored in depth in Chapter 4. Entrepreneurs can be intuitive by nature, yet in order to raise finance and achieve growth, they need a business plan, which may run contrary to their more intuitive nature. In addition, given their size and limited managerial capabilities, small firms sometimes cannot see the utility in using strategic management techniques in developing and

Table 13.3 Small firms' key distinguishing features and characteristics: some strategic tensions

Level	Features	Strategic tensions
Organizational	Liability of smallness Liability of newness Informality	Directly impacts on the knowledge and ability of smaller firms to invest in strategic management and planning techniques against the need to have a business plan to raise capital Can foster flexibility and facilitate innovation
Managerial	Centralized control Dynamics of ownership, e.g. familial relations Founder's influence and personal goals	Can lead to an unwillingness to delegate and introduce formal practices Can lead to quick decision making
Environmental	High levels of uncertainty Small market share Dependency on certain suppliers/customers	Strategic intent somewhat constrained and limited nature of choosing strategic options Opportunity to specialize, differentiate

growing their business. They will often see these as being of benefit only to larger, more complex organizations.

The second organizational tension centres on maintaining and fostering flexibility and facilitating innovation, as opposed to developing the more professional and mature organizational structures and managerial approaches that could enable the small firm to grow. This is an issue that we explored in Chapter 12 and one that requires delicate balancing, given the embryonic and fragile state of development of smaller firms. Here, much again depends on the mindset or 'organizational blueprint' of the owner-manager (Baron and Hannon, 2002).

The unwillingness of an entrepreneur/owner-manager to delegate activities and introduce new practices in a small firm can be a source of strategic tension, particularly if the desire is to grow and expand. The reality for owner-managers is that they cannot undertake all of the activities that they did when they first founded the business; as the business grows, they need to delegate. Underpinning this unwillingness to let go of control may be issues of trust and openness; owner-managers like to keep ideas and market knowledge 'close to their chests' and may not share strategic information freely with their staff, thereby reducing the openness required for sound strategic planning (Beaver, 2002). Another implication is that they may shun opportunities to grow or introduce formal practices, because they do not wish to risk losing direct control over their firm by delegating tasks or growing staff numbers (Gray, 1998: 21). For family businesses, the issue of succession or delegating core activities to non-family members can be a source of constant tension.

The second managerial tension is around quick decision making, which can enhance operational flexibility, but can prove damaging when dealing with core strategic issues of the business that encompass foundations and routes to advantage.

At the environmental level, the strategic tensions focus on strategic intent and choosing strategic options. Small firms may desire to grow and, in time, dominate or control the rules of competition. The nature of choosing strategic options (see Chapter 6) to pursue such strategic intent may lack analytical rigour and sophistication, and may be limited by the availability of resources. Tied to this strategic tension is the fact that the opportunity to specialize and differentiate may not exist to the extent that the small firm first envisaged. This, again, is tied to the resource availability of small firms. Strategy formulation and implementation influences how small firms utilize the resources that they have and identify the appropriate further resources necessary to grow and survive.

Some strategy formulation and implementation issues

In smaller firms, the domain questions of corporate level strategy (Chapter 7) and the market questions of business level strategy (Chapter 8) are usually conflated into one, because smaller firms usually only operate in a single market, or a limited range of markets with similar customer requirements (Beaver, 2002). Nonetheless, the questions of what business we are in and how we should compete have just as much importance in this context. Indeed, having a considered understanding of these strategic issues and exhibiting a coherency in direction may facilitate in mitigating some of the key reasons why small business fail (such as problems in raising capital, legitimacy problems, difficulties in attracting workers) (Baum and Oliver, 1996; Jennings and Beaver, 1997). However, the means by which these strategic questions are answered are likely to differ in smaller firms. It has long been assumed that formal strategic planning is an essential prerequisite for efficient performance in all business organizations, including smaller firms (McKiernan and Morris, 1994: 31). Yet the strategy-as-programming approach of the design school sits uneasily with the informality, limited resources, and environmental uncertainty faced by the smaller firm.

In these simple organizations, strategy is often an extrapolation of the personality of the owner-manager/entrepreneur (Mintzberg, 1979) or guided by founders' individual 'blueprints' of the way in which they wish their organization to compete (Baron and Hannon, 2002). In this sense, 'a lack of formal business planning in small firms does not mean that these firms are badly managed'

(Richbell, 2006: 498). Strategic thinking may be strategy planning, as the owner-manager synthesizes information from a variety of sources and moulds it into a vision of what direction the business should pursue. Often, formal planning is not explicitly contemplated in smaller firms until something goes wrong or evidence of it is required to gain capital, or legitimacy from customers or suppliers (Beaver, 2002).

In this context, it is also the case that 'attempts to measure the strategic health of such enterprises using standard evaluation methods are often inadequate and frequently misleading' (Beaver, 2002: 75). This is because even though small firms operate in the private, for-profit context, the instrumental objective of profit maximization may be subordinated to other goals. What constitutes successful performance may be something that is specific to each firm. For example, in a small-firm context, relative performance measures may include simply ensuring the survival of the firm, maintaining independence, being able to support one's family or ethnic group, or ensuring succession from one generation to the next (Aldrich and Cliff, 2003; Stanworth and Gray, 1991). In this context, sustainability may carry more weight than the quest for competitive advantage (D'Amboise and Muldowney, 1988). This is especially the case in family firms, in which continuity is a cherished ideal among family members, because most parents and their children want the business to remain in family hands (Griffeth *et al.*, 2006: 491).

Having reviewed key distinctions and characteristics of firms operating in different contexts, it is now possible to offer an overview by means of examining implications of the strategic management challenges in these contexts.

Strategic management challenges for NPOs, PSOs, and smaller firms

In Chapter 1, we identified the four strategic management challenges—orientation, **trade-off**, relevance, and change—and it is worth reflecting on these in the context of this chapter. Table 13.4 outlines how the strategic management challenges may apply in the context of NPOs, PSOs, and

Table 13.4 Strategic management challenges in the three domains

	Smaller firms	Not-for-profits	Public sector
Orientation challenge	Heavily linked to ownership Founders often have vision, and specific blueprints for success Survival vs competitive advantage	Clear vision, mission is driving feature Effectiveness and efficiency: doing well while doing good	Political wrangling, ambiguous goal Long-term support and smooth implementation difficult to ensure
Trade-offs	Shaped by liabilities of newness/smallness Informality, limited scope, more control of internal operations	What to conduct, often shaped by funding	Highly constrained by nature of public goods and by political mandates and/or professional values
Relevance	Focus on differentiating in unique niches	NPO's cause takes precedence	Normative and professional values, multiple stakeholder expectations
Change	Greater proximity to external environment, adaptability and flexibility important	Evolution vs revolution Pressures for accountability	Rarely radical Pressures for enhanced productivity, 'value for money' may alter the configuration of how the service is delivered

smaller firms. Each context presents a unique set of challenges for the strategists—in particular, managing continuing exchanges with the environment. The organizations operating in each domain are open systems, which depend very much on interaction and exchange with the external environment for their very viability and well-being. Gaining legitimacy, managing dependency relations, and in some cases simply meeting the table stakes necessary to survive are activities that consume the strategist's time and effort.

In reflecting on Table 13.4, we must be careful not to overstate differences and consequently treat the corporate sector, public sector, small business, and not-for-profit sectors as completely separate domains. While NPOs might be more likely to be visionary organizations, PSOs more likely to be bureaucratic, and smaller firms more likely to be simple structures (Mintzberg, 1979), it is best to speak of the extent of an orientation, rather than to assume there to be an ideal type. Overly mechanistic comparisons risk overlooking the key interactions between the various domains. It is clear that there are organizations that operate between the domains, such as a cooperative or mutual aid organization, which is somewhere between a private sector and public sector organization (Paton, 1992). Similarly, there is evidence of shifting boundaries: for example, privatization and tendering have seen aspects of public sector delivery stretch into the private and not-for-profit sectors. Public–private sector partnerships are an increasingly common way in which to produce government outputs (Boyne *et al.*, 2006). Likewise, NPOs can become involved with the private sector by means of sponsorship, partnerships, and service agreements (Paton and Cornforth, 1992: 37). Even those private sector organizations such as Ryanair, which claim to be exemplars of the positive impact of free market capitalism, in practice rely heavily upon regulation concerning landing slots and the government subsidies supplied to regional airports. Perhaps the best evidence of the blurred boundaries between domains can be found with the recent rise of social enterprises, which sell goods and services on a commercial basis, but have an explicit social objective, such as community transport, waste management, Café Direct, or the Fairtrade movement (Chell, 2007; Harding, 2004). Equally, private sector strategy may have much to learn from various contexts. For example, Peter Drucker (1989: 88) noted that 'in two areas, strategy and the effectiveness of the board, NPOs are practising what most [American] businesses only preach'. Similarly, Barney (2005: 945) argued that 'bringing strategic management theory to bear on social policy debates will benefit both the quality of many of these debates and the quality of the field of strategic management', while precisely because strategic management concerns the health and survival of firms, a basic understanding of how size influences competitive behaviour should be of paramount importance (Chen and Hambrick, 1995: 453).

Spotlight Charity needs a better foundation

Despite best efforts by corporate social responsibility activists, business is *not* philanthropic by nature. By contrast, philanthropic bodies, charities, and non-governmental organizations are, indeed, businesses in the eyes of the law. Yet, perversely, today's FTSE or Nasdaq companies are far more transparent, accountable, and responsibly governed than the typical wealthy foundation or charity. More damning, corporate results are measured in the marketplace, while philanthropic results are not. That invites mischief and mismanagement.

As grant-making institutions seek greater influence on public perception, policies, and practices worldwide, their need for greater openness and technical assessment has intensified. Good intentions should not excuse poor accountability. Philanthropic reform—not only new philanthropy—is essential. The trustees and directors should be every bit as accountable and liable as—if not more so than—their for-profit counterparts. UK shareholders, for example, have the right to vote on executive pay and perks; charitable donors to 'good causes' typically do not.

What role, then, should 'donor democracy' play in philanthropy's future? Environmental trusts demand that governments slash carbon budgets even as they profess ignorance of their members' carbon profligacy. US and European charitable foundations are notorious for bloated boards of fund-raising directors that—not unlike their 1990s corporate forebears—have become captive to their staff. Indeed, how does a bad philanthropic board get the sack?

The UK has begun addressing these concerns in a way that the USA has not. In November 2006, the UK Parliament approved the Charities Act even as US congressional efforts to mandate greater philanthropic accountability failed. While the British reforms take crucial first steps—for example, not granting charities the presumption that they act for the 'public benefit'—a disconcerting vagueness shrouds how regulators will assure effective transparency and transparent effectiveness.

'Of every $1,000 spent in so-called charity today,' observed a philanthropist whom both Warren Buffett and Bill Gates have described as an inspiration, 'it is probable that $950 is unwisely spent—so spent, indeed, as to produce the very evils it hopes to mitigate or cure.' The entrepreneurial billionaire who penned those words was Andrew Carnegie, the diminutive Scot and philanthropic giant, in his 1889 *Gospel of Wealth* manifesto. By today's standards, Carnegie's unusually transparent grant-making style puts contemporary foundation trustees to shame.

US corporate governance gurus such as Ira Millstein insist that top foundations grasp what the Enron debacle and the US Sarbanes-Oxley Act imply for their own institutional accountability. They have begun re-engineering their boards and flirting with transparency. Yet most philanthropic bodies appear operationally opaque, while providing no reliable assessment of their 'public benefit'. They seem to measure success more by how much is given to whom than by how much social or economic value they create. Any harm that their initiatives may cause—inadvertent or otherwise—is rarely discussed. This behaviour is no longer tolerated in the 'for profit' sector; why should charity be exempt?

Funders with the cash and conviction to proffer solutions for societal shortcomings should have a duty, if not the integrity, to disclose their own shortcomings. Global philanthropy would be more credible and productive if, say, the Ford, Rockefeller, and Soros Foundations and Wellcome Trust would publicly debate their greatest programmatic failures.

Freedom and fairness demand that individuals and institutions have a right financially to support lawful ideals and causes. That right does not entitle philanthropists to policies subsidizing inefficiency and opacity. In reality, well-intentioned tax subsidies have spawned foundations and charities that are more like mis-shapen creatures of tax advantage than healthy embodiments of public interest.

For any organization, preferential tax treatment should be contingent on performance measures that go beyond grant giving and wealth redistribution. Institutions unable or unwilling to proffer auditable results should lose their subsidy.

The urgency for innovative oversight reflects accelerating growth in non-profit assets and aspirations. Much as hedge funds and private equity have transformed global financial markets, entrepreneurial and institutional philanthropists are collectively investing billions to transform public policy. The Gates Foundation—by far the world's largest—is the colossus, but there are now literally tens of thousands of foundations with tax-supported ambitions to change the world. The global surge in mass affluence assures that this trend will accelerate. The next great philanthropic action in the West may be Chinese, Indian, and Russian.

Globalization and extraterritoriality—not just new wealth—have qualitatively complicated the altruism business. Philanthropic bodies increasingly serve as rivals and goads—rather than complements—to government. There is indeed a thin line between *noblesse oblige* and philanthropic imperialism. Crossing it is dangerous, but inevitably the insulated and unaccountable board and trustee will cross it. That is the regulatory story of twentieth-century philanthropy. Charitably put, in this emerging era, quality philanthropic governance is crucial to quality philanthropic leadership.

Source: Schrage (2007). Reproduced with the kind permission of Michael Schrage.

Implications for strategy practice

Strategy and strategic management approaches can offer real value in the context of NPOs, PSOs, and small firms. Applying such approaches and the resultant conversations help to clarify the visions and missions in these contexts, but also help in developing a more structured and analytical approach to understanding key choices. Such value can often be overlooked in these contexts, but is important to long-term sustainability, because it helps build ownership around the strategy—particularly among stakeholders who provide key sources of funding. The strategist in each of these contexts can vary, but they can shape, develop, and provide a much-needed blueprint for action, identity and motivation (particularly for volunteers in NPOs), legitimacy in introducing strategy practices and processes to secure appropriate resources, a lever with which to deal with political challenges, and a benchmark against which to evaluate performance. Strategists can directly influence practices, structures, approaches, and intent in these contexts in a manner that is clearly visible to key stakeholders.

In all three contextual settings, there is a requirement both to enhance productivity and operational effectiveness, and to ensure that the firm remains unique or offers a unique value proposition. While the means by which analysis occurs may differ, and while the strategy-formation process is likely to be influenced by multiple constituents, arguably the logic of Porter's (1996—Reading 1.1) argument still holds relevance.

In addition, it is important to consider the language, arguments, and rationale that strategists use to ensure legitimacy with respect to key stakeholders (a topic covered in Chapter 14). Strategists also have a role in defining what constitutes successful performance in contexts in which profit is not a primary goal. Defining operational effectiveness and the associated outcome metrics challenges strategists to develop new valuation and evaluation mechanisms that will impact recipients of services.

The role of the strategist can vary in these contexts and, in PSOs, there may be no explicit or obvious strategy roles. However, there is a real need in all contexts to develop strategy development capacities and to put in place robust strategy processes that really engage with key stakeholders, funders, and users of services alike. This forces a change in mindset, but not in core mission or focus. We must also bear in mind the appropriateness of some analytical tools to these contexts, but the value is in the strategic thinking that emerges. The nurturing and development of strategic capability and talented strategists are critically important for the sustainable development of these organizational contexts.

Finally, the role and influence of boards, particularly in these organizational contexts, must not be underestimated in support of strategy. For NPOs, an appropriate mix within a board is critical in achieving operational effectiveness, development of organizational procedures, and development of long-term strategic thinking about sustainability of activities around a core mission. Society is well served if PSO boards reflect the broad spectrum of managerial and strategic experiences necessary to deliver on their core objectives. Such boards can be powerful influencers, particularly with respect to long-term direction and supporting PSOs' management teams in overcoming short-term orientation and political influences. For small firms, bringing in outside expertise on an ad hoc basis or at board level can strengthen strategic capacity and capability, which can sharpen focus and direction. Such interactions can also provide much-needed support to owner-managers and management teams that have a consistent short-term intuitive focus. In all of the contexts discussed, organizational culture is likely to serve as a key **paradigm**, shaping what are judged as key threats and opportunities. The goal for the strategist is to leverage the benefit of unique cultural contexts and legacies, while also being cognizant of prospective weaknesses and blind spots that may emerge as a result.

Introduction to readings

Reading 6.1 is a classic conceptual piece by Christopher Hood, entitled 'A public management for all seasons?' (1991). This article brings together the key aspects of 'New Public Management' (NPM), tracing its origins and its claims to universality, as well as its different meanings and typical justifications for its use. Hood argues that, for criticism of NPM to be valuable, it must assess the nature of administrative values relating to what constitutes 'good administration'. Here, he captures three families of core values that relate to administrative design: sigma, theta, and lambda. Each has its own logic, and it is hard to satisfy all equally. How far does Hood's account help us to understand which value becomes dominant and why this may be the case? Hood's argument is based on the UK, but do these arguments hold in other contexts? Might it be that some parts of Europe, for example, have managed these tensions better or can do so? Or perhaps NPM is simply a language that is happily employed, but rarely enacted in practice—something that we will consider in the next chapter.

The second reading for this chapter, accessible via a link on the Online Resource Centre that accompanies this book, a research article on the smaller firm by Joyce and Woods (2003), considers the debate between Mintzberg's 'anti-planning' view of strategy in small firms, which, according to the authors, risks 'becoming fruitless and sterile', and a more rational planning approach. The authors seem to come down in favour of the rational planning approach—but does their research data support this? How does this argument fit with the view of small firms presented in this chapter? Is resolving the deficiency of strategic management tools in this context simply an issue of enhancing owner-manager knowledge and access? What of the unique characteristics of smaller firms?

Mini case study Success and longevity: The International Committee of the Red Cross *Ann M. Torres, J. E. Cairnes School of Business and Economics, National University Ireland, Galway*

Introduction

The International Committee of the Red Cross (ICRC), established in 1863, is a neutral organization that works towards ensuring humanitarian protection. The ICRC, headquartered in Geneva, Switzerland, operates in more than eighty countries and employs more than 12,000 staff (ICRC, 2005a). It is the world's oldest non-religious organization dedicated to humanitarian relief and it has a unique place in international law (Casey and Rivkin, 2005). The ICRC is mandated by public international law to assist victims of war and violence (Forsythe, 2005). The agreements that the ICRC establishes with the authorities of the countries in which its delegations and missions work mean that the ICRC avails of immunities and privileges that preserve its neutrality and freedom (ICRC, 2005a).

Organizational longevity

Under the Geneva Conventions, the ICRC initially focused on the welfare of wounded soldiers in international war. Now, the ICRC has expanded its remit to include 'civilian and military victims of armed conflicts and internal disturbances' (ICRC, 2005a: 1), as well as 'human rights issues that transcend conflict situations' (Forsythe, 2005: 2), such as 'disaster response, disaster preparedness, health and care in the community, and humanitarian principles and values' (Quelch and Laidler, 2003: 1). Since the end of the Cold War, the ICRC's activities have expanded considerably. As a consequence of its increased international presence, the ICRC has received more media attention, but as an organization it is still poorly understood. This lack of understanding persists despite the fact that the ICRC has won four Nobel Peace Prizes (1901, 1917, 1944, and 1963) (Forsythe, 2005). Such accolades raise the question: 'How has the ICRC existed for so long, and even expanded, when other organizations—even highly reputable ones ... —have foundered?' (Forsythe, 2005: 5).

History

Jean-Henri Dunant is the visionary behind the foundation of the ICRC. In 1859, Dunant, a Swiss businessman, came across a particularly brutal battle between the armies of Austria and the Franco-Sardinian alliance in Solferino, Italy, where 40,000 soldiers lay dead or dying (Quelch and Laidler, 2003). Dunant organized the local people of Solferino to attend to and comfort the wounded on both sides of the conflict (ICRC, 2005a). Dunant wrote an account of this experience, *A Memory of Solferino*, in which he made two solemn appeals:

> • for relief societies to be formed in peacetime, with nurses who would be ready to care for the wounded in wartime;
>
> • for these volunteers, who would be called upon to assist the army medical services, to be recognized and protected through an international agreement.
>
> (ICRC, 2005a: 6)

'By 1863 [Dunant] had garnered so much support that the Geneva Society for Public Welfare helped establish the International Committee for Relief to the Wounded', which in 1875 became the ICRC (Encyclopaedia Britannica, 2008). The emblem that the organization adopted was the inverse of the Swiss flag: a red cross on a white field (Quelch and Laidler, 2003).

Humanitarian mission

The ICRC's delegations and missions primarily employ nationals of the countries in which it works to carry out a range of activities, such as: assisting civilians, individuals deprived of their freedom, dispersed families, the wounded and sick of existing or emerging conflict; preventive action through cooperation with the National Societies; and humanitarian coordination and diplomacy (ICRC, 2007b). 'Delegations also act as early warning systems, which enable the ICRC to respond to needs quickly and effectively when conflict erupts' (ICRC, 2005a: 4). The ICRC and its societies work to uphold seven 'Fundamental Principles': humanity; impartiality; neutrality; independence; voluntary service; unity; and universality.

Humanitarian network structure

The Red Cross and Red Crescent Movement, also known simply as 'the Movement', encompasses three independent bodies: the International Committee of the Red Cross

(ICRC); the International Federation of Red Cross and Red Crescent Societies (IFRC); and the 186 National Societies. Each body has its own status and none has authority over the other (Quelch and Laidler, 2003). The ICRC is the founding body of the Movement; it manages the efforts of the National Societies and the IFRC. In times of conflict, the ICRC is the lead agency for international operations; it directs and coordinates international relief activities conducted by other members of the Movement. The ICRC acts as the custodian of the Geneva Conventions and promotes adherence to international humanitarian law (IHL). Central to instilling trust and confidence in the countries in which it works, the ICRC espouses three derivative principles: impartiality, neutrality, and independence.

International Federation of the Red Cross (IFRC)

In the aftermath of the First World War, it was recognized that greater cooperation was required among the various Red Cross Societies, which, 'through their humanitarian activities on behalf of prisoners of war and combatants, had attracted millions of volunteers and built a large body of expertise' (IFRC, 2007). The president of the American Red Cross War Committee, Henry Davison, proposed the formation of a federation of the National Societies. The IFRC 'acts as the official representative of its member Societies in the international field' (SCRCRC, 2001: 4). It 'works with National Societies in responding to catastrophes around the world. Its relief operations are combined with development work, including disaster preparedness programmes, health and care activities, and the promotion of humanitarian values' (IFRC, 2007: 4).

National Societies

The network of 186 National Societies forms the core of the Movement. The National Societies encompass 97 million volunteers, who 'provide a wide variety of services, ranging from disaster relief and assistance for the victims of war, to first aid training and restoring family links' (IFRC, 2007: 5). The volunteers support public authorities and their local knowledge enables the Movement to give assistance where it is required. Indeed, 'National Society volunteers are often the first on the scene when a disaster strikes and remain active within affected communities long after everyone else has come and gone' (ibid). It is this network of community-based volunteers that gives the Movement a distinct advantage in addressing humanitarian challenges.

Red cross and red crescent

Although the 'red cross' was meant to remain free of religious, political, or other associations, to some Muslims it was reminiscent of the Crusades. In response, 'the Ottoman empire declared that it would use a red crescent instead of a red cross as its emblem, although it agreed to respect the red cross used by the other side' (ICRC, 2007a: 2). The ICRC was the first to use the red crescent during the Russo-Turkish War between 1877 and 1878, and the emblem, which is the reverse of the Ottoman flag, was officially adopted in 1929.

Moves to create a third emblem were partly in response to the need for a neutral symbol that would be acceptable to all National Societies and states, and in particular to those that wish to use neither the red cross nor the red crescent. National Societies and states that did not use either of the official emblems were not recognized 'as full members of the Movement ... and raised the prospect that different emblems would continue to proliferate' (ICRC, 2007a: 2). The concern was that:

> if emblems grow more specific and more numerous, they will compromise the safety of those the Red Cross has sworn to protect. While soldiers in the heat of battle can be relied on to recognize perhaps two or three symbols of protection, expecting them to identify 200 or 300 isn't reasonable.
>
> (Giampietro and Smith, 2006: 1)

Additional reasons for considering a new emblem were highlighted in a July 2001 review of the Red Cross brand in fifteen countries by advertising agency Young & Rubicam (Griffin, 2005). The study found that while the Movement 'had a high status in all of the 15 countries, people weren't sure what the Red Cross actually did' (Griffin, 2005: 3). More importantly, the Movement began to reassess for what it wanted to be known. It was believed that a new emblem would provide the Movement with the opportunity to revitalize its brand (Quelch and Laidler-Kylander, 2005).

Red crystal

At the Diplomatic Conference of December 2005, the states party to the Geneva Conventions adopted the Third Protocol to the Geneva Conventions to endorse the red crystal: 'The red crystal, a square standing on one corner, is being promoted as a neutral third symbol that could bridge religious differences' (Griffin, 2005: 3). The red crystal does not replace the red cross or the red crescent; it simply broadens the choice of emblems and contributes to the universality of the movement (ICRC, 2007a). Because all three emblems have equal status under international law, it is hoped that, together, they will provide the Movement with a comprehensive and lasting solution.

Marketing and communications

Over the last few years, the ICRC's marketing unit has pursued a number of large-scale research studies so as to develop its communication strategies and to more effectively raise 'awareness and influence attitudes on issues of importance' (ICRC, 2006: 34). The ICRC has focused on two areas of research: examining the communication needs of key audiences, regionally and globally (ICRC, 2007b); and measuring 'perceptions of and attitudes towards humanitarian action, the humanitarian environment, [as well as] the ICRC logo and emblems' (ICRC, 2006: 34).

Organizational paradoxes

The ICRC is said to be an organization of paradoxes. It is hybrid in character, because it is neither a non-governmental organization (NGO), nor an inter-governmental organization (IGO) (Murphy, 2007). It is a private agency under the Swiss Civil Code, but it has an international legal profile, which affords the ICRC certain immunities and privileges, including UN Observer Status (Murphy, 2007). The ICRC places the welfare of individuals in conflict as its primary mandate, but it proceeds cautiously and generally with the consent of state authorities (Forsythe, 2005). It is non-political, but its activities make it 'inherently part of humanitarian politics. It professes impartiality and neutrality, but it calculates how to advance humanitarian policies that are in competition with other policies based on national and factional advantage' (ibid: 2). It is suggested that this inherent tension of opposites is what makes the ICRC a successful organization, perhaps spurring the organization to seek creative innovations to complex problems and situations.

Organizational strengths and weaknesses

The ICRC's most prominent strengths are its long experience and its established mandate, as well as its explicit values and organizational cohesiveness (DFID, 2003). The ICRC's organizational focus is abundantly clear: it is known for its humanitarian protection and assistance activities in situations of armed conflict, as well as for its relentless promotion of IHL.

Network relationships management

The ICRC's identity of independence is 'an essential strength as well as an operational weakness' (DFID, 2003: 9). Although the ICRC acknowledges the importance of coordination and cooperation among humanitarian agencies, 'it is reluctant to be coordinated by any other body, or to engage in relations that may compromise its perceived neutral status. Within this context the ICRC [needs] to establish how to engage more strategically with other concerned international actors' (ibid: 9). Given the network of organizations within the Movement, it is unsurprising that the ICRC is at times inconsistent in its manner of cooperating with National Societies and the IFRC. Consequently, the ICRC needs to clarify continuously and disseminate intensively its policy and guidelines in key areas of its work to ensure that all relevant field staff fully grasp its main objectives (ibid).

Because the ICRC is often perceived as a high-cost organization, attention to cost control management is in the ICRC's interest, particularly to demonstrate accountability to donors. The 'introduction of an analytical cost accounting system provides an instrument to the management at all levels to better appraise the costs of ICRC programmes and to achieve increased cost efficiency' (ibid: 10). However, it also must be recognized that the ICRC often works in difficult and hazardous situations, which require costly, labour-intensive methods.

Challenges ahead

The ICRC's experiential longevity is important because the nature of armed conflict is changing and, consequently, its approach for the twenty-first century is that of reflection. As the lead agency in the Movement, the ICRC is faced with the challenge of 'how best to reconcile the diverse domestic priorities and cultural particularities of the National Societies with its ambition to [engage] a global network for humanitarian action that works together effectively' (SCRCRC, 2001: 13)—that is, how all components of the Movement can function more cohesively in response to the changing contexts and new challenges (ICRC, 2007c). Most importantly, how can the ICRC ensure that the people requiring assistance remain at the heart of the Movement's activities, while simultaneously stimulating and cultivating humanitarian accountability (DFID, 2003)?

Sources: Casey and Rivkin (2005); DFID (2003); Encyclopaedia Britannica (2008); Forsythe (2005); Giampietro and Smith (2006); Griffin (2005); ICRC (2005a; 2005b; 2005c; 2006; 2007a; 2007b; 2007c); IFRC (2006; 2007); Murphy (2007); Quelch and Laidler (2003); Quelch and Laidler-Kylander (2005); SCRCRC (2001); VCCP (2006)

Questions

1. Outline the relevant distinguishing features and characteristics that could shape and influence the strategy of the ICRC.

2. Using Table 13.1, discuss the key strategic tensions—organizational, managerial, and environmental—of the ICRC.

3. How does the ICRC differ from other NPOs, and does this shape its core mission and direction?

4. Discuss how the issues that the ICRC faces are similar or dissimilar to those of any other large multinational organization.

Summary

Although this chapter has been able to provide only a brief overview of the role of various contexts in shaping strategy, their impact has been clear; each context has distinct features and characteristics, and the strategic tensions vary. It is evident that strategy can have real value and relevance to these contexts, and may be essential to organizational effectiveness. Yet, in many ways, we are at the beginning of the research journey of understanding the various facets of strategy in these complex organizational contexts. Such insights would benefit practitioners, society, and policymakers; as Mahoney and McGahan (2007: 79) note:

> the strategic management field has a relatively weak voice in the formulation of public policy, perhaps because we have not focused sufficiently on the important implications of our insights for managers in government and other non-profit domains. The very process of strategic thinking can be [as] important as certain outcomes.

As Beaver (2002: 75) has noted in relation to smaller firms, 'the process of strategic thinking and planning, rather than the plan itself appears to be the key driver of business performance'.

Engaging in a conversation about how domains differ, key underlying assumptions and common modes of operation are an important requirement for strategic management theory, else it can only ever be considered at best partial, and at worst biased and distorted. Too often, strategy and strategists are considered in a simplistic way as if they operate in a vacuum. It is important to question the assumptions of rational and classic views of strategy and strategic choice. This may involve more than a simple critique of rationality, but rather an enhanced understanding of what rationality actually means in different contexts. Following our review, it is even clearer that strategy may have much to learn from the missionary zeal of NPOs, the political and multiple stakeholder management required of PSOs, and the informal nature of smaller firms. The language of strategy has many tongues, and it is important to recognize the benefits and limitations of how it is spoken in different contexts.

Discussion questions

1. Is strategy relevant to all organizations? Do the arguments of strategic management hold in every context?

2. Compare and contrast the nature of the environment and the key strategic issues confronting:

   a) a global service organization listed on the stock exchange;

   b) a small manufacturing organization;

   c) a governmental department of health (such as the NHS); and

   d) a local cancer support charity.

3. What factors are associated with success in:

   a) NPOs;

   b) PSOs; and

   c) small businesses?

4. How do the nature and importance of evaluating performance differ across various contexts?

5. Who are the key strategists in each domain that we have explored in this chapter? What implications does this have for the organization's strategy?

Further reading

M. H. Moore (1995) ***Creating Public Value: Strategic Management in Government***, Boston, MA: Harvard University Press, is a classic, if contested, treatise on the value of applying the principles of strategic management to the public sector context.

W. Lasher (1999) ***Strategic Thinking for Small Business***, Oxford: Blackwell, offers an informative account of the process of strategy development in smaller firms and business units.

W. W. Powell (ed.) (1987) ***The Nonprofit Sector: A Research Handbook***, New Haven, CT: Yale University Press, provides a dated, yet extensive, range of contributions examining theories and research on NPOs.

visit the Online Resource Centre that accompanies this book to access more learning resources on this chapter topic at www.oxfordtextbooks.co.uk/orc/cunningham/

References

Aldrich, H. E. and Cliff, J. E. 2003. The pervasive effects of family on entrepreneurship: toward a family embeddedness perspective. *Journal of Business Venturing*, 18: 573–596.

Alford, J. 2001. The implications of 'publicness' for strategic management theory. In G. Johnson and K. Scholes (eds) *Exploring Public Sector Strategy*. London: FT/Prentice Hall.

Alvarez, S. and Barney, J. 2005. How do entrepreneurs organize firms under conditions of uncertainty? *Journal of Management*, 31(5): 776–793.

Barney, J. 2005. Should strategic management research engage public policy issues? *Academy of Management Journal*, 48(6): 945–948.

Baron, J. and Hannon, M. 2002. Organizational blueprints for success in high-technology start-ups: lessons from the Stanford project on emerging companies. *Californian Management Review*, 44(3): 8–37.

Baum, J. and Oliver, C. 1996. The institutional ecology of organizational founding. *Academy of Management Journal*, 39: 1378–1427.

Beaver, G. 2002. *Small Business, Entrepreneurship and Enterprise Development*. London: FT/Prentice Hall.

Berry, M. 1998. Strategic planning in small high tech companies. *Long Range Planning*, 31(3): 455–466.

Boyne, G., Meier, K., O'Toole, L., and Walker, R. (eds) 2006. *Public Service Performance: Perspectives on Measurement and Management*. Cambridge: Cambridge University Press.

Brown, A. and Iverson, O. 2004. Exploring strategy and board structure in nonprofit organizations. *Nonprofit and Voluntary Sector Quarterly*, 33(3): 377–400.

Bryson, J. 2004. What to do when stakeholders matter. *Public Management Review*, 6(1): 21–53.

Carland, J. W., Hoy, F., Boulton, W. R., and Carland, J. A. C. 1984. Differentiating entrepreneurs from small business owners: a conceptualization. *Academy of Management Review*, 9(2): 354–359.

Casey, L.A. and Rivkin. D.B. 2005. Double-red-crossed. *The National Interest*. 79: 63–69.

Chell, E. 2007. Social enterprise and entrepreneurship. *International Small Business Journal*, 25(1): 5–26.

Chen, M. and Hambrick, D. 1995. Speed, stealth and selective attack: how small firms differ from large firms in competitive behaviour. *Academy of Management Journal*, 38(2): 453–482.

Collier, N., Fishwick, F., and Johnson, G. 2001. The process of strategy development in the public sector. In G. Johnson and K. Scholes (eds) *Exploring Public Sector Strategy*. London: FT Prentice Hall.

Cornford, C. 2001. What makes a board effective? An examination between board inputs, structures, processes and effectiveness in non-profit organizations. *Corporate Governance*, 9(3): 217–227.

Courtney, R. 1996. *Managing Voluntary Organizations: New Approaches*. Hemel Hempstead: ICSA Publishing.

Curran, J. and Burrows, R. 1986. The sociology of petit capitalism: a trend report. *Sociology*, 20(2): 265–279.

Currie, G. and Lockett, A. 2007. A critique of transformational leadership: moral, professional and contingent dimensions of leadership within public service organizations. *Human Relations*, 60(2): 341–370.

D'Amboise, G. and Muldowney, M. 1988. Management theory for small business: attempts and requirements. *Academy of Management Journal*, 13(2): 226–240.

Dean, T., Brown, R., and Bamford, C. 1998. Differences in large and small firm responses to environmental context: strategic implications. *Strategic Management Journal*, 19(8): 709–728.

Department for International Development (DFID). 2003. *Working in Partnership with the International Committee of the Red Cross 2002–2006.* London: Stairway Communications for DFID.

Drucker, P. F. 1989. What businesses can learn from non-profits. *Harvard Business Review*, 67(4): 88–93.

Encyclopaedia Britannica. 2008. International Committee of the Red Cross. *Encyclopaedia Britannica Online*.

Feldman, M. S. 2005. Management and public management. *Academy of Management Journal*, 48(6): 958–960.

Ferlie, E. 1992. The creation and evolution of quasi markets in the public sector: a problem for strategic management. *Strategic Management Journal*, 13: 79–97.

Ferlie, E., Hartley, J., and Martin, S. 2003. Changing public service organizations: current perspective and future prospects, *British Journal of Management*, 14(1): 1–14.

Forsythe, D. P. 2005. *The Humanitarians: The International Committee of the Red Cross*. Cambridge: Cambridge University Press.

Francis, G. and Holloway, J. 2007. What have we learned? Themes from the literature on best-practice benchmarking. *International Journal of Management Reviews*, 9(3): 171–189.

Frumkin, P. and Andre-Clark, A. 2000. When missions, markets, and politics collide: values and strategy in the nonprofit human services. *Nonprofit and Voluntary Sector Quarterly*, 29(1): 141–163.

Garengo, P., Stefano, B., and Bititci, U. 2005. Performance measurement systems in SMEs: a review for a research agenda. *International Journal of Management Reviews*, 7(1): 25–47.

Giampietro, R. and Smith, K. 2006. Crystal power for the Red Cross. *Businessweek*, 13 January. Available online at http://www.businessweek.com/innovate/content/jan2006/id20060113_913948.htm?chan = search

Gray, C. 1997. Managing entrepreneurial growth: a question of control? In D. Deakin, P. Jennings, and C. Mason (eds) *Entrepreneurship in the Nineties*. London: Paul Chapman.

Gray, C. 1998. *Enterprise and Culture*. London: Routledge.

Griffeth, R., Allen, D. and Barrett, R. 2006. Integration of family-owned business succession with turnover and life cycle models: development of a successor retention process model. *Human Resource Management Review*, 16(Dec): 490–507.

Griffin, M. 2005. Emblem crossed out by a crystal. *The Age*, 19 September: 3.

Hansmann, H. 1987. Economic theories of non-profit organizations. In W. W. Powell (ed.) *The Nonprofit Sector: A Research Handbook*. New Haven, CT: Yale University Press.

Harding, R. 2004. Social enterprise: the new economic engine? *Business Strategy Review*, 15(4): 39–43.

Harris, M. 2001. This charity business, who cares? *Nonprofit Management and Leadership*, 12(1): 95–109.

Howard, R. 1990. Can small business help countries compete? *Harvard Business Review*, Nov/Dec: 88–103.

International Committee of the Red Cross (ICRC). 2005a. *Discover the ICRC*. Geneva: ICRC. Available online at http://www.icrc.org/Web/eng/siteeng0.nsf/html/p0790

International Committee of the Red Cross (ICRC). 2005b. *ICRC 2004 Annual Report*. Geneva: ICRC. Available online at http://www.scribd.com/doc/21795073/ICRC-Annual-Report-2004

International Committee of the Red Cross (ICRC). 2005c. *Working for the ICRC*. Geneva: ICRC. Available online at http://www.icrc.org/eng/resources/documents/misc/5r4jly.htm

International Committee of the Red Cross (ICRC). 2006. *ICRC 2005 Annual Report*. Geneva: ICRC. Available online at http://www.scribd.com/doc/21795073/ICRC-Annual-Report-2005

International Committee of the Red Cross (ICRC). 2007a. *Emblems of Humanity: The International Red Cross and Red Crescent Movement*. Geneva: ICRC. Available online at http://www.icrc.org/web/eng/siteeng0.nsf/html/p0876

International Committee of the Red Cross (ICRC). 2007b. *ICRC 2006 Annual Report*. Geneva: ICRC. Available online at http://www.icrc.org/Web/Eng/siteeng0.nsf/htmlall/section_annual_report?OpenDocument

International Committee of the Red Cross (ICRC). 2007c. *Report on the Strategy for the International Red Cross and Red Crescent Movement*. Geneva: ICRC. Available online at http://www.icrc.org/web/eng/siteeng0.nsf/htmlall/council-delegates-2007-strategy-151007?opendocument

International Federation of the Red Cross (IFRC). 2006. *Red Cross, Red Crescent, Red Crystal Emblems: Design Guidelines*. Geneva: IFRC. Available online at http://www.ifrc.org

International Federation of the Red Cross (IFRC). 2007. *The International Red Cross and Red Crescent Movement: At a Glance*. Geneva: IFRC.: Available online at http://www.icrc.org/eng/who-we-are/index.jsp

Jennings, P. D. and Beaver, G. 1997. The performance advantage of small firms: a managerial perspective. *International Small Business Journal*, 15(2): 63–75.

Johns, G. 2006. The essential impact of context on organizational behaviour. *Academy of Management Review*, 31(2): 386–408.

Kanter, E. M. and Summers, D. 1987. Doing well while doing good: dilemmas of performance management in nonprofits and the need for a multiple constituency approach In D. McKevitt, and A. Lawton (eds) *Public Sector Management: Theory, Critique and Practice*. Buckingham: Open University Press.

Kelman, S. 2007. Five public administration and organization studies. *Academy of Management Annals*, 1(1): 225–267.

Kong, E. 2008. The development of strategic management in the non-profit context: intellectual capital in social service non-profit organizations. *International Journal of Management Reviews*, 10(3): 1460–1545.

MacMillan, I. 1983. Competitive strategies for not-for-profit agencies. *Advances in Strategic Management*, 1: 61–82.

Mahoney, J. and McGahan, A. 2007. The field of strategic management within the evolving science of strategic organization. *Strategic Organization*, 5(1): 79–99.

McKiernan, P. and Morris, C. 1994. Strategic planning and financial performance in UK SMEs: does formality matter? *British Journal of Management*, 5: S31–41.

Melahi, K. and Wilkinson, A. 2004. Organizational failure: a critique of recent research and a proposed integrative framework. *International Journal of Management Reviews*, 5/6(1): 21–41.

Middleton, M. 1987. Nonprofit boards of directors: beyond the governance function. In W. W. Powell (ed.) *The Nonprofit Sector: A Research Handbook*. New Haven, CT: Yale University Press.

Miles, R., Snow, C., Meyer, A., and Coleman, H. 1978. Organization strategy, structure and process. *Academy of Management Review*, 3: 546–662.

Miller, C. and Cardinal, L. 1994. Strategic planning and firm performance: A synthesis of more than two decades of research. *Academy of Management Journal*, 37(6): 1649–1665.

Mintzberg, H. 1979. *The Structuring of Organizations*. London: Prentice Hall.

Mintzberg, H. 1996. Managing government. *Harvard Business Review*, May/June: 75–83.

Mintzberg, H., Lampel, J., Quinn, J. B., and Ghoshal, S. 2003. *The Strategy Process: Concepts, Contexts, Cases.* 4th edn. Harlow: Pearson Education.

Moore, M. H. 1995. *Creating Public Value: Strategic Management in Government*. Boston, MA: Harvard University Press.

Murphy, R. 2007. *International Red Cross and Red Crescent Movement: Lecture Notes*. Galway: The Centre for Human Rights, National University of Ireland.

Organization for Economic Co-operation and Development (OECD). 2005. *Small and Medium Sized Enterprises Economic Outlook*. Paris: OECD.

Oster, S. 1995. *Strategic Management for the Non-Profit Sector*. Oxford: Oxford University Press.

Oz, O. and Toker, A. 2008. Crafting strategy in not-for-profit organizations: the experience of an alumni organization, BUMED. *International Journal of Non Profit and Voluntary Sector Marketing*, 13: 167–175.

Paton, R. 1992. The social economy: value based organizations in the wider society. In J. Batsleer, C. Conforth, and R. Paton (eds) *Issues in Voluntary and Non-Profit Management*. Reading, MA: Addison-Wesley.

Paton, R. and Cornforth, C. 1992. What's different about managing in voluntary and non-profit organizations. In J. Batsleer, C. Cornforth, and R. Paton (eds) *Issues in Voluntary and Nonprofit Management*. Reading, MA: Addison-Wesley.

Poister, T. H. and Streib, G. 1999. Strategic management in the public sector: concepts, models and process. *Public Productivity and Management Review*, 22(3): 308–325.

Porter, M. 1980. *Competitive Strategy*. New York: Free Press.

Porter, M. 1985. *Competitive Advantage*. New York: Free Press

Porter, M. 1996. What is strategy? *Harvard Business Review*, Dec: 61–78.

Powell, W. W. and Friedkin, R. 1987. Organizational change in nonprofit organizations. In W. W. Powell (ed.) *The Nonprofit Sector: A Research Handbook*. New Haven, CT: Yale University Press.

Quelch, J. and Laidler, N. 2003. *International Federation of Red Cross and Red Crescent Societies*. Boston, MA: Harvard Business School Publishing.

Quelch, J. and Laidler-Kylander, N. 2005. *The New Global Brands: Managing Non-Government Organizations in the 21st Century*. Boston, MA: SouthWestern College Publishing.

Rhys, A., Boyne, G., and Walker, R. 2008. Reconstructing empirical public administration. *Administration and Society*, 40(3): 324–330.

Richbell, S. M., Watts, H. D., and Wardle, P. 2006. Owner-managers and business planning in the small firm. *International Small Business Journal*, 24(5): 496–514.

Robinson, R. and Pearce II, J. 1983. The impact of formalized strategic planning on financial performance in small organizations. *Strategic Management Journal*, 4: 197–207.

Robinson, R. and Pearce II, J. 1984. Research thrusts in small firm strategic planning. *Academy of Management Review*, 9(1): 128–137.

Rue, L. and Ibrahim, N. A. 1998. The relationship between planning sophistication and performance in small businesses. *Journal of Small Business Management*, Oct: 24–32.

Scase, R. and Goffee, R. 1987. *The Real World of the Small Business Owner*. 2nd edn. London: Routledge.

Schrage, M. 2007. Charity needs a better foundation. *Financial Times*, 15 February. Available online at http://www.ft.com/cms/s/0/881ef332-bc99-11db-9cbc-0000779e2340.html#axzz1Yhm x4Uv

Standing Commission of the Red Cross and Red Crescent (SCRCRC). 2001. *Strategy for the International Red Cross and Red Crescent.* Geneva: SCRCRC. Available online at http://www.icrc.org/web/eng/siteeng0.nsf/html/5N2HNT

Stanworth, J. and Gray, C. 1991. *Bolton 20 Years on: The Small Firm in the 1990s*. London: Paul Chapman Publishing.

Stonehouse, G. and Pemberton, J. 2002. Strategic planning in SMEs: some empirical findings. *Management Decision*, 40(9): 853–861.

Storey, D. 1994. *Understanding the Small Business Sector*. London: Routledge.

Tillett, A. 1970. C. I. Barnard and the theory of organizations. In A. Tillett, T. Kempner, and G. Wills (eds) *Management Thinkers*. Harmondsworth: Penguin.

VCCP. 2006. VCCP creates detention ad for ICRC. Press release, August. Available online at http://www.vccp.com/news/2006/aug.asp

Welsh, J. and White, J. 1981. A small business is not a little big business. *Harvard Business Review*, 59(4): 18–32.

Wheelen, T. and Hunger, D. J. 2002. *Strategic Management and Business Policy.* 8th edn. London: Prentice Hall.

14

The role of strategy agents

Consultants, management education, and strategy discourses

Believe those who search for truth. Doubt those who claim to have found it.

(André Gide, 1869–1961; winner of the Nobel Prize for literature, 1947)

Introduction

In this book, we have presented a relatively conventional account of strategy making and the role of **strategists** within organizations. A conventional last chapter would bring all of the book's ideas together and leave the reader happy in the knowledge that he or she has reviewed all of the components that constitute strategy. However, we have cautioned against simple and universal answers, and this is reflected in the opening quote from André Gide. If success could be reduced to a formula, companies would not need strategic thinking, but could rely on administrators to ensure that it was followed with precision. What makes **strategic decision making** so difficult, and therefore so valuable to companies, is the fact that there are no guaranteed keys to success (Rosenzweig, 2007). Too often, however, work on strategy reflects the assumptions of modernism: that the current view is the best; that ideas are progressing in a linear and cumulative fashion, drawing closer and closer to the 'truth'; and that an optimal balance or equilibrium is possible (Cummings, 2002; Townley, 2008). We have already acknowledged in Chapter 11 how chaos theory challenges some of these strategy truisms, and we have recognized the dilemmas and political realities that characterize the strategy process. All the while, however, we have remained largely grounded in a mainstream perspective. In this chapter, we relax these assumptions and start to explore some interesting questions concerning the role of various agents in the strategy process. For example, why is it that all top Fortune 100 companies employ the services of consultants? What is the nature of the values and ideas that we diffuse through management education, and do these really, or only, benefit businesses and practitioners? Why has the word 'strategic' come to be viewed with such reverence? What function does the language or **discourse** of strategy serve and to whose benefit?

This chapter seeks to ask a few critical questions of the assumptions built into strategic thinking. As Jones (2004: 491) notes, 'what is called the rhetoric of strategy—its persuasive power—is strong, and it is important to be appreciative of its strengths but also to be able to see where they originate, what assumptions they depend on and how they are constructed'. As an example, we have seen how our understanding of contemporary strategy and strategists is rooted in military warfare, but we have not considered the reality that there may be nothing heroic or glorious about such warfare (Carter *et al.*, 2008: 4). Rather than assuming an objective world 'out there' to be discovered and understood, this chapter draws on a social-practice perspective to explore how social reality is created and the purposes for which it is created. This involves stretching the scope of strategy beyond the organization. Often, strategy and strategists are considered in a simplistic way, as if they operate in a vacuum. In contrast, the line of inquiry that this chapter follows is more akin to the structure shown in Figure 14.1.

Figure 14.1 Strategy agents and discourses

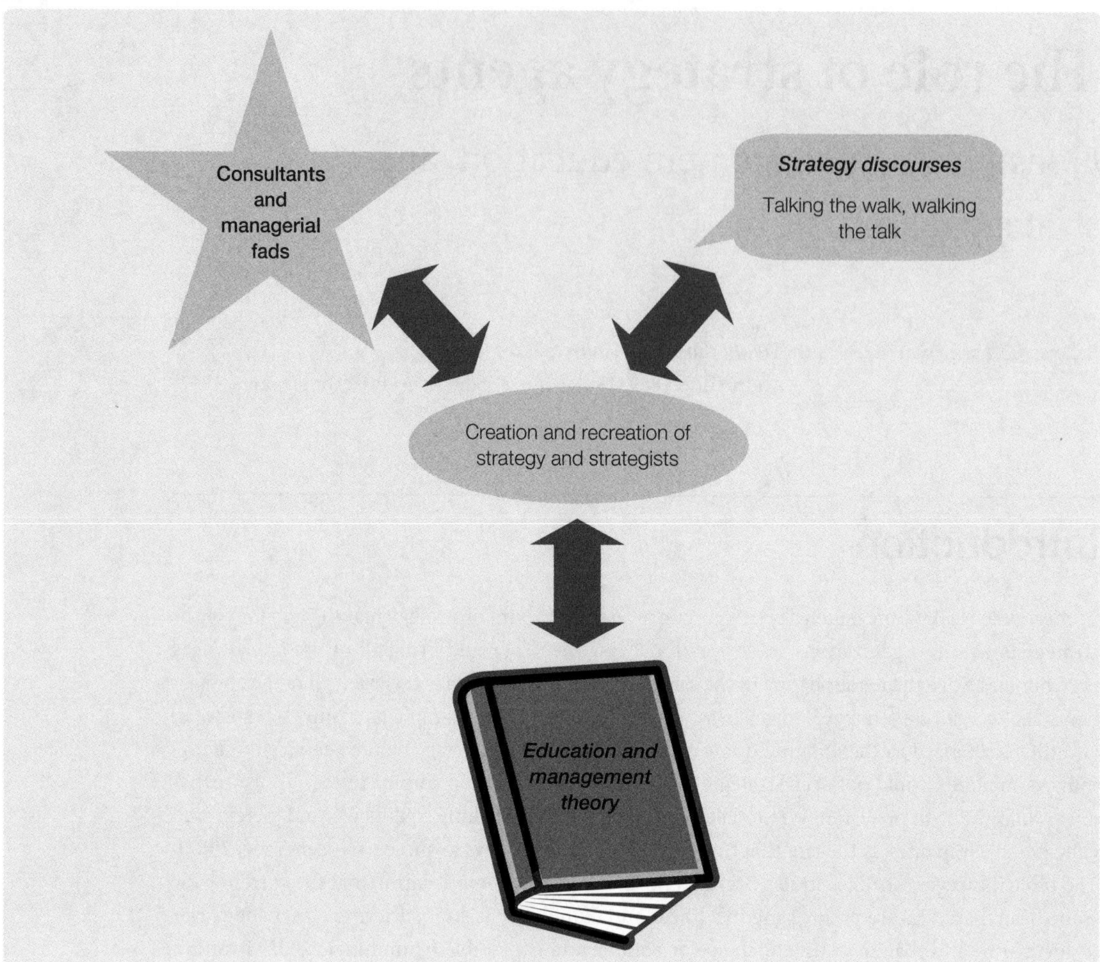

As Figure 14.1 suggests, strategy and strategists are continuously being created and recreated as a result of different influences (Kantola and Seeck, 2011). If strategists do not behave like mechanical toys that are simply wound up with the key of rational judgement and released to motor through predetermined steps, we should therefore question how they think and act. And even if they seem to portray such mechanical efficiency, we should consider who is turning the key and for what purpose. In this chapter, we consider, first, agents such as consultants and management gurus, who may have a role in shaping the practices and strategies actually deployed by organizations and utilized by strategists. This involves exploring the seductive nature of management fads and fashions, and why organizations seek the latest makeover in order to parade down the corporate catwalk (McKiernan and Carter, 2004: 11). Secondly, we consider the role of management education. Here, academic research—the processes by which ideas and theories are diffused, as well as the very nature and content of these theories—comes under scrutiny. We review these arguments and assess their implications for the debate on the rigour of research versus the relevance of ideas.

In the last section, we consider the discourse of strategy and the language that strategists use. The language of strategy can be viewed as a means of portraying **rationality**, legitimizing decisions to **stakeholders**, and defining social relations. In this broader purpose, the language of strategy also facilitates strategists in creating a sense of identity, reassurance, and professionalism. Some versions of this argument would hold that strategy is more about the management of meaning than the meaning of management.

The overall purpose of this chapter is not to provide definitive accounts of these ideas; indeed, some of these perspectives would question whether definitive accounts are possible. Instead, our purpose is to raise an awareness that such issues exist. We are usefully reminded that strategy as a social practice is often hotly contested and subject to the influence of numerous actors. Rather than succumbing to the hyperbole and false promises found in so much management writing, business strategists would do far better to improve their powers and capacity for critical thinking (Rosenzweig, 2007). While consideration of the agents, power, and discourse may not provide a means to *solve* the dilemmas presented in this text, they do provide a means to *dissolve* them. We sympathize with Leavitt (2007: 260), who urges the importance of making sure 'that our students get a few glimpses of what's backstage; that we alert them to crippling indignities and moral dilemmas that will inevitably accompany glowing promises'. We begin the chapter by focusing on consultants and managerial fashions and fads.

Consultants and managerial fads

Managers are often portrayed as fashion-conscious teenagers indulging in every passing trend so as to be seen as progressive, modern, and innovative (see Reading 6.2). We are now familiar with terms such as 'total quality management', 'Six Sigma', 'Japanese management', 'management by objectives', 'delayering', 'outsourcing', and 'offshoring'. The assumption that knowledge can be distilled and transferred like a commodity has fuelled an **industry** of management gurus and consultants offering seemingly objective advice on all aspects of organizational life (Cummings, 2002: 135). For example, the assumption that culture is something that an organization *has*, as opposed to something that an organization *is*, implies that culture is something that can be introduced in a managed way. Consultants market themselves on their ability to provide neutral, objective, and well-informed knowledge to managers too often consumed by specialisms or embedded in cultural factors to see the best route forward. The consultancy industry, in its very form and nature of interventions, is vast and permeates nearly every organizational existence—if not directly via interventions and advice, then indirectly via specialized magazines such as *McKinsey Quarterly*—and the diffusion of best practice. The relentless growth of management consultancy has been referred to as one of the 'the greatest phenomena of our times'. The proliferation of consultancy usage is a result of technological developments that have facilitated complex statistical analyses of performance, the emergence of a prescriptive quasi-science of management with readily marketable ideas, and increasing competition under the guise of globalization (Sturdy, 1997). Management literature has become part of popular culture, captured in 'airport book economies' including titles such as '10 Easy Steps to Avoid Global Depression' (Beinhocker, 1997). Subjects such as strategy have almost become a commodity, with many managers alluding to a sense of 'consultancy fatigue'—that is, a weariness, frustration, and cynicism about the activities of consultants (Gilbert, 1996).

Consultancy and consultants

Defining the precise nature of consultancy is difficult. Consultancy is a fragmented industry, providing advice in areas as diverse as strategic planning, implementing IT, or rewarding staff for performance. Overell (2002: 12) notes that the term is difficult to pin down, because consultancy provides 'a home to sole traders, occasional dabblers and out-and-out witchdoctors, just as much as it does to the big strategy boutiques'. In contrast, Greiner and Metzger (1983: 7) define consultancy as:

> an advisory service contracted for and provided to organizations by specifically trained and qualified persons who assist, in an objective and independent manner, the client organization to identify management problems, recommend solutions and help when requested with the implementation of solutions.

Given that, in most countries, consultancy is unregulated and there are few barriers to entry, it is unlikely that, in all cases, consultants will be specifically trained and qualified, and, as we note below, many strategists would take issue with the idea that they operate in a totally objective and independent manner.

External consultants have used their perceived expertise and unbiased perspectives as a selling point, exploiting the fact that managers often have very little exposure beyond their own specialisms (Canback, 1999). Larger organizations have set up internal consultancy practices, sometimes run as independent profit centres or centres of excellence, to diffuse knowledge and expertise throughout the organization. While external consultant interventions typically rely on expertise captured by the 'doctor–patient metaphor', whereby the consultant diagnoses the problem and offers a solution, internal consultancy is said to involve greater joint diagnosis of problems to establish consensus. While internal consultants are said to provide continuity in the process and more accountability for implementation, their ability to produce objective and insightful recommendations may be hindered by the internal politics of the organization. One of the most prominent arguments used against internal consultants is that they will be unable to free themselves from the cultural mindset and traditional ways of doing and looking at things in their organization—that is, the filter of the 'organizational **paradigm**' (Johnson, 1992). Berenbaum (1997) provides a useful way of determining the relative merits of using either internal or external consultants that is summarized in Table 14.1.

Fashions and fads

In 2008, Royal Bank of Scotland (RBS) engaged with every trendy business idea going, including 'employee pulse surveys' and a 'customer engagement index'. Absent, however, was a focus on what really mattered: the bank's risk assessment, cash flow and capital structure were dramatically deteriorating (Broughton, 2009). What makes managers so susceptible to the fashions and fads promoted by consultants and business gurus? Institutional theory would suggest that managers and firms are driven to introduce new practices as legitimacy-enhancing interventions, or as a consequence of 'mimetic isomorphism'—that is, simply because others have done so. Ironically, in some instances, simply having the new practice in place may be more important than whether the practice delivers value or not (Di Maggio and Powell, 1983). Here, it is important to acknowledge the active role of consultants and management gurus as suppliers who disseminate the ideals of best practices. Drawing on a fashion management perspective, Abrahamson (1996) notes how such suppliers:

Table 14.1 Relative merits of deploying external and internal consultants

Factor	External	Internal
New knowledge/experience	Yes	No
Fresh view of how things work	Yes	No
Personal bias	No	Maybe
Legitimacy	Yes	Maybe
Cost	High	Low/medium
Continuity	Unlikely	Yes
Share skills	Unlikely	Probably
Profit-motivated	Yes	Maybe

Source: Adapted from Berenbaum (1997)

1. sense the emergent collective preferences of managers for new management techniques;
2. develop rhetoric that describes these techniques as being at the forefront of management progress; and
3. attempt to disseminate this rhetoric among managers and organizational stakeholders in advance of other fashion setters.

While such fashions or fads may not necessarily have adverse consequences for organizations, this perspective does suggest that we should pay as much attention to the role of marketing as to content per se (Furnham, 2000). In their review of fads over forty years, Miller and Hartwick (2002) note eight elements or 'tell-tale signs' of **managerial fads**, as outlined in Table 14.2.

Miller and Hartwick (2002) note that classic management interventions differ from fads in that they instigate real changes, involve significant costs, and have lasting effects. They suggest some useful questions that may help companies to distinguish between what is real and novel in an approach and its effects, and what is the latest empty promise or fad being peddled by consultants and management gurus: 'Do the ideas or practices have a proven track record in similar companies?' 'Do they address problems or opportunities that are high priorities for our company?' Other observers claim that because best practices are so easily taken up and replicated, consultants and management gurus actually stifle difference and prevent creativity (Cummings, 2002: 135).

Highly standardized approaches are often overtly employed. Rational, static models still form the majority of the consultant's toolbox: Porter's 'Five Forces'; the 'Seven "P"s' of marketing; McKinsey's '7's; and the simplistic Boston Consulting Group (BCG) matrix (Sturdy, 1997). There is a tendency to create a 'can't do without' solution either through models, such as a star on the BCG matrix, phrases such as 're-engineering', or an unfounded set of claims (Weiss, 2003). In the process of **solution formulation**, consultants are actively involved in the construction, or redefinition, of problems in advance of offering themselves as a solution to them (Knights and Morgan, 1991). Success rests on their skill in identifying and manipulating key symbols and interests in order to provide a convincing performance (Williams, 2001). Essentially, consultancy is about impression management: constructing 'a reality which persuades clients that they have purchased a high quality service' (Clark,

Table 14.2 Tell-tale signs of a managerial fad

1. Simplicity	Easy to understand and communicate, e.g. business process re-engineering: 'Don't automate, obliterate'
2. Prescriptive	Normative in outlook; outlines specific actions or levers, e.g. Six Sigma, DMAIC (define, measure, analyse, improve, control)
3. Encouraging	Often falsely so or without grounded evidence, e.g. Peters and Waterman set out to discover what makes leading US businesses successful
4. 'One size fits all'	Assumed universal impact, e.g. Womack *et al.* (1990: 7–8) claimed that 'the principles of lean production can be applied equally in every industry across the globe ... [lean production] will truly change the world'
5. 'Cut and paste' elements	Organizations customize aspects and partially implement, e.g. despite claims of dominance, scientific management was very rarely implemented in the true form envisaged by Frederick Taylor
6. In tune with the zeitgeist	Relying on the business needs of the day, e.g. swings between cultural and rational techniques to match economic cycles
7. Novel, but not radical	Often simply an incremental evolution of what has gone before, e.g. quality improvement—from TQM and quality circles, to Six Sigma
8. Legitimized by 'gurus'	Typically associated with particular person, e.g. Demming—quality improvement; Hammer—business process re-engineering; Peters and Waterman—culture

1995: 118). Consultants have to convince clients of their **rationality**, that their ideas are progressive and linked to societal trends, and that they alone have the recipe for success.

But can we point the finger of blame solely at the sellers of ideas? Are managers simply puppets manipulated by consultants who create a demand for their product by socially constructing its desirability and necessity for competitiveness? Rather than treating managers simply as dedicated followers of fashion, perhaps we should draw attention to the conditions of dissemination and the needs of users rather than any intrinsic properties or claims to the truth inherent in models (Gabriel, 2002). Such an approach acknowledges the political utility offered by the supposed 'objectivity' and control promised by technical rationality (Sturdy, 1997). The depiction of managers as manipulated victims who seize on one panacea after another devalues the reciprocal nature of the consultancy relationship. Managers seek a sense of reassurance, control, or order, and this can be provided through interaction with consultants and the adoption of latest 'next or best practice'. Huczynski (1993), for example, argues that, as consumers, managers may utilize consultants for a range of reasons, as highlighted in Table 14.3.

While we have considered the role of consultants as 'sellers of ideas', Table 14.3 examines the potential motives and concerns of managers as 'consumers of ideas'. From this perspective, strategists may utilize consultant ideas in order to provide a solution to a critical organizational problem, thereby providing immediate security and reducing any sense of panic. Ideas can also be deployed in the service of motivating employees, or to enable change by providing new answers to old questions. Consultants may also be used as a way of rationalizing or legitimizing a predetermined course of action.

With respect to competition, the use of consultants may reduce the fear that the organization is missing out on something or giving away an advantage. Engagement with new ideas also indicates that the organization is being proactive and so appears to customers and employees alike to be ahead of the game. Consultants play a central role as managers are driven by institutionalized normative pressures to demonstrate their organization's commitment to progress and rationality. Decisions to use consultants and their practices are often taken to ensure conformity or because it is 'politically right', while their use indicates to stakeholders that the organization is trying to do the *right* thing (Abrahamson, 1996).

Finally, for an individual strategist, the adoption and championing of new ideas can provide visibility within the organization, thereby enhancing his or her career prospects. Likewise, engagement with leading ideas can help to legitimize the strategist's position as a member of the strategy profession. Moreover, by relying on external intervention, the strategist has inbuilt defence mechanisms: if no advantage is realized, blame can be attributed to the idea/consultant rather than to anything inherent to the strategist and his or her actions.

This indicates that it is important to pay attention to the dynamics of the relationship between consultants as the 'sellers of ideas' and managers as the 'buyers of ideas' (Huczynski, 1993; McGivern,

Table 14.3 Utilizing consultants: manager as consumer

Organizational	Perceived as solution to critical problem Internal motivational device Novel solution to a continuing problem Vehicle to assist organizational change
Competition	Fear of what competition might do To be seen to be ahead of the game vs competition Customer perceptions
Individual	Career enhancer Management defence Quick results to difficult problems Managerial status Boredom

Source: Created from Huczynski (1993)

1983). Managers clearly have an active role in the process and can resist interventions that they feel might threaten their career, identity, or power base. Consultants can be perfect scapegoats for failed projects, but they also provide managers with political utility: actions based on the recommendations of consultants can be presented as objective and politically neutral (Sturdy, 1997).

So far, we have illustrated the potentially contested nature of managerial knowledge and best practices, and how different agents will use knowledge to serve their own ends. This questions the assumption that there is simply one best way of getting better to be discovered 'out there'. In making this point, one cannot simply demonize consultants and management gurus; strategists are also key agents in the capitalist process and have their own agenda to ensure that their interests are realized (Sturdy, 1997; 2011). There is a need to move away from simplistic, stereotypical trivialization towards acknowledging that economic and social pressures have driven us to the point at which internal and external consultancy, from a client's or a consultant's perspective, is increasingly a war about meaning as much as a war about management. We now turn to the role of education and management theory in either exacerbating or bridging the gap between ideas and rhetoric and their actual relevance for management.

Education and management theory

One mechanism recently put forward to deal with the issues of fads and fashions is the concept of **evidence-based management**. Given its roots in clinical medicine, evidence-based management, as a means of rigorously assessing available evidence underpinning best-practice claims, is perhaps particularly appropriate to cure the 'ills' of current managerial practice. In building the case for evidence-based management, Pfeffer and Sutton (2006: 5) argue that 'if doctors practiced medicine the way many companies practice management, there would be far more sick and dead patients and many more doctors would be in jail'. They advocate that leaders should 'face hard facts and act on the best scientific evidence', thereby promoting healthy scepticism about what is currently being presented as 'best managerial practice'. Accordingly, they argue, the fault for the current malaise in management practice lies squarely at the feet of managers. While managers do actually *try* to act on the best evidence, this is often impeded by particular obstacles that evidence-based management can address.

This promise of evidence-based management movement is also evident in presidential addresses to the American Academy of Management, which have stressed the imperative of 'scientific knowledge as the basis for managerial policy and decision making' (Cummings, 2007: 356), arguing that such application would 'reduce the research–practice gap' (Rousseau, 2006: 256). Others note, however, that we should also focus attention on the origin of ideas: namely, the producers of education, and the values and ideals that they instill through both teaching and theories. The late Sumantra Ghoshal (2005: 75) commented on the self-fulfilling nature of theories: 'our own theories and ideas have done much to strengthen the management practices that we are all now so loudly condemning.'

There is little doubt that corporate scandals and the recent global financial crisis have done much to draw attention to the practices that are used to manage companies (Caulkin, 2011). Yet it would be disingenuous to criticize agents involved in the strategy process without looking at the values and interests that academics commonly diffuse among and promote to practising managers. Elsewhere, Jeffrey Pfeffer (2005: 99) notes that 'we ought to be both more explicit and more thoughtful about the values we are imparting by what we teach and how we teach it'. Indeed, partly as a result of a rigid focus on developing a scientific approach to the study of management, there is a concern that business schools have become 'uncoupled' from practice (Tushman *et al.*, 2007). This sense of burgeoning crisis in management not only refers to the way in which management knowledge is disseminated, but also questions the very basis of this knowledge in the first place. It is perhaps time that academics and managerial educators conducted their own cultural audit. As one of the most prominent writers on organizational culture notes, 'we are in grave danger of not seeing our own culture, our assumptions about methods, about theory, about what is important to study or not study, and, in that process, pay too much attention only to what suits our own needs' (Schein, 1996: 239).

In examining the diffusion of ideas, Henry Mintzberg (2004) was one of the first to offer a strong critique of contemporary management education. Mintzberg argued that Master of Business Administration (MBA) degree teaching favours strict analysis (science) over craft (experience) and art (vision), thereby leaving potential managers poorly equipped to manage in the real world. This tendency is perpetuated by the curricula of MBAs tending to be structured around the functions of business as opposed to the 'messy process' of management. The implications are that graduating students are ill-equipped to wrangle with complex, unquantifiable issues—in other words, the stuff of management (Bennis and O'Toole, 2005). Many commentators, however, have taken issue with Mintzberg's ideas, arguing that they apply only to specific types of MBA course in certain times and places.

Yet if Mintzberg's arguments can be brushed aside with the logic of 'It all depends', Sumantra Ghoshal's arguments strike at the heart of accepted business school wisdom by questioning the foundations behind most business management theory. Ghoshal questions the assumptions of much of the economic theory underpinning management research, noting the harmful effects that these assumptions can have on people and institutions (Ghoshal and Moran, 1996). Of critical concern is that a precondition for making business studies a science is often the explicit denial of any role of moral or ethical considerations in the practice of management (Ghoshal, 2005: 79). According to Ghoshal, this is evident in the malaise that haunts management practice today. Similarly, Ariely (2009) argues that assuming that decisions are made on a purely logical and rational basis is a flawed starting point. Management education does little to prepare managers for considering questions of power and responsibility (Alvesson and Wilmott, 1996). At the same time, there is little room for genuine **innovation** and creativity, as dominant (largely North American) business schools act as influential gatekeepers for new developments in business practice (Guest, 1990).

It must be acknowledged that business schools have provided a stable and structured occupational base for the study of strategy and organizations, and that they have yielded many successes in both the academic and practitioner contexts. What should be encouraged is more critical reflection on the assumptions, methods, and meaning of some of the knowledge and truisms that have perhaps been too easily taken for granted. The knowledge of what constitutes sound managerial practice and teaching methods is merely a creation of the last few decades, not perhaps the objective science that we assume it to be.

James March (2007: 17), one of the most influential contributors to writing and research on management, provided a timely reminder that 'the business school context is not a neutral one'. March noted the following potential implications of a narrow business school focus (ibid: 17–18).

- It can encourage the mutual isolation of business school scholars of organizations and disciplinary scholars.
- In so far as it encourages contact with the disciplines, it makes contact with ideas from economics more likely and contact with ideas from the sciences—psychology, sociology, or political science—less likely.
- It focuses research on the private sector, reducing attention paid to institutions in the public sector that characterized much early work in the field (see Chapter 13).
- It brings an emphasis on the audience of practitioners, on finding the correlates of organizational performance, rather than other organizational phenomena.
- It brings an orientation to the problems and possibilities of individual organizations (firms) and less attention to populations of organizations or to 'organizing'.
- It stimulates an emphasis on organizational strategies rather than societal strategies.

In addition, we can note that business education has craved for and been driven by attempts at pursuing hard scientific analysis. As Bennis and O'Toole (2005: 99) note, 'when applied to business—essentially a human activity in which judgments are made with messy, incomplete and incoherent data—statistical and methodological wizardry can blind rather than illuminate'. This is still the benchmark by which the majority of contributions are judged. Business studies remains romantically fixated on replicating the certainties of academic disciplines such as physics, rather than dealing with the practicalities of professions such as law and medicine. In this quest for scientific rigour, it is easy to see how one might lose sight on what is relevant and the 'reality' for most organizations. Our Spotlight piece explores whether this narrow logic might also have limitations for business schools themselves.

The argument about business schools can easily be extended to management researchers, who, as a community of explorers compete for discoveries and with financial backers eager for results, are often guided in certain directions (Mintzberg and Lampel, 1999). Journal guidelines and the paradigms of disciplines privilege certain accounts and methodologies, so that the pursuit of management knowledge is invariably a social process (Hackley, 2003). Management researchers are therefore servants of power, creatively selecting, presenting, and analysing in order to gain legitimacy. Hackley (2003) refers to 'bogus reflexivity' deployed by researchers to persuade audiences of the plausibility of their research findings and enhance their authenticity (Gill and Johnson, 2001: 172). Ultimately, while all data and findings must be interpreted to be succinctly communicated, researchers can deploy a range of techniques to give their work the status of rigour and 'objectivity'. Examples include using the passive voice, post-rationalization and of findings, or depicting the research process as logical, sequential, and progressive when in practice it may have been ad hoc, emergent, and full of blind alleys. For researchers, the reality is that future funding, visibility, career prospects, and professional status often rest on understanding and conspiring in the 'game-playing approach to publication'. Thus, rather than being purely the quest for some objective reality and universal best practice, the very conduct of management research is itself an inherently complex, social, and human performance (Giacalone, 2009; Golden-Biddle and Locke, 1993: 5). This focus on communicating research findings draws our attention to the importance of the nature of language and the role of various discourses in sustaining and creating meaning. Arguably, part of what business schools should encourage is 'inquiry into how and why we give priority to some vocabularies, meanings and artefacts while neglecting alternatives' (Starkey and Tempest, 2009: 579). This is the topic of the next section.

Strategy discourses and the role of knowledge and power

Successful strategy pivots on communication. Consider the response of financial investors and the effect on share prices if corporate decisions do not meet expectations, are not seen as rigorously grounded, or, irrespective of content, are not communicated in a coherent and logical manner. The sound justification and rationalization of results and corporate activities can be just as important as the actual content of strategy. Thus, from the viewpoint of the practitioner, the communication of a decision is everything: the decision that matters is that which is communicated through discourse (Hendry, 2000). The rhetoric and promise of change may be powerful enough to secure action, irrespective of whether the organization is delivering on the promise of initiatives (Eccles and Nohria, 1992). At the same time, Watson (2005) argues that strategic discourses—or what he terms 'business speak' (such as flexibility, engagement, and advantage)—may have become meaningless. By relying on a common and largely abstract vocabulary, companies may miss the chance to properly differentiate themselves. Mechanisms of communication are therefore of central importance to strategy, and 'the ability to describe and explain actions to the rest of the world in order for them to be accepted or appreciated' is a critical task for strategists (Brunsson and Olson, 1993: 63).

Some academics, such as Barry and Emles (1997), contend that most strategies and strategic decision making can be understood as a form of narrative storytelling. If we think about the way in which we communicate with each other, this appears to make a lot of sense. Whether intentionally or not, we tend to weave together a context for our story, recount events in a sequential, step-by-step manner, and finish with a conclusion or moral. Perhaps the same can be said of how organizations communicate and recount strategic events and happenings (Jacobides, 2010). This highlights the social nature of strategic knowledge. Both the process of telling the story and the actual story told reflect strategizing and strategy, respectively. This also begs the questions of who tells or narrates the story, what his or her purpose is, and why he or she recounts the story in a specific manner. Many accounts of strategy are provided *by* managers *for* managers and so any notion of conflicting interests, resistance, or difficulties in implementation are not recounted. This suggests that the processes of strategy are complex and multifaceted, and that, during interactions, certain meanings of strategy will be sustained or recreated. Too often, however, 'organizations are viewed as neutral, rational and technical, instrumental systems designed to convert inputs into outputs, and strategy is simply conceived as the determination of ends and the selection of means for achieving those ends' (Shrivastava, 1986: 371).

Strategy discourses affect what people see, how they see it, and labels that they use to interpret and communicate their reality (Ferraro *et al.*, 2005: 9). In this sense, discourses both reflect and shape the current social order. Strategic discourses are therefore particular ways of speaking and constructing social reality (Hardy *et al.*, 2005; Vaara *et al.*, 2004). While traditional methods provide insight into *meanings* of social reality, discourse analysis focuses on *its production* (Phillips and Hardy, 2002). As noted in the previous section, consultants and management gurus must present a discourse that is appealing to potential clients, novel, and yet must also connect with current perceptions of need and key issues (Thomas, 2003). Yet this is not the exclusive remit of external agents; internally, strategists shape discourses to their benefit. We clearly need a greater appreciation of the processes through which particular strategies as concepts, ideas, or narratives gain popularity and become legitimated and institutionalized. Vaara *et al.* (2004) present an interesting analysis of the extensive material on strategy discourse in airline **alliances**, pointing to a number of discursive practices that characterized strategizing in this context in the period 1995–2000, including:

1. the problematization of traditional strategies—by contrasting them with contemporary ideals of 'corporatization', 'globalization', and 'financialization';
2. the rationalization, objectification, and factualization of alliance benefits—with a specific focus on universal benefits for the 'customer'; and
3. the reframing of cooperation problems as 'implementation' issues.

In this instance, the ultimate objective of deploying these discursive practices was the naturalization of alliance strategies so that alliances appeared to be inevitable, logical, and progressive (Vaara *et al.*, 2004). This provides us with a pertinent example of how discourses were used to facilitate changes in the airline industry. At the centre of such accounts is the ability to persuade. Strategic discourses, after all, are instruments of persuasion. Strategists engage in a 'language game' as they shape and create reality to ensure legitimacy in the eyes of powerful stakeholders (Clegg *et al.*, 2004; McKiernan and Carter, 2004). From this perspective, the efficacy of strategy rests in its capacity to provide a means of organizational rationality rather than being able to determine an organization's future as it is traditionally depicted (Clegg *et al.*, 2004). This may involve deliberately ambiguous concepts, the meaning of which can be altered or stretched to suit the circumstances in which they are deployed. Indeed, much of the vocabulary of strategy is made up of poetic turns of phrase that arguably serve to conceal meaning rather than to reveal it, perhaps in order to hide impractical objectives or uncertainty as to real future direction (Caulkin, 2011; Rumelt, 2011: 37). For example, the notion of competitive advantage is at the heart of most strategic management writings and models, and yet one of its key proponents is quite vague about defining the term: 'despite the centrality of competitive advantage to his ideas, Porter does not clearly define what he means by the term' (Thomas, 2003: 790). Long case 8, 'Reassessing value in strategy' in Section 7 of this book, carefully dissects and deconstructs the discourse of 'value' as used in dominant strategy writing, opening up the term to alternative readings.

Overall, strategy discourse does not objectively 'discover', but socially 'creates', to focus minds and help people towards a particular course (Cummings, 2002: 215; Eccles and Nohria, 1992). In so doing, it provides a common language of strategy, enabling participants to converse strategically by offering a means by which complex options can be simply understood and communicated or mapped. At the same time, this may serve to gloss over ulterior motives of strategy discourse. Further, 'objectivity' and 'value-neutrality' are cultural domains that masquerade as natural, rational, and necessary. Strategic discourse may serve to create a commonality of purpose that silences any discontenting voices (Greckhamer, 2010: 863). Knights and Morgan (1991: 253) argue that 'a discourse is not simply a way of seeing; it is always embedded in social practices which reproduce that way of seeing as the "truth" of the discourse'. It is for this reason that Foucault (1980: 52) emphasizes the inseparability of power and knowledge. What constitutes knowledge can thus be seen to be socially constructed, subject to a continuous process of constitution, negotiation, and change, and bound up with the exercise of power. In taking this critical approach to examine the power effects of **corporate strategy**, Knights and Morgan (1991: 262–263) note that strategic discourse can serve the following purposes.

1. *Rationalization of failures* Everything is explicable in the end: strategic discourse, of competitive forces, can explain away failures.

2. *Sustains and enhances the rights of management and silences/ignores alternative perspectives on organizations* Strategy discourse emphasizes the professional and expert nature of managerial knowledge (Shirvastava, 1986) and diminishes the voice of third-party interest groups, such as trade unions. In strategy talk, sometimes understanding that which is left unsaid is more instructive than that which is carefully articulated (Carter *et al.*, 2008: 93).

3. *Generates a sense of personal and organizational security for managers* Strategy discourse provides a security blanket and a sense of purpose and identity for managers, or (phrased another way) 'chills out the existential dread that all senior management feel when charged with so much responsibility' (Carter *et al.*, 2008: 117).

4. *Can reflect and sustain a strong sense of gendered masculinity for male management* Aggressive and macho discourse and socialization may exclude women. Top-level strategizing is very much a gendered terrain (Hansen *et al.*, 2010).

5. *Demonstrates managerial rationality to colleagues, customers, competitors, government, and significant others in the environment* 'Strategy' talk has become a benchmark for legitimizing manager's activities (Darwin *et al.*, 2002: 129), leading to the construction and portrayal of managers as competent strategists.

6. *Facilitates and legitimizes the exercise of power* For example, the introduction of consultants can frequently be a device to legitimate a particular position taken within the company (Shirvastava, 1986).

7. *Constitutes the subjectivity of organizational members as particular categories of person who secure their sense of reality through engaging in strategic discourse and practice* Cultural change programmes in organizations have been criticized for manipulating employee sentiment and purpose to align their interests with those of the organization (Wilmott, 1993).

Taking this critical approach to discovering or rediscovering strategy and strategists enables us to analyse the power effects of strategic discourse and appreciate strategy as a performance (Biehl-Missal, 2011). The nature of the performance and the discourse will vary depending on the audience at which it is being directed. Dominant discourse can also be met with suspicion and subverted for people's own ends, or a counter-discourse can be developed. For example, in public sector contexts, a discourse of 'serving the national interest' may be articulated as a means to resist the interests of globalization and undertones of privatization (for example, Spicer and Flemming, 2007). Understanding discourses is therefore an interesting alternative route for understanding the meaning of strategy. In his critique of 'business speak', Watson (2005) argues that by conforming to the language of flexibility and value, meaning has become lost and organizations have missed the chance to properly differentiate themselves. Indeed, the omission of empathy, directness, and differentiation from strategic discourses with both customers and employees may mean that companies actually fail to build a proper and reliable bond (ibid). The attention that is paid to strategic discourses in existing strategy literature and research does not yet reflect this newly found importance (Brandenburger and Vinokurova, 2011).

Spotlight The business of business school rankings

The rise of business schools and the extent of investment in them have led to issues in terms of demonstrating accountability and performance. In recent times across the globe, the ranking of business schools in league tables has become commonplace. The most prominent examples include the Academic Ranking of World Universities (ARWU), commonly known as the 'Shanghai ranking', the *Financial Times* ranking, and those by *Asia Inc.*, *Business Week*, *US News & World Report*, and the *Wall Street Journal*. In the main, these rankings are largely dominated by US institutions. Given that business schools have typically extolled the virtues of competition, it is perhaps natural that this logic would also be applied to them. Business school ranking would seem to be a specific example of the argument that 'what gets measured gets managed'. Indeed, many observers praise rankings as a method of communicating business school 'performance', facilitating the development of a school's reputation, providing a means by which students can differentiate between schools, and serving to attract a high calibre of staff. This all seems positive and business schools, especially those performing well, welcome and praise the initiative. As Table 14.4 illustrates, rankings provide accountability to key stakeholders. They also help to focus strategic thinking and discussion of future direction within business schools, without which they might become complacent and ignore external trends and developments. There must also be some validity in the rankings—they are not based on subjective data and have been subject to rigorous scientific analysis. So why do some people take issue with them?

Some of the harshest critics of the rankings approach argue that it is not possible to put a quantifiable value on the nature of education: the logic of quantitative rigour does not hold in this context. Further, competition and rankings lead to short-termism, while students are treated as customers and resources are shifted away from undergraduate and other areas to more lucrative MBA programmes (most of the rankings are MBA rankings). As Zemsky (2008) argues, what happened to that old-fashioned notion that quality in education meant good teaching, engaged faculty, and industrious students? Other critics focus on methodological issues and the items that are included, such as graduation and retention rates, faculty and financial resources, and earnings of graduates. These do not allow for factors such as decisions by graduates to work in lower-paid jobs, in the not-for-profit sector, for example. Excluded also is information on the process of teaching, while by using numbers as the sole proxy for good institutions, there is also a failure to account for whether these are, or can ever be, indicants of better lives for students, faculty, and a pathway to societal well-being (Giacalone, 2009: 123; Morgeson and Nahrgang, 2008). Other critics, while accepting the factors that are included, question the weights attributed to them. While rating and accreditations by such organizations as the Association to Advance Collegiate Schools of Business

Table 14.4 Business school ranking advantages and disadvantages

Advantages	Disadvantages
Competition	Short-termism; students as customers; resource shifts to 'strategic areas'
Transparency/accountability	Methodology
Encourage strategic thinking	Limited attention to educational quality
Utility to prospective students	Limited base—mostly MBA rankings
Approximation truth to the rankings	Generation of knowledge vs dissemination of knowledge

(AACSB) or the European Quality Improvement System (EQUUIS) provide a benchmark, any number of business schools can pass these and thereby be labelled as more legitimate, or 'good'. A ranking approach produces a zero-sum game in the sense that the movement of one school has a ripple effect on the ranking of other schools. One consequence is that while there is often a shifting of places, there is little dramatic movement each year. The richer get richer and the poorer, on a relative scale, stay poorer.

In the USA, education activist Lloyd Thacker has made it his mission to restore educational values from what he calls an over-commercialized college selection process. Thacker has been circulating a letter calling on colleges to boycott a portion of the rankings, to stop using them for self-promotion, and to develop an alternative approach. Thacker describes his campaign as 'a test of character' for college presidents. He insists that many are eager to sign on, but face pressure from their boards of trustees, the members of which often come from the business world. But is Thacker's call realistic? Notably, despite his noble intentions, Thacker does not have the support of any of the top 100 universities. The issue is whether business schools should practise what they preach and labour under a ranking system. Operating like a business might yield the efficacy and output with which university administrators would be extremely pleased, but can this be achieved without sacrificing one of the true values of education: namely, the dissemination of knowledge for the public good?

Perhaps the consequence of greatest concern, however, is that the dominating presence, narrow agenda, and superficiality of the rankings have driven business schools to focus on image management (Gioia and Corley, 2002). Already, several media surveys try to prevent business school 'gaming' by incorporating results from past surveys into the current year's ranking and penalizing schools for overly exuberant coaching of students on their survey responses (Glick, 2008). We pointed out in Chapter 5 that there is debate over whether the business of business is business. Perhaps it is only natural that we ask whether the business of business schools should be business.

Implications for strategy practice

Some of the issues presented in this chapter may not sit very well with practitioners looking for a prescriptive 'how to' manual to orientate them in their practice of strategy. Strategists and managers will recognize that all never runs smoothly or as expected in business and that even the best-laid plans are seriously put to the test. This is why critical perspectives can prove so useful, because they facilitate engendering a level of questioning that may foresee or overcome the difficulties that can arise in the implementation of strategy ideas. Healthy cynicism is a positive thing. Too often, cultures are formed that prevent questioning 'the way in which we do things' or deny opportunities to communicate negative issues up the corporate ladder. This may not be intentional, but can come as a result of a fear of sharing negative knowledge and of non-communication practices that have become embedded over time. As discussed in Chapter 11 on strategic change, this is frequently something that occurs in successful organizations, which can become victims of complacency and ignore or hide information that counters or questions the basis of this success. This tendency is neatly captured in Barbara Ehrenreich's *(2009) Smile or Die: How Positive Thinking Fooled America and the World.*

Consultants can play a vital role in helping strategists and organizations to understand the issues that they are facing and the potential options that can be pursued. Bringing consultants into an organization affords an opportunity to deal with issues that strategists cannot explicitly address and which may be overlooked due to strong culture norms. Consultants may enable discussion of issues have been ignored or which could not have been discussed without outside intervention. Consultants may also have specialized expertise that the organization does not possess; employing their expertise may also benefit their processes and productivity. That said, there must be a clear objective for external intervention, while due attention should be paid to the managing the process from commencement through to aspects of learning and knowledge transfer.

The assumptions underpinning best practice, research results, and strategic decisions should always be aired and debated within organizations and by strategists. As John Milton (1608–74) commented: 'Where there is much desire to learn, there of necessity will be much arguing, much writing, many opinions; for opinion in good men is but knowledge in the making.' Rather than only make decisions, strategists should concern themselves with the nature of decision making, asking themselves the following questions.

- From where is evidence sourced?
- Is it from more than one independent source?
- Are the sources internal or external?

- What assumptions does this practice or strategy involve?
- Are these reasonable?
- Is there evidence of the practice or strategy working elsewhere in a similar company? Will in work in this context?
- How were the data collected?
- What form are they in (numbers—quantitative; or stories—qualitative)?
- What limitations are there to the data?

All strategists will employ key assumptions when conducting activities and unearthing these should be part of the essence of strategic thinking. This means that both academic research and 'best practice' promoted by consultants or management gurus should not be taken simply at face value. As we have seen in the Zara case study in Chapter 8, practices and activities from the fast-food industry have been deployed in the fashion industry—but that is not to say that they could be successfully applied in the construction or financial services sectors.

Finally, strategists should pay attention to the nature of strategic discourses that they employ. The language of strategy is often implicitly used, yet strategists would do well to consider the nature of the words that they are using with differing audiences. In essence, strategists should be consistent in how they describe the strategy of their business to any stakeholder group. Such consistency is important not only in terms of comprehension, but also in outlining a vision of the future and how this will be achieved. This consistency reinforces a sense of purpose throughout the organization—and presents a purposeful organization to the external community. Ultimately, a critical perspective, as presented in this chapter, brings us much closer to an understanding that 'managers are only as good as their ability to work things out thoughtfully in their own way' (Mintzberg, 2009: 16).

Introduction to readings

Reading 6.2, 'Strategy viewed from a management fashion perspective' by Timothy Clark (2004), seeks to contribute in an area usually left unexplored: namely, the role and influence of management consultants and external agents in the strategy process. Clark's paper is a good introduction to the purpose of this chapter, because it seeks to explore the 'full cast of players that extends well beyond the immediate confines of the management group within an organization'—or what he terms strategy's 'extended division of labour'. Clark uses the 'interpretative lens of management fashion' to account for those who engage in a race to sense managers' emergent collective preferences. Here, managers are judged akin to frantic teenagers sensitized and eager to grasp the processes and trends of fashion. Clark examines the role of different actors in the generation of management ideas, including management gurus, consultants, business schools, and publishers. His article finishes with three questions that provoke further reflection: who does what? Can external advice be a source of competitive advantage? What is the output? These in turn raise other questions touched upon in the chapter: if managers are involved in co-fabrication of ideas, why are certain ideas deployed? How are external agents and ideas selected? Clark's brief paper provides us with a long-overdue foundational understanding of the greater range of people and ideas impinging upon strategy processes.

The second reading for this chapter, accessible via a link on the Online Resource Centre that accompanies this book, an extract from Cummings and Angwin's excellent article 'The future shape of strategy: Lemmings or chimeras' (2004), builds on our understanding of what constitutes strategy knowledge and its applicability in the classroom setting and the business world. The authors argue that strategic analysis is framed by the same models and assumptions used in strategy's foundational works in the 1960s. These models are deemed overly top-down, static, and too simplistic to deal with the complex realities of today's business world. Instead, Cummings and Angwin suggest that the analogy of a chimera—'a creature with a single body and different formidable heads operating on many fronts'—can help us to understand how firms can confront numerous and often paradoxical challenges. Having explored why executives may cling to old strategy conventions and assumptions, the article utilizes a postmodern lens to cleverly re-examine globalization, motivation theory, and generic strategy, favouring a 'creative resolution of tensions' rather than simply abandoning old conventions for newer ones. The extract concludes with 'the value chimera': a multifaceted and multidimensional framework within which to assess how firms can manage their value-adding processes. This is a pragmatic tool and 'ten tips' indicate how it can be readily applied. Might strategists at last have an approach that enables them to capture corporate realities? We'll let you be the judge!

Reading 6.3, the concluding in-text reading for this section, is by Ezzamel and Wilmott and entitled 'Rethinking strategy: contemporary perspectives and debates' (2004). It builds and extends a social-practice approach to strategy by providing a Foucauldian analysis of strategy discourse. This involves asking two pertinent questions: how is sense to be made of strategy; and how do conceptions of strategy make sense of us? Alongside these questions, Ezzamel and Wilmott provide a brief, but useful, review of the origins of the strategy field and highlight the merits and limitations of the current phase, labelled 'post-rational analysis'. They acknowledge that the **strategy-as-practice** perspective is useful—for example, it promotes a methodology that questions the reliability of strategists' own accounts of their activities—but its downfall, together with that of other post-rational analysis, is that it assumes that there is a 'world out there' that is 'separate from and remains uninfluenced by' how this world is understood or theorized. In overcoming this perceived limitation, Ezzamel and Wilmott advance an analysis that seeks to understand how certain elements come to be constructed as 'the truth' and the 'natural order of things'. Rather than leaving matters in an abstract way, the authors draw on an empirical example of a strategic statement to offer one possible illustration of the kinds of discursive practice that compromise the micro-production of strategy in action. Overall, this account differs very much from mainstream interpretation of strategy, and many commentators take issue with the type of analysis that it proposes. Nonetheless, it is important to understand the types of argument that exist, if only 'to encourage a more reflexive understanding of what passes for knowledge of strategy'.

Mini case study Virgin consultants and the NHS: balancing spin with substance?

At the beginning of 2000, consultants from the Virgin Group, famous for revamping mature consumer product and service markets such as air and rail travel, cola, vodka, and banking, were called in by government ministers to report on Britain's hospitals. In an article in the *Sunday Times*, Secretary of State for Health, Alan Milburn, described Britain's publicly funded National Health Service (NHS) as 'a 1948 system operating in a twenty-first-century world'. 'That is why,' he explained, 'I have now asked Sir Richard Branson's award-winning Virgin Group to advise us on how hospitals can be made consumer friendly . . . It is about transforming the very culture of the NHS to make it a modern consumer service.' Press releases claimed that (then) Prime Minister, Tony Blair, would use the report to follow up on accusations made by his Health Secretary of the dire 'forces of conservatism' within the NHS and 'lambast the gross inefficiencies built into the system'.

The consultants visited nine hospitals and several general practitioners' surgeries over a twenty-six-day period and composed a damning report. They wrote of 'over-centralization', 'too much red tape', 'chaotic booking arrangements', and 'poor management'. They concluded that 'the patient is required to fit into the system, rather than the other way around', and that the 'dead hand of bureaucracy seems to stifle imagination and flair'. However, on the up side, they claimed that 'most [staff] are probably decent people who just need a little leadership and direction'. The actions they believed should be taken to remedy the situation included the sort of ideas that have become commonplace in many organizations: 'empowering workers to be more innovative'; making hospitals more 'consumer friendly'; and increasing transparency and accountability'. One recommended means of doing this was to allow patient representatives to go 'behind the scenes' and carry out 'snap inspections'. There was also talk of 'snack trolleys' and making hospitals 'more fun'.

However, NHS employees were critical of the Virgin report and the government's handling of it. Doctors felt that they were being blamed for poor public perception of the NHS, which, they argued, was caused by lack of funding. Stephen Thornton, chief executive of the NHS Confederation, accepted that declining standards needed to be addressed, but challenged 'the Virgin team to show me what they describe as a suffocating bureaucracy . . . Where on earth do they get ridiculous figures that imply there is one administrator to every two clinical staff?' Of all NHS staff, only 3 per cent were managers/administrators, compared with 44 per cent of staff who were nurses, 8 per cent who were doctors, and 17 per cent who were clerical; he asked, 'I wonder how many back-up staff it takes Virgin to get one pilot into the air?' In any case, he continued, 'many administrative and clerical staff undertake critical patient-related tasks. It is disingenuous to suggest these people hinder rather than help the treatment of patients'. Peter Hawker, chairman of the British Medical Association's Consultants Committee, similarly suggested that he was 'all for improving the services to patients but we need real resources, not an exercise in spin [doctoring]'.

These criticisms sparked a wider debate about the Blair government's use of consultants. A survey by the *Independent on Sunday* showed that the government had spent almost £1bn hiring private consulting firms in its first three years in office. It was revealed that the Department for Education and its agencies spent almost £10m between 1997 and 1999. In response, Nigel de Gruchy, general secretary of a prominent teaching union, claimed that 'The money could be much better spent. The government paid Hey McBer consultancies £3 million to come up with criteria for what makes a good teacher. We could have told them that for nothing'.

The Department of Health's spending on consultants in the same period was two-and-a-half times that of the Department for Education. According to one source, this could have paid for 2,327 heart bypass operations, 4,421 hip replacements, 737 full cancer treatments, and the wages of 1,133 junior doctors. A spokeswoman for the Unison health union said: 'It's an awful amount of money to spend on consultants, particularly if those consultants are at the expense of money going into front-line care. We generally know what the problems are; the difficulty is getting the government to listen to the people who are on the ground.'

Source: Reproduced by permission of SAGE Publications, London, Los Angeles, New Delhi and Singapore, Cummings (2002: 171–2).

Questions

1. Outline the strengths and weaknesses of bringing in external consultants to evaluate an organization such as the NHS.

2. Are the employees' criticisms of the Virgin report valid? Can you see any problems with any of the Virgin report's recommendations for the NHS?

3. How else might the government have gone about gaining insight into the problems that all parties seem to agree need to be addressed within the NHS?

Summary

Whipp (1996: 270) has described the lack of reflexivity in strategy as 'serious and potentially debilitating', adding that 'critical self-appraisal of motivations or core beliefs by those in the strategy literature is not widespread'. This chapter has analysed strategy and strategists through a more critical lens—one that is more aware of the socially constructed nature of much that we assume to be 'truth'. While it would be wrong to leave readers with the perception that all consultants and management gurus are simply witchdoctors peddling empty promises in an attempt to sell them to spellbound strategists, it would be equally mistaken to leave the impression that all knowledge and best practices are based on objective, efficiency-enhancing 'facts'. Likewise, while it would be wrong to universally question the purpose and value of management education, theory, and research, it would be misguided not to look in the mirror and reflect on its potential shortcomings. Lastly, given that strategic discourses are the mechanism by which strategy becomes real, our coverage would be incomplete if we were not to consider their role in creating, maintaining, and recreating the meaning(s) of strategy. Indeed, getting the 'right' decisions can depend less on the content of formal analysis and more on the ***display*** of classical rationality (Whittington, 2001). This chapter has put forward some ideas and perspectives to help us to better understand these neglected issues. While these do not *resolve* the challenges presented in other chapters, they do go some way to *dissolving* them by drawing attention to issues that underpin and inform them. Cummings (2002: 65) has spoken of the importance of approaches that engage with the interplay between modernist either/or hierarchies—for example, 'New is better than old', action versus reaction, global versus local—and explores how they may coexist. All strategic frameworks are valuable, but caution should be exercised so that they are not used in a rigid, universal, and non-questioning matter.

Overall, there is little doubt that both academics and practitioners should devote more attention to assessing the knowledge that they use, its purpose and assumptions, and whether it is relevant and appropriate (Grey, 2004). Pfeffer and Sutton (2006: 37) frequently suggest that one fruitful avenue is exploring 'companies that fail and why they fail, not just those that succeed'. Another is encouraging more active engagement and collaboration between academics and strategists. Ultimately, more complete understanding can come only from treating strategy as the messy and complex process that it actually is (Whittington, 2001). Strategy cannot be a given or fixed entity; organizations do not reach an end point at which they 'have a strategy'. The meaning and interpretation of 'strategy' are continuously negotiated and shifting in light of both external and internal factors. Strategy does not stand still, but is always in a state of flux. This is why it is so hard to research and understand, but ultimately why discovery and rediscovery of it can yield great advantages for strategists, organizations, and society.

Discussion questions

1. How do the ideas presented in this chapter challenge some of those presented in the earlier parts of the book?

2. Is it fair to depict strategists and organizations as fashion-conscious teenagers following the latest trends?

3. Should management education change to address the craft and art capacities of managers, as called for by Mintzberg (2004)?

4. Examine a piece of strategy research published as a peer review article. What assumptions are made, what methods are used, and how (if at all) is the argument made convincing?

5. Is an understanding of strategic discourse of relevance for the day-to-day practice of strategy and strategizing?

Further reading

M. Alvesson and H. Wilmott (1996) ***Making Sense of Management: A Critical Introduction***, London: Sage, provides an excellent introduction and overview to critical management studies, exploring what it means for management practice and research.

S. Cummings (2002) ***ReCreating Strategy***, London: Sage, offers an insightful account of strategy, depicting the pitfalls of its modernist heritage and providing a number of alternative means through which strategy and strategists can (and should) be considered.

P. D. Broughton (2008) ***What They Teach You at Harvard Business School***, 2nd edn, Harmondsworth: Penguin, is a fascinating read and a first-hand account of Broughton's experience as an MBA scholar at Harvard University. As part of the journey, Broughton documents the key ideas that were communicated, the nature of class dynamics, and the different modes of teaching and learning. All the while, Broughton is haunted by his own personal dilemma, contrasting the narrow ideals of key business ideas and practitioner insights with his own personal ideas about what constitutes 'success' and a meaningful career.

C. Carter, S. Clegg, and M. Kornberger (2010) 'Re-framing strategy: power, politics and accounting', ***Accounting, Auditing and Accountability Journal***, 43(5): 573–594, is a good overview, touching upon many of the issues discussed in this chapter. In particular, the authors call for a more sociological, critical, and multidisciplinary approach to examining strategy.

visit the Online Resource Centre that accompanies this book to access more learning resources on this chapter topic at www.oxfordtextbooks.co.uk/orc/cunningham/

References

Abrahamson, E. 1996. Managerial fashion. ***Academy of Management Review***, 21(1): 254–285.

Alvesson, M. and Wilmott, H. 1996. ***Making Sense of Management: A Critical Introduction***. London: Sage.

Ariely, D. 2009. The end of rational economics. ***Harvard Business Review***, July/Aug: 78–84.

Barley, S. and Kunda, G. 1992. Design and devotion: surges of rational and normative ideologies of control in managerial discourse. ***Administrative Science Quarterly***, 37(3): 363–399.

Barry, D. and Elmes, M. 1997. Strategy retold: towards a narrative view of strategic discourse. ***Academy of Management Review***, 22(2): 429–452.

Beinhocker, E. 1997. Strategy at the edge of chaos. ***McKinsey Quarterly,*** 1: 24–39.

Bennis, W. and O'Toole, J. 2005. How business schools lost their way. ***Harvard Business Review***, May: 96–104.

Berenbaum, R. 1997. Internal consultancy. In J. Neuman, K. Kellner, and A. Sheperd-Dawson (eds) ***Developing Organizational Consultancy***. London: Routledge.

Biehl-Missal, B. 2011. Business is show business: management presentations as performance. ***Journal of Management Studies***, forthcoming.

Brandenburger, A. and Vinokurova, N. 2011. Comment on 'Toward a behavioral theory of strategy'. ***Organization Science***, forthcoming.

Broughton, P. D. 2008. ***What They Teach You at Harvard Business School***. 2nd edn. Harmondsworth: Penguin.

Broughton, P. D. 2009. Harvard's masters of the apocalypse. ***Sunday Times***, 1 March.

Brunsson, N. and Olsen, J. 1993. ***The Reforming Organization***. London: Routledge.

Canback, S. 1999. Logic of management consulting. ***Journal of Management Consulting***, 10(3): 3–12.

Carter, C., Stewart, C., and Kornberger, M. 2008. ***A Very Short, Fairly Interesting and Reasonably Cheap Book about Studying Strategy***. London: Sage.

Caulkin, S. 2011. Swap the management-speak for plain English. ***Financial Times***, 9 May.

Clark, T. 1995. ***Managing Consultants: Consultancy as the Management of Impressions***. Buckingham: Open University Press.

Clark, T. 2004. Strategy viewed from a management fashion perspective. ***European Management Review***, 1(1): 105–11.

Clegg, S., Carter, C., and Kornberger, M. 2004. Get up: I feel like being a strategy machine. ***European Management Review***, 1: 3–13.

Cummings, S. 2002. *ReCreating Strategy*. London: Sage.

Cummings, T. G. 2007. Quest for an engaged Academy. *Academy of Management Review*, 32(3): 355–360.

Darwin, J., Johnson, P., and McAuley, J. 2002. *Developing Strategies for Change*. Harlow: Pearson Education.

Di Maggio, P. J., and Powell, W. W. 1983. The iron cage revisited: institutional isomorphism and collective rationality in organizational fields. *American Sociological Review*, 23: 111–136.

Eccles, R. and Nohira, N. 1992. *Beyond the Hype: Rediscovering the Essence of Management*. Boston, MA: Harvard Business School Press.

Ehrenreich, B. 2009. *Smile or Die: How Positive Thinking Fooled America and the World*. London: Granta.

Ferraro, F., Pfeffer, J., and Sutton, R. 2005. Economic language and assumptions: how theories can become self-fulfilling. *Academy of Management Review*, 30(1): 8–24.

Foucault, M. 1980. *Power/Knowledge. Selected Interviews and Other Writings 1972–77*. Brighton: Harvester Press.

Furnham, A. 2000. Secrets of success from the Heathrow school of management. *Business Strategy Review*, 11(3): 61–67.

Gabriel, Y. 2002. Essai: on the pragmatic use of organizational theory—a provocation. *Organization Studies*, 23: 133–51.

Ghoshal, S. 2005. Bad management theories are destroying good management practices. *Academy of Management Executive*, 4(1): 75–91.

Ghoshal, S. and Moran, P. 1996. Bad for practice: a critique of the transaction cost theory. *Academy of Management Review*, 21: 31–47.

Giacalone, R. 2009. Academic rankings in research institutions: a case of skewed mind sets and professional amnesia. *Academy of Management Learning and Education*, 8(1): 122–126.

Gilbert, K. 1996. Consultancy fatigue: symptoms and prevention. *Leadership and Organizational Development Journal*, 19(6): 340–346.

Gill, L. and Johnson, P. 2001. *Research Methods for Managers*. London: Paul Chapman.

Gioia, D. and Corley, K. 2002. Being good versus looking good: business school rankings and the Circean transformation from substance to image. *Academy of Management Learning and Education*, 1(1): 107–120.

Glick, W. H. 2008. Rain Man or Pied Piper? Moving business schools beyond media rankings with mass customization and stakeholder education. *Academy of Management Perspectives*, Feb: 18–23.

Golden-Biddle, K. and Locke, K. 1993. Appealing work: an investigation of how ethnographic texts convince. *Organization Science*, 44: 596–616.

Greckhamer, T. 2010. The stretch of strategic management discourse. *Organization Studies*, 31(7): 841–871.

Greiner, L. E. and Metzger, R. O. 1983. *Consulting to Management*. Englewood Cliffs, NJ: Prentice Hall.

Grey, C. 2004. Reinventing business schools: the contribution of critical management education. *Academy of Management Learning and Education*, 3: 178–186.

Guest, D. 1990. HRM and the American dream. *Journal of Management Studies*, 27(4): 377–97.

Hackley, C. 2003. We are all customers now: rhetorical strategy and ideological control in marketing management texts. *Journal of Management Studies*, 40(5): 1325–1352.

Hammer, M. 1990. Re-engineering work: don't automate, obliterate. *Harvard Business Review*, 68(4): 104–111.

Hansen, M., Ibarra, H., and Peyer, U. 2010. The best-performing CEOs in the world. *Harvard Business Review*, Jan/Feb: 104–113.

Hardy, C., Lawrence, T. B., and Grant, D. 2005. Discourse and collaboration: the role of conversations and collective identity. *Academy of Management Review*, 30(1): 58–78.

Hendry, J. 2000. Strategic decision making, discourse and strategy as social practice. *Journal of Management Studies*, 37(3): 955–976.

Huczynski, A. 1993. Explaining the succession of management fads. *International Journal of Human Resource Management*, 4(2): 443–463.

Jacobides, M. 2010. Strategy tools for a shifting landscape. *Harvard Business Review*, Jan/Feb: 77–84.

Johnson, G. 1992. Managing strategic change: strategy, culture and action. *Long Range Planning*, 25(1): 28–36.

Jones, G. 2004. Perspectives on strategy. In S. Segal-Horn (ed.) *The Strategy Reader*. 2nd edn. Oxford: Blackwell Publishing.

Kantola, A. and Seeck, H. 2011. Dissemination of management into politics: Michael Porter and the political uses of management consulting. *Management Learning*, 42(1): 25–47.

Knights, D. and Morgan, D. 1991. Corporate strategy, organizations and subjectivity: a critique. *Organizational Studies*, 12(2): 251–273.

Leavitt, H. 2007. Big organizations are unhealthy environments for human beings. *Academy of Management Learning and Education*, 62(2): 253–263.

March, J. G. 2007. The study of organizations and organizing since 1945. *Organization Studies*, 28(1): 9–19.

McGivern, C. 1983. Some facets of the relationship between consultants and clients in organizations. *Journal of Managerial Psychology*, 20(3): 367–386.

McKiernan, P. and Carter, C. 2004. The millennium nexus: strategic management at the crossroads. *European Management Review*, 1: 3–13.

Miller, D. and Hartwick, J. 2002. Spotting management fads. *Harvard Business Review*, 80(10): 26–28.

Mintzberg, H. 2004. *Managers not MBAs*. London: Prentice Hall.

Mintzberg, H. 2009. *Managing*. London: FT Prentice Hall.

Mintzberg, H. and Lampel, J. 1999. Reflecting on the strategy process. *Sloan Management Review*, Spring: 21–30.

Morgeson, F. and Nahrgang, J. 2008. Same as it ever was: recognizing stability in the *Businessweek* rankings. *Academy of Management Learning and Education*, 7(1): 26–41.

Overell, S. 2002. What is a consultant?, *Personnel Today*, 22 October, pp. 12–13.

Pfeffer, J. 2005. Why do bad management theories persist? A comment on Ghoshal. *Academy of Management Learning and Education*, 4(1): 96–100.

Pfeffer, J. and Sutton, R. 2006. *Hard Facts, Dangerous Half Truths, and Total Nonsense*. Boston, MA: Harvard Business School Press.

Phillips, N. and Hardy, C. 2002. Discourse analysis: investigating processes of social construction. *Sage University Paper Series on Qualitative Research Methods*, Vol 50, Thousand Oaks, CA: Sage.

Rosenzweig, P. 2007. *The Halo Effect ... and the Eight Other Business Decisions that Deceive Managers.* New York: Free Press.

Rousseau, D. 2006. 2005 Presidential Address: is there such a thing as evidence based management? *Academy of Management Review*, 32(2): 256–269.

Rumelt, R. 2011. *Good Strategy/Bad Strategy*. London: Profile Books.

Schein, E. H. 1996. Culture: the missing concept in organization studies. *Administrative Science Quarterly*, 41(2): 229–240.

Shrivastava, P. 1986. Is strategic management ideological? *Journal of Management*, 12(3): 363–377.

Spicer, A. and Fleming, P. 2007. Intervening in the inevitable: contesting globalization in a public sector organization. *Organization*, 14: 517–541.

Starkey, K. and Tempest, S. 2009. The winter of our discontent: the design challenge for business schools. *Academy of Management Learning and Education*, 8(4): 576–596.

Sturdy, A. 1997. The consultancy process: an insecure business. *Journal of Management Studies*, 34(5): 389–413.

Sturdy, A. 2011. Consultancy's consequences? A critical assessment of management consultancy's impact on management. *British Journal of Management*, 22: 517–530.

Thomas, P. 2003. The recontextualisation of management: a discourse-based approach to analysing the development of management thinking. *Journal of Management Studies*, 40(4): 775–803.

Townley, B. 2008. *Reason's Neglect: Rationality and Organizing*. Oxford: Oxford University Press.

Tushman, M., O'Reilly III, C., Fenollosa, A., Kleinbaum, A., and McGrath, D. 2007. Relevance and rigor: executive education as a lever in shaping practice and research. *Academy of Management Learning and Education*, 6(3): 345–362.

Vaara, E., Kleymann, B., and Seristo, H. 2004. Strategies as discursive constructions: the case of airline alliances. *Journal of Management Studies*, 41(1): 1–35.

Watson, D. 2005. *How Clichés, Weasel Words and Management Speak are Strangling Public Language*. New York: Gotham Books.

Weiss, A. 2003. Avoiding the tribalization of consulting. *Consulting to Management*, 141: 13–15.

Whipp, R. 1996. Creative deconstruction: strategy and organizations. In S. R. Clegg, C. Hardy, and W. R. Nord (eds) *Handbook of Organization Studies*. London: Sage.

Whittington, R. 2001. *What is Strategy and Does It Matter?* London: Routledge.

Williams, R. 2001. Client's role in the consulting relationship: is there a 'con' in consulting? *Managerial Auditing Journal*, 169: 519–522.

Wilmott, H. 1993. Strength is ignorance; slavery is freedom: managing cultures in modern organisations. *Journal of Management Studies*, 30: 515–552.

Womack, J., Jones, D., and Roos, D. 1990. *The Machine that Changed the World.* New York: Rawson Associates.

Zemsky, R. 2008. The rain main cometh—again. *Academy of Management Perspectives*, 22(1): 5–15.

Section 6 readings

Introduction

In this section, we have re-examined the key ideas of the text by exploring the role of strategy in public sector, not-for-profit, and small firm contexts, and by critically reflecting on the role of strategy agents.

- **Reading 6.1** by Christopher Hood, 'A public management for all seasons?' (1991), provides interesting perspectives on the ideology of new public management (NPM) and what constitutes 'good' administration. This reading provides much timely food for thought, as many national governments and societies rethink the role of the public sector in the wake of the global economic crisis. Strategy matters even more in public sector contexts, in which the associated changes shaped by budgetary issues and current societal debates will impact on all citizens.

- **Reading 6.2**, 'Strategy viewed from a management fashion perspective' by Timothy Clark (2004), and **Reading 6.3**, 'Rethinking strategy: contemporary perspectives and debates' by Mahmoud Ezzamel and Hugh Willmott (2004), provide a basis for reflection when considering the definition of 'strategy', how we understand strategy, and the role of different actors in shaping strategy in practice. Such reflexivity is consistently required by strategists and everyone involved in the strategic management field, both in academia and in practice. These readings also point to the subtle role of power and vested interests in shaping the ideas and meanings of what constitutes strategy.

Reading 6.1 A public management for all seasons? *Christopher Hood*

First published: (1991) *Public Administration*, 69: 3–19. *Public Administration*, Vol. 69 Spring 1991 (3–19). Reproduced with the kind permission of John Wiley and Sons Ltd.

The rise of new public management (NPM)

The rise of 'new public management' (hereafter NPM) over the past 15 years is one of the most striking international trends in public administration. Though the research reported in the other papers in this issue refers mainly to UK experience, NPM is emphatically not a uniquely British development. NPM's rise seems to be linked with four other administrative 'megatrends', namely:

(i) attempts to *slow down or reverse government growth* in terms of overt public spending and staffing (Dunsire and Hood 1989);

(ii) the shift toward *privatization and quasi-privatization* and away from core government institutions, with renewed emphasis on 'subsidiarity' in service provision (cf. Hood and Schuppert 1988; Dunleavy 1989).

(iii) the development of *automation*, particularly in information technology, in the production and distribution of public services; and

(iv) the development of a more *international* agenda, increasingly focused on general issues of public management, policy design, decision styles and intergovernmental cooperation, on top of the older tradition of individual country specialisms in public administration.

(These trends are discussed further in Hood 1990b).

NPM, like most administrative labels, is a loose term. Its usefulness lies in its convenience as a shorthand name for the set of broadly similar administrative doctrines which dominated the bureaucratic reform agenda in many of the OECD group of countries from the late 1970s (see Aucoin 1990; Hood 1990b; Pollitt 1990).

Although ill-defined, NPM aroused strong and varied emotions among bureaucrats. At one extreme were those who held that NPM was the only way to correct for the irretrievable failures and even moral bankruptcy in the 'old' public management (cf. Keating 1989). At the other were those who dismissed much of the thrust of NPM as a gratuitous and philistine destruction of more than a century's work in developing a distinctive public service ethic and culture (cf. Martin 1988; Nethercote 1989b).

NPM's rise also sparked off debate as to how the movement was to be labelled, interpreted and explained. What exactly was the public management Emperor now wearing? Where did the design come from, and did its novelty lie mainly in presentation or in content? Why did it find favour? Was it an all-purpose and all-weather garment? This article attempts to discuss these questions, with particular attention to the last one.

What the emperor was wearing: the doctrines of NPM

Different commentators and advocates of NPM have stressed different aspects of doctrine. But the seven overlapping precepts summarized in [Table 6.1.1] appear in most discussions of NPM. Over the last decade, a 'typical' public sector policy delivery unit in the UK, Australia, New Zealand and many other OECD countries would be likely to have had some exposure to most of these doctrines. But not all of the seven elements were equally present in all cases; nor are they necessarily fully consistent, partly because they do not have a single intellectual provenance.

Where the design came from: NPM as a marriage of opposites

One way of interpreting NPM's origins is as a marriage of two different streams of ideas. One partner was the 'new institutional economies'. It was built on the now very familiar story of the post-World War II development of public choice, transactions cost theory and principal-agent theory – from the early work of Black (1958) and Arrow (1963) to Niskanen's (1971) landmark theory of bureaucracy and the spate of later work which built on it.

The new institutional economics movement helped to generate a set of administrative reform doctrines built on ideas of *contestability*, *user choice*, *transparency* and close concentration on *incentive structures*. Such doctrines were very different from traditional military-bureaucratic ideas of 'good administration', with their emphasis on orderly hierarchies and elimination of duplication or overlap (cf. Ostrom 1974).

The other partner in the 'marriage' was the latest of a set of successive waves of business-type 'managerialism' in the public sector, in the tradition of the international scientific management movement (Merkle 1980; Hume 1981;

Table 6.1.1 Doctrinal components of new public management

No.	Doctrine	Meaning	Typical justification
1	'Hands-on professional management' in the public sector	Active, visible, discretionary control of organizations from named persons at the top, 'free to manage'	Accountability requires clear assignment of responsibility for action, not diffusion of power
2	Explicit standards and measures of performance	Definition of goals, targets, indicators of success, preferably expressed in quantitative terms, especially for professional services (cf. Day and Klein 1987; Carter 1989)	Accountability requires clear statement of goals; efficiency requires 'hard look' at objectives
3	Greater emphasis on output controls	Resource allocation and rewards linked to measured performance; breakup of centralized bureaucracy-wide personnel management	Need to stress results rather than procedures
4	Shift to disaggregation of units in the public sector	Break up of formerly 'monolithic' units, unbundling of U-form management systems into corporatized units around products, operating on decentralized 'one-line' budgets and dealing with one another on an 'arms length' basis	Need of create 'manageable' units, separate provision and production interests, gain efficiency advantages of use of contract of franchise arrangements inside as well as outside the public sector
5	Shift to greater competition in public sector	Move to term contracts and public tendering procedures	Rivalry as the key to lower costs and better standards
6	Stress on private-sector styles of management practice	Move away from military-style 'public service ethic', greater flexibility in hiring and rewards; greater use of PR techniques	Need to use 'proven' private sector management tools in the public sector
7	Stress on greater discipline and parsimony in resource use	Cutting direct costs, raising labour discipline, resisting union demands, limiting 'compliance costs' to business	Need to check resource demands of public sector and 'do more with less'

Pollitt 1990). This movement helped to generate a set of administrative reform doctrines based on the ideas of *'professional management'* expertise as *portable* (Martin 1983), *paramount* over technical expertise, requiring high *discretionary power* to achieve results ('free to manage') and *central* and *indispensable* to better organizational performance, through the development of appropriate cultures (Peters and Waterman 1982) and the active measurement and adjustment of organizational outputs.

Whether the partners in this union were fully compatible remains to be seen. 'Free to manage' is a rather different slogan from 'free to choose'. The two can conflict, particularly where the NPM revolution is led from above (as it was in the UK) rather than from below. The relative dominance of the two partners varied in different countries even within the 'Westminster model' tradition (cf. Hood 1990c). For example, in the unique circumstances of New Zealand, the synthesis of public choice, transactions cost theory and principal–agent theory was predominant, producing an analytically driven NPM movement of unusual coherence. But in the UK and Australia business-type managerialism was much more salient, producing a more pragmatic and less intellectually elegant strain of NPM or 'neo-Taylorism' (Pollitt 1990, p. 56). Potential frictions between these partners were not resolved by any single coherent or definitive exposition of the joint philosophy. Indeed, the New Zealand Treasury's *Government Management* (1987) comes closest to a coherent NPM 'manifesto', given that much of the academic literature on the subject either lacks full-scale elaboration or enthusiastic commitment to NPM.

Why NPM found favour: the acceptance factor

There is no single accepted explanation or interpretation of why NPM coalesced and why it 'caught on' (cf. Hood 1990b; Hood and Jackson 1991 forthcoming, ch. 8). Many academic commentators associate it with the political rise of the 'New Right'. But that on its own does not explain why these particular doctrines found favour, nor why NPM was so strongly endorsed by Labour governments ostensibly opposed to the 'New Right', notably in Australia and New Zealand. Among the possible explanations are the following four.

First, for those who take a sceptical view of administrative reform as a series of evanescent fads and fashions, NPM's rise might be interpreted as a sudden and unpredictable product of 'loquocentric' success (Minogue 1986). (Spann (1981) offers a classic statement of the 'fashion' interpretation of administrative reform.) 'Cheap, superficial and popular', like the industrial 'rationalization' doctrines of the 1930s (Hannah 1976, p. 38, fn. p. 34), NPM had many of the necessary qualities for a period of pop management stardom. A 'whim of fashion' interpretation has some attractions, and can cope with the cycles and reversals that took place within NPM – for instance, the radical shift in the UK, from the 'Heseltine creed' of *Ministers* as the hands-on public managers to the 'Next Steps' corporatization creed of professional managers at the top, with ministers in a strictly 'hands-off' role (cf. also Sturgess 1989). But equally, the weakness of a simple 'whim of fashion' explanation is that it does not account for the relative *endurance* of many of the seven precepts identified in [Table 6.1.1] over more than a decade.

An equally sceptical explanation, but one which better accommodates the recurring or enduring features of many aspects of NPM, is the view of NPM as a 'cargo cult' phenomenon – the endless rebirth, in spite of repeated failures, of the idea that substantive success ('cargo') can be gained by the practice of particular kinds of (managerial) ritual. Downs and Larkey (1986) describe a recurring cycle of euphoria and disillusion in the promulgation of simplistic and stereotyped recipes for better public management in the USA, which shows striking similarities with the well-documented cargo cults of Melanesia (Lawrence 1964; Worsley 1968). However, this explanation cannot tell us why the NPM variant of the recurring public management 'cargo cult' appeared at the time that it did, rather than at any other.

A third, less sceptical, approach might be to view the rise of NPM through Hegelian spectacles and interpret it as an epoch-making attraction of opposites. The opposites in this case are two historically distinct approaches to public administration which are in a sense fused in NPM. One is the German tradition of state-led economic development (*Volkswirtschaft*) by professional public managers, with its roots in cameralism (Small 1909). The other is the Anglo-Saxon tradition of liberal economics, allied with a concern for matching self-interest with duty in administration, that has its roots in utilitarianism (Hume 1981). But, like the 'cargo cult' interpretation, the 'synthesis of opposites' interpretation on its own does not help us to understand why those two distinct public administration traditions should have united *at this particular time* rather than at any other.

A fourth and perhaps more promising interpretation of the emergence of NPM is as a response to a set of special social conditions developing in the long peace in the developed countries since World War II, and the unique period of economic growth which accompanied it (see Hood 1990b and 1991 forthcoming). Conditions which may have helped to precipitate NPM include:

- changes in income level and distrimbution serving to weaken the 'Tocqueville coalition' for government growth in the electorate, and laying the conditions for a new tax-conscious winning electoral coalition (Tocqueville 1946, p. 152; Peacock 1979; Meltzer and Richard 1981);

• changes in the socio-technical system associated with the development of the lead technologies of the late twentieth-century Kondratiev cycle ('post-industrialism', 'post-Fordism'), serving to remove the traditional barriers between 'public sector work' and 'private sector work' (cf. Bell 1973; Piore and Sabel 1984; Jessop 1988).

• a shift towards 'new machine polities', the advent of a new campaign technology geared towards making public policy by intensive opinion polling of key groups in the electorate, such that professional party strategists have greater clout in policy-making relative to the voice of experience from the bureaucracy (cf. Mills 1986; Hood 1990c, p. 206).

• a shift to a more white-collar, socially heterogeneous population less tolerant of 'statist' and uniform approaches in public policy (cf. Hood and Schuppert 1988, p. 250–2).

The fourth explanation is somewhat 'overdetermined', but it seems more promising than the other three in that it has the power to explain what none of the others can do, namely why NPM should have emerged in the particular time and place that it did and under a variety of different auspices.

An all-purpose garment? NPM's claim to universality

Like many previous administrative philosophies, NPM was presented as a framework of general applicability, a 'public management for all seasons'. The claim to universality was laid in two main ways.

Portability and diffusion

First, much the same set of received doctrines was advanced as the means to solve 'management ills' in many different contexts – different organizations, policy fields, levels of government, countries. From Denmark to New Zealand, from education to health care, from central to local government and quangos, from rich North to poor South, similar remedies were prescribed along the lines of the seven themes sketched out in table 6.1.1. Universalism was not complete in practice; for instance, NPM seems to have had much less impact on international bureaucracies than on national ones, and less on controlling departments than on front-line delivery units. Moreover, much was made of the need for local variation in management styles – so long as such variations did not challenge the basic framework of NPM (Pollitt 1990, pp. 55–6). For critics, however, much of the 'freedom to manage' under NPM was that brand of freedom in which whatever is not forbidden tends to be compulsory (Larsen 1980, p. 54); and the tendencies to uniformity and 'cloning' under FMI points to possible reasons for the decline of FMI and its supersession by the corporatization creed of 'Next Steps.'

Political neutrality

Second, NPM was claimed to be an 'apolitical' framework within which many different values could be pursued effectively. The claim was that different political priorities and circumstances could be accommodated by altering the 'settings' of the management system, without the need to rewrite the basic programme of NPM. That framework was not, according to NPM's advocates, a machine exclusively tunable to respond to the demands of the New Right or to any one political party or programme (see, for example, Scott Bushnell and Sallee 1990, p. 162; Treasury and Civil Service Committee 1990, pp. ix, 22, 61). In this respect, NPM followed the claims to universality of traditional Public Administration, which also purported to offer a neutral and all-purpose instrument for realizing whatever goals elected representatives might set (Ostrom 1974; Thomas 1978; Hood 1987).

Counter-claims: critics of NPM

If NPM has lacked a single definitive 'manifesto', the ideas of its critics are equally scattered among a variety of often ephemeral sources. Most of the criticisms of NPM have come in terms of four main counter-claims, none of which have been definitively tested, in spite of the ESRC's 'Management in Government' initiative.

The first is the assertion that NPM is like the Emperor's New Clothes in the well-known Hans Andersen story – all hype and no substance, and in that sense a true product of the style-conscious 1980s. From this viewpoint, the advent of new managerialism has changed little, apart from the language in which senior public 'managers' speak in public. Underneath, all the old problems and weaknesses remain. Implicitly, from this viewpoint, the remedy lies in giving NPM some real substance in order to move from 'smoke and mirrors' to reality – for example, in making output contracts between ministers and chief executives legally binding or in breaking up the public service employment structure, as has happened in New Zealand (cf. Hood and Jones in Treasury and Civil Service Committee 1989–90).

The second is the assertion that NPM has damaged the public service while being ineffective in its ability to deliver on its central claim to lower costs per (constant) unit of service. Critics of this type suggest that the main result of NPM in many cases has been an 'aggrandizement of management' (Martin 1983) and a rapid middle-level bureaucratization of new reporting systems (as in the remarkable growth of the 'performance indicator industry'). Budgetary and control framework changes such as 'top-slicing' and 'creative accounting' serve to destabilize the bureaucracy and to weaken or destroy elementary but essential competences at the front line (see, for instance, Nethercote 1989b, p. 17; Nethercote 1989c). From this viewpoint, the remedy lies in applying to the NPM *system* the disciplines that it urges upon service-delivery bureaucracies but so signally fails to impose on itself – particularly in strict resource control and the imposition of a battery of published and measurable performance indicators to determine the overall costs and benefits of the system.

The third common criticism is the assertion that NPM, in spite of its professed claims to promote the 'public good' (of cheaper and better public services for all), is actually a vehicle for *particularistic* advantage. The claim is that NPM is a self-serving movement designed to promote the career interests of an élite group of 'new managerialists' (top managers and officials in central controlling departments, management consultants and business schools) rather than the mass of public service customers or low-level staff (Dunleavy 1985; Yeatman 1987; Kelleher 1988; Pollitt 1990, pp. 134–7). Implicitly, the remedy suggested by these criticisms is to have disproportionate cutbacks on 'managerial' rather than on 'operational' staff (cf. Martin 1983), and measures to 'empower' consumers, for instance by new systems of direct democracy (cf. Pollitt 1990, pp. 183–4).

The fourth line of criticism, to which most attention will be paid in the remainder of this paper, is directed towards NPM's claim of *universality.* Contrary to NPM's claim to be a public management for all seasons, these critics argue that different administrative values have different implications for fundamental aspects of administrative design – implications which go beyond altering the 'settings' of the systems.

In order for their counter-claim to have any significance, it must be able to survive obvious objections. First, it must be able to show that the objection is more than a semantic quibble about where the line comes between a different programme and a change of 'settings'. For that, it must be able to show that the incompatibility problem lies in NPM's 'hard core' research programme rather than in its 'elaborative belts' (Lakatos 1970). Second, it must be able to show that it is more than a trivial and obvious proposition. In order to survive this objection, it needs to show that there are different management-system implications of different *mainstream*, relatively orthodox values, without reference to values at the extremes of the orthodox belief spectrum (since it needs no elaborate treatise to show that different 'fundamentalist' values have different implications for public management). Third, the 'incompatibility' argument needs to rest on a plausible case that an 'all-purpose culture' either does not exist or cannot be engineered into existence. Unless it can do so, it risks being dismissed for mechanically assuming that there is a particular set of administrative design-characteristics which goes with the ability to achieve a particular set of values. Finally, it needs to show that the debate relates to *administrative* values – values that relate to conventional and relatively narrow ideas about 'good administration' rather than to broader ideas about the proper role of the state in society. Unless the critique of the 'all seasons' quality of NPM relates to administrative values in this sense, it risks being dismissed simply as an undercover way of advocating different *political values* from those currently held by elected governments. A case built on such a basis would not essentially be an administrative design argument, and would neither demonstrate that NPM is incapable of being adapted to promote alternative political values nor that NPM is a false recipe for achieving the narrow 'efficiency' values of the current orthodox agenda.

Most of the orthodox criticisms of NPM in this vein are vulnerable to counterattack from this last objection. Most academic attacks on NPM have questioned NPM's universality by focusing on the equity costs of a preoccupation with cost-cutting and a focus on 'bottom line ethics' (Jackson 1989, p. 173). For instance, a focus on outputs allied with heavy 'hands-on' demands on managers is often claimed to downgrade equity considerations, particularly in its implications for the ability of female managers to reach top positions in the public service (cf. Bryson 1987; Pollitt 1990, pp. 141–2). A focus on disaggregation and a private-sector PR style is likewise often claimed to reduce the accessibility of public services by increasing the complexity and opacity of government (Nethercote 1990c), and increasing the scope for buck-passing and denial of responsibility, especially for disadvantaged consumers. However, any simple dichotomy between 'efficiency' and 'equity' can be countered by NPM's advocates on the grounds that 'efficiency' can be conceived in ways which do not fundamentally conflict with equity (cf. Wilenski 1986), and that equity values could perfectly well be programmed in to the target-setting and performance indication process, if there was strong enough political pressure to do so.

Three clusters of administrative values

In administrative argument in the narrow sense, the rival values in play typically do not fall into a neat dichotomy. At least three different 'families' of values commonly appear in debates about administrative design, and these are summarized in [Table 6.1.2] (cf. Hood and Jackson 1991 forthcoming).

Table 6.1.2 Three sets of core values in public management

	Sigma-type values Keep it lean and purposeful	Theta-type values Keep it honest and fair	Lambda-type values Keep it robust and resilient
Standard of success	**Frugality** (matching of resources to tasks for given goals)	**Rectitude** (achievement of fairness, mutuality, the proper discharge of duties)	**Resilience** (achievement of reliability, adaptivity, robustness)
Standard of failure	**Waste** (muddle, confusion, inefficiency)	**Malversation** (unfairness, bias, abuse of office)	**Catastrophe** (risk, breakdown, collapse)
Currency of success and failure	**Money and time** (resource costs of producers and consumers)	**Trust and entitlements** (consent, legitimacy, due process, political entitlements)	**Security and survival** (confidence, life and limb)
Control emphasis	Output	Process	Input/process
Slack	Low	Medium	High
Goals	Fixed/single	Incompatible 'Double bind'	Emergent/multiple
Information	Costed, segmented (commercial assets)	Structured	Rich exchange, collective asset
Coupling	Tight	Medium	Loose

Broadly, the 'sigma' family of values relates to *economy* and *parsimony*, the 'theta' family relates to *honesty* and *fairness*, and the 'lambda' family relates to *security* and *resilience.*

The trio corresponds roughly to the management values used by Susan Strange (1988, pp. 1–6) in her account of the evolution of different regimes in the international sphere; and at least two of the three correspond to the groups of values given by Harmon and Mayer (1986, pp. 34–53) in their well-known account of the normative context of public sector organization. It cannot be claimed that these values are esoteric or extreme, or that they are not 'administrative' values.

Sigma-type values: match resources to defined tasks

In the 'sigma' family come administrative values connected with the matching of resources to narrowly defined tasks and circumstances in a competent and sparing fashion. Such values are central, mainstream and traditional in public management. From this viewpoint, frugality of resource use in relation to given goals is the criterion of success, while failure is counted in terms of instances of avoidable waste and incompetence. If sigma-type values are emphasized, the central concern is to 'trim fat' and avoid 'slack'.

Classic expressions of sigma-type values include:

(i) 'just-in-time' inventory control systems (which avoid tying up resources in storing what is not currently-needed, pushing the onus of accessible storage and rapid delivery on to suppliers);

(ii) payment-by-results reward systems (which avoid paying for what is not being delivered); and

(iii) administrative 'cost engineering' (using resources sparingly to provide public services of no greater cost, durability or quality than is absolutely necessary for a defined task, without excessive concern for 'externalities').

The principal 'coin' in which success or failure to realize sigma-type values is measured is time and money, in resource costs of consumers and producers.

It can be argued that an orthodox design for realizing sigma-type values would closely parallel the 'mechanistic' structures which have frequently been identified in contingency theory as applicable to defined and stable environmental conditions (cf. Burns and Stalker 1961; Lawrence and Lorsch 1967). Since the 'sigma' group of values stresses the matching of resources to defined objectives, the setting of fixed and 'checkable' goals must be central to any design for realizing such values. The fewer incompatible objectives are included, the more readily can unnecessary fat be identified and removed. Equally, the more that the control emphasis is on output rather than on process or input, the more unambiguous the waste-finding process can be. To make output control a reality, two features are necessary. One is a heavy emphasis on output databases. Such an emphasis in turn requires a technological infrastructure of reporting which will tend to make each managerial unit 'tightly coupled' in informational terms. The other is the sharp definition of responsibilities, involving separation of 'thinking' and 'executing' activities and the breakup of organizations into separate, non-overlapping parts, to come as close as possible to the ideal of single-objective, trackable and manageable units. It follows that information in such a control system will be highly segmented and valuable, so that it will be guarded with extreme care and traded rather than given away. These design characteristics map closely on to the recipes offered by the corporate management strain of NPM.

Theta-type values: honesty, fairness, mutuality

'Theta-type' connotes values broadly relating to the pursuit of honesty, fairness and mutuality through the prevention of distortion, inequity, bias, and abuse of office. Such values are also central and traditional in public management, and they are institutionalized in appeal mechanisms, public reporting requirements, adversary bureaucracies, independent scrutiny systems, attempts to socialize public servants in something more than 'bottom line ethics' or a high 'grovel count' (Self 1989). From this viewpoint, success is counted in terms of 'rectitude', the proper discharge of duties in procedural and substantive terms, while failure is measured in terms of 'malversation' in a formal or substantive sense. If theta-type values are placed at centre stage, the central concern is to ensure honesty, prevent 'capture' of public bodies by unrepresentative groups, and avoid all arbitrary proceedings.

Classic expressions of theta-type values include:

(i) recall systems for removing public officials from office by popular vote;

(ii) 'notice and comment' and 'hard look' requirements in administrative law (Birkinshaw, Harden and Lewis 1990, p. 260);

(iii) independent anti-corruption investigatory bodies such as the 1987–9 Fitzgerald Inquiry which effectively brought down the Queensland government in 1989 (cf. Prasser, Wear and Nethercote 1990).

The 'coin' in which success or failure is measured according to theta-type values may be partly related to 'balance sheet' items (insofar as dishonesty and abuse of office is often linked with palpable waste of resources), but also involves less tangible stakes, notably public trust and confidence and the ability to exercise citizenship effectively.

Putting theta-type values at the centre of the stage has implications for organizational design which are different from an emphasis on 'sigma-type' values. Where honesty and fairness is a primary goal, the design-focus is likely to be on process-controls rather than output controls. Goals, too, are less likely to be single in nature. 'Getting the job done' in terms of aggregate quantities is likely to be supplemented by concerns about *how* the job is done (cf. March and Olsen 1989, pp. 47–52).

Hence 'double bind' elements (Hennestad 1990) may be central to goal setting, with line management under complex cross-pressures and with control operating through a shifting-balances style (Dunsire 1978). The cross pressures and 'double bind' process may operate through the activities of independent adversary bureaucracies, rather than with corporate objectives settled in a single place – for example, in the Hong Kong style of independent anti-corruption bodies. Similarly, concern with process may cause the emphasis to go on the achievement of maximum *transparency* in public operations – for example, extensive public reporting requirements, 'angels' advocates' (the practice of incorporating representatives of 'public interest' groups on corporate boards), freedom of information laws, 'notice and comment' procedures, rather than simple 'bottom line ethics'.

Indeed, the logical conclusion of putting theta-type values first in designing public management would be to minimize the ability of those in high office to sell or distort public decisions as a result of 'capture' by particular groups – for example, by the entrenchment of adversarial processes within the bureaucracy or by greater use of direct democracy in public decision-making (Walker 1986; Pollitt 1990, pp. 183–4).

Lambda-type values: reliability, robustness, adaptivity

'Lambda-type' values relate to resilience, endurance, robustness, survival and adaptivity – the capacity to withstand and learn from the blows of fate, to avoid 'competency traps' in adaptation processes (Levitt and March 1988; Liebowitz and Margolis 1990), to keep operating even in adverse 'worst case' conditions and to adapt rapidly in a crisis.

Expectations of security and reliability are central to traditional public administration values, and have often been associated with the choice of public rather than private organization for the provision of a hazard-related task. Perhaps the classic historical case is of the Venetian arsenal and *Tana* as instruments for ensuring the security of Venice's maritime power by direct state production of ropes and vessels (cf. Lane 1966).

From the viewpoint of lambda-type values, success is counted in terms of resilience and reliability, while failure is measured in terms of catastrophe, breakdown and learning failure. If lambda-type values are placed at centre stage, the central concern is to avoid system failure, 'down time', paralysis in the face of threat or challenge.

Classic expressions of lambda-type values include:

(i) *redundancy*, the maintenance of back-up systems to duplicate normal capacity;

(ii) *diversity*, the maintenance of quite separate, self-standing units (to avoid 'common mode failure', whether in technical terms or in terms of 'groupthink'); and

(iii) *robustness*, use of greater amounts of materials than would ordinarily be necessary for the job (cf. Health and Safety Executive 1988, p. 11).

The 'coin' in which success or failure is measured in lambda-type values includes security, survival and the robustness of basic assumptions about social defence mechanisms.

Orthodox discussions of learning problems and catastrophes tend to focus on specific failings of individuals rather than systemic or structural factors in organizational design (Turner *et al.* 1989, p. 3). But some tentative pointers to the administrative design implications of putting lambda-type values at centre stage can be gleaned from three closely related literatures: 'contingency theory' ideas about structural factors related to highly uncertain environments (cf. Lawrence and Lorsch 1967); the literature on the organization of socially created disasters (Dixon 1976; Turner 1976 and 1978; Perrow 1984); and the developing and related literature on 'safety culture' (Westrum 1987; Turner *et al.* 1989).

Some of the ideas to be found in this literature about the engineering of adaptivity and error-avoidance are contradictory. A case in point is the debate about 'anticipation' versus 'resilience' (Wildavsky 1988). Moreover, Perrow (1984) claims that for some technologies, administrative design for error-avoidance is impossible, even if safety is highly valued. However, much of this literature tends to relate error-generation, capacity for resilience and learning failures to three elements of institutional structure

(i) degree of *integration* – the extent to which interdependent parts of the system are linked in decision and information terms rather than isolated into separate compartments, each trying to insulate itself independently against system failure;

(ii) degree of *openness* in the culture or management system, avoiding authoritarian barriers to lateral or systemic thinking and feedback or learning processes; and

(iii) the extent to which there are systemic pressures for *misinformation*, rather than sharing of information, built in to the organizational process.

From the perspective of this literature, an organizational design which maximized lambda-type values would need to involve: multiple-objective rather than single-objective organization (van Gunsteren 1976, p. 61); a relatively high degree of 'slack' to provide spare capacity for learning or deployment in crisis; a control framework which focused on input or process rather than measured output in order to avoid building up pressures for misinformation; a personnel management structure which promoted cohesion without punishing unorthodox ideas; a task division structure organized for systemic thinking rather than narrow compartmentalization; and a responsibility structure which made mistakes and errors admissible. Relatively loose coupling and an emphasis on information as a collective asset within the organization would be features of such a design structure.

Compatibility

From this discussion, as summarized in [Table 6.1.2], one fundamental implication is that these three sets of mainstream administrative values overlap over some of their range, like intersecting circles in a Venn diagram. For example, dishonesty frequently creates waste and sometimes leads to catastrophe. Frugality, rectitude and resilience may all be satisfied by a particular set of institutional arrangements in some contexts.

However, the discussion also suggests the hypothesis that any two out of the three broad value sets may often be satisfied by the same organizing principle for a set of basic administrative design dimensions; but that it is hard to satisfy *all three* value sets equally for any of those dimensions, and probably impossible to do so for all of them. Put simply, a central concern with *honesty* and the avoidance of policy distortion in public administration may have different design implications from a central concern with *frugality*; and a central concern with *resilience* may also have different design implications. If NPM is a design for putting frugality at centre stage, it may at the limit be less capable of ensuring honesty and resilience in public administration.

Implications for new public management

The work of the ESRC's Management in Government Initiative has helped us to identify the specific forms that NPM took in the UK and to trace its history. But, like many research initiatives, it has perhaps been more successful in prompting the critical questions rather than in answering them definitively. Two key questions in particular seem to deserve more examination, in order to 'put NPM in its place' intellectually.

First, NPM can be understood as primarily an expression of sigma-type values. Its claims have lain mainly in the direction of cutting costs and doing more for less as a result of better-quality management and different structural design. Accordingly, one of the key tests of NPM's 'success' is whether and how it has delivered on that claim, in addition to succeeding in terms of rhetorical acceptance. We still have remarkably little independent evidence on this point, and work by Dunsire *et al.* (1988) has some path-breaking qualities in that it is a serious attempt to develop indicators of organizational structure and control systems in a way that helps us to understand how privatization and corporatization works. It offers tentative evidence for the proposition that a shift in management structures towards decreased command-orientation

[1] I owe this idea to a suggestion by Dr. John Baker of John Baker and Associates.

and increased 'results-orientation' is associated with improvements in productivity. But the results obtained so far are only indicative: the study does not test fully for 'Hawthorne effects' or secular trends, and it has no control groups. We need much more work in this vein.

However, the critics' questioning of NPM's universality also offers a way of putting NPM in its place and involves crucial claims that need proper testing. Even if further research established that NPM was clearly associated with the pursuit of frugality, it remains to be fully investigated whether such successes are bought at the expense of guarantees of honesty and fair dealing and of security and resilience.

Broadly, NPM assumes a culture of public service honesty as given. Its recipes to some degree removed devices instituted to ensure honesty and neutrality in the public service in the past (fixed salaries, rules of procedure, permanence of tenure, restraints on the power of line management, clear lines of division between public and private sectors). The extent to which NPM is likely to induce corrosion in terms of such traditional values remains to be tested. The effects of NPM 'clones' diffused by public management 'consultocrats' and others into contexts where there is little 'capital base' of ingrained public service culture (as in many Third World countries and perhaps in Eastern Europe too) will be particularly interesting to observe. The consequences for 'theta-type' values are likely to be most visible, since the effects are likely to be quicker and more dramatic there than in countries like Australia and the UK which are still living off 'public service ethic' capital.

Equally, the extent to which NPM's precepts are compatible with 'safety engineering' in terms of 'safety cultures' deserves more analysis. NPM broadly assumes that public services can be divided into self-contained 'products', and that good public management requires de-emphasis of overarching externalities and emphasis on running services within given parameters. Whether the emphasis on cost-cutting, contracting-out, compartmentalizing and top-slicing is compatible with safety culture at the front line needs to be tested. The new breed of organizationally created disasters over the past fifteen years or so, of which some dramatic examples have occurred in the UK, suggest that the issue at least needs investigation.

Only when we can test the limits of NPM in terms of relatively narrow *administrative* values can we start to establish its proper scope and put it in its historical place.

References

Arrow, K. J. 1963. *Social choice and individual values.* New Haven: Yale University Press.

Aucoin, P. 1990. 'Administrative reform in public management: paradigms, principles, paradoxes and pendulums'. *Governance* 3, 115–37.

Bell, D. 1973. *The coming of post-industrial society.* New York: Basic.

Birkinshaw, P., I. Harden and N. Lewis. 1990. *Government by moonlight: the hidden parts of the state.* London: Unwin Hyman.

Bogdanor, V. (ed.). 1987. *The Blackwell encyclopaedia of political institutions.* Oxford: Blackwell.

Bryson, L. 1987. 'Women and management in the public sector', *Australian Journal of Public Administration* 46, 259–72.

Bums, T. and G. M. Stalker. 1961. *The management of innovation.* London: Tavistock.

Carey, B. and P. Ryan, (eds.) 1989. *In transition: NSW and the corporatisation agenda.* Sydney: Macquarie Public Sector Studies Program/Association for Management Education and Research.

Carter, N. 1988. 'Performance indicators: "Backseat Driving" or "Hands Off" Control' *Policy and Politics* 17.

Castles, F. G. (ed.) 1989. *The comparative history of public policy.* Cambridge: Polity.

Day, P. and R. Klein. 1987. *'Accountabilities'.* London: Tavistock.

Dixon, N. F. 1979. *On the psychology of military incompetence.* London: Futura.

Downs, G. W. and P. D. Larkey. 1986. *The search for government efficiency: from hubris to helplessness.* Philadelphia: Temple University Press.

Dunleavy, P. J. 1985. 'Bureaucrats, budgets and the growth of the state', *British Journal of Political Science* 15, 299–328.

—— 1989. The United Kingdom: paradoxes of an ungrounded statism', pp. 242–91 in F. G. Castles (ed.) *The comparative history of public policy.* Cambridge: Polity.

Dunsire, A. 1978. *Control in a bureaucracy*, Vol. 2 of *The execution process.* London: Martin Robertson.

Dunsire A., K. Hartley, D. Parker and B. Dimitriou. 1988. 'Organizational status and performance; a conceptual framework for testing public choice theories'. *Public Administration* 66, 4 (Winter), 363–88.

Dunsire, A. and C. C. Hood. 1989. *Cutback management in public bureaucracies.* Cambridge: Cambridge University Press.

Gustafsson, B. (ed.) 1979. *Post-industrial society.* London: Croom Helm.

Hannah, L. 1976. *The rise of the corporate economy.* London: Methuen.

Harmon, M. and R. Mayer. 1986. *Organization theory for public administration.* Boston: Little, Brown.

Health and Safety Executive. 1988. *The tolerability of risk from nuclear power stations.* London: HMSO.

Hennestad, B. W. 1990. 'The symbolic impact of double bind leadership: double bind and the dynamics of organizational culture'. *Journal of Management Studies* 27, 265–80.

Hood, C. C. 1976. *The limits of administration.* London: Wiley.

—— 1987. 'Public administration' in V. Bogdanor (ed.) *The Blackwell encyclopaedia of political institutions.* Oxford: Blackwell.

—— 1990a. Public administration: lost an empire, not yet found a role' in A. Leftwich (ed.) *New directions in political science.* Aldershot: Elgar.

—— 1990b. 'Beyond the public bureaucracy state? Public administration in the 1990s', inaugural lecture, London School of Economics, 16 January 1990.

—— 1990c. 'De-Sir-Humphrey-fying the Westminster model of governance' *Governance* 3, 205–14.

—— 1991 (forthcoming). 'Stabilization and cutbacks: a catastrophe for government growth theory' *Journal of Theoretical Politics.*

Hood, C. C. and G. W. Jones 1990. 'Progress in the government's Next Steps initiative'. Appendix 6 in HC 481, 1989–90, 78–83.

Hood, C. C. and M. W. Jackson. 1991 (forthcoming). *Administrative argument.* Aldershot: Dartmouth.

Jackson, M. W. 1989. Immorality way lead to greatness: ethics in government' pp. 160–77 in S. Prasser, R. Wear and J. Nethercote (eds.) *Corruption and reform: the Fitzgerald vision.* St. Lucia: Queensland University Press.

Jessop, B. 1988. 'Conservative regimes and the transition to post-Fordism', Essex *Papers in Politics and Government* No. 47, Department of Government, University of Essex.

Kast, F. E. and Rosenzweig, J. E. 1973. *Contingency Views of Organization and Management.* New York: Science Research Associates.

Keating, M. 1989. 'Quo vadis: challenges of public administration', address to Royal Australian Institute of Public Administration, Perth, 12 April 1989.

Kelleher, S. R. 1988. The apotheosis of the Department of the Prime Minister and Cabinet', *Canberra Bulletin of Public Administration* 54, 9–12.

Lakatos, I. 1970. 'Falsification and the methodology of scientific research programmes' pp. 91–196 in I. Lakatos and A. Musgrave *Criticism and the growth of knowledge.* Cambridge: Cambridge University Press.

Lakatos, I. and A. Musgrave. 1970. *Criticism and the growth of knowledge.* Cambridge: Cambridge University Press.

Lane, F. C. 1966. *Venice and history.* Baltimore: Johns Hopkins University Press.

Larson, E. 1980. *Wit as a weapon: the political joke in history.* London: Muller.

Lawrence, P. 1964. *Road belong cargo.* Manchester: Manchester University Press.

Lawrence, P. R. and J. W. Lorsch. 1967. *Organization and environment.* Boston: Harvard University Press.

Leftwich, A. (ed.) 1990. *New directions in political science.* Aldershot: Elgar.

Levitt, B. and J. G. March. 1988. 'Organizational learning'. *Annual Review of Sociology* 14, 319–40.

Liebowitz, S. J. and S. E. Margolis. 1990. The fable of the keys'. *The Journal of Law and Economics* 33, 1–26.

March, J. G. and J. P. Olsen. 1989. *Rediscovering institutions: the organizational basis of politics.* New York: Free Press.

Martin, J. 1988. *A profession of statecraft? Three essays on some current issues in the New Zealand public service.* Wellington: Victoria University Press.

Martin, S. 1983. *Managing without managers.* Beverly Hills: Sage.

Meltzer, A. H. and S. F. Richard. 1981. 'A rational theory of the size of government'. *Journal of Political Economy* 89, 914–27.

Merkle, J. 1980. *Management and ideology: the legacy of the international scientific management movement.* Berkeley: California University Press.

Mills, S. 1986. *The new machine men.* Ringwood: Penguin.

Minogue, K. 1986. 'Loquocentric society and its critics'. *Government and Opposition* 21, 338–61.

Nethercote, J. R. 1989a. The rhetorical tactics of managerialism: reflections on Michael Keating's apologia, "Quo Vadis"', *Australian Journal of Public Administration* 48, 363–7.

—— 1989b. 'Public service reform: Commonwealth experience', paper presented to the Academy of Social Sciences of Australia, 25 February 1989, University House, Australian National University.

—— 1989c. 'Revitalising public service personnel management'. *The Canberra Times* 11 June.

Niskanen, W. A. 1971. *Bureaucracy and representative government.* Chicago: Aldine Atherton.

Ostrom, V. 1974. *The intellectual crisis in American Public Administration.* Alabama: University of Alabama Press.

Peacock, A. 1979. 'Public expenditure growth in post-industrial society', pp. 80–95 in B. Gustafsson (ed.) *Post-industrial society.* London: Croom Helm.

Perrow, C. 1984. *Normal accident: living with high-risk technologies.* New York: Basic.

Peters, T. and R. Waterman. 1982. *In search of excellence.* New York: Harper and Row.

Piore, M. J. and C, F. Sabel. 1984. *The second industrial divide.* New York: Basic.

Pollitt, C. 1990, *Managerialism and the public services: the Anglo-American experience.* Oxford: Blackwell.

Prasser, S., R. Wear and J. Nethercote (eds.). 1990, *Corruption and reform: the Fitzgerald vision.* St, Lucia: Queensland University Press.

Scott, G., P. Bushnell and N. Sallee, 1990, 'Reform of the core public sector: New Zealand experience'. *Governance* 3, 138–67.

Self, P, 1989, Is the grovel count rising in the bureaucracy? *The Canberra Times* 14 April, p. 11.

Sparm, R, N. 1981. 'Fashions and fantasies in public administration', *Australian Journal of Public Administration* 40, 12–25.

Strange, S. 1988, States *and markets: an introduction to international political economy.* London: Pinter.

Sturgess, G. 1989, 'First keynote address' pp. 4–10 in B. Carey and P. Ryan (eds.). *In transition: NSW and the corporatisation agenda.* Sydney: Macquarie Public Sector Studies Program.

Thomas, R. 1978. *The British philosophy of administration.* London: Longmans.

Tocqueville, A, de 1946. *Democracy in America.* London: Oxford University Press.

Turner, B, A, 1976, 'How to organize disaster'. *Management Today* March 56–7 and 105.

—— 1978. *Man-made disasters.* London: Wykeham.

—— 1989. 'How can we design a safe organization?' paper presented at the Second International Conference on Industrial and Organizational Crisis Management, Leonard N. Stem School of Business, New York University, November 3–4.

Turner, B. A., N. Pidgeon, D. Blockley and B. Toft. 1989. 'Safety culture: its importance in future risk management', position paper for the Second World Bank Workshop on Safety Control and Risk Management, Karlstad, Sweden, 6–9 November.

Treasury and Civil Service Committee, 1990. Eighth report of Session 1989–90 *Progress in the Next Steps initiative*, HC 481, London: HMSO.

van Gimsteren, H. R. 1976. *The quest for control: a critique of the rational-central-rule approach in public affairs.* London: Wiley.

Walker, G, de Q. 1986, *Initiative and referendum: the people's law.* Sydney: Centre for Independent Studies.

Westrum, R, 1987. 'Management Strategies and Information Failure' pp. 109–27 in J. A. Wise and A. Debons (eds,) *Information systems failure analysis. NATO ASI Series F Computer and Systems Science, Vol. 3.* Berlin: Springer.

Wildavsky, A. 1985. Trial without error: anticipation vs. resilience as strategies for risk reduction' *CIS Occasional Papers* 13, Sydney: Centre for Independent Studies.

Wilenski, P, 1986. *Public power and public administration.* Sydney: RAIPA/Hale and Iremonger.

Wise, J. A. and Debons, A. (eds,) 1987. *Information systems failure analysis.* NATO ASI Series F, Computer and Systems Science, Vol, 3. Berlin: Springer.

Worsley, P, 1968. *The trumpet shall sound.* 2nd ed. London: MacGibbon and Kee.

Yeatman, A, 1987, The concept of public management and the Australian state in the 1980s', *Australian Journal of Public Administration* 46, 339–53.

Reading 6.2 Strategy viewed from a management fashion perspective

Timothy Clark

First published: (2004) *European Management Review*, 1: 105–111. Reprinted by permission from Macmillan Publishers Ltd: *European Management Journal*, (2004) 1, 105–111, published by Palgrave Macmillan.

Introduction

There is general agreement that strategy is a crucial and time-consuming activity. To a large extent, it determines the fate of many key institutions within society as practitioners develop and pursue innovative strategies in order to out-compete their rivals and secure long-term survival within a dynamic and ever-changing world. It is also a labour-intensive activity not only consuming hours, days, weeks and months of senior and middle management time, but also that of auditors, management consultants, investment bankers, public relations consultants, workshop and conference organizers, shareholder representatives and so forth. It is thus a very intensive, and expensive, activity involving a full cast of players that extends well beyond the immediate confines of the management group within an organization. However, a review of the ISI Web of Knowledge database indicates that when researchers come to analyse and review the drama of strategy they highlight, almost exclusively, the role of internal management. The other players within the strategy process, regardless of their importance, are ignored. This would suggest that they are generally viewed as incidental and/or irrelevant with little direct impact on the character of strategies that emerge. Yet a plethora of advice givers have had a critical impact on the nature of organizational life for many years (Clark and Fincham, 2002; Kipping and Engwall, 2002). But how they impact on and influence strategy is presently little understood.

In this article, I argue that if we are to amplify, extend and deepen our knowledge of strategy, we need to begin to conceive of it as a process built on an extended division of labour. We cannot continue with over-simplistic notions of strategy as being the preserve of a single elite group of individuals. One way to facilitate this shift is to begin to examine strategy through the interpretive lens of management fashion. This views ideas as the output of a community of fashion-setters. Managers are but one of a number of important actors involved in their production. With this in mind, the next section briefly identifies and reviews the main themes within the nascent management fashion literature. I then briefly identify the key members of the management fashion-setting community and describe their respective roles before outlining three areas of future research.

Management fashion

In recent years, there has been growing interest in the notion that management ideas and techniques are subject to swings in fashion in the same way that aesthetic aspects of life such as clothing styles, hair length, music tastes, furniture design, paint colours, and so forth are characterized by surges of popularity and then decline. Researchers have conceived of management fashions as ideas and techniques that fail to become firmly entrenched and institutionalized since organizations are attracted to them for a period and then abandon them in favour of apparently newer and more promising ones. These have included 'Excellence', Culture Change, Total Quality Management, Business Process Reengineering, Knowledge Management, Six Sigma and so forth. Drawing on Gill and Whittle (1993) these ideas are seen to progress through a series of discrete stages: (1) invention, when the idea is initially created, (2) dissemination, when the idea is initially brought to the attention of its intended audience, (3) acceptance, when the idea becomes implemented, (4) disenchantment, when negative evaluations and frustrations with the idea emerge, and (5) decline, or the abandonment of the idea. Within the extant management fashion literature three general strands can be discerned.

The first stream is concerned to identify and explicate patterns in the life cycle of the management fashion discourse. The lineage of this literature can be traced to Abrahamson's (1991, 1996a, b) seminal papers on the management fashion-setting process. Drawing on the innovation-diffusion literature (Rogers, 1983) and neo-institutional theory (DiMaggio and Powell, 1983) his theory argues that groups of interrelated knowledge entrepreneurs and industries, identified as management gurus, management consultants, business schools, and publishers, are characterized as being in a 'race' to sense managers' emergent collective preferences for new techniques. Rational and progressive norms are seen as governing the choice of managerial ideas and techniques. Rational normative expectations are that management techniques will be rational (i.e., efficient means to important ends), whereas progressive normative expectations are that management ideas will progress over time (i.e., be repeatedly replaced by new and better techniques). The members of the fashion-setting community develop rhetorics that 'convince fashion followers that a management technique is both rational and at the forefront of managerial progress' (Abrahamson, 1996a). Their rhetorics must therefore articulate why it is imperative that managers should pursue certain organizational goals and why their particular technique offers the best means to achieve these goals. Thus, within this model the management fashion-setting community is viewed as supplying mass audiences with ideas and techniques that have the potential for developing mass followings. These may or may not become fashions depending on fashion setters' ability to redefine fashion followers' collective beliefs about which management techniques are state-of-the-art and meet their immediate needs.

The plethora of empirical studies emanating from Abrahamson's (1996a) model of management fashion have focused primarily on the diffusion pattern of a range of fashionable discourses within the print media. Using citation analysis the number of references to a particular idea in a sequence of years are counted and plotted in order to identify the life cycle of a fashionable management idea.[1] The results of these studies demonstrate that the life cycles of a range of fashionable management ideas are characterized by an initial period in which the frequency of citations increases, peaks and then declines; although the shapes of the curves for different ideas are not necessarily identical nor symmetrical (i.e., they do not necessarily rise and fall at the same rate) and vary between countries (Abrahamson and Fairchild, 1999; Benders and van Veen, 2001; Spell, 2001; Gibson and Tesone, 2001). Furthermore, while the lifespans of recent management fashions are considerably shorter than those for ideas which came to prominence in earlier periods, their peaks are much higher. Carson *et al.* (2000) show that the period of time between the introduction of a fashionable management idea or technique and the peak in its popularity has fallen from a mean of 14.8 years in the 1950s–1970s, to 7.5 years in the 1980s, to 2.6 years in the 1990s.[2]

The second broad strand of literature has focused on identifying those factors that account for the popularity of particular management books and the ideas they seek to promote. Some commentators have focused on what Grint (1994) has termed the 'internalist' approach. That is, the popularity of a book is related to its novel and superior content when compared to previous ideas. Others have adopted the 'externalist' approach by seeking to determine '*why* the package is effective in its particular envelope of space and time' (Grint, 1994). From this perspective the key question is why do some ideas take off and engage particular audiences at certain times and not others? In answering it, the popularity and success of a book and its ideas is related to its ability to resonate with and be in harmony with the expectations and understandings of its target audience. If a book fails to convince its target audience of the plausibility and appropriateness of its ideas then it will probably not be bought in the quantities necessary to become a best-seller.[3] According to Grint (1994) 'for the "plausibility" to occur the ideas most likely to prevail are those that are apprehended as capturing the *zietgeist* or "spirit of the times"'.

Several writers have combined the two approaches distinguished by Grint (1994). For example, Kieser (1997) and Furusten (1999) have identified a number of common elements in best-selling management books. These include: a focus on a single factor; the contrasting of old ideas with the new such that the latter are presented as qualitatively better and superior; the creation of a sense of urgency such that the introduction of the ideas is presented as pressing and unavoidable; the linkage of the ideas to highly treasured management values; case studies of outstanding success, and a stress on an ideas' universal applicability. Even if all these elements are present, Kieser (1997) writes that they 'are useless if the timing is not perfect'. Hence, best-selling management books must not only present their ideas in certain ways, they must also appear plausible by speaking to their readers' immediate concerns.

The final strand of literature focuses on the individuals who are identified as the authors of popular management books and the progenitors of many fashionable ideas—the management gurus. It argues that the success and impact of their ideas is due to the form in which they are presented—their powerful public performances. To date, academic studies of the public performances of management gurus have largely consisted of theoretical discussions which, using the work of Lewin (1951) and Sargant (1997), have depicted the gurus as experts in persuasive communication who seek to transform the consciousness of their audiences through powerful oratory (Huczynski, 1993;

[1] Elsewhere I have pointed out that citation analysis is not without serious problems (Clark, 2004). Unless each article is read, it cannot indicate whether the idea is central or peripheral to the main topic or whether it is referred to positively or negatively. But, of greater importance is whether citation analysis actually captures the complete life cycle of an idea. Citation analysis is limited to the counts of references to an idea in selected sections of the print media, mainly leading academic journals, semi-academic journals and the popular management press. Such a method cannot determine the degree to which ideas are 'adopted' by organizations. Nevertheless, there is a tendency in the literature to assume that there is a symbiotic relationship between the pattern in the volume of discourse and trends in the adoption and rejection of ideas by organizations.

[2] See note 1 for limitations of these data.

[3] The processes that underpin people's decisions to purchase management books are complex. Gladwell (2000) has highlighted the importance of 'connectors', people who bring new products to the attention of large groups of people and persuade them of their importance. It is the actions of these individuals, he argues, that tip a product from being a minority taste to a mass fashion.

Clark, 1995; Jackson, 2001). More recent research has begun to empirically examine the live presentational techniques through which gurus convey their messages (Greatbatch and Clark, 2003a, b).

The importance of external agents

While there are undoubtedly a number of deficiencies with existing conceptual and empirical work on management fashion (see Clark, 2004), viewing strategy through this particular interpretative lens crucially foregrounds the importance of a previously ignored group of external agents who have impacted significantly on the evolving character of strategy within the modern organization. Fundamental to existing strategy theory and research has been the view of organizations as bounded, discrete and isolatable entities. Within these, managers are generally viewed as independent, self-sufficient agents with singular and absolute control over the process of strategy development and implementation. Whether research examines the identification of strategic issues, the initiation of strategic debates, the process of selecting between strategic alternatives, or the selling of key issues to decision makers, the focus is on the activities and roles of managers, more often than not the top management team. While a range of external influences, usually in the form of environmental contingencies, are identified as impacting on the shape and form of strategy, the role of external agents within strategic management has been almost completely neglected (for an exception, see Schwarz, 2003). This is despite the crumbling of organizational boundaries in response to the rise of what Castells (1996) has termed the 'network society'.

This disregard for the role of external agents in the strategy making process is strange given that some external agents have been in existence for as long as the modern corporation (Kipping and Engwall, 2002). For example, the origins of modern management consulting lie in the efficiency and time-and-motion studies pioneered by Charles Bedaux, Harrington Emerson, Frank and Lillian Gilbreth, and Frederick Taylor at the turn of the last century (McKenna, 1995; Kipping, 2002). Furthermore, strategy consulting, and its pre-eminent firms such as A.T. Kearney, Booz Allen & Hamilton, Boston Consulting Group, and McKinsey, was the prominent form of consulting activity between the 1930s and 1980s (Kipping, 2002). The activities of these firms have had a considerable impact on the nature of the bets that managers place on the future, the supporting investment, and the consequent directions that organizations have followed.

What I am questioning here possibly goes back to the origins of strategy and the foundational work of Alfred Chandler and his early successors. I am not so much concerned with the continuing epistemological resonances of these works and the constraints they may impose on contemporary research (see Whittington *et al.*, 2002). Rather my focus is on problematizing the notion implicit within this work, and much of that which has followed, that observed strategic choices and outcomes are exclusively the result of managerial action. Instead, I wish to highlight the importance of a range of external agents, which I shall term the management fashion-setting arena, in establishing the dominant strategic discourses and thus constraining and influencing management action. This group of knowledge entrepreneurs is concerned with the creation, fabrication and dissemination of ideas and techniques to the managerial audience. We should be under no illusion as to their influence since it is the ideas produced by this community that have come to dominate contemporary notions of the strategic ideal (Barley *et al.*, 1988; Gerlach, 1996; Whittington *et al.*, 2003). Their outputs govern to a large extent what is valued within the strategy field. As such they have a huge impact not only in determining the repertoires that are made available to academics and practitioners, but also the choices that are deemed legitimate. Theories and studies of management fashion are useful in that they both privilege and differentiate the role of the various agents within this community since, following Abrahamson (1996a), management fashions are conceived of as 'the product of a management-fashion-setting process involving particular management fashion setters—organizations and individuals who dedicate themselves to producing and disseminating management knowledge.' Within the lens of management fashion key strategic discourses, therefore, emanate from a management fashion-setting arena, the members of which are typically identified as management gurus, consulting firms, business schools and management academics, and publishers (see also Suddaby and Greenwood, 2001; Ernst and Kieser, 2002).[4] Generally, by scrutinizing the dynamic interplay between different sets of management fashion-setters and the management/client community, we will develop better insight into why particular strategy discourses emerge and become incorporated into the corporate repertoire. This will help us understand not only why certain bets are deemed more appropriate than others, but also how their relative merits are first evaluated and then enacted. In the remainder of this section, I briefly identify the key members of the management fashion-setting community and describe their respective roles as they are presently understood before outlining three areas of future research.

Figure [6.2.1] depicts the key actors within the management fashion-setting arena and their relationship to the

[4] This is a very simplified view of the membership of the management fashion-setting arena. I have argued elsewhere that agents, book editors, conference organizers and ghost writers are also important (Clark, 2004).

Figure 6.2.1 The dynamics of the management fashion-setting arena

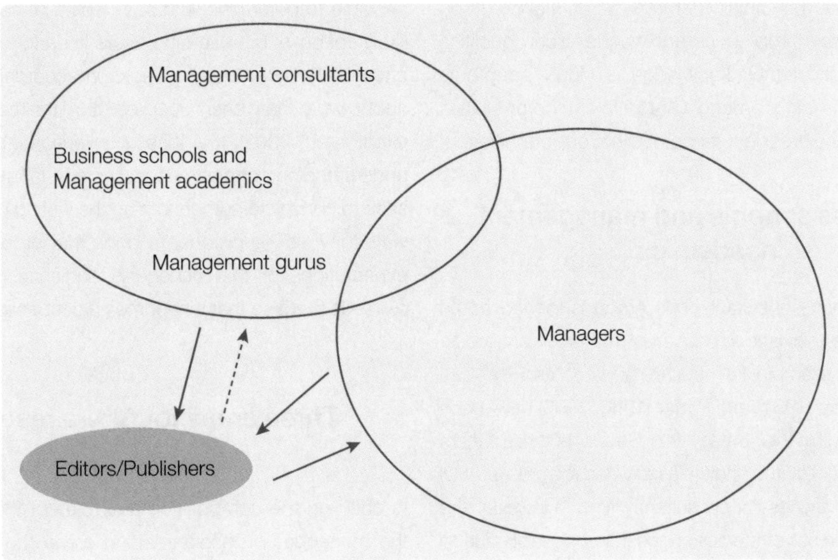

managerial audience. It differs in two important respects from previous conceptions of this arena. First, some fluidity with respect to the role and relationship between the members of the arena is acknowledged. This is because, as I develop below, multiple and simultaneous roles are possible. Second, the managerial audience, rather than being viewed as a passive, recipient audience, separate from production, is instead positioned in such a way as to recognize its active and mutual complicity in the co-fabrication of management ideas.

Management gurus

Management gurus are often viewed as the creators of innovative ideas. Through the publication of best-selling books, articles in leading business journals and talks on the international lecture circuit they have become the outstanding producers of popular strategic ideas. They are often the point of origin in the life cycle of a popular management idea. While it is mistaken to believe that they are solely responsible for the ideas they produce (Clark and Greatbatch, 2002, 2004), they nevertheless have a critical role in making particular ideas accessible and legitimate. Three types of management guru are commonly identified: (1) 'academic gurus' (e.g. Charles Handy, Gary Hamel, Michael Porter, C.K. Prahalad); (2) 'consultant gurus' (e.g. Peter Drucker, Michael Hammer, Tom Peters); and, (3) 'hero managers' (e.g. Lee Iococca, Luis Gerstner, Jack Welch). Thus, gurus cannot be compartmentalized into a single role. Rather, they straddle a number of communities depending on whether they derive their ideas from academic, consulting or management work. In this sense, gurus play a vital role as 'boundary spanners' translating management ideas between different communities.

Management consultants

Consulting firms are both significant consumers and producers of management knowledge. It is too simplistic to argue that they only draw upon the ideas that gurus create since many consultancies are in the business of positioning themselves as 'thought leaders' by actively creating in-house gurus. Furthermore, the larger firms have significant research capacities and systems of personal development—for example, the 'big four', in addition to niche firms such as Bain, McKinsey, Monitor, Strategos—which enable them to develop proprietary products that contain powerful and influential notions of strategy. They also draw upon the individual experience of consultants with clients for the benefit of the whole firm (Werr, 2002). This has been described as a 'people to documents approach' whereby experience is 'extracted from the person who developed it, made independent of that person, and reused for various purposes' (Hansen *et al.*, 1999). Consultancies contain powerful knowledge creation/management systems that support the generation of management knowledge that can be converted into commodified and commercial products. The outcome of these processes may be that a consultancy either 'builds a coherent arrangement of well-elaborated techniques around a leading mode' or 'builds up a collection of different, loosely coupled and multi-purpose tools that enhance flexibility and support the handling of a range of organizational problems' (Heusinkveld and Benders, 2002–3). In this sense, consultancies are fundamentally in the business of producing 'boundary objects' (Star and Griesemer, 1989). Knowledge is abstracted from a number of sources, codified and made portable so that it may be translated and reused in a broad range of situations. The resulting package is often reduced to a number of broad principles that lack situational precision since they remain ambiguous and vague. Such qualities ensure that consultancy knowledge is highly adaptable and so has meaning among very different communities thus ensuring the broadest range of client opportunities.

Business schools and management academics

Like management consultants, this group is viewed as an important consumer and producer of management ideas. The ideas of, for example, Barney (1991), Hamel and Prahalad (1994), Mintzberg (1991) and Porter (1980, 1990) have been very influential within the strategy field. Several of these writers have attained guru status and the associated rewards, as well as establishing successful consultancy firms. However, the findings of a number of studies suggest that possibly due to the lengthy peer review process and high rejection rates of academic journals, there is a tendency for many fashionable ideas to emerge initially in the business press (Barley *et al.*, 1988; Gibson and Tesone, 2001; Spell, 2001). In terms of reporting on fashionable ideas, the academic literature is generally seen to lag that of the business press. In this respect, academic theory and studies are perceived as following, rather than leading, management progress. Hence, those ideas with popular appeal and being disseminated by media organizations are primarily created by management gurus and consultants. In contrast, the ideas developed by business scholars are perceived to be less valid with the consequence that they are increasingly viewed as peripheral. Indeed, academic research tends to lag the popular management press, so that the research agenda is not being set by academics. Management academics increasingly research the outcomes of management actions that are influenced by the ideas of a small number of consultants and gurus.

Publishers

Publishers are concerned with identifying, producing and distributing ideas that are likely to have a mass appeal. In this respect, the role that book editors play in 'discovering' potential authors and popular ideas is similar to that of 'contact people' in other cultural industries. Publishing, film and music companies all employ people to locate new manuscripts, new film scripts and new singers. These people essentially go out into the field and act as scouts attempting to identify potential stars from the existing pool of talent that can then be signed up by their organizations. Book editors are key gatekeepers whose decisions can either facilitate or block the career of a would-be guru and idea with potential mass appeal. Editors work closely with authors helping shape their ideas prior to publication. Given the difficulty in predicting shifts in consumer tastes, it is not possible to determine with any degree of certainty what is likely to be a best-seller. Editors therefore minimize this uncertainty by producing books in accordance with rules about what has been successful in the past (Clark and Greatbatch, 2002). It is these conventions, based on their understandings of past successes and failures, which they seek to convey to authors during the writing process. In this way, they aim to produce a book that at least meets the expectations of the managerial audience, and hopefully exceeds them so that it becomes a best-seller.

Three areas for future research

Who does what?

In outlining the composition and roles of the members of the management fashion-setting arena the nature of the relationship with the management/client community has been overlooked. I have done this on purpose since we presently understand very little about the dynamics of the nexus of relationships between the community of knowledge entrepreneurs identified above and managers. There is a voluminous literature on the nature of the consulting industry, its history, and prescriptions relating to the management of the client–consultant relationship. There is an emerging literature on the management guru phenomenon. However, there is presently a void with respect to the role of the members of this arena in strategy. Given this lacuna there is a need to find out which members of the fashion-setting arena are involved in developing and implementing strategy. Why are they used and at what point? How do they all relate to one another? What facilitates and impedes the transfer of knowledge? To what extent is the character of the strategic ideas that emerge the responsibility of one or other, or both parties? What is the role of other groups, such as conference and workshop organizers (see Whittington, 2003)? By casting an intensive light on this system of actors, we will become more cognisant of the ways in which strategy emerges as the result of a series of collaborative relationships with a number of usually unseen heads and hands.

Is external advice a source of competitive advantage?

It is widely recognized that Barney's (1991) paper on the resource-based view of the firm has become the most influential framework for understanding strategy (Barney *et al.* (2001). In this article, he argued that sustained competitive advantage derived from the resources and capabilities a firm controls that are valuable, rare, imperfectly imitable, and not substitutable. These resources and capabilities can be viewed as bundles of tangible and intangible assets, including a firm's management skills, its organizational processes and routines, and the information and knowledge it controls.

When examining the role of external agents in the strategy process, researchers need to consider whether the use of these external resources contributes to a firm's competitive advantage. In order to answer this general question, research is needed that not only examines firms' capability with respect to selecting appropriate advice but also how this advice is generated in the relationship between the two parties and, where it is generic, adapted to meet the particular needs of the client. Conducting such research will enable us to determine the extent to which firms generate and sustain their own resources and capabilities and whether this in itself is of strategic significance.

What is the nature of the output from the management fashion-setting arena?

In turning our research gaze onto the activities of external agents within strategy, there is a critical need to examine the nature of their outputs. The intensity of competition and the rapid churning of products mean that producers within this arena have to generate almost instant positive customer awareness. This has a major impact on the nature of the ideas that are disseminated to the target audience. The successful actors—management consultants and gurus—capture managerial attention by producing ideas and techniques in which image predominates over substance (Clark and Greatbatch, 2004). More specifically, those ideas that gain popular appeal tend to express and exemplify broader social trends to which they are inextricably linked. They represent a central feature of communication in modern society, the pre-eminence of the image (Boorstin, 1961; Debord, 1967; Kellner, 2003). During production their connection to a concrete understanding of organizations is loosened as the form of presentation predominates since in an image-driven society perceptions of objects are more important than their actual substance. In the process of fabrication, the distinction between what is real and what is not becomes blurred. The 'real' is increasingly replaced by pseudo-forms, which are presented as authentic and whose content is governed by an entertainment/media logic. As such, these ideas are manufactured contrivances that are designed to have maximum impact on the intended audience and so gain broad appeal with the consequence that the contents are vivified and presented as a 'spectacular and glittering universe of image and signs' (Best and Kellner, 1999). They are thus packaged to be concrete, immediately graspable and most importantly to have instant impact. This is achieved by creating a realistic conceit (i.e., the 'pseudo' is presented as 'real') in which a product is produced in accordance with a set of general conventions so that it is what it is claimed to be. For example, convention dictates that ideas are designed in such a way that the intended audience believes that they will have a positive impact on their organization and working life. Thus, what is critical is not that the ideas actually work but that they are perceived to be of practical benefit and relevance.

Such a view of the character of the management ideas produced by sections of the management fashion-setting arena has several implications for strategy research. First, there is a pervasive notion that those strategy ideas that become adopted are initially evaluated in terms of being efficient and positive means to valued ends. They are therefore deemed to be superior to other competing ideas according to some objective criteria. Although fashion-setters extol the practical benefits of ideas and this is reinforced with references to and case studies of well-known successful organizations, their accessibility, immediacy and simplicity are also considered vital. Thus the form in which ideas are presented is as important as their technical content. Indeed, in an image-driven world the former is more important. The production system in seeking to enhance the aesthetic attractiveness of ideas is engaged in a process of beautification. If we are to better understand the impact of ideas and the choices that managers make, we need to move away from a focus on rational explanations and start emphasizing the aesthetic. The point here is not that theory can beautify the organizational world, as in the case of scientific management informing the principles of modernist architecture (Guillen, 1997), but that the very appeal of ideas may relate to their impact on our emotions and senses. To what extent are they viewed as beautiful or ugly and how does this impact on their selection? Exploring aesthetic judgements within strategizing represents a promising area for future research.

Second and relatedly, by aestheticizing strategy research the conventions deployed by the producers of popular ideas are foregrounded. It is these conventions that are at the heart of the spectacularization of fashionable management ideas because they determine the form in which they appear. They are based upon generalized beliefs about what makes a legitimate and successful management idea. As such they offer an opportunity to identify producers' understandings of the ingredients of a successful idea with the target audience. Such information may enable managers to make more discriminating decisions with respect to the authenticity and actual benefits of the ideas that are on offer. At the same time, the function of business school scholars will be elevated by providing a due diligence function in which academic research is 'devoted to testing the validity and reliability of managerial "concepts in use"' (Suddaby and Greenwood, 2001).

Conclusion

This article has argued for the greater inclusion of external agents within strategy research. Drawing on the emergent management fashion literature, it has conceived of these as a group of actors operating within a management fashion-setting arena. It is the outputs of this community that come to dominate conceptions of what are deemed legitimate strategic actions. They thus have a critical, if presently neglected, impact on the nature strategy. In order to fill this lacuna in strategy research three promising areas of research were outlined. However, to pursue this agenda a double shift in the priorities of strategy researchers is required. The first is to extend their notions of who is involved in the process of selecting, making and implementing strategy. This article has highlighted the usefulness of the management fashion perspective in supporting such a shift. The second relates to the nature of the research approach adopted. Whittington *et al.* (2002) have argued that strategy research is characterized by growing torpor and stagnation as it congeals around a modernist orthodoxy. They point out that the field is dominated by a deductive approach dependent upon large databases and sophisticated statistical tools which is unable to fully apprehend and understand the 'messy, shifting world of practice' (p. 476). This paper contributes to their general argument for a greater inclusion of inductive thinking, which they term 'after modernism', since to change what is being studied we also have to change the way it is viewed. Pursuing the three research agendas outlined in the article requires researchers to examine how strategy is produced, negotiated, transformed, and mobilized within a complex and shifting nexus of relationships. We thus need to pay attention to the actual practice of strategy, what Whittington (2003) refers to as the 'labour of strategy'. What localized skills and resources do people draw upon in order to achieve the work of strategizing? What are the embedded understandings that underpin the choice of partners and then enable people to work together? What are the features of relationships that facilitate and inhibit effective collaboration? How are the outputs of these collaborations consumed and communicated? Such questions imply a limited number of appropriate methodologies that are likely to be shaped by practical considerations such as time, available access, and in particular the unpredictable form and dynamics of live, emergent action and relationships. But whichever combination is chosen they will be inductive in character.

References

Abrahamson, E. (1991). Managerial fads and fashions: The diffusion and rejection of innovations. ***Academy of Management Review***, 16: 586–612.

Abrahamson, E. (1996a). Management fashion. ***Academy of Management Review***, 21: 254–285.

Abrahamson, E. (1996b). Technical and Aesthetic Fashion, in B. Czarniawska and G. Sevon (eds.) ***Translating Organizational Change***. Berlin: de Gruyter, pp: 117–137.

Abrahamson, E. and Fairchild, G. (1999). Management fashion: Lifecycles, triggers, and collective processes. ***Administrative Science Quarterly***, 44: 708–740.

Barney, J. (1991). Firm resources and sustained competitive advantage. ***Journal of Management***, 17: 99–120.

Barney, J., Wright, M. and Ketchen, D.J. (2001). The resource-based view of the firm: Ten years after 1991. ***Journal of Management***, 27: 625–641.

Barley, S.R., Meyer, G.W. and Gash, D.C. (1988). Cultures of culture: Academics, practitioners and the pragmatics of normative control. ***Administrative Science Quarterly***, 33: 24–60.

Benders, J. and van Veen, K. (2001). What's a fashion? Interpretative viability and management fashions. ***Organization***, 8: 33–53.

Best, S. and Kellner, D. (1999). Dedord, cybersituations, and the interactive spectacle. ***Substance***, 90: 129–156.

Boorstin, D.J. (1961). ***The Image***. New York: Atheneum.

Carson, P.P., Lanier, P., Carson, K.D. and Guidry, B.N. (2000). Clearing a path through the management fashion jungle: Some preliminary trailblazing. ***Academy of Management Journal***, 43: 1143–1158.

Castells, M. (1996). ***The Rise of the Network Society***. Oxford: Blackwell.

Clark, T. (1995). ***Managing Consultants: Consultancy as the Art of Impression Management***. Buckingham: Open University Press.

Clark, T. (2004). The fashion of management fashion: A surge too far? ***Organization***, 11: 297–306.

Clark, T. and Fincham, R. (2002). ***Critical Consulting: New Perspectives on the Management Advice Industry***. Oxford: Blackwell.

Clark, T. and Greatbatch, D. (2002). Collaborative Relationships in the Creation and Fashioning of Management Ideas: Gurus, Editors and Managers, in M. Kipping and L. Engwall (eds.) ***Management Consulting: Emergence and Dynamics of a Knowledge Industry***. Oxford; Oxford University Press, pp: 127–145.

Clark, T. and Greatbatch, D. (2004). Management fashion as image-spectacle: The production of best-selling management books. ***Management Communication Quarterly***, 17(3): 376–424.

Debord, G. (1967). ***The Society of the Spectacle***. London: Red and Black.

DiMaggio, P. and Powell, W.W. (1983). The iron cage revisited: Institutional isomorphism and collective rationality in organizational fields. ***American Sociological Review***, 48: 1457–1460.

Ernst, B. and Kieser, A. (2002). In Search of Explanations for the Consulting Explosion, in K. Sahlin-Andersson and L. Engwall (eds.) ***The Expansion of Management Knowledge: Carriers, Flows and Sources***. Stanford: Stanford University Press, pp: 47–73.

Furusten, S. (1999). ***Popular Management Books***. London: Routledge.

Gerlach, N. (1996). The business restructuring genre: Some questions for critical organization analysis. ***Organization***, 3: 425–453.

Gibson, J.W. and Tesone, D.V. (2001). Management fads: Emergence, evolution, and implications for managers. ***Academy of Management Review***, 15: 122–133.

Gill, J. and Whittle, S. (1993). Management by panacea. ***Journal of Management Studies***, 30: 281–295.

Gladwell, M. (2000). ***The Tipping Point: How Little Things Can Make a Big Difference***. Boston, MA: Little Brown.

Greatbatch, D. and Clark, T. (2003a). Laughing with the gurus. ***Business Strategy Review***, 13(3): 10–18.

Greatbatch, D. and Clark, T. (2003b). Humour and laughter in the public lectures of management gurus. ***Human Relations***, in press.

Grint, K. (1994). Reengineering history: Social resonances and business process reengineering. ***Organization***, 1: 179–201.

Guillen, M. (1997). Scientific Management's lost aesthetic: Architecture organization, and the Taylorized beauty of the mechanical. ***Administrative Science Quarterly***, 42: 682–715.

Hamel, G. and Prahalad, C.K. (1994). ***Competing for the Future***. Boston, MA: Harvard Business School Press.

Hansen, M.T., Nohria, N. and Tierney, T. (1999). What's your strategy for managing knowledge. ***Harvard Business Review***, 77(3): 106–116.

Heusinkveld, S. and Bender, J. (2002–3). Between professional dedication and corporate design: Exploring forms of new concept development in consultancies. ***International Studies of Management and Organization***, 32(4):104–122.

Huczynski, A. (1993). ***Management Gurus: What Makes Them and How to Become One***. London: Routledge.

Jackson, B. (2001). ***Management Gurus and Management Fashions: A Dramatistic Inquiry***. London: Routledge.

Kellner, D. (2003). ***Media Spectacle***. London: Routledge.

Kieser, A. (1997). Rhetoric and myth in management fashion. ***Organization***, 4:49–74.

Kipping, M. (2002). Trapped in their Wave: The Evolution of Management Consultancies, in T. Clark and R. Fincham (eds.) ***Critical Consulting: New Perspective on the Management Advice Industry***. Oxford: Blackwell, pp: 28–49.

Kipping, M. and Engwall, L. (2002). ***Management Consulting: The Emergence and Dynamics of a Knowledge Industry***. Oxford: Oxford University Press.

Lewin, K. (1951). ***Field Theory in Social Science***. New York: Harper.

McKenna, C.D. (1995). The origins of modern management consulting. ***Business and Economic History***, 24: 51–58.

Mintzberg, H. (1991). ***The Strategy Process: Concepts, Contexts, Cases***. London: Prentice-Hall.

Porter, M.L. (1980). ***The Competitive Strategy: Techniques for Analyzing Industries and Competitors***. New York: Free Press.

Porter, M. (1990). ***The Competitive Advantage of Nations***. London: MacMillan.

Rogers, E.M. (1983). ***Diffusion of Innovations***. New York: Free Press.

Sargant, W. (1997). ***Battle for the Mind***. Cambridge: Malor, (1st edn. 1957).

Schwarz, M. (2003). How do external consultants contribute to a firm's strategic review process? Paper presented at Annual British Academy of Management Conference, September, Harrogate.

Spell, C. (2001). Management fashions: Where do they come from, and are they old wine in new bottles? ***Journal of Management Inquiry***, 10: 358–373.

Star, S.L. and Griesemer, J.R. (1989). Institutional ecology, 'translations' and boundary objects: Amateurs and professionals in Berkeley's Museum of Vertebrate Zoology, 1907–39. ***Social Studies of Science***, 19: 387–420.

Suddaby, R. and Greenwood, R. (2001). Colonizing knowledge: Commodification as a dynamic and jurisdictional expansion in professional service firms. ***Human Relations***, 54: 933–953.

Werr, A. (2002). The Internal Creation of Management Knowledge: A Question of Structuring Experience, in M. Kipping and L. Engwall (eds.) ***Management Consulting: The Emergence and Dynamics of a Knowledge Industry***. Oxford: Oxford University Press, pp: 91–108.

Whittington, R. (2003). The work of strategizing and organizing: For a practice perspective. ***Strategic Organization***, 1(1): 117–125.

Whittington, R., Jarzabkowski, P., Mayer, M., Mounoud, E., Nahapiet, J. and Rouleau, L. (2003). Taking strategy seriously: Responsibility and reform for an important social practice. ***Journal of Management Inquiry***, 12: 396–409.

Whittington, R., Pettigrew, A. and Thomas, H. (2002). Conclusion: Doing More Research in Strategy, in A. Pettigrew, H. Thomas and R. Whittington (eds.) ***Handbook of Strategy and Management***. London: Sage, pp: 475–488.

Reading 6.3 Rethinking strategy: contemporary perspectives and debates *Mahmoud Ezzamel and Hugh Willmott*

First published: (2004) *European Management Review*, 1: 43–48. Reprinted by permission from Macmillan Publishers Ltd: *European Management Review* (2004) 1, 43–48, published by Palgrave Macmillan.

Introduction

One of the most instructive attempts to link the fields of organization studies and strategy comes in the recent work of Knights and Morgan (1991) [who argue that] the very language, symbols and exchanges around the subject of strategy have important outcomes. Strategy is a mechanism of power (Whipp, 1999).

How is sense to be made of 'strategy'; and how do conceptions of 'strategy' make sense of us?

Such questions are unfamiliar and puzzling to most students of 'strategy'. Nonetheless they are being posed by analysts who urge a more reflexive understanding of what passes for knowledge of strategy, contending that 'it is worth examining a little more closely how the discourse [of strategy] is formulated, how resources and cultural meanings are drawn into its service and what are its effects' (Knights and Morgan, 1991). 'Strategy' or 'strategic management' is conventionally studied as a distinctive field of activity that exists independently of efforts to specify its features and/or prescribe for its perfection. In contrast, discursive analysis attends to the presence and significance of discourse in the identification and realization of 'strategy'.

Discursive analysis, we argue in this paper, provides a theoretical lens that is sufficiently distinctive to justify its differentiation from more established ways of thinking about strategy. From the standpoint of Foucauldian discourse analysis, lay and academic analyses of strategy are not regarded as offering alternative – such as 'classical', 'evolutionary', 'processual' and 'systemic' (Whittington, 1993) – 'ways of seeing' a particular domain of activity. Rather, each such perspective on strategy is understood to be 'embedded in social practices that reproduce the 'way of seeing' as the 'truth' of the discourse' (Knights and Morgan, 1991). When adopting a discursive approach, 'strategy' is converted from 'a descriptive label' deemed to comprise a distinctive domain of researchable objects (e.g. 'strategies', 'environments' and 'competences') 'out there' in the world, to a discourse that is actively engaged in construing and constituting what strategy analysis commonsensically appears or aspires to capture or reflect:

> strategy as a discourse is intimately involved in constituting the intentions and actions from which it is thought to be derived. Strategy, then, is an integral part, and not independent, of the actions or practices that it is frequently drawn upon to explain or justify.
>
> (Knights and Morgan, 1991)

'Discursive analysis' of strategy is responsive – although perhaps not in ways that would be readily recognized or unequivocally welcomed – to the contention that 'many more theoretical lenses will be needed to explore the range of issues that the strategy field offers' (Prahalad and Hamel, 1994). In this paper, we seek to clarify and briefly illustrate its distinctive contribution by building upon the pioneering work of Knights and Morgan (1991) and Knights and Vurdubakis (1994) to provide a close reading of Foucault's conception of the relationship between power, knowledge and discursive practices. We then apply this understanding to analyse a fragment of empirical material that is drawn from a longitudinal study of a global retailing company (see Ezzamel and Willmott, 1998, for details). Finally, we reflect upon our main argument, alluding to what we identify as a paradox of doing discourse analysis.

Post-rational analysis: a critique

The field of strategy has been dominated by rational conceptions of its formulation and implementation, as exemplified in Michael Porter's thinking, where strategy is conceived as an outcome of a more or less rational calculation about competitive advantage in relation to buyers, suppliers, new entrants, the availability of substitutes as well as industry competitors. As Porter (1979) puts it, 'the corporate strategist's goal is to find a position in the industry where his or her company can best defend itself against these forces or can influence them in its favor'. Minimal attention is paid to the institutional context – such as the distinctive cultural values and organizational politics – within and through which decisions are actually made, including the values that bestow legitimacy upon rational models as a key component of top managerial ideology. Instead, the preference is for discerning the key factors or 'forces' that must be successfully disclosed and controlled for a successful strategy to be realized.

The past decade has seen some movement away from rational formulations of strategy, notably through the work of James Quinn and Henry Mintzberg in North America, and Andrew Pettigrew in Europe. Central to such post-rational analysis of strategy is an appreciation of its distinctive contexts and the role of values in the shaping of 'strategic intent' (Hamel and Prahalad, 1989), the nurturing of 'strategic thinking' (Mintzberg, 1994) and the making of 'strategic choices' (Child, 1972), developments that resonate with the growing influence of institutional theory in organization studies:

> the selection of strategy is primarily by means of management judgment and is likely to be bound up in a process of bargaining within the organization. Solutions are not so much likely to be adopted because they are shown to be better on the basis of some sort of objective yardstick, but because they are acceptable to those who influence the decision or have to implement it.
>
> (Johnson, 1987: 29)

Post-rational analysis directly challenges the coherence and credibility of models that represent strategic management as a logical series of steps that proceed from information gathering, through the rational identification of a strategic position to its systematic implementation. Rational models are criticized for their inadequate appreciation of the social embeddedness of the 'forces', including consideration of how the identification and management of such 'forces' (Porter, 1979) are subject to the *politics* of organizational action, entailing the activity of strategic decision-making. Adequate recognition and management of the local values and organizational politics, it is argued, is a necessary feature of strategic decision-making.

Post-rational analysis aspires to show how, in practice, strategic decision-making emerges from local understandings, recipes and routines, and is therefore resistant to, and subversive of, rational calculation and control. Strategy is conceived as *endemically* a negotiated outcome of competing values and conflicts of interest. Such features include the contextually specific values and processes of bargaining that are conceived to govern the formulation and acceptability of strategic visions and their practical implementation – features of decision-making that are unacknowledged, or treated as sources of 'noise' to be eliminated, in rational models of strategy.

In this light, Whittington's (2003) advocacy of a 'practice perspective' echoes the concerns of post-rational analysis as it commends a focus upon the practical business of strategizing, but with particular reference to 'the formal work of strategic and organizational design' (Whittington, 2003). His concern is to focus upon 'situated, concrete activity' (*ibid.*: 121) in order to discover what strategists actually do as 'a step to creating practical wisdom' (*ibid.*: 121) about the business of doing strategy. However, while the post-rational focus upon process is maintained, its attentiveness to culture and politics tends to be displaced by a preoccupation with the identification of skills, the tools and techniques that are used, and how the products of strategizing are consumed. Even the question of how specialists work together to craft strategies, or indeed become strategists, is abstracted from the examination of culture and politics (*ibid.*: 122). There is an underlying assumption that practices are 'shared' (Whittington and Melin, 2002: 44) rather than contested (see Contu and Willmott, 2003). Methodologically, the practice perspective departs from more established forms of processual analysis is in its skepticism about the reliability of actors' accounts of their strategizing, as generated through interview responses (see also Dingwall, 1997):

> While processual studies share the practice perspective's concern for close observation . . . the processualists expect much more from actors' accounts of their own actions.
>
> (Whittington and Melin, 2002: 46)

We have stressed how students of process and practice share an interest in a close-up examination of how strategy is accomplished, as contrasted with the arm's-length specification of the forces that are conceived in rational analysis to comprise an industry's structure and to condition strategists' efforts to establish a favourable position within it. Yet, an objectivist understanding is retained as strategy continues to be conceived as a set of elements of the world 'out there' to be captured by analysis – whether these are components of industry structure or constituents of practitioners' world views. Whittington (2003, emphasis added) counsels that the practice perspective is 'concerned with finding out what strategists' and organizers' jobs *really* are'. Mintzberg *et al* (1995: xi, emphasis added) commend a processual approach on the grounds that it provides 'a sophisticated understanding of *exactly what the context is* and how it functions'. They then use the analogy of engineering and physics to support this view:

> . . . one cannot decide reliably what should be done in a system as complicated as a contemporary organization without a *genuine* understanding of how that organization *really* works. In engineering, no student ever questions having to learn physics, or in medicine, having to learn anatomy. Imagine an engineering student's hand shooting up in a physics class, 'Listen, sir, it's fine telling us how the atom works. But what we really want to know is how the atom *should* work!'. Why should a management student's similar demand in the realm of strategy or structure be considered any more appropriate?
>
> (*ibid.*, first and second emphases added)

The point is well made that much rational analysis of strategy is governed by a normative compulsion to prescribe. The appeal to an example drawn from the natural sciences to lend authority to post-rational analysis is, however, unconvincing. Leaving aside the questionable choice of this particular example – since how atoms behave, as waves or particles, is conceived in quantum mechanics to depend upon how atoms are perceived/theorized – the problem is that the argument *pays no attention to*, and possibly denies, *the interrelationship of the subjects and objects of knowledge*. It is assumed that the world 'out there' is entirely separate from, and uninfluenced by, how this world is understood or theorized by imperfect and partial perspectives developed by researchers.[1]

The problem with the ambition to achieve 'a *genuine* understanding of how [an] organization *really* works' is that the reality of the object (e.g. 'organization' or 'strategy') is necessarily conditioned by the language used to articulate the preoccupations and perspectives of the subject (e.g. researcher): the use of language to describe the world is inescapably divisive, partial and incomplete. 'Old' (e.g. rational) and 'new' (e.g. processual and practice) conceptions of strategy share the presumption of being able to know what the world is 'really like' in advance, and independently of the generation of the knowledge to which the designation 'genuine' is (unreflexively) applied. This position assumes that the objects of 'observation' – that is, the constituent elements of the social world – are both transparent to, and unchanged by, the theory/methodology that accounts for them, thereby denying that how social theories are interpreted, evaluated and appropriated, arguably, influences the 'realness' of the world that the theories purport to describe and explain.

Discursive analysis

Discursive analysis is distinguished by its departure from a commonsense, dualistic conception of the language–reality

[1] Likewise, Pettigrew (1987 emphasis added) commends post-rational analysis for its capacity to provide 'a view of process combining political and cultural elements that *evidently has real power* in explaining continuity and change'. Mintzberg *et al.* (1995: xi) declare that, in contrast to orthodox conceptions of strategic management, their theoretical position 'tries to explain the world *as it is* rather than as someone thinks it is supposed to be'.

relationship in which language is conceived to reflect or capture reality. Foucault (1982) articulates this departure when he argues that discourse, such as that which is concerned with strategy, 'is not a slender surface of contact, or confrontation, between a reality and a language (*langue*)'. Nor, he argues, should language be treated as a group of 'signs (signifying elements referring to contents and representations) but as practices that systematically form the objects of which they speak' (*ibid.*: 49). To treat discourse as merely a sign that designates things is, Foucault contends, to disregard or neutralize its *constitutive* force. This neutralization occurs in both rational and processual models of strategy where their contribution to defining the phenomena that they aspire to study is disregarded.

Foucault's work invites us to explore an alternative approach in which the focus is upon 'a group of rules' or a 'grid of intelligibility' characteristic of particular discursive practices that operates to *identify and order objects in particular ways*. Such rules, which 'are immanent in a practice and define it in its specificity' (*ibid.*: 46), define 'not the dumb existence of a reality, nor the canonical use of vocabulary, but the ordering of objects' (*ibid.*: 49). Accordingly, the analytical focus is upon the truth effects of language in ordering the world in particular ways. Instead of understanding the language that comprises the field of strategy – such as 'firms' and 'markets' – as more or less accurate (and thus impartial) descriptions of an external social reality, such terms are understood to constitute the world in a particular, partisan, politically charged way: their use exerts truth effects insofar as they become widespread and institutionalized. Accordingly, the Foucauldian focus does not seek to specify what the practices (e.g. of strategizing) are but, rather, upon how the 'group of rules' comprising a discourse operates to constitute social practices, spawns their identification as 'strategy', and renders them intelligible in particular ways – notably, through the privileging of power–knowledge frameworks, such as Porter's 'five basic forces', that become hegemonic.

In the following section, we first interpret a fragment of empirical data to illustrate the argument of the previous sections. In doing so, we recognize that we are simultaneously appealing to a regime of truth – in the guise of strategy talk – that we aspire to scrutinize. We also acknowledge that our interpretations of the extract are constructed from our knowledge of other empirical data, including interviewees' accounts and company documents, that enacts *our* 'strategizing' about how to deliver our argument to an imagined audience. We appreciate how the identification of relevant data, as well as our own account of its significance, is inflected by a strategy discourse with which they engage in strategizing, and which enables them to present accounts of their strategizing activity.

Analysing strategy discourse

Consider the following statement by StitchCo's Chief Executive:

> I have had a unique opportunity to carry the company forward into the Nineties. It is a privilege to participate in this driving, entrepreneurial and creative environment and with so many people that have also been part of its history and development.
>
> (press coverage)

In this section, we first offer a possible understanding of this statement before reflecting upon alternative interpretations of its significance. The statement, we suggest, is illustrative of the kinds of discursive practices that comprise the micro-(re)production of 'strategy'. 'Strategy' is simultaneously absent and present. There is no direct reference to 'strategy', yet the CEO can be heard to invoke notions of strategy. We interpret his statement, reported in the press a few months after his appointment, as illustrative of how 'strategy work' is accomplished – in this case, by deploying the media to disseminate a view of the company for employees, customers, shareholders and others that characterizes it as 'driving, entrepreneurial and creative'. We take the production of this account to exemplify the mundane, social practice of (managerial) communication through which relations of power – between the CEO and his audience – operate to disseminate and promote a particular kind of knowledge, and membership, of the company. In this process, distinct subjects – notably, the CEO as occupier of the chief (and 'unique') executive position and objects, such as 'the company', its 'history' and 'environment' – are recurrently constituted, reproduced and transformed.

To the extent that such claims are accepted and normalized, they operate to (re)produce discourses of strategy and strategic management; they also act to forge a 'regime of truth', to use Foucault's phrase, that operates to discipline the thought and conduct of those who identify with its call. The statement alludes, we suggest, to the strategic management of StitchCo, both in its reference to moving 'forward', and in its association of this movement with a 'driving, entrepreneurial and creative environment'. Such discursive practices (of strategizing) act to position the activity and identity of employees within a process of 'carrying the company forward' and 'developing' it and within which the CEO ascribes to himself a key, and perhaps sovereign, role. The use of the term 'environment' is ambiguous: it construes an operating context that is 'driving', in the sense that the market disciplines those who fail to respond effectively to its changing demands; it also signals an aspiration and demand that StitchCo employees are themselves driving, entrepreneurial and creative. The strategy favoured by the CEO, we contend, seeks to harness entrepreneurship and creativity in ways that would build upon, rather than replace, a distinctive account of the history and development of the company.

This is just *one reading* of the CEO's statement. This statement may, of course, be interpreted in other ways. It could be read as a celebration of the implementation of a *rationalist conception of* strategy in which strategy is conceived to foster an 'entrepreneurial and creative' corporate culture capable of exploiting opportunities and parrying risks. Or, to draw upon our broader knowledge of the company, it could be heard to affirm an espoused strategy of 'product differentiation' combined with 'focus' (Porter, 1979) that was expected to revitalize the unique selling point ascribed to StitchCo merchandise. Alternatively, the CEO's statement could be interpreted as articulating a *processual conception of strategy* in which he is engaged in negotiating and promoting a particular vision based upon his 'recipe knowledge' of how to restore the fortunes of an ailing company. In such a reading, the opportunity of press coverage is interpreted as a way of disseminating a particular vision of strategy in which its dynamic ('carry forward', 'driving') meaning, and means of implementation, is given emphasis.

From a Foucauldian standpoint, however, whatever reading becomes dominant or 'taken for granted' evidences the play of power relations (e.g. by privileging particular discursive practices) rather than approximating what strategy 'is'. In this light, communications do not simply explain or justify the intentions or actions of managers to whom the task of formulating and implementing strategy is assigned. They also exert truth effects insofar as they operate to constitute employee intentions and actions that they are generally assumed to describe. The discourse can be read to signal an expectation or requirement that employees, the CEO included, will be assessed within, and will examine their own performance against a corporate and business 'environment' that is represented as 'driving, entrepreneurial and creative'. The implication is that employees who are construed as not demonstrating their commitment to, and delivery of, this discipline will no longer have the 'opportunity' to 'participate'. In this regard, the CEO is himself tied to, and disciplined (i.e. both constrained and enabled) by, a strategy discourse that he disseminates, and with which he and his appointees within StitchCo are strongly identified by the non-executive directors, major shareholders and media pundits, as well as its employees. The CEO's repeated and amplified articulations of the strategy fuelled the expectations of staff and investors that he would exemplify, demonstrate and deliver what it means to be 'driving, entrepreneurial and creative'.

Despite the power invested in such a knowledge of strategy, it should not be assumed that strategy discourse directly determines or unequivocally constrains either the actions of the CEO or other StitchCo employees. Other discourses and options are available that render such strategy discourse more or less credible and appealing. Investment in other discourses and associated identifications (e.g. family or career goals) can result in considerable scepticism, resistance or dramaturgical compliance with respect to proposed and enacted strategic change. At StitchCo, the terrain on which the new strategy discourse was propagated and distributed had previously hosted social relations and subjectivities to which the new CEO, an outsider, contrived to make selective appeals – for example, by acknowledging the impressive history of the company.

Conclusions

Discourses appeal to a context whose contours they invoke and reproduce. When interpreting the brief extract taken from some press coverage of StitchCo, the reader unfamiliar with the company is obliged to invoke a context – for example, a broad understanding of what businesses are and what CEOs do. As Fairclough and Wodak (1997, cited in Hardy *et al.*, 2000) contend, 'Discourse is not produced without context and cannot be understood without taking context into consideration ... Discourses are always connected to other discourses that were produced earlier, as well as those which are produced synchronically and subsequently.' It is to 'context' that we have necessarily appealed in constructing our interpretation of the CEO's statement.

That said, it is a mistake, from the standpoint of Foucauldian discourse analysis at least, to assume that 'context' and its interpreters can be independently or dualistically identified. This is where discourse analysis departs radically from the realist ontologies favoured by rationalist, processual and, indeed, certain forms of discourse analysis. Both context and discourse are understood to be continuously (re)identified through discursive practices. Knowledge of 'structure' and 'agency' undergoes construction and transformation in the discursive practicalities of its everyday use. This, to be clear, is not to deny the reality of what is discursively identified as 'history', 'context', 'structure', 'agency', etc. but, rather, to recognize how it is through discursive practices that we identify reality and, in doing so, effect its reproduction and transformation.

The analytical gauntlet thrown down by Foucauldian discourse analysis is to acknowledge and investigate the power/knowledge relations that are productive of *particular* ways of accounting for complex processes. It is not simply that discourse is contextually interpreted. Rather, it is *indexical* in the sense that discourses are rendered meaningful by connecting their claims to the discursively constituted contexts of their articulation. The CEO's statement is placed in the context of what is (discursively) constituted, for example, as the history of StitchCo and the position of its CEO. No discourse is capable of providing a closure in reflecting upon, or seeking to capture, StitchCo's past. Each possible history is identified through discursive work that is open to contest from alternative histories that it excludes or marginalizes. Discourse analysis exemplifies and stimulates an awareness of how the identification and privileging of particular historical, or contextual, conditions is necessarily the product of contingent, discursively produced ways of depicting the emergence of organizational (e.g. strategizing) practices.

The concern of discursive analysis is to better appreciate how, as forms of power-knowledge, strategy talk and texts are actively involved in the constitution of what, for example, rational and processual models contrive to prescribe or describe. In exploring a form of analysis that is more directly attentive to, and guided by, the reflexive quality of social relations, there is no aspiration to offer a substitute or corrective for rational or processual approaches to strategy. It is accepted that rational and processual analyses proceed from different assumptions, and that they each make distinctive contributions to the theory and practice of strategy. Their accounts of strategy are credible and valuable within their own terms of reference. For us, the shortcomings of rational and processual analysis reside in a lack of reflexivity (and humility) about claims to rationalize strategy or accurately reflect its processes and also in its disregard for its own truth effects, and not in the failure to embrace the discursive approach commended here. While the incorporation of greater reflexivity within rational and processual analysis would operate to qualify its objectivism – whether in respect of industry structures or 'managers' meanings – there would remain pragmatic or expedient reasons for minimizing consideration of their discursive production and political effects.

Analysis of 'strategy' as discourse is attentive to how the discourse of 'strategy' renders the world, including its experts and adopters, meaningful and tractable in particular ways. 'Strategists', as Knights and Morgan (1991) have noted, 'do not reflect upon the truth and disciplinary effects of their discourse'. In contrast to other accounts of strategy, it is not assumed that the 'object' of interest exists independently of its analysis. This approach, we acknowledge, is neither self-evidently valuable nor easily undertaken. This is not least because, in order to discuss any topic (e.g. strategy), it is necessary to treat the topic as if our knowledge of it exists independently of the discursive practices that identify and explore it as a topic. In addition, the truth effects of established strategic discourse, which find their echo in rational and processual models of strategy, are particularly powerful. These effects make it 'exceedingly difficult for us to disengage ourselves from such a view' (Knights and Morgan, 1991). Nonetheless, following the lead given by Knights and Morgan, we believe that by striving to do so, it is possible to open up and extend new ways of knowing strategy.

References

Child, J. (1972). Organization structure, environment and performances: The role of strategic choice. *Sociology*, 6(1): 1–22.

Contu, A. and Willmott, H.C. (2003). Re-embedding situatedness: The importance of power relations in situated learning theory. ***Organization Science***, 14: 283–297.

Dingwall, R. (1997). Accounts, Interviews and Observations, in G. Miller and R. Dingwall (eds.) ***Context and Method in Qualitative Research***. London: Sage, pp: 51–65.

Ezzamel, M. and Willmott, H. (1998). Accounting for teamwork A critical study of group-based systems of organizational control. ***Administrative Science Quarterly***, 43: 358–396.

Foucault, M. (1982). The Subject and Power, in H.L. Dreyfus and P. Rabinow (eds.) ***Michel Foucault: Beyond Structuralism and Hermeneutics***. New York: Harvester Wheatsheaf, pp: 202–226.

Hamel, G. and Prahalad, C.K. (1989). Strategic intent. ***Harvard Business Review***, May–June: 63–76.

Hardy, C., Palmer, I. and Phillips, N. (2000). Discourse as a strategic resource. ***Human Relations***, 53: 1227–1248.

Johnson, G. (1987). ***Strategic Change and the Management Process***. Oxford: Blackwell.

Knights, D. and Morgan, G. (1991). Corporate strategy, organizations and subjectivity: A critique. ***Organization Studies***, 12: 251–273.

Knights, D. and Vurdubakis, T. (1994). Foucault, Power, Resistance and All That, in J. Jermier, D. Knights and W. Nord (eds.) ***Resistance and Power in Organizations***. London: Routledge, pp: 167–198.

Mintzberg, H. (1994). The fall and rise of strategic planning. ***Harvard Business Review***, January–February: 107–114.

Mintzberg, H., Quinn, J.B. and Ghoshal, S. (1995). ***The Strategy Process***, European, edn. London: Prenctice-Hall.

Pettigrew, A. (1987). Context and action in the transformation of the firm. ***Journal of Management Studies***, 24: 649–670.

Prahalad, C.K. and Hamel, G. (1994). Strategy as a field of study: Why search for a new paradigm? ***Strategic Management Journal***, 15: 5–16.

Porter, M. (1979). How competitive forces shape strategy. ***Harvard Business Review***, 57(2): 37–145.

Whipp, R. (1999). Creative Deconstruction: Strategy and Organizations, in S.R. Clegg, C. Hardy and W. Nord (eds.) ***Managing Organizations: Current Issues***. London: Sage, pp. 11–25.

Whittington, R. (1993). ***What is Strategy – And Does it Matter?*** London: Routledge.

Whittington, R. (2003). The work of strategising and organizing: For a practice perspective. ***Strategic Organization***, 1(1): 119–127.

Whittington, R. and Melin, L. (2002). The Challenge of Organizing, in A.M. Pettigrew, R. Whittington, L. Melin, C. Sanchez-Runde Bosch, W. Ruigrok and T. Numagami (eds.) ***Innovative Forms of International Perspectives***. London: Sage, pp: 35–48.

Practitioner reflection

Padraig O'Ceidigh

Rediscovering strategy and strategists

My experience as an entrepreneur is that entrepreneurs are, first and foremost, intuitive strategists. They have an innate ability to selectively assemble key information, which, combined in an effective manner, creates relevant knowledge, allowing them to see a clear path forward to where they want to go.

Like all life skills, this one comes easier to some than it does to others. This fact does not go unnoticed with entrepreneurs and they continuously fine-tune this key attribute. They focus on developing their skills, similarly to an athlete preparing for the 2012 Olympics—the main difference being that the entrepreneurial athlete has to reach and maintain peak performance for sustained periods of time, with very few rest periods in between.

The initial instinct of an entrepreneur is, first, survival and, then, to grow to the next stage with his or her business. Thus, his or her initial focus is based on a short-term, close-up vision. This vision is based on creating a simple business model that is self-sustaining. The entrepreneur analyses the key requirements that will keep the business alive and also support him or her in getting to the next stage.

This short-term vision can be achieved only with the entrepreneur at the helm, being very much hands-on, and having a direct involvement and influence on every aspect of the business. Passion, commitment, and good, but subjective, decision making becomes the hallmark of survival, motivation, and growth. In almost all cases, entrepreneurs lack a number of key resources to get the business up and running. Therefore they focus on a small number of achievements that, they believe, will deliver the desired results. Growth and success happen one step at a time, and if you don't survive in the game long enough, then you will not be in a position to take those steps.

In most instances, the key achievements are:

- cash flow;
- product and team development; and
- customer attraction.

All of the above are actionable simultaneously. The entrepreneur requires the skills of a circus juggler, keeping a number of balls in the air at the same time, because he or she knows that if he or she drops even one ball, the show is over.

1. *Cash flow* Quickly turning sales into cash is the lifeline of any young enterprise, especially when capital investment is difficult to get.

Entrepreneurs continuously analyse and reshape their business models in order to ensure that they can maximize the levels of cash flow into the business, and keep hold of this money for as long as possible. They substitute cash flow income for capital investment, thus usually growth is internally funded.

2. *Production and team development* At the same time, they are acutely aware that they have to create and develop a product that, in their view, the market wants at a price that creates this positive cash flow. Entrepreneurs usually test their products from day one by selling to a small segment of the market. This facilitates the refinement of the product to better meet customer

needs. They usually do not have the luxury of time or finances to use consultants, advisers, or focus groups, so they go straight to the customer.

3. *Customer attraction* Entrepreneurs work very hard on creating a strong understanding of their customers. They always put themselves in the shoes and minds of potential customers by asking how, when, where, and why anyone would pay hard-earned cash to purchase the product or services offered.

Entrepreneurs analyse the current routes to market, their effectiveness, the emerging trends, whether they can fast-forward the route-to-market process by making purchase easier, and, at the same time, whether they can reduce the cost to the customer. Is there an alternative route to market that can be created that will produce a win–win for both the entrepreneur and the customer?

Entrepreneurs are constantly scanning the micro and macro environments in order to spot opportunities and interpret threats before they can cause real damage. This is the reason why entrepreneurs always look to niche markets: they offers the entrepreneur limited protection against the major competitors. Entrepreneurs constantly compare the world with their company and that of the world without their company. This indicates the added value and the uniqueness that they bring to the marketplace. Added value and uniqueness then become a driving force to facilitate growth in as protected a manner as possible.

Entrepreneurs realize the importance of relationships. They learn quickly that integrity, commitment, and flawless execution are fundamental to the creation and maintenance of powerful relationships. They take personal responsibility for this in their businesses. They are acutely aware of the importance of team and people in the realization of success with their business. They face the challenge of starting and creating a business at its most vulnerable stage while, at the same time, getting the best people possible committed to work in the company. This is particularly challenging, because very few employees leave a steady, reliable job to move to a high-risk, early-stage development business. Therefore many entrepreneurs offer equity incentives to such employees, to supplement a lower salary scale, and also to encourage all key employees to act and work as if they own the business.

During the early stages of growth, the business does not have formal structures, systems, or processes in place. Therefore the entrepreneur needs people who are self-starters, people who are willing to multi-task and who are self-motivating. In other words, the entrepreneur is again working on a number of objectives simultaneously, which are not, at least on first observation, congruent.

As we can see, the resources available to the entrepreneur are extremely limited and therefore he or she can create only a number of short-term objectives, analyse the risks involved with very limited information, and at the same time do what he or she can with those limited resources to achieve those objectives.

Frequently, the entrepreneur will have to modify his or her strategy for a number of reasons. The primary reasons for such modification would include:

- not being able to achieve initial objectives due to lack of resources and/or changing market conditions; and
- becoming aware of alternative opportunities that seem simpler to achieve with the resources available, while at the same time having the possibility of producing a stronger business model than the one originally envisaged.

Therefore entrepreneurial strategy is very much a continuously evolving process that is assessed constantly, and developed and modified at rapid speed. Remember: the entrepreneur does not have the time or money to procrastinate. Also, the marketplace is constantly changing, and that opportunity gap may disappear as quickly as it appeared.

The company then starts to develop the personality of the entrepreneur, as well as his or her vision. This is primarily due to two factors. In the first instance, the entrepreneur puts all of his or her energy into the business and, in almost all cases, becomes an integral part of that business. Secondly, the entrepreneur recognizes the importance of leadership and clarity of goals, so he or she becomes the catalyst for leadership and change.

Successful entrepreneurs realize the need to significantly change not only strategy, but also the manner in which strategy is created and executed as the business grows. They see that a different set of skills are required to lead the company forward: there is a far greater requirement for clear structures and lines of delegation, and industry best practice becomes a requirement.

At this stage, the entrepreneur should ask if he or she is the best-equipped person to lead the company to the next stage of growth. This is a critical point in the development of an entrepreneurial company.

In reflecting on the other contexts with which the authors deal in Chapter 13, what strikes me is that it is challenging to be a strategist and leader in any context—even more challenging to be entrepreneurial or innovative. Each context and organization has its own challenges. For not-for-profits, it is dealing with constant uncertainty about having sufficient resources to continue to operate. In public sector organizations, particularly in front-line services such as health care, dealing with personal crises requires a unique skill set and is even more challenging given the state of public finances in many countries post the international financial crisis.

Chapter 14 takes an interesting approach to the role of strategy agents in competitive markets. From my experience, management consultancy firms and individual management consultants can provide significant analytical support for managers and leadership teams in dealing with organizational issues. Their ability as outsiders to challenge the core assumptions about the business or the market is critically important. However, it would be fair to say that companies and managers have varying experiences of management consultants: some good; some bad. My view is that many companies are unclear and fuzzy about the core terms of engagement with a consultancy firm, and have an inflated expectation of what they can deliver and solve.

Finally, management fads come and go, as the authors rightly point out in Chapter 14, but I would suggest that these fads can be viewed as a way of testing the core assumptions about your business. Also, fads provide businesses with potentially new ways of viewing their activities: a prism of sorts. It is only after subjective and objective assessment that strategists and leaders can decide whether they buy into them. In my experience, being a strategist is all about being different and thinking differently.

Padraig O'Ceidigh is chairman of Aer Arann. From its beginnings as a small Irish island-hopping airline, O'Ceidigh has driven Aer Arann to its current position as one of the fastest growing regional airlines in Europe. Padraig trained as an accountant at the National University of Ireland, Galway, and has also worked as a teacher and solicitor. Padraig was named 2002 Ernst & Young Entrepreneur of The Year and went on to represent Ireland in the Entrepreneur of the Year awards in Monte Carlo in 2003.

Section 7

Long cases

Introduction

Case studies are a valuable means by which to assess the merit of strategic theories and tools while also serving to initiate debate around the key challenges and opportunities that strategists may confront. Each of our chapters closed with a mini-case which animated the key themes addressed in that chapter from the orientation and trade-off challenge at Hyundai in Chapter 1 to a critical consideration of the role of Virgin consultants in Chapter 14. This section presents a series of 10 more in-depth cases studies which will enable greater engagement, exploration, and debate around key strategic tensions and themes.

Details of the case studies can be found in the table of long cases and chapter themes on the following page. This table provides an indication of the key focus of the case (illustrated by two dots) and also the associated themes the case touches upon (illustrated by a single dot). Take for example our 'Book to bytes' case study. This is very much an examination of how technological trends are shaping the publishing industry and so aligns with our section on the foundations of advantage, and in particular the debate between markets and resources of Chapter 6. As a result of outlining the evolution of the industry the case also has implications for the routes to advantage available to firms, thereby touching upon the topic of Chapter 8. In contrast our Cloon Keen Atelier case has as its focus the viability of differentiation as a route to advantage (Chapter 8) in the context of a small firm (Chapter 13).

By definition the table of long cases is merely a general guide as case study topics can be interpreted in multiple ways and may open up discussion into a broad range of areas. To facilitate this we have included a purposefully a diverse range of case study contexts and approaches including:

- Case studies of companies (Cloon Keen Atelier, Macquarie, McDonalds, Renault–Nissan alliance);
- case studies of industries (publishing, grocery);
- case discussions of concepts (Ethical Trading initiative, Reassessing value)
- and case assessments of practice (City of London Police).

This collection reflects our belief that there is no one neat way to best understand strategy or single universal solutions. Instead our purpose should be to initiate strategy conversations which provide insights to guide practice. Another way of framing the case studies is on the basis of the key strategic management challenges they address.

Strategic management challenges and associated case studies

Orientation challenge	Who we are and where do we compete?	City of London Local Policing Plan 2006–9 Macquarie Bank Australia The Renault–Nissan alliance
Trade-off challenge	How do we compete?	McDonald's
Relevance challenge	What is our value proposition and for whom?	Cloon Keen Atelier Ethical Trading Initiative Reassessing value in strategy
Continuous change challenge	How do we adapt?	Book to bytes The UK grocery retailing industry

Long cases and related chapter themes

Section	Chapter	Long case 1 Books to bytes	2 City of London Local Policing Plan 2006–09	3 Cloon Keen Atelier	4 The Ethical Trading Initia-tive	5 Leadership: the Indra Nooyi way	6 Macquarie Bank Australia	7 McDonald's	8 Reassess-ing value in strategy	9 The Renault–Nissan alli-ance	10 The UK grocery retailing industry
1 Discovering strategy and strategists	Chapter 1 Discovering strategy	●		●			●●		●		
	Chapter 2 Discovering strategists					●●			●		
	Chapter 3 The process of strategizing					●					
	Chapter 4 Dynamics of strategy formulation		●●								
2 Foundations to advantage	Chapter 5 Purpose and values		●		●●				●●		
	Chapter 6 Market-based and resource-based approaches	●●		●	●			●		●	●●
3 Routes to advantage	Chapter 7 Corporate and global strategy						●●	●		●●	
	Chapter 8 Business and network strategies	●		●●						●	●

(continued)

Long cases and related chapter themes (Continued)

Section	Chapter	Long case									
		1 Books to bytes	2 City of London Local Policing Plan 2006–09	3 Cloon Keen Atelier	4 The Ethical Trading Initiative	5 Leadership: the Indra Nooyi way	6 Macquarie Bank Australia	7 McDonald's	8 Reassessing value in strategy	9 The Renault–Nissan alliance	10 The UK grocery retailing industry
4 Realizing advantage	Chapter 9 Levers for implementing strategy		●					●			
	Chapter 10 Interactions in executing strategy						●	●●			●
5 Sustaining advantage	Chapter 11 Strategic change					●●				●	
	Chapter 12 Innovation and corporate entrepreneurship			●							
6 Rediscovering strategy and strategists	Chapter 13 Managing strategy in context		●	●●					●		
	Chapter 14 The role of strategy agents								●●		

Case 1 Books to bytes: the competitive impact of e-books

Ann Brehony and Dr Ann M. Torres, Lecturer in Marketing, National University of Ireland, Galway

The evolution of the current business model

The publishing value chain has developed gradually since Gutenberg's 1455 production of the first printed Bible. In the market for printed materials, evolutionary survival of the fittest has prioritized the control of intellectual property rights and economy of scale as the tools for success. By the nineteenth century, publishers had established their roles as speculators, marketers, and producers of books, while niche-role companies began the work of organizing book production and distribution. The publisher began to focus more on the acquisition of intellectual property rights (IP) and the organization of its markets by means of literary reviews, commercial travellers, and catalogues (Feltes, 1986).

The arrival of the paperback

The twentieth century brought further refinement of this business model, with publishers now viewing themselves as adding value by conferring the authority of their brand on an author's work. Their function became one of sourcing, financing, producing, marketing, and selling the work of a list of authors. Allen Lane's development of the Penguin paperbacks is possibly the best example of successful twentieth-century publisher branding. Appalled by the poor selection of titles available at railway bookstalls, Lane decided that quality contemporary fiction should be available at accessible prices in a range of locations, such as railway stations, tobacconists, and chain stores.

Released in the summer of 1935, the first Penguin paperbacks included works by Ernest Hemmingway and Agatha Christie. At just sixpence, they changed both the way in which the reading public thought about books forever, and the way in which publishers added value to an author's work by expanding the exploitation of ancillary rights. The business strategy recognized that a piece of intellectual property could be exploited many times in a single territory. Titles could be established in hardback at a high price, with a smaller audience prepared to pay a premium for early access to the book, which was subsequently reissued in paperback at a lower price and sold to a wider audience. The hardback publisher would acquire all exclusive rights to publish an author's work for the full term of copyright. The hardback publisher's reputation guaranteed reviews for new releases; consequently their market always had access to the most talked-about titles. The paperback publisher reviewed the sales of the latest hardback titles and rushed to acquire the exclusive paperback licence for the best-sellers. The paperback model was fast-moving and mass market; titles were printed in monthly batches and operations were strictly sales-driven (Clarke and Phillips, 1994).

Publishers relied on their market knowledge to aid their assessment of what would sell. Firms began to find niche genres and subjects to attain critical mass in market segments; they employed editors who understood their niche and who had contacts with the appropriate authors. By the nineties, there was an international consolidation of the main English-language publishers and the market was rigorously segmented. The ancillary rights had widened to include television and film adaptations, and marketing and distribution became highly strategic, with higher concentration on 'saleable' books and authors, especially those who fit with the large retail chains' 'promotional plans' (Clarke and Phillips, 1994).

Table L1.1 Publishing timeline

1450	Johannes Gutenberg develops moveable type, revolutionizing the printing process and allowing books to become mass market commodities
1455	The first Gutenberg Bible is printed
1476	William Caxton establishes the first British printing press, his first publication being an edition of Chaucer's *Canterbury Tales*
1564	Birth of William Shakespeare
1868	Invention of the typewriter by US engineer Christopher Latham Sholes
1900	The Net Book Agreement (NBA) is introduced
1922	James Joyce's *Ulysses* is published
1928	The first *Oxford English Dictionary* is published
1935	First Penguin paperbacks are published
1966	ISBN numbers are introduced in the UK
1971	The world's first digital library, Project Gutenberg, is founded
1995	Amazon opens for business online
1997	The NBA is abolished
2006	The first e-reader is produced by Sony
2007	Amazon launches its Kindle reader
2010	Apple launches the iPad; Google opens the eBookstore
2011	Pottermore.com is launched to be an 'online reading experience' incorporating sales of e-books and Sony products that relate to the *Harry Potter* brand

The retail landscape

The book-retail space was also transforming: the eighties saw the arrival of Waterstones and the expansion of WHSmith into powerful chains of large well-stocked bookstores with highly tuned promotion and marketing techniques. Since 1900, publishers and booksellers had worked together under the Net Book Agreement (NBA), which set the prices for books. To challenge the NBA's fair trade practices, Waterstones and Dillons sold books below the agreed price, leading to legal battles, resulting in the 1997 Restrictive Practices' Court ruling that the NBA was against the public interest and illegal. Since the abolition of the NBA, the average book price has fallen by 60 per cent (Wilkinson, 2008). The large multiples' aggressive pricing strategy has led to the demise of over 500 independent booksellers and has shortened the shelf life of most novels (Jordison, 2010). The end of the NBA and the arrival of Internet retailers such as Amazon radically altered the book trade. Independent bookstores could not compete with the book retail trade behemoths and large chain supermarkets, which sold books at low margins as loss leaders to generate customer goodwill and to add quality to their core grocery stock.

The power structure began to shift from the publisher to the retailer. The produce-and-sell model demanded a faster turnaround of stock, which was being sold by larger chains in huge volumes, and the business model moved from being product-led to market-driven. The retailing chains exerted their power over the publishers by pushing for larger discounts and extended credit periods. Publishers needed to sell larger volumes to achieve their former NBA profit margins, which meant that they had to guarantee a bankable product. The bidding wars for best-selling authors led to high advance payments and the pressure to control international rights forced a consolidation of publishing companies into major media conglomerates, leading to the emergence of the 'Big Six': Hachette; HarperCollins; MacMillan; Pearson; Random House; and Simon & Schuster (see Table L1.2).

The Big Six sharpened their competitive edge by maximizing revenue from an increasingly segmented market with varied offerings across different formats and price points. For example, books with lower sales potential would not cover their costs if first published as lower-price-point paperbacks; they were dependent on sufficient

Table L1.2 The 'Big Six'

Hachette Book Group http://www.hachettebookgroup.com	Formerly known as Warner Books and owned by Time Warner, Hachette was acquired by Hachette Livre, a subsidiary of French media conglomerate Lagardère Imprints include: Little Brown & Company; Grand Central
HarperCollins http://www.harpercollins.com	The result of a merger between publishers William Collins and Sons & Co. Ltd and Harper & Row, now owned by Rupert Murdoch's News Corp Imprints include: Amistad; Avon; Rayo; William Morrow
MacMillan http://www.macmillan.com	Owned by the German publishing group Georg von Holtzbrinck Publishing, now based in New York Imprints include: St Martin's Press; Tor and Farrar; Straus & Giroux
Penguin Group http://www.pearson.com	The British conglomerate Pearson now owns this classic paperback brand Imprints include: Hamish Hamilton; Putnam; Berkley; Viking; Dorling Kindersley; Puffin; Ladybird
Random House http://www.randomhouse.com	Arguably the largest English-language trade publisher in the world, a subsidiary of a European media conglomerate, Bertlesmann Imprints include: Doubleday; Knopf and Crown
Simon & Schuster http://www.simonandschuster.com	Established as a producer of crossword puzzles in the 1920s, Simon & Schuster is now owned by the CBS corporation Imprints include: Pocket; Free Press; Scribner

hardback sales to create enough media interest to drive the later-released paperback formats. Television book clubs in the first decade of the twenty-first century, led by Oprah Winfrey in the USA and Richard and Judy in the UK, had ripple effects on the marketplace. In 2007, the forty-eight books endorsed by Richard and Judy's Book Club sold approximately 250,000 copies each (Wilkinson, 2008: 54). However, it became increasingly difficult to sell some categories of book in hardback, partly because these television book clubs reviewed only paperback editions.

The Big Six's brand identity made a statement about an author's commercial potential. This identity was aimed within the trade of publishing rather than at the consumer. An author's work taken on by a Big Six publisher informed agents who sought to supply similar books and authors. Big Six branding ensured media coverage and generated reviews. For trade buyers, the quantities ordered were determined by the publisher's brand. This collective access to the seat of power drove international media interest, which increased the value of ancillary income such as translation rights (Clarke and Phillips, 1994).

Since the Big Six knew the market trends, authors were selected to fill gaps in existing markets and to address future demands. These publishers had the expertise to determine the format and packaging to create the optiumum product. They also had the power to get the most competitive price for the IP, to which they could apply their size and market reach to ensure economies of scale across printing and distribution. Their knowledge of the retail chain and the market allowed them to meet book retailers' demands for faster, more reliable distribution in order to compete against other kinds of products (Clarke and Phillips, 1994). Although generating an increased output, the available range of books is the victim of this business model.

The potential financial worth of an author is rigourously assesessed from the outset, because all books are sold on a sale-or-return basis. The gamble on the size of a print run can mean a welcome windfall or a large debt. Word of mouth (WoM) is an important sales driver in the book market, but WoM is useless if the physical inventory is not in the retail stores at the time when the customer arrives to purchase the book. Sales momentum is crucial to get a book into an extended best-seller list, which generates attention in the form of reviews and media coverage. This formula creates 'breakthrough best-sellers': titles by authors who are not already established as best-sellers.

The arrival of digital devices

Amazon responded to industry inefficiency in 2007 with its electronic reader: the Kindle. By mid-2010, e-books accounted for 3–5 per cent of the publishing market for books (Richtel and Cain Miller, 2010). In May 2011, Amazon reported sales of 105 e-books for every 100 print books sold (Gabbot, 2011). Unlike traditional books, e-books require a piece of hardware to facilitate their consumption. In a merging of previously separate roles, Amazon, a book retailer, has become a digital printer, a publisher with its new imprint Encore, and a manufacturer of elelctronic devices.

The arrival of Apple's iPad in April 2010 may have completely changed the rules of the publishing game with a sales increase of 348.2 per cent predicted for 2011 (Evans, 2011). The iPad enters the market with an audience of 125 million loyal iTunes customers. E-books present opportunities and challenges for publishers, but it has been difficult for many to accept the changes in the publishing business. The digital format erodes the hardback-to-paperback template, because consumers need not purchase a hardback to acquire a book ahead of the mass market.

Because inventory is virtual, the ancillary rights to publish in different territories have become meaningless. There is a radical shift in book production and transmission in the form of the e-book. The twenty-first-century reader does not purchase an e-book; he or she merely licenses it and is therefore restricted in his or her ability to share, lend, or even display it. The issues around pricing will require a new analysis of the value proposition of this new format: will customers value the portability offered by an e-book over the permanence of a print title? The Big Six relied on the model of content being scarce; it required a capital investment to produce; consequently the model demanded a minimum audience to make publication viable. This model functioned well on the basis that money flows to scarcity. The Big Six need to devise new models for an era in which content is plentiful and the market is less willing to pay.

Consumer dissatisfaction with the range of product available on the high street has driven the customer online. Independent bookstores, which traditionally offered more choice and a greater range of niche titles, are finding it difficult to compete with the discounting on offer in the large chains. Mid-range authors are struggling to get their work published, and even if they manage a publishing contract, they are frequently dropped if sales quotas are not met. Authors and readers, the ends of the publishing value chain, are breaking free from the intermediary links of publishers and booksellers to explore ways of connecting directly with each other.

Low growth with low product differentiation

Although only two of the top ten publishing companies saw sales decline from 2008 to 2009, market growth was only 1.3 per cent (Jones, 2010). There is little value differentiation among the Big Six's products. To the average reader, the intrinsic quality and external value of a book is the same regardless of publisher. Mass-market paperbacks can arguably be described as commodities, but consumers are more likely to base their choice on author. Growth strategies in large publishing houses are contingent on retaining the rights to publish the best-selling authors. The digital marketplace with its inherent loss of ancillary territorial rights is making it harder for publishers to guarantee the same level of royalty return to their authors, who may look to the self-publishing route to ensure a larger share of the profits from their work.

Publishers use digital rights management (DRM) to lock consumers into their digital products. DRM prevents the customer from reading any book on any device other than the platform for which it was purchased. Arguably, the Big Six are competing for a diminishing share of a shrinking print market, rather than exploring ways of exploiting new opportunities presented by the expanding digital market. The notion of one format for written content is no longer valid and therefore the demands of an increasingly segmented marketplace require a variety of business models. Digital publisher Tim O'Reilly has found that e-books augment, rather than compete with, sales of its print titles; 60 per cent of sales of O'Reilly's e-books have come from countries in which the publisher had no physical book distribution, meaning that e-books have afforded it market expansion opportunities in new territories (Albnaese, 2010). It is difficult to determine when the industry will gravitate to a new set of business frameworks, or to speculate on who will be the winners and losers in this process. The competitive battle may see a realignment of the industry power structure, or could lead to the emergence of anything from a 'Big Four' to a 'Medium-sized 400'.

Changing access to raw material

In publishing terms, a best-selling author is unique and his or her brand is more recognizable than that of the publishing house. These authors do not have to compete with generic suppliers when they are topping the best-seller lists. Publishing has been dominated by franchise titles in the last decade, which has increased the power of the small number of agents who handle writers of this genre. The blockbuster strategy makes sense to the bottom line, but it does not increase the overall quality of supply. Of the sixty-one books published by Hachette's Grand Central Publishing in 2006 (the height of the authors' advances price wars), each title averaged a profit of almost US$100,000. However, without a US$5m best-seller, that average drops to US$18,000 (Kachka, 2008). The power of the supplier who can guarantee these sales cannot be underestimated.

The consolidation of publishing and retailing, while increasing the supply of published work, has reduced the variety of work available to the consumer. One of the largest book retailers in the USA is Wal-Mart, the customer of which is a 'Mom'; therefore, the inventory of books stocked is selected to cater for that customer and must pass the 'Mom litmus test' (James, 2009).

Commissioning editors are the creative force driving these blockbuster hits within the Big Six. Editors traditionally straddled the line between the needs of the market and the source of the product. They spent time nurturing talent in the hope of discovering the next break-through author. Gradually, their roles morphed into responding to the market. In this genre-specific, copy-cat environment, many editors believe that their judgement no longer counts and, regardless of success, the conglomerate bosses expect them to do better next year (Kachka, 2008).

Agents are conscious of the corporate demands placed on editors; this pressure has strengthened their hands in negotiations: contract terms are getting shorter, prices are going up and the royalties on e-books are hotly contested. The blockbuster era has made it difficult for publishing companies to retain their best-selling authors, whose agents are always seeking a better offer. Many agents have remarked the high turnover of editorial staff among the imprints of the Big Six has hindered their crucial role of fostering new talent. This role has reverted to agents, further increasing their power.

In an era in which IP will not be as valuable to a publisher as the audience that they can command, there may be cause to explore a contract model that allows for more dispersal of publishing options for the author and the publisher. Publishing consultant Mike Shatzkin refers to this shift as the 'control of IP versus the control of eyeballs'. He cites the example of publisher Hay House, a company specializing in the self-help, alternative health market. Hay House runs between thirty and 100 live events a year with its authors; it has over a million email addresses that it mines extensively to drive book sales. Speaking with an unnamed agent, Shatzkin reports how this agent sold a title to one of the Big Six and the book sold 12,000 copies; the agent sold the author's next title to Hay House, with which it sold 200,000 copies (Shatzkin and Cader, 2011).

The authors provide material, which in its raw state may not provide a marketable commodity; however, with the rise in self-publishing as a viable option, agents themselves are beginning to understand the investment required to shape this material into a saleable book. This investment extends beyond mere printing and binding costs. Both parties need to understand what each brings to the table, especially when that table is a new format.

New price arrangements

A difficulty with book pricing is the industry's own reluctance to identify its buyers. Tim O'Reilly, whose company O'Reilly Media publishes about 200 e-books per year, believes that the old publishing model, which lacks direct knowledge of the customer, is 'fundamentally flawed': publishing firms 'think their customer is the bookstore ... Publishers never built the infrastructure to respond to customers' (Auletta, 2010). The current landscape of change is shifting power back and forth between buyer and seller, with each party trying to estimate the value of e-books. Consumers are adapting to a new format and have yet to find a satisfactory price at which they receive value.

'Value' is decided by the market and not in the boardroom; since publishers do not sell directly to the reading public, they have little experience in establishing optimum book price points. Publishers have not experimented with price; instead, they have enclosed themselves into fixed pricing structures, which have accommodated retailers rather than allowed the industry to maximize profit by finding the optimum price. The e-book's arrival has seen the industry insist on repeating old habits: in late 2009 to early 2010, the listed price for most e-books in the US Amazon Kindle store was US$9.99. Although Amazon was paying in excess of this price to the publisher, it was prepared to use e-books as loss leaders to sell more devices and to gain market share. Amazon quickly found that if the same book was available in paper and digital form, 40 per cent of its customers ordered the digital version. Kindle customers, on average, buy 3.1 times as many books as they did twelve months ago (Auletta, 2010). Publishers were concerned that e-books were being devalued and that bricks-and-mortar bookstores would lose sales to the cheaper electronic outlets. Worried that customers would expect this level of discount forever, publishers felt compelled to act.

MacMillan was the first to suggest raising the Kindle price under an 'agency model'. Based on developments in the music industry, the agency model changed the publisher–retailer relationship to one of supplier and agent. Under the agreement, publishers would set the price and guarantee the agent a 30 per cent commission. Although this arrangement represented a loss of revenue in the short term for publishers, they believed it was the only way in which they could maintain their products' perceived value and retain industry profitability. If Amazon did not agree to these terms, then MacMillan would 'deeply window', or delay, the release of the Kindle edition so that electronic sales would not 'cannibalize' the more profitable hardback sales (Westerfeld, 2010).

However, in the digital marketplace, in which WoM on social networks is a huge driver of sales, this delay tactic was a risky strategy for MacMillan. HarperCollins had tried something similar in January 2010 with the release of the hardback edition of *Game Change* by John Heilemann and Mark Halperin. The first print run sold 70,000 units and sold out soon after its release on 11 January; since HarperCollins had made the decision to delay the release of the electronic edition until 23 February, there was a period of nearly three weeks during which bookstores had no copies in stock. This supply chain strategy, while trying to maximize the higher-priced sales from early adopters, actually managed to deprive the publishers of income as potential readers found other books to buy (Auletta, 2010).

Acutely aware of this example, Amazon took the drastic decision to de-list all of MacMillan's stock, both print and electronic, by removing the 'buy' buttons on its website; Amazon knew that MacMillan sells 14 per cent of its trade books and the vast majority of its e-books through the Amazon store (Auletta, 2010). Having built its business on comprehensiveness and without MacMillan's books, Amazon could no longer claim to be the world's best-stocked bookstore. Customers exercised their power in this situation and took their business to alternative sources of supply; switching costs were low and there was little inconvenience in shopping elsewhere. Fearing a wipe-out of its business model if other publishers were to follow MacMillan's lead, Amazon quickly recognized its suppliers' and buyers' power, and reluctantly agreed to MacMillan's terms, adopting the agency model of pricing. Books generate just under half of Amazon's revenue, of about US$25bn a year; the remainder is made up of other products such as DVDs and electrical goods (Auletta, 2010). According to the Big Six, Amazon treats publishers as dispensable and views books as a commodity to sell as cheaply as possible. All but one signed up to the agency model of pricing. Random House opted out in the belief that the agency model was developed in haste, and publishers were not taking the long-term view of the price situation. Interestingly, Apple's rise to supremacy in sale of content for the mobile reading device market and the growing use of Google Editions by independent retailers has made Random House review its policy on agency pricing, and saw it signing up to the new model in early 2011.

New disruptive threats

Publishers may look at disintermediation (that is, cutting out the middle man) as a future business strategy: networks and information will allow the buyer and the seller to interact directly, which would eliminate the intermediary bookstore and radically shorten the publishing value chain. Equally, authors could adopt this formula and cut the publisher out of the equation. These strategies made sense in other industries, such as aviation, in which most ticket purchases are now carried out online rather than through a travel agent. The logic of disintermediation suggests that book digitization puts the publishers' and booksellers' roles at risk.

Publishers also need to consider how to deliver value. Their core asset base is shifting from the IP that they control to the audiences they command. They are moving from selling content to selling audiences (Shatzkin and Cader, 2011). This fundamental shift in book publishing's value proposition is akin to media publishing. Innovation and new product development are creating publishing formats particularly suited to the digital marketplace. New entrants such as Diversion Books have emerged from established links in the value chain: in this case, literary agent Scott Waxman's recognition of the changing dynamic in the new digital middle ground opening up between corporate publishing and self-publishing. The capital-intensive demands of print distribution historically limited the self-publisher's access to market, and commercial publishers were not interested in self-published product because of its limited audience appeal. Diversion Books offers e-book publication and distribution, as well as print-on-demand (POD). Since Diversion Books operates an editorial and curatorial policy on the manuscripts that it accepts, Waxman describes Diversion's value proposition not as self-publishing, but as 'publishing support' (Deahl, 2010). Amazon and Barnes & Noble have also developed new self-publishing units. Significantly, Amazon has signed up mid-list crime author J. A. Konrath's latest novel *Shaken* under its new self-publishing imprint Encore. Konrath is best known for his crime series, featuring detective Jacqueline 'Jack' Daniels, published by Hyperion. His biggest sales were in 2004 for *Whiskey Sour*: 32,000 copies in mass-market paperback (Deahl, 2010). Under his deal with Encore, Konrath will be making an estimated 70 per cent return on the US$2.99 Amazon listed-price for the Kindle edition of *Shaken*. Amazon has committed to a paperback edition a year after the Kindle release—presumably when production costs have been recouped through digital sales.

The deal represents a realistic threat to the traditional Big Six value chain not in the form of Konrath's *Shaken*, which Konrath himself admits was rejected by the New York publishing houses, but in the implications for the royalty deals on offer from the Big Six. Shatzkin sees this deal as a 'significant jolt' to conventional publishing economics. Konrath's book sales will net him roughly US$2.10 a copy from the US$2.99 list price, which is a considerable increase on what he would have made on a US$9.99 e-book distributed under 'agency' terms and current Big Six royalty agreements. With the US$2.99 price point not being seen as barrier to sales and Konrath's brand already established, albeit with a niche of loyal crime-novel readers, the US$2.99 price will drive more sales than a US$9.99 price. To seriously threaten the Big Six, Encore merely needs to attract more high-profile authors with this increased author revenue share and their tied system of access to market through the Kindle reader on Amazon.

The market is launching e-readers and e-books with increasing regularity, which in turn spawns a whole new range of digital formats. Android smart phones are becoming the device of choice for Asian readers, with teenagers in Japan already known as *oyayubizoku* ('the thumb tribe'). These digital natives have grown up using mobile phones to communicate, shop, watch television, read books, and create content. Japanese media sharing sites, such as *Maho i-Land* ('Magic Island'), allow users to create and share their own novels in serialized format. These novels, posted over a period of days, create an intimate relationship between the writer and the reader, which is highlighted by the manner in which the reader receives the story daily to his or her phone, putting it on a par with a private text message or email. The distribution chain, although potentially limitless, is as immediate as it is intimate, with readers following an author's work as if they were friends. These mobile-phone novels are often subsequently published in print format: in 2007, four of the top five positions on the Japanese literary best-seller were originally serial mobile-phone posts (Goodyear, 2008). Suddenly, many of the Big Six value propositions appear somewhat redundant.

Changes in the business model

The *raison d'être* of any published document is content. Allen Noren, vice president of online and digital initiaves for O'Reilly Media, describes the current state of publishing flux as follows: 'The need for good content in all its forms is not diminishing. What is changing is the means of production and exchange, the business models and the rules of the game' (Clarke and Phillips, 1994: 72). With e-books and digital POD, the industry is returning full circle from a produce-and-sell model to the sell-and-produce model of the ancient hand-crafted manuscripts. All content goes through three simple processes: creation, transmission, and use. The digital revolution has removed the need for this process to be a linear transaction. Any user is now capable of becoming a creator or an intermediary, otherwise known as a 'prosumer'. Futurist Alvin Toffler predicted, in an age of mass production and standardization, the only way in which to continue to grow profit would be through a process of mass customization (Toffler, 1984). In a publishing context, mass customization is providing the means for the reader to produce and engage with the content.

The advantage of economy of scale is diminishing in its ability to provide a publisher with competitive advantage, and control of IP is more difficult in a digital medium. In the analogue era, technology and market forces ensured that illegal copies represented a significant capital investment by pirates. In the digital age, in which every copy can be classed as an original, even the term 'copyright' requires redefinition. Each link in the publishing, distribution, and value chain is required to re-examine its position. Authors and their agents are redefining publishing contracts; booksellers are engaging with publishers as agents rather than as retailers; wholesalers are becoming suppliers of POD services, with distributors carrying greater choice and less volume to bricks-and-mortar booksellers. The humble bookstore is consolidating into mass merchants (supermarkets), multinational chains, some independents, and large-scale online operations such as Amazon, iBooks, and Google. The specific needs fulfilled by books and the enduring staying power of the medium may suggest that e-books, similar to Lane's Penguin paperbacks, represent an addition to the range and spread of books. However, this new format is transforming the publishing value chain, with many links losing their potential to add value. The challenge for the Big Six is to devise a new business model to ensure their position in a market that is moving away from their core competency.

Case questions

1. How would you analyse the competitiveness of the publishing industry using Porter's Five Forces?

2. Outline the impact of the power shift between the major industry players: agents, authors, and retailers.

3. If you were the chief executive officer of a Big Six, how would you strive to reposition your brand in a digital marketplace?

References

Albnaese, A. R. 2010. The (Tim) O'Reilly Factor. ***Publishers Weekly***, 24 May. Available online at http://www.publishersweekly.com/pw/by-topic/industry-news/publisher-news/article/43267-the-tim-o-reilly-factor.html

Auletta, K. 2010. Publish or perish: can the iPad topple the Kindle, and save the book business? ***The New Yorker***, 26 April: 8–16.

Clarke, G. and Phillips, A. 1994. ***Inside Book Publishing, Vol. 4***. Abingdon: Routledge.

Deahl, R. 2010. Agents weigh the growth of alternate publishing options. ***Publisher's Weekly***, 24 May. Available online at http://www.publisher's weekly.com/pw/by-topic/digital/content-and-e-books/article/43276-agents-weigh-the-growth-of-alernate-publishing-options.html

Evans, J. 2011. Apple 2011: iPad sales hit 40 million. ***Computerworld.com***, 30 June. Available online at http://blogs.computerworld.com/18550/apple_2011_ipad_sales_hit_40_million

Feltes, N. 1986. ***Modes of Production of Victorian Novels.*** Chicago, IL: The University of Chicago Press.

Gabbot, A. 2011. Amazon and Waterstones report downloads eclipsing printed book sales. ***The Guardian***, 19 May. Available onlineathttp://www.guardian.co.uk/books/2011/may/19/amazon-waterstones-ebook-sales

Goodyear, D. 2008. I ♡ novels. ***The New Yorker***, 22 December. Available online at http://www.newyorker.com/reporting/2008/12/22/081222fa_fact_goodyear

James, S. 2009. Cheaper books come at a high cost to worthy literature. ***New York Times***, 27 November. Available online at http://www.nytimes.com/2009/11/27/us/27sfmetro.html?_r = 1

Jones, P. 2010. Pearson stays on top as world's largest book publisher. ***The Bookseller***, 21 June. Available online at http://www.thebookseller.com/news/121248-pearson-stays-on-top-as-worlds-largest-book-publisher.html

Jordison, S. 2010. Time to bring back the net book agreement? ***The Guardian***, 17 June. Available online at http://www.guardian.co.uk/books/booksblog/2010/jun/17/net-book-agreement-publishing

Kachka, B. 2008. The end. ***New York Magazine***, 14 September. Available online at http://nymag.com/news/media/50279/

Richtel, M. and Cain Miller, C. 2010. Of two minds about books. ***New York Times***, 1 September. Available online at http://www.nytimes.com/2010/09/02/technology/02couples.html?_r = 3&nl = todaysheadlines&emc = globaleua23

Shatzkin, M. and Cader, M. 2011. ***The Shatzkin Files.*** Available online at http://www.idealog.com/blog/

Toffler, A. 1984. ***The Third Wave.*** New York: Bantam.

Westerfeld, S. 2010. Amazon v MacMillan: free market fail. ***The Guardian***, 3 February. Available online at http://www.guardian.co.uk/commentisfree/2010/feb/03/amazon-macmillan-kindle-books?utm_source = feedburner&utm_medium = feed&utm_campaign = Feed%3A + theguardian%2Fbooks%2Frss + %28Books%29

Wilkinson, C. 2008. ***The Observer Book of Books.*** London: Observer Books.

Case 2 The City of London Local Policing Plan 2006–09

Modern-day policing is demanding, expensive, and unpredictable, as illustrated by the riots in London and other English cities during summer 2011. Police forces need to develop and support their officers to increasingly high levels. This involves investment in equipment, infrastructure, and ongoing professional development training. In the UK, police forces are subject to high levels of public scrutiny and are required to actively engage with the communities they serve in setting their strategic priorities. The City of London Local Policing Plan 2006–09 outlines the overarching aims of the force that is charged with policing one of the leading financial districts in the world. Events such as the royal wedding of Prince William and Kate Middleton in April 2011, the riots in London in August 2011, and the Olympic Games hosted in London in 2012 highlight the importance of having a police force supported by a clear strategic plan, which engages with and is relevant to multiple stakeholders, addressing issue of public safety and alleviating crime, through to issues of national security.

Our overarching aim

We will provide a high-quality police service in the City of London and work with the community, other organisations and agencies, to promote a safe, peaceful and crime-free environment.

Community cohesion, inclusion, consultation and working in partnership are consistent themes of this aim and directly support the Force's local policing priorities: Counter Terrorism; Economic Crime; Public Order; and Community Policing.

Our overarching aim and the individual priorities adopted by the Authority for policing the City, also supports and complements the City of London's vision for the City, which is [summarized in Figure L2.1].

Figure L2.1 City of London Police: vision

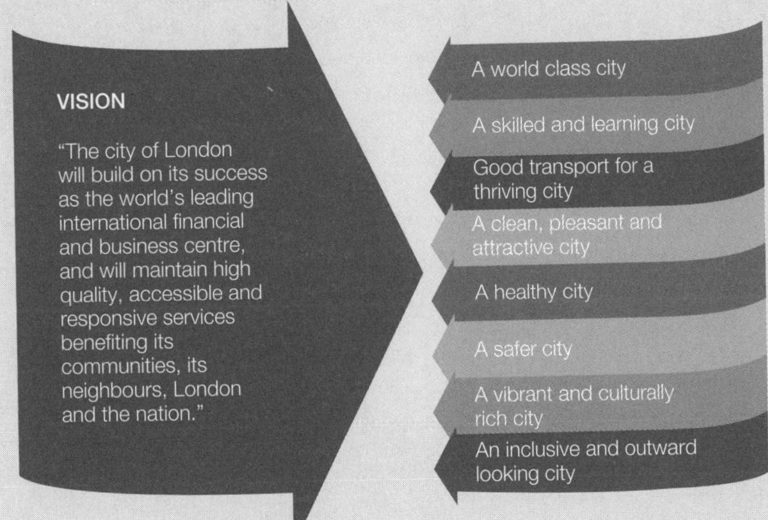

Our policing style

Table L2.1 Our policing style

Our values	Our management style
Be open, honest, sensitive, and polite to the public and our own staff	Consult with each other and our stakeholders, and communicate our intention
Acknowledge and value diversity	Empower and encourage staff to make decisions
Encourage equality of opportunity	Work in partnership with the Police Authority and City communities
Support participation and consultation	Be transparent in the way we make decisions
Encourage quality through continuous and lasting improvements	Be consistent in our approach to policy
Have pride in our service	Publicise our success and be honest about failure Maintain our position as one of the best urban police forces Recognise, praise, and reward success Value the diversity of our staff and the contribution different people make Focus policing priorities on community needs

Quality of service commitment

By November 2006, we will publish our Quality of Service Commitment to you. This will include detailed minimum standards and what you can expect from us in relation to the following:

- How easy is it to contact us
- How we will continue to provide you with a professional and high quality service
- What you can expect when you make an initial enquiry
- How you will be kept informed
- What you can expect from us if you are a victim of crime
- How you can engage with us, and influence policing in your area
- How complaints to us will be handled

The Force has not undergone any major re-structuring over the past year. The current structure [see Figure L2.2] is the most efficient way to support the policing priorities outlined within this Plan. Whilst the Force in its entirety supports all the priorities in different ways, having departments that specialise in Counter Terrorism and Economic Crime ensures that expertise and resources are readily available when needed. More detail about the work of the individual departments of the Force can be found in the Annual Report.

There is a danger that in any organisation with a defined departmental structure, 'silo management' could stifle co-operation and communication between the departments. To ensure that this cannot happen, we have introduced a structure in which each Department Head chairs a different committee [see Figure L2.3], and which in turn leads on a cross cutting functional area of the Force. This ensures lines of communication remain open between the Departments and promotes co-operation.

The 'Strategic' column [in Figure L2.4] shows those documents which both influence the Force's own strategic documents and which contribute to the Force's strategic direction; the Force's Control Strategy and Priorities fall out of these. The Priorities provide a focus for the Force's Divisions and Departments, as detailed in the upper half of the 'Tactical' column, in the delivery of policing in the City. The Committee structure, detailed in the lower half of the column, provides the framework within which the core, crosscutting functions of the Force are delivered.

The 'Operational' column [in Figure L2.4] shows how the Force's delivery performance is monitored and made accountable. At a national level, the Police Performance Assessment Framework is the structure whereby the Force's performance is compared with other forces, and is monitored by the Police Standards Unit, a division of the Home Office. Baseline Assessment is carried out throughout the year by HMIC to ensure forces are complying with all statutory provisions and guidance, and ensures that best practice is implemented and shared between forces.

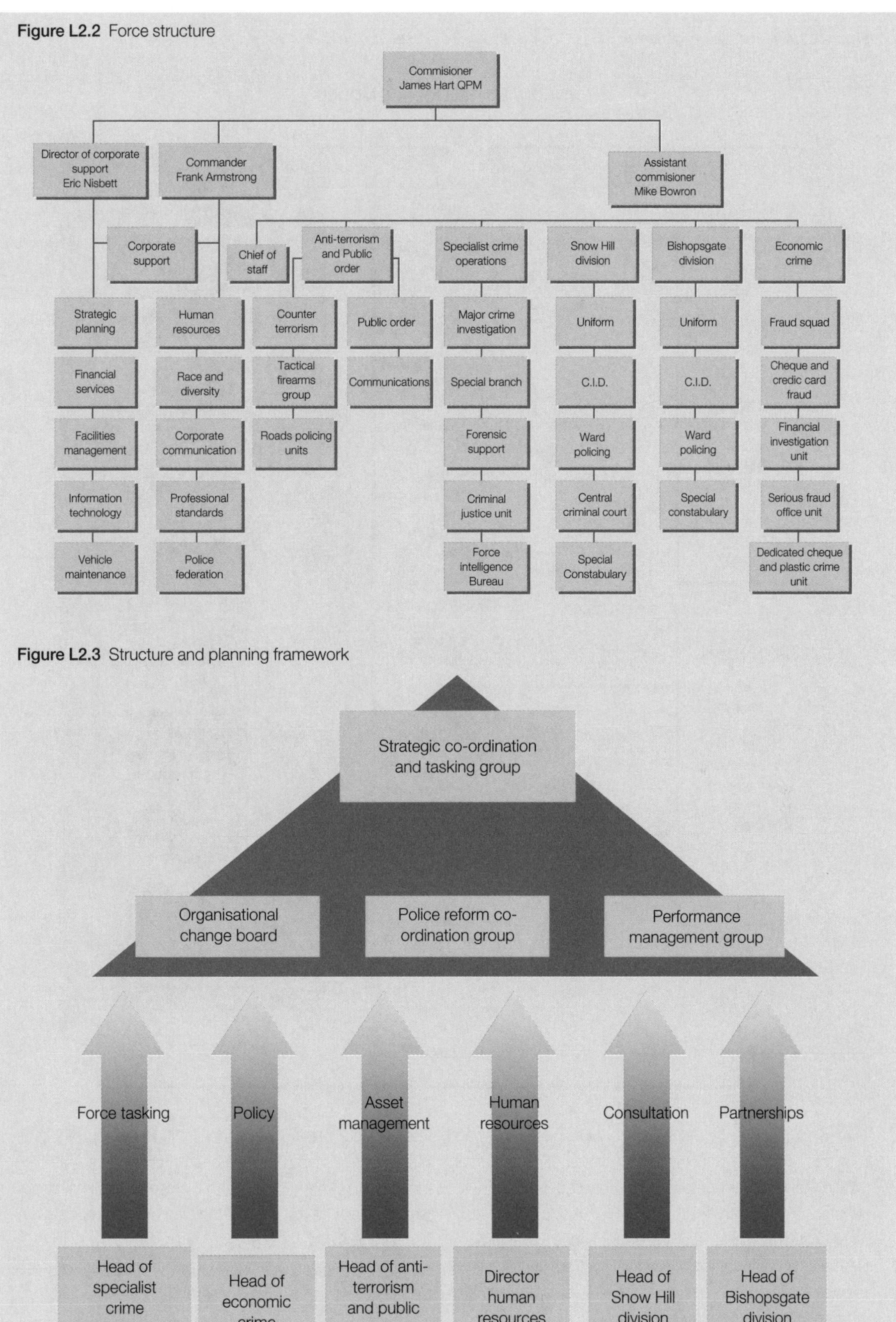

Figure L2.2 Force structure

Figure L2.3 Structure and planning framework

Figure L2.4 Force planning framework

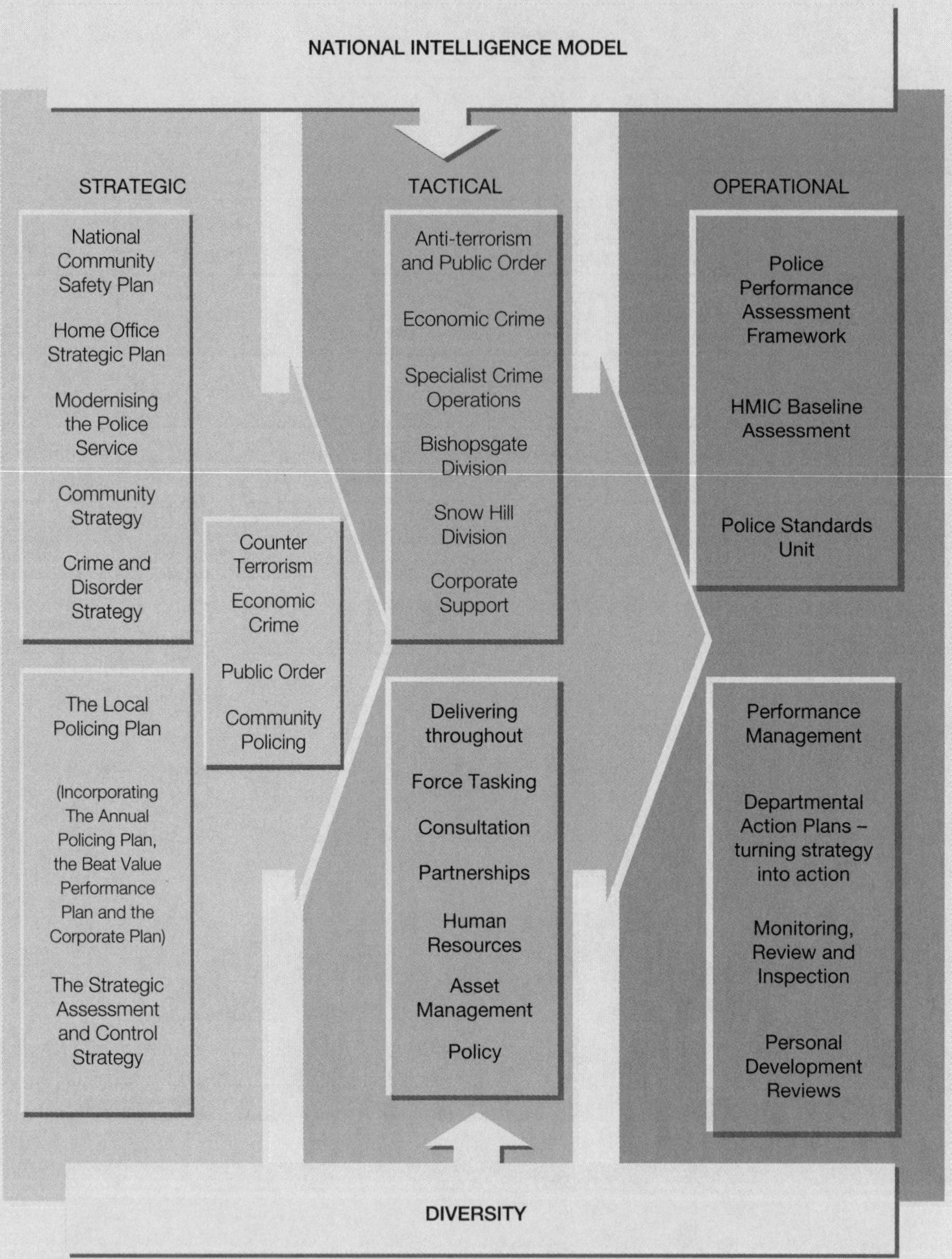

At a local level, the Performance Management Group monitors and drives Force performance. Departmental Action Plans provide details of how each department will develop and deliver its services over the coming year. Finally, on an individual level, the Performance Development Review is a competence-based system that identifies performance issues, and provides one of the means through which staff can be developed.

The National Intelligence Model (NIM) at the top of [Figure L2.4] illustrates how NIM has been integrated into all Force processes, from the strategic to the operational. In a similar way, Diversity, at the base of the diagram, underpins every aspect of policing.

Source: The extract is reproduced courtesy of the City of London Police and City of London Police Committee.

Case questions

1. Is the City of London Local Policing Plan a deliberate strategy as per Mintzberg's assumptions?

2. What are the limitations of this strategic plan?

3. How could the strategy process, as outlined in the plan, generate a more cohesive and bonded organizational culture that can react to external events?

4. Outline potential emergent strategies for the priority areas identified by this strategic plan.

Case 3 Cloon Keen Atelier: an SME's scent for a premium position

Dr Ann M. Torres, Lecturer in Marketing, National University of Ireland, Galway, with the generous cooperation of Cloon Keen Atelier

Introduction

Margaret Mangan, co-founder of Cloon Keen Atelier, always had a passion for scent; she believes scent forms the heart of her products. Cloon Keen develops high-quality products in which fragrance, design, and functionality are blended carefully to create a mood of authenticity and pleasure. The challenge for Cloon Keen, a small operator, is to pursue a strategy that reinforces its chosen market position as it develops new products and markets.

Place

In June 2002, Margaret Mangan and Julian Checkley established Cloon Keen Candles in Galway, Ireland, and began making their hand-poured candles. In the early days of their start-up, Margaret spent a number of weeks travelling around Ireland to find shops that are a good fit for Cloon Keen candles: primarily high-end gift and craft shops, as well as up-market interior and furniture shops with a modern flair. Margaret's sales drive was successful: she secured orders from over sixty retailers across the country. To its credit, Cloon Keen has retained about 90 per cent of its original retailers. Despite its achievement with retailers, the firm is shifting its focus toward developing its own retail initiatives, which are ultimately more profitable.

In August 2005, Cloon Keen Atelier opened its retail premises in the heart of Galway city at No. 3 Kirwin's Lane. In designing the shop interior, Mangan and Checkley took particular care in developing an atmosphere to reflect the brand. The shop has a warm, modern look that is clean and uncluttered, but not quite minimalist. An opening in Ceardlann Spiddal Craft Village in July 2006 was an opportunity for Cloon Keen to open another retail outlet in Spiddal, Co. Galway. Conveniently located 15 km from Galway city, Ceardlann is also a scenic tourist destination, where visitors can see Cloon Keen's master chandlers pour candles and purchase the finished product from the adjoining shop. Although the studio shop reflects aspects found in the Kirwan's Lane venue, the Ceardlann retail venue was tailored to showcase the craft studio and its environs. The effect is sufficiently similar that customers will recognize Cloon Keen's *look*, but suitably different to intrigue customers with variety.

Product

Cloon Keen employs the expertise of three perfumers to create fragrances exclusively for its range of thirty-five scented candles; it does not use generic scents. The quality of fragrance is especially important. Cloon Keen avails of authentic aromas, which do not smell harsh, bitter, or chemical. Superior-quality wax and cotton wicks are used to ensure optimum absorption and diffusion of fragrance. The craft for producing premium candles requires a highly scientific approach. For example, each scent requires a different wick to ensure that the candle burns effectively: spicy scents require a thicker cotton wick than sweet scents. Additionally, softer wax is more effective in scented candles, because harder wax poorly disperses fragrance. Cloon Keen assembles 300–400 units per week, which increases to 1,500–2,000 units per week during the busiest period between September and December (see Table L3.1).

Table L3.1 Cloon Keen Atelier's sales turnover for candles

Year	Wholesale unit sales	Cloon Keen's retail unit sales
2002	9,230	–
2003	22,189	–
2004	20,049	–
2005	22,313	–
2006	22,846	5,000
2007	23,900	7,500

Source: Cloon Keen Atelier

Cloon Keen produces two lines of premium-scented candles; these candles provide the maximum concentration of fragrance, with burning times of 50–65 hours. The gourmet collection, priced at €16.95 per unit, is packaged in tins and is a more playful, funky product. It comes in scents such as 'Basil and Lime Pesto', 'Crazy as Coconut', 'Just Baked Apple Pie', 'Fresh Linen', and 'Swedish Sauna'. Irish consumers generally prefer the softer floral scents in the gourmet range, such as 'Wild Irish Lavender' and 'Galway Honeysuckle'; these floral scents are among Cloon Keen's best-sellers. The spa collection of luxury candles, priced at €24.95 per unit, came into production in 2005. This line offers more sophisticated, subtle scents, such as 'Exotic Woods' and 'Fig Tree'; its sumptuous packaging reflects its more sensuous, indulgent qualities.

Another product venture was a line of Cloon Keen-branded soaps, creams, and lotions in two scents: 'Lavender' and 'Linden Blossom'. The prototypes were in development for two years and were put into production in spring 2008. Other products (such as shower gel, body scrub, bath oil, and shampoo and hair conditioner) were then added as a natural progression to the line. In time, the plan is to create a signature perfume to serve as the brand's hallmark.

Price

Cloon Keen's pricing strategy reflects its positioning as quality producer. However, its prices are more reasonable than products at the most exclusive price points. Margaret and Julian follow a policy of offering exceptionally high quality for the price that they charge and regularly monitor rivals' price levels to ensure that their products remain competitive. Cloon Keen's average sales per square foot is €430 and compares favourably with established competitors in the home interiors market, such as Yankee Candle, which earns average sales of €450 per square foot (Yankee Candle, 2007). With the launch of its personal care products, Cloon Keen expects average sales per square foot to increase to €650. Such a figure would enable Cloon Keen to compete more effectively with personal care competitors, such as The Body Shop, which has an average sales per square foot of €998 (Euromonitor, 2006b).

Brand and promotion

Margaret and Julian believe that Cloon Keen's brand values have greatly facilitated in generating word-of-mouth to build a loyal customer base. Cloon Keen's brand is based on offering accessible pricing for superior products and a unique store experience through its upscale store design, attentive customer service, and product presentation. Cloon Keen strives for authenticity in its branding approach. The combination of smell, touch, and sight in Cloon Keen's retail ambiance is meant to inspire and heighten the customer's experience. As a specialty retailer, Cloon Keen is being positioned as a worthy alternative to the high-priced designer brands offered in department stores.

Margaret and Julian avail of traditional media: primarily press features in quality news and fashion magazines, such as *Image*, *Irish Tatler*, and *The Gloss*. Select sponsorship, such as the launch of the new Irish Times building and the *Irish Tatler* magazine in October

2006, has been fruitful in generating awareness and opportunities for feature articles in the press. Merchandising within the shops, branding, and product packaging have been Cloon Keen's strongest forms of promotion. Margaret and Julian are interested in using electronic media to generate the opportunity for audience involvement. Interactivity can facilitate brand objectives and be a powerful tool for eliciting an immediate response from customers. Cloon Keen aims to build a website not only to serve as an online retail environment, but also as a platform to initiate a lifestyle blog, which would work as a source for stimulating viral marketing.

Customer profile

Even with its limited promotional efforts, Cloon Keen has garnered a loyal customer base, 80 per cent of whom are repeat customers. Cloon Keen's marketing efforts primarily target working women, aged 25–50, who have traditionally purchased premium scented candles and skincare products in department stores. They use these quality products on a daily basis as affordable luxuries. Cloon Keen's loyal customers are well travelled, have reasonably high levels of disposable income, are open to trying new products, and are increasingly seeking better pricing without sacrificing high quality and service. Cloon Keen's strategy has also been successful in attracting other consumers beyond its primary target, such as metrosexual males, who are attracted to the quality toiletries, as well as young teenage girls, who are attracted to Cloon Keen's gourmet range of candles.

Consumer trends in candles and home fragrances

Cloon Keen's candles primarily compete within the candles and home fragrances market. The notion of interior fragrances is said to originate in France, where the philosophy of a personal perfume is applied to home decor. The idea is to perfume the home to create an ambiance. Consumers who buy scented candles and home fragrances often do so to accent their home. An appealing fragrant environment is associated with mood enhancement; fragrance, or air care, has become the next big accessory for the home (Beck, 2004). For many consumers, scent is part of the style of their homes; it is a signature, just like their furnishings. Thus, the home *air space* has become a decorating space (Greene, 2006). Scented candles benefit from consumer perceptions of naturalness, at a time when consumers are increasingly put off by chemical-laden air-freshening products (Euromonitor, 2007c). The more successful air care products are those that position themselves as more natural alternatives in creating a harmonious environment rather than masking bad smells with powerful fragrances. Moreover, scented candles have the added advantage of being linked with aromatherapy.

Consumer trends in personal care products

Although traditional floral and spice notes will never go out of style, food-themed and food ingredient products are popular sellers. The popularity of food-scented products is encouraged 'in part that to an overstressed, emotionally frazzled society, food connotes comfort and safety'(La Ferla, 2001: 1). These scents are a salve: they make consumers feel cared for and energized. Food-based scents and ingredients in beauty products are also perceived as being healthier and coincide with the burgeoning consumer demand for an organic, eco-conscious style. *Conscious sensualists* are 'women who want to do the right thing for their health and the environment, but not at the cost of living well' (ibid) There is a substantial shift in the way in which consumers buy products; consumption is more reflective and concerned (Euromonitor, 2007b). An additional force catering for these conscious sensualists is a new aesthetic approach to product presentation. Although natural, organic, and eco-conscious products are in vogue, consumers also want to experience something exceedingly fine. Thus, conscious sensualists want products that are also stylish, edgy, and fashionable. Many working in the industry believe natural, organic, and eco-conscious products are an enduring trend (ibid). Organic Monitor estimates European sales of natural and organic personal care products to have increased by more than 20 per cent annually and exceeded €1bn in 2006 (Musselman, 2007). Increasingly, not only eco-conscious manufacturers, but also many other manufacturers throughout the industry are eschewing synthetic chemicals in favour of natural alternatives.

Personal care market in Ireland

Although the Irish grooming market is small, it is advancing rapidly. This highly fragmented market, which includes skin care and hair care products, colour cosmetics, and fragrances achieved annual sales nationwide in excess of €1.6bn in 2006 (Euromonitor, 2006a). In Ireland, the personal care sector was forecast to grow a further 25 per cent by 2010, reaching a value of over €2bn (ibid). Personal care products are a highly intimate purchase: consumers prefer to buy their own products than to receive them as gifts. In buying their toiletries, Irish consumers demonstrate a preference for expensive brands. A leading distribution channel for personal care products has been pharmacies, which accounted for 54.5 per cent of sales in 2005 (Datamonitor, 2006e). Specialist retailers and department stores account for only 18 per cent of personal care product sales (ibid). Retailers of personal care products are numerous and individually command a very small portion of the market. For example, Boots, with 13.7 per cent of the Irish personal care market, had the highest market share among retailers in 2005, while specialist retailers, such as The Body Shop and L'Occitane, held only 0.7 per cent and 0.4 per cent of the Irish market, respectively (Euromonitor, 2006a). Supermarkets accounted for 27.5 per cent of sales in 2005 and are becoming more important channels to access personal care products (Datamonitor, 2006e). Supermarket groups that operate as mixed retailers, such as Tesco and Dunnes, are increasing their presence within this market by offering a greater range of branded products, as well as by introducing their own lines of sophisticated private label brands (Euromonitor, 2007b).

Skin care market in Ireland

The Irish skin care sector was valued at €103m in 2009. Through its line of branded scented soaps, creams, and lotions, Cloon Keen is operating within the body care sub-sector of the skin care market. Products that have performed well in this sector are those that offer value-added benefits, such as intense moisturizing through the addition of natural ingredients such as ginko and shea butter, or the addition of vitamins and minerals to promote and maintain healthy skin, or which offer some cosmetic benefit through the addition of agents for self-tanning or toning and firming skin (Euromonitor, 2006d). These value-added innovations appeal to Irish consumers, who will pay premium prices for them.

Competitors

Cloon Keen also competes directly against specialty retailers of personal care products, including international chains such as The Body Shop and L'Occitane, as well as local specialty retailers, such as The Burren Perfumery. The number of specialty retail outlets selling personal care products has increased significantly in recent years, and the lack of significant barriers to entry may result in new competition, including possible imitators to Cloon Keen Atelier. Some of the firms that compete most closely with Cloon Keen are as listed in Table L3.2; all of these firms operate in *both* the candles and home fragrances markets, as well as the skin care sector of the personal care market. However, the firms are categorized according to the market in which each firm has a stronger presence.

Table L3.2 A selection of Cloon Keen's competitors

	Candles and home fragrances market	Skincare sector of the personal care market
International competitors	Sia; Yankee Candle	The Body Shop; Jo Malone; L'Occitane en Provence
Irish competitors	Fragrance Boutique	Burren Perfumery

The challenge ahead for Cloon Keen

The challenge for Cloon Keen Atelier is to find the optimum market position that provides a strategic advantage. Given the kinds of competitors identified, what are the strategic alternatives open to Margaret and Julian in developing their business? One consideration for Margaret and Julian is whether to open additional retail outlets and to what extent they should develop an online presence to pursue electronic sales. How could Cloon Keen leverage its competencies into competitive advantages to position itself successfully in the sectors that it pursues? For instance, Cloon Keen is known for its premium scented candles, but Margaret and Julian are starting to expand into the personal care market by creating their own line of skin care products and complementary accessories, such as body brushes, soap dishes, and soap dispensers. In outlining a specific strategic direction, Cloon Keen must consider the most effective and cost-efficient methods to target relevant audiences, which it believes is essential to establishing its lifestyle brand.

Appendix 1: Profiles of selected competitors

The Yankee Candle Company Inc. http://www.yankeecandle.com

In 1969, when he was 16 years old, Michael J. Kittredge made his first candle as a Christmas gift for his mother (Donovan, 2000)—'But a neighbour admired it so much he sold it to her [and] used the profits to buy wax and make more candles' (*Chain Store Age*, 1996: 70). By 1973, Kittredge's hobby had become a business, which went public in July 1999 (Donovan, 2000). Yankee Candle's headquarters is located in South Deerfield, MA, and has a staff of over 4,000 people. In the USA, Yankee Candle is one of the biggest manufacturers and distributors of scented candles (Yankee Candle, 2007). Through its global multi-channel network, Yankee Candle manages 420 retail venues, wholesales to 19,900 other retailers, and operates direct sales through its catalogues and websites (ibid). Yankee Candle offers over 2,900 types of candle in more than 200 scents, and also sells many other home fragrance products, such as electric fragrance dispensers, scented oils, room sprays, and automobile air fresheners, as well as home accessories (ibid). 'By building on its strong brand name, Yankee Candle has successfully extended its expertise and leadership in premium scented candles into fragranced products for the home and personal care' (*Worldwide Videotex*, 2003).

The SIA Group http://www.sia-homefashion.com

Sonja Ingegerd Andersson and Kjell Melander founded SIA in 1963 in Sweden. The SIA Group, an eminent brand within home decor, represents over €130m in annual sales, with distribution in thirty-nine countries throughout Europe, the USA, and Japan (Heinzen York, 2005). Its distribution channel includes fifty exclusive boutiques and over 330 points of sale through its network of partner stores (*Inside Franchising*, 2006). SIA creates two home fashion collections each year and offers 'over 3,000 items including accessories for the home, seasonal products, gifts and artificial flowers and plants. SIA has become a leader in European decorative home accessories, personal care and giftware' (Spring Fair Birmingham, 2007). Headquartered in Paris, the SIA Group employs approximately 300 people and the investment company Industri Kapital is its major shareholder.

Fragrance Boutique Ltd http://www.fragrance-boutique.com

Fragrance Boutique, established in 1987 by father-daughter team Roy and Sarah Donaldson, is located at the Malahide Marina in Co. Dublin, Ireland. Fragrance Boutique is a manufacturer of candle and scented giftware collections, including a range of soaps, candleholders, flower settings, body toiletries, and natural bath accessories (*Irish Independent*, 2000). Fragrance Boutique produces themed collections of decorated candles, pot pourri, and candle gift sets for the large retailers; 60 per cent of its turnover is attributed the export market (Shanley, 2005). The Millennium Candle was among the firm's most successful products. The design of the Millennium Candle, based on a fire-retardant transfer that burns more slowly than the wick, proved to be a hit with retailers and consumers (Devane, 2005). The Fragrance Boutique employs over thirty-five people, rising to seventy during the busy pre-Christmas period (*Irish Independent*, 2000). The John Hinde Group, a firm know for its postcards, bought Fragrance Boutique in 2003; the Donaldsons continue their involvement in the firm's operations and creative direction (Devane, 2005).

The Burren Perfumery http://www.burrenperfumery.com

The Burren Perfumery, located in Carron in the heart of the Burren, Co. Clare, is Ireland's first perfumery. Established almost forty years ago, Sadie Chowen and Edward Briggs are the perfumery's third owners (Kennedy, 2007). The perfumery's products are hand-produced using natural essences, plant extracts, and spring water. Given its location, the Burren Perfumery is also a tourist destination, where visitors can observe the traditional distillation and blending of perfumes (Drinkwater, 2006). Even though tour buses are not accommodated, visitors to the perfumery can number more than 300 a day in high summer (Amos, 2003). The Burren Perfumery produces cologne, perfume, shower gels, and soaps. Half of the perfumery's business is allocated to wholesaling to gift and craft shops in Ireland, Europe, and North America. The other half comes from people visiting the shop, and repeat business through mail order and online sales (Sweetman, 2002). In addition, the perfumery works with a number of hoteliers to provide aromatic toiletries for the guest bathrooms (ibid).

The Body Shop International plc. http://www.thebodyshop.com

In 1976, Anita Roddick established The Body Shop in Brighton, England. The Body Shop is known for its activism in social and environmental causes. The firm is generally credited with pioneering the use of natural ingredients in cosmetics and personal care products. The Body Shop frequently 'received more attention for its ethical stances, such as encouraging recycling, avoiding ingredients tested on animals, and forging partnerships with developing countries, than for its products' (Euromonitor, 2006b: 1). Another feature of The Body Shop's strategy was to rely on window displays, catalogues, and point-of-purchase product descriptions to attract and inform customers. In 1999, The Body Shop left manufacturing in favour of focusing on retailing (*International Directory*, 2002).

The Body Shop operates a broad, multi-channel network; there are more than 2,100 stores, two-thirds of which are franchised, across fifty-five countries (Anderson, 2007). Additionally, the firm sells products online, as well as through an in-home sales programme, The Body Shop at Home, in the UK, USA, Australia, and Germany in 2008 (Datamonitor, 2006d). The Body Shop has been differentiating itself by pursuing a *masstige* position, whereby it 'combines excellent [customer] service with a comprehensive range of naturally-inspired personal care products offering high performance benefits and competitive pricing' (ibid: 22). The Body Shop believes that product innovation successfully drives this strategy. Currently, the firm sells over 800 products, including skin care and sun protection products, hair care products, colour cosmetics, perfumes, home fragrances, men's grooming products, and accessories (ibid). In March 2006, The Body Shop was purchased for £625m and became a subsidiary of the L'Oréal Group (ibid). L'Oréal's skills in nurturing global brands should facilitate The Body Shop in communicating its unique position through higher profile methods to reach more consumers (Datamonitor, 2006c). However, consumers loyal to The Body Shop's ethical and natural branding may find it hard to believe that multinationals can trade ethically and that their products are as natural as those of smaller businesses (ibid).

Jo Malone Ltd http://www.jomalone.co.uk

The firm Jo Malone was established in London in 1983 by Jo Malone and her husband Gary. They founded the luxury skin care line with a single product: a nutmeg and ginger bath oil (*Soap, Perfumery & Cosmetics*, 1999). Jo Malone is known as a perfectionist perfumer, whose loyal customers appreciate her long-lasting fragrances. Today, the firm has well over 200 skin care, personal, and home fragrance products. The company's flagship store is in Sloane Street, London, but it has outlets in prestigious department stores in the USA, Canada, and Italy, as well as selling online and through catalogues (ibid).

Indeed, Jo Malone's select distribution strategy has meant that it has achieved high penetration in its online business to their overall total, because the products are so limited in the marketplace (*Fair Disclosure Wire*, 2007).

In October 1999, Estée Lauder acquired Jo Malone and, since its acquisition, has transformed Jo Malone into a top global brand by building heavily investing in its product range rather than promoting a personality (Datamonitor, 2006a). In every exclusive department store in which Jo Malone is sold, it ranks among the top five brands (*Fair Disclosure Wire*, 2007). In addition to its innovation in products, Jo Malone is innovative in its positioning strategy, whereby the firm is aggressively pursuing the gender-neutral fragrance market. Industry observers recognize that consumers are increasingly buying perfume that is neither conventionally masculine nor feminine (La Ferla, 2006). Through its neutral packaging (that is, chunky glass bottles with a white label with black lettering) and neutral sounding names (such as 'Lime Basil Mandarin' or 'Pomegranate Noir'), Jo Malone avoids being stereotyped. Moreover, the firm's marketing is distinct from how *unisex* scents were marketed in the late 1990s. Jo Malone circumvents the issue of gender by allowing customers to decide what is appropriate and by selling its products away from men's and women's fragrance counters (La Ferla, 2006). The gender-neutral approach has meant that Jo Malone has become highly desirable within the corporate gifting market (*Fair Disclosure Wire*, 2007).

L'Occitane en Provence http://www.loccitane.com

In 1976, Olivier Baussan founded L'Occitane, which is headquartered in Manosque in Haute Provence in the southeast of France. L'Occitane manufactures its own prestige line of skin care, hair care, men's grooming, and colour cosmetics products, as well as personal and home fragrance products, all of which are composed of essential oils and natural ingredients from the Provence area. Although the majority of Baussan' shares were bought by an investment fund, he still is L'Occitane's public ambassador: 'He promotes the company's perfume school for the blind in Provence and L'Occitane's Braille labelling' (Carvajal, 2006: 1). In a burgeoning personal care market, L'Occitane has abundant opportunity for expansion. Under the auspices of the investment fund over the last ten years, L'Occitane has grown from ten to over 750 shops across Europe, the USA, and Asia (Carvajal, 2006).

Within the natural cosmetics sector, L'Occitane inhabits a prestige position, but competitors such as The Body Shop are pursuing a more upscale position by remodelling stores and developing premium products for customers who appreciate personal luxuries (ibid). However, the mêlée is about perceived quality rather than price. Industry observers recognize that competitors at the premium end of the personal care market aim to achieve a distinct market position to minimize duplication (Cohen, 2000). Hence, even though customers of these high-end competitors may look similar according to demographics, they are quite distinct according to psychographics. Similarly to other prestige personal care firms, L'Occitane's customers are educated, well travelled, and wealthy. However, L'Occitane's customers have a psychographic profile within which they perceive themselves as worldly connoisseurs who appreciate quality products (ibid). L'Occitane is successful in attracting the male customer, who accounts for 30–35 per cent of its total customers (ibid). Its appeal to male customers is attributed to 'the store design, which evokes the French countryside rather than a boudoir, the vintage-style packaging, and the products themselves, which can be used by men or women' (ibid).

Case questions

1. What are Cloon Keen Atelier's strengths, weaknesses, opportunities, and threats (SWOT)? How well does Cloon Keen's business fit with current consumer and industry trends?

2. How should Margaret and Julian position Cloon Keen Atelier relative to those competitors that are most pertinent? After selecting Cloon Keen's market position, outline any changes required to implement such a positioning strategy.

3. Margaret and Julian believe that their hand-crafted premium scented candles provide Cloon Keen with a platform for entering other product markets and developing a lifestyle brand. What should Margaret and Julian do to establish Cloon Keen as a lifestyle brand?

4. How may Cloon Keen use electronic media to its best effect in promoting itself and its products? Moreover, how may electronic media facilitate or hinder Cloon Keen Atelier's communication efforts with its customers?

References

Amos, S. 2003. Scents of a place. *Country Living*, June. Available online at http://www.burrenperfumery.com/press/press-CL.html

Anderson, L. 2007. The Body Shop PLC. *Hoover's.* Available online at http://www.hoovers.com/body-shop/--ID__41856--/free-co-factsheet.xhtml

Beck, E. 2004. Under your nose: the next big thing? *The New York Times*, House & Home/Style Desk: 8.

Carey, B. 2007. Study uncovers memory aid: a scent during sleep. *New York Times*, 9 March. Available online at http://www.nytimes.com/2007/03/09/science/09sleep.html

Carvajal, D. 2006. Whiffs of combat waft over natural cosmetics. *New York Times*, 12 August, Business/Financial Desk: 1.

Chain Store Age. 1996. Retail entrepreneurs of the year. *Chain Store Age*, 72(12): 70.

Cohen, N. 2000. L'Occitane: an upscale flair in personal care. *Shopping Centers Today*. Available online at http://www.icsc.org/srch/sct/sct0500/07h.php

Datamonitor. 2006a. *Industry Comment: Market Watch—Personal Care*. London: Datamonitor Reports.

Datamonitor. 2006b. *Personal Care: Industry Update*. London: Datamonitor Reports.

Datamonitor. 2006c. *Market Watch: Global Round-up Industry Comment—Body Shop: Aiming to Satisfy a Worldwide Appetite for Natural Cosmetics*. London: Datamonitor Reports.

Datamonitor. 2006d. *The Body Shop International PLC: Company Profile*. London: Datamonitor Reports.

Datamonitor. 2006e. *Hand and Body Care in Ireland Industry Profile*. London: Datamonitor Reports.

Devane, M. 2005. Sweet smell of family success. *Sunday Business Post*, 21 August.

Donovan, D. 2000. Odor of magnitude. *Forbes*, 7 February, 165(3).

Drinkwater, C. 2006. Carol . . . meet Clare: Carol Drinkwater sets out to explore the glories of Co. Clare. *Mail on Sunday* (London): 94.

Euromonitor. 2003. *Boots on the Edge*. London: Euromonitor International.

Euromonitor. 2005. *Consumer Lifestyles: Ireland*. London: Euromonitor International.

Euromonitor. 2006a. *Country Market Insight: Retailing—Ireland*. London: Euromonitor International.

Euromonitor. 2006b. *The Body Shop International Plc: Retailing United Kingdom*. London: Euromonitor International.

Euromonitor. 2006c. *Home Furnishings: Ireland*. London: Euromonitor International.

Euromonitor. 2006d. *Skin Care: Ireland*. London: Euromonitor International.

Euromonitor. 2007a. *Hair Care: World*. London: Euromonitor International.

Euromonitor. 2007b. *Cosmetics and Toiletries: World*. London: Euromonitor International.

Euromonitor. 2007c. *Hair Care: Ireland*. London: Euromonitor International.

Fair Disclosure Wire. 2007. The Estée Lauder Companies Inc.'s Analyst and Investor Day: conference transcript. *Fair Disclosure Wire*, 6 March.

Greene, P. 2006. Accessorizing the air. *The New York Times*, 12 October, House & Home/Style Desk: 1.

Heinzen York, J. 2005. SIA selects one coast for U.S. distribution. *Home Accents Today*, 1 April. Available online at http://www.homeaccentstoday.com/article/CA525719.html

Inside Franchising. 2006. SIA home fashion franchise system profile. *Inside Franchising*.

International Directory of Company Histories. 2002. Encyclopaedia of company histories: about The Body Shop International Plc. *The Gale Group, Inc.* Available online at http://www.answers.com/topic/the-body-shop-international-plc

Irish Independent. 2000. Sweet smell of success for award finalist: the fragrance boutique. *Irish Independent*, 18 December, Business section.

Jacob, T. 2007. Olfaction: a tutorial on the sense of smell. Cardiff University, Wales. Available online at http://www.cf.ac.uk/biosi/staff/jacob/teaching/sensory/olfact1.html

Kennedy, E. 2007. Artisans: The Burren Perfumery. *The Sunday Business Post Online*, 11 February.

La Ferla, R. 2001. Beauty goes fruity. *New York Times*, 28 January, Style Desk Late: 1.

La Ferla, R. 2006. Scent of a person. *The New York Times*, 23 March, Section G: 1.

Lee, E. 2004. Marketers on the scent of increased retail sales: machines waft man-made smells—rotting corpse, skunk not popular. *Toronto Star* (Canada), Shopping: M04.

Musselman, F. 2007. Organics abound at Beautyworld. *Women's Wear Daily*, 9 February: 18.

O'Neill, M. 1991. Taming the frontier of the senses: using aroma to manipulate moods. *New York Times*, 27 November, Living Desk: 1.

Owens, M. 1994. Design credo: heed the nose. *New York Times*, 16 June, Section C: 1.

Porter, J., Craven, B., Khan, R., Chang, S., Kang, I., Judkewitz, B., Volpe, J., Settles, G., and Sobel, N. 2007. Mechanisms of scent-tracking in humans. *Nature Neuroscience*, 10(1): 27–29.

Shanley, V. 2005. Firing the ideas to shape the designs of tomorrow in a kiln of innovation: RDS showcase is a huge market stall for designers but it's a tough task to catch the eye of the international buyer. *The Sunday Tribune*, 23 January: 7.

Soap, Perfumery & Cosmetics. 1999. Lauder buys Malone. *Soap, Perfumery & Cosmetics*, November, 72(11): 3.

Spring Fair Birmingham. 2007. SIA (UK) Ltd. Available online at http://www.springfair.com

Sweetman, M. 2002. For one couple, making perfume in the isolated Burren is more a way of life than a business. *The Irish Times Magazine*, 27 July: 75.

Swengley, N. 1998. The woman with the perfect nose. *The Evening Standard*, 17 April: 26.

Van Toller, S. 1999. Assessing the impact of anosmia: a review of a questionnaire's findings. *Chemical Senses*, 24(6): 705–712.

Wilkie, M. 1995. Scent of a market. *American Demographics*, 17(8): 40–46.

Worldwide Videotex Update. 2003. Yankee Candle revamps e-commerce website. *Worldwide Videotex Update*, 22(8).

Wysong, P. 2002. Just a whiff of evidence for scents as therapy. *Toronto Star*, 20 December, Life: G02.

Yankee Candle Company Inc. 2007. The Yankee Candle Company Inc. *United States Securities and Exchange Commission, Form 8K Report*, 22 January.

Case 4 The Ethical Trading Initiative

Michael Blowfield, Teaching Fellow Organizational Behaviour, London Business School

Introducing the Ethical Trading Initiative (ETI)

Throughout the 1990s, supermarkets and major brands were under repeat criticism because of the allegedly poor labour standards in their supply chains. From the worldwide campaign against Nike, which started in 1990, to Christian Aid's Change at the Check-out report in 1997, companies that had benefited from the global supply chain revolution found themselves under assault from workers, non-governmental organizations (NGOs), trade unions, and consumers for alleged practices such as low wages, use of child labour, hazardous working conditions, slavery, and forced overtime.

The Ethical Trading Initiative (ETI; http://www.ethicaltrade.org) was established in 1998 as a response to this mounting criticism. The supply chains themselves were a product of economic globalization, which had created the conditions whereby famous-name companies could source from newly built factories in developing countries, from Indonesia, to the Dominican Republic, to Bangladesh. Although these companies had little or no manufacturing capacity themselves, they exercised considerable control over their suppliers, promising access to Western consumer markets in return for meeting stringent design, quality, delivery, and cost specifications. The global supply chain became quintessential to competitiveness for industries such as garments, footwear, agriculture, and electronic goods. It also represented a new model of governance that determined how material and human resources are allocated and the flow within the chain.

One increasingly observed feature of these chains was the labour conditions in the factories, fields, and packhouses in developing countries. Trade unions, NGOs, and the media all reported instances of low wages, excessively long hours, physical abuse, discrimination, child labour, and forced labour. Moreover, the same information technology on which companies relied to manage the chains efficiently was used by civil society organizations to disseminate news about abuses in what became global campaigns. The initial response of many multinational firms was that they did not own the factories and could not exercise control over their suppliers. Yet the success of the global supply chain model was predicated upon influence and control, and as allegations of human rights abuses increased, companies dependent on the reputation of their brands found it increasingly uncomfortable to deny responsibility and began to explore ways of managing labour conditions among their supply base, so that they did not contravene either international labour and human rights standards, or the ethical values of influential sections of Western society.

ETI was not the first attempt to tackle these issues: individual companies such as Levi Strauss and independent organizations such as Social Accountability International (http://www.sai-intl.org) had introduced codes of labour practice intended to be mandatory for manufacturers. What marked ETI out were two things: first, rather than introduce another labour standard into what was becoming a crowded governance space, its goal was to help companies to become better at monitoring labour conditions in their supply chains; secondly, rather than encouraging companies to seek competitive advantage from having the best labour conditions, it created a partnership in which not only companies, but also NGOs and trade unions could figure out together the most effective way of monitoring and improving the conditions of workers and their families in global supply chains.

The features of ETI

ETI is an alliance of companies, NGOs, and trade unions committed to identifying and promoting good practice in the implementation of codes of labour practice. As of 2011, it had seventy-two corporate members (including companies such as Gap Inc., Primark, Tesco, and WHSmith), fifteen NGOs, and three trade union federations representing 160 million workers worldwide. It is funded by companies and the British government's Department for International Development (DfID). Corporate membership is restricted to retailers and suppliers who source and/or sell food, clothing, and other products in UK markets, although the multi-stakeholder partnership model pioneered by ETI is accredited with inspiring the creation of similar initiatives in Scandinavia, and countries such as Kenya, South Africa, and Sri Lanka.

To understand ETI as a multi-stakeholder approach to supply chain governance, there are two features that are most important to understand:

- the Base Code of human rights and labour conditions; and
- the tripartite approach to governance and learning.

The ETI Base Code

ETI has a Base Code of labour practice and human rights, the provisions of which largely reflect internationally agreed declarations and conventions of the International Labour Organization (ILO) and the United Nations, and are therefore similar to those found in standards such as SA8000 and the Fair Labour Association (see Table L4.1). Corporate members of the ETI alliance commit to adopting the provisions of the Base Code as a minimum standard of labour practice in their supply chains. However, ETI is not an accreditation body that goes out to measure its members' performance against the Base Code; instead, the Code is used as the basis for companies to report to the ETI membership annually to show how well they are performing against the nine provisions of the Code. Therefore, although member companies commit to increasing the proportion of their supply chains to which the Code is applied over time, they are not expected to impose the Code everywhere from day one.

Consequently, while companies report on performance against the provisions of the Base Code, they also report on their progress in building the capacity to use the Code as a basis for supply chain management. This involves reporting against six criteria:

a. demonstrating commitment;

b. developing a credible monitoring system;

c. building support and skills within the company and its supply base;

d. ensuring that suppliers take action to improve workers' conditions; and

e. integrating ethical trade into the company's core business operations.

Tripartite approach to governance and learning

The Base Code informs, but does not explain, ETI's tripartite multi-stakeholder approach comprising business, trade unions, and NGOs. The tripartite alliance is reflected in the structure of the ETI board, and every pilot project (which, for a long time, were the main instruments for learning how to monitor supply chains) requires the three groups of the alliance to work together. This structure does not reflect the funding, which is primarily a mix of a grant from the UK's DfID (which has only observer status on the board), and annual subscriptions from corporate members on a sliding scale from £30,000 to £2,000, depending on size. Moreover, rather than have a large secretariat acting as an executive on behalf of the membership, members themselves take responsibility for much of the work (for example, pilots, working groups, guidance on monitoring, etc.).

Therefore, the concept of a multi-stakeholder alliance is not only a principle, it is also central to the day-to-day functioning of ETI, which is owned by its members. The board oversees the initiative's work and is chosen from the membership to represent the tripartite composition of the alliance. It is chaired by someone from outside of the membership and takes an active role in overseeing ETI's direction. In the debate about alternative approaches to global governance, there are divergent views about this type of alliance. For example, there are criticisms that such alliances can become dominated by one group or another (Stichele and Pennartz, 1996; Zeldenrust and Ascoly, 1998), and that they are difficult to manage and can be cumbersome. More optimistically, they might signify that companies, trade unions, and NGOs recognize that there are no off-the-peg solutions to the challenges of securing international labour standards for a globally dispersed workforce, and that ETI's advantage is to be able to offer a place to experiment, to fail as well as to succeed, and to avoid the spotlight of unrealistic expectation each time one tries to take a forward step (Blowfield, 2002).

Effectiveness of the ETI approach

NGOs, trade unions, and business each have their own criteria for membership, and ETI has been praised for demonstrating 'some considerable degree of sophistication and maturity as an organisation in the way it has handled a range of difficult membership issues as a whole', although there have been concerns that

Table L4.1 Provisions and criteria of the ETI Base Code

Heading	Criteria
Forced labour	• There is no forced, bonded or involuntary prison labour. • Workers are not required to lodge 'deposits' or their identity papers with their employer, and are free to leave their employer after reasonable notice.
Freedom of association/right to collective bargaining	• Workers, without distinction, have the right to join or form trade unions of their own choosing and to bargain collectively. • The employer adopts an open attitude towards the activities of trade unions and their organizational activities. • Workers representatives are not discriminated against and have access to carry out their representative functions in the workplace. • Where the right to freedom of association and collective bargaining is restricted under law, the employer facilitates, and does not hinder, the development of parallel means for independent and free association and bargaining.
Worker health and safety	• A safe and hygienic working environment shall be provided, bearing in mind the prevailing knowledge of the industry and of any specific hazards. Adequate steps shall be taken to prevent accidents and injury to health arising out of, associated with, or occurring in the course of work, by minimizing, so far as is reasonably practicable, the causes of hazards inherent in the working environment. • Workers shall receive regular and recorded health and safety training, and such training shall be repeated for new or reassigned workers. • Access to clean toilet facilities and to potable water, and, if appropriate, sanitary facilities for food storage shall be provided. • Accommodation, where provided, shall be clean, safe, and meet the basic needs of the workers. • The company observing the Code shall assign responsibility for health and safety to a senior management representative.
Child labour	• There shall be no new recruitment of child labour. • Companies shall develop or participate in and contribute to policies and programmes that provide for the transition of any child found to be performing child labour to enable her or him to attend and remain in quality education until no longer a child; 'child' and 'child labour' being defined in the appendices. • Children and young persons under the age of 18 shall not be employed at night or in hazardous conditions. • These policies and procedures shall conform to the provisions of the relevant ILO standards.
Living wages	• Wages and benefits paid for a standard working week meet, at a minimum, national legal standards or industry benchmark standards, whichever is higher. In any event, wages should always be enough to meet basic needs and to provide some discretionary income. • All workers shall be provided with written and understandable information about their employment conditions in respect to wages before they enter employment and about the particulars of their wages for the pay period concerned each time that they are paid. • Deductions from wages as a disciplinary measure shall not be permitted nor shall any deductions from wages not provided for by national law be permitted without the expressed permission of the worker concerned. All disciplinary measures should be recorded.
Non-discrimination	• There is no discrimination in hiring, compensation, access to training, promotion, termination, or retirement based on race, caste, national origin, religion, age, disability, gender, marital status, sexual orientation, union membership, or political affiliation.
Working hours	• Working hours comply with national laws and benchmark industry standards, whichever affords greater protection. • In any event, workers shall not on a regular basis be required to work in excess of 48 hours per week and shall be provided with at least one day off for every seven-day period on average. Overtime shall be voluntary, shall not exceed 12 hours per week, shall not be demanded on a regular basis, and shall always be compensated at a premium rate.
Security of employment	• To every extent possible, work performed must be on the basis of recognized employment relationship established through national law and practice. • Obligations to employees under labour or social security laws and regulations arising from the regular employment relationship shall not be avoided through the use of labour-only contracting, subcontracting, or home-working arrangements, or through apprenticeship schemes under which there is no real intent to impart skills or provide regular employment, nor shall any such obligations be avoided through the excessive use of fixed-term contracts of employment.
Harsh or inhumane treatment	• Physical abuse or discipline, the threat of physical abuse, sexual or other harassment and verbal abuse or other forms of intimidation shall be prohibited.

membership criteria are not always clear (Ladbury *et al.*, 2000: 4), leading to questions about why particular companies are entitled to join ETI while others' membership applications have been declined, and why some companies that come close to membership requirements refuse to join because they do not want to take on all of the membership criteria (ibid: 9). In 2001, for example, Waitrose and Nestlé sought membership, and claimed that they met the criteria applied to other companies. However, for various reasons, Waitrose's acceptance was deferred for several years until its parent company, John Lewis, was accepted. Nestlé has still not become a member. As Ladbury *et al.* (2000) observe, unwritten criteria for membership have emerged, a key one of which relates to the perceived ability of the applying company to gain the trust of all members of the tripartite alliance.

> Although there is a huge strength in ETI being an organisation built on trust and co-operation between companies, unions and NGOs it is almost inevitable that there will be some companies who will fail to engender that trust and confidence. Some corporate membership applications have been declined on this basis, even though the companies in question were acceptable on other grounds.
>
> (Ladbury *et al.*, 2000: 9)

One of the early expectations that advocates of improved labour conditions and of voluntary regulation of global supply chains had of ETI was that it would provide evidence of the benefits that such approaches can bring to workers and their communities. However, this has not proved easy. Initially, the benefits of the tripartite alliance were most apparent in the learning and the changes in member behaviour rather than in working conditions. Although there was evidence on a case-by-case basis of suppliers improving their performance in areas intended to benefit workers, overall it proved difficult to find data to answer questions such as how many workers were working fewer hours, or how many fewer women were being sexually harassed because of ETI. Furthermore, little was known about the inter-relationships between different criteria, such as whether any reduction in total hours was matched by increases in pay so that net incomes did not decline.

It is not necessarily that relevant data were unavailable, but the annual reports by member companies about what their monitoring revealed about labour practices in their supply chains was not (and still is not) made available beyond the membership. Indeed, there has often been a protracted negotiation process about what is made available amongst the membership. What companies have been more willing to disclose are changes in company behaviour that provide an indication that they are tackling labour issues. For example, early ETI annual reports highlighted that the percentage of the supply base being monitored by ETI's members grew rapidly. In 1999, members monitored over 1,500 suppliers, or 20 per cent of their supply base; in 2000, that number had grown to over 6,700, or 64 per cent. By 2006, that it had reached 35,000. Perhaps as significantly, companies were now recognizing that there many different tiers of supplier, and the number of second-tier suppliers monitored rose from 2,657 in 2005 to 12,211 a year later.

This monitoring takes various forms, but typically includes a mix of desk-based questionnaires leading to factory visits by the buyer or independent auditors. ETI's pilot projects, sharing of individual company experience through, for example, the joint-authored ETI handbook, and joint projects with other labour rights initiatives have together helped to identify what monitoring systems work best, and training in effective monitoring is one of the areas of performance that ETI has recently started to measure.

To a degree, enhanced capacity amongst corporate members and within their supply chains is held to be a proxy for actual improvements in labour conditions, at least in the short term. However, ETI recognized that assumptions about a causal relationship between company commitment and the benefits for workers needed to be substantiated, and in 2002 began to commission an impact assessment study, the results of which were first released in 2006. The study, carried out by the Institute of Development Studies at the University of Sussex, is amongst the first in-depth empirical study of how voluntary labour codes affect the lives of workers and their communities (Barrientos and Smith, 2006; 2007). At one level, it shows the difficulty of attributing causality to a particular company or initiative, because where there were positive or negative changes, the researchers found there to be multiple possible causes. But methodological difficulties aside, the assessment offers unique insight into how voluntary initiatives affect their intended beneficiaries.

The assessment examined the impact of company codes used by ETI's corporate members. These codes equal or exceed the provisions of the ETI Base Code. Findings on the impact of the codes at the worker level were mixed, as can be seen from the comparison of workplaces in three countries (Table L4.2).

In Table L4.2, 'major' refers to widespread and significant change found across some or all workplaces; 'minor' indicates that changes were reported at a few sites, or had minimal impact on workers. Thus, reductions in working hours or the introduction of health and safety

Table L4.2 Summary of impacts by the ETI Base Code principle at country study supply sites

Base Code principle	South Africa (Six worksites)		Vietnam (Six worksites)		India (Six worksites)	
	Management	**Workers**	**Management**	**Workers**	**Management**	**Workers**
Freedom of employment	None	None	None	None	None	None
Freedom of association	None	None	None	Minor	None	None
Health and safety	Minor	Minor	Major	Major	Major	Major
Child labour	Minor*	Minor*	Minor*	Minor	Minor	None
Living wage	Minor	None	Minor	Minor	Minor	Minor
Working hours	None	None	Major	Major*	Minor	Minor*
Discrimination	Minor	None	Minor	Minor	Minor	None
Regular employment	None	None	Minor	None	Minor	Minor
Harsh treatment	Minor	None	None	None	Minor	Minor

* An asterisk marks impacts that were considered negative by some respondents
Source: Adapted from Barrientos and Smith (2007)

precautions at over half the sites constitutes a major change, whereas the introduction of age documentation or the correct payment of annual leave observed at a few sites is a minor change. In some instances, both major and minor changes were viewed as negative by at least some workers (for example, because a reduction in working hours resulted in a decrease in take-home pay). 'None' indicates that no change was reported.

The assessment reveals that there are demonstrable impacts relating to certain aspects of the ETI Base Code, notably under the provisions on health and safety, and on legal employment entitlements such as the minimum wage, working hours, and deductions for employment benefits such as health insurance and pensions. At most workplaces, workers' physical and social well-being has been enhanced through health and safety improvements (such as information and training, fire safety, safety guards, protective equipment, improved toilets and drinking water) and reductions in working hours. Other improvements may have already occurred: for example, the assessment did not discover any child labour. Some improvements were limited to certain types of worker, so that, for example, there was evidence of improvement in the treatment of permanent and regular workers, but contract labour was still poorly treated in most countries.

The benefits were not limited to workers. For example, workers no longer took home their work clothes or touched their children after handling chemicals. Some permanent workers said that their houses were cleaner because of seeing improved factory conditions. Reduced working hours meant that workers had more time for relaxation and interaction with their families, and (especially for women) for domestic responsibilities. In addition to enhancing workers' sense of well-being, these changes may reduce their vulnerability to long-term health and social problems, with links to future income prospects.

However, there were other areas in which the impact was either mixed or unclear. This is especially true when considering process rights (that is, intrinsic principles of social justice that, under ILO Conventions, are what enable workers to uphold their rights). For example, codes have not led to wage increases through collective bargaining agreements, which, along with freedom of association, are considered a major process right. Without process rights, advocates argue, other changes do not follow. Codes have not led to a substantial increase in income in terms of guaranteeing a living wage, for example. Indeed, wages do not appear to have improved as a demonstrable result of the codes, and there are workplaces in which codes have led to a reduction in working hours and a resultant decrease in take-home pay (although this is not necessarily considered a negative outcome if there are other benefits, such as more leisure time).

In some areas in which codes may have had a positive impact, the benefits are limited to certain types of worker. For example, if suppliers pay into state insurance and pension schemes, workers' vulnerability to poverty in the event of childbirth, illness, or old age is reduced, but these types of employment benefit are often limited to permanent workers who constitute only a part of the workforce. This is also a reminder that lack of secure employment greatly increases workers' vulnerability to poverty, making the ETI Base Code's provision on security of employment an important element in improving worker well-being. However, this is not an area in which much impact is observed, and the assessment found anecdotal evidence that shortening lead times by ETI member companies had increased usage of temporary and contract labour in order to fulfil orders.

In addition to the lack of evidence for improvements relating to process rights, codes have had no impact on underlying patterns of employment based on gender, ethnicity, caste, and religion, although there is evidence of a connection to certain changes in relation to discrimination in some locations (such as employment benefits to women, access to training and promotion). There is an emergent awareness in ETI that these and other apparently intractable issues ultimately depend on achieving a balance between company power over suppliers, and empowerment of workers to have greater control over their lives. Hence, it is not enough to enforce codes: rather, there is a parallel need to help to build the capacity of workers and other local agents to implement a sustainable system of monitoring, enforcement, and remediation.

Along with building local-level capacity, ETI's membership has begun to recognize that the codes do not benefit all categories of worker, or get implemented equally in all types of workplace. Migrant labour, for example, is a common feature of the factories from which ETI's members source, and in most countries third-party contractors supply such workers on a highly flexible basis. Yet it is permanent and regular workers, not casual and migrant workers, who are more likely to benefit from code implementation. Addressing the conditions of these 'invisible' workers is therefore a significant challenge in the implementation of codes, not least because commercial pressures from buyers are intensifying their use.

Future challenges

As we obtain a fuller picture of ETI and related approaches using global supply chains to improve labour conditions, the lessons are starting to find their way into company behaviour towards suppliers. However, the suspicion remains that the success of these chains ultimately depends on the most powerful elements of the chain behaving in ways that serve the needs of shareholders and consumers, but not the majority of workers. While ETI continues to wrestle with its original challenge of helping workers and communities through the use of codes of conduct, it increasingly finds itself dealing as well with the wider characteristics of the supply chain, such as buyers' desire to drive down prices and to move to where costs are most competitive. Because the case for improved labour standards as an essential component of competitive advantage is not yet entirely convincing, ETI's members find themselves looking at intermediate steps. For example, faced with the reality that suppliers fear that companies will relocate in pursuit of lower costs, ETI's members have identified a few actions companies can take to reassure them, such as:

a. rewarding suppliers with good labour practices by continuing to do business with them;

b. collaborating with other sectors of society in the producing country to find alternatives to relocation if improved labour conditions seem to be driving up prices;

f. factoring the consequences for the country and workers into decisions about relocation;

g. building mitigation measures into their entry and exit strategies for each country; and

h. building mitigation measures into their contracts with suppliers.

Such ideas, along with thinking about how to better serve non-permanent labour and smaller producers, gain credibility when coming from ETI because even if it has not brought the black-and-white benefits for which some might have hoped, it is able to demonstrate a contribution to an area of continued corporate concern. Over ten years after it was established, ETI represents an interesting example of how a corporate responsibility initiative can influence companies and change their practices in different ways. We have seen that ETI's impact on workers is not straightforward, but it can claim to have had other types of impact on company behaviour, including:

a. improving its member organizations' and others' knowledge about how to monitor labour conditions amongst suppliers;

f. improving their knowledge about what to monitor and what the elements are of the chains;

g. raising member companies' awareness of labour rights issues;

h. influencing legislation;

i. increasing the overall level of monitoring of overseas' suppliers; and

j. building the capacity of companies and others to implement voluntary labour standards.

Case questions

1. What features of the multi-stakeholder approach distinguish it from other ways of protecting labour rights?

2. This type of approach is often cited as an example of voluntary self-regulation. In what way is it voluntary? Do you believe that it is genuinely voluntary?

3. What are the advantages and disadvantages of the multi-stakeholder approach compared to company or industry-specific initiatives to regulate supply chains?

4. What can be done to improve the impact of ETI for its intended beneficiaries?

References

Barrientos, S. and Smith, S. 2006. *The ETI Code of Labour Practice: Do Workers Really Benefit?* Brighton: Institute of Development Studies.

Barrientos, S. and Smith, S. 2007. Do workers benefit from ethical trade? Assessing codes of labour practice in global production systems. *Third World Quarterly*, 28(4): 713–729.

Blowfield, M. E. 2002. ETI: a multi-stakeholder approach. In R. O. Jenkins, R. Pearson, and G. Seyfang (eds) *Corporate Responsibility and Ethical Trade: Codes of Conduct in the Global Economy*. London: Earthscan.

Ladbury, S., Young, G., and Gibbons, S. 2000. *Mid-term Review: A Review of the Progress of the Ethical Trading Initiative for the UK Department of International Development*. Unpublished report. London: Department for International Development.

Stichele, M. V. and Pennartz, P. 1996. *Making it Our Business: European NGO Campaigns on Transnational Corporations*. London: Catholic Institute for International Relations.

Zeldenrust, I. and Ascoly, N. 1998. *Codes of Conduct for Transnational Corporations: An Overview*. Tilburg: International Restructuring in Industries and Services.

Case 5 Leadership: the Indra Nooyi way

Ranjani Jagannathan and Vivek Gupta, ICRM Center for Management Research

Leadership is hard to define and good leadership even harder. But if you can get people to follow you to the ends of the earth, you are a great leader. As a leader, I am tough on myself and I raise the standard for everybody; however, I am very caring because I want people to excel at what they are doing so that they can aspire to be me in the future.[1]

Indra Nooyi in a CNBC interview, June 2008

As someone who has always aspired to build a company committed to its people and to the world, I admire her determination to achieve sustainability at an established company like PepsiCo. And I believe that all socially responsible companies could learn from Indra Nooyi's style of leadership.[2]

Howard Schultz, President and CEO of Starbucks Coffee Company,[3] on presenting Nooyi the 2008 *Time 100 award*

Introduction

Indra Krishnamurthy Nooyi (Nooyi) became the first woman chief executive officer (CEO) of PepsiCo Incorporated (PepsiCo)[4] in 2006 at the age of 50. She was listed among *Time* Magazine's World's 100 Most Influential People in 2008.[5] In a poll conducted by *Forbes* Magazine for the World's 100 Most Powerful Women in 2008, she was ranked #3. In *Fortune* Magazine's annual ranking of America's leading business women titled *50 Most Powerful Women in Business*,[6] she was ranked #1 for three successive years in 2006, 2007, and 2008. (Refer to [Table L5.2] for awards and recognitions received by Nooyi.)

Nooyi joined PepsiCo as senior vice president (SVP), Strategic Planning, in 1994. As SVP, she directed the company's global strategy. She initiated and mapped out a number of PepsiCo's strategic decisions, including the spinning off of its restaurant business, the merger with Quaker Oats Company, an American food conglomerate, and the acquisition of Tropicana, among other contracts.

In 2000, Nooyi was promoted as PepsiCo's chief financial officer (CFO). She was also provided a seat on the board of directors and assigned the additional role of president with associated responsibilities for PepsiCo's corporate functions, including finance, strategy, business-process optimization, and information technology.[7]

In 2006, Nooyi became the fifth CEO of PepsiCo. As CEO, she continued to steer PepsiCo based on the vision of 'Performance with purpose'. She implemented a number of measures to improve the sustainability of the company's operations and image by focusing on improvements in the health implications of PepsiCo products. Measures such as removing trans fats from PepsiCo snacks, product innovation in the Quaker Oats brand to come out with a range of consumer-perceived healthy snacks, categorization of its snacks into three categories named '*fun for you*', '*good for you*', and '*better for you*' were undertaken under her leadership.

Nooyi's strategic measures to tackle the slow-down in the beverages and snack food industry included a productivity improvement programme, the benefits of which were expected to the tune of US$1.2bn over the next three years beginning 2009.[8] Other measures under her leadership included aggressive expansion into the

[1] Simon Hobbs, 'Indra Nooyi: Simon Hobbs meets the chairman and CEO of PepsiCo', http://enbceb.com, June 2008.

[2] 'The 2008 Time 100 Builders and Titans,' http://www.time.com, 2008.

[3] Starbucks Coffee Company is one of the world's leading coffee chains, which had a joint venture with PepsiCo to market and distribute Starbucks products.

[4] Headquartered in Purchase, New York, PepsiCo is a multinational snack foods and beverage company with revenues of US$39bn and over 185,000 employees as of 2008. PepsiCo owned five billion-dollar brands: namely, Pepsi, Tropicana, Frito-Lay, Quaker, and Gatorade.

[5] 'The 2008 Time 100 Builders and Titans,' http://www.time.com, 2008.

[6] 'Fifty Most Powerful Women in Business,' http://money.cnn.com/magazines/fortune

[7] 'Indra Nooyi named global CEO of PepsiCo,' http://www.thehindu.com, 15 August 2006.

[8] 'PepsiCo Press Release: Company reports third quarter 2008 results,' http://phx.corporate-ir.net, 2008.

emerging markets of Brazil, Russia, China, and India, and product and process simplification across the organization. (Refer to [Figure L5.1] for PepsiCo's organizational structure as of 2008.)

When Nooyi was SVP, the strategic measures that she planned and implemented resulted in a growth in PepsiCo's sales and profits. The company's overall sales increased from US$20,337m in 1996 to US$26,935m in 2001, and net profit doubled from US$1,149m to US$2,662m in the same period. After she became the CFO and president, sales recorded a further growth from US$25,112m in 2002 to US$35,137m in 2006, when she was promoted as the CEO. (Refer to [Table L5.3] and to [Table L5.4] for financial highlights of PepsiCo during Nooyi's tenure as CFO and CEO.)

However, Nooyi also had her share of critics, who found fault with what they called her lack of operational skills, her mercenary handling of the PepsiCo pesticide content issue in India, as well as her portraying PepsiCo products as healthy while, according to the health experts, they were not. Marion Nestle, Professor of Nutrition at the New York University and author of the books, *What to Eat* and *Food Politics*, criticized PepsiCo, saying: 'What PepsiCo is doing is shocking; it is aggressively marketing junk food as health food.'[9]

Nooyi as a strategist

Within two months of Nooyi joining PepsiCo as SVP, the company's restaurant business, which it had acquired a decade earlier and in which it had invested billions of dollars to build up, entered a sluggish phase with lower sales, volumes, and profits. Nooyi worked with Roger Enrico, chairman and CEO of Frito-Lay, who had been asked to take charge of PepsiCo's restaurant business as chairman and CEO of PepsiCo Worldwide Restaurants, and turn it around. Together, they investigated the problem and made efforts to analyse what was wrong with the business.[10] They concluded that the problem was with PepsiCo trying to adopt a management and distribution model that was more suitable for a packaged goods industry rather than a restaurant chain in the services industry. The management and distribution of a restaurant business required greater capital investment than its beverage and snacks business counterpart, and also generated lower returns than these businesses.[11] Nooyi believed the restaurant business had reached a stage at which it could be spun off into an independent business, because it did not fit in with the core PepsiCo businesses of snacks and beverages. It was this strategic decision that led PepsiCo to spin off its restaurant business into independent businesses.

In 1996, Nooyi found that PepsiCo's international beverages business had over-expanded and the repercussions were being felt on its balance sheet. PepsiCo's Venezuelan bottler was bought off by its competition, and two bottlers in Brazil and Argentina ran into financial problems. Consequently, PepsiCo's international business posted losses amounting to US$576m in special charges and asset impairments, international write-offs, and restructuring resulting in an operating loss of US$846m.[12] While PepsiCo's worldwide sales increased by 5 per cent to US$32bn, its earnings reduced by 28 per cent to US$1.1bn over 1995. However, excluding one-time charges, earnings dropped only by 6 per cent to US$1.9bn.[13]

Nooyi worked with Enrico on US$35bn worth of deals that included spin-offs and divestitures to put PepsiCo back on the fast-growth track. Enrico and Nooyi assessed strong brands, good cash flows, and a strong workforce as PepsiCo's strengths. Between 1996 and 1999, Enrico initiated rigorous financial controls to maximize PepsiCo's cash flows. The objective of this move was to ensure that management and financial resources were prioritized and judiciously used to expand the international business in core areas and emerging markets. In doing so, Nooyi's role of a strategist was utilized extensively to bring about money-spinning moves such as strategic mergers and acquisitions, emerging markets infrastructure development, and stock buy-back. These measures helped PepsiCo's performance to gradually improve.

[9] Patricia Sellers, 'The brand king's challenge when it comes to image making: PepsiCo is one of the smartest companies around—but it has never faced a problem quite like this,' http://money.cnn.com/magazines/fortune/fortune_archive, 5 April 2004.

[10] 'Nandan Nilekani chats up with Indra Nooyi,' http://economictimes.indiatimes com, 7 February 2007.

[11] 'PepsiCo's new generation Roger Enrico, PepsiCo's new CEO, has travelled a career path as curious as they come. but then, he says, "I think 'career path' are the two worst words invented"', http://money.cnn.com/magazines/fortune, 1 April 1996.

[12] 'Company history: PepsiCo Inc.', http://www.fundinguniverse.com, 2002.

[13] 'Letter from the chairman: PepsiCo Annual Report 1996', http://www.pepsico.com

In 1998, when Steve Reinemund, head of the Frito-Lay snacks business of PepsiCo, decided to revamp Frito Lay's distribution system, he asked Nooyi to help him out. Together, they created a new distribution system for PepsiCo that reduced overall costs and gave sales representatives more time with customers. The direct store delivery (DSD) system worked on the strategy of directly stocking the shelves of the retailers through its sales force. It also enabled the retailer to order supplies directly from PepsiCo. Under this process, the PepsiCo salesperson would frequent the store a fixed number of times in a supply chain cycle, spend a fixed number of hours, which would be divided into devoted time for selling the product to the retailer, stocking its shelves, taking orders for replenishment and fresh supplies, and also interacting with the consumer. This process had the dual advantage of reaching customers directly and helping PepsiCo to eliminate middlemen (distributors and wholesalers) to reduce costs. The strategy also enabled PepsiCo to gain an edge over Coca-Cola, which had a traditional distribution model.

Between 1994 and 2001, Nooyi used her experience in strategic planning and execution[14] to undertake a number of strategic initiatives at PepsiCo, which included the following.

The Tricon Restaurant spin-off

The restaurant chain business constituting Taco Bell, Kentucky Fried Chicken (KFC), and Pizza Hut was spun off into an independent company Tricon Global Restaurants, Inc., which was later renamed Yum! Brands Inc. This amounted to the divestiture of the company's larger restaurants to PepsiCo's existing shareholders, while its smaller restaurants such as Hot'n'Now, Chevys, California Pizza Kitchen, D'Angelo Sandwich Shop, and East Side Mario's were sold to new investors. This resulted in a loss of revenues of approximately US$10bn for PepsiCo, although it achieved Nooyi's desired objective of separating the service chain from the packaged goods businesses.[15]

Nooyi and Enrico had visited each of the restaurants across the country and also visited some of the competitors' restaurants to get a detailed bottom-up view of what had gone wrong with the restaurant chain, the profitability of which had come down drastically in the 1990s.[16] They found that the industry was saturated and the fast-food chains were competing aggressively with each other. Moreover, they also found that PepsiCo's restaurant chains did not make complete use of the scarce real estate in which they were housed. They catered only to breakfast or dinner or specific areas of dining, practically underutilizing the other slots. Subsequently, Nooyi argued with Enrico that PepsiCo could not add enough value to the fast-food industry with this service chain. The chain required higher capital investment, was labour-intensive, and also generated a lower level of returns as compared to PepsiCo's beverage and snacks businesses. Initially, PepsiCo had acquired these restaurants as small units and built them up into large self-sustaining chains. Therefore, these could now be spun off from the main PepsiCo business, she said. Even after the spin-off, however, PepsiCo continued to have a lifetime contract with these restaurants to stock its products. This decision helped PepsiCo to focus on its core areas of operations—namely, beverages and snacks—while providing the restaurant chain with the required level of autonomy to perform independently.

The Tropicana acquisition

Nooyi guided PepsiCo for the US$3.3bn acquisition of Tropicana, the world's biggest juice brand,[17] in 1998 from Seagram Company Limited.[18] It was the biggest acquisition in PepsiCo's history[19] and helped the brand's foray into the healthy beverages market. It also helped it to compete on an even footing with its arch-rival Coca-Cola,[20] which had acquired a rival juice brand named Minute Maid at that time. Nooyi put in a lot of effort on assessing the advantages of the Tropicana acquisition for PepsiCo not only in terms of improving the company's brand image as containing a healthy and convenient foods and drinks portfolio, but also in terms of its addition to PepsiCo's earnings. In the negotiation, she was

[14] Prior to joining PepsiCo in 1994 as SVP of strategic planning, Nooyi spent four years as SVP of strategy and strategic marketing for Asea Brown Boveri (ABB). Between 1986 and 1990, Nooyi was vice-president and director of Corporate Strategy and Planning at Motorola, where she had joined as business development executive for its automotive and industrial electronics group. Before joining Motorola, she spent six years directing international corporate strategy projects at the Boston Consulting Group.

[15] 'Nandan Nilekani chats up with Indra Nooyi,' http://economictimes.indiatimes com, 7 February 2007.

[16] Ibid.

[17] Constance L. Hays, 'PepsiCo to pay $3.3bn for Tropicana', http://query.nytimes.com, 21 July 1998.

[18] Seagram Company Limited, a Canadian company, was one of the world's largest distillers of alcoholic beverages as of 2000. It also sold other beverages and had entertainment and other business interests, all of which were sold off to companies such as PepsiCo and Coca-Cola. The company closed its distilleries and wound up operations in 2006.

[19] 'PepsiCo history', http://www.pepsico.com

[20] Established in 1888, The Coca Cola Company Inc (Coca-Cola) (turnover US$28.9bn; 90,500 associates worldwide in 2007) is the world's largest beverage manufacturing company, with a portfolio of 2,800 products sold across 200 countries, including 13 billion-dollar brands: http://www.thecoca-colacompany.com

even ready to settle for a lower return on investment (RoI) mainly because she had assessed that the brand possessed great potential to improve PepsiCo's bottom line.

The spin-off of PepsiCo's bottling operations into Pepsi Bottling Group

Nooyi had studied Coca-Cola's development strategies over the decade. She made a presentation to the PepsiCo's board on Coca-Cola's growth model and explained how the company had successfully reaped the benefits of higher margins by separating its bottling operations in 1986. The bottling business, she had found, required higher levels of investment and was very labour-intensive. She envisioned that if the bottling business were spun off into a separate business, PepsiCo could benefit from higher margins in the process. Nooyi initiated the spin-off of the company's bottling operations into Pepsi Bottling Group (PBG) in 1999. The initial public offering of PBG was valued at US$2.3bn. The company, however, continued to retain a majority stake in PBG. However, this move had a negative impact on PepsiCo's revenues to the extent of US$7bn.[21]

PepsiCo's revenues, which had declined from US$32bn in 1996 to US$22bn in 1998, increased to US$27bn in 2001. Operating margins improved marginally from 10 per cent in 1996 to 11.6 per cent in 1998 and further to 17.70 per cent in 2001. Operating cash flows also improved from US$1.5bn in 1996 to US$3.1bn in 1998 and US$4.2bn in 2001. Other positive trends included an increase in ROI from 15 per cent in 1996 to 18 per cent in 1998 and 26 per cent in 2001.

Nooyi becomes CFO

Nooyi was promoted as the CFO at PepsiCo in February 2000. A year later, she was promoted as the president and also provided a seat on the board of directors. As a CFO, she was responsible for innovation, finance, procurements, investor relations, strategy, and information technology functions.

The strategy that Nooyi adopted to achieve the objective of putting PepsiCo on the fast-growth track included acquisition and development of new products and achieving product synergies. For this purpose, Nooyi used the Quaker and Tropicana brands extensively to innovate and develop an entire range of snacks that could be positioned as healthy. Integrating the multiple brands, however, proved to be quite a challenge for PepsiCo.

When Nooyi was CFO, PepsiCo acquired popular non-carbonated beverage maker SoBe (South Beach Beverage Company[22]) for US$337m in 2001, beating Coca-Cola, which was the first to initiate talks with the company for its acquisition.[23] SoBe manufactured teas with herbal ingredients and a product called 'Life Water' that claimed to be enriched with Vitamins B, C, and E, in various fruity flavours,[24] and energy drinks that were popular among the American youth. It therefore constituted a prize acquisition to add to PepsiCo's beverage portfolio in the non-carbonated beverages segment.

The Quaker Oats merger

Nooyi was the key negotiator in the merger of Quaker Oats Company with PepsiCo at a cost of US$13.8bn in 2001.[25] Quaker Oats was expected to help PepsiCo to establish its presence in the healthy snacks and beverages business. The merger enabled the company acquire ownership of Gatorade, a leading sports drink that accounted for 83.6 per cent of the US retail market for non-carbonated beverages.[26] It also provided PepsiCo with a platform to launch snacks that were projected as healthy. Its existing Frito-Lay brand could not be used for creating a breakfast snack and be portrayed as healthy. The merger of Quaker Oats helped to bridge this gap.

[21] 'Nandan Nilekani chats up with Indra Nooyi,' http://economictimes.indiatimes com, 7 February 2007.

[22] South Beach Beverage Company (SoBe) founded in 1996, was a manufacturer of herbal teas, blended felt juices, and energy drinks. It was acquired by PepsiCo in 2000.

[23] http://www.pepsico.com

[24] 'North America bottled water market chronology.' Global Bottled Water. September 2008.

[25] 'The power of two at Pepsi', http://www.businessweek.com, 29 January 2001.

[26] 'Company history: PepsiCo Inc.', http://www.fundinguniverse.com, 2002.

While integrating Quaker Oats, PepsiCo faced a number of logistical problems. The two independent sales forces of Quaker and PepsiCo struggled to market the new products as a single force. Nooyi took charge of a business process optimization plan in February 2003 that involved combining the advantages of Frito-Lay's existing distribution systems with a few of Quaker's foundational management practices. Under this plan, it was decided that a few distribution centres would be merged and a common enterprise software platform adopted using Quaker's enterprise software implementation strategy and staff from the affected divisions apart from dedicated information systems staff. Although Nooyi had envisaged a cost reduction of US$800m between 2003 and 2005 as a result of the optimization programme, it ran into a lot of integration problems.[27]

The plan forced Quaker to stop its enterprise software implementation programme, which it had already partially completed, and to move back to its former systems, resulting in estimated losses of US$40m–US$100m to PepsiCo. However, Nooyi persisted in taking the acquisition and integration process forward, smoothing out the differences by tweaking PepsiCo's distribution chain DSD system and moving to a better pre-sell system, which separated the ordering and presales time of the sales force and combined it with the optimization programme and its 'Power of one'[28] strategy to achieve the required synergies.

Subsequently, PepsiCo posted a 7 per cent annual sales growth in 2002. The investment in the Quaker Oats and Tropicana brands and the divestiture of its non-core businesses began to pay off. The Gatorade brand provided PepsiCo with an edge in the non-carbonated beverages market, while its health foods segment helped its Frito-Lay business to expand beyond salty snacks.

Challenge of achieving double-digit growth rates

One of the major challenges for PepsiCo was to assess its new competitors, as Coca-Cola was no longer its sole rival in the markets it had ventured into. The new competition ranged from the food giant Kraft,[29] on the one hand, to other smaller drinks and snack food makers, on the other. To tackle these competitors, Nooyi created innovations in PepsiCo products and adopted fresh sales strategies to bridge the gap with its competition.

As a part of PepsiCo's growth strategy, Nooyi reorganized Frito-Lay's operating structure from its existing two divisions—Frito-Lay North America (FLNA) and Frito-Lay International (FLI)—to three broad units, by establishing two new companies—Frito-Lay Europe/Middle East/Africa and Frito-Lay Latin America/Asia Pacific/Australia—and integrating the existing FLI group into new operating companies. On the lines of existing units, FLNA, Pepsi-Cola North America, Pepsi-Cola International and Tropicana, each new company functioned as an independent unit, with its own president and CEO, and ultimately reported directly to Reinemund. Nooyi and Reinemund felt that by effecting this reorganization, the vast potential of all emerging markets for the snacks business could be tapped completely as individual businesses.

As of 2000, Frito-Lay operated in forty countries outside the USA and Canada. Frito-Lay Latin America/Asia Pacific/Australia spanned twenty-three markets and generated sales of US$3.5bn, and Europe/Africa/Middle East produced sales of US$2.4bn from seventeen countries from the UK to Africa, including joint ventures. The international salty snack market grew from US$10bn in 1990 to US$16bn in 2000, driven by Frito-Lay. Through a combination of internal growth and acquisitions, Frito-Lay's international business with revenue growth of 40 per cent became a significant contributor to PepsiCo revenues from 1996.[30]

The changes that Nooyi initiated, such as the acquisition of Tropicana and Quaker Oats and the spin-off of the Pepsi Bottling Group, helped to propel PepsiCo past Coca-Cola in market value in December 2005—the first time in its history that it had done so. PepsiCo entered the bottled water and sports drinks market earlier than its rival. In 2006, PepsiCo's Aquafina brand of bottled water had the largest market share, while Coca-Cola's Dasani took second place. In the sports drinks market, Gatorade

[27] 'Enterprise integration: The Pepsi challenge', http://wps.prenhall.com, March 2006.

[28] 'Power of one' was a strategy initiated by Roger Enrico, wherein PepsiCo decided to market its products in combination to encourage joint consumption and demand generation for its snacks and beverages.

[29] Kraft Foods Inc. (revenues US$42.2bn; 103,000 employees as of 2008) is a leading US-based snack foods and beverages company, with over nine billion-dollar brands including Kraft, Jacobs, LU, Maxwell House, Milka, Nabisco, and its Oreo brand, Philadelphia, and Oscar Mayer, and fifty additional brands with revenues of US$100m. About forty of Kraft's brands are over a hundred years' old. It is famous for its cheeses, ketchups, and snacks.

[30] 'PepsiCo announces moves to accelerate continuing growth momentum', *Market Wire*, February 2000.

Table L5.1 PepsiCo product portfolio categorization

Category	Type of product	Examples
Fun for you	Highly indulgent	Pepsi, Ruffles, and Lays
Better for you	Continued to taste good, but healthier alternative	Baked Lays, Low Fat Ruffles, and Rold Gold Pretzels
Good for you	When consumed, added back functionality into one's system	Tropicana with Calcium and Quaker Oats

Source: Adapted from PepsiCo Corporate Sustainability Report 2006-07

accounted for 80 per cent market share. PepsiCo's snack foods business also accounted for 60 per cent of the snack food market in the USA at that point in time.[31]

Analysts gave the credit to Nooyi as CFO for transforming the company's global strategy at a time when both Coca-Cola and Pepsi were facing a sluggish and saturated sales environment in their most vital market—the domestic market—for carbonated soft drinks.[32] The focus of the consumer had changed to health-conscious products and juices, and water sales had been substituted carbonated soft drinks, resulting in greater sales in the juices and bottled water segments. Gary Hemphill, senior vice president, *Information Services of Beverage Marketing*, a trade journal, commented: 'They were the first to recognize that the consumer was moving to non-carbonated products, and they innovated aggressively.'[33] According to analysts, after Nooyi became CFO in 2000, the company's annual revenues rose by 72 per cent over the period between 2000 and 2006, while the net profit more than doubled, to US$5.6m in 2006.[34]

Nooyi as CEO

In October 2006, Nooyi was promoted as PepsiCo's CEO. Analysts felt that her diverse knowledge of global markets and ethnic background were the reasons for her becoming CEO. On her appointment as CEO, Reinemund said: 'She not only co-authored our vision and drafted our strategic blueprint: she has a sharp talent for turning insightful ideas and plans into realities and for developing and replenishing our talent base.'[35]

Nooyi believed that, as CEO, she needed to present PepsiCo as a good, sustainable global company. She believed that corporations like PepsiCo had a responsibility to perform as ethical and sustainable companies as they were larger than some economies in size. She stated: 'Of the world's 100 largest economic entities, sixty-three are countries. The other thirty-seven are companies.'[36] Nooyi cited the examples of how a multinational corporation could damage its reputation in markets across the world by failing to adhere to ethics and sustainability norms.

Therefore, Nooyi adopted the vision of 'Performance with purpose', wherein the focus was not purely on profits, but on making PepsiCo one of 'the defining corporations of the twenty-first century'.[37] By this, she meant that PepsiCo must focus on the sustainability of the environment in which it operated and its workforce.

In 2007, PepsiCo's portfolio across its product segments of foods, snacks, and beverages consisted of three parts (Refer to Table [L5.1]). As a part of PepsiCo's sustainability efforts, Nooyi initiated changes in the composition of the company's product portfolio. This called for increasing the percentage of '*better for you*' and '*good for you*' snacks to 50 per cent, up from 30 per cent, as against its '*fun for you*' snacks group, and include more grains, nuts, and fruits in its product portfolio. By doing so, Nooyi had also helped to shape a model that enabled PepsiCo to innovate and bring out new products. In her words: 'We can be viewed as not just a lifestyle company that brings a slice of joy to you, but also as a nutritionally responsible company. That has been our acquisition trajectory over the last few years

[31] 'How Pepsi outgunned Coke', http://money.cnn.com, 1 February 2006.

[32] 'PepsiCo names first woman CEO', http://money.cnn.com, 14 August 2006.

[33] 'How Pepsi outgunned Coke', http://money.cnn.com, 1 February 2006.

[34] 'Indra Nooyi: Keeping cool in hot water', http://www.businessweek.com, 11 June 2007.

[35] 'PepsiCo names first woman CEO', http://money.cnn.com, 14 August 2006.

[36] Indra Nooyi, 'Performance with Purpose', Speech made at the World Business Council Summit for Sustainable Development, http://www.wbcsd.org

[37] 'Nandan Nilekani chats up with Indra Nooyi,' http://economictimes.indiatimes com, 7 February 2007.

and I think all our innovation, our strategic direction, is headed that way.'[38]

Under Nooyi's leadership, PepsiCo shifted its focus from the saturated US markets to the emerging global markets. Nooyi increased the size of her executive team to twenty-nine, allowing for a broader distribution of management decision-making power. She continued to emphasize the 'diversity' ideology of her predecessors by appointing an Italian native, Massimo d'Amore, to head PepsiCo's US soft drinks business, and recruiting a former Mayo Clinic endocrinologist to head PepsiCo's research and development (R&D) division. According to her: 'Succession planning is critical. Our succession planning process is designed to identify the kinds of experiences our leaders need. Once identified, we put people in assignments that enable them to build those skill sets.'[39]

Nooyi made sure that the talent PepsiCo recruited was diverse. This process, according to her, required an understanding of the specific needs of the diverse workforce. Nooyi stated: 'We set goals and time frames and held people accountable for getting to them. The first step was getting people in, but that's only half the problem because if they leave, it's more painful for the organization. Step two is inclusion. For example, if a woman says something, don't immediately interpret it as if a man said it, or expect a woman to react to a comment in the same way as a man. You will have a different dynamic with women, African-Americans, or Latinos because each group is a product of their socio-economic culture.'[40]

Nooyi believed that, while implementing strategic changes in the organization, it was important to communicate clearly the reasons for the change in order to take the employees with the organization through the change. When Nooyi clearly communicated the strategic rationale behind the spin-off of PepsiCo's restaurant business to the employees, there was no resistance to the resultant change. Nooyi emphasized that communication and if necessary, 'over-communication' was necessary at times to align the changes taking place in the organization with the goals and expectations of the employees. In her words: 'The first step is really understanding the points of view of each of the people that are involved and then trying to craft the new or better vision for them and then taking them along with you. It is communication all the time. I would say you might even argue that it is over-communication.'[41]

Nooyi believed in leading by example. She was also known as a tough negotiator who knew when to walk away and when she could shape the ideas of her management team into concrete strategies. She was known to expect high standards from her employees. According to Tim Menges, president of PepsiCo's Asia-Pacific region, an example of how Nooyi motivated employees to generate ideas was when she asked his team to find an inexpensive alternative to palm oil for PepsiCo's products in Thailand. He said: 'She kept pushing and pushing, saying, "I hear you, I hear you, so what's the right solution?" until we came up with one: rice bran oil. But don't try to delegate up, because she will bounce it right back in your face!'[42]

Strategic acquisitions as CEO

As CEO, Nooyi undertook a number of strategic acquisitions to bridge the gap in PepsiCo's product portfolio. These acquisitions were a part of her vision of 'Performance with purpose'. PepsiCo acquired: Bluebird Snacks (2006) and Izze (2006), a Brazil-based company that manufactured snack foods and drinks; Sandora, a Ukraine-based juice company (2007); and Naked Juice (2006), a US-based manufacturer of organic juices and soy drinks. PepsiCo also signed a ready-to-drink tea joint venture with Unilever and increased its presence in the healthy retail foods segment such as Whole Foods Market Inc., and introduced a vegetable and fruit-based snack called Flat Earth fruit and vegetable chips (2007).[43]

Nooyi also completed PepsiCo's biggest acquisition deal of Lebedyansky at a cost of US$13.8bn in 2008. Lebedyansky was a Russia-based juice company, deemed to be the largest in Europe and the sixth largest in the world in terms of market size.[44] She also announced PepsiCo's intention to invest US$1bn in China over four years beginning 2009, as a part of the objective of expanding into emerging markets and completing the gaps in its global product portfolio.

[38] 'Indra Nooyi, president and CFO, PepsiCo, CEO Speaker Series question & answer segment', http://mba.tuck.dartmouth.edu, 23 August 2002.

[39] 'Indra Nooyi's mantras for success', http://www.rediff.com, 12 September 2008.

[40] 'Indra Nooyi's views on US Prez', http://www.rediff.com, 22 May 2008.

[41] 'Indra Nooyi, president and CFO, PepsiCo, CEO Speaker Series question & answer segment', http://mba.tuck.dartmouth.edu, 23 August 2002.

[42] Betsy Morris, 'The Pepsi challenge', http://money.cnn.com, 18 February 2008.

[43] 'Indra Nooyi's Pepsi challenge: CEO puts her own brand on new products and global goals', http://www.marketwatch.com, 6 December 2007.

[44] 'Indra Nooyi's Russian coup: PepsiCo to buy 75% in top juice firm', http://www.indianexpress.com, 21 March 2008.

Table L5.2 Awards and recognitions received by Nooyi

Year/s	Organization	Awards, Rankings and Recognitions
2006, 2007, and 2008	*Fortune* Magazine	Ranked #1 in the World's 50 Most Powerful Business Women list
2003	US Pan Asian Chamber Commerce (USPAC)	Woman Pioneer Award
2006, 2007, 2008	*Forbes* Magazine Poll	#4, #5, and #1, respectively, in World's 100 Most Powerful Women
2006	Columbia University	India Abroad Person of the Year
2007	Government of India	Padma Bhushan Award, Indian government's third highest civilian award, for her contribution to global business
2007	US Citizenship and Immigration Services, US Government	American By Choice for her achievements as a naturalized American Citizen
2008	*Time* Magazine	World's 100 Most Influential People in 2008
2008	Chicago United	Chicago United Bridge Award 2008 honoring exemplary leadership in support of advancing diversity and inclusion

Source: Compiled from various sources

Response to global economic slowdown

PepsiCo faced a number of economic challenges in 2008. Spiralling fuel and energy prices, rising costs of raw materials and other commodities, and increased packaging costs across economies had become a cause for concern. PepsiCo announced that it would be raising its prices across product categories in April 2008, to offset the higher costs of cooking oil, oats, wheat, corn, and energy. Nooyi had expressed concerns that if corrective measures were not undertaken soon by the US government, it would significantly slow down consumer spending in the USA.[45] She, however, pointed out that PepsiCo had been recession-proofed by the fact that its '*good for you*' snacks, which comprised the largest share of PepsiCo's US product portfolio, acted as comfort food to consumers during the downturn, thus retaining their growth momentum.

By reorganizing PepsiCo to focus more on the growth in emerging markets, Nooyi justified that she was able to minimize and diversify the risks associated with the recession in the US economy. The company also adopted pricing measures to offset inflation, both through innovations and new product introductions and a combination of mix management, product weight-outs (for example, reducing the number of potato chips per bag, which is considered a legal alternative to raising prices of a product worldwide), and absolute price increase strategies.

In October 2008, Nooyi said in a press release: 'While we can't control the macro economic situation, we can enhance PepsiCo's operating agility to respond to the changing environment. To do so, we are implementing a broad-based productivity programme, which we expect will produce US$1.2bn in pre-tax savings over three years. The majority of the savings will be invested in our businesses. A primary focus will be restoring growth to our North American beverage business. We were adversely impacted by continued weakness in the US liquid refreshment beverage category, which resulted in disappointing performance in our domestic beverage business. We are taking important steps to revitalize our beverage portfolio. At the same time, we will increase our investment in developing markets, make selective investments to continue growing our global snacks business, and accelerate our global R&D initiatives to help to secure our future innovation pipeline. We firmly believe that now is the time to invest in our future growth.'[46]

[45] 'Nooyi slams US inaction on oil prices', http://economictimes.indiatimes.com, 12 June 2008.

[46] 'PepsiCo press release on 2008 financial results', http://phx.corporate-ir.net, 14 October 2008.

Figure L5.1 PepsiCo's organizational structure 2008

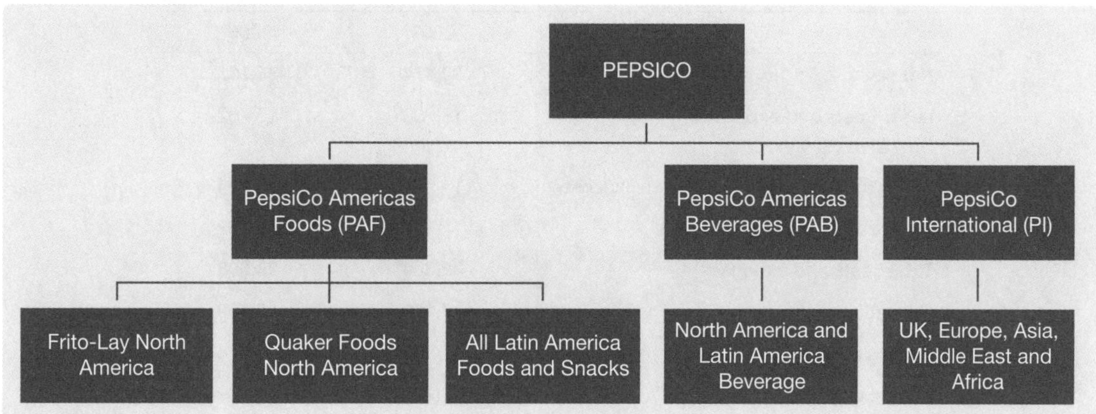

As of 2008, PepsiCo consisted of three main divisions: PepsiCo Americas Foods (PAF); PepsiCo Americas Beverages (PAB); and PepsiCo International (PI). PAF included Frito-Lay North America, Quaker Foods North America, and all Latin America food and snack businesses, including the Sabritas and Gamesa businesses in Mexico. PAB included PepsiCo Beverages North America and all Latin American beverage businesses. PI included all PepsiCo businesses in the UK, Europe, Asia, the Middle East, and Africa. PepsiCo manufactured and sold around 500 products catering to consumers of all age groups, in nearly 200 countries, and generated sales at the retail level inclusive of franchisees and partners of more than US$98bn in 2008.

Source: Adapted from http://www.pepsico.com

Table L5.3 Financial highlights of PepsiCo and its subsidiaries 2000–05 (US$m)

Statement of income	2005	2004	2003	2002	2001	2000
Net sales	**32,562**	**29,261**	**26,971**	**25,112**	**23,512**	**25,479**
Costs and expenses:						
Cost of sales	14,176	12,674	12,379	11,497	10,750	10,226
Selling, general and administrative expenses	12,314	11,031	9,460	8,958	8,574	11,104
Amortization of intangible assets	150	147	145	138	165	147
Merger-related costs			59	224	356	
Other impairment and restructuring charges	–	150	147	–	31	184
Total costs and expenses	**26,640**	**24,002**	**22,190**	**20,817**	**22,914**	**21,661**
Operating profit	**5,922**	**5,259**	**4,781**	**4,295**	**3,636**	**3,818**
Bottling equity income	557	380	323	280	160	130
Interest expense	–256	–167	–163	–178	–219	-272
Interest income	159	74	51	36	67	85
Income before income tax	**6,382**	**5,546**	**4,992**	**4,433**	**3,644**	**3,761**
Less: Income tax	2,304	1,334	1,424	1,433	1,244	1,218
Net income	**4,078**	**4,212**	**3,568**	**3,000**	**2,400**	**2,543**

Source: PepsiCo Annual Reports, http://www.pepsico.com

While announcing PepsiCo's quarterly results in October 2008, Nooyi said the company had introduced the 'Productivity for growth' programme to improve the company's productivity to combat the impact of the global slowdown. The programme involved simplifying all processes across segments of the organization for more effective and timely decision-making. In order to achieve these objectives, it planned to improve cost-competitiveness across its supply chain, and to upgrade and streamline its product portfolio.

The programme entailed eliminating 3,300 positions globally. Of these, 40 per cent related to the closing down

Table L5.4 Financial highlights of PepsiCo and its subsidiaries 2006–07 (US$m)

	2007	2006
Net sales	**39,474**	**35,137**
Less: Costs and expenses Cost of sales	18,038	15,762
Selling, general and administrative expenses	14,208	12,774
Amortization of intangible assets	58	162
Total costs and expenses	**32,304**	**28,698**
Operating profit	**7,170**	**6,439**
Bottling equity income	560	616
Interest expense	(224.00)	-239
Interest income	125	173
Income before income tax	**7,631**	**6,989**
Less: Income tax	1,973	1,347
Net income	**5,658**	**5,642**

Source: PepsiCo 2007 Annual Report, http://www.pepsico.com

of six plants and other capacity-rationalization actions. As a result of this, PepsiCo was expected to incur a pre-tax change of approximately US$550m–US$600m in the fourth quarter of 2008, comprising, severance and other costs of US$275m, asset impairments due to plant closures at US$200m, and other costs amounting to US$100m.

The criticism

Notwithstanding her successful stint in PepsiCo, Nooyi also had to face criticism on several fronts. She was criticized for her lack of operational experience. Nooyi had joined PepsiCo after six years in consulting and at PepsiCo too, and had worked as a strategist before becoming CFO and later CEO.

Critics believed that Nooyi was merely anticipating the regulations and following consumer trends rather than making conscious efforts to make PepsiCo's products healthy. A study conducted by the City University London, on the world's twenty-five largest food companies including PepsiCo, on their conformity to the new global diet and health agenda in 2006,[47] found that PepsiCo had not adopted the standards relating to limiting the portion size, on having a specific health policy on advertising, and on initiating staff health programmes. Nestle believed that PepsiCo was merely following health and nutrition standards to avoid obesity-related lawsuits. She said: 'They're going through the motions. The instant the [US Food and Drugs Administration] said they were going to require trans-fat labelling, Pepsi had the trans-fats out of its products and was advertising it. I don't think they're putting anywhere near the marketing effort into their healthier products. For me, it's a philosophical issue. Is a healthier junk food a better junk food?'[48]

Critics felt that the efforts taken by PepsiCo to reduce the adverse impact of its products on the health of its consumers were not enough. For example, the company's stance of limiting marketing to children aged below 12 years was cited by critics as leaving out a very important and growing category of consumers: high-school children. They were still targeted by PepsiCo, and vending machines in high schools continued to stock carbonated beverages. They further added that the existing non-soda alternatives offered by PepsiCo were low on nutrition, and contained high levels of sugar content and

[47] Tim Lang, Geof Rayner, and Elizabeth Kaelin, 'The food industry, diet, physical activity, and health: A review of reported commitments and practice of 25 of the world's largest food companies', http://www.city.ac.uk, April 2006.

[48] Angela Moore, 'Indra Nooyi's Pepsi challenge', http://www.marketwatch.com, 6 December 2007.

more calories than were recommended as part of a healthy diet for children.[49]

In 2003, PepsiCo came under attack from environmental groups in India for having high levels of pesticide content in its beverages. The groups claimed that the company was allowing pesticide residue to enter their locally manufactured beverages from the groundwater used by them. The groups even produced test results to back their claim that the pesticide residue content was higher than the prescribed standards in the world. It also showed that the results of these tests were within prescribed parameters for samples taken from the beverages marketed by the company in the USA, while for Indian samples they exceeded the norms.

Critics felt that Nooyi had been unable to put an end to these allegations even after becoming CEO. She disputed the results of the test and urged the Indian government to establish a procedure to carry out independent tests on PepsiCo's drinks for pesticide content—a costly and long-term project, and unlikely to be implemented soon by the government for these very reasons. While India accounted for a relatively small portion of PepsiCo's revenues, analysts felt that these allegations had had the impact of tarnishing the company's image worldwide.[50]

Case questions

1. How would you describe Indra Nooyi's leadership style?
2. Evaluate Indra Nooyi's role as a strategist.
3. Discuss the importance of sustainability in shaping PepsiCo's strategy.

References and suggested reading

'Fifty Most Powerful Women in Business', http://money.cnn.com/magazines/fortune, 2008, 2007, and 2006.

'PepsiCo press release: Company reports third quarter 2008 results', http://phx.corporate-ir.net, 2008.

'PepsiCo receives recognition for its water replenishment initiatives and wins the CII and UNESCO Award', http://wwwprdomain.com, 30 December 2008.

'Indra Nooyi wins leadership award for advancing diversity', http://economictimes.indiatimes.com, 11 November 2008.

James Ferre, '3,300 jobs to go as part of Pepsi's productivity program', http://www.ausfoodnews.com.au, 15 October 2008.

'Indra Nooyi's mantras for success', http://www.rediff.com, 12 September 2008.

'North America bottled water market chronology', *Global Bottled Water*, September 2008.

Mary Ellen Egan and Chana R. Schoenberger, 'The World's 100 Most Powerful Women', http://www.forbes.com, 27 August 2008.

'Life stories to inspire: Indra Nooyi—CEO, PepsiCo', http://changeminds.wordpress.com, 25 August 2008.

'In the spotlight: Indra Nooyi, PepsiCo', http://www.just-food.com, 13 June 2008.

Simon Hobbs, 'Indra Nooyi: Simon Hobbs meets the chairman and CEO of PepsiCo', http://cnbceb.com, June 2008.

Howard Schultz, 'The 2008 *Time* 100: Builders and titans', http://www.time.com, 1 May 2008.

'Indra Nooyi's Russian coup: PepsiCo to buy 75% in top juice firm', http://www.indianexpress.com, 21 March 2008.

Betsy Morris, 'The Pepsi challenge', http://money.cnn.com, 19 February 2008.

'PepsiCo announces initiatives with The Earth Institute and H20 Africa to drive sustainable water practices', http://www.prdomain.com, 22 January 2008.

'Indra Nooyi's Pepsi challenge: CEO puts her own brand on new products and global goals', http://www.marketwatch.com, 6 December 2007.

'PepsiCo looking beyond US for acquisitions this year: Nooyi', http://www.bloomberg.com, 26 July 2007.

'Indra Nooyi: Keeping cool in hot water', http://www.businessweek.com, 11 June 2007.

'Nandan Nilekani chats up with Indra Nooyi', http://economictimes.indiatimes.com, 7 February 2007.

'How Pepsi opened door to diversity: A 1940s all-black team targeted a new market and broke a barrier', *Wall Street Journal*, 9 January 2007.

'Indra Nooyi forges ahead as PepsiCo CEO', http://edition.cnn.com/2007/US/01/05/PYSK.nooyi/index.html, 8 January 2007.

'Indra Nooyi: New CEO at PepsiCo Inc', *Overseas Indian*, August 2006.

'Indra Nooyi named global CEO of PepsiCo', http://www.thehindu.com, 15 August 2006.

Diane Brady, 'PepsiCo shakes it up', http://www.businessweek.com, 14 August 2006.

'PepsiCo names first woman CEO', http://money.cnn.com, 14 August 2006.

'PepsiCo news release: PepsiCo's board of directors appoints Indra K. Nooyi as chief executive officer effective October 1, 2006 and Steve Reinemund to retire as chairman in May 20', http://phx.corporate-ir.net, 14 August 2006.

'Enterprise integration: The Pepsi challenge', http://wps.prenhall.com, March 2006.

'How Pepsi outgunned Coke', http://money.cnn.com, 1 February 2006.

Katrina Brooker, 'The Pepsi machine', http://money.cnn.com/magazines/fortune/fortune_archive, 30 January 2006.

[49] Melanie Warner, 'Critics say soda policy for school lacks teeth', http://www nytimes.com, 22 August 2005.

[50] PepsiCo products safest in the entire food chain, says Indra Nooyi', http://www.thainidian.com, 23 December 2007.

'PepsiCo flags up "healthy" products', http://www.nutraingrediants.com, 30 July 2004.

Patricia Sellers, 'The brand king's challenge when it comes to image making: PepsiCo is one of the smartest companies around—but it has never faced a problem quite like this', http://money.cnn.com/magazines/fortune/fortune_archive, 5 April 2004.

'Company history: PepsiCo Inc', http://www.fundinguniverse.com, 2002.

'Indra Nooyi, president and CFO, PepsiCo, CEO Speaker Series question & answer segment', http://mba.tuck.dartmouth.edu, 23 August 2002.

Nanette Byrnes, 'The Power of Two at Pepsi', http://www.businessweek.com, 29 January 2001.

'Nannette Byrnes, Steve Reinemund: Pepsi's new generation', http://www.businessweek.com/archives/2000/b3712060.arc.htm, 18 December 2000.

'The joy of lizards: Pepsi agrees to buy SoBe for $370 million', http://www.beverage-digest.com, 30 October 2000.

'PepsiCo's new formula', http://www.businessweek.com, 10 April 2000.

'PepsiCo announces moves to accelerate continuing growth momentum', ***Market Wire***, February 2000.

'Spin-off the bottler', http://news.morningstar.com, 30 April 1999.

Constance L. Hays, 'PepsiCo to pay $3.3bn for Tropicana', http://query.nytimes.com, 21 July 1998.

'PepsiCo Annual Report 1996', http://www.pepsico.com

'Letter from the chairman: PepsiCo Annual Report 1996', http://www.pepsico.com

Patricia Sellers, Suzanne Barlyn, and Kimberly Seals Macdonald, 'PepsiCo's new generation: Roger Enrico, PepsiCo's new CEO, has travelled a career path as curious as they come, but then, he says, "I think 'career path' are the two worst words invented"', http://money.cnn.com/magazines/fortune, 1 April 1996.

Indra Nooyi, 'Performance with Purpose', Speech made at the World Business Council Summit for Sustainable Development, http://www.wbcsd.org

Margaret Wommack, 'Private Carrier Pepsi embraces diversity amongst employees', http://ezinearticles.com

'Indra K. Nooyi biography', http://www.notablebiographies.com

http://www.pepsico.com

Case 6 Macquarie Bank Australia

Sophie Cacciaguidi and Martin Fahy

Introduction

Macquarie Group Limited (Macquarie) is one of a small number of Australian-owned investment banks that have, in the last decade, expanded internationally to become key players in the infrastructure-backed fund industry. Macquarie has successfully expanded beyond its home base using its comparative advantage in releasing value from large infrastructure investments, such as airports, toll roads, and office buildings. From its rather small beginnings in Sydney in 1985, Macquarie now has offices in some twenty-eight countries on six continents.

In Australasia, Macquarie is known as a market leader in investment and financial services. In Asia, it offers a wide range of investment, financial market, and advisory products and services; in Europe, the Middle East, Africa, and the Americas, the company focuses on specific business matters in which its field of expertise delivers maximum value to its clients.

A key stock on the Australian Securities Exchange (ASX) in recent years, the company has, in the past decade, expanded beyond investment banking to proprietary trading, fund management, retail banking and lending, real estate, and wealth management. While remaining a key player in the local strategic advisory market and investment banking, Macquarie has made its mark on the global stage creating investment funds and management companies based on acquired assets ranging from railroads to rail links (A-Train), seaports, airports, and motorways, to telecommunications networks and water treatment systems, etc.

History and evolution

Macquarie first began its operations in January 1970 in Sydney as Hill Samuel David Clarke, a subsidiary of the UK's Hill Samuel investment house. Hill Samuel itself had started life as a small business founded in 1832 by Marcus Samuel in London, at first as an importer of goods (specifically shells) from the Far East. By the middle of the nineteenth century, the firm (M. Samuel & Co.) had grown to become a considerable export business, shipping goods throughout Europe and to North America. By the late 1900s, the company had started trading oil and had become a major force in oil shipping operations, with its first designed tank steamers, the 'Murex', being the first ship in 1892 to cross the newly opened Suez Canal to deliver oil into reservoirs and make it readily available to consumers. While the original M. Samuel & Co. maintained its focus on investment banking and advice, the oil operations subsequently went on to form the basis of the Shell Oil Company.

The Sydney office of what was to become Macquarie began operations in 1970 with a staff of just three people. While Hill Samuel in the UK remained an important force in merchant banking markets, merging in 1985 with the TSB Group, and in turn ten years later with Lloyds Bank, Hill Samuel David Clarke grew strongly throughout the 1970s in the domestic Australian market and subsequently changed its name to Hill Samuel Australia.

In 1977, the company recruited David Moss, who, over the years, became a driving force behind the group's transformation into a global leading investment bank. Moss had spent his early career at the Australian Industries Development Corporation, before completing an MBA at Harvard Business School, where he was recruited by Hill Samuels' then chief executive officer (CEO) Tony Berg. Moss progressed up through the bank and, by 1984, had been made responsible for the bank's risk management activities. These same activities were to be a critical element in the international growth of the firm. For the remainder of the 1970s and 1980s, Hill Samuel

Australia remained focused on the Australian market and it was not until 1985 that the firm made its first foray into international markets, with the establishment of a presence in New Zealand.

One of the critical constraints on the bank for much of the 1970s was the Australian banking rules, which prohibited a bank under the control of a foreign company to provide full commercial banking services in the country. By the early 1980s, the Australian government proceeded to deregulate the country's banking system. It included a proposal permitting the establishment of a small number of foreign-controlled banks to set up operations in Australia. As a result of these impending changes, Hill Samuel Australia began preparations to transform itself into a focused investment bank. A key part of that strategy was to establishing itself as an independent Australian-based business in the hope of securing one of the much-coveted new commercial banking licences. As part of this move, Hill Samuel Australia petitioned the Australian federal government seeking a change in its shareholding structure so that it would be in a position to qualify for a licence to operate as an Australian trading bank. The authorization for Hill Samuel Australia to become Macquarie Bank Limited (MBL), an Australian bank, was obtained from the Federal Treasurer on 28 February 1985. The name of the new bank was inspired by one of the most well-known first governors of Australia, Lachlan Macquarie, an early pioneer of the country's economic development, whose forceful vision transformed Australia's penal colonies into a nation and a dynamic economy.

The newly established Macquarie Bank Ltd took over all of the existing activities of Hill Samuel Australia and began operations on 1 March 1985 from its premises in Sydney. This was quickly followed by the opening of operations in Melbourne a few months later, and in Brisbane in November 1986. Ten years later, on 29 July 1996, Macquarie Bank Ltd listed its fully paid ordinary shares on the ASX, and a few months later, on 30 October 1996, it entered the ASX's All Ordinaries Index with a market capitalization of over AU$1bn.

By the early 1990s, Macquarie Bank Ltd was expanding internationally, establishing its Security Capital Markets Group joint venture, later rebranded as the Macquarie Capital Partners (MCP), in the USA. By the beginning of the twenty-first century, MCP had originated transactions worth more than AU$33bn. It had also been instrumental in raising more than AU$25bn debt and equity capital. At that same time, recognizing the potential of infrastructure as an emerging asset offering long-term investment characteristics, it penetrated the Canadian market to become a key investor in the country's infrastructure, adding to its own portfolio of toll roads and airports.

In the decade to 2007, the Macquarie Infrastructure Group (MIG), became the world's largest operator of private toll roads internationally, as well as funds managed by the bank's subsidiaries invested in projects such as airports operating, for example, Kingsford Smith International Airport in Sydney, and Bristol International Airport in the UK. By 2011, Macquarie employed more than 15,500 people in some twenty-eight countries. At 31 March 2011, Macquarie had assets under management of AU$310bn.

Since its formation, Macquarie has created substantial shareholder value. As a result, in the period since listing (29 July 1996) to pre the global financial crisis, the total return to shareholders has by far exceeded that of any other company in the ASX top fifty. A shareholder who invested AU$1,000 in the Bank on listing in 1996 and reinvested dividends would have had an investment worth AU$19,136 as of 31 March 2007. By 2011, Macquarie had total revenues of over AU$7.644bn.

On 13 November 2007, Macquarie Bank Ltd was restructured and became the Macquarie Group Limited, a non-operating holding company, and the final listed parent for the Macquarie Group (ASX: MQG). By early 2008, the global financial crisis had led to unprecedented upheaval in the world's capital markets. Institutions that relied on short-term wholesale markets for their funding struggled to roll over their debt. In 2008, Babcock and Brown, an Australian firm that had sought to emulate Macquarie's innovative approach to infrastructure backed funds collapsed. As markets worldwide contracted, Macquarie engaged in aggressive cost management. In parallel with this, it sought to recalibrate its capital/funding. A key element in this was the use of the Australian government's wholesale funding guarantee, which allowed Australian banks, including Macquarie, to tap into wholesale funding markets using the government's AAA rating. This allowed Macquarie to maintain investor and market confidence. By early 2009, Macquarie, along with the other Australian banks, was recognized globally as having successfully negotiated the worst of the crisis. Emboldened by the challenges in international markets, Macquarie used the global financial crisis as an opportunity to acquire new capability in the areas of investment banking and funds management. Record levels of debt and equity capital raisings in the Australian market provided support to the group's revenue at a time when global markets remained anaemic. However, the ongoing uncertainty meant that merger and acquisition (M&A) deal flow was to remain weak and investors' share trading volumes were low.

Structure and operations

The Macquarie organizational structure consists of six operating groups: Macquarie Capital; Macquarie Securities Group; Fixed Income, Currencies and Commodities; Macquarie Funds Group; Banking and Financial Services Group; and the Corporate and Asset Finance Group. The executive committee, a central group comprising the managing director, deputy managing director, head of risk management, head of corporate affairs, and heads of Macquarie's major operating groups, manages the organization as a whole.

From the outset, Macquarie has had a flat operating structure, with central management giving operating divisions and business units a considerable autonomy. As a result, the firm has a strong entrepreneurial culture, with key operations managers directly responsible for the success of the business and rewarded accordingly. Macquarie's organizational style is intended to be non-hierarchical, with management of the day-to-day operations delegated to the executive committee. In addition, these business groups have considerable discretion in how they operate their businesses within overall guidelines parameters set by the board and executive committee. A defining feature of the firm is that all business activities are governed by a robust risk management approach.

As a result of this approach, Macquarie seeks to encourage a sense of entrepreneurship and commitment from its business managers. Business unit managers in the different geographies are encouraged to take ownership of the execution of strategy, with the central management team focusing on medium and long-term markets and industry risks.

Macquarie's fundamental strategy is to grow selectively by penetrating markets only where its specific knowledge and expertise offer real added value to its clients. This approach allows the company the strategic flexibility to penetrate new business sectors and regions as opportunities arise, while responding to the specialist requirement of individual local markets. In this way, Macquarie can ascertain key positions in a multiplicity of markets.

This management approach is reflected in Macquarie's global presence, with individual businesses working in discrete markets in twenty-eight countries. When entering a new country, Macquarie's strategy is to establish an alliance with a leading domestic provider, which allows it to combine its technical and specialist knowledge with the local providers' market presence and infrastructure.

Macquarie's international expansion

An important plank in Macquarie bank's growth strategy has been to build on its strong track record in infrastructure-based funds to selectively expand offshore. This expansion has seen total operating income from international activities expand significantly in the last ten years.

This expansion has involved setting up additional overseas offices to service clients and the creation of new businesses. While Europe and North America were the key focus of international expansion in the early years, the Asia Pacific region has been an important sphere of geographic expansion in recent years. As a result of these international activities, a growing percentage of Macquarie's business is now with clients outside Australia. Macquarie diversified its activities across the globe in a relatively short period of time. In 2004, Australia accounted for almost 75 per cent of revenues and over 50 per cent of total assets. By 2007, total international assets had expanded to AU$60bn and international revenues were in excess of AU$4bn.

It is important to understand that while Macquarie has expanded overseas, a substantial portion of the key management and strategic activities remain centred in Sydney. Macquarie's operations remain first and foremost Australian although the company has built a significant presence abroad, with operations in Europe (Germany, Austria, France, Italy, Switzerland, Ireland, and the UK), the Americas (the USA, Canada, and Brazil), Asia (China, Hong Kong, Japan, Korea, Singapore, Indonesia, Malaysia, the Philippines, Taiwan, and Thailand), the United Arab Emirates (UAE), India, South Africa, and New Zealand.

Two of the well-known recent acquisitions involve: Cook Inlet, now known as Macquarie Cook Energy, an energy trading and marketing operation based in Los Angeles and servicing North America's largest natural gas producers, utilities, industrial users, and other large wholesale energy sector participants; and RWE Thames Water Holdings, one of the world's largest water and wastewater services company supplying drinking water to 8 million people and sewage services to 13 million consumers. Today, Macquarie employs 15,500 people in over twenty-eight countries.

The global financial crisis

As global financial markets entered the second half of 2007, Macquarie was seen as well placed to continue to grow its international presence. With a diverse business mix and geography, a strong local regulator in the Australian Prudential Regulation Authority (APRA), good positioning in terms of its funding and capital adequacy, and a well-honed approach to risk management, Macquarie Bank was better placed than many of its peers globally to weather the impending storm that was to become the global financial crisis. During 2008, credit markets became extremely difficult and wholesale funding became more expensive. Volumes of trading in equity markets fell sharply from the very high levels of 2007, and, in line with global trend, M&A activity fell away in the face of increasing uncertainty. More worryingly, the crisis spread across the global real estate market and the listed infrastructure fund market, areas in which Macquarie had enjoyed success in the past. In the face of these difficult conditions, the Group was able to continue to perform relatively well, with strong contributions from its commodities-related trading businesses and also foreign exchange.

Faced with these turbulent conditions, the firm was successful in reigning in costs by keeping overheads and remuneration costs in line with business revenue. While global markets dealt with the upheaval of Lehman Brothers and the aftermath of Bear Sterns, Macquarie used its strong balance sheet to expand its international footprint in 2008 through a series of new funds, including a Russian infrastructure fund (a joint venture with Renaissance Capital) and an Indian infrastructure fund (based on a memorandum of understanding with State Bank of India). At the same time, it was recalibrating its asset allocation and undertook an AU$1bn on-market buy-back to facilitate the sale of partial interests in Copenhagen and Brussels airports. By 2009, international income was 52 per cent of total income and Asia Pacific accounted for almost a quarter of that total. Similarly, international staff made up 44 per cent of the total staff of approximately 12,500.

Key elements of the Macquarie Bank international strategy

Exploiting comparative advantage in infrastructure-backed investments

A key component of Macquarie's successful international expansion was its ability to leverage its expertise and comparative advantage in infrastructure-backed funds across different geographies. As Western governments sought to release capital from key infrastructure assets, Macquarie was able to use its early experience in the area to acquire and manage signature assets across the developed countries: specifically, in the USA, the UK, Europe, and Canada. As a result, it has positioned itself to exploit what some would view as key monopoly-type assets from which the company could gain significant economic rents generating in excess of normal returns. The subsequent incorporation of these assets into separate funds, which could in turn be sold to a wider range of investors, allowed Macquarie to maintain both growth and revenues by providing it with a stream of continuously renewed capital.

The corporate parenting style

While Macquarie now operates in some twenty-eight countries, its strong organizational culture has an important impact on its global operations. Risk management remains at the centre of all of the firm's activities and a key feature to the success of its investment strategy; the central team still maintains a close eye on all exposures. As a result, the firm can operate a paradoxically tight–loose approach to operations. Individual country teams have the flexibility to explore value creation opportunities, but within the constraints of tight capital rationing and risk management.

The most important risks identified by Macquarie are equity risk, credit risk, market risk, liquidity risk, operational risk, and legal compliance and documentation risk. While the Risk Management Group (RMG) oversees the appropriate identification, quantification, continuous assessment, and management of these risks within the company, individual businesses remain responsible. RMG also set prudential limits (centralized prudential management), ensuring that aggregated risks do not exceed the firm's economic capability to bear risk.

Successful portfolio management

As Macquarie grew internationally, it continued to expand its range of activities and manage its mix of revenues and assets. As a result, its exposure to individual sectors in specific geographies has been minimized. Over the important growth period from 2004 to 2009, the mix of revenues and assets across the different sectors has remained balanced. As such, the firm has chosen to expand internationally across a range of value propositions and has avoided relying on a narrow lending base for growth.

Strong focus on value creation and unwillingness to compromise standards

At the forefront of the expansion has been a desire to escape the relatively small size of the Australian market. This growth, however, has not come at the expense of cost control, quality of lending, margins, or shareholder value creation. In growing its balance sheet, Macquarie has avoided the trap of substandard lending or poor quality assets. The strong revenue streams also suggest that Macquarie has continued to avoid overpaying for infrastructure assets even in the face of increased bidding competition.

Conservative approach to risk management

Macquarie has, from its very earliest days, had a more conservative capital and funding profile than its peers, such as Babcock and Brown. As a result, when the financial crisis hit and wholesale funding markets dried up, it was able to weather the market shocks and set about recalibrating its activities to reflect the new realities. A key part of its risk management approach is to apply a stress test approach to all risk types and a detailed examination of the consequences of the worst-case outcomes. In addition, the firm determines the aggregate risk appetite by assessing risk relative to earnings rather than by reference to capital.

Conclusion

While the global financial crisis presented significant challenges for Macquarie, by late 2009, it was clear that its early robust response to cost control, funding challenges, and its strong focus on risk management would allow it to weather the crisis far better than many of its global peers. With the support of the Australian government, in the form of the wholesale funding guarantee, the group was able to continue its international growth aspirations. As a result, by 2009, 40 per cent of operating income was coming from businesses that did not exist in 2004.

In pursuing its international growth strategy over the past ten years, Macquarie has sought to deliver long-term value to shareholders by exploiting its comparative advantage in asset management, investment banking, and particularly in lending. The empowered entrepreneurial management ethos, combined with strong centralized risk management and close attention to maximizing deal fees and flows to Macquarie, has allowed it to gain a unique foothold in key overseas markets.

While the tyranny of distance often dogs the expansion plans of Australasian firms, Macquarie has shown that focusing on key sources of expertise and comparative advantage can yield results even in distant markets.

The challenge going forward for Macquarie is that, faced with increasingly turbulent capital markets, it needs to continue to attract and invest scarce capital in viable projects. The ability of the firm to continue to grow in the future is inherently dependent on the soundness of the strategic decisions of the past and the extent to which those expansions overseas continue to drive bottom-line operating cash flows. If the lending and asset management activities of the firm can avoid the worse aspects of the credit crisis, Macquarie is well placed to continue its future expansion. A strong balance sheet, combined with the ability to negotiate the cultures of new and less familiar markets, will remain a challenge.

Case questions

1. To what extent has Macquarie Bank's international expansion been successful and delivered value?

2. What lessons can be learned from Macquarie Bank's international expansion? Are these firm-specific lessons or would they hold relevance in other contexts?

3. What were the key factors likely to have enabled or constrained Macquarie Bank's corporate strategy?

4. What key challenges does Macquarie Bank now face going forward?

References

http://www.macquarie.com.au/mgl/au

Macquarie Bank Ltd. 2004. ***Macquarie Bank 2004 Annual Review***. Sydney: Macquarie Bank.

Macquarie Bank Ltd. 2007a. ***Macquarie Bank 2007 Annual Review***. Sydney: Macquarie Bank.

Macquarie Bank Ltd. 2007b. Result announcement for the year ended 31 March 2007: Presentation to investors and analysts. Sydney, 15 May.

Macquarie Group. 2009. ***Management Discussion and Analysis 31 March 2009***. Sydney: Macquarie Group.

Macquarie Group Ltd. 2011. ***2011 Annual Report***. Sydney: Macquarie Group.

Moore, N. and Ward, G. 2009. ***Macquarie Group Limited: Result Announcement for the Year Ended 31 March***. Sydney: Macquarie Group.

Case 7 McDonald's: still lovin' it?

Dr. Kerrie Fleming, Dublin City University Business School, Dublin, Ireland

This case study provides an example of how fast-food giant McDonald's has used franchising to ensure standardization and control through the efficient use of technology, offering an element of flexibility to adjust to changing consumer tastes while maintaining a significant market share across a global spectrum, as part of its 'Plan to Win' strategy.

Lonnell Buford, 38, of Montgomery County used to stop by the McDonald's near his Beltsville office every morning to order a steak, egg and cheese bagel, orange juice and coffee. But after his firm lost a contract in September, Buford lost his job as a forklift operator and had to move in with his mother. He cut back his McDonald's breakfast outings to twice a week and now orders from the dollar menu.

'I'm on a budget,' he said on a recent morning as he finished a \$2 meal of coffee and a sausage biscuit at a McDonald's on New York Avenue NW. 'I need to hold on to the little bit that I have.'[1]

Survival of the not so fittest

Every day, 64 million consumers, like Buford, eat in McDonald's restaurants across the world. The annual sales revenue of the company in 2010 was over US\$24bn, generated across its 32,737 restaurants in over 117 countries (see Table L7.1).

The business began its life in 1937 when two brothers, Richard and Maurice McDonald, developed food processing and assembly line techniques in a small drive-through restaurant in California. In 1954, Ray Kroc, a milkshake salesman, negotiated a franchise deal giving him exclusive rights to franchise McDonald's in the USA. The McDonald brothers sold the business in 1961 for US\$2.7m.[2] In the past decade, the McDonald's franchise has faced its greatest challenges since it was founded by Ray Kroc, such as changing consumer tastes, global recession, and strong competition. The famous 'golden arches' are a sight of joy for many young children across the globe, yet they have also become an object of scorn for protestors who suggest that they are a symbol of all that is wrong with global capitalism. In 2002, the company reported losses for the first time in twenty-nine years. Its public image was not helped by the sudden death of chief executive officer (CEO) Jim Cantalupo from a heart attack at a McDonald's convention in Florida in 2004; not long after his appointment, Cantalupo's replacement, Charlie Bell, was diagnosed with colon cancer and forced to step down. Critics seized on these events to highlight, albeit without any medical foundations, the consequences of a bad diet. At the same time, the growth and very viability of McDonald's business suffered something of a health scare. Having tactfully mastered global expansion, how can the golden arches deal with the changing demands of the consumer and yet still offer a fast, efficient, and reliable service? Is there room for the traditional fast-food take-away model in the face of increased criticism from health-conscious lobby groups? How can McDonald's protect its market share during uncertain economic times, in which disposable income has decreased, but consumer demands for variety and value have increased?

Table L7.1 McDonald's global revenues 2008–10

Geographic segment	2008 (\$bn)	2009 (\$bn)	2010 (\$bn)
USA	8,078	7,944	8,112
Europe	9,923	9,274	9,569
APMEA*	4,231	4,337	5,066
Other countries and corporate	1,290	1,190	1,328
Total revenues	**23,522**	**22,745**	**24,075**

*APMEA = Asia/Pacific, Middle East, and Africa
Source: McDonald's Annual Report 2010

[1] Mui, Y. 2010. 'Fast-food breakfast sales decline as fewer head to work', The Washington Post, 21 February.

[2] http://www.mcdonalds.com

McDonald's 'Plan to Win' strategy

In the introductory phase of its business operations McDonald's offered consumers low-priced food products, making eating out on a regular basis affordable for families.[3] This low-cost strategy worked well for a number of years, but a slide in profit margins and store sales revenue in 2002 demonstrated that the company had lost its way. This was reflected by a statement made at the time by the CEO, who said: 'We lost our focus; we had taken our eyes off the fries.' This low-cost strategy had been achieved through standardization, offering generic products at competitive prices and achieving market domination through expansion, constantly rolling out new stores across new locations, keeping competition out of an area. However, this expansion strategy caused a loss of focus on the core elements of the business and when Jim Cantalupo stepped in as CEO in 2003, he decided to shift the company's well-worn generic low-cost strategy of mass production for homogenous markets to one of greater differentiation. This strategy focused on marketing to turn around the negative publicity and offered customers a better overall fast-food experience, fulfilling the McDonald's mission to be 'our customer's favourite place and way to eat'. In more recent years, the company has faced a decline in the informal eating out (IEO) market, as well as shifting demographics and changing eating habits, which necessitates further strategic response. McDonald's has responded well to such changes, which are mostly led by consumer demand for convenience, value, and healthier and locally grown organic food. Efficient operations, effective marketing, and an ability to provide a fast service are all key drivers in ensuring survival in an industry that has become highly competitive. McDonald's 'Plan to Win' strategy centres on the five basics of a customer experience: people, products, place, price and promotion.[4] The strategy focuses on continuously increasing McDonald's relevance to consumers' everyday lives through optimizing the menu, modernizing customer experience, broadening accessibility, enhancing McDonald's food image, accelerating its interior and exterior re-imaging, and assessing its operational and financial activities.

In recent years, the interiors of McDonald's restaurants have been redesigned and hard plastic seats (originally designed to ensure a faster turnaround of customers) have been replaced with more comfortable chairs to encourage customers to stay longer and enjoy the McDonald's 'experience'. Different zones for different customers were created, including a den with wall-mounted flat-screen televisions, a play place for children, and a large high-top table with Wi-Fi access. The McCafe was introduced as a separately demarcated space inside the store, with a glass cabinet selling pastries and espresso-style coffees. This image redesign has paid off, strongly differentiating the brand from competitors such as Burger King and Wendy's.

Another part of the strategy that has boosted corporate profits is the extension of customer care facilities, which emerged from analysis of US demographic trends on informal eating behaviours. This included extending opening hours in some outlets across the USA. In the past decade, some restaurants have extended their hours from the basic 6 am–11 pm hours to all-night opening in some locations.[5] It is estimated that McDonald's has 40 per cent of the US morning breakfast market, which accounts for approximately a quarter of its revenue and 35 per cent of its profit. In 2011, the breakfast market grew by 5.7 per cent, with offerings such as coffee, fruit smoothies, frappes, and other cold drinks leading to the increase. These breakfast items are hugely profitable, because it takes an estimated US$0.35 worth of coffee to make a large frappe, for which McDonald's charges US$3.29. Other demographic trends also revealed the need for the availability of value items, so McDonald's introduced a breakfast version of its popular dollar menu, featuring five items: a sausage burrito, the sausage McMuffin, a sausage biscuit, hash browns, and coffee for US$1 each. The chain suggested that this offering promotes a strong national voice on the meal at a time when customers are concerned about value. Starbucks, Wendy's, and Dunkin' Donuts are working hard to challenge McDonald's in the breakfast market, launching hot breakfast sandwiches such as the 'Egg White Turkey Sausage Flat Bread'. Despite the strength of its competitors, McDonald's continues to command nearly half the US hamburger market, almost three times more than Wendy's and twice that of Burger King.

[3] Marino, L. and Jackson, K. B. 2006. 'McDonald's: polishing the golden arches', in A. Thompson, A. Strickland, and J. Gamble (eds) Crafting and Executing Strategy: Concepts and Cases, 14th edn, New York: McGraw-Hill/Irwin.

[4] http:/www.mcdonalds.com

[5] Businessweek. 2007. 'McDonald's 24/7', 5 February, available online at http://www.businessweek.com/magazine/content/07_06/b4020001.htm

Product innovation has also kept McDonald's on top: for example, the US$1.29 chicken snack wrap was intricately designed using a 16.5 cm tortilla wrap, which people can hold in one hand while steering a car with the other. The wrap also had a thick ranch dressing, as opposed to a thinner style dressing, to guard against spills whilst driving. These innovations have been extended to the ski slope, as illustrated by the opening of the first McSki restaurant in Lindvallen in Sweden, where customers can consume a Big Mac, hot chocolate, or apple pie without taking off their ski equipment. In 2006, McDonald's opened its first drive-through in Guangdong, China, reflecting the massive growth in Chinese car ownership. McDonald's in Australia has launched family boxes featuring popular items bundled together, competing with KFC, which traditionally offers buckets of fried chicken for family consumption.

Besides restaurant redesign, innovative menu modifications, and technological improvements, McDonald's has also worked hard on reducing its in-house costs. A reduction in carbon emissions and cost of fuel has been achieved by eliminating high-emissions vehicles from its company fleet. Media advertisers have also been pressed for lower rates on advertising and marketing the firm, while non-profitable stores have been closed across the globe. New stores have not been opened where neighbourhood developments appear weak.[6]

Ensuring consistency: franchising and technology

Almost 80 per cent of McDonald's business comes from franchising. Franchises are owned and operated by independent local businesspeople, while the remainder comes from directly operated restaurants. The purpose of direct operations are to maintain some in-house experience in order to continually develop and redefine operations, marketing, product, and pricing strategies, and to provide optimal direction for franchisees. Franchising is key to McDonald's international success, allowing it to license operators to use the full business package, including training, support, and corporate supplies.[7] McDonald's has a contractual or implied obligation to maintain its brand image through advertising, promotion, and the control of other participants in the franchisee system. The advantage for McDonald's is the ability to expand the standardized business model rapidly, and to spread costs and risks across its network of franchisees. For the franchisee, the main advantage is the established business model and one of the world's most recognized brands. For McDonald's, the franchisee is in a better position to understand local conditions and can handle cultural differences, language barriers, bureaucracy, and political problems more easily. The franchisee is seen not only as a source of revenue, but also as a conduit of information of the local environment. This domestic presence is seen as crucial for successful international expansion and the 'Think global, act local' approach is illustrated through the variations in McDonald's menus across its stores. In Israel, Big Macs are served without cheese, thereby permitting the separation of meat and dairy products required of kosher restaurants. In Germany, consumers demand beer with their Big Mac. In Japan, traditional McDonald's fare includes Teriyaki burgers. In Singapore and Malaysia, McDonald's underwent rigorous inspections by Muslim clerics to ensure ritual cleanliness, so that the chain could be rewarded with 'halal' or 'clean' certificates.[8] McDonald's also offers unique products, such as the Croque McDo, a traditional ham-and-cheese sandwich modelled after the French standard. The Chicken Maharaja Mac, a chicken patty version of the Big Mac, is produced in India for those consumers who do not eat beef.

Technology is also a key mechanism by which McDonald's retains control of operations and thereby ensures the consistency of its product. For example, in the Philippines, the management of operational functions such as monitoring inventory systems, application of management systems, document management, and hardware systems is done through efficient information and communications technology and infrastructure. Store systems in all branches must run efficiently at all times, so any trouble that may arise in one of the point-of-sale tills can be solved speedily to avoid service delays. In order to ensure this type of efficiency, McDonald's avails of technical support from Fujitsu

[6] Adamy, J. 2009. 'McDonald's seeks way to keep sizzling', Wall Street Journal, 10 March.

[7] Quinn, B. and Alexander, N. 2002. International retail franchising: a conceptual framework. International Journal of Retail and Distribution Management, 30(5): 264–276.

[8] Marino and Jackson, op cit.

Philippines Inc. (FPI), which provides each outlet with the use of a helpdesk service,[9] which solves any technical issues as quickly as possible in-store. The standardization model that has become iconic across each McDonald's outlet is one that allows the company an additional means of achieving fixed and specific goals through controlling its technical operations and products. Standardization is also a key feature of McDonald's operations, which can be viewed as an assembly line with a minimum amount of steps. Each step is intricate, from the precise arm motion for employees salting a batch of fries to the fact that, across all stores, one out of every two fries must measure 0.75 cm, meat for the Big Mac must weigh 45 g and contain 20 per cent fat, and buns must be 9.5–9.8 cm in diameter and 6 cm high. McDonald's has worked with Argonne National Laboratory near Chicago to devise a rapid frying system that reduces customer delivery time from 40 to 30 seconds.[10] Advances in automation are revolutionizing the fast-food industry, to reduce labour costs and increase speed of service. Customer interface technologies, such as touch-screen order systems, are being introduced across the globe, which release workers from counter duty. Most restaurants aim to process walk-in orders within 90 seconds and guarantee that customers never have to wait more than three-and-a-half minutes at a drive-through. This is measured by a wall-mounted timer, which counts down the minutes from when the order is placed to when it is handed to the customer. Service time charts are recorded by store managers and monitored by company representatives, who regularly inspect the outlets. The company also uses technology to assist with language and cultural differences through the use of pictographs on the point-of-sale terminals, which display the symbols of the products instead of words or numerals, allowing orders to be taken easily and with better accuracy. Self-order kiosks have been introduced in Germany, France, and Spain in 3,000 restaurants, which have added to the convenience of ordering and reducing labour overheads. These operational commonalities across the company allow the encompassing of knowledge, skills, training and induction, and standard procedures developing capabilities to compete quickly, with speed, routine, and standardization enabling cost reduction and economies of scale. Through the imposition of uniform technological control mechanisms and operational competencies across stores, McDonald's is constantly pursuing incremental innovations that lever its core competences and brand power.

McWorkers

In 2010, McDonald's employed 1.7 million people worldwide.[11] The company is committed to employing local staff and promoting from within. Some 37 per cent of McDonald's franchisee owners, 70 per cent of US restaurant managers, and 50 per cent of the company's US corporate employees all started as restaurant staff. There are three staff levels in McDonald's restaurants: hourly paid employees; junior business managers; and business management trainees. McDonald's has a training centre in Illinois, designed for managers, assistant managers, and franchisees, known as the 'Hamburger University'. Since its foundation in 1961, over 70,000 McDonald's employees have graduated from this institution. There are also training centres located in Munich, Tokyo, Sydney, London, and China. The curriculum concentrates on managing food processes, such as the temperature at which hamburgers need to be cooked and how to inspect restaurant facilities to ensure that quality standards are met. The company states that the experience gained in a McDonald's restaurant provides skills and values that last a lifetime, including teamwork, customer service, leadership, effective communication, and finance management.

In the past number of years, outlets in Brazil, the UK, and the USA have received prestigious awards such as 'Ten best companies for which to work', 'Top ten UK private sector performers in ethnic minority diversity', and 'Best company for minorities'. In 2006, a study of the company found that 83 per cent of crew members in five of the nine major McDonald's markets said that they would recommend working at McDonald's. However, despite its numerous accolades, some suggest that relations between the company and its employees can be fraught. A study of the company undertaken in Germany examining its human resources policy regarding unionization found that McDonald's is allegedly an active anti-

[9] http://www.fujitsu.com

[10] Vignali, C. 2001. McDonald's: 'Think global, act local'—the marketing mix. British Food Journal, 103(2): 97–111.

[11] http://www.aboutmcdonalds.com

union company. There were allegedly occasions on which the company has temporarily closed a restaurant and then reopened, employing only those who had shown no interest in unions or workers' councils.[12] McDonald's also prides itself in trying to achieve 100 per cent local control by local operators, but the term 'local' may refer only to the operator's proximity to the market, because human resource management practices appear to be subject to highly centralized control in the USA, which manifest as standard policies, conditions, and training.

A new McDonald's opens somewhere in the world every eight hours, and so recruitment is a major function for the company. In the past few years, the company undertook a strong recruitment drive with a campaign titled 'It's not just a job, it's a career' to offset the image of offering low-skilled positions without any serious career advancement prospects. McDonald's has worked hard to attract employees by offering perks such as above-average national minimum wage and 'weekend-only' positions to students. It also offers education scholarships of €1,500 to encourage people to pursue further education, as well as formal training programmes in which staff receive five days' training per year and managers receive twelve days, including both on-the-job and formal offsite training. These efforts appear to have paid off in Ireland, where, in 2011, the company was voted among the top fifty best places in which to work for the eighth consecutive year.

Challenges and reaction

Since the 1990's, McDonald's has been able to offset negative publicity with purposeful public relations campaigns and legal challenges. McDonald's has been at the forefront of anti-globalization campaigns, one led by British activists who distributed leaflets across London city entitled 'What's wrong with McDonald's?' McDonald's sued for libel and the case became known as 'McLibel'. In addition, books such as *Fast Food Nation*[13] accused McDonald's of using political influence to increase its profits at the expense of people's health and highlighted the poor social conditions of its workers. In France, a French farmer called Jose Bové led nine other farmers to wreck a half-built McDonald's restaurant in protest. When he was tried, 40,000 people rallied outside the courthouse. Bové said that the struggle was between real food from real farmers and industrial agriculture under corporate control. The targeting of children in McDonald's advertising campaigns has also been strongly criticized, but this potentially negative image has being offset through charity campaigns and corporate social responsibility projects. In 2006, during the company's fiftieth anniversary year, McDonald's donated US$50m to children's causes around the world. This was distributed through the Ronald McDonald House Charities (RMHC) and other children's organizations. In the USA, the company has supported care mobile programmes, which provide state-of-the-art vehicles to deliver cost-effective medical, dental, and health education services to children.

More recently, anti-fast-food campaigns have refocused attention on McDonald's, including the documentary *Super Size Me*, which documented an individual who consumed only McDonald's food for a month. He reportedly gained 24 lbs, became moody, and lost his sex drive. Such was the reaction to the film that McDonald's withdrew its Super Size meals and started to introduce healthier options, such as salads. To date, the company has sold 300 million premium salads in the USA, which equals 600 million servings of green vegetables. It has also introduced fruit and yogurts with children's Happy Meals. Its first Happy Meal for adults was launched in 2004, and included an exercise booklet and stepometer as part of the package. The company has also put nutritional information on its menu tray liners and also has food labelling. Although the ultimate decision to purchase and consume fast food lies with each individual consumer or, in the case of young children, with their respective guardians, governments initiatives to tackle obesity levels among children and adults will need to be strongly considered in the design of McDonald's future strategies for long-term survival.

[12] Royle, T. 1995. Corporate versus societal culture: a comparative study of McDonald's in Europe. International Journal of Contemporary Hospitality Management, 7(2/3): 52–56.

[13] Schlosser, E. 2001. Fast Food Nation. Harmondsworth: Penguin.

'I'm lovin' it' campaign

Justin Timberlake fronted the McDonald's 'I'm Lovin It' global campaign in 2003, which was the first campaign of its kind to feature a single set of commercials across 100 countries, incorporating the theme into advertising, promotions, public relations, restaurant merchandising, and overall brand communication initiatives. However, the direct translation of 'I'm Lovin It' in Japanese is 'As for me, there is that love', so McDonald's needed to localize its marketing communications and consider the enormous cultural and language differences within each country. In Beijing, McDonald's was advised not to advertise on television, because audiences have a tendency to switch to another channel during commercial breaks, meaning that adverts have little chance of being seen. Newspapers and popular magazines provided a more effective means of communicating the brand image in this region, where the company's mascot 'Ronald' was paired with a female companion known as 'Aunt McDonald', whose job it was to entertain children. An extension of this concept is seen across Beijing outlets, where public relations staff are available to answer customer questions. There are also several female receptionists to provide parents with a high level of courtesy. This is now being offered in other outlets in parts of Europe, where parental customers are provided with relief to care for their children during the 'McDonald's experience'. In recent years, the campaign has continued to promote McDonald's restaurants as a place in which to spend time with the family while enjoying the food, but it now includes advertising of value saver meal offerings for teenagers and young adults. One element of the marketing strategy that has been generic across the world has been the company's alliance with Walt Disney and DreamWorks, allowing McDonald's exclusive rights for everything from films to toys. This has led to McDonald's distributing toys in its Happy Meals for films such as *A Bugs Life*, *Toy Story*, and *Shrek*. The worldwide appeal of Disney and DreamWorks films and products has meant that this global marketing strategy has been a success, which is reflected in McDonald's financial success against all odds over the past few years.

McDonald's today

In 2010, CEO Jim Skinner reflected on McDonald's growth against the odds of global recession: 'We dug for deeper consumer insights, aligned our strategies, and strengthened the pace of our business.' He credited this success to the 'Plan to Win' strategy. This has been demonstrated by the increase in share price from US$58.91 per share in 2008 to US$76.76 per share in 2010. Global comparable sales increased by 5 per cent in 2010, which was the eighth consecutive year of same stores sales growth. In 2010, McDonald's served 200 million more customers than 2009, which resulted in a comparable sales increase in the USA of 3.7 per cent, while Europe comparable sales grew by 4.4 per cent in the same period. In 2010, the company returned US$5.1bn to shareholders through dividends and shares.[14] McDonald's has been able to achieve these financial results through its ability to create a flexible global brand and product range, which can be tinkered with to suit local cultural environments and markets.

Thanks to its 'Plan to Win' strategy, McDonald's has successfully weathered a number of challenges that have threatened its very existence, from a decline in profits and market share, to bad publicity. However, it remains to be seen whether McDonald's has developed the capability to survive the next stage of market evolution in a world that has become dominated by healthy eating, ethical behaviours, and carbon footprints. Was the change in low-cost focus to one of differentiation and customer focus a strategy forced upon McDonald's or did the company genuinely realize what the market really wanted? McDonald's now has to work hard to maintain the position of market leader, through developing future scenarios, which can incorporate elements such as customer convenience, customer value, and optimal operations. This could involve strategies to improve manufacturing systems inventory control, production planning, financial control, and operations. The future model might not be that of a service company, but one that serves as a family retreat, where parents can relax while children play with promotional toys or in increasingly elaborate indoor playground, with digital-media kiosks for burning CDs, developing iPhone applications, and interactive gaming facilities for young adults. Could the McDonald's experience actually be enhanced by replacing counter staff with touch-screen interfaces? Could more food production

[14] McDonald's Annual Report 2010.

processes be automated, freeing up restaurant staff to interact in more interesting ways with customers? Can developments in technology, such as the ability to order in advance from home or the car and the introduction of double-lane drive-throughs all enhance the customer experience? All of these are essential questions for McDonald's, which now needs to devise the successor to the 'Plan to Win' strategy, leading to the establishment of capabilities that will ensure survival and success for organizations in this era of kaleidoscopic change.

Case questions

1. Describe the methods that the company has used to ensure the consistency and success of its brand both globally and locally.
2. What has McDonald's done to ensure that it 'Thinks global, acts local'?
3. How did the McDonald's 'Plan to Win' strategy contribute to its recovery from losses in 2002?
4. Describe the key challenges that McDonald's now confronts.
5. How can McDonald's continue to achieve success in the context of an increasingly knowledgeable and demanding consumer?

Case 8 Reassessing value in strategy

Mishko Hansen, Doctoral Researcher, Judge Business School, University of Cambridge

Strategy is neither simple nor easy, but rather is best understood as confronting difficult truths and negating challenges (Beer and Eisenstat, 2004: 83; Rumelt, 2011). This text opened by discovering strategy and strategists and the challenges that they confront, while the latter chapters broadened and reframed the discussion by introducing differing contexts (Chapter 13) and critical perspectives on strategy and strategy agents (Chapter 14) in order to rediscover what is, or may be, meant by 'strategy' and 'strategists'.

The limitations of standard case studies is that they can imply a 'one a size fits all' solution or easily become abstracted from the power plays and politics that frame strategic thinking in practice. Consequently, in the spirit of fostering the type of critical conversations that we believe to be at the heart of strategy, we include a piece by Mishko Hansen, which serves to open up debate about what is seen by many as the essence of strategy: the notion of creating value. Linking with the theme of the purpose of business (see Chapter 5) and aligned with the logic of questioning characteristic of our rediscovering strategy and strategists chapters (see Chapters 13 and 14), the piece carefully dissects and deconstructs the purpose, use, and meaning of the term 'value' in strategy. In so doing, it offers a platform for debate, discussion, and reflection about what should be the true purpose of strategy and the appropriate moral template for strategists.

Reassessing value in strategy

Value is, in many ways, the single most important concept in strategy. When people talk and write about strategy, they almost invariably use terms such as 'adding value', 'creating value', and 'shareholder value'. Indeed, it is often stated (implicitly and explicitly) that the creation of value is the purpose for businesses existing in the first place. Companies, as a matter of course, describe how they intend to create value. Philip Clarke, group chief executive officer (CEO) of Tesco plc (2011), describes Tesco's purpose as being 'to create value for customers to earn their lifetime loyalty, and I want Tesco to put that at the heart of everything that it does'. His goal is for Tesco 'to be the most highly valued company, valued by our customers, valued by our staff, by the communities in which we work and by our shareholders'. ExxonMobil's core objective is 'to deliver long-term growth in shareholder value',[1] while Bayer's credo is 'working to create value through innovation and growth'.

The value proposition of Tesco, ExxonMobil, and Bayer seem easy to understand and conceptualize. Given this, you would think that there would be a clear theory of value within strategy. And yet this is very far from the case. In recent years, a number of prominent strategy thinkers have criticized the way in which value is conceptualized. For example, the late Sumantra Ghosal and colleagues (1999) proposed a 'new manifesto for business' based primarily on distinguishing between 'value creation' and 'value appropriation'. Similarly, the late C. K. Prahalad and V. Ramaswamy (2004: x) argue that the move towards increasingly networked business processes requires replacing the traditional value paradigm with one based on the 'co-creation of unique value with customers'. From a more critical perspective, Henry Mintzberg and colleagues (2002), in a piece provocatively titled 'Beyond selfishness', questions the attractiveness of strategy based on a narrow vision of value-maximization. Recent writing on corporate social responsibility has also emphasized the need to re-examine 'value'. For example, John Elkington and colleagues (2006: 7), the originator of the influential 'triple bottom line' concept, has argued that the increasing awareness of the need to account for non-financial dimensions of corporate performance and impacts requires 'new thinking about value creation appropriate to the very different circumstances of the 21st Century'.

[1] http://www.tescoplc.com/media/142254/business-for-a-new-decade-transcript.pdf; http://www.exxonmobil.com; http://www.sustainability2006.bayer.com

Current uses of value in strategy

As these concerns suggest, there are tensions and ambiguities about the way in which value is used in strategy. Why is this? And should it be of concern to you? To explore these questions, let us take a closer look at some of the assumptions that underlie the mainstream notion of value and the kind of issues that are at stake. Although it may be true that strategy lacks an adequate definition of value, it is not to say that there is no dominant definition. To see this, let us look at two examples of the use of value by leading management strategists: Michael Porter, and Kim and Mauborgne. As discussed by Cummings and Angwin (2004), many—perhaps most—managers from around the world have been influenced in how they think about strategy by Porter's 'Five Forces' model, and his concept of the value chain. In both *Competitive Strategy* and *Competitive Advantage*, Porter is clear on the importance of value. Indeed, competitive advantage, he asserts, 'grows fundamentally out of the value a firm is able to create for its buyers' (Porter, 1998: 3). So how does Porter define value? He defines it as 'what buyers are willing to pay for a product or service' (ibid: 3, 132). This, in turn is based on 'their level of satisfaction or meeting their needs'. So, logically Porter is saying that value *equals* the level of satisfaction and meeting needs. In some ways, this sounds quite reasonable. And, to be fair to Porter, he is much more explicit in this than most strategy (and management) writers—for whom it is usually simply assumed.

A similar account can be seen in Kim and Mauborgne's influential bestseller *Blue Ocean Strategy*. The cornerstone of this strategy, they explain (Kim and Mauborgne, 2005: 12, 7, 79), is 'value innovation', which focuses on 'making the competition irrelevant' by creating 'uncontested market space' through 'open[ing] up unprecedented customer utility'. By 'utility', Kim and Mauborgne are referring to (as with Porter) a level of satisfaction or meeting their needs. Combined with the right pricing and cost structure, significant new customer utility ensures that the firm can 'create a leap in net buyer value, where net buyer value *equals* the utility buyers receive minus the price they pay for it'. Through this formulation, we can see that, for Kim and Mauborgne, 'customer utility' and 'buyer value' are, in fact, interchangeable terms, and that both can be measured financially, since they can be 'netted' by subtracting their financial cost.

By efficiently creating customer utility, the firm also (Kim and Mauborgne, 2005: 119) 'creates a leap in value for itself in the form of profit—that is, the price of the offering minus the cost of production'. So, we can see that Kim and Mauborgne are also saying that value *equals* the level of satisfaction and meeting needs *equals* the amount that people are willing to pay for a product are service. Again, Kim and Mauborgne are unusual, since they make explicit the value framework that they are using. Are there any problems with this definition of value? We will return to this later, but first let us look at things from a slightly wider perspective.

What is crucial to see is that both Porter and Kim and Mauborgne are articulating their versions of value within a wider 'story of value' that is of immense influence, not only in strategy and thinking about business, but also in broader economic and political decision making. This story is fundamentally a story about free exchange for mutual gain, one that begins, and in a sense ends, with consumers. Buyers, faced with limited resources, act in such a way as to get the most satisfaction and 'utility' from their purchases. Responding to this, businesses create products and services that are valued by buyers. By efficiently supplying these offerings to the market, a business is able to pay its employees and suppliers and make a profit, thereby creating value for itself and, in doing so, its shareholders as well. This, in turn, creates a platform for offering more and better products in the future. Society benefits from all of these activities, because it is made up of individuals who, at different times, take on (or have the opportunity to take on) the role of buyer, employee, supplier, shareholder, and so on. Together, these processes form the virtuous circle that is at the centre of free market capitalism. This basic schema is depicted in Figure L8.1.

In this 'story of value', corporations have a crucial role. By pursuing and achieving competitive advantage, corporations are the major drivers of innovation and increased standards of living. This is true at a national level and also internationally. The ideal vision of globalization imagines that, with the dismantling of trade barriers and the embracing of corporate-led capitalism all over the planet, it is only a matter of time before the products, services, jobs, and increasing levels of wealth that a vibrant economy brings are spread to people everywhere. So creating value is about achieving a better world! No wonder there are no strategy books that suggest that creating value is not really that important, or might not be worth pursuing.

It is because of this background 'story of value' that Kim and Mauborgne (2005: ix) can assert that efficient value innovation is key to building 'a future where customers, employees, shareholders, and society win'. Similarly, in *Competing for the Future* (one of the most influential strategy books of the 1990s), Hamel and Prahalad (1994: 38) depict business competition as

Figure L8.1 The virtuous circle of free market capitalism

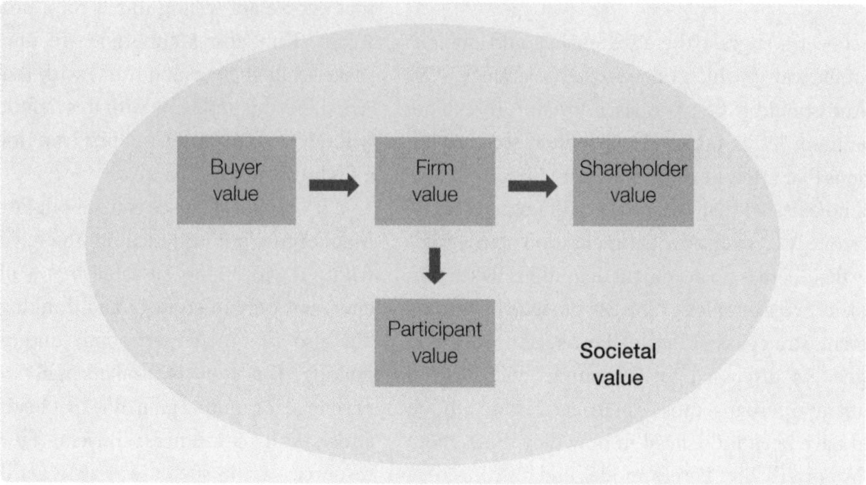

revolving around 'creating the future' based on delivering 'new and profound customer benefits'. The strategic foresight that this requires, they argue (ibid: 112–114), comes when company executives are able to 'empathize with basic human needs', and strive to 'better the human condition' and 'make a difference in people's lives'. More recently, Ian Davis (2005), CEO of McKinsey, has argued that 'the ultimate purpose of business as the efficient provision of goods and services that society wants. This is a hugely valuable, even noble, purpose'. For Davis, this does not, however, seem to require significant change in business practices, but rather a re-articulation of the existing 'social contract', so as to make existing corporate contributions to society clearer. All the while, shareholder value 'should continue to be seen as the critical measure of business success'. Indeed, in mainstream strategy thought, value creation—even in the narrowly defined form of shareholder value—is usually taken to be directly linked to human well-being. Stewart's *The Quest for Value* (1991), one of the first books advocating a narrow shareholder value focus for corporate strategy, shows this familiar presumed linkage between 'value' as measured in market transactions and the well-being of individuals and society.

> It is easy to forget why senior management's aim must be to maximize its firm's current market value. ... [A] greater value rewards the shareholders ... But, and this really is much more important, society at large benefits too ... Although there are exceptions to this rule, most of the time there is a happy harmony between creating stock market value and enhancing the quality of life.
>
> (Stewart, 1991: 1)

The story then, is one in which business success is based on creating value. Value is based on customer utility, and the higher the utility, the more people are willing pay. Therefore, increasing 'value' as identified in market transactions is predicated on increasing 'customer value'. In this way, business success is described as emanating from 'unprecedented customer utility', 'satisfaction', meeting 'basic human needs', 'new and profound customer benefits', 'bettering the human condition', enhanced 'quality of life', 'social benefit', and other similarly excellent-sounding things.

Questioning value

Having sketched out the mainstream use of value in strategy and the 'story of value' of which it is part, the question to consider is what is wrong with this picture? Why are so many people, even within management itself, challenging it? To explore this, let us examine two major criticisms that are often made against the 'strategy' concept of value. The first, which is at the heart of the increase in interest in corporate social responsibility in the past several years, can be called the *market failure* critique of value. The second, which is generally less articulated (within management-related writing at least), can be called the *failure of markets* critique of value. Because the first is better known and less radical in its implications, we will look at it more briefly. But, as we will see, the kinds of market failure that are often pointed to in calling for greater corporate social responsibility become all the more important if you agree, even in part, with the *failure of markets* approach.

The market failure critique of value

There are numerous critiques of value based on market failure. Despite their differences, all are based on the fundamental insight that the welfare-enhancing outcomes that are assumed to flow from the 'creation of value' depend upon markets working properly. What is meant by 'properly'? In essence, the economic theory that underpins the 'story of value' outlined above assumes certain features of markets. In their classical formulation, this includes assumptions such as there being no product differentiation, that no market participants have greater power than others to influence price, that all market participants have perfect and complete information, that everyone has access to the same technologies and resources at the same prices, and that there are no barriers to industry entrance or exit. In economic models, if all of these conditions were to hold, then markets could be said to be functioning 'perfectly', and collective social welfare would be maximized, all else being equal. Although no one thinks that these conditions are achieved in reality, if markets approximate these conditions to a reasonable degree, then they can be thought of as working 'properly'. However, when significant deviations arise from these assumptions and social welfare is damaged in a systemic way, a 'market failure' is said to exist.

The most visible form of market failure critique relates to 'externalities'. Externalities are said to occur when the parties to an economic exchange do not take into account costs or benefits that accrue to 'outside' stakeholders. A typical example would be a company the production of which pollutes the water in the river next to its factory. In this case, the pollution exits the factory and then goes downstream, causing potential problems for human (and animal) life, but no direct damage to the company itself (in the absence of appropriate legal frameworks and regulatory measures). Similarly, the customers who buy the company's products get the benefits of using the product, but do not also have to accept the pollution that accompanied the making of the product (unless they live downstream from the factory). So both the company and customers are ignoring costs that are *external* to their immediate concerns.

What is important to see is that almost no one really believes that there are no market imperfections or 'failures', or that markets never provide useful information at all. There is, however, a great deal of contestation over how important market failures are. For many people concerned about the environment, it seems clear that the tendency to ignore environmental costs has led to a potentially catastrophic trajectory for our global economy. This is why, for example, the seminal Stern Review (commissioned by the UK government) argued that climate change represents 'the greatest market failure the world has seen'.[2] Here, we have an economic trajectory that could potentially undercut the very viability of life on earth, and yet each step towards this unenviable future has been called an increase in 'value'. If we take such environmental concerns seriously,[3] factoring in the *full costs* of products and services might show that many successful and admired companies are destroying value rather than creating it!

To use a concrete example, if we believe the mainstream story of value, then finding the companies that have done most to 'improve the human condition' is easy: we just have to look at the Fortune 500 list of the world's largest global companies, and find those with the largest revenue. Number two (in 2007), was Exxon. Of course, Exxon has satisfied a huge volume of people's 'needs and wants'—it would not have sold so much oil if that were not the case. And anyone who has driven a car, or been on a bus, train, or plane lately, can attest to this. But then there are the externalities. Most simply, the use of Exxon's products (directly and indirectly) has allegedly caused a great deal of pollution and unleashed greenhouse gasses. Another example is Wal-Mart, the largest company in the world by revenue, which has provided low prices to customers, but in the process come under a barrage of criticism for everything from allegedly destroying local communities to providing dead-end 'McJobs', as well as—through its global supply chain—employing vast numbers of workers in alleged 'sweatshop' conditions, and representing a massive ecological footprint from the high volume of cheap, low-cost products it sells. So, is Wal-Mart the huge value 'creator' that it appears to be in strategy terms, or is it a value 'extractor' that is prospering despite (or because) of the external social and environmental costs that arguably never enter it or its customers' decision making?[4] There are many other examples of possible market failures that could be examined. A particular

[2] The entire Stern Review on The Economics of Climate Change can be downloaded at http://www.hm-treasury.gov.uk/independent_reviews/stern_review_economics_climate_change/stern_review_report.cfm

[3] For a sobering recent account of the state of the world's environment, see United Nations Environment Programme (UNEP). 2007. Global Environment Outlook (GEO 4): Environment for Development. Available online at http://www.unep.org/geo/geo4/report/GEO-4_Report_Full_en.pdf

[4] In the case of Wal-Mart, the company has recently adopted an unusually proactive social and environmental stance, recognizing that substantial market failures are possible, and that it has the power and the responsibility to do something about them.

Figure L8.2 The market failure critique of value

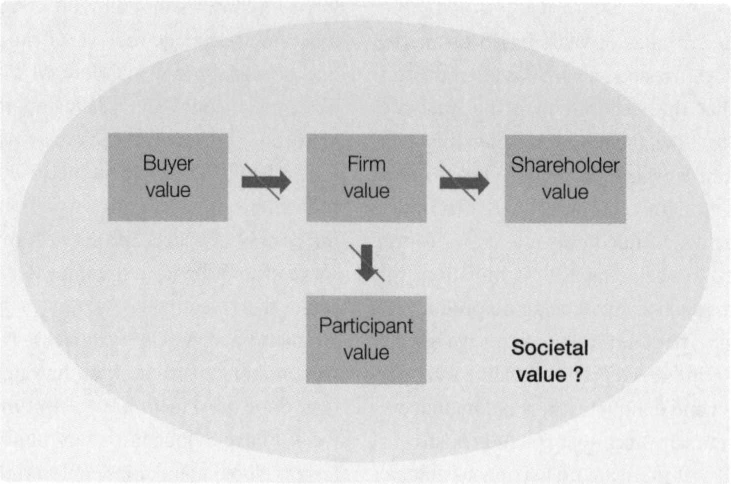

area relates to questions of the differences in power and access to technology, capital, and other resources possessed by market participants. For example, can multinational corporations trading with impoverished farmers in developing markets be considered to be engaging in 'free exchange'? The rise of the Fairtrade initiative (described in Chapter 5) is, in many ways, premised on trying to correct such perceived inequalities of power in the global marketplace.

For the purposes here, suffice it to say that there are many concerns about how closely the reality of corporate-led capitalism equates to the kind of beneficial outcomes assumed in the 'story of value'. As Figure L8.2 illustrates, in the market failure critique of value, there are breaks between all of the value linkages of the story—and, depending on how seriously you take them, this might lead you to support efforts to 'internalize' more costs (through a carbon tax, for example, or higher global labour standards), and to introduce greater equality into market relationships (through Fairtrade and related initiatives), or to it might lead you to turn away altogether from the idea that the strategy view of 'creating value' is a very good indicator of welfare enhancement.

Without picking one side or the other, let us assume that there are market failures in the real world, that, although some may not be that serious, others are, and that therefore a degree of regulation and legal frameworks that mitigate some of these potential failures is reasonable. Furthermore, from such a perspective, there seems to be a case for corporations taking their social responsibilities seriously and thereby reducing market failures without the need for such extensive formal rules and regulation. But, with these things in place (and it is a matter of debate how much change in 'business as usual' that would imply), there are still some serious concerns with the mainstream theory of value—concerns that go beyond 'tweaking' markets on the edges to make them more efficient.

For this reason, we will investigate the *failure of markets* critique of value. There are a wide variety of such critiques—and they are often made indirectly rather than directly—but many revolve around a fundamental observation. If there is one basic assumption within the strategy 'story of value', it is this: the more value that is created by a company, and the more broadly within an economy,[5] the greater should be the customer's—and, more broadly, the citizen's—level of satisfaction and well-being. The problem with this is that, for the most part, the more this claim is investigated empirically, the more this assumption appears to be poorly supported.

The failure of markets critique of value

With the *market failure* critique, it was important to see how value had to be placed within a wider set of assumptions about the functioning of markets; to explore the *failure of markets* critique, it is necessary also to focus more narrowly, in particular on the assumptions about human nature upon which the strategy view of value is based. One way in which to unpack this is to look a little bit more closely at the concept of 'benefit' or 'utility', which many strategy thinkers claim is the source of value creation and the foundation of competitive advantage. Like many key ideas in management thought, this idea is in fact taken from economic theory, in which the theory of utility plays a foundational role.

[5] Note that measures of economic output, such as GDP, are made up of the value-added of all economic participants.

According to an overview of utility theory, 'The term utility has been historically used by economists to refer to personal feelings such as pleasure, satisfaction, lack of pain, etc., led by consumption' (Coto-Millán, 2003: 7). In the eighteenth and nineteenth centuries, the theory of utility developed jointly with the idea of 'economic man', which conceived of human beings as needing, desiring beings, for whom increasing consumption possibilities (bringing more benefit, more utility) would lead to a happier life. In principle, however, this connection to the value of consumption was open to being questioned, and many leading economists of this period, such as Adam Smith and J. S. Mill, saw little necessary connection between well-being and consumption. In the twentieth century, however, the idea of 'revealed preference' was introduced in economics, which suggested that we have no access to the internal 'utility states' of individuals, but that the best proxy we can have for these states are through people's preferences, as revealed through the economic choices that they make. This shift was supposed to make economics more 'scientific'—and it coincided with a move towards making economics a primarily mathematical discipline. But what it also did, to paraphrase Daniel Kahneman and colleagues (1997),[6] is make utility into a 'black box' in which the presumed linkage between satisfaction and well-being that arose from consumption became a working assumption—something that was assumed rather than investigated. The result was that levels of consumption, as measured through financial transactions, became increasingly taken as the focus for thinking about well-being. This implied that—as for Porter and Kim and Mauborgne—that increasing value *equals* increases in what people are willing to pay *equals* increases in well-being (via the black box of utility). So, the theory of utility came to underpin what could be called an 'aggregative' conception of human well-being in which the more people are able to 'get' (consume), both in terms of the quality and quantity of products and services, the happier and more satisfied they should be. But is this assumed relationship actually borne out in real life?

Subjective well-being

'Subjective well-being' is the general term for a growing body of research that seeks to understand and measure people's sense of happiness or life satisfaction. Its starting point directly contradicts the idea that utilities cannot be measured. Increasingly, it appears that self-reported and third-party assessments of well-being in surveys, interviews, etc. are more stable and consistent than originally thought. So let us briefly investigate a number of the key findings of subjective well-being research that seem to have direct relevance for thinking about 'value'.

One of the most dramatic and consistent findings in this research is that, in direct contrast to the central premise of 'the story of value', there seems to be little connection between the increasing value of market transactions and people's happiness. In other words, there seems to be a *consumption disconnect*. What the studies show is that, aside from the very poorest of countries and those facing disruptions caused by war, political turmoil, etc., per capita gross domestic product (GDP) and well-being measures show little correlation (Diener and Suh, 2000; Frey and Stutzer, 2002; Layard, 2005). Similarly, within individual countries such as the USA, UK, and Japan, for which life satisfaction data has been collected for several decades, there appear to have been negligible shifts in people's level of experienced well-being despite dramatic increases in per capita GDP. So, despite the vast increases in 'value' as represented in the products and services that companies produce (and in people's consumption), this does not seem to have translated into any heightened level of satisfaction or well-being.

Another important finding of subjective well-being research is that although absolute levels of wealth do not seem to matter very much, relative levels do. On average, people who are relatively well off compared to others in the society in which they live consistently report higher levels of subjective well-being than those who are relatively poorly off. What this underlies is the importance of status (Frey and Stutzer, 2002) and the ability for people to access a 'normal' standard of living within their particular society. This result is important for two reasons. First of all, such status and access issues are obviously relational. No matter how much money everyone makes, and how significant their life achievements, there will always be those with more and those with less. So, as far as status goes, no combination of products and services can raise everyone's status together. Secondly, while it is in each individual's own interest to raise his or her level of status, if everyone is trying to do the same, then on average no one is able to improve his or her own level. What this suggests is the danger of a 'status race' in which there can be no overall winners, only a continued raising of the stakes (Frank, 2000).

Besides the relative nature of status and access, it appears that human adaptability is also a major reason why additional flows of products and services do not seem to lead to greater happiness. The 'hedonic' or 'satisfaction'

[6] Winner of the Nobel Prize in Economics in 2002.

treadmill (Frey and Stutzer, 2002) seems to work very dependably with each increase in income, each new product or service consumed soon becoming part of people's normal life patterns and eliciting no special level of enjoyment.

Layard (2005: 63) suggests that subjective well-being research to date points to seven main factors influencing happiness:

- family relationships;
- financial situation;
- work;
- community and friends;
- health;
- personal freedom; and
- personal values.

As he points out, all except for financial situation and health are based on the quality of people's relationships. And, indeed, even financial situation appears to be relevant only relative to others in one's community, or to the level to which one was previously used, as opposed to any absolute level (Layard, 2005: 42). Perhaps surprisingly, health itself also seems to have a strong relative component, with the better off within a particular culture on average consistently enjoying better health than the worse off.

So, the study of subjective well-being suggests that, beyond a basic subsistence level, the story of 'unprecedented buyer utility' leading to a better life (at least if reported life satisfaction is taken as a proxy for this) simply does not hold. In other words, it suggests that a *failure of markets* is taking place. New products are being introduced at an ever-increasing pace, corporations are getting leaner and meaner, many people around the world are richer and have more lifestyle options than ever before, and yet if consumers are no more satisfied with their lives than they were before mobile phones, SUVs, stock index futures, easy international travel, low-cost high-quality goods, etc., then what is this 'value' that corporations are creating really all about?

This is a big question and a variety of fields, including anthropology, sociology, psychology, and philosophy, all provide alternative ways for thinking about 'value'. An example of this would be in looking at consumption more in terms of the meanings that it has for people, and way in which it enters into the formation of their identity and sense of self. Such a perspective might take us away from an aggregative view of human well-being—in which more and higher quality products and services are the key—to what could be called a 'relational', or 'harmonizing', view of well-being. In this case, as with Layard's suggestions of the causes of happiness mentioned above, it would seem that whether companies are 'adding value' or not would depend in some way on the degree to which the products and services that they bring to market are helping people to have a greater sense of the coherence of their lives and more balanced sense of identity. Indeed, to a degree, the recent shift towards thinking about 'creating value' in terms of the experiences of consumers incorporates some of these considerations—but without it seems to be moving away from the idea that experiencing 'more' is better.

There are many other versions of the *failure of markets* critique of value, but hopefully this brief discussion raises some clear questions about the 'story of value' in strategy. As Figure L8.3 indicates, the *failure of markets* critique acknowledges the processes by which companies are made more valuable from a resources perspective and valuable to shareholders in a financial sense, but questions the nature of the buyer value and societal value that is supposed to accompany this.

Summary

We have considered the concept of value in strategy, and have tried to show that value is assumed to correlate with happiness, well-being, quality of life, and other such states, which are given a positive *normative* value. It is for this reason that creating value and achieving competitive advantage can be thought of in some way as the purpose of business, as something that the employees, managers, and directors of businesses *ought* to be doing—and that the government, civil society, and other stakeholder groups *ought* to support. But we have seen that the *failure of markets* critique of value calls the linkages between what businesses usually do (produce, compete, innovate,—add value), and how people achieve positive life outcomes into question. At the same time, this does not imply that creating value is in any way a negative for human well-being. Perhaps running businesses is just something that humans do together—like cooking and eating food, spending time with friends, engaging in politics, building institutions, celebrating festivals, making music, getting married, and raising children. And indeed, as touched on above, there is an emerging area of strategy that thinks about business competition very much in terms of socio-cultural processes, in which innovation is akin to engaging in group artistic expression such as theatre, and corporations and other constellations of networked actors stage experiences in co-creation processes in which the boundaries of producer, supplier, and consumer are all blurred (as in the networked innovation perspective in Chapter 1).

Figure L8.3 The failure of markets critique of value

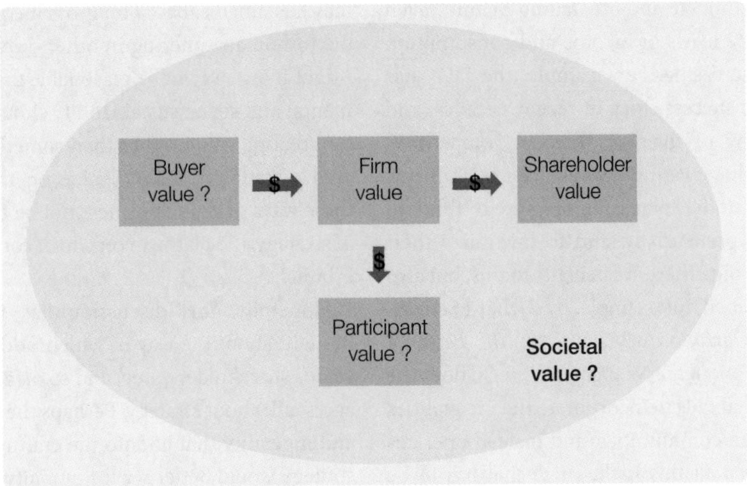

But if, to a degree at least, 'value' and human well-being are uncorrelated, might not that mean that the concerns that underlie the *market failure critique* of value take on a more pressing aspect? Let us take for an example the area of environmental degradation and climate change. The arguments for what action to take on these issues always tend to revolve around what the trade-offs are in terms of *value*. Typically, for example, economists and policymakers try to calculate how much GDP would have to be spent (or forgone) in order to reduce carbon and the carbon trajectory of the economy. It is usually viewed as a terrible burden if GDP[7] growth were to be slowed to any considerable degree or if any substantial costs were to have to be borne by consumers. But does this make any sense? Does this not involve trading off the production of more products and services, which have no noticeable well-being impact for consumers,[8] with the continuing increase in greenhouse gas concentration in the atmosphere? In other words, is there a real trade-off, or are the market failures that environmental externalities represent simply losses for humanity (not to mention for the animals, plants, and integrity of the world's ecosystems)?

Similar considerations relate to issues of inequality and power. The products and services that 'value' represents in strategy could no doubt benefit people in many of the poorest countries in the world. But, unfortunately, the logic of competitive advantage involves focusing on the most profitable potential customers—hence the theme of Bill Gate's speech at The World Economic Forum in 2008,[9] in which he argued that much more money is spent researching how to address the minor problems of affluent than is spent trying to solve life-threatening conditions that affect vast numbers of the populations of poor countries. The problem is that, in the world of 'value', people count as much as they have money to spend. The situation in which employees in the developing world work for minimal wages (often under extreme pressures) to produce goods for developed-country consumers is often portrayed as part of a trade-off, in which severe inequalities are part of the price that needs to be paid to ensure that economic growth will continue as quickly as possible. But again, is this a real trade-off? If heightened consumption in affluent countries has no well-being impact, then is tolerating the degree of inequality and injustice that is seen around the world not simply a loss for humanity?

There is another perspective on inequality as well, one that relates more closely to people living in wealthy countries themselves. If you recall that one of the consistent findings of subjective well-being research is that people who are *relatively* poor in comparison with others around them tend to be less happy and satisfied with their lives. One of the persistent themes of the neoliberal economic policies that have become so dominant in the world in the past few decades is that social inequality is necessary to incentivize people to compete, innovate, and work hard. And, indeed, the trajectory of many of those economies that have taken the neoliberal route suggests that this can work. However, the widening inequalities around the world, as well as within particular

[7] Remember that GDP is composed of the aggregate 'value' created by all the producers in the economy—foremost among which are the highly competitive companies about which strategy textbooks usually talk.

[8] In the wealthier countries at least, which still represent the bulk of value creation and consumption.

[9] The full text of Bill Gates' speech 'A new approach to capitalism in the 21st century' can be found online at http://www.microsoft.com/Presspass/exec/billg/speeches/2008/01-24WEFDavos.mspx

countries, has also led to more people feeling that they are struggling to compete and are 'falling behind', even while their absolute levels of income and consumption may indeed be increasing. For example, the USA has been an economic success story in recent decades, and has spawned many of the world's most competitive, innovative and 'value creating' companies—but US citizens have also felt under increasing pressure to think of their careers entrepreneurially, and to maximize their own 'value' or lose out. There are benefits to this, but also real costs, as described, for example, by Richard Sennett in his book *The Corrosion of Character: The Personal Consequences of Work in the New Capitalism*. So does the creation of value that fails to incorporate the inequalities within and between communities, and instead operates on the assumption that this is the price that has to be paid to maximize growth, not perhaps involve an ethical bias that marginalizes the interests of many of the people living on this planet?

The point here, once again, is not to argue that the creation of value by companies is a bad thing in itself, but to highlight that the mainstream strategy conception of value has at its heart noble concepts such as improving 'the human condition', and people's well-being, and yet all too often seems to take no account of whether the products and services being produced are environmentally sustainable, based on gross inequalities, or contribute to human suffering in other direct or indirect ways. Might it instead not be reasonable to think that environmental and social sustainability should be a prerequisite for creating value rather than something that is considered a trade-off against value on the margin? Should these ways of doing business not be the beginning point of strategy, the platform on which competitive advantage is built?

Hopefully, this discussion has provided food for thought about the way in which 'adding value', 'creating value', 'shareholder value', and so on are used when managers talk about strategy. Perhaps the tremendous efforts and ingenuity that go into the crafting and execution of strategy would better serve humanity if 'value' were to be reassessed and allowed to underpin a broader vision of business purpose. As the corporate governance crusader Bob Monks put it, 'In order for 'value' to be an acceptable concept for corporate conduct, we need to have an overall accounting revision that takes a holistic approach, or what I call long-term economic value rooted in the social good' (quoted in Trammell, 2004). It is left for you to decide the degree to which such a revision in the mainstream view of value is desirable, or indeed necessary.

Case questions

1. Do you believe that a revision of the mainstream notion of 'value' is necessary?
2. What are the merits and limitations of the market failure and failure of markets critique of value?
3. As a strategist working for a company with which you are familiar, suggest ways in which you might align value and well-being.
4. Discuss how markets or customers incorporate value into their evaluation of companies.
5. Does value create value and for whom? Discuss.

References

Beer, M. and Eisenstat, R. 2004. How to have an honest conversation about your business strategy. *Harvard Business Review*, Feb: 82–89.

Coto-Millán, P. 2003. *Utility and Production: Theory and Applications*. Heidelberg/New York: Physica-Verlag.

Cummings, S. and Angwin, D. 2004. The future shape of strategy: lemmings and chimeras? *Academy of Management Executive*, 18(2): 21–36.

Davis, I. 2005. What is the business of business? *McKinsey Quarterly*, 3: 104–113.

Diener, E. and Suh, E. M. 2000. *Culture and Subjective Well-being.* Cambridge, MA: MIT Press.

Elkington, J., Emerson, J., and Beloe, S. 2006. The value palette: a tool for full spectrum strategy. *California Management Review*, 48(2): 6–28.

Frank, R. H. 2000. *Luxury Fever: Money and Happiness in an Era of Excess.* Bryn Mawr, PA: The American College.

Frey, B. S. and Stutzer, A. 2002. *Happiness and Economics: How the Economy and Institutions Affect Well-being.* Princeton, NJ: Princeton University Press.

Ghoshal, S., Bartlett, C. A., and Moran, P. 1999. A new manifesto for management. *MIT Sloan Management Review*, 40(3): 9–20.

Hamel, G. and Prahalad, C. K. 1994. *Competing for the Future.* Boston, MA: Harvard Business School Press.

Kahneman, D., Wakker, P., and Sarin, R. 1997. Back to Bentham? Explorations of experienced utility. *The Quarterly Journal of Economics*, 112(2): 375–405.

Kim, W. C. and Mauborgne, R. 2005. *Blue Ocean Strategy: How to Create Uncontested Market Space and Make the*

Competition Irrelevant. Boston, MA: Harvard Business School Press.

Layard, P. R. G. 2005. *Happiness: Lessons from a New Science.* New York: Penguin Press.

Mintzberg, H., Simons, R., and Basu, K. 2002. Beyond selfishness. *MIT Sloan Management Review*, 44(1): 67–74.

Porter, M. E. 1998. *Competitive Advantage: Creating and Sustaining Superior Performance.* New York: Free Press.

Prahalad, C. K. and Ramaswamy, V. 2004. *The Future of Competition: Co-creating Unique Value with Customers.* Boston, MA: Harvard Business School Press.

Rumelt, R. 2011. *Good Strategy/Bad Strategy*. London: Profile Books.

Stewart, G. B. 1991. *The Quest for Value: A Guide for Senior Managers.* New York: HarperBusiness.

Trammell, S. 2004. The path of a pioneer. *CFA Magazine*, 37–41.

Case 9 The Renault–Nissan alliance: not just a handshake[1]

Dr Merieke Stevens, Assistant Professor, Purchasing and Supply Management, Erasmus University, Rotterdam School of Management

Introduction

The global automotive industry is a very different place now from that which it was in 1908, when the first mass-produced automobile rolled off the line at Ford's factory in Detroit. The famous quote attributed to Henry Ford, that customers could have cars in any colour they liked as long as it was black, poignantly characterizes the business climate of the early 1900s. Mass production had just been born and incredible gains could be made from improving operational efficiency. Moreover, the demand for automobiles seemed insatiable for many decades to come.

A century later, not much remains of this favourable climate. Consumers have become ever more demanding; in developed markets, the supply of automobiles by far exceeds demand; and emission rules have become more and more stringent. Globalization and trade agreements, moreover, mean that car manufacturers cannot hide behind national borders anymore. How to cope in such a climate was a question that both Nissan and Renault repeatedly faced during the 1990s. There were two apparent facts of which both were aware, at least to some extent: that operational efficiency is important, but not sufficient to be profitable; and that to survive in the volatile global market, a company must have global presence. How to actually achieve these goals was less clear. Considering their respective positions as strong regional players—Nissan in Asia and North America, and Renault in Western Europe—finding a partner appeared almost a necessity for both carmakers. Nevertheless, there was no apparent rationale to find each other.

Looking back at the years that have passed since June 1998, when then Renault chief executive officer (CEO) Louis Schweitzer first wrote to Nissan's president Yoshikazu Hanawa, the choice to ally and the path that subsequently unfolded seem straightforward and secured of success. The geographical presence of Nissan and Renault was complementary to a great extent: Nissan possessed the admired Japanese operational excellence from which Renault could still learn, while Renault had the corporate managerial strengths that Nissan clearly lacked at the time. However, even though there seemed to exist an 'almost miraculous complementary relationship between the two companies',[2] when the alliance agreement was signed in 1999, the situation was controversial and far from guaranteed of success.

A brief history of Renault[3]

Renault was founded in 1899 by Louis Renault (1877–1944) and his two brothers Marcel and Fernand. Their initial success was based on their racing victories in self-build cars. At the turn of the nineteenth century, Renault had sales outlets and subsidiaries in several European countries, as well as the USA. The strategy of Renault during the first half of the twentieth century consisted of vertically integrating the production of most components in order to decrease dependency on outside firms. World War II brought a turbulent period to Renault's history, when German forces occupied Renault's main factory and British Royal Air Force (RAF) bombers consequently reduced it to ruins. The occupation by the Germans of Renault factories made

[1] Remark made by Nissan's chief operating officer Toshiyuki Shiga, when interviewed by Korine et al. (2002).

[2] Comment by Georges Douin, member of the Renault–Nissan board of directors, in Douin (2002).

[3] Based on official Renault company documentation.

Renault an 'instrument of the enemy' in the eyes of the French government, and Louis Renault was jailed as a traitor, while his company was nationalized and given the official national duty to provide labour to the French population.

World War II had greatly damaged the industrial infrastructure of Europe, and American carmakers continued to dominate the industry at this time. Subsequent leaders at Renault attempted to gain a foothold in the profitable US market, but such attempts were never quite successful, even despite an alliance with American Motors Company (AMC) in the 1970s. In Europe, Renault continued to grow and, with the production of 2 million vehicles in 1980, became Europe's largest carmaker. During this time, the financial aspect of Renault's ambitions always seemed to be a secondary concern and consequently bankruptcy loomed in 1984. Together with its main shareholder, the French government, a turnaround policy was announced in which a refocus on Renault's core business—automobiles—took centre stage. The government at this time recognized that Renault's duty to provide jobs was no longer tenable, and a workforce reduction of 21,000 was announced and the possibilities of privatization explored.

Nevertheless, Renault still largely depended on its sales in Western Europe—a difficult market that was slowly reaching saturation. It became increasingly clear that it had to become a global player and that, in order to realize this transition, finding a global partner would be a sensible approach. In 1990, Renault and Volvo of Sweden announced an alliance that was to result in the merger of the two firms in 1993. This plan, however, met with great resistance in Sweden both within Volvo and amongst Volvo shareholders, and eventually fell through, resulting a substantial financial loss for both companies and much negative publicity.

One realization that came out of the failed merger with Volvo was that privatization of Renault would increase its flexibility and thereby strengthen its future prospects of finding an alliance partner. The French state reduced its majority share in Renault to a minority share of 46 per cent in 1996—the last year in which Renault would record a loss. Further reductions of the French government's share followed and, by 2008, it held only 16 per cent of Renault. Other aspects that contributed to Renault's turnaround were its investments in emerging economies and the increased streamlining of its production facilities. Renault also had several hit models, such as the Espace, the Clio (European Car of the Year 1990), the Twingo, and the Scenic (European Car of the Year 1996). Still, the need to become more global did not subside and, in 1998, Renault's CEO Louis Schweitzer started to write directly to potential partners. One of the people who received a letter from Schweitzer was Yoshikazu Hanawa, president of Nissan.

A brief history of Nissan

When the first Japanese entrepreneurs ventured into the automotive industry in the 1920s and 1930s, their American and European counterparts had already made tremendous gains in productivity and efficiency. The limited demand for automobiles in Japan was mainly supplied by American producers. Nevertheless, Nissan's founder Yoshisuke Aikawa (1880–1967) believed that there was an opportunity for Japanese carmakers and he set out to produce his first automobile. As had been a worry of Louis Renault, Aikawa realized that he could not simply match the operational supremacy of the American carmakers; he decided to acquire technology as a package from outside the firm, importing American tools, designs, and engineers to Japan. Aikawa could sustain this approach because the Japanese militarization of the 1930s and 1940s resulted in the closure of the domestic market to foreign producers, and an increase in army orders for trucks (Stevens and Fujimoto, 2009).

Aikawa participated in the industrial build-up for World War II and, like Louis Renault, was imprisoned as a war criminal after the war. He was freed when Cold War fear increased among the American occupiers and they needed strong national leaders to keep Japan out of Communist hands. Aikawa, however, did not regain formal control over Nissan. Due to its support of national goals during the war, Nissan found itself close to governmental funds that were available for the post-war rebuilding of Japan's economy. In the decades to follow, Nissan became known as the 'darling' of Japan's leading Ministry of International Trade and Industry (MITI). In support of national economic goals, during this time Nissan focused on operational excellence and export; as a consequence, cost control and profitability became secondary concerns. Such an approach was tenable because of Nissan's technological strengths and innovativeness, the surge in international demand for fuel-efficient Japanese cars after the oil crises of the

1970s, and the ready availability of governmental funds.

Nissan's operational orientation prevented it from taking the necessary decisions on a strategic level to avert financial distress when markets started to contract at the end of the 1980s. As a consequence, Nissan made losses and saw its global market share decreasing almost every year during the 1990s. While the Japanese government provided Nissan with life-saving capital injections on several occasions, Nissan was looking for an affluent partner that would bail it out and help it to redesign its corporate strategy. One candidate partner that presented itself to Nissan was DaimlerChrysler. CEO Jürgen Schrempp was one of the prime architects of Daimler's *Welt AG* (World Corporation), which aimed to be present in every automotive market of the world. While Nissan had diminished bargaining power due to the state in which it found itself, being absorbed by a foreign company was extremely unattractive. Nissan is an abbreviation of *Nihon Sangyō*, which means 'Japan Industries', so at a national level there was also great reluctance to forever bury the brand name 'Nissan'. Ultimately, however, after examining Nissan's books, DaimlerChrysler considered its financial situation too precarious to save the company and pulled out of the negotiations in March 1999.

While Nissan conducted its initial talks with DaimlerChrysler, the negotiations with Renault had also started. First, several one-to-one meetings between Nissan CEO Hanawa and Renault CEO Schweitzer took place (see Table L9.1 for an overview of strategic milestones). When talks between DaimlerChrysler and Nissan were terminated, Schweitzer and Hanawa started to discuss a possible framework for cooperation in more detail. Gradually, they built a relationship of trust that is considered to have been a central aspect of the successful take-off of the Renault–Nissan alliance (Korine *et al.*, 2002). The main agreement reached between Schweitzer

Table L9.1 Renault–Nissan Alliance strategic milestones

1998	
June	Renault CEO Louis Schweitzer writes to Nissan CEO Yoshikazu Hanawa; twelve one-to-one meetings between Schweitzer and Hanawa follow
July	Joint Renault–Nissan teams study the possibilities of cooperation
November	Based on the findings of the joint study teams, Renault's Louis Schweitzer, Carlos Ghosn, and Georges Douin present the benefits of an alliance to the Nissan board
1999	
March	Schweitzer and Hanawa sign the alliance agreement in Tokyo
May	Renault takes a 37 per cent equity stake in Nissan Motors and a 15 per cent stake in Nissan Diesel
June	First meeting of the Global Alliance Committee (GAC) in Paris; monthly meetings alternately in Paris and Tokyo follow Carlos Ghosn (chief operating officer), Patrick Pelata (executive vice president, product planning and corporate strategy), and Thierry Moulonguet (senior vice president, deputy chief financial officer) of Renault join the Nissan board of directors
October	Ghosn announces the Nissan Revival Plan (NRP) in Tokyo
2000	
January	Renault Mexico is established, with the support of Nissan
July	Sales of Renault vehicles start in El Salvador and Honduras, with the support of existing Nissan facilities
October	Nissan Brazil is established with the support of existing Renault facilities Renault Morocco purchases Nissan's Moroccan distributor
November	Sales of Renault vehicles start in Ecuador, with the support of existing Nissan facilities
2001	
April	A joint purchasing organization, Renault Nissan Purchasing Organization (RNPO), is established
May	Renault re-enters the Australian market in cooperation with Nissan
June	Renault Argentina becomes a Nissan importer Carlos Ghosn becomes CEO of Nissan
November	Distribution of Renault vehicles in Indonesia through the local Nissan distributor starts

Table L9.1 Renault–Nissan Alliance strategic milestones (Continued)

2002	
March	Renault increases its stake in Nissan to 44 per cent Nissan acquires a 13 per cent stake in Renault (increased to 15 per cent in May 2002) A common strategic management structure is established, the Renault-Nissan BV (RNBV), and incorporated in the Netherlands
April	Ghosn joins the Renault board of directors
May	The Alliance Board, replacing the Global Alliance Committee, meets for the first time
July	A joint IS/IT organization, Renault Nissan Information Systems (RNIS), is established
2003	
July	Itaru Koeda joins the Renault board of directors, succeeding Hanawa
2004	
January	RNPO Phase III, enlarging the scope of activities and geographic spread of common purchasing, begins
2005	
February	Toshiyuki Shiga is appointed chief operating officer of Nissan
March	Renault sells its stake in Nissan Diesel
April	Ghosn is appointed president and chief executive officer of Renault
2007	
February	Renault and Nissan, together with Mahindra & Mahindra, announce the construction of a 400,000 unit capacity production site in Chennai, India
September	Renault and Nissan announce the establishment of a business centre providing product and manufacturing engineering, purchasing, design, cost management, and information system design in Chennai
2008	
January	Mahindra & Mahindra discontinues its involvement in the establishment of a new production site in Chennai Cooperation with Renault through an earlier established joint venture continues
February	Renault and Nissan start the construction of a 400,000 unit capacity production site in Tangiers, Morocco
April	RNPO expands its scope to include 90 per cent of all parts purchased by Nissan and Renault

Source: Renault–Nissan joint press releases; Stevens (2009)

and Hanawa was that Renault and Nissan would remain separate brands, which would cooperate on an equal footing. The Alliance charter signed in July 1999 by Schweitzer and Hanawa underlines the balanced nature of the cooperation between the two carmakers, and stresses the importance of mutual trust and respect, as well as loyalty between the two firms in their pursuit of performance.

Key trends and strategies in the automobile industry

At the beginning of the twenty-first century, the automotive industry went through several important transitions, the most notable of which included the near saturation of the European and American markets, the tremendous growth in developing markets such as India, China, and Russia, and the increasing awareness of environmental issues leading to a surge in the importance of alternative propulsion techniques to replace the internal combustion engine. In addition to these developments, consumers have become more and more demanding, requesting increased quality for reduced prices. In dealing with these trends, there are many similarities, but also important differences between the major automotive players (see Table L9.2

Table L9.2 Top twenty automotive producers by global sales and market share, 2006

Carmaker		Global sales	Global market share
1	Toyota	8,808,000	12.8%
2	General Motors	8,679,860	12.6%
3	Ford	6,008,000	8.7%
4	Volkswagen	5,720,096	8.3%
5	DaimlerChrysler	4,748,500	6.9%
6	Hyundai-Kia	3,753,437	5.5%
7	Honda	3,550,000	5.2%
8	Nissan	3,477,799	5.1%
9	PSA/Peugeot-Citroen	3,365,900	4.9%
10	Renault	2,433,372	3.5%
11	Fiat	2,288,284	3.3%
12	Suzuki	2,174,000	3.2%
13	BMW	1,373,970	2.0%
14	Mitsubishi	1,258,000	1.8%
15	Mazda	1,233,661	1.8%
16	Avto Vaz	860,448	1.3%
17	China FAW	681,964	1.0%
18	Isuzu	650,734	0.9%
19	Fuji Heavy Industries	601,773	0.9%
20	Dongfeng	459,516	0.7%

Note: Sales include mini vehicles, passenger cars, light, medium, and heavy commercial vehicles, and buses.
Source: Automotive News 2007 Global Market Data Book

for an overview of the top twenty carmakers by global market share). A general response to these trends that can be discerned is consolidation into ever larger, but fewer, global groups.

In answer to the saturation of their home markets that many established manufacturers are facing, a surge in globalization is taking place. Carmakers move to growth regions not only to benefit from lower labour costs, the availability of cheap parts, and less stringent environmental rules, but also to be present in markets in which there is growth. All carmakers in Table L9.2, apart from the Chinese Dongfeng and FAW, and the Russian Avto Vaz, have established joint ventures with Chinese firms, while most are attempting to enter the increasingly open Russian market. Renault and Nissan, for example, concluded joint ventures with Dongfeng and Avto Vaz. Most of the top twenty carmakers are present in India, while Renault–Nissan plans to open a vehicle plant in Chennai.

On 10 January 2008, Indian carmaker Tata Motors revealed the Nano, a basic entry-level vehicle costing 1 lakh (INR100,000 or approximately US$2,500), with which it hopes to capture the vast market of Indian families who now mainly use motorcycles for transportation. While ultra-low-cost vehicles are being built by other carmakers as well—most notably Toyota, General Motors, Fiat, Suzuki, and Renault–Nissan—except for the Renault Logan, most of these vehicles are stripped-down versions of existing models. Moreover none is as cheap as the Tata Nano. Tata forecasted the initial volume of the Nano, available from the latter half of 2008, to be 250,000 units annually, but allegedly it is asking its suppliers to prepare for the production of 1 million units a year (Snyder, 2008). The global volume of below US$5,000 vehicles has been predicted to be 15.7 million units annually by 2020, approximately the entire domestic US demand.[4] If these predictions are accurate, Tata might be the prime mover in a very lucrative automotive segment.

Nevertheless, being successful in only one segment, like being successful in only one region, is usually not sufficient to be a profitable global player. While carmakers in general are known not to be equally strong in all segments, clear weaknesses are not permitted for global players. Alliances are a common approach with which to address this situation, but they are not the only solution. This is exemplified by Toyota. In 2006 and 2007, it was the largest carmaker by sales and by far the most profitable carmaker. While Toyota has a history of cooperation with other carmakers, it has not taken the step to ally with one of its local partners as Renault and Nissan had done. When Toyota decided to expand its product line-up by moving into the luxury market, it did not cooperate with an existing firm, as for example Ford did with Jaguar, but instead built its Lexus luxury brand from scratch. A notable exception to the approach of offering a full-range of vehicles is BMW, which sold its Rover mass-production operations in 2000 and embarked on a very profitable strategy that focused exclusively on the premium segment.

A volume producer that follows a go-it-alone approach similar to that of Toyota is Honda. Honda has been able to produce a very profitable range of volume cars without feeling a need to find a foreign alliance partner. During the early years of the twenty-first century, Honda has been especially successful in the USA, while retaining its domestic popularity. Two successful groups that also refrained from forming alliances are Volkswagen and Peugeot-Citroen. Contrary to Toyota and Honda, however, the success of these two groups mainly depends on their strong market positions in Europe, and while neither is experiencing the troubles of pre-alliance Nissan and Renault, the saturation of the European market is a real concern for both groups.

At the opposite end of the strategic spectrum is the *Welt AG*, or 'World Corporation', of Daimler's Schrempp. The idea of the *Welt AG* was to be present as a main player in every automotive market of the world, growing through mergers and acquisitions of local firms in regions in which it previously was not present, and always maintaining the *Welt AG* brand name. The dissolution of ties between Daimler and Chrysler in 2007 poignantly showed that this approach might be just a bit too sweeping. A more moderate, but nevertheless still bold, approach to achieving global presence was followed by Ford and General Motors. In order to increase their global presence and benefit from growth in different regions, both American carmakers acquired stakes in European and Japanese carmakers. While this piecemeal approach prevented large-scale disasters like the Daimler and Chrysler dissolution, the troubles and decreasing sales and market shares of Ford and GM show that they also might have stretched themselves too thinly.

Renault and Nissan chose to ally in order to regain their competitiveness. Their approach, however, was one of equality and mutual respect, with no partner taking a dominant position and with both brand names remaining unchanged. The piecemeal approach of getting to know each other through discussion and productive cooperation resulted in a strategy somewhere in between the go-it-alone approach of Toyota and Honda, and the *Welt AG* approach of Daimler. The Renault–Nissan approach can be called 'focused partnering' because moves are well researched and the partners slowly, but steadily, work towards achieving mutual goals without forcing cooperation where individual action would make more sense.

The relationship between Ford and Mazda, which dates from 1969 when the American carmaker and its Japanese counterpart embarked on a joint project in which Nissan was also involved, is another example of cooperation between a Western carmaker and a Japanese firm. Ford's influence on Mazda's corporate management, however, has not been as far-reaching or visible as Renault's influence on Nissan. Moreover, the difference in size between Ford and Mazda and the fact that Ford has important strategic ties to many more automotive companies gives the Ford–Mazda alliance less of an outlook of a partnership between equals than the Renault–Nissan partnership.

In addition to the shift of growth markets, a second important trend in the automotive industry is the increased importance of alternative propulsion techniques. With the increased awareness of environmental costs, the hegemony of the internal combustion engine as dominant design is slowly starting to change. Toyota has been a first mover in this area, with the hybrid Toyota Prius being a huge success. Ghosn, in 2005,[5] announced that Nissan would systematically pursue all alternatives to the internal combustion engine: diesel, ethanol, hydrogen, electric, and hybrid cars. It was criticized, however, for being a late adopter and for jeopardizing its 1970s' and 1980s' image of being a technological leader.

[4] A.T. Kearney Consulting, cited in Snyder (2008).

[5] Carlos Ghosn, in a 2005 speech at the Foreign Correspondents Club, Japan.

Complementarities between Renault and Nissan

At the end of twentieth century, Renault and Nissan were faced with the fact that, in order to survive global competition in the next century, their regional strengths were not sufficient. Having a complete line-up of vehicles in every class, as well as global presence, was considered to be essential for volume producers. Once the alliance team had started to discuss the complementarities between the two carmakers, it quickly became clear that great synergies could be reached between the two and that both carmakers would significantly enhance their chances of succeeding as global players. Most evidently, there was great complementarity between the geographical market presence of Renault and Nissan. Renault had a strong presence in both Western and Eastern Europe, as well as in Latin America, whereas Nissan was strong in Asia and North America. Both companies were volume producers under their own brands, while Renault also produced entry-level vehicles under the Dacia brand and Nissan made luxury vehicles under the Infiniti brand. In addition, Renault had a strong presence in the commercial vehicle market, while Nissan did not, whereas Nissan produced several SUVs and light trucks, which Renault did not. These complementarities provided great opportunities for cooperation and mutual learning through common manufacturing projects (see Table L9.3).

The greatest complementarity between Renault and Nissan was less tangible, and although anticipated during the initial talks, became evident only when the alliance charter had already been signed: the complementarity between Renault's corporate management skills and Nissan's operational skills. Renault had gained valuable experience in cost control and profitability when it was faced with bankruptcy in 1984, and Nissan's situation in 1998 did not seem miles apart from Renault's state in the 1980s. Nissan, on the other hand, had operational and technological strengths from which Renault could learn. Similar to Renault's official duty to provide labour, Nissan, as a large Japanese enterprise, had a lifetime employment scheme that was extended to the majority of its white-collar employees. Another strategic commonality between the two carmakers was their extreme diversification into various sectors that were unrelated to their core business of producing automobiles. And, similarly to 1984, when the French government saved Renault from the brink of bankruptcy, being close to the government in Nissan's case also meant being saved from a financial crisis that would have caused the collapse of most unsupported companies. For both companies, having strong historical ties with their respective governments resulted in inflexibility and a lack of profit focus that was seriously hampering in the era of globalization.

The failed merger with Volvo in the early 1990s had provided Renault with valuable insights into alliances. One important lesson that Renault had learned was that being a national company is often unattractive for global partners. Secondly, it learned that time matters in creating momentum for an alliance, and the fact that three years passed between the initial agreement with Volvo and the proposed merger of Volvo and Renault meant there was plenty of time for resistance against the cooperation to develop. Thirdly, Renault learned that cultural differences between two global partners should not be underestimated and have to be given sufficient attention.

After in-depth research that was executed in close cooperation between employees at all levels in Nissan and Renault, the Nissan Revival Plan (NRP) was announced in October 1999 by Renault manager Carlos Ghosn, appointed by Schweitzer to become Nissan's chief operating officer (COO). The fact that a foreigner announced the NRP clearly showed that a different turn had been taken at Nissan. In Japan, a tradition exists of relying on *gaiatsu*, or 'foreign power', to realize changes that everybody knows are necessary, but for which no one is able or willing to take the visible responsibility. Ghosn, in this respect, has been compared to Commodore Perry, who forcibly opened Japan to world trade in the 1850s, and to the American occupiers who forced Japan to democratize after its defeat in World War II (Stevens, 2009). Ghosn's foreign audacity was especially needed for the dismissal of employees and the breaking of decades-long ties with suppliers—measures that, at a managerial level at Nissan, were known to be necessary.

Ghosn came to Nissan with the nickname 'Le Cost Killer', earned at Renault for his involvement in the restructuring of Renault's European facilities, which involved the much-publicized decision to close the Renault assembly plant in the Belgium town of Vilvoorde, rendering 3,500 employees obsolete. Ghosn's image as ruthless restructurer was transformed into a much more favourable one when Nissan's performance dramatically improved during the first two years of the alliance. Subsequently, Ghosn became known as the 'Nissan Saviour'. Ghosn carefully used the media in building his image of committed leader of Nissan and, in 2001, had his first autobiography published in Japanese,

Table L9.3 Renault–Nissan Alliance productive milestones

2000	
December	Production of the Renault Scenic at the Nissan Cuernavaca plant in Mexico begins
2001	
November	Production of the Renault Clio at the Nissan Aguascalientes plant in Mexico begins
December	A common Renault–Nissan commercial vehicle (LVC) plant is inaugurated in Brazil
2002	
March	Sales of the double-badged Nissan Interstar/Renault Master begin in Europe Production of the Nissan Platina, derived from the Renault Clio sedan, begins at the Nissan Aguascalientes plant in Mexico Sales of the Nissan March, the first vehicle built on common platform B, begin in Japan Sales of the Renault Vel Satis, fitted with a Nissan 3.5-litre V6 petrol engine, begin
September	Sales of the Renault Megane II, the first vehicle built on common platform C, begin in Europe
October	Production of the first cross-manufacturing project in Europe begins at the Nissan Barcelona plant in Spain, sold as the Renault Trafic/Nissan Primastar/Opel-Vauxhall Vivaro
December	Sales of the Nissan Almera, fitted with a Renault 1.5-litre diesel engine, begin
2003	
January	Sales of the Nissan Micra, the European version of the Japanese March built on common platform B, begin in Europe
March	Sales of the Nissan Primera, fitted with a Renault 1.9-litre diesel engine, begin
April	Sales of the new Nissan Micra, fitted with a Renault 1.5-litre diesel engine, begin in Europe
October	Sales of the double-badged Nissan Kubistar/Renault Kangoo begin in Europe
2004	
June	Sales of the Renault Master, fitted with a Nissan 3.0-litre diesel engine, begin in Europe
September	Sales of the Renault Modus, Renault's first vehicle built on common platform B, begin in Europe Sales of the Nissan Tiida, built on common platform B, fitted with a common 1.5-litre petrol engine, and the first vehicle with a co-developed navigation and communication system, begin in Japan
December	Sales of the SM7, the third Renault Samsung model built with the technical support of Nissan, begin in South Korea Sales of the Nissan Lafesta, Nissan's first vehicle built on common platform C and fitted with a common 2.0-litre petrol engine, begin in Japan
2005	
April	A joint parts warehouse is established in Hungary
May	Sales of Nissan Serena, based on common platform C and fitted with the common 2.0-litre petrol engine, begin in Japan
September	Sales of Renault Clio III, based on common platform B and fitted with a common six-speed manual transmission, begin
2006	
January	Sales of Nissan Tiida, fitted with the common six-speed manual transmission begin
December	Cooperation on electric vehicle (EV) development is announced
2007	
September	Sales of Nissan Aprio, a subcompact car based on the Renault Logan and built in the Renault plant in Brazil, begin in Mexico

Source: Renault–Nissan joint press releases; Stevens (2009)

to be followed by dozens more, as well as several French and English volumes, plus innumerable articles in the popular, business, and academic media. One of Ghosn's main strengths appeared to be his image of personal commitment to his professional task—a characteristic highly valued in Japan. When Ghosn announced the NRP, he promised that he would resign if his targets were not achieved.

During the 1990s, the main problem at Nissan had been a misplaced focus on operational excellence and production volume for export, which drew attention away from its dire financial state and actual customer demand. Organizationally, Nissan appeared to be burdened mostly by a lack of cross-functionality in its organizational structure. The most urgent task that faced the Renault–Nissan alliance team was the financial revival of Nissan and, as a first step, Renault paid €5bn to acquire a 37 per cent stake in Nissan (33.4 per cent is a controlling stake according to Japanese law), which was increased to 44 per cent in 2001 when Nissan also acquired 15 per cent of Renault stock (without voting rights).

Subsequently, the streamlining of Nissan commenced: 21,000 jobs were cut worldwide, of which 14,000 in Japan; land, securities, and non-core assets were disposed of; companies in which Nissan held shares were reduced from 1,394 to only four. Capacity was planned to be reduced by 30 per cent; three out of seven domestic production plants were closed; and purchasing costs would have to be reduced by 20 per cent, lead times by 50 per cent, administration and sales costs by 20 per cent, distribution subsidiaries by 20 per cent, and retail outlets by 10 per cent. Renault's capital injection, in combination with the income generated by these restructuring measures as well as improved performance, resulted in the alleviation of Nissan's debt in 2001. With Nissan's solvency restored, the two carmakers from that point onwards could fully focus on reaching the synergies anticipated in the early meetings between Schweitzer and Hanawa.

Successes of the Renault–Nissan alliance

One of the main operational successes of the Renault–Nissan alliance, as was anticipated in the early stages of their negotiations, was the tremendous increase in global reach for both carmakers. From January 2000 onwards, the mutual use of global facilities commenced. Examples are the sale of Renault vehicles in El Salvador, Honduras, and Ecuador through Nissan's local partner, the production of Renault cars in a Nissan plant in Mexico, the distribution of Renault vehicles in Indonesia through Nissan local distributors, the establishment of a Nissan plant in Brazil with the help of local Renault dealers, the purchase of a Nissan distributor in Morocco by Renault Maroc, and the importing of Nissan vehicles by Renault Argentina (see Table L9.3).

Another area of successful operational cooperation is the development of shared vehicle platforms.[6] Before the alliance, Renault and Nissan had a combined number of thirty-four platforms, which was planned to be reduced to only ten by 2010, resulting in great research and development (R&D) cost reductions. The development of the first common platform exemplifies the approach of equality and respect between the two partners. Soon after it was decided to develop a platform for the small/medium segment, it became clear that there were fewer shared vehicle components than initially expected, and that the wheelbase proposed by Nissan was too small and had a lower level of performance than that needed by Renault for the three vehicles that it planned to build on the platform (Segrestin, 2005). Differences in culture and language, plus more than 10,000 kilometres between Paris and Tokyo, added to the initial difficulties. In the spirit of the alliance, however, the equality between the two partners was maintained and no formal platform management team was assigned. In cases in which consensus could not be reached, it was decided to develop specific components separately (Segrestin, 2005). While certain components were excluded from the project and designed individually by the two carmakers, the main benefits of the first joint development project were of a managerial nature: a standardization of purchasing methods was formulated; procedures were devised to share information; and a joint research programme was developed in order to synchronize protocols and development procedures (Segrestin, 2005). In March 2002, sales of the Nissan March, the first vehicle built on a commonly designed wheelbase for subcompact cars, started in Japan (see Table L9.3).

Nissan's crisis of the 1990s had proven that strategic management was not one of Nissan's strengths, and Renault's corporate management were called upon to assist Nissan in transitioning into a global player. The first step in redesigning Nissan's management structure was the despatch of three Renault executives to Nissan's board of directors in June 1999. The next step was the assignment of 200 Nissan employees from Japan, the USA, and Europe to nine cross-functional teams (CFTs), each of which was to address one specific topic, such as

[6] Vehicle platforms, or wheelbase systems, include the axles and wheels, as well as defining interfaces for other parts of the vehicle.

purchasing, R&D, or marketing and sales.[7] In order to prevent the CFTs from reverting to Nissan's previous complacent approach, members of each CFT were purposefully selected from different departments and different positions within the company. In September 1999, an additional seventeen Renault managers were assigned to Nissan. The CFTs set out on a rigorous examination of Nissan and made problems explicit that were implicitly understood inside the company, but which were not articulated because of Nissan's complacent culture and hierarchical structure.

By communicating clearly to Nissan's employees that a different turn had been taken and that Nissan's previous company culture had contributed to Nissan's problems, it was then attempted to create a company-wide sense of urgency that would enable the steady overhaul of deeply ingrained habits. The two most striking changes were the replacement of the traditional Japanese system in which pay and promotion are based on seniority with a system in which bonuses and promotion would be based on personal achievements, and the breaking down of boundaries between departments that previously had resulted in conflicting interests between such groups as purchasing and R&D, which ideally should closely work together. The reforms instigated by the Renault-sent managers did not meet with great resistance, because all Nissan employees understood that bankruptcy had been a serious threat.

When the NRP goals were reached in 2001, a year before the deadline, strategic cooperation was deepened with the establishment of organizations for common purchasing (the Renault–Nissan Purchasing Organization, or RNPO) and information services (Renault–Nissan Information Services, or RNIS). In March 2002, an Alliance strategic management company (Renault–Nissan BV) was founded and incorporated under Dutch law. Nissan and Renault both hold 50 per cent of Renault–Nissan BV, which in its turn holds 100 per cent of joint companies such as RNPO and RNIS. According to Ghosn, it is irrelevant to put numbers behind the benefits that result from having common purchasing and information services or using each other's facilities abroad, because it is clear that these are significant.[8]

Areas to be improved

The one area of cooperation between Renault and Nissan in which the reforms did not reach the anticipated synergy is purchasing. After initial research by the alliance board, it became clear that Renault paid 20–25 per cent less for its parts, while Nissan suppliers were known for the high quality of their products. In an attempt that earned Ghosn the name '*keiretsu* killer', sweeping reforms of Japan's traditional supplying system were announced, starting with the sale of shares in all but four of 1,394 affiliated companies. While the initial cost reductions of 20–30 per cent requested from Nissan suppliers in NRP still met with a certain amount of acceptance on the side of suppliers due to their awareness of the state that Nissan was in, the fact that Nissan in 2001—when it had alleviated its debt and had fulfilled its reform goals in two rather than three years—did not let is suppliers share in its regained strengths, but on the contrary asked them for additional cost reductions. This resulted in unwillingness on the part of suppliers to invest in the relation with Nissan, and in 2003 Nissan set up the Administration for Affiliated Companies (MC-AFL) headed by executive vice president Itaru Koeda.

Renault–Nissan alliance in the era of consolidation

In 2006, Renault and Nissan together sold almost 6 million vehicles and thereby, as a group, took the position of fourth largest carmaker in the world with a combined global market share of 9 per cent. This position is not uncontested and both carmakers did not deliver on all of their respective growth targets. The question remains whether Renault–Nissan can keep the momentum of their alliance. While there are examples of successful automotive alliances—such as Volkswagen and Skoda, Citroen and Peugeot, and Volvo and Ford—failure is more common, such as Daimler and Chrysler, Jaguar and Ford, and Saab and GM.

The main trends affecting the automotive industry at the turn of the twenty-first century are increasingly demanding consumers, the saturation of developed markets and growth in developing markets, and the importance of alternative propulsion techniques because of increasingly stringent environmental regulations. Three main types of approach to these challenges exist: a go-it-alone approach, the *Welt* approach, and an inbetween approach of focused partnering.

[7] Nissan Revival Plan official presentation.

[8] Interview with Carlos Ghosn by Shimokawa et al.(2003)

Case questions

1. In what circumstances would you follow which approach? (i.e. go it alone, Welt, or focused partnership)

2. Describe why Renault and Nissan chose the approach that they did.

3. Why is operational efficiency, as introduced by Ford, not sufficient anymore?

4. Has Tata found the answer to survive the cut-throat competition between carmakers?

References

Automotive News. 2007. Global Market Data Book. Available online at http://www.autonews.com

Douin, G. 2002. Behind the scenes of the Renault–Nissan alliance. *Journal de l'Ecole de Paris du Management*, 38: 3–10.

Johnson, C. 1998. *MITI and the Japanese Miracle: The Growth of Industrial Policy, 1925–1975*. Stanford, CA: Stanford University Press.

Korine, H., Asakawa K., and Gomez, P. Y. 2002. Partnering with the unfamiliar: lessons from the case of Renault and Nissan. *Business Strategy Review*, 13(2): 41–55.

Segrestin, B. 2005. Partnering to explore: the Renault–Nissan alliance as a forerunner of new cooperative patterns. *Research Policy*, 34: 657–672.

Shimokawa, K., Konno Y., Heller D. A., and Kato, H. 2003. Nissan jidousha ribaibaru puran to Nissan jidousha Hanawa kaichou, Ghosn shachou intabyuu kiroku [Memo on Interviews with Chairman Hanawa and President Ghosn of Nissan Motor Co. Ltd. and the Nissan Revival Plan]. *Hosei Journal of Business*, J40(3):45–85 (in Japanese).

Snyder, J. 2008. Tata Nano changes low-cost development. *Automotive News*, 14 April.

Stevens, M. 2009. Foreign influences on the Japanese automobile industry: the Nissan–Renault mutual learning alliance. In R. Rasiah, Y. Sadoi, and R. Busser (eds) *Multinationals, Technology and Localization: Automotive and Electronics Firms in Asia*. New York: Routledge.

Stevens, M. and Fujimoto, T. 2009. Nissan: from the brink of bankruptcy. In M. Freyssenet (ed.) *The Second Automobile Revolution: Trajectories of the World Carmakers in the 21st Century.* London: Palgrave MacMillan.

Case 10 The UK grocery retailing industry

Ciara Fitzgerald, Centre for Innovation and Structural Change, National University of Ireland, Galway

Introduction

Grocery shopping, by tradition, is perceived as a necessary, yet dreaded, chore. The typical weekly grocery shopper struggles with intimidating aisles of endless jars, tins, and ready meals as he or she hustles his or her way through heaving crowds of fellow frazzled shoppers. The grocery shopping experience is no longer limited to mere food and drink products. Shoppers can now purchase non-food items on the supermarket shelves, ranging from *Twilight* books through to the latest Lady Gaga album. As well as this, retailers such as Tesco are offering one-stop shops, providing insurance and petrol. It is for this reason that grocery retailing is one of the chief economic sectors of the UK.

Development of the grocery retailing industry in the UK

The UK grocery industry has seen radical changes over the past thirty years. Traditionally, the UK industry consisted of small corner shops, run by local independents. They placed an emphasis on providing a high level of personal service. Although the corner shop is still in existence, predominantly in ethnic communities, it has been largely replaced by supermarkets, superstores, online shopping, and convenience stores, with an emphasis on size, choice, and efficiency of operation.

Key milestones

Post-1945, farming subsidies and retail liberalization stimulated the birth of the supermarket. Rising affluence following post-war hardship created demand for new emerging trends in the grocery retailing industry. The concept of shops selling a variety of different products developed in contrast to the traditional sweetshop, butcher, etc. Sainsbury's had been operating as a chain of dairy produce shops since the late nineteenth century, but began expanding into other product types in the 1920s, such as fresh meat and packaged own-brand groceries. Tesco opened its first store in Burnt Oak, North London, in 1929. In 1930, Marks & Spencer (M&S) opened its flagship store in Marble Arch, London, and started selling food products a year later. As grocers discovered the gains from increasing size, they began the trend that continued for decades: The total number of shops declined, but the average size increased.

The 1960s and 1970s witnessed a focus on price competition in the UK grocery retailing industry, which in turn created a major shift in consumer behaviour and shopping patterns. The supermarket chains expanded and spread to become national chains throughout the 1960s. The dominant retailers expanded by building larger stores. Consequently, larger product ranges were offered by such retailers. A number of changing society trends favoured the popularity of larger supermarkets. At this time, cars were becoming a household item, which increased the volume and frequency of grocery shopping, as problems of transport logistics were less of an obstacle for shoppers. Additionally, suppliers were beginning to source food globally at a fraction of previous costs. Furthermore, planning law relaxation facilitated the diffusion of retailers into out-of-town retail park sites in the 1970s and 1980s. Also during this time, retailers began producing imitations of manufacturer's brands under their own names, known as 'own labels'. Own-label products were perceived as cheap, low-quality versions of national brands and posed a serious threat only to the weak, unadvertised manufacturer brands.

At the end of the 1980s, UK entered a period of recession. Tesco, Sainsbury's, and Safeway became engaged in serious expansion of the superstore across the UK landscape. These retailers made huge investments into building off-centre superstores.

Different retail formats

Today, grocery stores operate in a competitive environment that includes a number of different retailing formats. Each of the retail formats is unique in its own way (see Table L10.1).

Grocery industry today: some trends

Supermarkets have become an important phenomenon of the twenty-first century. Across the adult population in the UK, 79 per cent regularly shop for food and groceries. The UK industry is it its most inherently competitive phase since the advent of self-service in the 1960s. Discounters, successful in their home markets, have entered into the UK market. In spite of a slow start to their popularity, 2008 witnessed an increase in shoppers as customers heavily favoured their low-price offers. Weak traditional retailers are being acquired and the market has become more consolidated. For example, in March 2009, the Co-operative Group completed the acquisition of Somerfield plc. The changes in the grocery retailing industry today have been shaped by the dramatic changes in British social patterns. For example, the rise of the TV celebrity chef, such as Jamie Oliver, has helped to broaden food tastes. Rapid uptake of the Internet prompted the launch of a new home shopping service and increasing levels of car ownership have all helped to fuel growth in the industry. The economic downturn in the economy in 2008–09 led to consumers eating out less, while also being more aggressive in buying products on deal. Innovative 'dine in' promotions were introduced by retailers to offer customers restaurant-quality meals at home. Such promotions enjoyed huge success, as reflected by M&S's sales of over 15 million 'dine in' meals in 2010. Also, consumers were increasingly trading down to own-label and value brands. Nevertheless, issues around obesity and labelling, food inflation, environmental awareness, own label, and non-food diversification pose clear threats to the industry.

Table L10.1 Description of different retailing formats in the UK grocery retailing industry

Retail format	Description
Supermarket	Larger in size and has wider selection than a traditional grocery store Smaller than hypermarket or superstore
Superstore/Supercentre	Physically large chain stores Located in large-scale shopping malls on edges of towns/cities
Out-of-town retail park	Grouping of many retail warehouses and superstores Found on fringe of most large towns and cities, in highly accessible locations
Hypermarket	Superstore/supercentre combined with a department store
Convenience store	Small shop or store Often located alongside busy roads or petrol stations Frequently located in densely populated urban neighbourhoods Prices higher than supermarkets for less choice

Obesity and labelling

Obesity figures have grabbed government attention and driven change to promote healthier eating trends. In the UK, nearly a quarter of adults and nearly a fifth of children are obese, after sharp increases in the last decade. Experts have warned that the number could soar unless action is taken. Some predictions suggest that 60 per cent of men, 50 per cent of women, and 25 per cent of children in the UK could be obese by 2050 if action is not taken (Foresight, 2009). As a result of these shocking reports, a £372m strategy aimed at cutting levels of obesity in England was launched by the UK government. Announcing the strategy, former Health Secretary Alan Johnson said that food labelling was central to helping people to eat well. There are currently two food labelling methods, with the government backing the 'traffic lights' approach rather than labelling showing the percentages of guideline daily amounts (GDAs) that a product contains. While Sainsbury's, Asda, and Waitrose opted for the traffic-light labelling, Tesco went for the rival GDA system, which was advocated by many of the big food manufacturers.

Food inflation

Furthermore, concerns of food inflation have impacted the current industry and it is predicted by analysts that food inflation is the greatest challenge facing farmers and the food processing industry, as food inflation rose by 12 per cent in 2007 (Ball, 2008). The economic crisis of 2008–09 has brought the food inflation issue to the fore, with an increasing percentage of the UK population not being able to afford basic food essentials.

Environmental awareness

In light of increasing environmental awareness among consumers, supermarkets have been putting considerable effort into portraying a greener and more neighbourly image: they no longer compete on price alone, but also on ethical perception. Tesco's green efforts include promises to install wind turbines and solar panels, to source more food locally, and to encourage healthier eating. Asda and Sainsbury's have unveiled similar initiatives and M&S unveiled a £200m environmental plan in 2007, which included a pledge to become carbon neutral and to send no waste to landfill by 2012. The trend towards becoming 'green grocers' was kick-started in 2005 by Lee Scott, president of the vast Wal-Mart discount chain in the USA and the parent company of UK chain Asda. Mr Scott made a US$500m (£254m) commitment to use 100 per cent renewable energy, create zero waste, and cut greenhouse emissions by 2009.

Own label

Own-label has also become an important phenomenon within the grocery industry and has its roots as a cheap alternative to the recognized household brands. It has moved to a position in which consumers perceive some own-label brands to be as least as good as the manufacturers. Retailers use their own-label range in their positioning strategies, trying to differentiate themselves from competition. M&S led the field in development and use of own-label: first in clothing; then in food. Today, all of the main retailers, including Sainsbury's, Tesco, and M&S, compete in their use and sophistication of their own-label offer. Own labels became an even more importance source of competitive differentiation during the economic crisis of 2008–09, as competitors used attractive own-label pricing strategies to retain old and attract new customers.

Non-food diversification

Diversification into non-food products is a symptom of maturity of the UK retailing industry. The non-food offer of supermarkets is extremely wide: financial services, CDs, clothing, books, electrical goods, and even real estate have been added to retailers' ranges. Fashion in particular has become a strong seller for the supermarkets, which have persuaded customers to overcome their perception of supermarket clothes in the same way as they did for their own-label products; Asda is leading the way, with its George clothing range, and Tesco is also enjoying success with its Florence & Fred (F&F) brand.

The increase of leading grocers in the convenience sector has raised the profile and consumer expectations of convenience stores. Whilst some of the major chains have been opening ever-larger format stores, with Asda and Tesco in particular opening hypermarkets, at the same time Tesco and Sainsbury's have diversified into smaller format convenience stores to try to gain a growing share of an increasing consumer trend towards convenience shopping. This translated to over 50,814 convenience stores in the UK (IGD Research, 2007) and this industry is a still highly fragmented market with a large number of operators present. Sainsbury's, Tesco, M&S, and the Co-operative Group were the initial major chains to operate convenience stores. However, Waitrose and Morrisons soon caught up on the trend, and have also opened such stores.

There are a number of enablers that have facilitated the evolution of the grocery retailing industry, including technology developments, supply chain transformation and government regulation.

Technological developments

Technology has been at the core of the change in the UK grocery retailing industry. The major retailers that now dominate the industry have been able to use technology to their advantage by deploying websites, sophisticated store technology, and loyalty cards. Britain's big four retailers—Tesco, Sainsbury's, Morrisons, and ASDA—have deployed standardized electronic point of sale (EPOS) and other computerized equipment that allow relationships to be drawn nationwide, between such factors as store size, location, and outputs in terms of trading profit. Additionally, the larger retailers have sought to roll out increasingly standardized store formats across the country, creating the advantage of economies of scale. The loyalty card is another benefit of increased technology. Some of the retailers constantly draw down point-of-sale information about transactions and, when a loyalty card is used, they can match that with actual customer identification. Bar codes and scanning are now commonplace, but they were revolutionary when they first appeared in supermarkets in the 1980s. For the first time, retailers could measure in real time exactly what was being sold. Online shopping sites have contributed to the success of some of the larger retailers. The success of this retail format is such that Tesco opened an online-only store in Croydon, London. The store, outwardly similar to a normal Tesco store, is closed to the public and filled with trained employees executing online orders for the whole of south London.

The boundaries of food technology themselves have expanded in response to scientific development and ever more sophisticated customer demand. Food development must now address the delicate issue of genetically modified (GM) foods—that is, foods produced from genetically modified organisms (GMO) that have had their DNA altered through genetic engineering. GM foods were first put on the industry in the early 1990s. The most common modified foods are derived from plants: soybean, corn, canola, and cotton seed oil. Controversies surrounding GM foods and crops commonly focus on human and environmental safety, labelling and consumer choice, intellectual property rights, ethics, food security, poverty reduction, and environmental conservation.

Supply chain transformation

Another facilitating factor in the development of the UK grocery retailing industry has been rapid technological and organizational innovations in the process of bringing food to the consumer. Pre-1980, the dominant method of distribution to stores was for manufacturers to store products at their factories or warehouses for multiple drops to numerous small shops. Over time, retailers invested in regional distribution centres to consolidate deliveries from suppliers for onward delivery to stores. This created a market for third-party logistics service providers. The major retailers either constructed their own large-scale, high-tech facilities, or outsourced to the major logistics companies with world-class facilities. Most of the major retailers deploy a combination of 'in-house' and contracted distribution systems. Buying and distribution became a headquarters' activity. The three key features of supply chain management have become quality, volume, and logistics, with a particular emphasis on the scale of operations and the system required to ensure adequate quality control. Centralization has changed the relationship between the individual store managers and the local suppliers. Suppliers are no longer in a position to arrange their own local supply deals; all supply deals now are arranged through the central depot, which consequently has transformed the nature of the supply chain.

The dynamics of the supply chain in the UK grocery retailing industry has changed significantly over the last three decades. As the dominant retail customers drive for higher quality at competitive prices, they are pressurizing suppliers for lower costs. The power in the distribution channel has shifted away from branded goods manufacturers towards retailers. During the 1990s, retailers began to focus on their primary distribution networks and implemented just in time (JIT) principles under which they demanded more frequent deliveries of smaller quantities (Fernie and Sparks, 2004). Also the abolition of resale price maintenance (RPM) in 1994 empowered retailers to negotiate supplier deals, and to manage prices and margins across a full product offer. Nowadays, retailers are much more global in their outlooks and so supply chain logistics are equally international, in effect increasing supply-side capacity. Larger chains have reduced the number of suppliers through their selective choice of products and identification of preferential suppliers, particularly for unique products such as retail brand ranges. Some suppliers feel that they cannot complain about supermarket practices because of fears that they will lose their contracts and the market for their produce. Some of these activities could be seen as anti-competitive. This has fuelled concerns that British grocery retailers are exploiting their market power to the detriment of suppliers and consumers. In the mid-to-late 1990s, amid widespread concerns, the government ordered a Competition Commission investigation of the sector. Whilst the Commission found little evidence of abuse of market power in terms of pricing and profits, it did express concerns over treatment of suppliers (Competition Commission, 2000). The media and other commentators remained wary about retailer power. However, a change may be afoot for suppliers: as retailer giants scramble to reduce their carbon footprint in an effort to compete on ethical perceptions, they are increasingly supporting their local producers.

Government regulation

UK industry regulatory factors have assisted the changes in the UK grocery retailing industry. The abolition of RPM in 1964 enabled retailers to offer price discounts through bulk purchasing and bulk sales. The widespread tendency to ignore 'fixed' or 'manufacturer's recommended prices' had started somewhat earlier in food retailing. With the RPM removed, manufacturers could not control the prices at which retailers could sell their goods to the public. Also, in the late 1990s, planning regulations were tightened with the introduction of measures to protect town centres and to limit out-of-town retail growth. Previous to this, a series of laissez-faire government planning and inconsistent local policy had created a high street starved of many formal local shops. These regulations have played a pivotal role in rejuvenating town centres, to which large retailers have returned in the new guise of convenience stores. Moreover, considerable media attention focused on issues surrounding obesity and healthy eating has increased consumers' awareness of the food that they eat. The UK government introduced a 'five a day' initiative to provide a clear and consistent message of the need to eat five portions of fruit and vegetables a day in an effort to increase awareness among consumers on the benefits of healthy eating.

Competition: the fight for market share

The grocery retailing industry in the UK is characterized by a small number of companies, growing in size, to gain increasing shares of the market, and a small share remaining for independent businesses and small shops. In the UK, the grocery retailing industry is dominated by a number of large supermarket retailers. There is intense rivalry and competition among the key players, as each attempt to gain market share at the expense of the others. The 'Big Four'—Tesco, Sainsbury's, Morrisons, and ASDA—have, in recent years, asserted their dominance y. Collectively, these retailers accounted for 80 per cent of main users in 2009 (see Table L10.2). Table L10.2 shows the proportion of food and grocery shoppers that mainly use each given retailer for food and groceries products. Main users are individuals who identify a retailer as their main store for food and groceries—in other words, they spend more with this retailer that they do at any other retailer.

Asda Wal-Mart

Asda was formed in 1965, so it is a relative newcomer compared to Sainsbury's and Tesco. It was the pioneer of the superstore format. Its early strategy consisted of quality groceries at a low price. It expanded in the 1970s and 1980s, in 1989 buying rival chain Gateway's superstores for £705m. This move overstretched the company and it found itself in deep trouble, trying to sell too many different products. It came close to going bankrupt and had to raise money from shareholders in both 1991 and 1993. New management under Archie Norman re-established Asda's price reputation as it refocused on meeting the weekly shopping needs of ordinary working people and families. It stood out from the crowd by being significantly cheaper than its rivals. Since 1999, Asda has been wholly owned by Wal-Mart, the infamous US retailer. The takeover should be seen as part of a long process: Asda had been mirroring Wal-Mart's strategy for some years before the takeover happened. It prized itself on its low-price advantage. The key focus continues to be on value, but the company is continuously looking at how else it can position itself. In April 2006, Asda launched a new format called 'Asda Essentials', focusing primarily on own-brand products, only stocking branded items that are perceived to be at the 'core' of a family's weekly shop. This type of retailing was an attempt to address competition from discount supermarkets such as Aldi and Lidl. However, in January 2007, it was announced that the initial trial Essentials store would close within a month after only ten months of trading. In 2009, its operations approached 400 stores (including ASDA Living and stand-alone George

Table L10.2 Percentage share of active food and groceries shoppers using a given retailer as their main store, 2005–09

Main users (%)	2005	2006	2007	2008	2009
Key players in the UK grocery retailing industry					
Tesco	30.7	30.9	31.0	33.0	31.1
Asda	22.9	22.5	22.8	20.4	22.1
Sainsbury's	13.3	1.5	16.6	15.9	14.5
Morrisons	9.7	11.8	11.7	12.4	12.6
Co-op	3.7	2.8	2.2	2.4	2.7
Somerfield	2.6	3.1	2.8	2.6	2.3
Waitrose	2.0	1.8	2.8	2.0	2.7
M&S	1.1	1.2	1.3	1.4	1.2
New entrants: hard discounters					
Aldi	0.9	1.2	1.3	1.3	2.4
Lidl	0.9	1.0	1.3	1.7	1.7

Source: Adapted from Verdict Research (2009)

clothing stores, which primarily sell groceries and apparel). The stores also sell CDs, books, videos, and housewares. Since being bought by Wal-Mart, Asda has set off a price war in the UK by initiating Wal-Mart's aggressive 'price rollback' programme and converting stores to Wal-Mart's supercentre format under the ASDA/Wal-Mart banner. Asda also has a strong presence online, where its online shopping stores boast a range of services including Asda Travel, an optician, and a pharmacy.

Future plans Asda Wal-Mart is continuing with an aggressive expansion strategy, concentrating on Asda Living stores as the retailer focuses on the non-food sector.

Marks & Spencer

M&S boasts an iconic heritage in UK retailing and its commitment to quality over price. The rise of M&S from market stalls to become one of the world's most respected retailers is well known. As a relentless innovator, it has led many new developments in food retailing, especially chilled prepared food. Principles of partnership with its suppliers and supply chain management learned in its clothing business have been applied to food, with a revolutionary effect. For 125 years, M&S exclusively sold its own-label products, which are renowned for offering excellent quality at a fair price. However, in 2009, it announced the move to stock other brand products. The decision can be seen as a repositioning for M&S, as it tries to be seen as a store to use for a full weekly shop, rather than the occasional source of luxury items. The strategic decision to broaden its range will also heighten the rivalry between M&S and its closest competitor, Waitrose, which already sells the big brands alongside its own-label foods. M&S has always been and still is predominantly a textiles company. In 1948, a food development department was set up. Applying the principles that served it so well in clothing, M&S was extremely thorough, examining everything from pest control to the provenance of raw materials. It also successfully launched the ready-made sandwich and diversified into flowers and wines. In the early 2000s, M&S sales were not as healthy as desired and an aggressive reinvigoration strategy was put in place under the watchful eye of Sir Stuart Rose. The company returned to its core values of quality, value, service, innovation, and trust. As of 2009, Marks and Spencer had over 600 UK stores, including Simply Food franchise stores, as well as an international business. The Simply Food retail formats include franchise stores in BP Connect forecourts, motorway service stations, railway stations, and airports. The international business consists of the stores in Ireland and Hong Kong, together with franchised operations in over thirty countries. In February 2007, M&S announced the opening of the world's largest M&S store outside of the UK at the Dubai Festival City. M& S also has a strong online shopping channel.

Future plans While, Marks and Spencer's future strategies include developing trading space, their long term focus appears to be channelled into their multi-channel operations.

Morrisons

Morrisons Supermarkets plc is the fourth largest chain of supermarkets in the UK. From its beginnings as an egg and butter stall, 'Victoria', its first supermarket, was opened in Bradford in 1961. Hereafter, it developed a strong culture and loyal customers in parts of Northern England. On 8 March 2004, the takeover by Morrisons of Safeway plc was completed. Morrisons proceeded to rebrand the supermarkets under its own name and the convenience stores were initially rebranded as 'Safeway Compact'. In 2011, there were 455 Morrisons stores across the UK. Following the integration of Safeway, Morrisons was well placed to drive organic sales growth beyond its core northern market. Acquiring Safeway gave it access to a more upmarket wealthy demographic in the south of England. Having successfully extended its sales-led, value-driven proposition beyond its Yorkshire heartland, Morrisons focused on delivering robust shop-keeping standards and driving sales and business efficiencies through its optimization plan. Morrisons announced in 2011 the opening of its first convenience store, branded 'M-local', with an emphasis on fresh food. As of March 2008, all of the fresh beef sold in Morrisons stores nationwide is 100 per cent prime and 100 per cent British. This means that Morrisons is the only top supermarket in the UK in which all of the fresh beef, lamb, pork is 100 per cent British-sourced. Morrisons has revealed an evolution of its brand identity as the company sharpens its positioning to be 'the food specialist for everyone' and to make the most of its key strengths of freshness, service, and value; highlighting its brand proposition, 'fresh for you every day'. Morrisons does not operate an e-shopping channel and does not have a market outside of the UK. Because it did not diversify aggressively into non-food products, it was in a better position to weather the economic downturn of 2008–09.

Future plans Morrisons' strategy for the future is built on three core values of offering fresh food, at competitive value, through a quality service. Future avenues for growth may be the growth of non-food products and the development of an online shopping presence.

Sainsbury's

For much of the twentieth century, Sainsbury's was the market leader in the UK supermarket sector. John James Sainsbury started the business in 1869. From the very beginning, it was quality that set Sainsbury's apart from the competition. It was the supermarket of choice, offering quality and value. It introduced a range of own-label products, the quality of which solidified its premier-class reputation. However, in 1995, it lost its place as the UK's largest grocer to Tesco; in 2003, it was pushed into third by ASDA. The company's fortunes have improved since the launch of a recovery programme by CEO Justin King in 2004. The retailer is taking a proactive stance to drive growth, with ongoing investment in lowering prices and revamping its premium food offer. Significant improvements to availability, product quality, and range architecture have enabled Sainsbury's to better differentiate itself from rival grocers, as evident from its latest slogan campaign, 'Try something new today'. Despite predictions that Sainsbury's would regain second position, ASDA has continued to outperform it on market share. In 2011, Sainbury's boasted 934 UK stores. A typical Sainsbury's store offers complementary non-food products and services. It also launched a 'Feed your family for a fiver' campaign in response to increasing concerns over tightened household budgets in March 2008. Sainsbury's launched the initiative in conjunction with celebrity chef Jamie Oliver, who has worked with the group for the previous eight years. An Internet-based home delivery shopping service became available to nearly 90 per cent of UK households from 2009. Sainsbury's briefly had a presence in the east coast US market, but in 2004 it sold its US chain and has since operated solely in the UK. It also offer a Sainsbury's bank service.

Future plans Sainsbury's plan to aggressively target the convenience sector and also the non-food areas are a conscious effort to regain its title as number one UK grocery retailer. In 2007, it identified five areas of focus to take Sainsbury's from recovery to growth—namely: great food at fair prices; accelerating the growth of complimentary non-food ranges; reaching more customers through additional channels; growing supermarket space; and become active in property management.

Somerfield/Co-operative Group

Somerfield is a chain of small-to-medium-sized supermarkets operating in the UK. It was initially part of Somerfield Ltd, formerly Somerfield plc, which also included the Kwik Save chain of discount food stores until February 2006. In 1998, the company took over the rival Kwik Save chain. Kwik Save focused on the low-cost segment of the retail market. However, it transpired that Kwik Save had over-expanded with a badly focused portfolio of stores, many in poorer areas, and the company was in a worse state than Somerfield's management had

...ized. The original plan was to transfer all Kwik Save stores to Somerfield, but it quickly became clear that many outlets were not suitable for conversion, either due to size or location. Instead, the larger Kwik Save stores were converted, some were sold or closed, and the chain became a trading division of Somerfield Stores Ltd, sharing its supply chain and back-office systems with Somerfield. Somerfield proceeded with trading primarily from secondary sites and high-street locations, trying to prove that the smaller store had a rightful place among the retail giants such as Tesco and ASDA. It prided themselves on offering a welcome alternative to the overwhelming experience of the mammoth superstores. However, in 2008, Somerfield was taken over by the Co-operative Group. This move doubled the Co-operative Group's market share in 2008 to almost 8 per cent and made it the UK's fifth largest supermarket chain after the Big Four. Set up in 1844, the Co-operative Group aimed to make food available to working people at a reasonable price. Any profits are returned to members as a dividend (or 'divi'). The Co-operative Group also has interests spanning financial services, pharmacy, funerals, travel, and farming. The Co-operative Group is a unique family of businesses run by almost 6 million members. It operates over 5,000 trading outlets and also offers an online shopping service. It promotes values of honesty and social responsibility, with ethical trading at the core of its brand.

Future plans Somerfield stores was rebranded as The Co-operative Food, and plans to leverage on its increased economies of scale and stronger buyer power to focus on lowering cost for the customer. Continued expansion plans are in place to increase its presence in the UK by opening more stores.

Tesco

Tesco is the indisputable leader of the UK grocery industry, with a runaway market share (over 30 per cent) and the only UK-based supermarket chain to be a major international company. Tesco became the industry leader in 1995 and has continued to increase its market share ever since, reaching a staggering 31.5 per cent market share in 2007, and taking 12.5 per cent of total consumer spend in the UK, resulting in it being named as the most admired UK company around the world (Verdict, 2009). Tesco founder Jack Cohen, who, from 1919, sold groceries in the markets of the London East End, acquired a large shipment of tea from T. E. Stockwell and made new labels by using the first three letters of the supplier's name and the first two letters of his surname forming the word 'Tesco'.

By 2011, Tesco was either number one or two in eight of its thirteen markets outside the UK. The company's impressive growth has been underpinned by its unrivalled understanding of customers and its ability to respond quickly to changing patterns of consumer demand. In 2009, Tesco responded more aggressively than competitors to the threat from fast-expanding heavy discounters, by offering 'discount brands at Tesco'. These factors have been supported by the retailer's world-class management team, a consistent corporate strategy, innovative marketing, flexible store formats, substantial physical expansion, and a strong reputation for value. Few retailers can boast an all-encompassing and inclusive customer base such as that of Tesco. Originally specializing in food, it has diversified into areas such as discount clothes, consumer electronics, consumer financial services, selling and renting DVDs, CDs and music downloads, Internet service, consumer telecoms, consumer health insurance, consumer dental plans, and budget software. It even entered into the housing market, with a self-advertising website called Tesco Property Market. However, due to the declining trade in the property market, this operation has since ceased. In 2011, Tesco introduced Tesco Tyres, Video on Demand, Gold Exchange, Your Beauty Salon, and its own record label, further strengthening its diversification strategy.

The retailer has been at the forefront in responding to changing consumer dynamics with a much-improved organics and fresh food offering in recent years, in addition to outstanding progress with its non-food development. Tesco Clubcard was launched in 1995. With the tightening of planning regulations, Tesco began to open high-street stores, the first in June 1992 called 'Tesco Metro' in Covent Garden. Tesco has also been moving towards hypermarkets through the Tesco Extra format and it has also diversified into the convenience store sector with its Express format, partly by acquiring a number of chains, including T&S. T&S owns convenience stores through the One Stop and Day & Nite chains. Tesco is also looking outwards and has opted for Europe, the developing markets of the Far East, and the USA. However, market maturity has had an impact on Tesco. While Tesco extended its lead over its rivals impressively in 2009 for the eleventh successive year, its market share gain was the smallest since 2002. This could be interpreted as a sign that Tesco is beginning to falter or it could be indicative of a stronger competitor set. However, in December 2010, Tesco increased its market share to 30.7 per cent.

Future plans For Tesco, the challenge is to stay ahead. In order to accomplish this, it has devised a seven-part strategy concentrating on becoming an international retailer, whilst maintaining a strong core UK business. It is also focusing on becoming as strong in non-food as in food. Community responsibly is also a core feature in Tesco's future strategy.

Waitrose

Waitrose is the supermarket division of the John Lewis Partnership, with 243 branches as of 2011. Like the Partnership's department stores, Waitrose is targeted at a middle-class market, emphasizing quality food and customer service rather than low prices, as its slogan reflects: 'Quality food, honestly priced.' The company has a royal warrant to supply groceries, wine, and spirits to the Queen. After taking important first steps to becoming a true national player in 2004–05, Waitrose reported strong organic sales growth for the 2006–07 financial year, with sales up 5.3 per cent. A focused food offer, comfortable store environments, and high levels of customer service have facilitated Waitrose in increasing its main user share. Waitrose has proved increasingly popular among shoppers seeking haven from the growing complexity of rivals such as Tesco and ASDA. Having ramped up the size of its store estate in recent years, Waitrose has improved its visitor share faster than any of its main competitors. It executes a high commitment to real and fresh food. Waitrose was the first to sell organic products in supermarkets. The high-quality retailer benefited from the current trend amongst UK consumers of putting greater emphasis on the quality of food.

Future plans Waitrose plans to strengthen its non-food offering of clothing and housewares in its Food & Home store. The up-market supermarket also plans to invest on new product development and plans to launch a convenience food brand to grow its convenience business.

Table L10.3 summarizes the key features of the main retailers, as discussed.

New market entrants

Recent new entrants to the UK grocery retailing industry came in the form of hard discounters. The strategy of discounting, and hence the industry in which such firms operate, is quite different from that of the typical UK supermarkets. Aldi and its imitators spotted a market gap in the UK. The attack on the British industry from the discounters came in a variety of forms and formats.

Aldi has been quick to respond to changes in the UK grocery retailing industry. As the first European hard discounter to enter the UK industry in 1990, Aldi has built an extensive store network with a presence of over 400 stores, as recorded in 2009. While it was the pioneer of hard discounting in the UK, more recently it has led the pack in moving to a softer discount proposition. The retailer has worked hard to introduce premium ranges and to extend its coverage of fresh and organic products.

Despite entering the UK market four years after rival Aldi, Lidl has targeted space growth more aggressively, expanding its portfolio to over 530 stores, as recorded in 2009. In line with recent consumer trends and rivals' activities, Lidl has moved from a pure price-driven proposition to a good-value proposition. As the figures show in Table L10.2, shoppers are warming to the European powerhouses and they may become a real force for change in the UK industry.

Future plans Both new entrants will continue to have an impact on the UK retail industry as they drive growth aggressively, as well as broaden product ranges and maintain their low prices.

Competition concerns: the Competition Commission

The Competition Commission conducted a two-year investigation into whether the dominant players abuse their market position, drive small rivals out of business, or abuse their suppliers. In a statement of proposed 'remedies' designed to improve competition in the £123bn grocery industry, the Competition Commission suggested changes to the way in which planning decisions are made to encourage competition and bring an end to supermarkets imposing conditions on land that they sell off, which currently prevent rivals setting up stores. The watchdog requested a new ombudsman to help to protect small suppliers and farmers, and supermarkets may have to appoint in-house compliance officers to ensure that their buyers treat suppliers in accordance with a new and wider-ranging code of practice. The new code is expected to ban supermarkets from changing contract terms retrospectively. However, the report findings were not welcomed by all. Lobby groups and

Table L10.3 Retailer cross-comparison

Name of company	No. of employees approx	No. of UK stores approx	Market diversification	Online shopping channel
Asda Wal-Mart	143,000	500	Worldwide via Wal-Mart	Yes
Marks and Spencers	78,000	700	Europe; Middle East; Asia	Yes
Morrisons	132,000	450	UK only	No
Sainsbury's	146,000	870	UK only	Yes
Co-operative Group	85,000	2,800	UK only	No
Tesco	470,000	2,700	Europe; Asia; USA	Yes
Waitrose	42,000	250	UK only	Yes

Source: Collated from company corporate websites accessed 31 December 2010

campaigners accused the watchdog of failing to protect small retailers and opening the door for hundreds of new supermarkets. Policy director Andrew Simms commented: 'Instead of doing the job they were given, which was to break the stranglehold of the big four supermarkets ... they propose measures, such as weakening current checks and balances on planning, that will tighten their grip.' Tesco has nearly a third of the UK grocery industry and the Big Four together control three-quarters of the market. It is thought that some supermarkets are being allowed to achieve monopoly status in the UK food marketplace and in many other countries. Tesco is the chief target of this attack. 'Tescopoly' (Simms, 2007) is a campaign run by UK anti-poverty and environmental campaign groups, aimed at highlighting environmental and social impacts attributed to British supermarket chains. The campaign uses the slogan 'Every little hurts', a play on the slogan used by Tesco, 'Every little helps'.

One change proposed is a 'competition test', which local planning authorities will have to consider before giving the go-ahead to new stores. It is intended to make it easier for rival stores to set up in towns dominated by a single grocery chain. The Commission identified 200 locations in which more competition was needed. However, grocers with 60 per cent of a local market will still be allowed to go ahead with a new store. The Commission is also taking action on 'restrictive covenants', which grocers attach to land that they buy and sell to prevent rivals using it to build stores. The watchdog said that such covenants must be released and will be banned in future. Independent retailers and smaller supermarket chains had campaigned for the big grocers to be forced to sell off their vast landbanks and had hoped that some grocers—Tesco in particular—would be forced to sell off stores to rivals. The new code of practice, setting out how supermarkets must deal with their suppliers, will extend to all grocery retailers with a turnover of more than £1bn. Previously, it applied only to the Big Four chains, but will now include M&S, Waitrose, Lidl, and Aldi, among others. The Campaign to Protect Rural England (CPRE) accused the Competition Commission of 'a narrow obsession between a few giant retailers', and warned that the proposals 'could spell disaster' for local shops and their communities.

Future of the UK grocery industry

Today, UK supermarkets trade in a market that sells higher levels of convenience, greater choice in both price and quality, and in different product ranges. The UK food market is one of the most concentrated in Europe. As people's lives become more crowded, supermarket alternatives that will save time or effort may be attractive. During 2009, price competition in the industry intensified due to the economic crisis. Many competitors invested in growing own-label or value brands.

Whilst the grocery industry has enjoyed huge success over the last few decades, there are some serious threats to the industry as a whole. The proliferation of out-of-town supermarkets has been blamed for the disappearance of smaller, local grocery stores, and for increased dependency on the car and the consequent increase in traffic. These smaller businesses have been closing at accelerating rates over the past few decades, causing a parliamentary group to speculate in January 2006 that, by

2015, there may be barely any independent small shops left at all. Furthermore, the industry is conscious of the welfare of food. The vulnerability of the food industry was highlighted by the BSE crisis, which was, single-handedly, the most traumatic food scare in UK history.

The choice of goods in UK supermarkets is staggering. Retailers have been instrumental in promoting competitive pricing, albeit sometimes at the expense of local traders. But how will retailers cope with offering continued price competitiveness as food inflation rises? Also, in the current retailing climate, customer loyalty is harder to maintain. Consumers expect not only good food quality and value, but also ethical standards and an acceptance of social responsibilities from their food. Will fresh food be the battleground for retailers as they aggressively compete to attract and retain the all-elusive grocery shopper?

Finally, is the shopping experience the same as it was thirty years ago? Is it a question of a mature industry that has learned all of the tricks? Arguably, we have experienced the introduction of online grocery shopping and there is a heightened focus on convenience shopping, but have these radical initiatives revolutionized our shopping experience? Self-service, supermarket, superstore all transformed the shopping experience in their time, but what will come next? Will Tesco continue its reign of dominance? What will it take for the rest of the field to catch up? Should the retailers be taking a 'helicopter' perspective or focus on day-to-day efficient operations? Is there room for niche players? Is there any reason why a successful niche strategy should not be extended globally? Or will discounters, such as Lidl and Aldi, rise and reign?

Case questions

1. What are the sources of competitive advantage in the UK grocery industry?
2. Carry out an analysis of the UK grocery industry. What are your main conclusions? Is this an attractive industry?
3. From your industry analysis, develop three scenarios for the grocery industry for the next three years.
4. Using a strategic group map, do you envisage the competition in this industry will change radically over the next ten years?
5. Undertake an analysis of the UK grocery market from a resource perspective. What are your main conclusions? Do core competences explain the competitive dominance of Tesco?
6. What are the key intangible assets within the UK grocery industry?

References

ASDA. 2009. ***Annual Report 2009***. Available online at http://www.asda.co.uk

Ball, J. 2010. Retail prices: inflation returns pushing prices up 2.8% in a month. *The Grocer*, 30 January.

Competition Commission. 2000. ***Supermarkets: A Report on the Supply of Groceries from Multiple Stores in the United Kingdom***. Available online at http://www.competition-commission.org.uk/rep_pub/reports/2000/446super.htm

Cooperative Group. 2009. ***Annual Report 2009***. Available online at http://www.cooperative.coop/corporate/groupoverview/Somerfield

Fernie, J. and Sparks, L. 2004. ***Logistics and Retail Management: Insights into Current Practice and Trends from Leading Experts***. London: Kogan Page.

Foresight. 2009. ***Obesity Report***. Available online at http://www.foresight.gov.uk/Obesity/Obesity_final

IGD Research. 2007. ***Global Convenience Retailing: Maximising the Opportunity***. Available online at http://www.igd.com/index.asp?id = 1&fid = 2&sid = 2&cid = 262

Marks and Spencer. 2009. ***Annual Report 2009***. Available online at http://corporate.marksandspencer.com

Sainsbury's. 2009. ***Annual Report 2009***. Available online at http://www.jsainsburys.co.uk/ar09/index.shtml

Seth, A. and Randall, G. 1999. ***The Rise and Rise of the Supermarket Chains***. London: Kogan Page.

Simms, A. 2007. ***Tescopoly: How One Shop Came Out on Top and Why it Matters***. London: Constable and Robinson Ltd.

Tesco. 2009. ***Annual Report 2009***. Available online at http://www.investorcentre.tescoplc.com/

Verdict. 2009. ***UK Food and Grocery Retailers***. Available online at http://www.verdict.co.uk/eMarketing/vr160/vr160aonsite.htm

Waitrose. 2009. ***Annual Report 2009***. Available online at http://www.waitrose.presscentre.com/content/default.aspx?

Wm Morrison. 2009. ***Annual Report 2009***. Available online at http://www.morrisons.co.uk/Corporate/Investors/

Glossary

acquisition The buying or taking ownership of another entity

alliance A partnership between two or more organizations working together towards a common objective

balanced scorecard A holistic approach to measuring organizational performance that complements traditional financial measures with those related to customer satisfaction, organizational learning and innovation, and internal process improvement

business ecosystem A network of organizations (including competitors, suppliers, customers, and distributors) spanning industry boundaries that work either in competition or collaboration to support economic value creation

business model A system-level means of analysing the scope and scale of activities conducted by an organization in order to 'do business', including the means by which value is created and captured

business-level strategy A strategic stance that reflects the basis on which an organizational business unit has chosen to compete in a given market

core competencies A distinct group of activities and processes, embedded within behaviours and routines, which enable an organization to excel in meeting key client or customer requirements

corporate entrepreneurship Refers to the process of creating new business within existing organizations in order to improve organizational profitability and/or to facilitate the strategic renewal of existing business

corporate governance The system by which organizations are directed and controlled; the corporate governance structure specifies the distribution of rights and responsibilities among different participants in the corporation, such as the board, managers, shareholders, and other stakeholders; the corporate governance structure also provides the rules and procedures for making decisions on corporate affairs, in particular the key interests and priorities that the organization should serve in order to ensure accountability, responsible behaviour, and adequate levels of performance

corporate social responsibility (CSR) An umbrella term capturing all of those corporate activities devised to ensure that the organization and its actors act in an ethical manner and pay appropriate attention to broader social issues

corporate strategy A higher-level strategy examining the nature of businesses and industries in which an organization should operate

discourse Texts, language, and/or forms of communication that serve to signify or sustain specific meanings

diversification A significant extension of the scope of organizational activities as a result of introducing new products or services or by entering new markets; depending on the extent to which diversification complements existing activities, it can be judged to be 'related' or 'unrelated' diversification

dynamic capabilities Refers to the firm's ability to integrate, build, and reconfigure internal competencies in order to rapidly address changing external circumstances and thereby stay ahead of the competition

empowerment The process of delegating control, sharing ideas and information, and facilitating the autonomy of others so that they can follow their own initiative

evidence-based management An approach to strategic decision making that is explicitly focused on and driven by the best research evidence available

evolutionary change A type of change that occurs gradually over time, typically within an existing frame of reference

formulation The process of devising and evaluating available strategic options with the intention of choosing the most appropriate course of action with which to create advantage

hyper-competition A term capturing the intensity of competition and speed of environmental change characteristic of the modern era

industry recipe The business-specific world view of a set of organizations that has evolved over time, and which serves to frame assumptions about the competitive environment and nature of industry forces

industry A group of firms that compete in a similar competitive space producing outputs that serve the same broad function

innovation The generation and exploitation of new products and services or the introduction of new ways of operating

joint venture Refers to an instance in which two organizations come together to form a partnership that shares the risk or expertise required of a specific project

key success factor (KSF) A key dimension in which it is of critical importance to outperform competitors

managerial fad A popular and attractive managerial innovation or idea that is unlikely to bring sustainable success to an organization

merger The creation of a new legal entity by bringing together two or more independent companies, typically on a voluntary basis

mission statement A statement of what an organization does and how it does it

not-for-profit organization (NPO) An organization that does not issue stock shares or distribute its surplus funds to owners or shareholders (termed the 'non-distribution constraint'), but instead uses funds to help it to achieve societal goals; the status of an organization as an NPO is typically conferred by legislation

organizational learning The means by which an organization absorbs knowledge and experience to adapt and increase the likelihood of enhanced future performance

paradigm A frame of reference shaped by legacy, history, and culture, which can filter or distort both individual and organizational perceptions of both the internal and external environment

parenting style The approach or style of leadership deployed by a corporate parent in managing its business units

portfolio The scope of strategic business units controlled by a diversified corporation; can also be used to refer to the portfolio of products or services offered by an organization

public sector organization (PSO) An organization that is part of the state and deals with either the production, delivery, or allocation of goods and services by and for the government or its citizens

rationality An approach to analysis founded upon a deliberate and objective reasoning

resource Something that an organization owns, controls, or can access over a period of time; resources can be tangible, such as physical infrastructure, or intangible, such as brand name

resource-based view An approach to understanding organizational advantage that suggests that the essence of advantage resides internally within the firm

revolutionary change A type of change that emphasizes transformation and a dramatic change of direction or new frame of reference

scenario planning The process of devising contingency plans exploring the impact of a limited number of future possible occurrences

stakeholder An individual and/or group with an interest, material or otherwise, in the purpose, activities, and outcomes of an organization's activities

strategic decision making The process of making decisions on critical issues likely to have a long-term impact on the viability and success of an organization

strategic group A group of firms within an industry that compete on the same basis; enables identification of direct competitors

strategic metaphor An image deployed by management that can facilitate in communicating the purpose and meaning of an organization to both internal and external stakeholder groups

strategist An individual or a group skilled in strategy and tasked with responsibility for organizational strategy

strategy-as-practice An emerging approach to understanding strategy that focuses on the activities, processes, and people that constitute the strategy process; a strategy-as-practice perspective emphasizes strategy as something that an organization does rather than something that it simply has

sustainable competitive advantage An organizational advantage that continues to exist over a period of time, even after attempts at replication by competitors

trade-off A conscious decision made by an organization to conduct only those activities seen as central to differentiating the organization from competitors

Index

A

B

C

D

E

F

G

H

J

K

L

N

O

P

Q

T

U

V

W

X

Y

Z